CS

FOURTH EDITION

Success Studybooks

Advertising and Promotion
Book-keeping and Accounts
Business Calculations
Chemistry
Commerce
Commerce: West African Edition
Communication
Economics
Electronics
European History 1815–1941
Information Processing
Insurance
Investment
Law
Managing People
Marketing
Politics
Principles of Accounting
Principles of Accounting: Answer Book
Psychology
Sociology
Statistics
Twentieth Century World Affairs
World History since 1945

First published 1974
Second edition 1983
Third edition 1989

This edition first published 2001
by John Murray (Publishers) Ltd
50 Albemarle Street
London W1S 4BD

Layouts by Wearset, Boldon, Tyne and Wear
Artwork by Wearset

Typeset in 10.5/12pt Sabon by Wearset
Printed and bound in Great Britain by The Bath Press, Bath

A CIP catalogue record for this book is available from the British Library

ISBN 0 7195 7207 X

SUCCESS IN

ECONOMICS

FOURTH EDITION

CHRIS NUTTALL
DEREK LOBLEY

Acknowledgements

The author and publishers would like to give special thanks to Andy Graham and Derek Orton for their comments and advice on the text and for their very valuable contributions, particularly in Units 13 and 14.

The Publishers would like to thank the following for permission to reproduce copyright material.

Written Material:
The Bank of England p. 280
David Batty/The Big Issue, March 1999 p. 11
Business Review, November 1997 pp. 226–227
R. Wild, *Essentials of Production and Operations Management* (Cassell, 4th edn 1995) Reproduced by permission of Cassell plc., Continuum International Publishing Group p. 68
By permission of the Division for Sustainable Development, United Nations p. 449
Excerpts from Comparative Economic Systems, second edition, by H. Stephen Gardner, copyright © 1997 by the Dryden Press, reprinted by permission of the publisher pp. 27, 136
Economics for a Developing World, 1992 p. 444
Adapted from Robert Nutter, 'Exam boards – Monopoly or Oligopoly?', *Economics Today*, September 1998 p. 211
© The Economist Newspaper Limited, London (February 2000) p. 425
Encyclopaedia Britannica (1999) pp. 20, 315–316
Friends of the Earth, 1998 p. 448
Milton and Rose Friedman, *Free to Choose* (Harcourt, Brace and Company, 1980) p. 370
'Reproduced from an article by Patrick Dunne in the April 1999 issue of *Management Today* with the permission of Haymarket Management Publications Ltd' p. 65
Adapted from *Lloyds TSB Economic Bulletin*, December 1998 (Internet edition) p. 173
Adapted from B. Jewell, *An Integrated Approach to Business Studies* (Longman, 3rd edn 1996) Addison Wesley Longman Ltd p. 196
D. Begg, *Economics* (McGraw-Hill, 5th edn 1997) pp. 96, 100
'National Accounts', National Statistics © Crown Copyright 2000 pp. 56, 58, 60, 63, 286, 291, 308, 311, 313, 330, 332, 333, 378, 389
Office of the European Parliament and the Representative of the European Commission in the United Kingdom pp. 228, 420, 414–415
The Affluent Society by John Kenneth Galbraith (Hamish Hamilton, 1958, 4th edn 1984) copyright © John Kenneth Galbraith, 1958, 1969, 1976, 1984. Reproduced by permission of Penguin Books Ltd p. 83
The New Industrial State by John Kenneth Galbraith (Hamish Hamilton, 1967) copyright © 1967 by John Kenneth Galbraith. Reproduced by permission of Penguin Books Ltd p. 55
Professional Manager, May 1998 p. 365
Reproduced by permission of the Stationery Office Ltd p. 424
© Fiona Kennedy, Tesco Stores Limited p. 259
© Times Newspapers Limited, 24th March 1998 p. 16

Photographs:
p. 15 Efe pygmy camp of the Ituri Forest, Democratic Republic of Congo: Picture courtesy of Robert C. Bailey, University of Illinois at Chicago; **p. 49** *clockwise from top* Science Photo Library, Science Photo Library, Oxford Scientific Films, Oxford Scientific Films; **p. 71** Hulton Getty; **p. 227** Paula Solloway/Format; **p. 240** Hulton Getty; **p. 350** Hulton Getty.

Every effort has been made to trace all copyright holders, but if any have been inadvertently overlooked the Publishers will be pleased to make the necessary arrangements at the earliest opportunity.

Contents

Introduction: studying economics

Success in Economics is an up-to-date and lively textbook that has been designed to cover the new A and AS level syllabuses. It is based on current ideas and theories and does not assume any prior knowledge of the subject. There are many recent examples taken from familiar sources, including the media and everyday life, to give relevance to the theories and principles of economics. It is hoped that this will make *Success in Economics* both interesting and easy to use, while also covering all the key syllabus areas, some of which represent new areas of study for economics at A and AS level.

How to use this book

Success in Economics is divided into units to provide a manageable and, it is hoped, logical coverage of the topic areas of GCE A and AS level courses in economics. Each unit provides comprehensive coverage of its area. This breakdown of material is appropriate both for those following a 'terminal' exam route and those taking a modular approach.

However, there is a danger of seeing economics as a discipline of separate parts, rather than as a unified body of theory. Major areas such as demand and supply cut right across and lie at the heart of all other areas of study within economics. Questions and assignments you will tackle during your course, or in your exam, will require responses which touch on more than one topic area or unit of this book. For example, inflation may be linked to demand and supply, interest rates and employment. You should therefore be prepared to use the units in a flexible manner and be aware of the need to apply your knowledge and understanding appropriately to the issues raised. Many of the *Think about it* and *Something to do* boxes, which appear in all units, will require you to make links between related areas of economics.

References to other sources

Economics is concerned with analysing and making sense of information about the needs and wants of society and about how society tries to satisfy those needs and wants from available resources. Much of the information is in the form of statistics, and there have been many attempts to analyse the situations behind the statistics. Some of the theories that have been put forward have been intended to support a particular political theory or approach.

It is not possible or practical to include in this book detailed statistical sources or accounts of economic theories relevant to all of the themes of the units. Key statistics and theories are given and explained in detail. Full reference details are given in the 'Bibliography and Internet sources' list on page 471. These will enable you to investigate further the themes of each unit and provide useful resources for your coursework.

Success in Economics *and your syllabus*

Success in Economics has been written for students on GCE A and AS level economics courses. It is an accessible introduction to the world of economics and assumes no prior knowledge of the subject.

The present edition is a revision of Derek Lobley's original well-respected text, bringing it up to date and making it relevant to the latest syllabus changes. It is equally appropriate for linear and modular courses.

The book aims to prepare you for all exam board requirements in respect of syllabus coverage and types of questions. Make sure you have a copy of, or access to, the syllabus for the course you are following. You should study this carefully to ensure you are aware of the specific knowledge that is required. The following tables show how the units of *Success in Economics* cover the topic/module areas in the different A/AS level syllabuses.

OCR AS/A level content	S. in Economics units
Module 2881 The Market System	**1, 3–5**
Managing scarce resources - the reasons for choice and its consequences	1, 3
Competitive markets and how they work	3, 5
Firms and how they operate	4
Module 2882 Market Failure and Government Intervention	**7, 10**
Economic efficiency within competitive markets	7
Why markets may not work efficiently	7
Making choices and the impact of government intervention on market outcomes and efficiency	7, 10
Module 2883 The National and International Economy	**5, 7, 9–13**
Government macro-economic policy objectives and indicators of national economic performance	9, 10, 12
Aggregate demand and aggregate supply: the determinants of output, employment and prices	5, 7, 11
The application of macro-economic policy instruments	10, 12
Structure and essential determinants of international transactions	13
Module 2884 Economics of Work and Leisure	**2, (5), 7, 10, 11**
Nature of work and leisure and trends in employment and earnings	11
Theories of market structure and competitive behaviour in markets for leisure	(5)
Labour demand, supply and wage determination	2
Market failure and the role of the government and unions in the labour market	7, 10, 11
Module 2885 Transport Economics	**(5), (7), (10)**
Transport, transport trends and the economy	–
Theories of market structure and competitive behaviour in transport markets	(5)
Resource allocation issues in transport	(10)
Market failure and the role of the government in transport	(7), (10)
Module 2886 Economics Of Development	**14**
The concept of development	14
Economies at different stages of development	14
Theories and models linked to development	14
Problems of developing economies	14
Policies to promote development	14
Module 2887 The UK Economy	**9, 10**
The performance of the UK economy	9

OCR AS/A level content	S. in Economics units
Controlling the performance of the UK economy	10
Modelling the economy	–
Policies to improve economic performance	10
Conflicts, current issues and controversies	–
Module 2888 Economics in a European Context	**13**
The 'New Europe'	13
The Single European Market (SEM) and Economic and Monetary Union (EMU)	13
The transition economies of Europe	13

AQA AS/A level content	S. in Economics units
The Economic Problem	**1**
The nature and purpose of economic activity	1
Economic resources	1
The economic objectives of individuals, firms and governments	1
Scarcity, choice, and the allocation of resources	1
Opportunity cost, the margin, trade-offs and conflicting objectives	1
Value judgements, positive and normative statements	1
The Allocation of Resources in Competitive Markets	**3, 5**
The determinants of the demand for goods and services	3
Price, income and cross elasticities of demand	3
The determinants of the supply of goods and services	3
Price elasticity of supply	3
The determination of equilibrium market prices	5
Causes of changes in equilibrium market prices	5
Applications of demand and supply analysis to particular markets	5
The interrelationship between markets	5
How markets and prices allocate resources	5
Monopoly	**5**
Monopolies and the allocation of resources	5
Production and Efficiency	**(1), 2, 4, 7**
Specialisation, division of labour and exchange	2
Economies of scale	4
Economic efficiency	1, 7
Market Failure	**(1), 7, 10, 11**

AQA AS/A level content	S. in Economics units
Positive and negative externalities in consumption and production	7
Public goods	7
Merit and demerit goods	7
Market imperfections	7
Inequalities in the distribution of income and wealth	1, 10, 11
Government Intervention in the Market	**10**
Rationale for government intervention	10
Methods of government intervention to correct distortions in individual markets	10
Government failure	10
The impact of government intervention on market outcomes	10
The National Economy: Performance of the UK Economy and Government Policy Objectives	**9–14**
Indicators of national economic performance	9
The objectives of government economic policy	10
Economic growth	14
Inflation	13
Employment and unemployment	11
The balance of payments	13
How the Macro-economy works	**1, 3, 6, 10, 11**
Aggregate demand/aggregate supply analysis	3, 11
The determinants of aggregate demand	3, 11
Aggregate demand and the level of economic activity	3, 11
The determinants of aggregate supply, free market and interventionist views	3, 5, 6, 10
Short-run and long-run aggregate supply curves	3
The Main Instruments of Government Macro-economic Policy	**10**
Fiscal policy	10
Monetary policy	10
Supply-side policies	10
European Union	**13**
The deepening of European integration	13
The opportunities of the single market	13
The euro	13
The widening of European integration	13
The regional dimension of the EU	13
The reform of the EU	13
Economic problems: the European dimension	13
Globalisation and the EU	13
EU aspects of global problems	13
Theory of the Firm	**4–6**
The objectives of firms	4
The divorce of ownership from control	4
The law of diminishing returns and returns to scale	4
Fixed and variable costs, marginal, average and total costs, short-run and long-run costs	4
Economies and diseconomies of scale	4
Technological change, costs and supply in the long-run	4
Total, average and marginal revenue	4, 6
Profit	4, 5
Competitive Markets	**5**
The model of perfect competition	5
Competition and the efficient allocation of resources	5
The dynamics of competition and competitive market processes	5
Concentrated Markets	**3–5, 7**
Monopoly and oligopoly	5
Price makers and price takers	5

AQA AS/A level content	S. in Economics units
The growth of firms	4, 5
Sources of monopoly power	5
The model of monopoly	5
Collusive and non-collusive oligopoly	5
Interdependence in oligopolistic markets	5
Price discrimination	3
Consumer and producer surplus	3
Contestable and non-contestable markets	5
Market structure, static efficiency, dynamic efficiency and resource allocation	7
The Labour Market	**(1), 6, 11**
The demand for labour, the marginal productivity theory	6
Influences upon the supply of labour to different markets	6
The determination of relative wage rates in competitive markets	6
The influence of trade unions and monopsonistic employers in determining wages and levels of employment	6
Discrimination in the labour market	6
The distribution of income and wealth	(1), 6, 11
Government Intervention in the Market	**1, 5, 7, 10**
Market failure and government failure	7
Competition policy	5, 10
Public ownership, privatisation, regulation and de-regulation of markets	1, 7
Notions of equity	10, 11
The problem of poverty	1, 10
Government policies to alleviate poverty and to influence the distribution of income and wealth	10
Cost-benefit analysis	1, 7
Government Policy, the National and International Economy: Growth of the Economy and Cyclical Instability	**10, 14**
The nature and causes of fluctuations in economic activity	14
The trend rate of economic growth	14
The costs and benefits of economic growth	14
The use and limitations of national income as an indicator of changes in living standards	9
Inflation and Unemployment	**11, 12**
The causes and consequences of unemployment	11
The natural rate of unemployment hypothesis	11
The Phillips curve	11, 12
The causes and consequences of inflation	12
Monetarism and the quantity theory of money	12, 10
Managing the National Economy	**10**
Monetary policy, the money supply and interest rates	10
The exchange rate as a target and instrument of economic policy	13
Taxation and public expenditure	10
Fiscal policy	10
The interrelationships between fiscal and monetary policy	10
Possible conflicts of policy objectives	10
The International Economy	**13, 14**
The pattern of trade between the United Kingdom and the rest of the world	13, 14
Trade with developing economies	13, 14
The principle of comparative advantage	13, 14
The benefits and costs of international trade	13, 14
Protectionism	13, 14

AQA AS/A level content	S. in Economics units
The balance of payments account	13
The determination of exchange rates	13
Exchange rate systems and their implications for the conduct of economic policy	13
European monetary union	13

Edexcel AS/A level content	S. in Economics units
Unit 1: Markets – How They Work	**1–6, 10, 13**
Positive and normative economics	1
Scarcity and opportunity cost	1
The production possibility boundary or frontier	1, 2
Specialisation and the division of labour	2
Economies of scale	4
The advantages of international trade: the principle of comparative advantage	13
Consumer and producer surplus	3
The price mechanism as a means of allocating resources	3, 5
The role of the price mechanism in resource allocation in free market and mixed economies	5
The supply of, and demand for, goods and services	3
The concept of elasticity with respect to both supply and demand	3
Applications of supply and demand analysis in the product and factor markets	5, 6
Entry and exit of firms	4
Government intervention in markets: rationale for such intervention and the effects on consumers, producers and the government	10
Indirect taxes and subsidies	10
Unit 2: Markets – Why They Fail	**7, 10**
Market failure	7
Types of market failure	7
Remedies for market failure	7, 10
Government failure	7, 10
Unit 3: Managing the Economy	**3, 9–11, 13, 14**
Measures of the economic performance of countries:	3, 9–11, 13, 14
• The Retail Price Index	9
• The level of unemployment	11
• The balance of payments	13
• Gross Domestic Product	9
Economic growth	14
Aggregate demand	3, 11
Aggregate supply	3
The relationship between aggregate demand and the price level and between aggregate supply and the price level.	3, 5
The equilibrium level of real output	3
Macro-economic policy objectives in an EU context	13
Conflicts between these objectives	13
The relative merits of supply side and/or demand side policies as means of realising policy objectives	10
Unit 4: Industrial Economics	**1, 3–5, 7, 10, 13**
The birth and growth of firms	4
The motives for the growth of firms	4
Internal and external growth	4
Alternative motives of firms	4

Edexcel AS/A level content	S. in Economics units
• Productive efficiency	4
• Allocative efficiency	4, 7
Measures of market concentration	5, 7
Pricing and output decisions under different market structures and different motives	5, 7
The conditions necessary for price discrimination in monopoly	5
Pricing and non-pricing strategies	5
Barriers to entry and exit	3, 4
Contestable markets	5
Competition policy in the UK and EU	5, 10, 13
Regulation of privatised industries	1, 4
Unit 5A: Labour markets	**2, 4, 6, 10, 11, 13**
The supply of labour: the working population	2, 6
The demand for labour. Labour as a derived demand	2, 6
Wage determination in competitive markets	6
Differentials in different occupations; between men and women; skilled/unskilled workers: ethnic groups. Discrimination	6
The role of trade unions	6
Government intervention in labour markets	10, 11
The case of monopsony	6
Unemployment and labour market imperfections	6, 11
Government policies to influence geographical mobility and occupational mobility	4
The changing structure and flexibility of UK and EU labour markets	4, 13
Ageing populations in developed economies	6
Factors influencing the distribution of income and wealth	1, 10
Changes in the distribution of income and wealth	1, 10
Aggregate and disaggregated data	11
Policy issues associated with poverty and inequality	10, 11
Unit 5B: Economic development	**14**
Indicators of development in developing countries in sub-Saharan Africa, Asia and Latin America	14
The causes of economic growth in developing countries	14
Differences between developing countries	14
The costs of economic growth	14
Constraints on economic growth	14
Development strategies	14
Sources of external finance	14
Unit 6: The UK in the global economy	**10–14**
Factors contributing to globalisation	13
International exchange	13
Trade liberalisation and protectionism	13
Sources of possible conflict between trading blocs and the role of the World Trade Organisation (WTO)	13, 14
The balance of payments	13
International competitiveness	13
The UK's changing international competitive situation	13,14
Balance of payments disequilibrium	13
Exchange rate systems	13
European Monetary Union	13
Inward foreign investment by MNCs	13, 14
External shocks to the global economy	14
Public expenditure and taxation	10
The working of fiscal, monetary and supply side policies	10
Unemployment and inflation in an EU and global context	12, 13
The relationship between real output and the non-accelerating inflation rate of unemployment (NAIRU)	11, 12

Study skills

Note-taking

Note-taking is an extremely important skill for advanced level students, and one that will be useful for life, but it needs to be undertaken efficiently. The first point to remember is that note-taking is not the same as essay writing! Long, detailed notes are rarely useful for revision purposes and are virtually impossible to remember. When you take notes from a book, article, class talk or lecture, you are trying to make an *accurate summary* of what you are reading or hearing. You should tailor your notes for an immediate task (for example, writing an essay) and also to be of use to you later (perhaps for revision).

To help you develop the skill of note-taking, a list of DO's and DON'Ts is provided below.

Do	Don't
• Aim to sort out the **main points** of a lecture or a written source. **Ignore what is irrelevant**.	• Don't attempt to write virtually everything down without thinking about it and its possible future use.
• Listen or look for **key words**, **concepts** and **short phrases** which can be efficiently and swiftly recorded.	• Don't make notes in sentences or as slightly reduced versions of the original, e.g. copying long phrases.
• Adopt a system of **abbreviations** (see below).	• Don't write long words in full, unless these are new key words or concepts.
• **Leave space** between points (and across the notepad for future additions, references, etc.).	• Don't clutter the notepad or jumble your notes making them difficult to understand (or add to later).
• Use **numbers**, **letters**, etc. during or after note-taking to sequence and provide a structure to your notes. Develop a logical, simple system for identifying key items, for example underline, CAPITALS, circle, box.	• Don't rely on memory or a rambling set of notes.
• Make a record of all your **sources**.	• Don't mix up different sources without identifying them.

You may find the following list of common abbreviations useful for note-taking.

Symbol	Meaning	Abbreviation	Meaning
∴	therefore	NB	note
∵	because	i.e.	that is
...	implies, it follows from this	wd	would
>	is greater than	cd	could
<	is less than	shd	should
=	equals, is the same as	b4	before
≠	does not equal, is not the same as	c.	about, approximately
"	ditto	v	versus
@	at	+	also, in addition to
e.g.	for example	→	leads to, led to, causes
c.f.	compare/cross-reference	←	is caused by, depends on

Always look after your notes carefully – perhaps file them with your class notes. Organise your file well, using file dividers. Reorganise it regularly.

Essay writing

Answer the question!

Relevance is vital. No matter how interesting or well-written your essay is you will not be given credit unless you answer the specific question that has been set. Make sure you understand what the question is asking and what you are required to do before you begin to write.

Provide a clear structure

Your essay should follow a carefully thought-out plan. The points made should be logical, you should make clear the relations between issues and you should state directly the connection between what you are writing and the question set.

Data response and structured questions

Data response questions

These questions contain an item or items of data that may be written, pictorial, numerical or diagrammatic and may be from an economic or other source. Questions based on the data may be divided into subquestions or subsections; most require you to refer to the data in your answer. Mark allocations for the various parts are shown. These are important as they give you an indication of the length of time and depth required for the responses. Data response questions are sometimes referred to as stimulus-response questions.

Structured questions

Structured questions, as above, may include text, diagrams, numbers and charts. They may be from economic or other sources. However, some structured questions do not contain any data or stimulus materials. Questions are divided into subquestions or subsections to provide a logical sequence for the development of your answers. Mark allocations for the various parts are shown and, as indicated above, are very important in answering the questions.

Exam preparation and technique

Revision

Efficient exam revision takes months and should certainly not be left until the evening (or even the fortnight!) before the exam.

- Use syllabus notes for guidance.
- Use past papers.
- Use your own coursework and notes.
- Do not rely on certain questions being in the paper – there are no guarantees!
- Prepare more than the minimum necessary topic areas in case of difficult or unusual questions.
- Fix your material in your long-term memory, so that you can recall it days or weeks later.

Simply re-reading your notes or textbook is not enough to fix material in your memory. Memorising is much more active – you need to seek out the meaning of what you are reading, think it through and structure it in the way you feel is most relevant. Once you have read a unit:

- run through it in your mind
- write down the key points
- make sure you understand key terms (in **bold** in the text); use the Glossary on pages 451–470.

This reinforces the information and helps you restructure it in your thoughts.

Start your revision several months before the exam, reminding yourself regularly of the key points. Every time you re-read material it will take less effort and you will be storing information in your long-term memory.

Beating boredom

The biggest obstacle to learning is often boredom. Try to overcome it by asking challenging questions and disputing what the author has written. If you can find points for discussion, the material will start to become more interesting. Vary the activity and the way you are trying to learn the material.

You learn best when your mind is working on the material, transforming it in different ways. Visualisation is a very active and useful process – take notes in the form of illustrations, diagrams or charts.

Know your paper

Before the exam make sure you know the number of questions you will have to answer, whether there are compulsory questions and the time and length of the exam. Knowing how long to spend on each question is a crucial factor in your exam performance.

Exam technique

When you receive the exam paper, check that the instructions for answering it are as you expected. Ask the exam room invigilator if there are any matters that concern you.

Choice of questions

Spend some time looking through the questions and identify those that you think you can answer. Cross through any questions that you cannot answer or do not fully understand. Look carefully at all parts of each question.

Planning your answer

- Read through the question again, carefully.
- Try to get behind the question – what is it really asking?
- Decide and note down what you intend to cover and in what order, so that your answer has a logical structure.
- Pay careful attention to the amount of time you have for each answer. Do not over-plan and use up your writing time. If you have 45 minutes for an essay, allow about 30–35 minutes for the actual writing and the rest for planning and checking your answer.
- Remember to answer the question that is set: stick to the point and do not stray from it. However good and interesting your answer, unless it actually answers the question set, you will get no marks.
- When the time you have allowed for the question is up, draw it to a conclusion and begin the next. If you have not quite finished an answer, leave space on the page so that you can come back to it and improve your answer if you have time left after answering the other questions.

Key skills

Key skills are generic, or non-specific, skills that are useful in education, work and life in general. Many employers value key skills highly, when recruiting staff, and therefore evidence of achievement in key skill areas can be important to your future career. Key skills are also important in the areas of self-employment and your personal life, because they can help you organise your life and your work, and help you handle money and information, and work with others. For these reasons, assessing key skills is a part of the A and AS level assessment process in all subject areas.

In economics, an ability in key skills is important because it will aid your learning as well as enabling you to understand, handle and interpret data, and express yourself clearly.

The key skills areas in which you will be assessed are

- communication
- application of number
- information technology
- working with others
- problem solving
- improving own learning and performance.

While you cannot learn key skills from this textbook alone, since they are freestanding areas of learning, studying economics for A or AS level will provide many opportunities for developing key skills.

For example:

- discussing topics with others, and making a presentation in front of your class and tutor will provide evidence towards the key skill of **communication**
- obtaining and interpreting numerical data, and making calculations using different formulae, will provide evidence towards the key skill of **application of number**
- producing and presenting information using a computer package will provide evidence towards the key skill of **information technology**
- planning an activity and working with others to achieve the desired outcome will provide evidence towards the key skill of **working with others**
- identifying a problem, suggesting two ways of solving it, and planning and trying one of these will provide evidence towards the key skill of **problem solving**
- setting targets for your own learning, planning how to achieve these and monitoring your progress will provide evidence towards the key skill of **improving own learning and performance**.

It is important that you familiarise yourself with the criteria for each key skill, and the type of evidence needed to demonstrate your achievements in these. As you work through the activities in *Success in Economics*, look out for opportunities to produce the evidence you require.

Finally, we hope that you find this book a useful and enjoyable guide to economics. Good luck!

1 What is economics?

Introduction: scarcity and choice

Economics is the study of how society produces the goods and services that provide its material well-being. Much of the information that economists use is in the form of statistics, often displayed as a table, chart or graph. Economics itself, however, is concerned with understanding the real situations behind the statistics – the problems society has in meeting the needs and wants of people, and how these are solved by governments, businesses and people themselves.

The basic problem that economics deals with is that while people have potentially infinite wants, the resources from which their wants can be satisfied are limited and capable of alternative uses. Economists describe this situation by saying that the resources needed to produce the goods and services that will satisfy society's wants are **scarce**. Not all wants can be satisfied from the scarce resources available, therefore. Society must choose which wants to satisfy and allocate resources to the production of the particular goods and services that will meet those wants. It must also decide how much of each good or service to produce and who gets what – how goods and services will be allocated amongst its members. As a social science, economics looks at the behaviour of society in choosing how to allocate its scarce resources, and at the effect of such decisions on society's material well-being.

In this unit, we consider the implications of **choice** in the economy. In particular, we look at

- how scarce resources are allocated
- opportunity cost, trade-offs and conflicting objectives
- different types of economy and the role of government
- the tools of economic analysis
- positive and normative economics.

What is economics about?

Most of us are aware of the kinds of things that economics deals with. Hardly a day goes by without television or the newspapers telling us that inflation is up (or down), the Bank of England has raised (or cut) interest rates, a large manufacturing company is making a number of workers redundant, or that in America a CD of your favourite band would cost you less than you can buy it for in the UK. But what do these simple facts mean to us and to society as a whole?

HOMELESSNESS

'BIG ISSUE' VENDOR SHOWS OFF HIS IDEAL HOME – A PUBLIC TOILET

■ BY DAVID BATTY

ROBERT FENNELL AND HIS CONVERTED CONVENIENCE

Robert Fennell's home stands on a hill overlooking affluent Hampstead Village in North London. But he isn't a millionaire – he's a *Big Issue* vendor and lives in a public toilet.

Fennell, 38, a qualified carpenter, has transformed the interior of the disused WC. After knocking down three toilets and ripping out the urinals, he built a bed from a cubicle door, made shelves from salvaged plywood and turned an old oil drum into a fireplace.

While his neighbours get their food delivered from Harrods, Fennell lives a 'Third World life-style', collecting his water from a standpipe and foraging for firewood on Hampstead Heath with his dog Samson. 'My customers call me the mountain man,' he jokes.

He became homeless after returning from Yugoslavia where he had fled with his wife, a Croatian, who was refused asylum by the Home Office. Southwark Council said he did not qualify for rehousing as he had made himself 'intentionally homeless'. He found the toilet six years ago after being evicted from a shop doorway on the village High Street.

His neighbour, Bernard Green, is more hospitable, praising his work clearing paths and trimming trees. He even gave Fennell a gas heater and cooker.

Green, 84, a retired company director, believes Fennell should be given the rights to the property. 'Before he was there it was a filthy mess,' he says. 'It's a pleasure to have someone there to prevent the place being used as a knocking shop.' He vowed to mount a protest if anyone tried to evict Fennell.

But a spokesman for Camden Council, which owns the toilet, said it had recently received a complaint about someone living there and was investigating the matter.

Source: *The Big Issue*, 15–21 March 1999

Something to do

- Read the article on homelessness.
- Write notes on the kinds of economic issues you think are involved. Consider in particular:
  - What are the implications for society of the situation described in the article?
  - In what respect is the article about the allocation of scarce resources?
- You should try to get into the habit of regularly reading newspapers for articles and news stories about economic events and facts. Read especially the 'broadsheets' such as *The Times*, the *Financial Times*, the *Independent*, the *Daily Telegraph* and the *Guardian*; and magazines such as *The Economist*. Take a copy of any articles that you think concern economic issues and keep them in a special file. You may want to create separate sections in your file for different topics such as unemployment, inflation, international trade, etc.

Making choices

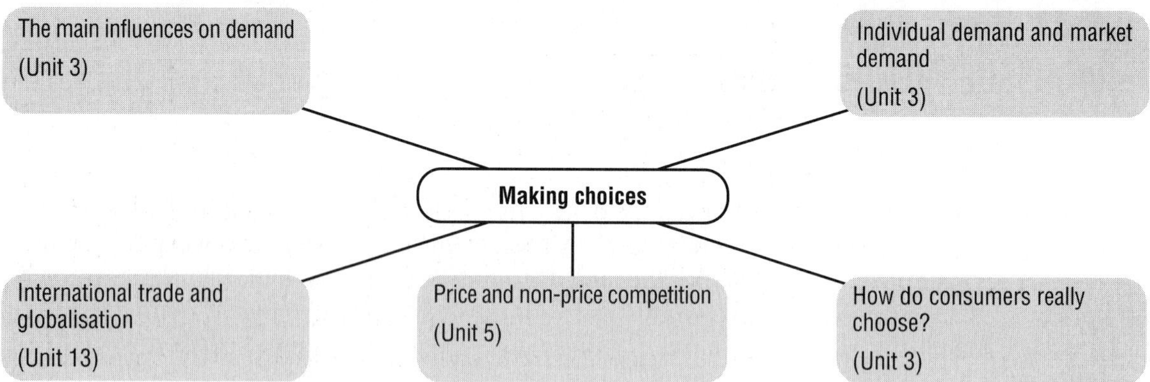

Consider the graphs in Figure 1.1. These show that while, over the years, the UK car industry has increased its output, people are buying an increasing proportion of foreign-made cars. This trend has been accompanied by a reduction in the number of people employed in the UK motor manufacturing industry.

Fig. 1.1 The UK motor industry

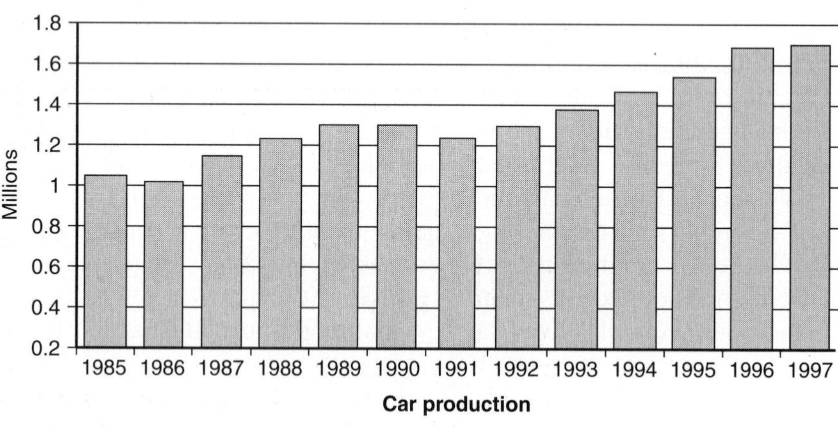

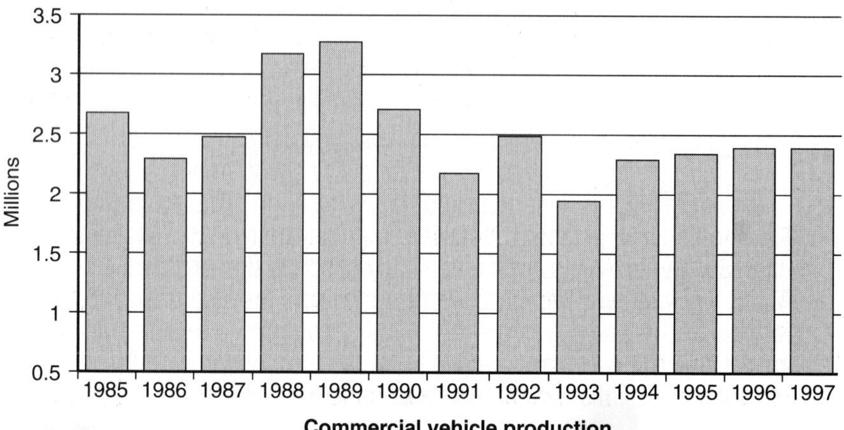

Fig. 1.1 (continued)

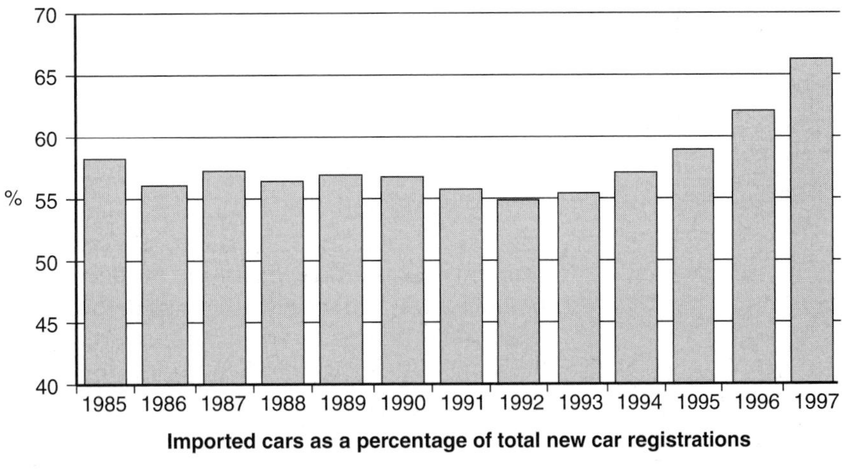

Imported cars as a percentage of total new car registrations

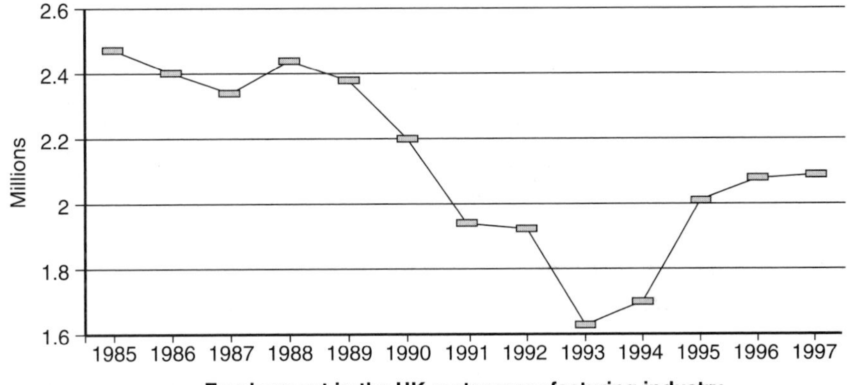

Employment in the UK motor manufacturing industry

Deciding whether to buy a British car or a foreign car involves making a choice. Choice is at the heart of economics. Why most cars bought in the UK are imported cannot readily be seen from the graphs in Figure 1.1 – it is probably down to factors such as price, quality or design, or a combination of these. But if sales of British cars fall because more people choose to buy foreign cars, it seems obvious that fewer British cars will be produced, less labour will be required and employment in the British car industry will fall.

The reduction in employment may, however, also be the result of a different type of choice. Motor manufacturers have increasingly chosen to use machines rather than people to produce cars.

Think About It

- Why do you think motor manufacturers increasingly use machines rather than people to produce cars? Can you tell the reason from the graphs in Figure 1.1?
- Do you think society benefits from using machines rather than people to manufacture goods such as cars?
- Discuss your answers as a class.
- Summarise your discussion and explain the conclusions you have reached.

The statistics alone cannot tell us *why* cars are increasingly being produced by machines, but we can assume that the manufacturers believe that this is more cost-effective and efficient.

Statistics such as the rate of inflation, impending redundancies, the differences in costs of items bought in different countries, and those on the motor industry in Figure 1.1, merely describe situations. They do not analyse them, and they cannot explain how they have arisen or show what will happen in response to any action intended to improve those situations. Economics, however, is concerned with the situations behind the statistics. Ultimately it is about how people in society choose to satisfy their wants: how they use their skills and knowledge to produce the things – such as clothes, food, houses, cars and computers – that they want, and how these choices affect the material well-being of society.

We need each other

Economic dependence

We live in a world where the vast majority of us depend on others to produce the things we want. We rely on farmers to produce the food we eat, doctors to make us well when we are sick, and companies such as Ford or General Motors to produce cars for us to drive. Of course, the farmer usually relies on farm workers to help him on the farm; the doctor relies on the practice staff to help her practice run smoothly and provide the service we want; and Ford relies on its employees to run the machinery and make the cars it produces. As individuals, we work in organisations such as these and are paid wages that enable us to purchase the goods and services we choose.

This **economic dependence** also crosses national borders (see Figure 1.2). Look at the produce on the shelves of any supermarket and you will find items such as coffee from Kenya and Brazil, pasta and tinned tomatoes from Italy, wines from France and Chile, and lamb from New Zealand. As consumers, we want the goods produced by other countries, while other countries need to sell their products to the UK in order to get money to buy the goods and services they want but do not produce themselves. Societies that are economically independent, for example some tribes of the Efe, who still live as hunter-gatherers in the tropical rainforest of Zaire, are rare.

Fig. 1.2 The flow of international trade between Brazil and the UK

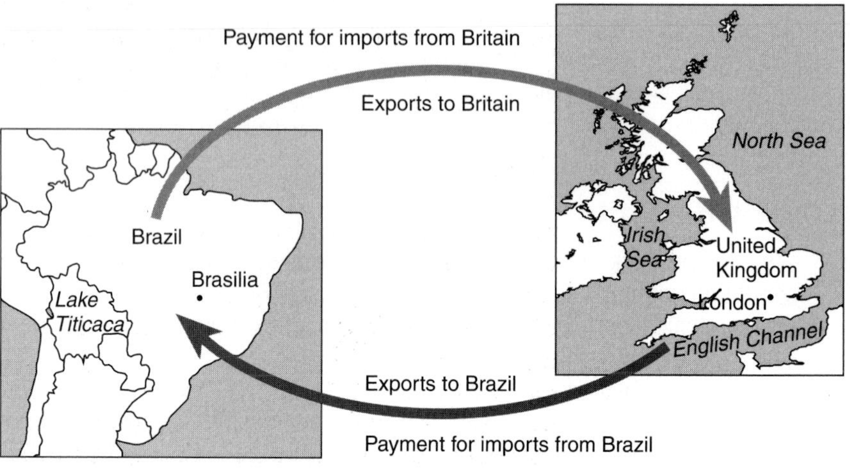

Efe village, Zaire

Using available resources

Any society, whether it is economically dependent or independent, must produce everything it wants from the **resources** that are available to it or to those countries with which it trades. The resources available to the Efe are very limited, so if they are to be satisfied, the wants of the Efe must be few. A society such as that in modern Britain, on the other hand, is able to satisfy a wider variety of wants because the resources available to it, and to the other societies and countries on which it depends, are far greater. In order to provide all the things society wants, however, Britain has had to develop a complex **economy** of interrelated factors. Action affecting one factor in the economy has effects on other factors.

Key Points

- *An* ***economy*** *is a system of interrelated factors that combine to satisfy the needs and wants of society.*

If people choose to buy more foreign cars, for example, this affects not only demand for British cars, which in turn results in fewer British cars being produced and a consequent reduction in employment in the British motor industry, but also demand for other British-made products that the now redundant car workers would have bought with their wages. By reducing interest rates, the Bank of England may be able to encourage motor manufacturers to reduce their prices or to buy new machinery that will produce higher quality cars more cost-effectively. Either could lead to a higher demand for British cars, increased employment, increased demand for other British goods and lower inflation.

The basic economic problem: scarcity, choice and the allocation of resources

Only space is infinite (as far as we know). Everything found on Earth is finite or, in other words, in limited supply. This is as true of naturally occurring resources such as water and the human labour required to operate water treatment plants in order to make the water fit to drink, as it is of the money used to finance the water treatment plants, pay the wages of the employees or enable the customers to pay their water bills.

Of course, the supply of some resources, such as the air that we breathe, while finite, is plentiful enough to satisfy everyone's needs. These are called **free resources**, or economically free goods. But the supply of most resources is limited in relation to the demands people put on them, and, where this is the case, the resource is said to be scarce. This is so even in the case of resources such as trees or wheat, which are renewable and replace themselves either naturally or through careful management.

Processing free resources – added value

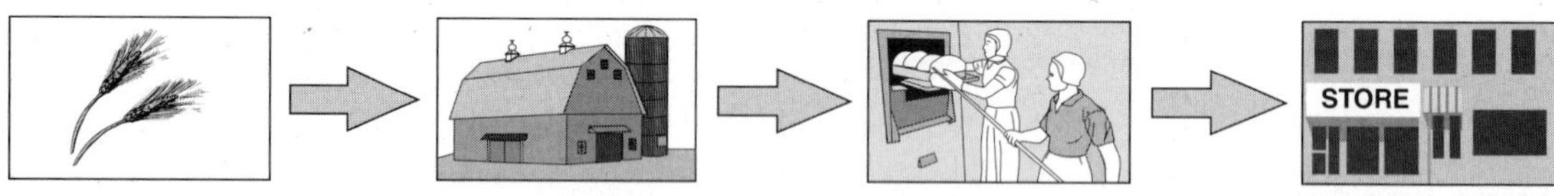

Wheat, which in its wild state is a free resource, is grown and harvested on the farm, with the aid of fertilisers, farm machinery and the farmer's labour. It is then turned into flour, and sent to bakeries, where it is turned into bread. Finally, the bread is delivered to shops, where it is sold to customers. At each stage of the production process, value is added to the original free resource, and this must be reflected in the final selling price.

Something to do

- Make a list of all the free resources you can think of that are provided by nature. Identify those that are **renewable** and those that are **non-renewable**. What does this tell society about using those resources?

1BN LITRES OF WATER MISSING

There is far less water good enough to drink in England and Wales than was previously supposed, the Environment Agency claims in a report today.

A new assessment concludes that a billion litres less is available from rivers, lakes and aquifers each day than was estimated in the early 1990s. The study, which has looked more closely at rainfall patterns over recent years, says that the North-West, Thames Valley, the West of England, and Wales are the hardest-hit areas.

Giles Phillips, the agency's head of water resources, said yesterday that the study underlined the need for small but important investment in better water treatment works, pumping equipment and less leaky pipes. The report will be especially worrying for water companies and their customers if the recent years of drought are continued and global warming forecasts prove sound.

"The new yields do show up concerns over the resilience of some water supply systems in the face of severe drought," Dr Phillips said.

The Government has asked the agency for advice on how water supplies can be better managed into the next century. Water companies have been asked to submit draft water resource and management plans by June this year.

Source: *The Times*, 24 March 1998

Think about it

- To what extent can water be said to be a scarce resource?
- What effect(s) do you think the widespread installation of water meters will have on the problem mentioned in the article?

Key Points

- ***Scarce resources*** *are those of which there is a limited supply, so that demand for them would exceed supply if they were freely available.*

Because the resources necessary to produce the goods and services that people want are scarce, individuals, firms and even governments can only obtain a certain amount of a resource to satisfy those wants at any one time. Also, the same resources that are used to produce one type of good or service cannot also be used to produce another. A tree that has been cut down and the timber used to produce furniture cannot be pulped to make paper. In the same way, if you have £50 to spend, you can purchase a pair of trainers costing £49.99, but you cannot also buy a CD costing £15 because you have already used your money resource. Similarly, the government cannot train additional doctors in an attempt to cut hospital waiting lists with the money it has already put into refurbishing schools.

Needs and wants

While resources are scarce, people's wants, on the other hand, are potentially unlimited.

People have basic needs that must be satisfied in order to sustain life, such as the needs for food, warmth, shelter and clothing. In addition, people have various psychological and social needs, such as the need for security, the need to belong to a family or social group, the need for recognition and esteem and the need to develop and achieve goals.

Basic needs can be satisfied in several ways. You can satisfy your need for clothing, for example, by buying a smartly tailored suit or a T-shirt and jeans. Your need is for clothing, but the suit or the T-shirt and jeans are what you want.

Key Points

- ***Basic needs*** *must be satisfied in order to sustain life.*
- ***Wants*** *are the ways in which we choose to satisfy our needs, and also to gain a level of satisfaction and enjoyment.*

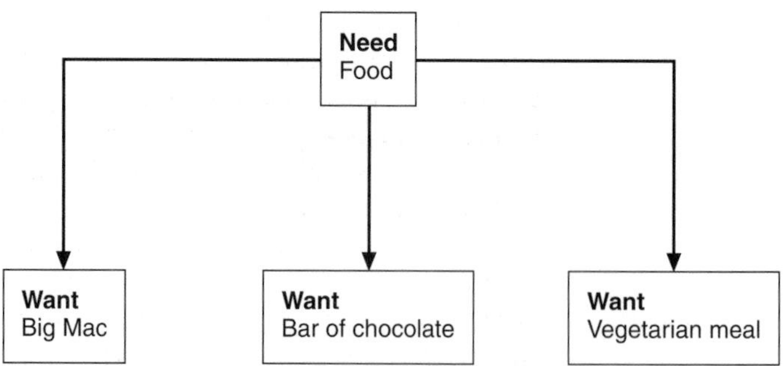

Fig. 1.3 The need for food can be satisfied in several ways

There are three principal reasons why people's wants usually exceed the ability of resources to satisfy them:

- Most things people buy eventually wear out and need to be replaced.
- As technology develops, new or improved products become available.
- People's tastes and fashions change. Generally, people will want new things that will satisfy their tastes and/or are in fashion.

What is effective demand?

Your wants will not be satisfied unless you have the money and are willing to pay for the things you want. **Effective demand** is created when people want something and are both able and willing to pay for it. In this way, demand is cumulative: the greater the number of people who want something and are able and willing to pay for it, the stronger will be the demand for it. The stronger the demand, the more likely a business or other organisation will be prepared to supply the item demanded. **Demand** and **supply** are important economic concepts; we look at them in detail in Unit 3.

Key Points

- ***Effective demand*** *is that part of society's wants that is supported by the willingness to pay an economic price. Effective demand for a product is measured in relation to the quantity of the product that is purchased over a particular period of time at a particular price.*

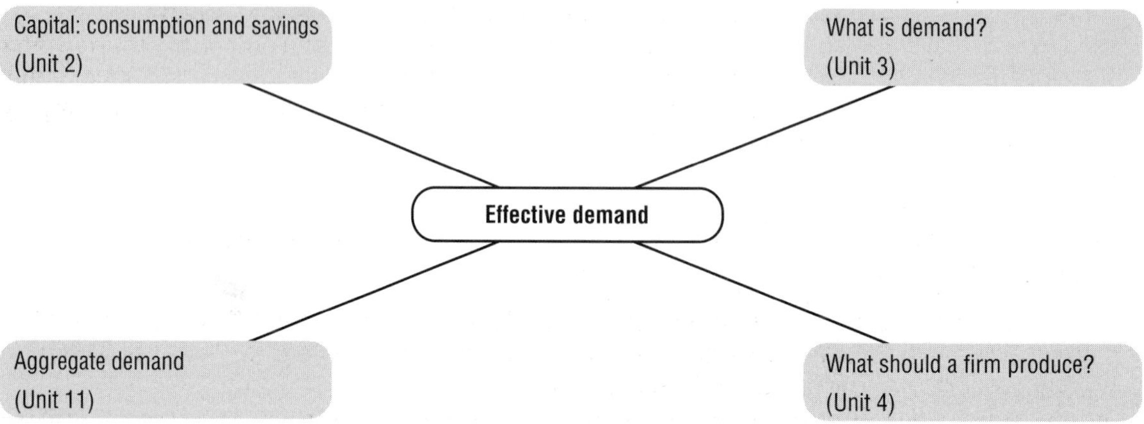

For example, in Britain, many people would like to own a Rolls Royce. To this extent they create a demand for Rolls Royces. But Rolls Royces are luxury motor cars, and cost a great deal to manufacture – so much, in fact, that few people can afford them. The demand created by those people who would like a Rolls Royce but cannot afford one, or would rather spend their money on something else, is obviously ineffective. No one is going to make a car that a lot of people want but will not buy. Fortunately for Rolls Royce, however, there are enough people who can both afford the price and are willing to pay it, so that over a period Rolls Royce is able to manufacture a quantity of their cars and to sell them to eager customers.

Three key questions

It is clear that satisfying our wants from scarce resources involves a choice. For us as individuals, the choice is: which of our wants do we satisfy? For example, if you want both a new pair of trainers and a CD, but only have enough money to buy one, you have to choose between them. This choice, although it may not be easy to make, is fairly straightforward. For society as a whole, however, the choice is far more complex. There are three basic questions that must be answered:

1. What should society produce, and how should resources be allocated?
   This is called the **allocation problem**. If a government allocates resources to providing accommodation for the homeless, the same resources cannot be allocated to improving healthcare for the elderly. Similarly, if labour and steel has been allocated to the production of cars, the same labour and steel cannot be used to produce up-to-date rolling stock for the railways.
2. How should goods and services be produced?
   This is called the production problem. For example, banks are rapidly introducing new technology to help them provide better and more cost-effective services for their customers. However, the new technology also means that there are fewer employment opportunities in the banking sector, thus increasing the level of unemployment in society.
3. Who should get the goods and services that are produced?
   This is called the **distribution problem**. Many people are unable to afford all the things that they need. Many elderly people, for example, cannot afford to heat their homes properly in the winter. Should heating for elderly people be provided by the State? Should single parents receive free childcare to enable them to find employment?

Think about it

- To what extent do you think the government should become involved in deciding how the allocation, production and distribution problems ought to be solved in the case of transport?
- What about essential items such as food and clothing?

Such questions must be answered by every society, no matter what its level of development. Even the Efe must decide whether to use the branches they gather for heating or for building homes. As we shall see, different societies address the 'three key questions' in different ways. The way a society chooses largely depends on its system of government and the type of its economy.

Food, glorious food

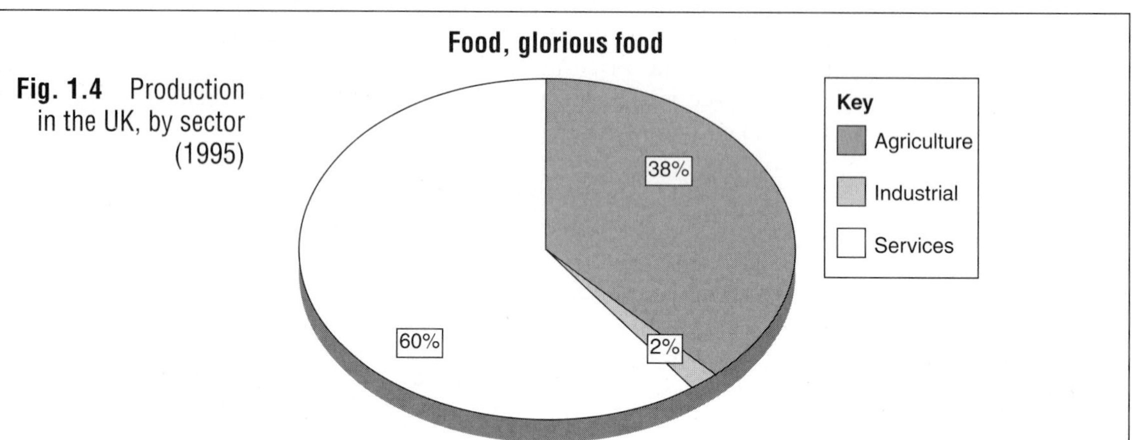

Fig. 1.4 Production in the UK, by sector (1995)

Food is one of the basic things people need in order to sustain life. It is essential for the survival of society, therefore, that some resources are allocated to the production of food, and that food is distributed in such a way as to enable everybody to obtain at least enough to live on.

In the United Kingdom, the production of food has to compete for available resources with all the other products that society wants. In fact, agricultural production (the basic source of food) accounts for less than 2 per cent of total production (see figure 1.4).

In 1995, this included 14 400 000 metric tons of wheat; 8 125 000 metric tons of sugar beet; 6 900 000 metric tons of barley; 6 445 000 metric tons of potatoes; 1 330 000 metric tons of rapeseed; 769 000 metric tons of cabbage; 750 000 metric tons of carrots; 600 000 metric tons of oats; 29 484 000 sheep; 11 868 000 cattle; and 7 879 000 pigs. The fish catch (1993 figure) was 905 656.

Both agriculture and industrial production have declined as percentages of total UK production. In 1976, agricultural production accounted for 3 per cent and industrial production nearly 43 per cent of total UK production. The decline in agricultural production is due to two basic factors affecting the way resources are allocated: increasing demand for land to be used for non-agricultural (and more profitable) purposes; and the tendency for people to look for work in non-agricultural occupations (where wages are higher). These factors have been partly offset through addressing the production problem by changing from labour-intensive methods to capital (machine) intensive methods. The increasing use of technology has also made agricultural land more productive. In addition, some food products are imported.

However, the decline in agriculture in the UK might give concern that sufficient food is available and distributed to those who need it. In the main, food is distributed throughout society in response to effective demand. This does, however, mean that whilst much of society is able to purchase all the food they need (if not all the food they want), there are some sections of society who would have difficulty doing so without help. These include the elderly; the long-term and short-term sick and disabled; single-parent households; the unemployed; and others on low incomes. In order to ensure the equitable distribution of food to these and other sections of society, therefore, the government makes welfare payments (pensions, incapacity benefits, unemployment benefit, etc.) in accordance with the perceived needs of individuals.

Source: *Encyclopaedia Britannica*, 1999

Economic systems and the role of government

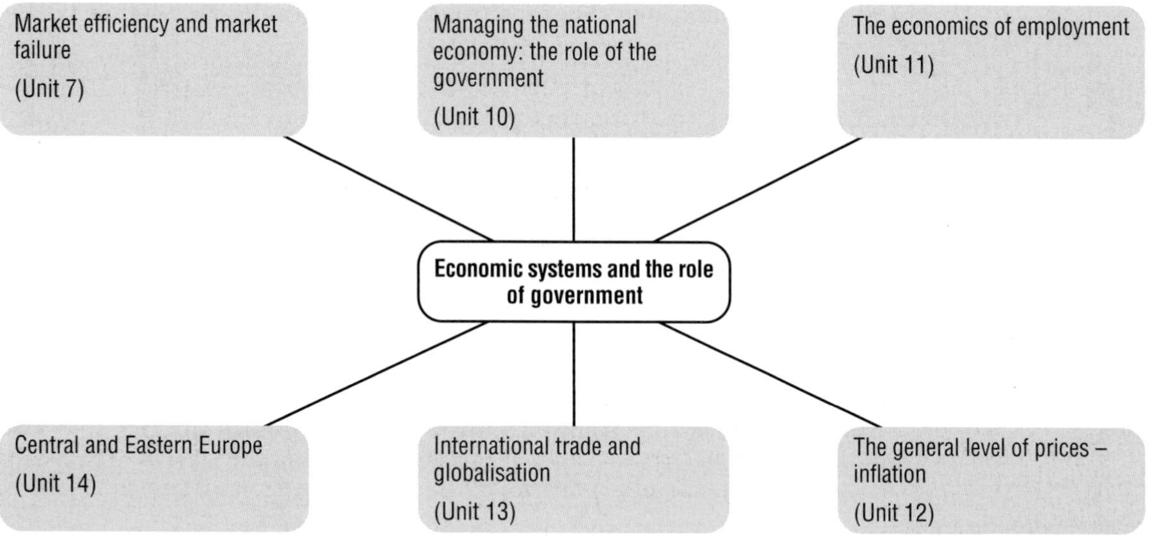

The people and institutions that combine together to convert resources into finished products and distribute them to users collectively form the economic system or the economy. As we have seen, a modern economy is a complex system. While no two economies are exactly the same, it is possible to identify three general types of economic system or economy:

- the **market economy**
- the **centralised** or command economy
- the **mixed economy**.

Each type of economic system is characterised by the role played by its government in taking decisions and influencing the operation of the economy. Figure 1.5 illustrates the relationship between the type of economy and the level of government intervention.

Fig. 1.5 The continuum of government intervention in an economy

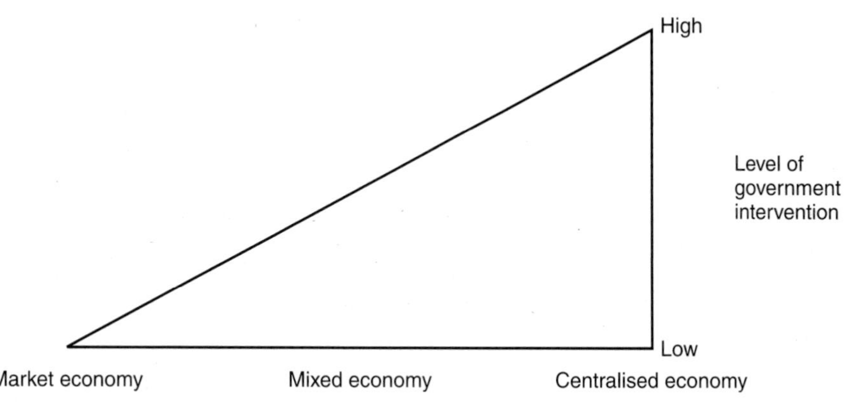

The market economy

A market economy is one in which consumers (buyers) choose which goods and services they want, and producers (sellers) decide what they are going to supply – and, therefore, how economic resources are allocated – without any government control or interference. Three conditions are necessary for goods or services to be produced in this economy.

1. There must be an effective demand for the goods or services – people must be willing and able to buy them at prevailing prices.
2. Producers must be able to sell their goods and services at a profit – there is no point in producing goods at a cost of £2 each and selling them for £1.50 each.
3. There must be a means by which potential buyers and producers can communicate their intentions.

In general, in such an economy consumers can be expected to buy the goods that they can afford, that will satisfy their wants and that will give them the best value for money. Producers will supply those goods that they can sell and that will provide them with a profit. Those producing goods that consumers do not buy, or which are not sold at a profit, are likely to go out of business. Thus, in a market economy, the following hold true:

- Consumers, by choosing what they want to buy, influence how resources are used: the resources are employed in industries that produce goods that consumers will buy.
- Industries and businesses that produce goods that consumers are not willing to buy will go into decline and their resources (labour, land and capital) will become unemployed or be allocated to other types of production.

> ***Think about it***
>
> - What services do you use that are provided by the State, so that you do not have to pay for them? Think of items such as roads, and services such as your local reference library.
> - What would happen if these were not produced or made freely available to you and other users?
> - What do you think would be the effect of a decision by the government that in future everyone who used services and other items provided by the State had to pay the actual cost of using them?

Producers who are sellers in one market are buyers in other markets: they have to purchase the resources they need. Like consumers, they want to obtain the best value for money. If labour becomes too expensive, for example, employers may buy machinery instead. In this way, they aim to produce goods as efficiently as possible.

In the market economy, this combination of consumers seeking the best value for money and producers seeking efficient and cost-effective production determines the use of resources. In practice, however, there are many obstacles that prevent the smooth working of the market system. For example, producers may get together to fix prices so that consumers do not have a free choice. Another problem is that some essential goods or services may be too expensive for many consumers. In cases such as these, the market is said to have failed. We consider **market failure** in more detail in Unit 7.

Think about it

- Many industries, such as banking and farming, have introduced new technology. This has often resulted in fewer people being employed in these industries, because the new technology has enabled one employee to do the work that previously required several employees. Do you think this has benefited
  - society
  - the industries involved?

The centralised or command economy

Some societies do not trust the market mechanism, and in extreme cases they abandon it completely. Although the reason for this may be mainly political, there are clear economic implications.

Instead of the market determining what is produced and how it is produced, decisions are taken by the government, or by agencies appointed by the government, covering:

- production (what goods and services should be produced); this involves the allocation of economic resources such as labour
- distribution (who should receive the goods and services that are produced).

The basic economic problem is the same: there are insufficient resources to produce everything that is wanted. Choices have to be made. It is unlikely that the pattern of production will be the same when the decisions about what should be produced and how resources should be allocated are made by governments as it is when such decisions are left to consumers and producers. This is because a government is likely to have different priorities to those of individuals. An ordinary citizen might prefer to spend all his or her income on food, drinks, clothes, housing and holidays. A government, on the other hand, might decide that a proportion of everyone's income should be spent on defence and that expenditure on holidays is less essential.

While this kind of economy can avoid what some see as the waste associated with market economies (the money spent on advertising virtually identical products, for example), it does have the important disadvantage of needing a large number of administrators to make decisions. This might be just as wasteful as some of the activities of the market economies.

What has happened in practice is that most economies have developed as a mixture between the market economy and the centralised economy.

The mixed economy

Here an attempt is made to strike some kind of balance between the market economy and the government-controlled economy. The balance between the two will vary from country to country, the degree of government involvement depending on the political objectives of the government itself.

There are a number of ways in which the government may move the economy away from a free-market situation:

- The government may itself supply certain goods or services directly to consumers. Education and medicine are examples where governments may feel that the services are too important to be left to the market – or where market prices may be too high for some consumers.
- The government may set up special organisations to supply some basic goods or services, such as postal services. These organisations need not be required to make a profit.
- The government may, through its taxation policy, discourage the consumption and therefore the production of some goods, such as cigarettes and alcohol.
- Similarly, a government may encourage the production of other goods by contributing to or subsidising part of the costs of production. Some governments encourage food production in this way.
- Finally, the government may affect all kinds of economic activity by means of legislation. For example, the minimum wage that must be paid by employers in Europe has been established by law (see Unit 13). Other laws control the use of dangerous materials such as asbestos.

Fig. 1.6 Examples of today's economies

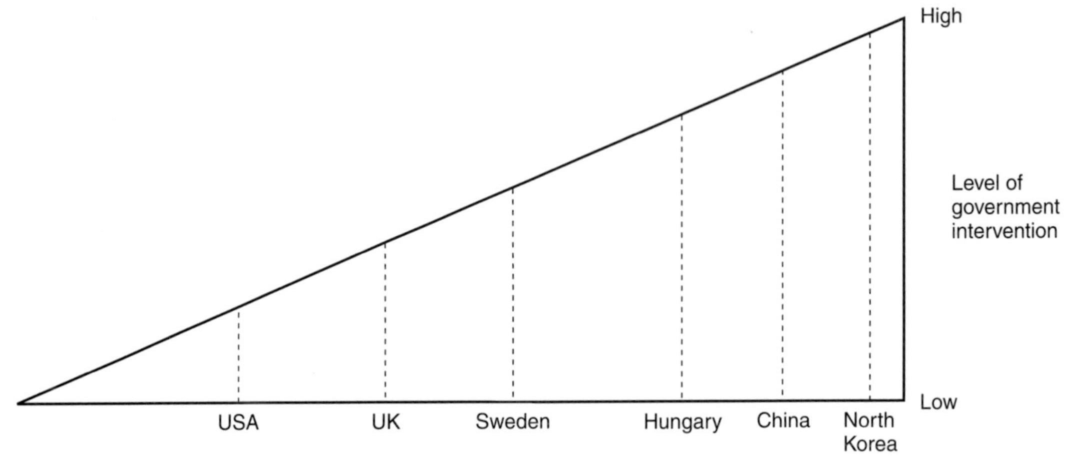

From the free market to central control – examples of today's economies

While no economy is completely controlled by either government or market forces, economies can be identified as being market-based or centralised (see Figure 1.6). The economy of the USA is left largely to the influence of the market, while North Korea has what is probably the closest approach to a completely controlled economy that currently exists in the world. The UK economy is a mixed economy, in which the government intervenes both by influencing demand (and therefore the provision of goods and services) through welfare payments and by itself providing goods and services. Services such as health and education are provided both by the State and privately, while services such as social security are provided almost exclusively by the State. There is some direct control of industrial production, through nationalised industries, although since the 1980s the tendency has been to return nationalised industries to private ownership.

Sweden is an exemplar of a social-welfare state, in which income is redistributed by the government through welfare payments, and around one-third of Sweden's **gross domestic product** (see Unit 9) is devoted to public social protection (maternity benefits, family allowances, free childcare, education, healthcare, vacation grants for housewives, free marital counselling, pensions, home help, etc.). On the other hand, governmental control of production through measures such as nationalisation has never played a large part in Sweden's economic policy.

In Hungary, although the old-style control of the Stalinist regime was abandoned in the 1950s, the State still owns all important industrial and other organisations such as banks, and the government intervenes to a large extent in business and the economy through subsidies, price controls and foreign exchange.

China is an economy in transition. For many thousands of years, the economy has been centralised, partly due to the need for co-ordination of such services as irrigation. However, in 1992, Deng Xiaoping embarked on a programme designed to lead China to become a 'socialist market economy' in which State-owned institutions would remain the mainstay of the economy, but included in the system would also be market-led institutions providing financial services, real estate and information technology. Even in North Korea, total control of the economy by the Communist regime is an impossibility. North Korea is not self-sufficient in food production, and persistent food shortages give rise both to commercial fishing along the east coast and a flourishing black market. Commercial forestry is also well developed, especially in the forested northern mountain regions.

EAT TV, DRINK TV, SLEEP TV – AN EXAMINATION OF CURRENT DEVELOPMENTS IN TELEVISED SPORT

Rob Lightfoot and Simon Chadwick

THE traditionally regulated environment within which sport is televised no longer offers the certainty that spectators, organisers or television companies were once able to take for granted. Although there have been calls for a renewed system of government regulation, the globalisation of world television markets and the operation (and success) of free markets may prove to be irresistible. If regulation is the key, then a considered response will be a must. Making a case for implementing restrictions on the amount of coverage, listing of events or quality of the coverage would seem to be a difficult task. From a free-market perspective there is little reason to over-burden the market with excessive controls. Nevertheless, it wouldn't be unreasonable to consider the merits of some price control to ensure that the welfare of the consumer isn't compromised. Prices are, however, apt to reflect the development costs that accrue to the broadcaster, and consequently there is a fine balance to be struck. Quite how a domestic government might regulate global corporations such as News International (owners of BSkyB) is open to question; the use of domestic or continental competition possibilities is one option, but it is unlikely that technology will allow a return to the monopoly or duopoly of previous years.

Some have taken a slightly less serious view of the form that future regulation should take. J. Duncan suggests that the armchair sports fan should indeed be protected against changes in television sport. Amongst his suggestions for statutes are that the music by the Lightning Seeds should be reinstated to the goal-of-the-month competition on *Match of the Day*, that pay-for-view should be a two-way street and that viewers should receive bonuses of 50 pence for each time a football commentator didn't understand the laws of the game. If only it were that simple for a single viewer, company or government to exercise such control!

Source: Adapted from *Teaching Economics and Business*, vol. 2, no. 3, Autumn 1998

Think about it

Increasingly, the rights to televise major sporting events are being bought by privately owned television companies and broadcast on a 'pay-per-view' basis. In their article 'Eat TV, Drink TV, Sleep TV', Lightfoot and Chadwick suggest that while there have been calls for a renewed system of government regulation, this would prove difficult and may be ineffective.

- Do you think that the right to televise major sporting events should go to the highest bidder?
- Should the owner of the rights to televise an event such as the World Cup be able to charge viewers to watch each match?
- If a company such as BSkyB buys the rights to televise sporting events and then charges viewers for watching, what are the implications for (a) sports fans and (b) sporting events?

The role of government

Governments can play a significant role in influencing and directing the economy of a country. The actual role played by a particular government, and the amount of economic control exerted, will largely depend on its political views and policies. However, the economic activities of most governments are directed towards four aims:

1. supplementing the **market forces** of demand and supply, to ensure that those goods and services considered important to the well-being of society, for example, defence, law and order, the fire service, are produced and made available to those sections of the community who need them. These are termed 'collective goods' since they affect the well-being of society as a whole. At the same time, a government will prohibit, or control, the production of goods and services considered undesirable or harmful to society
2. ensuring fair play in the market place by regulating the activities of producers and suppliers in order to protect the interests of consumers
3. helping economically disadvantaged sections of the community by redistributing income through taxation and welfare benefits. These are 'merit goods' and are benefits which every person should enjoy.
4. providing assistance for producers and suppliers. This assistance may be in the form of grants and subsidies, or improved opportunities such as those provided by the European Union and trading agreements with other countries.

Economics can be divided into micro-economics and macro-economics.

- **Micro-economics** analyses the various economic principles, such as demand and supply (see Unit 3), or the theory of the firm (see Unit 4).
- **Macro-economics** looks at how these micro-economic principles affect society in areas such as unemployment (see Unit 11), inflation (see Unit 12), and international trade (see Unit 13).

The economic objectives of governments are usually macro-economic.

Market and planned economies

In a market economy, co-ordination of demand for and supply of goods and services is principally achieved through the free and spontaneous movement of market prices which themselves react to the forces of demand and supply (see Unit 3). Any shortage (or surplus) of a commodity will cause its relative price to rise (or fall). This will result in an increase (or decrease) in the quantity supplied and a decrease (or increase) in the quantity demanded, and the shortage (or surplus) will be reduced or eliminated.

Ideally, a market economy also provides for consumer sovereignty. Consumer demand determines what is produced in the economy. Of course, the consumer may be manipulated by the marketing of producers and suppliers. Nevertheless, if consumers cannot be convinced to buy a particular product, production of that product will ultimately cease.

This is not always true in centrally planned economies, where shortages and surpluses may arise from a mismatch of planners' priorities and consumer demand. A planned economy is, quite simply, one in which the co-ordination of long-run and/or short-run decisions is attempted by means of a central plan, which is designed to guide the economy towards certain goals or objectives.

Directive planning (or command planning), which has been employed in the former Soviet Union, China, Eastern Europe, and the US military, is a system whereby the most important long-run and short-run decisions are made by the central planning authority and are then passed down to subordinates in the form of instructions, directives or commands. A directive plan typically includes an annual target for each factory and each important product, and compliance is compulsory. A centrally planned economy (CPE) is a country that employs directive planning as its predominant co-ordinating mechanism. Countries that are attempting to replace directive planning with market institutions are now commonly known as transitional economies (TEs).

Source: Adapted from H.S. Gardner, *Comparative Economic Systems* (Dryden Press, Fort Worth, Texas, USA, 2nd edn 1998)

What are economic resources?

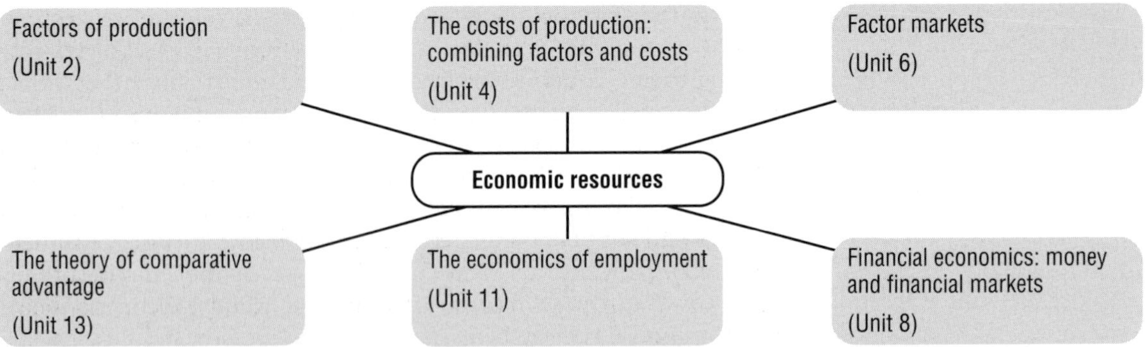

We have seen that society uses **economic resources** to produce the goods and services it wants. Because they are essential to all forms of production, these resources are frequently referred to as **factors of production.** There are four basic categories of factors of production: land, capital, labour and entrepreneurship (see Figure 1.7).

Fig. 1.7 Combining the factors of production

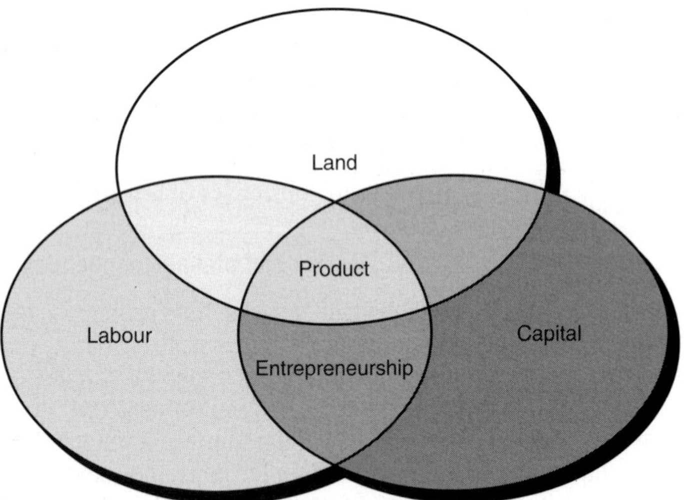

Land

Here the term land is used in its broadest sense. It consists of all **natural resources**, including

- agricultural and building land
- mines and quarries
- rivers, oceans and the atmosphere
- mineral deposits
- forests and crops.

A feature of land is that it involves no **cost of production**, although there may be a cost of extracting, refining or growing the resource. Oil, for example, is freely available in the sedimentary rocks of the Earth's crust. However, extracting the oil, refining it and making it conveniently available to customers is a very expensive process, and this is why, although the oil itself may be free when it is still in the rock, it is expensive to buy when it is in the garage.

Some land resources, such as air and seawater, are plentiful and freely available to everyone. These are called **environmental free goods**. Other resources, such as oil, are limited and may be used up in the foreseeable future. Resources such as wheat and trees are renewable, at least in the long run, in that new stocks can be grown.

Modern society relies heavily on the large-scale consumption of natural resources, so there is a real danger of these resources being used up. Some renewable resources, such as fish stocks, are being consumed faster than they can be renewed. In some urban areas, for example Tokyo, the emission of waste products is polluting the atmosphere, so that even environmental free goods such as air to breathe are becoming scarce. Conservation of natural resources is, therefore, of increasing concern to modern society.

Something to do

- Select a non-renewable land resource, such as coal or oil, and find out the current estimates of how long it will be before your chosen resource runs out.
  Useful sources of information are yearbooks and works of reference such as the *Encyclopaedia Britannica*, magazines such as *The Economist* and newspapers such as *The Times* and the *Independent*. Information about specific resources may also be obtained from commercial producers, such as Esso (oil) and RJB Mining (coal), and non-commercial organisations such as Friends of the Earth. Many of these have Internet sites that might help your investigation.
- What will be the consequences to society when the resource does run out?
- What should we be doing *now* to lessen the effects of the resource running out?

Capital

Unlike land, **capital** is an **artificial resource**. That is, it is made by people to help in the production of other goods and services. There are two types of capital:

- **Working capital** is made up of raw materials, goods being processed and finished goods not yet sold. Working capital, or **variable capital**, is sometimes also called **circulating capital**, as it 'circulates' in the production process while it is being changed from raw material to finished good (see Figure 1.8).

Fig. 1.8 The flow of working capital

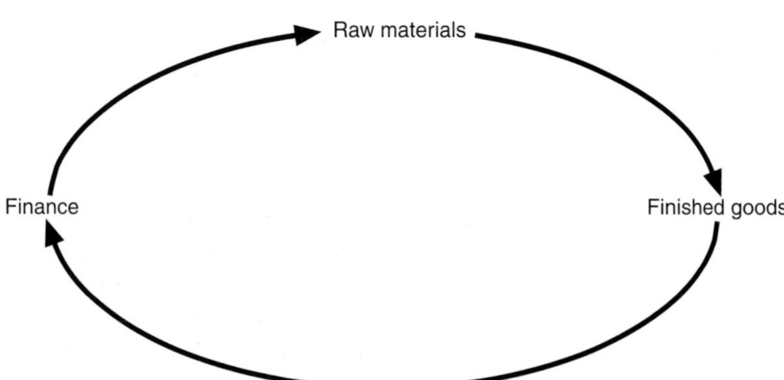

- **Fixed capital** includes those goods that are part of the production process but are not used up in producing individual units. Plant and machinery, factories and office buildings, electricity pylons and so on are all fixed capital. Roads, schools and hospitals are also types of fixed capital. Since they are not used directly in the production of goods and services, however, but are part of the nation's stock of assets, they are called **social capital.** Social capital makes an important indirect contribution to the production of goods and services, and to the well-being of society.

Labour

Labour is work performed by the world's population, and includes not only labour performed in exchange for a wage or salary payment, but also work undertaken within the family or household. All kinds of human occupation and effort are included here, both physical work and skilled mental effort. The skills acquired by a trained workforce constitute human capital.

Entrepreneurship

An **entrepreneur** is a person who takes risks by investing his or her own money in a project with a view to making a profit. He or she makes all the major decisions, and takes all the profits or, if necessary, meets the losses. In a large business, these roles are divided between various people (see Unit 2).

The above division of the factors of production is fairly arbitrary, and there is often an overlap between some of them. We might, for example, consider a newly discovered region purely as land. But if we were to use it for agriculture, the land might then contain a considerable amount of capital in the form of artificial fertilisers. Or suppose the land contains rich mineral deposits: we might then consider these to be a part of our capital. Labour also contains an element of capital: the skills that a trainee learns in training may be regarded as an investment that will contribute to future production. Clearly, too, entrepreneurship is not totally separate from labour. To avoid this kind of overlap it is sometimes more convenient to divide the factors of production into only two groups:

- human economic resources
- non-human economic resources.

However economic resources are classified, the whole point of economic activity is to use these resources to produce the goods and services that society requires. The resources *currently available* are a stock of wealth that has been accumulated from past production. We look at economic resources, or the factors of production, in more detail in Unit 2.

Something to do

- Identify the economic resources that are used in your school, college or place of work.
- Where do they come from and how are they obtained?

Production

Production can be defined as the process of combining factors of production to convert raw materials into finished goods and services. Since there is a limited amount of each factor of production, there is a limit to what can be produced.

Fig. 1.9 Production possibilities

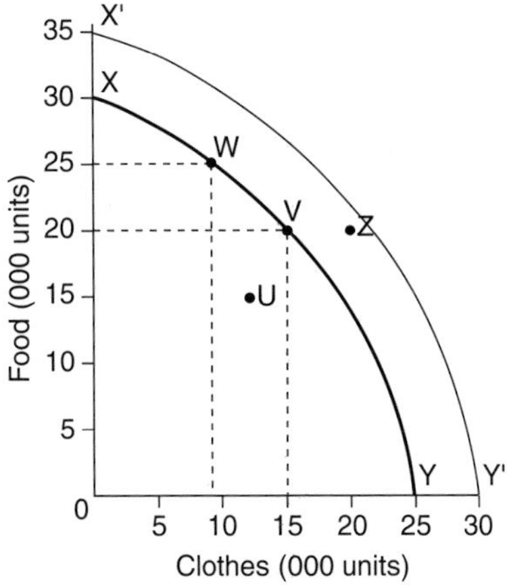

Production possibility curves

Consider the situation illustrated in Figure 1.9. This represents a country that uses all its resources to produce food and clothes. If only food was produced, it could produce 30 000 units; if all the resources were used for clothes, 25 000 units could be produced. The line XY, therefore, shows all the combinations of food and clothes that could be produced in this country.

Somehow the community has to decide what combination of the two goods to produce. To make the best use of its resources, the country will need to be somewhere on the line XY, otherwise it will be producing less than it is capable of. Thus it could be at point W, producing 25 000 units of food and 9000 units of clothes; or at point V, producing 20 000 and 15 000 units. Notice that if production is anywhere on the curve XY, the output of one type of good can be increased only by reducing the output of the other. The line XY shows the maximum levels of production and is known as the **production possibility curve** or **production possibility frontier.**

Production cannot, therefore, be at point Z, which represents an output of 20 000 units of each product. It is impossible to produce both food and clothes in these volumes using currently available resources. Therefore, there must be a mechanism that allows a choice to be made, so that a desirable combination of the two goods is produced.

However, an increase in the availability or productive efficiency of resources could push the production possibility frontier to the right, to give a new possibility frontier X'Y', allowing a higher level of production to be achieved.

Think about it

- In the example in Figure 1.9, why can't both food and clothes be produced in greater quantities? How can an increase in available resources alter this?

If production was at point U, on the other hand, the country would be producing below capacity, since production of both clothes and food can be increased. Less than full-capacity production may be caused by unemployment, by unused facilities, such as empty factories, by unused machinery or other resources, or by inefficient production processes.

You should note that the production possibility frontier is a curve. This is mainly because some resources are more suitable to the production of one type of good than another, thus, as more of one good is produced, proportionately more of its alternative must be sacrificed to achieve an increase. In this example, some resources, such as cotton, sewing machines and the labour of skilled tailors, will be more suited to producing clothes than food. As resources are reallocated from producing food to producing clothes, the first resources to be reallocated will be those most suited to a change in use, for example land used to grow cotton may be used to grow wheat. As more and more resources are reallocated, they will be less and less suited to producing the new commodity. This is an example of the principle of **diminishing returns**, which we examine in more detail in connection with land in Unit 2.

Economic efficiency

The term **economic efficiency** (explained in Unit 7) is used to describe the effectiveness of the allocation of factors of production in an economic system to meet the needs and wants of society. In order to assess the economic efficiency of a particular economy, therefore, we must

- find out which goods and services will yield the greatest satisfaction to society, and their relative importance
- establish the factors of production required to produce those goods and services, and in what proportions
- use those factors of production as efficiently as possible.

In the economy represented in Figure 1.9, therefore, for optimum economic efficiency to be achieved production needs to be at the point on line XY that reflects society's relative demand for food and clothes. Production at any other point would represent less than optimum efficiency.

Something to do

The following table shows the production of consumer goods and producer goods that a country can achieve using existing resources.

Product	Units produced		
Consumer goods	10 000	6 000	0
Producer goods	0	3 800	6 000

- Use the data to produce a production possibility curve. The vertical axis on your chart should represent consumer goods and the horizontal axis should represent producer goods. The scale on each axis should be the same and begin at 0. Current production is 6000 units of consumer goods and 3800 units of producer goods.
  - If production of consumer goods was increased to 8000 units, what would be the effect on production of producer goods?
  - If production of consumer goods was 5000 units and production of producer goods was 3400 units, what would you conclude from this?

What does society really produce?

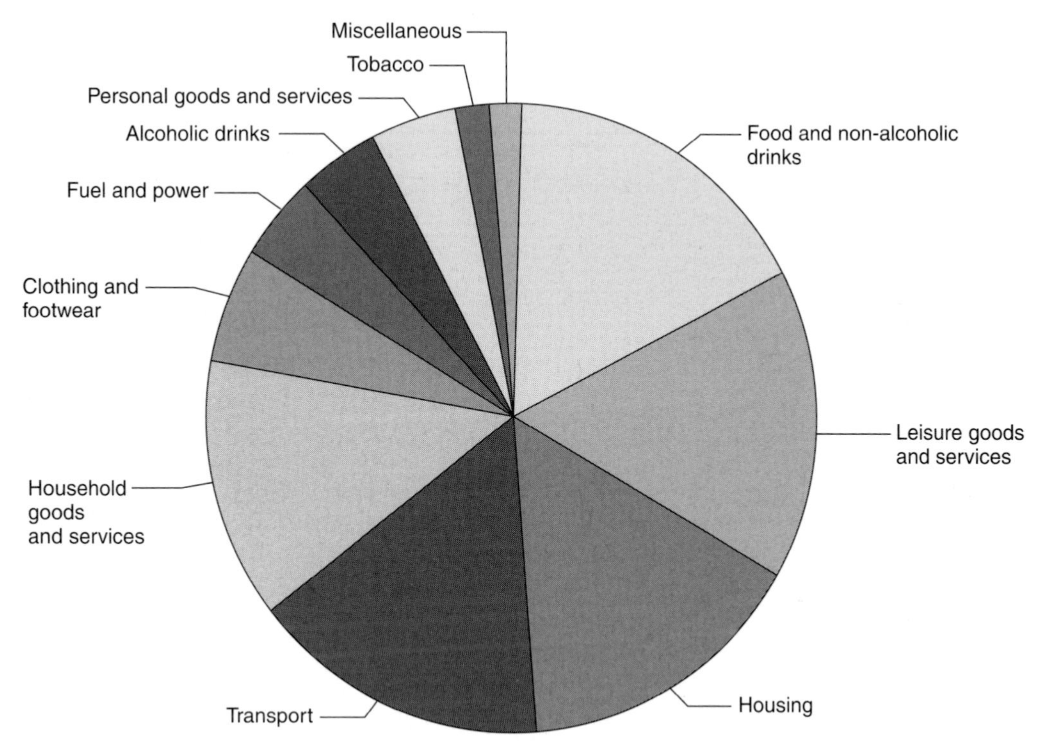

The pie chart shows the types of goods and services produced by society, and on which consumers spend their incomes. Each segment represents the proportion of total average weekly household expenditure spent on each type of product in the UK during 1996/7. From this it can easily be seen that a household can only spend more – that is, allocate more of its financial resources – to one commodity by spending less on another with its existing income. Spending more on, say, clothing and footwear, will increase the size of that segment of the chart, squeezing the other segments.

Source: Adapted from *Economics Today*, vol. 6, no. 3, January 1999

Costs in economics

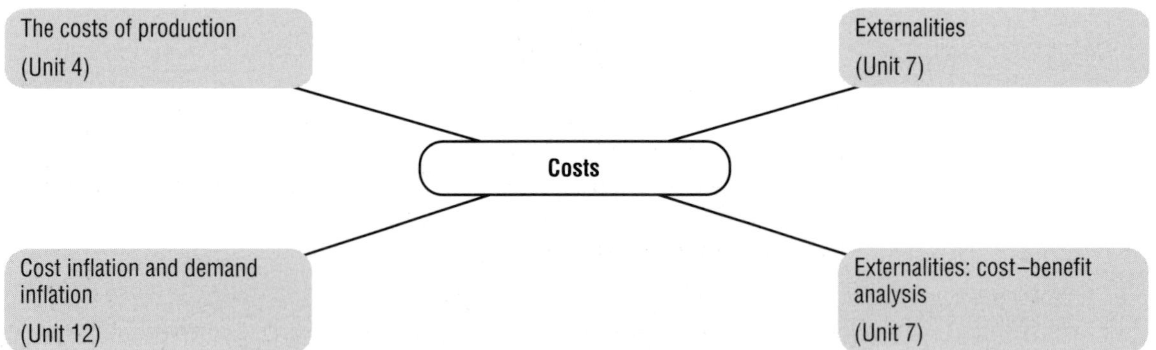

Costs may be expressed in different ways:

- **accounting costs**, which are expressed in terms of money
- **opportunity costs**, which are expressed in terms of alternatives sacrificed
- **private costs**, which are the costs to individuals and organisations
- **social costs**, which are borne by the whole of society.

Accounting costs

In everyday language, the cost of something is measured by the amount of money required to purchase it or to buy the factors of production needed to produce it. For example, the cost of a magazine might be £2. This £2 is the amount required to pay for the labour and other resources used in the production of the magazine, including an element of profit for the entrepreneur. Clearly this is an important way of measuring costs, and it is convenient for both individuals and businesses to compare the money costs of two different lines of activity. We may regard such costs as accounting costs in that they are the figures that an accountant would use to measure the costs of production.

Key Points

- ***Accounting costs*** *are the costs of factors of production necessarily incurred in the production process.*

Types of accounting costs include

- labour
- raw materials
- overheads
- advertising
- the costs of transporting and delivering goods.

Opportunity cost

As well as accounting costs, there is a further real cost of any particular action. Suppose that you have £15 to spend and are undecided between buying a CD and a book. Eventually you decide to purchase the book, so you cannot buy the CD. The benefit or enjoyment you would have obtained from the CD is the opportunity cost of purchasing the book instead.

Similarly, if some economic resources are used to produce motor vehicles for one group of people, those resources cannot be used to produce the refrigerators required by other people. Thus the fundamental principle is that society cannot produce anything without denying itself something else. This is the idea of opportunity cost, which derives from the unavoidable scarcity of economic resources.

Key Points

- ***Opportunity costs*** *are the benefits that would have been obtained from the next best alternative use of scarce resources.*

Opportunity cost can be shown in graphical form on a production possibility curve. It is the amount by which the level of production of one type of good is affected by changes in the level of production of a second type of good. Thus, in the example on page 31, if the current level of food production is 20 000 units, the effect of raising this to 25 000 units is a reduction in the level of clothes production from 15 000 units to 9000 units. We can therefore say that in this example, the opportunity cost of choosing to increase food by 5000 units is 6000 units of clothes.

Think about it

- In the production possibility curve you produced for the activity on page 32, if the current production of producer goods is 2800 units, what is the opportunity cost of increasing this to 3600?

Decisions are often complicated by conflicting objectives, however, which may lead to compromise and trade-offs. For example, the government may want to attract more people into nursing and see raising the general level of nurses' pay by 4 per cent as one way of doing this. However, another objective of the government may be to improve care for the elderly by building new day centres in every community. Clearly, with limited resources, these objectives conflict: one cannot be achieved without sacrificing the other. The government cannot raise the level of nurses' pay by 4 per cent *and* build its intended number of day centres. The government therefore has to trade off one objective against the other, so that the optimum benefit to society and use of resources is achieved.

Private, social and external costs

There is another respect in which the accounting costs considered above are an incomplete way of measuring the true costs of many types of economic activity. This arises because some kinds of production incur costs that the accountant does not consider. For example, when a road haulage company sends a lorry from London to Birmingham, it must charge a rate that gives an adequate profit. This will take account of such costs as the purchase price of the vehicle, the fuel, the driver's wages and insurance. These are **private costs** – costs that have to be covered by the road haulage company.

> **Key Points**
>
> - ***Private costs*** *are those costs that are directly borne by a supplier in producing goods or services. They can normally be expressed quantitatively in terms of money.*

But there are other costs associated with the journey that the company itself does not have to bear. These include the lorry's contribution to traffic congestion, atmospheric pollution and noise pollution, the effects of which are difficult to quantify or give a money value. Costs such as these are borne not by the operator but by society as a whole, although society may impose taxes on the operator so that some kind of contribution is made.

> **Key Points**
>
> - ***Social costs*** *include private costs and the external costs that may be by-products of the production process and are borne by society as a whole. They may be expressed in qualitative rather than quantitative terms.*

Social costs = private costs + external costs

> *Something to do*
>
> - As a class, or in pairs, discuss what you think are the social costs of
>   - constructing a new bypass to avoid a rural market town
>   - producing coal
>   - opening a new supermarket on an out-of-town site.
> - Are there any social *benefits* that might counterbalance these costs? Discuss what these might be, and whether you think they outweigh the social costs in each case.

Social costs and social benefits are examples of **externalities**, which is the name given to the situation which occurs when the people or institution not directly involved with an activity are nevertheless affected by it, either favourably or unfavourably (see also Unit 7, pages 242–267).

Production and consumption

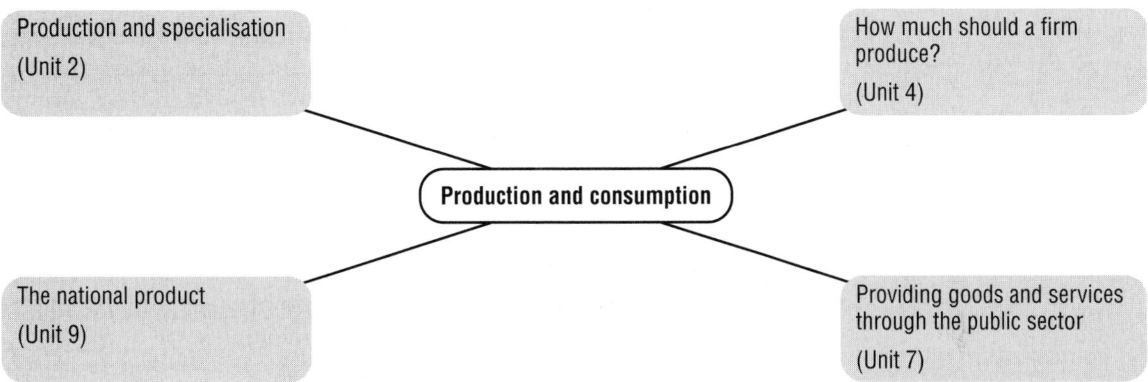

In most developed economies, the choice of what is produced depends largely on the consumer's ability and willingness to buy. To be willing to buy a product, the purchaser must expect to obtain some satisfaction from that product. Manufacturers will only be able to sell, and therefore will only produce, goods that give satisfaction to consumers.

Utility

Another way of looking at this is to say that consumers will consider buying goods only if they will be able to derive some **utility** from them. The word 'utility' is used here in a technical economic sense and means the ability to satisfy consumers' wants or desires. Something that has utility is not necessarily useful. People wear decorative jewellery not because it is useful but because it gives them satisfaction. Although many goods – known as **producer goods** – are brought not by consumers but by manufacturers to help in the process of production, the same argument can be applied. A firm will buy a machine only if the machine can yield satisfaction by producing the goods that the firm wishes to sell.

Key Points

- *Utility is the amount of satisfaction to be obtained from the purchase of one unit of a product.*

The object of production, therefore, is to convert factors of production into goods and services that yield satisfaction to consumers or other producers. Any good that ceases to give utility or satisfaction will, in a free market, soon cease to be produced, as no one would buy it. For example, tastes in the fashion industry change rapidly; last season's clothes no longer give utility and so are no longer produced, as there is no demand for them and they would not be sold. We return to the concept of utility in our discussion of 'demand' in Unit 3.

Basic concepts and tools of economic analysis

We have established that economics is concerned with how scarce economic resources are allocated to the production of the goods and services wanted by society. There are various ways in which an economist might investigate the processes that occur within an economy:

- An economist might simply observe what is going on and record it. It would be a relatively straightforward business to determine how many cars or houses had been produced and how many people were employed in each industry at a particular time.
- If this information were collected for a number of years it might become more useful – the economist could analyse it and perhaps detect certain trends in the economy. It might become apparent that the output of some industries was expanding while that of others was in decline. Still, this is an examination only of what has already occurred. This is the kind of information shown in Figure 1.1.
- A third, more important, and more technical possibility is to use observations of what has happened in the past, of how people and organisations have behaved, to formulate theories about the effects or consequences of future economic policies or actions. Theories are general statements that try to explain relationships and events in the world around us. In this respect, an economist is a social scientist and as such is in a more difficult position than a physical scientist, such as a physicist or a chemist, who is able to create the conditions required to test a particular theory in the laboratory.

When investigating the operation of an economy, an economist is dealing with people, and people are not only different, they are unpredictable. A physicist or a chemist is able to carry out carefully controlled experiments in a laboratory. Variables such as temperature or the presence of oxygen can be eliminated, other factors introduced and the effects observed. On the strength of these observations firm assertions can be made about how the world behaves. An economist, however, cannot put people into a laboratory to carry out controlled experiments on them. What he or she must do is examine society as it is, study its reactions to past experiments in economic policy, and on this basis try to forecast its response to new policy initiatives. In this way, the economist builds **economic models** that highlight aspects of economic life.

What is an economic model?

An economic model is a representation of an economy (or part of an economy) which enables the relationship between certain causes and effects to be examined. For example, the total demand for a product depends on a large number of factors, such as

- the price of the product
- the price of related products
- the level of consumers' incomes
- advertising
- government policies
- the weather.

A firm may want to know the likely effects on the demand for its product if consumers' incomes rise. This will be difficult to determine if at the same time as incomes rise all other influences are changing as well. An economist could, however, construct a model allowing all influences to be held constant except consumers' incomes. Using this model, the economist could then examine the likely impact of a change in income on the quantity demanded. (This is known as the principle of ***ceteris paribus***.) That would be a very simple economic model, but it could subsequently be made more sophisticated and complex by allowing other influences to change.

It is important to be clear about the value of economic models. They do *not* tell us what should be done: their purpose is to describe a situation and predict the consequences of certain actions. For example, the government might wish to reduce the burden of taxes by a billion pounds. This might be achieved in a number of ways: a reduction in the basic rate of income tax, a reduction in the higher rate of income tax, a decrease in value added tax or excise duties, or a combination of these.

Think about it

- Figure 1.8 on page 29 shows a simple economic model. What does it tell us about working capital and how working capital is used?

The Treasury has a very complex model of the economy, which allows projected changes to be fed into it so that the likely consequences of each can be assessed. It is then a political decision as to which course of action is taken, based on the policies of the government. It is not a matter of a unique correct answer to the problem being shown by the model. The economist can point out the likely effects; the politician must balance advantages against disadvantages before deciding which course of action to take.

Why do economists disagree so often?

Economists, like politicians, often disagree. One reason is that the statistics and other data they have to work with are insufficient, out of date, or contain inherent inaccuracies. For example, unemployment figures are collected in different ways in different countries. In America, a household survey method is used and only those who say they are actively seeking work are counted; by contrast, most Western European countries simply count those registered unemployed or claiming benefit. There are obvious discrepancies and inadequacies in these methods that can give rise to disagreements between economists investigating unemployment.

Think about it

During the 1980s and early 1990s, the Conservative Government changed the basis on which unemployment figures were calculated more than twenty times. Each change resulted in a reduction in the level of unemployment statistics.

- Why do you think that this might have led to disagreement among economists over the resulting unemployment figures (the changes were themselves proposed by economists)?
- Do you think the last change would necessarily have produced the most accurate statistics?

Positive and normative economics

Positive economics

In addition, economists frequently disagree about matters of policy – what is the right course of action in a particular situation. Many economists believe that, as a science, economics should deal only with facts – data that can be measured, recorded and checked – and the possible consequences of those facts. This is **positive economics**. Positive statements describe a situation, or say what would happen if a particular course of action was followed. For example, the statement 'the level of unemployment has fallen over the past three months' is a positive statement. It is based on verifiable data that can be checked (the data may be incorrect).

Positive economics makes use of two scientific approaches based on the methods of logic:

- **induction** – where the facts are observed and recorded; a causal relationship between them is then sought to lead to general truths
- deduction – where the explanation of a particular situation is sought by making hypothetical assumptions about the situation and constructing economic models to test those assumptions.

An example of induction would be if an economist noticed that more Christmas trees are sold during the first three weeks of December than at any other time. This would be coupled with an increase in demand for Christmas trees at that time, and may lead to a generalisation that demand for some products can be affected by the season.

Deduction, on the other hand, would lead to the conclusion that as more Christmas trees are always sold during the first three weeks of December, and Christmas Day has always fallen on 25 December, assuming Christmas Day falls on 25 December next year, more Christmas trees will again be sold during the first three weeks of December.

Normative economics

Normative economics uses the assumptions and hypotheses of positive economics as a base for statements about what ought to be done in particular circumstances. An example of a normative statement is 'the way to reduce unemployment is to reduce interest rates and encourage production'.

Normative statements tend to be about value judgements and policies, and often involve politics. Indeed, this branch of economics used to be called 'political economy'. While those who subscribe to the purely scientific approach to economics may feel normative statements are outside the scope of economics, there are two principal reasons why a normative approach is frequently adopted by economists:

- Value judgements are difficult to avoid, and it is hard to see how any economic activity can be undertaken without some value judgements. For example, on page 32 it is stated that in order to assess the economic efficiency of a particular economy we must find out which goods and services will yield the greatest satisfaction to society and their relative importance. However, since there can be no absolute measure, deciding on the relative importance to society of different goods and services necessarily involves a judgement.
- Unless economic investigation is used as a basis for value judgements and deciding political economic policy, it loses much of its purpose and use as a social science.

Something to do

- Identify which of the following statements are positive statements and which are normative statements.
  - (a) Harvinder studied hard and obtained an 'A' grade in economics.
  - (b) To obtain an 'A' grade in economics you should study hard.
  - (c) The economic development of Third World countries is being held back by huge international debts.
  - (d) The economically developed countries of the world should help the economic development of Third World countries by cancelling their debts.
  - (e) Statistics show that since there seems to be a connection between the inflation rate and the level of unemployment, the way to reduce unemployment is to control inflation.

2 Economic resources, production and specialisation

Introduction: types of resources

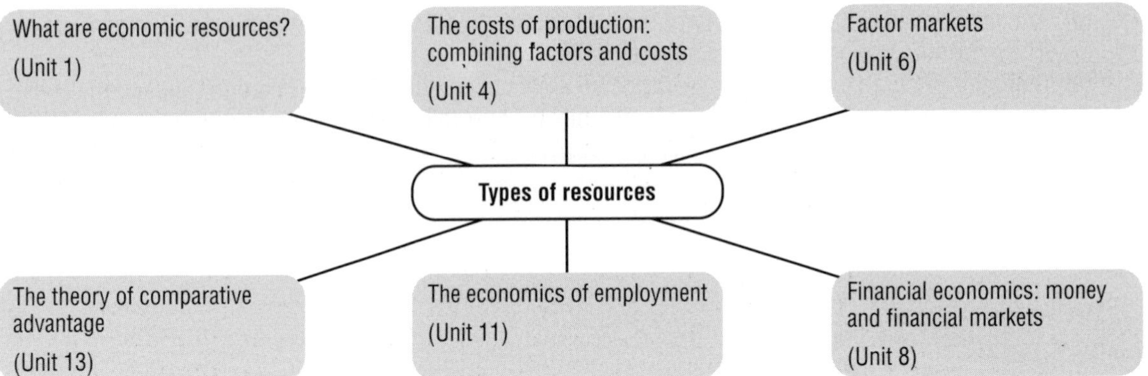

In Unit 1 we saw that production of any kind involves the use of economic, or scarce, resources. These resources are known as **factors of production**. They are combined in the production process to produce the goods and services that society wants (see Figure 2.1). Factors of production are generally classified as

- land
- capital
- labour
- entrepreneurship.

Fig. 2.1 Combining the factors of production

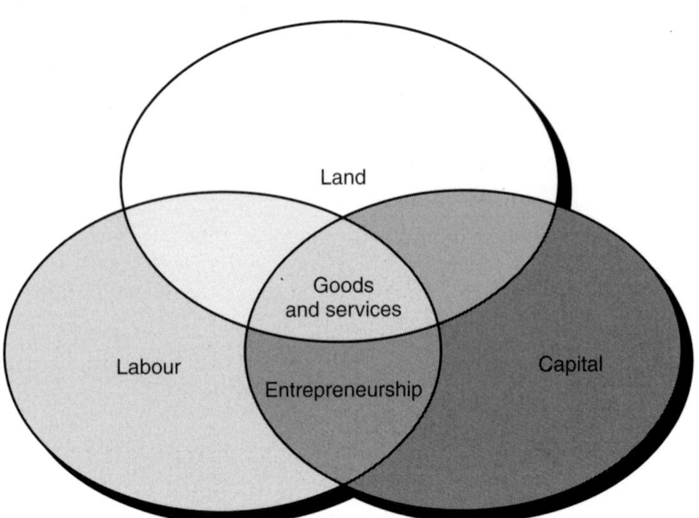

In terms of their supply, resources can be said to be fixed, renewable or non-renewable.

Fixed resources

The supply of some factors of production is fixed, which means that, while they will not disappear or be used up in the production process, they cannot be increased.

One such factor is land. Land used for farming continues to exist when the crops are harvested and the livestock sent to market. While an individual farmer may increase the amount of land he farms, there is only a certain amount of land on the Earth's surface.

Renewable resources

Other factors of production are not in fixed supply. They are **renewable** and can be replaced or even increased over time, either through natural processes or by careful management. For example, the wheat that the farmer harvests this year, and is eventually turned into bread, will grow again next year.

Some renewable factors of production, however, may only be replaced or increased over long periods. Forests take many years to reach maturity; trees that are cut down for timber, perhaps to end up as furniture or the frame of a house, take several years to replace. This is why resources that can only be replaced in the long run must be carefully managed to ensure a continuous supply.

Non-renewable resources

Some factors of production will eventually run out completely. They are **non-renewable** and must be conserved and used with care in order to ensure that society gains the most benefit from them. Oil, for example, is an important fuel in industry and society. Without oil, cars and lorries would not run, and electricity generating stations would not supply the electricity to light our lives or drive computers and machinery. An immense quantity of oil is obtained from naturally occurring reserves within the Earth and used by individuals and business organisations every day. The amount of oil that is now left to society, although vast, is finite. Once used, it cannot be replaced. Although oil is expected to continue in plentiful supply, at least during the early part of the twenty-first century, unless new deposits are discovered, or a synthetic substitute is developed, production is likely to decline.

In this unit we consider each factor of production – land, capital, labour and entrepreneurship – in more detail. In particular, we look at

- the supply of each factor of production
- the different types and uses of each factor of production.

Individual factors are often more suited to one purpose than another. Therefore, after a look at the process and types of production, we will consider specialisation in the production process and see how the various factors of production are combined and used to produce those goods and services for which they are most suited.

Factors of production

Land

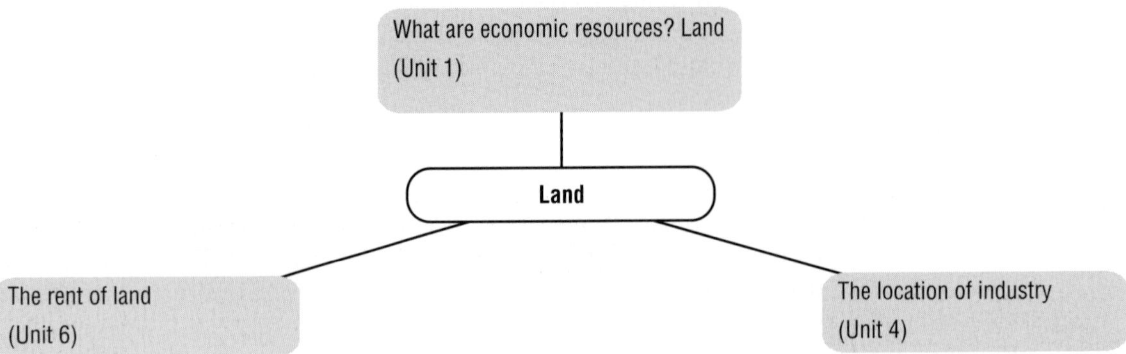

Land, as a factor of production, consists of all naturally occurring resources, including

- the actual land surface of the Earth
- the rivers, seas and oceans
- naturally occurring resources found on or within the Earth, such as mineral and chemical deposits, forests, animals and fish stocks.

Whether or not it is currently inhabited – or even habitable – the entire land surface of the Earth is theoretically available for use as a factor of production. As such, therefore, the supply of land is fixed. The amount of land available within the boundaries of the UK is approximately 244 000 square kilometres.

The uses of land

As a factor of production, land can be used in various ways:

- for agriculture and farming
- as a factor in manufacturing and service industries
- for recreational purposes.

Thus, in the UK, some of the 244 000 square kilometres available is used for farming; some for offices, shops, factories and other industrial purposes; while some is kept as open spaces for recreation or else designated areas of natural beauty to be freely enjoyed by everyone (see Figure 2.2). In addition, land is required by the government for schools, hospitals and other state enterprises, as well as for roads and other forms of social capital that benefit the community. One of the more important and difficult tasks of governments today is confining the use of land for industrial purposes to certain clearly defined areas in order to maintain a balance between the various uses of land.

Think about it

- Look at Figure 2.2 opposite. To what extent do you think that the use of land in the UK should be decided by the government rather than by those who are willing to pay the highest price for it?

Fig. 2.2 The principal uses of land

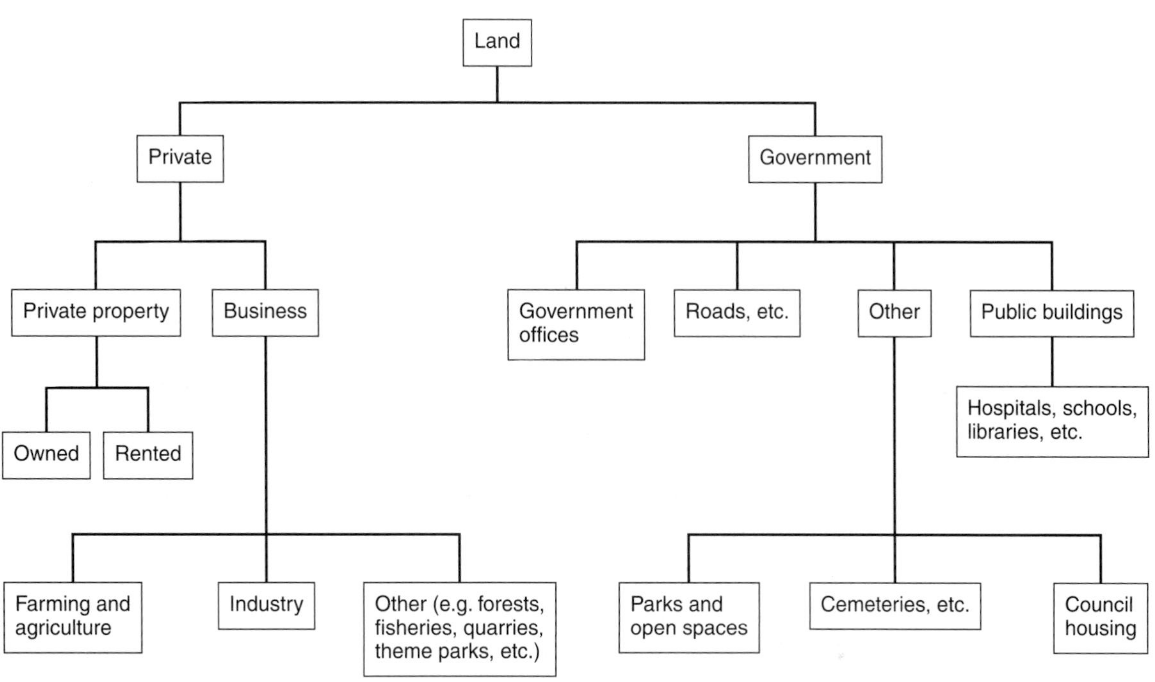

Land and the principle of diminishing returns

The principle of **diminishing returns** is one of the fundamental theories of economics. It is a principle to which we return in this and other contexts in later units. According to the theory, when one factor in the production process is increased while other factors are held fixed, a point will eventually be reached where additional units of that input yield progressively smaller, or diminishing increases in output.

An example of diminishing returns can be seen in the case of a market gardener who owns six acres of land. Working on her own to cultivate the land and grow produce, she is unable to fully exploit all her land. In fact she calculates that she is only able to achieve 35 per cent productivity from her land. She therefore employs another gardener to help her. In this way she is able to double the produce she obtains from her land. Her return from employing one extra unit of labour (the variable factor of production – see page 65) is therefore a 100 per cent increase in output from her land (the fixed factor of production).

However, even by employing one additional unit of labour, our market gardener sees that her land is still not being fully exploited. Production is still only 70 per cent of the land's capacity. She therefore employs a second gardener to help her. This time, the impact of the additional unit of labour (the second gardener) is less than the impact of the first. By employing the first gardener, she was able to double the production of her land to 70 per cent, whereas the maximum by which the second gardener can increase productivity is 30 per cent. This is less than the increase she obtained from employing the first gardener, and represents a decrease in the return obtained from the additional unit of labour (from 35 per cent to 30 per cent).

There is a similar effect when extra units of land are brought into cultivation. The most suitable land, quite naturally, tends to be cultivated first. Therefore, additional units of land tend to be less suitable, and less productive, than land already in use. For example, a farmer may grow wheat and also keep sheep. The best land will be used for growing wheat, as this will produce the best crop, and inferior land will be used for grazing sheep. However, if the farmer wants to increase production of wheat because this is what his customers require, he can do this only by changing the use of some of the inferior land, previously used for grazing, and growing wheat on it. The inferior land, while perfectly adequate when used for grazing sheep, will not yield as good a crop of wheat as the best land.

The eighteenth-century economist Thomas Malthus first noted this effect when he observed that productivity fell as inferior land was brought into cultivation to meet the growing need for food. While early economists developed the concept of diminishing returns in connection with agricultural land, the principle also applies to other factors of production, as shown in the following diagram.

The principle of diminishing returns

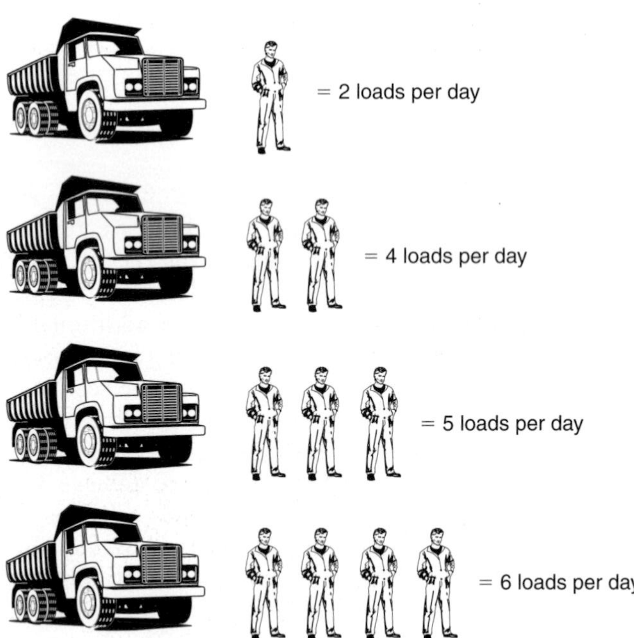

- A dumper truck with one driver can deliver two loads in an eight-hour day.
- Two drivers can increase the time the truck is in use to a maximum time of 16 hours, and therefore double the productivity of the truck.
- A third driver can help with loading the truck for a quicker turnround of the vehicle, increasing the number of deliveries to five.
- A fourth driver can help with the loading, and ensure minimum downtime of the truck during lunch breaks, etc. This gives a total number of deliveries that can be made by all four drivers of six per day.
- The return per driver has therefore diminished from two loads per 16-hour day for a single driver to $6 \div 4 = 1.5$ loads per 16-hour day per driver when four drivers are employed.

Changing the supply and productivity of land

While the area of land available for production may appear to be fixed, there are various ways in which both the supply and **productivity** of land may change.

- Although the scope for exploration and discovering new land is virtually exhausted (at least on our own planet), the great advances in road, rail, sea and air communications during the twentieth century have increased the accessibility (and therefore the amount that can be used) of agricultural and other land throughout the world.
- Modest amounts of land may be reclaimed from the sea, especially in low-lying coastal areas such as the Fenlands of England or the Netherlands.
- Land previously useless for agriculture may be cultivated by the application of modern technology, including fertilisers and artificial irrigation.
- Misuse may reduce the supply and productivity of land. For example, intensive unscientific cultivation in America and India has left arid and unproductive areas which need very heavy investment to restore fertility.
- Poor land management and natural forces such as wind and rain can cause serious erosion. Today, Palmyra in Syria, once an important grain-producing area, is surrounded by desert due to the prevailing wind. In hilly and mountainous areas, heavy rainfall can remove the fertile topsoil, so that vulnerable slopes have to be protected. Activities such as deforestation can also leave large areas of land unprotected and susceptible to erosion.

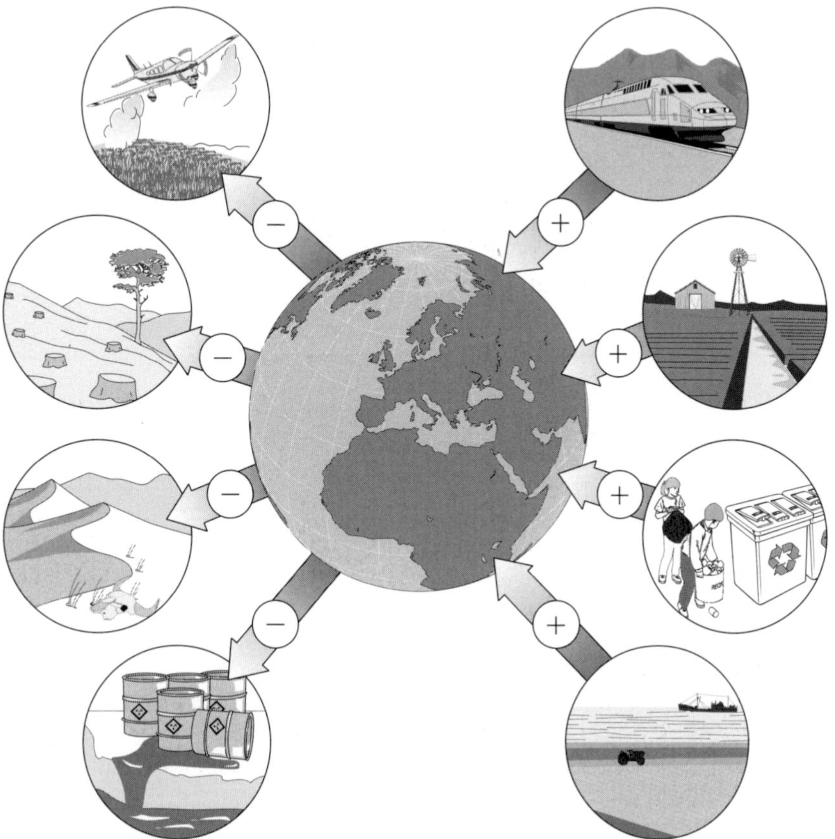

Fig. 2.3 Factors affecting the usable land surface of the Earth

Factors tending to *reduce* the Earth's usable land area	Factors tending to *increase* the Earth's usable land area
• misuse • poor cultivation methods • intensive use of pesticides • deforestation • weathering • erosion • dumping of toxic waste	• improved communications by road, rail, sea and air • land reclamation schemes • technological developments • new, natural fertilisers • artificial irrigation • better waste disposal methods, including recycling • better land and crop management

Naturally occurring resources

If we consider land as consisting of all natural resources, it is apparent that many of these resources are not in fixed supply. For example, industries such as coal mining and oil production have steadily reduced the known supply of coal and oil. As we have seen, resources such as these, which once used up are gone forever, are known as non-renewable resources. Other natural resources, such as crops, fish stocks and forests, are renewable resources in that they can be replaced either naturally or through careful management. Crops such as wheat may be replaced each year, in a regular cycle of planting, growth and harvesting (see Figure 2.4), whereas other renewable resources, such as forests, may take many years to replace.

Existing supplies of non-renewable resources, and resources that take a long time to renew, are now used more carefully and intensively in order to conserve stocks. In many cases developments in technology allow a better use of natural resources. For example, modern furnaces allow much more energy to be harnessed from coal than was previously possible.

Think about it

- Are the following resources renewable or non-renewable?
  - iron ore
  - wool
  - rice
  - salt
  - gold
  - leather
  - china clay
  - coal
  - honey
  - people
- Are the following products made from renewable or non-renewable resources?
  - plastic carrier bags
  - windows
  - trainers
  - books
  - car bodies
  - tyres
  - computers
  - ball-point pens
  - sweatshirts

Fig. 2.4 The crop cycle for wheat

(**a**) The wheat is sown

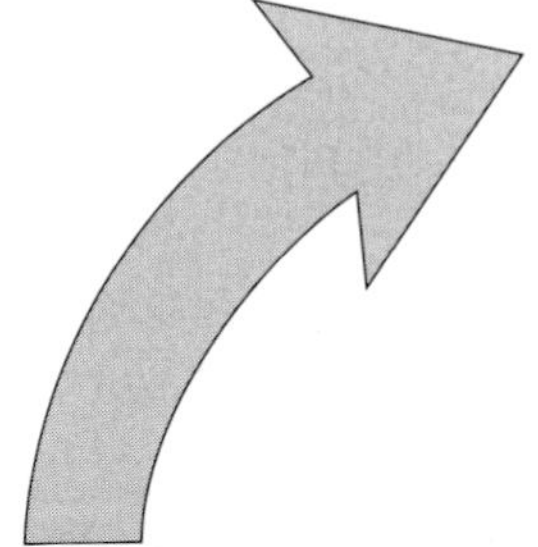

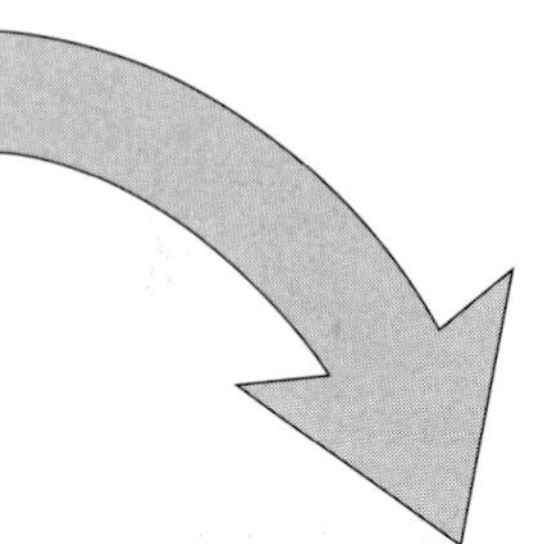

(**d**) Some seed is kept for sowing the following year

(**b**) The wheat is harvested

(**c**) After harvesting the ground will be left fallow for resowing

Capital

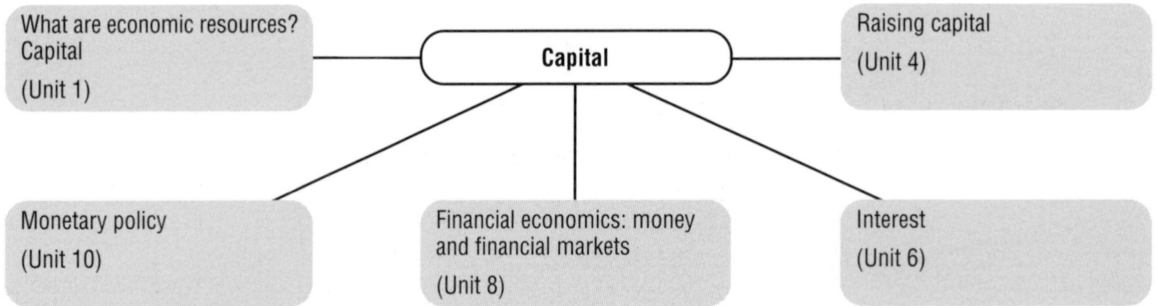

Capital, wealth and income

Unlike land, capital consists of resources that have been produced rather than those that occur naturally. Capital may be physical or financial.

- Physical capital consists of those factors of production that have been created in the past and are still available for use. Items of physical capital are called assets.
- **Financial capital** consists of money, such as cash or deposits in banks and building societies, and investments that can be converted into cash, such as shares. Financial capital may be available to purchase physical capital when required.

The capital of a person, business or country is their wealth. Confusion often arises over the distinction between wealth and income. We frequently say of someone that they are wealthy, when what we mean is that they have a large income. The distinction can perhaps be most easily understood by considering that

- wealth is a stock of money or goods existing at one moment
- income is a flow of money or goods over a period.

Thus a person's wealth is what he or she actually owns at a given point in time, while their income is what they receive over a given period (for example a year). Thus, a person may have much wealth (land, art treasures) but low income (monthly salary).

Only capital is considered as a factor of production. A company such as British Energy, for example, owns physical capital in the form of power stations and offices, and equipment such as turbines, gas circulators and computers. These are the physical **assets** of the company since they are long-lasting and not used up in the production process. They are **productive assets** as they are used to produce the electricity supplied by the company.

British Energy also owns financial capital (or financial assets) in the form of deposits at its bank and elsewhere. However, financial capital has value only in as far as it can be used to purchase physical capital and other factors of production. In addition, as we shall see, the financial assets of businesses and individuals are usually invested with a financial institution such as a bank or building society. This money is then used by the financial institution to make loans to third parties (usually individuals or businesses) so that they can themselves buy physical assets.

Thus, in counting the stock of capital in an economy, there is a danger of double counting if we include both physical capital and financial capital. Only physical capital is therefore included in the calculation of a country's stock of capital.

Consumption and savings

Both as individuals and as a community, we have the choice of

- spending all our money income on goods and services for immediate consumption, for example items such as food, travelling or holidays
- purchasing physical assets, such as houses or cars, to add to our stock of capital assets that will last for the foreseeable future
- saving some money for future use, perhaps in a bank or building society where the money we save will be pooled with that saved by others and may be lent to yet others so that they may buy capital assets.

Capital is thus accumulated by forgoing current consumption in favour of saving for future use. The government also diverts some money from immediate consumption through taxation. Although money saved for future use is often referred to as capital, it is not capital in the economic sense. Rather, it is used to purchase capital.

Many individuals, for example, deposit their savings with financial institutions such as banks. The financial institutions in turn use the large amounts of money deposited with them to provide loans to businesses and other organisations, enabling them to buy productive assets such as plant and machinery. It is these productive assets, which allow the production of goods and services to take place, that form a large part of economic capital.

Fig. 2.5 The flow of savings and investment

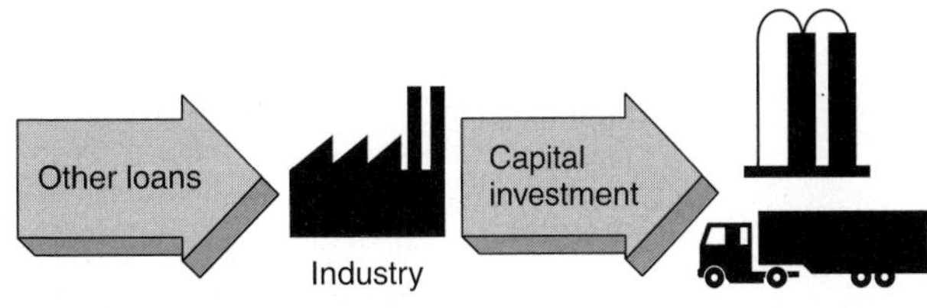

A house is not (just) a home

People buy houses to live in, and the type and size of house they buy will depend on their needs and their income. A house is a physical asset that is likely to last for a long time without significant deterioration, and therefore forms a significant part of the owner's wealth. Indeed, a person's house is likely to be at the same time

- their largest item of capital
- their largest item of total expenditure
- their largest liability (in respect of mortgage)
- a significant part of their current expenditure (in loan repayments).

The house is likely to be their largest liability, since – as houses are so expensive – the great majority of people in the UK have to take out loans in the form of mortgages in order to be able to afford them. These days, mortgages in excess of £100 000 are not unusual.

One of the reasons that people have always been prepared to borrow up to 80 per cent or even 100 per cent of the price of a house is that they have been confident that the value of the house will rise, so that over time the ratio of the outstanding loan to the value of the house will reduce. In addition, as a person's income increases, the burden of mortgage repayments will become less.

The tendency for house prices to rise over time is common to most developed economies, and is related to growing populations, rising real incomes and the increase in the cost of land. During the mid-1980s, however, house prices in many parts of the UK began to rise at an alarming rate. This was due to high tax relief on mortgage repayments, the ready availability of funds from lenders competing with each other for a share of the mortgage market, and relatively low interest rates, making house purchase easy and attractive. The result was rapidly increasing demand for houses, which could not easily be met from the existing stock, and new houses took time to build.

The boom in house prices was brought to a halt when interest rates peaked at 15 per cent in 1990, more than double their level in the mid-1980s. People could no longer afford the repayments on mortgages at this rate of interest, and were especially unwilling to commit themselves to the purchase of a new house during the uncertainty of the recession that was just beginning to bite. House prices levelled off, and actually began to fall. Those who had taken out large mortgages while interest rates were low were in a particularly invidious position. Unable to afford the repayments on their mortgages, they found that the value of their houses had in many cases fallen to less than the amount they owed. This is a situation known as 'negative equity'. In 1989, the Department of the Environment estimated that 36 per cent of first-time buyers had mortgages in excess of the value of their property.

Such a situation had never been experienced on this scale before. Worried mortgage lenders – building societies and banks – were swift to protect their interests by repossessing houses where the borrower had defaulted on the mortgage. Such houses were sold, frequently at a loss, so that the owner not only lost their home but their capital as well. The number of properties taken into possession in this way increased from 4900 in 1981 to 75 500 in 1991, and was still at a level of almost 50 000 in 1995.

This was a lesson that house buyers and prospective house buyers are unlikely to forget. House prices, like the return on any other form of investment, can go down as well as up.

Types of capital

The accumulated stock of capital is the wealth of the community. Most capital is in the form of **producers' goods**. These are assets that are available for use in the production process, and include

- machinery and equipment of all kinds used to produce goods and services
- buildings, such as factories and offices, where production takes place
- stocks of raw materials, components and finished or part-finished products.

Capital items such as machinery, equipment and buildings are known as **fixed capital**, since, although they may wear out over a number of years, they are not used up in the production process. Items that are used up in the production process, such as raw materials and components, are known as **variable capital** because the amount of them that a business has at any one time varies with the level of production. Thus, a manufacturer has the same factory, offices and machinery whether it produces one unit a day or twenty. However, the manufacturer is likely to have at any given time greater stocks of raw materials and components, and possibly of finished and part-finished units, the higher its level of production.

Raw materials, components and finished or part-finished products are also known as **circulating capital** (or **working capital**) since they 'circulate' in the production process (see Figure 2.6).

Fig. 2.6 Circulating, or working, capital

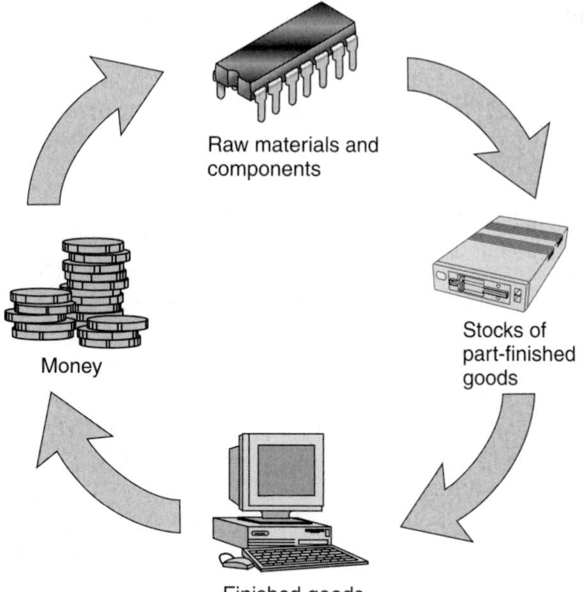

As capital goods have become more sophisticated through technological development, they have also become more specialised. The caveman's axe would have served a variety of purposes, but this is not the case with much modern machinery and equipment which may have been developed to perform one specific task in a particular industry. Oil rigs are not much use for anything other than drilling for oil. Other equipment may perform a variety of functions. A transit van, for example, may be used to carry a variety of different types of goods or passengers.

It is not only business organisations that are involved in the accumulation of capital. The government, too, provides many goods and services and has to invest in capital assets. Sometimes, as with investment in the nationalised industries (for example, the purchase of new computer equipment for the Post Office), such capital investment is similar to the capital investment of private businesses. Much government investment, however, is **social capital**, which includes

- hospitals
- schools
- roads, motorways and motorway bridges
- leisure centres.

These are provided for the benefit of the whole community. Like all real investment, they are made available through forgoing current consumption. This is sometimes undertaken voluntarily, when people lend money to the government (for example, through National Savings schemes); sometimes involuntarily, through taxes on individuals and organisations. In effect, the satisfaction of some current wants is sacrificed for the anticipated greater satisfaction of wants in the future.

Individuals, besides contributing their savings towards various kinds of capital investment, also invest in capital for their own use. The main type of individual capital investment is in the form of house purchase (which itself may be financed by borrowing the savings of others that have been deposited in banks and building societies). While houses are not productive assets in the economic sense, this kind of investment is important in that, if people buy their own houses, the State does not have to provide them. However, private house purchase means that large amounts of money are diverted away from other forms of productive investment.

Fig. 2.7 Capital in the economy

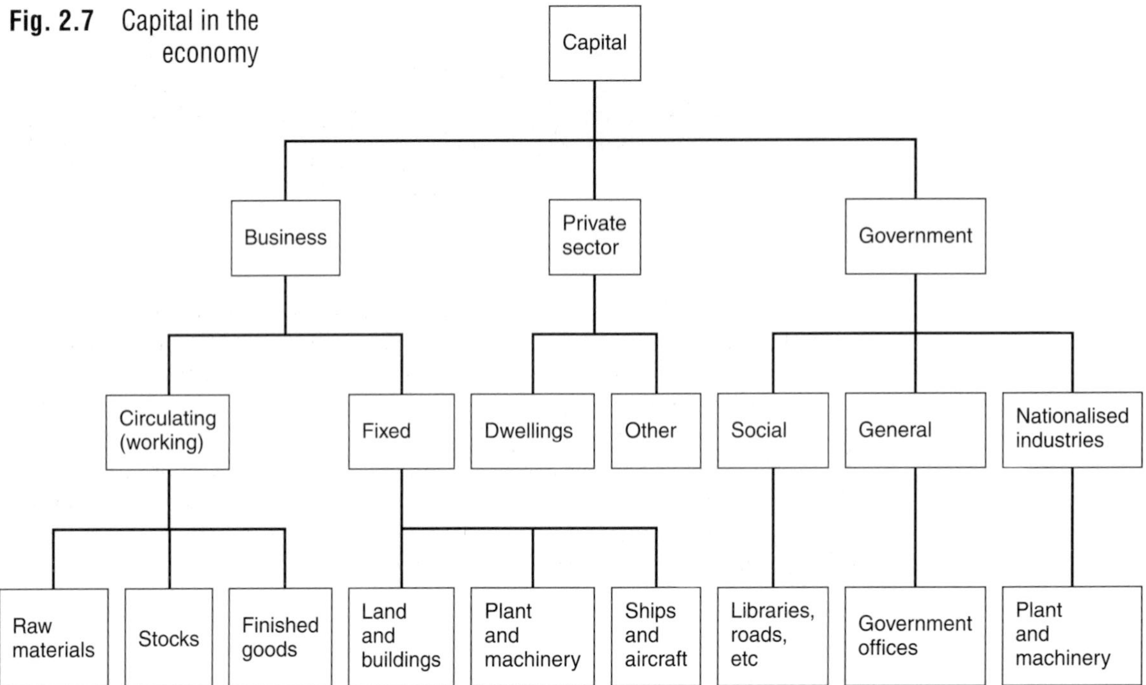

The importance of capital

Modern methods of production require considerable investment in productive assets, and today's society depends on social assets such as transport and communications networks. For many developing African and Asian countries, which often have an abundance of labour and other natural resources, the greatest obstacle in their development is a shortage of capital as a factor of production. **Capital deficiency** can be a vicious circle (see Figure 2.8). Low productivity means that almost the whole national income/production is required for current consumption. There is almost no scope for saving, little investment can occur, and so production remains low. Any increase in production is needed for current consumption by an expanding population.

Fig. 2.8 The vicious circle of capital deficiency

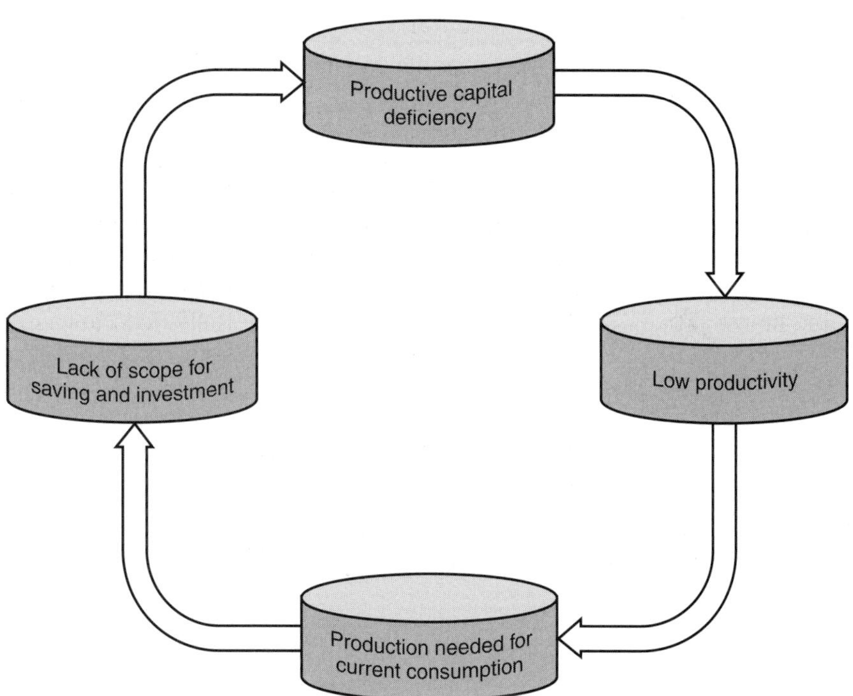

In order to develop, therefore, such economies must try to obtain capital so that productive output may be increased sufficiently to generate enough savings to sustain investment. The rapid expansion of economies such as Japan and the so-called 'Tiger' economies of Asia show that, while this is difficult, it can be done. Many developing countries borrow on the international money markets in order to finance capital investment. The downside to this, as we see in Unit 14, is that massive interest payments on the debt often cause an additional drain on current expenditure, thus making it harder to break out of the vicious circle.

Capital and power

No subject has been more faithfully explored by economists than the relation between what anciently have been called the factors of production – land, labour, capital and the entrepreneurial talent which brings these together and manages their employment. Until recently, the problem of efficiency in production – that of getting the most from the available productive resources – was envisaged, almost entirely, as one of winning the best combination of these agents. The elucidation by means of diagrams of the arcane problems inherent in factor combinations remains one the prime pedagogical rites of economics. Economists have been equally concerned with the way in which the prices of the factors of production – rents, wages, interest and profits – are determined. Indeed, in the classical tradition, the subject was thought of as falling in two parts: the problem of value having to do with the determination of the prices of goods and the problem of distribution or how the resulting income was divided between landlords, workers, capitalists and entrepreneurs.

One aspect of the relationship between the factors of production has, however, been less examined. That is why power has been associated with some factors and not with others. Why did ownership of land once convey plenary power over the dominant form of productive enterprise and, therewith, in the community at large?

Why, under other circumstances, has it been assumed that such authority, both over the enterprise and in the society at large, should lie with the owner of capital? Under what circumstances might such power pass to labour?

It is a puzzling neglect. On coming on any form of organised activity – a church, platoon, government bureau, congressional committee, a house of casual pleasure – our first instinct is to enquire who is in charge. Then we enquire as to the qualifications or credentials which accord such command. Organisation almost invariably invites two questions: Who is the Head? How did he get there?

Source: Adapted from J. K. Galbraith, *The New Industrial State*, chapter 5 (Penguin, 1967)

Capital formation in the UK

The amount of its annual income that an economy sets aside for real investment or capital formation varies between countries and from time to time in any single country.

Table 2.1

UK gross domestic fixed capital formation											
	1986	**1987**	**1988**	**1989**	**1990**	**1991**	**1992**	**1993**	**1994**	**1995**	**1996**
Total GDFC	65	75.2	91.5	105.4	107.6	97.7	93.6	94.3	100.3	108.7	114.6
Gross national product (GNP)	389	427	476	519	552	575	602	634	679	712	752
Investment as a % of income	16.7	17.6	19.2	20.3	19.4	17	15.5	14.9	14.8	15.2	15.2

Source: *UK National Accounts* (The Stationery Office, 1999)

Table 2.1 shows the amount that was spent on gross domestic fixed capital formation – that is on all kinds of physical assets in the UK – in each year from 1986 to 1996 (line 1 – total GDFC) and the total level of production of goods and services by UK citizens and organisations during each year (line 2 – GNP). Line 3 – investment as a percentage of income – shows that until 1990, an increasing percentage of **gross national product** (GNP) was invested. This declined slightly after 1990, however, probably due to the effects of the **recession.** A recession is a period of at least six months when a country's output and income are both falling: if a country's income is falling it has less available, after spending on current consumption, assuming that it maintains its level of consumption, to invest in capital items. Some countries manage to invest a greater proportion than this, others less. In the period following the Second World War, it became evident that countries such as Japan, which invested heavily, made the strongest economic progress.

Think about it

During a recession firms tend to reduce their level of investment in capital goods as most of the money they have available is required either to pay for current operations or else to save for unforeseen problems.

- What do you think the long-term effects of this will be
  - for the firm
  - for the country as a whole?

Table 2.2 (see pages 58–59) shows how funds were invested in the UK between 1986 and 1996. As you can see from the first half of the table, total investment rose by 176 per cent, from £65 billion to £114.6 billion. The second half of the table shows what the amounts would have been at prices prevailing in one given year (in this case 1990), and this enables us to compare the volume of investment, eliminating the effects of inflation. These constant-price columns show that the increase in investment in real terms was smaller – a rise of 124 per cent from £83.7 billion to £104.1 billion – but still a useful improvement.

Over the period 1986–96, there was an increase in the amount of private-sector investment and a decline in that of the public corporations (nationalised industries) partly because the process of privatisation (see Units 4 and 7) has resulted in fewer public-sector businesses.

Human capital

There is one kind of investment that does not result in any increase in tangible assets, and that is investment in people. Human capital may be regarded as the accumulated skills of the workforce. Like other forms of capital accumulation, investment in human capital can be expected to show some kind of dividend or benefit in the future. When a company invests in new machinery, it expects to make a profit from its investment. If an individual spends three or four years obtaining a degree, it is likely that he or she will receive a dividend in the form of a higher income or standard of living. The economy overall will also benefit from investing in labour, which may be a good economic reason for education being provided by the State.

Table 2.2

		Gross domestic fixed capital formation (£ million)										
		1986	**1987**	**1988**	**1989**	**1990**	**1991**	**1992**	**1993**	**1994**	**1995**	**1996**
At current prices												
By type of asset	Buses and coaches	125	166	199	179	164	139	116	149	142	142	141
	Other road vehicles	5 329	6 754	7 677	8 603	8 013	6 532	6 807	7 559	8 497	9 710	10 333
	Railway rolling stock	95	126	187	242	377	363	504	591	393	224	158
	Ships	162	239	116	122	234	500	119	363	684	695	84
	Aircraft	511	520	670	1 178	1 478	1 113	1 164	1 338	1 783	419	1 134
	Plant and machinery	24 690	27 073	31 504	36 382	36 762	34 677	33 854	34 565	37 311	42 967	44 252
	Dwellings	14 140	16 355	20 297	22 988	21 439	18 501	18 734	19 974	21 224	22 255	22 538
	Other new buildings and works	16 514	19 874	24 794	31 368	34 855	31 759	29 398	26 279	26 411	28 842	31 779
By industry group	Agriculture, hunting, forestry and fishing	1 196	1 265	1 420	1 485	1 368	1 063	1 070	1 167	932	939	1 126
	Mining and quarrying including oil extraction	3 636	3 226	3 536	4 055	4 700	5 958	5 743	4 904	3 810	4 463	4 623
	Manufacturing (revised definition)	10 105	11 040	12 415	14 248	14 227	13 183	12 433	12 410	13 534	15 775	15 388
	Electricity, gas and water supply	2 792	2 798	3 119	3 943	4 742	5 608	6 365	5 910	5 221	5 085	4 567
	Construction	609	763	1 142	1 111	965	585	563	650	727	821	1 165
	Wholesale and retail trade, repairs, hotels and restaurants	6 269	7 687	9 456	9 468	9 136	8 352	8 225	7 936	8 263	10 744	11 362
	Transport, storage and communication	5 683	6 840	7 875	9 604	9 453	9 279	9 175	10 667	12 545	11 937	13 192
	Financial intermediation, real estate, renting and business activities	8 197	11 534	15 532	20 372	21 170	15 360	12 675	10 746	13 334	15 952	19 615
	Other services	8 939	9 599	10 652	13 788	16 122	15 695	15 713	16 454	16 855	17 283	16 843
	Dwellings	14 140	16 355	20 927	22 988	21 439	18 501	18 734	19 974	21 224	22 255	22 538
Transfer costs of land and buildings		3 466	4 051	5 456	4 381	4 255	4 163	2 946	3 475	3 807	3 482	4 204
Total		**65 032**	**75 158**	**91 530**	**105 443**	**107 577**	**97 747**	**93 642**	**94 293**	**100 252**	**108 736**	**114 623**

Table 2.2 (continued)

		Gross domestic fixed capital formation (£ million)										
		1986	**1987**	**1988**	**1989**	**1990**	**1991**	**1992**	**1993**	**1994**	**1995**	**1996**
At 1990 prices												
By type of asset	Buses and coaches	163	193	233	190	164	151	124	131	154	142	134
	Other road vehicles	7 454	8 672	9 083	9 422	8 013	5 963	6 029	6 567	7 246	8 228	8 502
	Railway rolling stock, ships and aircraft	876	981	1 056	1 619	2 089	1 894	1 634	2 029	2 474	1 080	1 092
	Plant and machinery	27 512	29 086	33 770	37 925	36 762	33 955	32 602	31 749	33 705	36 352	37 074
	Dwellings	20 170	21 807	25 247	24 789	21 439	17 919	18 335	19 661	20 371	20 322	19 909
	Other new buildings and works	21 913	25 603	29 222	32 806	34 855	33 424	33 677	32 665	32 783	32 411	33 215
By industry group	Agriculture, hunting, forestry and fishing	1 461	1 491	1 587	1 537	1 368	1 049	1 074	1 161	904	861	977
	Mining and quarrying including oil extraction	4 513	3 898	4 047	4 252	4 700	6 101	6 383	5 565	4 243	4 491	4 415
	Manufacturing (revised definition)	12 097	12 641	13 846	14 984	14 227	12 803	11 828	11 230	11 997	13 181	12 442
	Electricity, gas and water supply	3 404	3 304	3 490	4 094	4 742	5 612	6 561	6 115	5 337	4 687	4 021
	Construction	771	907	1 287	1 180	965	568	557	598	654	708	986
	Wholesale and retail trade, repairs, hotels and restaurants	7 681	9 056	10 638	9 923	9 136	8 331	8 490	8 095	8 304	10 056	10 329
	Transport, storage and communication	6 767	7 811	8 768	10 100	9 453	9 108	9 002	10 357	11 730	10 535	11 248
	Financial intermediation, real estate, renting and business activities	9 770	13 523	17 331	21 387	21 170	15 637	12 831	11 333	14 233	15 829	19 249
	Other services	11 454	11 904	12 370	14 505	16 122	16 178	17 340	18 687	18 960	17 865	16 350
	Dwellings	20 170	21 807	25 247	24 789	21 439	17 919	18 335	19 661	20 371	20 322	19 909
Transfer costs of land and buildings		5 597	5 997	6 553	4 719	4 255	4 097	3 572	3 784	4 045	3 714	4 164
Total		**83 685**	**92 339**	**105 164**	**111 470**	**107 577**	**97 403**	**95 973**	**96 586**	**100 778**	**102 249**	**104 090**

Source: *UK National Accounts* (The Stationery Office, 1999)

Labour

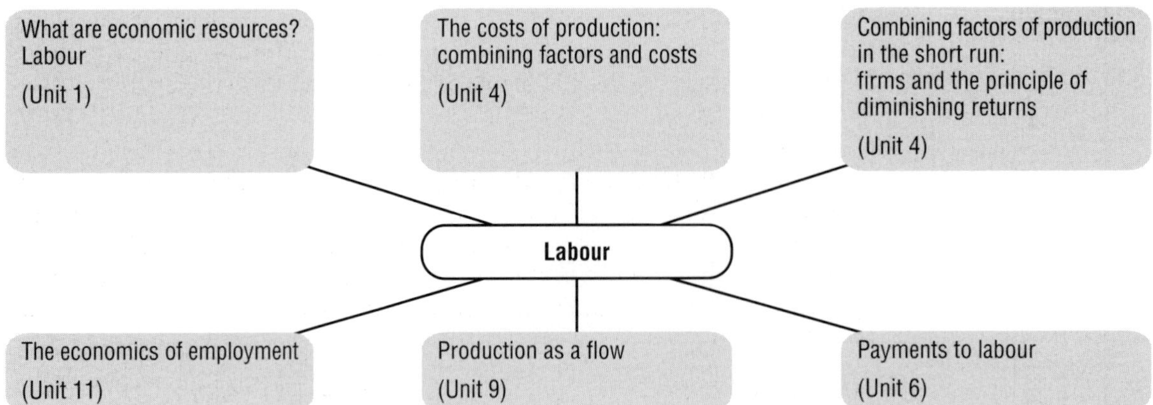

All human work or effort can be considered to be labour. Nothing can be produced without labour; labour is an essential factor of production – even when it only involves pressing a button on a computer panel. The availability of labour is related to the size and structure of the population. Before we consider labour as a factor of production, therefore, it will be useful to examine these aspects of the population.

The population

The population and its structure form the backcloth against which all economic activity takes place, for the population is made up of people, and people are both the producers and the consumers of goods and services.

The population of the UK has shown an almost continuous rise since the middle of the eighteenth century. Most other countries have seen similar population increases. Indeed, the growing world population is putting increasing pressure on other resources.

Table 2.3

Population[1] of the UK (thousands)							
	1961	**1971**	**1981**	**1991**	**1996**	**2011**	**2021**
England	43 561	46 412	46 821	48 208	49 089	51 161	52 484
Wales	2 635	2 740	2 813	2 891	2 921	2 989	3 043
Scotland	5 184	5 236	5 180	5 107	5 128	5 059	4 993
Northern Ireland	1 427	1 540	1 538	1 601	1 663	1 720	1 724
UK	**52 807**	**55 928**	**56 352**	**57 808**	**58 801**	**60 929**	**62 244**

1 Data are mid-year estimates for 1961 to 1996 and 1996-based projections for 2011 and 2021.

Sources: Office for National Statistics; Government Actuary's Department; General Register Office for Scotland; Northern Ireland Statistics and Research Agency

Something to do

- From the figures in Table 2.3, construct a graph showing population growth in the UK. You can do this using a computer spreadsheet package such as Excel or Quattro.
- Write notes explaining what the graph shows, and give reasons why you think the curve is the shape it is.

In the UK, a census (that is, a count of the population) is taken every tenth year. The first census was taken in 1801. Prior to that estimates of the size of the population were made: in 1688, the population was estimated to be approximately 7 million. The fastest rate of growth occurred during the first half of the nineteenth century, but the growth rate has nearly always given cause for concern.

Now, in fact, the growth rate is slowing down, but this is also a cause for concern in that it is likely to give rise to an ageing population – a situation in which the proportion of older people to younger is growing. This has serious implications for employment (fewer people coming onto the labour market) and for services such as healthcare and leisure (older people need special healthcare, and when people retire they have more time to enjoy leisure pursuits).

<u>What size should a population be?</u> The idea that there is an **optimum population** for a country has been developed in connection with the problems of over-population. A country's optimum (or best) population is the size of population that can both be supported by and fully exploit the other available factors of production and the level of technical knowledge in the country and any addition to, or subtraction from, this level would reduce the average standard of living.

A country such as China may seem to be over-populated in that it may be possible to increase its living standards if it had a smaller population; whereas a country such as Canada is probably under-populated – its natural resources could support a larger population. However, it is usually very difficult to determine whether a country's population is above or below the optimum. There are several reasons for this:

- Changes in technology will alter the level of population that can be supported.
- The optimum level may be affected by changes in the age structure of the population (for example, how many people are of working age) (see pages 61–65).
- In countries where women are not expected to undertake paid work, the sex distribution of the population will affect its optimum size.
- The effects of additional units of labour on the production possibilities of an economy are difficult to estimate.
- The optimum population for production may be different from the optimum population for consumption; an advanced technology may require a small labour force, but a large number of consumers for the goods it produces.
- The level of production depends on many things other than the combination of factors of production; a government's economic policies may be beneficial or detrimental in this respect.

<u>The age structure of the population</u> One of the main determinants of the size of a country's labour force at any time is the age structure of the population. It is common practice in developed industrial economies to divide the population into three age groups:

- under 16
- 16 to 64
- 65 and over.

Although these groupings do not correspond exactly with those in full-time education, those of working age and those of retirement age, changes in the proportions of the groupings are important indicators of the sizes of the **working** and **dependent populations**. Such changes have several implications for the economy:

- Changes in age distribution will change the pattern of demand – demand for medical facilities for older people, for example.
- Changes in demand require changes in the allocation of resources, which may be difficult as resources become more specialised.
- If the dependent (non-working) population becomes a greater proportion of the total and productivity per worker does not increase, there will be a greater burden on the working population. The government will have to provide more services, and individuals who are in work will have to pay more in taxes in order to maintain standards.
- Changes in the age structure of a population may also bring changes in the capital market – as more people move into the retirement age group, for example, they begin to live on the savings they have accumulated in earlier years.

It must be remembered that changes occur gradually and are almost imperceptible as they arise. Over a period of years, however, the ways in which resources are used will change to reflect the changing age structure of the population.

The projected population Social and economic planning must be based on a firm assessment of the size and needs of the future population. In the UK, this is provided by the Office of the Registrar General. Population forecasts are calculated by applying current and anticipated birth and death rates to the current population. This sounds a fairly simple process, but population forecasts have to be treated with the utmost care. One difficulty is that an assessment must be made of future changes to birth and death rates, not just for the population as a whole, but for each age group and sex.

The figures in Table 2.4 show how the projections of future population have had to be amended at various times. The assumptions on which the projections are based are more likely to be wrong if a long time-period is involved. Developments in medical science and changes in lifestyle can change birth and death rates, and it is impossible for forecasters accurately to predict these and similar influences.

Table 2.4

Projected population of the UK (millions)					
Year of forecast	**1976**	**1981**	**1991**	**2001**	**2011**
1971	56.6	57.7	60.3	63.1	–
1975	56.0	55.9	57.3	58.3	–
1979	–	56.0	57.1	58.4	–
1986	–	–	57.4	58.9	–
1988	–	–	57.5	59.2	–
1998	–	–	–	59.6	60.9
Actual population	55.9	55.9	57.8	–	–

Table 2.5

	Distribution of the workforce at mid-June each year (thousands, seasonally adjusted)										
	1987	**1988**	**1989**	**1990**	**1991**	**1992**	**1993**	**1994**	**1995**	**1996**	**1997**
Workforce	28 083	28 430	28 731	28 813	28 614	28 483	28 279	28 160	28 113	28 184	28 107
Males	16 460	16 527	16 557	16 511	16 388	16 240	16 030	15 873	15 791	15 620	15 515
Females	11 623	11 903	12 174	12 302	12 226	12 242	12 248	12 288	12 323	12 564	12 592
Unemployed	2 836	2 294	1 786	1 615	2 301	2 734	2 919	2 644	2 313	2 150	1 600
Males	1 978	1 599	1 276	1 191	1 744	2 095	2 242	2 024	1 764	1 631	1 222
Females	857	694	510	424	557	639	677	620	549	519	377
Workforce in employment	25 248	26 137	26 945	27 198	26 313	25 749	25 360	25 517	25 800	26 034	26 507
Males	14 482	14 928	15 281	15 320	14 645	14 146	13 789	13 849	14 027	13 988	14 292
Females	10 766	11 208	11 664	11 878	11 669	11 603	11 571	11 667	11 773	12 045	12 215
HM Forces	319	316	308	303	297	290	271	250	230	221	210
Males	302	300	291	286	278	270	252	232	214	206	195
Females	16	16	16	18	19	20	19	18	16	16	15
Self-employed persons (with or without employees)	3 042	3 223	3 515	3 562	3 413	3 230	3 190	3 302	3 357	3 291	3 338
Males	2 301	2 447	2 698	2 723	2 612	2 444	2 391	2 485	2 550	2 469	2 487
Females	741	776	817	839	801	786	799	816	807	822	851
Employees in employment	21 576	22 255	22 660	22 909	22 250	21 904	21 588	21 663	21 987	22 340	22 792
Males	11 702	11 977	12 001	12 051	11 538	11 226	10 951	10 941	11 115	11 201	11 507
Females	9 874	10 278	10 659	10 858	10 713	10 677	10 636	10 723	10 872	11 139	11 285
of whom Total, production and construction industries	6 335	6 395	6 408	6 285	5 756	5 395	5 082	5 060	5 108	5 122	5 247
Total, all manufacturing industries	4 815	4 858	4 851	4 733	4 319	4 096	3 913	3 923	4 026	4 068	4 111
Work-related Government-supported training programmes	311	343	462	423	353	325	311	302	225	181	167
Males	177	205	291	260	217	205	195	191	147	112	104
Females	134	138	171	163	136	120	117	111	78	69	64

Note: Because the figures have been rounded independently, totals may differ from the sum of the components. Also, the totals may include some employees whose industrial classification could not be ascertained.

Source: *Employment Gazette* (The Stationery Office, 1999)

The working population Other things being equal, the larger the number of people in the 16–64 age groups, the larger the working population. In the UK, the Department for Education and Employment (the DfEE) regularly monitors the size of the working population; some recent figures are given in Table 2.5.

The definitions of some categories are changed from time to time, but there are some points to be clear about:

- The working population includes all those in civilian employment, the self-employed, those in the armed forces and the registered unemployed.
- From 1987 to 1996 the number available for work remained at the same level overall, while the number in employment increased by 500 000.
- The increase in the number in employment relates to women rather than men. The number of men in employment actually decreased over the same period. This could be for a number of reasons:
  - the decline in manufacturing industry, where men have always been predominant
  - the expansion of those industries, in particular service industries, offering better employment opportunities for women
  - the greater availability of women for employment.
- There was a significant increase in the number of self-employed people (10 per cent). Again, a number of factors could explain this, including:
  - unemployed people using redundancy payments to start their own businesses
  - government and other schemes to help people establish their own businesses.

Fig. 2.9 The UK labour force, by age (1997 and 2002)

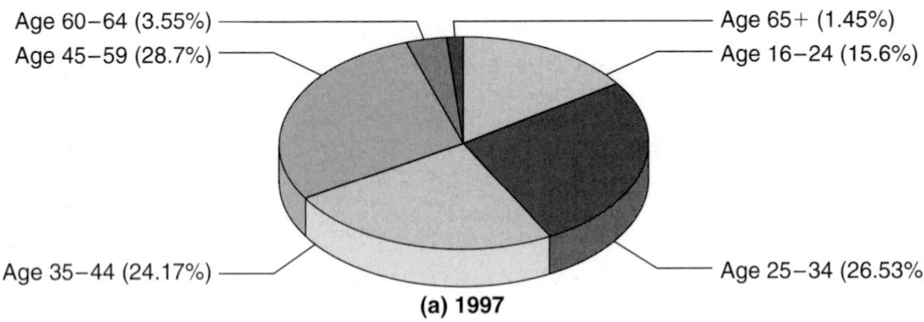

(a) 1997

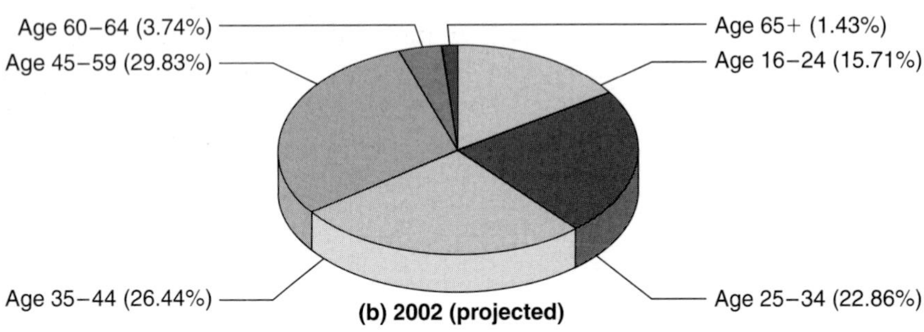

(b) 2002 (projected)

There are problems in the way such statistics are compiled. For example 'employees' includes people on various government training schemes. While the figures in Table 2.5 are perhaps the nearest we can get to an official estimate of the supply of labour, the figures on their own are inadequate. They do not tell us about the number of hours worked per week, the weeks worked per year or whether work is full time, part time, temporary or permanent. (In general, in the UK, there has been a decline in the number of hours and weeks worked, and a decline in full-time work over a long period.) Nor do the figures say anything about the quality of labour – increasingly, industry and commerce need skilled and qualified employees. It is not just the size of the working population that is important, but the skills to exploit ever-developing new technology.

Fixed and variable factors of production

While some factors of production may be easily varied in response to need, other factors may be fixed in that they cannot easily be varied, at least in the long run. As we see in Unit 4, the fixity of some factors of production may dictate how many goods a firm produces, or how it produces them. For example, if a firm needs to increase production of its goods in order to meet an unexpected increase in demand, it may be able to do so by asking employees to work overtime, by taking on temporary workers and by buying additional raw materials and parts. These factors of production are therefore variable: the overtime and temporary workers being variable labour, the additional raw materials and parts being variable capital.

In order to fully meet the new demand for its product, however, the firm may need new machinery and even a larger factory to house the machinery and the larger workforce required to operate it. Clearly it is not so easy to buy new machinery or a new factory. The machinery may have to be made to the firm's requirements, and the factory may have to be built. This may take several months, or even longer. These are therefore **fixed factors of production**, in that they cannot be varied in the short run.

Entrepreneurship

It is common practice to consider entrepreneurship as a separate factor of production. An entrepreneur provides, or arranges, the capital necessary for a business, takes decisions and risks, and, if the entrepreneur actually owns the business, benefits from any profits (or bears any losses) at the end of the year.

The growth of large business organisations, however, has given rise to a division of entrepreneurial functions, which are carried out by managers. Management may be considered a form of labour, but since it is responsible for the *organisation* of production rather than for production itself it may still be treated as a separate factor. This view is reinforced by industrial conflicts over things such as wage claims, which can resolve into battles between labour and management rather than between labour and the owners of capital.

REMOVING THE FOUNDER

THESE days, it is no longer enough to start your own business – no matter how successful it is. An entrepreneur must learn to manage their business if they are to continue to lead it. While entrepreneurs like Richard Branson are held up as examples of the best of British business leaders, many others fall victim to their own success as entrepreneurs but failings as managers, as Patrick Dunne explains in this extract from his article 'Building to last: removing the founder'.

DILEMMA ***A successful company has outgrown one of its founders. Although well-liked, the executive lacks the skills or the motivation to help lead the business through its next period of change and expansion.***

ISSUES ***Most fast-growth companies are eventually faced with this dilemma and the problem is often exacerbated when the founder is also the chief executive, chairman or major shareholder. Succession is one area of boardroom behaviour where we can learn much from animals. When tension mounts in a chimpanzee pack, the stronger members become less tolerant of the weak.***

Similarly, in business, past triumphs are overlooked and bloody battles become hard to avoid if the matter isn't dealt with swiftly. There is little to be gained from waiting until it is clear to all that the executive is out of his depth or is underperforming.

Source: 'Building to last: removing the founder', *Management Today*, April 1999

Production and specialisation

The purpose of economic activity is to produce the goods and services wanted by society. In doing this, the factors of production are combined in the production process. Some factors are particularly suited to specific types of production; **specialisation** takes place when those factors are used in the production – or processes within the production – of goods and services for which they are most suited.

Production

Production is the process of converting raw or basic materials originally extracted from the Earth, sea or atmosphere into forms that yield utility or satisfaction to consumers. This must be done at a time and place convenient to consumers.

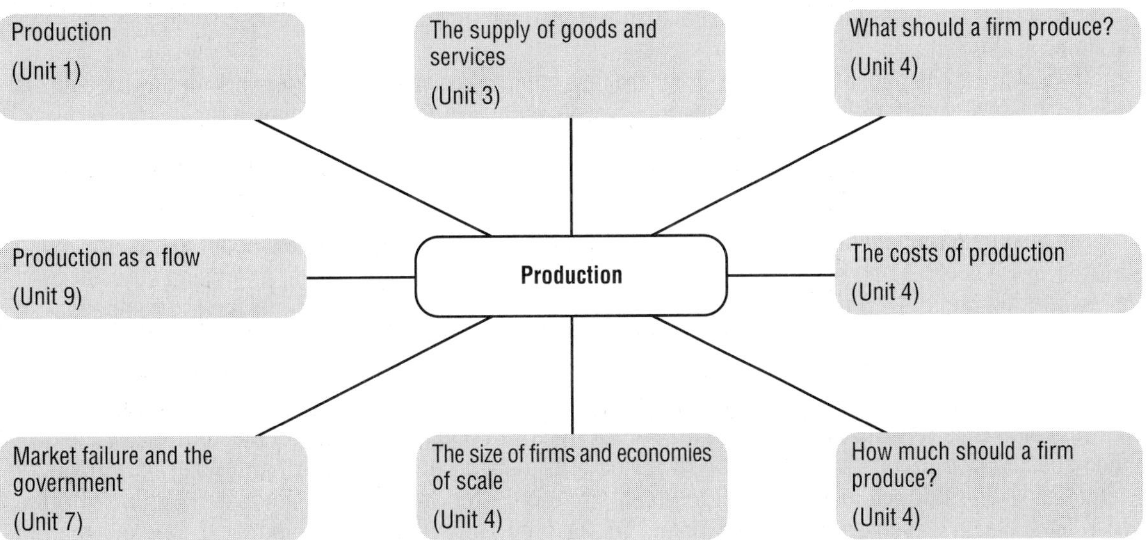

Land, labour and capital are combined in various proportions by entrepreneurship to bring about this conversion. Sometimes goods are produced using a high proportion of labour to other factors of production; for example, the National Health Service and education are both **labour intensive**. Motor manufacturing, on the other hand, with its emphasis on using robots and other hi-tech equipment in the production process, is **capital intensive**.

Many developing countries with large populations but little investment in machinery are particularly dependent on labour-intensive methods, whereas in countries with more developed economies each unit of labour may be assisted by a large amount of capital equipment and their methods of production are capital intensive. For example, in the UK, farming is capital intensive, involving the use of machinery, scientifically developed seeds and artificial fertilisers, whereas farmers in Ethiopia do not have the same capital resources available and rely much more on human labour.

Pokhara weavers

Pokhara is a large lakeside town in Central Nepal. Although its population is only 60 000 it is second in size and significance only to Kathmandu, the capital, 200 km to the East. The main crossroads in Pokhara is known as Prithvi Chowk. There, located virtually at the junction, is a group of people creating a variety of woven bamboo products. They occupy a piece of land about 10 m × 10 m at the side of the road. In addition, they have a small area to display finished goods at the side of the road, at the junction. Goods, materials, etc. are stored, where necessary, in a hut at the rear of the main site.

The goods produced are mainly baskets of various sizes and floor mats. Except for the final weaving operation, all operations are common, irrespective of the end product. The common operations together convert long pieces of bamboo into the raw materials for the final weaving process.

The description below focuses on the weaving of large floor mats approximately 3 m square.

The operations

Bamboo poles, cut locally, are brought to the site by hand or cart. They are typically 2.5 m long and 12 cm in diameter.

Usually it is necessary to cut off the solid end of the pole; this is done on the floor with a large heavy knife used as a hatchet.

The poles are then split, lengthwise. They are first cut in half with a heavy knife driven down by blows from a piece of wood until the pole splits into two. Each half is then split further by the same process, but now the knife can usually simply be pushed down the split pole. The number of splits determines the width of the final weaving material. Splitting each half into six (i.e. twelve pieces in total) produces pieces approximately 2.5 cm wide.

The next operation involves the cutting of thin flat strips from the split poles. Again this is done with a knife which is run along the poles but at right angles to the previous cut – i.e. producing strips at right angles to the radius – along the natural laminations of the bamboo. The material 'peels' quite easily in this way, but not always over the full pole length, so the strips produced are of different lengths. All but the strips from the outside of the pole are the same yellowish colour on both sides. The outer strip is green on one (the outer) side. All strips are approximately 2 mm thick.

The material is now ready for weaving. This, for mats, is done horizontally on the floor with considerable speed and dexterity, new strips being joined into the weave in either section (along or across) as required, until a full mat is obtained. The green strips are used to introduce a squared pattern into the mat. Each mat is woven one quarter at a time, i.e. the first quarter is woven, then the second is added to make a half mat, then the third and finally the last quarter to complete the square. Finally the strips are trimmed off, and all edges are bound.

There are other occasional operations, i.e. occasional sprinkling of water on to the waiting strips to keep them flexible; removal of finished products; removal of waste material; measuring of mats during weaving; and sharpening of knives.

Manning

When busy, five people undertake the above operations, as follows:

1 trimming ends and splitting poles
1 making strips
2 weaving products
1 supervising; helping out; moving materials between workers and occasional jobs.

During quiet times, all operations are undertaken by two or three people. With manning, and making no other items in the site area, approximately five or six large mats could be made in one day.

Source: R. Wild, *Essentials of Production and Operations Management* (Cassell, 4th edn 1995)

Types of production

The distinction between labour-intensive and capital-intensive production corresponds to the distinction that can be made between two types of production:

- direct production
- indirect production.

Fig. 2.10 Types of production

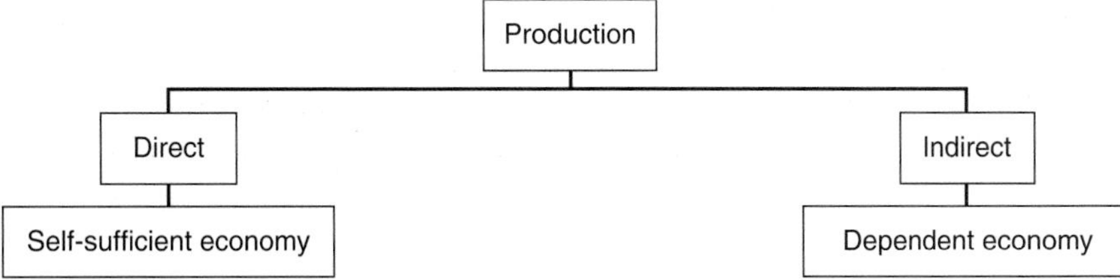

Direct production

Under this system, the basic economic unit – a family or village, for example – produces all it needs for itself. It is self sufficient. Methods of production are likely to be traditional and labour intensive, output is likely to be mainly agricultural, and productivity (measured by output per person) is likely to be low. Workers may each perform a variety of jobs during the year, developing no great expertise in any of them.

Since output is low, an important characteristic of systems of direct production is a lack of developed markets. A market is a system that enables consumers to satisfy their wants by purchasing the surplus output of producers. If there is no surplus output to sell, there is no need for a market. It follows from this that if there is no market in which to sell surplus output, there is no profit to set aside for future investment in better production techniques. This means that it is very difficult to break away from a system of direct production. This is one of the obstacles hampering the economic growth of developing countries.

Indirect production

As we saw in Unit 1, in a modern industrial economy no one is self sufficient. Virtually everything we use or buy only becomes available through the combined efforts of a great many individual people at home and abroad. We acquire the goods we need indirectly. For example, a pilot earns money by flying planes for an airline. The pilot uses the money earned in this way to obtain goods and services that are produced by other people, including items such as food and clothing. This can only be achieved through the co-operation of others and requires a complex system (the economy) that enables **trade** to take place. Thus people working in the clothing industry produce more clothes than they require for themselves, and can sell their surplus production at a profit – to the pilot and others who want clothes but cannot produce them themselves. The clothing workers in turn earn money from the clothes they have sold and are able to buy the things they want, but cannot produce themselves, which are provided out of the surplus production of others.

Something to do

- The economy of the Efe (see Unit 1) is based on a system of **direct production**. Write notes on what might be the advantages and disadvantages to their society of changing to a system of **indirect production**.

Categories of economic activity

There are three broad categories of economic activity:

- The **primary sector** consists of the extraction of raw materials from the land, sea or atmosphere. Typical industries in the primary sector include agriculture, mining or quarrying, forestry and fishing.
- The **secondary sector** takes the raw materials produced by the primary sector and processes or refines them or else manufactures finished goods from them. Typical industries in the secondary sector include building and construction, all forms of manufacturing, food processing and oil refining.
- The **tertiary sector** consists of service industries. Most tertiary sector industries, such as leisure and tourism, health, financial services, and other services such as hairdressers, retailers and home appliance repairers, provide services to private individuals. A growing segment within the tertiary sector, however, consists of firms that provide services to business. These include accountants, business consultants, computer consultants and so on. This segment is now so important in the UK economy that it is sometimes called the **quaternary sector.**

The chain of production for oil

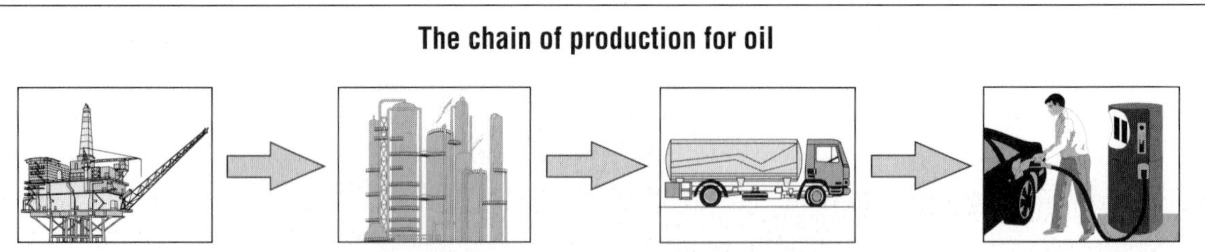

The crude oil is extracted from the Earth by an oil company operating in the primary sector. It is then transshipped, usually by pipeline, to a refinery, operating in the secondary sector. The refined oils are then transported by road to the garages where they are sold to the final consumers. Road transport and garages are both services in the tertiary sector. Although the process of oil production passes through all three sectors, often the oil rig, refinery, road tankers and garages are owned by one large company.

As a general rule, the balance between the three sectors gives an indication of the stage of development of an economy. Figure 2.11 shows the structure of civilian employment by sector in the UK for 1997.

Fig. 2.11 Structure of civilian employment in the UK, 1997 (% of total)

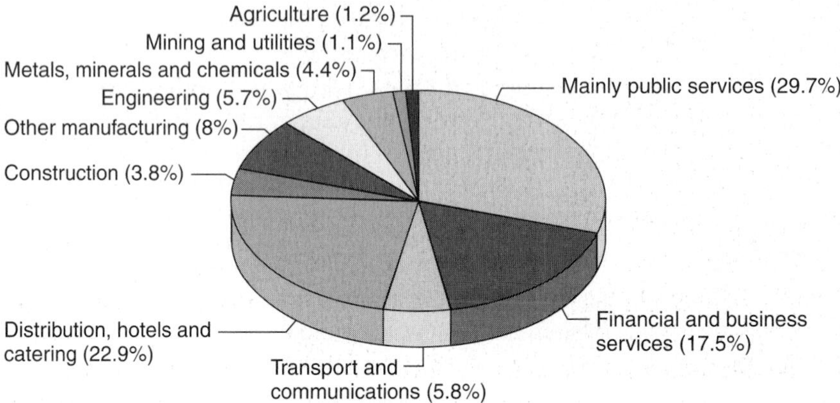

Think about it

- There is a continuing trend towards a greater proportion of the UK labour force being employed in tertiary rather than primary or secondary industries. What do you think are the implications of this for manufacturing, the economy and education in the UK?

Specialisation and the division of labour

The eighteenth-century economist Adam Smith first drew attention to the importance of specialisation and the **division of labour** in his book *The Wealth of Nations* (1776). He was primarily interested in seeing how the productivity of a particular industry increased when the manufacture of its products was broken down into specialised activities.

Specialisation and the division of labour depend on the concept of exchange. A business is able to specialise in the production of one good or service because its owners are able to exchange that good or service for other goods and services. Similarly, the employees of a business are able to specialise in one type of activity, such as accountancy or operating a machine, since they are able to exchange their labour for goods and services that they need. This type of exchange has been facilitated by the development of money as a medium of exchange (see Unit 8).

Adam Smith (1723–90)

Adam Smith, who was born in Kirkaldy, Scotland, became one of the first and most influential of British economists. He was educated at Glasgow and Oxford Universities, and lectured on language and literature in Edinburgh between 1748 and 1751, when he became first Professor of Logic, and then Professor of Moral Philosophy at Glasgow University.

His first writings were on moral philosophy, in which he was influenced by Continental philosophers whom he met during a tour of France and Switzerland. He was appointed Lord Rector of the University of Glasgow in 1787, and a year later became Commissioner of Customs in Edinburgh.

Smith's major work, *An Investigation into the Wealth of Nations* (1776), was the first real attempt to establish economics as a science in its own right. In it he attempted to show that wealth was created and distributed most effectively without any government interference. In doing so, he also first proposed the advantages of the division of labour, in a passage analysing the operations in a pin factory, which has been held as a fundamental principle in economics ever since. An extract is reproduced below.

Of the Division of Labour

The greatest improvement in the productive powers of labour, and the greater part of the skill, dexterity, and judgement with which it is anywhere directed, or applied, seem to have been the effects of the division of labour. The effects of the division of labour, in the general business of society, will be more easily understood by considering in what manner it operates in some particular manufactures. It is commonly supposed to be carried furthest in some very trifling ones; not perhaps that it really is carried further in them than in others of more importance: but in those trifling manufactures which are destined to supply the small wants of but a small number of people, the whole number of workmen must necessarily be small; and those employed in every different branch of the work can often be collected into the same workhouse, and placed at once under the view of the spectator. In those great manufactures, on the contrary, which are destined to supply the great wants of the great body of the people, every different branch of the work employs so great a number of workmen that it is impossible to collect them all into the same workhouse. We can seldom see more, at one time, than those employed in one single branch. Though in such manufactures, therefore, the work may really be divided into a much greater number of parts than in those of a more trifling nature, the division is not near so obvious, and has accordingly been much less observed.

To take an example, therefore, from a very trifling manufacture; but one in which the division of labour has been very often taken notice of, the trade of the pinmaker; a workman not educated to this business (which the division of labour has rendered a distinct trade), nor acquainted with the use of the machinery employed in it (to the invention of which the same division of labour has probably given occasion), could scarce, perhaps, with his utmost industry, make one pin in a day, and certainly could not make twenty. But in the way in which this business is now carried on, not only the whole work is a peculiar trade, but it is divided into a number of branches, of which the greater part are likewise peculiar trades. One man draws out the wire, another straights it, a third cuts it, a fourth points it, a fifth grinds it at the top for receiving, the head; to make the head requires two or three distinct operations; to put it on is a peculiar business, to whiten the pins is another; it is even a trade by itself to put them into the paper; and the important business of making a pin is, in this manner, divided into about eighteen distinct operations, which, in some manufactories, are all performed by distinct hands, though in others the same man will sometimes perform two or three of them. I have seen a small manufactory of this kind where ten men only were employed, and where some of them consequently performed two or three distinct operations. But though they were very poor, and therefore but indifferently accommodated with the necessary machinery, they could, when they exerted themselves, make among them about twelve pounds of pins in a day. There are in a pound upwards of four thousand pins of a middling size. Those ten persons, therefore, could make among them upwards of forty-eight thousand pins in a day. Each person, therefore, making a tenth part of forty-eight thousand pins, might be considered as making four thousand eight hundred pins in a day. But had they all wrought separately and independently, and without any of them having been educated to this peculiar business, they certainly could not each of them have made twenty, perhaps not one pin in a day; that is, certainly, not the two hundred and fortieth, perhaps not the four thousand eight hundredth part of what they are at present capable of performing, in consequence of a proper division and combination of their different operations.

Source: A. Smith, *The Wealth of Nations* (1776)

Levels of specialisation

Specialisation occurs at many levels, and may take place without any actual division of labour. (The term 'division of labour' is usually used to mean the practice of dividing a specific job or process into several smaller jobs or processes.)

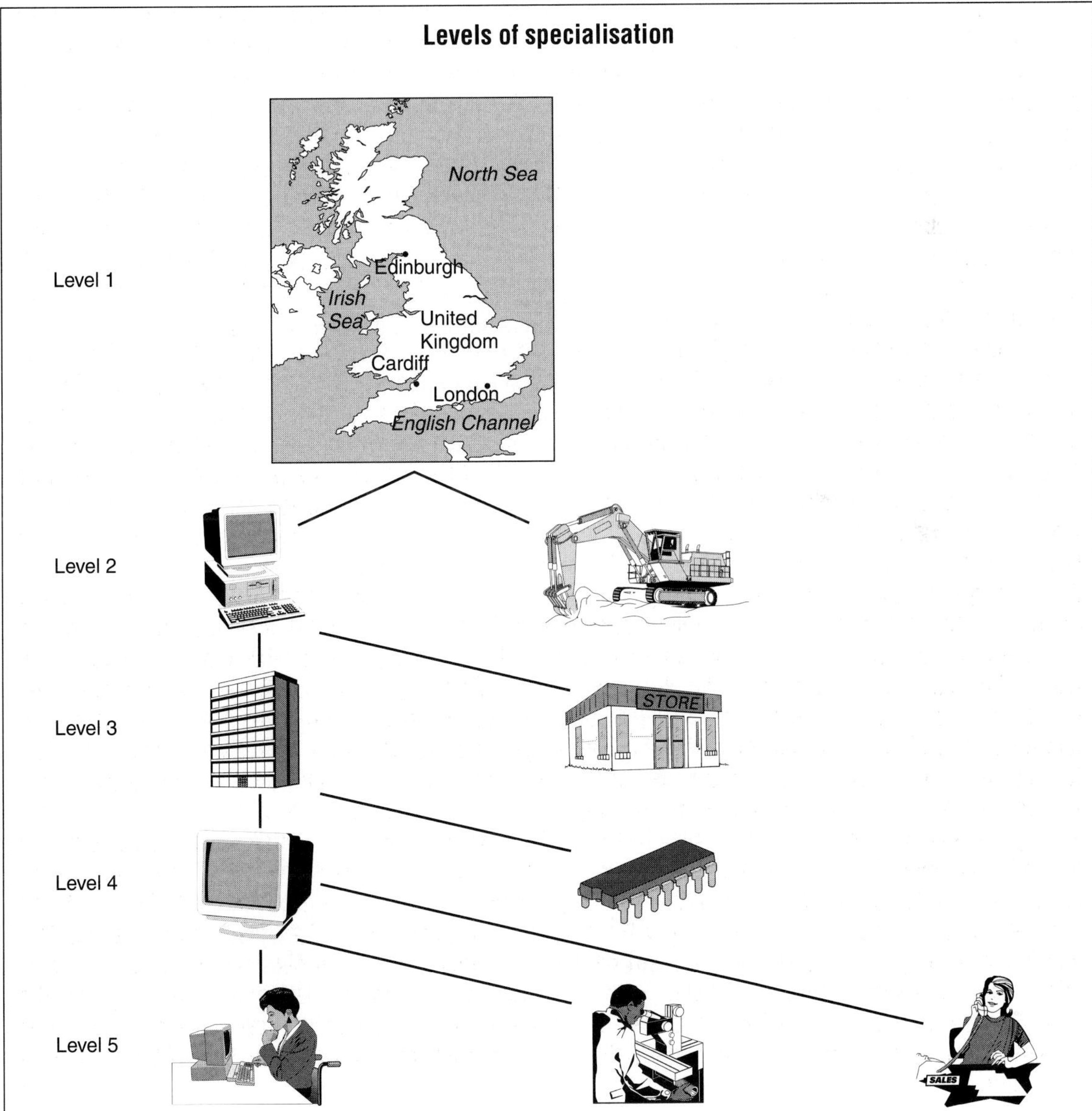

At the highest level, countries may specialise in the production of those goods in which they have a natural advantage. Within a country, industries will specialise in the production of certain types of goods (level 2). Individual firms specialise in, for example, production and retailing (level 3), and a firm may have different factories or plants to manufacture different parts of the product (level 4). Finally, people working for a firm will specialise in the type of work in which they have particular skills or abilities. For example, some employees will work in administration, others in production and yet others in selling (level 5).

International specialisation

Geographical, geological and climatic factors make some areas of the world more suitable than others for the production of certain goods. Tropical fruits cannot be produced economically in Northern Europe, and copper cannot be mined in countries where there are no deposits. In addition, there are often acquired differences between countries, arising from investment in machinery and other capital goods, or the supply of cheap labour. Factors such as these often influence the goods a country produces, and most countries specialise in producing those goods in which they have a natural advantage.

Something to do

The European Union consists of a number of individual member states (currently fifteen, although this is likely to increase in the future). The members vary greatly in terms of culture, size, natural resources and technological development.

- In groups, select two member states to investigate.
  - Which goods does the UK export to your chosen countries, and which goods does the UK import from them? Why do you think this is?
  - Write notes on your conclusions and discuss them with other groups of students who have investigated other European Union member states.
- You will find useful sources of information on the European Union in your school, college or central library (see also page 413). Get used to using your library and find out about the resources it has. These will probably include not only books but newspapers and magazines, CD ROMs and Internet access.

Regional specialisation

Similar considerations often lead to specialisation between areas or regions within a country. The availability of factors of production, such as a labour force with skills appropriate to a particular industry, and economic history have often combined to concentrate industries in particular areas. The result is that it is often very difficult for competitive plants to be established outside those areas.

Specialisation between industries

Individual industries tend to concentrate on producing a particular type of product. This enables them to concentrate on building up capital and expertise particularly suited to producing that type of product. In this way they are able to produce goods efficiently and cost-effectively, gaining a good reputation for themselves and their product.

While it is common practice to talk of distinct industries, such as the motor industry, in practice it is often very difficult to draw boundaries between industries. Should the manufacturers of electrical components, or the firms supplying upholstery for car seats, be included in the motor industry? If they are included, what about that part of their output that supplies the shipbuilding or domestic appliance industries?

In the UK, the Standard Industrial Classification (SIC) system tries to overcome such difficulties, and is used in the collection of all relevant official statistics. The whole economy is classified into 22 broad groups and each firm allocated to a group on the basis of its main product. These classifications are divided into various trades, each of which may be further subdivided.

Specialisation between firms

Industries are made up of a number of individual business organisations, or firms. As we see in Unit 4, a firm is an entity that is regarded in economics as a unit of control since, through its management, it can take decisions that have a considerable influence on an economy. Individual firms are often highly specialised even within an industry. For example, the transport industry contains many individual firms. While some firms will carry most items for various customers, other firms will specialise in carrying particular types of goods, such as livestock or nuclear waste.

Specialisation between factories

One firm often has many factories or plants. These are called the **units of production**. The firm determines the specific product each factory or plant produces; individual plants often specialise in making a particular part of the final product. Thus a motor manufacturer may have one plant that manufactures engines, another car bodies and so on. In this way, each plant can accumulate machinery and skilled labour that is entirely suited to the type of production it carries out.

Specialisation within plants

An individual plant may produce more than one item. A manufacturer of household soaps may find it cost-effective and efficient to produce washing-up liquid and shampoo in the same plant, especially if they require many of the same basic raw materials. Although they are both produced in the same plant, however, the production processes may well be kept separate, each dedicated to producing its own type of product with machinery and equipment that has been specifically designed to help in the manufacture of that product.

The division of labour

While the division of labour is at the most detailed level of specialisation, it is the most important form of specialisation, and the form on which all other levels depend. Every individual has their own particular skills and aptitudes – the things they can do best, and perhaps better, than other people who do other things best. These skills and aptitudes may be inherent in a person, or may be learned through training or experience. Thus a person may have a natural aptitude for working with figures, or they may have learned to work with them by taking a course such as the Association of Accounting Technicians, or they may have aptitude simply because working with figures has become an important part of their job.

> ***Think about it***
>
> Each of us has particular skills and aptitudes that suit us for a particular type of job or career.
>
> - Identify and make a list of your own particular skills and aptitudes.
> - What types of work do you think you should specialise in?

Adam Smith discovered the effectiveness of the division of labour when he investigated the production of pins in a factory (see the extract on page 72). He found that by breaking down the process into eighteen distinct operations carried out by different employees, production was far higher than when each employee produced a complete pin. Modern industrial production is based on this principle, often breaking down complex production into a large number of specific operations, which are carried out by employees who may have the skills and aptitudes that are appropriate to carrying out those operations. Thus, in a manufacturing plant, some employees will operate the machines to produce the product, while others will receive and store raw materials, some will check and pack the finished product and yet others will deal with its dispatch to the customer. Among those who actually produce the goods, some may operate specific computer-controlled machines, while others have the skills to hand-finish the product.

> Your own school or college presents an example of the division of labour. Overall management and running of the establishment is the responsibility of the Principal or Head, who is a specialist in college or school management. Other people are employed to do the school or college administration, and some may specialise in accounting or record keeping. Employees who have skills in maintenance work and cleaning see that the building is safely maintained in a good and clean condition, while other employees may be employed to ensure the security of the premises and those who work or study in them. There may be separate departments for subject areas as diverse as business, humanities, science and technology, each department with its own complement of tutors who are specialists in their subjects.

Division of labour in this way is not just confined to plants and factories. In order to operate efficiently and successfully, all firms need back-up services such as marketing, administration and financial management. In small firms, one person may have to undertake several of these functions. In larger firms, however, where each function becomes more complex, specialists may be employed to carry out a specific function, such as human resource management.

3 Demand and supply

Introduction: demand, supply and the market

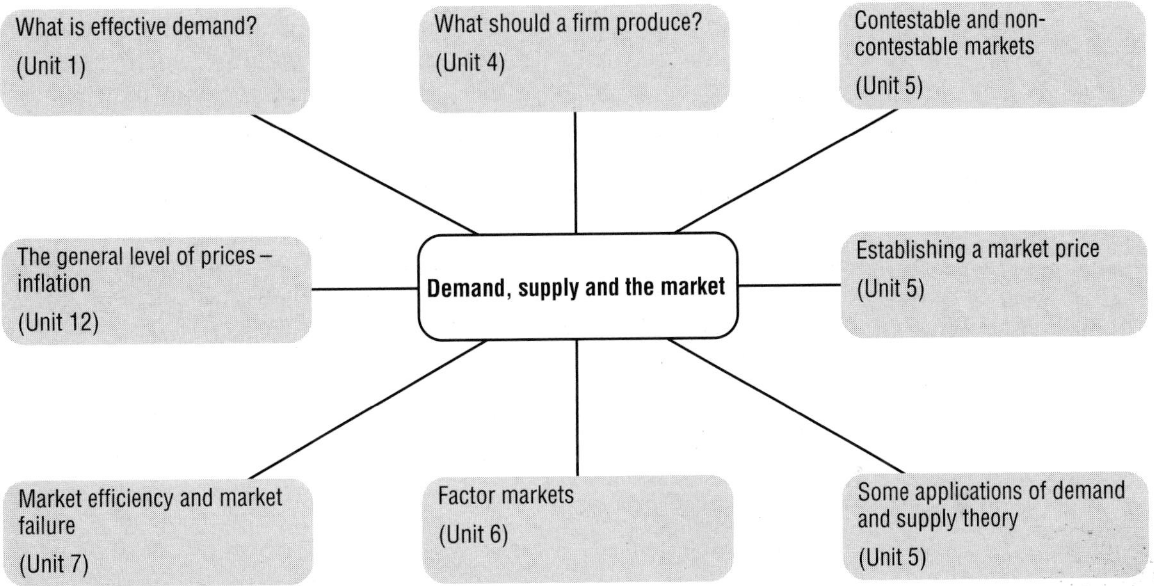

All economies depend on three basic ingredients or mechanisms:

- **demand** for goods and services
- **supply** of goods and services
- a **market mechanism** whereby goods and services can be exchanged or bought and sold (exchanged for money).

Demand is created when people in society want specific goods or services. However, as we shall see, firms and other organisations are only prepared to supply goods and services in response to **effective demand,** which is demand backed up by the willingness and ability to pay for the goods and services. The willingness of a consumer to pay for a particular good or service depends on its price and the utility, or satisfaction, he or she will derive from it compared with the utility provided by alternatives at the same price. A consumer's ability to pay for a particular good or service depends on his or her level of income. Demand, then, is very much influenced by price, and, generally speaking, the lower the price of a product the more of that product consumers are likely to be prepared to buy.

The price of a product also influences how much of a product firms are prepared to supply. All production involves costs, as we saw in Unit 1. Firms will not produce goods or services unless the price they receive at least covers their costs. Assuming that a firm is aiming to maximise profit, the greater the amount by which the price the firm can sell its products for exceeds the costs of producing them, the more of its products the firm will be prepared to supply at that price.

However, the operation of these two effects – the lower the price, the greater the demand; the higher the price, the greater the supply – gives rise to a conflicting situation that is solved by the intervention of the market. A market is a place or arrangement whereby the suppliers and buyers of goods and services come together. Without a market which enables buyers to get the things they want and suppliers to sell their products, recover their costs and so in turn be able to buy the things they want, the forces of demand and supply would be ineffective. The market plays such an important part in bringing together the effects of demand and supply, that when it operates successfully it dictates the prices of goods and services and the quantities in which they are bought and sold.

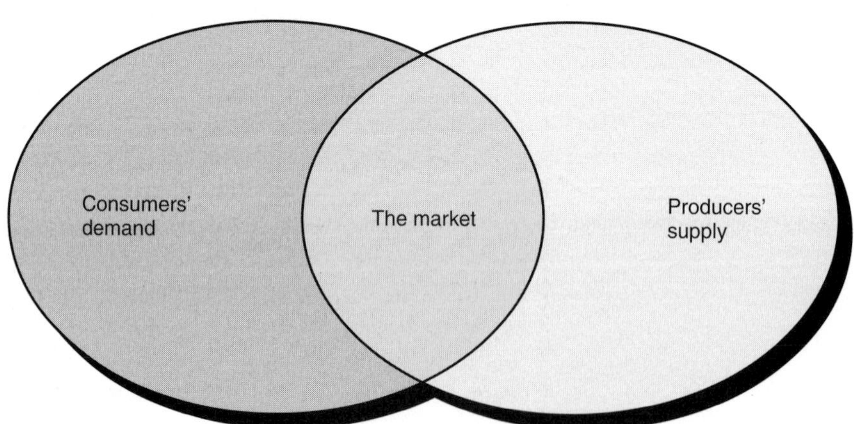

Fig. 3.1 The relationship between demand, supply and the market

In this unit, we examine the essential mechanisms of demand and supply and see the influences on them. In particular, we consider:

- what constitutes demand, and the factors that influence it
- utility, or the satisfaction obtained from goods and services
- changes in demand
- indifference curves
- what constitutes supply, and the factors that influence it
- changes in supply
- elasticities of demand and supply.

We then look at firms – the organisations that actually produce and supply the goods and services society wants – in Unit 4, before returning to examine the operation of markets in more detail in the following units.

What is demand?

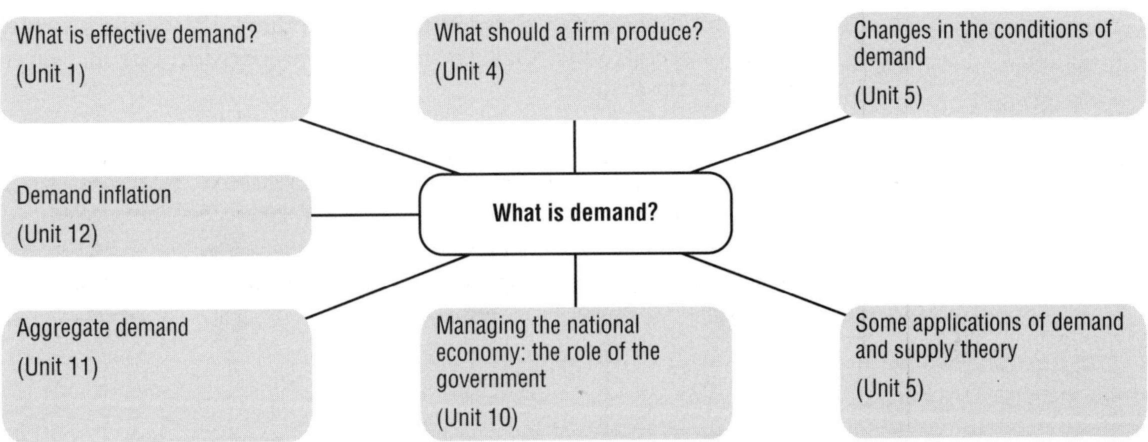

Demand is created whenever someone wants something. However, in economics we are interested in effective demand, and this cannot be equated simply with wants or desires.

Key Points

- ***Effective demand*** *is created when people want something and are willing and able to pay a price for it which makes it worth producing and selling.*

Time is also important in establishing demand. To say 'the demand for trainers is 30 pairs' is meaningless: we need to know whether it is 30 pairs per day, per week, per year or per any other period.

Something to do

- Research the demands of your fellow students, colleagues, family or friends. Try to obtain information from at least ten people.
  - Select two items that you know they all use or buy regularly, such as cans of soft drink, burgers, public transport or magazines.
  - Check the prices of your chosen items (in the case of something like public transport you may want to identify the cost of a particular journey – for example, to college or work – or else the average cost per mile).
  - Find out the quantity demanded at the price you have identified and over a specific period (say a week or a month) by the people whose demand you are researching.
  - Construct a table showing each person's demand for each product over the period you have chosen. Remember the quantity demanded must be for the product at the price you originally identified.
  - Keep your table, as you will need it to complete the activity on page 88.

An individual consumer's demand for a given product is their **individual demand.** If we add together the individual demands of every consumer (whether a person, government or firm) for a particular product, we can obtain the total or **market demand** for that product. This is the quantity or quantities of a product that consumers are prepared to buy in a given period at various prices.

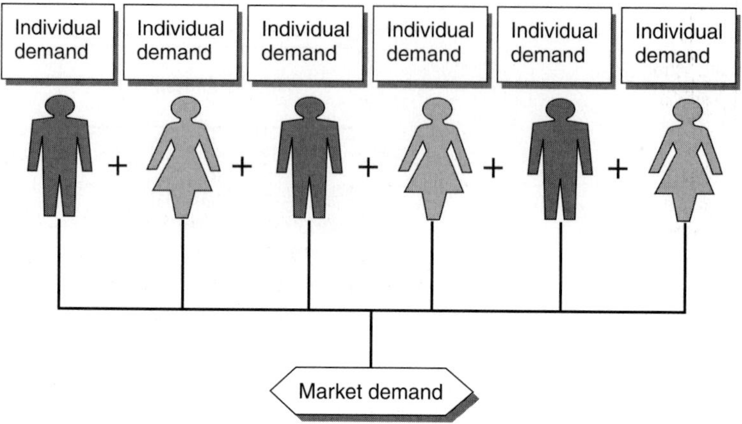

Fig. 3.2 Individual demand and market demand

The main influences on demand

A number of factors may affect both individual demand and market demand:

- **Price:** Some products are outside the price range of most consumers and are dismissed from their consideration. Other goods complete for consumers' attention, and their prices can significantly affect the demand for them. Generally, the higher the price, the lower the quantity demanded. When the price rises, some consumers will think the goods are no longer worth buying at the higher price. If the price falls, more people will consider the goods value for money and be prepared to buy, or buy more of them. The significance of price changes varies from product to product.
- **Income:** Effective demand must be supported by the ability to pay, and therefore an individual's demand partly depends on their level of income. Some goods are too expensive for most consumers. Equally, an individual's income may be such that he or she is not affected by considerations of price, particularly in respect of certain goods such as coffee, cars or houses. As levels of income change, so do patterns of demand. This is as true of an economy as it is of an individual.
- **Taste:** Consumers' tastes and preferences help to determine individual and market demand. Many factors influence taste, including fashion, lifestyle and personal preference. For example, fashion in clothes changes from year to year, and last year's fashions may no longer be in demand. The trend towards healthier lifestyles has increased the demand for foods containing higher proportions of unsaturated fats at the expense of those containing saturated fats. If you like the colour blue, you are more likely to buy a blue T-shirt than a red one.
- **Prices of other goods:** Demand for one product may depend partly on the prices of other products. Some goods are necessary for other goods to function, or yield utility, properly. These are called **complementary goods.** For example, video recorders require video-

cassettes. A fall in the price of video recorders may considerably increase demand for them, and this in turn would lead to an increase in demand for videocassettes. A change in the price of videocassettes, on the other hand, would have little effect on demand for video recorders. Other goods are substitutes for each other. Tapes may be considered substitutes for CDs, and a rise in the price of CDs may mean that many people switch to listening to tapes instead, resulting in decreased demand for CDs and increased demand for tapes.

- **Population:** Demand is influenced by changes in the size and structure of the population. For example, in Britain we have an ageing population, which means that the proportion of older people to younger people is increasing. The effect of this will be that more services and products, such as medical and leisure services, aimed at older people will be required. Changes in demand due to changes in population are unlikely to be significant over a short period, but over a number of years the pattern may change considerably.
- **Government policy:** Demand for some goods is affected by government policy towards them. In the UK, cigarettes and alcohol are taxed highly, partly in order to control demand for these products, while drugs such as cannabis are prohibited by law.

Think about it

- Do you think the government is right to try to control demand through taxes or legislation, or is this an unethical constraint on people's freedom to choose? Consider the demand for products such as tobacco, alcohol, drugs and pornography.
- Is government action to control the demand for and supply of these goods effective?
- What about the continuing demand for prohibited substances, or the development of a black market or smuggling?

- **Seasonal factors:** Demand may vary according to the time of year. Thus demand for ice cream increases in a hot summer, while demand for Christmas trees only occurs over the few weeks leading up to Christmas. Expectations of an increase in tax on alcohol may lead to considerably increased demand for wines, spirits and beers on the eve of the Chancellor's Budget.

Fig. 3.3 The influences on demand

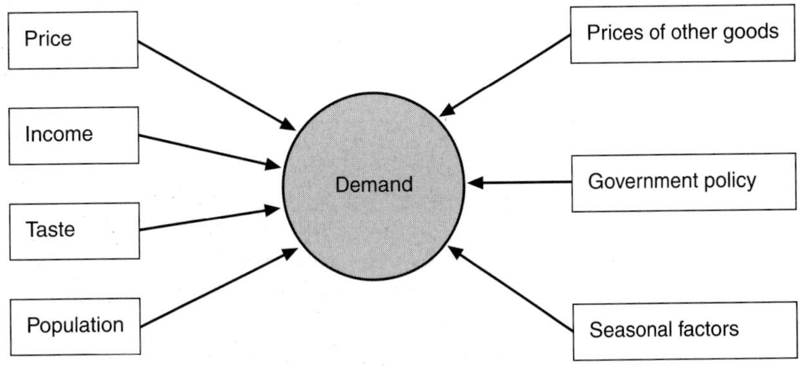

All these factors can influence demand at the same time. However, as we are principally interested here in the effects of a *change in price* on quantity demanded, we can simplify matters by assuming all other factors (known as the **conditions of demand**) remain the same (the principle of ***ceteris paribus*** – see Unit 1). We consider changes in the conditions of demand in the section beginning on page 90.

Individual demand and market demand

When you go shopping you have two types of decisions to make.

- What goods and services will you buy?
- In what quantities will you buy them?

Utility

Some goods will have no appeal for you, since you would get no satisfaction from using or consuming them. If you are not interested in stamp collecting, you will not be tempted to bid at a stamp auction in the town hall. If you train regularly at your local running track, however, you may well call in at a sports shop to buy some new running shoes. This is because you will derive some **utility** from the running shoes, whereas you will derive none from the stamps.

As we saw in Unit 1, utility is not the same as usefulness, but it is the underlying determinant of individual demand. People buy pictures because they like them. Pictures are not useful, but they do provide utility. On the other hand, if your bike has a flat tyre, a pump is useful and also yields utility. A consumer will not buy a product unless he or she expects to obtain utility from it. The utility obtained from a particular product may vary with time and place. An ice cream is more likely to yield utility to someone in London on a sweltering day in July, than to someone on Snowdon in January.

Marginal utility

The amount of utility you expect to derive from a product is important in determining how much of the product you will buy. In general, the greater the utility you expect, the higher the price you are prepared to pay.

Let us suppose that a student, Judy, is thirsty and wants a cup of coffee in her college refectory. The price is 60 pence a cup. Judy will only buy the coffee if she expects to derive at least 60 penceworth of satisfaction, or utility, from it. If she thinks she will derive more than 60 penceworth of utility from the coffee, it seems a good buy and so she spends her money. If she thinks she will derive less than 60 penceworth of utility from it, she will not buy the coffee. (Of course what goes on in Judy's mind is just the feeling of 'Is it worth it?'.) Let's assume that Judy thinks she will derive 60 penceworth of utility from the coffee and so buys a cup.

Having drunk this, what are the chances that she will now buy a second cup of coffee? She has already satisfied the need for a drink to some extent, so it is unlikely that she will expect to obtain as much utility from a second cup as she did from the first. If, for example, she only expects to obtain 55 penceworth of utility from the second cup, she will not be prepared to pay 60 pence for it. It will, however, be a reasonable purchase if she can negotiate a price of 55 pence for it.

This is the principle of **diminishing marginal utility**.

Key Points

- *The principle of **marginal utility** states that the more a consumer already has of a product in a given period of time, the less utility he or she will anticipate from further units and the less he or she will be prepared to pay for those further units.*
- ***Marginal utility** can be defined as the satisfaction received from possessing or consuming one extra unit of a commodity, or the satisfaction lost by not possessing or consuming it.*

The word 'margin' means 'extra'. Most economic decisions are made 'at the margin'. We all buy some clothes and some food, for example. What an economist is interested in is whether, when we have the money, we buy an *extra* unit of food or an *extra* unit of clothes.

From *The Affluent Society*

In the contemporary United States, the supply of bread remains plentiful. The yield of satisfactions from a marginal increment in the supply is small. Measures to increase the supply of bread or wheat have not, therefore, been a socially urgent consideration of publicly concerned citizens. Having extended their bread consumption to the point where its marginal utility is very low, people in the industrial countries have gone on to spend their income on other things. Since these other goods entered their consumption pattern after bread, there is a presumption that they are not very urgent either – that *their* consumption has been carried, as with wheat, to the point where marginal utility is small, or even negligible. So it must be assumed that the importance of marginal increments of all production is low and declining. The effect of increasing affluence is to minimise the importance of economic goals. Production and productivity become less and less important.

Source: J. K. Galbraith, *The Affluent Society* (Penguin Books, 1991)

Think about it

- Read the extract from *The Affluent Society* by J. K. Galbraith.
- Galbraith argues that because in industrial countries there is no shortage of goods to supply people's needs, the additional production and supply of other goods and services is increasingly less important. Do you agree?
- In view of the economic interdependence of societies (discussed in Unit 1), what are the implications of this argument for
  - the unemployed
  - other developing countries?

Table 3.1 shows the circumstances in which our student, Judy, would be prepared to purchase various numbers of cups of coffee during a day. She thinks she would obtain 60 penceworth of utility from the first cup and is therefore prepared to pay 60 pence for it. (If the price were higher, she would not buy it.) On the other hand, if she has already had two cups of coffee, she will be prepared to offer only 40 pence for a third, since this is all the extra utility she expects to obtain from it. If she is asked to pay 50 pence for a third cup of coffee, she will refuse and spend the money on something else that will give at least 50 penceworth of utility. To maximise satisfaction, consumers will always behave in this way, ensuring that the price paid for each product purchased is proportional to its marginal utility (see page 82).

Table 3.1

Utility of cups of coffee		
Cups of coffee	**Utility (penceworth per cup)**	**Total utility (penceworth)**
1	60	60
2	55	115
3	40	155
4	20	175
5	5	180

When consumption rises, there is an increase in total utility, which rises even though marginal utility declines. This diminishing marginal utility is shown in Figure 3.4. In practice, of course, Judy will not be able to pay less for her second cup of coffee than for her first. She will have to pay the prevailing market price for each cup she buys and it is up to her to decide how many she wants and can afford.

Fig. 3.4 Increasing total utility

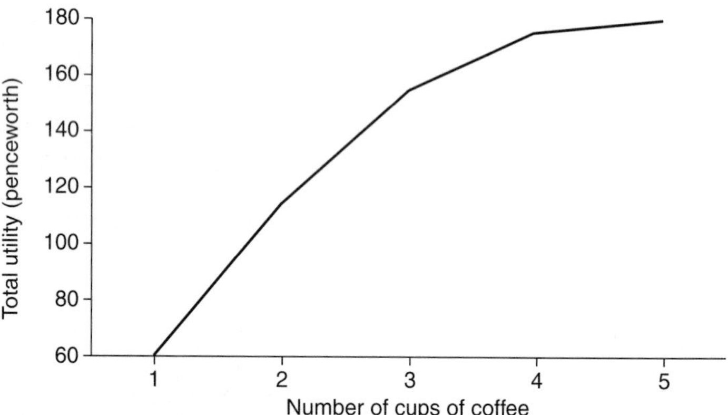

In some cases marginal utility is actually negative and therefore reduces the total satisfaction obtained from all units bought up to that point. For example, if Judy chose to buy chocolates instead of coffee, the marginal utility she obtained from buying an additional bar may increase total utility until she had bought and consumed perhaps three bars. Too much chocolate, however, may make her feel sick and therefore a fourth bar would reduce the total utility she obtained from the chocolate she had consumed.

Demand schedules and demand curves

Individual demand

The table of Judy's diminishing marginal utility for coffee illustrates an important underlying principle of the theory of demand: the more a consumer already has of a good, the less utility they will anticipate from further units of it and the less they will be prepared to pay for those units. This is because of the principle of diminishing marginal utility. Table 3.2 illustrates this principle in respect of an imaginary product – scrails.

Table 3.2

Diminishing marginal utility			
No. of scrails (per week)	Total utility (penceworth)	Marginal utility (penceworth)	Maximum price offered (pence)
1	40	40	40
2	71	31	31
3	97	26	26
4	119	22	22
5	139	20	20
6	157	18	18
7	173	16	16
8	188	15	15

Table 3.2 shows the circumstances in which a consumer would be prepared to purchase various numbers of scrails per week. This consumer expects to obtain 40 penceworth of utility from the first unit, and is therefore prepared to pay 40 pence for one scrail. If the price were higher, the consumer would not buy any. On the other hand, if the consumer already has three scrails, he will be prepared to offer only 22 pence for a fourth, since this is all the extra utility he expects to obtain. If the consumer is asked to pay 25 pence for the fourth scrail, he will refuse and spend the money on something else that will give him at least 25 penceworth of utility. In order to maximise satisfaction, a consumer will always behave in this way, ensuring that the price paid for each unit of a product is proportional to its marginal utility.

When consumption rises there is an increase in total utility, which rises even though marginal utility declines, as shown in Figure 3.5.

Fig. 3.5 Diminishing marginal utility and increasing total utility

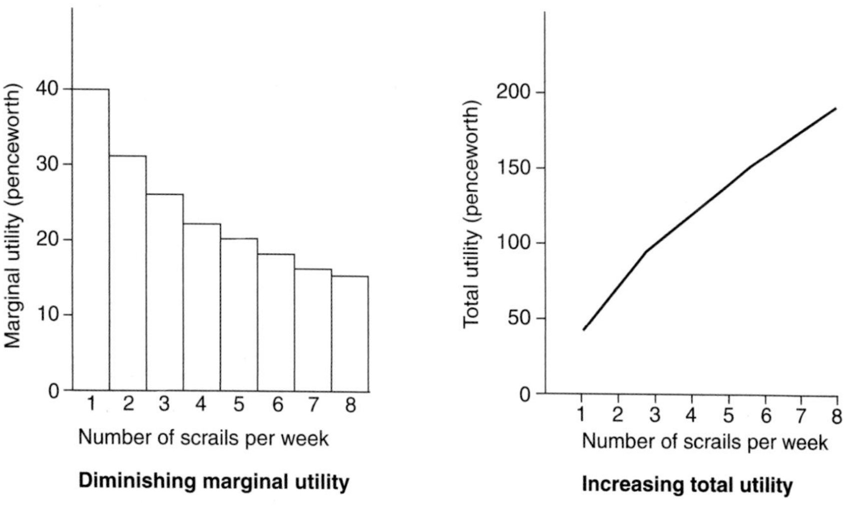

Notes: 1. For any level of consumption, total utility = the sum of the marginal utilities.
2. Total utility will increase until marginal utility = 0.

In practice, of course, the consumer cannot pay less for the second scrail than for the first. Like our student, Judy, he will have to pay the prevailing market price for each one, and it is up to him to decide how many he wants and can afford. If the price is 20 pence he will buy five, as the price then corresponds to the marginal utility he will get from a fifth unit. This implies not that his requirements are fully met, but that at prevailing prices a sixth scrail would yield too little utility – or, in other words, would not represent value for money.

We may now take the important step of converting our table of diminishing marginal utility (Table 3.2) into a demand schedule. This is shown in Table 3.3.

Table 3.3

Individual demand schedule for scrails	
Price (pence)	**Quantity per week**
50	0
40	1
31	2
26	3
22	4
20	5
18	6
16	7
15	8

This demand schedule assumes that changes in demand are entirely due to changes in the price of scrails – it is based on the principle of *ceteris paribus* (see page 39).

As we have established that our consumer is prepared to pay a price equivalent to the marginal utility he derives, we can say that when the price is, for example, 18 pence, he will buy six scrails. If the price rises to 50 pence, however, he will refuse to buy any and will spend his money on something else. The same information can be shown graphically in an individual **demand curve** (see Figure 3.6). This records price along the vertical axis and quantity demanded along the horizontal axis.

Fig. 3.6 Individual demand curve for scrails

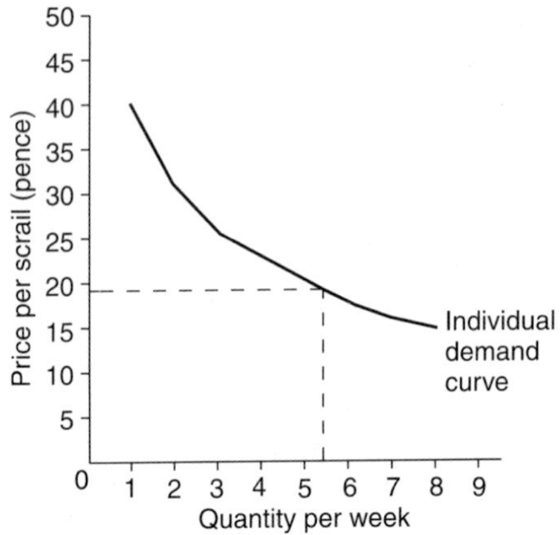

Notes: 1. If the price is 19 pence, quantity demanded is 5.4 units. If these are actually purchased, total expenditure would be 19 × 5.4 pence = 102.6 pence.
2. What would be the total expenditure if the price were 25 pence?

From Figure 3.6, we can find the number of scrails that, on average, our consumer will buy at any particular price. Both Figure 3.6 and Table 3.3 show that as price falls, the quantity demanded rises. We can now see that the reason for this is that as consumption rises, the marginal utility to be derived from an extra unit falls and a consumer can only be persuaded to buy more units if the price is reduced. There is no point spending £10 to get £5 worth of utility – and no sense in buying additional units of a product at all when the further supply would be a nuisance and lead to less overall satisfaction.

There are likely to be thousands of other purchasers of scrails, and each will have their own demand curve for them. Some examples are given in Figure 3.7. Each curve represents a person of distinctly different habits from the others. In Figure 3.7a, the consumer doesn't come into the market until the price is as low as 20 pence, while the consumer in Figure 3.7b is prepared to buy two scrails at 49 pence, and would no doubt still be in the market for them if the price rose above 50 pence. So would the consumer in Figure 3.7c, although this consumer cannot be persuaded to buy more than four units per week in any circumstances. The consumer in Figure 3.7d will buy twelve if the price falls to 8 pence, even though they will not enter the market at all until the price falls to 30 pence.

Fig. 3.7 Other individual demand curves for scrails

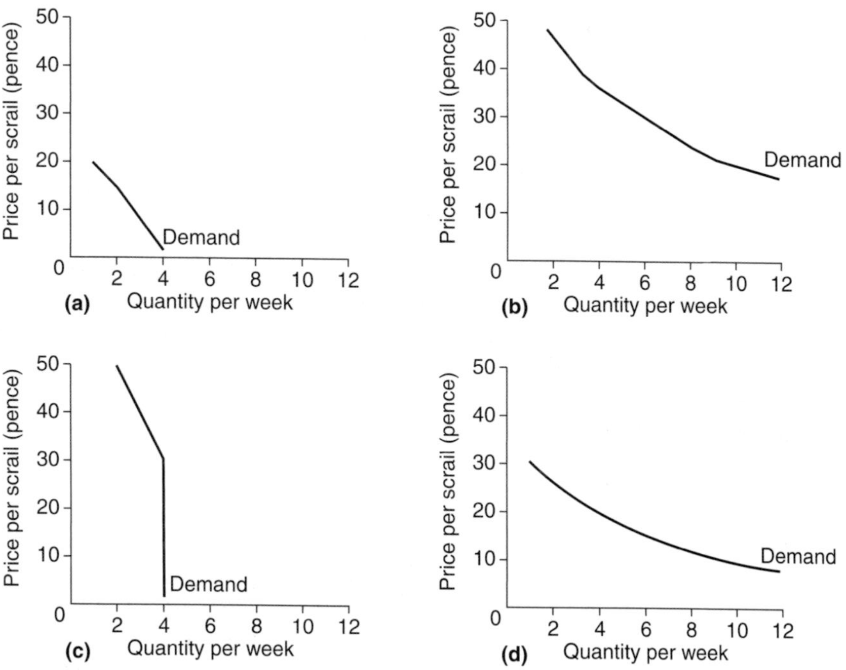

Market demand

So far we have looked at individual demand. Economists, however, are more concerned with the overall level of demand for a product (as are suppliers of those products). The level of demand can be obtained by adding together the demands of all individuals at each price. This gives a market demand schedule, which can be shown graphically as a market demand curve. The market demand schedule and curve for scrails are shown in Table 3.4 and Figure 3.8.

Table 3.4

The market demand schedule for scrails	
Price (pence)	**Quantity per week (000s)**
50	4
45	6
40	8
35	10
30	12
25	15
20	20
15	30
10	50
5	90

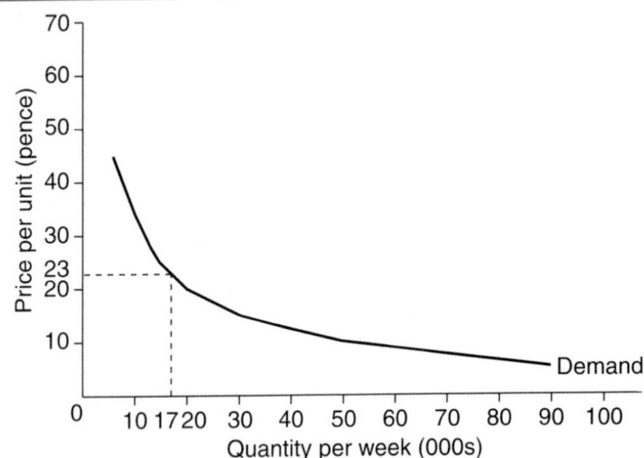

Fig. 3.8 Market demand curve for scrails

Notes: 1. There are two aspects of this curve: (a) it shows the price per unit that a g level of output can be sold for; (b) it shows the quantity that can be sold a particular price. For example, if producers have 17 000 units to sell, then a of 23 pence will dispose of them. The alternative view is that if the price is pence, then 17 000 units can be sold.

2. Total expenditure for consumers (total revenue for producers) is calculate price and quantity. Thus, if price is 23 pence, then total expenditure is 23 pence × 17 000 = £3910.00.

Something to do

- For the activity on page 79, you collected people's demands for a range of products *at a specific price* (the current price). Choose one of the items you selected and research the effect that a change in price would have on demand. For example, if you choose to research the demand for public transport, and you have identified that the current average price for a journey is 10 pence per mile, find out what people's demand would be at 6 pence, 8 pence, 10 pence, 12 pence and 14 pence per mile (you may want to convert this into the fare for a specific journey). You can either use your original sample of people to find out what their demand for the product or service would be at each price, or choose a new sample of people.
  - Construct individual demand schedules and curves for each person in your sample.
  - Construct a market demand schedule and curve based on your sample.
  - Compare the individual demand curves with the market demand curve: how do they differ? Can you suggest reasons for this?
- Keep your graph as you will be adding to it later.

When discussing the principles of demand in general, we may use a *generalised* demand curve, which characterises all normal demand curves without being concerned with the details for particular products. A generalised demand curve is shown in Figure 3.9. From this we can see that

- when price = OP, quantity demanded = OQ
- a price of OR will be low enough to persuade consumers to buy OV units
- total consumer expenditure at price OP = OPAQ (price multiplied by quantity).

Fig. 3.9 A generalised demand curve

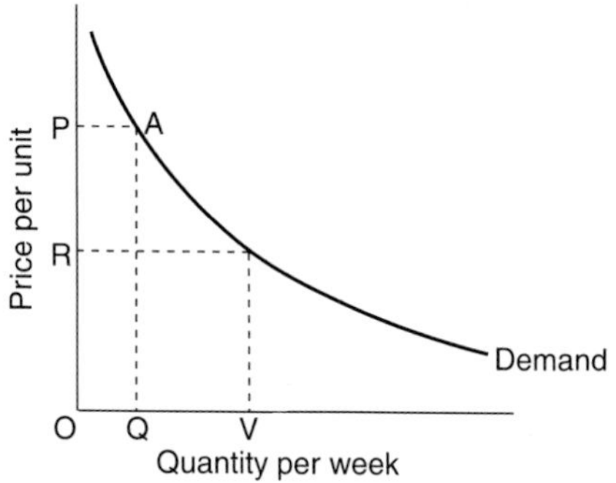

Consumer surplus

We have seen that if the price of scrails is 22 pence, our consumer will buy four units, since this will equate price and marginal utility. Thus the consumer will spend 88 pence. Four scrails, however, will provide the consumer with 119 penceworth of utility (the sum of their marginal utilities) and if the scrails had been sold at auction he would have been prepared to pay this amount for them. The 31 penceworth of utility gained in addition to the utility paid for is known as the consumer surplus, and is shown as the shaded area in Figure 3.10. The consumer surplus is the satisfaction that the consumers receive but do not pay for and is often the target of tax collectors. We return to this in Units 10 and 14.

Fig. 3.10 Consumer surplus

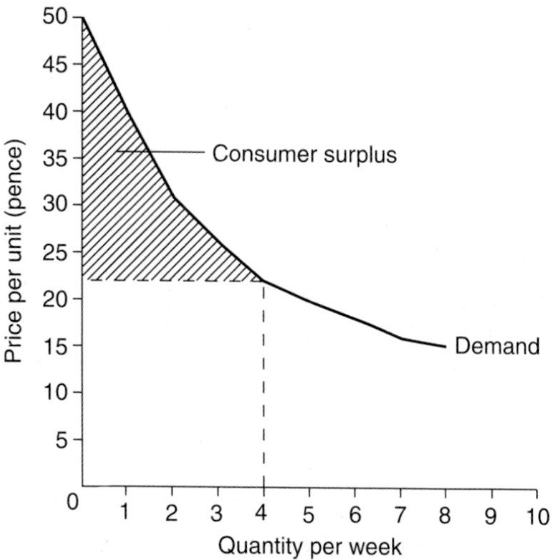

Note: The consumer pays 22 pence for each unit, but he would have been prepared to pay more than 22 pence for each of the first three units because they give him higher marginal utility. The shaded area shows the extent of this utility: consumer surplus.

Changes in the conditions of demand

In looking at the effects of price changes on demand, we have had to hold constant all other influences that might also affect demand. These influences are known as conditions of demand, and, as we have seen, include factors such as

- incomes
- the prices of other goods
- changes in taste and fashion
- population size and structure.

If the conditions of demand for a product change (see page 90), the demand curve for that product will also change. The following examples demonstrate this.

A change in incomes

In Figure 3.11, the market demand curve at one level of income for a product is shown by the line DD, so that at a price OP consumers are prepared to buy OQ units.

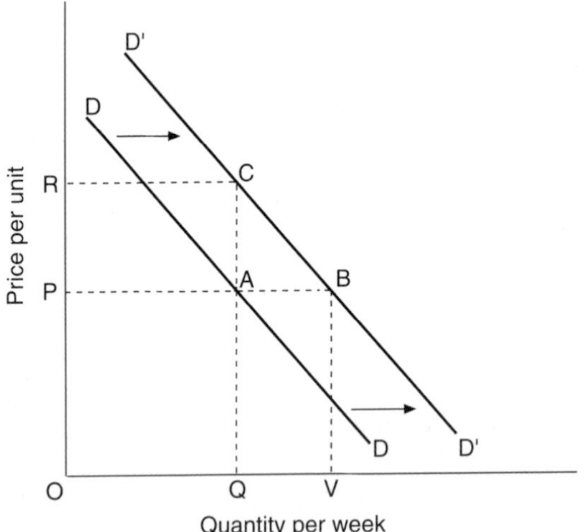

Fig. 3.11 A change in the conditions of demand

- If incomes in general rise, existing consumers may demand more of the product at any given price and new consumers may enter the market. This will have the effect of moving the curve to the right, D'D' in Figure 3.11, so that at price OP consumers are now prepared to buy OV units. (Alternatively, the price could be raised to OR with demand remaining the same.)
- A fall in incomes may move the demand curve to the left (from D'D' to DD).

Demand for some commodities is not affected in this way, however. For example, the demand for salt is unlikely to be affected by a change in the level of incomes because expenditure on salt forms an insignificant proportion of most people's total expenditure, and the marginal utility of further units of salt is likely to be zero – they already have all the salt they need.

Where a good is regarded as an inferior substitute for another, an increase in income may lead people to buy more of the superior good and less of the inferior good, for example, a rise in income might lead to a fall in demand for supermarket 'economy' brands and an increase in demand for brand names.

A change in the prices of other goods

- Except in the sense that all goods are competing for consumers' attention, demand for some goods is independent of the demand for other goods. These goods are said to have a neutral relationship to each other. An example is salt and petrol. A change in the price of salt is unlikely to have an effect on the demand for petrol.
- If two goods are **substitutes** (see page 81), however, the demand curve for the first is likely to move to the right in response to an increase in the price of the second (or to the left in response to a decrease in the price of the second). An example of substitute goods might be two brands of washing powder.
- If the two goods are **complementary** (see page 80), as the price of one rises, the demand curve for each is likely to move to the left; moving to the right in response to a decrease in price of one of the complementary goods. An example of complementary goods might be fountain pens and ink.

A change in tastes

Consumers' tastes are moulded by advertising and other forms of publicity. One aim of advertising is to shift the demand curve for the advertised product to the right, reflecting increased demand for the product at each price. Conversely, a successful government anti-drugs campaign will shift the demand curve for drugs to the left.

Something to do

- What would happen to the market demand curve you constructed for the activity on page 88 if
  - the level of people's incomes rose?
  - people's tastes changed?
- Construct new curves on the same graph to reflect these changes.

Shifts in demand curves

As we have seen, when the conditions of demand for a product change to produce an increase in demand for that product, the demand curve moves, or shifts, to the right. This indicates that because of the new conditions of demand, more of the product is demanded at any given price. Similarly, when the conditions of demand change to produce a decrease in demand for a product, the demand curve shifts to the left. This indicates that less of the product is demanded at any given price because of the new conditions of demand.

Figure 3.12 shows an increase in demand for a product. There are two basic ways in which this can happen:

- a fall in price from OP to OR, in which case the consumer moves along the curve DD from point A to point B. This is called an extension of demand. The reverse move, in response to a price increase, is called a contraction of demand
- a change in the conditions of demand, shifting the demand curve from DD to D'D'. In this case, consumers move from point A on DD to point C on D'D'. This is called an increase in demand (the reverse being a decrease in demand).

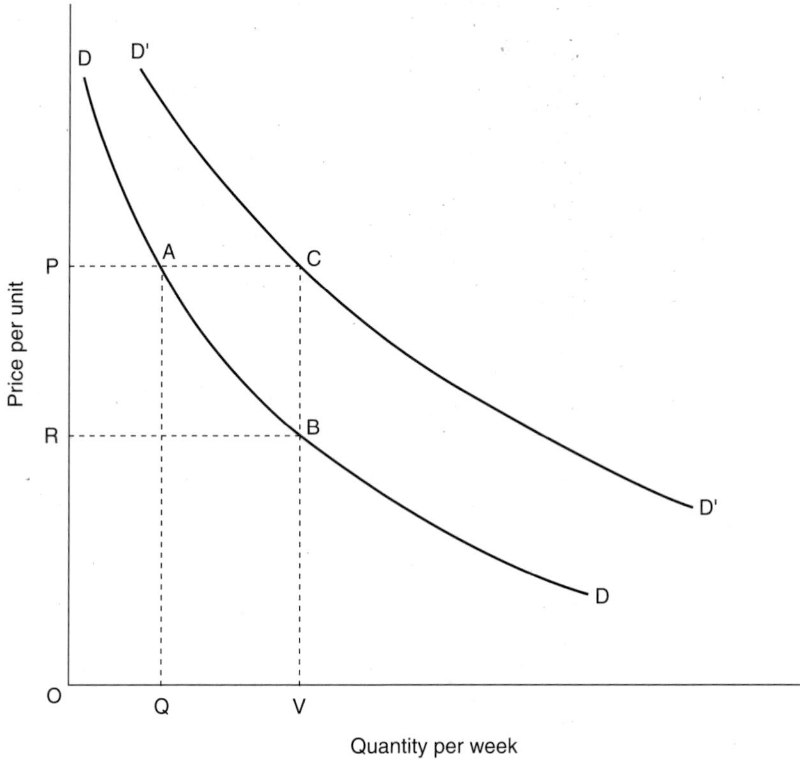

Fig. 3.12 An extension in demand and an increase in demand

Price elasticity of demand

In some cases the response of demand to changes in price is quite marked. For example, a small reduction in the price of one brand of petrol will induce many consumers to buy it in preference to other brands. A similar change in the price of all brands of petrol, however, would have little effect on the total demand for petrol. The concept of **price elasticity of demand** (PED) lets us quantify the *degree* to which the quantity of a product demanded responds to a change in the price of the product. This is called the proportionate responsiveness of demand to price.

It is important to distinguish between demand for a product in general, demand for a particular brand, and demand at a particular outlet. If the price of a brand of dog food is 50 pence per tin, and you normally buy seven tins per week, your weekly expenditure on dog food is £3.50. If you discover that a certain shop is selling the same brand at 40 pence per tin, you are likely to buy dog food there rather than at your usual shop. Other consumers are likely to do the same and this will increase demand at the new shop at the expense of other local retailers. Similarly, if the price of a different brand of dog food is reduced to 10 pence below that of your normal brand, you are likely to switch to the cheaper brand, along with other consumers. Neither scenario, however, will alter total demand for dog food, nor is it likely that a general reduction in price will increase total demand for dog food.

Something to do

The concept of elasticity is an important one in economics. It is used by businesses and governments in deciding pricing and economic policy.

- Consider the following situations and give reasons.
  (a) Why might Tesco want to know the elasticity of demand for its bottled water in response to price changes (i) if there is an increase in the cost of plastic bottles and (ii) if a major competitor reduces the price of its bottled water? Consider the effects on Tesco's sales and profits.
  (b) Why might the government want to know the elasticity of demand for cigarettes in response to price changes if it wants to reduce smoking in society by increasing the tax on tobacco products?
  (c) Why might the government want to know the elasticity of demand for houses in response to price changes if it wants to increase employment in the housing industry by adjusting tax relief on mortgages?

The coefficient of price elasticity

If we assume the change in demand for dog food at the shop offering it at the lower price is as shown in Table 3.5, the price elasticity of demand can be measured using the formula

$$\text{price elasticity of demand (PED)} = \frac{\text{\% change in quantity demanded}}{\text{\% change in price}}$$

In the case of our retailer, we obtain

$$\text{PED} = \frac{+75\%}{-20\%} = -3.75$$

This is called the **coefficient of price elasticity**. Although price elasticity can be positive or negative, it is usually negative, and the minus sign is frequently omitted. We follow this convention here.

Table 3.5

Change in demand for dog food at a single retail shop		
Price per tin (p)	**Quantity demanded (per week)**	**Total outlay by consumers (£)**
50	200	100.00
40	350	140.00

The shopkeeper's total revenue from dog food rises from £100 to £140 when the price is reduced. An increase in revenue always results from a fall in price when the value of the PED is greater than 1. The same thing is shown graphically in Figure 3.13, the reduction in price resulting in a loss of revenue of £20 on the 200 tins that could have been sold at 50 pence (represented by rectangle *A*) and a gain in revenue of £60 on the extra 150 tins sold as a result of the change in price (rectangle *B*).

Fig. 3.13 Price elasticity of demand and total revenue

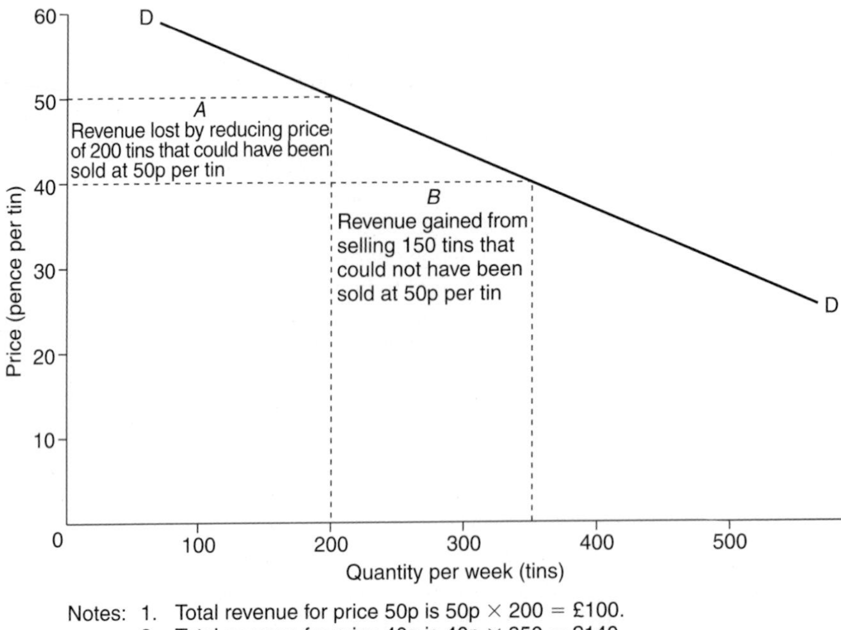

Notes: 1. Total revenue for price 50p is 50p × 200 = £100.
2. Total revenue for price 40p is 40p × 350 = £140.
3. The increase of £40 is accounted for as follows:
reduction on original 200 = 200 × 10p = −£20
gain on extra 150 = 150 × 40p = +£60
net change = +£40

There are five categories into which price elasticity can be divided:

1. **Price elasticity of demand** = 0 (Figure 3.14a): Here the quantity demanded neither expands nor contracts when the price changes from OP to OR and a producer can increase price without losing customers. Demand for petrol or addictive drugs may behave like this over moderate price ranges. The demand curve is vertical over the relevant range. A fall in price leads to a fall in revenue, since rectangle *B* shown in Figure 3.13 does not exist. Demand in this case is said to be perfectly inelastic.

Fig. 3.14 Price elasticity of demand

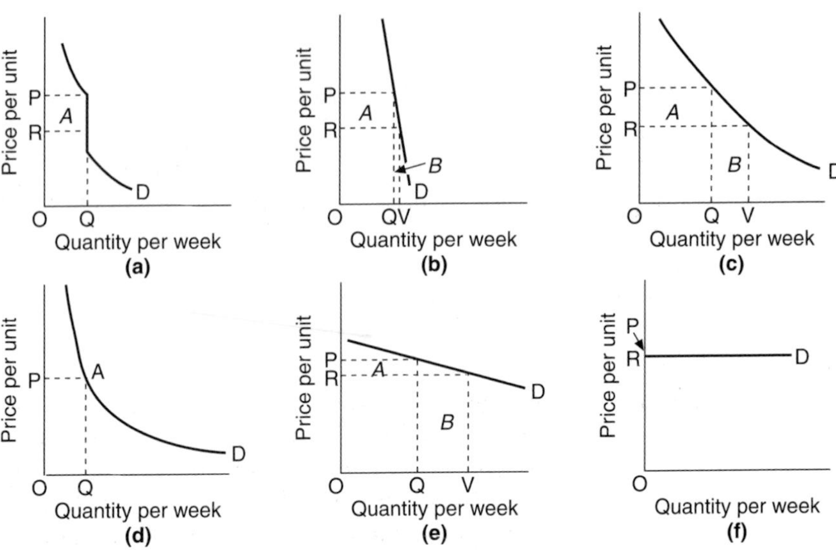

2. **Price elasticity of demand is greater than 0 but less than 1** (Figure 3.14b): In this case a particular percentage fall in price results in a smaller percentage extension of demand. The net result is that total revenue (for the producer) or expenditure (for the consumer) falls when the price falls and rises when the prices rises. Rectangle *B* is smaller than rectangle *A*. Demand is said to be inelastic for this commodity.
3. **Price elasticity = 1:** In the case shown in Figure 3.14c, we find that the percentage fall in price is perfectly matched by the percentage extension in demand, and so revenue remains constant. Rectangles *A* and *B* are equal in area. Demand is said to have unit elasticity.
   There is no particular reason why elasticity should equal 1 any more than it should equal 0.1 or 1.1, but we should appreciate the shape of the curve in Figure 3.14d. This rectangular hyperbola is of interest, in that any rectangle drawn from it to the axes will be of equal area to OPAQ so that producers' revenue (or consumers' expenditure) is the same for any price.
4. **Price elasticity of demand is greater than 1 but less than infinity** (Figure 3.14e): The quantity of goods demanded changes by a greater proportion than the change in price, and accordingly total revenue rises when price falls (rectangle *B* is larger than rectangle *A*). Demand is elastic.
5. **Price elasticity of demand equals infinity** (Figure 3.14f): This concept is of more use in constructing economic models than it is in practice. The demand curve is horizontal, indicating that at price OP the demand is zero but if the price falls slightly the producer can sell as many units as he can produce. Again a fall in price leads to a rise in revenue. Rectangle *A* does not exist and the size of rectangle *B* depends on the amount sold. Demand is said to be **perfectly elastic.**

Most demand curves are likely to have elasticities which vary along their length corresponding to category 2 or 4 above. The technique of comparing total revenue at two different prices can only indicate whether elasticity is greater or less than 1.

Something to do

- Use the market demand schedule you constructed for the activity on page 88 to calculate the coefficient of price elasticity of demand for each product at the current price and the next higher price in your schedule.
- What does this coefficient tell you?

Some pitfalls surrounding elasticity

Arithmetic measurement When we measure elasticity we are measuring the slope of the demand curve at a particular point. Since price changes in the UK must of necessity be of at least 1 penny, which may represent a high percentage of the price, we have to measure elasticity over a *range* of points. There is no great difficulty if we are consistent in measuring for a fall or rise in price, but confusion can arise if measurements are not consistent. When using the data in Table 3.5 we found the elasticity was 3.75 when the price fell. In this case a 20 per cent fall in price led to a rise of 75 per cent in quantity demanded. But suppose we regard the price as having risen from 40 pence to 50 pence. Now the quantity demanded falls by

$$\frac{150}{350} \times 100\% = 42.8\%$$

owing to a rise in price of 25 per cent, and the elasticity is given by

$$\text{PED} = \frac{42.8\%}{25\%} = 1.7$$

The demand curve seems to behave differently for a rise and a fall in price! In our example, this difference was large because of the large percentage price change.

Let us now examine a section of a different demand schedule (Table 3.6).

Table 3.6

Estimates of price elasticities of demand in the UK			
Good (general category)	**Demand elasticity**	**Good (narrower category)**	**Demand elasticity**
Fuel and light	−0.47	Dairy produce	−0.05
Food	−0.52	Bread and cereals	−0.22
Alcohol	−0.83	Entertainment	−1.40
Durables	−0.89	Expenditure abroad	−1.63
Services	−1.02	Catering	−2.61

Source: D. Begg, *Economics* (McGraw-Hill, 5th edn 1997)

If the price of computers falls from £1500 to £1485, the price elasticity of demand may be calculated as follows:

$$\text{PED} = \frac{\%\text{ change in quantity (Q)}}{\%\text{ change in price (P)}} = \frac{+2/500}{-15/1500} = \frac{+0.4\%}{-1\%} = -0.4$$

We have included plus and minus signs to show the direction of change.

Let us now suppose that the price of computers rises from £1485 to £1500. Elasticity is calculated as follows:

$$\text{PED} = \frac{\%\text{ change in Q}}{\%\text{ change in P}} = \frac{-2/502}{+15/1485} = \frac{-0.398\%}{+1.01\%} = 0.394$$

This is slightly lower than the previous figure, but the difference is much narrower than that which we had in connection with Table 3.5 – this is because we are dealing with a much smaller percentage change in price. If you substitute £1490 for £1485 in Table 3.7, you will find that the difference in calculated elasticity when a price fall and price rise are considered is even smaller.

Table 3.7

Hypothetical demand schedule for computers	
Price (£)	**Quantity (per week)**
1 500	500
1 485	502

Optical illusions

A glance at the two demand curves shown in Figure 3.15 suggests that (a) is elastic while (b) is inelastic. A more careful examination shows that they convey exactly the same information and thus have the same elasticity! We must be very careful not to label curves elastic or inelastic without considering the scales involved.

Fig. 3.15 Two demand curves conveying the same information

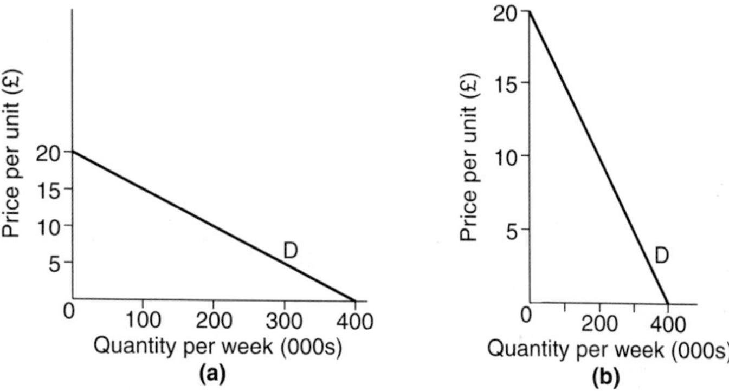

Changing elasticity

In only three circumstances will a demand curve have constant elasticity over its entire length (see Figure 3.14d): absolute elasticity, absolute inelasticity and unit elasticity along the whole curve. The elasticity of the curve in Figure 3.16 varies from infinity to zero as we move from top to bottom.

Fig. 3.16 Varying price elasticity of demand

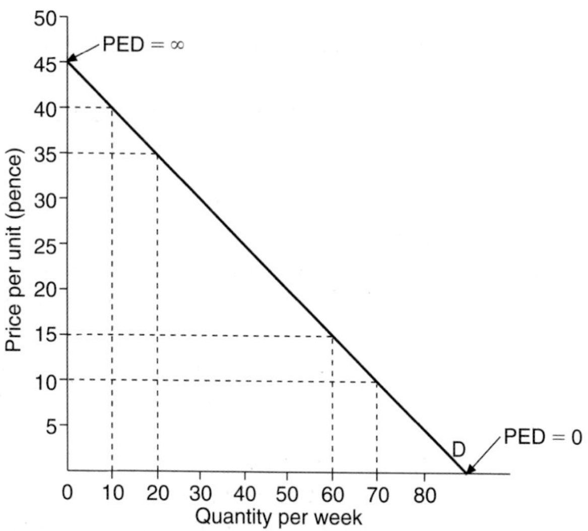

Notes:
1. At price 40p and price 15p a fall in price of 5p extends demand by 10 units.
2. When price falls from 40p to 35p, PED = 100% ÷ 12.5% = 8.
3. When price falls from 15p to 10p, PED = 16.67% ÷ 33.33% = 0.5.
4. In fact PED varies from infinity at price 45p to zero at price = 0.

What determines price elasticity of demand?

The main factors that determine the price elasticity of demand for a commodity are as follows:

- **The availability of substitutes** (see page 91): If we have a commodity 'food' which includes everything we eat, demand for it is likely to be inelastic. If we have a commodity 'Brussels sprouts', however, the demand for it is likely to be fairly elastic as there are other green vegetables that can be substituted for it if its price rises.
- **The consumer's budget:** In general, if consumers spend only a small proportion of their income on a commodity, price elasticity of demand for it will be low. Even doubling the price of matches, for example, will hardly reduce demand significantly.

Cross-elasticity of demand

It is sometimes necessary to estimate the effect of a change in the price of one product on demand for another. This is particularly true of substitute or complementary goods (see pages 80–81). The way demand for one good responds to changes in the price of another is called the cross-elasticity of demand. It is calculated by the formula

$$\text{cross-elasticity of demand} = \frac{\text{\% change in quantity of A demanded}}{\text{\% change in price of B}}$$

- In the case of substitutes, cross-elasticity will be positive – a rise in the price of product B will be followed by a rise in demand for product A.
- If the goods are complementary in demand, cross-elasticity will be negative, since an increase in the price of product B will result in a reduction in demand for product A.

This concept may be useful to producers estimating the effects of changes in the prices of competitors' goods on demand for their own. A high positive cross-elasticity will indicate the desirability of maintaining stable prices when competitors increase theirs, as consumers readily switch from one product to another. (We return to the concept of cross-elasticity of demand in the context of indifference curves on page 102.)

Something to do

A shop that sells cameras finds that average demand for its best-selling 35mm compact camera is 25 per week, while average demand for the new digital camera it has just started selling is ten per week. The price of the 35mm camera is £240, while the price of the digital camera is £275. When, as part of a special promotion, the price of the digital camera is reduced to £250, demand for it increases to fifteen, while demand for the 35mm camera drops to 22. (The reason that overall demand for both cameras has increased is that the promotion on the digital camera has actually increased the number of customers.) At the same time, demand for 35mm colour films drops from an average 200 per week to 190 per week.

- Calculate the cross-elasticity of demand for the 35mm camera and for colour films.
- Are the cameras and films complementary or substitute goods?

Normal goods, inferior goods and the value of income elasticity for a product

- Normal goods are those goods for which demand falls as incomes fall. This includes most goods, such as cars and books, televisions and washing machines, shoes and wine. Normal goods therefore have *positive* income elasticity of demand (that is, demand for them rises as income rises) although this is usually less than one.
- With **inferior goods**, demand actually increases as incomes fall. Inferior goods are typically cheap goods that people buy when they cannot afford more expensive normal goods. Inferior goods may be second-hand cars and library services, television and washing machine repairs. When incomes are low, consumers tend to purchase second-hand rather than new cars, borrow books from the library rather than buy them, and put off buying new televisions and washing machines by having their existing ones repaired to prolong their lives. In general, inferior goods are low-quality necessities that people must buy, but for which higher quality alternatives exist. Inferior goods have *negative* income elasticity of demand (that is, demand for them falls as income rises – because consumers can afford the more expensive alternatives they would prefer).

The value of income elasticity for a particular product is therefore dependent on whether the product is a normal good or an inferior good, and how much of a necessity the product is.

It is also useful to distinguish between necessities and luxury goods:

- All inferior goods are necessities, since their income elasticities of demand are negative, as are normal goods with positive income elasticities in the range 0 to 1.
- Luxury goods are those goods that have an income elasticity of demand that is higher than 1. They tend to be high quality products for which cheaper but perfectly adequate alternatives are available.

It is only when incomes rise to a fairly high level that they affect demand for luxury goods, but above that level a 1 per cent rise in incomes results in a higher than 1 per cent rise in demand for luxury goods. For example, demand for Rolls Royce cars is fairly constant regardless of normal variations in income levels. However, it is possible to suppose a situation where a substantial rise in incomes led to more consumers being able to afford Rolls Royces. (This is, of course, unlikely and would probably be met by substantial increases in the prices of their cars as Rolls Royce tried to maintain their position as manufacturers of luxury cars.)

Income elasticity of demand

A change in the incomes of consumers will normally lead to a change in the level of demand for some goods. The extent of this change is known as the **income elasticity of demand.** It is calculated by the formula

$$\text{income elasticity of demand} = \frac{\%\ \text{change in quantity demanded}}{\%\ \text{change in income}}$$

Income elasticity, which is positive except in the case of inferior substitutes, is not of great importance where individual consumers are concerned, but it is significant for particular industries. We might expect the income elasticity of demand for food to be low, because once an adequate level of consumption has been reached there is no need to buy extra food as income rises. Income elasticity for leisure activities, however, tends to be high. This helps explain the growth of tourism among people in the wealthy countries of the developed world. Industries for which demand is income-elastic keep a close eye on levels of income and employment when planning their market strategies.

Something to do

As a result of a new factory opening in an area, employment in the area has increased, and average take-home pay has risen from £300 per week to £325 per week (other employers in the area have had to raise wages in line with the new factory). A local theatre has noticed that its auditorium, which can seat 1000, is now on average 95 per cent full on Friday nights, rather than 82 per cent full as it was prior to the opening of the new factory.

- Calculate the income elasticity of demand for theatre tickets.
- Why might the income elasticity of demand for theatre tickets at this theatre not be a good guide to the income elasticity of theatre tickets generally?

Table 3.8

Estimates of income elasticities of demand in the UK			
Good (general category)	**Income elasticity of demand**	**Good (narrower category)**	**Income elasticity of demand**
Tobacco	−0.50	Coal	−2.02
Fuel and light	0.30	Bread and cereals	−0.50
Food	0.45	Dairy produce	0.53
Alcohol	1.14	Vegetables	0.87
Clothing	1.23	Travel abroad	1.14
Durables	1.47	Recreational goods	1.99
Services	1.75	Wines and spirits	2.60

Source: D. Begg, *Economics* (McGraw-Hill, 5th edn 1997)

Think about it

- Using Table 3.8 consider the following goods and services. Do you think they are income elastic? Why?
  - passenger rail transport
  - *The Times* newspaper
  - a high-interest investment account
  - the services of your local NHS hospital

Regressive demand curves

While most demand curves slope down from left to right, occasionally we find examples like those shown in Figure 3.17 which do not fit into the pattern.

Fig. 3.17 Regressive demand curves

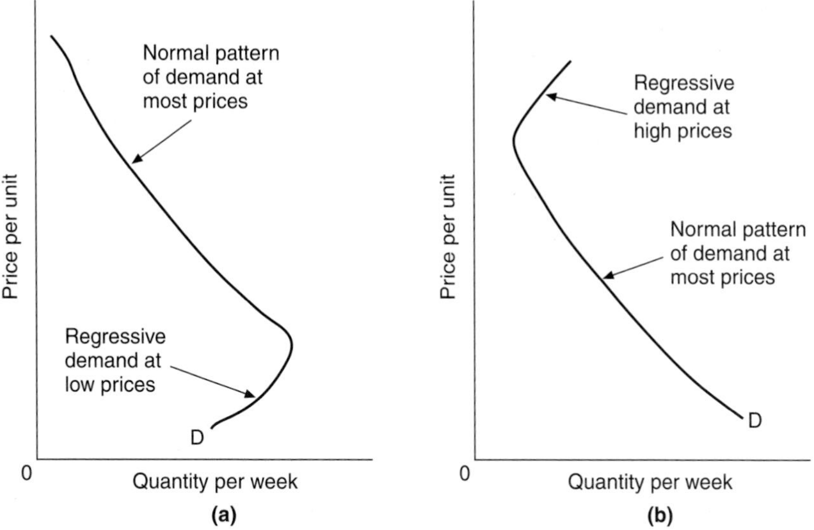

- **Giffen goods** (Figure 3.17a): Giffen goods are those basic items consumed by people on very low incomes which consumers regard as very inferior substitutes for something they want but can't afford. Demand for a Giffen good actually rises when the price rises because consumers on very low incomes maintain their former level of purchases and, finding that they can no longer afford other goods, increase their purchases of the Giffen good. Giffen goods are called after Sir Robert Giffen (1837–1910), who noticed this phenomenon while studying how the Irish peasants had behaved during the potato famine in the 1840s.
- **Goods of ostentation** (Figure 3.17b): Some consumers believe that the higher the price the better the product. In some circumstances a producer can exploit this by raising the price of goods and attracting consumers who would otherwise reject the goods as being too cheap. Such goods are purchased not for their intrinsic value but to emphasise status. Examples of such goods are jewellery and certain makes of cars. At a lower level, a brand name can give a product the effect of a good of ostentation, especially if the brand name is long established and well known for quality. For example, most larger supermarket chains sell own-label products such as breakfast cereals. However, Kellogg, Nabisco and other manufacturers are able to sell their own higher priced products through the same supermarket chains, where they will be bought because they are familiar to consumers, and many consumers will believe that in paying a higher price for the same product they must be getting better quality.

How do consumers really choose?

Weaknesses of demand curves

Demand curves as a way of analysing market demand have weaknesses. They are really more useful to a firm or industry analysing the probable effects of changes in the price of its product than to an economist trying to explain consumer behaviour, or to consumers themselves. Consumers cannot really measure utility quantitatively and are unlikely to make adjustments to their expenditure patterns every time there is a small change in the price of one of the commodities they consume. A consumer is more likely to say that one commodity yields more utility than another, rather than to try to put a value on utility per unit of different commodities. (Putting commodities in order of preference is called the ordinal approach, whereas assigning a numerical value to the utility derived from each unit consumed is called the cardinal approach.)

Another weakness of demand curve analysis is that it rests heavily on the rather artificial assumption that conditions of demand remain constant. It does not allow prices and incomes to change at the same time, for example. Nor, when the price of a product falls, does the demand curve indicate the causes of the extension of demand that follows. It cannot show whether consumers buy more because they feel they are now getting a better bargain and so switch from some other commodity (the **substitution effect**) or because they now have a higher real income and so can buy their former quantities and still have money remaining for further purchases (the **income effect**).

Indifference curves

To overcome some of these difficulties, the technique of indifference curve analysis has been developed. This builds a pattern of individual consumer indifference curves, each curve showing a number of choices between alternatives that yield equal satisfaction.

Assume that a consumer buys food and clothes, and that in a given period she currently buys 25 units of food and 2 units of clothes. This combination gives her a certain level of utility. If she reduces her expenditure on food by 5 units, total utility is also reduced. Increasing her expenditure on clothes may, however, restore it – perhaps an additional 2 units of clothes will compensate for the loss of 5 units of food. She could then be said to be indifferent to the two combinations: 25 units of food and 2 units of clothes, or 20 units of food and 4 units of clothes. Table 3.9 shows a number of other combinations of food and clothes giving our consumer the same amount of utility as the original combination. This is known as an indifference schedule, and can be used to plot an indifference curve for the consumer.

Table 3.9

A consumer's indifference schedule	
Units of food*	**Units of clothes**
25	2
20	4
15	7
10	12
5	28
0	55

* The amount of food could have been reduced by 1 unit at a time, but the larger reductions make it easier to see what happens to the demand for clothes.

Something to do

- The following is the indifference schedule of a consumer who buys computer games and goes to the cinema. Construct the consumer's indifference curve.

Computer games	Visits to the cinema
5	63
10	50
17	38
30	25
70	13
138	0

Diminishing marginal utility and the rate of substitution

The schedule (Table 3.9) shows diminishing marginal utility because the more units of clothes our consumer has, the more she wants to compensate for the loss of each further unit of food. This is the principle of the diminishing marginal rate of substitution.

Key Points

- *The **diminishing marginal rate of substitution** states that the greater the amount of a commodity that a consumer has, the more easily he or she may be compensated for the loss of a marginal unit.*

Fig. 3.18 A consumer's indifference curve

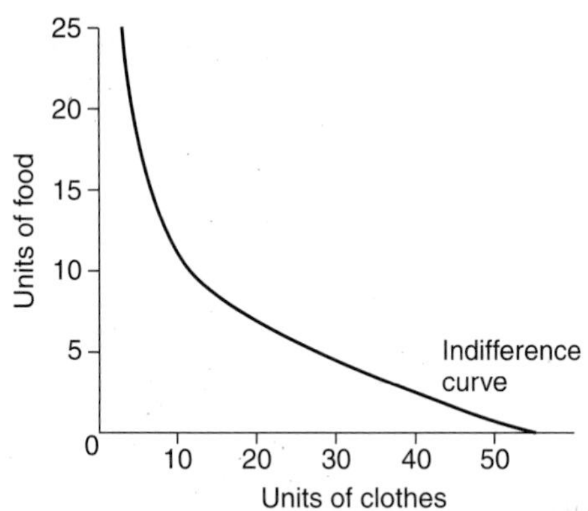

The schedule (Table 3.9) and curve (Figure 3.18) apply to one consumer. Another consumer is likely to have a different scale of preference, even though the initial combination of food and clothes may be the same. He might, for example, enjoy his food more and require 10 units of clothes to compensate for the loss of 5 units of food. In this case the indifference schedule and curve would both be different from those of the first consumer. They would still, however, display the same principle of a diminishing marginal rate of substitution.

Figure 3.19 shows the indifference curves of two consumers. The slopes of the curves are different because of their different tastes. At point *a* they are each consuming OM units of food and ON units of clothes, but require different amounts of clothes to compensate them for the loss of ML units of food. Consumer 1 requires only NR whereas consumer 2 requires NV.

Fig. 3.19 Indifference curves relating to different consumers

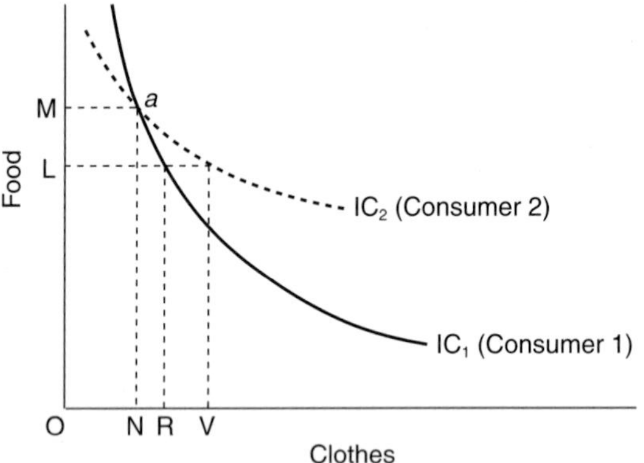

If our original consumer had started from a situation in which she had one more unit of clothes or food, she would have obtained more utility than with 25 units of food and 2 of clothes. Her indifference curve would then have been above and to the right of the first curve. This is shown as IC_2 in Figure 3.20. Each curve, representing various combinations of goods between which the consumer is indifferent, is part of a family of such curves unique to that consumer (see Figure 3.20). Total utility is constant along the length of any one curve, but is greater along curves to the right (further from the origin) since each combination on a curve further from the origin gives more of both goods.

Fig. 3.20 A family of indifference curves

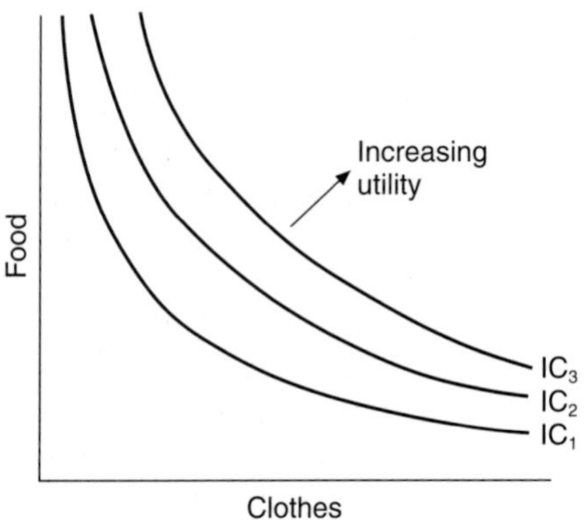

Obviously, no consumer only purchases two types of goods. This is usually overcome by plotting the amount of a single commodity along one axis and using money income to represent all others and plot this on the other axis, as in Figure 3.21. In this case, if the consumer is at point *a*, we know he or she is buying ON units of clothing and still has OM units of money to spend on all other goods. Note that this does *not* indicate that the consumer is paying OM units of income for ON units of clothes. If the consumer moves to point *b*, then we know that, compared with *a*, MR units of money have been sacrificed to obtain an additional NV units of clothes.

Fig. 3.21 An indifference curve incorporating all goods consumed

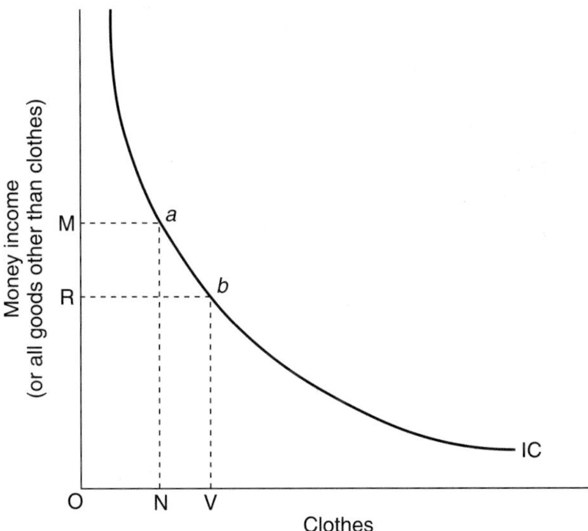

The budget line

We can assume that a consumer will want to be on as high an indifference curve as possible as this will maximise utility from spending income. In Figure 3.22, a consumer has an income of £200. If a unit of clothing costs £5, we can plot a line AB joining the point at which no income is spent on clothes and that where all income is spent on clothes. This is the consumer's budget line, and shows all the possible combinations of clothing and money income that the consumer can enjoy. The consumer could, of course, be placed anywhere in the triangle OAB, but would then have some unspent income and would not be maximising satisfaction.

- If the consumer's income increases by £25, the budget line will move away from its original position to a parallel line CD. This shows that the consumer can now obtain more satisfaction by spending more money on clothes or other goods or both. A reduction in income has the opposite effect and moves the budget line to the left.
- If the price of clothes changes, on the other hand, the consumer can buy more units of this commodity. This is shown in Figure 3.22 by the new budget line AE, which is not as steep as AB. In this case the price of a unit of clothes has fallen to £3.33, which enables the consumer to buy a maximum of 60 units.

Fig. 3.22 The budget line

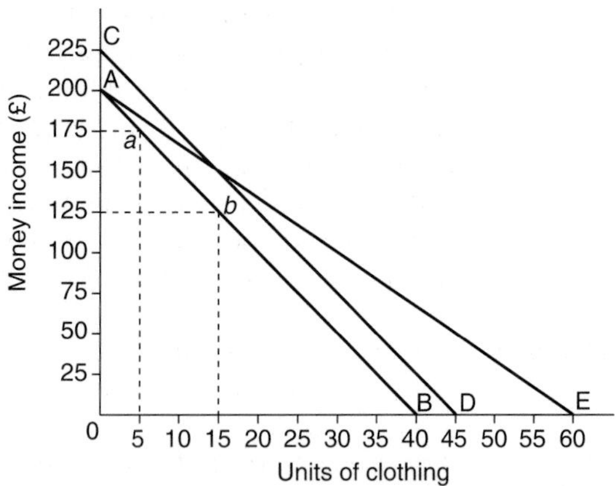

> *Something to do*
>
> - Select a product you purchase regularly, such as clothes or CDs. Construct your own budget line for your chosen product. Show what would happen if
>   - your income increased by 10 per cent
>   - the price of your chosen product decreased by 20 per cent.

Consumer equilibrium

Figure 3.23 combines a budget line with three indifference curves. The consumer is able to take up a position anywhere along the budget line AB. At A the consumer buys no clothing and is on an indifference curve to the left of IC_1, and so gains less satisfaction than would be obtained if IC_1 could be reached. As the consumer moves down the line AB, IC_1 is eventually reached at *a*, so by giving up an amount AM of other goods the consumer is able to buy some clothes.

Fig. 3.23 Consumer equilibrium

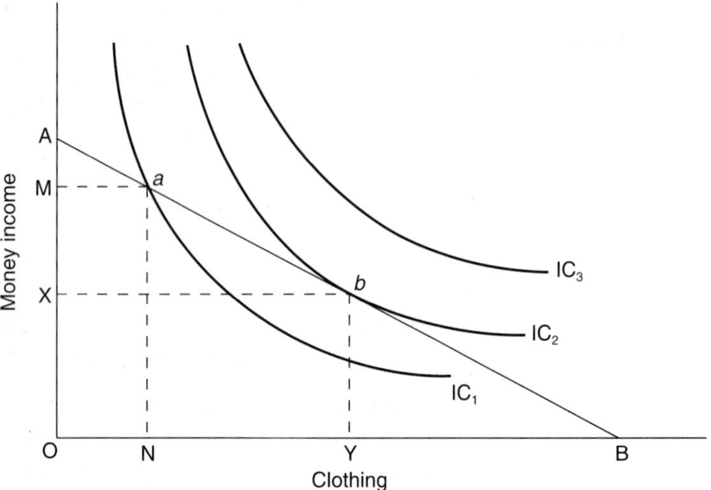

We can see from Figure 3.23 that the consumer could be in a better position by moving beyond *a*. Indeed, a move to the right of *a* will put the consumer on a higher indifference curve (the spaces between the curves shown could be filled with an infinite number of other indifference curves). As the consumer continues to buy clothes at the expense of other goods, the position *b* is reached, where the budget line forms a tangent to the indifference curve IC_2. At this point the consumer buys OY units of clothes for XA units of income, retaining OX units of income to spend on other things. However, we can see that any further move along the budget line will take the consumer into a lower indifference curve, yielding less satisfaction. Therefore *b* is the best position the consumer can reach with an income of OA, and at this point the consumer is said to be at equilibrium.

Changes in income

As income rises, the budget line moves progressively further from the origin. This enables the consumer (see Figure 3.24) to increase purchases of clothing from OW units to OZ units, and at the same time to increase purchases of other goods from OR to OU. The line joining the points of tangency *a*, *b*, *c* and *d* is known as the income consumption curve and shows how the consumer's purchases change as income rises. In this case the curve slopes upwards in a straight line from the origin, showing that the consumption of a commodity rises in proportion to income, and also that consumption of other commodities rises as well.

Fig. 3.24 The effect of increases in income

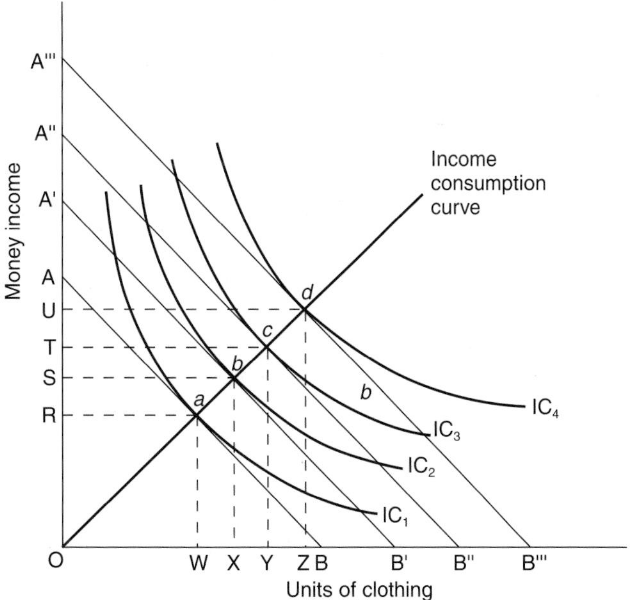

The slope of a consumer's income consumption curve varies according to the type of goods covered (see Figure 3.25).

- In Figure 3.25a, the income consumption curve is rather flat and tends to level off. This is the curve of a luxury good such as jewellery or a luxury car, for which demand rises more than proportionately with income.
- In Figure 3.25b, the steepness of the income consumption curve shows that consumption of the commodity measured along the horizontal axis does not increase in proportion to income. In this case the axis has been labelled 'Newspapers', but it might as easily have been labelled 'Salt' or 'Food'.

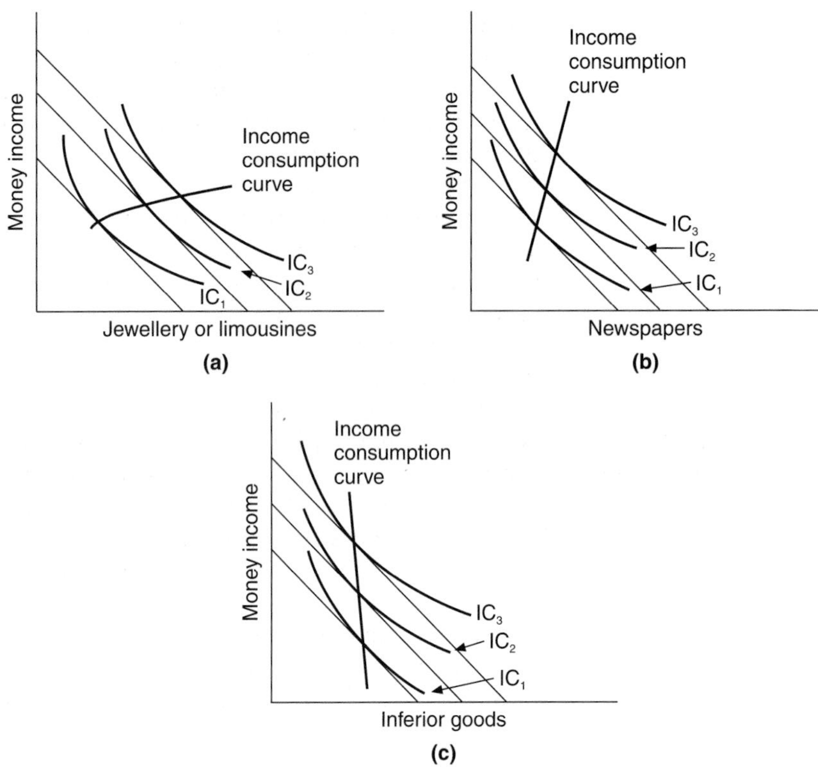

Fig. 3.25 Three other income consumption curves

- Figure 3.25c is a rather special case, for the income consumption curve slopes backwards, showing that consumption of this commodity actually *declines* as income increases. Such commodities are inferior goods (see page 99). A special type of these – Giffen goods – was discussed on page 101.

Inferior goods and Giffen goods

As we have seen, inferior goods are those which consumers buy when their incomes are relatively low, but discard as their incomes rise. As a further example, people on low incomes tend to use public transport more, since they cannot afford cars. As their incomes rise to a level at which they can afford a car, however, their use of public transport falls, even though they could afford to use it more. A similar situation arises with package holidays. People on lower incomes tend to go on mass-market package holidays, sometimes at all-in prices, to popular destinations such as Spain, Greece and Turkey. As their incomes rise, they often prefer to go on more tailor-made holidays to destinations such as Barbados, Sri Lanka or Kenya.

The distinction between Giffen goods and inferior goods is important. Giffen goods are those for which demand rises when their price rises. For example, as the general level of food prices rises, more basic foods tend to be bought and consumed. Inferior goods are considered in relation to the consumer's income.

The income consumption curve may be used to show how consumption changes with income. It enables us to measure income elasticity of demand (see page 99):

$$\text{income elasticity of demand} = \frac{\%\ \text{change in quantity demanded}}{\%\ \text{change in income}}$$

This is a calculation demand curves do not permit. In most cases the income elasticity will be positive as the quantity demanded rises when income rises. The main exception is the instance of inferior goods, where quantity demanded falls as income rises. In this case income elasticity of demand will be negative.

While an individual's income elasticity of demand may not be of great significance, the combined income elasticities of all consumers of a particular product may be very important to producers and planners. For example, if it is known that income elasticity of demand for holidays abroad is high, and a rapid increase in incomes is expected, then a holiday company has every reason to invest in making more foreign holidays available.

What happens when prices change?

Figure 3.26 shows what happens when the price of a commodity (in this case clothes) falls. The new budget line AC is less steep than the previous one AB, reflecting the lower price of clothes, and the consumer can obtain increased satisfaction by moving to IC_2, this time at *a*. In this particular case, the consumer not only increases consumption of clothing from OW to OX but also spends a greater amount, OY rather than OV, on other goods. As money income is constant, we know that the consumer must be spending less on clothing than at the previous higher price, so we know that the consumer's demand for clothing is price inelastic.

Fig. 3.26 The effect of a fall in price on consumer equilibrium

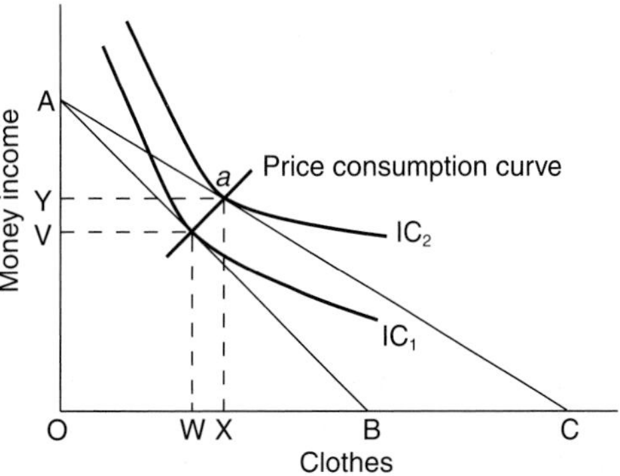

The curve joining the points of maximum satisfaction is referred to as the price consumption curve. Again, other types of curve are possible (see Figure 3.27).

- Where one product (in this case clothes) is considered to be such a good buy relative to other products when the price falls that the consumer actually retains less income to spend on other goods, the price consumption curve slopes downwards (Figure 3.27a). In such a case, price elasticity of demand is greater than unity.
- In Figure 3.27b, the price consumption curve is horizontal. A fall in price leads to increased consumption of clothing (OX units instead of OW), but in this case the money income retained to spend on other goods remains constant at OV. As income is fixed at OA, total expenditure on clothing must remain constant, and price elasticity of demand equals unity.

- In the case of Giffen goods (Figure 3.27c), a fall in price reduces consumption from OW to OX units, as consumers prefer to spend a greater amount of income on other products even though the Giffen good has fallen in price. The reason for this is that real income has increased and thus the consumer is able to buy a wider variety of products than before. This is one instance where the price elasticity of demand is greater than one.

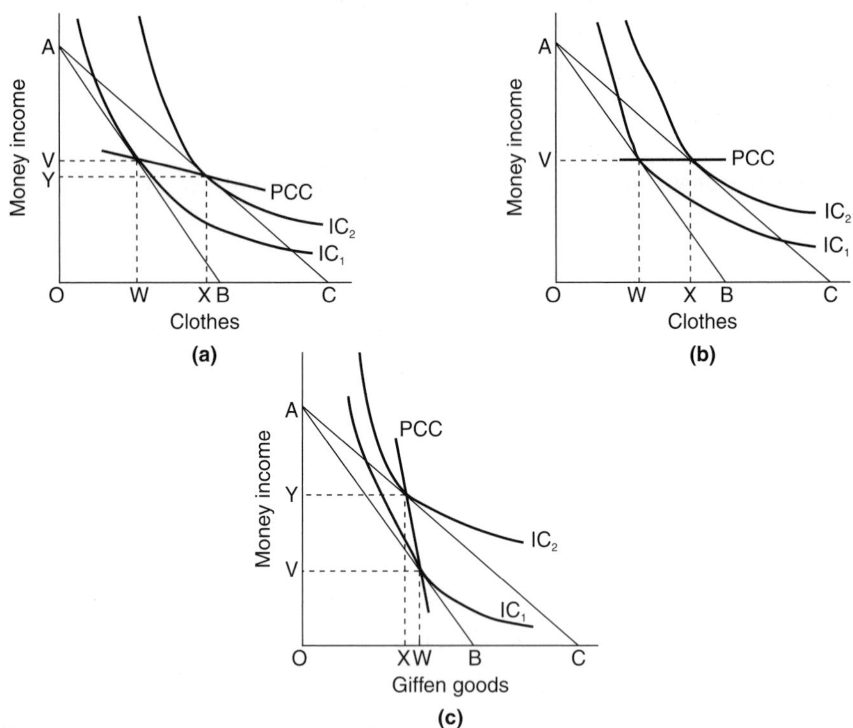

Fig. 3.27 Some other price consumption curves

Income and substitution effects of a fall in price

The changes in demand shown in Figure 3.24 on page 107 were the result of changes in money income and also (since prices were assumed to remain constant) in real income, which is measured by the volume of goods and services that money will buy. Such a change in demand is called the income effect, and except in the case of inferior goods may be expected to lead to an increase in demand (if anything).

The changes in Figures 3.26 and 3.27 on page 109 and above were the result of a fall in price. A fall in price (with money income constant) leads to an increase in real income as the consumer is able to purchase as many goods as at the previous price and still have money left to spend on extra goods. Part of the increase in demand that occurs when prices fall is therefore also due to the income effect. The remainder of the increase is attributable to the substitution effect. This is the tendency of the consumer to increase purchases when the price of a commodity falls, as the commodity then represents a better bargain when compared with other goods. Demand curve analysis does not allow us to distinguish between the income and substitution effects of a fall in price, but indifference curves may.

Think about it

- How significant do you think the substitution effect is on demand for the following items?
  - chocolates
  - video recorders
  - CDs
  - public transport
- Why is this important to suppliers of these products?

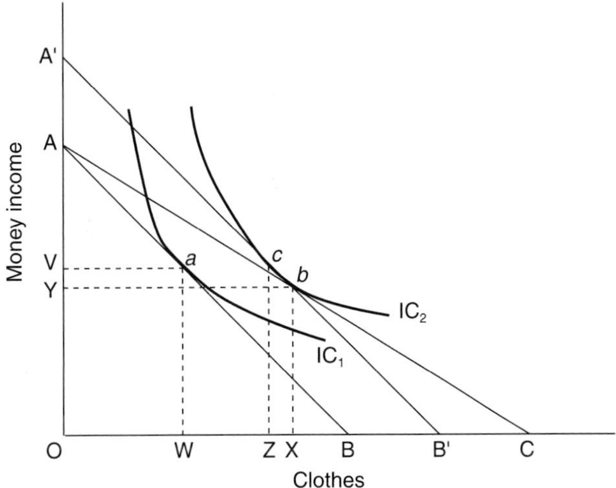

Fig. 3.28 The income and substitution effects of a fall in price

The budget line shows the price of a product. For example, in Figure 3.22 on page 106, with an income of £200 the consumer was able to purchase 40 units of clothing. The price of clothing is therefore £200 ÷ 40 = £5 per unit. In Figure 3.28, the price of clothing is OA/OB. When this is the case, the consumer maximises satisfaction at *a* by buying OW units of clothing and OV units of other goods. A fall in price to OA/OC enables the consumer to reach *b* on IC_2 and buy OX units of clothing and OY units of other goods. More utility is now obtained than was possible at the higher price.

The consumer could, however, have reached IC_2 in another way. If the price of clothing had not fallen, but income had increased by an amount AA', the budget line would have moved to A'B', enabling the consumer to settle at *c* on IC_2. This move from *a* to *c* would allow consumption of clothes to increase from OW to OZ.

- The same increase resulting from a fall in price rather than an increase in income is the income effect of the fall in price and is attributable to a higher real income.
- The associated move along IC_2 from *c* to *b*, allowing consumption to rise from OZ to OX, is the substitution effect of the fall in price.

The substitution effect will always be positive, moving the consumer down the indifference curve, and will normally be reinforced by a positive income effect. The explanation of the fall in demand for Giffen goods when price falls is attributable to the positive substitution effect being outweighed by a negative income effect.

Substitute goods

Figure 3.29a represents the community indifference curves (the sum of individual curves) for two brands of petrol, which can be considered substitutes. The price consumption curve (PCC) slopes down, showing that if the price of brand A falls with respect to brand B, enabling consumers to buy OC rather than OB if they wish, they actually increase their purchases from OW to OX. This reduces demand for brand B from OV to OY. Thus a fall in the price of brand A leads to a fall in the demand for brand B. By attaching numerical values to each axis it would clearly be possible to establish the precise cross-elasticity of demand for brand B. It will be positive, as the price of brand A and the demand for brand B move in the same direction.

Fig. 3.29a Cross-elasticity of demand, substitute goods

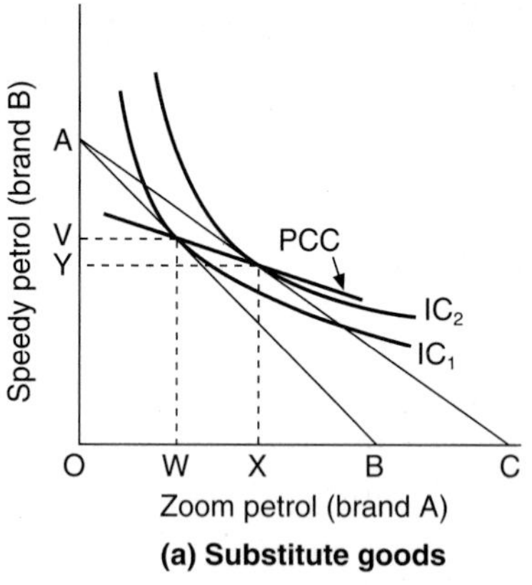

Complementary goods

In Figure 3.29b, which represents community indifference curves for the complementary goods cars and petrol, the price consumption curve slopes upwards. This is because a fall in the price of cars leads to a greater demand for cars but lower expenditure on them (AY instead of AV). As people are buying more cars they will also buy more petrol, and the cross-elasticity of demand is negative (an increase in demand associated with a fall in price).

Fig. 3.29b Cross-elasticity of demand, complementary goods

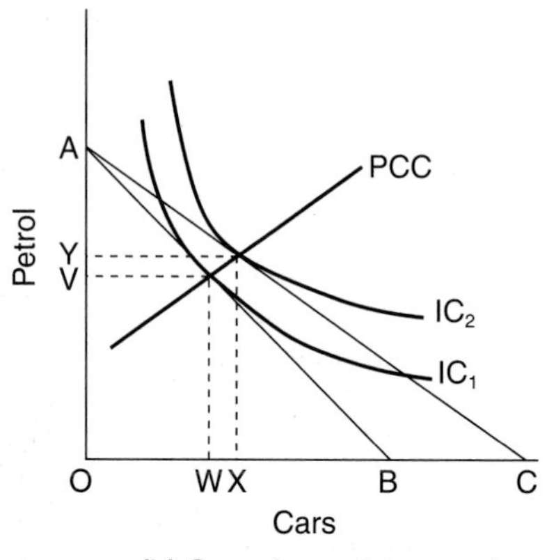

The supply of goods and services

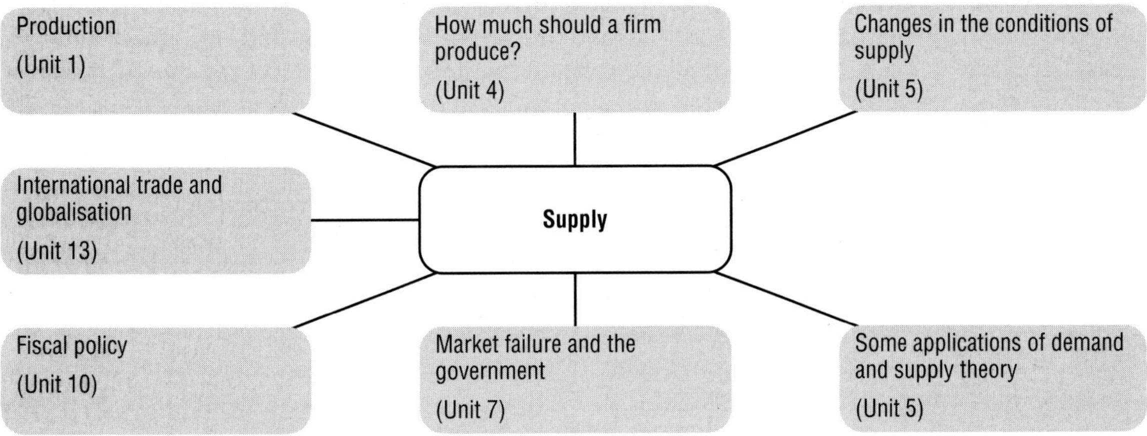

So far in this unit we have examined the demand for goods and services. The consumers who create demand for goods and services form one side of the market, while those people and enterprises who supply goods and services form the other.

In the same way as it is possible to draw demand curves, it is possible to draw supply curves, both for individual suppliers in a market and for the market as a whole. The supply curve shows the relationship between price and the quantity supplied, but again this quantity is influenced by factors other than price. In order to isolate the effects of price on quantity supplied, these factors, known as **conditions of supply**, must be held constant. The most important conditions of supply are

- the scale of production
- production techniques
- the costs of factors of production
- government intervention
- the price of other products.

The influence of changes in these is discussed below, but first we consider supply curves assuming the above conditions to remain constant.

Fig. 3.30 Factors affecting supply

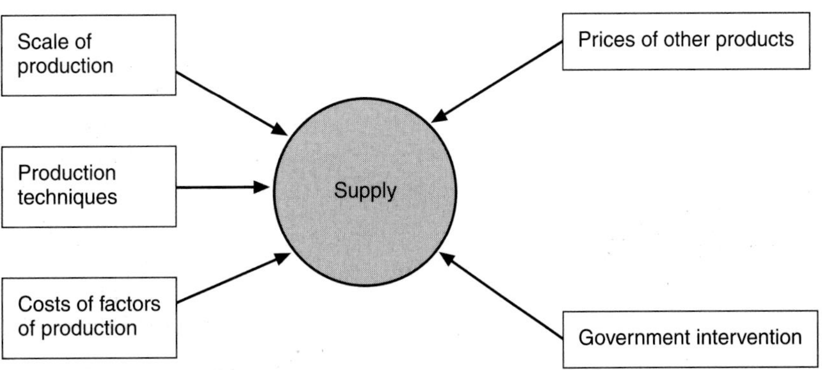

Individual supply curves

Individual suppliers have their own supply schedule for their product. Generally, as price increases, a supplier will be prepared to supply a greater quantity. Obviously, the price must cover the basic costs of production. Three possible **individual supply** schedules are given in Table 3.10, with the corresponding individual supply curves shown in Figure 3.31.

Table 3.10

Individual supply schedules for scrails			
Price (pence)	**Quantity supplied (per week)**		
	Firm A	**Firm B**	**Firm C**
50	15 000	5 000	375
45	12 000	5 000	350
40	8 000	5 000	200
35	5 000	3 000	100
30	3 000	2 000	–
25	2 000	1 000	–
20	1 200	500	–
15	700	–	–
10	300	–	–
5	100	–	–

- Firm A is an important supplier in the market and is prepared to supply some units even at very low prices. As the price rises, however, firm A is able to expand production and take advantage of the more profitable sales.
- Firm B is a fairly high-cost producer and finds it unprofitable to supply units when the price is below 20 pence. The capacity of the plant is well below that of firm A, so whatever the price offered firm B cannot supply more than 5000 units per week using existing equipment. (In the long run, of course, it may buy more machinery and take on more labour in order to increase its productive capacity.)
- Firm C is a much smaller concern altogether. Here costs are so high that the firm will enter the market only when the price offered is 35 pence. A subsequent increase in price from 45 pence to 50 pence can induce the firm only to produce an additional 25 units, so it must be running close to full capacity.

Fig. 3.31 Individual supply curves

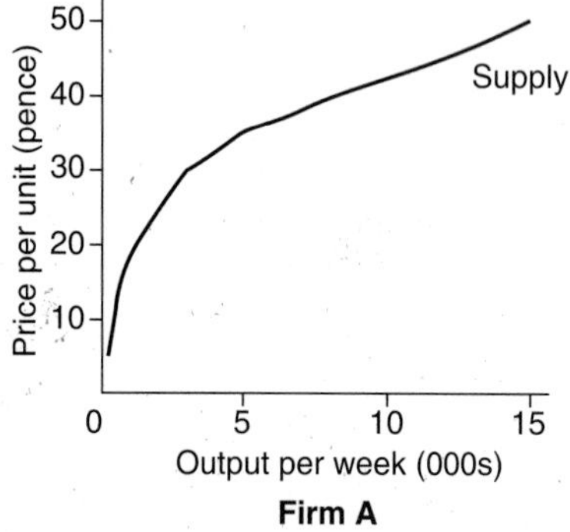

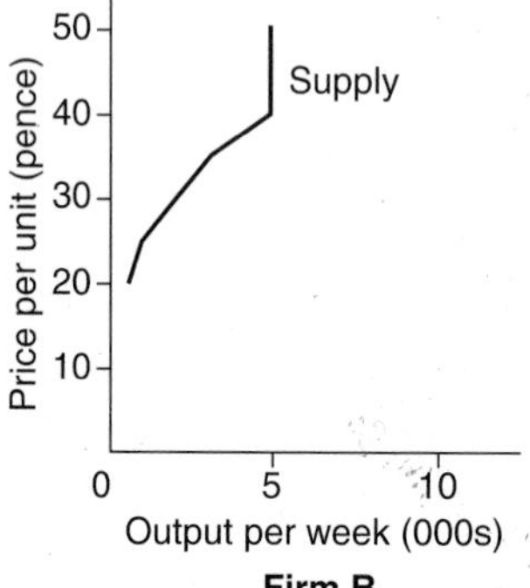

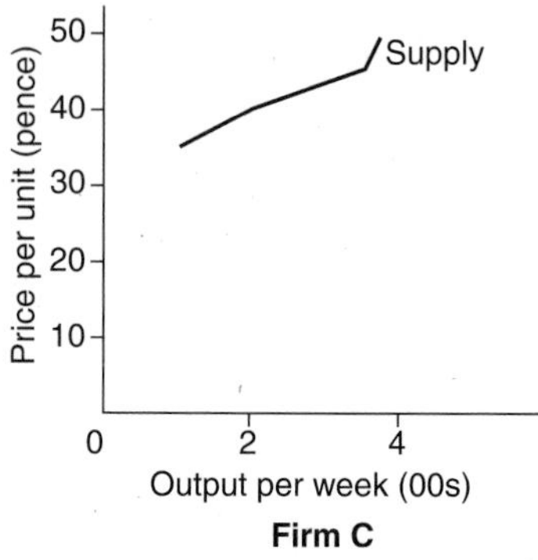

The market supply curve

The **market supply** curve for a product is calculated by adding together the supply schedules of all the individual suppliers in the market. Thus, if Table 3.10 shows all the firms supplying that market, we can easily find the quantity supplied at any price. If the price is 25 pence, then 3000 units will be produced, while at a price of 50 pence 20 375 units will be on offer. In most cases there will be more than three firms supplying the market, however. Competition is also likely to come from abroad, particularly – in the case of the UK – from firms within the European Union. When these factors are taken into consideration it is possible to construct the market supply schedule (Table 3.11) and curve (Figure 3.32). Remember that Figure 3.32 is a short-run supply curve drawn on the basis that other conditions of supply remain constant. If the conditions of supply change, the position of the supply curve must be reconsidered.

Table 3.11

Market supply schedule for scrails	
Price (pence)	**Quantity supplied per week (000s)**
50	25
45	20
40	14
35	10
30	8
25	7
20	6
15	3
10	2
5	1

Fig. 3.32 Supply curve for scrails

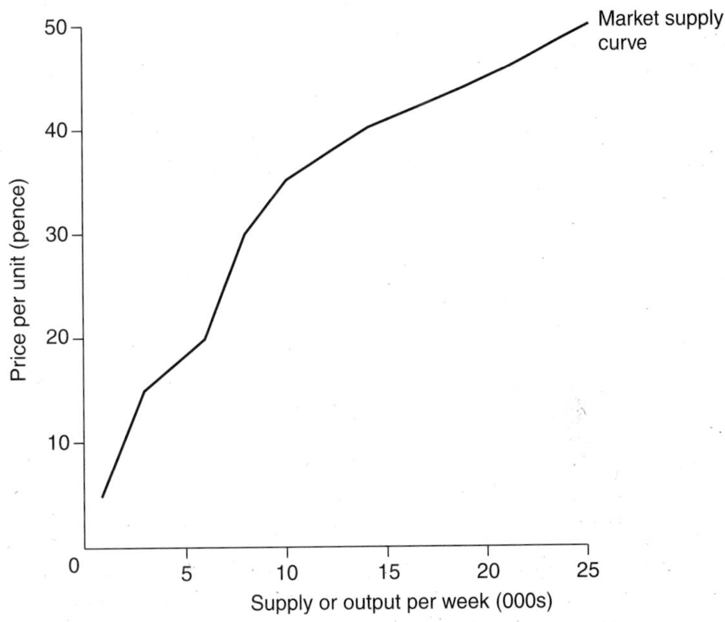

Producers' surplus

Figure 3.33 shows the supply curve for a product of which no units will be supplied at a price of OA or below. The curve shows the prices necessary to supply given quantities of the product. At price OP producers will be prepared to supply OQ units.

If producers received only the amount of money required to induce the production of each extra unit of output, their total revenue for an output of OQ would be OAEQ. In fact they actually receive OPEQ since they sell the whole output at the market price of OP. The difference between the two areas, APE, is known as the **producers' surplus.** It is comparable to the concept of consumer surplus (see page 89), and we return to it in the contexts of taxation and economic welfare in Units 10 and 14.

Fig. 3.33 Producers' surplus

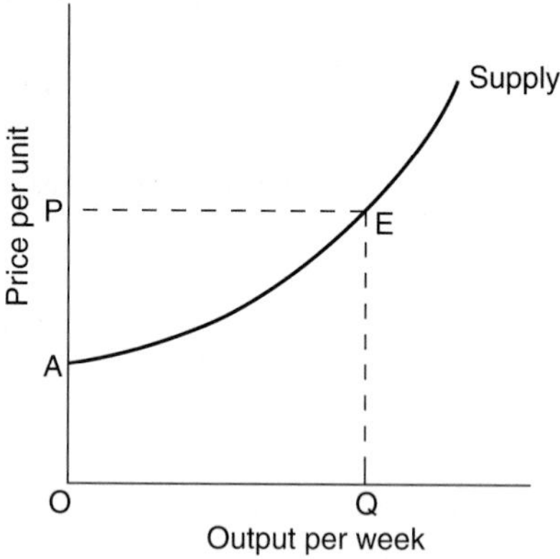

Changes in the conditions of supply

The scale of production

We have seen that supply is affected by factors other than price, called conditions of supply. Changes in these alter the supply curve.

The size of an industry may increase as new firms enter or as existing firms expand and install new equipment. In this case more units are likely to be supplied at each price. The supply curve will therefore move to the right, as shown in Figure 3.34a. Here the two curves are not parallel, and there is no reason why they should be. In fact, if the increase in supply is attributable to the entry of new, relatively high-cost firms to the market, the supply curves may even merge at low prices where the new firms will produce nothing (Figure 3.34b). If firms leave the market, or reduce the scale of their operations, the supply curve will move to the left.

Fig. 3.34 An increase in supply

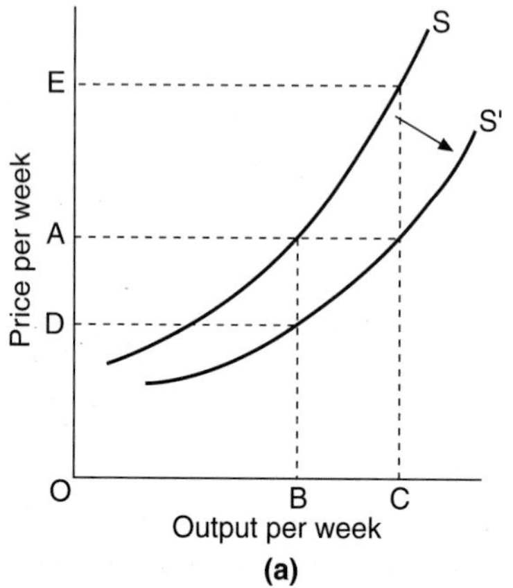

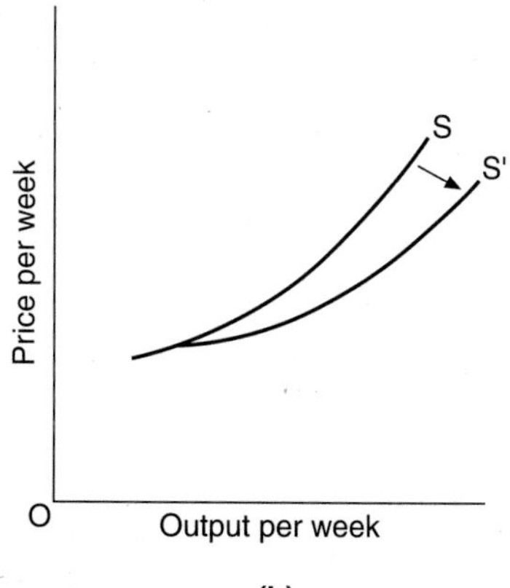

As the move from OB to OC has been achieved by the firms shifting to a new supply curve, this is an increase in supply. A quantity OC could also have been produced by the price rising to OE, with the capacity of the industry remaining unchanged. Such a move is an **extension of supply**.

Production techniques

Even if the size of the industry does not change, it may be possible to secure an increase in supply by reorganisation, using new production techniques or equipment. This frequently happens when new technology is introduced to an industry. In such cases the supply curve will shift in the same way as in Figure 3.34.

The cost of factors of production

One of the most important influences on supply is the cost of the factors of production (see also Unit 4). If there is an increase in wages, for example, and such an increase is not matched by extra output, the additional cost will almost certainly have to be covered by a higher price for the product, causing the supply curve to move to the left (from S' to S on Figure 3.34). The extent of the move depends on

- the willingness of the producer to absorb the extra costs, perhaps by improving efficiency or reducing profits
- the size of labour costs as a proportion of total costs.

A wage increase in a capital-intensive industry, such as electricity generation, would not normally be expected to lead to a significant increase in prices. A similar percentage rise in salaries in a firm of accountants, where the cost of labour comprises a far greater proportion of total costs, would lead to a much larger price increase.

It is not only labour that can increase in price, of course. The cost of raw materials may rise, shareholders may press for higher dividends, or the price of power may increase. In all these cases the supply curve for the industry will move to the left.

Government intervention

The government can intervene in many ways that will affect the supply of goods and services. These are discussed in detail in Units 9–14. However, one of the most significant ways in which governments influence supply is through the taxation of goods and services. If the government imposes a tax of 20 pence per unit on a commodity, the producer will normally pass this on to the consumer. The quantity of goods previously supplied at £1.00 per unit will now be offered at £1.20. The whole supply curve will therefore move to the left by an amount representing 20 pence per unit.

Something to do

- Write notes explaining the effects of the following on the position of the supply curve of cars.
  (a) The trade unions secure a large rise in wages without a corresponding rise in output.
  (b) The government removes indirect taxation from cars.
  (c) The price of raw materials increases.
  (d) There is an increase in the demand for cars.
  (e) Technology increases the productivity of labour.

Price elasticity of supply

As we have seen, price elasticity is a useful concept when considering demand. In the same way, it is useful to measure the price elasticity of supply. This is the responsiveness of supply to a change in price. The formula for calculating the price elasticity of supply is

$$\text{price elasticity of supply (PES)} = \frac{\text{\% change in quantity supplied}}{\text{\% change in price}}$$

Thus, if the price of a product falls from 25 pence to 24 pence, and the quantity supplied falls from 100 units to 90 units, then

$$\text{PES} = \frac{10/100}{1/25} = \frac{10\%}{4\%} = 2.5$$

In most cases, price elasticity of supply is positive, since the changes in price and quantity are normally in the same direction (but there are exceptions – see the section on regressive supply curves, page 121). As with elasticity of demand, there are five broad categories of elasticity of supply (see below). In each of the following, elasticity is calculated assuming a rise in price.

1. **Price elasticity of supply equals infinity** (Figure 3.35a): In this case the industry is unwilling to supply anything at a price of 25 pence, but if the price rises to 26 pence then it is prepared to supply as much as anyone is prepared to buy. In this case an infinite change in quantity is associated with a 4 per cent change in price. The elasticity equals infinity and is an example of perfect elasticity. This sort of elasticity is unlikely to occur in real life.

Fig. 3.35 Price elasticity of supply

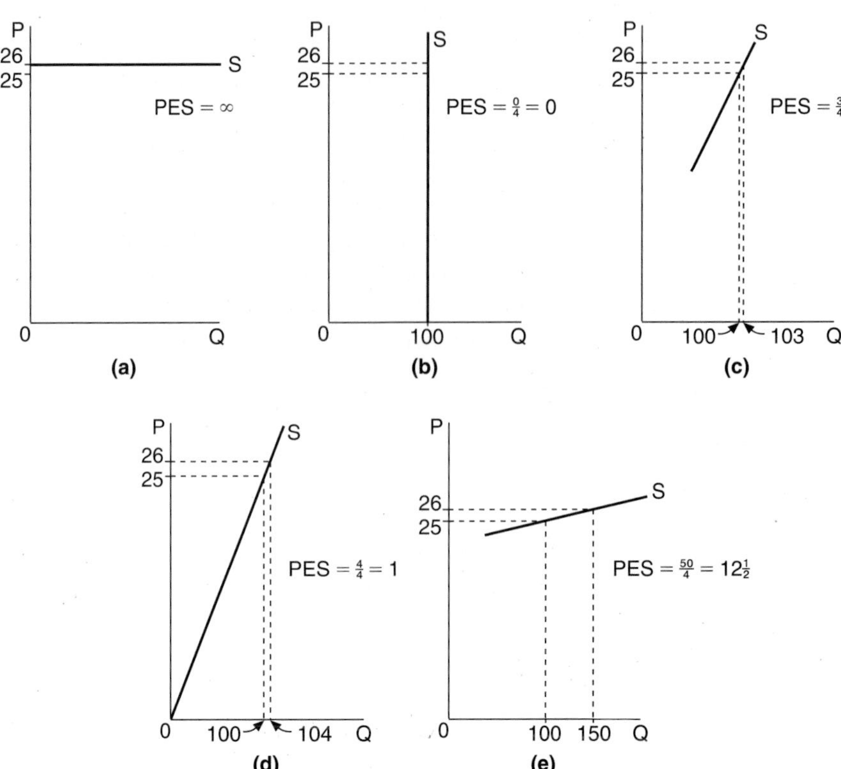

2. **Price elasticity of supply equals 0** (Figure 3.35b): At the other extreme to infinite elasticity is zero elasticity, where supply is perfectly inelastic. Here the increase in price has no effect on quantity supplied.

While neither of the above two examples is likely to be found in practice, they do provide limits towards which most real-world supply curves will approximate. Example 1 is the extreme towards which manufacturing industry approximates, while example 2 is more representative of primary production where it is not so easy to transfer resources from one product to another.

3. **Price elasticity of supply is greater than 0 but less than 1** (Figure 3.35c): Here an increase in price of 4 per cent leads to an increase in supply of 3 per cent so that elasticity is $\frac{3}{4}$. This is an example of an industry that has difficulty increasing its output. Supply is inelastic.
4. **Price elasticity of supply equals 1** (Figure 3.35d): This is a rather special case. The price and the quantity supplied each rise by 4 per cent. In fact this curve has an elasticity of 1 along its entire length. This will be true of any straight-line supply curve that passes through the origin, but not of other straight-line supply curves, whose elasticity decreases from left to right.
5. **Price elasticity of supply is greater than 1 but less than infinity** (Figure 3.35e): In this case a 4 per cent rise in price induces a 50 per cent increase in output. This is an industry that can easily expand its output to meet an extra demand for its product. The supply is elastic.

What determines the price elasticity of supply?

The main determinants of price elasticity of supply include the following:

- **The intensity of use of the fixed factor in the short run:** In Figure 3.36a, an increase in price from OP to OR stimulates very little extra output. This is because the plant (the fixed factor) is already being used very intensively and very little extra production can be squeezed from it even if an abundance of variable factors is available. In Figure 3.36b, the supply can be increased fairly easily because the firm is operating a long way below full capacity. Firm A may be working a three-shift system and running machines at nearly full capacity. Firm B, on the other hand, may only be operating for eight hours a day, and even then not at full capacity.

Fig. 3.36 Price elasticity of supply and spare capacity

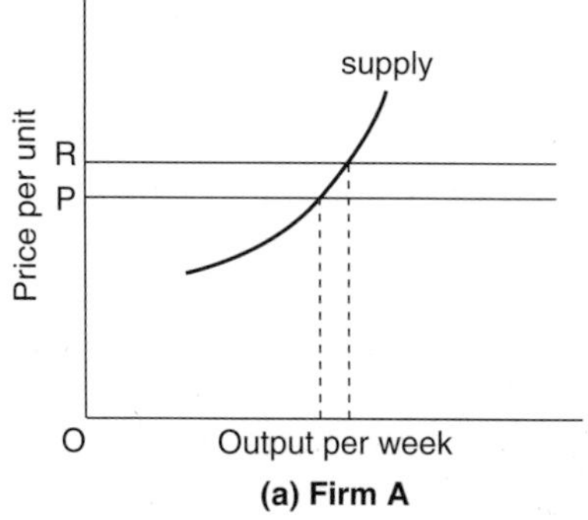

(a) Firm A

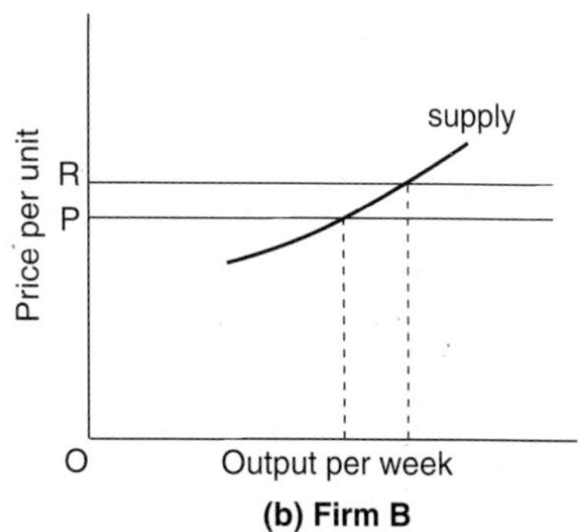

(b) Firm B

- **The availability of other factors:** If extra units of the variable factors required for production are not available, price elasticity of supply will be low even if the plant is under-utilised. Even a considerable rise in the price of a product will have little effect on the quantity supplied if raw materials and components are unobtainable or in short supply.
- **Specific factors of production:** If a productive process requires very specific factors of production, such as complex chemical equipment, then price elasticity of supply will be low when the existing plant is at full capacity. When a productive process depends mainly on non-specific factors, then the price elasticity of supply will be much higher as extra units of the factors will be more easily obtainable.
- **The time factor:** The time factor is one of the most important influences on elasticity (see below).

Short-run and long-run PES While it may be difficult to increase supply in the short run, due to the lack of availability of additional factors of production, in the long run all factors can be increased, thus increasing productive capacity. For example, we have already said that the firm in Figure 3.36a is operating at full capacity, working a three-shift system and running its machines at nearly full speed. In the short run, it is difficult for the firm to increase production. In the long run, however, it could take on and train more labour and buy additional machines. In the example shown in Figure 3.37 the maximum supply in the short run is OM, but in the long run extra units of the factors of production can be employed, enabling the industry to move onto a new short-run supply curve with a maximum supply of ON.

Fig. 3.37 Short-run and long-run price elasticity of supply

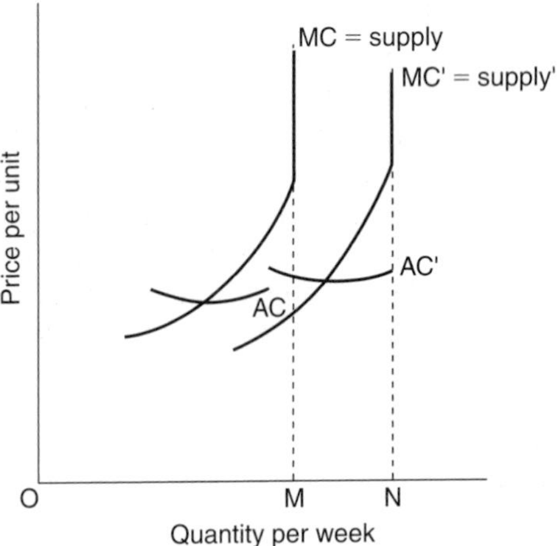

Firms do not always respond immediately to a short-run rise in price. Suppose a company is geared to the production of 100 000 cans of cola a week. The cans are produced one week and sold the next, and the firm will be employing sufficient quantities of its factors of production to achieve this output. If it becomes apparent that a change in market conditions has meant that it will now be profitable to sell 110 000 cans, the firm cannot put this amount on the market today because this week's supply is fixed by last week's output. In the very short run, supply (market supply) is absolutely fixed. It will take at least a week to provide sufficient variable factors (raw materials, etc.) to increase supply by

10 000 units. The market supply period ends when this is achieved and the short-run supply period then begins. If the rise in demand is permanent, however, it may be necessary in the long run to employ more fixed factors of production, or new firms may enter the market.

It follows from this that

- market supply is less elastic than short-run supply
- short-run supply is less elastic than long-run supply.

As time goes by, the supply curve gets flatter, showing a larger percentage rise in supply for a given rise in price.

The long and the short of it

Economists distinguish between events that happen, or circumstances that can change, in the short run, and those that can change in the long run. While there is no set limit to where the short run ends and the long run begins, the short run refers to a period of time during which at least one of the factors of production is fixed. In the long run, on the other hand, all factors of production can be changed.

For example, if a college wants to increase its intake of students, in the short run it can employ temporary, part-time lecturers and utilise classrooms during periods in which they might otherwise be unused, and perhaps make use of other parts of the college. The college is still, however, limited in the number of additional students it can accept in this way. In the long run, however, the college can expand by building additional classrooms, or even buying or renting suitable premises away from its main site.

The time scale of the short run and the long run varies from business to business. For a corner shop, it might be a couple of hours while the owner goes to the local Cash-and-Carry to restock the shelves. For an oil refiner, the short run may be several years while a new refinery is constructed.

Regressive supply curves

There are some circumstances in which the supply curve may be regressive (backward sloping) over part of its length. Where labour is concerned (see Figure 3.38), for example, an increase in wages may actually result in a fall in supply. When wages are at OW, OM hours are worked; but when wages rise to OV, the same total wage can be earned for less work and the supply of labour falls from OM to OL. This phenomenon was observed in the coal industry in the UK in the 1940s. As miners' shift bonuses increased they worked fewer hours, since they could earn a reasonable income whilst enjoying more leisure time.

Fig. 3.38 The regressive supply curve of labour

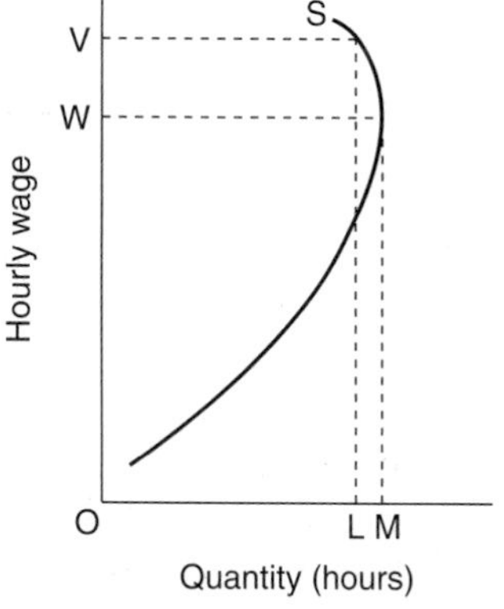

The labour market and markets for other factors of production are considered in detail in Unit 5.

4 The theory of the firm

Introduction: the firm as a unit of supply

In Unit 3 we saw how goods and services are supplied in response to demand. Here we look in detail at the business organisations that actually produce those goods and services.

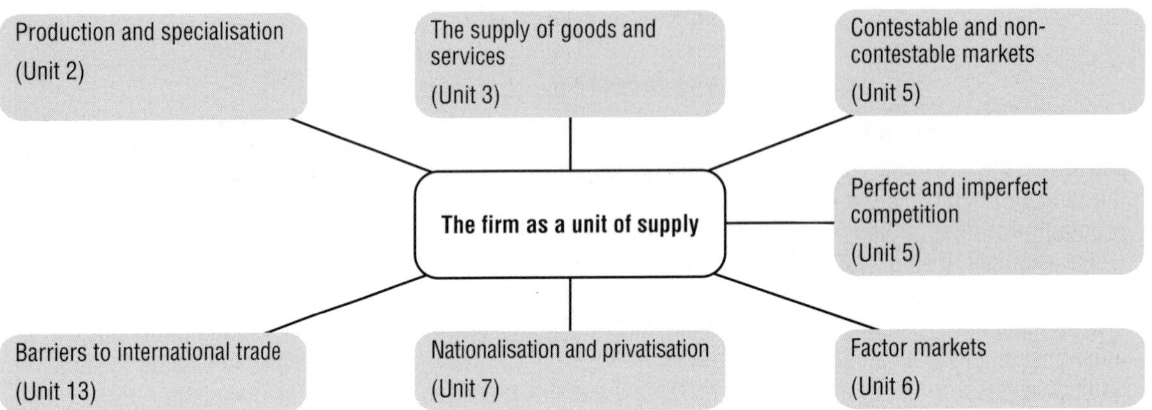

Business organisations, or firms, can be considered as systems for changing inputs into outputs (see Figure 4.1). The inputs are the factors of production, and the outputs are the goods and services produced, plus finance to pay for the factors of production and provide a profit.

Fig. 4.1 The firm as a system for change

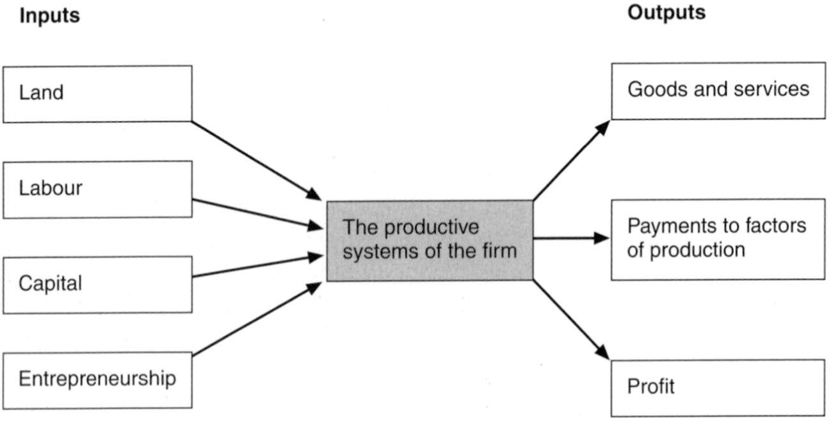

In this way, individual business organisations are the units that produce and supply the goods and services that are wanted by society. As we shall see, there are many different types of business organisations, ranging from small businesses such as local tradespeople, shops and freelance artists, for example, to giant multinational companies such as Microsoft and Coca-Cola. To simplify matters, businesses are classified according to the purpose for which they have been set up and who owns them.

When starting a business, or firm, there are several decisions that must be taken, including:

- What goods or services will the firm produce?
- How much will it cost to produce the goods or services?
- How much will the business receive from sales of its product?

The **costs of production** depend on various factors, such as the cost and availability of factors of production and the development of technology. The **revenue** the business will receive from its sales depends on the demand for the product of the business as shown by its demand curve (see Unit 3); revenue is therefore influenced by the price at which the product can be sold. Any excess of sales revenue over costs of production is profit. The higher the price at which the product can be sold, the higher the profit that the business can make. One of the main objectives of most businesses is profit maximisation, or making the highest possible profit.

However, there are other questions that must be answered:

- How will the capital for the business be raised?
- What legal form should the business take?
- How much should the business produce?
- How large will the business be?
- Where should the business be located?

We begin this unit by looking at the decision of what to produce. We then discuss the different types (legal forms) of business organisation that exist, and the reasons for their existence – the objectives of firms. This is followed by an analysis of the costs, revenues and profits of businesses to see how they affect decisions about the size of a firm's output. Finally, we examine the advantages and disadvantages of size and growth, and the factors influencing decisions on location.

What should a firm produce?

We saw in Unit 1 that people in society have a potentially infinite number of needs and wants. It would seem, therefore, that a business could be set up to produce almost anything, and people would buy it. Indeed, when you look around at the immense variety of goods and services that is available, it is difficult to believe that there is anything that is not being produced already.

However, the decision as to what to produce is a vital one. If a firm is to be successful it must sell enough of its production at least to cover its costs. (We examine this in more detail later.) For this situation to be achieved, two conditions must be met:

- There must be an **effective demand** (see Unit 1) for the product.
- The firm must be able to compete with any other firms already producing and selling the same product. (Competition is examined in Unit 5.)

To find out whether these conditions are met, a business, or those wishing to establish a new business, must undertake comprehensive market research into both the product and the market for the product. (Markets are examined in Unit 5.)

Market research

If it is to produce a product that it can sell, a firm must identify something that consumers want and are prepared to pay for. The firm must also know whether there is enough scope for it to sell its product, or whether consumer demand for the product is already being met. Sometimes, even though consumer demand for a product is currently being met by other firms, there is still scope to enter the market, perhaps by supplying the product at a cheaper price, or by supplying a product that more closely meets consumer requirements.

Market research is undertaken

- to identify a possible gap in the market for a product to meet a demand not currently being satisfied
- to find out what other firms are already supplying a product and how difficult it will be to compete with them
- to establish what consumers really want from a product in terms of quality, what the product will do, and the price consumers are prepared to pay.

Thus, market research is used both by

- firms starting up, to ensure that they will be able to sell their product and make a product
- existing firms, to check that their product is what consumers really want and that it has a competitive edge over other firms' similar products in terms of quality, price or use.

Market research can be primary research or secondary research.

Primary research involves obtaining data, or information, first hand and involves going to the actual source of that data. The main methods of primary research are

- personal investigation
- interviewing
- questionnaires
- observation
- experimenting, perhaps launching a new product to find out consumers' reactions to it.

Secondary research, sometimes called desk research as much of it can be done from the researcher's desk, involves obtaining data that already exists, either in the form of published statistics and other information, or in the form of historical records. Published statistics and other information will usually have been collected originally for other purposes. Examples are

- government statistical publications such as *Social Trends* and *Annual Abstract of Statistics*
- publications of the Statistical Office of the European Union
- publications of other organisations such as the Bank of England, *The Economist*, the *Financial Times*.

Many sources of valuable secondary data are now available on the Internet.

Historical sources of data include a firm's existing records, such as sales records, accounts and customer purchase orders.

Types of business organisations

The legal form of a business

Business organisations are classified according to who owns them. This defines their legal form. As the business develops, its legal form may be changed, usually to protect its owners, to obtain additional sources of finance, or to take advantage of the benefits of growth (see pages 160–163, economies of scale). Most businesses are owned by private individuals, either on their own or in groups. These are **private-sector** businesses. Some business organisations, however, are owned by the State, on behalf of the community. These are said to be in the **public sector**. Also included in the public sector are those organisations owned by the government and run on business principles – public corporations such as the BBC, nationalised industries such as the Post Office or the nuclear fuel industry, as well as local authorities and government departments.

Something to do

- Identify which of the following are private-sector and which public-sector businesses.
  - Barclays Bank
  - the Post Office
  - Microsoft
  - your school or college
  - Eton College
  - British Airways
  - Heathrow Airport
  - the Co-operative Bank
  - Granada Television
  - the BBC

Fig. 4.2 Types of business organisation

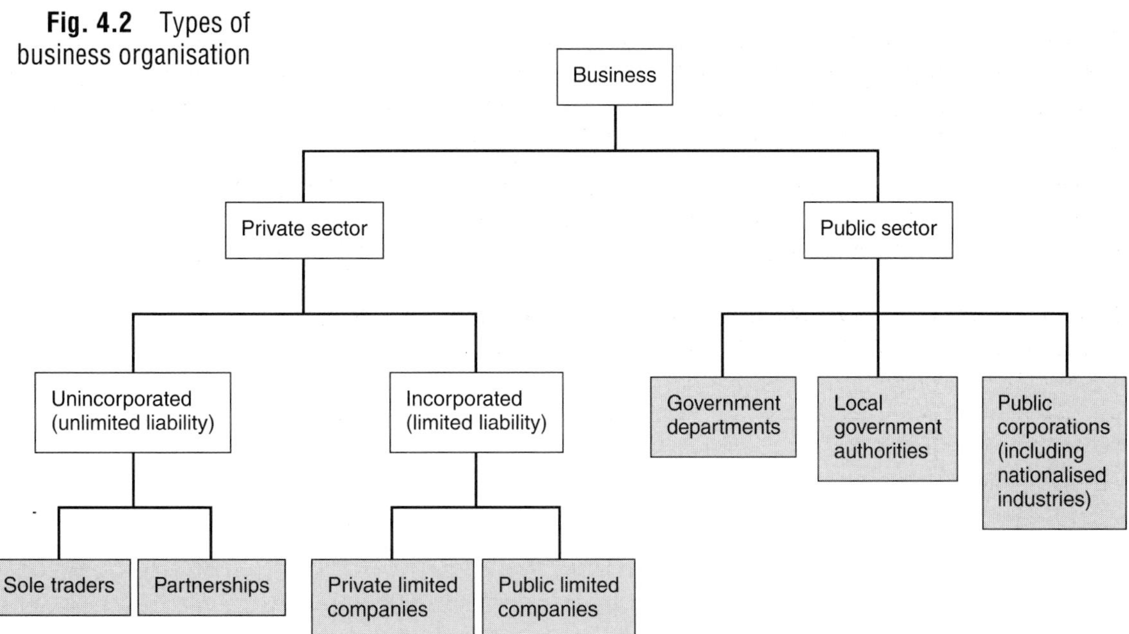

Private-sector businesses

Businesses in the private sector may be either unincorporated or incorporated.

- An **unincorporated business** has no legal existence separate from the owners of the business. The affairs of an unincorporated business are thus considered to be the affairs of its owners.
- An **incorporated business** *does* have a legal existence separate from its owners.

Whether a business is established as an unincorporated or incorporated business depends on a number of factors, including the need for finance, the objectives of the owner, the degree of control an entrepreneur wants to exercise and various legal and tax implications. An important consideration is the liability of the owners of the business. The owners of a business have either unlimited or limited liability.

- **Unlimited liability** is where the owners of a business are legally responsible for the affairs of the business. This means that all the profits of the business belong to the owners, who can use them as they wish – to put back into the business or to draw on for their own personal expenditure. However, unlimited liability also means that the owners of the business are responsible for any debts the business incurs. If the business is unable to pay its debts, the money owed may be recovered from the owners of the business, whose personal possessions, including their homes, may be sold for this. Owners of unincorporated businesses normally have unlimited liability.
- **Limited liability** is where the owners of a business are responsible for the affairs of the business only to a limited extent. Normally, owners with limited liability are only entitled to a percentage of the profits of the business proportionate to their share of the business. The total profit of the business will rarely be distributed to the owners, however, as some will be retained within the business to cover future costs and investment. Should the business fail and be unable to pay its debts, on the other hand, the liability of the owners is limited to the value of their share of the business (in reality the amount they originally paid for their share of the business). Owners of incorporated businesses have limited liability.

The main types of business to be found in the private sector are shown in Figure 4.2. They are described in more detail in the chart on pages 127–9.

The main types of business organisation in the private sector

Type of business organisation	Characteristics	Advantages	Disadvantages
Unincorporated businesses with unlimited liability			
Sole trader	• Typically a small business owned and run by one person (the proprietor) • Often established with the minimum of capital	• The owner retains total control of all decision-making in the business, and can dispose of profits as he or she wishes. • Simple to set up, with few legal formalities	• Most sole trader businesses are small, with little scope for growth due to few sources of capital other than the personal funds of the proprietor. The failure rate of sole-trader businesses is very high. • Unlimited liability means that the proprietor is personally liable for all the debts of the business.
Partnership	• Owned by two or more partners • Common form for professional firms, such as architects, doctors and solicitors • May be set up with a legal Deed of Partnership setting out roles and responsibilities of each partner. If no Deed exists, the partnership is covered by the Partnership Act 1890.	• Partners share control of the business and disposal of the profits, although a 'senior' partner may have overall authority. • All partners may contribute to the capital of the business, giving more scope for growth. • Simple to set up, with few legal formalities, except the Deed of Partnership. • Because there are more owners, specialisation is possible, and the responsibility for decision-making is spread, with cover for illness, etc.	• Unlimited liability means that all partners are equally responsible for the liabilities of the business. In the event of default by one of the partners, liability for his or her share will rest with the other partners. • Sources of capital are still restricted, although more sources may be available than for a sole trader. • Personal conflicts between partners may affect the running of the business.

Type of business organisation	Characteristics	Advantages	Disadvantages
Incorporated businesses where owners have limited liability	• Limited companies are considered legal entities in their own right, separate from their owners. • The owners of limited companies buy shares in the company, which entitle them to a say in the overall running of the company and a share in the profits (normally a 'dividend' on their shares). • The owners of the business appoint directors to manage the business and take day-to-day decisions on their behalf.	• Limited liability means that shareholders are only responsible for the liabilities of the business to the extent of their shareholding. • The larger capital base provided by shareholders gives greater scope for growth. • Some major plcs (public limited companies) are among the largest commercial organisations in the world, operating internationally and with production facilities and outlets in many different countries. • Their greater size and capital base usually gives limited companies access to more sources of funds, both for growth and for survival in times of difficulty.	• The separation of ownership from management of the company means that the owners do not have day-to-day control of decision-making, or of the distribution of profits. This may lead to a conflict of objectives. • The availability of shares, especially when they can be freely traded on the stock market, leaves plcs particularly vulnerable to take-over by other companies. • Not all take-over bids are hostile, however, and may in fact provide the funds necessary for a company's survival or expansion.
Private limited companies (Ltd)	• In private limited companies, the number of shareholders is restricted, and shares can only be sold or transferred privately with the agreement of all the shareholders. • The shareholders in private limited companies are usually closely involved with the business, and are often the directors themselves.	• Original owners run less risk than in a plc of losing control of the business by a takeover bid.	• Limited number of shareholders sets a limit on expansion.

Type of business organisation	Characteristics	Advantages	Disadvantages
Public limited companies (plc)	• Shares in public limited companies may be freely bought and sold by the general public on the stock market. • Owners of plcs are therefore rarely closely involved with the business.	• Ability to expand and benefit from economies of scale.	• Potential management problems in large organisations. • Danger of takeover. • Danger of shares losing value through fashion and rumour.
Franchises	• A franchise is a licence to trade under the name and in the products of another company. • The franchisee (often a sole trader or small private limited company) buys the franchise from the franchisor (sometimes, but not always, a major multinational company). • In addition to the purchase price, the franchisee may have to pay a percentage of turnover or profits.	• A franchisee trades under the name of a well-known company with recognised products, and often a ready market. • The franchisor often undertakes national advertising, from which the franchisee benefits. • The franchisor may offer training in areas such as business development, administration and marketing. • By buying a franchise, a small company may benefit from the economies of scale normally only enjoyed by major national and international companies.	• The franchisor may place restrictions on the activities of the franchisee, who is tied to the products and suppliers of the franchisor. • Lack of ability to make decisions • Part of the franchisee's profits or turnover must be paid to the franchisor. • Franchisor's fee may be based on turnover rather than profit.

Something to do

Two of your friends are thinking of opening their own health food shop, and have asked you to join them in the venture. They hope in time to open more shops. One of your friends has suggested forming a limited company, but the other wants to keep it as a partnership, feeling that this will be less formal.

- Write notes for a meeting with your friends at which they have asked you to advise them on the advantages and disadvantages of different legal forms of business.

Public-sector businesses Public-sector organisations are owned and run by the government on behalf of the community instead of being owned by private individuals or groups. They include

- government departments, such as the Department of Social Security or the Department for Education and Employment
- nationalised industries such as British Waterways and public corporations such as the Post Office and the BBC.

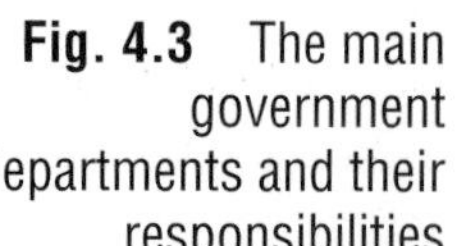

Fig. 4.3 The main government departments and their responsibilities

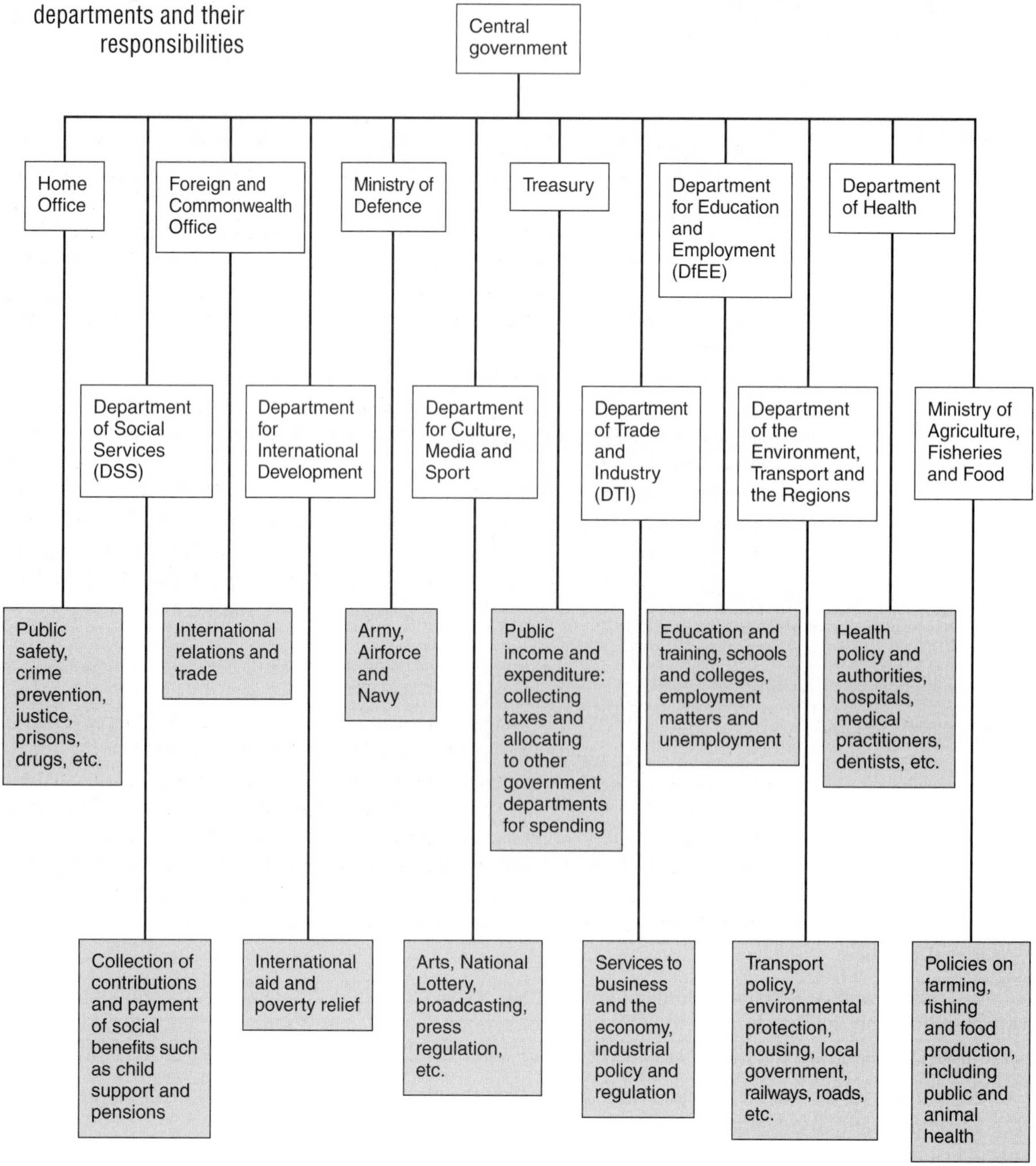

Government departments exist to carry out the policies of government. Different departments are responsible for, for example, collecting taxes, providing free education and health services, and distributing welfare payments (see Figure 4.3).

Something to do

- Make a list of the different types of fixed and working capital that is used by either your school or college, or your place of work.

The purpose of organisations in the public sector is to provide goods and services that are considered too important for the security of the country or the general welfare of society to be left to profit-motivated firms in the private sector. In 1979, Margaret Thatcher began a period of Conservative government which continued under John Major until 1997. During this period, a policy of returning nationalised industries to private ownership drastically reduced the number of industries in public ownership.

While at the time of writing there are only a few nationalised industries left, there is still considerable debate over whether some of these, including the Post Office and London Underground, should be privatised. This is very much a political matter, and a change in the political climate of the UK could even see a return to nationalisation in the future. Other countries have different policies on the nationalisation/privatisation issue, and therefore it is important to have some knowledge of the arguments for and against nationalisation or privatisation (see the section beginning on page 132).

Raising capital

To a large extent, the most appropriate form for a business depends on its need for capital. Once a suitable product has been identified and it is known that the product can be sold at a price and in sufficient quantities to make a profit, a business organisation can be set up to produce and sell the product. Setting up and running a business requires capital in the form of finance to pay for the factors of production the firm will require. The finance a firm requires is of two types: **fixed capital** and **working capital** (see Unit 1, pages 29–30 and Unit 2, pages 44–66).

Fig. 4.4 Sources of finance

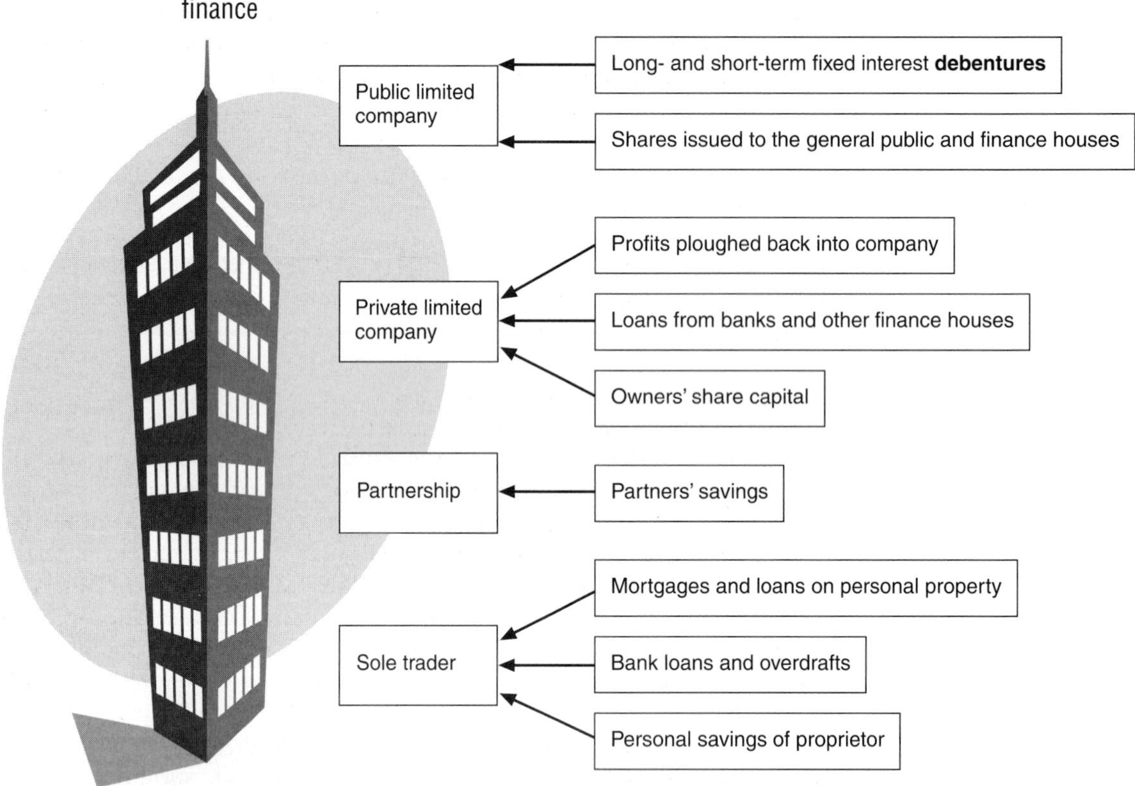

Sources of finance

There are various sources of finance for both new and existing businesses. The finance for a start-up business, especially when on a small scale, is often provided by the entrepreneur setting up the business. Indeed, small businesses often have few other sources of finance, as they lack the security or prospects of large profits that bigger organisations have. Other sources of finance include banks and other finance houses (see Unit 8), as well as finance generated by the firm (including trade credit, **retained profit**, deposits from customers) and the government (in the form of regional assistance and subsidies, tax credits, and schemes such as the Business Start-Up Scheme, which provides a weekly allowance for people starting new businesses).

Nationalisation and privatisation

Why industries were nationalised

There are a number of reasons why certain industries in the UK have been nationalised in the past. While strong economic arguments can be and were put forward, there is usually also an underlying political belief that public ownership of some essential services is desirable. The main motives for nationalisation include the following:

- **Ideological** The Labour Government elected at the end of the Second World War nationalised many industries as an essential part of its socialist policies. In this way, it sought to exert control over the economy by nationalising the Bank of England as well as industries such as electricity, gas, coal and transport. At the same time, social welfare was brought into the public domain through the establishment of the National Health Service.

- **National security** It was felt that leaving certain key industries, such as power, transportation, steel production and telecommunications, in private hands posed a potential threat to national security, since ownership and therefore control of these could be transferred into hostile hands and the country held to ransom or prevented from effectively defending itself.
- **Failing industries** might be nationalised in order to maintain levels of investment or employment. At the end of the Second World War, the railways in Britain had become run down and needed considerable investment in track and rolling stock. Such investment had to be provided by the government. British Railways was therefore formed as a nationalised industry in order to ensure the maintenance of the railways as an important and viable system of transportation. In the 1970s, the motor companies Rolls Royce and British Leyland faced bankruptcy. They were nationalised in order to avoid the high levels of unemployment that would result from their collapse. In contrast, when the Chrysler Corporation in America was faced with collapse in 1980, the US government ensured its survival as a private company with a package of loan guarantees and wage concessions.
- Some industries were considered **natural monopolies**. These were mainly services covering the whole country, such as the postal and telephone services, gas, electricity and water. Such services are typically supplied through a network system and were considered difficult to divide between different suppliers. Again, this contrasts with the American tendency to leave such natural monopolies in private hands and to regulate them.
- **Market failure** (See also Unit 7.) There is a belief that market forces alone will not ensure that some services essential to the well-being of society will be provided to everyone who needs them if they are left in private hands. This type of good is often termed a 'merit good' – something that everyone should have in a civilised society, regardless of their income. Examples are education and healthcare. What may or may not be a merit good is a political value-judgement.
- **Investment decisions** in private-sector firms are taken on the basis of whether the firm expects to increase its profits. Firms thus assess a potential investment in new machinery from a straightforward appraisal of the expenditure involved and the additional income the new machinery can be expected to produce. In the public sector, however, other considerations may be taken into account. For example, in purely financial terms, building a new bypass that avoids a rural market town may be uneconomic. When other non-financial benefits associated with the project (such as easing the flow of traffic and congestion in the market town) are able to be taken into account, a decision to go ahead with the investment may be justified.
- **Prices** Private-sector firms will normally set their prices so as to maximise their profits. Nationalised industries, however, may be set other objectives by the government and thus be able to keep prices down. Whilst they are required to make a surplus sufficient to cover their costs, and provide investment capital, they are not required to maximise their profit.

Privatisation Privatisation takes several forms, including

- the sale of State-owned assets, such as council houses
- the sale of government shareholdings in private companies such as BP
- contracting-out to private companies services normally provided by local or national government, such as the collection and disposal of household rubbish
- the sale of nationalised industries either to private individuals, as in the case of British Telecom, or to private companies, as in the case of British Rail. The table below shows the main British nationalised industries that have been returned to private ownership.

Table 4.1

Nationalisation and privatisation in the UK		
Industry/organisation	**Year nationalised**	**Year privatised**
British Petroleum	1913	1979
British Aerospace	1977	1981
Britoil	1976	1982
National Freight	1969	1982
Associated British Ports	1963	1983
Cable and Wireless	prior to 1900	1983
British Telecom	prior to 1900	1984
Jaguar Cars	1975	1984
British Gas	1949	1986
Royal Ordnance	prior to 1800	1986
British Airports Authority	1966	1987
British Airways	1946	1987
Rolls Royce	1971	1987
British Steel	1951	1988
Water Authorities	1983	1989
Regional Electricity Boards	1948	1990
British Coal	1947	1995
British Rail	1948	1996
BBC	1927	–
British Nuclear Fuels	1971	–
British Waterways	1948	–
Post Office	prior to 1850	–

The principal reasons why successive British governments since the 1980s have followed a policy of privatisation are as follows:

- There was a belief that large monopoly organisations, such as British Telecom, wielded too much power and did not respond to the needs of consumers.
- With no competition, and with the guarantee that the government would continue to fund them, critics claimed that nationalised industries became poorly managed and inefficient.

- Poor management and inefficiency were compounded by interference in the running of nationalised industries by successive governments based on political rather than business objectives.
- Nationalised industries suffered from under-investment by governments that had other priorities in the allocation of public funds.
- There was a belief that the interference of government in the provision of goods and services should be kept to a minimum.
- Proceeds from the sale of nationalised industries enabled governments to meet the public sector's net cash requirement (PSNCR) without having to raise taxes (see also Unit 10).

As you can see from Table 4.1 on page 134, the majority of industries that were nationalised have been privatised again since 1979. There is also increasing involvement of private industry in raising finance for public sector projects such as major construction projects, through the private finance initiative (PFI), and forming partnerships with public sector organisations. Nevertheless, there is still discussion over privatisation of some of the remaining nationalised industries, most notably the Post Office and Air Traffic Control.

Something to do

In recent years government policy in the UK has been towards the privatisation of industries that had previously been nationalised.

- Arrange a class debate on the topic of whether the gas, electricity and water supply industries should remain in private hands, or whether it would be better to return them to state ownership.
  Decide who will speak in favour of industries remaining in the private sector and who will speak in favour of them being renationalised. Write down the arguments for and against each side and read them out at the beginning of the debate. At the end of the debate, a vote should be taken.
- Individually, write notes on the debate and the arguments put forward, and record the result of the vote. Did you agree with the result? If not, give your reasons.

Central Eurasia: Results of Privatization

For the region as a whole, the private sector share of GDP increased from 11 per cent in 1989 to 50 per cent in 1995. The most aggressive programs were undertaken in East-Central Europe, the Baltic States, Russia, and Albania. Least aggressive were Belarus, Tajikistan, and Turkmenistan.

What has been the deeper significance of these privatization programs? It is too early to answer this question definitively, but a few points are clear. First, on a macroeconomic level, the privatization programs have provided temporary revenues for governments during critical stages of transition, and have distanced governments from money-losing enterprises, allowing them to reduce budgetary subsidies. In Bulgaria, the Czech Republic, Hungary, and Poland, the share of subsidies in GDP declined from an average of 16 per cent in 1989 to 3 per cent in 1994.[1]

On a macroeconomic level, it is not yet clear that privatization programs have made major contributions to the efficiency of enterprise operations in Central Eurasia. Evidence of efficiency gains is strongest for small retail and service enterprises that have simple systems of ownership and governance.[2] However, even in small enterprises, efficiency gains tend to be small when a new private company is left in the hands of an old Soviet-era manager. A recent study of managerial practices in 452 small shops in seven Russian cities found that restructuring requires new people who have new skills more suitable to a market economy. About 30 per cent of the shops in the study were, in fact, transferred to new owners and managers. When privatization only served to strengthen the property rights of existing managers, this was not found 'particularly effective in bringing about significant change'.[3]

The impact of large privatizations on microeconomic efficiency is even more ambiguous. When ownership of an enterprise is given or sold to 'insiders' (workers or managers), the change in performance usually is very small. When ownership is transferred to the general population, old enterprise directors are frequently able to exercise effective control and make a few changes.

The results of privatization are sometimes dramatic, however, when foreign investors are willing and able to participate. In 1991, for example, a Polish lighting company was purchased by a Dutch businessman. The new owner invested heavily in training and new equipment. After three years the company reportedly was able to maintain employment at about 3000 persons, raise its salaries by about 10 per cent each year, reduce its prices by about 25 per cent, double its sales, reduce environmental emissions, and move from losses to profits.[4]

Notes: 1 International Monetary Fund, World Economic Outlook, May 1996, 81

2 Daniel Gross and Alfred Steinherr, *Winds of Change: Economic Transition in Central and Eastern Europe* (New York: Longman, 1995), 285–7

3 Nicholas Barberis, Maxim Boyco, Andrei Schleifer, and Natalia Tsukanova, 'How Does Privatization Work? Evidence from the Russian Shops,' *Journal of Political Economy* 104 (August 1996): 788

4 World Bank, World Development Report 1996, 63–4

Source: Adapted from H.S. Gardner, *Comparative Economic Systems* (Dryden Press, Forth Worth, Texas, USA, 2nd edn 1998)

The rest of this unit concentrates mainly on firms in the private sector.

Why do firms exist?

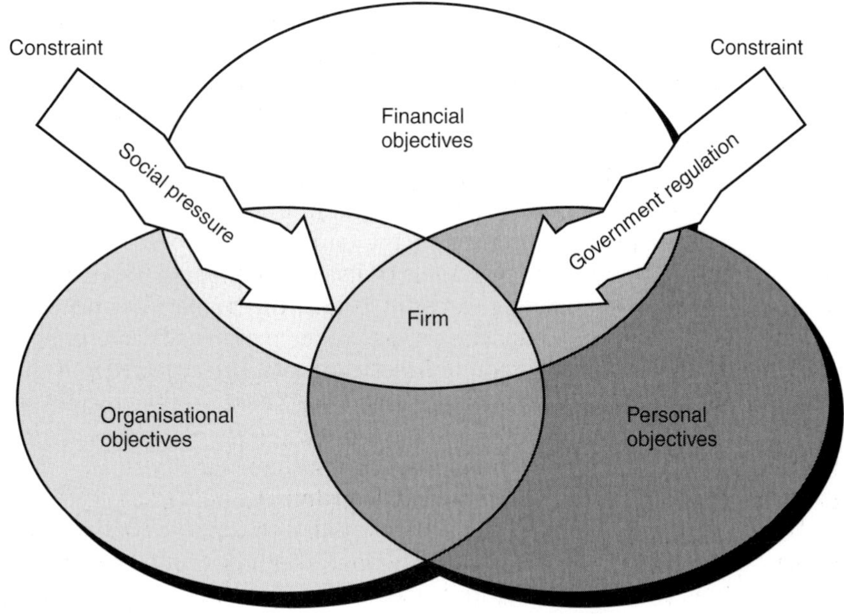

Fig. 4.5 Objectives of a firm and the constraints on them

The objectives of firms

Financial objectives

Making a profit is a prime objective of the majority of businesses in the private sector. Unless it makes a profit, a firm is unlikely to survive and will go out of business.

In the short term, a business may be able to survive if the revenue it receives from sales just covers its costs. In the very short term, a business may be able to survive even when it is making a loss. This is often the case with a new business that has high set-up costs, which may not be recovered until the business has established itself in the market.

In the long term, however, the owners of the business expect it to make a profit and so provide a return on their investment. If it doesn't, they will probably close the business and do something else that will provide the return they are looking for. Banks and other institutions that have helped to finance the business will also be likely to call in loans and cancel overdraft facilities if the business is not making a profit – especially if it is having difficulty keeping up repayments on the loan.

Not all organisations are expected to make a profit, however. Charities, for example, are established to distribute the money they receive amongst those for whom the charity has been set up. Similarly, the main objective of most organisations in the public sector, such as schools and hospitals, is to provide a service to society. Even these organisations, however, must break even (that is, they must cover their costs) if they are to continue to survive.

Personal and organisational objectives

While financial objectives are essential to the survival of any private-sector organisation, they are not the only objectives a business has. Other objectives of a business can be identified as either personal or organisational.

Personal objectives are those of the individual employees who work in the firm. Where the person who manages the firm is also its owner, personal objectives are especially important. They may, for example, include position or respect within the community, power, status or good labour relations.

In limited companies, especially large public limited companies, ownership is separated from management. This may mean that the objectives of the employees who actually run the company differ from the objectives of its owners. While the owners of the business – its shareholders – want profit, the managers may want security, power, status, high salaries and other perks such as company cars. Often such objectives conflict. For example, the objectives of the production manager may be to maximise production. If this results in diminishing returns (see pages 144–146), profits – which are the main objective of the owner of the company – may suffer.

Sometimes government and social constraints will influence a firm's objectives or its ability to achieve them. For example, the introduction of a minimum wage has reduced a firm's control over its wage bill and therefore its costs. This may mean that the firm has to increase the price of its product. However, if the price elasticity of demand for its product is high, the firm may have to absorb some of the costs involved in paying the minimum wage, so reducing its profits. Similarly, a large manufacturing company may have to invest in equipment that will reduce emissions harmful to the environment, either in response to government regulation or because of social pressure. Here again, the additional costs of the equipment may prevent the company from achieving its objective of profit maximisation.

Think about it

- A firm of civil engineers has been contracted by the government to build a bypass around a market town. In what ways might the objectives of the owners of the firm conflict with those of the government, the firm's employees and society? What are the economic and social implications of these conflicting objectives, and what action might be taken to resolve the conflicts?

Whatever the objectives of a firm, however, or the constraints imposed, it must cover its costs in order to survive. In the next section, we examine the types of costs that firms incur.

Costs

As we saw in Unit 1 (pages 34–36), all forms of production involve three types of costs:

- accounting costs
- opportunity costs
- private and social costs.

Here we are concerned primarily with accounting costs, which are the financial costs that a firm must cover from revenue.

The costs of production

Combining factors and costs

Production is the process of combining the factors of production in order to convert raw materials into a product that is wanted by consumers. However, it is rarely necessary to employ factors of production in fixed proportions to produce a given output. For example, a certain amount of wheat may be produced by what are called extensive methods in the prairies of Canada or by intensive methods on the wheat farms of East Anglia, the proportion of land to other factors of production being higher in the former case than in the latter.

The proportions in which factors are combined will normally reflect their relative costs and availability:

- If land is plentiful, and therefore cheap, extensive agriculture will normally prevail.
- If there is a shortage of land, and its price or rent is high, then more intensive cultivation would develop.

The same principle applies to manufacturing industries, and also to services. As labour becomes relatively more expensive, employers tend to substitute other, relatively cheaper, factors for it.

In a productive process at any given time, however, there will be some factors of production that cannot easily be increased, while others may be varied on a day-to-day basis. In the refining of crude oil, the amount of capital equipment employed is fixed over fairly long periods. It is true that it can be reduced merely by the refining company refusing to use it, but even in this unlikely event the costs of the equipment are still borne by the firm. An increase in capacity of 20 per cent by the installation of new equipment may take anything up to five years to achieve, once the design has left the drawing board; the time since the original decision to increase production will be even longer. Thus, capital is regarded as a **fixed factor of production**.

The fixed factors of production are those which cannot be changed in the short run. No precise time span can be allocated to the short run, since this varies greatly between industries. It may be several years in industries such as oil refining or the generation of electricity, but only a matter of weeks or even days in a car-hire business where the main units of capital, motor vehicles, are easy to acquire. In this case, the fixed factor of production is more likely to be the land required for offices, garages and maintenance services.

Think about it

- Consider the following industries and identify their fixed factors. How long do you think the short run is in each case?
  - banking
  - aeroplane manufacture
  - computer games development
  - a pop group
  - a hospital

In most industries the factor of production most easily altered in quantity is labour. Labour is a **variable factor of production.** Other important variable factors are raw materials and fuel supplies, which can usually be increased or decreased quite smoothly. There will, however, be degrees of variability. While some labour is hourly paid and perhaps subject to a week's notice, monthly paid staff may have contracts which entitle them to up to three months' notice or, in the case of some senior employees, even longer.

In the long run, all factors of production are variable, so an industry may secure an increase in output by employing more units of each factor in their existing proportions or by taking on more of the variable factors and using the fixed factors more intensively.

As we can categorise factors of production as fixed or variable, we may also allocate costs in the same way. In this context, we consider costs in the accounting sense of money spent on the various factors of production, rather than in the broader economic sense discussed in Unit 1.

- **Fixed costs** are those which (in the short run) do not vary directly with output; for this reason they are also known as **indirect costs.** These costs have to be paid, whether or not the firm produces any goods. They include annual rent payable for land, interest on capital and the replacement of capital objects, hire or rental charges for equipment for which notice of cancellation is required, and the salaries of many employees which must be paid regardless of output. (Fixed costs are also sometimes called overhead costs.)
- **Variable** or **direct costs** are those which do vary directly with output. If a firm is not producing anything, it can quite easily reduce its expenditure on power, raw materials and direct labour. If the break in production is prolonged, then other costs initially regarded as fixed will become variable – the salaries of monthly paid staff, for example.

Fig. 4.6 Fixed and variable costs

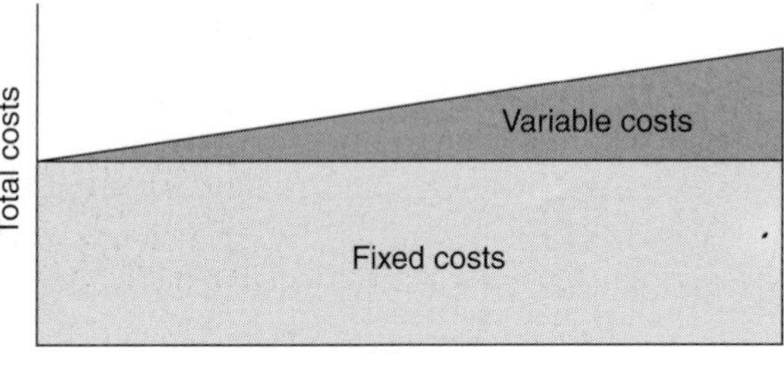

While the fixed costs of a business do not vary with production, the variable costs increase as production increases.

Something to do

- The main costs of a commercial transport company are listed below. Identify which are fixed costs and which are variable costs. Do any contain elements that might be fixed and elements that might be variable?
  - drivers
  - vehicles owned by the company
  - trailers rented by the company
  - road tax
  - fuel
  - office buildings
  - insurance
  - office staff
  - maintenance

Costs, revenues and profits

In order to recover its costs of production, a firm must sell its products. The value of the sales of its product is the firm's income or revenue.

- If the revenue a firm receives from selling its goods is less than its total costs, the firm makes a loss.
- If the revenue the firm receives exactly equals its costs, the firm will break even.
- If the revenue the firm receives exceeds its costs, the firm will make a profit equal to the amount by which revenue exceeds costs.

This is illustrated diagrammatically in Figure 4.7.

Fig. 4.7 Costs, revenues and profit

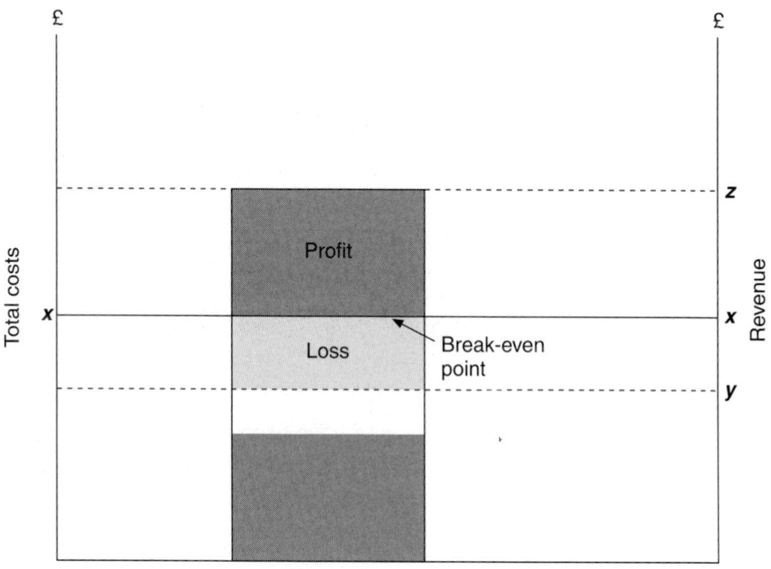

If the total costs of a business are at point ***x***:

- the business must have a revenue of ***x*** to break even
- with a revenue of ***y***, the business will make a loss of ***x*** – ***y***
- a revenue of ***z***, however, will generate a profit of ***z*** – ***x*** (total revenue less total costs).

Profit versus cash flow

An important distinction must be drawn between profit and **cash flow**. Once a sale has been made, the value of that sale forms part of the firm's revenue for the period, and is counted towards any profit the firm makes.

However, it is often the case that goods are not paid for at the time of purchase. It may be that the supplier sends the customer an invoice with a request that the invoice is paid within 30 days, or by the end of the following month. Some firms will delay making payment for goods they have bought for as long as possible. Alternatively, goods may be bought on credit and paid for in monthly instalments over a period of several months or even years. Where this is the case, a firm does not receive the money for products it has sold until some time later. Although the firm will likewise pay for products it has purchased some time after it has bought them, there are various expenses it must still pay straight away. These include items such as wages, tax, insurance, telephone and electricity charges, rent and so on. Obviously, a firm's ability to pay these expenses depends on its receiving sufficient money to cover them, regardless of the actual value of sale it has made. A firm that cannot pay its bills, even though it may be profitable, can be made bankrupt and go out of business.

It is essential, therefore, that firms not only ensure that their revenues cover costs, but also that their cash flow – that is, the timing of receipts and payments of actual cash – enables them to meet expenditure as it becomes due. Many basically sound businesses have failed because of poor management of their cash flow.

Key Points

- *Profit is the value of a firm's sales less its costs in a given period.*
- *Cash flow is the flow of actual cash received and payments made by a firm during a given period.*

Something to do

Advanced Business Solutions Limited is a small company providing secretarial services to local businesses. At the end of its first year of trading, it has made a profit of £25 000. However, the company's bank is concerned that it has run up an unarranged overdraft of £8000 and can no longer pay its bills. The company cannot understand how, when it has made a profit, it cannot pay its bills.

- You work for the company's bank, and have been asked by your manager to draft a letter explaining to the managing director of Advanced Business Solutions the difference between cash flow and profit, and the importance of maintaining a healthy cash flow in the pursuit of profit. Draft the letter.

How much should a firm produce?

Combining factors of production in the short run

In order to decide how much it should produce so as to best achieve its objectives, a firm must take account of the principle of diminishing returns (see Unit 2).

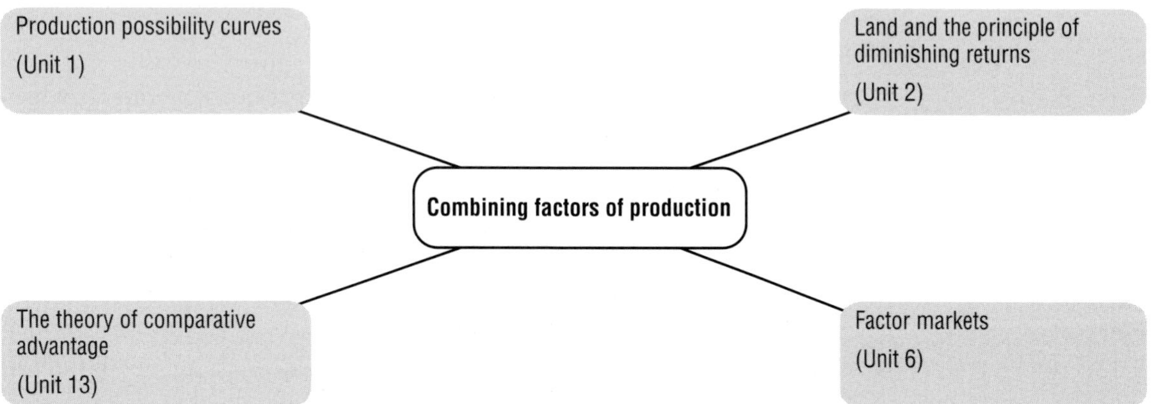

> **Key Points**
>
> - *The **principle of diminishing returns** states that as increasing amounts of a variable factor of production are used in conjunction with fixed amounts of other factors of production, marginal product and average product at first increase but eventually decline.*

The principle must be examined more carefully in the context of a firm's production, but first certain terms must be defined.

Average and marginal product

- **Average product** is the total output (or product) divided by the number of units of the variable factor. If, for example, a farmer employs ten men to produce 2000 kilograms of wheat, the average product is 200 kilograms.
- **Marginal product** is the increase in total product resulting from the employment of an extra unit of the variable factor (which, in the case of the above farmer, is labour). If the farmer employs a further (eleventh) man and output rises to 2100 kilograms, then the marginal product is 100 kilograms, the amount added by the extra man. (Note that 'marginal product' is also sometimes referred to as 'marginal physical product'.)

The concept of the margin is fundamental to a study of the theory of production, and it is essential that its characteristics are clearly understood. As we have seen above, marginal product is the amount that is added to total product by the efforts of one more unit of a factor. The sum of the marginal products therefore gives the total product.

- If no worker is employed, output will be nil.
- If the employment of one man increases the output to ten units, both the total product and the marginal product are ten.
- If the employment of a second man increases total product by a further fifteen units, then the total product rises to 25, which is the sum of the marginal products (10 + 15).
- If the marginal product was negative, then the total product would be reduced.

Marginal product exercises an important influence over average product:

- If the marginal product is greater than the previous average product, the average product rises.
- If the marginal product is less than the previous average product, the average product falls.

It may be helpful to think of this in terms of the average age of a class of students. Suppose that there are ten students in a class, whose average age is 20 (that is, their combined ages total 200 years). If an extra student who is aged 25 joins the class, the average age becomes $\frac{225}{11} = 20.45$. If the new student was aged 18 years, then the average age would fall. If the new student were aged 20 years (that is, the marginal item is the same as the existing average), the average age would neither rise nor fall. The same is true of both marginal product and average product.

Something to do

Healthy Office Catering is a small catering service that makes prepared meals for local office staff. The sandwiches and meals are prepared during the morning and delivered to the offices at lunch time. To begin with, the business was run by the two partners, Harvinder Singh and Anne Sale, who between them prepared 200 sandwiches and meals a day and delivered them using two vans. Realising the potential for growth, however, they employed an assistant and are now able to prepare and deliver 275 meals a day.

- Calculate the average product per worker.
- Calculate the marginal product of the additional employee.

Firms and the principle of diminishing returns

Let us now return to the principle of diminishing returns and imagine that a farmer with a fixed amount of land experiments to discover the effects of employing different amounts of labour for wheat production (see Table 4.2 and Figure 4.8).

When one worker is employed the total product, marginal product and average product are all the same (assuming that is nothing is produced with no employees), but as the number of employees increases, the three quantities diverge. The least important from our point of view is total product, but we may notice that up to the employment of the tenth worker total product rises but at a decreasing rate after the employment of the fifth worker. This is what is meant by diminishing returns: there is an increase in output from successive applications of the same amount of factor, but the increase eventually becomes smaller. If this were not so, economic problems would not exist as it would be possible to produce the entire world's food requirements in one field!

Table 4.2

Application of successive units of labour to a fixed amount of land										
1 No. of workers	2 Total product (kg)	3 Marginal product (kg)	4 Average product (kg)	5 Fixed costs (£)	6 Variable costs (£)	7 Total costs (£)	8 Marginal cost per unit (£)	9 Average fixed cost per unit (£)	10 Average variable cost per unit (£)	11 Average total cost per unit (£)
1	5	5	5.0	50	10	60	2.00	10.00	2.00	12.00
2	12	7	6.0	50	20	70	1.43	4.17	1.67	5.83
3	23	11	7.6	50	30	80	0.91	2.17	1.30	3.47
4	36	13	9.0	50	40	90	0.77	1.39	1.11	2.50
5	48	12	9.6	50	50	100	0.83	1.04	1.04	2.08
6	58	10	9.7	50	60	110	1.00	0.86	1.03	1.89
7	65	7	9.3	50	70	120	1.43	0.77	1.08	1.85
8	68	3	8.5	50	80	130	3.33	0.74	1.18	1.92
9	70	2	7.7	50	90	140	5.00	0.71	1.29	2.00
10	71	1	7.1	50	100	150	10.00	0.70	1.41	2.11
11	71	0	6.4	50	110	160	–	0.70	1.55	2.25

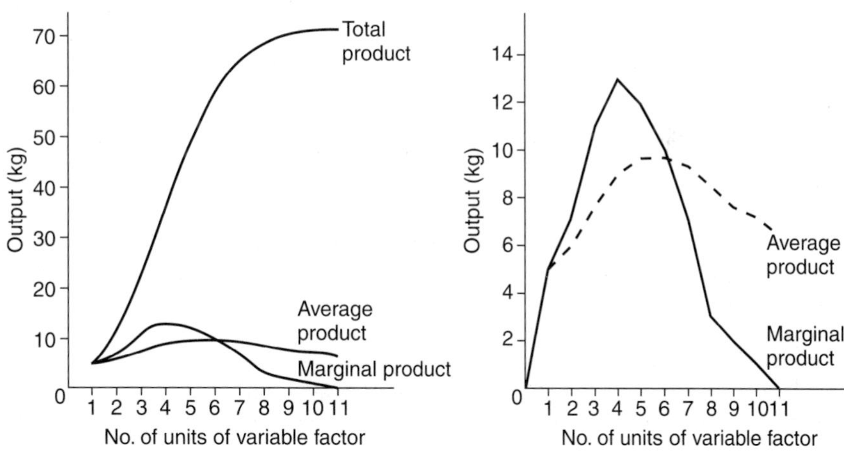

Fig. 4.8 Graphical representation of Table 4.2

Another way of expressing the growing difficulty of increasing total output (or product) is to say that marginal product eventually falls – marginal product being the increase in total product added by each additional unit of a factor of production. We notice that when employment is doubled from one worker to two workers the marginal product rises from 5 kilograms to 7 kilograms. This is a case of increasing returns, since a 100 per cent rise in the output of labour results in a more than proportionate rise in total output – from 5 kilograms to 12 kilograms.

We must not make the mistake of thinking that the second worker is more productive than the first – the marginal product of 7 kilograms is partly attributable to the first worker, since some specialisation is possible with two workers, and so the fixed factor can be more fully exploited. Similar considerations arise from the employment of the third and fourth workers: division of labour promotes greater efficiency in the use of the land.

From this we can see that the marginal product is not the actual output of the marginal unit of the factor, but is the increase in the total product obtained from the employment of the marginal unit of the factor and is attributable to all units of the factor. When the fifth worker is employed, the marginal product declines from 13 kilograms to 12 kilograms, and this shows that the benefits of division of labour are becoming exhausted. The employment of a tenth worker gives an increase in output (marginal product) of only 1 kilogram, not because the tenth unit of labour is any less hard-working than the previous nine, but because no amount of extra effort can squeeze further output from the fixed amount of land. On a more fertile piece of land, marginal product might still be rising with ten employees, but we can be certain that diminishing returns would eventually set in.

The average product does not rise as rapidly or as far as marginal product. The reason is clear if we consider the rise in employment from one worker to two. The extra employee increases total output to 12 kilograms. The marginal product concept allocates the whole of the increase of 7 kilograms to the second worker, even though we know that it is partly attributable to the first person, but when we measure average product we divide the total product of 12 kilograms equally between those units of the variable factor; hence the average product (6 kilograms) rises less rapidly than marginal product (7 kilograms). When marginal product is less than average product, average product declines less rapidly than marginal product since the effects are again spread thinly over all the units of the variable factor rather than being concentrated on the marginal unit.

The relationship between marginal product and average product is such that they are equal when average product is at its maximum. This follows from our discussion of average and marginal concepts above (see pages 143–144). So long as marginal product is greater than average product, the latter must be rising even if marginal product is falling. When marginal product is less than average product, the latter must be falling. When average product is neither rising nor falling but is at its maximum, then it must be equal to marginal product.

The principle of diminishing returns does not apply only to agriculture. We may imagine the production line in a motor factory designed for a workforce of perhaps 300 workers. If the owner tries to operate with just one employee, the total product, marginal product and average product would each be negligible. As the workforce is increased, output will rise and average product may be expected to reach its maximum when 300 workers are employed. Further increases of labour lead to a rise in total output but a fall in average and marginal product, until the production line is saturated with labour and the employment of perhaps the four hundredth worker results in a marginal product of zero or even a fall in total product if the extra employee ends up getting in the others' way. (See also the example given in Unit 2, page 46.) The point is that the fixed factor eventually becomes saturated with the variable factor. When this happens very quickly we say that diminishing returns set in early; when it takes much longer we may say that diminishing returns are delayed.

The importance of marginal product

Since diminishing returns are bound to set in at some point, a firm will want to know whether at any given point it is worth employing extra units of labour or any other variable factor. The answer depends on the aims of the firm.

If its main objective is to maximise production, it will continue to employ additional units of labour until the marginal product falls to zero. To proceed beyond this point would result in negative marginal product, and reduce total product. If the firm's main objective is to maximise profits, however, it will employ extra units of labour as long as it adds more to total revenue than it does to total costs.

The assumption underlying the theory of production is that the principal objective of most firms is to maximise their profits. Here we consider the implications of this assumption in terms of Figure 4.9, where the marginal product curve from Figure 4.8 is shown in a more generalised form.

Fig. 4.9 The limit to the employment of a variable factor

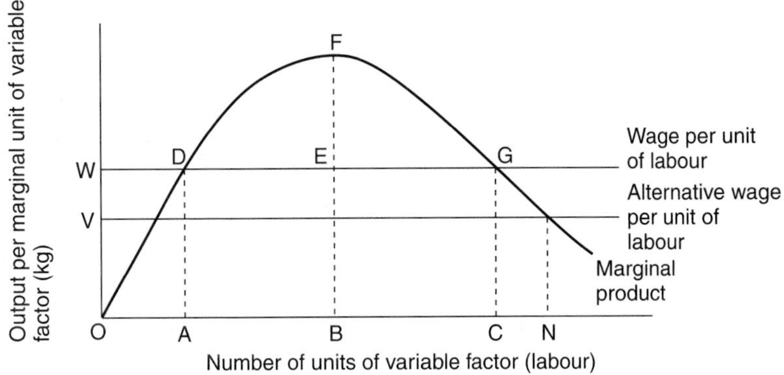

To avoid the complications arising from the use of money, we will assume that each worker receives a wage in the form of part of what they have produced (OW), and that there are no other costs involved.

If OA units of labour are employed, the total wage bill will be represented by the area OWDA, but the total product is only ODA (the sum of the marginal products). There is therefore a loss of OWD. When further units of labour are employed, the marginal product rises by more than the additional costs of employing them. For example, when OB people are employed, the wage of the marginal employee is BE (= OW) but the marginal product is BF. Until OC people are employed, the increases in total product (shown by the marginal product curve) are greater than the rises in the wage bill (OW), and there is a surplus of DFG on employing the units of labour between A and C. (The total product derived from employing these people is ADFGC, where total wages are ADGC.) If there are more than OC employees, profits will be reduced, since the addition to output will be less than the wages payable to extra units of labour. It would, therefore, be inconsistent with the aim of profit maximisation to employ more than OC men.

From this we can see that profits are maximised when the addition to total output falls to the point where it only just equals the cost of the last person, and in our example that profit is measured by the area DFG minus OWD (that is, the profit from employing units of labour between A and C minus the loss from employing the initial units OA).

Although we may see OC as being the profit-maximising level of employment, there may be circumstances in which it is a loss-minimising situation, since the area OWD may be greater than DFG. It will be the best position for a firm if the level of wages and the productivity of workers are fixed. If wages change, then it would be best to employ a different amount of labour. At wage OV, for example, it is worth employing ON units of labour, but if the wage rate rises above OW fewer people should be employed.

The cost curves of the firm

The discussion so far has been conducted in terms of units of output and units of labour, but each firm will need precise estimates of its costs and revenues in monetary terms. In Table 4.2, the last seven columns deal with costs. We have assumed quite arbitrarily that the firm has to meet fixed costs of £50 per productive period and variable costs of £10 per unit of labour employed. We can easily arrive, therefore, at the figure for the total cost of producing any particular output. For example, if the firm wants to product 70 kilograms it needs to employ nine people. The wage bill will be £90 (£10 × 9), and since there are fixed costs of £50, the total cost is £140.

Average and marginal cost

In Figure 4.8, we isolated average product and marginal product, but we must now identify **average cost** and **marginal cost.**

- Average cost – or, more precisely, average *total* cost – is found by the formula

$$\text{average total cost (ATC)} = \frac{\text{total cost}}{\text{output}}$$

That is, when output is 70 kilograms, the average total cost is £140/70 = £2 per kilogram.

- The precise definition of marginal cost is 'the increase in total cost when output is increased by one unit'. In practice, it is difficult to employ labour in sufficiently small amounts to produce just one extra unit, and Table 4.2 does not allow this. However, we can get a good approximation of marginal cost by using the formula

$$\text{marginal cost (MC)} = \frac{\text{increase in total cost}}{\text{increase in output}}$$

Consider an increase in the number employed from three to four. This involves £10 in extra variable costs and a rise in output of 13 kilograms; therefore

$$\text{MC} = \frac{£10}{13} = £0.77$$

It is also possible to calculate average fixed costs and average variable costs.

- Average fixed cost is found by the formula

$$\text{average fixed cost (AFC)} = \frac{\text{total fixed cost}}{\text{output}}$$

- Average variable cost is found by the formula

$$\text{average variable cost (AVC)} = \frac{\text{total variable cost}}{\text{output}}$$

In Figure 4.10 the relationship between the various curves is shown diagrammatically.

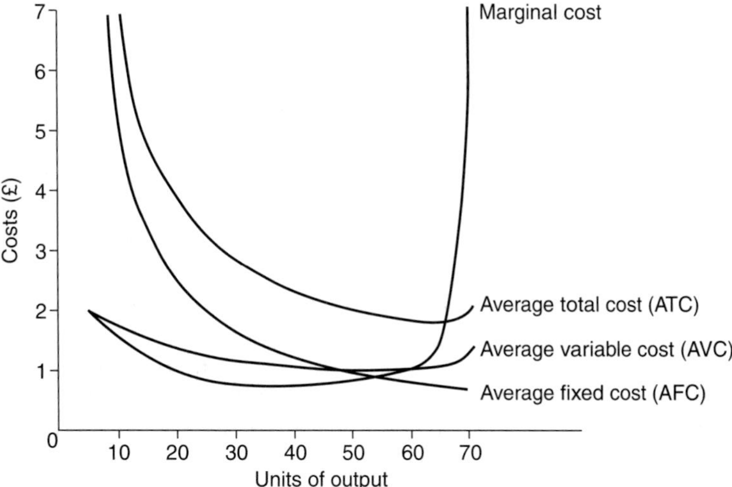

Fig. 4.10 The cost curves of the firm

With reference to Figure 4.10, note especially the following points.

- As output rises the AFC curve falls, since the fixed costs are spread more thinly over a larger output. The AFC curve is the same shape as a demand curve with an elasticity of 1 over its entire length (see Unit 3, pages 94–95). All rectangles drawn from the curve to the axes will be equal in area, showing that the total fixed costs do not alter.
- The marginal cost curve is U-shaped, due to the operation of the law of diminishing returns. When a second worker is employed, total costs rise by £10 (the worker's wage), and output rises by 7 kilograms. On our definition, therefore, marginal cost is £10 ÷ 7 = £1.43. With the third employee, total cost still rises by £10, but output increases by 11 kilograms, so marginal cost is now £10 ÷ 11 = 91 pence. This fall in marginal cost reflects the more efficient use of labour and the more economic use of the fixed factor as more people are employed. The employment of a fourth person gives a further fall in marginal cost, but when the fifth employee is taken on there is a fall in the marginal product which causes the marginal cost curve to rise. The curve continues to rise until marginal product falls to zero when the eleventh person is employed.
- The ATC curve is also U-shaped. The fall in its early stages is due in part to influences discussed above which result in average or variable cost falling. The fall is also partly due to the fact that average fixed costs fall as output expands. Average total cost continues to fall after marginal cost begins to rise. The relationship between these two is exactly parallel to that between average product and marginal product, and the ATC curve is cut by the marginal cost curve when average total cost is at a minimum because when marginal cost exceeds the existing average cost it will raise the overall average. When average total cost does begin to rise, it is because the rise in average variable costs more than offsets the continuing fall in average fixed costs.

- It is essential to distinguish between marginal cost and average variable cost (AVC). Marginal cost relates an *increase* in output to an *increase* in variable costs, whereas average variable cost relates *total* output to *total* variable costs. Therefore, when we measure average variable cost we are interested in all the production that has taken place, whereas measurements of marginal costs relate only to increments of output.
- An important element has until now been left out of our calculation of costs. An entrepreneur will not remain in business unless he or she is making a profit, and, in the study of economics, profit is seen as a cost of production that has to be met in the same way as wages or raw materials. While the actual amount of profit that is necessary to keep any firm in a given industry cannot be estimated precisely, it is generally known as a **normal rate of profit**. Anything less than a normal rate of profit will induce firms to leave the industry as equipment wears out. If profits are higher than a normal rate, however, new firms will be attracted in and existing firms will be tempted to expand. Profit was left out of Table 4.2 partly because of the uncertainty regarding the appropriate level and partly due to the difficulty of allocating it to fixed or variable costs. This is a matter of some debate. However, the generalised cost curves that will be used from now on should be regarded as including a normal rate of profit, that is, the rate of profit which is just enough to keep the firm in business.

The curves drawn in Figure 4.10 are derived from Table 4.2. The marginal cost curve is by far the most important in fixing the output of the firm.

Something to do

In the activity on page 144, you calculated the average and marginal product for Healthy Office Catering when they had three workers and produced 275 meals per day. The fixed costs of the business are £50 per day plus £32 wages per worker, while variable costs are 35p per meal.

- Calculate
  - average total cost per day
  - marginal cost of the additional employee per day
  - average fixed cost per day
  - average variable cost per day.
- Construct the appropriate cost curves.

Think about it

- What are the implications of the marginal cost curve fixing the output of a firm for the government wanting to improve the provision of health services by employing more nurses in the NHS?

The firm's supply curve

The firm's cost curves show how much it costs on average to produce a given output (average total cost curve) or how much total cost increases when output is increased (marginal cost curve). The actual amount that the firm produces will depend on changes in total cost and changes in total revenue. Consider the case in Figure 4.11.

Fig. 4.11 The output of the individual firm

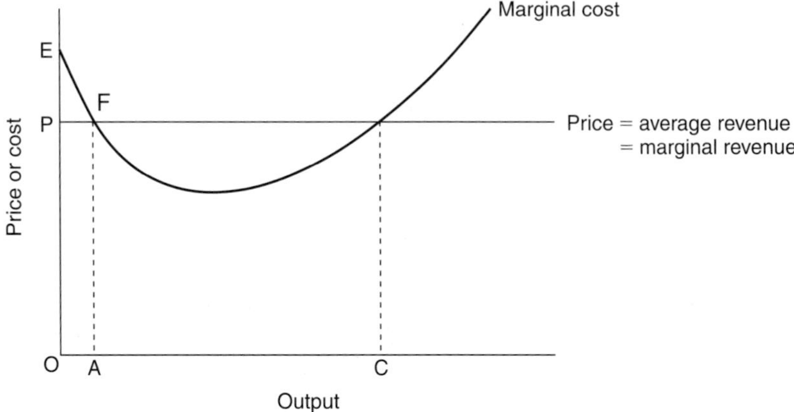

Here we are assuming that the price is fixed at OP and the firm (a profit maximiser) can sell as much as it wishes at that price. In these circumstances, the firm knows that its **marginal revenue** is always constant. Marginal revenue (MR) is the increase in total revenue resulting from the sale of an extra unit of product. In Figure 4.11, MR is equal to price.

In the light of our discussion on pages 147–151, it is a straightforward matter to establish the most profitable output, remembering the cost curves include a normal rate of profit. If the entrepreneur decided to produce OA units, total variable costs (the sum of the marginal costs) would exceed total revenue by PEF (OEFA minus OPFA). For all the units of output between OA and OC, the addition to total revenue (marginal revenue) is greater than the addition to total cost (marginal cost) and so the increase in output is profitable. The expansion of output beyond OC, however, pushes marginal cost above marginal revenue and therefore reduces profits. OC is thus the profit-maximising output.

Fig. 4.12 The firm's supply curve

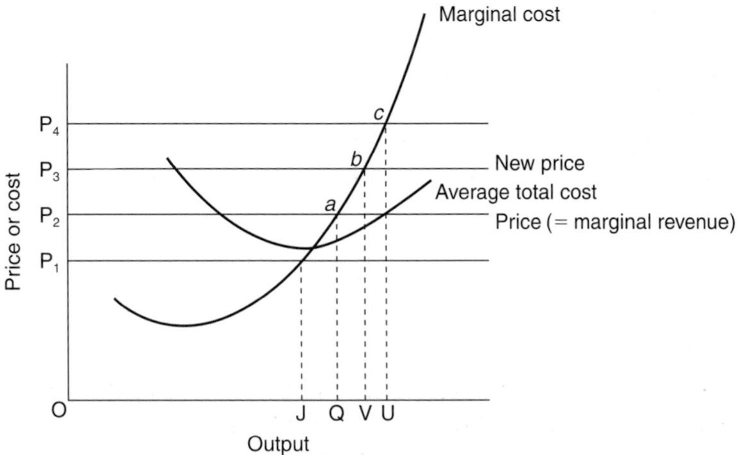

Figure 4.12 shows what will happen if price changes. Let us suppose that the original price is OP_2. By equating marginal cost (MC) with price (which is the same as marginal revenue) at *a*, the firm fixes output at OQ and maximises profits. If the price now rises to OP_3, OQ is no longer the profit-maximising output since MR is greater than MC at that price. It is therefore worth expanding output to OV, thereby adding more to total revenue than to total costs and attaining a new profit-maximising position at *b*. A further rise in price to OP_4 gives yet another profit-maximising output, OU, whereas a fall in price to OP_1 gives an output of OJ.

Key Points

- *In each case, as the price changes, the firm moves along the marginal cost curve in order to determine its output. We can conclude, therefore, that* ***the marginal cost curve is also the supply curve of this particular firm.***

The supply curve shows the relationship between the quantity supplied and the market price. It shows the price that is necessary to induce the firm to put a particular quantity of its product on the market, or – looking at this in a different way – it shows the amount that will be produced at any given price.

Key Points

- *To be more precise, we can say that the part of the marginal cost curve which is above the average total cost curve forms the supply curve.*

If price fell to OP_1 in Figure 4.12, the firm's best output would be OJ, but in this case average total cost (including a normal rate of profit) is higher than the price received and the firm could not afford to stay in business for very long.

Short-run and long-run costs

The cost curves discussed in the preceding section are short-run cost curves which have been drawn up on the basis that at least one factor of production is fixed in supply. In this case the only way to increase output is by employing more units of the variable factor so that the fixed factor is used more intensively. This will be quite adequate to meet temporary fluctuations in demand. If the firm is faced with a permanent increase in demand, however, it may decide to increase its employment of all factors of production. If the firm does this, it may choose between a variety of short-run cost curves.

Consider the possibilities shown in Figure 4.13.

- In Figure 4.13a, we have a firm which has doubled its use of a factor that is fixed in the short run. It may, for example, have installed a second production line. We have therefore drawn two average total cost curves and the two associated marginal cost curves. Up to an output of OA units, average total cost is lower if the capacity of the firm is restricted – it is wasteful to install the second production line to meet a demand of OB, since a very large amount of excess capacity would remain. (A firm with excess capacity is operating at below optimum output – that is, the output where average cost is at a minimum.) The output OC, however, can be more efficiently produced by installing new equipment than by trying to squeeze extra output from existing equipment. The average total cost is OD using the original capacity but only OE if extra equipment is brought into use.

Fig. 4.13 Employing extra units of all factors

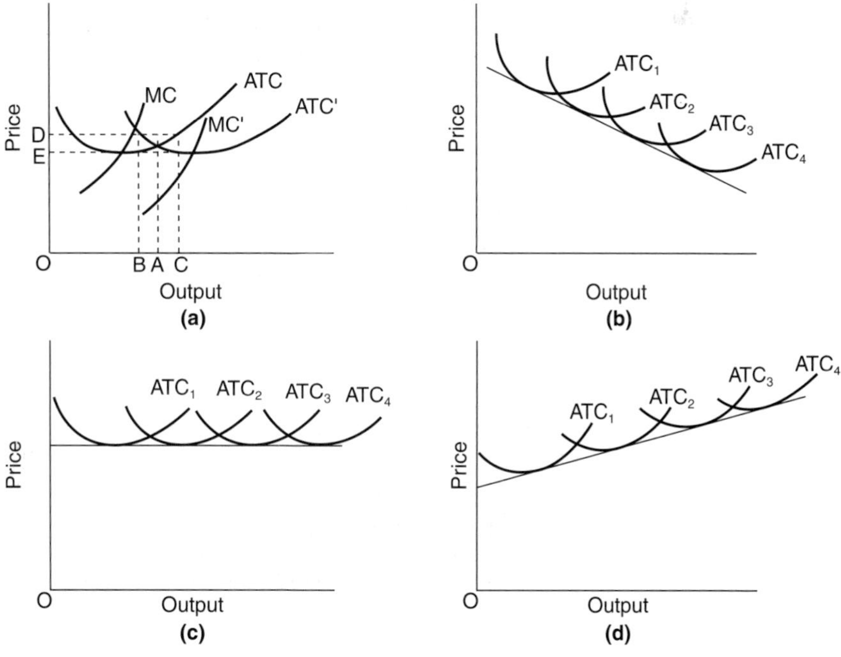

- The installation of extra capacity cannot normally be achieved overnight, however. This may take months or years. It is customary, therefore, to regard the two combined short-run average total cost curves as giving the long-run average total cost curve ATC showing costs when both old and new equipment are in use. Figures 4.13b–d indicate the possible trends of the long-run average total cost curve.
- In Figure 4.13c, as we increase capacity, the optimum output increases but the average cost of that output is constant. This is a case of constant costs or constant **returns to scale**.
- In Figure 4.13b, as optimum output increases, the cost falls. This is a case of decreasing costs or increasing returns to scale.
- In Figure 4.13d the rising trend indicates increasing costs. This is a case of diminishing returns to scale.

Returns to scale or economies of scale?

It is important to distinguish between returns to scale and **economies of scale**.

- Returns to scale are a feature of the long-run cost function. In other words, as the cost of production varies, so too does the revenue produced.
- Economies of scale, on the other hand, are a feature of the long-run production function. This means that as a firm increases its production or size, it is able to benefit from advantages that larger firms can enjoy, such as higher discounts on the greater quantities of raw materials purchased.

  *Dis*economies of scale are the disadvantages of increasing in production or size, such as the tendency of large firms to develop cumbersome and wasteful bureaucracies.

Fig. 4.14 Long-run average total costs

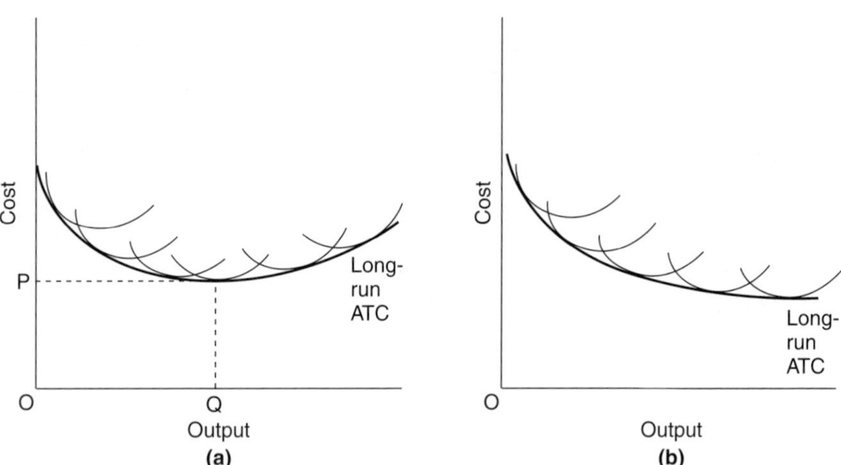

The shape of the long-run average total cost curve will depend very largely on the availability of technical and managerial economies of scale (see also pages 160–163) and on the rapidity with which **diseconomies** associated with the scarcity of labour or raw materials, or with managerial deficiencies, set in. In Figure 4.14a, we find what many economists regard as a typical long-run average total cost curve with costs falling in the early stages of expansion down to a long-run optimum level of OP, at output OQ, then perhaps a period of constant costs followed by rising costs as diseconomies and bottlenecks in production offset earlier economies.

Figure 4.14b shows a downward-sloping long-run average total cost curve. In industries such as motor manufacturing and oil refining, technological progress is so rapid and persistent as to allow average total costs (measured at constant prices) to show a considerable fall over a long period.

Something to do

- Write notes outlining the relationship between short-run and long-run costs for
  - a local authority leisure centre
  - a market stall trader.

The size of firms and economies of scale

It is evident that different individual units of production – both firms and plants – vary considerably in size, and in general it is not difficult to attempt some classification of firms as large or small. Firms such as BT and Marks & Spencer are usually regarded as being large, while Joe's Pizzas or Lisa's Mobile Hairdresser are small by most standards. Sometimes, however, it is necessary to support this kind of intuition with a more objective measure. There are various possibilities, but usually we measure either the input of factors of production or the output of goods and services.

Table 4.3

Largest firms in the UK (private sector), 1997 (£ million)

	Turnover	Capital employed	Pre-tax profit	Equity market capital*
1. BP	44731	20554	3667	39591
2. Shell	32831	20987	4347	33536
3. HSBC Holdings	18481	26947	4524	34462
4. National Westminster Bank	14590	15505	1122	11877
5. British Telecommunications (BT)	14446	17484	3019	21926
50. British Land Company	287	4002	62	1666

* Value of paid-up shares

FTSE 100

Table 4.3 gives details of the five largest private-sector firms, and for comparison the fiftieth, in the UK in 1997, ranked on the basis of their annual sales (turnover). This is the most useful way to measure the size of firms in different industries in terms of output, since money is the only common denominator for the production of firms such as BP and BT. It might be possible to use units of production to compare the size of firms in the same industry, but even here care is necessary. Two fast-food restaurants each serving 1000 meals a day might well be equal in size, but this is not true of two firms each producing 1000 motor cars if one produces luxury limousines while the other produces family saloons.

Had the companies in Table 4.3 been arranged on the basis of other measures, a different order would have arisen. In terms of capital employed, BP would have dropped to third place, while the equity market valuation for HSBC Holdings would have taken it higher than Shell, although this is not a reliable measure since the value of shares can fluctuate for various reasons.

How do firms grow?

Many industries are dominated by large firms. However, none of these began life as an industrial giant. Each has grown to reach that status, often over a long period of time. Their growth may have been of two kinds:

- internal growth
- external growth.

Internal growth

Sometimes a firm grows larger because it maintains its share of an expanding market. Further growth could result from the active development of new markets for the firm's products, perhaps overseas.

Equally important may be the development of new products. Thus the development of pocket calculators, compact discs, new improved kitchen equipment, and so on, can result in individual firms growing in size.

This kind of internal, or organic, growth can be a slow process. The markets for most goods grow slowly – some hardly at all. New products may involve many years of research, development and testing before they can be marketed. Aggressive companies may want to increase the scope of their activities more quickly. This has led to the expansion of the process of external growth.

External growth

Basically this involves a merger with another business. The terminology here is sometimes confusing, but in the long run not important. A take-over indicates that one company gains control of another despite resistance on the part of the latter. A merger suggests that two companies come together by mutual agreement – sometimes establishing a new distinct business, sometimes retaining their separate identities. In what follows, the term 'merger' is used to cover both take-overs and mergers.

Fig. 4.15
Diagrammatic summary of mergers

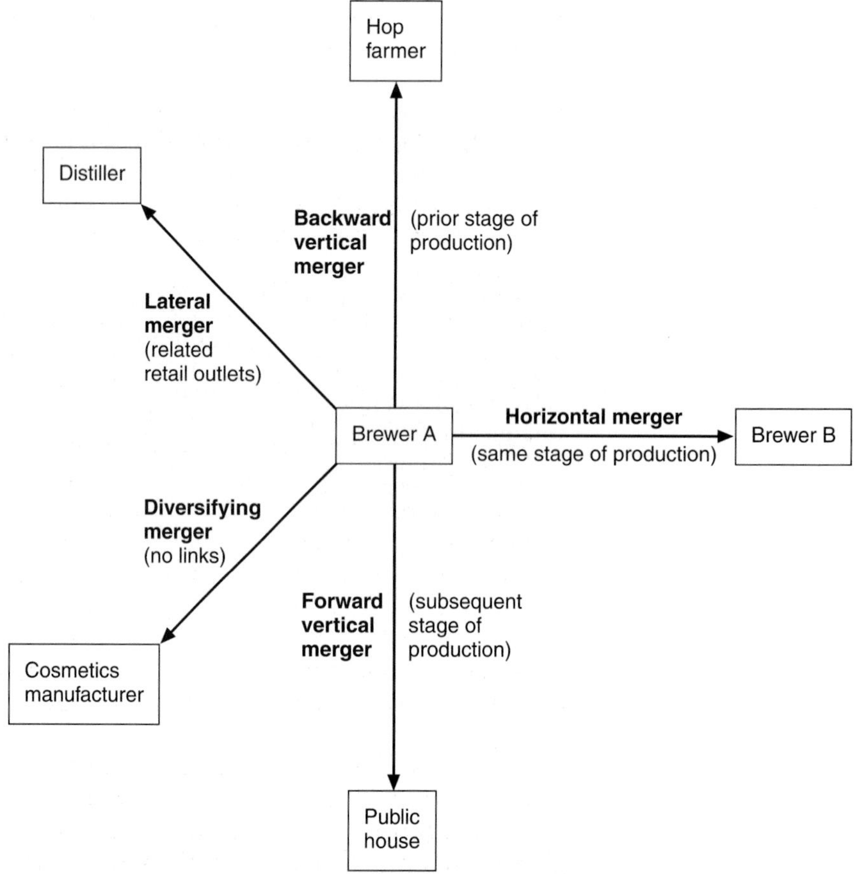

<u>Horizontal mergers</u> These occur where the two companies are engaged in the same stage of production of the same good. The merger of two brewers or bakers or motor-vehicle assemblers would be an example of a horizontal merger. The aim of such mergers is often to take advantage of economies of scale (see page 154), thus reducing the cost of production per unit of output. The extent to which the cost savings are passed on to customers will depend largely on the degree of competition that remains in the industry.

Horizontal mergers are often accompanied by statements about rationalisation. Rationalisation means reorganising production to achieve a given level of output by using fewer resources. It is likely to lead to redundancies as some services are centralised. At the very least, the merger will reduce the amount of advertising and sales staff that are required.

<u>Vertical mergers</u> These occur between two companies engaged in different stages of the production of a good. In the brewing industry, for example, we may distinguish backward vertical integration, when the brewer takes over the supplier to safeguard his raw materials, and forward vertical integration, when the brewer acquires public houses to facilitate the distribution of his product or to safeguard his retail outlets. To some extent backward integration allows the producer to bypass purchasing in the markets and this can lead to economies. Similarly, forward integration and control of the market allow production to be planned with greater confidence. Both types of vertical integration are likely to lead to rising profits.

<u>Lateral mergers</u> These involve two companies which produce related goods that do not compete directly with each other. The common link may be at one end of the process only: distilling and brewing are two distinct and separate techniques, but the lateral merger of brewers with distillers should lead to important marketing economies.

<u>Conglomerate or diversifying mergers</u> These occur where the products of the companies involved are unrelated. The acquisition of a cosmetics or potato-crisps manufacturer by a tobacco company constitutes a diversifying merger. Such mergers are frequently defensive, or in anticipation of a decline in the acquiring company's principal market.

Many diversifying mergers are of a more aggressive nature, stemming from financial manipulation, and they give rise to a holding company, which may be defined as a company controlling a number of other companies by holding at least 51 per cent of their ordinary shares but not necessarily taking an active part in their management. In this way companies in a variety of industries may benefit from the financial skill and prestige of the holding company without losing their separate identities. By careful selection, a holding company can establish a closely integrated group with each section complementary to others.

A series of diversifying mergers can, however, result in the establishment of a very large firm with interests in many different industries. These industries will be located in a number of different countries, giving rise to the phenomenon of multinational businesses.

Fig. 4.16 Simplified organisational structure of a large general retailer

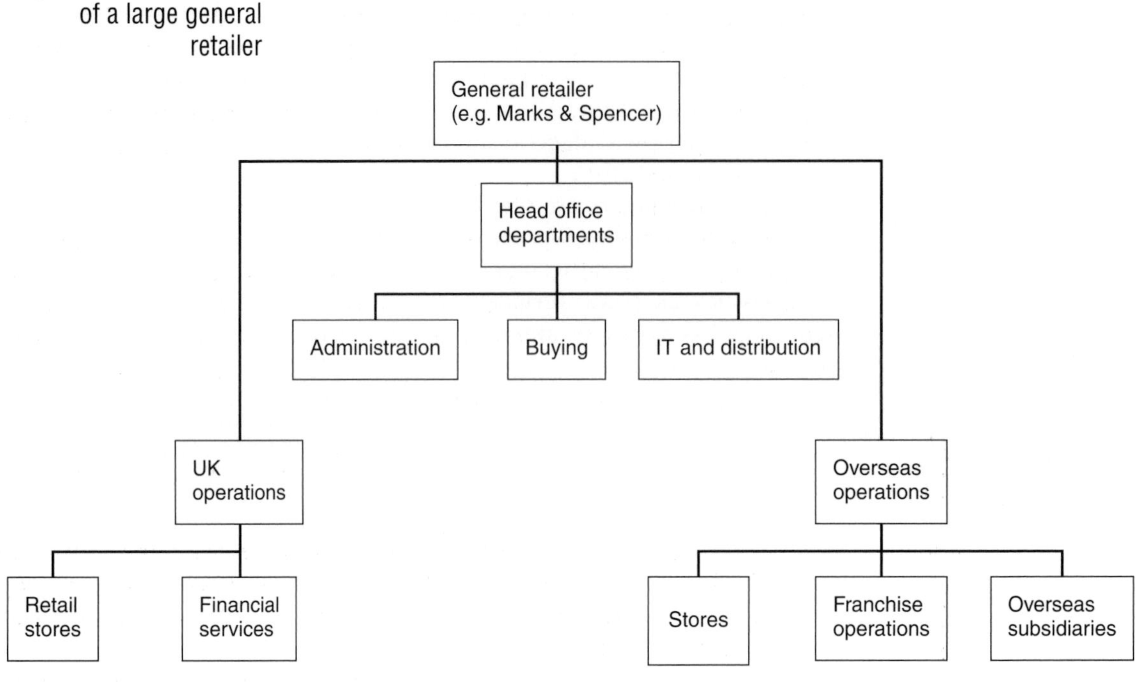

Think about it

- Consider the following mergers and identify what type of merger was involved:
  - the *Daily Mail* newspaper owning forests in Canada
  - Walmart taking over ASDA
  - a furniture manufacturer merging with a chain of high-street furniture stores
  - Unilever owning frozen-food producers and soap-powder manufacturers
  - a computer software developer taking over an Internet service provider.

Multinational businesses

A multinational company may be defined as one which has productive facilities in countries other than that in which it is based. Important examples are Unilever (which operates in over 50 countries) and BP Amoco (which operates across six continents). Some of the largest multinationals are American-based and include businesses such as Exxon (which owns Esso) and Ford. The annual sales of these multinationals are larger than the total output of many individual countries, so such companies have a lot of influence in the countries in which they operate. In developing countries, the establishment of a multinational may well cause more problems for the host country than it solves. Before considering why this is so, however, we should think about the reasons for the growth of multinational companies.

Reasons for the growth of multinationals

Other things being equal, most firms would prefer to expand in their domestic market rather than abroad. Limits to the size of the home market, however, mean that extra sales can eventually be achieved only by selling abroad. Since there may be obstacles, such as trade barriers and import taxes (see Unit 13), placed in the way of exports from one country to another, companies may seek the alternative route of actually producing goods in those other countries. If there is local competition, the multinational will hope to prevail through its greater size or superior technology or efficiency.

Sometimes, though, the establishment of overseas factories may be dictated by other considerations. Essential raw materials or cheap labour may attract the multinational; or tax advantages and other incentives may be offered by governments anxious to attract investment. Operating in more than one country may help to spread risk and give more options in the choice of sites for production units.

Economic effects of multinationals

The principal economic effects of the development of multinationals are as follows.

- Employment should increase in the host country. Labour will be required first to build the new plant and then to operate it. This may, however, be at the expense of employment or potential employment in the home country.
- Every country has financial and economic dealings with other countries. These are summarised annually in the country's **balance-of-payments** statement (see Unit 13). By their very nature, multinational companies are involved in international transactions, and these will to some extent affect the balance of payments of both the home and the host country. Initially, capital will be transferred from the home country to the host country. This will be harmful to the balance of payments of the former and helpful to the balance of payments of the latter. Later, when profits are made on the investment and returned to the home country, the balance-of-payments gains and losses are reversed.

  There may be further balance-of-payments effects. Exports from the home country to the host country may be reduced, since the goods can now be produced in the host country. Since its imports are reduced, the host country benefits; that benefit will be increased if the new factory itself begins exporting.
- Multinationals can be credited with the transfer of technology from one country to another, thus facilitating economic progress. It can generally be expected that the level of economic activity in the host country will increase, and this can be seen as desirable.

But not all the consequences of the multinationals are beneficial:

- If a company is located solely in the UK, for example, developments that benefit the company will probably also benefit the whole UK economy. If the company increases its exports, this helps both the company's profits and the UK's balance of payments. This 'coincidence of interests' does not always exist with multinational firms; they may decide to fulfil extra export orders from one of a number of plants, and they will do what is best for the company, not for a particular economy.

- Multinationals may take advantage of their situation to minimise their taxation. Suppose a company has two factories in two countries, A and B, and that the factory in A supplies components to the factory in B. If profits are taxed at 50 per cent in A, and at 10 per cent in B, it is beneficial for profits to arise in B rather than A. The company can therefore arrange for the factory in A to sell goods cheaply to the plant in B, so that profits in A are kept to a minimum, while profits are increased in B. A reversal of tax rates would lead to a reversal of pricing policy.

This is only one example of the way in which large firms might get round government policies. When they are located in developing countries, they may even be in a position to dictate to governments anxious not to jeopardise valuable overseas investment (this is discussed further in Unit 13).

As the scale of economic activity increases and large multinationals spread even wider, governments find it necessary to co-ordinate their policies in relation to such companies, so that their possible disadvantages do not outweigh their benefits.

Economies of scale

One of the effects of growth is that firms may enjoy the benefits of economies of scale. Economies of scale arise when the cost per unit of production falls as the size of a firm or plant increases. It is customary to divide economies of scale into two groups:

- internal economies, relating to a single firm
- external economies, which may benefit a large number of different firms or industries.

Internal economies of scale

A number of different types of internal economies of scale may be identified.

<u>Technical economies</u> Technical economies of scale are those found primarily in individual plants. Here, neither the capital costs nor the running costs of plants increase in proportion to their size. For example, a shipping company that can justify using a 250 000-tonne bulk oil carrier gains in two respects: the capital cost per 1000 tonnes of capacity is similar to that of a 100 000-tonne tanker, and neither the size of the crew nor the amount of fuel required by the vessel increases in proportion to its size. Similar considerations apply to the inland distribution of oil and account for the increasing size of road tankers. Chemical engineers use a rule of thumb in connection with the size of plant, which they call the 0.6 rule. This means that, on average, a 100 per cent increase in the capacity of a machine or plant leads to a rise in costs of approximately 60 per cent.

Large firms may enjoy other technical economies by locating specialised plant on one site or by using the same plant to make parts of different products.

An important source of technical economies in the mass-production industries is the intensive use of equipment in order to spread fixed costs over as large an output as possible. Since a motor manufacturer will spend millions of pounds on the development of a new model before the first car comes off the production line, he must sell a very large number in order to reduce the development costs per vehicle to a minimum.

Managerial or administrative economies The cost of processing large orders is not likely to increase in proportion to the size of those orders. Sales personnel, typists and accounts clerks can deal as comfortably with orders for 1000 units as they can with orders for 100 units. This kind of administrative economy is really an extension of the technical economy of spreading fixed costs (see page 140) over large outputs. In multi-product firms, many administrative costs may be shared between products, but this is impossible in a single-product firm. The principal managerial economies, however, are likely to be those derived from specialisation and division of labour: the large firm can employ specialist accountants, marketing managers, sales personnel and production engineers, each of whom, by devoting all his or her attention to a relatively small part of the company's work, may do much to increase productivity.

Financial economies Large firms have not only a large turnover but also many assets. When it comes to raising capital for the purchase of new plant or for investment in stocks of raw materials, the valuable assets of the large firm give it a further advantage. Investors in ordinary or preference shares or purchasers of debentures are likely to be more impressed by the status and achievements of a large nationally known company than by those of a small relatively unknown one. Moreover, the actual administrative costs of raising money through the capital market would be proportionately lower for large firms since the costs do not increase in proportion to the size of the share issue. Large firms also have the advantage when it comes to short-term finance. An examination of the published accounts of many public companies will reveal bank overdrafts of hundreds of thousands of pounds. A small local business, on the other hand, may have difficulty in persuading the bank manager to part with even a few hundred pounds. The borrowing difficulties of small and medium-sized firms have resulted in the formation of a number of government-sponsored bodies whose main task is to channel funds towards deserving firms.

Marketing economies These may be available both in the purchase of raw materials and components and also in the sale of the finished products. A large firm may not only receive normal discounts for bulk purchases, but may also be able to dictate very advantageous terms as it constitutes a large proportion of the supplier's market. To the extent that advertising increases the size of the market for a firm's products and allows further division of labour in production, it too may lead to further economies of scale. The large firm is better able to support the advertising costs of launching new products and of keeping representatives in the field to maintain or expand its market share.

Social economies Social economies may be divided into two groups: those that build up the goodwill of the community in general and thus attract custom, and those that develop the loyalty of the firm's employees. The former may be regarded as an extension of the marketing effort and are the responsibility of the public relations department. They involve, for example, the sponsorship of football or cricket competitions or the subscription of money to good causes, and they may be expected to result in increased turnover. The latter consist of recreational facilities, housing, superannuation schemes, Christmas bonuses, and any projects designed to make workers feel that they are an integral part of the firm and to win their loyalty. Larger companies are more likely to have the resources to finance such schemes, which are often seen as a means of compensating for the lack of personal contact between the owners and the employees.

External economies of scale

External economies of scale are those available to all the firms in a particular industry, and indeed may be of advantage to a number of firms in different industries. They can be grouped as follows:

Economies related to a particular industry Many of these are derived from the concentration of an industry in one locality (see also pages 166–168). They include the provision of specialist maintenance or training facilities in local technical colleges, or the development of a pool of labour with the skills appropriate to the industry. Other external economies may relate to a trade association. This is an association of producers or suppliers of services, corresponding to, though not normally parallel to, a trade union. Examples of such associations are the Society of Motor Manufacturers and Traders and the Brewers' Society. Economies obtained from membership of a trade association might include joint or generic advertising: 'Join the tea-set' was intended to increase the consumption of tea in general, not one particular brand of tea. Technical information and market trends may also become available from the association, which may be able to organise trade fairs or other marketing facilities beyond the scope of any single manufacturer.

Economies related to industrialisation Areas of high economic activity always include a number of firms dependent on the major companies of the area but providing an essential service to them. Thus the motor industry is served by a host of small firms which provide components and maintenance services to them and other industrial concerns. The activities of the services sector multiply, providing advantages to firms in the area compared with those in less developed regions.

Economies related to society The provision of roads, railways, housing, schools, hospitals and other social services is largely the responsibility of the State. As industrialisation proceeds, the provision of these items of social capital increases and makes an area more attractive to firms and potential employees – in many cases also giving further advantages to firms already in the area. Better housing attracts better workers at all levels, and better communications facilitate purchases and sales.

It is not likely that any one firm will be able to enjoy all the economies of scale, both internal and external, at the same time, but the possibility of it taking advantage of them as it grows larger raises two important questions. Why is that many industries are not dominated by one large firm? How do thousands of small firms manage to survive? We try to find answers to these questions below.

The limits to growth: diseconomies of scale

As a firm expands its activities and takes advantage of economies of scale, it is able to reduce the unit or average cost of production. Beyond a certain size, however, the unit cost may begin to rise again owing to the effects of internal or external diseconomies of scale.

Internal diseconomies of scale

Technical diseconomies These occur as the size of plant increases. Bulk oil carriers, for example, need special berthing facilities, the cost of which may go a long way towards offsetting the savings made by the use of larger units. A further difficulty which applies to all kinds of vessels and carriers is that more expensive materials may have to be employed in construction as the capacity increases.

In the chemical industry, enormously complicated plant is required for the production of some plastics. It may be more economic to have two relatively small plants rather than one double the size, partly because the construction problems are greater with large plants and partly because the failure of one of two plants does not bring production to a halt.

Administrative diseconomies These arise in the large organisation through the minute division of managerial labour. It may be very expensive to inform staff of routine matters through internal memoranda; changing production techniques or market structures may render a given management structure obsolete and wasteful; and customers' inquiries may be routed through many managerial channels before a decision is reached. Such complex structures may mean that a large firm is slow to respond to changes in the market or other external factors.

External diseconomies of scale

These may arise as a result of the overcrowding of industrial areas and the consequent increase in the price of the land, labour and services. An obvious and important example is provided by the congestion costs resulting from high traffic densities.

The survival of small firms

There is no one way of deciding what constitutes a small firm. The last full inquiry into the issue of small firms (by the Bolton Committee, which reported in 1971) concluded that there was no satisfactory universal measure. It used different criteria in different industries:

- the size of turnover
- the number of employees
- the share of the market.

The difficulty can be understood if we consider just two areas: oil refining and the operation of taxi services. We might devise a method for measuring the size of firms in the oil-refining business. Whichever method is used – turnover, market share or employees – we can be fairly sure that the smallest firm in that industry will be far bigger than the largest firm in the taxi industry. This is why different measures have to be used.

For the purpose of the submission of accounts, the Companies Act 1985 defined small companies as private companies meeting two of the following criteria

- not more than 50 employees
- assets not exceeding £700 000
- turnover (or sales revenue) not exceeding £1.4 million.

These are updated regularly. Whatever measures are devised, however, and despite the fact that the biggest firms continue to increase in size, there is a large and growing small-firms sector which is vital to the economy of the UK. Small firms are especially active in the service sector, where they have the largest share of the market.

In spite of many advantages of growth, there are several reasons why small firms continue to thrive.

- The entrepreneurial spirit of people who value independence and who may make a greater contribution to the economy by running their own businesses than they would if submerged in a larger organisation. Many firms could expand but do not do so because their owners wish to retain control or do not want the worry of a larger organisation.
- Small and geographically dispersed markets are best served by small firms, in which the optimum size of a unit of production is small. Large firms are often not interested in producing custom-made goods. A large construction firm that normally builds motorways or power stations will not want to waste resources building an extension to your kitchen, which is the type of job ideally suited to a small builder.
- Small firms frequently provide an important service to large firms, not only by providing them with components but also by relieving them of the need to organise the production of those components. This enables the larger firm to concentrate on its main tasks.
- Small firms can be an important source of innovation. The management of small firms is closer to the market than top management in large firms and may be quicker to spot and appreciate the significance of new developments. Decisions can be taken quickly, without the need for a large bureaucracy. Small firms are more flexible, and perhaps more amenable to the wishes of their clients.
- Assistance is available to people considering starting their own business. Various grants, subsidies or tax advantages ensure that activity in the small-firms sector is maintained. The government's main reason for such support may be the hope of reducing unemployment, since recent experience suggests that most new jobs are created in small businesses.

The number of small firms in an economy is not constant. Each year many fail, others succeed and perhaps are no longer small, while more are established for the first time. There seems to be no end to the flow of people prepared to start their own businesses.

The optimum size and returns to scale

We may imagine a firm gradually increasing in size, at first enjoying the benefits of economies of scale with the average cost per unit of production falling, and later meeting diseconomies of scale and rising costs. At the point where the costs per unit of production are at a minimum, the firm is said to be operating at its optimum size.

As a firm increases in size, there are three possible effects on unit costs:

1. They may fall: in which case the firm is said to be operating under decreasing costs or increasing returns to scale. For example, a building firm may employ a certain amount of labour and capital to build new houses. If demand for houses rises unexpectedly, this may partly be met in the short run by employing additional labour. The firm will find, however, that only a certain number of new houses can be built on the land it owns, and so diminishing returns set in. In the long run, the firm can purchase more land to the extent that doubling the input of factors of production may more than double the output (doubling the amount of labour enables the workforce to work more efficiently together in teams, so more than doubling the number of houses they can build).
2. They may be constant: a case of constant costs or constant returns to scale. For example, the building firm will find that at a certain level any increase in factors of production will be met by an exactly proportionate increase in output. A doubling of inputs exactly doubles the output (twice as many employees, using twice as much equipment and materials, can build twice as many houses: additional employees merely work together in teams on additional houses).
3. They may rise: a case of increasing costs or decreasing returns to scale. Beyond a certain point, decreasing returns will set in. Here a doubling of inputs will fail to double the output. It may, for example, be that one factor of production cannot be increased sufficiently: the building firm may grow too large, so that the owner is no longer able to run it efficiently.

Obviously the merits of expansion will depend partly on whether the firm is operating under increasing, decreasing or constant returns to scale.

The location of industry

While the scale of economic activity may be important in determining economic efficiency, the geographical distribution of industry also has an effect on performance. In this section, we examine

- the principal influences affecting the location of industry
- the extent to which the principal influences have changed
- the problems arising from a changing pattern of location
- the attempts made by governments to ease the problems.

Factors influencing choice of location

In the absence of any government interference, there are a number of factors which influence a firm's decision on where to locate its activities. It would be convenient if we could assume that the firm, in seeking to maximise its profits, weighed up all the factors associated with various sites and then selected the best. Such rational locations are rare, however, if they exist at all, but no firm will set up production or establish a factory without taking some account of most of the following factors.

Power All businesses need a source of energy. This is not a problem in the UK or other industrial economies since electricity, gas and oil are widely available and easily distributed. In the nineteenth century, however, the availability of coal was an important determinant of industrial location. Coal was expensive to transport, so there were savings to be made by locating near to the coalfields. In some countries, it is still the case that location of industry is restricted by the availability or non-availability of local fuel supplies.

Raw materials Like coal, raw materials may be expensive to transport, so they have often exerted an important influence on industrial location. Iron ore as a raw material is heavy, and its cost of transport is important in location decisions. In the nineteenth century, the UK iron industry flourished as coal and iron were found in close proximity to each other. The exhaustion of the ore deposits and the discovery of new supplies in other areas led to changes in industrial location. Today, a large proportion of ore is imported into the UK, and coastal locations have assumed a new significance – as they have for oil refining, whose basic raw material was almost all imported until recently. The cement industry in the UK is situated mainly in the South-East, where the chalk of the Chiltern Hills and the North Downs is readily available.

Labour There is no point in building factories where the supply of labour is inadequate. In the geographically compact UK this is not usually a major problem in terms of numbers, but it may be a problem in terms of quality. Businesses requiring employees familiar with techniques based on new technology may not immediately find them in areas of high unemployment where labour has perhaps been released from declining coal mines or steel works. Heavy investment in retraining may be necessary to equip the quantity of labour with the necessary skills.

Markets In the nineteenth century, industries were located near raw material sources. In the first half of the twentieth century, with fuel widely available, the proximity of markets (see Unit 5) became a more important factor in location decisions. Materials and components for manufactured goods can be gathered from a wide variety of areas, none of them exercising strong attraction, so industries have tended to move towards major centres of population – notably the South-East – which have the further advantage of offering a good supply of labour.

Transport At any point in time the location of raw materials and markets is fixed. The location decision may then be seen in terms of transport costs. The nineteenth-century sociologist Max Weber developed the theory that industries using weight-losing raw materials (iron ore and many other minerals) would be situated near the materials to avoid the transport of waste, while industries using weight-gaining materials would be expected to develop near the market. Bread-making provides an example here, for although flour is bulky it gains considerable weight when water is added. Such a theory must, of course, take account of the value of materials or finished products in relation to their weight or bulk. It is important for pressed car bodies to be produced near the car assembly point since they are difficult and relatively expensive to transport. It matters little, however, whether printed electrical circuits are produced in Basildon or Bolton for delivery to London, and the price of Swiss watches is not much affected by transport costs to the United States of America.

While transport costs may exercise an important influence on location when transport is inefficient and expensive, improvements in communications reduce the emphasis attached to this factor, and a large proportion of industry in the UK may be regarded as 'foot-loose' and free to settle almost anywhere in the country without materially affecting costs. This accounts, in part, for the increasing concentration of production found in some industries. It is no longer necessary for each town to have its own brewery or large bakery: production can be centralised in large plants, benefiting from economies of scale, with the goods being distributed over a wide area by increasingly efficient transport systems.

Telecommunications These days it is not just communications in the form of transport that are important. Telecommunications permit organisations to be in contact with each other almost instantaneously. Documents can quickly be sent from one office to another electronically. Executives – perhaps in different countries – can hold conferences through the telephone system. These developments would seem to have two effects. First, they give a company greater freedom in the location of new factories or offices, since even remote or overseas branches are almost next door in many respects. On the other hand, the new communications system may have encouraged an even greater concentration of financial organisations in London. Money, capital and commodity markets depend on the rapid availability of information. The networks providing such services and the necessary maintenance services are to be found in London, and so are the firms that are dependent on them.

<u>Industrial inertia</u> Although the original advantages of particular locations have disappeared, new firms or plants tend to become established in traditional areas. This is largely due to the availability of external economies of scale such as labour, training facilities, maintenance services and marketing institutions. Such a tendency is called industrial inertia.

Once a firm has become established in an area it will be reluctant to move elsewhere when expansion is necessary, because of the problems of co-ordinating the activities of different plants and of persuading key personnel to move from one area to another.

There are thus many factors influencing the choice of location, though it is unlikely that most actual location decisions take all those factors into account. Indeed, many locations may be haphazard in that a factory may be established in an area simply because its founder lives there, or because the site has become available in one area before any others. There is one factor, however, which no firm can ignore nowadays when making its location decision, and that is government policy.

Government intervention and regional policy

The need for government intervention

In the 1930s, it became apparent that there were wide differences in the level of unemployment in the various regions of the UK. Unemployment overall was high, and this was not unique to the UK. Important traditional industries were, however, experiencing particular difficulties:

- Coal-mining was in decline because industry and shipping were turning to more convenient fuels.
- The textile industry was losing out to low-cost overseas producers.
- Shipbuilding was more or less at a standstill. The demand for new vessels had declined because of the trade slump.
- Iron and steel suffered because of the decline in shipbuilding and other heavy engineering activities and competition from abroad.

Unemployment of this kind, resulting from a permanent decline in demand for a product, is known as **structural unemployment** (see also Unit 11) and is not a serious problem provided that there are other expanding industries to absorb the unemployed. However, these declining industries worked in close proximity to each other – mainly on coalfields – and there were no expanding industries. The result was heavy **regional unemployment**. What new industry there was tended to look for sites in the South-East and the Midlands.

The government first intervened in 1934 (the Special Areas Act) with a view to reducing the differences in regional unemployment. Differences in the level of employment are, however, usually accompanied by other inequalities: educational opportunities, health and housing expectations are all likely to be lower in areas of high unemployment. Thus the policy now has a broader objective than it originally had.

Types of government intervention

The government may intervene in a positive or a negative way, for example, by encouraging industrial development in areas of high unemployment, while blocking development on 'green belt' areas surrounding larger cities. The main thrust of its policy, however, has been positive, by way of offering grants and incentives of various kinds. The main aspects of regional policy have been as follows:

- **To identify areas in need of assistance:** There has been a significant reduction in the number of assisted areas since 1980. The main adjustments were made in 1984, and reflected the fact that unemployment in non-assisted areas had increased. Rather than add these areas to those receiving assistance (and thus increase the costs of the programme), the government removed many previously assisted areas from the scheme, on the grounds that unemployment in those areas was no longer significantly above average. The plan was that assistance would be concentrated on the most needy areas.
- **To offer incentives to firms moving to, or expanding in, the assisted areas:** In 1988, the government launched a new scheme, the Enterprise Initiative, to promote regional private-sector activity, particularly among small firms. For example, new firms in the assisted areas employing up to 25 people may receive 'innovation grants' of up to 50 per cent of their capital costs up to £250 000. Assistance is also available through the European Regional Development Fund.
- **Government employment:** The government can have some direct effect on regional unemployment through the location of its own activities. The Inland Revenue headquarters are at Middlesbrough, the Royal Mint is in Wales, and the National Insurance head office is at Newcastle. In general, though, it has proved difficult to move the main administrative activities away from London.

Weaknesses of the regional policy

- The policy had long been subject to criticism on the grounds that it was expensive in terms of jobs created – perhaps £25 000 or £30 000 per job – and many of these would be jobs that would have been created elsewhere anyway.
- Many firms receive the automatic regional development grants even though they would have gone ahead with their investment without the grants.
- Since the assistance was generally linked to capital investment, it was not necessarily very effective in creating jobs. The policy faced a dilemma here: the long-term interests of an area require efficient industries which tend to be capital intensive; in the short term the region is looking for employment, but labour-intensive industry may have a short lifespan.
- Much of the money devoted to regional assistance ultimately helped businesses outside designated areas, many of them of abroad, since businesses in the areas had to acquire machinery and other equipment from outside.
- There may be a more general argument against inducing firms to build new plant in areas they would not choose of their own accord. Such firms may lose some of the benefits of their traditional location and, in the long run, incur extra costs.

Other arguments based on economic theory have also been put forward against government intervention in the location of industry. These are based on the view that in a free-market economy, the market forces of supply and demand will eventually result in a more equal distribution of employment, wage levels and productivity between regions. The two principal arguments are that under a free-market system

- firms will be tempted to move into regions where unemployment is high, by low wage levels. This will result in an increase in employment and wage levels in these regions
- workers will tend to move into areas where demand for the goods produced in that area is strong, and therefore levels of employment and wages are high. This will have a levelling effect on both employment and wages.

Benefits of the regional policy

In practice, there will always be imperfections in a free-market system. Labour is not freely mobile between one region and another, and firms that have invested heavily in one region, perhaps to locate close to a source of raw materials or customers, will be reluctant or unable to relocate. Some government intervention may therefore be necessary to equalise regional differences. In addition, intervention may bring other benefits. Reasons for intervention may include the following.

- In cases of great regional imbalance, problems may be created in the areas of high economic activity. Heavy congestion might impose great pressure on social capital so that local taxpayers have to finance an increase in that capital. In other areas, social capital is under-utilised – public investment is wasted.
- There is a danger of decline becoming self-perpetuating. Industries don't move in; the younger energetic people move out; the area becomes less attractive to industry. So to secure a better use of national resources, the government intervenes.
- Sometimes more general economic policy measures would be inappropriate. If there is full employment in one area, there is no point in giving incentives to all firms. Some kind of selectivity is necessary.
- If the policy of regional assistance is successful to any degree in creating employment, there are likely to be social benefits as well – perhaps reduced crime rates and better educational opportunities

A change of emphasis

In 1988, government policy towards industries, and especially the regions, was changed. Automatic regional development grants were discontinued, but the assisted areas were retained. Henceforth grants were to be discretionary: those applying for them had to show that the project concerned would not go ahead without the financial assistance. This was represented not as a reduction in regional aid but as a reallocation. Emphasis was placed on assistance to small firms (those with fewer than 25 employees) in the development areas, who are eligible for grants of 15 per cent of the cost of new investment up to the maximum of £15 000. This was seen as part of the much broader Enterprise Initiative designed to encourage greater efficiency in industry.

The principal means of helping industry in the regions is now regional selective assistance (RSA). This is discretionary and covers both manufacturing and service industries. It is project-based and may be granted to assist in either creating jobs or providing capital for projects of any size. Aid is also available from the European Regional Development Fund (ERDF) of the European Union. This comes directly out of the EU budget, and is allocated directly to the governments of member states. There has, however, been criticism that some member states have used the fund to replace rather than supplement the regional assistance provided by national governments. By 1999, the UK had received more than £10bn from the fund.

In 1997, the new Labour Government under Tony Blair established nine regional development agencies (RDAs) to develop and implement economic strategies aimed at improving the competitiveness and industrial strength of the regions. These are responsible for advising the DTI on administering RSA and also developing support services for industry such as advice on inward relocation, recruitment and training. A network of local Business Link agencies was formed in July 1998, offering industry in an area a single point of contact as a source of business information and support, including a range of business consultancy services. These agencies indicate a trend towards encouraging industry to develop and become more efficient and competitive through advice and training, including management training, rather than simply providing financial assistance.

5 Markets

Introduction: what is a market?

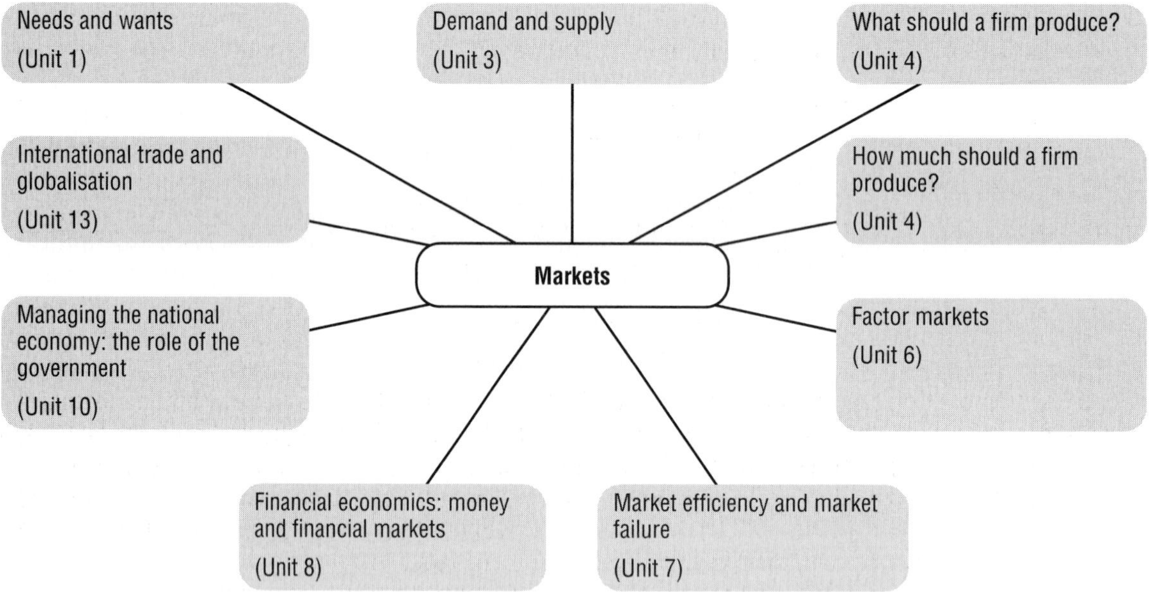

A market is a system that brings people and organisations together in order to buy and sell goods and services. Originally, all markets had a physical location – somewhere that people with produce to trade could meet other people who wanted that produce, and maybe had produce of their own to trade. Many towns still have market places, and in a sense all shopping centres are markets. Some markets are of national and even international importance. Billingsgate Fish Market and Smithfield Meat Market, both in London, are national markets, supplying traders throughout the UK, while Lloyds of London is an international insurance market that supplies insurance to individuals and organisations all over the world.

The development of new methods of communication has meant that the markets for some products have grown up without the need for a single physical location. This is especially the case where the product being sold cannot conveniently be transported to a physical location where the buyer can take possession of it, or where buyers and sellers in the market are too geographically widespread to be able to gather in one place. For example, the housing market exists partly in the columns of local newspapers and partly in the various offices of estate agents, while the foreign exchange market consists of offices throughout the world linked by telephone, fax, e-mail and other channels of communication.

A major influence in most markets is price. As we saw in Unit 3, consumers are only prepared to buy (demand) and suppliers only prepared to sell (supply) if certain conditions on pricing are met. The market can therefore be said to be the number of people or firms willing to buy or sell a given quantity of a product at a particular price. So important are demand and supply in the operation of markets that they are known as **market forces**. As economists, we are primarily interested in how many buyers and sellers there are in a market, and how prices of goods and services are fixed.

In this unit, we investigate

- different types of market
- different types of competition
- how market prices are established
- the influence of demand and supply
- the effects of intervention in the operation of markets
- perfect and imperfect competition.

IT and the 'new economy'

➜ Advocates of the 'new economy' believe that IT has transformed the economy, enabling a golden period of rapid growth that will bring rapidly rising standards of living. In fact, the jury is still out, though the recent performance of the US economy lends weight to the new economy arguments.

➜ IT accounts for a rapidly rising share of the economy. In recent years it has accounted for nearly half of all US economic growth. In the UK, computer services has outgrown all other parts of the economy and accounted for 10% of all new jobs in the last five years.

➜ During the next three years, the number of Internet users in Europe is likely to double every eighteen months, thereby beginning to catch up on US penetration rates. But because early Internet users tend to be affluent, such figures understate the likely impact on the economy.

➜ The increasingly important role of IT in the economy will change fundamentally the economics of business in large numbers of sectors. When change comes it will be shockingly rapid for incumbent players.

➜ Some markets that have been characterised by slow evolution will instead see sudden change. Rather than supporting many sellers, some markets will change to 'winner takes all'.

➜ Other markets will become much more competitive, with many sellers competing increasingly across national boundaries. The combination of European Monetary Union and the Internet will be much more effective in breaking down barriers than either would be in isolation.

➜ As the Internet becomes more significant as a distribution channel, understanding the market will become even more important, because on the Internet your rival is a click away from your website. Fortunately, the Internet also makes market research much easier.

Source: Adapted from *Lloyds Bank Economic Bulletin*, December 1998 (Internet edn)

Think about it

- Read the extract from Lloyds Bank's *Economic Bulletin*.
- In what ways does it describe information technology as both a market and a market place?
- How will the Internet encourage competition? Do you think this will be good for society and the economy?

Contestable and non-contestable markets

Someone deciding to set up in business for themselves, whether as a business consultant or as a florist, would have little difficulty doing so as long as they had the necessary skills and finance, access to customers and a base from which to operate. This is because there is no restriction on prospective suppliers entering those markets, which are therefore open to anyone who feels they can make a profit by supplying customers in the market. Of course, a firm that did enter a market must compete for customers with other firms already in that market. For example, when Dixons Group launched its new Internet service, Freeserve, in 1998, it had to compete with other providers of Internet services already in the market, including major companies such as America Online, Compuserve and Microsoft, as well as smaller companies such as Demon Net and Clara Net. A firm will be tempted to enter a market if it sees that other firms already in the market are able to make more than normal profits (see Unit 4, page 150).

- **Contestable markets** are those which firms are able to enter and leave without restriction.
- **Non-contestable markets** are those to which there are barriers (or difficulties) to firms entering or leaving.

Barriers to entry and exit

Barriers to a firm entering or leaving a particular market may be deliberate (where they are purposely erected by firms already in the market) or innocent (where they are not). The main barriers to entry and exit are as follows:

- **Legal barriers:** Many industries are regulated by laws that restrict entry to the market. For example, betting offices, hairdressers and taxi services must be licensed to carry out their business.
- **Restrictive practices:** Firms in many markets, individually or collectively, operate what are known as restrictive practices. These include, for example, suppliers forcing retailers to sell their entire range of products, such as chocolate or ice cream, and not just one high-profile brand name. Entry to other markets may be restricted by trade or professional associations who are able to limit the number of firms in a market, through setting qualifications for membership or withholding approval of firms.
- **Branding:** Where a well-known brand name exists in a market, it is often difficult for new and unknown firms to compete on an equal footing. A firm entering a market in competition with a high-profile brand name will have to undertake extensive – and expensive – marketing of their product. (See also page 196.)

- **Capital costs:** In some industries requiring the use of expensive equipment and machinery, the capital costs involved in setting up are high and may not be recovered for a considerable time. Where this is the case, a firm intending to enter the market for that industry's goods needs access to funding to cover its capital costs. Such funding may not be available to any but large organisations that already have a successful track record.
- **Sunk costs:** Sunk costs are costs that are not recoverable by a firm if it fails. For example, setting up in business may involve considerable expenditure on administration, research and development, marketing and producing a product. Such costs will include staffing and labour, materials, equipment and so on. Unless a firm is confident that it will see a return on these costs within a set time, it may be unwilling to risk the expenditure necessary to enter the market.

A high level of costs can be a barrier to an existing firm leaving a market, just as much as to a new firm entering it. Once a considerable amount of money has been spent setting up and developing a firm, there may be a reluctance to close the firm or stop production even though profits are not as high as anticipated. As long as the firm is not actually making a loss, it may be felt that some return on the investment is better than none. (See also the section beginning on page 201, 'Leaving the industry'.)

Something to do

- Identify the possible barriers for firms wanting to enter or leave the markets for
  - household electrical goods such as washing machines and televisions
  - computer games software
  - private hospital care.

Where there are no entry or exit barriers to a market, **perfect competition** may be said to exist in the market. We examine the concept of perfect competition in the section beginning on page 197. First, however, we must examine how the market price of a product is established and the different policies firms adopt when competing for customers.

Establishing a market price

Table 5.1

The weekly market for scrails		
Price (pence)	**Quantity demanded per week (000s)**	**Quantity supplied per week (000s)**
50	5	25
45	6	20
40	8	14
35	10	10
30	12	8
25	15	7
20	20	6
15	30	3
10	50	2
5	90	1

Fig. 5.1 The market for scrails

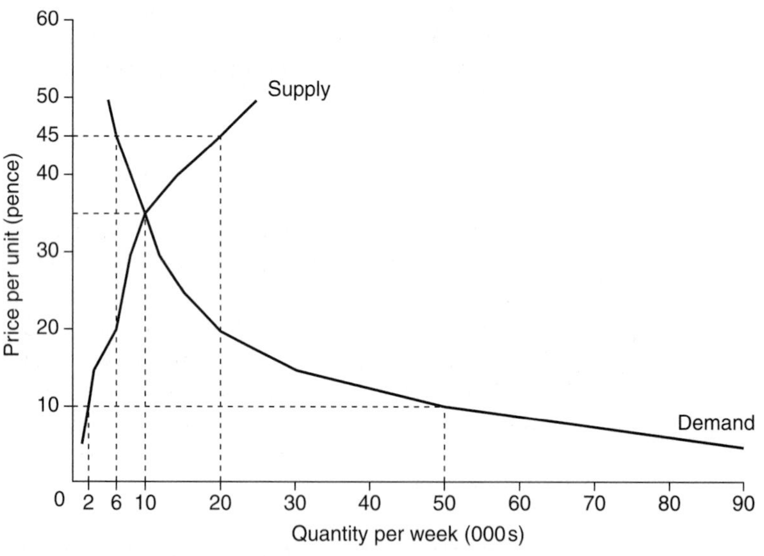

Table 5.1 and Figure 5.1 show the quantities of a product, scrails, demanded and supplied at various prices. Consider what would happen if the price of the product was arbitrarily set at 45 pence per unit. At this price, even relatively inefficient producers will find it worthwhile to enter the market, while efficient producers already in the market at lower prices will expand in the hope of further profits. The result is that producers are prepared to supply 20 000 units.

Think about it

- In the example given in Table 5.1 and Figure 5.1, what do you think would happen if producers were to produce and supply 20 000 units of the product per week?

Consumers, on the other hand, will relate the price of 45 pence to the amount of utility (see Unit 3) they expect to derive from the product. At a price of 45 pence, people who are only prepared to buy the product at a lower price will not be interested. Thus the demand for the product is 6000 units in that week. This means that there is an excess supply of 14 000 units. At the end of the week, this excess supply will have been produced but not sold, and will therefore be left on the suppliers' hands.

During the following week, suppliers will not produce so many, as they do not want to get left with large unsold quantities of the product again. At the same time, since they are anxious to get rid of the stocks they have now, suppliers will compete with each other by cutting prices. There will be no need for them to reduce supply by the full 14 000, since more consumers will find it worthwhile to enter the market, or purchase more units of the product, as the price falls. Gradually, demand will extend until it is equal to supply at a price of 35 pence per unit.

Key Points

- *Therefore, an **excess supply** leads to a **downward pressure on price.***

If, on the other hand, the price of the product has been set at 10 pence, producers will only be prepared to supply 2000 units, since it is difficult to make a worthwhile profit at this price. But at this price the product is such a bargain in relation to the amount of utility consumers expect to get from it, that demand reaches 50 000 units. This means there is an excess demand of 48 000 units. In such circumstances, suppliers will rapidly increase the price of the product in order to take advantage of the shortage in the market. As prices rise, it becomes more attractive to suppliers and production will expand. The increase in prices will also cause demand to fall until, at a price of 35 pence, demand and supply are equal.

Key Points

- *In the above example, **excess demand** results in an **upward pressure on price.***

In this way, an **equilibrium price** is established which will remain in force in the absence of any change in the conditions of supply and demand. A change in those conditions, however, will lead to a new equilibrium price. Where there are a large number of buyers and sellers in a market, and competition is fierce, price adjustments leading to a new equilibrium are swift. In many markets, however, the process of adjustment may take a considerable time.

The prices of good and services in a market or market economy therefore serve three basic purposes. These are summarised on page 178.

Purposes of market prices

1. They **signal the relative costs of purchasing** those goods and services, providing a measure against which customers can compare the utility they will obtain.
2. They **provide an incentive** for customers to purchase and for suppliers to provide the goods and services wanted by society.
3. They serve to **regulate the allocation of resources**. If the price of a product is too high, customers will not buy it as they will not obtain sufficient utility. The resources that would have been allocated to that product will then be allocated to the production of something else that will provide consumers with utility and suppliers with a profit.

Think about it

- How do you think the principle of equilibrium or market price applies to services such as transport, health and education? Write notes analysing how you think the following prices are set:
  - fares on private bus services
  - government funding of the National Health Service (this is the price the government pays on behalf of UK citizens for this service).

Changes in the conditions of demand

Increase in demand

Let us assume that the market is in equilibrium at a price OP and quantity OQ, with consumers just absorbing each week's supply. This position is shown in Figure 5.2.

A favourable change in the conditions of demand (see Unit 3) will cause the demand curve to move to the right, so that at price OP consumer demand is now for OU units. In the short run, firms are unable to supply more than OQ units, however, since this week's supply is determined by last week's production. In a competitive market we may therefore expect the extra demand to be temporarily stopped by a rise in price to OT. This allows suppliers a very good profit, however, and in response to such a price increase producers will expand their output until a new equilibrium is established at price OR and quantity OV.

Fig. 5.2 An increase in demand

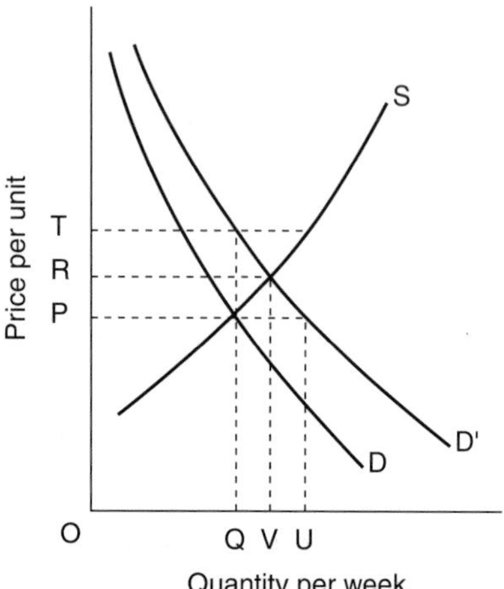

There are, however, instances where the effect of the demand curve moving to the right is not to increase both equilibrium price and **equilibrium quantity**. These are shown in Figure 5.3.

- In Figure 5.3a, supply is perfectly inelastic and the only effect of an increase in demand is a corresponding increase in price.
- In Figure 5.3b, supply is perfectly elastic and, as consumers can purchase as many units as they wish at the price OP, the only effect is that the equilibrium quantity increases.
- In all other cases with an upward-sloping supply curve, the effect of an increase in demand is to increase both price and quantity supplied. Figure 5.3c shows two supply curves passing through the same point at the original equilibrium price. On the less elastic curve S_i, a change in the conditions of demand causes a larger rise in price and a smaller rise in quantity than is the case with the more elastic supply curve S_e.

Fig. 5.3 The importance of price elasticity of supply when conditions of demand change

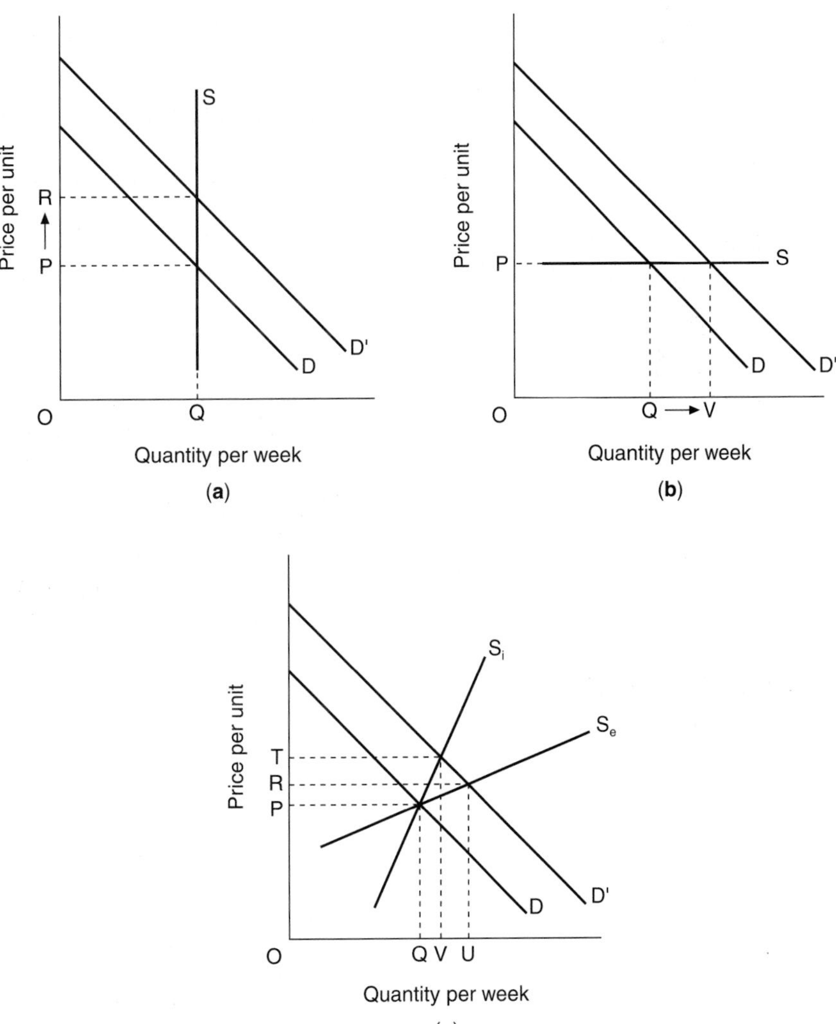

Thus the effect of a given change in the conditions of demand depends on the elasticity of supply.

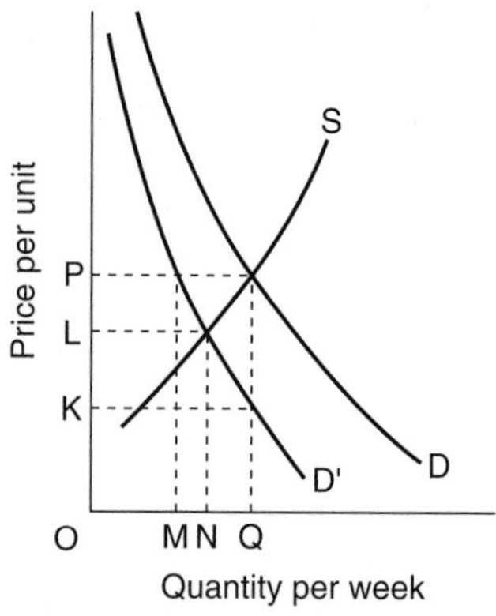

Fig. 5.4 A decrease in demand

Decrease in demand

The effects of a decrease in demand are shown in Figure 5.4. Here we have a market where production has been geared to the equilibrium output OQ. When the demand curve shifts to D', the only way to dispose of the excess supply MQ is to allow the price to fall to OK. This does not bring the market to equilibrium, since there is excess demand, but a new equilibrium is reached at price OL with a quantity of ON units. The price elasticity of supply will, of course, be as significant here as it is when the demand increases (the greater the price elasticity of supply, the greater the change in quantity following a change in price).

> *Think about it*
>
> - In Unit 2, we saw the importance of the age structure of the population (see the section beginning on page 60). The birth rate in the UK is now declining – in other words, fewer children per thousand of the population are being born. How might this affect the provision of primary education in the UK?

Changes in the conditions of supply

Increase in supply

Figure 5.5 shows a situation in which an increase in supply has arisen. This may be due to the entry of new firms into the industry, which is now prepared to supply OV units rather than OQ at the original equilibrium price OP. However, an excess supply of QV units exerts a downward pressure on prices until a new equilibrium is established at price ON and quantity OR. Thus the increase in supply leads to a lower equilibrium price and a higher equilibrium quantity.

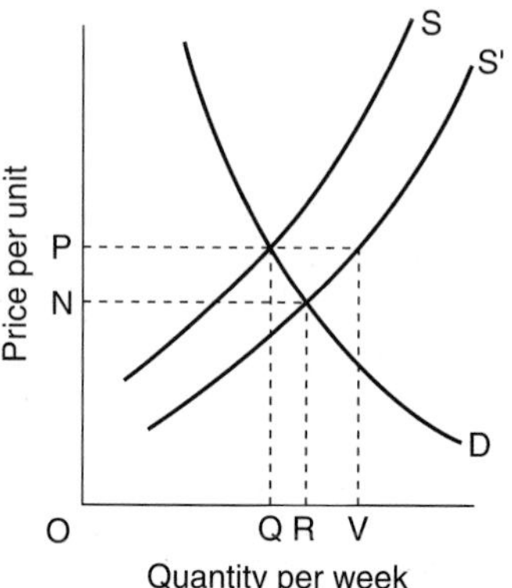

Fig. 5.5 An increase in supply

There are, however, instances where this is not the case. Once again, elasticity is important – in this case, elasticity of demand. Examples are shown in Figure 5.6.

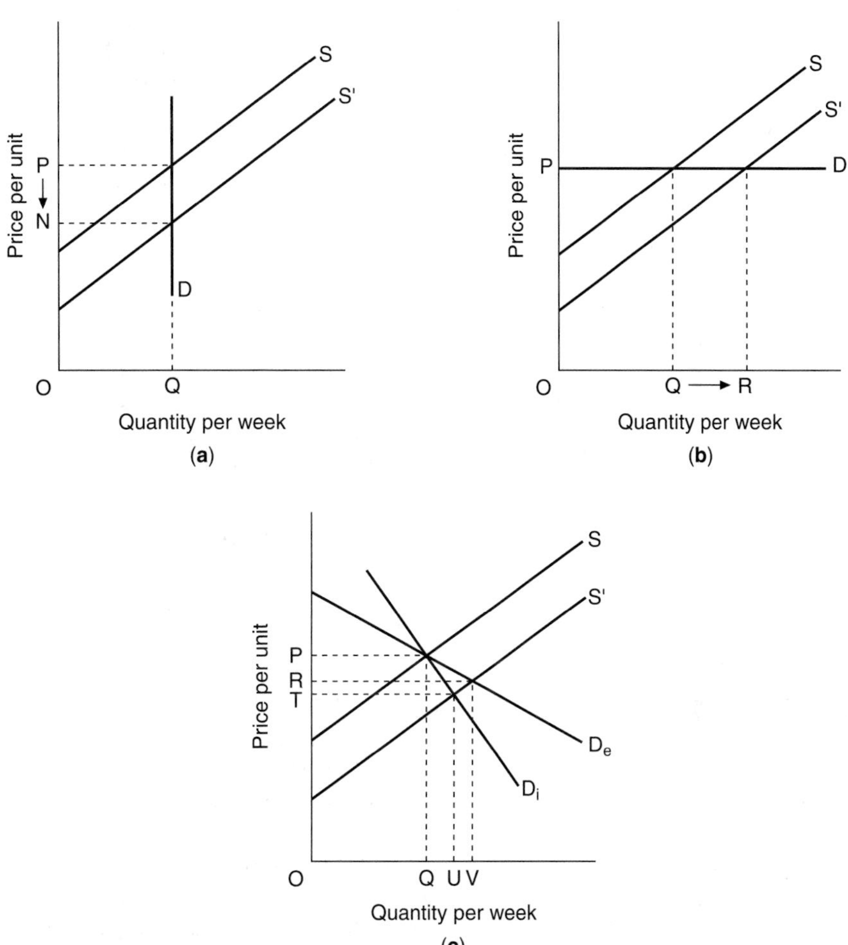

Fig. 5.6 The importance of price elasticity of demand when conditions of supply change

- In Figure 5.6a, demand is perfectly inelastic and, although the price may fall, consumers cannot be persuaded to buy more than OQ. Thus quantity remains the same and price falls.
- Figure 5.6b, on the other hand, shows a situation in which consumers are prepared to buy as much as they can at a price OP, so there is no need for producers to reduce prices to sell the extra output and only the equilibrium quantity changes.
- Neither of the above cases is likely to occur very often in the real world. Most cases will be similar to those shown in Figure 5.6c, where we have two demand curves associated with the same change in supply with an equilibrium price of OP and quantity OQ. When demand is relatively inelastic (D_i) the increase in supply leads to a smaller change in quantity but a larger change in price than when demand is relatively elastic (D_e).

Decrease in supply

Figure 5.7 shows a situation in which there is a decrease in supply. This may be due to a rise in the cost of factors of production. The supply curve moves to the left, showing that a smaller quantity will be produced at each price. Thus the original equilibrium quantity OQ will be put on the market for a price of OV rather than OP. But at this price equilibrium is impossible, since there is excess supply of MQ, so forces are set up which establish a higher equilibrium price at OR and a smaller equilibrium quantity ON. There will not be a change in both price and quantity unless the demand curve slopes downwards. The reasons for this are explained in the next section.

Fig. 5.7 A decrease in supply

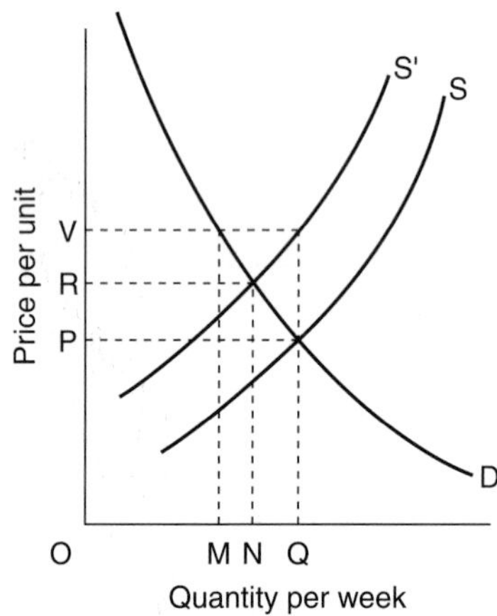

Effect of changes in market conditions on equilibrium price and quantity

Change	Effect on equilibrium price	Effect on equilibrium quantity
Increase in demand	Rises	Rises
Decrease in demand	Falls	Falls
Increase in supply	Falls	Rises
Decrease in supply	Rises	Falls

Changes in the conditions of demand and supply

The changes in conditions described so far are short-run changes, in that after the initial change in the conditions of demand or supply no subsequent changes occur. In fact, however, when the demand curve shifts it is also likely that in the medium to long term the supply curve will move. There are two possibilities to consider.

An increase in demand and an increase in supply

In Figure 5.8, an increase in demand, after forcing the price up to OT, changes the equilibrium price and quantity from OP and OQ to OR and OV. This adjustment is made by a movement along the supply curve. If the price OR is sufficiently attractive, new firms will enter the industry, causing the supply curve to move to the right and the equilibrium price to fall below OR and the equilibrium quantity to rise above OV. We are unable to predict the extent of the change in supply yet; but in Figure 5.8, the curve moves just far enough to offset the increase in demand

and the original price is restored, but a greater quantity (OW) results. In different circumstances, the new equilibrium price might be above or below the original equilibrium price, depending on whether there are diseconomies or economies of scale (see Unit 4, pages 155–165).

Fig. 5.8 An increase in demand and supply

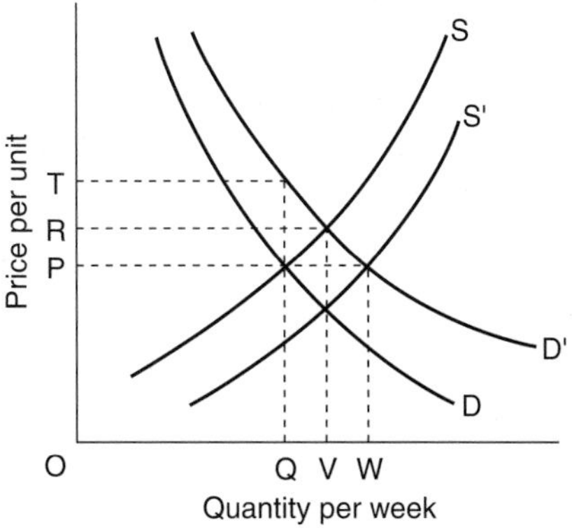

A decrease in demand and a decrease in supply

In the situation shown in Figure 5.9, after forcing the price down to OT, the decrease in demand leads to a lower price OR and a lower output OV. Some firms will not now be able to compete and will leave the industry. As they do this, the supply curve moves gradually to the left, thus moving up D' and establishing another equilibrium price. Once again, we have made this equal to the original equilibrium price, but there is no reason why it should not be different.

In the case of the original change being a change in the conditions of supply, there is no economic reason why the demand curve should shift as well. If it does shift (by coincidence), however, it will affect the long-run equilibrium price.

Fig. 5.9 A decrease in demand and supply

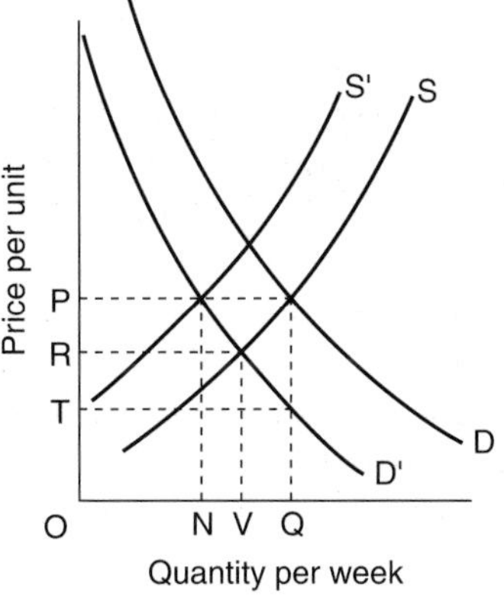

Demand relationships

Complementary demand

Many goods need to be consumed in fixed or nearly fixed proportions, and a change in the market position of one of them will almost certainly influence the market price of the others. CDs and CD players, cars and petrol, and gas fires and natural gas are examples. As we saw in Unit 3, these are referred to as **complementary goods**. Here we consider the effects of changes in the conditions of demand and supply on the market for natural gas and gas fires.

Fig. 5.10 A change in market conditions with complementary goods (only equilibrium conditions shown)

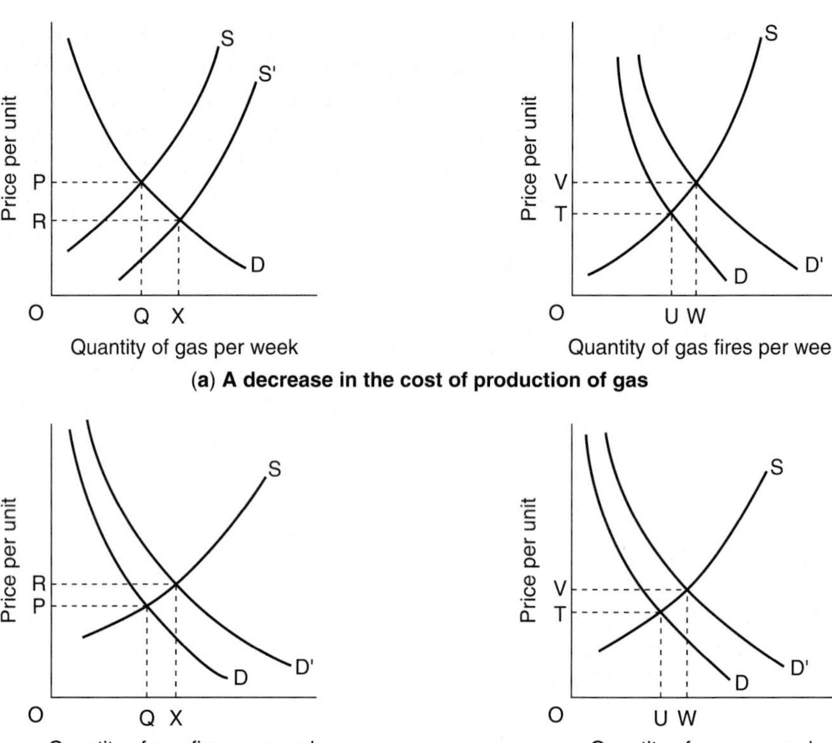

- In Figure 5.10a, we assume that the price of gas has fallen, perhaps as a result of the discovery of new reserves of natural gas or because of increased competition from suppliers now that British Gas is no longer the only supplier of natural gas. The supply curve moves down to the right, reflecting the lower price at which any given quantity will now be supplied. The demand curve for gas does not move, because the conditions of demand for gas have not changed, but we now have a lower equilibrium price for gas (OR). The conditions of demand for gas fires have changed, however, and we may expect some consumers to switch from electricity to gas for cooking and heating. This will obviously not occur overnight, but there will be a gradual movement of the demand curve leading to a higher equilibrium price and quantity for gas fires. Now that a higher price is obtainable for producing gas fires, it is likely that new firms will be attracted to enter the industry. This will cause the supply curve for gas fires to move to the right.
- In Figure 5.10b, the demand for gas fires has increased, perhaps because of a change in taste or fashion in favour of gas fires. The demand curve moves to the right, giving a higher equilibrium price and quantity. If people buy more gas fires, they will obviously need more gas, and the demand curve for gas moves to the right as well, giving a higher price and a larger quantity.

Remember that a new demand curve is drawn only when the conditions of demand change, and a new supply curve is drawn only when the conditions of supply change.

Derived demand Some goods are needed only when others are in demand. While such cases bear a close resemblance to complementary goods, they are usually referred to as cases of **derived demand**. The best examples are among the factors of production. The demand for thatchers falls as the demand for thatched roofs falls; the demand for computer programmers increases as the demand for computers increases. Thatchers and computer programmers are both examples of labour as a factor of production.

Competitive demand Many goods are substitutes for each other (see Unit 3) and are therefore competing with each other in the market place. A change in the price of gas is likely to affect the market for electricity; the direction of the changes is indicated in Figure 5.11.

Fig. 5.11 A change in market conditions with substitute goods (only equilibrium positions shown)

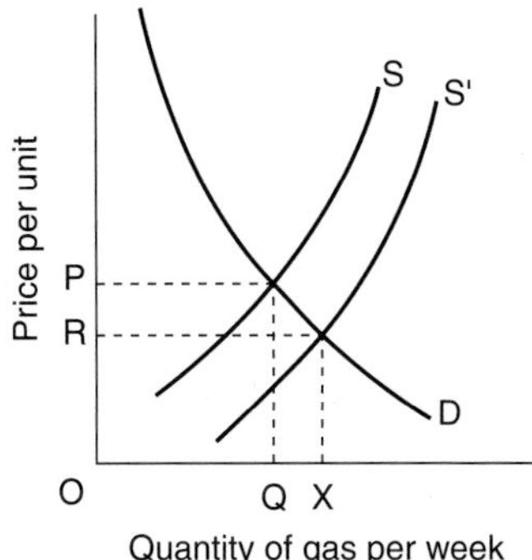

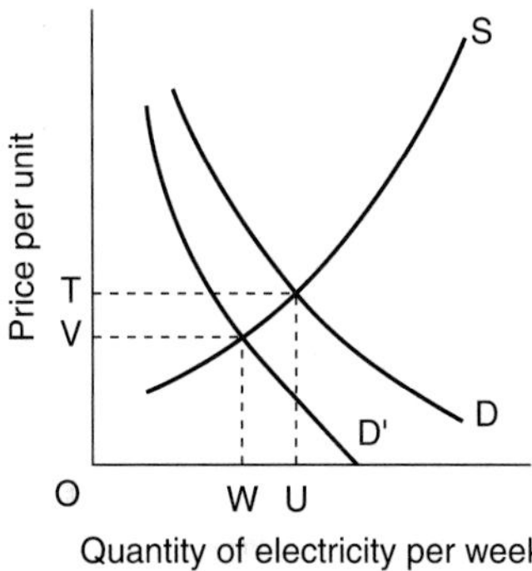

(a) A decrease in the cost of production of gas

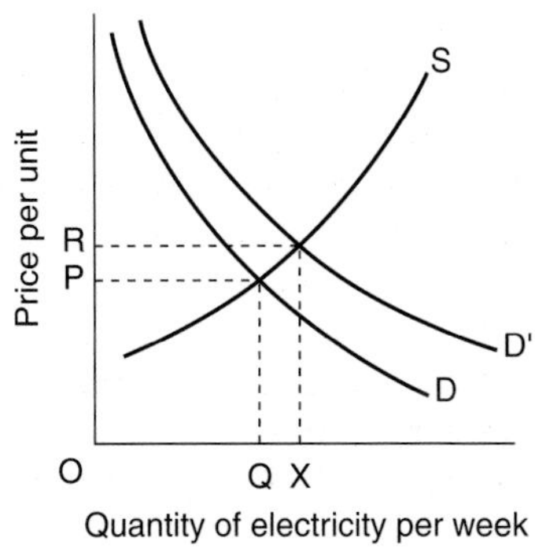

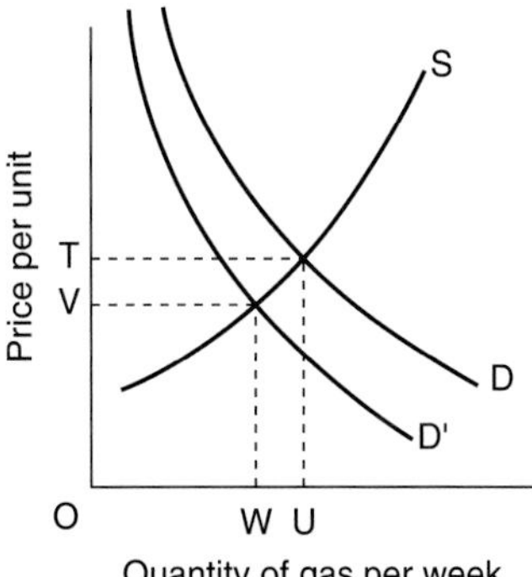

(b) An increase in the demand for electricity

- In Figure 5.11a, a fall in the cost of supplying gas leads to a decrease in the demand for electricity and a lower equilibrium price and quantity.
- In Figure 5.11b, a change in taste in favour of electricity leads to a higher price for electricity and a decrease in the price of gas as the demand curve moves to the left.

Think about it

- Not all goods that are in competitive demand are perfect substitutes for each other. If fountain pens and wristwatches are often bought as presents rather than for the purchaser's own use, what would be the effect of an increase in the price of wristwatches?

Cross-elasticity of demand

In Unit 3, we saw that cross-elasticity of demand measures the sensitivity of demand for one commodity to a change in price of another commodity:

$$\text{cross-elasticity of demand} = \frac{\text{\% change in quantity of A demanded}}{\text{\% change in price of B}}$$

Our analysis of substitute and complementary goods (see pages 80–81) showed that in the case of substitutes cross-elasticity will be positive (an increase in the price of gas causing an increase in demand for electricity), and that the closer the substitutability, the higher the cross-elasticity. So a small rise in the price of one brand of cigarettes would result in a large increase in demand for a competitive brand but a smaller increase in the demand for pipe tobacco, which is not so complete a substitute. With complementary goods, the cross-elasticity of demand is negative (a rise in the price of gas fires leads to a fall in the demand for gas).

Independent demand

Some goods are totally unrelated. We should not, for example, expect the market for travel alarm clocks to be very much affected by a change in demand for electric drills. However, if the community is spending a greater proportion of a fixed income on electric drills, it has less money remaining to be spent on other things – so the conditions of demand for travel alarm clocks are changed slightly. But the link between the two is, at best, tenuous. We must leave it to common sense to distinguish between independent goods and substitutes.

Supply relationships

There are many products that have to be produced together. Sometimes this is for natural reasons. For example, farmers cannot produce more lamb without producing more wool, although they can alter the proportions in the long run by breeding different kinds of sheep. The production of extra beef increases the supply of hides. Sometimes **joint supply** occurs because the producer wants to avoid waste: during the process of refining crude oil into petrol, for instance, the oil refiners produce a multitude of by-products.

Figure 5.12 shows the markets for lamb and wool on the assumption that they are, at least in the short run, produced in fixed proportions. If the demand for lamb rises, perhaps because of successful advertising campaigns by the producers, the demand curve moves to the right, causing a rise in price and quantity. As the supply of lamb rises from OQ to OT, the supply of wool also increases and, as the conditions of supply for wool have changed, a new supply curve is established to the right, giving a lower equilibrium price of OV and a higher equilibrium quantity OW.

Fig. 5.12 Joint supply – the markets for lamb and wool (only equilibrium positions shown)

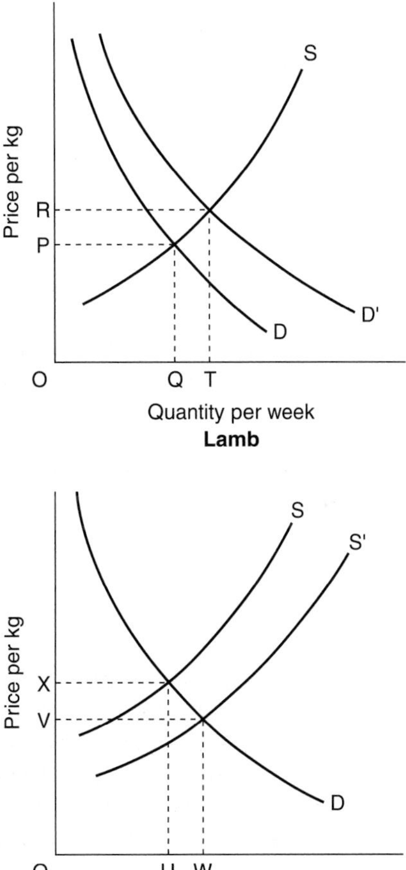

If the increase in the price of lamb had come about because of a decrease in the supply of lamb, then the supply curve of wool would also have moved to the left, causing a higher equilibrium price and a lower equilibrium quantity.

Some applications of demand and supply theory

The incidence of taxes on expenditure

When the government levies **excise duties** on goods, it normally collects the tax from the producers of the goods and leaves it to the producers to recover the money from their customers. Such taxes are called **indirect taxes** because the government does not collect them directly from the people or organisations who actually pay the tax. Some consumers may avoid paying the tax by forgoing the product altogether.

In Figures 5.13 to 5.16, we first examine the general effect of imposing an **expenditure tax** (indirect tax) and then consider the importance of elasticity of demand and supply in determining the final effects of the tax.

Fig. 5.13 The incidence of taxation

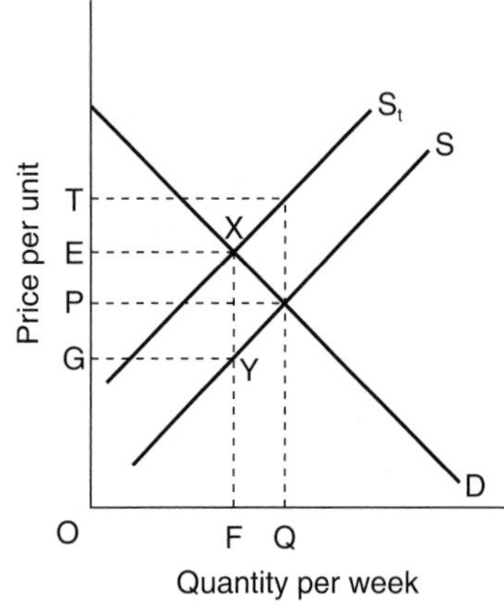

Specific and *ad-valorem* taxes

In Figure 5.13, the free-market equilibrium price and quantity are OP and OQ. If the government were to impose a tax of PT per unit on the product, this would have the effect of moving the whole supply curve vertically upward by PT as the producer tried to shift the burden of the tax onto consumers. As the tax is PT per unit whatever the price, it is a **specific tax**, charged at a set amount per unit, rather than an ***ad-valorem* tax**, which is levied as a percentage of the value of the goods. The new supply curve S_t is therefore parallel to the original supply curve. (In the case of an *ad-valorem* tax, the new supply curve would rise more steeply than the original.)

The producers now try to sell the quantity OQ at a price OT i.e. the price that would have been charged before the tax, plus the tax, but the excess supply forces equilibrium price and quantity down to OE and OF. For each unit sold, the producer must remit to the government the amount of the tax GE (= PT, since S and S_t are parallel). The final effects of the tax are therefore:

- a rise in price to the consumer of PE per unit
- a fall in the receipts of producers of GP per unit
- a revenue to the government of GEXY (the amount of the tax multiplied by the number of goods sold)
- a fall in the level of resources employed in the industry from the level required to produce OQ units to the level required to produce OF units.

The effect of taxation on goods and services

The effects of a tax are called the incidence of the tax. In the case of taxes on expenditure, the incidence is determined by the elasticities of demand and supply. Various possibilities are explored in Figures 5.14, 5.15 and 5.16.

- In Figures 5.14a and 5.14b, the two demand curves are identical, and so are the equilibrium prices and quantities (OP and OQ). The supply curves, however, have different elasticities – relatively high in (a), lower in (b). The imposition of the same tax XY per unit in each case has different effects. In (a), where supply is relatively elastic and therefore easy to adjust, there is a large fall in the equilibrium quantity (QF), a large rise in price (PE) for consumers, and a small fall (PG) in the revenue per unit for producers compared with (b).

Fig. 5.14 The incidence of taxation – differing elasticities of supply

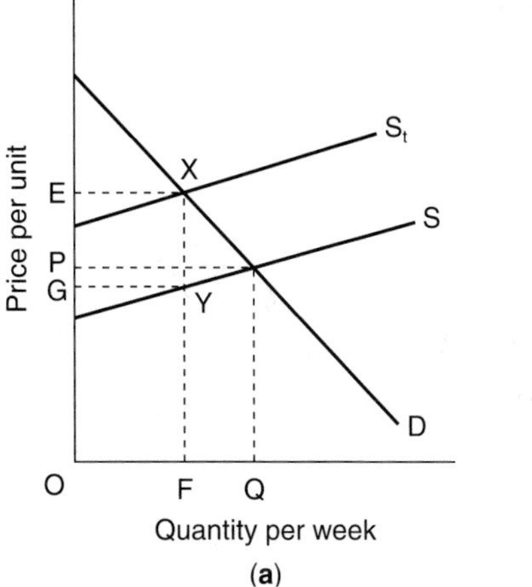

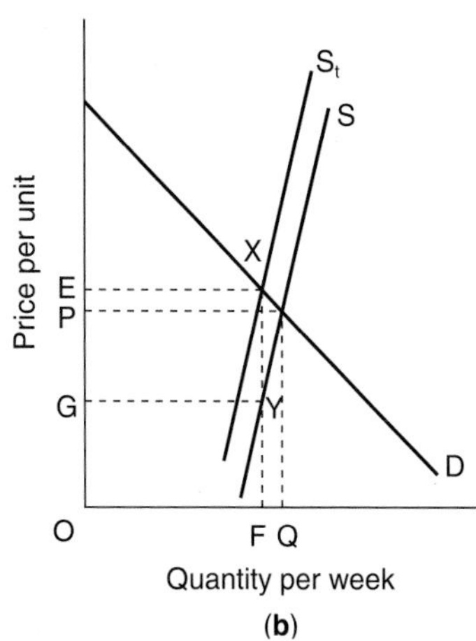

- In Figures 5.15a and 5.15b, it is the elasticity of demand that is different in each case, while the supply curves and the original equilibrium prices and quantities are the same. In this case, when demand is inelastic, the rise in price to consumers is higher, the fall in producers' revenue per unit is lower, and the fall in quantity is lower than is the case with high elasticity. The point here is that most consumers are prepared to buy the good even after the tax has been imposed. This is why, for example, the government can impose high taxes on alcohol and tobacco and still receive large sums in revenue from them.

Fig. 5.15 The incidence of taxation – differing elasticities of demand

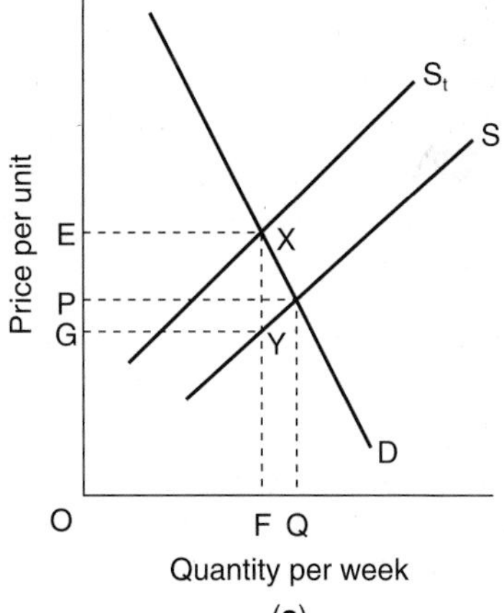

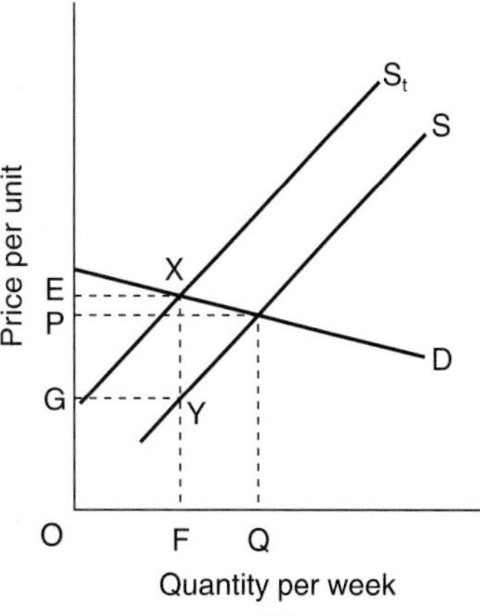

- Figures 5.16a and 5.16b show two markets: one where both elasticities are high and the other where they are both low. As you might expect from the above discussion, the more elastic market experiences a much greater reduction in output when a tax is imposed, partly because consumers react quickly to higher prices and partly because output is easily adjusted when supply is elastic. While this is the case with many manufactured goods, it is less easy with, for example, agricultural crops, where supply is relatively inelastic.

Fig. 5.16 The incidence of taxation – extreme examples

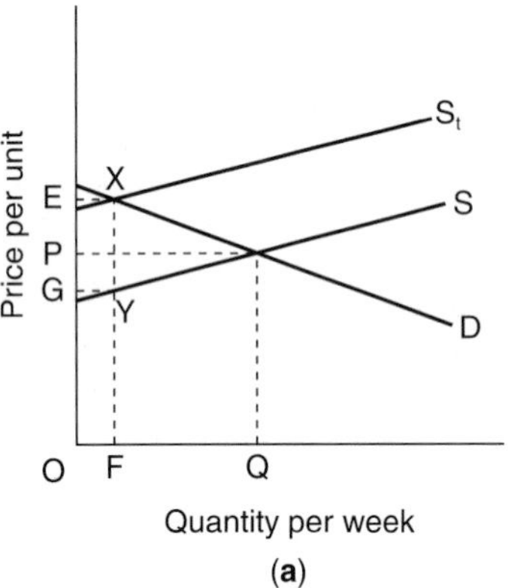

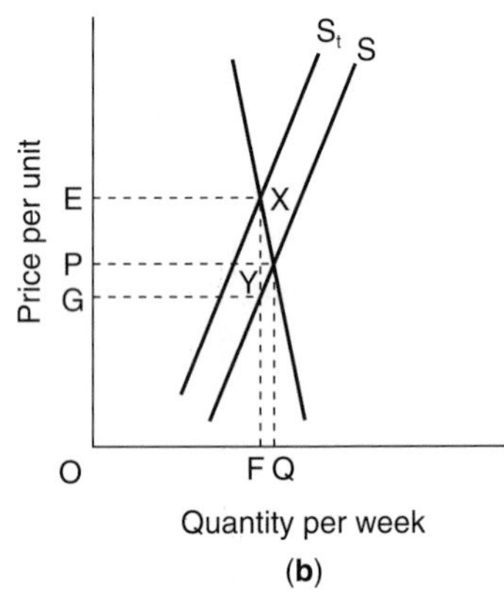

The effect of expenditure taxes on consumer and producer surplus

- In Figure 5.17a, with market price established at OP, there is a consumer surplus (see Unit 3) of PBE as the consumers obtain a total utility of OBEQ for which they spend only OPEQ. There is a producer surplus of APE, showing the surplus revenue received by suppliers above that absolutely necessary to induce them to supply the amount OQ.

Fig. 5.17 Consumer and producer surpluses

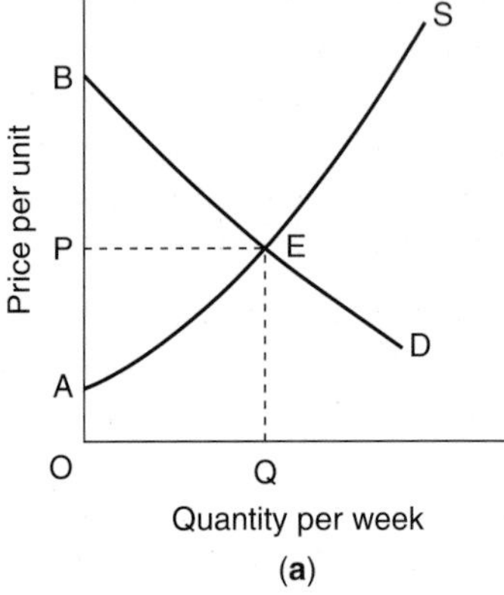

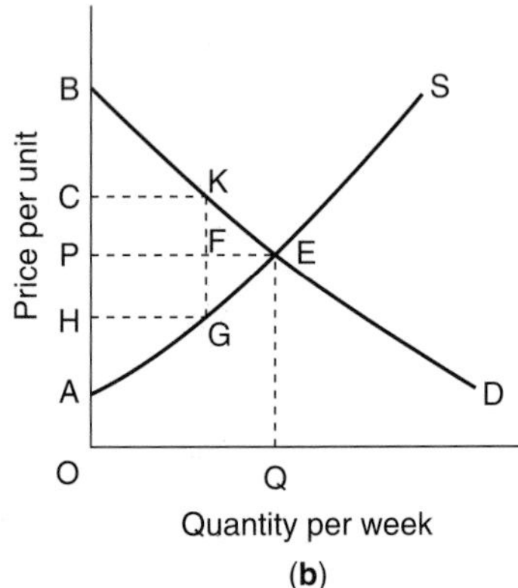

- Figure 5.17b shows what happens when the imposition of a tax establishes the new equilibrium price OC (the second supply curve going through K has been omitted to simplify the diagram). The consumer surplus is reduced by PCKF to CBK, and the producer surplus is reduced by PFGH to AHG. The triangle GKE represents the consumer and producer surplus that is lost because of the tax: neither the parties concerned nor the government are able to benefit from it. The higher the tax, the greater this amount of loss.

It is the extent of this loss that prompts many commentators to find income tax preferable to expenditure taxes.

Subsidies

Governments generally impose taxes in order to raise revenue for **public expenditure**, although as we see in Units 9–14 this is not always the case. The government may also give **subsidies**, which can be regarded as negative taxes. The main objectives of government subsidies are

- to reduce the price of essential goods to consumers
- to increase the supply and availability of these goods
- to enable the producers of such goods to compete with overseas producers.

Fig. 5.18 The effects of a subsidy

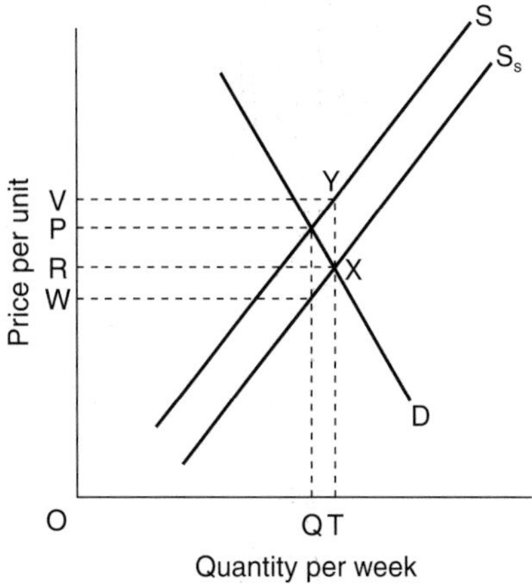

The general case is illustrated in Figure 5.18. The free-market price and quantity are OP and OQ. The government, believing the price to be too high or that consumers are getting insufficient quantities of the product, decides to subsidise the producers to the extent of PW per unit. The supply curve accordingly moves down by this amount to S_s, indicating that any given quantity will be put on the market at a lower price than before. A new equilibrium is established at a price OR and quantity OT. The effects of this are as follows:

- Consumers pay OR per unit instead of OP.
- Producers receive OV per unit instead of OP, of which OR is paid directly by the consumers and RV by the government (or indirectly by taxpayers).
- The government spends RVYX on the subsidy.
- A greater amount is supplied than would be without the subsidy.

Something to do

- Construct diagrams to establish whether the following are true:
  (a) If the elasticity of demand is taken as constant, the reduction in consumers' price and the increase in output resulting from a given subsidy increases as the price elasticity of supply increases.
  (b) If the elasticity of demand is taken as constant, the reduction in price to consumers will be greater and the increase in output following the award of a subsidy will be smaller as the price elasticity of demand decreases.

Price controls

Sometimes the forces of supply and demand work erratically or lead to hardship when prices rise owing to shortages. At other times, circumstances may depress prices to the detriment of producers. In such cases the government may intervene to establish maximum or minimum prices. The schemes that may be operated by the government are often complicated, but there are two straightforward cases:

- statutory minimum prices
- statutory maximum prices.

Minimum prices

Figure 5.19 indicates that in the free market the equilibrium position is reached at price OP and quantity OQ. If the government feels that a price of OP gives producers insufficient return on their investment, it may establish a minimum price at OT. The effect of this is to bring about a greater output of OR, but to reduce consumer demand to ON, hence producing excess supply. It is clear that if the government interferes with the market by establishing a minimum price it must also intervene and establish an agency to buy up the surplus output. The 'line' ABX is in effect the demand curve for the industry's product if the government enters the market to buy the surplus.

Fig. 5.19 Statutory minimum prices

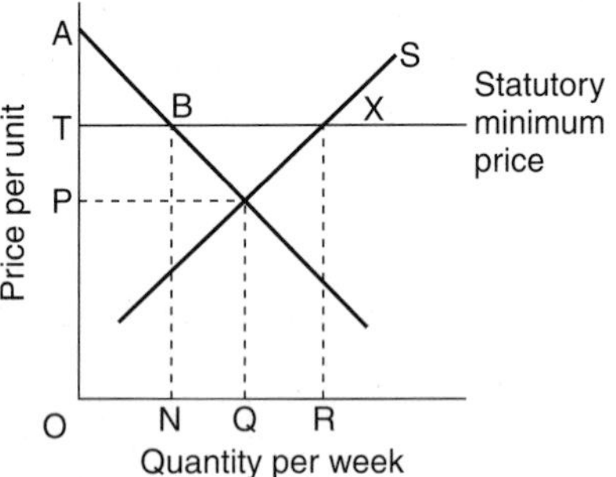

Of course, we have only considered the short-run supply curve and it may be that a price of OT is so attractive that more producers will be drawn into the industry, causing an even greater excess supply. If the product is not perishable, the buying agent may store it for a time in the hope that supply will fall; but if it is perishable, or if there is always an excess supply, then the agency must either destroy the surplus, sell it overseas or give it away to those who cannot afford to buy it.

In many ways the fixing of artificially high statutory prices is characteristic of the EU common agricultural policy (CAP): see Unit 13.

Maximum prices

Whereas statutory minimum prices lead to excess supply, statutory maximum prices, as we can see from Figure 5.20, result in excess demand – in this case NR, when the price is fixed at OT. The danger of this scheme is that it will lead suppliers to attempt to direct their output onto the black market, leaving shortages on the open market. An extensive system of inspection becomes necessary to enforce the scheme and to prevent the black-market price reaching OL. Also, as with statutory minimum prices, interference in one area leads to an essential intervention elsewhere. Unless consumers are going to be served on a first-come-first-served basis, a rationing scheme must be established to ensure equality of treatment. One possible method would be to allow potential customers a fraction ON/OR of what they would buy at price OT – that is, if the consumers and their demands can be identified.

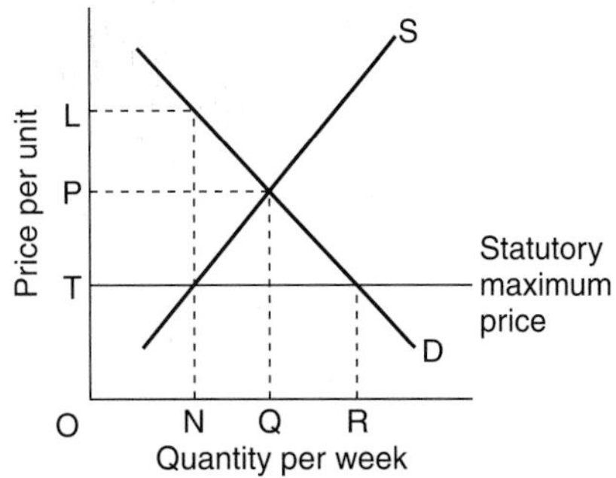

Fig. 5.20 Statutory maximum prices

There are many other situations where demand and supply are important in analysing the effects of economic policy, which we return to later.

The price mechanism

The interaction of the forces of demand and supply is often referred to as the **price mechanism.** While it does show how prices are determined in a free market, its underlying function is to allocate economic resources between industries. Thus, under competitive conditions, an increase in the demand for video recorders will lead to a rise in price and greater profits for that industry, so producers will bring more resources into the industry. These resources will have been attracted away from other industries whose products are not so popular.

Other subsidiary functions of the price mechanism include

- providing a crude rationing system: where goods are in short supply, price rises and some consumers are excluded from the market
- indicating consumers' preferences to producers: so that the most desirable pattern of production is developed
- influencing methods of production, by fixing the relative prices of factors of production.

Think about it

- Is the price mechanism an efficient and fair way of setting prices? Is it satisfactory for services such as the National Health Service, public transport (even in the private sector) or education?

Ideally a situation is reached where consumers maximise satisfaction (so the ratio of marginal utility to price is the same for everything a consumer purchases – see Unit 3), and where producers maximise profits (at the point where marginal cost equals marginal revenue – see Unit 4). In the real world, however, the system does not work smoothly and it is often necessary for the government to intervene to avoid problems that would derive from the uncontrolled operation of the price mechanism.

When the price mechanism breaks down, the market system no longer works efficiently in allocating resources and providing those goods and services that are needed by society. This is **market failure.** Both market failure and market efficiency are discussed in Unit 7.

Price and non-price competition

Firms in a competitive market will develop various policies of competing for customers. Some of these will be based on the price they charge customers for their product, while others will relate to the product itself.

Price-based competition

In the real world the price actually charged for a product to a large extent depends on the objectives of the supplier in relation to its overall goals and what it hopes to achieve in the market both in the short run and in the long run. Competition can be based on price or non-price factors. With **price-based competition**, suppliers use the price charged to customers as the major factor in their competition policy.

While there are constraints on a firm's pricing policy, including the costs of production and the price elasticity of supply for the product, the objectives of a pricing policy may be

- to maximise profits
- to maximise sales
- to maintain the status quo.

Fig. 5.21 Strategies of price-based competition

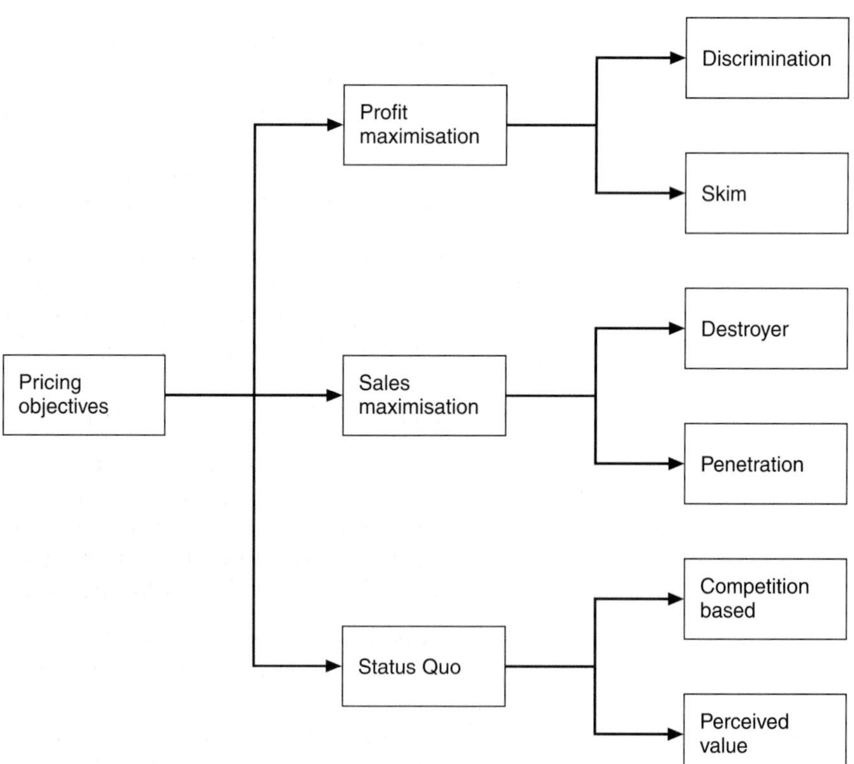

The main pricing policies that a firm can adopt are as follows:

- **Price discrimination:** Where demand for a product is inelastic for some consumers but more elastic for others, a supplier may adopt a policy of charging a different price to the segment of the market where demand is inelastic from that charged to the segment where demand is elastic. For example, telephone companies discriminate between business users, private users and mobile-phone users. They also charge at a higher rate during weekdays, when a large number of business calls are made and demand is inelastic; and a lower rate after 6p.m. and at weekends, when most use of the telephone is by private individuals whose demand for making telephone calls is far more price elastic. (See also page 118.)
- **Skim pricing:** In the case of a totally new product, it may be possible to charge an inflated price initially in order to obtain a high profit from those customers who want to be the first to own the product, whatever the price. Suppliers of high-technology products such as computers often use skim pricing, coupled with the frequent and rapid introduction of new product developments. The success of this strategy depends on there being sufficient customers willing to pay the high price for the product.
- **Destroyer pricing:** Destroyer pricing is a policy that can be adopted if the objective of a supplier is to eliminate the competition. It is a very aggressive pricing policy that involves setting a very low price in the knowledge that it cannot be met by competitors. Customers will be attracted away from competitors, who will therefore lose sales and market share, eventually leaving the market altogether.
- **Penetration pricing:** Where skim pricing is inappropriate, penetration pricing is a strategy based on charging a low initial price for a product in order to attract sales and penetrate, or establish a position in, the market. This pricing strategy is often adopted for new part-work magazines, where the first few issues are sold at reduced prices, often coupled with the offer of free gifts with later issues.
- **Competition-based pricing:** In markets where competition is high and products are similar, suppliers' prices tend to be based far more on the market price and the prices charged by competitors. Suppliers in these markets are known as price-takers, since they have to take the price established by the market (see also Figure 5.22).
- **Perceived-value pricing:** Where demand is known to be price inelastic, the price of a product may be set according to the customers' perception of value for money. This may result in either a high price for goods of ostentation, for example a Porsche, or a low price, where customers look for a bargain, as with high-volume household goods.

Non-price-based competition

Not all competition between suppliers is based on price, however. It may be that there is little scope for charging other than the market price; or consumer demand may be more responsive to non-price factors, such as the following.

- **Unique selling point:** The unique selling point (USP) of a supplier's product is the factor that makes it more attractive to customers than the products of competitors. Thus the USP of a building society investment account may be its rate of interest, or easy accessibility to depositors' money.
- **Brand name:** An identifiable and respected brand name can be important in attracting and keeping customers, especially where competing products in a market are homogeneous (similar). Gordon's Gin, for example, maintains its position as the leading brand of gin largely because it is a well-known name. A brand name may be linked in consumers' minds with other factors such as value for money, quality or service.
- **Quality:** Product quality is of increasing importance to consumers, and can be a significant factor in influencing consumer demand for different products.
- **Service:** Of equally increasing importance to consumers these days is the service provided by suppliers. It is no longer sufficient to provide a quality product. These days customers expect suppliers to provide more in the way of customer service, including giving information and after-sales service.

Kotler's price–quality strategy mix

		Price of product		
		High	**Medium**	**Low**
Quality of product	**High**	Premium	Penetration	Superbargain
	Medium	Over-pricing	Average price, average quality	Bargain
	Low	Hit and run	Shoddy goods	Cheap goods

Source: Adapted from P. Kotler, *Marketing Management* (Prentice Hall, 1976)

The choice of strategy will depend on

- the market segment being targeted
- the stage in the product life cycle
- the likelihood of repeat purchase
- competitive circumstances.

Source: Adapted from B. Jewell, *An Integrated Approach to Business Studies* (Longman, 3rd edn 1996)

Perfect and imperfect competition

In the remainder of this unit, we look at two types of market:

- markets in which there is **perfect competition**
- markets in which there is **imperfect competition.**

We begin with an analysis of perfect competition – a concept that never occurs in reality, but which helps us to build a model of how competition affects the operation of markets.

Fig. 5.22 Types of competition

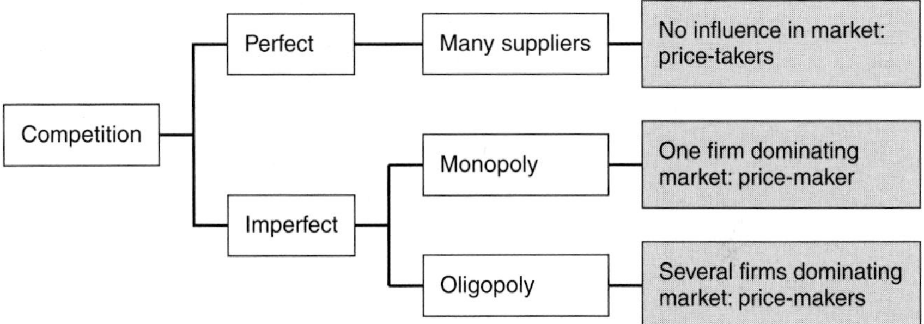

What is perfect competition?

Perfect competition exists in a market when a number of suppliers are competing on an equal basis for the same customers, without any supplier or customer being able to influence the market, and without there being any obstacles to new suppliers entering the market on the same terms. For perfect competition to develop, several conditions must be met.

- All the firms in an industry are trying to maximise their profits.
- There is a large number of producers supplying a market, but no single firm is sufficiently large to be able to influence market price. In this situation, a single firm entering or leaving a market would not have a significant effect on ordinary demand or supply curves.
- There is a large number of buyers, none of whom is large enough to influence market price.
- Each consumer in a market is trying to maximise his or her individual satisfaction and has no loyalty to particular suppliers.
- All firms supplying a market are supplying a product that is similar in all respects.
- New suppliers are free to enter the market on equal terms, and there are no obstacles to existing suppliers leaving the industry. The same applies to buyers.
- All sellers and all buyers have perfect knowledge of the prices being asked and offered by other sellers and buyers.

Wholly perfect competition does not occur in the real world, since in reality all the above conditions are never fulfilled. There are several reasons, however, why it is useful to consider perfect competition as an economic model.

- It is a standard against which other models can be assessed.
- It allows us to review what is happening in a market by using the model of perfect competition and introducing modifications later.
- It is relatively straightforward, allowing important ideas to be introduced at the outset and leading on to more advanced theories.

The demand for a firm's product

The shape of the demand curve for an individual firm's product is derived from the assumption that no single firm in a market is large enough to influence market price. In this case, the firm must accept the ruling price as determined by the forces of supply and demand. It can sell as much as it wishes at this price.

Fig. 5.23 The perfectly competitive firm's demand curve

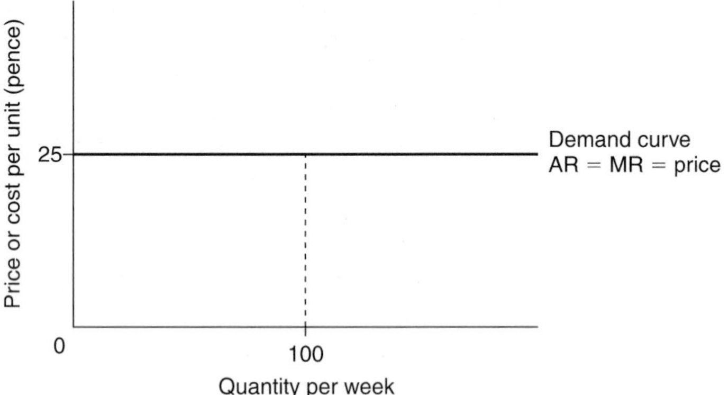

In Figure 5.23, the prevailing price of the product is 25 pence. The firm can sell as many units at this price as it wishes, and so the demand curve for its product is horizontal. If the firm decides to sell 100 units, its **total revenue** will be £25, and its **average revenue** (total revenue divided by the number of units sold) will be equal to the price, 25 pence. If the firm tried to charge 26 pence, it would have no sales, since its customers would buy elsewhere at the lower price. Since the firm is trying to maximise its profits, and can sell as much as it wishes at 25 pence, there is no incentive for it to try to gain extra customers by reducing price. The most important consideration for the firm is that its **marginal revenue** curve, showing the increase in total revenue derived from the sale of an extra unit of the product, coincides with the average revenue or demand curve (see Unit 4). For example, if it sells 101 units, its total revenue will be £25.25, an increase of 25 pence over the total revenue from selling 100 units. This will be the case for all levels of output, so:

average revenue = marginal revenue = price
in conditions of perfect competition

Fig. 5.24 The situation facing the perfectly competitive firm

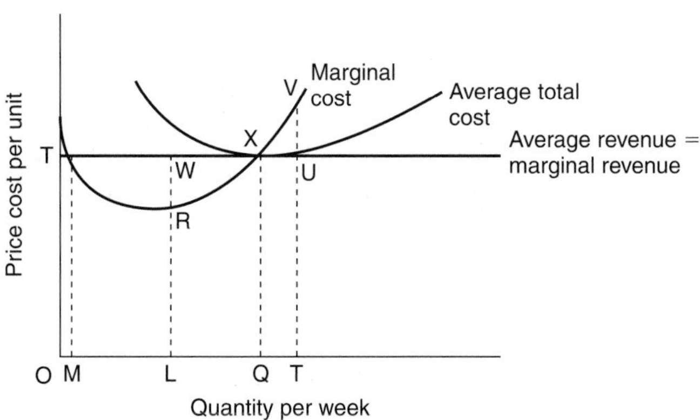

In Figure 5.24, the short-run cost curves and the revenue curve are shown. As long as the revenue from selling an extra unit of production is greater than the cost of producing that unit (as long as marginal revenue is greater than **marginal cost**), a firm will increase output as this will help to maximise profits. In terms of Figure 5.24, this will apply at any stage between OM and OQ. (It is necessary to produce the unprofitable OM units in order to reach the profitable units beyond M.) Thus, producing OL, the firm adds LR to its costs and LW to its revenue, and its surplus of marginal revenue over marginal costs increases. For any output beyond OQ (OT, for example), the increase in costs (TV) is greater than the increase in revenue (TU), and units are being produced which add more to costs than they gain in revenue. The firm will be justified in increasing output up to OQ but not beyond. Thus profits are at a maximum where the marginal cost curve cuts the marginal revenue curve from below. In this way, the marginal cost curve can be used to show the entrepreneur when to cease expanding output. The primary function of marginal curves is to show the most profitable level of output.

The relationship between average total cost and average revenue gives information about the level of profits. Average total cost and marginal cost curves include a normal rate of profits (see Unit 4). In Figure 5.24, total costs and total revenue are equal at OPXQ, since average total cost and average revenue are both equal at OX (= OP). The firm is thus making a normal rate of profit and is in a state of equilibrium, for, given its cost and revenue curves, it could not be in a more profitable position. If all the firms in an industry have the same cost curves, then the industry is in equilibrium, as all firms just make normal profits and are in a position where

marginal cost = marginal revenue =
average total cost = average revenue = price

Figure 5.25 shows the situation of a single firm in a perfectly competitive industry. The vertical scales of the two diagrams are the same, but the horizontal scales are different. In Figure 5.25b, OV represents several million units of output; in Figure 5.25a, OQ represents only a few hundred units.

Fig. 5.25 Expansion in perfect competition

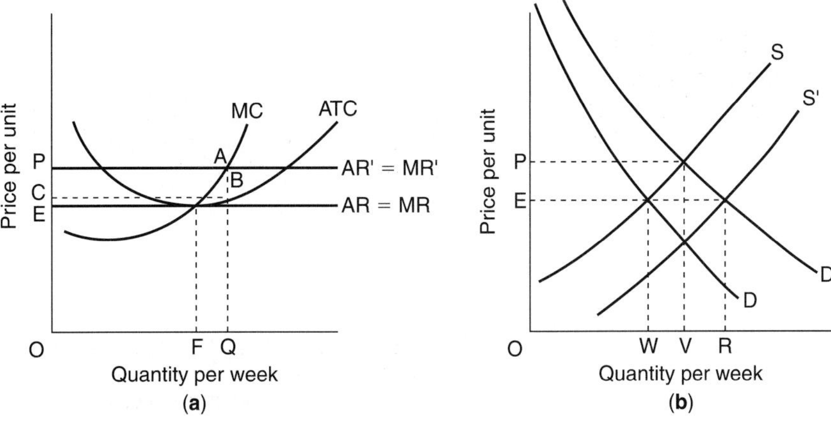

The original equilibrium price and quantity for the industry are shown in Figure 5.25b by the intersection of the demand and supply curves to be OE and OW. The firm has to accept the price OE and, equating marginal cost and marginal revenue, produces OF.

If there is now an increase in demand for the product, the market price rises to OP, which the firm now accepts. This produces OQ instead of OF units and the firm makes abnormal profits of CPAB, the extent to which total revenue (OPAQ) exceeds total costs (OCBQ). As new firms enter the industry, the market supply curve gradually moves to the right, reducing market price until the abnormal profits are eliminated. If the supply curve moves to S', the old equilibrium price of OE is restored and the industry is experiencing constant costs. It would be unrealistic not to expect the firm in Figure 5.25a to join in the general expansion of the industry and we should therefore draw another set of cost curves to the right of the original pair with minimum average total cost remaining constant.

If abnormal profits were eliminated before the supply curve moved as far as S', the new equilibrium price would be between OE and OP. This would indicate that costs were increasing as the industry expanded, and the new cost curves for the firm would be above and to the right of the old ones.

The third possibility is that even when the supply curve reaches S' there will still be abnormal profits because of the emergence of economies of scale (see Unit 4). New firms will continue to enter the industry until, at a price below OE, abnormal profits are finally eliminated and the industry reaches a new equilibrium. In this case, the new cost curves of the firm will be to the right and below the original curves (see Figure 4.13 on page 153), indicating decreasing costs.

Fig. 5.26 A perfectly competitive firm: less than normal profits

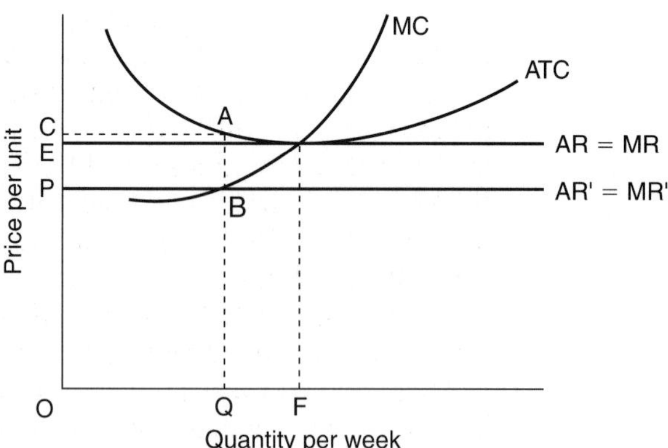

The firm in Figure 5.26, and firms like it, will eventually have to leave the industry in the circumstances discussed in the next section. It may have been operating for some time in equilibrium at price OE and quantity OF when a fall in demand leaves it to face a price of OP, which is insufficient to cover its average costs of production. As firms leave an industry, the market supply curve moves to the left, causing the price to rise until the remaining firms are again in equilibrium and making normal profits. This time the new equilibrium price will depend on the extent of the leftward movement of the supply curve.

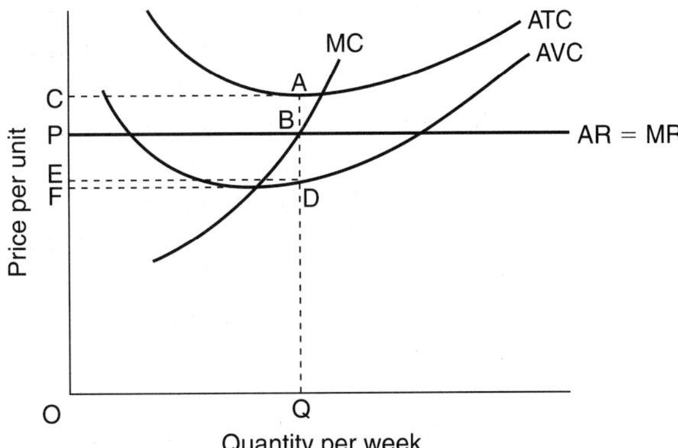

Fig. 5.27 Leaving the industry

Leaving the industry If a firm cannot cover its average costs, it will eventually have to leave the industry. The timing of its exit will depend on the extent of its deficit and the age of its fixed factors of production (see Unit 4). Figure 5.27 shows a firm's average total cost curve (ATC) and the average variable cost curve (AVC). The gap between the average total cost curve and the average variable cost curve indicates average fixed costs, and this is therefore smaller at high outputs than low outputs. The firm has determined its output by equating marginal cost with marginal revenue, but has had to sell at price OP, below average cost OC. Profits are therefore below normal to the extent of PCAB. If the firm continues in business for the time being, this is the weekly or monthly deficit that must be met.

If the owners of the business decide to cease production immediately and close down, they will still have to meet their fixed costs in the short run, for by definition these are the same whether output is zero or a million. In this case the firm, producing nothing, would be spending ECAD (average fixed cost × previous output) on such things as interest charges, rates, rent, standing charges and some salaries while the business was being wound up. It is obviously better to remain in production in the short run and lose PCAB, than to close down production and lose ECAD. If the short-run price falls below OF, however, the firm would have to close down immediately, for not only would it be failing to cover its fixed costs but it could not even pay its variable costs. If the price remains at OP, the best time for the firm to leave the industry would be when fixed factors of production had to be replaced.

Of course, if there are other firms in the industry operating at a loss, it may be that, when some of them close down, prices will rise sufficiently for other firms in a similar position to be able to survive.

Think about it

One result of firms leaving an industry can be a rise in unemployment, at least in the short run, as employees made redundant do not have the appropriate skills to find alternative employment. Over the years, this has been particularly the case in industries such as shipbuilding and mining.

- What action might the government or private industry take to lessen the social effects of this kind of unemployment?

Imperfect competition

In practice, competition in markets is far from perfect. There are many problems in real-world markets that result in various degrees of imperfect competition. At the opposite extreme to perfect competition (many firms, identical product, freedom of entry and exit) is **monopoly**, a situation where one firm produces the total market supply of a good. Between the two extremes are various degrees of competition. In the remainder of this unit we examine the operation of imperfect markets.

The characteristics of monopoly

A monopolist is literally the only supplier of a product. Monopolists can therefore charge whatever price they like, or restrict output. What they cannot do, however, is fix both price and output: if one is fixed, the market will determine the other.

To some extent, almost all producers are monopolies. For example, the only producer of Ford motor cars is the Ford Motor Company. The Ford Motor Company is not, however, the only producer of motor cars and it is not, therefore, a true monopolist: it is operating under conditions of monopolistic competition (see pages 207–208). Ford has a degree of monopoly power but must nevertheless consider the activities of its competitors who produce substitute goods.

Even if Ford was the world's only manufacturer of motor cars, we might still not consider the company as a monopolist, for there would still be substitutes for cars, including cycles, motor cycles and public transport. It is important, therefore, to be clear about the market under consideration (Ford operates in both the market for motor cars and the wider market for transport). It is more accurate to speak of degrees of monopoly.

The Competition Commission (known until April 1999 as the Monopolies and Mergers Commission) has defined a monopolist as a firm that controls at least 25 per cent of the market in which it operates; the questions of what is meant by 'controls', and how to define a particular market, however, give rise to much debate and often controversial decisions.

Types of monopoly

There are several types of monopoly.

- **Natural monopolies:** Natural monopolies fall into two groups. The first consists of firms that are the sole owners of natural resources, such as minerals or energy. Very few of this type of natural monopoly exist. De Beers, for example, has a near monopoly in the supply of diamonds from South Africa. Until recently, the supply of water, gas and telecommunications in the UK were in the hands of nationalised industries with either a regional or national monopoly.

  The second group consists of firms that supply those goods and services considered to be more efficiently produced and distributed under monopoly than under competitive conditions. Examples of natural monopolies that fall into this second group include services such as national defence and policing.

By operating as large, single organisations, natural monopolies are not subject to the constraints of competition and a free market. They avoid the duplication of resources and administration – such as factories, offices and equipment, stocks of raw materials and finished goods, advertising and personnel – that is implicit in a free-market economy where there are many competitors. This serves to increase the efficient allocation of resources. Large organisations are also able to benefit from economies of scale (see Unit 4).

- **Technological monopolies:** Many large manufacturing companies enjoy a high degree of monopoly power because of the vast amounts of complex capital equipment they employ. It would be very difficult for any new firm to begin the mass production of motor cars and hope to compete with existing producers. Thus, although they compete vigorously with each other, the motor manufacturers enjoy a degree of monopoly power.
- **Statutory monopolies:** These are established by the government. In general, public corporations and nationalised industries are the most important statutory monopolies, but you could also include the patent rights of inventors and the copyright of authors and composers who enjoy a legal, if temporary, monopoly.
- **Cartels:** A cartel is a group of firms acting together to reduce competition between themselves and from other firms. The firms in a cartel may, for example, agree to charge the same price for their goods, or to limit their output, perhaps on a quota basis. In the worst cases, they may conspire to prevent new firms entering the industry by exerting pressure on the suppliers of components or raw materials or on potential customers.

Something to do

- Construct a table with columns for each type of monopoly. To complete your table, identify as many examples of each type of monopoly as you can. Keep your table and continue adding examples as you go through your course. Your table may look something like this:

Types of monopoly			
Natural	**Technological**	**Statutory**	**Cartel**
	Microsoft		

The monopolist's equilibrium

The demand or average revenue curve of a monopolist will be different from that of a perfectly competitive firm. The demand for the monopolist's product is the same as the demand for the industry's product, and the curve will therefore slope downwards from left to right. The fact that the average revenue curve slopes downwards, showing that the monopolist can increase sales by reducing price, has an important implication in relation to the marginal revenue curve. Marginal revenue will always be below average revenue and slope down more steeply.

Fig. 5.28 Average revenue and marginal revenue for the monopolist

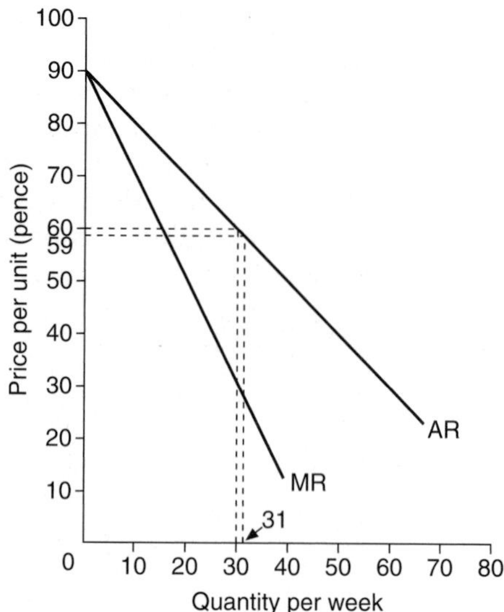

Imagine that the monopolist in Figure 5.28 sells 30 units per week at 60 pence per unit. To sell one more unit per week it must reduce the price by one penny. The monopolist will therefore lose 30 pence on the 30 units that could have been sold at 60 pence, and will gain 59 pence on the 31st unit, which could not have been sold at a price of more than 59 pence. Total revenue increases by 29 pence – and this is, of course, the marginal revenue, which is considerably below the average revenue of 59 pence.

Figure 5.29 shows the situation facing the monopolist. In Figure 5.29b, only the two marginal curves are drawn so that we can see that the monopolist, like the perfectly competitive firm, will fix output at the point where MC = MR.

Fig. 5.29 Monopoly equilibrium

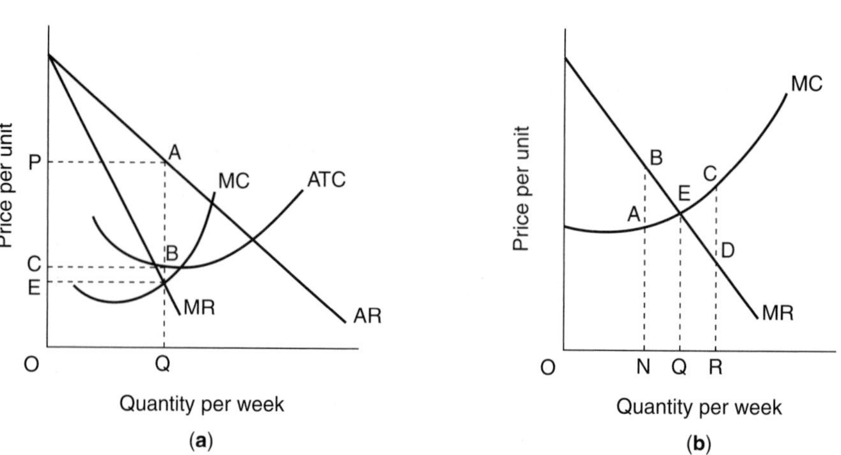

If the firm produces less than OQ units – for example, ON – it would forgo some profits, in this case ABE. If more than OQ is produced – for example, OR – profits are reduced by an amount ECD. Therefore OQ must be the profit-maximising output.

Having determined the most profitable level of output, the monopolist charges what the market will bear for the product. In this case, the average revenue curve in Figure 5.29a shows that consumers will pay OP per unit for a quantity OQ, and this is what is charged. You should notice that this is considerably above OE, the marginal cost of producing OQ units. It is also considerably above OC, the average total cost of producing OQ units. The monopolist is thus able to make an abnormal profit of CPAB. This is sometimes referred to as **monopoly rent.**

In economics, 'rent' has the special meaning of being any payment above that required to keep factors of production employed in their present occupation. In this case the monopolist could be making a normal profit at a price of OC and would be prepared to remain in the industry if price fell to that level. The monopolist is thus receiving a rent of CPAB. (We return to the concept of rent in Unit 6.)

Since the firm is by definition a monopolist, new firms are unable to enter the industry and the abnormal profits can continue indefinitely. This is in contrast to the perfectly competitive situation, where abnormal profits attract new firms to enter the industry until those profits disappear.

Elasticity of demand and monopoly equilibrium

There is an important relationship between the equilibrium output of the monopolist and the **price elasticity** of demand for its product. In order to explore this, we must first examine a different method of measuring price elasticity of demand.

In Figure 5.30a, it can be seen that the price elasticity of demand (PED) at point A may be measured simply by measuring the distances a and b and dividing a by b. Thus, at a point half-way along the demand curve, a and b will be equal and elasticity will be 1; three-quarters of the way along the curve at B, elasticity will be $\frac{1}{3}$. If the demand curve is not a straight line, elasticity at any point can still be measured by drawing a tangent to the curve at the relevant point and then assessing the ratio of the two parts of the tangent, as in Figure 5.30b.

Fig. 5.30 Point price elasticity of demand

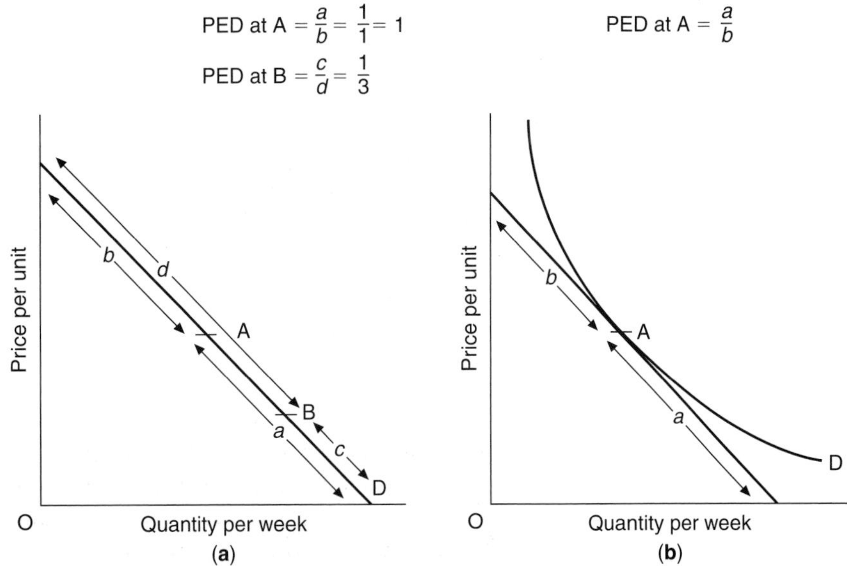

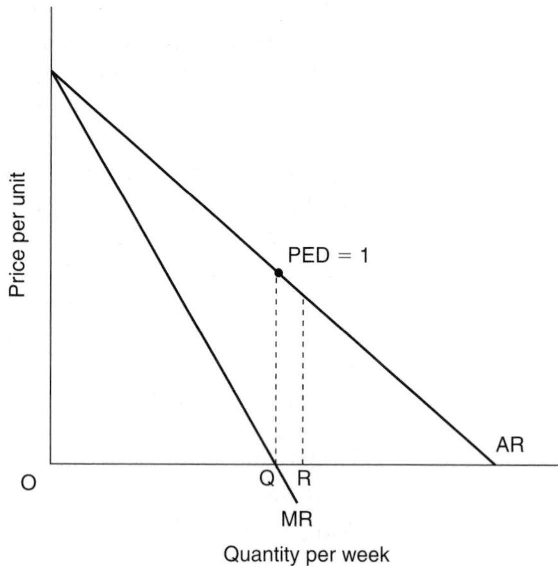

Fig. 5.31 Price elasticity of demand and marginal revenue

In Figure 5.31, when output is OQ, marginal revenue is zero. Therefore elasticity of demand is 1 (since total revenue must be constant if marginal revenue is zero and we already know that, if total revenue is constant following a change in price, price elasticity of demand is 1 – see Unit 3, page 92). We also know that price elasticity is less than 1 to the right of Q, because marginal revenue is negative, so total revenue would fall following a reduction in price. The monopolist could not, therefore, be in a profit-maximising position at an output greater than OQ. It would be more profitable, for example, to reduce output from OR, as this would reduce costs while increasing total revenue. Accordingly, we can conclude that the monopolist can only be in equilibrium to the left of Q, and that is when demand is elastic.

Discriminating monopoly

In Unit 3, we saw that consumers receive a surplus of satisfaction, known as the consumers' surplus, when they buy goods at the prevailing market price. It may be possible for a monopolist to reduce this by charging different consumers different prices. A monopolist who can do this is known as a **discriminating monopolist**. There are three conditions necessary for price discrimination to take place:

- The market for the product must be capable of being divided into distinct parts, or segments, and consumers buying in a segment where price is low must not be able to sell in another segment where price is high.
- The price elasticity of each market segment must be different: the object of price discrimination is to sell at a high price where demand is inelastic, and sell at a lower price where demand is elastic, so that in each case revenue is increased.
- The cost of selling to each market segment, and of keeping them separate, must not be so high as to wipe out the extra profit.

In Figure 5.32, we can trace the effects of price discrimination. Figure 5.32a shows that the monopolist maximises profits by selling 1000 units at 10 pence each, giving total revenue of £100. The monopolist knows, however, that some consumers would not be put off by a higher price. If the market is divided into two parts, one with inelastic demand (Figure 5.32b) and one with elastic demand (Figure 5.32c), then total output can be divided between them so as to increase profits. This is done by equating the marginal cost of the whole output to marginal revenue in each segment of the market. Only a small reduction in price in the elastic segment is necessary to increase sales. When elasticity of demand is greater than 1, a fall in price leads to an increase in total revenue. In this case, 700 are sold for £63. In the inelastic segment of the market, a considerable increase in price does not produce a great change in quantity and again total revenue increases. In this segment, 300 units are sold for £45. Total revenue over both market segments is now £108 instead of £100.

In this example, one of the elasticities is greater than 1 and the other less than 1. In fact, gains will occur as long as the elasticities are different, even if both are greater, or both less, than 1.

Fig. 5.32 Monopolistic discrimination

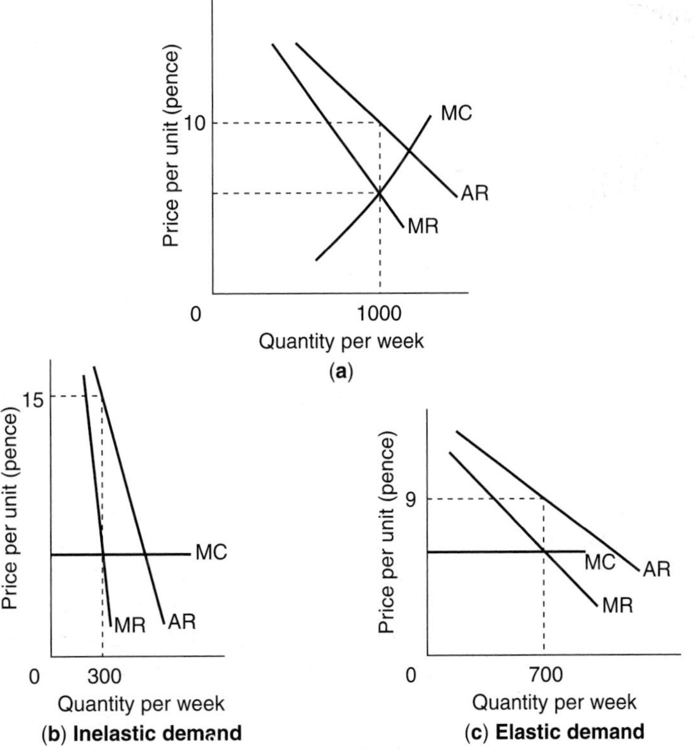

Monopolistic competition

In an industry with imperfect competition, each firm will be producing basically the same product, but will try to distinguish it from its rivals through product differentiation. The difference may only be a matter of packaging, but each manufacturer sets out to establish their product as something different from the products of other manufacturers even though they may in fact be very close substitutes.

Think about it

- How do oil companies, high-street banks and manufacturers of soap powder differentiate their products in order to increase demand for them?

By differentiating its product from those of its competitors, the firm in an imperfectly competitive market will be able to increase its sales by reducing prices. The firm faces a demand curve similar to that of the monopolist (see Figure 5.29). This situation is shown in Figure 5.33.

Fig. 5.33 Monopolistic competition

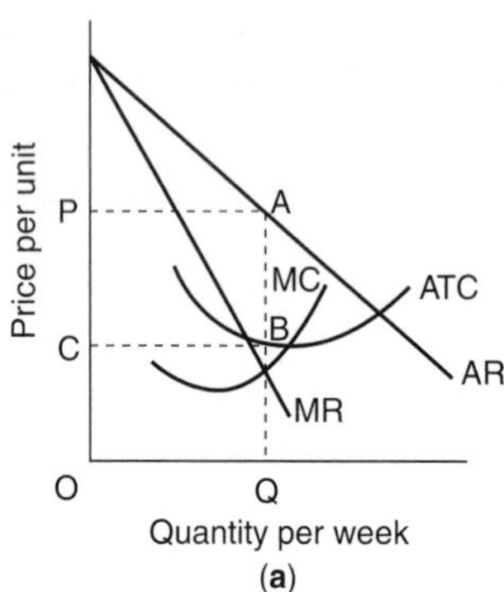

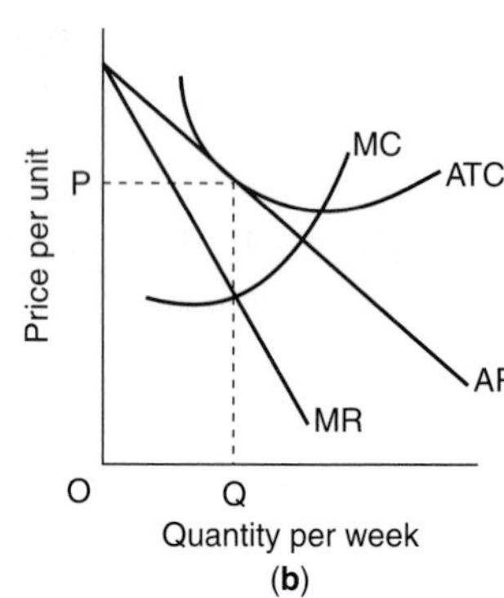

The short-run equilibrium position of the firm is identical to that of the monopolist, and the firm is able to make abnormal profits of CPAB. Under conditions of monopolistic competition, however, new firms are free to enter the market, and we can expect them to attract some customers away from existing firms with the result that the average revenue curve of each existing firm moves to the left. The extent of the leftward movement depends on the success of each firm in maintaining the loyalty of its customers, but the limit of the movement is indicated in Figure 5.33b, which shows the long-run equilibrium of the firm. In this case, the average revenue (AR) curve has moved far enough to the left to become a tangent to the average total cost (ATC) curve. Thus, at the profit-maximising output of OQ, the firm is just making a normal rate of profit and is operating some way below the optimum size (because AR is not tangential to ATC at its lowest point).

Oligopoly

An **oligopoly** is a situation where there are just a few firms competing with each other in a market. Examples in the UK include motor vehicle manufacture, brewing, petrol refining, the production of household detergents and banking. The characteristics of an oligopoly are as follows:

- There are just a few suppliers competing with each other for the whole market.
- There is usually limited entry to the market, for example due to high set-up costs.
- Firms in an oligopoly tend to avoid damaging price-based competition, preferring to come to an agreement on pricing in order to achieve profit maximisation throughout the industry and often relying on non-price competition to maintain or increase their share of the market.

A firm in such an industry must be especially careful in determining its commercial policy. This is clear if we think of the extreme example of oligopoly – an industry comprised of just two firms (a **duopoly**). While most firms proposing a change in the price of one of their products will try to predict the reactions of their customers, the duopolist will also have to make an assessment of how its competitor will react. If one firm in a duopoly plans to increase price, it can expect demand for its product to contract. The amount by which demand contracts depends largely on how the firm's competitor reacts to the price increase. The competitor may maintain its own price, hoping to attract much of the first firm's business, or it may follow the lead of the first firm by increasing its price. Only by considering the reactions of its competitor, therefore, can a duopolist formulate its own pricing strategy.

Fig. 5.34 The oligopolist

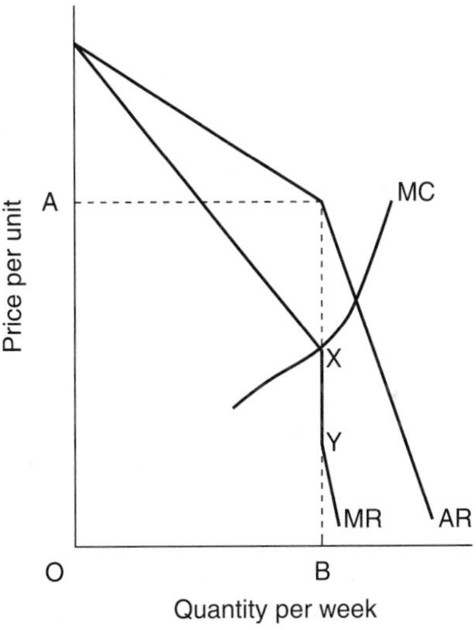

This leads to one of the main theories of the behaviour of oligopolists, illustrated in Figure 5.34. You will notice that the demand curve (or average revenue curve) is an unusual shape. The firm is in equilibrium at price OA, producing OB. If it increases price, it may expect a significant drop in demand because its few competitors do not follow, hoping to pick up extra sales for themselves by maintaining their prices. On the other hand, if our firm reduces its price, it might gain relatively few extra sales as its competitors also reduce their prices, fearing a loss of sales to the first price-cutter. Thus, once the oligopolist is in an equilibrium position, it is probable that the elasticity of demand is higher for an increase in price than it is for a reduction in price.

A further peculiarity of the oligopolist's position, if the kinked demand curve is an accurate reflection of this, is that the marginal revenue curve is discontinuous (shown by the 'step' in Figure 5.34). This implies that if the marginal cost curve crosses the marginal revenue curve anywhere between X and Y, the price will not alter. Of course, if the AR curve moved, so would the MR curve, together with the profit-maximising quantity and price.

This view of the oligopolist's behaviour is not universally accepted. Some argue that the demand curve is inelastic when price rises, as rival firms follow the increase in price. The above analysis rests on the assumption that the firms involved act independently. In fact, the firms in an oligopoly may find it in their own interests to co-ordinate their activities. Generally, the smaller the number of firms in a market, the greater the chances of such co-operation being successful.

A united front?

The extreme possibility in an oligopoly is that the firms will act in concert, as if they were a single decision-making body (in effect a monopoly). They could then restrict their combined output to force up prices and so obtain abnormal prices. The difficulty would be to ensure that all firms in the market adhered to the agreed price: there would be an advantage to an individual firm if it reduced its price to attract customers from the other firms. A weakness of OPEC (the Organisation of Petroleum Exporting Countries) is that it has been unable to maintain its stipulated crude oil price.

Individual members frequently undercut the price in order to dispose of surplus output. However, the advantage is not long lasting, since other producers normally respond by cutting their prices, too. The result is that the profits of the industry are reduced overall.

In practice, it is largely illegal for firms to conclude formal agreements that fix prices or levels of output (see restrictive practices, Unit 7, page 257). In this situation, various arrangements may emerge. One possibility is that a dominant firm may be informally recognised as a price-leader. Prices are stable, though not necessarily identical, until the price-leader decides that it is time for a price increase. When that occurs, other (probably smaller) members of the industry increase their prices. They tend not to raise prices independently in case they lose too much custom to the dominant firm. They also tend not to reduce prices independently in case they provoke the larger firm into aggressive competition.

One of the dangers for oligopolists is that they can easily find themselves involved in a price war for customers that does not increase the industry's sales volume, but does reduce profits and may result in the eventual closure of some firms. It is perhaps a reflection of the general desire to avoid this situation that firms avoid vigorous price competition and try to maintain or increase their market share through methods of non-price competition, such as advertising, competitions, coupons offering selected benefits, and sponsorship of various activities.

Think about it

Read the article about competition and prices in the examinations market.

- Why do you think exam boards do not, or cannot, compete by price competition?
- Is the public examination a natural monopoly, as suggested in the conclusion to the article?
- What are the advantages of competition to
  - the exam boards themselves
  - schools, colleges and candidates?

Competition and Prices in the 'Examinations Market'

The new market structure in examining is an interesting subject for testing economic theory.

1. Is *oligopoly* the ideal market structure to serve the interests of the consumers: the schools, colleges and ultimately the candidates?
2. Is increased market concentration to be welcomed? Would a monopoly be more desirable, i.e. one exam board only?
3. How do these exam boards compete?
4. Is the examining system a *contestable market*?

Until comparatively recently, the exam boards had a relatively loyal set of customers among schools and colleges. Schools tended to enter their pupils for exam papers set by the board in their geographical area. Thus the majority of schools in the North of England taking A levels used the JMB because this examining board was based in the Universities of Sheffield, Manchester, Leeds, Liverpool and Birmingham.

In recent years, schools and teachers within them have looked for a syllabus and hence an exam board which best suited their own pupils, the resources of the school and the particular interests of the teachers. By the early 1990s the exam market had become much more *demand led* and the boards had to compete much more aggressively for their market share. Schools were under pressure to raise standards and teachers sought those syllabi which gave the best chance to their pupils.

The exam boards were faced with a highly competitive position and suddenly had to market their product to 'discerning customers'. Schools often now use a number of exam boards for both GCSE and A level – twenty years ago they would probably have used only one. Although exam boards are not essentially profit-making companies, they do have to cover costs and operate commercially. In the jargon of economics they probably seek to make *normal profits*. The market has also had to adapt to the possibility of new entrants despite the high *entry barriers* that exist.

How have the exam boards adapted to their new situation? Essentially they have to remain competitive and to do this they must try to maintain their market share. This could be defined by entries per subject as a percentage of the total national entry. Many oligopolists compete by *non-price competition*, others may compete on price alone. The latter is more likely when the product is homogeneous, which different exam syllabi in the same subject are not. Close examination of the fees charged by the examining boards to schools and colleges for GCSE and A level reveal remarkable similarities.

If the exam boards do not or cannot compete by price competition then market share can only be increased or maintained by non-price competition.

The non-price competition takes many forms. Schools and colleges are now seen as consumers and syllabi are devised with their interests in mind – *market led* rather than *producer led*. Teachers are offered extensive training in teaching the GCSE A level courses on offer. The boards provide mark schemes and examiners' reports on past papers. They also allow teachers and students to question examiners about recent papers. The examiners provide conferences for students who are preparing for the examination and give out helpful hints. The boards offer different ways to take the same A level, linear or modular, with or without coursework, etc. Schools and colleges are bombarded with glossy brochures about courses, conferences, and new syllabi.

Conclusion

The boards fight for their market share where the consumer is king!

Has the new, highly concentrated oligopoly been a success? Clearly the recent mergers have removed the duplication of too many GCSE and A level syllabi, but there is still plenty of choice in a competitive market. However, are standards being maintained? In their rush to attract more candidates have exam boards started to make mistakes? Exam re-marks were at record levels in 1997 as thousands of candidates appealed against their grade.

As a brief letter to *The Times* said recently, "Why do we need more than one Examination Board for what are supposed to be national examinations of the same standard?" Is the public examination system a *natural monopoly*?

Source: Adapted from Robert Nutter, 'Exam Boards – Monopoly or Oligopoly?', *Economics Today*, September 1998

Something to do

Daily newspapers are constantly trying to find ways of competing and increasing their own circulation and share of the market. In the past this has led to crippling price wars.

- Make a list of the different ways in which they compete now.
- How does this attempt to avoid the self-destruction involved in waging a price war?

Criticisms of the theory of imperfect competition

Modern industrial firms are not obsessed with marginal changes in costs and revenue. Indeed, it is very difficult to calculate marginal costs in many industries. Today's industrialist is more likely to try to establish the average variable cost of producing a product and then add a fairly arbitrary percentage to cover fixed costs, including profits.

Pricing in practice

Pricing in the public sector and in the privatised utilities such as water, gas and electricity provides particular difficulties. Many services are provided to consumers free of direct charges, being financed out of taxation. Others, such as NHS prescriptions, are subject to arbitrary fixed charges. Yet others, such as the charges made by the public corporations – for example, the BBC licence fee – are subject to many influences. There are two main approaches to this type of pricing, based on average total cost and marginal cost.

- **Average total cost:** Total costs of production are estimated and divided by the anticipated sales. While this has the merit of simplicity, it does lead to the problem of cross-subsidisation of some consumers by others. In the electricity industry, for example, peak demand occurs at about 8.00a.m. and 6.00p.m. The electricity companies must have sufficient generating equipment to meet demand at these peak times. Some of this equipment will be idle for much of the time, and less equipment would be needed if demand for electricity were spread evenly throughout the day. It follows that a person who consumes electricity only at off-peak periods imposes less of a burden on the electricity company than the person who uses electricity at peak times. If both users are charged the same price per unit, there is cross-subsidisation of the peak-time user by the off-peak user.
- **Marginal cost:** To overcome the problem of cross-subsidisation, a system of marginal cost pricing would be necessary. This would result in peak-period users paying higher charges than off-peak users, since they are the consumers who necessitate the installation of extra generating plant. It is technically possible to record not only a consumer's total consumption, but also the time of consumption. Consumers could then be charged retrospectively for their electricity, paying more for peak-period consumption than for off-peak.

There are difficulties inherent in this, however. First, it would lead to a great increase in the administrative costs of the electricity company. Second, it is in practice very difficult to estimate marginal costs precisely. Accordingly, electricity companies compromise by charging a lower price to consumers taking electricity overnight – for example, for night storage heaters. There is also the problem that it costs the electricity companies more to supply a remote homestead than it does to supply, say, a house on a large modern estate. Marginal costing would lead to heavy price rises for farmers and those living in rural areas.

Long-run costs

A further criticism of the theory of imperfect competition lies in the argument that the modern industrialist does not recognise the U-shaped cost curves familiar to economists. This is an argument concerning the long term rather than the short term. It is impossible for short-run cost curves not to be U-shaped, owing to the operation of the law of diminishing returns (see Unit 4). It is also quite possible that technical and managerial economies will lead to a falling or horizontal average total cost curve up to very large outputs, in which case the long-run marginal cost curve will also be horizontal. But it is also extremely likely that managerial diseconomies, if nothing else, will eventually lead to rising costs so that the U-shaped long-run curve will be replaced by a saucer-shaped one.

Other objectives

Most of what has been said about the behaviour of firms has assumed that the overriding aim is the maximisation of short-term profits. This is not always the case.

- A firm will often be prepared to sacrifice short-term profits for higher potential long-term profits. For example, a firm may undertake an expensive marketing campaign, or under-cut competitors' prices in the short-term in order to gain more customers, and thus increase profits in the long-term.
- An objective of some firms might be to maximise sales or share of the market. This may be the case in large companies where the owners (the shareholders) have a very remote say in the running of the business. Here the decision makers (the management) may consider that higher sales and hence market share will benefit them individually more than higher profits. Thus a sales manager will look to maximising sales, and a production manager will look to maximising production. Both may lead to a drop in profits if the increase in sales leads to an increase in unit costs, or the increase in production means that expensive stock is left unsold in warehouses.
- Short-term profit maximisation may also be restrained by the desire to develop a favourable public image or a reputation for reliability. The success of a firm such as the Body Shop, for example, is built on its reputation for concern for the environment. It is essential for the long-term success of the business that this reputation is maintained, even if this means additional costs and therefore reduced profits in the short term.

6 Factor markets

Introduction: factor incomes

We have seen that all production involves the employment of **factors of production**. The factors of production therefore must be supplied by their owners and purchased by the firms that require them in the production process. Markets for factors of production exist in the same way as markets for other goods and services, and the price of each factor is to a large extent decided by the forces of demand and supply. The prices paid for factors of production are referred to by economists as **factor incomes**. The four types of factor incomes are

- **wages** paid for labour
- **rent** paid for land
- **interest** paid for capital
- **profit** paid for entrepreneurship.

Firms pay for the factors of production that they use out of the income they receive from selling their products. If we assume that there is no tax on expenditure to divert a part of a firm's income to the government, then when a product is sold the full purchase price will eventually be paid to all the factors of production that have been combined in the production of the product and its delivery to the final customer.

In this unit, we investigate the influences that determine the payments to each of the factors of production.

Payments to labour

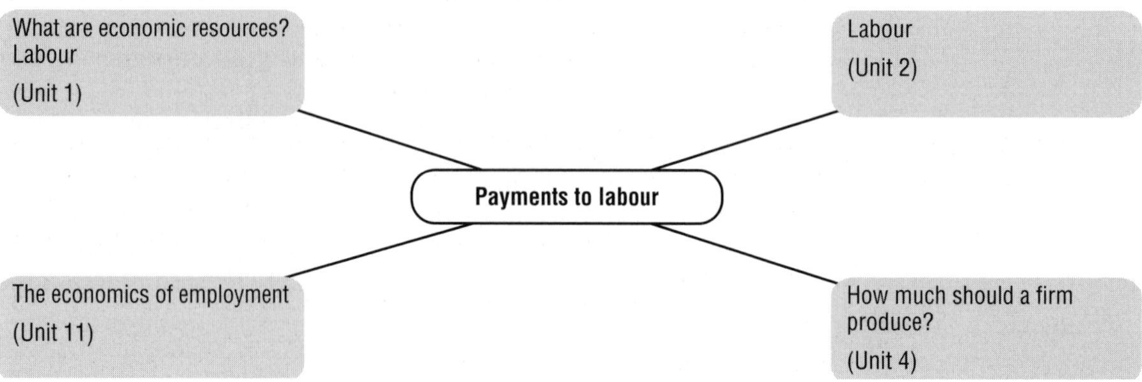

There are three principal ways in which payment is made for labour. These are as follows:

- **Time rates:** The simplest method of paying for labour is in relation to the amount of time for which it is employed. An employer may pay for labour at so much per hour or week, or, in the case of salaries, so much per year. In the last instance, the employee will normally receive the salary in twelve equal monthly instalments. Time rates are most appropriate where it is difficult to measure the work done, or where quality is more important than quantity.

The disadvantage is that, without adequate supervision of labour, time wages may become mere attendance payments and the employer may not get full value for the expenditure.

- **Piece rates:** The main alternatives to time rates are piece-rate systems. Here the worker is paid according to the number of units, or pieces of work, completed. Thus earnings increase in direct proportion to work. Such a system is appropriate where the work is easily measured and where quantity is more important than quality.

  There are many types of piece rate, and one of the disadvantages of paying wages in this way is the difficulty of establishing a system appropriate to a particular process, and of setting rates for particular jobs. Although quantity may be more important than quality, payment by the piece necessitates the employment of inspectors to ensure that workers are not paid for inefficient low-quality work.
- **Fees:** Solicitors, architects and many other professional workers charge fees for their labour. The methods of assessing such fees vary – sometimes they are related to the amount of work involved, and sometimes to the value of the transaction concerned.

Think about it

- Many professional workers, such as barristers and business consultants, are paid high fees. These are often based on an hourly rate in the same way that the wages of an operative in industry are calculated – only the rate is very much higher in the case of the professional than it is in the case of the factory worker. In view of the fact that professional workers rarely produce any real goods, do you think that the discrepancy between the fees earned by a professional worker and the wages earned by an industrial worker is justified? If so, on what basis? If not, why not? In answering these questions, consider factors such as scarcity, demand and supply, elasticity and costs.

In economics, all payments to labour are normally called **wages**. In this section, we first examine the basic theory of wages and then look at the way practice seems to differ from theory.

The marginal productivity theory

In perfectly competitive conditions, wage levels will be determined by demand and supply. Table 6.1 shows successive units of labour being applied to a fixed amount of land. For convenience, we shall assume that the workforce receives its wages in the form of 10 kilograms of its product or output.

At first, marginal product rises, but with the introduction of the fifth worker it begins to fall. This is due to the principle of diminishing returns (see Units 2 and 4). In order to maximise profits, the employer will try to equate marginal cost with marginal product. Therefore, as long as the addition of each worker increases production by not less than 10 kilograms (in other words, as long as marginal product is not less than 10 kilograms), the employer will continue to add to the workforce. Accordingly, the firm will employ six workers. If wages were increased to 12 kilograms (wage 6), it would be wasteful to employ a sixth worker, who will only add 10 kilograms to the total output. In this case, only five workers would be employed.

Table 6.1

The law of diminishing returns again				
No. of workers	Total product (kg)	Marginal product (kg)	Wage per worker (kg)	
			(a)	(b)
1	5	5	10	12
2	12	7	10	12
3	23	11	10	12
4	36	13	10	12
5	48	12	10	12
6	58	10	10	12
7	65	7	10	12
8	68	3	10	12
9	70	2	10	12
10	71	1	10	12

If we present the same information graphically, as in Figure 6.1, we can see that the downward-sloping part of the marginal product curve is the firm's demand curve for labour, and that the higher the price, the smaller the quantity of labour employed. The industry's demand curve for labour can, of course, be obtained by adding together all the individual demand curves (see also Unit 3, page 84).

Fig. 6.1 The firm's demand for labour

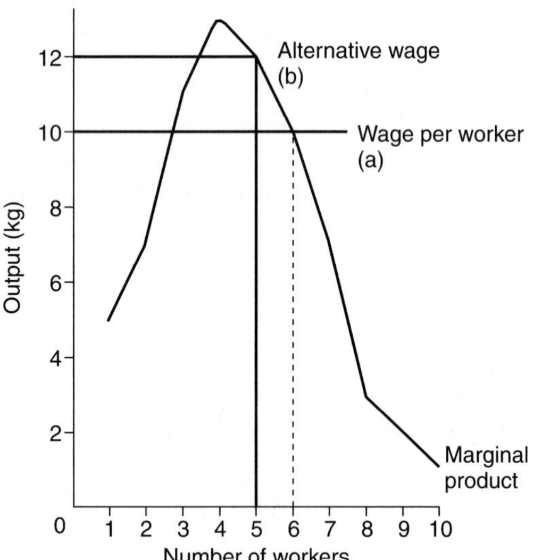

In the real world, of course, employees are paid in money rather than product, and firms are more concerned with the extra revenue they will receive from sales of additional product than they are with the marginal product (or marginal physical product) produced by each additional unit of labour. Additional labour is employed because it will contribute to total revenue. The additional revenue contributed by each additional unit of labour employed is called the marginal revenue product (MRP) of labour to distinguish it from the marginal *physical* product shown in Figure 6.1.

As we saw in Unit 3, under conditions of perfect competition (see Unit 5), a firm can sell any quantity of its product at a given price. MRP is therefore calculated using the equation

$$\text{marginal revenue product (MRP)} = \text{marginal product} \times \text{price}$$

If we assume that the price of the product in Table 6.1 is £10 per kilogram, we can calculate the MRP as shown in Table 6.2. It is then possible to construct an MRP curve using the MRP figures as shown in Figure 6.2. Since, under conditions of perfect competition, a single firm cannot influence the cost of labour, the marginal cost of labour must equal the average cost of labour, which is the current wage rate. This is shown in Figure 6.2 as the horizontal line W at £70 per week.

Table 6.2

Marginal revenue product			
No. of workers	**Marginal product (kg)**	**Price (£)**	**Marginal revenue product (£)**
1	5	10	50
2	7	10	70
3	11	10	110
4	13	10	130
5	12	10	120
6	10	10	100
7	7	10	70
8	3	10	30
9	2	10	20
10	1	10	10

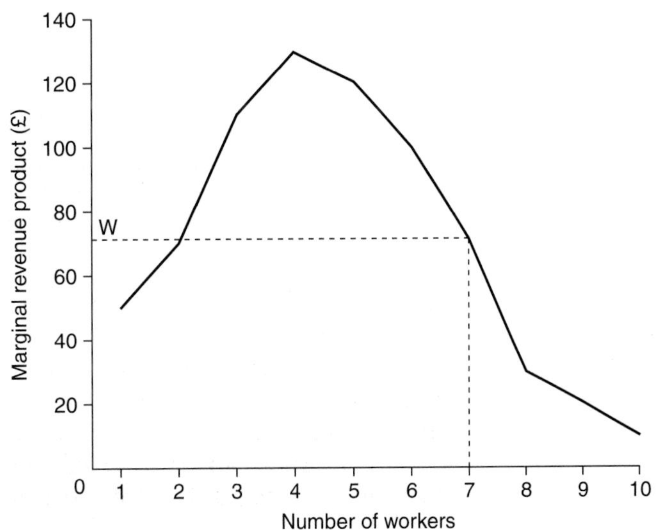

Fig. 6.2 Changes in marginal revenue product

A firm will try to equate MRP and the current wage rate, and the firm in Figure 6.2 will therefore employ seven workers, since if fewer than this were employed, the firm could add to revenue by employing more, while the cost (MC) of employing more than seven would exceed the additional revenue (MRP) obtained.

Derived demand

We should notice here that the demand for labour – and indeed for all the factors of production – is a **derived demand**. Factors are demanded not for their own sake but for what they can produce. If the demand for public transport is high, so too will be the demand for bus drivers. But the demand for a factor does not depend only on demand for the product. As techniques of production change, so the proportions in which the factors of production are hired will alter. For example, modern navigational systems reduce the size of crew needed by ocean-going vessels, even though these vessels carry more cargo.

We saw in Unit 2 that the overall supply of labour depends mainly on the size and structure of the population. The supply curve of labour, however, is likely to slope upwards from left to right as more labour is forthcoming at higher wage rates. In these circumstances, the market for labour is comparable with other markets examined in Unit 4, and the pressures of supply and demand discussed in Unit 3 will establish an **equilibrium wage** (price of labour) as in Figure 6.3.

Fig. 6.3 Competitive determination

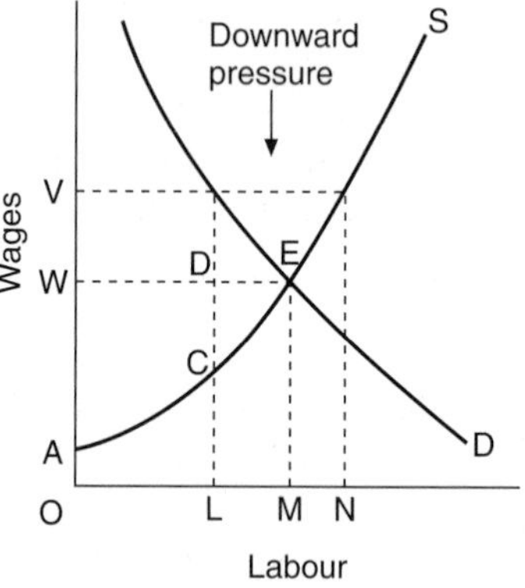

Figure 6.3 is an outline of the **marginal productivity** theory of wages, and it goes some way towards explaining the real-world situation. There are many examples of the sources of demand and supply influencing wages, and it is clear that no employer will pay workers more than the value of their marginal product. But there are obvious weaknesses to the theory when proposed as an explanation of real-world adjustments.

Problems with the marginal productivity theory

So far, we have dealt only with wages and a commodity called labour, with the implication that labour will move from low-wage activities to high-wage activities so that equilibrium will be established. However, it is really necessary to consider wages together with other benefits and disadvantages of a particular job – or the 'net advantages', including hours and conditions of work. Also, we know there is not a single commodity called labour but thousands of different working people, endowed with a huge variety of talents and skills but not easily interchangeable between jobs.

The implication of the first of these considerations – the variety of benefits and disadvantages of a particular occupation – is that the net advantages of an occupation should be equated with the marginal product. Thus a university lecturer with generous holidays and congenial working conditions might be expected to accept a lower money income than a similarly qualified geologist working long and inconvenient hours in difficult terrain searching for oil. The implication of the second consideration – the different talents of the working force – is that those with very scarce talents may well earn more than the value of their marginal product because of their scarcity.

Other problems with the marginal productivity theory include the following.

- Most employers would find it very difficult to calculate the marginal product of a particular type of labour. Any theory based on the assumption that such calculations are possible must be too precise to explain what actually happens in the labour market. The measurement of marginal productivity is particularly difficult in the case of new machinery, where there is an increase in productivity per worker. It would be wrong to attribute the whole of the increase in output to labour, especially as there may actually be less work involved.
- The theory necessarily assumes that labour is mobile between jobs, and can easily move from low-wage employment to high-wage employment. In practice such mobility is likely to be restricted.
- The assumption of perfect markets is clearly unrealistic. Important monopoly interests influence both sides of the labour market: trade associations on the one side, trade unions on the other.

Think about it

- Why do you think the mobility of labour is restricted? What can or should be done about the situation?
- Consider the development and impact of new technology. What effect do you think this is having on labour mobility?

Before we examine the practical difficulties associated with the operation of the labour market, there is a further concept that needs clarification – that of economic rent.

Economic rent

In the situation shown in Figure 6.3, a wage of OW would be established and OM people would be employed in the industry. Changes in the conditions of demand for or supply of labour would have effects similar to those explored in Unit 3.

This enables us to examine the idea of **economic rent**. The early theory of economic rent was developed in relation to land, but it may be applied to all factors of production. Economic rent is the term applied to any payment received by a factor of production over and above what is necessary to keep it in its present occupation. Thus, if a singer with a band earns £1000 per week but could earn £200 per week in his or her next best job, then £800 of the singer's earnings may be regarded as economic rent and the remaining £200 as his or her **transfer earnings.** If the singer is offered less than this for singing, he or she will probably transfer to the other occupation.

In the labour market illustrated in Figure 6.3 no one is willing to work for less than OA. Consider the position of a person at OL. The curve shows that they would be willing to work for a wage of LC, but the established wage received is LD (= OW). Thus the person's transfer earnings are LC, and they receive economic rent of CD. Only the marginal unit of the factor OM receives no rent, but the workforce as a whole receives economic rent of AWE, which represents the difference between what the employer actually pays for labour (OWEM) and what would have been paid if it had been possible to negotiate with each employee separately (OAEM).

Economic rent and price elasticity of supply

It is clear from Figure 6.4 that the proportions of economic rent and transfer earnings in a factor's income depend on its price elasticity of supply.

- In the case of Figure 6.4a, the supply of the factor is completely inelastic: whatever the price offered for it, the quantity supplied is constant. If income falls to zero, the factor will still not leave its present occupation, as there are no alternatives available. In this case all the earnings are economic rent and there are no transfer earnings. It is, of course, a theoretical limiting case and has little practical significance, as there are usually alternative uses for most factors of production.

Fig. 6.4 Elasticity of supply and rent

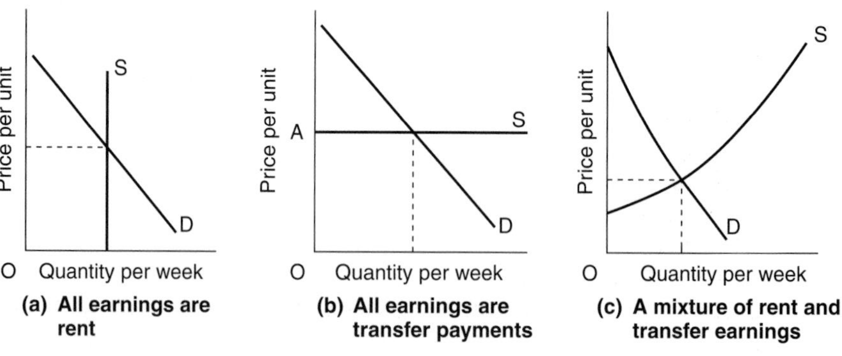

- At the other extreme, Figure 6.4b shows the position where the supply of the factor is perfectly elastic. Producers can employ as much as they wish at a price OA but could obtain none at a lower price. This might represent the position of a single firm employing labour at a fixed price under an agreement with a trade union. In this case, as no one is willing to work for less than OA, total earnings are all transfer earnings and no economic rent is payable.
- In between these two extremes will be the majority of cases, where the elasticity of supply is greater than zero but less than infinity. There will be elements of both transfer earnings and economic rent in the factors' incomes, as in Figure 6.4c.

Economic rent and scarcity

Sometimes a factor of production may receive payments above its transfer earnings because of a temporary shortage of that factor. In this case at least part of the surplus can be expected to disappear as the supply of the factor increases. This kind of temporary surplus is known as **quasi rent**, or **temporary rent**; it has been earned in the recent past by computer programmers. It is likely to occur wherever there is a lengthy period of training involved before extra workers become available to meet an increase in demand.

In general, rent tends to be related to scarcity. The reason why an international footballer may earn over £30 000 per week is that there is a shortage of people with his ability. He earns the rent because of his scarce ability and his revenue-earning potential as a 'crowd puller'. Sometimes the supply of particular types of labour is deliberately restricted to ensure that rent is earned. Professional associations such as those of accountants or lawyers might adopt such a policy. (This is similar to the abnormal profits that are earned by monopolists – see Unit 5 – and is sometimes called 'monopoly rent'.) The labour market provides many examples of such rent.

The labour market

It does not take much research to discover that there are large differences in people's wages. To some extent these conform to what we expect from knowledge of market forces: where there are scarcities, wages are high;
are low. Thus, people in different
for the same work – those wages
nent.

Something to

- In groups o
  - commerc
  - nurses
  - solicitors'
  - accountan
  - garage me
  - computer
  Sources of in … wspapers, Jobcentres and
  employment
- To what exter … and, and to what extent the
  value of the w

not operate smoothly: people
arn different wages. In theory,
he high-wage work, bringing
ce the differences remain. This
ket which prevent the market
t the operation of the labour
escribed below.

Immobility of labour While it is easy enough to move labour from one industry or occupation to another in a textbook, it is more difficult in practice.

- Occupational immobility exists because changing jobs may involve retraining. People may be unwilling to undertake such retraining, particularly as they grow older. Such immobility allows wage differences to persist.
- Geographical immobility of labour may help to account for regional differences in pay for people in similar jobs. Geographical mobility involves people moving home when they change jobs. There are often strong economic and social forces acting against this; the contrast between low house prices in areas where there are few jobs and high house prices in areas with more jobs is enough to prevent many such moves; family and other ties will also often be a deterrent. (The levels of regional unemployment in the UK are shown in Figure 6.5.)

Both types of mobility may be inhibited by a lack of knowledge of the opportunities in other industries or areas.

Fig. 6.5 Regional unemployment in the UK, July 1996 (000s, seasonally adjusted)

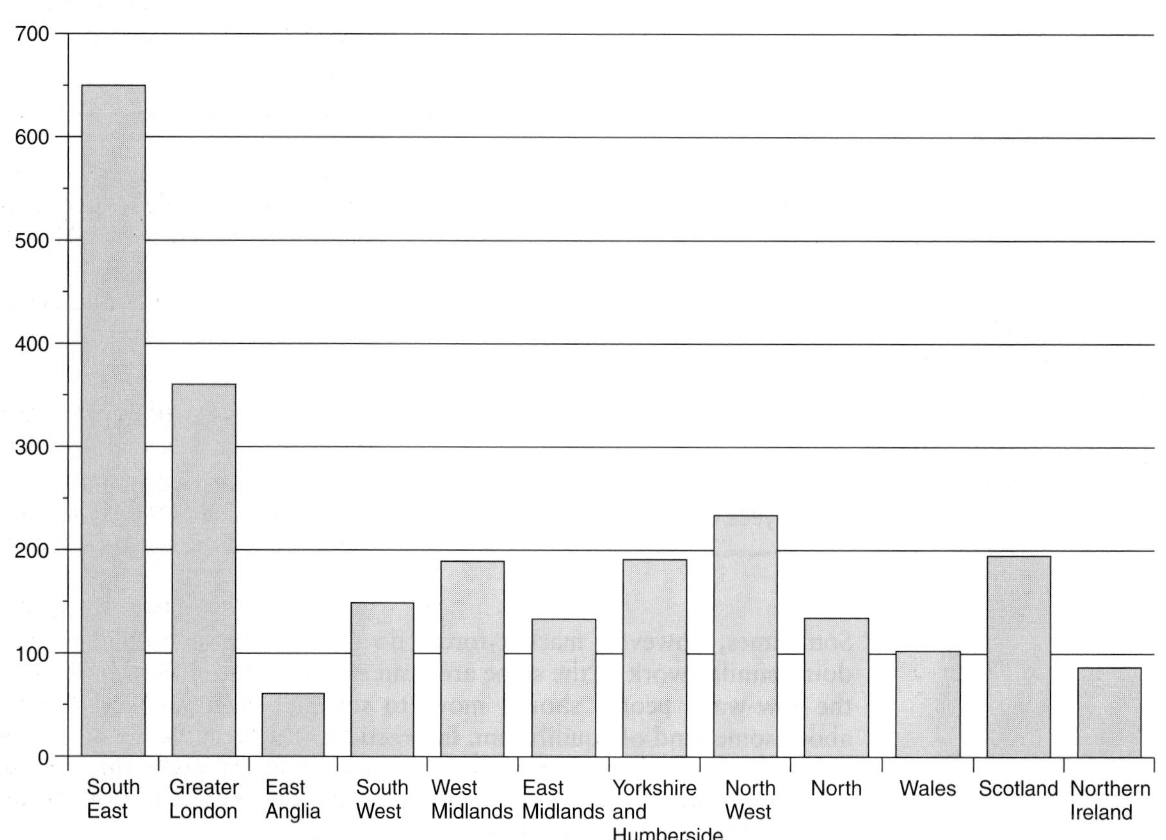

Employers In Unit 5 we examined the problems associated with monopolists (the only sellers of a product). Some employers are **monopsonists,** or single buyers, and may be in a position to prevent wages rising since their employees cannot find work elsewhere. Even if an individual employer is not in this position, a group of them may be. Many employers belong to a trade association, such as the Freight Transport Association for road hauliers. (A trade association is a kind of employers' trade union.) While trade associations have other functions (research and advertising, for example), they often negotiate wages rates on behalf of all members, adding to their overall bargaining power.

The largest employer in the UK is the government. For economic and political reasons, which override its aims as an employer, however, it may seek to hold down wages, and frequently does so. Many of its employees, including nurses and teachers, are in a weak position for finding alternative work due to their specialised skills.

Trade unions Like trade associations, **trade unions** have many functions relating to the working conditions of their members and to the economy in general. In the context of this unit, their most important function may be considered as the negotiation of wages.

Think about it

The purpose of trade unions in negotiating wage levels with employers is to obtain the highest wages they can for their members. While this is a valuable service for their members, it may also be construed as blackmailing the employers, especially where there is a threat of strikes or other industrial action.

- Do you think this type of interference with the economy is justifiable? If so, why?

In many industries today the determination of wage levels is the outcome of the interaction between monopolistic (single-seller) trade unions and monopsonistic (single-buyer) trade associations. This is particularly so in the public sector.

Factors favourable to a trade union in negotiating an increase in members' wages include the following:

- If wages constitute a small proportion of total cost, an employer may be willing to concede a wage claim rather than risk industrial action which will have an adverse effect on production while heavy overhead costs still have to be met.
- Where the demand for the product is buoyant and inelastic, a wage claim may be conceded in the knowledge that extra costs can be passed on to consumers.
- In cases where workers are able to show that their productivity has increased, or will increase, a wage claim may be successful. In this connection 'productivity bargains' are frequently associated with above-average wage increases. The workforce agrees to give up traditional and outmoded methods of working and to adopt more flexible and productive attitudes and methods in return for higher pay. At the same time, surplus labour may be induced to leave the firm by the offer of redundancy payments.

- Sometimes the nature of the product may be significant. If the workers supply an essential good or service, the disruption of which would cause immediate inconvenience to the community, then the pressure of public opinion may force the employer to a quick settlement.
- Where wages for a job are below those offered elsewhere for similar work, it is often possible to bring pressure to bear on employers to secure a proper adjustment.
- A successful wage claim in one firm may set the scene for successful claims elsewhere.
- The organisation of the union itself and the structure of the industry may be significant. Where the majority of the workforce is concentrated in large plants and belongs to a single union, the chances of successful wage claims are probably higher. But when the workforce is thinly spread over a very large number of establishments and is perhaps in close daily contact with the employer, there may be a great reluctance to take industrial action and wages settlements are likely to be lower.
- The control that the union has over the supply of labour may be a major influence. If an employer can easily obtain non-union labour, the position of the union is, of course, weakened. If the union controls the supply of labour, the chances of success are correspondingly greater.

All the above factors may help trade unions in their pay negotiations. There are fewer advantageous factors for employers, especially if they negotiate as individuals rather than as members of a trade association:

- In conditions of high unemployment, when demand for goods and services is depressed, employers should be able to resist excessive wage claims, particularly if the industry employs mainly unskilled labour.
- A monopolist that need not fear losing its market to competition during a strike may be expected to resist wage increases vigorously (though it is, of course, the monopolist that is more likely to be able to pass on wage increases to consumers in price rises).
- In the same way, a firm that is the sole buyer of a particular type of labour will be able to hold down wages, as the supply of labour is inelastic and workers may not easily find alternative employment.
- In a period of relatively constant prices, wage demands are likely to be moderate and excessive claims will be easier to resist.
- If it is easy to substitute machinery for labour, the employer is in a strong position. Workers will be restricted in the pressure they can exert.

Traditional differentials

Although the determination of wages will depend on the interaction of trade unions and employers, there are several other factors that help to determine the pay for a particular job, including traditional differentials and, since 1999, the introduction of a **minimum wage**. Workers generally like to maintain their place in the wages league. Normally this means maintaining their best place in the league rather than their average place! Sometimes this is difficult – especially when production methods have changed, so that earlier skills are no longer required. This is the kind of situation that is sometimes resolved only after major industrial disputes.

Something to do

- Imagine you are employed by a large manufacturing organisation, and it is your job to negotiate a wage increase for all employees. Make a list of the factors you will need to obtain information on in order to be in a strong negotiating position.
- If you worked in the NHS, would your approach be different? Give your reasons.

The globalisation of the labour market

The labour market is increasingly being affected by the **globalisation** of business and the interdependence of economies. We saw in Unit 4 the trend towards multinational business organisations, and in Units 13 and 14 we examine the international effects of trade and development. Here it is important to appreciate the effects of the globalisation of business and trade on the labour market.

There are two principal ways in which globalisation has an impact on the labour market:

- First, as firms grow and become multinational organisations, with operations in several countries, employees from the firm's base country are increasingly required to travel to other countries in which the firm operates. This may be, for example, in order to co-ordinate the activities of the firm, to meet or train the firm's employees in other countries, so as to ensure a uniform culture and standard of quality throughout. Or sales executives from the firm's base country may be required to visit and sell to foreign customers, or attend foreign trade fairs and other events.
- Second, as trade and other barriers between countries come down, particularly within the European Union, it is increasingly possible for workers in one country to seek employment in another. For example, there is now free movement of labour and access to employment throughout the EU for both workers and employers.
- Third, it may affect the relative bargaining strengths of employers and unions. Employers may threaten to move operations to another country, and unions may form international links.

This trend towards globalisation means that workers employed, working in or visiting foreign countries must be aware of the customs of that country, especially regarding business and trade. In addition, they must be fluent in the language of the country they are operating in. Working conditions in different countries also vary, and this has an important aspect on employment and the willingness of employees to move to other countries.

The government and the labour market

We have seen that the government is involved in the labour market as a major employer. We have also identified some imperfections in the labour market. It is in connection with these that the government has a further involvement: the responsibility to encourage the smooth working of the market. There are many aspects of this involvement, the most significant of which are outlined below.

The minimum wage

In April 1999, a minimum wage was introduced in the UK. This takes labour at the lower levels out of the free market where it is solely subject to the forces of demand and supply. It also introduces an additional cost to firms employing labour at the minimum wage rate that would otherwise be paid at a lower wage rate.

THE MINIMUM WAGE

***Gwen Coates** outlines how the minimum wage works and considers the arguments for and against its introduction in the UK*

During the last year, there has been much discussion in the press, in parliament and among the business community about the implications of introducing a national minimum wage. The government is committed to introducing a minimum wage and to this end has appointed a Low Pay Commission to determine the appropriate level at which such a wage should be fixed.

What is it and which countries have one?

The introduction of a national minimum wage usually means that all employees are entitled to receive a minimum hourly rate of pay. The rate is normally a proportion of the average male hourly rate of pay.

Different minimum wage systems have been in operation. Some are statutory (in France, Greece, the Netherlands and Portugal), some are based on collective agreement (in Belgium, Germany and Spain) and some cover selective industries only (for example Wages Councils in the UK before 1993).

In Belgium, Denmark, Germany, Greece, the Netherlands and Portugal, minimum wages are set at approximately 70% of average earnings. In France, Luxembourg and Spain they are set at 60% of average earnings, while in the US it is 33%.

Minimum wages and the UK

In the UK, the Trades Boards Act of 1909 made some attempt to introduce minimum wages in those industries with extremely low wages and poor conditions. This legislation was repealed in 1945. Over 50 Wages Councils with powers to set pay and conditions in a range of low-pay industries were created. Wages Councils were abolished in 1993 in an attempt to reduce distortions in the labour market and encourage a more competitive environment. The government decided that Britain should opt out of the Social Chapter with its requirement to introduce a national minimum wage. The government argued that, with the exception of equality at work and health and safety issues, other conditions of work including pay should be determined by market forces and not by law.

The implications of introducing a minimum wage in the UK

Arguments for

(1) The free market theory predicts that a minimum wage will lower employment because it raises the price of labour (see Figure A). Studies in the United States have suggested that the opposite is true. In a free market, firms which set very low wages often have high labour turnover rates and longer periods in which they cannot find workers. In the short run, such low wage rates may boost profit margins, but not in the long run. In the fast food industry, the introduction of minimum wages has reduced staff turnover, raised the skill level of employees and increased employment. This stems from the fact that employers have come to value their employees more. Employees have become a more expensive resource. Firms therefore need to ensure that they enhance the productivity of their employees in terms of skills and flexibility and also reduce the likelihood of them leaving.

Burger King, the fast food chain, which was involved in a recent low pay scandal where it caused staff to take unpaid breaks when business was quiet, has now indicated its readiness, along with Tesco the supermarket chain and many other businesses in relatively low-pay sectors, to accept a national minimum wage.

(2) Many of the very low paid are in receipt of in-work state benefits to subsidise their low pay. An increase in their income due to the introduction of a minimum wage might reduce the taxation required to fund government spending on such benefits, which currently stands at approximately £3 billion per annum. Without a minimum wage, taxpayers are, in effect, subsidising firms which pay very low rates of pay. Taxpayers in this context include not only individuals but also those firms who pay higher wages to their workforce.

(3) On the assumption that unemployment decreases or that total wages rise, a positive multiplier effect may occur in the economy. An increase in the general level of income due to the introduction of a national minimum wage may result in an increase in the demand for goods and services. This in turn may give rise to an increase in employment which may lead to an increase in income and so forth.

(4) Concerns about rising prices and unemployment were expressed about Equal Pay legislation introduced in the 1970s. These proved unfounded.

Arguments against

(1) In a free market, the price of a good or service is determined by supply and demand. Wages are the price of labour, and thus the wage in any given occupation will be determined by the supply of labour (coming from those who wish to work) and the demand for labour (arising from firms who wish to employ people).

The equilibrium or market wage for a particular job is determined where the supply of labour and the demand for labour are equal. A minimum wage that is set above this equilibrium wage will increase the supply of labour but reduce the demand for labour. More people will offer themselves for work when wages rise, however employers

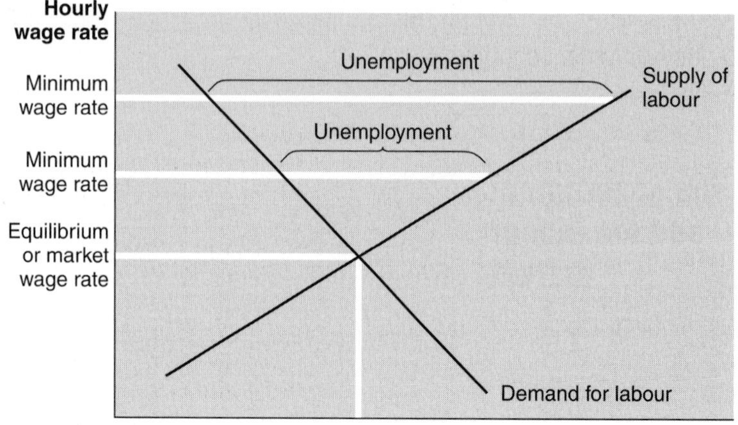

Minimum wage rates set above the equilibrium wage rate increase the supply of labour, but reduce the demand for labour, resulting in unemployment.

Fig. A *Effect of minimum wage on employment*

will try to reduce the number of employees they require when wages rise. The result – unemployment. From Figure A it can be seen that the higher the minimum wage, the greater the gap between the demand for and the supply of labour. This indicates that the higher the minimum wage, the greater the amount of unemployment created – hence the current debate about the level at which a minimum wage should be fixed.

(2) As costs of production increase, firms may need to increase prices if they are to maintain their profit margins. This in turn may make them less competitive in both export markets and against imported products in the UK. In the long term, the effect could be more unemployment.

(3) In both Europe and the United States, research suggests that minimum wages have resulted in high levels of youth unemployment. In France youth unemployment levels are twice as high as in the UK, and in Belgium one and a half times as high – both countries have minimum wages. In the US, studies have shown that in retailing a 25% rise in the legal minimum wage for 18 and 19-year-olds led to a 16–25% drop in employment among this group.

(4) Workers higher up the pay ladder may push to restore their differentials if the lowest paid receive a pay rise. If this were to occur, costs of production would rise and more jobs might be destroyed. A wage/price spiral might be triggered with serious implications for inflation.

(5) Many companies are already involved in outsourcing part of their production to countries where labour is cheap. Some commentators suggest that the introduction of a minimum wage may encourage more companies to consider this in order to maintain their profit margins and to remain competitive.

(6) Finally, it would be difficult to enforce a minimum wage. Individuals are unlikely to take cases to tribunals for an extra few pence an hour, and the costs of policing such a policy might be huge.

Fig. B *Stacking fruit in Tesco—along with many other businesses in relatively low-paid sectors, Tesco has indicated its readiness to accept a national minimum wage*

Conclusion

There are many arguments for and against a minimum wage and it is generally possible to find as much research to support one view as to support another. Most research suggests that, in general, job losses are likely to be greatest in industries where there are a large number of low-paid workers; where product markets are very competitive; where low-wage labour is easy to replace with capital, and where low-wage labour contributes a high proportion of total costs. This would suggest that industries like textiles are likely to be hardest hit, and groups such as the young and unskilled.

The impact of minimum wages on the structure of wages and employment depends upon the level at which a minimum wage is set relative to average wages and the coverage of minimum wages across the workforce. In most countries in Europe, minimum wages cover 5–8% of the workforce. Much of the debate on minimum wages in the UK involves figures of approximately £3 to £4.50 per hour. Approximately one quarter of workers in Britain earn less than £4 per hour. Thus it is likely that a minimum wage in the UK will cover many more workers than in Europe. The implications of its introduction will therefore be more wide ranging.

Clearly, the crucial issues involved in the introduction of a minimum wage concern the level at which it will be set, the time-scale for its introduction and the general level of economic growth in the economy.

Gwen Coates *is a Senior Lecturer at Staffordshire University Business School and one of the editors of* Business Review.

Source: *Business Review*, November 1997

Think about it

- Read the article about the minimum wage.
- Do you think that a statutory minimum wage harms the competitiveness of the UK, as the Conservative Government under John Major argued when it refused to sign the Social Charter of the Maastricht Agreement in 1991?

Mobility of labour Immobility of labour may be occupational or geographical (see page 222). The government's main effort is directed towards occupational immobility, principally through the work of the Department for Education and Employment. This includes

- providing information through the nationwide network of Jobcentres and the more specialised Professional and Executive Register
- providing training through a wide range of schemes including retraining for those out of work.

Your career opportunities?

There are special programmes aimed at opening up opportunities for you to travel, study and/or gain work experience in another European Union member state. Under EU rules qualifications gained in one country must, in general, be recognised in another. It is also your right to receive the same job opportunities, terms and conditions of employment, or to set up a business anywhere in the EU. Help is also given to small independent companies and businesses which would like to sell their products in other countries. On a personal level, EU health and safety rules protect you from hazards in the workplace, such as excessive noise, exposure to dangerous substances or prolonged work at computer screens.

Source: *The European Union – a guide for students and teachers* (Office of the European Parliament and the Representative of the European Commission in the United Kingdom, 1998)

Think about it

The above extract emphasises the commitment of the European Union to equal training and career opportunities for the citizens of all member states.

- How far do you think these measures will go towards
  - increasing the mobility of labour
  - equalising wage rates throughout Europe?

Working conditions Mobility of labour is not the only issue that has attracted the government's attention, though in other areas the government's interest is more social or political than economic. The Employment Protection (Consolidation) Act 1978 requires that most employees must receive written details of their terms of employment, gives protection against unfair dismissal, and provides for the legal right to organise trade unions. Discrimination between employees or potential employees on the grounds of race, gender, disability or marital status is unlawful in respect of training, promotion, remuneration or any other employment matters.

Trade union law The Employment Acts of 1980 and 1982 govern trade union activity. As a result of the 1980 Act, the government was permitted to issue codes of practice on picketing, and it made funds available to finance postal ballots of members in case of disputes. The 1980 Act included some protection for workers not wishing to join a trade union. In 1982 this was extended so that it became unfair to dismiss anyone for not joining a union unless a secret ballot had shown that 80 per cent of the relevant workforce was in favour of compulsory union membership (known as a **closed shop**).

In 1984 the Trade Union Act further increased the rights of individual workers: they each have a right to vote in a secret ballot for members of their executive, and to vote on the same basis before a strike is called or other industrial action taken.

Disputes The final involvement of the government is assistance in the resolution of industrial disputes. The extent of government activity in this matter is a political decision. Since 1979, the government has left it to the Advisory, Conciliation and Arbitration Service (ACAS) to mediate in disputes, either when ACAS feels it has a contribution to make or at the request of the parties involved.

Other factor incomes: interest, profits and rent

Producing goods and services is made very much easier by using machinery and equipment. This can be bought with income saved from one period and not spent during that period. A firm or an individual who forgoes consumption may receive a reward for his or her savings in the form of **interest**. The person or firm who uses those savings (whether they are their own or someone else's) for productive purposes is taking a risk that their project may be a failure. The reward for such risk-taking is profit.

In the next two sections we look at the nature, determination and importance of interest and profits. Then, in the final section of this unit, we turn to a further aspect of the theory of rent: the payment made for the use of land.

Interest

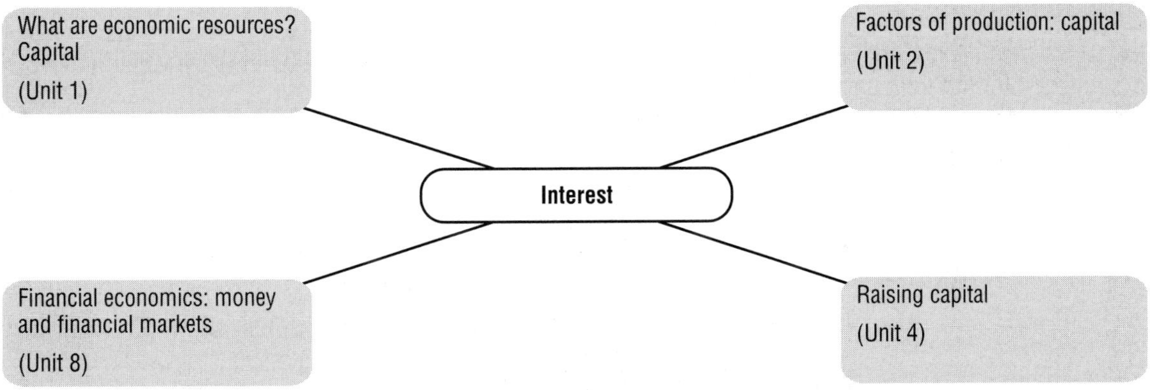

What are economic resources? Capital (Unit 1)

Factors of production: capital (Unit 2)

Interest

Financial economics: money and financial markets (Unit 8)

Raising capital (Unit 4)

Interest is the payment made for the use of someone else's money. If the payment is to be regarded purely as interest there should be no risk involved for the lender. Where there is a risk of default, part of the payment should be regarded as profit – this is the reward for enterprise or risk-taking. In practice, it is difficult to disentangle the two components. What is perhaps of more importance is to consider the factors which influence the rate that will have to be paid on a particular loan. These factors include the following.

Degree of risk The rate of interest that is paid for a loan will to some extent reflect the degree of risk involved. The bank will probably lend money to companies such as ICI or Marks & Spencer at a lower rate than it would charge to personal borrowers, because there is less risk of those companies defaulting on payment. If you wish to borrow money to buy a car, the rate that you pay will vary according to the source of the loan. A credit company or finance house (see Unit 8) will normally charge a higher rate than one of the high-street banks. The justification for this is that the finance house pays a higher rate to its depositors because, in theory, the depositors are taking a greater risk. (In practice this is not likely – many finance houses are subsidiaries of the banks anyway.)

The period of the loan The return that depositors receive on their money or the interest that borrowers have to pay will also reflect the time for which the loan is arranged: the shorter the period of the loan, the lower the rate of interest. Money lent to **discount houses** 'at call and short notice', for example, will command a lower rate of interest than the money advanced to the government for 91 days against **Treasury bills** (see Unit 8). Local authorities are frequent borrowers and offer depositors a range of different rates of interest according to the length of the loan, paying more for a long-term loan than for a short-term loan. The extra reward is compensation to the depositor for the loss of liquidity over a longer period. (The more easily an asset can be turned into cash, the more liquid it is said to be.)

Determining the rate of interest

A glance at the financial columns of a newspaper will indicate the prevailing rates of interest on different kinds of loan. It will normally be clear how those rates are related both to risk and to the loss of liquidity.

Something to do

- From the financial columns of a newspaper such as the *Financial Times*, find out the current rates of interest for different types of loans.
- Write notes analysing how far you think these relate to risk and liquidity.

We must now consider the factors determining the rate prevailing in a particular market at a particular time. There are two theories of the rate of interest to consider.

- The **loanable funds** theory stresses the supply of funds and the demand for them in a particular market.
- The Keynesian **liquidity preference** theory concentrates on the demand or preference of individuals and institutions to hold their assets as money rather than in any other form.

At any one time there will be a large number of different rates of interest. However, we assume here that there is just one rate and we consider how that rate is determined.

The loanable funds theory The loanable funds theory examines the rate of interest in the same way that we analysed other markets in Unit 5, by looking at the demand for funds and the supply of funds.

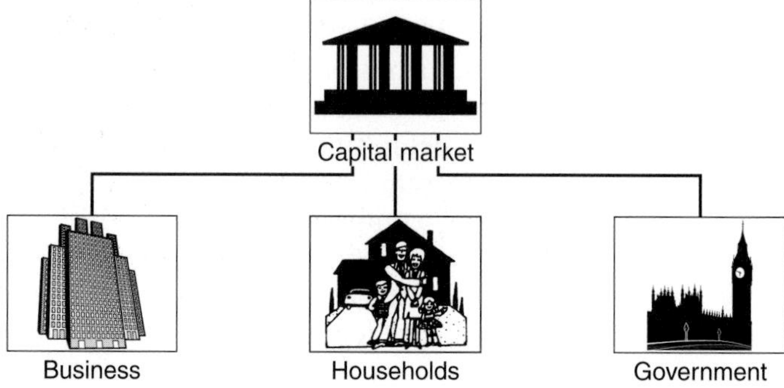

Fig. 6.6 The capital market and the demand for funds

<u>The demand for funds</u> Demand for funds comes from three main directions: business organisations, private individuals and the government. To some extent each group provides some of its own funds and need not enter the capital market to acquire them. A company may finance all of its current investment out of past profits; an individual may buy a new car out of his or her past savings. But frequently each group will resort to the **capital market.**

- **Business borrowing:** A company's demand for capital depends on its prospects of using the funds profitably. It will therefore estimate the likely trend of costs and revenue associated with a projected investment and establish the likely profit. If this is greater than the prevailing rate of interest, then the investment is likely to go ahead. If it is smaller, however, the project will probably be deferred. Accordingly, one of the main determinants of the demand for funds is the rate of interest: a reduction in the rate causing an extension of demand.

  The emphasis on the expectations of the company reminds us that the demand for capital is a derived demand (see page 218), however, and, while changes in the rate of interest may cause extensions or contractions in demand, changes in the underlying conditions of the economy will cause shifts in the demand schedule. In general, a very active economy will raise entrepreneurs' expectations and move the demand curve for funds to the right, while a depressed economy with many thousands unemployed will cause the demand curve for funds to move to the left. Indeed, such influences may be more important in determining the level of demand for funds than the price of borrowing. This is particularly so where the anticipated level of profits is high in relation to the rate of interest, since a modest change in the interest rate will not make much difference to the overall prospects of the project.
- **Personal borrowing:** Personal demands for capital resources may be divided into two categories: the demand for funds to finance house purchase, and the demand for funds to finance the purchase of consumer durable goods, especially cars. In the first case, there is little indication that the rate of interest is a major determinant of the demand for funds – the level of income, the shortage of rented accommodation, and the price of houses are far more important. In the second instance, the level of interest rates is more important, but other conditions relating to credit agreements, such as the level of the initial deposit and the period allowed for repayments, are equally significant.
- **Government borrowing:** The government enters the capital market as a borrower when it cannot raise enough through taxation to meet its capital expenditure. The factors governing public expenditure are very complicated and may only loosely be related to economic conditions. The building of hospitals or schools, for example, is not something that can be dictated by ordinary economic criteria, although it is safe to say that the government endeavours to borrow most heavily when the interest rate is low.

<u>The supply of funds</u> The immediate sources of loanable funds are the institutions mentioned in Unit 8, but, as we shall see, they derive their resources in much smaller instalments from business organisations and members of the public.

- One of the factors that determine the supply of funds will be the reward offered for forgoing liquidity – the rate of interest itself. The higher the rate of interest, the greater the supply of loanable funds.

  In practice, slight changes in the rate of interest are unlikely to cause much change in the supply of funds. Few savers react to an increase in interest rates by saying 'Now that the rate is 9 per cent instead of 8 per cent we will save more.' Much greater changes in the rate would be necessary to induce such a response. (Of course, where the relative rates obtainable in different markets change, savers may switch their savings from one area to another.) Some people may even respond to an increase in interest rates by reducing their savings, since they can earn the same amount from a smaller deposit.
- More important than the interest rate is the level of individual and national income. Wealthy societies and individuals have more opportunity for saving, and within any community it is the wealthy who are responsible for the bulk of saving.
- The institutional framework can also influence the supply of funds. We may interpret this in its broadest sense to include the nature of society itself. If it is prone to political upheaval, savings will tend to be low, since no one will risk leaving money in institutions that may be subject to political dispute. In a society like the UK, with a large number of institutions specially geared to encourage savings, the supply of loanable funds is likely to be greater than in a society whose capital market and financial institutions are rudimentary.
- Other factors of importance are the risks and liquidity factors (see pages 233–235), and the possibility of inflation. The latter is considered more fully in Unit 12. Here we may note that if the rate of interest is 5 per cent, a person depositing £100 for one year will receive £105 at the end of the year, but is worse off in real terms if prices have risen by 10 per cent during the year. This is because the purchasing power of the money has been reduced by this amount. In such circumstances savers may seek alternative outlets for their funds.

<u>The equilibrium rate of interest</u> When the demand and supply curves for loanable funds have been established, we can find the **equilibrium rate of interest** at the point of intersection of the two curves. At this point, savings (the supply of funds) and investment (the demand for funds) will be equal and the market will be in equilibrium.

If borrowers change their view of things, the demand curve will shift and, as in other markets, a new equilibrium price (rate of interest) will be established. The supply curve will move if savers take a different view.

In practice, there may be imperfections in the market, which prevent it working completely smoothly. An important factor is government influence. For reasons of economic policy the government may want to see interest rates move up or down. While interest rates in the UK are set by the Bank of England, the government can use its influence as a major borrower, active in the financial markets, to help achieve this objective. However, this tends to confirm the operation of forces of demand and supply: when funds are plentiful, interest rates tend to fall; when funds are scarce in relation to demand, rates rise.

The basic 'market' explanation of interest rates concentrates perhaps too much on price – on the rate of interest as a determinant of the demand for and supply of funds, rather than the outcome of the interaction of demand and supply. There is an alternative approach: the liquidity preference theory.

The liquidity preference theory

While the loanable funds theory emphasises the importance of demand for and supply of funds, it says nothing about the overall supply of money in the economy. The economist John Maynard Keynes was primarily interested in the control of the cycles of economic activity, which were features of nineteenth- and early twentieth-century capitalist economies. In the course of his work, which is more closely examined in Unit 11, he developed his own theory of interest that relates the supply of money to the wish to hold it. Unlike the loanable funds theory, this does not bring savings and investment into equilibrium.

<u>The supply of money</u> The supply of money may be regarded as fixed at any one time. It is not a quantity that can easily be controlled by the authorities, for, as we shall see (Unit 8), the banks have considerable power to create credit. Keynes was primarily concerned with short-term policy, and changes in the supply of money in the short term may be disregarded.

<u>Liquidity preference – the desire to hold money</u> If the supply of money is fixed, then, according to this theory, the rate of interest will depend on the desire of the public and of business and financial organisations to hold their assets as cash.

> *Think about it*
>
> - Why might (a) private individuals and (b) business organisations want to hold their money as cash, perhaps in a current bank account, rather than invest it?

Fig. 6.7 The uses of cash

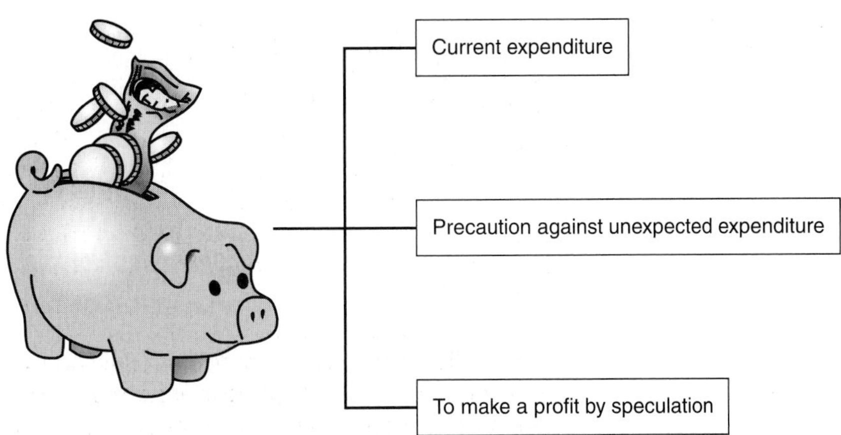

Keynes identified three motives for holding cash:

- **The transactions motive:** Most people receive their incomes either weekly or monthly. Since they do not spend all their money the moment they receive it, but spread expenditure over the period between paydays, they need to hold some income in money balances either in cash or in bank accounts. The average amount held in this way will depend partly on the frequency of paydays (the more frequent they are, the lower the average holding of cash) and partly on the level of income of the individual (the wealthy generally hold more than the poor). In addition, all kinds of businesses will need to hold some cash assets to meet their day-to-day commitments. In the case of both individuals and businesses, the balance that is held for transaction purposes is likely to be fairly stable, each of them knowing their probable commitments for the next few weeks and holding cash accordingly.
- **The precautionary motive:** The careful individual and the prudent business will hold a further reserve of cash to meet irregular or unexpected expenditure. A sudden rise in the cost of raw materials might otherwise find a business short of cash, and an individual might be somewhat embarrassed by an expensive repair to their car. Once again, however, the amount held in the form of money will probably be fairly stable and will depend mainly on the level of income. In many respects, in fact, we can regard the precautionary motive as part of the transactions motive. Beyond holding cash for the type of reasons cited above, it might be sensible for firms and individuals to invest their money to earn a return, and the majority of them do so.
- **The speculative motive:** Wealthy individuals and many financial institutions have a further reason for holding assets in the form of cash – it is possible to make profits by speculating on the price movements of (mainly) government bonds (see below).

Government bonds

Government bonds, or **gilt-edged securities**, are issued in £100 units at a fixed rate of interest. Thus the owner of a £100 bond issued at 5 per cent knows that each year £5 will be received. We can assume that when the bond was issued, the market rate of interest was 5 per cent because a lower rate would not have attracted enough buyers and 5 per cent was sufficient to raise the necessary money.

If the market rate of interest rises to 10 per cent and the holder now wants to sell the £100 5-per-cent bond, they will only receive £50 for it – the amount that would yield the purchaser 10 per cent (£5 ÷ £50 × 100%), the equivalent of the new market rate of interest. No one would pay £100 for the bond to earn £5 when they could buy a new bond and earn £10.

If the market rate falls below 5 per cent, however, the price of the bond will rise above £100. The basic formula for establishing the price is:

$$\text{market price} = £100 \times \frac{\text{original rate of interest}}{\text{market rate of interest}}$$

So, if the market rate of interest fell to 3 per cent, the price of the bond would be £166.66. Notice that the rate of interest and the price of bonds move in opposite directions.

It now becomes clear why cash may be held for speculative purposes. If the market rate of interest is low, the price of bonds will be high and speculators will want to hold cash in anticipation of a rise in interest rates, which will bring down the price of bonds. When this happens, speculators will buy bonds, reducing their cash holdings and receiving a greater yield on their bonds because they have bought at lower prices. At high rates, most of their cash is tied up in the form of bonds that they hope to sell when interest rates fall and the price of bonds rises. For this reason the liquidity preference curve (L) slopes downwards in Figure 6.8. It levels at a very low rate of interest since it is unlikely that speculators would allow the rate to fall to zero before demanding extra cash for speculative purposes, or that anyone would be willing to part with the liquidity unless some interest were payable. In Figure 6.8, if the supply of money is fixed at OM, the equilibrium rate of interest would be OA. An increase in the money supply to ON reduces interest to OB. Changes also occur as a result of changes in tastes or income distribution, and these cause the liquidity preference schedule to move.

Fig. 6.8 Liquidity preference

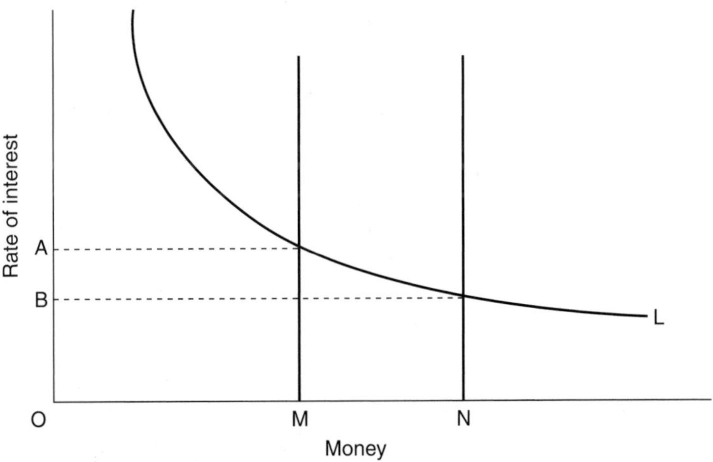

The chief significance of the liquidity preference theory of interest is that it shows quite clearly how the authorities can influence rates by altering the supply of money, a topic to which we return in Unit 10.

Something to do

- Look in the financial columns of a daily newspaper such as *The Times*, *Financial Times* or *Daily Telegraph* and find out the current prices of government bonds.
- Construct a table showing the original prices of the bonds, their current prices and the prevailing bank rate (or market rate of interest).
- Track the changes in the prices of bonds and interest rates over time. Identify and explain any correlation between these.

Profits

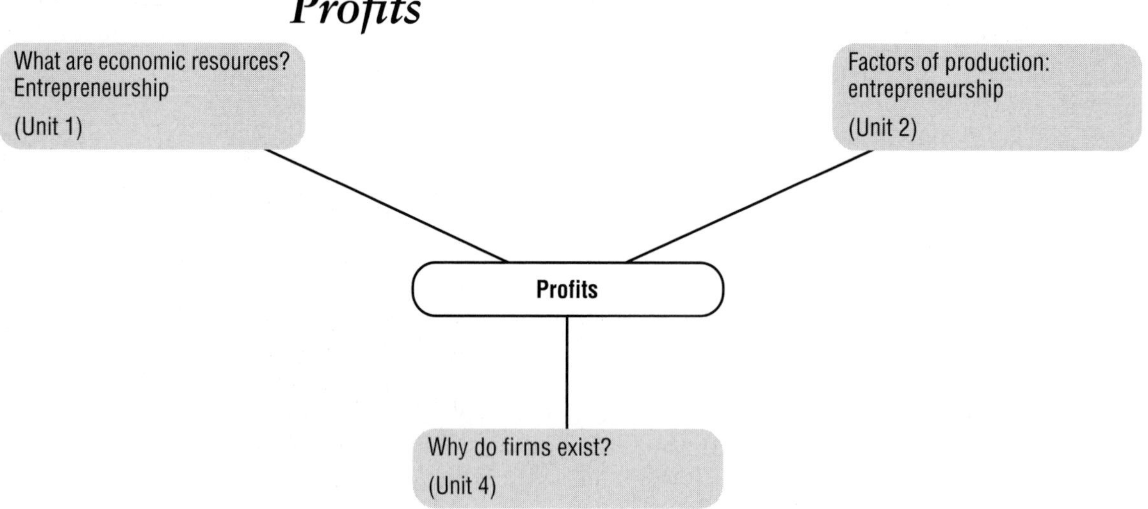

We noted on page 229 that the interest paid to some investors incorporates an element of profit, rewarding the investor not for the loss of liquidity but for the risk taken that the investor might lose the money altogether. That risk is the possibility embodied in any industrial or commercial project that it will fail for any one of a number of reasons, including the following:

- The managers of the enterprise may have misjudged the market and, by the time their product is on the market, tastes and the pattern of demand may have changed in favour of something else. Clearly, such risks will be greater in, say, the fashion industry than in many branches of the food industry; but the wise manufacturer, whatever his or her field, will make a careful survey of the likely market before committing to produce the goods for it.
- In many industries it will be some years before a particular investment pays for itself. There is always the possibility in such cases that changes in technology will render the original investment obsolete, at considerable cost to the company concerned.
- Social and political changes may reduce the chances of profit or, if the business were to be nationalised or re-nationalised, eliminate them altogether.

During the industrial revolution, the risk of loss through such cases was borne by the entrepreneur. Today it is largely borne by the holders of ordinary shares in a limited company, or partners or sole proprietors in smaller businesses. As compensation for this risk or uncertainty, they expect an element of profit to be included in their income. Profit, though, is not only the reward of risk-taking: it may also be regarded as the reward for enterprise – for identifying an opportunity and taking advantage of it. It is this rather than the risk that explains the relatively high profits that accrue to the developers of some fairly simple inventions. (Other inventors, of course, whose inventions are less commercial, die penniless.)

Fig. 6.9 Revenue, costs and profit

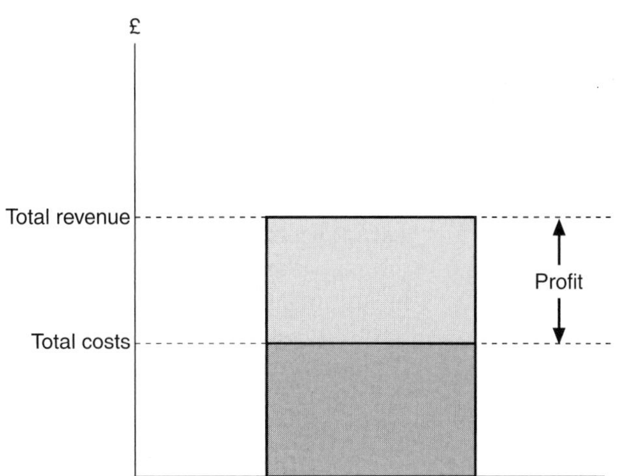

The nature of profit

Although profit is a reward to one of the factors of production, it differs in several respects from the income payable to the other factors:

- Profit is a residual reward payable to the entrepreneur – in other words, profit is what remains after all the other costs of the business have been met. Whereas labour can normally be certain of its weekly wage or monthly salary, and the bond holder can be fairly certain of his or her interest, there is no guarantee that the ordinary shareholder will receive a dividend. There is no contractual obligation on the part of a company to pay a dividend.
- It may sometimes be impossible for the company to pay a dividend if profits are negative and loss is incurred. While it is impossible not to pay wages to employees, the company may survive for some time without actually making a profit, as we saw in Unit 5.
- Although profit, in an accounting sense, is a residual payment to capital, the economist regards it as a cost that has to be met if the firm is to stay in business. While the firm may survive one year and perhaps two without making a profit, it will in the long run go out of business if it cannot pay a dividend to its shareholders.
- Just as interest sometimes embodies an element of profit, the payment that is itself referred to as profit may, especially in the small business, have several components. Consider the case of the local grocer who, at the end of the year, having paid all his bills and the wages of the staff, has a surplus of £15 000. To describe this all as profit is to exaggerate the extra payment the grocer is receiving for enterprise or risk-taking. The following modifications must be made:
  - The entrepreneur could probably have earned £10 000 per year in some other occupation. This opportunity cost should be set against the £15 000 before a realistic assessment of profits can be made.
  - The money that the entrepreneur has invested in the business could have earned an income in the form of pure interest if it had been invested in gilt-edged securities.

The role of profits

Traditionally, profits have particular functions in the economy:

- **Profit encourages risk-taking:** If there were no extra reward for enterprise or risk-taking, no one would invest in anything but pure interest-yielding stock. The risk inherent in investing in plant and machinery to meet future demand – which might or might not materialise – must be balanced by the prospect of a return higher than that available on risk-free investment. It is the prospect of this higher return, or profit, that gives rise to the succession of large and small businesses, each making its own contribution to the growth and development of the economy.
- **Profit serves as a guide to resource allocation:** The fact that profit may be either positive or negative allows it to serve as a useful guide to the allocation of resources. Where an industry is expanding to meet an increase in demand, its profits are likely to be buoyant and the funds necessary for the further development will be easily acquired. Often this demand will not necessitate the entry of new firms but simply the expansion of existing ones. As more capital is employed, seeking a share in the profits available in the industry, so extra units of other factors of production may be employed. On the other hand, unprofitable firms will find it difficult to attract extra capital, or even to renew their existing capital equipment, and will therefore release resources as they decline. It needs no single decision-making body to decide where funds should be allocated or when they should be withdrawn: the votes of consumers as expressed by their purchases will determine this.

Think about it

- Should the profit motive serve as a guide to resource allocation in the privatised transport industry?
- What about utilities such as gas, electricity and water?

The profit motive is not infallible in allocating resources. There are many activities in which it is almost impossible for private capital to make a profit and operate on a scale large enough to meet the public's requirements. In these circumstances, the industry may be left in private hands but receive a subsidy from the government – this is the case with shipbuilding in some countries. More frequently, as in the case of public services such as road-building, they are taken over by the State. On the other hand, the profits in many firms, and the resources employed in those firms, are excessive because those firms do not have to meet all the costs of production. The social costs of environmental pollution, for example, fall on all taxpayers and business ratepayers, not solely on the consumers or manufacturers.

- **Profits may be a measure of efficiency:** In competitive industries, profits may be regarded as a sign of efficiency, since profits will be larger if costs are kept to a minimum. But we must be wary of assuming that the firms making the largest profits (however measured) are necessarily the most efficient. They may be in fairly strong monopolistic positions or they may be members of a cartel able to cover their inefficiency by charging exorbitant prices.

Where do profits go?

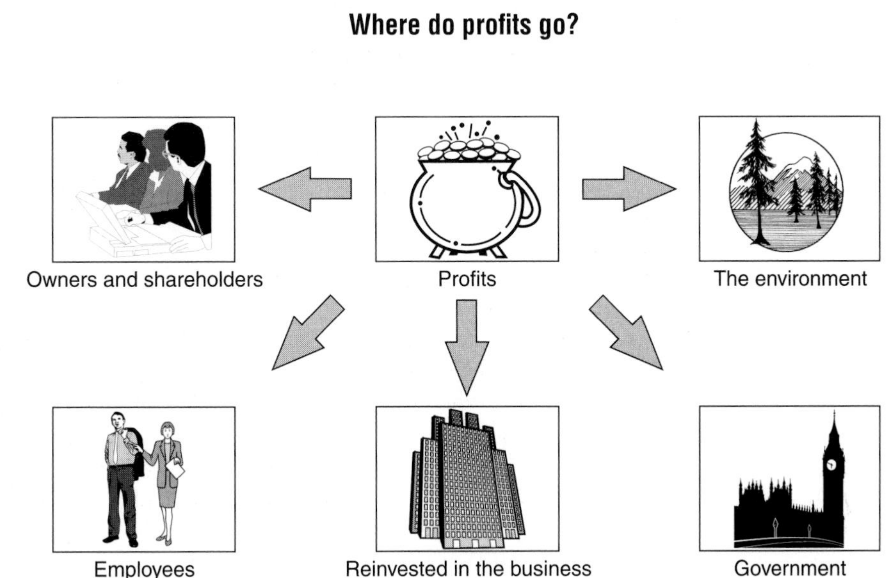

The profits of a business can be distributed in several ways:

- Some will go to the owners of the business, as a reward for investing their money.
- Some may be shared among employees, perhaps as bonuses or profit-related payments, as a reward for their efforts and labour.
- Some may be reinvested in the business to boost the success of the business in the future.
- The government will take a share of the profits in taxes.
- The business may use some of its profits to invest in the environment or the local community.

Some failings of profit-motivated capitalism

While profit may perform the functions mentioned above, there are a number of problems associated with a capitalist system based on the profit motive. These include the following:

- A clear weakness of an economy dependent on its profits is that only those goods or services that yield a profit will be available.
- Some services regarded as essential to everyone in a society whatever their income, medical care for example, may be too expensive for some consumers if delivered and charged for on a profit-based formula.
- Other services, such as defence and law enforcement, would not be provided at all because they cannot be broken down into individual units. These are known as 'public goods'.
- The unrestricted pursuit of profit may result in an undue emphasis on goods such as tobacco and alcohol at the expense of others such as education.
- The pursuit of private profit may generate long-term social costs, for example pollution, not borne by the firms who cause them.

It is for such reasons that the government intervenes, through taxation or in other ways, to try and ensure that essential services are provided even if they are unprofitable.

The rent of land

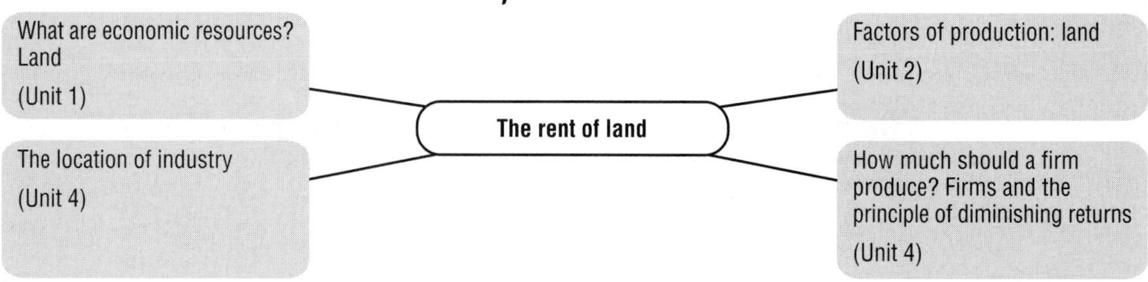

The reward earned by the factor land, like that earned by labour and capital, depends on the conditions of supply and demand. We have already examined the concept of economic rent as a surplus payment to any factor of production (see page 219). In order to distinguish the rent of land from economic rent, we call it **commercial rent.**

David Ricardo, who developed the early theory of economic rent, regarded it as a surplus in much the same way as we now regard economic rent. This was because, in common with his contemporaries, he believed that the value of a product depended on the labour embodied in it and on nothing else. Moreover, the supply of agricultural land was fixed and had virtually no other use. Accordingly, anyone who received rent for land was receiving a payment which had not been earned and which was only received because land was in short supply. It was regarded as 'pure rent'.

David Ricardo (1772–1823)

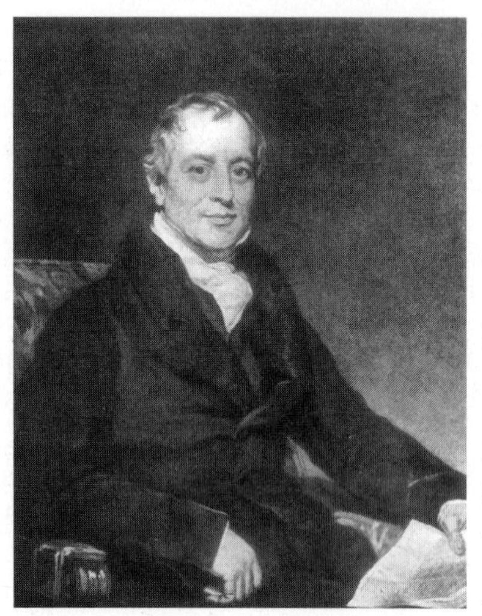

David Ricardo was born in London and attended schools in England and Holland. When he was fourteen, he joined his father's brokerage house, where he was able to make a fortune on the stock market.

His first published work on economics, *The High Price of Bullion, a Proof of the Depreciation of Bank Notes*, developed out of letters to the *Morning Chronicle*. It was about the depreciation of paper currency, which was still not totally trusted some 70 years after the South Sea Bubble scandal rocked the British economy. In it, Ricardo argued for basing the value of money on metal. This brought him into contact with such influential figures in the realms of philosophy and economics as Thomas Malthus, James Mill and Jeremy Bentham.

His major work, *Principles of Political Economy and Taxation*, published in 1817, applied deductive logic to an analysis of monetary principles. He believed that increases in the population would lead to a shortage of productive land and developed a theory of rent based on the relative productivity of land. He also developed a labour theory of value in which wages are based on the price of food, which is itself determined by the cost of production, including labour. Thus the cost of labour determines value.

Ricardo entered Parliament in 1819 as member for Portarlington. As an MP, he argued for parliamentary reform, voting rights and old age pensions, as well as economic and monetary issues, until his death on his estate in Gloucestershire.

Something to do

- Find out about the South Sea Bubble.

It became apparent during the late eighteenth and early nineteenth centuries that, as more and more land was brought into cultivation to meet the demand for wheat, the owners of the most suitable land were able to increase the rent they charged to farmers. The reason for this was that the price of wheat was determined by the cost of producing it on the least suitable land and the increasing demand for wheat. No one would farm the land if they could not at least cover their costs. The farmers on the most suitable land were then making very high profits, not because they were better farmers but because they happened to be farming on the most fertile land. These high profits Ricardo regarded as being attributable to 'the original and indestructible properties of the soil' and it was these that the landlord was able to absorb in rent.

Under these conditions rents are clearly determined by the price of the product – the higher the price of wheat, the higher the rent chargeable. But the payment of rent also depends on the shortage of land. Early settlers in America and Australia paid no rent because there was no shortage of land. This is very different from the position on land for housing purposes in the UK today. Landowners can deliberately withhold land from the market, waiting for the price to rise, and by contributing to the shortage ensure that rents rise in the face of heavy demand. When the demand for housing is highest the price of land is highest, and thus rents in London are higher than those in less populated places such as Devon. Landlords in London are therefore able to command a high rent because of the shortage of land and accommodation there.

Although rents in general seem to be determined by demand, it is also possible to regard them as determining price. A new business taking a site in London will have to include the rent paid as part of total costs and it will be embodied in the prices charged for the products of the business. Similarly, a landowner will be faced with a number of alternative outlets for his or her funds and will only invest these funds in property if he or she can earn at least as much from it as in the best alternative occupation. So the cost that the proprietor has to meet will be at least as high as the transfer earnings (see page 220) of the landowner.

We have seen that, with the possible exception of profit, where special circumstances apply, the principles of demand and supply are important in determining the level of rewards to individual factors of production. In the case of labour, we linked the demand for the factor to its marginal product: we saw that there is no point in paying £200 per week to someone who adds only £150 to the week's revenue. This is equally true of the other factors of production: they will be employed only if their contribution to output more than covers their costs.

However, if factors of production are to be employed at all, they will have to be paid for. This requires the existence of money, which we consider in Unit 8. First, though, we conclude our examination of markets by looking at market failure (Unit 7).

7 Market efficiency and market failure

Introduction: market forces and market intervention

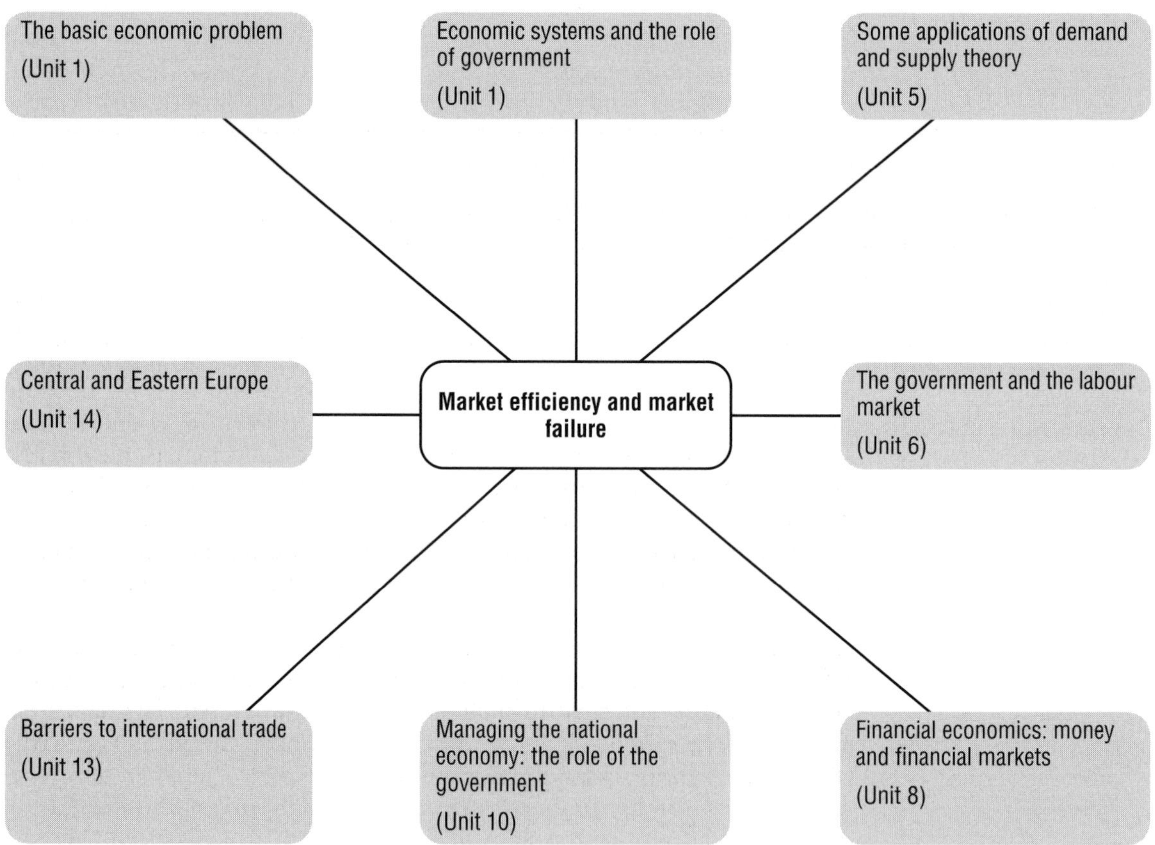

We have seen that a market is a structure that brings people and organisations together in order to buy and sell goods and services. Through the operation of the price system, a market allows resources to be allocated, and goods and services to be produced and distributed in accordance with the market forces of demand and supply.

This raises the question: are markets the most efficient way of solving the key questions of allocation, production and distribution? In Unit 1 (see pages 16–20), we posed three key questions:

- What should society produce and how should resources be allocated?
- How should goods and services be produced?
- Who should get the goods and services that are produced?

If market forces are unable to provide the best solution to these questions, we must ask: why not? And: what should be done to improve the situation?

Think about it

- From what you have read about markets so far, do you think that leaving everything to market forces is the most efficient way for society to solve the problems of the allocation, production and distribution of resources?
- Why?/Why not?

This takes us out of the strict objective bounds of **positive economics** (the facts and data that can be measured, recorded and checked) into the subjective realms of **normative economics** (what should be done under particular circumstances). (See Unit 1.) In this unit, we discuss whether a market system is the best way of solving these problems, or whether there should be an element of control and direction in the operation of markets. If a market *is* the best way of solving the allocation, production and distribution problems, then the market can be said to be efficient. If, however, it is felt that in order to obtain the greatest benefit to society some element of control is required, the market can be said to have failed. This in itself involves normative decisions, such as

- what is the greatest benefit to society?
- who decides?
- how can it be measured?

In particular, we look at the following topics:

- what makes a market efficient
- why markets fail
- the externalities, including pollution and the need for conservation, that may give rise to the need for intervention in markets
- how cost–benefit analysis enables objective decisions to be taken
- the role of the government.

Market efficiency

If the purpose of production is to meet society's demand for goods and services, and markets exist to bring people and organisations together in order to buy and sell those goods and services in accordance with the forces of demand and supply, then it would seem that a market can be considered efficient if everyone who has an effective demand (see page 18) for a particular product is able to satisfy their demand in the market. This will be achieved through the operation of the price system and the principle of marginal utility (see Unit 3).

It follows from this that an efficient market economy is one in which resources are allocated, and goods and services produced and distributed in such a way that any change would result in someone being worse off. This is known as **equity**, or the equal distribution of goods and services between members of society.

Fig. 7.1 Equity

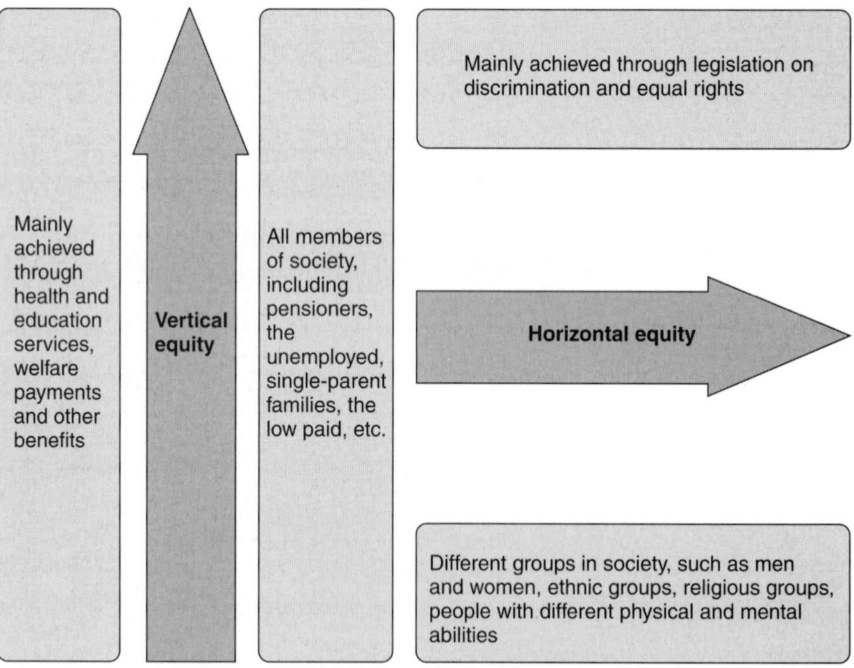

- **Vertical equity** is the equal distribution of goods and services (including incomes and wealth) between people whose abilities to contribute to and obtain goods and services (including incomes and wealth) from the economy are different.
- **Horizontal equity** is the equal distribution of goods and services (including incomes and wealth) between people whose abilities to contribute to the economy are the same but whose abilities to obtain goods and services (including incomes and wealth) from the economy are different.

So vertical equity is concerned with inequalities in the distribution of essential goods and services *due to inequalities in income or wealth*. One of the government's economic objectives is to correct this failure of the market to satisfy everyone's needs by redistributing income through raising taxes and making welfare payments such as unemployment benefits, winter fuel payments to old age pensioners, and payments to single parents, as well as providing services such as health and education.

Horizontal equity, on the other hand, is concerned with inequalities in the distribution of essential goods and services and the ability to obtain these *due to unequal treatment*, including employment opportunities, through discrimination of race, gender or disability. The government attempts to correct such inequalities through legal statutes – for example, the Sex Discrimination Act 1975 or the Disability Discrimination Act 1999.

Think about it

Most people in modern Western society accept that horizontal equity in an economy is right. However, many find some attempts at vertical equity less desirable, especially when their own spending power is reduced through higher taxes so that others in society may benefit. For example, every taxpayer, whether or not they have children, pays for the State to provide primary and secondary education which is enjoyed only (at least, directly) by those with children of school age; and single people and married couples without children contribute through taxation to the child benefit payments that are made to families with children. In this way there is a measure of redistribution of income in society.

- How many other forms of income redistribution can you think of?
- Do you think that redistributing income in this way, from the 'haves' to the 'have nots', is right or fair?
- How far do you think the principle of income redistribution should be carried?

Efficiency in the allocation of resources in an economy is therefore achieved when the maximum possible satisfaction, or utility, is obtained by society as a whole. This involves allocative efficiency, productive or technical efficiency and economic efficiency.

- **Allocative efficiency** exists where the combination of all goods and services produced in an economy provides the greatest possible utility for society as a whole (that is, for every member of society), and no additional *overall* gain in utility can be obtained by distributing goods and services differently (in other words, no one can become better off without someone else becoming worse off and resulting in a loss of total utility for society as a whole).
- **Productive** or **technical efficiency** exists where the factors of production are allocated in such a way as to provide the maximum possible output of the goods and services wanted by society for the minimum possible cost in terms of usage of those factors of production. (The concept of productive efficiency also applies to the individual firm – see Unit 4.)
- **Economic efficiency** exists where the combination of goods and services that is produced from the scarce resources available to a society is that which provides the maximum possible utility for that society.

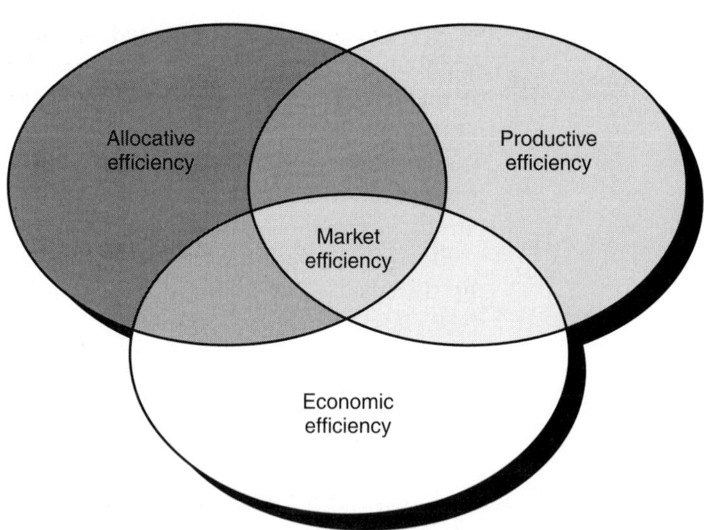

Fig. 7.2 Allocative, productive and economic efficiency

Something to do

- In Unit 1, we saw that the maximum production of different types of goods from the same resources can be shown on a production possibility curve (see pages 31–32). Write notes explaining how the position of an economy's production on the production possibility curve may be influenced by and influence the allocative, productive and economic efficiency of that economy.

Efficiency and perfect competition

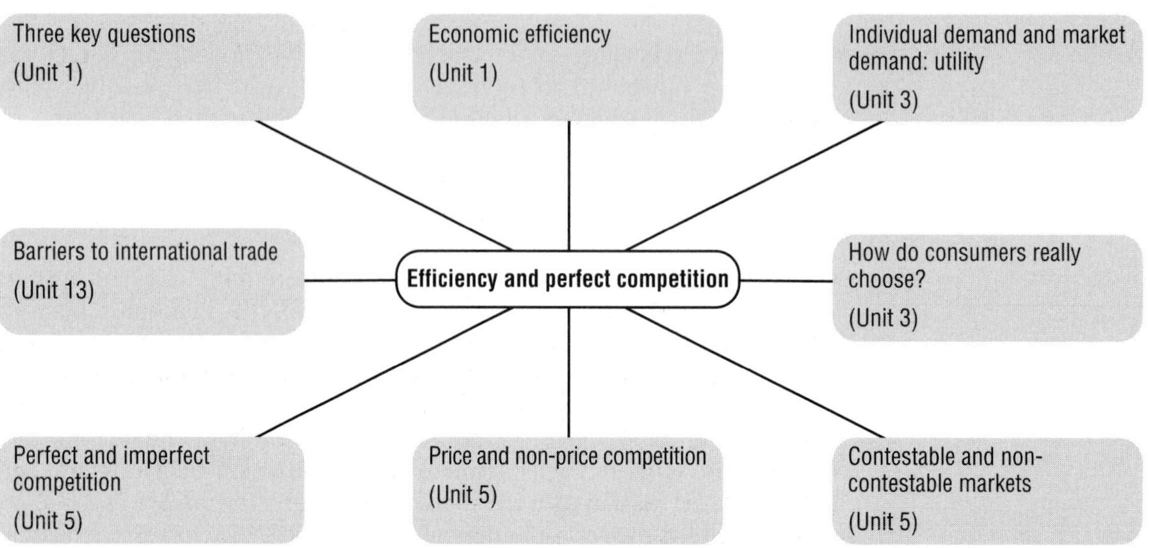

In a market economy, allocative efficiency can be achieved because consumers correlate their marginal utility for different goods and services to the prices of those goods and services, so that

$$\frac{\text{marginal utility of A (MUa)}}{\text{price A (Pa)}} = \frac{\text{MUb}}{\text{Pb}} = \frac{\text{MUn}}{\text{Pn}}$$

where n = the number of goods and services produced in an economy. This can be expressed

$$\frac{\text{MUa}}{\text{MUb}} = \frac{\text{Pa}}{\text{Pb}}$$

Complete allocative efficiency is, however, only possible in conditions of perfect competition (see Unit 5), since it is only under these conditions that consumers can maximise their utility. As there will be a single price consumers can pay for various goods and services, it follows that they will buy enough of a particular product to maximise their marginal utility from that product. For example, if some consumers in a society have a higher marginal utility for product A than others, they will be prepared to pay more for it. Those consumers with a lower marginal utility, on the other hand, will choose to spend their money on product B, where their marginal utility is higher. In effect, they will exchange product A for product B while retaining the same overall utility in society as a whole.

Similarly, in a market economy, suppliers combine scarce resources in order to produce the goods and services wanted by society. The proportion in which the different factors of production are combined depends on relative prices in the factor market, which are themselves determined by demand based on

- the price of the finished product
- the relative productivity of each factor.

Thus the quantity of each factor of production employed will be

$$\frac{\text{marginal physical product of factor A (MPPa)}}{\text{price of factor A (Pa)}} = \frac{\text{MPPb}}{\text{Pb}} = \frac{\text{MPPn}}{\text{Pn}}$$

and this can be expressed as

$$\frac{\text{MPPa}}{\text{MPPb}} = \frac{\text{Pa}}{\text{Pb}}$$

Again, in conditions of perfect competition, there will only be one price for a factor and it therefore follows that firms will combine factors of production in the proportion that will enable them to maximise profits. If the marginal physical product of a factor is higher in one type of production than another, demand for the factor in that type of production will be higher, pushing up the price of the factor. Firms in other types of production will then substitute other factors of production and the equilibrium of demand and supply for each factor of production will be maintained overall.

Efficiency and the allocation of resources

In Unit 5 (pages 197–201), we saw that firms in an industry make normal profits when price equals marginal cost (P = MC). It can now be seen that P = MC is also allocatively efficient. Since under conditions of perfect competition price is also equal to the marginal utility of consumers (P = MU), if the price of a product is higher than its marginal cost (P > MC), it will also be higher than the marginal utility of consumers (P > MU). In this case, consumers will buy less of the product, resulting in a fall in supply to meet the new level of demand. Resources no longer used in the production of that product will be allocated to the production of other goods and services (where P < MU), and the price of the product will fall until P = MU = MC once more.

Pareto efficiency

An efficient allocation of resources may be said to exist in an economy with a given set of consumer tastes, resources and technology, when it is impossible to make anyone in society better off by allocating resources differently without at the same time making someone worse off. This was the position argued by Vilfredo Pareto in his book *Manuel D'Economie Politique*, published in 1909, and such an allocation of resources is said to be **Pareto efficient.**

For example, a government, believing that people wanted CDs rather than books, may feel that society overall would be better off by reallocating resources from the production of books to the production of CDs. This would lead to a drop in the production of books, with a consequent increase in their price, and an increase in the supply of CDs, with a consequent drop in their price. However, while this would obviously make those members of society who wanted more CDs than books better off, since more CDs would be available at a lower price, members of society who still preferred books would find that there were fewer available and that they would have to pay more for them. They would therefore have been made worse off. In this way, the reallocation of resources between books and CDs would be inefficient, although some members of society would undoubtedly benefit.

Static and dynamic efficiency

However, any given set of consumer tastes, resources and technology will only exist in an economy at a specific point in time. Consumer tastes are constantly changing, as we saw in Unit 3. Technology also changes, enabling new ways of producing goods and increasing the productivity of factors of production. Any allocation of resources in response to consumer tastes, resources and technology applying at a particular time is therefore static and results in **static efficiency**, taking no account of changes in these. Obviously, true efficiency must take account of these changes, and respond to trends in these factors. Such efficiency in the allocation of resources is known as **dynamic efficiency**.

Think about it

- How might a tour operator, offering a selection of package and tailor-made European and worldwide holidays, apply the different types of efficiency described above in order to maximise profits?

Why do markets fail?

Since an efficient allocation of resources and production can be achieved through market efficiency in conditions of perfect competition, it may be asked: why do markets fail?

There are three principal reasons for **market failure**:

- Conditions of perfect competition may not exist.
- Some economic goods cannot be effectively priced in the market.
- There may be external benefits or costs.

Conditions of perfect competition may not exist

The conditions of perfect competition are discussed above and in Unit 5. Here we may note that it is only when there is perfect knowledge in a market, a condition of perfect competition, so that prices are at equilibrium, that P = MC (see page 199). The same applies to factor markets and to markets for goods and services. Since this is one of the criteria for market efficiency, its absence will lead to market failure.

Economic goods not priced in the market

Where a market system exists, the equilibrium price of a product is arrived at on the basis of demand and supply. However, this price is only a true equilibrium if utility from the product is only enjoyed by consumers who actually purchase the product. There are some goods and services, however, the enjoyment of which cannot be confined to a certain set of consumers who have paid for the privilege. For example, defence services are provided by the government for society as a whole out of taxation, since it would be impossible to provide defence purely for those who were prepared to pay for it and exclude others. Goods and services of this nature may be paid for by the government (out of taxation), by an institution such as a charity (out of donations or subscriptions), or by private organisations (for example, by sponsoring).

Fig. 7.3 Payment for goods and services not priced in the market

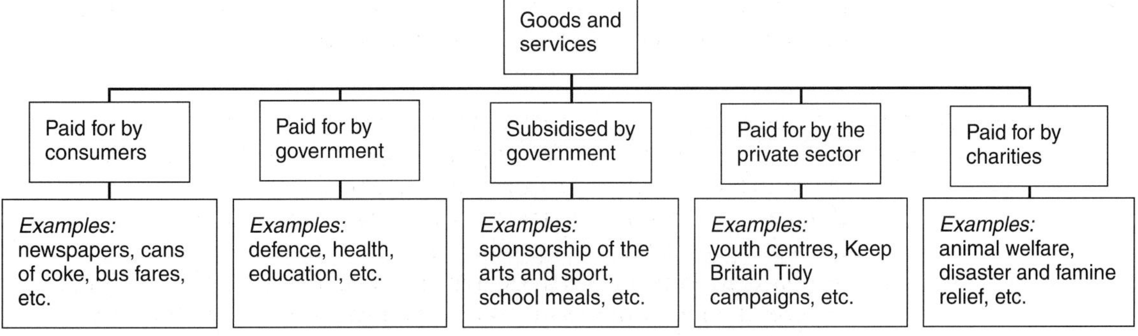

Something to do

The following are all economic goods that are not priced in a free market:
- food and medical supplies flown in to a country following a natural disaster such as an earthquake
- the National Health Service
- performances of the Royal Shakespeare Company.

- Identify the ways in which they are paid for, and who pays for them.
- What do you think would happen if they were not paid for in these ways?

Externalities

In Unit 1 we saw that the production of some goods and services involves costs that are borne not only by the supplier of those goods and services. For example, a cement factory may increase production by using a new chemical fuel. This will reduce its total costs. However, the burning of the chemical fuel may add to the pollution of the atmosphere, which is an increased cost to society.

Similarly, a householder may decide to increase their enjoyment of their home by growing a tall hedge around their garden, so ensuring their privacy. Buying and planting the hedging plants costs the householder money, but they believe that the increased utility they will obtain from their garden will be worth the cost. However, there may also be an external cost to their nextdoor neighbour, who may lose the benefit of the sun shining into *their* garden for a large part of the day.

Not all externalities are costs – they may equally be benefits. For example, a farmer may decide to grow crops without the use of artificial fertilisers, in order to maximise his profits by targeting the growing market for organic foods. However, the farmer's actions may have the added benefit of improving the habitat of birds and other wildlife which impacts on the enjoyment of the countryside by members of society.

Figure 7.4 illustrates how a single project involves both external costs and external benefits.

Fig. 7.4 Externalities associated with a new bypass

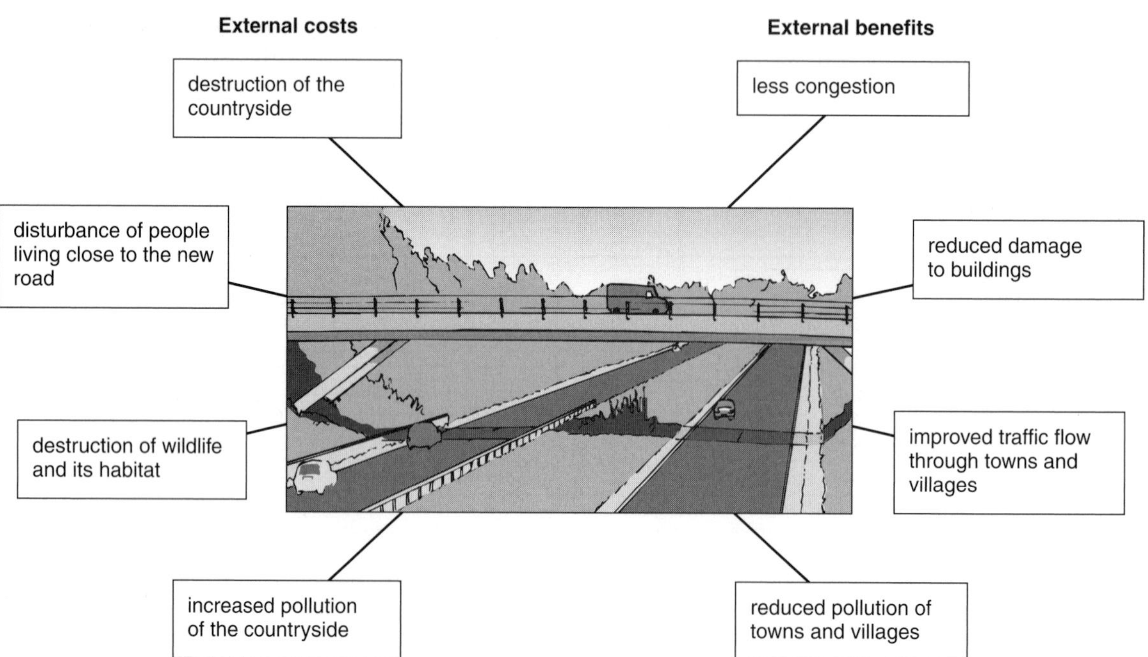

The effect of externalities

In order to assess the effect of externalities on allocative efficiency, we consider the case of the cement factory using a chemical fuel that increases pollution of the atmosphere. The pollution caused in this way is a cost of production; were the true costs of production to be borne by the factory it would have to pay the cost of converting the fuel, or screening emissions, so that it was rendered harmless. This additional cost would then be passed on to the factory's customers in the form of higher prices for the product and this would result in a reduction in demand for the factory's cement so that resources were reallocated to other types of production.

This is a clear instance of the distinction between private costs and social costs, which we examined in Unit 1 (see pages 34–36). Social costs are ***negative* externalities** in that they are not a direct cost to the firms producing the goods or services.

We may similarly distinguish between private benefits and social benefits.

- **Private benefits** are those benefits generated by the production of goods or services that accrue directly to the supplier or customer.
- **Social benefits** are those benefits generated by the production of goods and services that accrue to society as a whole. Like social costs, they may be by-products of the production process and expressed in qualitative rather than quantitative terms. Social benefits are ***positive* externalities.**

Since externalities introduce additional costs or benefits of production, they change the conditions of allocative efficiency described on page 245.

Where production involves external costs, the social marginal cost is added to the private marginal cost (PMC) to obtain the true marginal cost to society as a whole, which must equal the true price to society:

$$PMC + SMC = P$$

This is shown in Figure 7.5.

Fig. 7.5 Externalities causing over-production at the free-market price

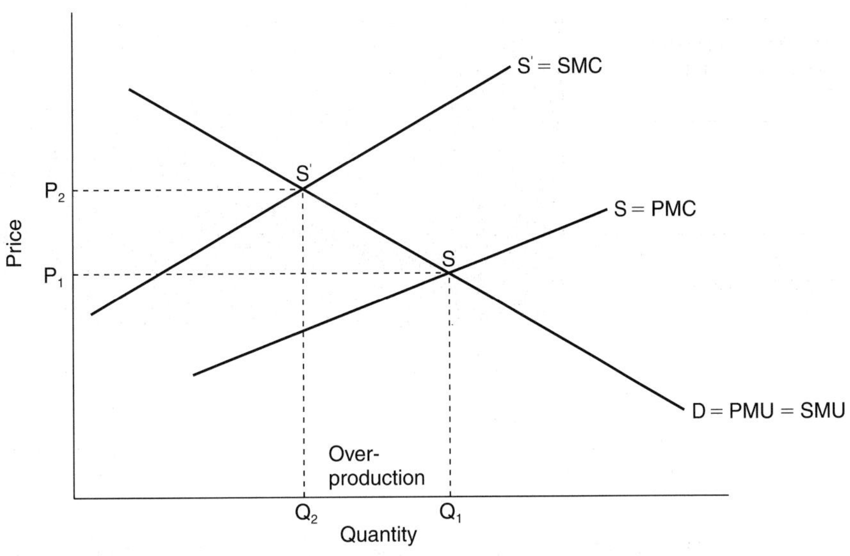

Here D is the cement factory's demand curve, which is the same as the consumer's private marginal utility curve (D = PMU). In the absence of externalities (in this case the costs of pollution), this would also be the social marginal utility or benefit curve (SMU).

The **private cost** of producing additional units of the factory's product is shown by the private marginal cost curve (PMC). Demand and supply are therefore at equilibrium at point S. This means that the factory is prepared to supply Q_1 units of product at a price of P_1, and consumers are prepared to purchase Q_1 units of product at a price of P_1.

Since the pollution of the atmosphere represents an additional **social cost**, however, a new *social* marginal cost curve (SMC) must be constructed to include both private and social marginal costs. This gives a reduced equilibrium supply and demand of S', at which the factory is prepared to supply, and consumers prepared to purchase, Q_2 units of product at the higher price of P_2.

This means that an excess of supply and consumption has occurred as, since the actual price of the commodity does not include the externality, MC + SMC > P, resulting in an inefficient allocation of resources.

When social benefits, rather than costs, are involved, the converse is true. In Figure 7.6, we see that the additional social benefits to be derived from a product shift the demand curve for that product from D(PMU), where consumers are prepared to purchase, and suppliers supply, Q_1 units of product at a price of P_1, to D' (SMU), where consumers are prepared to purchase, and suppiers supply, Q_2 units of product at a price of P_2. This is because demand for the product at the actual price of P_1 does not reflect the externality, so that PMU + SMU > P. The result is under-production of the product, and again, an inefficient allocation of resources.

Fig. 7.6 Externalities causing under-production at the free-market price

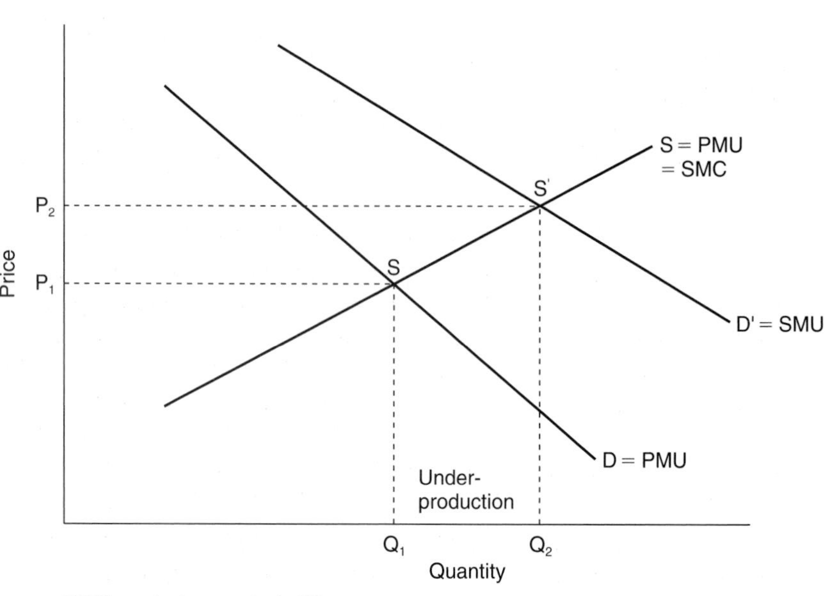

Dealing with externalities

Externalities can be addressed in various ways, including the following:

- **Internalisation**, whereby the supplier accepts responsibility for the externality and absorbs the cost of putting it right. For example, a construction company building a new road may pay the costs of excavating, removing and restoring a Saxon settlement in a new location.
- **Pressure groups**, such as Greenpeace, can demand that governments and private firms take externalities into account when contemplating a major project such as building a nuclear power station (of course, the pressure group may not get their way).
- **Private action** by firms or individuals is often intended to improve their own public image, but may go a long way towards paying for social costs. Examples of such action might include, for example, a football club paying for the policing of the neighbourhood around their ground at match time, or a private firm sponsoring a youth club.
- **Government action** to cover externalities includes
  - taxation and subsidies
  - introducing a pricing system, such as parking meters and tolls
  - direct controls, such as planning controls and licensing
  - providing goods and services through the public sector, either free or at subsidised rates which may be related to ability to pay.

Cost–benefit analysis

An obvious difficulty with achieving an efficient allocation of resources in the face of externalities is how can externalities be measured?

Cost–benefit analysis (CBA) is a procedure that seeks to take the subjectivity out of making decisions about projects which involve significant externalities, by attempting to draw up a 'balance sheet' of costs and benefits, including social costs and benefits, in financial terms. It is mainly used in connection with major public projects such as the construction of a bypass or expenditure on the NHS, where there is no price system to give an indication of utility. The basic procedures are:

- identification of all costs and benefits associated with a project, including future costs and benefits
- quantifying the costs and benefits in terms of money
- comparing overall costs with overall benefits
- reaching a conclusion: if benefits exceed costs, the project should proceed; if costs exceed benefits, the project should be cancelled (at least for the present, since the relative weight of costs and benefits may change in the future).

Difficulties may arise when trying to carry out a cost–benefit analysis:

- Many projects provide benefits for some and costs for others. For example, a new housing estate will benefit the families who will live there, but present a cost to others who gained enjoyment from the green-field site. Only if such losers are fully compensated by the gainers so that there will have been no overall loss of utility can we be satisfied that society's resources are being efficiently allocated.
- In the case of the state provision of services, and government projects, where there is no market price, it is practically impossible to calculate marginal utility or compare opportunity costs.
- Some social costs and benefits cannot be given a value. For example, how can you put a value on saving human life, protecting a species of wild orchid, or maintaining an historic building?

While cost–benefit analysis is a useful technique and can help in decision-making, it is not without problems. These must be taken into consideration when using cost–benefit analysis to weigh up the costs and benefits of a particular project. It must also be remembered that many public-sector projects are the result of political decisions that may render any cost–benefit analysis irrelevant.

Something to do

- Carry out a simple cost–benefit analysis of each of the following:
  - building a new community sports hall at your school or college
  - restoring a historic house and opening it to the public
  - constructing a bypass to take traffic away from a rural market town through the only known habitat of a rare species of snail.
- Would you proceed with the projects? Justify your answers.

Government and the environment

There is a growing awareness of the impact of economic activity on the environment and an increasing involvement of the government to try to reduce the problem.

The environment provides society with natural resources (for example, minerals), amenity resources (for example, landscapes), a life-support system (for example, the air we breathe) and a waste-absorption system (for example, forests absorb CO_2). Individual economic decisions concerned with private costs and private benefits rarely take into account the impact on the environment. The main problem usually lies with the sum total of individual actions, making it difficult to allocate responsibility. For example, the use of CFCs in millions of refrigerators can have a detrimental effect on the environment as a life-support system. Similarly, large-scale fishing and the ever increasing use of packaging for consumer goods are threatening the capacity of natural resources to renew themselves quickly enough to allow such practices to continue at their present levels.

Governments are increasingly being seen as the agents for control of the impact of economic activity on the environment. A variety of measures are available, including taxation, legislation, the funding of research programmes and international agreements.

Something to do

- In what ways does the increasing use of the car have an impact on the environment? Suggest what the Government could do to halt the rise in car use and car ownership.

Market failure and the government

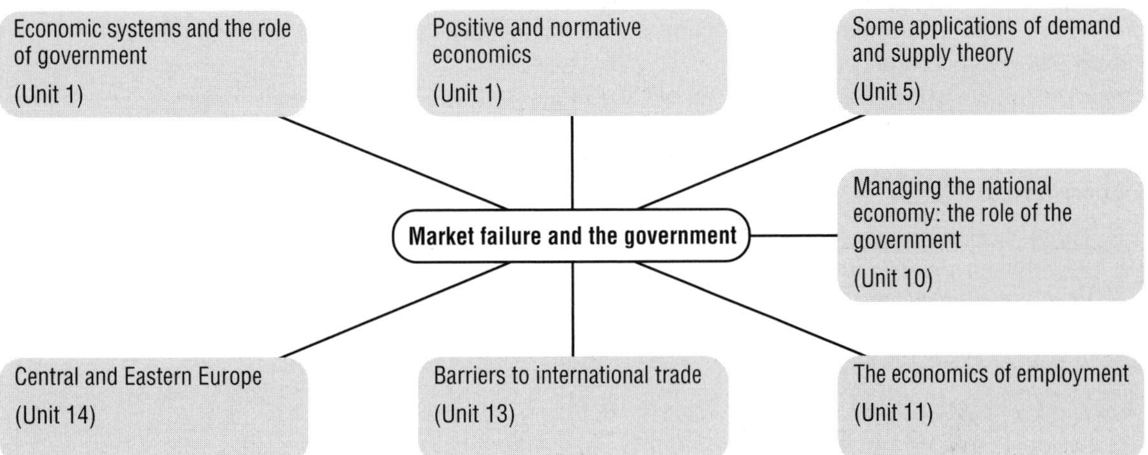

Market failure results from, and produces, an allocation of resources that may be both inefficient in meeting the demands of society and inequitable in its distribution between members of society. One of the roles of government is to intervene in the operation of markets to improve the efficient working of the economy. This involves not only making normative judgements about the distribution of goods and services, but also developing policies to achieve employment and inflation objectives, among others. These will be examined in detail in later units, but the economic objectives of a government generally fall into three key areas:

- the efficient allocation of resources
- economic stability
- the equitable distribution of income.

In order to achieve these objectives, a government may intervene in the operation of markets either through industrial and competition policies, or by providing and distributing goods and services itself through the public sector (see also Unit 10).

> *Something to do*
>
> The Government can only take appropriate action concerning a perceived market failure if it has timely and accurate information regarding both the cause of the market failure and the likely results of any action.
>
> - Make a list of at least three types of information that the Government might need in order to take appropriate action.

Industrial and competition policy

Governments and competition

While large firms may benefit from economies of scale (see Unit 4, pages 160–163), they may also use their size to dominate the market and restrict competition. Accordingly, in the UK, the government has normally tried to establish a legal framework that encourages competition and restricts the growth of monopoly power, and, as a member of the European Union, the UK also works within the EU's anti-monopoly and cartel laws.

Think about it

- Why do you think governments, especially since the Thatcher governments of the 1980s and early 1990s, have considered that competition is important in raising output and lowering prices?
- Is this view necessarily correct?

Something to do

- Try to check newspapers and magazines, such as *The Economist*, regularly for reports of government action to influence the economy. Copy or cut out any reports or articles about government measures aimed at increasing competition. Write summaries analysing the Government's actions and the intended outcomes. Keep these in a file for future reference.

In practice there are two problems to deal with:

- the basic monopoly problem of a single large firm dominating a market (see below)
- the situation where a number of independent firms co-ordinate their activities in various ways, thus restricting the operation of market forces, to the detriment of consumers (see the section on restrictive practices below).

Policy in the UK has perhaps concentrated on the latter problem, but we consider them here in the order given above.

The single-firm monopoly

In 1948, the Government established a Monopolies Commission to investigate situations where one firm had more than one-third (now one-quarter) of the domestic market. Initially, its most important evidence related to firms co-operating to control markets, and it was this kind of evidence that led to controls on such restrictive practices (see also Unit 5 and below).

As far as large firms were concerned, although the government had powers to investigate their behaviour, it had no power to prevent mergers leading to more large firms. Such power was conferred by the Monopolies and Mergers Act 1965. The government could then delay any proposed merger which would result in a firm controlling one-third (since revised to one-quarter) of the domestic market or involving the transfer of assets of £5 million or more (since revised to £30 million).

The provisions of the 1965 Act were strengthened by the Fair Trading Act 1973, which allowed the Monopolies and Mergers Commission to investigate those markets where a number of firms appear to be colluding to influence prices or output. The Act also provided an indication of how public interest might be taken into account by the Commission. The policy was further extended by the Competition Act 1980, which brought public-sector bodies within the scope of the Monopolies and Mergers Commission, the government hoping that the Commission would review the policies of all the nationalised industries. On 1 April 1999, the Monopolies and Mergers Commission was replaced by a new **Competition Commission.**

Restrictive practices

The early investigations of the Monopolies Commission produced extensive evidence of firms operating **restrictive practices** to prevent the free operation of the market. This led directly to the Restrictive Trade Practices Act 1956.

The 1956 Act established a Registrar of Restrictive Practices who keeps a register of all collective agreements that restrict the freedom of the parties to decide the price of their product, the size or quality of their output, or the destination of their product. It is the Registrar's duty to bring the parties to an agreement before the **Restrictive Practices Court**, especially established for the purpose, where the onus is on them to show that the agreement is not against the public interest. They may accomplish this by showing one of the following:

- The agreement is necessary to protect the public against injury.
- The agreement ensures that the public receives some specific and substantial benefit which would disappear if the agreement were ended.
- The agreement is necessary to enable small firms to compete with large firms.
- The agreement is necessary to prevent small firms from being exploited by very large customers or suppliers.
- The agreement is necessary to maintain the level of employment in particular areas or industries.
- The agreement is necessary to maintain exports.
- The agreement is necessary to maintain another restriction already approved by the Court.

Even if an agreement satisfies one or more of these points, it must still be shown that the benefit from it outweighs any general detriment to the public from the agreement as a whole.

The Fair Trading Act 1973 transferred responsibility for the control of restrictive practices to the Director General of Fair Trading, and at the same time brought the provision of services within the same framework of control. As a tidying-up process, the various aspects of the policy were pulled together in the Restrictive Practices Act 1977.

Effectiveness of the policy

As is often the case, it is difficult to be precise about the impact of the policy on competition because we can only guess what would have happened without the legislation.

As far as the single-firm monopoly and merger situation is concerned, however, it can be said that since the 1965 Act only about 3 per cent of relevant mergers have been referred to the Commission. Of this 3 per cent, about two-thirds did not eventually go ahead, either because the parties decided not to proceed, or because of discouraging reports from the Commission. In any case it should be noted that the Commission can only make recommendations and it is up to the government to decide whether to accept them and act on them.

When it has investigated large firms, the Commission has not been over-critical. The main charge against such firms tends to be that of excessive profits derived from their dominant market position. The Commission has often found that such profits are the result of greater efficiency or the reward for risk-taking in the development of new processes or products.

With respect to restrictive practices, more than 5000 agreements have been registered, and the majority of them voluntarily abandoned. Of those that have been taken before the Court (fewer than 40), only about a dozen have been upheld as being in the public interest.

Of course, the fact that so many formal agreements have been ended does not preclude the possibility that a wide network of informal agreements exists. These are, of course, more difficult to detect and control.

Think about it

- Do you think government economic policy has been effective in increasing competition between firms? What about restrictive practices?
- How has government action on monopolies and mergers, and restrictive practices benefited consumers?
- What action do you think the Government should take now?

Price-fixing

One aspect of the policy against restrictive practices seems to have been more successful than most. This is the abolition of the practice of resale price maintenance (RPM), where a group of firms jointly fixed the retail prices of goods and took action to ensure that retailers observed them. The 1956 Act specifically outlawed collective RPM. Individual firms were allowed to set the retail prices of their goods until 1964. Since the Resale Prices Act of that year, prices can only be fixed with the approval of the Restrictive Practices Court.

In 1995, one of the last remaining examples of price-fixing – the Net Book Agreement, under which books had to be sold at their cover price as fixed by their publishers, and could not be discounted – was abolished. This enabled retailers such as supermarkets to start selling books at cut prices so that shoppers could buy them with their everyday shopping rather than having to go to a bookshop. Other retailers which always sold books, such as WH Smith, soon followed and began to offer selected books at a discount in order to compete with the supermarkets.

Manufacturers of medicinal products that can be bought 'off the shelf' successfully defended their right to fix the price at which their products could be sold when a supermarket tried to sell a brand of proprietary headache pills at a discount in the early 1990s.

Some firms try to get around the Resale Prices Act by not supplying retailers who are going to discount their products. This applies especially to some manufacturers of designer fashion-wear, such as jeans, and expensive perfumes, who argue that their customers expect to pay high prices and not to see their goods available cheaply in supermarkets and similar stores.

BOOKS AT TESCO

Fiona Kennedy

THE increased presence of books in supermarkets is a trend which has provoked a mixture of reactions in the book trade. For some people, supermarkets represent a new and positive arena for selling books; for others, they are a destructive, destabilising influence on the traditional book trade. In reality, although it is true to say that a proportion of book sales in supermarkets are sales which would otherwise have gone through traditional book retailers, a more significant proportion are sales which the book trade would not have had at all.

The huge advantage which supermarkets have over traditional bookshops is store traffic. An astounding 9.5 million people whiz round Tesco every week, and this creates a massive opportunity for the book industry. The fact is that a large number of people are intimidated by traditional bookshops – the range can feel too overwhelming, and the environment too studious. Supermarkets on the other hand are places they visit frequently, and which therefore feel comfortable and familiar to them. This means that supermarkets have access to a very significant group of potential book buyers which traditional bookshops cannot reach, and this makes the supermarket sector very important to the future of the book industry. No one is better placed to increase the market than the supermarkets, and not surprisingly Tesco intends to be the driving force.

Of course the demise of the NBA has made the book market much more appealing for Tesco than it was previously. Price competitiveness is a crucial aspect of supermarket retailing, and while there was no flexibility on price, books remained a relatively limited opportunity. The range consisted almost entirely of bargain books which was the only means of conveying a value message. In the music and video markets, on the other hand, Tesco was already a major player and had proved very convincingly that entertainment products were viable in a supermarket environment. With the NBA no longer in place, books could be treated in the same way and this opened up enormous opportunities.

But how best to exploit the opportunity? We weren't about to remove baked beans from the shelves in order to make room for thousands of book titles. In fact, the amount of space allocated to books in an average Tesco store is tiny compared to a traditional bookshop, meaning that we can only buy a very small proportion of the total number of books which are published. We had to determine how to use this space in a way which was commercially effective and which also made sense for the customer. Our conclusion was that rather than attempt to do a bit of everything, we should identify several clear sectors which were particularly relevant to our consumer base and to our core business. The logical areas were cookery books, children's books, fiction and general bestsellers. Within these segments, our objective is to offer well-presented, credible ranges at highly competitive prices. Price is a particularly important element in this positioning. It is important to recognise that Tesco is not a destination store for books. People buy books in Tesco on impulse, and because of this, books need to be priced at a level where the customer can include a book in their shopping trolley without there being any discernible difference to the ultimate bill. Clearly this means that some titles are out of our price range. With time, however, as Tesco becomes more established as a book retailer, we expect to reach a situation whereby customers start to put books on their shopping lists, and to budget for spending money on books.

This is already beginning to happen with children's books. There are very clear indications that parents are increasingly concerned about their children's education, and are more motivated than ever to spend money on books if it is going to give their child an advantage. We are keen to ensure, therefore, that our children's book ranges do not just consist of innumerable tie-ins to the latest Disney release, but also include books with a clear educational benefit. The aim is to create a 'fun to learn' feel – a range of books which is responsible and helps children's learning skills while also appealing to the children themselves.

Another issue we have to consider is the frequency with which customers are visiting our stores. Many people are visiting Tesco every week, or at least every two weeks. So, for them, our book ranges can quickly become boring and tired and we need to ensure that we change and refresh these ranges regularly. In practice this means that around 30–40% of each range is removed and replaced every six weeks, with the exception of the paperback bestseller section which is changed every two weeks. This gives us the opportunity both to introduce new and recently-published titles and to pull out lines which have under-performed.

So what is the next stage? Tesco is serious about the book market, and we aim to establish ourselves as a major player in our chosen segments of the market – particularly cookery books, which so neatly support the core business. Clearly this means allocating more space to books in order to offer more range and greater choice. The danger, however, is that we end up creating another bookshop-type environment, thereby diluting our competitive advantage. The solution lies in integrating books with other product areas, not segregating them. Simple mechanics such as siting Rick Stein's *Fruits of the Sea* next to our fish counters has had a dramatic effect on sales and market share. At a broader level, positioning children's books with toys and children's videos, or cookery books with utensils, makes books much more integral to the customer's shopping trip. There are also seasonal events such as Mother's Day or Valentine's Day, where books can be merchandised alongside cards, chocolates, flowers and so on.

All these things expose more books to more people, and this can only be good news for the book trade.

The author is Senior Book Buyer at Tesco, and a judge of the 1997 Orange Prize for Fiction.

Source: *The Author*, Spring 1997

Providing and distributing goods and services through the public sector

Besides intervening in the operation of markets and the way firms behave, the government also provides some goods and services and arranges their distribution through the public sector (see Unit 4). The public sector consists of

- **government departments**, supplying services such as policing and prison services, and distributing welfare payments
- **government agencies**, such as the Stationery Office (formerly HMSO) and the Royal Mint
- **quangos** (quasi autonomous non-governmental bodies), such as Training and Enterprise Councils and 'watchdogs' such as Ofgas and Oftel, which are sponsored by the government but run by non-government personnel
- **nationalised industries**, which are run by public corporations, such as the Post Office and the BBC.

Fig. 7.7 Types of public-sector organisations

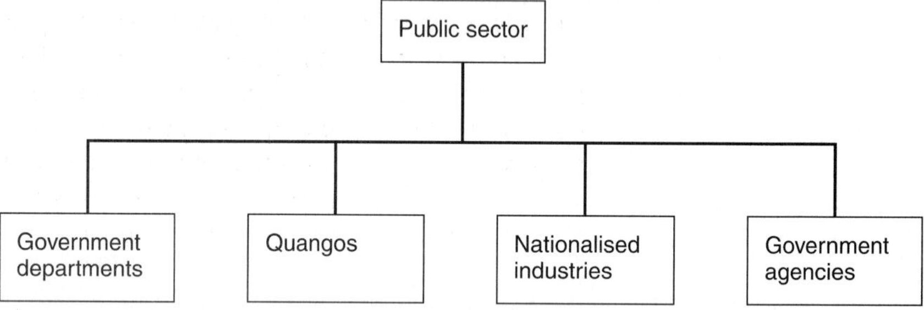

Goods and services provided and distributed by the public-sector organisations fall into two main categories:

- **public goods**, such as defence and street lighting, which if provided must be provided for the whole community
- **merit goods**, such as education and health services, which it is generally considered *ought* to be consumed by everyone in society.

Public goods

Public goods are those goods and services that cannot be provided to be consumed by one person alone. It is impossible, for example, for street lighting to be provided so that only one person can enjoy it: it must be there for everyone or not at all. This aspect of public goods is called **non-excludability**, which means that when the good or service is provided for one person, it is impossible or impractical to exclude other people from enjoying it.

Non-excludability leads to another feature of public goods – non-rivalry. Non-rivalry means that all people can enjoy the public good to the same extent. In other words, the enjoyment of that good by one person does not diminish the amount of the good available to others. The armed forces, for example, provide the same level of defence for everyone in the community.

These characteristics of public goods make them unsuitable for provision under a free-market system. If left to the free market, the supply of public goods would depend on demand for and price of those goods. However, because of the non-excludability and non-rivalry of public goods, the price system must break down. No one will be prepared to pay individually for a good that, when supplied, will be equally available to everyone in society, whether they have paid for the good or not. People who enjoy a good without paying for it are called **free-riders**. In a free-market situation where it is impossible to exclude free-riders, the price of the product will settle at zero, since this is the price at which consumers are able to maximise their utility from a good and is therefore the price they are prepared to pay for it. Obviously, however, at a price of zero, supply will also be zero, since at this price a firm will derive no profit. Public goods may not therefore be provided under market conditions, and in order to ensure allocative efficiency (see page 245), their supply and distribution must be undertaken by the government and paid for through taxation.

In principle it may be possible to introduce a measure of exclusion from some public goods by imposing fees or tolls. Road traffic wanting to cross the Thames using the Dartford Tunnel or Bridge, for example, must pay a toll charge. This excludes all traffic unwilling or unable to pay the toll. Similarly, it may be possible to charge the general public for entering parks and other open spaces, or for using motorways such as the M1. Such goods are **quasi-public goods**. In practice, however, it is often impractical to charge for providing these goods and services since doing to may lead to their under-use, exclude members of society who would benefit from them, and in any case cost more in administration to collect the charge than the revenue generated.

Merit goods

Merit goods are those goods and services, such as education, health and social services, which are considered to be socially desirable, but which may be inadequately provided through the market system, leading to under-production and under-consumption. Unlike public goods, merit goods may be provided through the market (as with private education and medical treatment), but where this is the case they are not equally available to everyone, usually because their price restricts effective demand to those with higher incomes. Some merit goods are therefore made available both through the market system, for those who are willing and able to pay the market price, and through the public sector, for those who are not.

Another reason for the government providing merit goods through the public sector is that some merit goods involve huge capital costs that would not be borne by the private sector. Major construction projects, such as building new motorways or urban renewal schemes, are goods of this type, where the capital cost must be borne by the government. These have large externalities which, while the private sector would not be prepared to take them into consideration, will influence a government's decisions on expenditure, especially where such a decision may have a political dimension. For example, safety on the railways is an area of concern to society and the government. Proposals for improving this are often announced by the government's Transport Minister, and the government's achievements in fulfilling these proposals become a measure by which its success is judged. Improvements to the railway system therefore become a political matter, and the government will be prepared to invest heavily in such improvements in order to be seen to be fulfilling its promises.

Unlike merit goods, **demerit goods** are goods and services that are considered to be socially undesirable. These include tobacco, drugs and pornography. Demand for these is likely to lead to allocative inefficiency over-production in the market, and therefore over-consumption. The government therefore takes measures to control or prevent the production of demerit goods, by, for example:

- levying a high level of duty on them, so increasing their price and reducing demand
- licensing their production or distribution
- prohibiting them by law.

Think about it

- Are the government's restrictions on pornography, drugs and tobacco really in the interests of society as a whole, and what people want, or are they an unwarranted intrusion into people's behaviour?
- What would happen if the supply of these goods was left to market forces, and would it be a good or a bad thing (and in whose opinion)?

Balancing economic efficiency and accountability

Under a market system, the supply of goods and services is determined by price. Provision of goods and services by the public sector, on the other hand, is largely decided on the basis of the needs of society. Assessing the real levels of needs in society and how scarce resources should be allocated between competing needs, however, is a difficult and subjective process which in the end must be based on normative – often political – values.

Whereas a private firm is accountable to its owners for making a profit by supplying goods and services, organisations in the public sector are accountable to the general public, through the government. The general public are in the special position of being both the providers of the finance for production (through taxation) and the consumers of public-sector goods and services. The government, which makes decisions on production and distribution of goods and services by the public sector, is also responsible to the general public, who show approval or disapproval of the government's decisions and actions through the voting system.

A balance between the economic efficiency and accountability of the private sector must therefore be reached. For example, as consumers, the general public wants the maximum provision of social services. In as far as they provide the finance for the public sector, however, taxpayers want their money to be used efficiently to improve the use and allocation of resources within the economy. The balance between economic efficiency and accountability is achieved in different ways by different types of public-sector organisation:

- Where a high degree of public accountability is required, for example in the provision of services of national importance such as defence and education, these are normally provided by government departments. The department is run by a minister who is responsible to Parliament, and through Parliament to the people. However, the high degree of accountability required may conflict with strict economic efficiency.
- Government agencies such as the Royal Mint and the Stationery Office require less accountability but must place greater emphasis on economic efficiency in the provision of goods.

- Nationalised industries are organised as public corporations that are accountable to a minister, but are given their own responsibility for the economic efficiency of day-to-day operations and decisions on such matters as pricing, output, levels of expenditure and so on. Accountability is maintained through submitting an annual report to Parliament and the responsibility of the minister for general policy directives, but some accountability is surrendered in the interests of economic efficiency.
- Where minimal accountability is required, the provision of a good or service may be allocated to a quango.

Think about it

- Where should the balance between economic efficiency and accountability be drawn in respect of
  - education
  - the National Health Service?

Paying for the public sector

Under a market system, the provision of goods and services is paid for by the consumers who actually buy and use those goods and services. As we have seen, however, such a system is not appropriate for most goods and services supplied by the public sector. Therefore, other sources of finance have to be found.

- **Taxation** is the main method of financing public expenditure. Taxes are collected by the government from the general public in several forms (see Unit 10), either as a levy on income or as a tax on expenditure. This form of finance is especially suitable where non-excludability or non-rivalry exists.
- **Borrowing** is only really appropriate in the case of projects requiring large initial capital expenditure, such as building hospitals or fighter aircraft, where taking such expenditure from tax revenue would reduce the ability of the government to meet its day-to-day expenditure. The long-term need for borrowing to finance public expenditure is known as the public sector borrowing requirement (PSBR). However, in practice some government borrowing is needed in order to balance current income and expenditure, as we shall see in Unit 10.
- **Charges** are levied on some goods and services provided by the public sector. In the case of nationalised industries, these charges, such as the BBC licence fee, have to cover the costs of providing the service. In other cases, such as road tolls and NHS prescription charges, the charge is intended as a contribution towards costs in order to ease the burden on the public purse. Charges can also help to counter over-consumption, especially when elasticity of demand is such that meeting demand at zero price would result in inefficient allocation of resources. Some charges can have a regressive impact, discriminating against those who would most benefit from the good or service. Thus, if a charge was to be made for education, this would especially hit low-income families with children of school age – the very consumers that the provision of state education is intended to benefit most. One way of avoiding the regressive impact of charges is to discriminate in their application. NHS prescription charges, for example, are waived for old age pensioners, children and some others who would find payment difficult.

Nationalisation and privatisation

As we saw in Unit 4, **nationalisation** is the taking of an industry, or firm, into public ownership. For example, the railway industry comprised a number of privately owned regional companies. When it was nationalised in 1948, the government, on behalf of the State, took over the different companies, compensating their original owners with the agreed value of their company.

Reasons for nationalisation

The programme of nationalising certain UK industries was started largely as a result of Labour policies after the Second World War. There were several reasons why the Labour Government believed that nationalisation of these industries would increase the economic efficiency of the UK and help to correct market failure.

- Basic industries, such as steel and coal production, should be run for the benefit of the country as a whole rather than a few private industrialists.
- Nationalisation of basic industries, and making them accountable to and controllable by the government, would facilitate the management of the economy, including areas such as unemployment.
- Many key industries, such as the railways, were run down after the Second World War. They needed considerable investment if they were to run efficiently. This could most effectively be provided by the government.
- Industries such as gas, electricity and water were considered to be natural monopolies, belonging to the nation and not appropriate for private ownership.
- State-owned industries were more likely to consider social needs, and not just the needs of shareholders.
- The effective co-ordination of essential services, such as power and transport, was likely to improve if these services were provided by central government rather than diverse private firms.

Nationalisation did not, however, turn out to be the answer to managing the nation's economy, or to solving the allocation problem, as the Labour Government had hoped, and was the subject of severe criticism. In the early 1980s, the Conservative Government, under Mrs Thatcher, began to take a route towards **privatisation** again.

Reasons for privatisation

The reasons for this change in policy (which was largely along party political lines) were as follows:

- The nationalised industries were believed to be poorly managed and inefficiently run.
- They did not respond effectively to the needs of customers, being product- rather than market-orientated and providing the type and standard of service they felt consumers should have, rather than the type and standard of service consumers actually wanted.
- Nationalised industries, being accountable to government, suffered from too much government interference in the way they were run, often on political rather than economic grounds. This added to their inefficiency.

- Because nationalised industries were both funded by and expected to contribute to the public purse (in reality most nationalised industries were sources of expenditure rather than income), they had to compete with other areas of public expenditure, such as the National Health Service and the police. As a result, nationalised industries in general suffered from under-investment.
- Public-sector trade unions had become too powerful; and because they represented employees in key industries such as electricity, gas, coal and waste disposal, they were able to hold the country to ransom.
- The general philosophy of the government at the time reflected an underlying belief in the role of the free market rather than state intervention.

With so many difficulties, the Conservative Government believed that nationalised industries actually made the economy less stable and easy to manage than if they were privately owned. Private firms seeking to maximise their profits would be more likely to be well run, provide the service that consumers want, and allocate resources efficiently according to the needs of society as required by the price system.

Ways to privatisation

Privatisation of the production and distribution of services in the 1980s and 1990s took various forms:

- Some state-owned assets, such as council houses, motorway service areas, and some forests previously owned by the Forestry Authority, were sold to private buyers.
- Major government shareholdings in public limited companies, such as British Aerospace and BP, were sold.
- Some services provided by national and local government, such as refuse collection and the cleaning of schools and hospitals, were put out to tender (that is, private companies were allowed to put in competitive bids to carry out the work, which was then allocated according to merit).
- Nationalised industries were sold, either by public subscription for shares (as in the case of British Gas and the regional electricity boards), or by tender (as in the case of British Coal and British Rail).

In addition, both the Conservative Government under John Major and the Labour Government elected in 1997 have encouraged competition, between private and state-owned industries and also with newly privatised industries. For example, licensing restrictions have been relaxed to allow some competition within the radio broadcasting industry, while telecommunications has been opened up to allow companies such as Vodafone and Hutchinson Telecommunications to compete with BT. Whilst the major period for privatisation appears to have been from the mid-1980s to the mid-1990s, more recent government actions and proposals indicate that the policy is still being pursued.

The rail system has been privatised, the possibility of privatising the Royal Mail has been investigated and the Labour Government elected in 1997 considered the privatisation of Air Traffic Control and the London Underground. In addition, a role for the private sector in owning and running more prisons or bringing in private management companies to run failing schools are amongst suggestions which could see both a deepening and a widening of the privatisation concept.

A further measure intended to break the monopoly power of some privatised industries has been the establishment of 'watchdog' bodies to oversee the activities of these industries and ensure that they provide the services customers require, at reasonable prices. These 'watchdogs' include Ofgas to oversee gas suppliers, Ofwat to oversee the water companies, and Oftel to oversee the telecommunications sector.

A more recent way of involving the private sector in areas which were previously considered the domain of the public sector has been the private finance initiative (PFI), also referred to as public–private partnerships. Essentially, these involve the public sector deciding what capital projects it would like to be built (for example, a new hospital or a new prison) and then persuading the private sector to provide the necessary expertise and finance to take on the task. The State then leases back the buildings for, say, a twenty- or thirty-year period. In this way, the new prison or hospital is provided without the State having to draw on public funds (through taxes or borrowing), whilst the private sector receives a commercial rent and has ownership of a capital resource. There is controversy over the policy, not least because of the potentially high cost to the government in the long run.

Market failure or government failure?

We began this unit by considering the problem of market failure. However, it is apparent from the nationalisation/privatisation debate that it is not only markets that can fail to achieve economic efficiency. Nationalisation was a programme of government intervention in markets, intended to correct market failure and achieve economic efficiency. However, in as far as it has failed to fulfil its objectives and has now led to a policy of re-privatisation, the programme of nationalisation can be considered to have been a **government failure**. Government failure occurs when economic inefficiency arises due to too much government interference in the operation of markets, in other words when government intervention results in greater inefficiencies than if no intervention had taken place. The role of government in influencing the economy comes largely from the theories of John Maynard Keynes (see Unit 11). However, some economists, such as the Austrian Friedrich von Hayek and the American Milton Friedman, believe that too much government intervention is the threat, rather than too little, and that in general markets operate best when left alone.

Reasons for government failure

There are several reasons why government failure may arise. These include:

- **lack of accurate or appropriate information** – as, for example, when decisions about the allocation of resources are based on imperfect information about society's wants or the technological needs of individuals

- **too great an emphasis on political policies** such as state welfare or nationalisation, so that political programmes are pushed through because they are part of the government's political ideology, rather than because they are economically efficient. An emphasis on state welfare, for example, can lead to both a distortion of effective demand and an over-dependence of individuals on welfare payments. This gives rise to situations such as those in which unemployed people may receive more in state benefits than they would in work, so that the benefits paid – which are intended to support people without jobs while they find work – in fact provide a disincentive to work
- **increasing bureaucracy** resulting in inefficient operations, where a burgeoning civil service hinders the rapid response of the government to economic conditions, or impedes the implementation of government policies
- **too much regulation** of individuals or firms, resulting in firms being unable to respond efficiently to the needs of society, or individual consumers being unable to maximise their utility
- **conflicting objectives**, either within government or between government and society. For example, the government may wish to develop a transport policy that involves a programme of road construction, but finds that this conflicts with its stated policy of preserving the countryside. Or society may look to the government for cuts in the rate of income tax, so that individuals can spend their wages as they wish; the government, on the other hand, may consider that an increase in income tax and expenditure on the NHS may be of greater benefit to society. Conflicting objectives such as these are usually resolved by a trade-off
- government interference in a market can lead to the distortion of that market. For example, subsidising a firm or industry may lead to unfair competition, and perhaps the subsidising of an inefficient operation. Providing subsidies for firms to move into and create jobs in certain areas of high unemployment can enable those firms to compete unfairly with similar firms in other areas, by allowing them either to make abnormal profits or to supply at below the market price.

8 Financial economics: money and financial markets

Introduction: what is money?

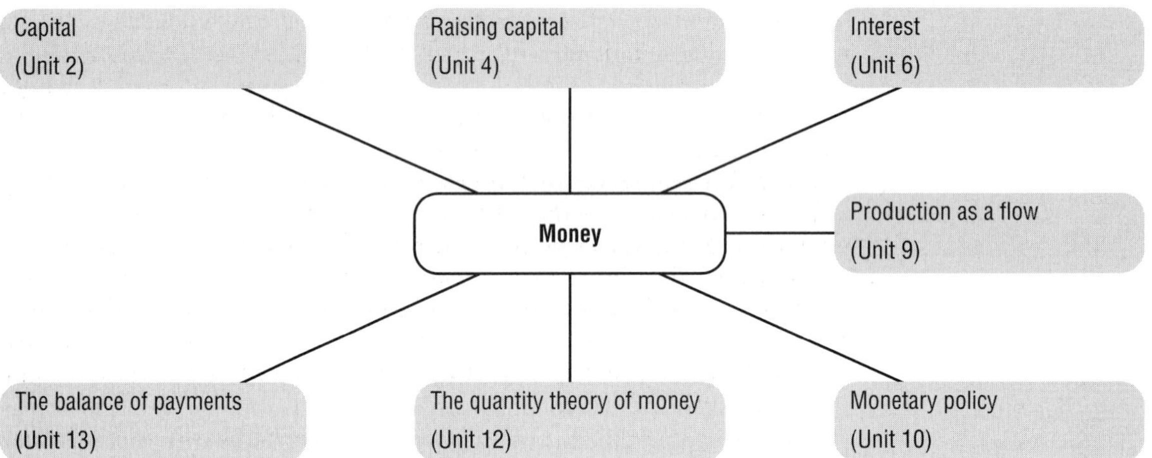

An essential element in the operation of any developed economy is money. Money serves many purposes, perhaps the most important of which are as

- a means of exchange
- a measure of value.

But what exactly is money, and why does it play such a vital part in modern society?

Money may be defined as anything that can be generally accepted in exchange for goods and services. In different societies in the past – and in some isolated communities still – cattle, cocoa beans, maize, beeswax, pigs, shells, teeth and other items have all been used as money. Most economies, though, have eventually settled on metal as the basis of their currency, though not always in the form of coins that we would recognise. Gold rings, iron swords, metal shells, copper crosses and axe heads have all served as money.

In this unit, we consider the functions and purposes of money and its development in the UK, before looking at the financial institutions and markets that have grown up around the use of money. In particular, we examine

- the functions and purpose of money
- the value of money
- the role of the Bank of England and other financial institutions
- the creation of credit
- the capital market and the Stock Exchange.

The functions and purpose of money

We all know what money is, but we are so familiar with it that we tend to take it for granted. However, the very existence of our complex economic structure depends on the existence of money and it is one of the major areas of concern to economists. An understanding of the functions and purpose of money is therefore essential.

A means of exchange

In the absence of money, goods would have to be bartered – or swapped – directly for each other. Children swap comics, stamps, autographs or coins with little difficulty. A considerable amount of barter goes on in international trade. Here, however, although money does not change hands, it plays an essential part in determining the amounts of different commodities that should be swapped for each other.

Imagine, however, an employee on a production line in a car factory being offered wages in the form of a starter motor. Even if this form of payment was accepted by the employee in exchange for their labour, he or she would then have the problem of exchanging the starter motor for food or clothes. It may be simple to find a grocer anxious to dispose of surplus food or a tailor selling clothes, but unless either of them was prepared to accept a starter motor in exchange, the employee would be unable to deal with them.

The most important function of money, therefore, is to eliminate the need for this 'double coincidence of wants' – that the person or organisation whose products you want happens to want the goods you are offering in exchange. So the employee on the car production line is paid with money, which can be exchanged for food and clothes; the grocer and tailor can then use the same money to buy the goods that they want. In this way, money serves as a means of exchange.

A measure of value

An employee who is paid with starter motors may well disagree with his or her employer over the number of starter motors their labour is worth. Once agreement is reached, the employee will then have to agree appropriate **exchange rates** of starter motors for food and clothes. Meanwhile, the grocer and tailor will be negotiating exchange rates with customers offering books, pottery, leather goods and a thousand other items in exchange for food and clothes. Everyone would have to carry a host of exchange rates in their head in order to trade effectively. So the second function of money is to serve as a measure of value or **unit of account**. Comparisons of the value of goods are made easier by reducing them all to a single monetary standard. It thus becomes much easier to recognise a bargain and to avoid paying excess prices.

Think about it

- Try to think what it would be like if we *did* live in a world without money. Imagine you were out with a friend and wanted to go to McDonald's for a Big Mac. When you got there, the only thing they wanted in exchange for the meal was a CD you had. Do you think that would have been a fair exchange? How many Big Mac meals would you expect for your CD? How would you decide?
- Now consider the money price of a CD and a Big Mac. How many Big Macs can you buy for the price of a CD? Do you think the money price is a fair measure of the value of each?

A store of wealth

People may not wish to spend the whole of their income within a few days of receiving it. If they are paid in some durable engineering product it is possible to keep it until a later date, perhaps to save towards buying an expensive item such as a car or a house. If they are paid in the form of a perishable commodity, however, such as corn or livestock, saving their income becomes more difficult. In this way, money acts as a store of wealth, which allows saving to take place.

A standard for deferred payments

Most people do not in fact hold their savings in the form of notes and coins, largely because it yields them no interest. They place their money with one or more of a number of financial institutions, such as banks and building societies, which promise to repay the money deposited with them on demand or subject to specific notice and to pay interest on it in the meantime.

In this way, a person depositing money with a bank or building society is in effect lending it to them, and deferring repayment until a later date. Again, money is used to fix the repayments and the interest. Thousands of other agreements to settle loans and debts at a future date also depend on money serving as a **standard for deferred payments.** Wage agreements and mortgages are important examples.

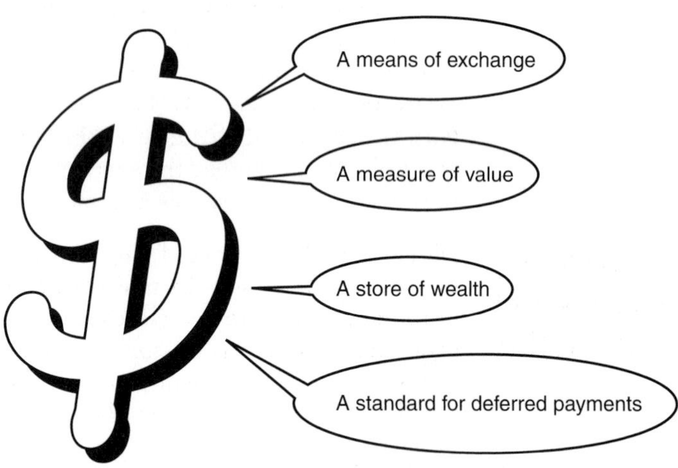

Fig. 8.1 The functions and purposes of money

By fulfilling each of the above functions, money allows the economy to develop.

- Since money serves as a means of exchange, it permits division of labour and specialisation to occur. Each worker is confident that he or she is no longer dependent on the achievement of a double coincidence of wants to exchange their surplus output.
- Money as a standard of value permits the speedy settlement of transactions and thereby acts as a stimulus to trade.
- In its role of a store of wealth and a standard for deferred payments, money permits and even encourages savings, which are the very source of economic achievement.

Essential attributes of money

For any commodity to be effective as money, it has to meet four essential criteria.

Acceptability

Money has to be generally acceptable. Items were originally used as money because they had intrinsic value to the communities in which they were used – that is, they were desirable for their own sake as well as being a means of exchange for acquiring other goods. This is why precious metals have frequently been used as money, and until recently were used to make coins. Today, the notes and coins in your pocket generally have no intrinsic value, but you can use them in the knowledge that other people will accept them in exchange for goods.

Stability of value

Money has to have stability of value. We should be less eager to accept something as money if we expected the value to fall by 50 per cent by the end of the day. Indeed, when this happens and people anticipate that rapid price rises will erode the value of money, the monetary system may collapse. This happened in Germany in 1923, when a vast amount of extra money in the form of notes was printed and put into circulation. The problem arose because there were no extra goods to buy with the increased amount of money in people's pockets, which meant more money was chasing the same amount of goods. In most economies, prices normally rise by only a small percentage each year, so while no modern money has complete stability of value, its value does not change at such a rate that we lose confidence in it.

Durability, divisibility and portability

Money should be long lasting, capable of being divided into convenient units of exchange, and small enough to be carried around. It should be durable and not deteriorate over time – one of the disadvantages of livestock. It should also be readily divisible, so that small payments can easily be made. It is also helpful if money is easily portable.

Uniformity

Money has to be uniform. Perhaps a minor consideration these days is that money should be uniform in quality. This is to prevent 'bad money driving the good out of circulation'. For example, if you have two coins, one with an intrinsic value of 10 pence and the other with no intrinsic value, then you may be tempted to spend the latter and keep the former. This is the principle known as Gresham's law, after an Elizabethan finance minister, Sir Thomas Gresham (1519–79). In this connection it is worth noting that money should be difficult for counterfeiters to copy, which is why banknotes are given such ornate designs.

The development of money in the UK

By Norman times, coins were already in widespread circulation. They bore the stamp or effigy of the monarch, and this guaranteed their value so that people accepted them as the general means of exchange. Control over the supply of money (the number of coins in existence) was negligible. One of the great weaknesses of the currency was the ease with which the king could debase it in order to increase his personal income by calling in existing gold or silver coins, melting them down, adding perhaps 20 per cent of base metals, then reissuing the same number coins with the same face value and keeping the balance of gold or silver for himself. The only merit of this policy was that it accustomed the community to accept money whose intrinsic value was less than its face value.

Paper money first developed in the seventeenth century. Wealthy traders began to leave (or deposit) their holdings of gold or silver coins at local goldsmiths for safekeeping. The goldsmiths issued receipts or promises to pay in return. It was not long, however, before these goldsmiths' receipts themselves began to be used as money. In order to pay for goods or services, to settle a debt or repay a loan, a depositor could simply endorse with his signature the receipt he had been given by the goldsmith rather than draw the gold or silver coins from the goldsmith's vaults. In this way the person who had deposited money with the goldsmith transferred his claim against the goldsmith to his own creditor. Sometimes a receipt might change hands many times and could properly be regarded as money, although it would normally only circulate on a local basis. At this time, the notes or receipts were fully backed by gold or silver: for every £100 worth of receipts issued, the goldsmith held £100 in gold or silver coin.

During the eighteenth century, the goldsmiths, who already charged a fee for looking after gold deposits, developed a far more profitable technique. It had become obvious that most traders were willing to use notes issued by the goldsmiths – or bankers, as we may now call them – in their everyday transactions, and would redeem them only on rare occasions. So a banker might notice that, on average, perhaps only 20 per cent of the depositors' gold coins was withdrawn during a week – and most of this was quickly redeposited. By holding gold and silver coins equivalent to 20 per cent of the total number of notes he had issued, a goldsmith could, therefore, always meet the demand of his customers for money. As a consequence, it became common practice to write notes in excess of deposits held and to issue them to customers who wanted to borrow money. The goldsmith would keep an account of the transactions, called a **balance sheet**. The balance sheet of such a banker might look like that in Table 8.1. The 'Liabilities' side shows the value of the notes that the banker had issued to customers. Thus customers holding notes issued without coins being deposited had exactly the same claim against the bank as those who had actually left coins with the bank.

If all note-holders tried to redeem their notes simultaneously, then the banker would be unable to meet his liabilities, but this event was unlikely to occur if the banker kept a prudent reserve of gold. Some greedy bankers, however, issued notes far in excess of deposits, and on many occasions legitimate requests for cash led to bank closures and losses for depositors when a bank was unable to meet its commitments. Despite such setbacks, the system of **fractionally backed notes** survived. ('Fractionally backed' is the term used when the notes in circulation have a nominal value greater than the value of gold held by the bank.)

Table 8.1

A balance sheet			
Assets	**£**	**Liabilities**	**£**
Gold coin	1000	Promises to pay gold on demand	5000
Customers' promises to repay	4000		
Total	**5000**	**Total**	**5000**

Something to do

- On checking its transactions over the past year, Willowbrook Central Bank finds that customers' cash deposits have averaged £15 000 000, while withdrawals have averaged £1 650 000. On this basis, calculate the percentage of cash deposited that the bank should keep in reserve to meet customers' demands.
- Assuming cash deposits increased by 17 per cent in the next year, following an aggressive marketing campaign, calculate how much the bank could lend to customers, while keeping the same cash reserve ratio.

It became necessary to control the indiscriminate issue of fractionally backed notes by what became known as country banks. The Bank Charter Act of 1844 limited the issue of notes by such banks but allowed the Bank of England an unlimited issue so long as the notes issued did not exceed the Bank's gold holdings by more than £14 million. This £14 million was known as the **fiduciary issue** – meaning it was backed only by faith. When banks amalgamated, their note issues were taken over by the Bank of England. As there were many amalgamations in the second half of the nineteenth century, the Bank issue increased and that of the country banks gradually disappeared. Throughout the period, however, notes were convertible into gold by the issuing bank on demand. This practice ceased in 1914 with the outbreak of war, but was re-established in 1925 for sums of £1700 or more. It was finally abandoned in 1931 when the **gold standard** collapsed. Since then, notes have been of only token value, although British coins containing a high proportion of silver were minted until 1946.

Alongside these developments in the note issue, even more fundamental changes occurred within the banking system. As we have seen, the early bankers lent to their customers by giving promise to pay – which could be used as money – but in the nineteenth century their lending techniques became more sophisticated. When customers wished to borrow, the bank would make entries in the ledger showing the sum available to each customer, who would be free to transfer his deposit in one of two ways:

- by withdrawing cash
- by instructing the bank via a **cheque** to transfer sums to another account.

Banks are described more in the section beginning on page 275, but we must note here that the bulk of today's **money supply** consists of entries in bank ledgers and has no tangible existence.

Financial institutions

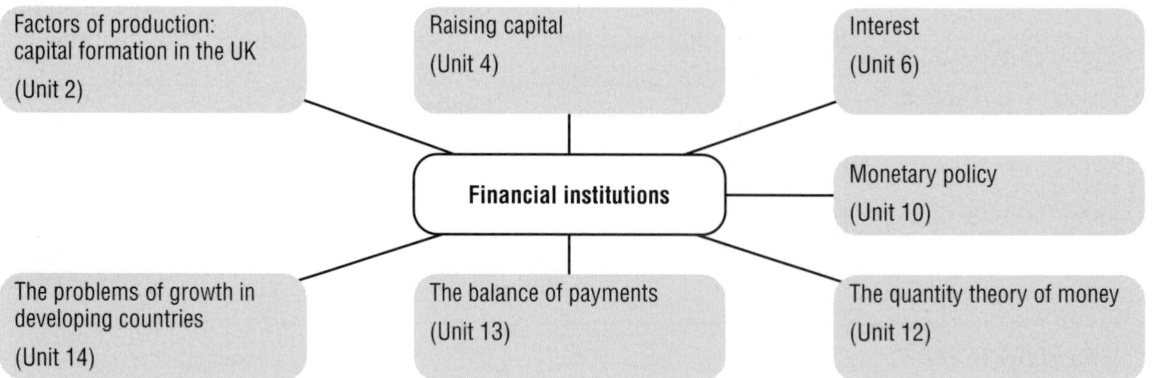

The financial markets

All markets have three essential factors: buyers, sellers and a market price. In financial markets the buyers are seeking the use of money, the sellers have surplus money that they are willing to supply, and the price is the rate of interest charged. Financial markets are complex, but it is convenient to identify two sectors:

- the **money market**, where funds are bought and sold on a short-term basis. Particularly involved in the money market are the Bank of England, the retail banks and specialist institutions such as discount houses and accepting houses (see later sections of this unit). These all have an important role in bringing lenders and borrowers together.
- the **capital market**, where borrowers want the use of money for long periods – sometimes permanently.

Fig. 8.2 Financial markets

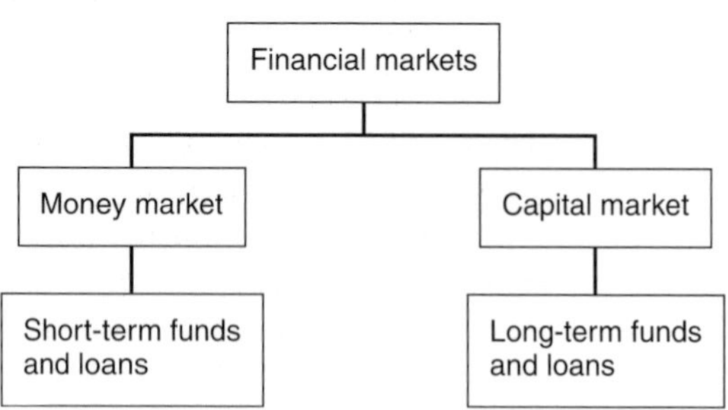

A common feature of the markets is that those people (and it is individuals who are the main suppliers of funds) who lend money normally want to be able to reclaim it at short notice, while borrowers frequently want the use of money for longer periods. A clear example is provided by building societies whose depositors want to be able to draw their money out subject to at most a few days' notice but whose borrowers want to repay over 25 years. It is the job of the building society to reconcile these two conflicting aims. All financial intermediaries, as they are called, have the same problem.

We begin our examination of the financial institutions by looking at the work of the familiar retail (or high-street) banks.

Commercial or retail banks

These banks – also known as the clearing banks – are the main links between ordinary citizens and the financial system. Their forerunners in the seventeenth and eighteenth centuries were the goldsmiths who developed a means of creating credit for their customers. This is a process that is carried out by the banks today, and it is this that sets them apart from other financial institutions.

Credit creation

A single-bank system

Imagine an economy in which there is only one bank. Soon after beginning business, it finds that individuals and firms have placed £10 000 of cash with it for safekeeping. Its balance sheet (ignoring the shareholders' capital or property owned by the bank) would appear as in Table 8.2.

Table 8.2

Balance sheet 1			
Assets	**£**	**Liabilities**	**£**
Cash in hand	10 000	Customers' deposits	10 000

Something to do

- Construct a balance sheet for Willowbrook Central Bank (see the activity on page 273) after its customers have deposited the first £15 000 000 with it.

The balance sheet is in effect a snapshot of the bank's financial position at a particular point in time.

- The **liabilities** are the amounts that the bank may be called on to provide to its customers.
- The **assets** are the cash and other resources available to the bank to meet its liabilities.

At this stage the bank has only received deposits from customers and issued receipts, or promises to pay, in return. It is clear that the bank has sufficient cash to meet any demands made by its customers.

In practice, customers prefer to settle their debts with each other by cheque, ordering their bank to transfer money from one account to another. Thus if Adams and Brown each have an account at the bank, and Adams owes Brown £100, he can settle his debt by writing a cheque which instructs the bank to reduce his account by £100 and to increase Brown's by the same amount. No cash changes hands. The bank still has obligations to its customers of £10 000: there has simply been a slight adjustment of those obligations.

If all the bank's depositors were always prepared to settle their debts in this way, the bank could ignore its holdings of cash, since all transactions would be carried out by transferring money in ledgers. Customers usually need to draw certain amounts of cash from the bank each week to make small payments, however, and to pay those people who prefer not to use the banking system. If the bank discovers that, at the most, the weekly withdrawal of cash amounts to 10 per cent of total deposits, and that this is quickly redeposited by traders accepting cash payments from customers, then the most cash the bank needs to meet demands from its customers with deposits of £10 000 is actually only £1000. The remaining £9000 can be used to make loans to other customers.

Let us imagine that another customer, Clarke, approaches the bank for a loan of £1000. The bank manager is agreeable and opens an account for him with a credit balance of £1000. Clarke can now write cheques to the value of £1000, transferring money out of his account, although he has deposited no money with the bank: he simply promises to repay the £1000 plus interest. The bank's balance sheet now shows a different picture (see Table 8.3).

Table 8.3

Balance sheet 2			
Assets	**£**	**Liabilities**	**£**
Cash in hand	10 000	Customers' deposits	11 000
Loans to customers (or promises to repay by customers)	1 000		
Total	**11 000**	**Total**	**11 000**

The bank now has insufficient cash to supply all its customers if they wish to withdraw their deposits. However, the bank knows that the most that is likely to be withdrawn is £1100 (10 per cent of deposits). It can therefore go on making loans (or creating credit, which is the same thing) until the cash that is held is equivalent to only 10 per cent of deposits (see Table 8.4).

Table 8.4

Balance sheet 3			
Assets	**£**	**Liabilities**	**£**
Cash in hand	10 000	Customers' deposits	100 000
Loans to customers (or promises to repay)	90 000		
Total	**100 000**	**Total**	**100 000**

Something to do

- Construct a new balance sheet for Willowbrook Central Bank on the basis that the bank has loaned the full amount it was able to while retaining its cash reserve ratio (which you calculated in the activity on page 273).

So far as a customer is concerned, the standing of his or her account is the same whether he or she has opened the account by depositing cash or by taking out a loan. Similarly, when someone accepts money in payment for goods or services, it makes no difference whether that payment is made out of cash that has previously been deposited with a bank or a loan that has been granted by the bank. In creating credit, the bank has in fact added to the supply of money, or money in circulation.

In practice, a bank will not create deposits for customers merely on the strength of promises to repay. The bank will check customers' creditworthiness (the likelihood of them being able to repay the loan when it is due) and will often insist on a prospective borrower providing some kind of security which can be sold to raise cash in the case of default by the borrowers. Such security might be the borrower's house or other personal possessions, or something that can be converted into cash, such as stocks and shares or an insurance policy with sufficient surrender value to cover the loan.

A more important refinement must be made in respect of the duration of loans and the commitment of customers to repay. In the case mentioned above, the bank could meet cash withdrawals of £10,000 because it had established a **cash reserve ratio** of 10 per cent. The cash reserve ratio (sometimes referred to simply as the 'cash ratio') is the ratio of cash held to deposits received.

We must now consider what would happen if customers withdrew £1000 which was spent but *not* then redeposited by other customers (see Table 8.5).

Table 8.5

Balance sheet 4			
Assets	**£**	**Liabilities**	**£**
Cash	9000	Customers' deposits	99000
Loans to customers (promises to repay)	90000		
Total	**99000**	**Total**	**99000**

Something to do

- Redraw the balance sheet of Willowbrook Central Bank to show the position if customers withdraw £10000 which is not redeposited with the bank.

Since £1000 has been withdrawn, the bank's assets have fallen by £1000 and its obligations to depositors have fallen by the same amount. But its holdings of cash have fallen by a greater percentage than its deposits: the ratio of cash to deposits is now

$$\frac{£9000}{£99,000} \times 100\% = 9.09\%$$

If the bank wishes to maintain a ratio of 10 per cent, then it must be able to replenish its cash holdings quickly. When granting loans to customers, the bank will therefore stipulate the period of the loan and will often include a clause requiring repayment at perhaps seven days' or three months' notice. Sometimes it will lend subject to repayment on demand. In these circumstances, the balance sheet in Table 8.4 might be redrawn as in Table 8.6.

Table 8.6

Balance sheet 5			
Assets	**£**	**Liabilities**	**£**
Cash	10 000	Customers' deposits	100 000
Loans repayable within 3 months	20 000		
Longer-term loans	70 000		
Total	**100 000**	**Total**	**100 000**

If customers draw out cash which is not quickly redeposited and the cash ratio becomes too low, as in Table 8.5, then the bank can demand repayment of some short-term loans, and thus restore its holdings of cash to the appropriate level.

The distribution of a bank's assets may in practice be determined in two ways:

- It can be left to the individual bank to determine the balance between cash, short-term loans and longer-term loans.
- The government, through the Bank of England, can lay down rules so that the relationship between the categories is fixed within narrow limits.

In either case, a bank must keep sufficient **liquid assets** to ensure that it can meet the legitimate demands of their depositors. Liquidity in this case means 'nearness to cash'.

Our calculations of credit creation were all made on the basis of cash, but a bank may use a different base in establishing its lending policy, such as a range of short-term assets including short-term loans and loans repayable on demand. The principle is the same, in that an increase in the bank's holdings of the base assets allows a bigger increase in total deposits and lending. The lower the stipulated ratio, the greater the increase in lending following an increase in the credit base.

Something to do

- Calculate the new ratio of cash to deposits (that is, the cash ratio) shown in the balance sheet for Willowbrook Central Bank that you constructed in the activity on page 277.
- If the bank wanted to maintain its previous cash to deposits ratio, how much of the amount loaned would it have to be able to call in at short notice?

A multi-bank system

The system outlined above is workable because when Adams pays Brown or Clarke by cheque they use the same bank (which we will call X) and only a ledger adjustment is necessary. In reality, of course, there is more than one bank accepting deposits from and making loans to customers. What, then, would happen if Brown or Clarke paid Adams's cheque into an entirely different bank (which we will call Y), which insisted on bank X handing over the appropriate amount of cash so that bank Y could meet the requirements of its own customers?

If the cheque was for £100, then bank X would lose this amount and bank Y would receive it. Bank X could not afford to let this happen on a daily basis, as it would eventually run out of cash. But, of course, some of bank Y's customers would no doubt write cheques in favour of bank

X's customers and these would cancel out those going from bank X to bank Y. So long as the cheques going in each direction more or less balance, the banks have nothing to fear. Also, as long as the banks followed the same policy of credit creation, the required balance will be achieved. If one bank operates with a cash ratio of 10 per cent and another with a cash ratio of 50 per cent, however, the former will gradually lose cash to the latter. An adjustment in lending policies will have to be made.

The banks' balance sheet

The banks are central to the smooth running of the economic system. Although their methods of operating may have changed since the days of the goldsmiths, their basic functions are unaltered. These are

- to provide a place of safekeeping for their customers' money
- to make loans
- to provide what are known as cash-transmission facilities.

Table 8.7 (on page 280) shows the combined balance sheet of the UK retail banks. (Some of the items are explained in detail in the following section.) This helps us to identify the basic banking roles and also the balancing act that the banks carried out.

The arrangement of assets is deliberate. They are in order of increasing liquidity (nearness to cash) and increasing profitability, which reflects the balance the banks strike between their obligations to their customers and the requirements of their shareholders. Generally, the less liquid the asset the more profitable it is.

Customers need the assurance that they can withdraw cash when they need it. If withdrawals are heavy, cash reserves might fall so low as to encourage speculation that the banks cannot meet their customers' requirements. To prevent this, the banks arrange their assets so that they always have a flow of cash coming in from short-term loans. Since these loans are short term, they earn little interest and so do not contribute heavily to the banks' profits. The banks' shareholders, though, want a dividend on their shares, so other bank assets are designed to produce the necessary profits. Higher interest can be earned on advances to customers, but they are not liquid – they can only gradually be turned into cash.

Functions of the retail banks

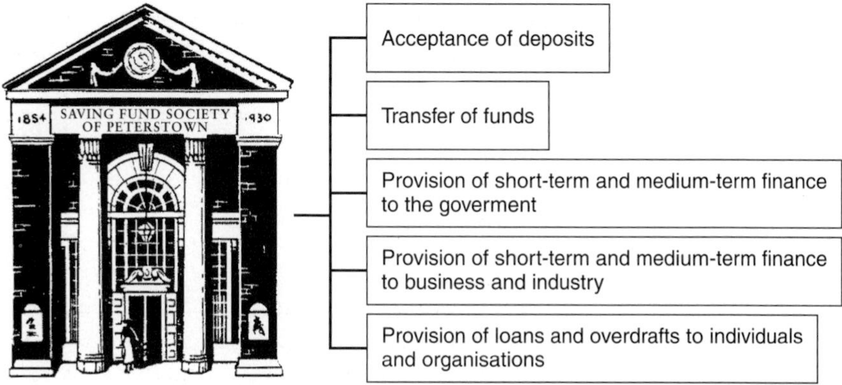

Fig. 8.3 The functions of clearing banks

Table 8.7

Retail banks: balance sheet (December 1988–December 1995)					
		31/12/88 (£ mn)	**31/12/90 (£ mn)**	**31/12/92 (£ mn)**	**31/12/95 (£ mn)**
Sterling assets					
Notes and coins		3375	3926	4293	5329
Balances with Bank of England		749	1032	829	1200
Market loans:	Secured money with LDMA	5220	7375	4947	4420
	Other UK banks	17639	31748	43743	58372
	UK banks CDs	4201	8469	9161	13300
	UK local authorities	738	226	297	318
	Overseas	3573	5258	7265	12464
Bills:	Treasury bills	1502	2469	1762	9900
	Eligible local authority bills	388	31	24	—
	Eligible bank bills	6060	10064	7997	9809
	Other	137	150	217	334
Advances:	UK public sector	702	527	348	524
	UK private sector	147920	234239	248871	300732
	Overseas	5284	4599	2380	3101
Banking dept. lending to central government (net)		956	1657	1227	−1801
Investments:	British government stocks	3547	3226	2571	12 353
	Others	5122	10 785	17 839	30 670
Other currency assets					
Market loans and advances:	UK banks	10007	9395	16911	18536
	UK bank CDs	178	736	729	951
	UK public sector	—	18	2575	5
	UK private sector	7648	10 980	12 541	18 139
	Overseas	30391	38020	53437	61823
Bills		436	1153	3540	2732
Investments		6198	11675	20499	46500
Miscellaneous (all currencies)		20 999	28355	28016	27967
TOTAL ASSETS		282974	426114	492009	637679
Sterling liabilities					
Notes issued		1407	1678	2084	2576
Deposits:	UK banks	20165	27830	31383	48233
	UK public sector	4185	4550	4233	7235
	UK private sector	137362	218053	237471	299478
	Overseas	17609	26730	22386	27399
	Certificates of deposit	11965	21354	22732	28765
Other currency liabilities					
Deposits:	UK banks	6373	6903	11268	14341
	Other UK	6883	10371	15402	23019
	Overseas	26437	37346	60419	80422
	Certificates of deposit	3549	6690	13666	22160
Sterling and other currencies		47038	64609	70965	84051
TOTAL LIABILITIES		282974	426114	492009	637679

Source: The Bank of England

We will now examine how some of the items in the balance sheet (Table 8.7) are related to the functions of the retail, or commercial, banks.

- **Deposits** were conventionally divided into **current accounts** (which did not earn interest) and **deposit accounts** (which did). However, competition between the banks themselves and from building societies has led to interest being paid on many current accounts, now known as **sight deposits**. These are the deposits that are available for immediate withdrawal. They amount to about 50 per cent of the total deposits. The remainder are **time deposits**, which usually earn a higher rate of interest and can be withdrawn only after an agreed period (the interest rate increasing with the notice period).
- **Notes and coins:** Banks are obliged to keep a certain amount of cash in their tills in order to meet the daily demands of their customers. Since this does not earn interest, the banks keep their till money as low as possible.
- **Balances with the Bank of England:** Banks are obliged to keep some cash at the Bank of England. They use this in much the same way as an individual uses a current account (except that they cannot overdraw). The cash at the Bank of England is used to settle inter-bank indebtedness and to replenish cash in the banks' tills if necessary. The amount that has to be held in the form of cash in their tills or cash at the Bank of England varies from time to time. From the banks' point of view, the smaller the amount required the better, since neither item earns them any interest.
- **Secured loans to discount houses:** Discount houses are specialist institutions in the money markets (see pages 290–292). Their importance to the banks is that they are prepared to take very short-term loans from the banks – often known as 'money at call and short notice'. These loans are used to finance the purchase of Treasury bills, bills of exchange and other securities. They earn little interest but the banks can make them with the certain knowledge that discount houses would always make repayments on time, so the banks are clear about their liquidity.
- **Market loans: other banks and institutions:** There is a wide variety of financial organisations in the money market other than the discount houses, including overseas banks and securities dealers. The banks also advance short-term loans to these, though probably at a rate of interest which is slightly higher than that charged to the discount houses.

  Also included here are **certificates of deposit** (CDs). These are issued by the banks in return for large deposits (£50 000 or more) made for a fixed period of time at a fixed rate of interest. Since a certificate of deposit is a promise from a bank to pay a set sum on a given day, it is highly marketable and the original owner can easily transfer the certificate to another person if he or she wants their money before the certificate matures. Since these certificates appear on the assets side of the balance sheet, we can conclude that the banks have acquired them from previous holders in exchange for cash. Any certificates that the banks themselves issue to depositors are, of course, included as certificates of deposit in the liabilities section of the balance sheet.

- **Treasury bills** are another important liquid asset, although they are of declining significance. The majority of the bills, which are sold by tender every Friday, are acquired by the discount houses (see pages 290–292). The number of bills issued each week depends mainly on the estimated excess of government expenditure over receipts for the following week. A Treasury bill is a promise by the Treasury to pay the holder a sum of money, say £10 000, 91 days after the issue of the bill. Bills are allotted to the highest bidders, and holders make profits by paying the government perhaps £9750 today, holding the bill for three months, and then receiving £10 000. Thus by lending £9750 for three months the holder makes a profit of £250 or just over 2.5 per cent of the outlay. This is equivalent to an annual rate of just over 10 per cent.

  The bills acquired by the discount houses are usually passed on to the clearing banks before they reach maturity. (There is a convention that the banks do not bid directly for the bills themselves.) In this way the bank can acquire bills of the exact maturity or liquidity they require. For example, if a bank has cash surplus to its requirements for the next 26 days, it can utilise the money by buying Treasury bills 65 days old (bills mature in 91 days). The price it pays must lie somewhere between the original purchase price and the redemption price and in the case of a bill issued for £9750 might be £9928.57, allowing the discount house a profit of £178.57 (£250 × 65 ÷ 91) and the bank (if it holds the bill for 26 days) a profit of £71.43 (£250 × 26 ÷ 91).

  The price of Treasury bills is related to other rates of interest. The **yield** will be higher than the rate paid for money at call and short notice, since the discount houses, having borrowed money at call at one rate, will re-lend only at a higher rate.
- **Other bills:** Equally liquid – though slightly less desirable than Treasury bills, since they do not carry a government guarantee – are other **bills of exchange** used in the finance of commerce and trade. Where the purchaser of goods requires temporary credit which the seller cannot afford, the latter may draw a bill of exchange setting out the debt and demanding payment in (usually) three months' time. The purchaser acknowledges his or her debt and at the same time promises payment in three months by signing the bill. If the purchaser has a good name in the business world, the bill may be accepted by an accepting house (see page 292) or clearing bank, which will then endorse it. This means that, in the event of the purchaser failing to meet the debt on the due date, the seller can look to the accepting house or clearing bank for payment.

  It is unlikely that the seller will hold the bill for three months, however. He or she will probably sell it to a bank at a discount in order to receive the money earlier. The bank then collects the money at the end of three months from the original purchaser and makes its profit. The rate of discount on commercial bills of this kind will be slightly higher than on Treasury bills – this reflects the slightly greater risk involved. Properly accepted commercial bills are widely bought and sold by the Bank of England in the course of its open-market operations.

You should note the differences between a **rate of discount** and a **rate of interest**. If a three-month £100 bill is bought for £97.50, in other words at a discount of £2.50, or 2.5 per cent, the annualised rate is 2.5% × 4 = 10% per annum.

Something to do

- A bank pays £4900 to a discount house for a £5000 bill of exchange redeemable in three months. The annual rate of interest is 9 per cent. Has the bank made a good short-term investment?

- **Advances:** The most profitable assets of banks are their advances to private- and public-sector customers. These may be in the form of **overdrafts**, whereby customers are allowed to draw cheques in excess of the money they have deposited, up to an agreed limit, and pay interest only on the amount overdrawn; or in the form of **loans**, whereby customers' accounts are credited with the amount of the loan, and interest is payable on the whole amount. Providing advances is a most important function of the banks and one without which industry and trade could not flourish.
- **Investments:** As an alternative to lending to customers in the way outlined earlier, the banks may lend to the government by taking up **bonds**. In this case the banks' liabilities are increased as they credit the account of the government with the value of the bonds bought.

Government bonds

Government bonds are known as **gilts** or **gilt-edged securities**. When the British Government wishes to borrow money over a long period of time it will issue a bond, for instance for £10 000, with a fixed rate of interest and state the year in which it will be paid back or redeemed. (Some bonds are undated, which allows the government to redeem them at any date.) These bonds are known as gilts because it is certain that the interest will be paid and that they will be redeemed. Therefore, they are a very safe buy for investors. However, the return on them is likely to be lower than for other financial investments.

It is not, of course, necessary for the banks to acquire bonds directly from the government since they are always available in substantial numbers on the Stock Exchange (see page 296). It is difficult to be precise about the earnings made from government securities since they pay a fixed rate of interest, which means that their yield varies according to the price paid. (The yield on an asset or investment is measured by calculating the income received as a percentage of the price paid.)

Suppose that, in year 1, £100 of government stock was issued at 5 per cent. This means that the long-term rate of interest was 5 per cent and that anyone who buys the stock receives £5 per year in interest payments. If, by year 3, the long-term interest rate in the financial market has risen to 10 per cent, the holders of the fixed-interest government stock will still only receive £5 per year. But if they wished to sell the stock, no one would now offer them the £100 they paid for it, since new stock could be bought for £100 and earn £10 per year. The highest price payable for £100 of the original stock is that which will give the new owner of it a yield of 10 per cent. This can be calculated as

$$£100 \times \frac{5\%}{10\%} = £50.$$

This relationship is an important feature of the **gilt-edged market** (the market in government securities) and one to which the banks must pay careful attention.

Summary of the functions of the clearing banks

- The acceptance of deposits and their transfer via the cheque system and other methods which have been devised by the banks
- The provision of short-term finance to the government, indirectly through money at call, and by the acquisition of Treasury bills
- The provision of medium-term finance to the government by the acquisition of government bonds
- The provision of short-term finance to industry and trade through the discounting of bills of exchange
- The provision of medium-term finance to individuals, industry and trade by the system of overdrafts and loans.

The ultimate objective of all this activity, as well as a whole range of non-banking services such as taxation advice, executorship and many others which do not concern us here, is of course to produce profits for the banks' shareholders. This is achieved in two ways:

- by obtaining funds at one rate of interest (often zero) and lending these funds at a higher rate
- by charging for services provided.

The government and the banks

The main banks are in a powerful position. Through the process of credit creation they can be a major influence on the total amount of money in the economy. Since the amount of money available has an important influence on the performance of the economy, the government seeks to control the amount of new money that is created. This is the principal objective of **monetary policy**, which is discussed in Unit 10.

The main link between the government and the retail or clearing banks is the Bank of England. We consider the principal functions of the Bank of England in the next section.

The Bank of England

We have seen that the retail or clearing banks are not entirely free to create credit as they wish. The government has overall responsibility for the management of the economy, and this includes controlling the supply of money. The **Bank of England** is its agent in operating monetary policy and is the link between the government and the retail banks. In this respect, the Bank of England acts as a **central bank**. Founded in 1649, and nationalised in 1946, the Bank of England was given operational independence in 1997.

The Bank of England's balance sheet

The Bank of England regularly publishes its balance sheet (see Table 8.8).

The division of the balance sheet into two sections (the Issue Department and the Banking Department) is longstanding but no longer reflects the way in which the Bank is organised. Its work is too extensive and too complex to permit such a simple division. However, we can see some of the main functions of the Bank reflected in its balance sheet.

The government's bank

Bank accounts

One of the most important functions of the Bank is to administer the principal bank accounts of the government. These appear under the heading 'Public deposits' in the balance sheet. It would be an exaggeration to say that all government receipts and payments pass through the accounts held here, for some government departments hold accounts elsewhere for convenience. Control of the flow of government funds is centred here, however.

In view of the volume of government receipts and payments, it is perhaps surprising that public deposits at the bank are so small. This is a matter of deliberate policy on the part of the authorities (in this instance the Treasury and the Bank). Rather than allow a substantial balance to accumulate in the form of public deposits, they would prefer to pay off part of the national debt (see below and page 343). On the other hand, the Bank does take steps to ensure that there is always enough in the accounts to meet the requirements of the government and, on rare occasions, the Bank itself lends to the government on an overnight basis in the form of **ways and means advances**.

Managing the issue of notes and coins

The government reserves the right to issue banknotes and coins, and these reach the public via the Bank of England. The notes actually reach the general public from the retail or clearing banks, who acquire notes from the Banking Department of the Bank of England, thereby reducing the bankers' deposits there. The Banking Department receives notes from the Issue Department. Notes are backed by UK Government securities and the securities issued by other governments. Coins reach the public by a similar route, but originate at the Royal Mint.

The national debt

The government raises most of its money through taxation. When it needs more, it borrows from the public, thus adding to the **national debt**. This is the accumulated outstanding borrowing of the government from its citizens and, to a lesser extent, from overseas. In 1997 the national debt stood at around £300 billion.

Table 8.8

The Bank of England: balance sheet (£ million)												
		December										
		1986	**1987**	**1988**	**1989**	**1990**	**1991**	**1992**	**1993**	**1994**	**1995**	**1996**
Issue Department	Liabilities:											
	Notes in circulation	14119	14654	16071	16849	17283	17466	17542	18218	20055	21262	22407
	Notes in Banking Department	11	6	9	11	7	4	8	12	5	7	12
	Assets:											
	Government securities	2718	9783	10339	13946	14672	11791	7808	6816	11468	14552	16524
	Other securities	11412	4877	5741	2914	2618	5679	9742	11414	8592	6717	5896
Banking Department	Liabilities:											
	Total	2606	3059	3203	5398	8613	5825	5623	11095	6192	7114	6229
	Public deposits	86	100	94	69	44	104	97	6205	938	1159	1001
	Bankers' deposits	932	1064	1310	1750	1842	1813	1553	1700	1855	2001	2021
	Reserves and other accounts	1574	1880	1784	3565	6713	3894	3959	3175	3385	3941	3193
	Assets:											
	Total	2606	3059	3203	5398	8615	5825	5623	11095	6192	7114	6229
	Government securities	474	559	882	1354	1432	1346	1237	1174	1050	1090	1232
	Advances and other accounts	701	1064	661	726	2146	2443	3935	9411	4696	5499	2339
	Premises, equipment and other securities	1420	1430	1651	3307	5030	2031	443	498	441	518	2646
	Notes and coin	11	6	9	11	7	5	8	12	5	7	12

Source: *Annual Abstract of Statistics* (The Stationery Office, 1999)

<u>PSBR and PSDR</u> In the Budget each year, the Chancellor of the Exchequer estimates the amount of money that will be raised through taxation over the coming twelve months, and the proposed state spending over the same period. If spending exceeds income, the difference will be borrowed. This is known as the PSBR (Public Sector Borrowing Requirement). If income is to exceed spending, then the difference can be used to pay off government debts from previous years. This is known as the PSDR (Public Sector Debt Repayment). Over the past decades, total borrowing has exceeded total repayments and thus the State has built up a national debt. If the next Budget requires a PSBR, then the national debt will increase by the amount borrowed. If it leaves a PSDR, then the national debt will decrease by the amount paid back. If there is a balanced budget, (that is, income = expenditure), then the national debt will remain unchanged.

Most of us own part of the national debt, the basic sterling components of which are shown below.

<u>Marketable debt</u> The bulk of the debt is marketable debt. It is marketable because it can normally be bought and sold on the Stock Exchange. The majority of the debt consists of fixed-interest government stocks issued in £100 units. When the government borrows money, it will issue bonds in return, promising two things:

- to pay interest at a stated annual rate
- to repay the loan to the holder of the bond when it matures.

Since the bonds carry a government promise of repayment, they are completely safe, which means they can always be sold – though not at a guaranteed price. The price will be affected by the rate of interest paid in the private sector.

A high proportion of the government bonds, or gilt-edged securities, is held by financial institutions of various kinds. It is through organisations such as insurance companies, unit trusts and pension funds (see pages 295–296) that most citizens have an indirect interest in, and part-ownership of, the national debt.

Part of the marketable debt, known as the **floating debt**, is in the form of Treasury bills. These are short-term loans to the government arising when the government is temporarily short of funds (see page 282).

<u>Non-marketable debt</u> The non-marketable debt grows when people lend money to the government by purchasing Premium Bonds, National Savings certificates and similar documents. If you have a Premium Bond and want to recover the money, you cannot sell your Premium Bond to someone else. It is non-marketable and the money can be recovered only by redeeming the bond (which means the bond will be bought back by the government).

The Bank of England undertakes the administration of the national debt on behalf of the government. It is responsible for the issue of new securities, either to replace those maturing or to raise extra money for the government. The Bank keeps a register of the holders of government stock, paying them interest on appropriate days and repaying them as the stock matures.

If interest rates are high but are expected to fall during the next two or three years, the Bank may feel that it would be unwise to issue twenty-year stock, for example, and commit itself to paying a high rate interest for the whole period. The Bank would rather issue two-year stock and hope to make a longer issue at a lower rate of interest in two years' time. If it does this, of course, many of the administrative costs are doubled. These costs may also be important in deciding whether the government should raise, say, £1000 million by one issue or by two separate issues. A further important administrative problem is the timing of the redemption of stocks. The Bank is not always happy at the prospect of redeeming, say, £1000 million of stock on a given date because, unless £1000 million of new stock is taken up on the same day, the cash holdings of the clearing banks will dramatically increase as the money from redeemed stock is deposited with the banks. This may be overcome in two ways:

- The Bank may buy up stock for some months in advance of its redemption date, in the course of its ordinary market operations.
- No fixed date for repayment may be given.

Thus, one of the current issues is 7.75 per cent Treasury stock 2012–2015, giving the Bank a degree of flexibility in making repayment.

Monetary policy

Perhaps the most important of the Bank's functions as the Government's bank is the implementation of monetary policy in pursuit of the broad economic objectives of the government of the day. This involves controlling the supply of money and the price of money (the rate of interest), and it is the most difficult of the Bank's jobs. Up until 1997, the responsibility for deciding the interest rate lay with the Chancellor of the Exchequer, although the Governor of the Bank of England acted as the primary advisor. In that year, the new Labour Government transferred the responsibility to an independent Monetary Policy Committee (MPC), under the chairmanship of the Governor. (Monetary policy is discussed in Unit 10.)

Lender of the last resort

We have seen that the clearing banks arrange their assets so that they always have access to liquid resources which can be converted into cash on demand. The most liquid of their assets (other than actual cash and balances at the Bank of England) consists of money at call – that is, redeemable on demand – with the discount houses (see page 230). Normally the Bank's management will be such that they do not have to insist on repayment of their 'call money' at times when this is likely to embarrass the discount houses. There are, however, occasions when the banks' holdings of cash are dangerously low and, to ensure that they can meet the requirements of their customers who want cash, they do then demand repayment of call money by the discount houses. The discount houses spend most of their call money in buying Treasury bills, so, not having cash available, they may have to seek funds from other financial institutions. If no one else can oblige them, they turn, as a last resort, to the Bank of England. The Bank is always prepared to advance money to the discount houses, either by re-discounting Treasury Bills or by lending against acceptable security, and will fix the rate it charges the discount houses according to market conditions. The mechanics of the process are quite simple. The Bank of England, in re-discounting bills for the discount houses, credits their accounts at the Bank (part of bankers' deposits) with the appropriate sum, which they are then free to transfer to the clearing banks in order to discharge their obligations. In this way the Bank ensures that the market never goes short of cash.

External functions

On behalf of the government, the Bank of England also discharges a number of functions that may properly be regarded as belonging to the international economy rather than to the domestic economy:

- The nation's gold and foreign currency reserves are held at the Bank in the Exchange Equalisation Account. It is from this account that the foreign currency needed by an importer to buy goods, or the spending money needed by a traveller going abroad, ultimately comes, and into which receipts are paid.
- Exchange-control regulations are operated by the Bank. The government may wish to limit the amount of foreign currency spent abroad by British citizens, and it is the Bank that will supervise arrangements in this connection. The British Government has, however, removed almost all such controls over the movement of sterling. The Bank is also responsible for maintaining orderly exchange rates against other currencies, in the light of government policy. This is explained in more detail in Unit 13.
- The Bank's expertise is often called for in international monetary negotiations, particularly in connection with the International Monetary Fund (see Unit 13).
- The Bank's governor represents the UK at the European Central Bank (the central bank of the EU).

The bankers' bank

As an essential aspect of its linking role between the government and the banking system, the Bank of England acts as banker to the banks. This function is reflected in the item 'Bankers' deposits' in Table 8.8. All institutions in the monetary sector are required to keep cash at the Bank of England, and some international organisations may also hold accounts with the Bank which appear under this heading.

The role of the Bank as the bankers' bank is important in facilitating the settlement of inter-bank debts and in contributing to the smooth running of the money market in general. The accounts that the banks hold at the Bank of England may be regarded as current accounts, but they cannot be overdrawn.

In this role the Bank takes a guiding role, advising them on policies and activities.

Other accounts

Although the Bank does not compete with the clearing banks, it does run a number of ordinary accounts for private customers. These are mainly long-established accounts or accounts for Bank employees. This is done largely to give Bank staff some training in the principles of commercial banking. Such accounts appear under the heading 'Reserves and other accounts' in Table 8.8. Also included here are the accounts of a number of international banks and banks under foreign control.

Other financial institutions

While the retail banks and the Bank of England are the most prominent of the financial institutions, there is a wide variety of others meeting the requirements of different groups of lenders and borrowers. Some of these, such as the discount houses, are primarily concerned with short-term borrowing and lending in what we may regard as the money market (see page 274). Others, such as the building societies and the Stock Exchange, deal in longer-term funds and form part of the capital market. However, it is impossible in practice to draw a firm boundary between the money market and the capital market, since many organisations work in both sectors.

Discount houses

We have seen that the **discount houses** play an important part in the issue and distribution of Treasury bills. A glance at their balance sheet, as shown in Table 8.9, will give an indication of the extent of their activities.

The balance sheet covers the money-market dealing counterparts of the Bank of England, authorised under the Banking Act.

The discount market

The discount market became important in the nineteenth century in connection with the financing of trade by means of bills of exchange which were a major means of trade credit. Its function today involves gathering funds that are temporarily surplus to the requirements of other financial institutions and channelling them towards other organisations in the public and private sectors temporarily short of money. The discount houses, therefore, act as middlemen, providing an important service to both sides of the market. Those with surplus funds do not have to seek those who want to borrow; they simply lend to the discount houses, and those wanting to borrow can go direct to the discount houses.

Most of the discount houses' funds come from the clearing banks, although 'Other UK banks' in Table 8.9 covers money from industrial and commercial firms with funds available for a short period. It can give us a good idea of the importance of the discount market if we imagine a situation where it has liquid cash of £1 million on its hands. What could it do with it?

- **Treasury bills:** The discount houses might spend their £1 million on Treasury bills, for which they tender every Friday, specifying the day on which they wish to take up the bills. Such bills are guaranteed by the government and carry no risk whatsoever, and the discount houses can make a modest but certain profit on them. In most countries, Treasury bills are sold direct to the banks, but the London Discount Market survives because *its* members guarantee to take up the whole issue of Treasury bills each week, so the government knows that its borrowing needs will be met. It is in return for this guarantee that the Bank of England acts as lender of last resort to the discount houses; the latter then release the bills to the banks in the quantities and of the maturity required.

Table 8.9

Discount houses: balance sheet (£ million)													
			December										
			1986	1987	1988	1989	1990	1991	1992	1993	1994	1995	1996
Assets	Total		9 539	11 608	12 027	15 276	15 193	11 857	9 743	10 551	10 581	12 495	21 954
	Treasury bills		240	261	647	940	415	158	248	91	1	661	420
	Other bills:	Sterling	4 073	5 351	4 205	6 006	5 384	3 851	2 902	1 953	3 042	3 163	4 470
		Other currencies	30	25	51	45	80	13	—	—	—	—	—
	British Government securities		21	33	8	4	13	61	72	187	292	250	508
	UK banks CDs:	Sterling	3 022	3 705	4 304	4 338	5 753	5 408	4 546	5 251	4 753	4 581	9 491
		Other currencies	124	38	33	137	138	134	63	51	6	—	—
	Building society CDs and time deposits		348	747	897	1 270	1 768	978	510	569	497	159	320
	Local authority securities		13	2	—	—	—	—	—	—	—	—	—
	Other assets:	Sterling	1 428	1 417	1 738	2 307	1 399	1 136	1 291	2 248	1 788	3 551	6 626
		Other currencies	168	119	136	218	244	116	110	202	202	130	119
Borrowed funds	Total		9 246	11 312	11 727	14 926	14 911	11 604	9 482	10 338	10 382	12 274	21 667
	Bank of England, banking department		—	45	35	113	43	—	—	332	—	—	—
	Other UK banks:	Sterling	6 983	8 064	8 182	10 192	10 861	8 871	7 571	7 049	7 939	6 795	7 160
		Other currencies	129	59	68	145	92	66	52	94	82	20	7
	Other sources:	Sterling	1 988	3 019	3 294	4 219	3 559	2 472	1 743	2 710	2 241	5 349	14 345
		Other currencies	146	125	148	258	357	196	115	152	120	109	156

Source: *Annual Abstract of Statistics* (The Stationery Office, 1999)

- **Other bills:** The historical outlet for the discount houses' funds was in the discounting of bills of exchange ('Other bills' in Table 8.9). As we saw on page 282, such bills are used when a purchaser requires credit which the vendor cannot afford to grant. If the bills have been accepted in the way described on page 282, then the discount houses will regard them as **bank bills** or **fine bills** and will discount them at the minimum rate (that is, they will make very little profit on them). Bills not so accepted are called **trade bills** and, as they carry a greater degree of risk, they are discounted at a higher rate. Discount houses frequently do not discount them and they are instead discounted directly by the drawer's bank. A further disadvantage of trade bills is that the Bank of England will not normally accept them as security for loans, nor will it usually re-discount them.
- **Certificates of deposit (CDs):** The discount houses have joined in the expansion of these certificates. Since they are assets here, they represent money lent to other parties.
- **Time deposits:** Although loans for up to three months are the main business of the discount houses, they do hold some long-term investments. Since nearly all their money is repayable at short notice, however, they must be careful about this kind of investment. Any government stocks they hold are likely to be close to their maturity date so that they can more easily be redeemed at the Bank of England.
- **Other assets:** These include funds lent to organisations such as building societies and local government authorities.

Summary of the role of the discount market

- The provision of short-term finance for industry and trade through bills of exchange
- The provision of short-term finance for the government through the acquisition of Treasury bills – in particular, the guarantee to the government that all Treasury bills will be taken up each week
- The provision of safe, liquid assets to the banking system as and when they are wanted
- The channel through which the Bank of England acts as the lender of last resort to the banking system
- The provision of finance to local authorities and other bodies. (This ability to branch out into markets other than their traditional ones stems directly from the discount houses' high standing and reputation for integrity.)

Think about it

- Do discount houses provide a valuable service, or are they just another form of financial intermediary, making profits by moving money around?

Merchant or investment banks

There is no formal definition of what constitutes a **merchant bank**. The foremost are sometimes known as **accepting houses** and include such famous names as Morgan Grenfell, Rothschild and S.G. Warburg. Accepting houses grew to prominence because of their skill in accepting the bills of exchange used in the finance of international trade. We have seen that discount houses will advance money against bills of exchange, but they are more willing to do so if the bill has been accepted by one of the major accepting houses, thus rendering it a bank bill or fine bill. As the acceptance of a bill is a guarantee that the acceptor will meet the debt in case of default, the accepting house clearly needs a detailed knowledge of the traders involved. In the nineteenth century, only the most skilful accepting houses survived. Today their most important function in the money market is still to guarantee the value of paper securities, for which they charge commission.

Nowadays merchant banks – often called investment banks – have many other activities, however. They are an important financial intermediary for industrial concerns. When a company wants to raise new long-term capital, it will normally ask a merchant bank in its capacity as an **issuing house** to arrange the issue of shares. In general, merchant banks perform the role of financial advisers to their industrial clients, guiding them not only in connection with new share issues but also on the timing and scale of investment and on the merits and tactics of take-over bids and mergers. A merchant bank itself might make medium-term loans to its clients, perhaps to finance the installation of new machinery which does not require the raising of extra long-term capital. If not, it will make arrangements for such loans, or possibly purchase machinery and lease it to the client.

The merchant banks do not compete directly with retail banks for deposits. Their depositors are to be found in commerce and industry, and in the monetary sector. Only about a quarter of their deposits are sight deposits (see page 281). Merchant banks are closely involved in lending and borrowing in the money market, often through the use of certificates of deposit, but they also have a foot in the capital market through their management of unit trusts, investment trusts and pension funds (see pages 295–296).

It should be noted that the old merchant banks face increasing competition in many of their activities from subsidiaries of retail banks who have set up their own merchant banking organisations. One area where all are involved is the so-called 'parallel market', alongside but closely involved with the main money market, which consists of retail banks, discount houses and the Bank of England.

In the 1960s and 1970s, there grew up an increasing demand for funds from new sources – local authorities and finance houses, for example. There also developed a large number of organisations striving to meet this demand, including overseas banks, which rapidly established offices in London, and consortium banks, which are jointly owned by groups of retail banks who established these subsidiaries when restrictions were placed on their principal companies. The outcome was seen in the form of new flows of money and the development of new markets, the most significant of which include the local authority market, the market in certificates of deposit and the inter-bank market. The latter can involve any of the institutions in the **monetary sector**, and provides a facility through which those temporarily short of funds can obtain them from those in surplus. The market thus contributes to the smooth running of the overall market for short-term funds.

The capital market

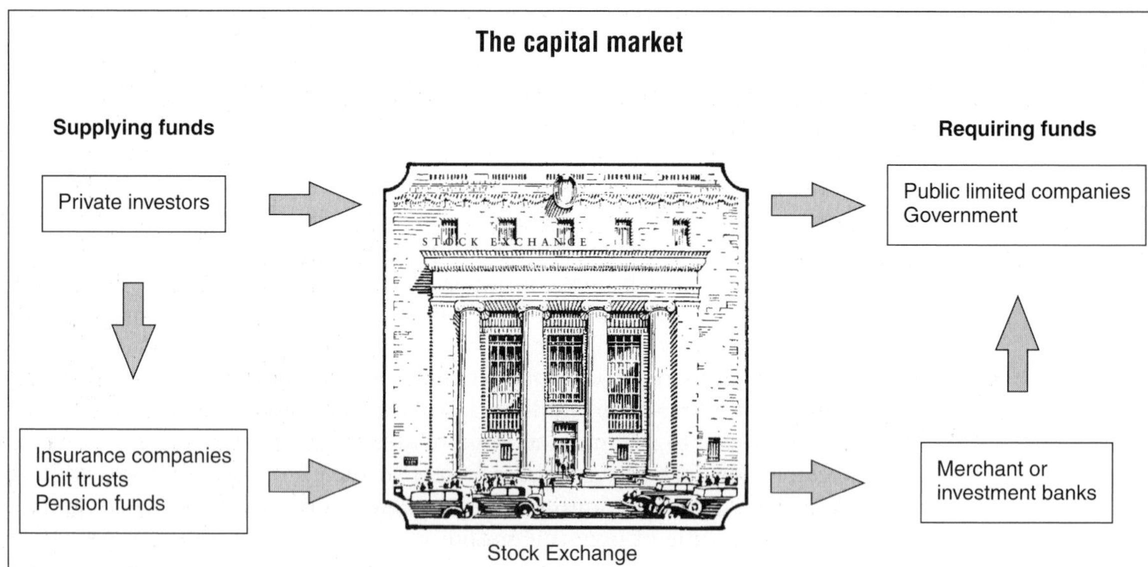

Stock Exchange

While there is no clear boundary between the money market and the capital market, since many firms are active in both markets, the capital market caters for those who want to raise money on a long-term basis – perhaps indefinitely. So a manufacturer wishing to raise a million pounds to finance the import of raw materials that will be made up and sold within six months enabling him to repay his debt at that point, will seek the assistance of the money market. If the same manufacturer were seeking several million pounds to finance the installation of new machinery which would not pay for itself for ten years, then he would look to the capital market.

At the centre of the capital market is the Stock Exchange (see page 296), where stocks and shares are bought and sold. On one side of the market, supplying funds to it, is a number of institutions, such as insurance companies, unit trusts and pension funds, each of which gathers resources from a large number of subscribers, and invests them. There is also an increasing number of individuals who invest directly on the Stock Exchange, bypassing these institutions. On the other side of the market are those requiring funds to finance industrial and commercial development or social improvement. These include the public limited companies (frequently represented by the merchant banks) and the government. The capital market exists to meet the requirements of these various components, and its most important function is to channel funds towards the business community through the new-issues market.

All businesses require capital, but only the public limited companies are allowed to appeal directly to the public for their funds. When a private company is on the point of going public, it will normally consult an issuing house (a specialist merchant bank) about the best approach. Issuing houses advise clients on the scale, structure and timing of the raising of capital, and help to decide whether the money should be raised mainly by loans or by the issue of ordinary shares.

An important aspect of a share issue is the guarantee that the funds will be raised. If a company needs £35 million for a project and the share issue raises only £25 million, the project may have to be cancelled. The issuing house therefore arranges the **underwriting** of the issue. Underwriters are basically insurers. In return for a commission, they guarantee to buy that portion of the share issue not otherwise taken up. In this way the raising of the necessary finance is guaranteed in advance.

The underwriters are not full-time underwriters, but financial intermediaries who are mainly occupied in other activities relating to the capital market. They might, for example, include insurance companies, unit trusts, investment trusts and superannuation (pension) funds.

Something to do

- Consider the following and decide whether the prospective borrower is more likely to go to the money market or the capital market:
  - someone wanting a mortgage to buy a house
  - a firm requiring finance to cover this week's wage bill
  - a discount house requiring cover for long-term investment
  - the government seeking to finance a new hospital.

Insurance companies

Many people have a life insurance policy for which the insurance company collects weekly, monthly or annual premiums and undertakes to pay a lump sum either on a specific date (the maturity date) or on the death of the insured person. The company is able to repay more than it collects in premiums because it invests those premiums in securities which yield interest or dividends.

The majority of the funds that reach industry and commerce via the insurance companies would not be available for productive investment without the existence of these companies, as individually contributions would be too small to be worth investing in securities.

Unit trusts

While a part of many people's savings reaches the Stock Exchange via the insurance companies, the number of people who invest in unit trusts is much smaller. Small savers are able to buy units in a fund, and the managers of the fund then use the investors' money to buy shares of companies in the particular sectors of industry to which the trust is committed. (Unit trust deeds indicate the area to which funds will be applied.) All earnings on the shares are payable to the trust managers. Such earnings are then redistributed to unit holders, who may elect to convert them into further units.

The main advantage of a unit trust is its security. This comes from the fact that it can spread its investment across a large number of companies and industries, thereby eliminating the danger of complete loss if one company collapses. But precisely because of the trust's pattern of widespread assets, unit holders cannot normally expect spectacular returns on their investment, though holders do have the advantage of expert professional advice in the handling of their money.

Investment trusts

These are really limited companies that use their capital to buy shares in other businesses in order to make a profit for their shareholders. Shares in investment trusts are bought in the same way as shares in other businesses and are therefore not so easy to obtain as units in a unit trust.

Like unit trusts, investment trusts apply their funds mainly to industrial investment, and approximately 90 per cent of the capital is invested in ordinary shares. The main advantage of the investment trust over the unit trust is that it is less restricted in its activities by a trust deed, and thus retains greater flexibility for switching funds from relatively unprofitable to more profitable uses.

Pension funds

Pension funds operate on broadly the same principle as insurance companies, collecting weekly or monthly contributions from employees and their employers and guaranteeing the future payment of a pension. A high proportion of their money is invested in shares.

These organisations are among the most important financial intermediaries gathering funds for the capital market and making them available to industry and commerce for the purchase of factories, machinery and equipment.

The Stock Exchange

But what happens if an investor in a company – either an institution or an individual – wants to withdraw his or her money when the company has already spent it on machinery and cannot therefore repay? The Stock Exchange resolves this situation by providing the mechanism through which the investor can turn his or her assets into cash without damaging the company in which he or she has invested. Stockbrokers and licensed dealers can always be found who will buy second-hand shares. They will not however, guarantee the price – this will depend on market conditions.

Without the Stock Exchange, companies would have difficulty in raising capital. Few of us would commit money to a company if subsequently we had independently to find buyers for our shares.

The Stock Exchange is also important in other respects:

- Its strict rules provide a safeguard for investors' funds. The Stock Exchange will not permit dealings in the shares of companies unless the companies have been closely investigated.
- The price movements provide an important indication of the performance and prospects of individual industries and of the economy in general.
- It is of crucial importance to the government in financing the national debt. While most publicity seems to concentrate on the trade in company securities, most transactions involve the buying and selling of government stock. Like commercial concerns, the government might find it difficult to borrow if there were not a ready market for second-hand stocks.

Other capital-market institutions

National Savings

To some extent the government is fortunate in that it can access a subsidiary part of the capital market. Through National Savings, the government can make use of the personal savings of millions of individual citizens. These savings bypass the main capital market and are directly available to the government. Although they are diverted from the main capital market, however, they are not without competition.

Building societies

One of the most important avenues for personal savings is the **building society** sector, where a significant proportion of the personal sector's liquid assets are lodged. They were not originally public limited companies, as the retail banks are, but mutual societies, owned by lenders and borrowers. Until the 1980s, building societies had always been outside the main money and capital markets, raising money from individual citizens and lending almost entirely for house purchase. This contrasts with retail banks, which raise their money from many more sources and lend only a small proportion for house purchase.

The situation began to change in the 1980s, when the first building societies ended their long-standing cartel arrangements and started to compete vigorously with each other. The building societies and the banks then began to compete with each other's traditional services. The banks developed new personal savings schemes and increased their mortgage lending for house purchases, while the building societies looked for alternative sources of and outlets for funds and also started to provide money-transmission services (for example, cheque accounts) for their customers.

The Building Societies Act 1986 acknowledged these developments and opened the way for the societies to expand their services and compete more effectively with the banks. Many of the restrictions on their lending policies were removed, and – more important in the long run – a mutual society became free to convert itself into a limited company with the agreement of its members. The Abbey National Building Society did this in 1989, since then others have converted. This change increases the availability of capital which the society might require to expand its activities. Such expansion typically occurs on two broad fronts: services directly linked to mortgage activities – estate agency and conveyancing – and, in more direct competition with the banks, lending for general purposes, the growth of ordinary current-account services, and even the development of pension services or the administration of unit trusts.

There has, however, been much controversy within and outside mutual societies about conversion to plc.

The financial markets are always changing, but the institutions we have examined (with perhaps the exception of the Bank of England) have one thing in common: they all lend money for a longer period than they borrow it. They therefore have to strike the balance between liquidity and profitability.

Because of the changing nature of the financial markets, it has proved difficult for the authorities to follow a steady monetary policy. We examine their problems in this respect in Unit 10.

9 Measuring the national economy

Introduction: macro-economics

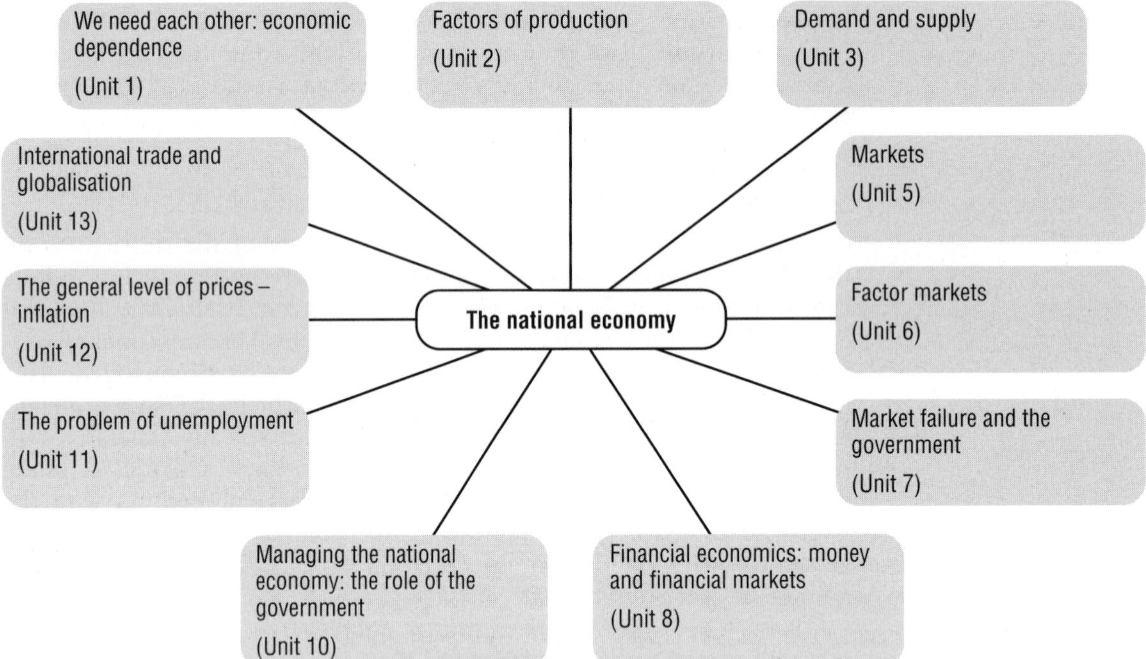

So far we have concentrated on various parts of economic activity and have looked at individual economic units such as banks, single industries and factors of production – all aspects of **micro-economics**. Yet each of these contribute to the overall performance of the economy and has an effect on such things as the general level of employment, the rate of inflation or the balance of payments. These concepts belong to the field of **macro-economics** – the study of the whole economy.

In the remaining units of this book, we examine the issues of macro-economics and the field of public economic policy. We examine the main macro-economic problems and the policies which a government might use in its attempt to achieve its broad economic objectives. These objectives are likely to be as follows:

- **An adequate level of employment:** Until the 1970s, an 'adequate' level would have been regarded as a situation where unemployment was not more than 3 per cent of those seeking a job. Since then, there have been times when unemployment has been much higher than this and there has been much discussion of what constitutes 'full employment' (see Unit 11).
- **Price stability:** The process of **inflation** (the situation of persistently rising prices) has various unsettling effects on an economy (see Unit 12), so governments generally follow policies aimed at keeping inflation under control.

- **Economic growth:** The economic growth of a country is what enables its people to enjoy a higher standard of living, since in a growing economy more goods are produced each year (see Unit 14).
- **A balance-of-payments surplus:** It is generally preferable if a country's overseas payments are lower than its receipts from overseas (see Unit 13). A balance-of-payments surplus enables domestic economic objectives to be the main priority of a government.
- **A more equal distribution of income and wealth:** This may be achieved through taxation and welfare payments (see Unit 10).

While there may be general agreement in society about the first four of these, there are often differences of opinion about the commitment of a government to the last.

Fig. 9.1 The macro-economic objectives of a government

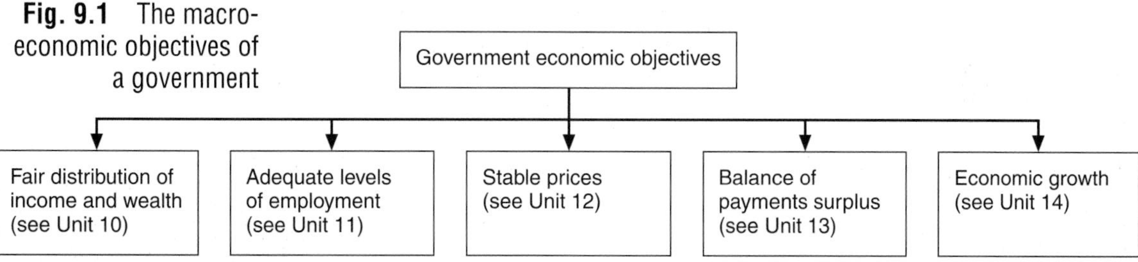

Think about it

- Why do you think there might be differences of opinion about the economic objective of achieving a more equal distribution of income and wealth?
- How important do you think this is as an objective?
- Do you think it is currently being effectively achieved? Give your reasons.

Something to do

- Remember to keep reading newspapers and magazines for articles and news stories about economic events and facts. File the articles in separate sections according to topic. Create an index for your file, or a cross-referencing system.

One of the problems facing a government is that the main objectives of economic policy are not always compatible. A reduction in unemployment, for example, may lead to inflation, as we see in Unit 12, while further economic growth may also contribute to inflation and this could adversely affect the balance of payments. These and other conflicts make the formulation of economic policy difficult and often results in a trade-off of objectives. We therefore need to look at the main objectives of governments and the methods available for achieving these, before considering actual policies.

Before that, however, we need to establish an indicator of the general level of economic activity and welfare. This involves valuing all the goods and services produced in the economy and arriving at what is called the **national product**. This is what concerns us in this unit.

The national product

The **national product** may be defined as the income a country receives from the goods and services it produces during a period. It is important in that it provides a measure of economic activity within a country, and therefore a guide to that country's prosperity.

To calculate a country's national product, it would be possible simply to compile a list of the goods and services produced in the economy over a period of a year. Such a list would be very complicated, however, and difficult to use for comparison with previous years or with other countries. To make the calculation and comparison easier, a common measure must be found for all goods and services. The most convenient common measure is money (see Unit 8); if we calculate the money value of all the goods and services produced within a country in a year we obtain the value of the **gross domestic product** (GDP), a widely used economic indicator.

Key points

- *GDP may be fully defined as the aggregate monetary value of the goods and services produced in one year by factors of production located and paid for within the economy, even if they are owned abroad.*

Sometimes a closely related concept, the **gross national product** (GNP), is used instead.

Key points

- *GNP may be defined as the aggregate monetary value of all the goods produced during the year by factors of production owned within the economy even if they are located overseas.*

The term 'gross' here indicates that no allowance is made for **depreciation**, or the extent to which capital has been used up in the year. If that allowance is made, we arrive at the **net domestic product** or the **net national product**.

Production as a flow

The economy can be regarded as a vast production line with raw materials and labour being fed in at one end and finished products flowing out at the other. The process is continuous and has no regard to time, so it is only for convenience that we cut into the flow to measure its value every twelve months. Unless it is specifically stated to the contrary, national product figures refer to a calendar year, although there is no reason why daily, weekly or monthly measures should not be taken. Whatever the time interval selected, there are bound to be difficulties. For example, at the end of any period there are some goods in the course of production, while others are finished but awaiting delivery. Some goods in stock at the beginning of the year may still be in stock, and the value of stocks may have changed. Those who are responsible for calculating the **national product** must find ways of overcoming all these and many other problems.

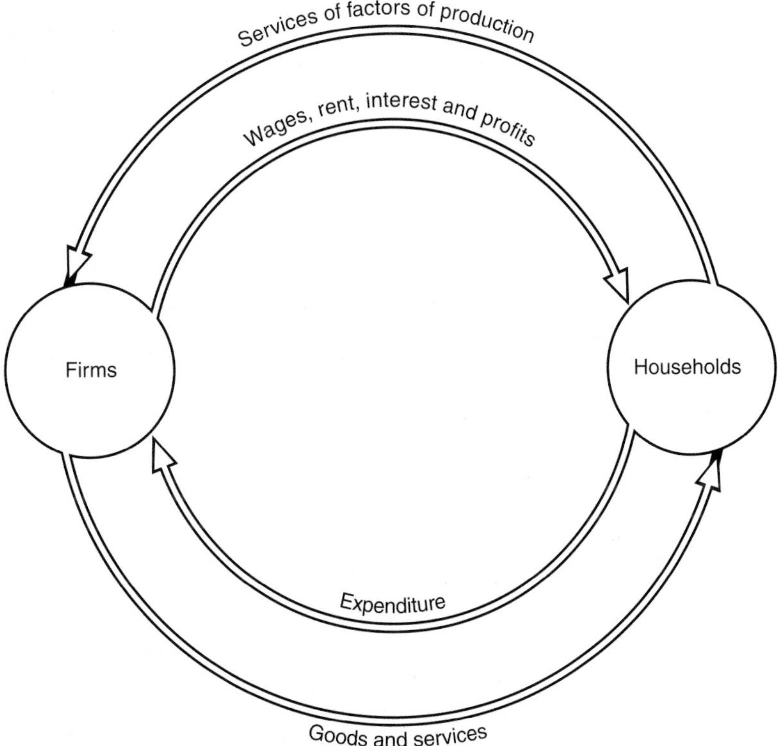

Fig. 9.2 The circular flow of production and income (simple model)

A simple model of the economy represents it as a continuous flow (see Figure 9.2). This gives a simplified outline of the economy which will take on greater sophistication in later units. This simplified model does, however, contain the essential economic elements:

- the **household** (or personal sector), which owns factors of production and supplies them to the firms (or corporate sector) in exchange for incomes
- the **firms**, which combine the factors of production to produce goods.

As well as helping to produce goods and services by supplying factors of production, the household has another important function – spending the income it has earned on the goods and services it has helped to produce. In this way, firms acquire the money necessary to finance the next cycle in the process.

Measuring the national product in a simple economy

Let us imagine an economy in which the following transactions happen in the course of a year.

1. Farmer Adams sells wheat grown by his own and his employees' efforts to miller Brown for £100.
2. Brown grinds the wheat and sells the flour to baker Clark for £150.
3. Clark sells the flour, when made into bread, to retailer Davis for £200.
4. Davis sells the bread to the consumers for £250.

Something to do

- Construct a simple model of the economy using the above transaction.

In this economy, as in a real economy, the national product may be measured in three ways, based on

- output
- expenditure
- income.

The output method

As we are trying to measure the value of the national product, the most obvious approach would be to establish the output of every firm and add them together to obtain the value of the national output. The gross value of the output of the four firms in the economy in the example discussed above amounts to £700. But it would be quite wrong to conclude that this is the value of the national product, for the community has only £250 of bread to show for its efforts. The mistake which has been made is that the wheat has been measured several times. If we add together both Adams's £100 of output and Brown's £150, we are counting the value of the wheat twice. In order to avoid this, we must add only the **value added** at each stage – that is, the value of output minus the cost of raw materials. If we assume that Adams obtained his seed free, then the value of the national product becomes £100 + £50 + £50 + £50, or £250, which is the amount spent by the consumers on bread, the finished product.

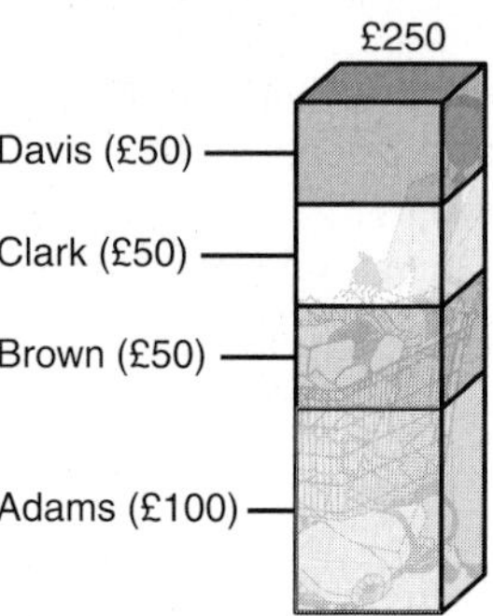

Fig. 9.3 The output method of calculating national product

This answer leads us to the second method of measuring the national product, the expenditure method.

The expenditure method

Instead of standing, as it were, at the farm or factory gate, clipboard in hand, measuring the value of each firm's output, we can establish how much everyone has *spent* on goods and services during the past year. Once again, however, care must be taken to avoid double-counting and only final expenditure must be counted – all intermediate expenditure must be omitted. The expenditure of Brown, Clark and Davis must not be added as well as the final expenditure of the consumers, or we shall again arrive at the misleading figure of £700. By counting only final expenditure, we obtain a national product of £250 – the value of the bread produced.

The income method

The third method of measuring the national product is to establish the incomes of the owners of factors of production. Adams and his employees have £100 to share among themselves; the miller and her employees have £50 to share out; the baker will also have £50 to share between himself and his employees, as will the retailer and his staff. Thus total (aggregate) income amounts to £250, which is the value of the national product.

Fig. 9.4 The expenditure method of calculating national product

Consumers pay a total of £250 to Davis for the bread. Out of this:

- Davis pays Clark £200 for the bread
- Clark pays Brown £150 for the flour
- Brown pays Adams £100 for the wheat

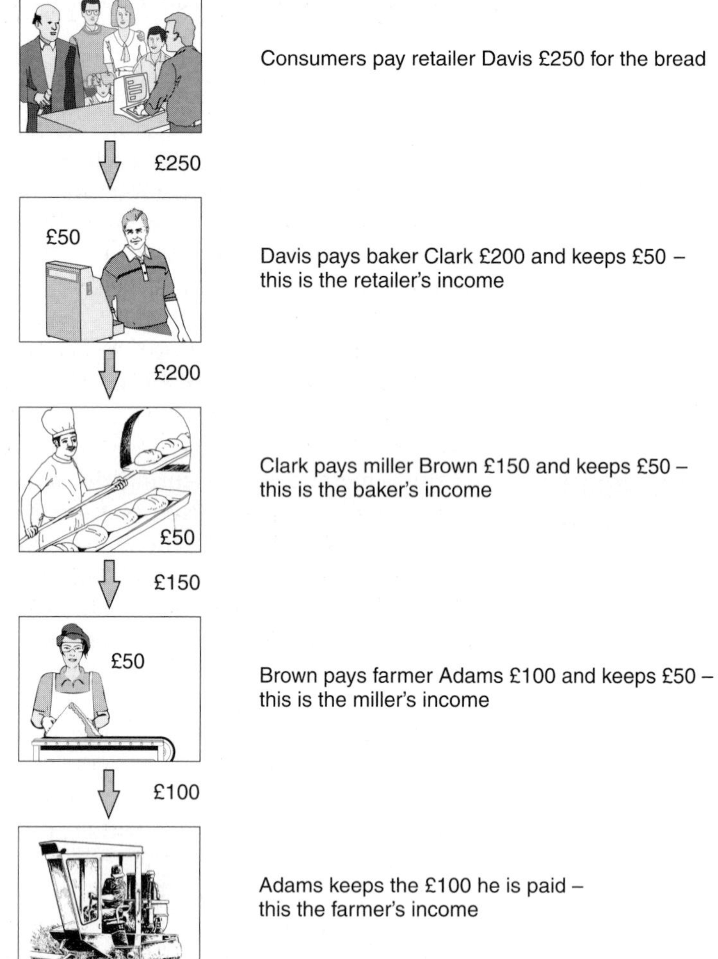

Consumers pay retailer Davis £250 for the bread
£250
£50
Davis pays baker Clark £200 and keeps £50 – this is the retailer's income
£200
Clark pays miller Brown £150 and keeps £50 – this is the baker's income
£50
£150
£50
Brown pays farmer Adams £100 and keeps £50 – this is the miller's income
£100
Adams keeps the £100 he is paid – this the farmer's income

Fig. 9.5 The income method of calculating national product

We can see from these measurements that the value of the national product is the same, whichever of the three methods is used. In its simplest form, the relationship between the three different aspects of the economy (output, expenditure and income) can be expressed as the following identity:

national output ≡ national expenditure ≡ national income
(where ≡ means 'is identical to')

Something to do

In a simple economy, primary industries produce raw materials which they sell to manufacturing industries for £15 000 000. The manufacturing industries then turn the raw materials into finished goods at an additional cost of £20 000 000; and sell the finished goods to retailers at a profit of £5 000 000. The final consumers then buy the goods from the retailers for £65 000 000.

- Using the national output, national expenditure and national income methods of calculating national product, produce workings to demonstrate that they are equal.

Real-world complications

In a real economy, the measurement of the value of goods and services is a good deal more complicated than in our simple model, for several reasons.

- **The government:** The government undertakes a wide range of economic activities, imposing taxes and also providing goods and services. It runs some industries. Thus there are in fact three sectors, not two (as in Figure 9.2), to consider in the economy: the personal, the corporate and the public sectors.
- **Transfer payments:** Many people receive an income, although they do not produce anything. As we are trying to measure the value of the goods produced, the calculated national product would be exaggerated if these non-productive incomes were included. An example of such an income is that of retirement pensioners, who provide no economic service in exchange for their pensions during the period in which they receive them. All such incomes are transfer payments (not to be confused with 'transfer earnings' – see Unit 6), the transfer of money from one source to another without the donor receiving any productive service in return. Further examples of transfer payments are pocket money given by parents to their children, and the money won on a football pool or on a national lottery – such wins involve the transfer of money from all the losers to all the winners.
- **Unmarketed services:** Many goods and services do not reach the market place and are therefore not automatically included in national product calculations. They therefore become the subject of arbitrary decisions about their inclusion, which may make comparisons over time or between countries difficult. It is not easy to put a value on the services that a household provides for itself without any prices being involved. Routine housework, decorating, gardening and repairs would probably cost thousands of pounds if outside contractors were employed, yet these services are not included in the national product because they are not (usually) marketed. However, where outsiders *are* employed to perform these tasks, the measured national product increases. It is likely that this sector, outside the market, will be of greater significance in poorer countries, where markets are not so fully developed.

  In one important case, however, the imputed (or estimated) value of an unmarketed service *is* included in the national product. This is the estimated rent value of owner-occupied houses. If such a house were rented from a landlord rather than occupied by the owner, then the occupier would have to pay rent and this would appear as part of the national product. When compiling the final **national accounts**, it is normal to include the imputed rent of such dwellings. If this were not done, then the size of the national product would depend partly on the number of owner-occupiers, which would give the wrong impression.
- **Imports and exports:** The UK economy, like others, is really an open one. It depends heavily on imports, exports and international investment. In calculating national income, these factors must be taken into consideration. For example, much of the expenditure by UK residents is on imported goods that are produced in other countries, while

many goods produced in the UK are sold abroad. In the first case, money earned in the UK goes out of the country (this is called a **leakage** from the economy), while in the second case, money earned abroad comes into the UK (this is called an **injection** into the economy). Adjustments have to be made for both these factors. In the same way, a part of many incomes is interest, dividends or rent obtained from overseas investment. When calculating the national product using the expenditure or output method, allowance must be made for all these instances if the results are to be compatible with the result obtained through the income method.

- **Timing:** Timing creates a minor problem. It is obviously not possible to stop the economy at a given time, such as midnight on 31 December each year, and make the necessary calculations for measuring the national product. For, at any one time, many goods will have been produced but not sold (it is convenient to regard these as having been purchased by the producer), while some incomes earned by producing goods in one year will not be received until the following year.

It can be seen that the model of the economy shown in Figure 9.2 needs to be considerably refined to take account of all these factors. A more sophisticated model is shown in Figure 9.6.

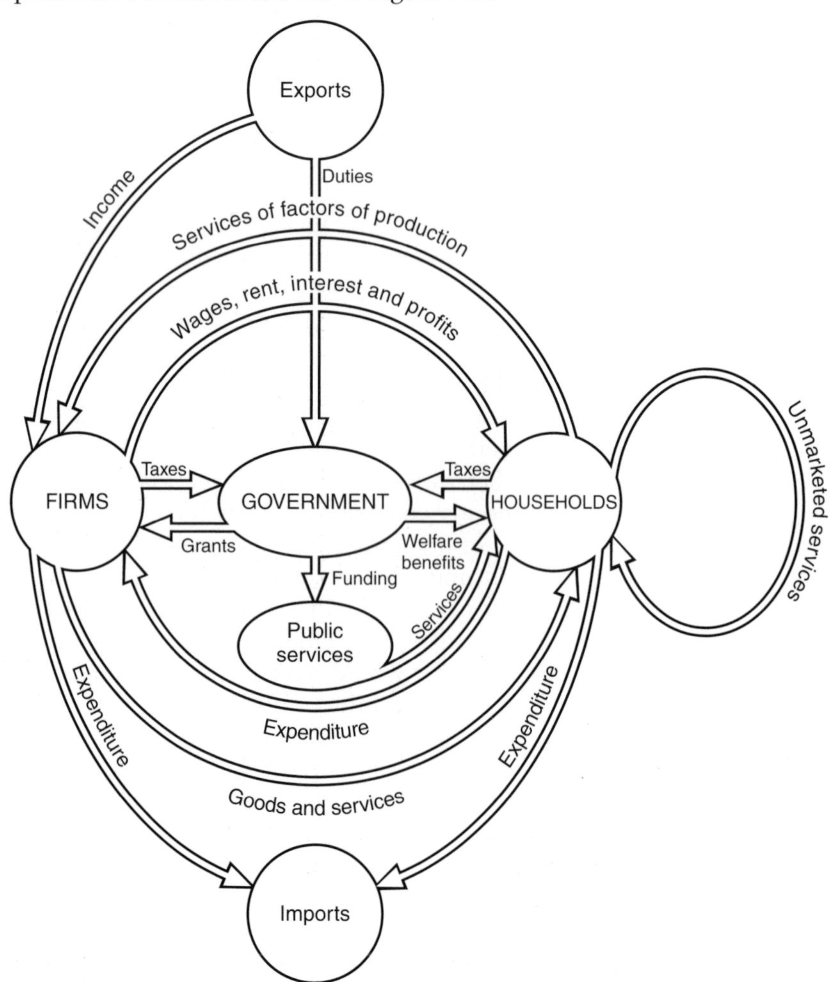

Fig. 9.6 The circular flow of production and income

National product by category of expenditure

Table 9.1 shows the main components of the UK's GDP on an expenditure basis for the years 1986 to 1996.

- Consumer expenditure on goods and services (£473 509 million) accounts for the bulk of total expenditure.
- The government itself (including local government) also buys goods and services (£155 732 million), which are included.
- While the above cover current expenditure on goods and services for immediate use, we must take account of investment in machinery and other fixed assets that are needed to facilitate the future production of goods and services, and also expenditure on producing goods that have not yet been sold, or completed, and are therefore held as stock or work in progress. The first, investment in machinery and other assets, is known as gross domestic fixed capital formation (GDFCF) and added another £114 623 million to total expenditure in 1996, while the value of the physical increase in stocks and work in progress (the difference between the value of these at the beginning and end of each year) was £2 917 million. Thus total domestic expenditure (the total amount spent by people and organisations in the UK in 1996) was £473 509 million + £155 732 million + £114 623 million + £2 917 million = £746 781 million.
- This still does not represent the total demand for British goods. During the twelve-month period there were exports of £217 147 million. When these are included, we arrive at total final expenditure of £963 928 million.

  However, some domestic expenditure is used to buy imports and, since imports are not part of UK output, this outlay (£222 603 million) must be deducted to arrive at a gross domestic product at market prices of £741 325 million. This is an estimate of the value of all the goods and services produced in the UK in 1996 valued at their market prices. A statistical error (see note 2 to Table 9.1) required an adjustment of £975 million to the published figure, giving an adjusted gross domestic product at market prices of £742 300 million.
- In order to arrive at the actual or **factor cost** of producing these goods and services, it is necessary to make an adjustment for taxes on expenditure and for subsidies. The prices of most goods and services, for example, include **value added tax (VAT)** of 17.5 per cent. This must therefore be deducted to arrive at the factor cost. Similarly, other goods are subsidised by the government, so the subsidy must be taken into account in arriving at their factor costs.

  If we make adjustments for taxes and subsidies, we arrive at a figure for gross domestic product at factor cost of £642 916 million. This is the value of all the goods and services produced in the UK at their actual cost of production.

Something to do

- If total consumer expenditure in a closed economy is £500 billion, including VAT at 17.5 per cent on £300 billion goods, and a further £1 billion goods including a subsidy of 25 per cent, calculate
  - total VAT
  - total government subsidy
  - the effect of these on the figure of £500 billion as gross domestic product.

Table 9.1

National product: by category of expenditure (£ million)											
	1986	**1987**	**1988**	**1989**	**1990**	**1991**	**1992**	**1993**	**1994**	**1995**	**1996**
Categories of expenditure at current market prices Consumers' expenditure	241 554	265 290	299 449	327 363	347 527	365 469	383 490	406 569†	427 394	446 169	473 509
General government final consumption	80 911	87 045	93 641	101 796	112 934	124 105	131 875	137 756†	144 068	149 208	155 732
of which: Central Government	50 331	53 736	57 522	63 294	70 108	76 985	82 259	89 074†	93 190	96 027	101 140
Local authorities	30 580	33 309	36 119	38 502	42 826	47 120	49 616	49 682†	50 878	53 181	54 592
Gross domestic fixed capital formation	65 032	75 158	91 530	105 443	107 577	97 747	93 642	94 293	100 252†	108 736	114 623
Value of physical increase in stocks and work in progress	682	1 228	4 333	2 677	−1 800	−4 927	−1 937	329	3 708†	4 748	2 917
Total domestic expenditure	388 179	428 721	488 953	537 279	566 238	582 394	607 070	638 947†	675 422	708 861	746 781
Exports of goods and services	97 885	106 397	107 273	121 486	133 165	134 289	142 497†	160 464	176 602	199 675	217 147
of which: Goods	72 627	79 153	80 346	92 154	101 718	103 413	107 343	121 398	134 664†	153 077	166 340
Services	25 258	27 244	26 927	29 332	31 447	30 876	35 154†	39 066	41 938	46 598	50 807
Total final expenditure	486 064	535 118	596 226	658 765	699 403	716 683	749 567†	799 411	852 024	908 536	963 928
less Imports of goods and services[1]	−101 221	−111 737	−124 796	−142 808	−148 285	−141 009	−150 651†	−168 408	−182 955	−204 380	−222 603
of which: Goods	−82 186	−90 735	−101 826	−116 837	−120 527	−113 697	−120 447	−134 858	−145 793†	−164 659	−178 938
Services	−19 035	−21 002	−22 970	−25 971	−27 758	−27 312	−30 204	−33 550	−37 162	−39 721	−43 665
Statistical discrepancy (expenditure adjustment)[2]	—	—	—	—	—	—	—	—	—	—	975
Gross domestic product[3]	384 843	423 381	471 430	515 957	551 118	575 674	598 916	631 003†	669 069	704 156	742 300
Net property income from abroad	4 629	3 927	4 566	3 502	1 269	150	3 124	2 595†	9 667	7 920	9 652
Gross national product[3]	389 472	427 308	475 996	519 459	552 387	575 824	602 040	633 598†	678 736	712 076	751 952
Factor cost adjustment Taxes on expenditure	62 872	68 971	76 039	79 980	78 298	85 416	87 521	90 336	96 418†	103 697	108 484
Subsidies	6 301	6 265	6 037	5 782	6 066	5 995	6 737	7 203	7 484†	7 631	9 100
Factor cost adjustment (taxes *less* subsidies)	56 571	62 706	70 002	74 198	72 232	79 421	80 784	83 133	88 934†	96 066	99 384

[1]Excluding taxes on expenditure levied on imports.
[2]The statistical discrepancy (expenditure adjustment) is part of the residual error.
[3]Including taxes on expenditure levied on imports.

Source: *Annual Abstract of Statistics* (The Stationery Office, 1999)

Sometimes the concept of gross *national* product is preferred to GDP. The only difference between the two concerns

- incomes derived from property owned abroad (including investments and profits from businesses), and
- property in this country owned by people overseas.

Some people in the UK receive an income from overseas investments, and this is added to GDP. Similarly, some of the profits of businesses located in the UK are sent to overseas owners, and these are subtracted from GDP. To convert GDP to GNP we must also add property income from abroad and subtract property income paid abroad. Thus

$$\text{GNP} = \text{GDP} + (\text{net property income from abroad}) - (\text{property income paid abroad})$$

In 1996 (see Table 9.1), the net value of all property income was £9652 million, so GNP exceeded GDP by this amount.

An individual business always makes an allowance for depreciation when calculating its costs. Depreciation is an estimate of the extent to which fixed assets have been used up during the year. This is also estimated for the entire economy. In 1996, it was £77 billion, and, as we have seen (page 300), if this is deducted from the gross domestic product or gross national product figures, we obtain the net domestic product or net national product for the year.

'National products'

We have identified a number of different 'national products'. The relationship between them is summarised in Figure 9.7. The smallest of the figures is 'net national product at factor cost' and it is this that is known as **national income**, although this term is often loosely used to describe any national product figure.

Fig. 9.7 National product relationships

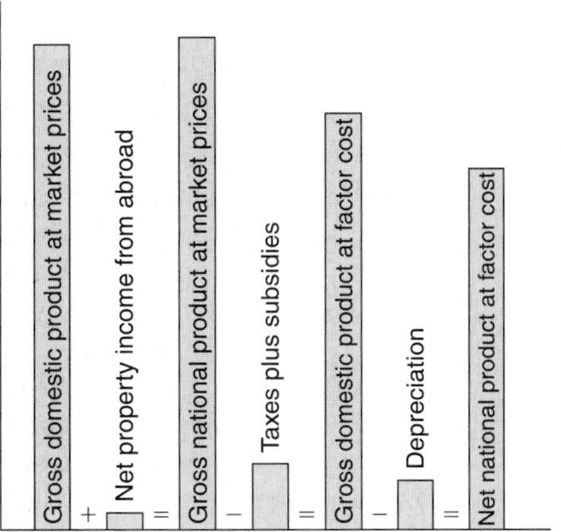

Think about it

- What is the difference between the various 'national products'? Why might each of them be useful?

National product by factor incomes

Table 9.2 shows the main components of the UK's GDP on an income basis for the period 1986 to 1996.

- **Income from employment** includes both wages and salaries, which are measured at their gross (tax-inclusive) value. This gives the costs of employment of labour to the individual firm. Taxation on incomes is thus ignored, as otherwise the level of national product would vary with changes in the level of income tax and National Insurance.
- **Income from self-employment** includes an element of wages and profits which have accrued to the self-employed person.
- **Profits** are allocated in various ways. A portion of the profit of a business becomes the personal income of the owners of the business, often in the form of dividends paid on shares held in the company. Part of a business's profits must be paid to the government in the form of tax, while another part will be retained by the business to build its reserve fund. Similarly, any trading surplus of public corporations are either reinvested in the business or returned to the government.

  To clarify the treatment of taxation, let us imagine an economy operating without money. In this economy, a firm produces 1000 tractors. It is taxed at the rate of 10 per cent on its output and keeps 5 per cent of its output in reserve. The firm will therefore have to hand 100 tractors to the government as a tax and will keep 50 tractors in reserve. When assessing the firm's contribution to the national product, these 150 tractors must be included, otherwise the national product will be underestimated. In exactly the same way, the money value of output paid in tax or kept in reserve must be included.
- **Rent** includes not only commercial rent received by private landowners or house owners, but also rent received by the government from various sources, and the **imputed rent** of owner-occupied houses (see pages 240–241).
- **Stock appreciation:** Goods produced early in the year and valued at £5 at the time of production may be worth £5.50 by the end of the year. To include such goods at £5.50 would exaggerate their costs, so stock appreciation of 50 pence must be deducted.

This method of measuring the national income does not give the same results as the expenditure method, so a small adjustment may have to be made for errors and omissions. This is called the **residual error**. It arises because this method uses different source statistics from the expenditure method.

This gives us the gross domestic product at factor cost ('factor cost' represents the actual costs of employing factors of production, irrespective of taxes and subsidies), which can be converted to other national product measures by adjusting for taxes, subsidies, property income from abroad and depreciation.

Table 9.2

National product: by category of expenditure (£ million)											
	1986	**1987**	**1988**	**1989**	**1990**	**1991**	**1992**	**1993**	**1994**	**1995**	**1996**
Factor incomes Income from employment	212 380	230 208	256 537	284 878	315 471	331 967	342 608	351 561	365 035	381 208	400 354
Income from self-employment[1]	35 104	39 361	45 829	51 440	56 727	54 735	55 862	60 110	65 296	68 915	69 898
Gross trading profits of companies[1,2,3]	47 339	59 453	64 377	67 880	66 103	60 191	63 168	75 908	88 398	92 530	101 409
Gross trading surplus of public corporations[2,3]	8 213	6 993	7 554	5 951	3 426	1 410	1 699	2 438	2 698	4 230	3 959
Gross trading surplus of general government enterprises[1]	155	−75	−32	199	12	−36	206	193	495	623	681
Rent[1]	23 848	26 155	29 904	34 467	38 887	45 633	52 160	56 092	58 466	61 230	63 850
Imputed charge for consumption of non-trading capital	3 068	3 307	3 634	4 005	4 391	4 363	4 207	3 918	3 890	4 115	4 333
Total domestic income[1]	330 107	365 402	407 803	448 820	485 017	498 263	519 910	550 220	584 278	612 851	644 484
less Stock appreciation	−1 835	−4 727	−6 375	−7 061	−6 131	−2 010	−1 778	−2 350	−4 143	−4 761	−973
Statistical discrepancy (income adjustment)	—	—	—	—	—	—	—	—	—	—	−595
Gross domestic product at factor cost	328 272	360 675	401 428	441 759	478 886	496 253	518 132	547 870	580 135	608 090	642 916
Net property income from abroad	4 629	3 927	4 566	3 502	1 269	150	3 124	2 595	9 667	7 920	9 652
Gross national product	332 901	364 602	405 994	445 261	480 155	496 403	521 256	550 465	589 802	616 010	652 568

[1]Before providing for depreciation and stock appreciation.
[2]Including financial institutions.
[3]Figures for companies and public corporations are affected by privatisation.

Source: *Annual Abstract of Statistics* (The Stationery Office, 1999)

Gross domestic product by output

The last method of calculating the national product is to add together the output of every firm or organisation. As stated above, since different firms produce different goods and services, the only way of doing this is to value each firm's output in terms of value added. Table 9.3 shows the national product calculated in this way, categorised by industrial sector (in other words, the output of each firm in an industrial sector is added together to give the total output for that sector) for the period 1986 to 1996.

Since value added figures are derived from income figures, when we add together the value added by each sector, we arrive at the GDP at factor cost (income based) of £642 916 million for 1996 (see Table 9.2). This is the same as the GDP (expenditure based) excluding taxes on expenditure and subsidies (see Table 9.1).

Note that no special provision is made for international trade in the output figures. This is because goods for export are already included in the net output of each firm, and imports are automatically excluded. GDP by output can be converted to GNP by adding the net property income from abroad (£9652 million – see Table 9.1) to give a total GNP of £652 568 million excluding taxes on expenditure and subsidies.

Table 9.3

Gross domestic product by industry[1] (£ million)											
	1986	**1987**	**1988**	**1989**	**1990**	**1991**	**1992**	**1993**	**1994**	**1995**	**1996**
Agriculture, hunting, forestry and fishing	6680	7120	7153	8324	8943	8964	9738	10092	10231	11544	11790
Mining & quarrying including oil & gas extraction	13533	14128	11488	11260	11318	11203	11674	12261	13591	14986	18068
Manufacturing (revised definition)	81252	88623	98784	107166	111315	106896	109811	115719	123941	131701	137006
Electricity, gas and water supply	9407	9918	10263	10583	10583	13388	13558	14902	14815	14092	13606
Construction	19916	23158	28121	32911	34568	31506	29797	29030	30902	32241	33746
Wholesale and retail trade; repairs; hotels and restaurants	45617	49451	56050	62343	68271	71755	74742	78860	83212	87633	93091
Transport, storage and communication	27247	30037	34238	37356	40523	42191	43782	46327	49042	50837	54056
Financial intermediation, real estate, renting and business activities	71330	79499	89939	102549	114506	118813	129179	138481	152350	156164	164282
Public administration, national defence and compulsory social security	22604	24368	26000	28028	31676	34257	36774	37925	37273	37123	38244
Education, health social work	31645	34731	39674	46633	51744	58371	62998	66601	72082	77199	81876
Other services including sewage and refuse disposal	13326	14482	16198	16077	17928	18387	19221	20482	21969	23379	24713
Total	342557	375517	417907	463229	501377	515731	541275	570681	609406	636899	670479
less Adjustment for financial services	14285	14841	16479	21473	22489	19478	23143	22811	29271	28809	26968
Statistical discrepancy (income adjustment)	—	—	—	—	—	—	—	—	—	—	−595
Gross domestic product	328272	360675	401428	441759	478886	496253	518132	547870	580135	608090	642916

[1]The contribution of each industry to the gross domestic product before providing for depreciation but after providing for stock appreciation.

Source: *Annual Abstract of Statistics* (The Stationery Office, 1999)

What are national product figures used for?

Fig. 9.8 Uses of national product figures

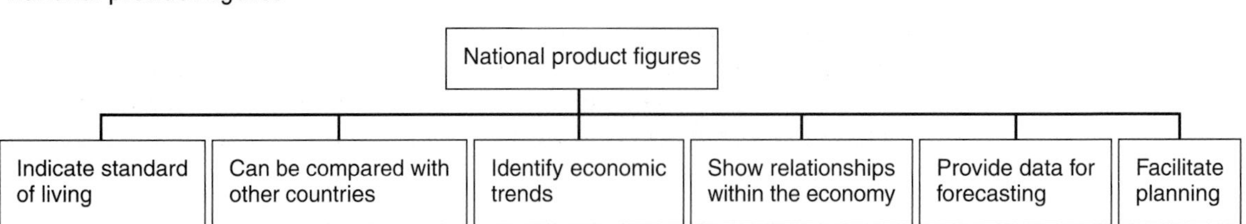

Compiling the national income statistics (known as the process of **social accounting**) is a fairly long and complex operation. The figures are published in the autumn following the year to which they relate in *The United Kingdom National Accounts* (known as the Blue Book, because it is published in blue covers).

Once they are published, they do have a number of important uses. These are summarised below and in Figure 9.8.

Uses of national product figures

- They provide an indicator of the overall **standard of living** in a country. While income cannot be equated with well-being, it is a convenient standard.
- They allow **comparisons** to be made with the economies of other countries.
- They enable **economic trends** to be identified.
- They highlight relationships between **different parts of the economy**.
- They help the government in **planning** economic policy.
- They help businesses and other organisations to **forecast** future levels of economic activity.

In using national income statistics for these purposes, however, it is important to be aware of complications that arise. These include the following:

- An increase in national income over time may be partly due to inflation rather than exclusively to increased output.
- An important factor to consider is the size of the population. The average national income or gross domestic product *per head* may give a more meaningful indication of a society's standard of living. Even more meaningful is the actual *distribution* of income.
- The production of some goods for defence (tanks, war planes) may appear as an increase in national product, but since these goods have no immediate welfare benefit their production may decrease consumer prosperity.

- It is important to consider the balance of production between consumer and producer goods: an increase in the production of producer goods may not affect the standard of living of individuals, although it may have an effect on, for example, the quality of consumer products.
- National income statistics are affected by the balance of imports and exports.
- National income statistics exclude externalities.
- In comparing the national income of different countries, it must be remembered that currency exchange rates and the relative costs of factors of production may make such a comparison difficult.

Think about it

- The table below has been compiled by the Government of Ruritania to show that it had a higher standard of living than Hofland in 1999. What additional information would you need to verify this?

Country	GNP in 1990 (£)	GNP in 1999 (£)
Hofland	10 000 million	30 000 million
Ruritania	5 000 million	50 000 million

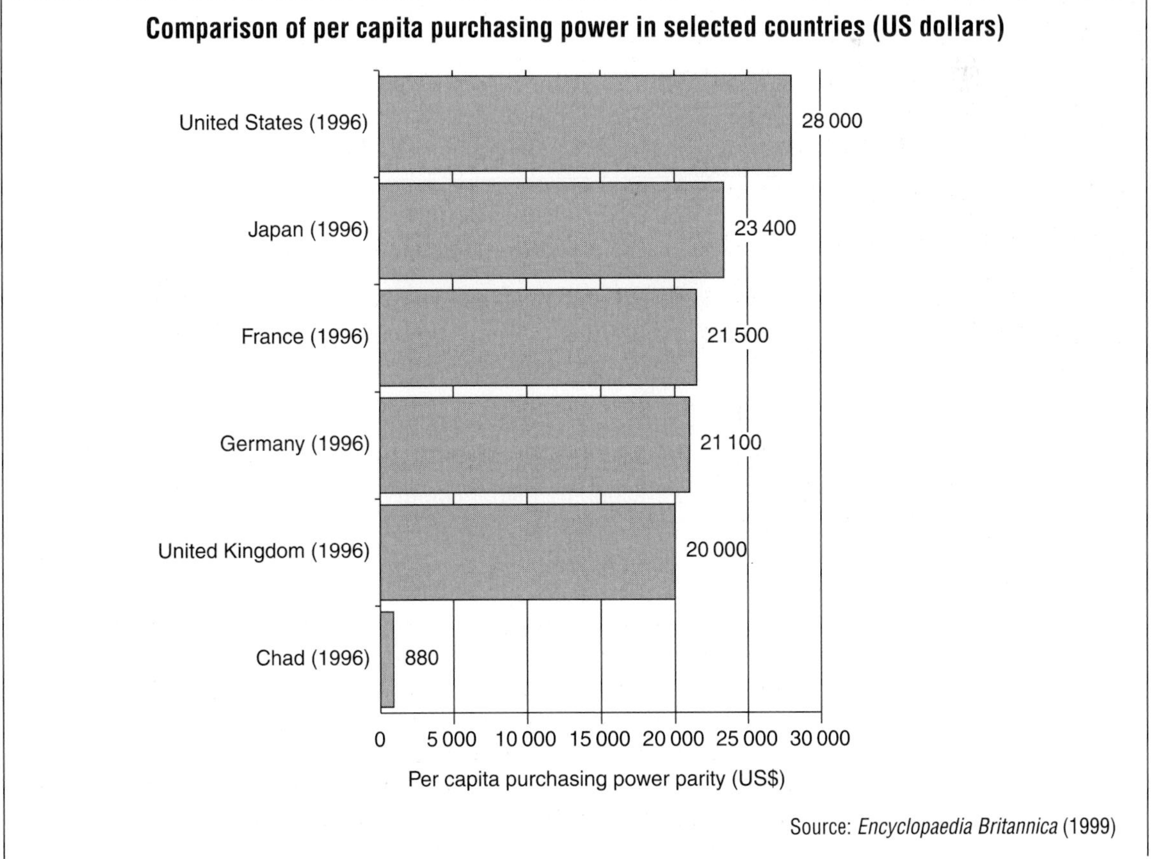

Source: *Encyclopaedia Britannica* (1999)

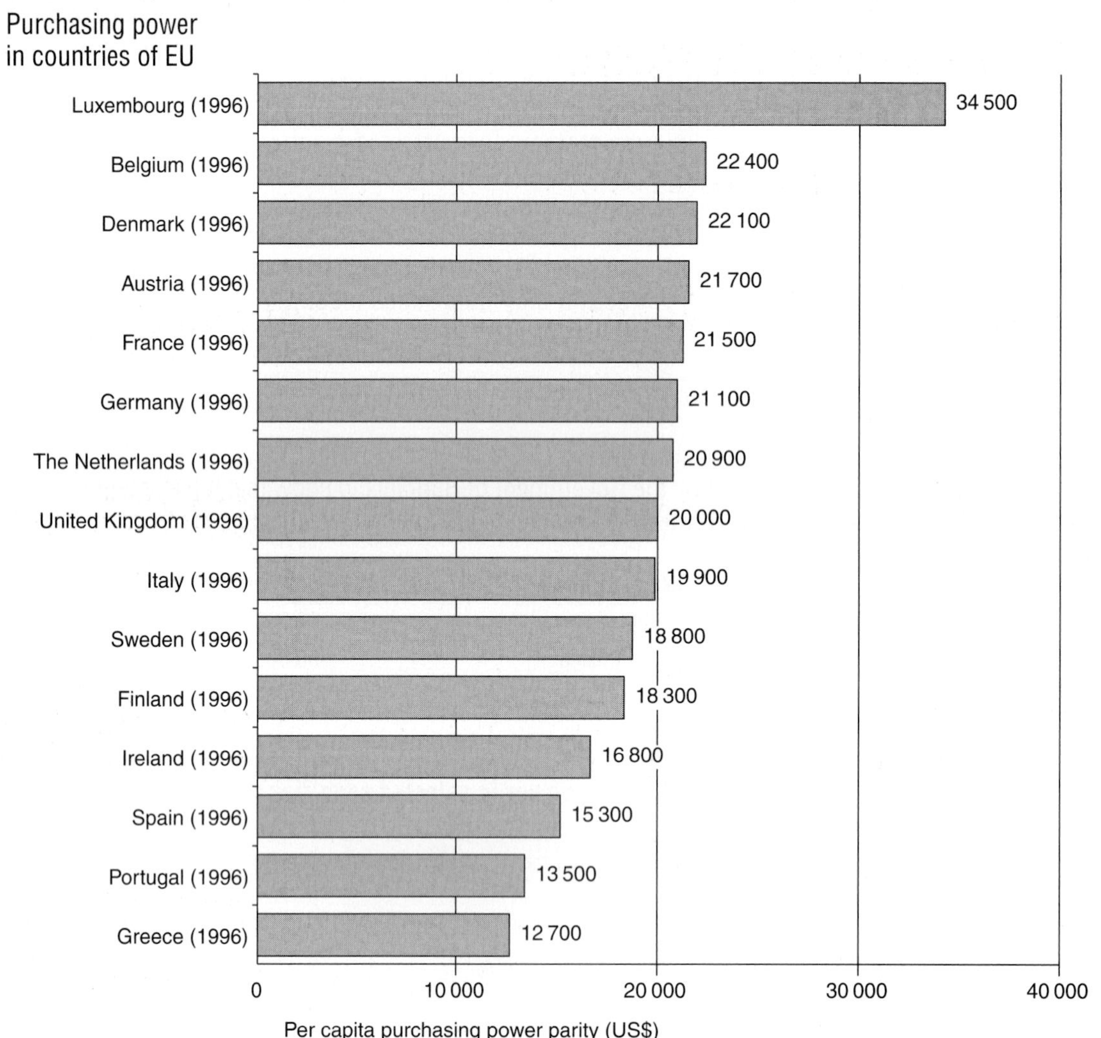

Source: *Encyclopaedia Britannica* (1999)

1. GNP figures have been converted into US dollars in order to facilitate comparison.
2. Per capita figures are found by dividing GNP by the total population. They are important, since a country with a high GNP and low population may have a stronger economy than a country with the same GNP but a larger population. Demographic factors such as age structure have a significant impact on per capita GNP.
3. Even per capita GNP figures are misleading, because they do not reflect the level of prices or **purchasing power** of money in the economy. Some comparative statistics are given in the two graphs.

10 Managing the national economy: the role of the government

Introduction: the problem

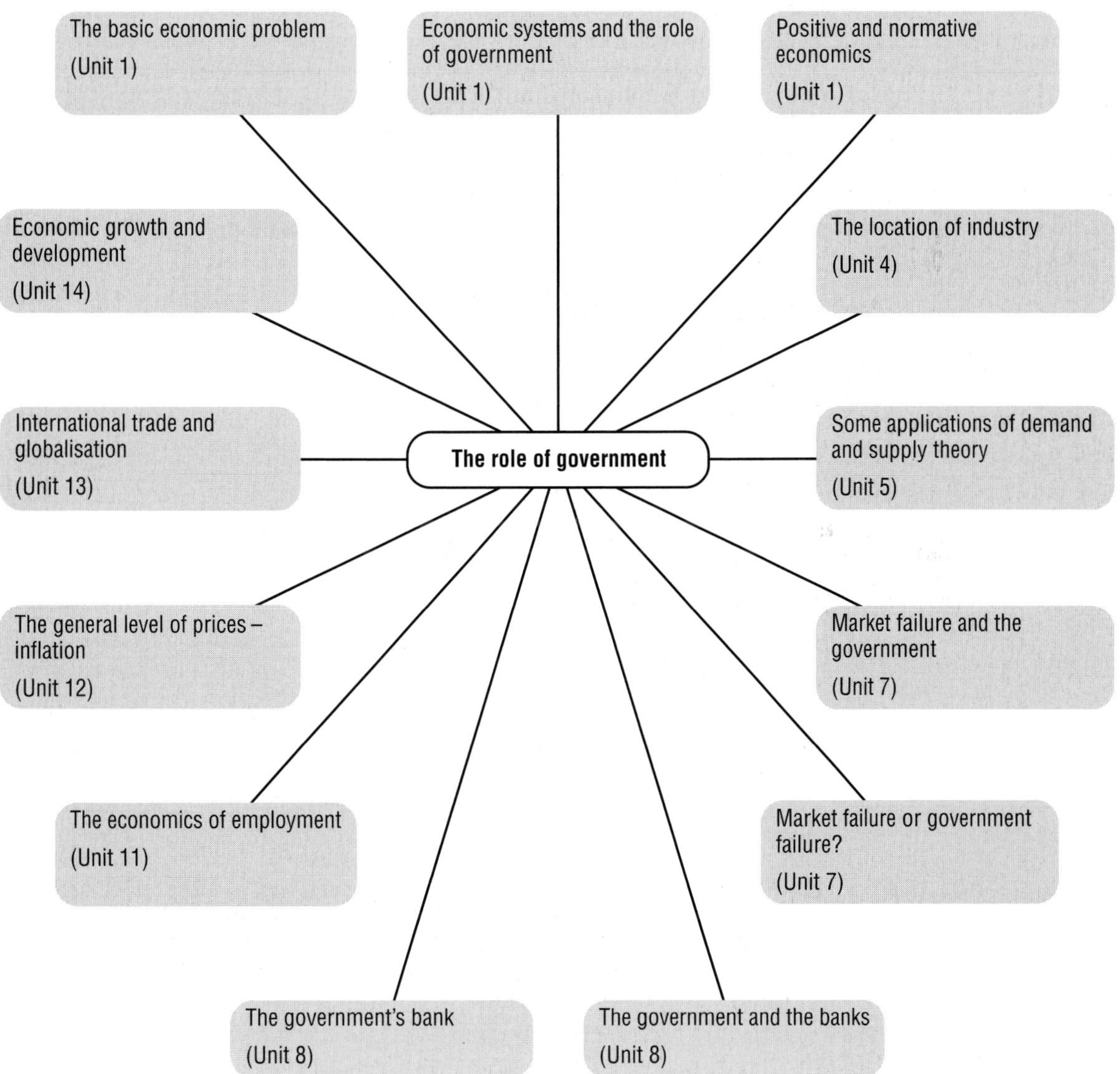

In Unit 9, we identified a number of government economic policy objectives:

- an adequate level of employment
- economic growth
- price stability
- a balanced international trading position.

Experience suggests that left to itself the economy will not achieve all these objectives together. Instead, it will tend to move in cycles, generating, for example, higher employment together with inflation, followed by lower employment and lower inflation.

Since 1945, it has been regarded as a function of government to influence the economy in such a way as to minimise fluctuations in the level of economic activity. The methods used to do this may be divided into three groups.

- **direct control** of prices and incomes and the use of resources: UK governments have made a number of attempts at establishing statutory or voluntary controls over pay and prices. Most have succeeded in putting a brake on inflation only for lost ground to be recovered once the controls were removed. Such policies were not used after 1980, except in so far as the government has resisted high pay claims in the public sector
- **fiscal policy**, which uses the levels of taxes and **government expenditure** to influence the level of economic activity
- **monetary policy**, which is used to control the amount of money in the economy and the price of money (that is, the rate of interest).

Fig. 10.1 Types of government economic policy

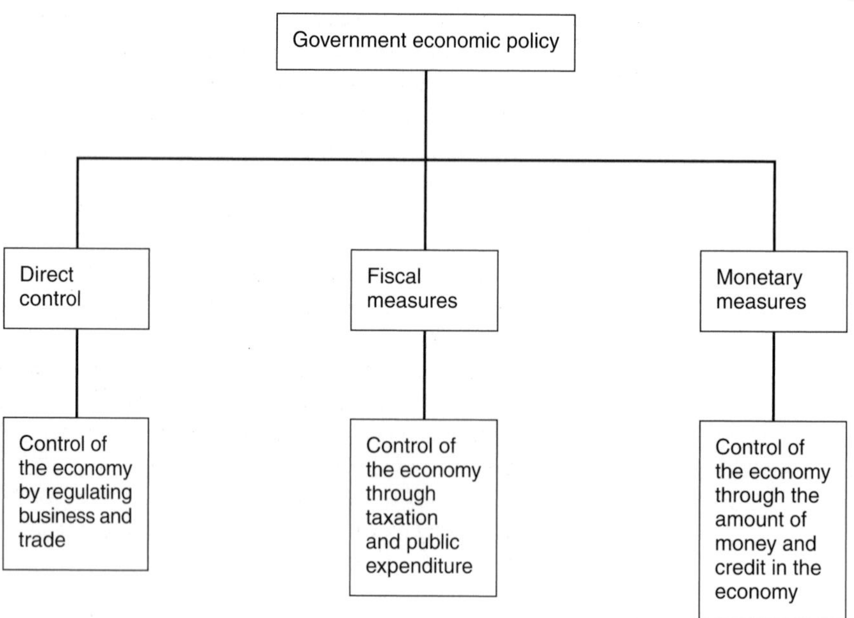

For most of the post-war period the UK government has sought to control the level of economic activity through fiscal policy, using monetary policy mainly to create the general economic atmosphere. In this unit, we examine these two key areas of government policy, including the role of the monetary policy committee (MPC). We also look in some detail at taxation, both general and local; the role of the Budget; and government borrowing. The unit ends with a brief look at supply-side measures.

Monetary policy

The money supply

The objective of monetary policy is to influence the level of economic activity through the control of the **money supply** – the amount of money there is in the economy. First we need to define the concept of the money supply. On the face of it this may seem straightforward, but it is a process that is surrounded by problems. The Bank of England has a number of different measures of the money supply, and these have been amended over the years to reflect changing circumstances – for example the change in status of some ex-building societies, such as Abbey National, Halifax and Alliance and Leicester, to become banks. The Bank of England differentiates between **narrow money** and **broad money**, as described below.

Narrow money

- **M0** is the monetary base. It consists of notes and coins in circulation outside the Bank of England, plus the banks' operational deposits at the Bank of England. The personal money supply of most people includes more than just notes and coins, however, so it is necessary to include other elements.
- **Non-interest-bearing M1 (nib M1)** consists of notes and coins in circulation plus private-sector sterling sight deposits with the banks (see Unit 8). This represents an effort to assess the amount of money held for transactions purposes (as opposed to savings). However, since the main banks all now offer interest on current accounts, any link between nib M1 and the general level of economic activity is likely to be reduced. Accordingly, a further measure of 'transactions' money is required.
- **M2** consists of notes and coins held by the public sector, plus private-sector non-interest-bearing sight deposits at the banks, plus other accounts subject to withdrawal by cheque, plus other deposits due to mature within one month, plus National Savings Bank ordinary accounts.

  M2 acknowledges that transactions money is not confined to one group of institutions or accounts. The spread of such money is likely to increase as competition between financial institutions increases and they allow easier withdrawal of their long-term deposits. Although it is placed among the narrow measure, M2 is in fact rather broad, bringing in far more deposits than nib M1. However, there are still broader definitions.

Broad money

- **M4** replaced M3 as the principal broad money concept in 1989, when the inclusion of ex-building society deposits in the money supply created such a break in the series that M3 had to be discontinued. M4 covers all the following sterling items held outside the public sector other than by banks and building societies:
  - notes and coins
  - non-interest-bearing bank deposits
  - interest-bearing retail-bank deposits
  - other interest-bearing deposits up to five years' original maturity
  - building society shares and deposits
  - other building society deposits up to five years' original maturity.

M4 really takes the money supply beyond a purely transactions concept, for it includes some items which are clearly for savings purposes. Surprisingly, perhaps, it excludes National Savings ordinary accounts, which are included in M2.

- **M5** consists of M4 plus most National Savings ordinary accounts and instruments, plus some money market items such as Treasury bills and bank bills.

Fig. 10.2 Measures of money supply

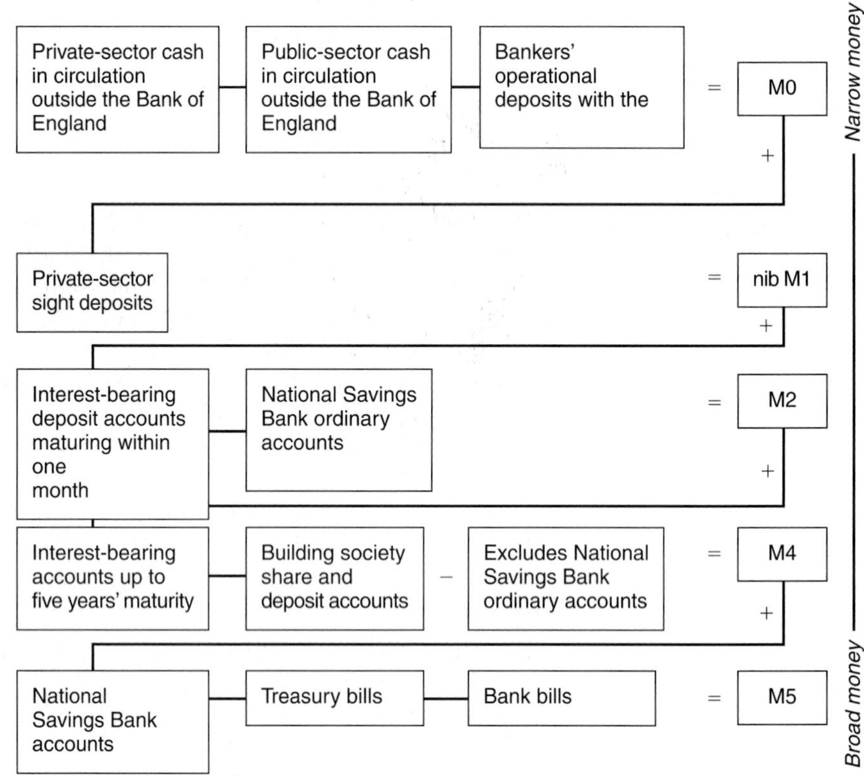

> ***Think about it***
>
> - Compare the different measures of money supply. Which do you think gives the most accurate value of total purchasing power in the UK? Why?

The number of measures of the money supply reflects two areas of concern:

- The first is quite simply to have an assessment of the purchasing power in the economy. This is not easily determined. If you consider a single individual, their immediate personal money supply consists of the notes and coins they hold plus any bank current account they have. However, they might also have money in a deposit account at the bank and a deposit account in a building society – all easily available to spend. In addition, they might have money invested in National Savings which can be converted into cash quite readily and even some shares or other assets which could be sold and the proceeds spent.

The problem, then, is to determine what constitutes money, not as far as the individual is concerned, but as far as the whole economy is concerned. This is what will largely determine the overall spending power in the economy – something that the government will want to keep under control, since spending power influences demand and therefore affects inflation, unemployment and economic growth.

- The second is that, over the years, monetary policy has developed along the lines of establishing targets for the quantity of money in the economy. The quantity of money in the economy must be related to the national product (see Unit 9). Targets may be set for all or any of the measures of money supply.

The role of monetary policy

In the late 1980s and early 1990s, the UK experienced a period of rising inflation accompanied by a rapid increase in the amount of money in the economy. While cause and effect were not easy to determine, attempts were made to ensure that the supply of money did not grow or fluctuate sufficiently to cause unwanted changes in the economy.

At one stage, the main thrust of economic policy seemed to be to ensure that the supply of money – whichever measure is used – did not grow beyond a predetermined target. It became apparent, however, that there is no definite link between, say, M4 and the rate of growth in the demand for money in the economy. Other steps may therefore be required to control the growth of demand for money. The control of growth in the money supply is still important.

In particular, managing the supply of money in the economy is important in controlling inflation (see Unit 12) and deflation.

- **Inflation** occurs where there is a general increase in the level of prices, and this can happen when the growth in the money supply is greater than the growth in GNP. For example, if more credit is made available by mortgage lenders in response to an increased demand for house purchase, this could lead to inflation. In effect, a greater amount of money (initially in the form of mortgages) would be chasing the same quantity of goods.
- **Deflation**, on the other hand, occurs when a fall in general demand for goods – perhaps in response to rapid price increases – leads to an actual reduction in GNP due to firms cutting down on production in the face of the reduced demand. Such deflation can lead to a lack of confidence among businesses, lower capital investment and unemployment (fewer new machines or employees are needed when production is being reduced).

Control over the money supply can be exercised in many ways, and the methods used have varied considerably over the years. Much anti-inflationary policy is now the responsibility of the Bank of England's independent monetary policy committee (MPC) – see also Unit 12, page 382. However, there are various other measures that the government can take. It is unlikely that the government – or any monetary authority – would use all the following measures during the same period.

Basic monetary policy techniques

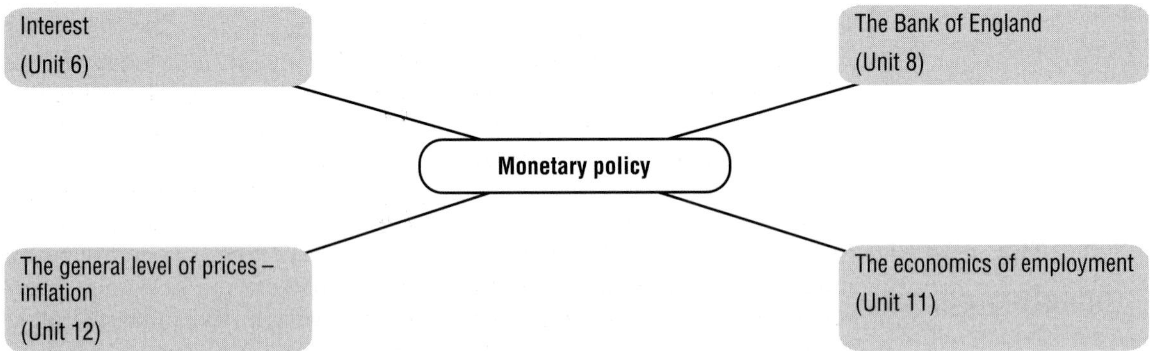

We have seen that most of the money supply consists of book entries made by banks. In Unit 8, we saw that goldsmiths first created money beyond the size of their gold deposits and that today's banks can create deposits (and therefore money) in excess of their holdings of cash. The extent to which this can be taken depends on the credit base that is used. Until 1971, the banks observed a ratio of cash reserves to deposits of 8 per cent; from 1971 to 1981, the ratio was 12.5 per cent. There is now no formal published requirement – the banks operate on a prudential basis agreed with the Bank of England. If the authorities want to control the level of bank deposits, and thus the money supply, they must be able to control the credit base. A reduction in the base brings a much greater reduction in the permitted level of deposits. If the ratio of cash to deposits is 8 per cent, for example, a reduction of £100 in those assets will cause deposits to fall by £1250. If the ratio is 12.5 per cent, deposits will fall by £800.

The basic monetary techniques are therefore geared to control the growth of stipulated bank deposits. For the purposes of this discussion, the exact definition of those assets is not important, since the processes involved are the same. We will assume a 10 per cent ratio.

Open-market operations

A fundamental method of controlling the money supply is known as **open-market operations**. The Bank of England orders the government broker to buy or sell government securities on the Stock Exchange. When the broker is instructed to buy £1000 of securities, he or she will always be able to find a vendor by setting the price sufficiently high. The seller of the securities receives a cheque for £1000 drawn on the Bank of England, which he pays into his account at a retail (or clearing) bank. His deposit at the bank thus rises by £1000. The bank presents the cheque for payment to the Bank of England, which credits the clearing bank's account (held at the Bank of England under the heading 'Bankers' deposits' – see Table 8.8) with £1000. As a result of this, on the basis of the 10 per cent ratio, the clearing bank can create further deposits of £9000. Not all of the extra money will go directly into the hands of the public, of course, for, as we know, many of the loans created will be highly liquid and made principally to other financial institutions. Some will be invested in securities by the banks themselves. The effect of open-market operations working in this direction is therefore to add both to the money supply and to the level of **aggregate monetary demand** (or the total level of demand for goods and services – see Unit 11, page 350). The banks are happy to co-operate in this expansion since they can please the government, oblige their customers who require loans, and at the same time satisfy their shareholders, who require profits.

When the government is selling securities in the open market, however, the cash base of the bank is reduced, so their lending powers are also reduced. One way of frustrating this aspect of government policy is for the banks to hold a disproportionately high level of liquid assets. When their cash base is reduced, they can then quickly restore it by turning the appropriate amount of liquid assets into cash.

Something to do

- If the Bank of England wanted to increase aggregate monetary demand by £1 billion, what value of government securities would the government broker have to buy or sell on the Stock Exchange, assuming that the retail banks keep to a cash ratio of 10 per cent and that 75 per cent of any increased money supply would go directly into the hands of the public?

Special deposits

In order to stop banks holding disproportionately high levels of liquid assets, the system of **special deposits** was introduced. By this, the Bank of England can call for special deposits from clearing banks in order to reduce their holdings of liquid assets and their powers to create credit. Such deposits are frozen at the Bank of England and are not in any circumstances available to the banks, although the banks do receive interest on these special deposits, equivalent to that which they would have received had the money been invested in Treasury bills.

The system of special deposits has not been used as a method of controlling the money supply in the UK for many years.

Funding

Where banks have liquid assets as well as cash, as they usually do, their ability to increase deposits can be restricted by **funding** – a process by which the Bank of England either redeems some of its short-term debt and issues new longer-term securities, or, where new loans are concerned, issues longer-term rather than short-term securities; thus, by changing from short-term liquid assets to long-term securities the potential liquidity base is reduced. It may be necessary to offer a high rate of interest in order to sell the longer-term bonds, however, and this will impose a limit on the process.

Requests and directives

Use may be made of requests and directives to the clearing banks concerning the level and direction of their lending. The directives might indicate that loans should be available to finance investment or exports but not to finance personal consumption.

Variable reserve–assets ratio

Rather than attempting to control the size of the credit base, the Bank of England could change the required ratio – a higher ratio of cash reserves to deposits would reduce the power of the banks to create credit. In fact, a variable ratio has not been used in the UK.

Interest rates

The above measures all try to directly influence the level of deposits. The Bank of England may also influence the level of bank lending indirectly by altering the price of borrowing – the rate of interest.

Historically, the Bank did this openly by publishing the rate of interest at which it was prepared to deal with the discount houses. Originally this was the **bank rate** – the rate at which the Bank would re-discount bills of exchange. (It is by doing this that the Bank acts as the lender of last resort.) In 1972, the bank rate was replaced by the **minimum lending rate**, which was intended to reflect the forces of demand and supply operating in the money market – as opposed to the authorities arbitrarily determining the bank rate.

In 1981, the minimum lending rate itself disappeared. The Bank declared that from then on it would influence market rates through its operations in the markets, with no formal announcement of the interest rate. Broadly speaking, when there is a shortage of funds in the money market – perhaps because large payments have been made to the government – the Bank informs the discount houses that it will buy Treasury bills and other bills of exchange from them. The discount houses then offer bills to the Bank at prices they hope the Bank will accept and which normally reflect the prevailing market rate of interest. The higher the price the discount houses ask for the bills, the lower the rate of interest that is implied (see Unit 6, pages 230–231, and Unit 8, pages 290–292). If this rate suits the monetary policy that the Bank is following, it will buy the bills – acting as lender of last resort. If the Bank thinks the price of the bills is too high (the rate of interest is too low), it will refuse to buy them. The discount house will then reduce the price and effectively endure a higher rate of interest. If the Bank seeks a significant rise in rates, it may refuse to buy the bills at all. This forces the discount houses to borrow directly from the Bank, at a rate of the Bank's choice.

The Bank can similarly engineer a reduction in short-term rates by agreeing to buy bills at a higher price. If there is a surplus of funds in the market which threatens to induce an unwanted fall in interest rates, the Bank will probably sell Treasury bills to absorb the surplus cash.

There are two points in particular to remember.

1. The Bank operates directly only on very short-term rates of interest.
2. If these short-term rates increase, effects will soon spread to other rates of interest. This is because an increase in the rate at which the Bank deals would involve the discount houses in losses which they will not want to persist.

Consider the following:

A discount house borrows £1 million at call from a retail bank, at 9 per cent. (This, like all interest rates, unless otherwise stated, is an annual rate and will be scaled down for shorter-term loans.) The discount house uses the £1 million to buy Treasury bills yielding 10 per cent.

Assuming that it keeps renewing the call-money loan, the discount house expects to pay interest over three months of

$$£1\,000\,000 \times \frac{9}{100} \times \frac{1}{4} = £22\,500$$

(The $\frac{1}{4}$ occurs because the period is one-quarter of a year.)

The discount house expects to earn from the Treasury bills

$$£1\,000\,000 \times \frac{10}{100} \times \frac{1}{4} = £25\,000$$

which gives a profit of £2500.

However, suppose that the retail bank demands intermediate repayment of its loan. The discount house seeks the help of the Bank of England, but has to pay 10.5 per cent to raise £1 million. The interest on this is £26 250, so the bank makes a loss of £1250 (£26 250 minus £25 000) instead of a profit of £2500.

Something to do

- Calculate the loss to a discount house which borrows £750 000 for three months at call from a clearing bank, at a rate of interest of 5.75 per cent, and buys £750 000 Treasury bills yielding 6.0 per cent, if the clearing bank demands immediate repayment of its loan and the discount house has to borrow £750 000 from the Bank of England at 6.25 per cent.

Reverting to our example, the fact that the Bank of England is now demanding 10.5 per cent is a clear sign to the discount houses. They will now increase the rates that they charge for loans. Before long, money market rates in general will move upwards, filtering through to the rates charged on loans and overdrafts to the public.

In fact, though, private-sector borrowing does not respond readily to changes in interest rates. Sometimes when rates rise, lending continues simply because the banks have the resources available. This has led the authorities on occasions to sell more government securities than necessary to finance the government's borrowing requirement – a practice known as over-funding, which reduces the banks' lending powers.

The effectiveness of monetary policy

There are basically two components of monetary policy:

- the control of the credit base through the sale and purchase of securities by the Bank of England
- the control of bank lending through the adjustment of interest rates.

In general, the policy has been operated on the basis of setting target rates of growth for the measures of money supply and trying to manage policy so as to meet those targets. The targets have tended to be fairly broad – perhaps aiming at a growth rate of between 4 per cent and 7 per cent for one of the measures. Experience has varied, but targets have more often been missed than achieved.

Before 1981, monetary policy was directed at the main banks, but there was an increasing number of banks outside the immediate control of the Bank of England. This made it difficult for the Bank to control the money supply. The definition of the 'monetary sector' in 1981 remedied this. Over 300 organisations come within the sector. They have an obligation to leave a small proportion of their funds with the Bank of England, which in return is prepared to deal in bills accepted by these organisations.

Having gathered most of the appropriate financial institutions into the monetary sector, the Bank hoped to be able to use market forces to achieve its objectives in meeting monetary targets. Virtually all quantitative controls over the banks have disappeared – there are no longer any cash or reserve ratios. However, the banks do guarantee to make sufficient secured loans to the discount houses for them to operate efficiently.

Whatever the framework, however, there are bound to be difficulties in using monetary policy. The difficulties fall into two groups

- immediate objectives
- policy objectives.

Difficulties with the immediate objectives

- The objective of controlling the money supply is itself vague. As we have seen, there are several different measures of money supply. The authorities are often uncertain as to which should constitute the main target. Evidence of this can be seen in the number of times the government itself has decided to target different quantities.
- Changes in the behaviour of the markets change the significance of the targets. For example, M4 includes both interest-bearing and non-interest-bearing sight deposits.
- If the authorities decide to restrict the growth of certain liquid assets to prevent the expansion of the credit base, the banks themselves might encourage the growth of other assets. A reduction in Treasury bills might be balanced by an increase in ordinary bills of exchange.

- In this connection, the banks may be able to make restrictive action by the Bank ineffective by themselves holding more liquid assets than is strictly necessary. Then a given amount of open-market selling will not produce the desired reduction in credit creation.
- Though it would be more difficult within the post-1981 monetary sector arrangements, there have been occasions in the past when credit restrictions were circumvented by the use of organisations outside the monetary sector, for example, overseas banks and markets in foreign currency loans.

Despite these problems, the market approach to monetary policy seems not to have caused too much difficulty in recent years.

Difficulties with the policy objectives

The government does not try to control the supply of money as a kind of academic exercise: the purpose is to ensure that the real economy moves along an appropriate course. Even if the policy objectives are restricted to a low level of unemployment and a low inflation rate, it has to be conceded that monetary policy alone is not likely to achieve these objectives. Fiscal policies, involving taxation and government spending, are necessary to influence demand which in turn impacts on levels of employment and inflation (see Units 11 and 12). When economic policy consisted solely of monetary policy (under the gold standard and balanced budgets), periods of high unemployment were experienced.

The difficulties include the following.

Interest rates

Suppose the objective is to reduce inflationary demand. To reduce borrowing through the use of interest-rate policy would need very high interest rates. For a number of reasons, this might not appeal to the authorities.

- While demand inflation might be reduced in the long term, cost inflation might be encouraged, for the cost to businesses of borrowing to finance stocks and expansion will have increased.

> **Key points**
>
> - ***Demand inflation*** *is caused by consumers demanding more goods and services than are currently available, leading to increased prices.*
> - ***Cost inflaton*** *is caused by a rise in the costs of production being passed on to consumers in the form of higher prices.*

- The increase in interest rates will have an effect on **foreign exchange rates**. Money will be attracted to London, and sterling will appreciate. This will reduce the price of imports and increase the price of exports, neither of which will necessarily be welcomed by the government. (See also Unit 13.)
- Rising interest rates will have a depressing effect on the stock market (initially on gilt-edged securities, but eventually throughout) and will increase the government's borrowing costs.

For these reasons, it would be inappropriate for interest rates to be allowed to fluctuate too widely.

The control of interest rate fluctuation is now the job of the Monetary Policy Committee (see page 321), which is an independent body that meets once a month to determine the 'base rate' around which it will operate, which affects all short-term interest rates. In effect, therefore, the setting of interest rates now lies with an independent panel of experts and not with a government minister: this, in theory, protects it from political interference.

Selectivity

It is difficult for monetary policy to be selective in its impact. To return, briefly, to interest rates: it might be necessary to encourage an increase in interest rates to reduce or slow down rising consumer demand. At the same time, it might be desirable to have low interest rates to encourage investment by industry. This combination is not possible – if interest rates are high in one sector, they are high in all sectors. Some discrimination may be achieved through taxation, but monetary policy alone will not achieve it.

This lack of discrimination is not confined to interest rates. Restrictions on bank lending may have a random effect, especially when there are no overall controls or directives covering lending policy. The restrictions would apply equally to a consumer wishing to purchase a Japanese television set and to a manufacturer wishing to buy some machinery made in Birmingham. The banks may find one party more creditworthy than another, but monetary policy does not distinguish between them.

Cause and effect

The link between money supply and economic performance is by no means clear cut, so the government cannot be over-reliant on monetary policy. It might be that unemployment fell following a fall in interest rates, but there is no way of being certain that the fall in interest rates actually led to the change in unemployment. A government could not therefore rely on a further fall in interest rates being followed by another reduction in unemployment, since many other factors might have been at work. There is also a time element – it is uncertain how long it takes for a given monetary policy change to work its way through the economy.

Taxation

To some extent the success of monetary policy – and indeed its structure – is dependent on fiscal policy (see below). If the government cannot raise the money it needs through taxation, it must either reduce its expenditure or borrow the money. The means by which it borrows to a certain extent determines monetary policy (or at least restricts it) so that it perhaps cannot pursue certain objectives.

There are thus a number of problems associated with monetary policy. It needs to be remembered, however, that the policy is not intended to deal with the 'fine tuning' of the economy; its primary function is to provide a general economic atmosphere of restriction or expansion or stability, within which other policy initiatives may flourish. The most important of these other policy initiatives is fiscal policy, which we consider next.

Fiscal policy

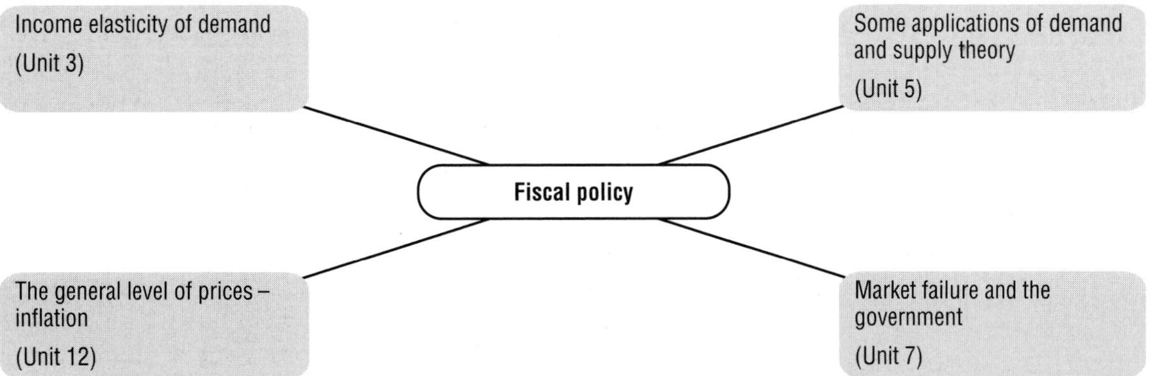

Taxation and government expenditure

Broadly defined, fiscal policy is the use of taxation and government expenditure to influence the country's economic activities. **Public finance** covers the methods employed by the government to raise revenue and the principles underlying government expenditure. The government's expenditure plays just as large a part in economic policy as taxation.

Table 10.1 gives broad indications of the level of the government's income and expenditure.

- Taxes on income and expenditure are the main source of government income. Although social security contributions are not strictly taxes, if these are added to central government taxes on income and expenditure the total for 1996 is £249 439 million – well over half of all income.
- As for expenditure, almost half the total is accounted for by grants of various kinds.

Note that expenditure exceeded income by £20 128 million. This **deficit** is covered by borrowing.

Before considering the sources of government income, we examine the need for government expenditure.

The need for government expenditure

Public goods

Two of the State's primary functions are defence and the maintenance of internal law and order. Each of these can be regarded as a collective service or **public good** in that it is necessarily provided to all members of the community at the same time. As it is impossible for individuals to opt out of using or benefiting from defence, it would not make sense to talk of a market price for the commodity. Accordingly it must be supplied and paid for by the community as a whole. Similarly, since we all benefit from the maintenance of law and order, the cost of the police service is met by taxpayers and ratepayers rather than by those who happen to be willing to pay for protection. An exception arises when a private organisation specifically requests police protection or assistance. For example, large numbers of police officers are on duty in football stadiums on Saturday afternoons, and, since they are there at the request of the football clubs, the latter are charged for the service.

Table 10.1

General government: summary account (£ million)												
		December										
		1986	**1987**	**1988**	**1989**	**1990**	**1991**	**1992**	**1993**	**1994**	**1995**	**1996**
Current receipts	Taxes on income	51 973	55 658	61 723	70 000	76 875	75 178	73 716	73 248	80 675	90 694	94 685
	Taxes on expenditure	62 872	68 971	76 039	79 980	78 298	85 416	87 521	90 336	96 418	103 697	108 484
	Social security contributions	26 165	27 663	30 682	33 333	34 457	36 216	36 975	39 267	42 086	44 371	46 270
	Community charge/council tax	—	—	—	586	8 629	8 128	7 907	8 038	8 450	9 151	9 906
	Gross trading surplus[1]	155	−75	−32	199	12	−36	206	193	495	623	681
	Rent, etc.[2]	4 101	4 347	4 117	3 902	4 255	4 565	4 736	5 363	5 540	5 630	5 757
	Interest and dividends, etc.	5 738	5 802	6 071	6 990	6 397	5 663	5 247	4 842	5 072	5 264	5 339
	Miscellaneous current transfers	266	363	394	431	504	545	419	617	704	713	632
	Imputed charge for consumption of non-trading capital	2 583	2 804	3 110	3 448	3 806	3 763	3 603	3 354	3 287	3 455	3 653
	Total	**153 853**	**165 533**	**182 104**	**198 869**	**213 233**	**219 438**	**220 330**	**225 258**	**242 727**	**263 598**	**275 407**
Current expenditure	Current expenditure on goods and services	78 328	84 241	90 531	98 348	109 128	120 342	128 272	134 402	140 781	145 753	152 079
	Non-trading capital consumption	2 583	2 804	3 110	3 448	3 806	3 763	3 603	3 354	3 287	3 455	3 653
	Subsidies	6 301	6 265	6 037	5 782	6 066	5 995	6 737	7 203	7 484	7 631	9 100
	Current grants to personal sector	49 454	50 798	52 175	54 033	58 939	69 287	80 052	88 537	92 630	96 168	98 611
	Current grants paid abroad (net)	2 233	3 277	3 248	4 278	4 596	1 083	4 834	4 908	5 077	7 089	4 933
	Debt interest	17 243	18 026	18 279	19 010	18 786	17 022	17 120	18 515	22 250	25 917	27 159
	Total current expenditure	**156 142**	**165 411**	**173 380**	**184 899**	**201 321**	**217 492**	**240 618**	**256 919**	**271 509**	**286 013**	**295 535**
	Balance: current surplus[1]	−2 289	122	8 724	13 970	11 912	1 946	−20 288	−31 661	−28 782	−22 415	−20 128
	Total	**153 853**	**165 533**	**182 104**	**198 869**	**213 233**	**219 438**	**220 330**	**225 258**	**242 727**	**263 598**	**275 407**

[1]Before providing for depreciation.
[2]Includes royalties and licence fees on oil and gas production.

Source: *Annual Abstract of Statistics* (The Stationery Office, 1999)

Merit goods The State provides other services which *could* be sold on an ordinary supply and demand basis. Education and health services are examples. However, these are generally regarded as being too important to be left entirely to market forces, and so they are provided either free or at a low direct cost to the consumer. This is partly because there are **externalities** involved – that is, it is not only the consumer who is affected by the service concerned. We all benefit from children being educated so that everyone uses the same language and the same numerical system; similarly, society as a whole benefits from individuals being in good health. If these services, or **merit goods**, were only provided privately, many individuals might not take advantage of them as they might rather spend their money on other things in accordance with their own scales of preference. On the other hand, many people might find such goods or services too expensive for them. Social and humanitarian considerations dictate that the services should be provided free of direct charge, or at least be heavily subsidised by the State. This is both for the benefit of the individual, and so that society may make the best use of its resources.

The more important the public benefits obtained from the private consumption of services, the greater the degree of government **subsidy** is likely to be. Primary and secondary education are now provided free of direct charge, while some direct charges are made for courses in technical colleges and universities. In the health service, prescription and other charges are made both as a deterrent to consumption and to slow down the increase in public expenditure, thus reducing the burden on the taxpayer.

Think about it

- Is the government right to intervene in the provision of merit goods such as health, education, housing and shelter, food and transport?
- Is the way the government intervenes fair?

Economy A further group of services taken over and provided by the government without direct charge are those for which the cost of collecting revenue directly from users would be disproportionately high. It would, for example, be possible to finance road building and road maintenance via a complex system of tolls covering all roads. Since this would be expensive, road building is financed out of general taxation, to which, it is true, the motorist makes a substantial contribution. Similarly, proposals to charge for NHS prescriptions according to the value of the drugs prescribed meet with opposition partly because of the high administrative costs involved.

Minimum living standards Through the social security system, the government has an obligation to ensure that everyone has at least a minimum standard of living. A combination of taxation and government expenditure aims at producing a more equal distribution of income and wealth. For reasons which are explained below (see the section on 'The scale of government expenditure' on page 332), an increasing proportion of government expenditure is devoted to social security and welfare payments.

Industrial and employment policy

While there may be broad agreement about the need for government expenditure under the above headings (although there may be arguments about the amounts involved), there is less agreement about industrial expenditure. Some governments opt for a close involvement with industry, making heavy subsidies in order to maintain employment or develop new industries. Others distance themselves from industry, leaving the private sector to determine the scale and direction of their expenditure.

An important example of differences between political parties here is the extent to which governments pursue policies of nationalisation or privatisation (see also Units 4 and 7).

The scale of government expenditure

Clearly there is ample scope for the government to spend money. Indeed, a worrying feature of the economy for some commentators is the scale of government or public expenditure (see Figure 10.3) and the difficulty of controlling it.

Fig. 10.3 General government expenditure as a percentage of GDP[1]

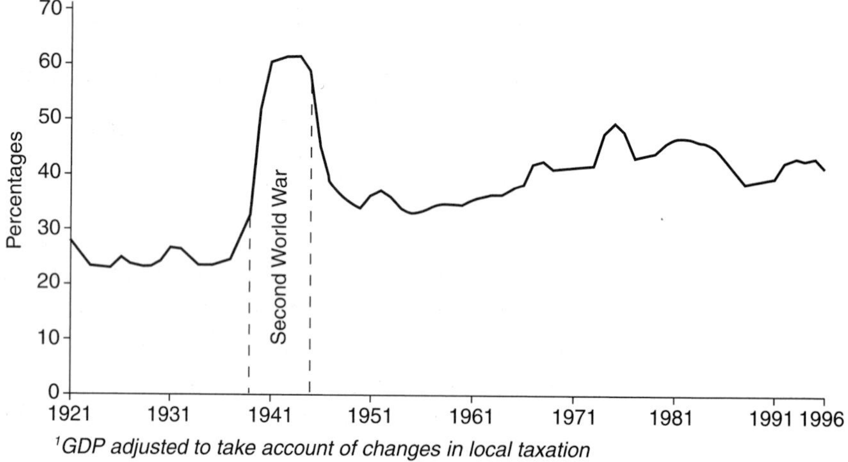

[1] *GDP adjusted to take account of changes in local taxation*

Source: Office for National Statistics, 1999

A noticeable characteristic of the UK economy since 1945 has been the steady increase in government expenditure, in absolute terms, despite many attempts to restrict its growth. While government expenditure has grown as a percentage of GDP since the 1920s (see Figure 10.3), it has in fact fallen somewhat since the early 1970s and shown a considerable reduction from the levels of the mid-1970s to the mid-1980s. There are several reasons for the absolute increase:

- The size of the population has increased, so more services have to be provided.
- The range of services and payments – particularly social services and social security payments – has increased.
- The continuing problem of unemployment necessarily incurs government expenditure, both in the form of unemployment benefit payments and in attempts to reduce the level of unemployment.
- The age structure of the population ensures that social security expenditure will continue to rise as the proportion of retired people increases.

Table 10.2

General government expenditure in real terms[1]: by function (£ billion at 1996 prices)						
	1981	**1986**	**1991**	**1994**	**1995**	**1996**
Social security	64	80	85	104	107	107
Health	28	31	36	41	42	43
Education	29	31	34	38	38	39
Defence	26	30	27	25	24	23
Public order and safety	9	11	15	16	16	15
General public services	9	10	13	14	15	13
Housing and community amenities	15	13	10	11	11	10
Transport and communication	9	6	8	7	9	8
Recreational and cultural affairs	3	4	5	5	5	5
Agriculture, forestry and fishing	3	3	3	3	4	5
Other expenditure[2]	46	41	28	38	44	37
All expenditure	**241**	**259**	**264**	**302**	**314**	**306**

[1]Adjusted to 1996 prices using the GDP market prices deflator adjusted to remove the distortion caused by the abolition of domestic rates.
[2]Includes expenditure on mining, manufacture, construction, fuel and energy and services, as well as all other expenditure not allocated to a specific function.

Source: *Social Trends* (The Stationery Office, 1998)

The trends in some of the main areas of expenditure are shown in Table 10.2.

Given the efforts made by successive governments to contain or reduce public expenditure, it is perhaps surprising that the level of such expenditure has been so nearly constant as a proportion of GDP. Two questions arise:

- Is there an ideal balance between public and private expenditure?
- Given the nature of the UK economy, is there a limit to the level of public expenditure?

Something to do

- Obtain the latest edition of *Social Trends*. (You will find this either in your own school or college library, or in your nearest central library.)
  - Find out the latest government expenditure figures in the categories shown in Table 10.2.
  - Construct a pie chart to show each category as a proportion of total government expenditure.
- If you were the Chancellor of the Exchequer and had to reduce general government expenditure by £10 billion, what do you think would be the best way of achieving this?
- What would be the main results of your actions? Do you think they would be popular or unpopular?

Limits to government expenditure

In practice, the balance between public expenditure and private expenditure is a political matter.

- Those who favour more private expenditure put their faith in market forces to bring about an adequate distribution of resources. The Conservative Governments in the 1980s took such a view, believing that competition would provide the spur to efficiency and extra output, which would bring about generally improved standards of living.

Increasingly, too, people were charged for services which had previously either been provided free of direct charge or been heavily subsidised.

- Those who favour more public-sector expenditure concentrate on the failures of the market system, which might not provide an adequate level of essential services at reasonable prices or ensure basic living standards for everyone.

The future trend will depend on a number of factors, including:

- the **age structure of the population** (see Unit 2): an ageing population increases public expenditure on health care and social security
- **unemployment** (see Unit 11): rising unemployment increases government expenditure
- **inflation** (see Unit 12): rising prices can lead to unemployment, and to an increase in welfare benefits to those in need in order to meet the higher prices.

Whatever happens in these directions, government expenditure will remain an important factor in the economy, and there will be demands that the government does not meet. The problem is that all the services provided by the State could be improved if more resources were made available. Even the Chancellor of the Exchequer does not have unlimited resources; and may in any case choose to set limits to government spending even when extra money *is* available. In effect, the Chancellor must then make a choice between various policies:

- improve some services at the expense of others, keeping overall expenditure constant
- increase expenditure in general, financing it through extra tax revenue or borrowing
- transfer the provision of certain services from the public sector to the private sector
- impose charges for some services
- provide as many services as possible, if necessary increasing taxation in order to do so.

As we know, the tendency has been to opt for reduction in the scope and level of services provided within the public sector. For example, the government has become more selective in giving assistance within the social security system. Many political disputes arise over the question of selectivity in awarding benefits. One view is that benefits should be available to everyone as a right. This is partly due to the administrative complexity and expense of establishing which cases are needy or deserving. An opposing position is that, since resources are limited, they should be concentrated where they will achieve the greatest benefit and be withheld from those whose marginal utility from benefits is low. This is reflected in schemes for charging for NHS prescriptions, with exemptions for certain categories such as schoolchildren and pensioners.

However, in one sense we are running ahead of ourselves, as before he (or she) can allocate expenditure between departments the Chancellor needs to know where his revenue is coming from. Before we consider other aspects of public expenditure in connection with the Budget (see the section beginning on page 341), then, we must examine the income – 'current receipts' – part of Table 10.1.

Taxation

Classification of taxes

As noted on page 329, the government's main source of income is **taxation**. Taxes may be classified in various ways. One possibility is to divide them into **direct taxes** and **indirect taxes**.

- A **direct tax** is a tax that is levied (imposed) on specific individuals or institutions, on whom the burden of the tax falls.
- An **indirect tax** is levied on the activities or products of individuals or institutions and the burden of the tax may be shifted to the final consumer.

When an employee is assessed for **income tax** (a direct tax), for example, the employee must bear the burden (it is the employee who has to pay the tax). But when **excise duty** (an indirect tax) is levied on a whisky distiller, the distiller is able to recoup the tax by increasing its prices so that the final consumer pays the additional tax.

While such a distinction is clear in some cases, however, it is not so clear in others. Local authority rates on businesses, for example, may be passed on to final consumers in the form of higher prices, even though such rates are a direct tax. Accordingly, it is now common simply to divide taxes into two groups:

- taxes on income or wealth, and
- taxes on expenditure.

We look at these in more detail on pages 337–340. First, though, we need to note a further way of classifying taxes, according to whether they are **progressive, proportional** or **regressive.**

- Progressive taxes are those which are arranged so that rich people not only pay more tax than poor people but also hand over a greater percentage of their income in tax.
- Proportional taxes are those in which all taxpayers hand over the same proportion of their income in tax, which means that rich people pay a greater sum than poorer people.
- Regressive taxes are those which force poorer people to part with a greater proportion of their income than rich people.

Principles of taxation

When Adam Smith (see Unit 2) first discussed the principles of taxation in *The Wealth of Nations*, he said that taxes should be levied on people according to their ability to pay. Since there was no income tax at the time, he was probably thinking of proportional taxes on property. Today, however, fairness is usually taken to mean that the tax system overall must be progressive. This means that the tax system should have the characteristics of **vertical equity** – the tendency for the percentage of income or wealth paid in tax to rise as income or wealth rises. This is really based on the principle of diminishing marginal utility. The more income you have, the less importance you attach to an extra £1, so the greater amount of tax you can afford to pay on that £1.

In the early 1990s, the top 20 per cent of income earners in the UK earned over 40 per cent of total income and the bottom 20 per cent earned less than 7 per cent. In terms of total wealth, the most wealthy

50 per cent of the population owned over 90 per cent of total wealth. Distribution of income and wealth tells us much about how a society shares its 'cake' (the national income cake or GDP). Governments take an interest in this: if distribution is too uneven, then this can lead to social problems and political instability, whereas if governments intervene too much, by redistributing via taxation, they may stifle enterprise and reduce the overall size of the 'cake'.

The other aspect of equity in taxation is **horizontal equity** – the requirement that people with the same income and the same commitments should pay the same amount of tax.

We return to the concept of equity in the next section.

The other principles laid down by Adam Smith were that

- tax should be payable at a time and place convenient to the taxpayer
- the taxpayer should be certain of his liability in advance (in other words, there should be no retrospective taxation)
- tax should be economical to collect.

While these principles of taxation provide a suitable framework for the tax system, there are other desirable characteristics for modern systems:

- The system should be flexible. It should be easy to increase or decrease taxes to meet the requirements of economic policy.
- It is sometimes argued that taxes should be neutral in their impact. This follows from the free-market idea that the best allocation of resources is achieved if consumers and producers are left to their own devices. We have seen, though, that there are weaknesses in the market mechanism. The government might actively discourage the purchase of some products through high taxation. Alcohol and tobacco are obvious examples, though here the British government is in a difficult position since these produce a large proportion of annual revenue.
- It is desirable that the taxation of incomes does not act as a disincentive to labour. High tax rates may have an effect at both ends of the income scale. Those at the top of the scale may refuse promotion or extra responsibility if extra income is subject to tax at 60 or 70 per cent. Alternatively, they may find ways of avoiding the tax (which is legal) or evading it (which is illegal). At the bottom of the scale, the combination of losing social security benefits and paying income tax might dissuade some people from accepting employment. This situation forms what is known as the **poverty trap**.
- It is becoming increasingly important to make sure that UK rates of taxation are compatible with those in the rest of the European Union. The EU stipulates, for example, that minimum requirements on VAT have to be met and all member countries have to take into account the Single European Market with its emphasis on competition and a 'level playing field'. Governments, of course, can and do have different tax rates (for example, petrol prices vary throughout Europe, mainly due to different tax regimes) but they need to be aware of the impact their taxation policies will have now that firms and people can move across internal EU national borders without hindrance.

Taxes on income and wealth

Income tax Income tax is the largest single source of revenue for the government. Once a clearly progressive tax, income tax has now become more of a proportional tax. There is now only slight acknowledgement of the idea of vertical equity. This is achieved by allowing taxpayers an initial slice of their income free of tax and then taxing any additional income at only two or three different rates.

The policy in recent years has been one of the gradual simplification of the structure of income tax. This makes tax systems conform more closely to the basic principles outlined by Adam Smith. The taxpayer can have a better understanding of the system and be more certain of his or her liability. The authorities find the system easy to administer when there are fewer tax rates.

Think about it

- To what extent is it desirable for the government to follow a policy of reducing income tax?
- How do you think this might be achieved, and what would be its effects?

National Insurance Although National Insurance contributions are not in fact taxes, it is appropriate to consider them here. All employees and self-employed people pay a contribution of a percentage of gross income between upper and lower limits. If income rises above the limit, no further payments are made.

Corporation tax Companies have to pay a percentage of their profits, after deducting various allowances mainly to encourage investment, in the form of corporation tax. If part of a company's profits are distributed to shareholders as a dividend, the company must pay the income tax involved, which can then be set against its corporation tax liability.

Capital gains tax If you buy shares or other assets at one price and sell them at a higher price you have made what is known as a **capital gain** (your capital has increased). In effect, this is extra income for you, and is taxable once the overall gains in a tax year reach a certain threshold.

Some of the capital gains that are realised are attributable to inflation, however. For example, assets bought for £1000 and sold for £1200 show capital gains of £200 (20 per cent). But if prices in general have risen by 5 per cent the real gain is only £150. The tax is **index linked** (linked to inflation) so that it is levied only on the real gain.

Inheritance tax Some countries have a specific tax on wealth. This has the effect of broadening the tax base and may be considered more equitable. Suppose that two citizens have the same income and pay the same amount of tax, but one of them has personal wealth of £200 000 and the other one assets of only £50 000. It might be argued that the former can afford to contribute more to the Exchequer than the latter. This form of wealth tax has never been attempted in the UK. The nearest approach is inheritance tax.

On the death of an individual, their estate is valued and if its value is less than a prescribed threshold no tax is payable. The portion of the estate in excess of the threshold is taxed.

The economic effects of taxing income and wealth

- The conventional advantage of taxing income or wealth is that the tax can be made progressive, and in this way income can be redistributed.
- Higher marginal rates of income tax may be disincentives to effort. One of the principles of taxation is to collect revenue with a minimal impact on the allocation of resources. This may be achieved by reducing higher tax rates. The reason for this is that while reducing higher tax rates may be an incentive to effort since people with higher incomes will be able to keep a greater percentage of those incomes, since they may also save rather than spend the extra money, the effect on overall demand for goods and services will be small. Of course, the other possibility is that a given net income can be obtained from a smaller gross income: some people may not need to work so hard.
- Lower personal taxation permits both increased effective demand and higher personal savings. Increased demand can lead to greater production and a reduction in unemployment. It can also lead to inflation. Higher personal savings can lead to more investment by firms, since a large proportion of personal savings is placed with finance houses which make the funds available to industry. Such investment by firms also yields increased production and can reduce unemployment. Not all personal investment, however, will benefit the UK economy since some may be placed overseas.
- Heavy taxes on wealth tend to lead to the break-up of large estates. By imposing a relatively low rate of inheritance tax, the government limits this effect. The desirability of this depends on the view taken of inherited wealth!

Given the levels of unavoidable government expenditure, it would be impossible to raise the necessary revenue solely through taxing expenditure, so taxes on income and wealth must remain a central feature of the tax system.

Taxes on expenditure

Taxes on expenditure fall conveniently into two categories:

- taxes collected by the customs and excise authorities
- taxes collected by other agencies.

Taxes on expenditure are called indirect taxes since, although they are levied on the manufacturer or wholesaler, they are passed on to the ultimate consumer by means of price rises.

> *Think about it*
>
> *'Taxes on expenditure are fairer than taxes on income, because if you don't buy you don't pay.'*
>
> - Comment on this statement.

Customs duties Customs duties are levied on imported goods on an ***ad-valorem*** basis (that is, according to the value of the goods). They may be divided into

- **protective duties** (designed to protect home industry from foreign competition), and
- **revenue duties** (designed to raise revenue for the government).

<u>Excise duties</u> Excise duties are levied on a fairly narrow range of home-produced goods. They are normally specific duties (that is, levied at so much per kilogram or litre). Taxes on alcohol, tobacco and petrol are examples. The price elasticity of demand for these goods is very low and the rates of tax are very high. About half the retail price of petrol is accounted for by tax, and a bigger proportion for alcoholic spirits.

<u>Value added tax (VAT)</u> was introduced in 1973 as part of the comprehensive reform of the UK tax system undertaken by the Conservative Government. The standard rate of VAT in the UK is 17.5 per cent, and this rate applies to all transactions except those that are specifically defined as coming within one of the following two categories:

- Some businesses, goods and services are exempt from the tax. They include small businesses whose taxable turnover per year is lower than a given threshold; transactions in land, insurance, postal services, betting, gaming and lotteries; financial services; educational services; and burial and cremation services. Traders in these categories do not have to charge any tax for the value they have added to their goods, though they will not be able to reclaim any input tax they have paid on goods and materials purchased. This input tax will be added to the retail price. (Insurance premiums are subject to a separate tax.)
- Other goods and services are zero rated. A business selling zero-rated goods will not charge its customers VAT. It can, however, reclaim tax paid on its purchases of materials, so the goods are in effect sold tax free – the tax is not passed on to the customer.

Apart from the distinction over reclaiming tax paid, the main difference between these two categories is the necessity for the seller of zero-rated goods to keep the appropriate records to reclaim tax paid.

Think about it

- Is VAT a progressive, proportional or regressive tax? To what extent? Do you think VAT could be made more equitable?

The economic effects of taxing expenditure

- The most important aspect of expenditure or outlay taxes is that they are normally regressive. The tax on a packet of twenty cigarettes is a much greater burden to a person who earns £5000 a year than it is to someone on a £30 000 salary. It is true that the lower-paid person does not *have* to buy cigarettes but if they do smoke, they are voluntarily bearing a disproportionate tax burden and thereby reducing the degree of vertical equity in the system. Against this, however, such taxes do spread the burden of taxation and bring into the tax net people who might otherwise remain outside.
- The discriminatory nature of excise duties imposes a disproportionate burden on those who consume alcohol or tobacco or who drive cars. About 40 per cent of customs and excise duties are raised via taxes on alcoholic drink, tobacco and petrol.
- The pattern of expenditure taxes affects the allocation of resources (see Unit 3). The greater the elasticity of demand and supply, the greater the effect of outlay taxes on the allocation of resources.

- Expenditure taxes are likely to have inflationary effects. An increase in VAT, like all tax increases, may in itself be regarded as deflationary since it reduces demand. However, workers may respond by demanding higher wages and depending on how successful they are, there may be an increase in costs and prices and further encouragement to inflation. Thus while demand inflation may be reduced, cost inflation is encouraged. (Inflation is examined in detail in Unit 12.)
- The burden of expenditure taxes is often hidden. Consumers are not always aware of the amount of tax that they are being asked to pay, so these taxes probably do not have the same disincentive effect on effort as income taxes. Also, the government revenue from *ad-valorem* taxes such as VAT rises with inflation, so the government does not have to risk unpopularity by adjusting the rate of tax.
- Because they are discriminating, indirect taxes can easily be adjusted to meet certain policy objectives. Thus the government can tax undesirable activities, or it may award subsidies to desirable activities. Indirect taxes on petrol and fuel, including taxing cars at different rates based on fuel efficiency, for example, are increasingly being used in an attempt to reduce pollution. Such taxes, intended to promote conservation of the environment, are often called 'green taxes'.
- The most obvious effect of VAT is to broaden the base of expenditure taxes, so that a given amount of revenue can be raised by taxing a wide range of goods at lower rates, while the severe rates of excise duties are retained on a narrow range of goods.
- Although expenditure taxes are normally regressive, the application of different rates to different goods (0 per cent to 17.5 per cent) probably makes VAT in the UK slightly progressive, in that lower-income groups are likely to spend a greater proportion of their income on zero-rated goods and services. It would be possible to have a VAT system with a large number of rates designed to make the tax more progressive, but the administrative complexity makes this undesirable. Ideally, VAT is best operated as a flat-rate tax on all transactions.
- VAT has the merit of taxing services as well as goods. Before the introduction of VAT, there was no effective tax on services and it was a weakness of the tax system that different kinds of consumer expenditure were treated in different ways.
- Expenditure taxes directly affect the allocation of economic resources through the price mechanism. Since VAT is levied on a wide range of goods, its impact on any one industry is minimised. If the government is anxious to reduce the demand for some goods, however, it can impose higher rates of tax, for example excise duties on tobacco.
- One respect in which VAT might seem to be unfair is that the consumer is sometimes required to pay VAT on taxes that he or she is paying already. Thus petrol is subject to both excise duty and VAT: if the excise duty rises by 20 pence, the total tax rises by 23 pence (20 pence excise duty + 3 pence VAT).
- Administratively, VAT is a complex tax because it is a multi-stage tax levied in three different ways and payable by VAT-registered businesses four times a year. It is not too expensive to the government, however, since much of the work involved falls on those firms or individuals who have to remit the tax to the government.

The role of the Budget

The government exercises the right to raise through taxation the revenue it needs to meet its commitments. Its proposals are normally embodied in the Budget statement made in March each year. The original purpose of the Budget was simply to raise sufficient revenue to cover government expenditure, and the government was expected to set a good example to the community by living within its income. But it became clear, particularly through the work of John Maynard Keynes (see Unit 11), that the significance of the Budget far exceeded its role in the government's housekeeping. The Budget is the most important economic regulator, since the overall fiscal policy – the balance between government income and expenditure – has a vital part to play in determining the performance of the economy.

The macro-economic role of the Budget

The level of economic activity depends basically on the level of aggregate monetary demand (see Unit 11, page 352). The government may therefore influence the level of activity by varying its own expenditure.

Boosting the economy

In conditions of high unemployment, the government may run a budget deficit (that is, it will spend more than it takes in taxation) in an effort to get more people working. The difference between what it spends and what is raised in taxation must be found by borrowing or, as a very dangerous last resort, by printing money. Deficit financing will also probably involve lower taxation, which will leave consumers with more money to spend than they previously had. From the point of view of employment, the taxes that should be reduced are those that will give the greatest stimulus to demand, though by doing this there is a danger of also stimulating inflation – see also Unit 11.

Something to do

- Make a list of taxes that the government should adjust if its objective were to stimulate demand in the economy.
- What would the actual and immediate effects of reducing them be?

If the government wishes to increase consumption, they might cut expenditure taxes or else adjust income tax to benefit those who tend to spend a large proportion of their income on good and services – mainly low income earners who only just qualify to pay income tax. On the other hand, investment might best be encouraged by reducing company taxation and adjusting investment incentives. The important point is that it is not just a question of reducing taxes and hoping that demand will rise. A careful assessment must be made of the amount by which, and the directions in which, demand needs to rise. An injection of extra government expenditure will not have a once-and-for-all effect but will have a variety of effects. (This is discussed in detail in Unit 11.) Moreover, an increase in government expenditure of, say, £500 million is likely to have a more beneficial effect on the level of employment than a reduction in taxation of £500 million, since part of the tax reduction will be saved by those who benefit and a substantial part may be spent abroad.

Calming the economy

When the economy suffers from over- rather than under-activity and inflationary pressures are being generated, the government must budget for a **surplus** and reduce its own expenditure, as well as reducing that of consumers by raising taxation. The difficulty is that, whereas consumers are likely to be happy to co-operate in expanding the economy by spending their higher after-tax incomes, they are not normally so eager to accept less money as taxes are increased. Public reaction to smaller pay packets (when income taxes rise) or to higher prices (when expenditure taxes rise) is normally to demand – and often secure – wage increases which more than compensate for the higher tax burden and so add another twist to the inflationary spiral.

Prioritising objectives

If the Chancellor's only task was to budget either for a surplus or for a deficit according to whether inflation or unemployment was the main problem, then his job would be a simple one. The government must place the various macro-economic objectives in order of priority, however, and consider the effects of fiscal policy on each of them. It may be that the main problem is inflation and so the Chancellor decides to run a large budget surplus by increasing taxes. Increases in taxation have a depressive effect on the economy and on business confidence, so investment is likely to decline. But investment increases productivity and so contributes to the fight against inflation and stimulates economic growth.

Enough has been said to indicate the complexity of the Chancellor's task in respect of macro-economic policy. There are further complications to be considered when he assesses the micro-economic effects of his measures.

The micro-economic role of the Budget

Once the general macro-economic strategy has been determined, the Chancellor must determine how any overall change in the balance between taxation and expenditure is to be accomplished. Suppose that the strategy is to inject an extra £1000 million into the economy, by increasing government expenditure or by reducing taxation or by a combination of the two. The Chancellor will be faced by an infinite range of choices as to how to disperse the money. First he must choose the balance between tax cuts and expenditure increases; then which taxes to cut – expenditure taxes or income taxes – and, if the latter, what aspects of the taxes? Would extra expenditure be more beneficial if it were used to increase nurses' pay or to clear derelict industrial sites? There is no clear answer to these or other related questions. The Chancellor's decision is a matter of political choice – the only thing about which the Chancellor can be certain is that, whatever decisions he comes to, he will not please everyone.

Government borrowing

The need for borrowing

- If the government cannot – or prefers not to – raise all the revenue it requires through taxation, a budget deficit results. This has to be financed through borrowing, and the accumulated borrowing makes up the national debt (see Unit 8, page 285). Any annual borrowing is known as the public sector borrowing requirement (PSBR). The PSBR is thus the difference between public-sector expenditure and public-sector revenue (almost entirely from taxation).
- Sometimes governments have no option but to borrow if the economic cycle dictates that they have a shortfall in their income due to recession (assuming they do not want to increase taxes). This is because during a recession tax revenues fall but expenditure on social security rises. Conversely, when the economic cycle is more favourable the government may find itself with more revenue than expenditure. In this case a PSBR is turned into a PSDR – public sector debt repayment – and money is used from this to pay off parts of the national debt.
- At other times, the government may decide to borrow, regardless of the economic cycle, because it is actively engaged in manipulating the economy to achieve certain objectives (such as a reduction in the level of unemployment) and needs extra money to do so. This is called 'discretionary' or 'active' fiscal policy.

Funding the borrowing

There is a difference in funding the PSBR and funding the national debt.

The PSBR

To finance the PSBR, the government can borrow from four sectors and in each case it does so on the strength of selling government 'securities' – for example, Treasury bills, bonds and National Savings certificates.

1. It can borrow from the non-bank private sector, e.g. pension funds.
2. It can borrow from the Bank of England.
3. It can borrow from the private banking sector.
4. It can attract finance from abroad.

Borrowing from the Bank of England or the private banks can lead to increases in the money supply and prove inflationary, so the government often tries to avoid this. (In fact, during the 1980s, the government, concerned about inflation, used the full-fund rule: it attempted to issue long-term stock instead of short-term and did not resort to 'printing money' by borrowing from the Bank of England.)

The national debt

The national debt is ongoing, bonds (long-term debt) and bills (short-term) are bought and sold each day by the Bank of England, as people and institutions cash in their securities on the maturity date. The PSBR is added to accumulated PSBRs over the years and this is, in effect, the national debt. However, occasionally the Chancellor is able to pay off parts of the national debt when he has a PSDR (public sector debt repayment). This does not happen very often because it depends on government revenue exceeding government spending. This was the case in the late 1980s and again in the financial year 2000/01 due to growth in the economy and a resulting surplus of funds in the Treasury.

The effects of government borrowing

The effect of government borrowing depends on how the borrowing occurs.

One possibility is for the government to offer such attractive terms to savers that money moves out of building societies and other private-sector institutions into the public sector. There are at least two problems associated with this.

1. High interest rates may be necessary to attract funds and these high rates may contribute to cost inflation (see Unit 12, page 374) and slow down the investment necessary for economic growth.
2. If the government attracts too high a proportion of savings, the private sector will have difficulty raising the funds it requires – it will have been crowded out.

If high interest rates are ruled out, the government has to resort to short-term borrowing. This will quickly lead to an increase in the money supply, again with the danger of inflationary pressure.

Local taxation

Many services are provided by local authorities on behalf of the government. The general feeling behind this is that locally elected bodies have a greater awareness of the needs of local people than central government.

Expenditure by local government is largely determined by legal requirements. For example, local authorities cannot opt out of the provision of basic education services. Nor can they spend excessively, for the government would counter this by imposing limits on the amounts that could be raised through local taxation. (This imposing of limits on local taxation is known as 'capping'.)

Until 1990, rates were the main source of revenue available to local authorities independent of central government. The amounts levied on each property depended on its rateable value, which in turn reflected its annual rental value – the amount for which it could be let. This was the amount that a tenant might be expected to pay for its use; thus the rateable value of a terraced house in the industrial heart of a town might be £100, while that of a five-bedroom detached house set in three acres of land on the outskirts might be £900. Each spring, the rating authority estimated the expenditure to be met from the rates for the following twelve months and divided this by the total rateable value of an area to establish the rate per pound to be levied. Thus if the total rateable value of the town was £10 million and the projected expenditure was £15 million, the rate per £1 of rateable value would have been £15 million ÷ £10 million = £1.50 in the pound.

For many years there was dissatisfaction with the rates system, for a number of reasons. These are summarised below.

Disadvantages of the rates system

- Rates were only loosely related to ability to pay. Since they were levied on property and not people, the system did not distinguish between wealthy and poorer households. A property with four or five wage-earners was assessed for the same amount as an identical house occupied by a pensioner.
- They were not specially related to the use of local services.
- Their burden often varied inversely between rich and poor areas. Wealthy areas might have needed fewer services than poorer areas. Less money was therefore required.
- They constituted an arbitrary burden on industry, which, it was said, was driven away from high-rate areas.

Such problems led to calls for an alternative form of local taxation. Two possibilities – a local sales tax and a local income tax – were considered and rejected since they would have been expensive to administer and could have created problems between adjacent areas – people travelling to shop in low-tax (and probably wealthy) boroughs. Instead, in 1990, the domestic rating system was replaced by the community charge or 'poll tax', which was levied, with few exceptions, at a fixed amount per adult in each area.

While the community charge overcame the weakness that the rates did not discriminate between single and multi-occupied houses, it had the disadvantage of being regressive: identically sized families – say, two adults and one grown-up child – in the same borough paid the same amount irrespective of their ability to pay. It is true that there were some exemptions from the tax – prisoners, monks and nuns, and the homeless – and some discounts, up to a maximum of 80 per cent, but in principle the tax was payable by everyone over the age of eighteen, even students.

By its nature, a poll tax cannot be imposed on businesses, even though businesses and their employees use local services. Businesses therefore continued to be assessed on the old system, except for the rate in the pound which is fixed nationally rather than locally – the uniform business rate, which was set at 34.8 pence in the pound for 1990/1 and index linked to the **retail price index** for subsequent years. Rateable values were re-assessed for 1990/1 in an attempt to ensure that the burden of the business rate was equitable.

The council tax

There remained a great deal of dissatisfaction with both the community charge and the uniform business rate. In April 1993, the community charge was replaced by a new **council tax**.

The main features of the council tax are as follows:

- It is designed to reflect the capital value of a property.
- It is based on occupation of property by two adults, with a 25 per cent reduction where there is only one occupier.
- Payment for property in the most expensive band is restricted to three times that in the least expensive band.
- There are discounts for the less well-off, with no minimum contribution, and for people with disabilities.
- A second home qualifies for a 50 per cent discount.

Think about it

- Do you think that the council tax is more equitable than the rates system or the poll tax?
- How do you think the present council tax might be improved to make it fairer to, for example, one-parent families, the low paid or pensioners?

Something to do

- Find out from your local council
  - how much council tax is paid by a householder in each tax band, and
  - what discounts are available to pensioners, disabled people, students and other less well-off sections of the community.
- Use this information to demonstrate to what extent the council tax is a progressive tax.
- Do you think the council tax is a sufficiently equitable tax? Justify your conclusions.

Supply-side measures

We have been looking at how the government can raise revenue and use that revenue to spend on areas in the economy that it feels are important. In doing so, the government hopes to manipulate the economy to fulfil its 'macro' and 'micro' objectives. Fiscal policy and monetary policy are broadly used to control aggregate demand in the economy but this is not the government's only interest. We now turn our attention to **supply-side** policies.

Supply-side policies were much in evidence during the last two decades of the twentieth century. This was partly a result of high inflation in the 1970s, with the associated industrial unrest and economic crises of that decade. In 1979, the Thatcher Government came to power determined to reduce the role of government in economic affairs and to reinstate the role of the 'free market' in allocating resources. The argument was that government had become 'too big' and that Keynesian economics (aggregate demand management policies – see Unit 11, page 350) had contributed to high inflation. The new emphasis was therefore placed on the 'supply-side', with the idea being to increase 'aggregate supply' in the economy, stimulating production, improving efficiency and increasing competition in order to boost output and tackle the problem of rising prices. Successive governments since 1979 have continued this policy.

What does supply-side policy involve?

Supply-side economists believe that free markets are the most efficient way to organise an economy. Adam Smith (the eighteenth-century economist – see page 71) wrote of an 'invisible hand' which, left to itself, would guide the economy to its most efficient use of resources. Therefore, supply-side economists believe in keeping the role of government in economic affairs to a minimum, restricted to setting the framework within which the role of demand and supply is allowed to work properly. These economists argue that when governments intervene in markets they have the effect of distorting those markets, resulting in economic inefficiency. Supply-side polices, then, are about improving the workings of free markets.

Supply-side policies can operate in any area of the economy. Opposite, we look at examples of supply-side measures in the labour market.

- **Reducing the power of trade unions via legislation passed in Parliament** Trade unions can abuse their power and thereby distort labour supply and wage bargaining. Legislation to curb their power is a supply-side measure intended to remove an 'imperfection' in the labour market.
- **Cutting welfare benefits** An over-generous welfare system means that some people may stay on state benefits longer than they would otherwise. Making it more difficult to get social security benefits and reducing their real value over time is a supply-side measure intended to motivate people into employment.
- **Reducing income tax** The idea behind this supply-side measure is to provide an incentive for people to seek employment opportunities and, when in work, to encourage them to work harder so that productivity increases and the individual is rewarded by being allowed to keep more of what he or she earns.
- **Promoting training and education** By encouraging 'life-long learning' and introducing more work-related qualifications (such as National Vocational Qualifications – NVQs) the government hopes to make people more employable and flexible in the labour market. Furthermore, the redundant worker from an industry in decline (such as mining or the car industry) needs to be retrained. Youth unemployment also needs to be tackled, hence policies such as the 'New Deal' in 1998 to get those under the age of 24 into training programmes.
- Encouraging the setting up of small businesses with the aid of grants, allowances or the removal of some legal restraints.

Of course the goods market has also been opened up to supply-side measures. Since the early 1980s many industries have been privatised in order to foster a culture of competition, based on the belief that firms in the private sector will strive to be more efficient and cost-conscious (because they have to keep private shareholders rewarded). Examples of privatisation include the telecommunications industry, the water companies, electricity generation and distribution, and many more – see also Unit 7. **Deregulation** of markets has also taken place. This involves making it easier for firms to compete by abolishing certain controls and regulations. For example, local bus services are now provided by the private sector who bid for licences from local authorities. As well as privatisation, governments have also cut state subsidies to industry. Generally the view is that if firms cannot compete in the market place then they should not be helped out by government.

These are just some examples of what governments have been doing in recent decades to free up markets and allow the interplay of demand and supply to allocate resources to their most efficient use. By increasing competition, costs fall, supply increases and this helps governments achieve other targets such as low inflation and higher productivity.

Something to do

- How might the government's target setting for schools and other educational institutions help improve the supply-side of the economy?

11 The economics of employment

Introduction: economic influences on employment

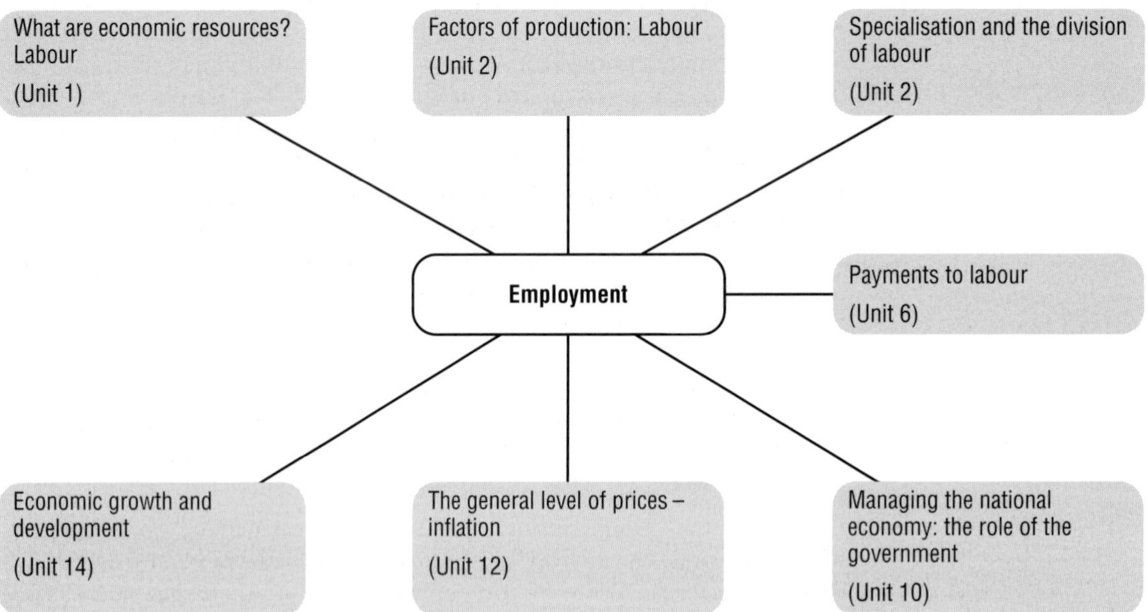

As we have seen, one of the aims of economic policy is to generate an adequate level of employment. Quite what is regarded as adequate may vary from time to time, and is a question that is examined in this unit. Before considering that issue, and the policies that governments use to influence the level of employment, however, we must examine the economic influences on employment.

In this unit, we consider the three main theories of employment: classical, Keynesian and new or neo-classical. In particular, we look at the influence of wage rates and aggregate demand (consumption, investment and other factors) and consider how they influence the level of employment. Finally, we examine the causes and types of unemployment and look at how governments may try to achieve full employment in the UK.

Theories of employment

The classical theory of employment

We saw in Unit 6 that a single firm's demand curve for labour slopes down from left to right, indicating that when wages are low the number of workers employed will be higher. Not surprisingly, it was held for a long while that the way to cure unemployment was to reduce wages and induce employers to take on more labour. At times of high unemployment such a solution was widely advocated.

The **classical theory of employment** is mainly derived from the theories of classical economists such as Adam Smith, David Ricardo and John Stuart Mill.

The influence of wage rates

According to classical theory, full employment will be achieved when the real wage rate is at the level required to clear the labour market – in other words, at a level at which employers are prepared to offer a job to everyone who wants one, and at which everyone who wants a job is prepared to accept the wages offered. If the general level of wages offered is too low, people are not prepared to work for them, while if the wages demanded by workers are too high, employers cannot afford to pay them and unemployment results.

Fig. 11.1 The classical theory of employment

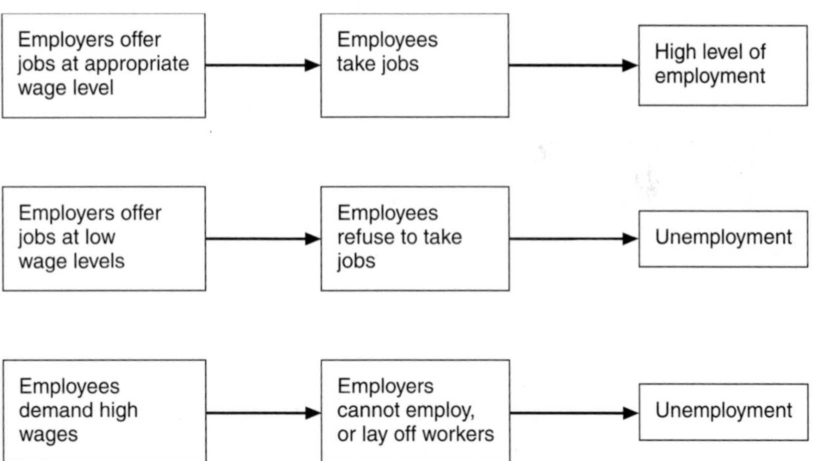

There are three principal reasons why the general level of wages might be too high to clear the labour market:

- Institutions such as trade unions may use their strength to secure a high wage.
- Employers, competing for the same employees, may offer a wage or salary that is above the norm.
- A minimum wage imposed by the government or the EU may be above the level required to clear the labour market.

Think about it

- To what extent do you think that the wages of employees such as nurses, teachers, police officers and those serving in the armed services should be dictated by the demand for labour in the private sector?

The Keynesian theory of employment

In his book *The General Theory of Employment, Interest and Money*, first published in 1936, John Maynard Keynes, later Lord Keynes, pointed out that the theory outlined above overlooked the fact that the demand for labour is a **derived demand** based upon existing prices and costs, and that people have a dual role in the economy: they are both workers and consumers. When no one wants to buy the products of an industry, then that industry must rid itself of some of its factors of production, including labour, thus causing a rise in the number of unemployed. If sufficient people are forced to accept wage reductions, their purchasing power is reduced and the level of demand for some products must also fall, producing a rise in unemployment.

John Maynard Keynes

John Maynard Keynes, 1st Baron Keynes of Tilton (1883–1946), was born in Cambridge and educated at Eton and Cambridge University. In *A Treatise on Money* (1930), he attempted to explain why economies went through cycles of boom and depression. These were believed to be self-correcting in as far as during a recession interest rates would fall, encouraging business to invest and the economy to expand. However, his analysis failed to address the problem of prolonged depressions; he turned to the problems of these in his major work, *The General Theory of Employment, Interest and Money* (1936). He suggested that prolonged recessions were not self-correcting and that government spending must take the place of investment by businesses in order to increase the flow of income through the economy. Following the Second World War, Keynes led the British delegation to the United Nations Monetary and Financial Conference. His theories have had a profound influence on the economic policies of many governments on both sides of the Atlantic.

This brings us back to the dual role of people as factors of production. On the one hand they have the task of producing the goods and services required by society, but on the other, as members of that society, they spend their incomes on the goods and services they have helped to produce. If they decide to save some of their income rather than spend it, production may exceed demand so that goods will be left in warehouses and employers will be forced to lay off labour as stocks accumulate. This applies not only to a single factory or industry, but also to the economy as a whole. If no one wants to buy the goods a factory produces, then it cannot afford to continue employing the factors of production. In the case of the economy as a whole, it is the total demand for the goods and services produced by its factors of production that is important.

The influence of aggregate demand

Keynes argued that the level of employment in the economy depends on the total level of demand for goods and services, which he called **aggregate monetary demand,** but which is commonly referred to as aggregate demand. This can be broken down into four components

- consumption
- investment
- exports
- government demand for goods and services.

If we can identify factors that determine each of these, we will know what determines the level of employment and may be able to suggest policies that will influence it.

New classical theories of employment

Followers of Keynes's theory of employment have more recently met opposition from economists, called 'new' or 'neo-classical' economists, who have favoured theories based on those of the classical economists. Whereas Keynes's theory is largely based on employment levels being influenced by the demand for goods and services, so that an increase in demand will lead to increased production and consequently increased employment, new classical economists believed that supply itself influences employment, since an increase in total output of goods and services (aggregate supply) will lead to increased total expenditure to buy those goods and services (aggregate demand).

The mining industry in the UK

In the past many different metals, including gold, lead and tin, were mined in the United Kingdom. Now, however, most mines have been closed because the supply of metals has run out or become too expensive to extract. Customers in the UK buy these metals from abroad, where supplies are more plentiful and cheaper to obtain. In the eighteenth century, for example, Cornwall had a flourishing tin-mining industry employing thousands of miners. It was among the most important tin-mining areas in the world. Today there are no miners and only the ruins of disused mines are left as the UK buys all the tin it needs from as far away as Bolivia and Malaysia.

The type of mining mainly associated with the UK nowadays is coal mining. However, activity in this area has also declined in recent years, with coal production falling from around 90 million tonnes a year in the mid-1980s to less than 60 million tonnes a year in the mid-1990s.

The decline in the coal industry is due to several factors. Most of the coal reserves in the UK can only be extracted from deep mines which are expensive to operate. This, coupled with uncertainty about supply during two major strikes by British miners (1974 and 1984), led large coal users such as the electricity-supply industry which operates many coal-fired power stations to look for new sources of coal and also investigate alternative fuels, including nuclear power.

Coal is now imported from countries such as Colombia where wages and other costs are lower than in the UK. In addition, demand for UK coal has fallen because of the increasing use of other cheaper, more efficient and more environmentally friendly sources of energy such as natural gas. As a result of the decline in demand for UK coal, and therefore the reduction in output, the average total number of employees on colliery books has fallen from 175 000 in the 1980s to just over 35 000 in the mid-1990s.

Think about it

- Read the above extract. Unemployment is a continuing problem and point of debate in the UK economy. What do you think are the main causes of unemployment? Do you think there are any effective measures that could be taken by the government, industry or society to reduce unemployment?

Aggregate demand

The employment of factors of production, including labour, depends on the production of goods and services. These may be for consumption, investment, purchase by the government or exports. The level of production in turn depends on the level of aggregate demand. In considering aggregate demand we shall ignore imports and exports. For the moment, the government's demand for goods and services will also be excluded, partly because it is determined by social and political as well as economic factors, and partly because the government may regulate its demand according to the level of consumption and investment.

This leaves us with a model of an economy in which aggregate demand depends on the demand for consumer goods and the demand for investment goods, which is known as a **closed economy** with no government and no foreign trade. In the short run, the level of employment in such an economy will therefore also depend on consumer and investment demand, since the level of employment depends on aggregate demand.

We have seen in earlier units that short-run increases in output result from an increased employment of the variable factors of production, while in the long run increases may come about through the use of extra machinery which can lead to less labour being employed (see Unit 10). We are concerned here with the short run, however, and it is an acceptable approximation to say that an increase in gross domestic product is accompanied by (and may depend on) an increase in the level of employment. It follows from this that, if we know what determines the level of consumption and the level of investment, we will also know what determines the level of employment.

The propensity to consume

'Consumption' covers all personal expenditure on goods and services except the purchase of houses, which is regarded as investment. We saw earlier that the demand for any individual good is related to its price; however, an individual's total expenditure does not depend on the price of any single good – if one is too expensive, the consumer will buy something else. We therefore need to consider other influences on consumption. These include

- the level of income
- the distribution of income
- institutional factors
- expectations of rising prices
- life-cycle influences.

The level of income

In Figure 11.2 the line OE, drawn at 45 degrees, links all the points where the whole of income is spent on consumption. We may regard any point on this line as an **equilibrium position**. (The word 'equilibrium' indicates that change will only occur if an external factor is introduced.) Thus, if income is £30 million, expenditure is also £30 million; that is, income of £30 million generates expenditure of £30 million, which in turn generates income of £30 million, and so on.

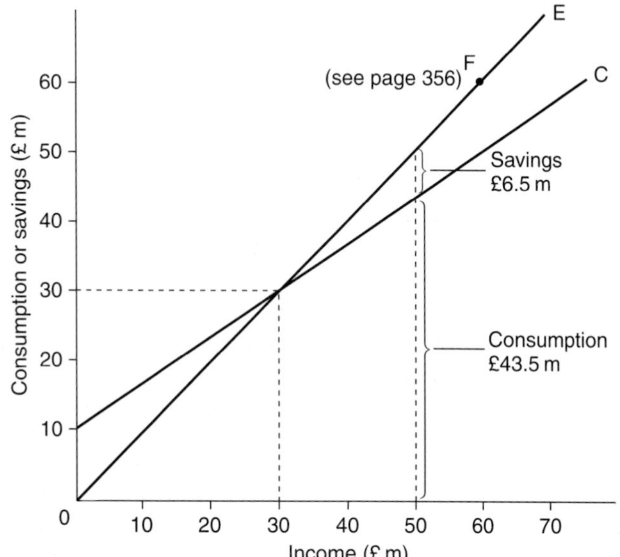

Fig. 11.2 The propensity to consume

In Figure 11.2 the population's intended expenditure on consumption at different levels of income is shown by the line labelled C. This is known as the **consumption function** or the **propensity to consume** curve. At low levels of income (less than £30 million), consumption is actually greater than income – for example, if income is £20 million, consumption is about £23 million. This is because there are certain basic items people must buy in order to survive. When incomes are low, people will supplement them by drawing on savings or borrowing so that they can at least buy these basic items. At high levels of income, consumption is lower than income as people can afford to save. For example, if income is £50 million, consumption is £43.5 million and savings are £6.5 million, since at this level of income, the current needs of people are covered with a margin that can be put to one side for future needs.

We can see from Figure 11.2 that as income rises so too does consumption, but the proportion of income spent on consumption falls. Thus, when income is £30 million, it is all spent on consumption, but when income rises to £60 million, the proportion spent on consumption is 83.3 per cent, and with income at £65 million, 81.5 per cent is spent on consumption.

- The relationship between the level of consumption and the level of national income is known as the average propensity to consume (APC). It is always expressed as a fraction of 1:

$$\text{APC} = \frac{\text{C}}{\text{Y}}$$

where C = consumption and Y = national income.
Thus, from Figure 11.2, when national income is £40 million,

$$\text{APC} = \frac{37}{40}$$

- The proportion of income not spent on consumption is known as the average **propensity to save** and is likewise expressed as a fraction. In this case it is $\frac{3}{40}$.

The sum of the average propensity to save and the average propensity to consume is always 1 in a closed economy with no government.

The marginal propensity to consume (MPC) and the marginal propensity to save (MPS) must not be confused with the average propensities.

- The **marginal propensity to consume** is that proportion of an increase in income which is spent on consumption:

$$\text{MPC} = \frac{\text{rise in C}}{\text{rise in Y}}$$

  Thus, if income rises by £1 million and consumption by £600 000, the marginal propensity to consume is $\frac{3}{5}$.
- The marginal propensity to save, which is the proportion of an increase in income which is not spent on consumption, is $\frac{2}{5}$.

If the consumption line is straight, as it is in Figure 11.2, then the marginal propensity to consume is constant and whenever income increases by a specific amount, then consumption rises by a smaller constant amount. This is an approximation to actual behaviour which need not worry us too much. The consumption function is more likely to resemble that in Figure 11.3, where it rises steeply at first and then flattens out. This is because at very low levels of income a community will spend the majority of any increase in income on consumption, while at very high levels the bulk of a similar increase will be saved (thus giving a low MPC).

Fig. 11.3 Diminishing marginal propensity to consume

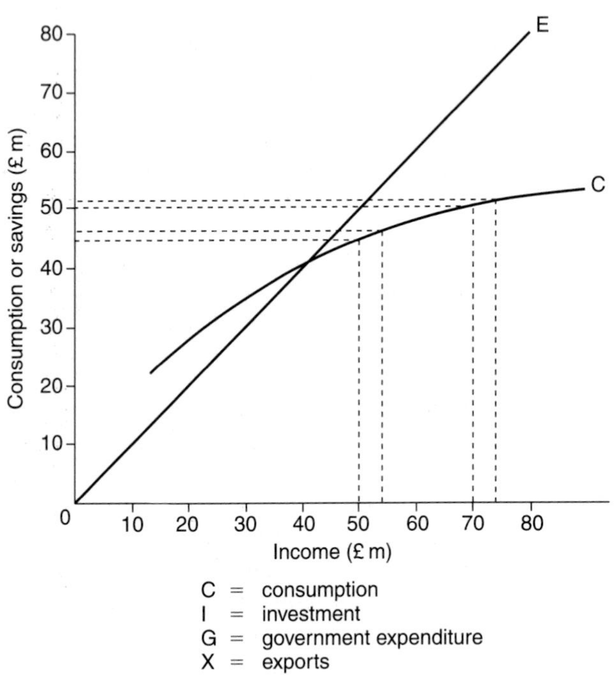

In Figure 11.3, for example, if income rises by £4 million from £50 million, consumption rises by £2 million and MPC = $\frac{1}{2}$. A similar rise in income from £70 million to £74 million, however, causes consumption to rise by under £2 million, MPC at this level of income being less than $\frac{1}{2}$. Similar conditions apply to sections of a given community – consider, for example, the likely reactions of retirement pensioners and millionaires to an increase in income of £1 per week. However, the important general rule is that consumption increases as income increases, but by a smaller amount, leaving more scope for savings.

The distribution of income

While the level of national income is the most important determinant of the level of consumption, the distribution of that income between different income groups will also exert an influence. If income is concentrated largely in the hands of the relatively wealthy, then we would expect the average propensity to consume to be lower than if income was more evenly distributed. The government's taxation policy will also have some influence on the level of consumption. Let us suppose that the very rich, who have a marginal propensity to consume of $\frac{1}{2}$, are forced to pay extra taxes of £1 million. As they would have saved £500 000 of this anyway, they cut their consumption by only £500 000. If the £1 million spent in taxes is used to increase social security benefits for those with a marginal propensity to consume of 1, the whole of the £1 million will be spent and the net effect is that consumption will rise by £500 000. By such a policy, the government can move the consumption function vertically upwards or downwards.

Institutional factors

These are of significance. We saw in Unit 6 (pages 230–235) that the supply of savings will depend partly on the encouragement given by financial institutions. Accordingly, we can say that the position of the consumption function depends on the encouragement given to savings in the community. If the members of the community increase their propensity to save, then their propensity to consume will decrease and the consumption function accordingly moves downwards.

Expectations of rising prices

These will persuade consumers to buy today rather than tomorrow, causing an upward movement of the consumption function. In the same way, consumers will delay their purchases if prices are expected to fall, thus causing the consumption function to fall.

Life-cycle influences

A number of economists (for example, Modigliani, Aldo and Friedman) have argued that individuals do not base their current consumption on their current income, but on their likely long-term income and their present stage of life. Thus, a young person who is both training to be a professional and is likely to inherit wealth is prepared to consume well above current income. This is because he or she is confident of having sufficient income in the future to pay off loans used to finance current consumption. On the other hand, a middle-aged factory worker with a family and little prospect of higher income through promotion or wealth will tend to limit his or her consumption to ensure sufficient money is being saved for when he or she retires. A changing structure of population, both by age and circumstance, can have an impact on both average propensity to consume and marginal propensity to consume.

To simplify our investigation we shall assume that consumption varies directly with income and that the other factors discussed above are constant.

Returning to Figure 11.2, if consumption is the only kind of expenditure, then the equilibrium level of national income must be £30 million. Once again, by equilibrium we mean a situation which is unchanging, and if national income in a given period is £30 million, then the consumption function shows that the £30 million will be spent and, since every expenditure generates a corresponding income, this will generate income in the next period of £30 million and so on until a factor is introduced from outside to disturb the equilibrium. As long as consumers' spending levels remain the same, equilibrium will be at £30 million. If for some reason consumers revise their plans, a new equilibrium will be established. For example, if they increase their purchases of consumer goods this will be reflected by an upward movement of the consumption function, the new curve crossing OE to the right of £30 million and giving a higher equilibrium income. A downward movement of the consumption curve, following a decrease in purchases of consumer goods, would give a lower equilibrium income.

However, let us return to our original position. If national income is £30 million, employment within the economy must be at the level required to produce £30 million worth of goods and services at current prices and costs, although there is no reason why this should constitute anything approaching 'full employment'.

Let us assume there is a direct relationship between national income and the level of employment, and that a national income of £30 million leads to an employment rate of 50 per cent, and that £60 million should constitute the full employment level. To achieve this higher level of income, and therefore full employment, the consumption function must pass through point F in Figure 11.2. One possibility is that the government will intervene. It may, for example, cause the consumption function to move upwards by redistributing income. Before we consider that line of approach, however, we must consider the other part of aggregate demand – investment.

Something to do

There are 1 million unemployed people in Agraria, which is a closed economy with a GDP or national income of £30 000 million. It has been established that the marginal propensity to consume of the economy is constant at $\frac{1}{2}$ and that an increase of £1 million in the GDP reduces unemployment by 200 000.

- What increase in income is necessary to reduce the level of unemployment to 200 000?

The level of investment

In order to produce consumer goods, firms need to buy machinery and equipment. These are goods purchased for investment rather than consumption: in other words, they are goods that will last and not be used up in the production process. The demand for investment goods (or gross domestic fixed capital formation, as it is called), like the demand for consumer goods, creates employment, and the greater the level of investment the greater the level of employment in the industries producing investment goods. (Note that we are only concerned with investment in new, productive assets since it is only this kind of investment that influences employment – the purchase of second-hand machinery or of securities has no direct impact on the level of employment.)

The level of investment is determined by the following factors:

- **Replacement needs:** Some investment occurs regularly as existing equipment wears out and has to be replaced. In flourishing firms this causes few problems, but in less profitable firms it may be subject to the same considerations as new investment (that is, expectation of future profits and the marginal efficiency of capital).
- **Expectation of future profits:** This is the most important factor in the determination of investment. Firms will only invest if the investment is likely to lead to increased profits. In calculating the prospective yield from an investment, a firm will make estimates of its future costs, the future price of its product, sales forecasts, possible competition from new products, changes in government policy, and the likely future state of the economy.
- **The marginal efficiency of capital:** This is the rate at which prospective annual yields from the investment must be discounted to bring them into line with the supply price of the asset (see below).

Think about it

- Which would have the greatest effect on unemployment – investment in a new lorry or investment in government securities? Why?
- How might the provision of personal savings schemes by organisations such as Marks & Spencers and Virgin affect levels of unemployment?

In practice, the relationship between the prospective yield on the investment and the rate of interest might not be a very close one. There are a number of reasons for this:

- It might need a significant change in the rate of interest to alter a firm's investment plans.
- As we have seen, some investment is replacement investment and has to occur if the business is to continue.
- This year's investment might be part of a five-year plan, so its postponement would be very difficult.
- The government and its agencies are responsible for much investment, and some of this may be determined by non-economic factors, so it will not respond to changes in the rates of interest.

Discounting

Discounting can be a complicated business, but the situation may be understood from the point of view of a firm considering the investment of £50 000 in a new lorry.

Calculations suggest that after paying for the lorry and covering all the running costs, the firm will be left with a profit of £6250 each year for the next five years. This represents an annual yield of 12.5 per cent. (Remember this will only come about if the calculations are correct.) One thing that doesn't have to be estimated is the amount that could be earned by investing the £50 000 in government securities or some other form of interest-bearing saving. If the yield on this kind of investment is 14 per cent (£7000 per year), since this yield is certain, the rational thing to do is invest in the government stock. On the other hand, if the yield of the securities is less than 12.5 per cent, the firm will be prompted to buy the lorry.

The level of investment would therefore seem to be determined by the relationship between the prospective yield on the investment and the rate of interest.

We cannot, therefore, be very precise about the determinants of investment. There are many factors involved. Experience suggests that investment rises as the gross national product rises (wealthy nations do not need to spend all their income on consumption). However, it will simplify our discussion if we assume that investment is constant for all levels of income. This is done in Figure 11.4, which shows the same situation as Figure 11.2 except for the introduction of investment of £10 million.

Fig. 11.4 A move towards the full-employment equilibrium

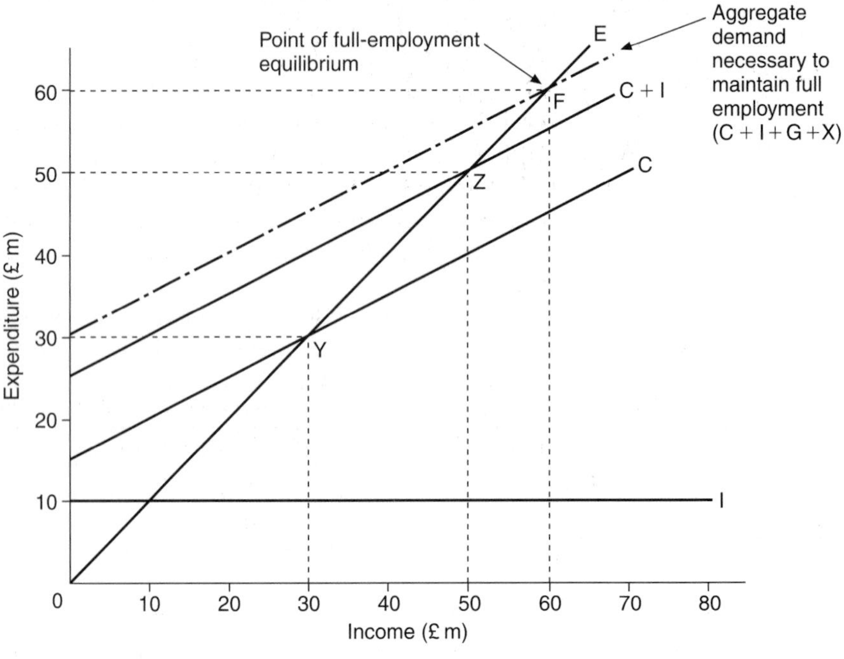

Towards full employment

In Figure 11.4, the horizontal line I represents a constant level of investment of £10 million, and line C the level of consumption at various levels of national income. Line C + I therefore represents expenditure on both investment and consumption at various levels of national income. This line is parallel to C, but a constant £10 million above it. Again, line E represents expenditure at various levels of national income. Notice that while total expenditure rises by £10 million (from C to C + I) the equilibrium level of expenditure has risen by £20 million from £30 million to £50 million (the previous equilibrium level – see Figure 11.2). This is largely due to a feature called the **investment multiplier**, and before considering Figure 11.4 further, we shall look at the effect of this.

The multiplier effect

As an example to illustrate the process, we will assume an economy which has been in equilibrium for some time. It has a national income of £20 000 million with constant average and marginal propensities to consume of $\frac{4}{5}$. Thus the national income consists of £16 000 million of consumption and £4000 million of investment. (Savings are also equal to £4000 million; we return to this equality later.) What will happen if investment rises by £1000 million? The owners of factors of production employed in the investment goods industry receive an increase in incomes of £1000 million, as all expenditure creates a corresponding income. (In practice, there may be long time-lags before some of these incomes are received, but for simplicity we ignore this here.) We know that the marginal propensity to consume is $\frac{4}{5}$, and therefore the recipients of the extra £1000 million of income will spend £800 million and save £200 million. This expenditure will be largely on food and clothes, televisions, computers and cars, and the owners of the factors of production working in these industries will then receive extra incomes of £800 million. This means that the following year's national income will rise by £800 million which, at the MPC of $\frac{4}{5}$, leads to a rise in consumption of £640 million and a rise in savings of £160 million. The application of the multiplier continues in the same way in subsequent years, as shown in Table 11.1.

Table 11.1

The multiplier in action: effect of extra investment of £1000 million with MPC = $\frac{4}{5}$

	Rise in income (£m)	**Rise in consumption (£m)**	**Rise in savings (£m)**
Year 1	1000.0	800.0	200.0
Year 2	800.0	640.0	160.0
Year 3	640.0	512.0	128.0
Year 4	512.0	409.6	102.4
	–	–	–
	–	–	–
	–	–	–
Total	**5000.0**	**4000.0**	**1000.0**

Each increase in consumption leads to successively smaller increases in income, and eventually national incomes in fact rise by £5000 million as a direct result of the increase in investment of £1000 million. The ultimate rise in the level of national income depends on the size of the marginal propensity to save. If the community is so rich that its marginal propensity to consume is zero, then the rise in national income will be the same as the rise in investment, since the recipients of the original £1000 million will save it all and will not generate a secondary increase in income. But if the marginal propensity to consume is 1, then there will be no end to the rise in national income, at least in money terms.

We could continue to work through the process begun in Table 11.1 until the increases in income became very small indeed, and the total approximated to £5000 million. However, it is easier to use a formula to calculate the ultimate increase in income. The basic formula is

$$\text{rise in income} = \text{rise in investment} \times \frac{1}{\text{marginal propensity to save}}$$

or

$$\text{rise in Y} = \text{rise in I} \times \frac{1}{\text{MPS}}$$

The fraction $\frac{1}{\text{MPS}}$ is the **multiplier.**

In our example, we obtain

$$\text{rise in income} = £1000 \text{ million} \times \frac{1}{\frac{1}{5}} = £5000 \text{ million}$$

Table 11.2 gives some examples assuming a rise in investment of £1000 million.

Table 11.2

The effect of the size of MPS on the rise in national income

Rise in investment (£m)	MPS	Multiplier	Rise in national income (£m)
1000	$\frac{1}{5}$	5	5000
1000	$\frac{1}{4}$	4	4000
1000	$\frac{1}{3}$	3	3000
1000	$\frac{1}{2}$	2	2000

The multiplier works both ways, and a fall in the level of investment will lead to a larger fall in the equilibrium level of national income. The extent of this fall will again depend on the size of the marginal propensity to consume.

Something to do

- Identify reasons why there might be a fall in the level of investment in a country's economy.
- If the level of investment in the economy shown in Table 11.1 fell by £250 million per year, what would be the effect on national income over a period of five years?
- What would be the effect if the marginal propensity to save was $\frac{2}{7}$?

Before returning to Figure 11.4, we may note that other **injections** of expenditure into the economy, such as a rise in exports or a rise in government expenditure, will also give a multiplier effect. Nor are savings the only way in which money **leaks** from the economic system. As far as the employment of factors of production is concerned, money taken by taxation and not spent on goods and services and money spent on imports are both equivalent to savings, for they cannot create employment in the domestic economy. (For more on injections and leakages, see pages 305–306.)

The model in Figure 11.4 has been constructed so that the multiplier has a value of 2 and the initial investment of £10 million leads to an ultimate rise in income of £20 million, to £50 million. At the new equilibrium level of income, consumption is £40 million and savings are £10 million. Another way of looking at this is to say that the consumer goods industries are producing £40 million worth of goods and there is investment of £10 million. As the nation's savings and investment are undertaken by two different sets of people, we might ask the question: 'Why are they equal?' In fact this question has almost been answered in the analysis of the multiplier effect. In order to clarify the process by which equality comes about, a distinction should be made between *planned* savings and investment and *actual* savings and investment.

There is absolutely no reason why planned savings on the part of households should be equal to planned investment by firms. The only real equality is between actual savings and actual investment. If we look back at the economy in the past we can see that the savings and investment that have occurred are equal in amount. There is no great mystery about this, as the terms are just different names for that part of the national product which is not spent on consumption. If we suppose that an economy is at point Y in Figure 11.4, with an equilibrium of £30 million and no savings or investment, planned savings are zero. If entrepreneurs decide to spend £10 million on investment, planned savings and investment at the start are unequal, but actual savings and investment are equated by the rise in income resulting from the multiplier. This allows savings of £10 million to be made out of the new national product of £50 million. On the other hand, if the economy is at point Z with planned savings of £10 million, and entrepreneurs decide to invest nothing, then the negative multiplier will reduce income to £30 million so that actual savings will fall to zero.

Injections and leakages

The economy we have been discussing has been unrealistic in so far as there has been no foreign trade and no government interference. The introduction of either of these, however, does not materially alter the theory. Any **injection** of expenditure into the economy leads to a higher level of aggregate demand; any **leakage** leads to a lower level of aggregate demand. Each of the movements is associated with the appropriate multiplier effects.

- Leakages from the economy consist of savings, taxation and expenditure on imports. These may be lumped together since each of them indicates that money is taken out of circulation and no longer contributes to aggregate demand in the domestic economy.
- Investment by industry, financed through profits or borrowing, government expenditure, and the demand for exports are all injections into the economy. They all increase aggregate demand and thus generate more employment.

Returning to Figure 11.4, the introduction of investment of £10 million left us in equilibrium at point Z. (Remember, all points on the 45 degree line OE are positions of equilibrium.) If we assume that full employment would be achieved with a national product of £60 million, we need the aggregate demand line to pass through point F. For it to remain in such a position, certain conditions must be fulfilled, though it is no longer necessary for savings and investment to be equal. However, the withdrawals or leakages from the economy – savings (S), taxation (T) and imports (M) – must equal the injections into the system – investment (I), government expenditure on goods and services (but not transfer payments) (G) and exports (X). Thus, in equilibrium,

$$S + T + M = I + G + X$$

If S + T + M is greater than I + G + X, the economy will be moving to a lower equilibrium. If S + T + M is smaller than I + G + X, so that there are net injections into the economy, then it will be expanding and moving towards a higher equilibrium income.

The achievement of full employment

As a result of the introduction of investment into our economy, national income has increased to £50 million and employment is much nearer the target of full employment. However, there is still a deficiency of demand of £10 million below the full-employment level. This is known as the **deflationary gap**. (Where there is demand in excess of the full-employment level, there is said to be an **inflationary gap**.)

Government activity

The responsibility of a government committed to full employment is to ensure that the aggregate demand curve passes through point F (arbitrarily assumed to be the full-employment equilibrium). There are two broad courses of action open to the government:

- It may add its own demand for goods and services to that of households and entrepreneurs by increasing public expenditure on, for example, road building or defence equipment, or services such as the National Health Service. This will cause the aggregate demand curve to move upwards. There will, of course, be multiplier effects from any such injection of expenditure.
- It may use its monetary and fiscal policy to encourage higher consumption and investment expenditure, for example by reducing income tax rates, which will cause the aggregate demand curve to move upwards.

Demand for exports

To complete the picture we should mention the demand for exports. A further way of increasing the level of demand is to persuade countries overseas to buy more of our economy's goods.

The equilibrium of the economy can now be achieved at an income of £60 million generated by consumption, investment, government expenditure and exports, so that aggregate demand goes through point F in Figure 11.4. If demand rises above £60 million, which represents the physical limit of the output of the economy, then inflation will occur. This is discussed in Unit 12.

Something to do

- Calculate what would happen to employment and the labour market if aggregate demand in the model economy described in Figure 11.4 rose above £60 million.

The problem of unemployment

It is convenient in the Keynesian model outlined on pages 350–351 to interpret the term 'full employment' literally, as the position in which everyone who is able and wants to work is employed. In practice, this does not occur; there is always some unemployment. Figure 11.5 shows the development of unemployment in the UK since 1970. Prior to this, during the period of 1945 to 1970, unemployment was around 500 000, or between 1 per cent and 3 per cent of the labour force.

Fig. 11.5 UK unemployment, 1970–97

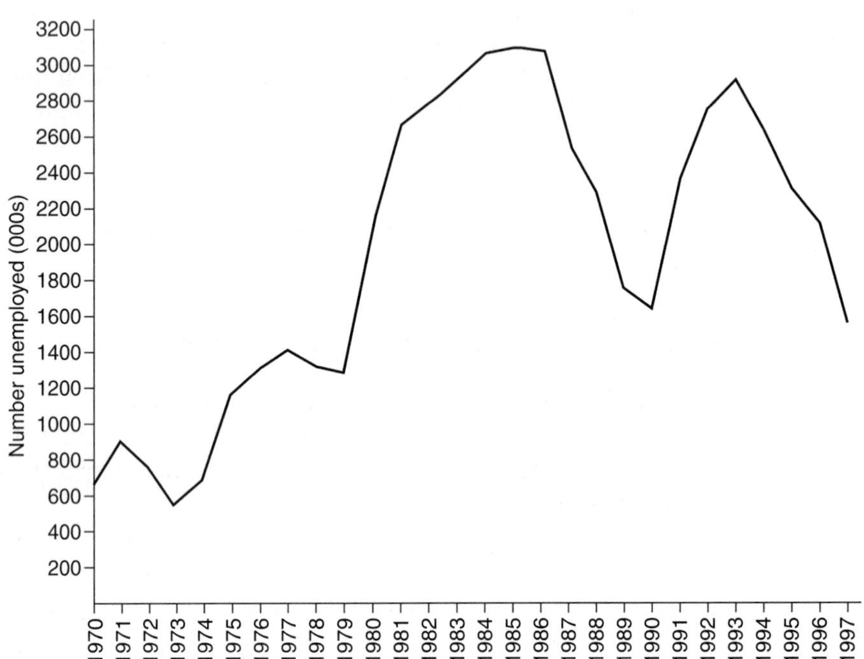

Measuring the rate of unemployment

Measuring the rate of unemployment is itself full of uncertainties. Theoretically, unemployment levels can be calculated by dividing the number of people of working age who are without jobs and are seeking employment by the total population of working age and multiplying by 100 (to arrive at a percentage). The official unemployment rate in Britain is calculated by dividing the number of people who are claiming Job Seekers' Allowance by the total number of employees, self-employed people, benefit claimants, those in HM forces and those on training schemes, and multiplying by 100.

An obvious problem with this method is, of course, that a government can manipulate the official unemployment rate simply by changing entitlement to benefit. The Conservative governments of the 1980s and early 1990s altered the way in which the unemployment rate was calculated more than twenty times. Each change resulted in a reduction in the 'official' unemployment rate.

Do unemployment figures work?

Unemployment figures quoted in the media provide only a partial picture of UK joblessness. Moreover, current methods of calculating unemployment may place the UK at a disadvantage in the allocation of European grants.

An 18-month study funded by the Economic and Social Research Council carried out by Anne Green and Terence Hogarth of the Institute of Employment Research at the University of Warwick questions the value of relying solely on conventional unemployment measures. With changes in the industrial and occupational structure, claims Anne Green, the rise in the number of women in employment, and the growth of part-time and other forms of flexible working, the boundaries between employment, unemployment and inactivity are increasingly fuzzy.

Conventional unemployment measures do not, for example, include those on government schemes, those defined as economically inactive who would like a job and those in part-time work because they could not fund a full-time job.

''Any notion of a single true measurement of unemployment is flawed,'' said Anne Green.

Her research suggests a range of alternative measures of non-employment at the local and regional scale, and argues the case for a battery of cumulative and overlapping measures which serve different objectives. Adopting broader measures of unemployment would also reveal greater regional differences.

Source: *Professional Manager*, May 1998

Think about it

- Read the article above.
- What categories does it suggest should be included in measures of unemployment? Do you agree?
- Do you think there are any other categories that should be covered?
- What difference do you think including those categories would make (a) to the unemployment figures and (b) to government economic policy, assuming the government's intention is to reduce the level of unemployment?

The costs of unemployment

Whatever formula is used to calculate the level of unemployment, however, unemployment carries with it costs to the unemployed individual, to his or her family and to the nation. These are summarised below.

The costs of unemployment

For the individual and his or her family	For the nation
• a fall in income	• higher taxes to pay for unemployment benefit
• a lower standard of living	• the opportunity cost of using public money spent on benefits in other ways
• possible hardship and difficulty in meeting even basic needs of food and heating	• loss of revenue to the government in terms of the taxes they would have received had the unemployed been earning
• a loss of self-esteem	• loss of output
• stress.	• a reduction in aggregate demand.

Types of unemployment

General or cyclical unemployment

If the overall level of aggregate demand falls, we can expect unemployment throughout the economy. In our earlier example, this will occur if the level of aggregate demand falls below £60 million (see Figure 11.4). When aggregate demand rises again, unemployment falls. The UK economy has a history of booms, when aggregate demand increases, and slumps, when it falls. This is known as the **trade cycle**, and for this reason unemployment associated with changes in aggregate demand is called **cyclical unemployment**. This is the type of unemployment Keynes was concerned about, and which did seem to have been eliminated by the use of policies of demand management between 1945 and 1970. However, one of the components of unemployment in the 1980s and early 1990s was general or cyclical unemployment. A problem with increasing aggregate demand is that it can lead to inflation.

Classical unemployment

Classical unemployment occurs if the real wage rate is above the level necessary to clear the labour market. Disequilibrium exists in the labour market when the price of labour is above or below the level necessary to clear it. If the rate is too low, then although jobs may exist, prospective employees are not prepared to accept them at the wages offered. If the rate is too high, firms will be unable or unwilling to offer sufficient employment to clear the labour market.

There are three main reasons for the wage rate being too high:

- institutional factors, such as trade unions or professional associations using their power to secure higher wages for their members
- employers offering high wages in order to attract highly skilled or experienced employees
- government legislation, such as the imposition of a minimum wage rate, or social benefit arrangements leading to the so-called 'poverty trap' where the financial benefits of being employed are little more than the benefits of being unemployed.

Structural unemployment

Structural unemployment results from a permanent decline in demand for an industry's product. In the UK, employment in manufacturing industries has fallen significantly since the 1970s. This is largely due to increasing competition from Europe and the rest of the world.

Sometimes structural unemployment leads to **regional unemployment**. This occurs when an industry which is a major employer in an area goes into decline. For example, in many areas of Leicestershire, Nottinghamshire and Yorkshire, sizeable villages grew up around the coal mines where most of the villagers were employed. The decline of the coal-mining industry has led to the closure of many of these mines and as a result unemployment in these areas has risen steeply, there being no suitable alternative employment readily available. A similar situation has arisen in areas associated with shipbuilding, textiles and steel production.

Technological unemployment

While structural unemployment results from a change in the pattern of demand, **technological unemployment** derives from a change in the methods of production. New technology is continually reducing the need for labour. The increased use of machines requiring fewer people to operate them while improving production rates originally affected manufacturing industries, but more recently this has spread to service industries such as banking, retailing and even other minor service industries such as car parks. This leads to an excess of labour in the market which is increasingly difficult to absorb into other areas of the economy; hence more unemployment.

Frictional unemployment

Frictional unemployment covers people moving from one job to another. It is a natural process in a growing economy. This type of unemployment, if short-term, presents no cause for concern and is one of the factors contributing to a 'natural' rate of unemployment (see below).

Seasonal unemployment

Seasonal unemployment occurs particularly in agriculture, construction and the leisure industries. The demand of each of these for labour is partly governed by the season and weather conditions. For example, demand (and therefore employment) in the UK hotel industry increases during the summer months and at holiday times such as Christmas and Easter.

Something to do

- Identify the type of unemployment that is operating in the following cases:
  - Maria has left her job and is taking a few weeks' break before starting her new one.
  - Joe is a coal miner. He has been unemployed for six months, since the colliery where he worked closed down.
  - During the last recession Sheraz, a textile worker, was made redundant due to cutbacks at his firm.
  - Aliena worked at the local branch of a high-street bank. A new cash dispenser has just been installed, and she has been made redundant as fewer cashiers are now needed to serve customers.

Is there a natural rate of unemployment?

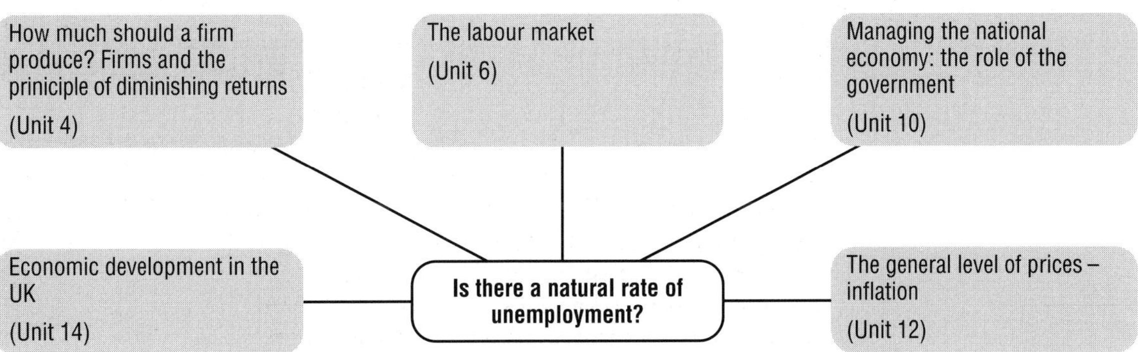

In 1958, A.W. Phillips investigated what he believed to be a possible correlation between the levels of unemployment and changes in wage rates in the UK. Plotting the data on a scattergraph, he found that there was in fact a reverse correlation. He constructed a line of best fit for the data; this is now known as a **Phillips curve** (see Figure 11.6). Phillips then went on to show that there was a further correlation between changes in wage rates and inflation and therefore a reverse correlation between unemployment and inflation.

Fig. 11.6 Phillips curve

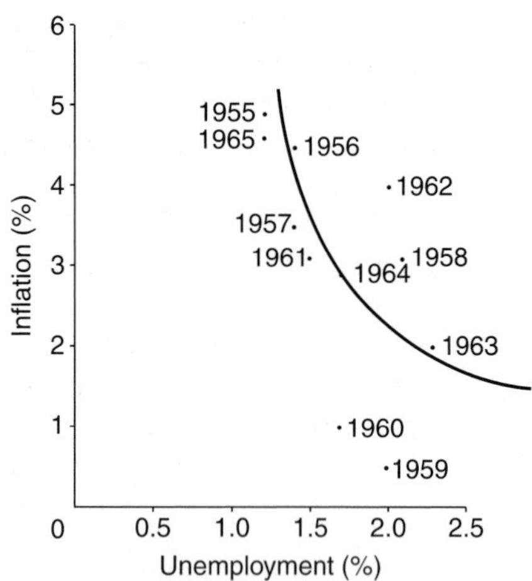

At first, his findings seemed broadly to support the Keynesian model: in times of low unemployment (and therefore high aggregate demand) inflation tended to be high, and vice versa (see also Unit 12, where inflation is discussed in more detail). Data collected from around the mid-1960s onwards, however, seemed to show no such correlation. Inflation continued to rise despite increasing unemployment.

It was Milton Friedman, a supporter of the classical theory of employment, who found that it was possible to construct a Phillips curve to fit the data, but that the curve was vertical and showed a long-run rather than a short-run correlation. This is shown in Figure 11.7. From this, Friedman calculated what he called the **non-accelerating inflation rate of unemployment** (**NAIRU**), which he believed to be the **natural rate of unemployment** which cannot be reduced without causing inflation.

Fig. 11.7 Vertical Phillips curve

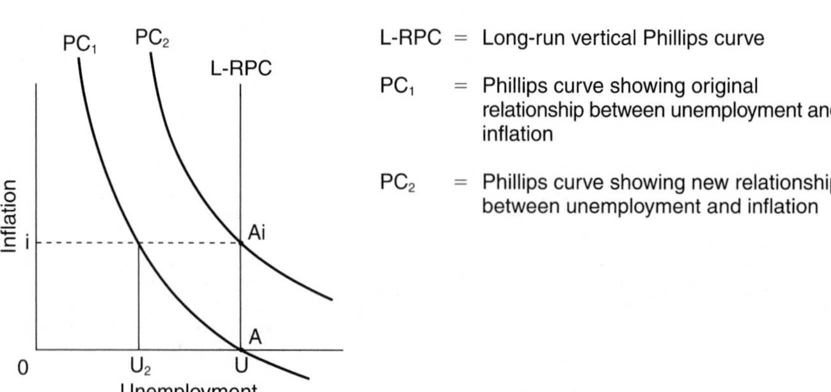

The economy in Figure 11.7 is at point A with zero inflation and unemployment at U, its so-called natural rate. An increase in aggregate demand will cause firms to take on more workers to meet the demand for more goods and services. This will reduce unemployment in the short run to U_2. To attract more workers, however, the level of wages must be increased, and the cost of the wage increase passed on to consumers in the form of higher prices. This causes inflation to rise to i, which in turn has an adverse affect on aggregate demand. As a result, unemployment reverts to U but prices remain at the higher level to maintain profits. Thus inflation is accompanied by reduced aggregate demand and unemployment, and the economy moves to point Ai, its new equilibrium point on the long-run Phillips curve. Note that the two Phillips curves, PC_1 and PC_2, show the relationships between unemployment and inflation at the original and the new equilibrium points.

Reducing unemployment

As we have seen (page 349), classical economists believe that unemployment occurs when wage rates are too high for firms to offer sufficient employment to clear the labour market. According to this view, unemployment can be most effectively reduced by lowering wage rates. However, lowering wage rates is not easy, especially if prices have risen. Those in employment are unwilling to accept lower wages, and many of the unemployed will not be prepared to take jobs at the lower rate.

Keynesians, on the other hand, believe that the way to reduce unemployment is to increase aggregate demand. A government might do this, for example, either by reducing taxes and leaving people with more money to spend on goods and services for consumption, or by increasing government spending. This is called **demand-side** economics, as it takes the view that the way to solve economic problems is by managing demand.

New or neo-classical economists, however, argue that increasing demand will only be successful in reducing unemployment in the short run. In the long run, it will cause inflation accompanied by a rise in unemployment. They believe that there is a natural level of unemployment, and barriers exist to prevent unemployed people from accepting jobs at the wage rates necessary to clear the labour market. Some of these barriers, and the policies a government might adopt to overcome them, are summarised below. This view considers that unemployment should be tackled from the supply side of labour, rather than trying to manage demand. Supply-side policies for the reduction of unemployment have been adopted by successive UK governments since the early 1980s.

Barriers to employment and policies to overcome them

Problem	Solutions
• People cannot afford to accept low paid jobs	• Increase income tax thresholds, or reduce rates in the lowest tax band; increase the level of the minimum wage
• People are unwilling to take low paid jobs because the loss of benefits will make them worse off	• Reduce benefits to the unemployed (Job Seekers' Allowance, National Insurance credits), or pay top-up allowance to those unemployed who accept low paid jobs (Welfare to Work initiatives)
• Workers lack the necessary skills to make it worthwhile for firms to employ them	• Increase the skills of the unemployed by providing training opportunities both in full-time work and education (such as New Deal)

12 The general level of prices – inflation

Introduction: historical perspective

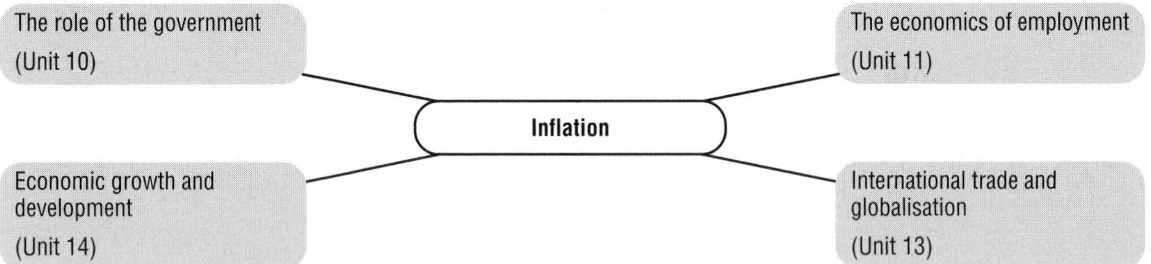

The implementation of Keynesian policies of demand management in the UK between 1945 and 1970 was associated with a period of more or less continuous full employment and relatively stable prices. We saw in Unit 11 that in the 1970s unemployment rose rapidly and we know that this was accompanied by much higher rates of inflation. Much economic policy since then has been aimed at reducing the rate of inflation and the distortions it causes.

In this unit, we consider first the causes and types of inflation, including an explanation of the quantity theory of money. We then turn to the measurement of inflation and the difficulties involved in the construction and use of index numbers. We are then able to examine the distortions that inflation – and deflation – cause in an economy, before ending with a section on efforts to control inflation.

The proximate cause of inflation

Inflation is a disease, a dangerous and sometimes fatal disease that if not checked in time can destroy a society. Examples abound. Hyperinflations in Russia and Germany after World War I – when prices sometimes doubled and more than doubled from one day to the next – prepared the ground for communism in the one country and nazism in the other. The hyperinflation in China after World War II eased Chairman Mao's defeat of Chiang Kai-shek. Inflation in Brazil, where it reached about 100 per cent a year in 1954, brought military government. A far more extreme inflation contributed to the overthrow of Allende in Chile in 1973 and of Isabel Perón in Argentina in 1976, followed in both countries by the assumption of power by a military junta.

No government is willing to accept responsibility for producing inflation, even in less virulent degree. Government officials always find some excuse – greedy businessmen, grasping trade unions, spendthrift consumers, Arab sheikhs, bad weather or anything else that seems even remotely plausible. No doubt businessmen are greedy, trade unions are grasping, consumers are spendthrifts, Arab sheikhs have raised the price of oil, and weather is often bad. All these can produce high prices for individual items; they cannot produce rising prices for goods in general. They can cause temporary ups or downs in the rate of inflation. But they cannot produce continuing inflation for one very god reason: none of the alleged culprits possesses a printing press on which it can turn out those pieces of paper we carry in our pockets; none can legally authorize a bookkeeper to make entries on ledgers that are the equivalent of those pieces of paper.

Source: Milton and Rose Friedman, *Free to Choose* (Harcourt, Brace and Company, 1980)

Causes and types of inflation

Demand inflation: the Keynesian model

In Unit 11 the market economy was pushed into a position of full-employment equilibrium through the introduction of various kinds of demand for goods and services, and we assumed that in this position it was physically incapable of producing any more goods and services per production period. (Of course, it might be possible to overcome this by the introduction of more efficient machinery, but this is a long-run process and here we are concerned mainly with the short run.)

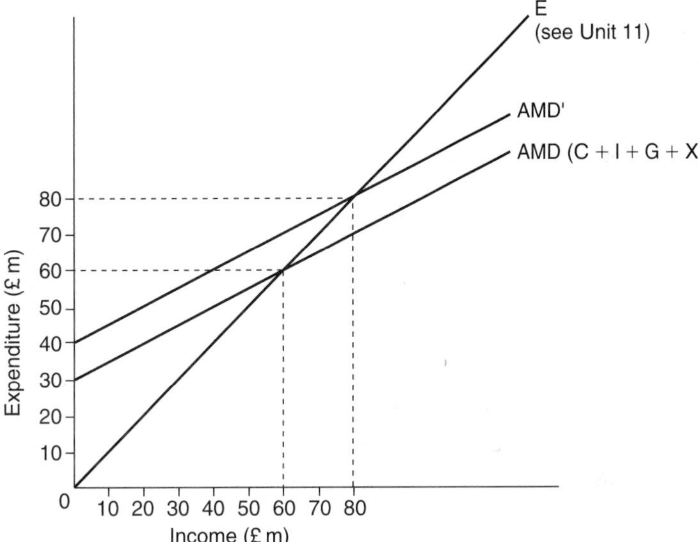

Fig. 12.1 An inflationary increase in aggregate monetary demand

The model economy is reproduced in Figure 12.1, and is again in a position of full-employment equilibrium at £60 million. (Turn back to Unit 11, page 350, to remind yourself of how aggregate monetary demand or AMD is arrived at.) What would now happen if there was an increase of £10 million in the demand for machinery?

Extra orders are placed with manufacturers of machinery – but we know that they are physically incapable of producing more goods. In Unit 3, we saw that, in conditions of excess demand, firms and industries choke off the extra demand by increasing their prices. In practice the process will be accelerated as buyers try to jump the queue by offering higher prices than those being asked. As a result, factors of production employed in producing machinery receive higher money incomes and can in turn bid up the prices of consumer goods.

There is in effect a change in the **conditions of demand** in individual consumer goods markets, and so the demand curves move to the right (see Unit 3, pages 90–91). The multiplier works itself out in the same way as before (see Unit 11, pages 359–361), except for the fact that the rise in national income is a monetary rise only. At the new national income equilibrium of £80 million, the economy is producing the same number of goods as it was when equilibrium was £60 million and the *real* national income remains unchanged.

Something to do

Milton Friedman is an influential American economist. During her time as Prime Minister, Margaret Thatcher put considerable trust in him as her economic advisor. Much of modern monetary theory is based on Friedman's work.

- Read the extract from Milton and Rose Friedman's book *Free to Choose* and answer the following questions:

(a) What does Friedman believe is the underlying cause of inflation?
(b) Why do you think Friedman has come to this conclusion?
(c) What other causes of inflation are there?
(d) Do you think Friedman's view of the cause of inflation is correct? Justify your answer.

Fig. 12.2 A simple model of inflation

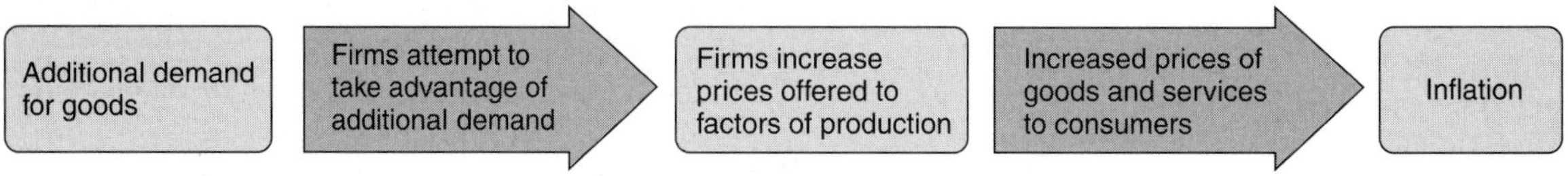

Additional demand for goods → Firms attempt to take advantage of additional demand → Firms increase prices offered to factors of production → Increased prices of goods and services to consumers → Inflation

Something to do

- Construct a new aggregate monetary demand curve for the economy in Figure 12.1, showing an increase in the demand for machinery of £15 million.

Key points

- *Although no economy is likely to reach the position of absolutely full employment, it is not uncommon for a position to be reached where an increase in AMD leads to a relatively small increase in output and a relatively large rise in prices. This leads many people to regard* ***inflation as a condition of excess aggregate monetary demand over aggregate supply in conditions of full employment.***

We know through experience that inflation can also occur in conditions of considerable unemployment. The importance of the above definition of inflation (for it is not the only one) lies in the fact that it draws attention to aggregate *monetary* demand and consequently to the supply of money. The relationship between the supply of money and the level of prices has long been of interest to economists. The best-known expression of the relationship is known as the **quantity theory of money**. This has many variations, but below we examine it in its simplest form.

The quantity theory of money

The quantity theory is based on the belief that the general level of prices depends on the supply of money: if the money supply increases without a corresponding increase in the quantity of goods and services produced, then prices tend to rise.

Imagine a simple economy that produces 1000 units of output a year, which are all purchased by the residents. The money supply in the economy consists of 200 £1 coins, and the goods are priced at £1 each. As the goods are all bought, it follows that each £1 coin is involved in five transactions on average. The value of all the transactions is equal to the supply of money multiplied by the number of times each unit of money changes hands. Another way of looking at the total value of the transactions is to consider the average price of the goods sold (the general level of prices in our simple economy) and the number of transactions that occur (here, £1 × 1000).

These two aspects of the same event constitute the basis of the quantity theory of money. If we call the money supply M; the average number of times that each unit of money changes hands (the **velocity of circulation**) V; the general level of prices P; and the number of transactions T, then we may summarise the previous paragraph by saying that

$$PT \equiv MV$$

The sign '≡' indicates that these two items are exactly the same. We are not proving anything; we are just looking at the same transactions from two different angles. If we divide each side by T, however, we obtain

$$P \equiv \frac{MV}{T}$$

This implies that the general level of prices, P, is related to the supply of money, the rate at which that money changes hands, and the number of transactions that occur. It is clear that an increase in prices *might* follow from an increase in the money supply, or its velocity of circulation, or a reduction in the number of transactions: but there is nothing in the theory to say that an increase in the supply of money *will* lead to a rise in the general price level, since a rise in M may be compensated by a fall in V, or prices may rise merely because the velocity of circulation increases. Moreover, the money supply may be increased in conditions of high unemployment, which would lead to an expansion of output without rising prices. Thus the quantity theory of money is important in drawing attention to one aspect of inflation, but it does not fully explain how inflation occurs.

Something to do

- Calculate the effect of the above simple economy minting an additional 200 £1 coins, in order to reduce the number of times each coin was used.

Cost inflation and demand inflation

While acknowledging the importance of money supply to the inflationary process, it is useful to consider other forces which make their contribution to rising prices. The standard distinction here is between **cost-push inflation** and **demand-pull inflation**. The names indicate the main causes of the particular inflation, although it is possible for one kind of inflation to lead to the other kind in a particularly unpleasant circle.

Fig. 12.3 Cost-push inflation

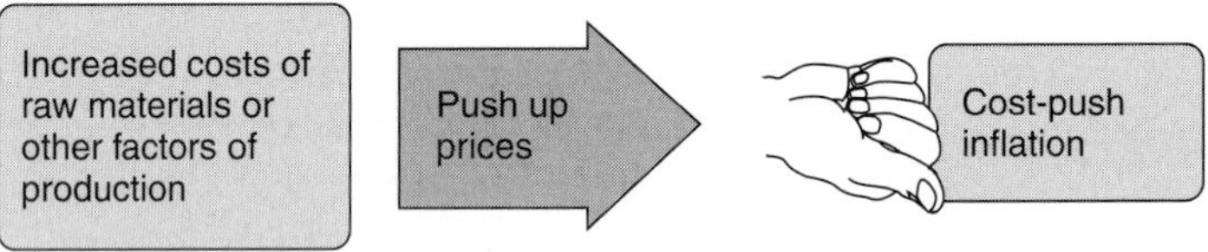

Cost inflation

This occurs when prices rise as a result of the costs of production increasing more rapidly than output. An increase in the cost of imported raw materials, a rise in wages unmatched by a rise in output, or an increase in profits to meet the demands of shareholders would each tend to push prices up. If prices rise for any of these reasons over a broad front of the economy, then workers and shareholders whose incomes have not increased will find their real incomes fall (they will be able to buy fewer goods from their current income) and they will demand extra payments as compensation. If this second round of pay rises is not accompanied by at least proportional rises in productivity, then more prices will rise and so the spiral will continue.

Demand inflation

If cost inflation develops, labour will probably seek higher wages to compensate for the fall in real incomes. This may have two effects:

- If unaccompanied by increased output, it will give further impetus to cost inflation.
- To the extent that wages rise faster than output, workers will have more money to spend and this will lead to demand inflation.

Fig. 12.4 Demand-pull inflation

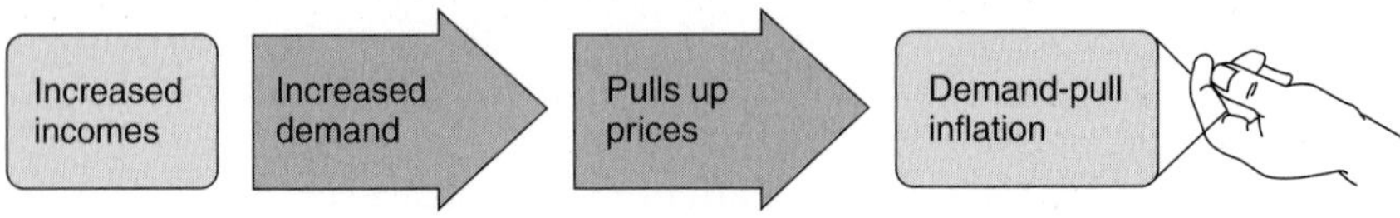

It may be, of course, that the initial impetus to inflation comes from the demand side. If the banks freely create credit for consumers, these people will be able to spend in excess of their current income, or consumers may save less and spend more of their existing income. Aggregate monetary demand is then likely to rise ahead of output, prices will increase, and the trade unions will demand wage increases to compensate. These wage increases will lead to further price increases, and again the spiral will continue.

The Phillips curve

A formal analysis of the relationship between the level of demand, as measured by the level of employment, and the rate of inflation was published by Professor A.W. Phillips in 1958 (see also Unit 11, page 367). Figure 12.5 illustrates his findings, which were based on statistics for the British economy between 1862 and 1957.

Fig. 12.5 The Phillips curve

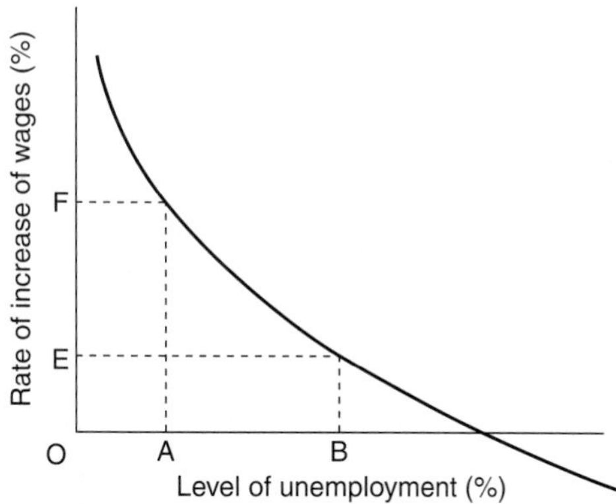

At the point where the Phillips curve crosses the horizontal axis there is zero wage inflation. Since there is high unemployment, labour cannot easily secure a wage increase. As unemployment falls, the rate of inflation rises; so with unemployment at OB per cent, wages rise at OE per cent. As the economy moves nearer to full employment, wage inflation proceeds at an accelerating rate (the curve becomes steeper). Thus, there seems to be a kind of choice between inflation and unemployment: if we want lower inflation we have to accept higher unemployment. This trade off between inflation and unemployment was not so apparent in the 1970s and the 1980s, when inflation and unemployment tended to move in the same direction. Unhappily this did not fit into the Keynesian explanation of the economy, which allowed economic policy to seek a balance between inflation and employment.

However, a further explanation was developed, and it depended on the *expected* rate of inflation. In terms of Figure 12.6, suppose unemployment is OB. Our original (lower) Phillips curve shows wage inflation of 3 per cent. The higher Phillips curve is drawn on the basis that workers expect price inflation to run at 4 per cent, and at the given level of unemployment (OB), wage inflation is now 7 per cent so that the real wage is maintained. Clearly there could be any number of these curves, and the unemployment rate of OB could be associated with various levels of wage inflation. This, of course, reflects the behaviour of workers who seek to protect their real wages by anticipating inflation.

The implication of this analysis is that above the 'natural rate' (see Unit 11) a given level of employment can only be maintained at the cost of an ever-increasing rate of inflation.

Fig. 12.6 Expectations and the Phillips curve

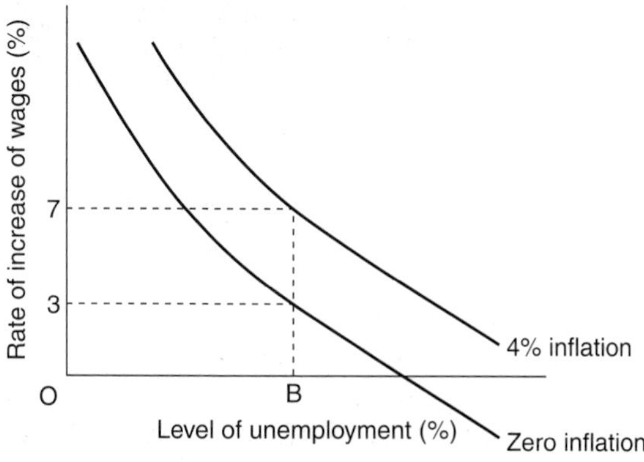

Measuring inflation

In order to assess the rate of inflation and thus the scale of the problem, and to judge the success of any policies to reduce the rate, it is necessary to measure the change in the value of money. This is normally done by means of an index of prices, which tries to measure the average change in prices and thus (when prices are rising) shows the fall in the **purchasing power** of money.

Index numbers

The object of a price index is to measure the average change in prices. It cannot include every price change, so the compilers take a representative basket of goods, covering the expenditure of an average family, and trace changes in the prices of those goods included in the basket. In the first year – the **base year** – each individual price is taken as a figure of 100, which is known as the **price relative**. Suppose that the index contains three goods – food, shirts and petrol – whose prices in year 1 are £1 per kilogram, £10 per shirt and 70 pence per litre. Each of these prices is regarded as 100 in year 1. Subsequent changes are related to this 100. If the price of food rises to £1.20 in year 2, then its price relative becomes 120, an increase of 20 per cent. When petrol falls to 56 pence, its price relative becomes 80, a fall of 20 per cent. Shirts at £11 give a price relative of 110. These changes are summarised in Table 12.1.

Table 12.1

A hypothetical prices index

Commodity	Actual prices (£)		Price relatives		Weight	Expenditure relatives	
	Year 1	Year 2	Year 1	Year 2		Year 1	Year 2
Food	1.00	1.20	100	120.0	6	600	720
Shirts	10.00	11.00	100	110.0	1	100	110
Petrol	0.70	0.56	100	80.0	3	300	240
Index number			100	103.33		100	107

A simple index may be obtained by averaging the price relatives for year 2. In our example, the index has risen from 100 to 103.33 which suggest that retail prices have risen by 3.33 per cent over the period and that the value of money has fallen. This procedure may be repeated to measure subsequent changes. However, it oversimplifies the task of measuring changes in the value of money unless consumers divide their expenditure equally between the three commodities in the basket.

In order to make the index more realistic, we must give **weights** to each commodity according to their relative importance in household expenditure. (The government's **retail price index** has a total weighting of 1000 divided between various goods and services on the basis of the pattern of expenditure.) If the investigation showed that consumers' expenditure is divided between food, shirts and petrol in the ratio 6:1:3, then the price relatives for each year are multiplied by the weights to give **expenditure relatives**, and the overall index is calculated by dividing the sum of the expenditure relatives by the sum of the weights. Thus, in our example, the index moved from 100 in year 1 to 107 in year 2. When compared with the index calculated purely on the basis of price relatives, more emphasis is given to the rise in the price of food, which is responsible for 60 per cent of household expenditure.

Something to do

The index for a given year is found by the equation

$$\text{index for a given year} = \frac{\text{value for that year}}{\text{value for base year}} \times 100$$

- Using this equation, index the following data, using 1995 as the base year:

Price of scrails					
1995	**1996**	**1997**	**1998**	**1999**	**2000**
35p	37p	40p	44p	50p	52p

- What has been the yearly percentage inflation rate in the price of scrails?

Difficulties of constructing and using index numbers

In practice, the construction of an index is more complicated than the above description. The main difficulties include the following:

- **The contents of the basket:** The compilers must decide what goods to take into account. Then decisions must largely depend on the purpose of the index: there is no point including mink coats, for example, if the index is meant to indicate changes in the value of money for the general public.
- **The weighting of the contents of the basket** also poses problems. In the case of the retail price index (RPI), the weights are frequently changed to reflect the growing importance of some goods and the relative decline of others in the average family's budget. Over a long period the usefulness of the index is reduced by such changes. The index also cannot take account of changes in quality or the introduction of new goods or services.
- **Measuring prices:** It is unlikely that the same goods would be sold at the same prices all over the country. This can be overcome only to a limited extent by recording changes in a number of different centres.
- **The choice of base year** will affect the subsequent movements of the index. If prices are high in the base year, then increases in the index in following years may be damped down.

The current retail price index (RPI)

Table 12.2 shows the weights given to different categories of expenditure in the 1996 retail price index for the UK.

We can see that the items carrying the most influence are housing, food and motoring; a change in the price of any of these will have a greater effect on the index than a change in the price of tobacco or bus fares, for example.

Table 12.3 shows the monthly movements in the retail price index for 1996. During the year, prices overall rose by about 2.9 per cent.

Table 12.2

Weighting of the 1996 retail price index	
Group	**Weight**
Housing	190
Food	143
Motoring expenditure	124
Alcohol	78
Household goods	72
Leisure services	65
Clothing and footwear	54
Household services	48
Catering	48
Leisure goods	45
Fuel and light	43
Personal goods and services	38
Tobacco	35
Fares and other travel	17
All items	1 000
All items except housing	810
All items except mortgage interest payments	958

So that the changes can be put into context, Figure 12.7 shows how prices have changed from 1961.

Table 12.3

Retail price index 1996 (13 January 1987 = 100)	
January	145.3
February	146.2
March	146.9
April	147.9
May	148.4
June	148.5
July	147.7
August	148.7
September	149.6
October	149.6
November	149.7
December	149.5

Fig. 12.7 Retail price index, 1961–97

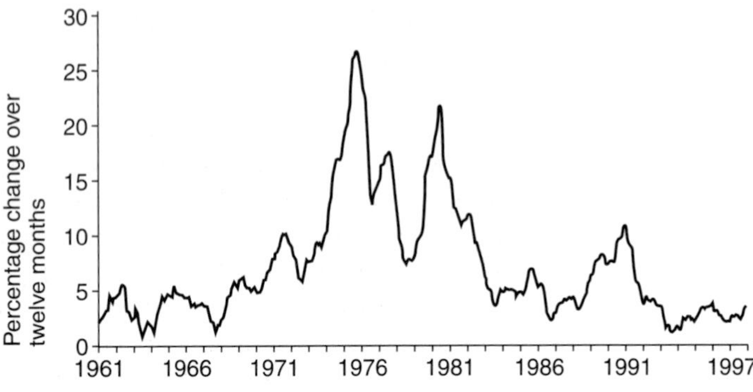

Source: Office for National Statistics

The effects of inflation

While there is a view that a degree of inflation is a necessary stimulus to the economy (slightly rising prices encouraging investment), the strenuous efforts of governments to restrain its pace suggest that it produces many undesirable side-effects. The main effects of inflation are as follows.

Fear of rapid inflation

Lurking in the background are fears that moderate inflation will give way to very rapid inflation and a complete collapse of confidence in the monetary unit. If prices rise at 2 per cent per year, it is 35 years before they double; but if they rise at 15 per cent per year, they double in less than seven years. Once prices start rising rapidly, wage rises begin to anticipate price rises.

Table 12.4

The effects of inflation on the long-term value of money			
The value of £1000 over different periods at different inflation rates			
Period	**Inflation rate**		
	4 per cent	**7 per cent**	**10 per cent**
10 years	£676	£508	£386
15 years	£555	£362	£239
20 years	£456	£258	£149
25 years	£375	£184	£92

Real-income levels

The effect on the distribution of real income is, however, of greater immediate importance. Inevitably some groups of workers are able to negotiate larger pay rises than others. Some manage to keep ahead of inflation because of a strong bargaining position (their real incomes increase), while others fall behind and their real incomes fall. Also, the balance between different forms of income may be altered. Wages may increase at the expense of profits, or vice versa. In the absence of government intervention, those in the most exposed position include people receiving social security benefits, who have no bargaining power. In general, such benefits are indexed to the inflation rate so that their real value is maintained – though, since such increases are retrospective, the real value soon falls. Similar distortions occur with other forms of income: those receiving fixed-interest payments on gilt-edged securities lose, whereas holders of a similar investment in ordinary shares will possibly find their dividends keeping pace with inflation and may have the compensation of rising capital values.

Taxation

One of the effects of inflation is to drag into the tax net some people who previously did not pay income tax. Suppose the first £2000 of income is tax free and then income tax is payable at a rate of 25 per cent. If, in year 1, your income is £2000, you pay no tax. By year 2 prices have risen by 10 per cent, and so has your income, which is now £2200. You now have to pay 25 per cent tax on £200, which reduces your money income to £2150. Since £2150 will not purchase as much in year 2 as £2000 did in year 1, your real income will have fallen. Tax allowances are normally increased annually to prevent this occurring.

Expenditure taxes are affected in different ways. The revenue from VAT, which is a percentage tax, increases automatically as prices rise. The real burden of excise duties, which are a fixed amount per unit, falls as prices rise and so these duties are periodically increased.

Borrowing and savings

The real burden of borrowing money is reduced by inflation, since repayment is made in money of reduced purchasing power. Inflation thus encourages people to borrow and is a disincentive to save. It has other effects on the capital market as well. One hundred pounds invested in gilt-edged securities might yield £7 or £8 per year, but if prices are rising at 10 per cent per year the holder of such securities is in a worse position at the end of the year than at the beginning, even if they can still sell the securities for £100. Consequently, during periods of inflation, savings may be diverted away from the orthodox channels provided by the financial institutions into non-productive channels such as vintage cars, postage stamps, or anything else that can be expected to yield capital gains. While this is fine for the individual, it does not improve industrial investment or growth and in the long term may be one of the more harmful aspects of inflation.

Balance of payments

It is not only the domestic effects of inflation that demand government action, for a rapid rate of inflation also has an adverse effect on the balance of payments (see Unit 13). Imagine two countries whose trade with each other is in equilibrium. When the level of prices in one country rises rapidly, our knowledge of the principles of demand indicates that it will now be more difficult for that country to sell its goods abroad. Also, imports will now be more attractively priced in relation to home goods and the demand for imports will increase. In this way inflation may lead to a **balance-of-payments deficit** and, as we see in Unit 13, difficulty for the government.

The effects of deflation

The term **deflation** is commonly used to refer to a situation in which inflation is slowing down (that is, the rate of increase is decreasing), whilst for economists it strictly means that the general absolute price level between one period and another has fallen. Deflation can bring as many problems as inflation. The last time the UK experienced this phenomenon was during the Depression of the 1930s, when the consequences of a continuing fall in the general price level (which includes consumer prices, wages, property prices and financial assets) led to such uncertainty and redistributive effects as to cause severe economic and social problems.

Controlling inflation

Monetary and fiscal policies

The conventional way of reducing inflationary pressure is to reduce the level of aggregate demand through monetary policy (higher interest rates and lower bank lending) and through fiscal policy (higher taxes and lower government expenditure). Experience shows that such policies can be counter-productive. Higher interest rates increase the cost of borrowing for industry, and these costs may be passed on in the form of higher prices. Increases in taxes such as value added tax lead to higher prices and may encourage people to seek wage increases – the opposite of what is needed. Similarly, an increase in income tax will reduce real income. If people obtain pay rises to restore the position, inflation may continue. As a result, governments have sometimes resorted to other policies. These take the form of direct controls over prices or incomes or both.

Direct controls over incomes or prices

At various times in the UK, attempts have been made to impose a freeze on incomes or to set a statutory limit for income or price rises, or to encourage voluntary restraint. The former involves the establishment of some organisation to police the system; the latter soon breaks down!

The principal difficulty surrounding a formal **incomes policy** is the establishment of appropriate criteria for increases in income. It is usual for the government to set a basic norm – the average increase that should occur. This immediately becomes the accepted minimum increase. Increases above the norm are allowed to those showing increases in productivity or to those who are significantly underpaid. Difficulties arise in respect of certain groups whose productivity is not measurable in meaningful terms but who live in the same inflationary world as everyone else and have the same need to maintain their real wages. Civil servants, doctors, nurses, teachers and members of the armed forces are examples of such groups.

It is even more difficult to cope with the problem of the low paid with an incomes policy designed to fight inflation. As a result of the implementation of a **minimum wage** in the UK in 1999, cost and demand inflation could both see considerable impetus, particularly when 'the league table effect' begins to exert itself and each group of employees wants to maintain its best position in relation to others. A further difficulty is the timing of the introduction of incomes policy: it is never the right time, because there is always a group which has to be the first to be subjected to restraint.

In practice, incomes restraint eventually builds up distortions in the patterns of pay, and the relaxation of restraint is likely to be followed by another round of inflationary pay increases.

The encouragement of increased efficiency

Too much emphasis on restraint, as has already been suggested, obscures the more sensible alternative approach to the problem of inflation: the encouragement of increased efficiency. The long-term solution to the UK's problems lies in a higher level of productive investment – other policies are only holding operations.

Recent government policy – the MPC

The control of inflation has been the key macro-economic policy objective of recent governments. The incoming Labour Government of 1997 made clear its commitment to low and stable price increases by immediately giving the Bank of England sole operational responsibility for setting interest rates to achieve an inflation target set by the Government. At the time of writing, the target is 2.5 per cent for retail price inflation excluding mortgage payments.

In effect, the Bank of England has been made semi-independent of the government and a monetary policy committee (MPC) meets regularly to decide the Bank's rate of interest. There are nine members of the MPC, each with one vote. They examine the latest economic statistics, using a range of variables, and make a judgement about the net effect of these on the general price level over the coming months. Their job, therefore, is to decide whether inflationary pressures are building up and whether altering interest rates will reduce these pressures. It can be seen as a pre-emptive monetary policy. The fact that individual members of the MPC do not always agree, some voting for a change and others not, only goes to show that economic management is not an exact science.

13 International trade and globalisation

Introduction: the reasons for international trade

So far we have considered economic problems and the monetary and fiscal policies the government has for dealing with them as they apply within the UK. The extent of such problems, however, and the effectiveness of government policies are often limited by the repercussions they may have on the international trading position of the nation. In fact it has frequently been the UK's **balance of payments** (the annual summary of the UK's international trading position) rather than the level of unemployment or the rate of inflation that has dictated the direction of government economic policy.

The pattern of world trade is so complicated that no single explanation can be given as to why international trade has become such a vital influence on an economy. The most obvious reason for trading with other countries is to obtain goods that either cannot be produced in the home country or can only be produced at great expense.

Climatic and geological differences account for a proportion of international trade, and for a large proportion of the exports of the poorer countries of the world. Thus, oil is exported by the UK, where it is found in deposits under the North Sea, and wines are **imported** into the UK from France and other countries, where the climate is more suitable for growing vines.

Less obviously, perhaps, differences in the skills of labour and in the accumulation of capital account for some of the exports of the wealthy countries. For example, industrialised countries such as the UK have accumulated the capital equipment and labour skills to produce items such as cars and machinery. Less industrialised economies, on the other hand, tend to have an abundance of unskilled labour and little capital equipment. Many of their exports are agricultural goods produced by labour without the help of modern machinery.

It was such differences in the distribution of factors of production that underlay the traditional pattern of world trade, with manufactured goods from the UK being exchanged for food and raw materials from Commonwealth countries. This, pattern, however, is being superseded, since the majority of world trade now involves the exchange of manufactured goods between industrial countries. Countries frequently import goods that they can quite easily produce for themselves. For example, over half of the new cars purchased in the UK are manufactured abroad and an enormous amount of industrial machinery is imported, while overseas countries have a considerable demand for British manufactured goods, in particular electrical goods.

In this unit, we examine the basis of international trade, the balance of payments and how international trade is financed. In particular, we look at:

- the theory of comparative advantage
- the terms of trade
- obstacles to international trade
- the structure and meaning of the balance of payments
- ways in which international trade is financed
- the European Union.

The unit ends with a consideration of the trend towards globalisation and internationalism.

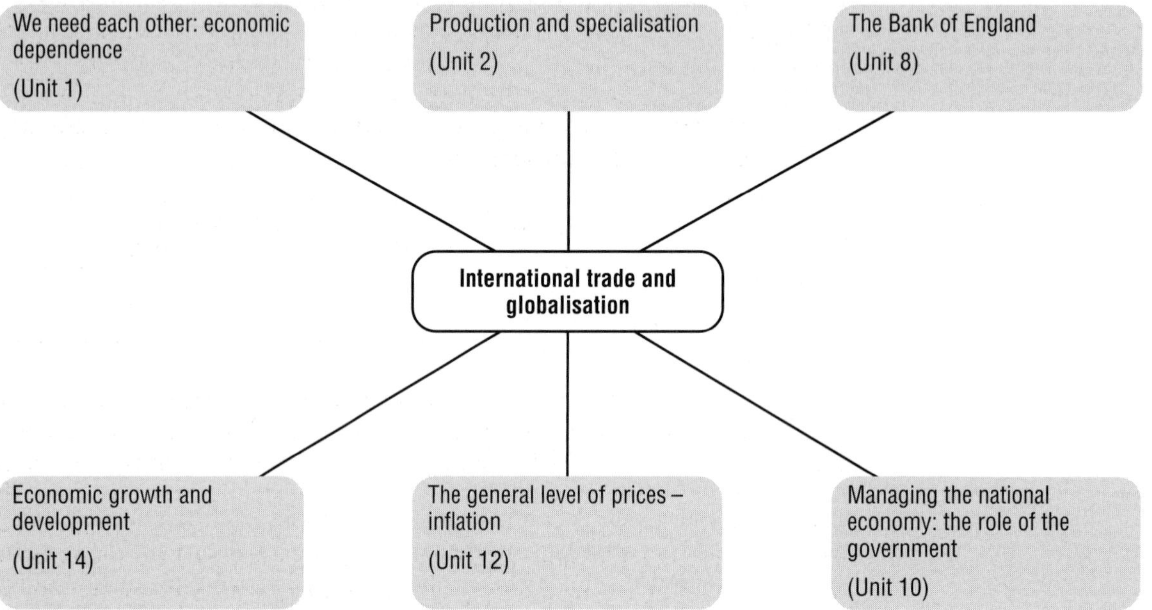

Something to do

In Unit 1, we met the Efe tribe, who live in the Ituri Forest of Zaire. The Efe exist in almost total isolation, having very little trade with the outside world.

- Do you think that the Efe tribespeople would benefit from trade with other countries? Give your reasons in terms of ethics and material standards of living.
- Make a list of the commodities you think the Efe have, or could produce, that other countries might want.

The theory of comparative advantage

The theory of **comparative advantage** shows that even where one country is more efficient than other countries at producing everything – that is to say, it has an **absolute advantage** in all industries – gains will be available to it from international trade so long as it transfers resources towards the industry in which its absolute advantage is greatest. It will then sell the surplus to other countries which in their turn will channel resources towards those industries in which their deficiency is least.

But first let us consider a more simple case. Assume a world with only two countries, Industria and Agraria, which each produce two goods, food and machines. Industria is an efficient producer of machines but finds food production expensive as there are land shortages. Agraria is an efficient farming nation but is backward in producing machines. In order to avoid the major complication of international trade, that of exchange rates of domestive currencies, we shall deal in terms of 'days' of labour when measuring the costs of production and prices of goods. We assume that the following cost pattern is established in each country in the absence of international trade:

Table 13.1

	No. of days' labour in Industria	No. of days' labour in Agraria
One unit of food	2	1
One unit of machinery	3	4

Each country thus has an absolute advantage in the production of one good, but the reasons for trade are best explained in terms of the comparative costs within each country. If the domestic comparative cost ratios ($\frac{2}{3}$ and $\frac{1}{4}$ in this case) are different, then trade is beneficial to each country. Agraria can produce 4 units of food by giving up the production of 1 unit of machinery and transferring resources to agriculture. Industria produces 1 unit of machinery by giving up the production of $1\frac{1}{2}$ units of food and using the resources for machinery. If Agraria can acquire more than 1 unit of machinery in exchange for the 4 units of food that it now produces instead, it will be better off. If Industria can acquire more than $1\frac{1}{2}$ units of food in exchange for one machine, it too will be better off. They can obviously meet each other's requirements: Agraria produces an extra 4 units of food, keeps perhaps 2 units for domestic consumption, and exchanges 2 units for one machine produced in Industria. Industria then has $\frac{1}{2}$ unit of food more than it did in isolation.

The total gains from trade will depend on

- the size of the two economies
- the extent to which specialisation occurs
- the relative strengths of demand in the two countries for the two traded commodities.

If we assume that each country has 1000 days of labour at its disposal and that in the absence of trade each divides its resources equally between the production of food and machines, total production could be summarised as follows:

Table 13.2

	Output of food	Output of machines
Agraria	500	125
Industria	250	166⅔
Total	**750**	**291⅔**

(Each output figure is obtained by dividing the total days allocated to the production of a commodity by the number of days required to produce a single unit.)

If complete specialisation occurs, with each country concentrating on the product which it can produce most efficiently, output is increased:

Table 13.3

	Output of food	Output of machines
Agraria	1000	—
Industria	—	333⅓
Total	**1000**	**333⅓**

Thus the maximum gains, given the distribution of factors before trade began, are 250 units of food and 41⅔ machines.

While one would expect trade to give general benefits where each country had an absolute advantage in one commodity, it is perhaps a little more surprising to find that each country can benefit when one of them has an absolute advantage in both products.

Suppose that the cost pattern in the two countries is as follows:

Table 13.4

	No. of days' labour in Industria	No. of days' labour in Agraria
One unit of food	2	3
One unit of machinery	1	4

Industria has an advantage in each product, but the advantage is greatest in the production of machinery, and it is on this that Industria should concentrate. In the absence of trade, with each country dividing its 1000 days equally between the two industries, output would be:

Table 13.5

	Food	Machinery
Agraria	166⅔	125
Industria	250	500
Total	**416⅔**	**625**

Because of Agraria's relative inefficiency, complete specialisation would result in a fall in food output:

Table 13.6

	Food	Machinery
Agraria	333⅓	0
Industria	0	1000
Total	**333⅓**	**1000**

This is unrealistic. The world will, presumably, want at least as much food as before. Let us suppose that food output remains at $416\frac{2}{3}$ units. Some of this will have to be produced by Industria, giving output as follows:

Table 13.7

	Food	Machinery
Agraria	$333\frac{1}{3}$	0
Industria	$83\frac{1}{3}$	$833\frac{1}{3}$
Total	**$416\frac{2}{3}$**	**$833\frac{1}{3}$**

To keep world output of food at $416\frac{2}{3}$ units, Industria has to devote $166\frac{2}{3}$ days to agriculture, so has $833\frac{1}{3}$ days for the production of machinery. Thus the increase in output is $208\frac{1}{3}$ machines ($833\frac{1}{3} - 625$).

If it were decided to keep the output of machinery at its pre-trade level of 625 units, Industria would have 375 days to devote to food, giving output of:

Table 13.8

	Food	Machinery
Agraria	$333\frac{1}{3}$	0
Industria	$187\frac{1}{2}$	625
Total	**$520\frac{5}{6}$**	**625**

This is an increase in food output of $104\frac{1}{6}$ units.

The reason why gains are possible even though Industria has the advantage in both products is that the internal cost ratios are different. The effects of this may be summarised as follows:

- If Industria gives up the production of 1 unit of food, 2 extra machines can be produced. If these machines can be exchanged for anything more than 1 unit of food, Industria will have gained.
- If Agraria gives up the production of 1 machine, $1\frac{1}{3}$ units of food can be produced. If the food can be exchanged for more than 1 machine, Agraria will have gained.

In fact it can be shown that if the goods are exchanged at a rate which lies between the two internal cost ratios, both countries can gain. The internal cost ratios are:

- for Industria, 1 unit of food costs 2 machines (because it has to give up 2 machines to produce 1 unit of food)
- for Agraria, 1 unit of food costs $\frac{3}{4}$ of a machine (because the 3 days needed to produce 1 unit of food would produce $\frac{3}{4}$ of a machine).

The rate at which trade takes place must lie between 1 unit of food for 2 machines and 1 unit of food for $\frac{3}{4}$ machine. Thus, if 1 unit of food is exchanged for 1 machine, Industria gives up 1 unit of food to produce 2 machines, exports 1 machine for 1 unit of food, and so gains 1 machine. On the same basis, Agraria gains $\frac{1}{3}$ of a unit of food.

The actual rate of exchange that is established will depend on the strength of demand for the two products in the two countries.

Notice that if trade is conducted outside these rates, one of the countries would be better off if it were not trading. Suppose the rate is 1 unit of food for 4 units of machinery: Industria exports 4 units of machinery and receives 1 unit of food in exchange. But if it had not produced those machines in the first place it could have used its resources to produce 2 units of food itself. Similarly, if the rate of exchange were 1 unit of food to $\frac{1}{2}$ a unit of machinery, Agraria would best serve its own interests by transferring resources back to the machine industry and producing $\frac{3}{4}$ of a machine for each unit of food forgone.

The rate at which goods are actually exchanged is known as the terms of trade. We return briefly to this concept on page 389.

Something to do

- The following are the costs of production (in terms of hours of labour) of coal and steel in two countries. Calculate the benefits to each country of international trade with each other, if each country spends 10 000 hours of labour equally distributed between the two products.

	Hours of labour in country A	**Hours of labour in country B**
One unit of coal	24	16
One unit of steel	32	8

The limitations of the comparative cost theory

The theory outlined above depends on the existence of certain rarefied conditions, and complications arise if these conditions are relaxed.

- There are, of course, more than two countries in the real world and more than two commodities. Although the introduction of more countries and commodities complicates the exposition of the theory, it does nothing to deny the basic principle that a country should concentrate on the production of the good or goods for which its comparative advantage is greatest (or its disadvantage least).
- We have implicitly assumed that factors can transfer freely from one industry to another. This process is in practice likely to take many years and necessitate considerable retraining of labour. In these circumstances, the benefits of trade may be reduced, and will almost certainly be delayed.
- We have also assumed constant costs during the transfer of resources from one industry to another. This means that the transfer of a given amount of resources from one industry to another always results in the same rise of production. In fact, if the expanding industry in each country is subject to decreasing costs (increasing returns to scale) the gains from trade will be greater than we have so far implied. In conditions of increasing costs in each country, the benefits available will similarly be reduced.
- Transport costs, which we have ignored, will also limit the benefits available, as will the introduction of **tariffs** and other obstacles to trade (see pages 392–393).
- Some of the greatest problems of international trade are connected with currencies. By omitting this aspect from our picture, we have exaggerated the smoothness with which trade can occur.
- Finally, there are frequently political, social or strategic reasons why countries do not trade freely with one another.

The terms of trade

In the previous section, we spoke of the terms of trade in relation to the quantity of goods that could be acquired for a given volume of exports, and it is these *real* terms of trade that are important. Since the UK imports and exports thousands of different goods each year, it is impossible to obtain a meaningful measure of the real terms of trade, so we have to resort to a monetary measure. We can use the formula

$$\text{terms of trade} = \frac{\text{index of export prices}}{\text{index of import prices}} \times 100$$

In the base year, the index of both import prices and export prices will be 100 (see page 376), and the terms of trade will be 100. If in the following year the import prices index rises to 102 while the export prices index remains at 100, the terms of trade will become 98, showing a deterioration in the terms of trade – a greater volume of exports is now needed to pay for a given volume of imports. A figure above 100 indicates an improvement – a given amount of exports will purchase a greater amount of imports.

Recent movements in the UK's terms of trade are shown in Table 13.9.

Table 13.9

UK terms of trade, 1989–95 (base year = 1990)

Year	Index of export prices	Index of import prices	Terms of trade
1989	96.5	97.7	98.8
1990	100	100	100
1991	101.4	101.2	100.2
1992	103.5	102.1	101.4
1993	116.2	112.3	103.5
1994	118.6	116.1	102.2
1995	126.4	127.8	98.9

Source: *Annual Abstract of Statistics*, 1999

An improvement in the terms of trade does not necessarily benefit the economy: since it means that exports are less competitive and imports more competitive, it may mean a deterioration in the balance of trade. The outcome is likely to be related to the price elasticity of demand for imports and exports.

Barriers to international trade

We have seen how the opening up of trade between countries leads to greater world production of traded goods and, by implication, to an increase in economic welfare. Conversely, any measures which inhibit trade between nations may be expected to reduce the volume of output and the level of economic welfare.

Despite this, every government takes steps to control the volume of imports entering its country. This is done for a variety of reasons and invites retaliation from its trading partners. There are a number of ways of protecting the home economy from overseas competition. Those most frequently used include the following.

Tariffs A **tariff**, or import duty, is a surcharge imposed on the price of goods entering a country. The effect is to increase the price of the goods so that, unless demand is perfectly inelastic, the quantity purchased will fall. This can be illustrated with a supply and demand graph, as shown in Figure 13.1.

Fig. 13.1 The effect of tariffs

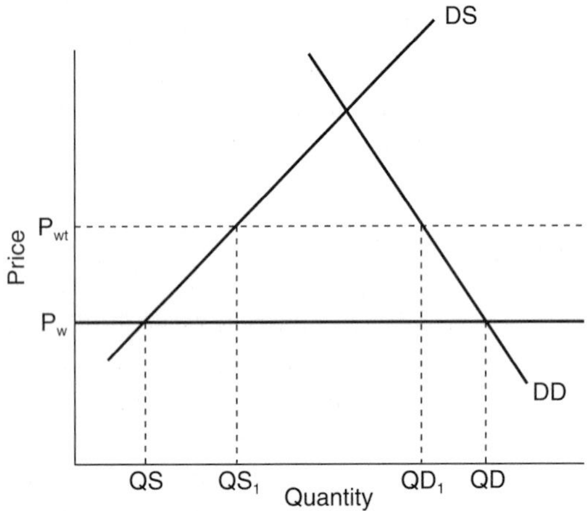

In Figure 13.1, DD shows the domestic demand for, and DS shows the domestic supply of, a product P. The world price of P is P_w. Under conditions of free-trade equilibrium, domestic producers supply at quantity QS, and domestic consumers consume at quantity QD. The quantity of product P that must be imported is therefore QD – QS. If a tariff is imposed on imports of product P to raise the domestic price of imports of the product to P_{wt} (world price P_w plus the tariff), the price of the product supplied by domestic producers will also rise to this level. At this price, demand for the product falls to QD_1, while the quantity that domestic producers are prepared to supply increases to QS_1 Domestic output of the product therefore increases, and imports fall to $QD_1 - QS_1$ Imports fall from CG to EF.

Tariffs may be either

- **specific** – say 50 pence per unit imported, or
- ***ad valorem*** – perhaps 10 per cent of the price of the good.

The former type is less significant as prices rise, while the latter increases in proportion to price rises.

While the imposition of a tariff enables home producers to compete more effectively than foreign producers, and also increases demand for home-produced goods, not all tariffs are imposed for protective purposes. Many are essentially revenue tariffs, which are designed to provide revenue for the government and may be imposed on goods for which there is no effective domestic substitute.

Subsidies

When these are granted to home producers, the effects are similar to taxes on overseas goods. If, for example, American wheat costs £80 a tonne delivered to the UK and British farmers need £90 to cover their costs and make a living, then they clearly cannot compete. The government can assist British agriculture either by imposing a tariff of £10 on American wheat or by giving the British farmer a subsidy of £10 a tonne to enable him or her to sell at £80 and thus be able to compete.

While the form of protection that is chosen will make little difference to the ultimate pattern of trade, it does have an important effect on the direction of support for home agriculture. If tariffs are imposed on imports, the consumer supports home agriculture directly by paying a higher price than he or she would in the absence of the tariff; but if home producers receive a subsidy, the support for agriculture comes indirectly from the taxpayer. As most tax is paid by the relatively wealthy, support through the taxpayer may be considered preferable to direct support from consumers, many of whom have very low incomes.

Quantitative restrictions (quotas)

Tariffs seek direct influence on the price at which goods are sold, but an alternative form of protection – quantitative restrictions, or **quotas** – seeks to control the level of imports and allows them to find their own price. The main difference between this kind of protection and tariffs is that, whereas with a tariff the government gains extra revenue, with quota restrictions the benefit of the higher price from limited supply goes to the seller of the goods, unless the government takes prior steps to prevent this. The easiest way is to auction import licences so that the highest bidders pay the government for the licence to sell the volume of goods required. Alternatively, licences may simply be sold (or merely issued) to overseas suppliers on the basis of the pattern of supplies in earlier years.

Non-tariff barriers

Until recently, the commercial barriers to trade were assessed purely in terms of tariffs and quantitative restrictions. With the complete removal of such barriers within the European Union, the significance of non-tariff barriers to trade has increased. These may take the form of discriminatory administrative practices, such as deliberately channelling government contracts to home companies even where their tenders are not competitive or insisting on different technical standards. In a common market of fifteen members, this could force producers to manufacture to fifteen different sets of technical specifications if they wished to sell in each member country, and to yet more specifications if they wished to sell outside the area. Steps are under way to eliminate such situations within the EU, but their existence will probably remain a hindrance to world trade in general for a long while.

Exchange controls

As an alternative to imposing various limitations on traded goods, governments may reduce the flow of those goods by restricting the amount of foreign exchange (currency) available for their purchase. If the government wishes to reduce the flow of imports from America, it may set limits to the amount of US dollars that its citizens can acquire to buy American goods. In the past, the British government restricted the amount of currency available to people wishing to take holidays overseas so that it could be used for more essential purposes. The governments of developing countries frequently conserve foreign currency in this way.

Whichever restraint is employed, the intention (except in the case of purely revenue-raising tariffs) is to increase the demand for home goods at the expense of foreign suppliers. The implication is normally that foreign producers can market goods in the country concerned more cheaply than home producers can. By imposing tariffs or other controls, the government enables home producers to maintain or increase their sales, maintain employment in the industry, and perhaps increase profits. While those connected with the protected sector benefit partly at the expense of overseas producers, they also benefit at the expense of home consumers, who are forced to pay a higher price than would be necessary in conditions of free trade. Since one (perhaps small) sector benefits at the expense of two other groups, it is worth looking at the arguments advanced in defence of tariffs and other obstacles to international trade.

Think about it

- Restricting the amount of foreign currency that holiday makers are allowed to take out of the country enables more of the country's foreign currency reserves to be used for other purposes that the government think are more important. In view of this, do you think that such exchange controls are justified? Consider
  - the restrictions on the individual's freedom to spend their money where and on what they choose
  - the effects on both the tourist trade and tourism in the UK.

Why are tariff barriers erected?

The balance of payments

Tariffs and other controls may be imposed as a short-term method of correcting a deficit in the balance of payments (see pages 400–401). The extent to which this is successful will depend on the elasticity of demand for imports. The higher the elasticity the greater the saving of foreign currency, though as long as the elasticity of demand is greater than zero there will be a reduction in foreign-currency expenditure if there are no other changes. In fact, however, a tariff is likely to invite retaliation, so that the long-term effects are unpredictable.

Anti-dumping

Closely connected with the balance-of-payments motive is the imposition of a tariff to counteract the practice of **dumping.** This is the situation where prices are kept artificially high in the home market by restricting supply there and selling the surplus abroad at a price which undercuts those charged by domestic sellers abroad. While it is often difficult to prove that dumping occurs, it is generally agreed that it is unfair and that governments are entitled to impose protective tariffs to counter it.

Infant industries In developing countries, tariffs are frequently imposed to protect new or infant industries until they are strong enough to meet foreign competition. The case for such tariffs seems reasonable enough; the difficulty is that, once the tariff is established, the protected industry can always find very good reasons for its continuation and many infant industry tariffs still protect full-grown but relatively inefficient industries.

Employment In the past, an important reason for the imposition of tariffs on imports into the UK has been to reduce unemployment. Tariffs can be set so high that they virtually exclude all imports. In the same way, tariffs can be selectively applied to individual industries in which there is high unemployment. A disadvantage of such protection, however, is that it may delay the changes that are necessary for domestic industry to become internationally competitive again.

Strategic tariffs These are imposed to protect industries whose products may be essential in times of war or international crisis. Governments do not like to be entirely dependent on foreign suppliers for essential materials and equipment. In the UK, for example, the production of aircraft and defence equipment and shipbuilding have been subsidised by the government to ensure that the appropriate skills and technologies remain available.

Low-wage imports It is sometimes argued that governments should impose tariffs on imports from countries where wages are very low. Very often this may be a political or ethical rather than an economic argument. In terms of the use of economic resources, if labour is cheap it should be used; if capital is cheap it should be used.

The gains and losses from tariffs are unpredictable. In general,

- consumers in the protected economy lose, since prices are higher
- producers in the protected economy gain, since demand increases
- overseas producers lose since they are deprived of a market.

The theory of comparative costs suggest that losses will outweigh gains.

GATT – reducing tariffs

The General Agreement on Tariffs and Trade (GATT) was founded in 1947, and since then has accomplished a steady reduction in the level and number of trade tariffs. There are currently more than 120 members of GATT, who collectively represent about 90 per cent of international trade.

GATT has a permanent staff who try to supervise the level of restrictions on trade, and organise periodic meetings, or 'rounds', of members at which tariff reductions are negotiated. There has been success in securing reductions on a broad front, though on a number of occasions exceptions have been made to deal with special circumstances such as acute balance-of-payments problems or infant industries. Generally, a member of GATT has to offer the same tariff treatment to all other members, but notable exceptions to this are necessary if the integrity of trading groups such as the European Union is to be maintained. Similarly, concessions are sometimes made to developing countries who are not in a strong trading position.

At the 'Uruguay Round', between 1986 and 1994, tariffs were reduced on agriculture and on services such as banking and insurance. The World Trade Organisation was set up to monitor observance of the agreement which will provide an estimated 2 per cent increase in GDP for the UK by 2005.

The balance of payments: its structure and meaning

In our analysis of comparative costs, we confined ourselves to trade by barter, excluding any idea of money or currency. In practice, it is the use of different currencies that causes many of the problems associated with international trade.

First of all we must consider the differences between a purely domestic transaction and an international purchase. In day-to-day transactions we simply hand over cash in exchange for goods and services. The cash has no intrinsic value but only exchange value; it is acceptable to vendors (sellers) because they know that they will subsequently be able to exchange it for other goods and services.

The British importer of a £15 000 German car will find, however, that his German supplier will not have much use for £15 000 sterling and will insist on payment in Deutschmarks or euros. It is this fact that distinguishes international transactions from domestic trade. The importer will instruct his bank to buy £15 000 of Deutschmarks or euros from the foreign-exchange market. The currency is provided essentially by the Bank of England in its role as custodian of the foreign-exchange reserves. The Bank's holding of foreign currency falls and its holding of sterling rises by £15 000. The importer's sterling balance falls by £15 000 but he can now use the Deutschmarks or euros to pay for his car.

If many people are buying foreign goods, the Bank of England may have difficulty in meeting demands for foreign currency. In general, however, the demand for foreign currencies is approximately balanced by the supply of foreign currency to the market from those overseas residents who need sterling to buy goods from British exporters. It is only in cases of considerable imbalance that the government is forced to intervene.

All the transactions between one country and the rest of the world that involve an exchange of currency are brought together annually under the heading of the balance of payments. This in effect summarises the country's financial and economic transactions with the rest of the world during the preceding twelve months.

The reasons for measuring the balance of payments

To measure performance

A country's balance of payments may be likened to the annual income and expenditure of a household. The household receives income by supplying the services of factors of production and spends that income on the purchase of goods and services it requires. If the household spends all its income, no more and no less, it is in the same position as a country whose balance of payments just balances. If it spends more than its income, either by borrowing or by drawing on past savings, the household has a balance-of-payments deficit for the year. If its expenditure falls short of income, it may regard itself as having a balance-of-payments surplus.

This illustrates one reason for assessing the balance of payments: it shows whether or not the country as a whole is paying its way in the world. If Agraria produces £10 000 million of goods, exports £2000 million of them and imports £3000 million, its inhabitants have consumed more goods than they have produced. On the other hand, the inhabitants of other countries must have consumed fewer goods than they have produced – a situation which, as we shall see, cannot continue indefinitely. (Again the comparison with the household is appropriate.) The government needs an assessment of the balance of payments in order to check that the community is living within its means.

To protect the foreign-currency reserves

If a household has an income of £1200 per month and spends £1400 per month, it has a deficit of £200 per month. That £200 must have come from somewhere. One possibility is that £200 has been borrowed from the bank or a credit card company. This cannot continue for too long, since the household will not be able to borrow indefinitely; repayment will soon have to be made. Alternatively, the household may have been using its savings from previous months. Again this cannot go on forever, since the savings will be used up. The household will need to change its policy so that income is greater than expenditure and previous loans can be repaid or savings can be restored.

There is a similar problem for the government in relation to the nation's foreign transactions. If as a nation we spend more abroad than we earn, the difference can be financed by borrowing from other countries or by using previously earned foreign currency. Since there is a limit both to overseas borrowing and the stock of foreign currency, the government monitors foreign transactions so that, if necessary, policy can be changed to reverse the balance between earnings and expenditure, which will restore the foreign-exchange reserves.

Think about it

- If you spend more than your income, you can borrow money to cover the shortfall, at least in the short term. If, however, you do not repay the money, the person or organisation from whom you borrowed it can sue you, repossess some of your property and if necessary have you declared bankrupt. Similarly, a government can borrow money in order to cover a trading deficit. It is more difficult, however, to sue a country for repayment of the debt or seize its goods if it defaults on repayment. What do you think would happen if a country refused to pay a large debt
  - to private investors and bankers within the country itself
  - to foreign governments and organisations?

The balance-of-payments accounts

The balance of payments is divided into two parts: the **current** (or **trading**) **account** and the capital account. The position for the UK in 1997 is summarised in Table 13.10. The term 'capital account' is in fact slightly inaccurate since it covers short-term transactions as well as long-term ones. In theory, the two parts of the accounts should cancel each other out. For example, if a British company exports goods worth £1000, this is shown as a credit of +£1000 in the current account. Payment will probably not be immediate, so there is an increase in Britain's external assets of £1000 (the money owed by the foreign importer). This *increase* is shown by a *minus* sign in the capital account (−£1000). Thus the two aspects of the transaction are self-cancelling. If the goods had been paid for immediately, the increase in the asset of cash would have been shown by a minus. This can be confusing, but remember that in the capital section a minus sign indicates an increase in assets or a reduction in liabilities, and a plus sign shows a decrease in assets or a rise in liabilities.

Table 13.10

UK balance of payments, 1997 (£m)	
Current account	
Visible trade	
Exports	+171 783
Imports	−183 695
Balance	−11 912
Invisible trade	
Credits	+68 237
Debits	−50 183
Balance	+18 054
Balance on current account	+6 142
Capital account	
Transactions in external assets and liabilities	−6 455
Balancing item	−313
Overall balance	0

The current account

Visible trade During 1997 goods exported were worth £171.8 billion while imports were nearly £183.7 billion, showing a deficit of nearly £12 billion. A visible trade deficit is the normal situation for the UK.

Invisible items The invisible items shown in the current account in Table 13.10 are broken down into three groups in Table 13.11:

Table 13.11

UK invisible transactions, 1997 (£m)	
Services balance	11 881
Investment income balance	10 950
Transfers balance	−4 777
Total	**18 054**

- Services are what are sometimes referred to as 'invisible imports and exports'. Included are payments for such things as transport and tourism and – most important – banking, insurance and other financial services. The surplus of almost £12 000 million derives mainly from the last group and is attributable to the continuing predominance of the City of London as a financial centre. If overseas residents or firms run a bank account in London, any charges that they pay are a credit in the UK balance of payments. Transactions in transport and tourism are substantial but their net effect is less significant than that of financial services. In connection with transport and tourism, it is important to remember that when people from the UK go abroad for a holiday the payment made to hotels constitutes an invisible *import*, a debit in the balance of payments, because money is leaving the country.

- People and firms in the UK have investments all over the world. Any income from these investments (shares, factories, houses) appears under the heading 'Investment income balance'.
- Transfers have nothing to do with trade but, by convention, appear in the current account. On a personal level, people living in the UK may transfer money to relatives in other countries. More important, however, are government transfers which represent, for example, the UK's contributions to the EU or other international organisations.

It has always been the case that the invisible items show a surplus for the UK, and this normally more than covers a deficit on visible trade. It should be noted, however, that the invisible items are becoming relatively weaker, partly because other countries are increasingly providing for themselves services which were previously obtained from the UK.

The capital account

Any changes in the size of external assets held by people in the UK (or firms or the government) will be recorded in the capital account, as will any changes in overseas liabilities.

We saw earlier that one group of transactions is the monetary aspect of importing or exporting. When a UK resident buys goods from abroad, the goods are a debit to the visible account. If the goods are bought on credit, there is an increase in overseas liabilities in the form of trade credit; if the goods are paid for immediately, there is a reduction in overseas assets because we now have less foreign currency. While it has not been a problem in the UK in recent times, an important aspect of balance-of-payments management is to ensure that there is an adequate amount of foreign currency available for those wishing to import goods. Sometimes governments restrict the uses to which foreign currency may be put so as to conserve it for essential purposes.

The creation of trade credit or the payment for goods arises because we trade with other countries. The capital account, though, also contains several other kinds of borrowing and lending:

<u>Short-term borrowing and lending</u>

- **Financial markets** are now international, linked 24 hours per day. Banks and others can move funds from one centre to another at will, often for short periods to take advantage of perhaps a higher rate of interest in Tokyo than in New York.
- **The government**, through the Bank of England, may borrow from other governments or lend to them if necessary, perhaps because of a temporary shortage of particular currencies.

<u>Investment</u> Investment may be either direct, where for example a company owns a production plant overseas, or indirect, where individual or institutional investors put money into bank accounts or stocks and shares in another country.

The earnings from such investments may be inflows, where British investors receive profits from overseas production facilities or income from investments from overseas bank accounts or stocks and shares, or outflows, where the earnings are paid to overseas owners of plant in the UK or investors in UK bank accounts or stocks and shares.

The balancing item It was shown earlier that the current account and the capital account should cancel each other out, because each transaction has two aspects. Table 13.10 shows a difference of £313 million between the two parts of the balance of payments, and this is entered as the **balancing item.**

There are several factors which account for the discrepancy between the two sections of the balance of payments and thus explain what the balancing item covers:

- The sheer size of the task of collecting and collating the figures in itself makes some errors inevitable.
- The time-lags which occur between goods being delivered and payment being effected account for part of the difference, and may make it difficult to match purchases with payments.
- Sometimes it is difficult to identify trade credit, and there is no doubt that much of this is concealed in the balancing item.
- A further problem arises if the exchange rate of sterling against another currency alters between the goods being delivered and payment being made.

The difference between imports and exports is known as the **balance of trade.**

Fig. 13.2 UK exports, 1985 and 1995

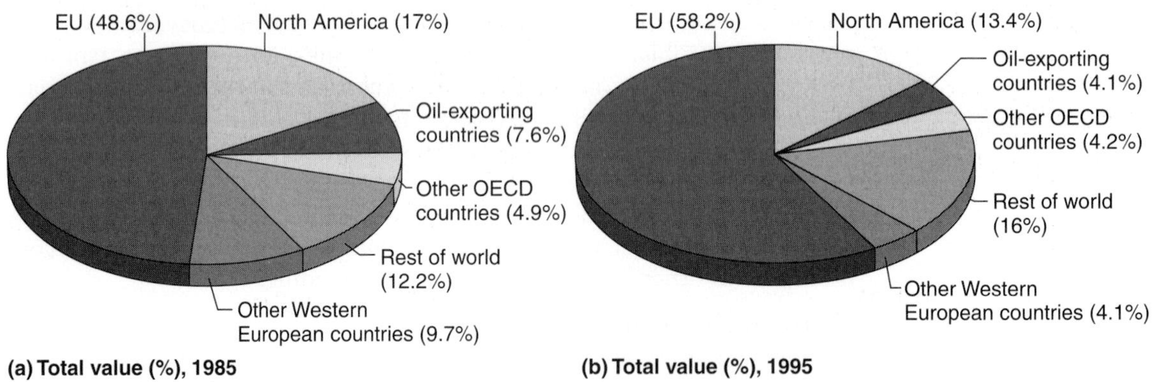

(a) Total value (%), 1985

(b) Total value (%), 1995

Finished manufactured (41.2%)
Unclassified (2.7%)
Food, beverages, tobacco (6.3%)
Basic materials (2.7%)
Fuels (21.5%)
Semi-manufactured (25.6%)

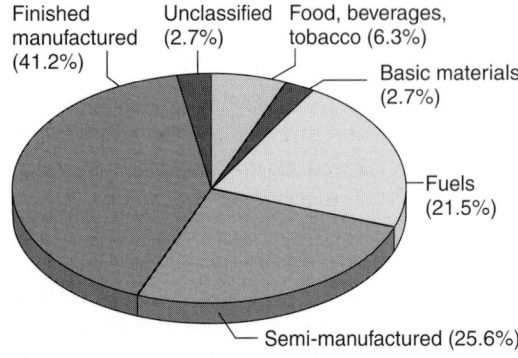

(c) Commodity type (%), 1985

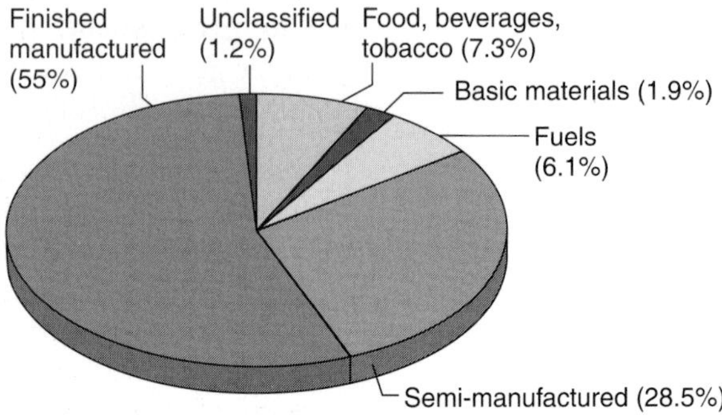

(d) Commodity type (%), 1995

UK visible trade

Historically, the UK has exported manufactured goods and imported mainly food and raw materials. Figures 13.2 and 13.3 show the structure of external visible trade in 1985 and 1995.

Fig. 13.3 UK imports, 1985 and 1995

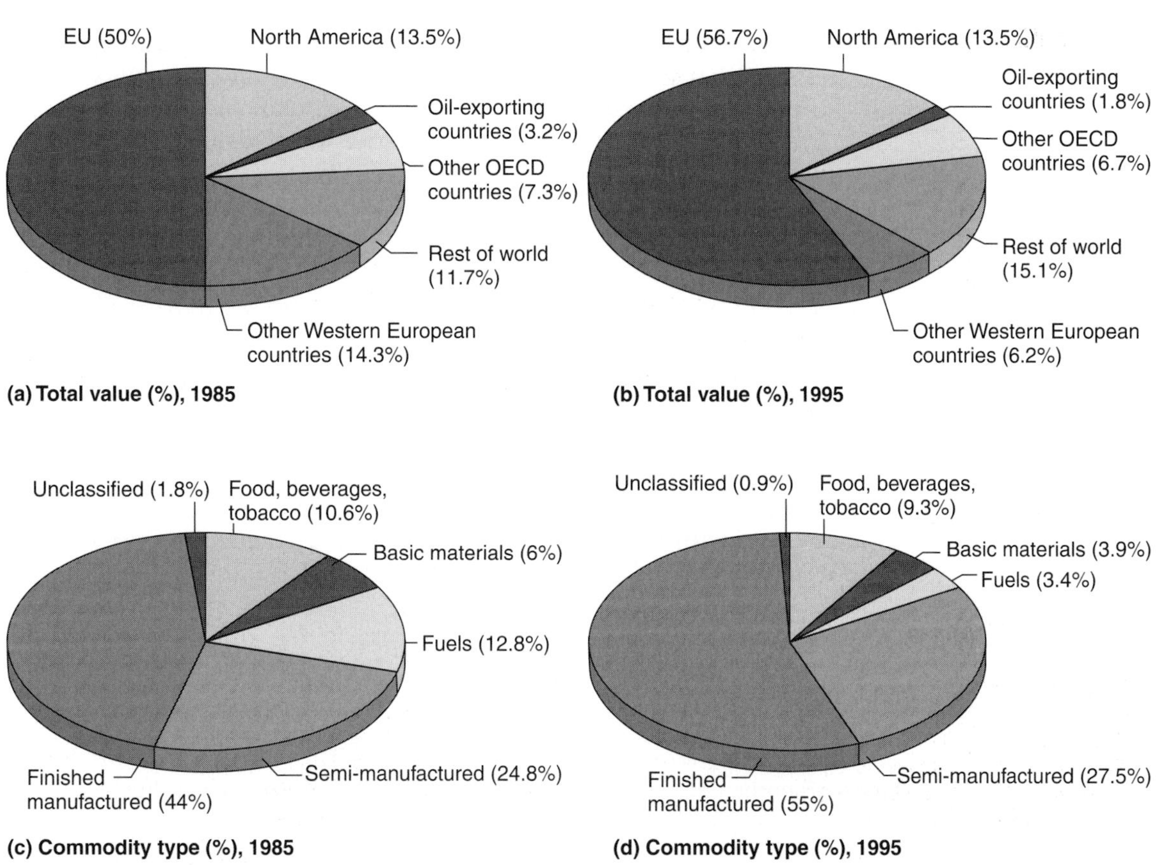

It is clear that the pattern of trade has changed. In 1985, 68.8 per cent of UK imports were manufactured or semi-manufactured goods, a figure that rose to 82.5 per cent in 1995. A number of factors may account for the changing pattern of trade:

- The UK is increasingly self-sufficient in agriculture.
- The demand for food does not increase in proportion to income. As incomes rise, we tend to buy about the same amount of food but devote extra expenditure to consumer durable goods (often imported) and services.
- Synthetic products have tended to replace basic raw materials.
- The development of North Sea oil has reduced the need for imported oil.
- One reason for the increase in semi-manufactured imports is the tendency of raw material producers to process those raw materials to some extent before exporting them. (This also accounts in part for the relative decline in the import of basic materials.)

UK exports continued to be dominated by manufactured and semi-manufactured goods. These actually showed an increase between 1985 and 1995 as a percentage of total exports. The following points should be noted, however:

- The structure of the UK economy has changed. There has been a severe shake-out in manufacturing. Many of the goods previously exported are no longer produced.
- Increasingly, other countries are turning to manufacturing. This is especially true in the Far East: the UK imports large amounts of textiles from Indonesia, and all kinds of sports equipment and footwear from South Korea and Taiwan. Audio-visual equipment is largely imported.
- It has at times been the case that the exchange rate of sterling has been too high, making exports uncompetitive and encouraging imports.

Geographically, UK trade is dominated by its links with Europe and industrialised countries elsewhere. This is not surprising given the changes that have occurred in the goods which are traded, and the increasing importance of the European Union in world trade. Since the goods that are traded are increasingly manufactured goods, the UK's trade is inevitably with manufacturing countries. By 1995, the EU accounted for 58.2 per cent of exports and 56.7 per cent of imports. Compared with these figures, North America accounted for just 13.4 per cent of exports and 13.5 per cent of imports.

The significance of the oil-exporting countries as both suppliers and importers has declined with the increase in UK off-shore oil, mainly from oil fields in the North Sea.

Something to do

- Food forms a substantial proportion of both UK imports and UK exports. Make notes giving reasons for this. Identify some foodstuffs that are imported and some that are exported. Why do you think this is so?

Correcting a balance-of-payments deficit

Taken as a whole, the balance of world trade – that is, the total imports and exports of all countries – must be equal. Some individual countries will have deficits, however, while others will have surpluses.

There are several reasons why a country might have a balance-of-payments deficit:

- Consumers in the country may prefer foreign-produced goods. For example, car buyers in the UK generally prefer foreign cars to British cars.
- Lack of competitiveness, for example on price or quality, may induce consumers to buy foreign imports. If buyers of television sets in the UK think that Japanese televisions are better quality and represent better value for money than televisions made by British companies, they will tend to buy the Japanese product. Such lack of competitiveness may, of course, be based on perceived rather than real differences.

- A decline in the comparative advantage of a country in producing certain goods may be brought about, for example, by improved technology and methods of production. This has affected much of British manufacturing over recent years.
- The exchange rate, or value of the home currency compared to other currencies, can be too high, so that foreign-produced goods are comparatively cheaper than home-produced goods. This situation was prevalent in the UK throughout much of the late 1990s, where a high value of the pound meant cheaper imports into the UK, while other countries had to pay more for UK-produced goods.
- There may be insufficient domestic productive capacity to meet domestic demand. This may be as a result of a preference for foreign goods, or for some other reason. There is now insufficient capacity for textile production in the UK, for example, to meet demand. This is largely due to cheaper imports of textiles from abroad.
- If a country is reliant on exporting an important commodity, fluctuations in the price of and demand for that commodity can have a strong effect on the country's balance of payments. As a net exporter of oil, the UK is particularly susceptible to fluctuations in the international price of oil.

There are several measures that a country facing a balance-of-payments deficit can take. These fall into two types:

1. **Expenditure-reducing policies** are designed to give consumers less income to spend on imports, thus reducing demand for imports. The two principal methods of reducing the incomes of consumers are
   - increasing income tax in order to reduce disposable income
   - raising interest rates to reduce demand.
2. **Expenditure-switching policies** are designed to encourage consumers to switch their demand away from imports towards home-produced goods. The principal way of doing this is to increase the price of imports in comparison with home-produced goods. Methods of encouraging expenditure switching are
   - introducing tariffs and other import controls (see page 392)
   - reducing inflation to a level below that of other countries (see pages 394–395)
   - reducing the costs of production of domestic firms, for example through subsidies (see page 391)
   - bringing about a **devaluation** or depreciation of the exchange rate thus making imports more expensive.

Paying for imports

Perhaps the most important difference between domestic trade and international trade is the intervention of foreign currency. Importers need to be able to change their domestic currency into that of the exporters or into some other currency acceptable to the authorities in the exporting country.

Assuming that the machinery exists to make the necessary currency available, there is the further problem of the rate of exchange.

While these matters are of concern to individual traders, the government itself may be concerned about the total amount received from overseas in relation to total payments.

Foreign exchange

International prices are made up of two elements: the domestic price of the goods and the exchange rate against foreign currencies. For example, if £1 exchanges for $1.5, goods exported from the UK with a domestic price of £100 will cost 100 × $1.50 = $150 in the USA. There are two ways of altering the price of the goods in the USA. If their cost of production in the UK was reduced to £90, they would sell for $135 in the USA; or if the exchange rate fell to £1 = $1.4, the price in the USA would fall from £150 to £140.

The international market for foreign currencies is enormous, with by far the largest foreign exchange (FOREX) market being in London. While some of the foreign currency traded is to pay for imports, there is also a significant amount of speculative investment that takes place, and this increases the volatility of the market. Fluctuations in exchange rates can be caused by several factors. Taking sterling as an example, these are:

- **demand for sterling** created by exports, investment in the UK by foreign investors, support of sterling by the Bank of England buying pounds, and speculation on the FOREX markets with investors buying sterling
- **supply of sterling**, which is influenced by the volume of imports, foreign investment by UK investors, foreign central banks supporting their own national currencies by selling sterling, and speculation on the FOREX markets with investors selling sterling
- the **balance of payments**, which, if UK exports are strong, will lead to a demand for sterling to pay for them
- **economic growth**, which can lead to a rise in the exchange rate, particularly when the growth is 'export-led'
- **interest rates**, which, when they are high, can attract foreign investment to UK banks and finance houses, driving up demand for sterling and causing a rise in the exchange rate
- **inflation**, which, if higher than in other countries, will lead to increasing prices and falling demand for exports. This may require a fall in the exchange rate to correct.

There are three principal ways in which attempts have been made to achieve stability of exchange rates:

- the **gold standard**, whereby exchange rates are rigidly fixed and adjustment comes about through expenditure-reducing policies
- **floating exchange rates**, whereby the exchange rates may vary from day to day and adjustment is achieved through expenditure switching
- **managed flexibility**, which is a compromise between the gold standard and fully floating exchange rates and allows for adjustments by means of both expenditure-reducing and expenditure-switching policies.

We examine each of these in turn, taking as our example the exchange rate between the British pound and the US dollar. The situation within the EU is considered on pages 413–421. However, the principles outlined in the following sections apply whether the currencies used for comparison are the British pound and the euro or the euro and other world currencies such as the US dollar or the Japanese yen.

The gold standard

Although it is now largely of only historical interest, the gold standard is important in illustrating the effects of sacrificing domestic economic balance to external balance. Under the gold standard, the balance of payments had to be given absolute priority over the domestic aims of full employment and economic growth – although these were not at the time regarded as the government's responsibility. Although there were many possible variations of the gold standard, each would have had to comply with the following rules:

- The monetary authorities of each country must fix the value of their domestic currency in terms of gold, and be prepared to exchange gold for notes at the fixed rate.
- No restrictions must be placed on the import or export of gold.
- The domestic money supply must be closely linked to the supply of gold, so that an increase in the supply of gold (because of a balance-of-payments surplus) results in a rise in the domestic money supply, while an outflow of gold leads to a reduction in the domestic money supply.

The implication of each monetary authority fixing the value of its own currency in terms of gold is that exchange rates between currencies become fixed within very narrow limits which are determined by the cost of shipping gold between the two countries. If the pound sterling is fixed at £1 = $\frac{4}{35}$ ounce of gold and the American dollar at \$1 = $\frac{1}{35}$ ounce of gold, then the exchange rate between the two currencies will be £1 = \$4. If it moved far from this, it would be worthwhile buying gold in one country and shipping it to another country. Thus the rate of exchange under the gold standard can be taken as being fixed.

If the exchange rate is fixed, adjustment to the balance of payments has to be achieved by altering the relative domestic price levels in the countries concerned. In the days when the gold standard operated, governments also always sought to balance their budgets, so this adjustment had to be achieved through monetary **deflation** in the case of deficit countries or inflation in the case of surplus countries.

Consider the process in the deficit country:

1. It suffers a loss of gold as it is shipped out to settle the deficit.
2. The loss of gold forces the authorities to cut back the supply of money in the economy. The extent to which the domestic money supply is reduced depends on the ratio that the authorities are required to maintain between the gold reserve and the note issue. If the ratio of gold to total note issue is thought adequate at 10 per cent, then a reduction in the gold reserves of £1000 leads to a fall in the note issue of £10 000. (This is achieved by means of open-market operations – see Unit 10.) Bank credit becomes more difficult to obtain, since the base for creating credit is reduced. As it is more difficult to acquire loans, the level of demand falls and with it the demand for imports – causing some improvement in the balance of payments.
3. This movement will be reinforced by the rise in interest rates which will have occurred owing to the reduction in the supply of money. Some consumers or entrepreneurs will postpone expenditure, and

there will also be a beneficial balance-of-payments effect of attracting money from abroad in search of higher interest rates.

4. The fall in the level of domestic demand will lead to a rise in unemployment (with the accompanying negative multiplier effects discussed in Unit 11). This will result in cuts in wages, lower costs of production and lower prices in the deficit country.
5. The outcome will be an increase in exports, since prices are now more competitive, and a fall in imports, since incomes have fallen. Together with the inflow of capital, this causes the balance of payments to improve.

This process is shown diagrammatically in Figure 13.4.

Ideally, the surplus country will have been implementing policies diametrically opposite to those outlined above (see Figure 13.5).

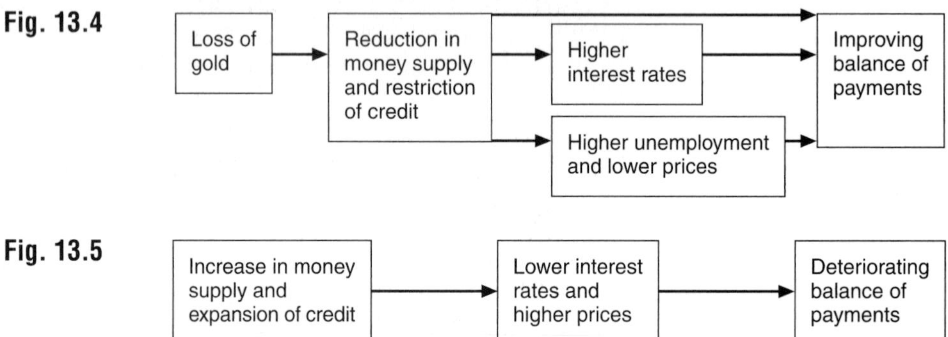

Fig. 13.4

Fig. 13.5

If both countries (or all countries) stuck to the rules of the system, the gold standard did provide an automatic means of adjustment to the balance of payments and did not allow deficits to become too large before corrective action was taken.

> ***Think about it***
>
> - Why do you think that gold was chosen as a standard against which the values of different currencies should be fixed?

Weaknesses of the gold standard

Despite the apparent smoothness with which the gold standard could operate, it was finally abandoned in 1931, having shown itself inadequate to meet the requirements of the international economy. The main weaknesses which had been revealed were as follows:

- There was no pressure on surplus countries to obey the rules. An inflow of gold could be frozen and not be allowed to swell the domestic money supply. After all, why should the economy be inflated specifically in order to create balance-of-payments troubles? But if surplus countries refused to inflate, the pressure on deficit countries became much greater: the whole burden of adjustment fell on them and necessitated massive domestic deflation, with consequent cuts in living standards and political and social difficulties as workers found themselves unemployed.

- Millions of units of output were lost merely to maintain an arbitrarily established exchange rate. Public opinion became gradually less tolerant of such an order of priorities.
- The smooth working of the system depended on wage costs being flexible in a downward direction. From the 1920s, the trade unions were less prepared to accept the cuts in wages necessary to secure a balance-of-payments surplus. Their resistance weakened the gold standard. Moreover, it was more difficult to cut prices since industry was becoming gradually more capital-intensive and consequently fixed costs formed a higher proportion of total costs. In many cases what was required to cut unit costs was an increase in output, not reductions.
- Ultimately it was the absolute rigidity of the exchange rate linked to gold – a metal almost irrelevant to economic welfare – and the changing order of political and social priorities that led to the abandonment of the system in 1931.

Something to do

- Explain to someone with no knowledge of economics how a balance-of-payments deficit can be eliminated under the gold standard.
- What were the weaknesses of the system?

When the gold standard was abandoned in 1931, it was replaced temporarily by a system of floating exchange rates – a regime to which the UK returned in the 1970s.

Floating exchange rates

While adjustment under the gold standard was achieved by policies designed to reduce expenditure in deficit countries and increase expenditure in surplus countries, a system of floating exchange rates would achieve adjustment by alterations in the exchange rate brought about by market forces and resulting in expenditure being switched towards the products of the deficit country.

Under such a system the price of one currency in terms of another would be determined by the forces of supply and demand for the two currencies, which in turn depend largely on the level of demand for each country's exports. Suppose that the UK and the USA have been trading in equilibrium at an exchange rate of $2 = £1 for some time. The implication is that British importers supply £1000 to the foreign exchange market to buy necessary dollars, and US importers supply $2000 to acquire sterling. If the currencies are supplied to the market in these proportions, then the rate of $2 = £1 will be maintained. What will happen if the market changes, however?

This is illustrated in Figure 13.6, where the original equilibrium of $2 = £1 is shown at the intersection of the original demand curve and the supply curve. For some reason the demand curve moves to the left from D to D' (perhaps Americans are buying goods from Germany or Japan instead of the UK). Now at $2 = £1 only £675 are demanded while £1000 are supplied. If, for some reason, the British government wanted to maintain the exchange rate at $2 = £1, it would have to purchase the surplus sterling, £325, by supplying $650 to UK importers. But it is more likely that the market will be left to make the adjustment: it will move to a new equilibrium at $1.75 = £1, with £750 being supplied and demanded. This means that Americans are supplying $1312.5 (£750 × 1.75$/£).

Fig. 13.6 The foreign-exchange rate

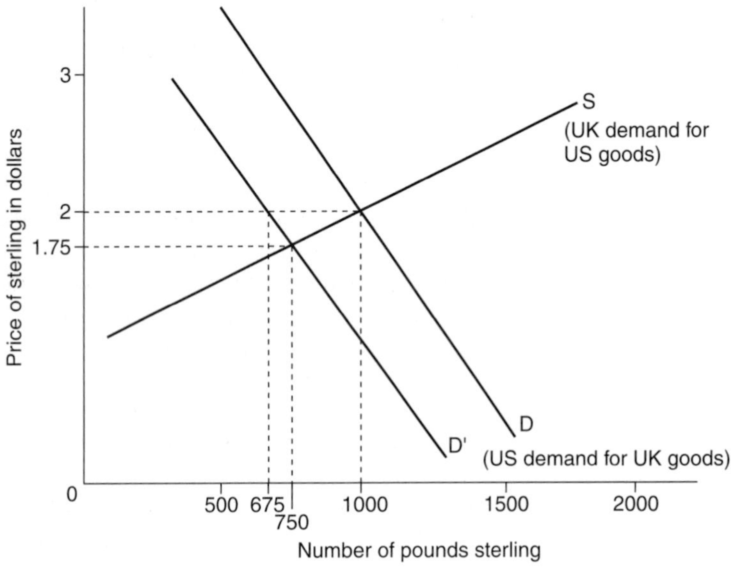

Two things have happened during the move from one equilibrium rate to the other:

- As the rate has fallen from $2 towards $1.75, importers in the UK have realised that American goods have become more expensive (because each pound buys fewer dollars) and some people have reduced their demand for imports, so the supply of sterling has been reduced.
- At the same time, British exports cost fewer dollars for the Americans, because each dollar purchases more pounds. There is an expansion in the demand for UK exports as a result.

Of course, starting from the original equilibrium point, either the demand curve or the supply curve could move in either direction, but the market will readjust following the principles outlined above.

An important implication of this is that the amount of foreign currency available is shared out, at a price, between those who are prepared to pay for it. This means that, under this system, the problem of a shortage of currency doesn't exist. In turn this means that the government does not *have* to make the balance of payments the priority in economic policy, since, if necessary, the market will make the necessary adjustment.

Thus, while the gold standard provided automatic adjustment through domestic economic policy, floating rates achieve that adjustment through the exchange rate. This seems an ideal arrangement. However, there may be problems.

Difficulties with floating exchange rates

- Floating exchange rates introduce an extra element of uncertainty into international trade. Suppose that a UK manufacturer invoices an American customer for £1000 when the exchange rate is $2 = £1, and that the customer pays with a draft for $2000. By the time the exporter receives the draft, the exchange rate may have altered to $2.50 = £1 and the exporter will then receive only £800 ($2000 ÷ 2.5$/£) when he converts it into sterling and so does not make his expected profit. If the exporter had insisted on payment of £1000 in sterling then the risks associated with an alteration to the exchange rate would be transferred to the American importer, for if on the day he wished to settle the account the rate had become $2.50 = £1 he would have to hand over $2500 rather than $2000 dollars to acquire £1000. If the rate moves, exporters or importers can make windfall gains.

  It is possible to insure against such fluctuations in the exchange rate by buying or selling the currency in advance, but this adds extra costs, which are likely to discourage some of those traders whose profit margins are small.
- The exchange rate is not the outcome only of trading activities. Assuming that the government does not intervene in the market, there are two other important influences:
  - Transactions in assets and liabilities (mainly capital items). People who wish to invest in foreign countries have to acquire the appropriate currency in the foreign-exchange market. Depending on the direction of the investment, either of the curves in Figure 13.6 may move – causing the exchange rate to alter if the investment is sufficiently high.
  - Speculators may bring about changes in the exchange rate. If £1 = $2 and sterling is expected to depreciate, speculators may sell £1000 today and buy $2000. If enough people do this the pound will depreciate to, say, $1.90. The speculators can then buy back £1000 for $1900, showing a profit of $100. Meanwhile the exchange rate has temporarily moved away from its equilibrium trading rate.
- If fluctuations in the exchange rate are to be kept within reasonable limits, the price elasticity of demand for imports and exports needs to be quite high. The adjustments in demand can then occur quite rapidly. If the price elasticity of demand is low, however, the exchange rate may have to alter considerably before it has a marked effect on the pattern of trade. This will be accompanied by large changes in domestic prices.
- Free exchange rates tend to be inflationary. As we have seen, one of the main reasons for controlling inflation is to prevent a heavy balance-of-payments deficit. Because the exchange rate itself rations the available currency, under free exchange rates, a deficit cannot occur and so a powerful incentive for inflation control is removed. Moreover, if imports rise more rapidly than exports, causing a depreciation in sterling, the price of imports rises – so giving additional impetus to inflation.

- Finally, and in some ways most important, the depreciation of the exchange rate of a deficit country causes the terms of trade to move against it as the price of its exports falls in international markets and the price of its imports rises. If the country is heavily dependent on imported raw materials, this will almost certainly lead to a new round of price increases, which will again lead to a reduction in the demand for its exports. This will then lead to a further depreciation of the exchange rate and the cycle will be repeated.

It is unlikely that the government will permit the exchange rate to be determined only by market forces. If it wants the pound to appreciate, it will instruct the Bank of England to buy pounds and sell foreign currency. To bring about a depreciation, the government will sell pounds.

In May 1997, the Chancellor of the Exchequer in the incoming Labour Government announced clear responsibilities for monetary policy. In particular, a Monetary Policy Committee (MPC) of the Bank of England now decides on short-term interest rates. The MPC meets monthly and its task is to set interest rates which it judges will meet the government's inflation target. Up until May 1997, the Bank of England advised the government as to what the interest rate should be, but it was the Chancellor of the Exchequer who decided whether or not to change the rate. By making the Bank of England independent in this way the temptation for governments to take political considerations into account when deciding on interest rates is removed (for example, who will benefit or suffer most from a change and how this might affect the popularity of the government). At the same time, it makes it less likely that the value of sterling will decide short-term interest rates, since it is the government's inflation target which has the greatest influence.

Think about it

- Why do you think governments are frequently unwilling to allow exchange rates to be determined solely by market forces?

Managed flexibility

This system was devised at the end of the Second World War as a compromise between the rigidity of the gold standard and the flexibility of the system of floating exchange rates. It was supervised by the International Monetary Fund (IMF), which had to deal with three distinct problems: exchange rates, international liquidity and convertible currencies.

Exchange rates

It was agreed that the value of the American dollar, the strongest currency at the end of the war, should be fixed at $\frac{1}{35}$ of an ounce of gold. The par (or declared) value of other currencies was then to be set in terms of the dollar. A small degree of flexibility was built in, as currencies were allowed to fluctuate within 1 per cent above or below their declared par value.

In the UK, the job of maintaining the rate within the permitted limits was entrusted to the exchange equalisation account (EEA), a department of the Bank of England. The EEA retained (and still retains) a stock of foreign currencies and sterling. When the price of sterling in the foreign-exchange market approached its ceiling (that is, its par value plus 1 per cent), because it was in heavy demand as overseas importers wanted to buy British goods, the EEA would announce its willingness to sell sterling at a price fractionally below the official ceiling. It thereby ensured that the price did not rise higher, for if the Bank of England would sell £1 at $2 no one would pay a higher price to someone else. When the price of sterling fell towards its lower limit (that is, its par value minus 1 per cent), the EEA would undertake to buy at a price fractionally above the official limit, thereby fixing the floor below which the price would not fall.

Changes in the par value itself were to be allowed only in cases of fundamental disequilibrium, which might be indicated by persistently large deficits or surpluses but which was not defined by the agreement.

The original post-war declaration of par values was a fairly arbitrary matter, with little relationship to economic realities. In consequence, the parity of the pound was declared at $4.03, a rate which made it virtually impossible for British exporters to compete with American producers and which led to devaluation in 1949 to $2.80, a rate which was maintained until 1967.

There are really two ways to establish the 'correct' exchange rate if one wants a fixed rate between two currencies:

- The first is known as the **purchasing power parity** theory. This says that the exchange rate should be such that if a given representative bundle of goods costs £1000 in the UK and $3000 in the USA, the exchange rate should be $3 = £1. If the prices subsequently rise by 10 per cent in the UK but are stable in the USA, the rate should alter to $2.72 = £1 ($3000 = £1100). In practice, this is subject to all the difficulties associated with the compilation of index numbers (see Unit 12, pages 376–377) – especially the problem of finding a representative bundle of goods.
- The second way of establishing the rate is much simpler: it is to allow market forces to operate freely for a few weeks or months in order to establish the equilibrium on the basis of which the new par value can be declared.

International liquidity – the role of the International Monetary Fund

As we have seen, with a system of floating exchange rates the need for currency reserves is minimised since available currency is allocated through the price mechanism. (In practice, some reserves are required to insure against sudden shortages of particular currencies.) If, however, rates are fixed within very narrow limits, the government of a deficit country will need to provide foreign currency to importers in that country to the extent of the deficit. It may be able to do this from currency acquired in the past, but if the deficit is large this may not be possible. The IMF was designed to help in this respect.

The Fund consists of a large pool of different currencies contributed by members and its principal function was originally to make those currencies available to members with temporary balance-of-payments problems.

The Fund's resources were often used not simply to finance trading deficits but also to fight off speculation against a currency – especially sterling – so maintaining exchange rate stability, which was a primary aim of the Fund. Periodically, the Fund had to make large sums of dollars available to the UK so that the government could buy the sterling that overseas holders, fearing a fall in its value, were anxious to dispose of.

The channelling of foreign currency through the Fund did not increase the amount of foreign exchange or liquidity available for the finance of international trade. It did, however, gather the money together so that it was more easily available, and it thereby obviated the need for deficit countries to try to borrow from the surplus countries.

The provision of currency to countries in difficulty arose directly from the IMF's determination to maintain stable exchange rates. If sterling was fixed at $2.80 but speculators thought it was worth only $2.20, they would sell sterling. The only way to prevent it falling towards $2.20 was for the EEA to buy sterling in large amounts. The only place to obtain such large amounts was from the IMF.

Convertible currencies

One further aspect of the Fund's work is in connection with convertible currencies. During the period 1931–45, a method used to safeguard the balance of payments was the imposition of limitations on the convertibility of a country's currency. Thus a government could impose a variety of exchange controls to prevent its residents buying goods abroad.

Just as GATT was established to secure the removal of tariffs and other commercial barriers to trade, one of the tasks of the IMF was to secure the full convertibility of currencies, since restrictions on convertibility are just as effective as are tariffs in distorting patterns of trade in one country's favour. The task was a difficult one, owing to the overwhelming trading superiority of the USA, and it was not until 1958 that sterling finally became fully convertible to foreign holders and not until 1979 that all controls on the use of sterling were removed.

The collapse of the managed flexibility system

The system operated from 1945 to 1973, though it was in a poor state from 1971. It had several weaknesses which related to exchange rates and international liquidity.

Exchange rates

The very name of the system – 'managed flexibility' – indicates that its founders intended exchange rates to be flexible, but flexible in a managed or orderly way. In practice, the exchange rates of the major trading nations – and especially of the USA and the UK – proved extraordinarily inflexible. The pound was devalued in 1949 and then again in 1967, but the dollar maintained its pre-war gold value until the end of 1971. Such rigidity was the fault of the users of the system rather than of its designers.

With economies growing at different rates – and especially prices inflating at different rates in different countries – alterations to exchange rates must occur if distortions to individual economies are to be avoided. Suppose that in 1949 the rate of \$2.80 = £1 was exactly right, in that goods produced in the UK for £100 could compete on level terms with similar American goods produced for \$280. If over the next ten years, UK prices doubled while those in the USA rose by only 50 per cent, the goods that could be traded on level terms in 1949 would now cost £200 to produce in the UK and \$420 in the USA. If British goods were now exported at that rate they would cost \$560 in the USA, while American goods would cost £150 in the UK. It is clearly very difficult for UK producers to compete if the exchange rate is fixed permanently at \$2.80 = £1. If the pound were devalued to \$2.10 = £1, however, the goods could again be traded on level terms.

Whether the devaluation is successful or not depends on the price elasticity of demand for exports and imports:

- Devaluation reduces the overseas price of British exports. Suppose goods cost £100 in the UK and the exchange rate is \$2.50 = £1; their price in the USA would then be \$250. If the pound is now devalued by 20 per cent to \$2.00 = £1, the price of the goods in the USA is now \$200. The UK's foreign-currency earnings will increase only if the USA's price elasticity of demand for the goods is greater than 1.
- Similarly, the price of American goods in the UK will rise following the devaluation of sterling, and expenditure will fall only if the price elasticity of demand in the UK is greater than 1. (The balance of trade will improve if the sum of the two elasticities is greater than 1.)

Because the IMF discouraged devaluations, when they did eventually occur they were large and perhaps destabilising.

International liquidity

A consequence of the refusal to devalue an obviously weak currency was that it gave rise to one-way speculation and put pressure on international liquidity. Enormous amounts of foreign currency had to be made available during 1963–67 to support sterling at an artificially high rate. Following the devaluation of sterling in 1967, doubts arose about the long-term viability of the managed flexibility system, dependent as it was on the dollar which by then was a relatively weak currency for two reasons:

- Other economies were much stronger than in the immediate post-war period and their currencies were therefore stronger.
- The USA had sustained a series of balance-of-payments deficits which were financed by the issue of paper dollars to creditor countries. It was this outflow of dollars that undermined confidence in the system.

The four kinds of international liquidity

1. **Gold** is historically the most important means of settling international debts, though its significance as a proportion of world liquidity has declined over recent years. As long as the system of managed flexibility continued, one way of increasing liquidity was to increase the price of gold (devalue the dollar), but this was resisted until the system was on the verge of collapse in 1971.
2. **Reserve currencies** The shortage of gold for monetary use and the reluctance to increase its price led to a greater dependence on reserve currencies as internationally liquid assets. For a number of historical reasons, countries became willing to accept payment in paper dollars or sterling on the understanding – but not with the guarantee – that they could be converted on demand into gold at a fixed rate of exchange. The success of such a system depends on the confidence of overseas holders of dollars and pounds that the issuing governments have sufficient liquid assets to pay on demand. If that confidence is lost, the system comes under great pressure.
3. **IMF drawing rights** are discussed (see pages 409–410) and we need only note here that, while the Fund has played an important part in channelling liquidity in the right directions, it is only in recent years that it has engineered the introduction of a new form of liquidity.
4. **Special drawing rights** The increasing reluctance of all countries to hold reserve currencies accelerated the introduction of special drawing rights (SDRs) as a new method of adding to the liquid reserves of IMF members. SDRs are book entries credited to members of the Fund. These credits are regarded by members as part of their reserves and they are transferable between governments. For example, if the UK has a balance-of-payments deficit with Canada, it may, with the approval of the Canadian Government, transfer SDRs from its account at the IMF to the Canadian account in exchange for Canadian dollars, which would then be placed in the foreign-exchange reserves of the UK. The dollars could then be placed at the disposal of people wishing to pay for their imports from Canada. The success of the scheme depends on the willingness of surplus countries to accept SDRs in exchange for currency. They have no obligation to accept further SDRs once their holding of them is equal to 300 per cent of their original allocation by the IMF.

   Originally the SDRs had a gold guarantee: now their value is determined by a weighted average of the five main trading currencies (dollar, sterling, Deutschmark, French franc and Japanese yen) and is expressed in dollars.

   SDRs may be used between governments to settle their mutual indebtedness, and they are used as a unit of account for some official transactions.

After 1967, confidence in paper dollars declined. Non-Americans holding dollars began to cash them in. American gold reserves came under pressure, and eventually the dollar was devalued in 1971. This meant that it was no longer worth $\frac{1}{35}$ ounce of gold, and that the world monetary system was sure to move towards greater flexibility.

The floating pound

Since the UK withdrew from the European exchange rate mechanism (ERM) in 1992, the pound has floated freely on the foreign exchange markets. This allows the value of the pound to be determined by the forces of demand and supply alone. There is no exchange rate target set by the government. This has meant that the value of the pound has risen making UK exports less competitive.

Something to do

- Make a list of the policies a government could pursue in order to prevent the floating pound from making UK exports less competitive.

The European Union

The European Union (EU) was first established as the European Economic Community (EEC) by the Treaty of Rome in 1957. At that time, the member states were France, Germany, Italy, Belgium, the Netherlands and Luxembourg. In 1973, the original members were joined by the UK, Denmark and Ireland. Greece joined in 1981, Portugal and Spain in 1986, and Austria, Finland and Sweden in 1995, to give the Union its present fifteen members. The total population of the EU is around 370 million. At the time of writing, there are proposals to expand the EU to include Poland, Hungary, the Czech Republic, Slovenia, Estonia and Cyprus. Other countries have submitted applications to join.

Aims of the EU

The main aim of the Union is to 'bring about lasting peace and prosperity for all its citizens'. To further the economic aspect of this aim, the EU established its macro-economic objectives through the Maastricht Treaty (1993):

> *'to promote throughout the community a harmonious, balanced and sustainable development of economic activities, a high level of employment and of social protection, equality between men and women, sustainable and non-inflationary growth, a high degree of competitiveness and convergence of economic performance, a high level of the quality of the environment, the raising of the standard of living and quality of life and economic and social cohesion and solidarity between member states.'*

There are four main areas of EU activity intended to achieve the overall goal of peace and prosperity for all citizens:

- the **single European market** (SEM)
- European social policy
- European monetary union (EMU)
- the European **common agricultural policy** (CAP).

We look at each of these in turn on pages 416–421.

Something to do

- How familiar are you with the structure and institutions in the EU? Read the following extract from an EC publication. Try to present the information diagrammatically.
- Find out more about EU institutions by visiting the website mentioned at the end of the extract.

How does the EU work?

Governing the EU

Like any government, the European Union is a system for making decisions and spending money on a joint rather than individual basis. The Member States of the Union nominate members of the Commission and judges to the Court of Justice. Representatives of each government sit in the Council of Ministers. Members of the European Parliament (MEPs) elected by the voters in each country sit in the European Parliament and a taxpayers' representative from each Member State sits in the Court of Auditors. Between them these five 'institutions' plus the European Council make, interpret and monitor the laws of the European Union.

The European Council

The European Council or summit consists of the Heads of State or Government of each Member State, who usually meet twice a year to give overall direction to the EU's programme.

Under the treaties Europe is managed by five different institutions:

The European Commission

The European Commission is made up of 20 Commissioners appointed by the national governments of each Member State. There are two Commissioners from each of the larger countries and one from each of the smaller ones. Each Commissioner is responsible for a particular area of Community policy. For example, one Commissioner from a larger country may be responsible for common commercial policy and external relations with North America, Australasia and the Far East, and the other for transport. Each policy area has a Director-General and staff to carry out and oversee the implementation of that policy. The Commission proposes new laws, manages common EU policies to make sure they run smoothly, and acts as guardian of the treaties setting up the Union, by making sure that the Member States implement their decisions effectively. The European Commission is based in Brussels, and is organised into 25 Directorates-General, dealing with all policy areas from agriculture to overseas development.

The Council of Ministers

The Council of Ministers, comprising government ministers from each Member State, discusses the proposals put forward by the European Commission and ensures that national interests are represented. This Council then decides what form these proposals should take, amends the proposals if necessary and decides whether or not the proposals should become law. The Council is based in Brussels, and the presidency changes every six months, for example, July to December 1997 Luxembourg; January to June 1998 UK; July to December 1998 Austria; January to June 1999 Germany; July to December 1999 Finland; January to June 2000 Portugal; July to December 2000 France.

The European Parliament

The European Parliament consists of 626 MEPs democratically elected from each Member State. There are 87 MEPs from the United Kingdom. If you are not sure who your MEP is, you can find out by looking in the telephone directory or phoning your local council offices. An election is held every five years; [the most recent European elections were held in June 1999.] Parliament meets in Strasbourg for one week every month in plenary session.

Its 20 specialist committees meet in Brussels and some additional plenary sessions are also held there.

MEPs sit in multinational political groups. The Party of European Socialists includes the UK's Labour

MEPs; the European People's Party includes British Conservatives. British Liberal Democrats sit in the European Liberal, Democratic and Reformist Group and Scottish Nationalist MEPs sit in the European Radical Alliance.

MEPs are consulted on proposals from the European Commission, give their opinion, suggest amendments and in some cases jointly decide legislation with the Council of Ministers. They are their constituents' voice in Europe.

The European Court of Justice

The European Court of Justice decides whether actions taken within the EU are against European law. The Court sits in Luxembourg, and there is one judge from each Member State. A proportion of these judges is replaced every three years.

The Court of Auditors

The Court of Auditors, on behalf of taxpaying citizens, monitors all financial transactions in the EU. It is the Court's job to guarantee that certain moral, administrative and accounting principles are respected, and to make sure the European Union's money is actually used for the purposes for which it is intended. The Court also publishes reports on the financial management of the EU.

There are various procedures for passing laws, each involving the European Commission, the Council of Ministers and the European Parliament in the process. The process always starts with a formal proposal or draft directive from the Commission; this may be at the request of a Member State government, the Council of Ministers, the European Parliament, industry or at the Commission's own initiative. It must, however, be related to an area covered by the treaties. This is then scrutinised in detail in one of the European Parliament's 20 specialist committees and debated in plenary session before the Council of Ministers votes on the amended proposal. Sometimes proposals have a second reading in the European Parliament and in a limited number of cases Parliament and Council decide jointly on a proposal. When there are disagreements over the interpretation of European Union laws, between a Member State, a company, or an individual and the institutions, the European Court of Justice in Luxembourg may be called on to adjudicate. If an individual citizen feels his or her rights have been infringed through maladministration by the institutions, they can take their case to an Ombudsman, elected by the European Parliament.

The all-important European Union rules are made not by bureaucrats but by our own and other Member States' national ministers, who are appointed to sit on the Council of Ministers. They have the final say about whether or not something should become EU law.

To find out more:
Ask in your school/college or public library if they have: Bainbridge, T. and Teasdale, A., *The Penguin Companion to the European Union*; and European Commission publications about the European Union institutions.
Contact your local MEP's office or European resource centre and ask for information about the European Parliament and the institutions of the EU.
Look at EU institutions on the Internet at http://europea.eu.int/inst-en.htm

Source: 'The European Union – a guide for students and teachers', pp. 16–19 (Office for Official Publications of the European Commission)

The single European market

The **single European market** (SEM) was established in 1992, but is still developing especially in respect to European monetary union, which is an essential and integral part of harmonisation of the market. It is both a customs union and a free-trade area, the aim of which is to encourage economic growth and employment within the Union. Essential to the SEM is the free movement of goods, services, capital and labour between member states, and common external tariffs on goods coming into the EU.

Reduced formalities for goods crossing frontiers between member states have resulted in lower costs and increased competition. This has brought about benefits to consumers in terms of lower prices and increased efficiency. The single market rivals the US in terms of numbers of consumers, and this has led to the development of large Pan-European multinationals that can benefit from economies of scale. Large US and Japanese companies are also setting up production and distribution facilities in the EU – many of them in the UK – in order to have a foothold in the single European market.

Just as UK competition policy has sought to ensure that the domestic economy maximises the benefits it can achieve from a market economy, so the EU has established similar policies to ensure the same for the European market.

The EU seeks to harmonise customer laws amongst member states and prohibits all agreements and practices which may inhibit trade between member states. The aim is a level playing field for all buyers and sellers. Thus, attempts by national governments to subsidise a firm will usually be prevented by EU law because of the unfair advantage it has gained over other European firms in the market.

Opening up the movement of labour between member states has shown less marked benefits. The mobility of labour, especially between countries, is limited, and the formation of Pan-European companies has led to some job losses. In 1997, however, the Monti Report found that between 300 000 and 900 000 jobs had been created within the single European market since 1992.

Think about it

- What opportunities and threats does the establishment of the single European market hold for a small manufacturing company in the UK?

European social policy

European social policy is an area of increasing EU activity, although it is one that the UK views with suspicion, arguing that it imposes unacceptable costs on British industry that make them uncompetitive in Europe.

In 1993, the Conservative Prime Minister negotiated the UK's opt-out from the Social Chapter of the Maastricht Treaty, arguing that the flexibility of the UK labour market would be harmed and that increased power for trade unions would lead to higher costs for business which would in turn lead to increased unemployment.

The Social Chapter covers

- the rights of workers within the EU
- equal rights for employees, including fair pay
- improvements to working conditions, including hours
- the right to training
- social security provision for those on low incomes or unemployed
- freedom of association with the right to collective bargaining
- health and safety at work
- the provision of employment opportunities for young people, disabled people and those over compulsory retirement age.

In 1997, the new Labour Prime Minister, Tony Blair, signed up to the Social Chapter, with the provision that no new EU laws should damage the competitiveness of British firms.

Think about it

- Why do you think that John Major, as Prime Minister, thought that signing up to the Social Chapter would make British firms uncompetitive? Do you think he was right? Justify your answers.

In addition to the Social Chapter, a European social fund (ESF) was set up in 1993 with the aim of funding projects aimed at improving employment and social conditions in areas designated as being of special economic need, where GDP is less than 75 per cent of the EU average. The European social fund takes around 10 per cent of the total EU budget. The UK is a major receiver of funds from the ESF.

European monetary union (EMU)

European monetary union (EMU) is designed to harmonise the economies of EU member states through the adoption of a single currency (the euro), one interest rate set by a European Central Bank, and eventually other measures such as common rates of tax. EMU is part of a move towards greater political integration in the EU.

The euro was launched as a single European currency on 1 January 1999, when eleven of the fifteen EU member states adopted it. Denmark, the UK and Sweden opted out of the currency and Greece failed to meet the criteria of economic stability that had been set. At the time of writing, countries that have adopted the euro are continuing to use their own currencies, but the exchange rates for those currencies have been 'irretrievably and irrevocably' fixed.

Most countries have adopted a system of 'dual pricing', where prices of goods and services are shown in the currency of the country and in euros, until the national currencies of all those countries that have adopted the euro are withdrawn in 2002.

In 1999, with the UK opted out of the euro, the Prime Minister declared that there must be a referendum about whether to join. However, in or out, the euro has important implications for the UK:

- British firms trading with the EU will be forced to deal in euros.
- A volatile exchange rate of the pound against the euro may adversely affect Britain's trade in Europe.
- London's position as the leading foreign exchange market could be threatened by euro capitals such as Paris or Frankfurt.
- The transparency of prices throughout Europe may lead to some British firms having to change their pricing strategies.
- Foreign investors may favour countries using the euro rather than the UK.

Should Britain join the euro?

Arguments in favour	Arguments against
• The removal of exchange rate uncertainties must benefit UK firms.	• Currency unions have collapsed in the past.
• Joining the single currency for Europe will bring an end to currency transaction costs for UK exporters and tourists (and for non-UK European exporters and tourists selling and travelling to the UK).	• Without full economic integration between countries adopting the euro, interest rates may be set at too high a rate in order to reduce inflation in one member state, thereby damaging the economy of others.
• This may lead to an increase in trade within the euro area.	• Britain would lose her right to devalue sterling in order to restore international competitiveness.
• Unless it adopts the euro, Britain could lose out on some benefits to be obtained from EU membership.	• Some of the stronger EU economies, such as France and Germany, may try to dominate EU economic policy.
• 'Transparency': trade with EU countries will not require the comparison of different exchange rates, making informed choice of customer or supplier easier.	• The Euro may weaken against other world currencies.
• A single currency may facilitate the movement of factors of production to areas where they will be used most efficiently.	• Because of language and cultural differences, labour will not move easily from one area to another.
	• The UK chancellor will lose more control over economic policy to the European Bank.

The Labour Chancellor of the Exchequer, Gordon Brown, suggested five economic tests before a decision should be taken on Britain joining the euro. These are as follows:

- Britain should achieve sustainable economic convergence with other countries that have adopted the euro.
- Britain's economy should show a sufficient level of flexibility.
- It must be established that adopting the euro will lead to better long-term decision-making.
- There must be no adverse effects on financial services.
- Adopting the euro must benefit employment.

Ultimately, the success of the euro will be judged on criteria such as:

- Has it led to lower long-term inflation and interest rates?
- Has it encouraged sustainable economic growth throughout the area of its adoption?
- Has it helped to reduce unemployment and improve living standards in member states?
- Has it led to closer economic, political and social integration?

Something to do

- Research the performance of the economies of those members of the European Union that have adopted the euro. Basing your answer on the criteria for the success of the euro outlined above, do you think the common European currency is proving to be a success? Justify your conclusions.

The European Central Bank

The European Central Bank is an essential ingredient of European monetary union. Based in Frankfurt, under the presidency of Wim Duisenberg, its main aim is price stability throughout the area covered by the euro. It has set a target of a 2-per-cent year-on-year increase in the 'harmonised index of consumer prices' – the EU equivalent of the retail price index. Like the Monetary Policy Committee of the Bank of England, the Council of the European Central Bank meets monthly to set interest rates. Council votes are split between the countries that have adopted the euro on the basis of a simple majority vote. Unlike the Bank of England's MPC, however, the European Central Bank will not publish the minutes of its meetings, or its inflation forecasts. The national central banks of euro countries are now agencies of the European Central Bank.

The European Community budget

The 1997 budget of the European Community is ECU ([1]) 82.365 billion ([2]).

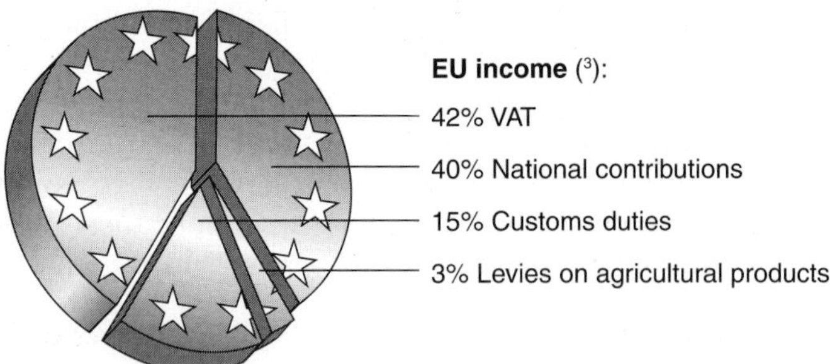

Where does the money come from?

As you can see the most important source of income is from VAT. Each member has to pass on the equivalent of a 1.4% VAT rate to the Community budget. For example, if the UK charges a VAT rate of 17.5%, that means approximately 16.1% goes to the UK budget and 1.4% to the Community budget.

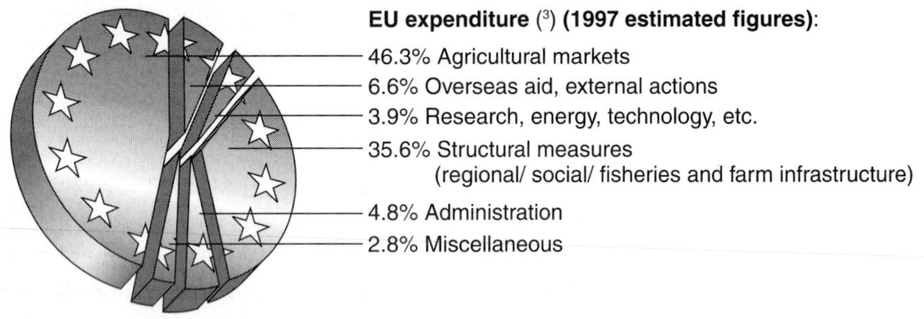

Where does the money go?

The UK and Germany are termed 'net contributors' to the EU budget, because they put in more money than they take out.

Some countries, like Ireland, Greece and Portugal, receive large grants but are not able to give so much, and often receive more in financial terms than they contribute.

([1]) ECU 1 = GBP 0.732974 (at exchange rate in February 1996).

([2]) *The European Union and its citizens: questions and answers.* Available from http://europa.eu.int/en/comm/dg10/qa/qa.html

([3]) *General budget of the European Union for the financial year 1997: the figures.* Office for Official Publications of the European Communities, 1997, Brussels.

Source: 'The European Union – a guide for students and teachers', p. 22 (Office of the European Parliament and the Representation of the European Commission in the United Kingdom; London, 1998)

The European common agricultural policy

The common agricultural policy (CAP) is one of the longest-standing policies of the European Union, and one that over the years has been open to abuse and often become synonymous with butter and grain mountains, wine lakes and the green pound (where subsidies mean that a £1 sale is worth more to a farmer than it is to an industrialist).

When the EEC was formed in 1957, over 20 per cent of its working population was employed in agriculture, and each of the six members had its own protective policy, some of which conflicted with each other. To ensure fair trade in agriculture, it was necessary to formulate a new policy. While there are variations for different commodities such as beef and grain, the policy generally operates as follows:

- The EU farming ministers establish a target price for a commodity designed to give producers a fair return on their investment.
- They establish an intervention price well below the target price at which the EU will purchase surplus output.
- They establish a threshold price. This is used as a base price for assessing the levies (taxes) imposed on food imported from outside the EU to ensure that its price does not undercut EU producers.

In general, the guaranteed prices have been high enough to result in surplus production that has to be purchased by the Agricultural Fund, stored (a notoriously expensive process) and eventually sold, usually overseas at low prices.

Criticisms of the CAP

The policy has attracted criticism on a number of grounds:

- The excess production implies a waste of economic resources.
- Prices are artificially high. In effect, consumers and taxpayers subsidise farmers.
- The overseas sale of surplus output means that the EU subsidises foreign governments and consumers.
- More important is the effect of the policy on other producers. First the EU imposes levies on imported produce, so reducing the demand for the produce of overseas farmers, even though they may be more efficient. Then surplus output is sold cheaply overseas, thus depriving other producers of sales in third markets. This highlights one of the general effects of the single European market – and indeed of tariffs in general – that of **trade creation** and **trade diversion.** Trade is 'created' behind the tariff barrier as consumers are encouraged to buy home-produced goods. At the same time, trade is diverted from its normal channels as overseas producers lose their traditional markets. In assessing the growth in output and trade within the single European market, these losses elsewhere must be considered.
- The CAP currently consumes almost 50 per cent of the total EU budget – when less than 6 per cent of the EU workforce is now employed in agriculture – leaving insufficient funds for other policies.

Achievements of the CAP

Despite the above criticisms, we should remember the achievements of the CAP:

- The EU has become largely self-sufficient in those products that can be grown in Europe. This was one of the objectives of the CAP.
- Agricultural efficiency has increased significantly. The Agricultural Fund is used not only for supporting prices but also to encourage extra productivity through improved technology and agricultural methods.

Reform of the CAP

There is widespread recognition that the system needs reform. In March 1999, the EU farming minister agreed new measures, including

- a 20 per cent staged reduction in the intervention price for beef up to 2002, with the introduction of a private storage aid scheme. In 2002, there will be increased subsidies for bulls (£105 per head) and steers (£147 per head), with regional ceilings on the number of animals eligible
- a 15 per cent cut in intervention prices for butter and skimmed-milk powder
- a 20 per cent reduction in the intervention price for cereals by 2002.

Globalisation

One of the most important developments in business and economics towards the end of the twentieth century has been the trend towards **globalisation** and internationalisation. In Unit 4, we looked at the way in which firms grow and become multinational organisations, with production facilities in several countries. The term 'internationalisation' is used to describe the increasing involvement of large firms in activities that cross national boundaries.

Globalisation, on the other hand, refers to the process whereby large firms actively seek to produce and market their products on an international basis, without adapting to the conditions that prevail in any particular country. This approach to international production and marketing is based on the belief that as the world is developing economically it is becoming more homogeneous so that individual variations in national markets are disappearing.

It has long been the subject of jokes, particularly among business travellers, that the hotels of international chains such as Hilton International or Holiday Inn are so similar that when you are staying in one you don't know whether you are in London, Istanbul or Kuwait. However, globalisation and the provision of one product in all national markets is by no means restricted to hotels. Car manufacturers, such as Ford or Renault, produce and market the same models throughout the world. McDonald's sell the same Big Mac in Birmingham as they do in Paris and Moscow, although recent protests by French farmers have resulted in Roquefort Burgers being put on the menu in their French restaurants.

This trend towards globalisation has affected the nature of international competition. It has also had a profound effect on the global balance of economic power. While the strategies of General Motors and Coca-Cola have little overall impact on the economies of major industrialised nations such as the USA and Japan, or on influential trading groups such as the European Union, such companies have turnovers that dwarf the economies of less developed countries such as Chad or Nigeria. The decision to establish a base in one of these countries can therefore have a great influence on the economic policies of the country, particularly in areas such as business taxes, employment and interest rates. Even a major economy like the UK is prepared to offer significant incentives to persuade companies such as Nissan to build a new plant in the home country rather than in France or Germany.

The globalisation of business has been facilitated by developments in technology and in particular information technology which allow the implementation of processes and policies to be applied throughout the world. The growth of trading groups such as the European Union and the North American Free Trade Agreement (NAFTA), and the easing of barriers to international trade through the General Agreement on Tariffs and Trade, have also meant that business could develop on a global scale, taking advantages of the global market and benefiting from economies of scale.

The impact on labour has been less impressive. Global firms often base their productive facilities where labour is cheap, using their economic strength to keep wages low. For many firms the process of globalisation has meant merging with firms in other countries. This has often led to the duplication of jobs, with resulting redundancies. Employees in key positions sometimes find themselves having to travel frequently between operating sites in different countries, with the associated stress and lack of time to spend with their families.

External shocks and the global economy

Why is it that events in one country can have such a major impact in so many countries? Let us look at why a big fall of share prices on the Tokyo Stock Exchange is likely to have such an impact around the world.

The immediate impact of the fall in share prices is that a large number of Japanese investors suddenly become less wealthy. Why does the impact not end here? First of all, a fall in Tokyo share prices indicates that the financial value of Japanese companies has fallen significantly. If the companies are not valued so highly, they will find it much more difficult to find the funds for planned capital investment and expansion because they have less **collateral** to offer. In fact, the opposite is likely to be true and they will be forced to contract. However, because the ownership and control of Japanese companies are not restricted to locations in Japan, the contraction and failure to go ahead with planned capital investment is likely to affect many other countries, including the UK. This will have implications for employment in those countries, both because of the contraction of Japanese controlled companies and the withdrawal of orders for capital goods.

At the same time, the fall in share prices is unlikely to be limited to the Tokyo Stock Exchange. Shareholders around the world will be influenced by the falls. Why are Japanese shareholders selling such vast quantities of shares while very few wish to buy? Shareholders begin to wonder whether it is because of recession, poor management, growing competition or some other reason. Given that Japan is an important trading market for other countries, then the fears underlying the Japanese market must surely apply to other countries too. Therefore, shareholders elsewhere are likely to consider that it may be time to sell shares and, before long, falls on other stock markets occur. The impact on American, Asian and European companies of major falls in their paper value is likely to be similar to that described above for their Japanese counterparts. Therefore, a further impact on employment and investment, both domestically and internationally, could result.

All of these impacts can be traced to the internationalisation and globalisation of so many markets.

Think about it

- What do you consider would be the impact on the UK and the rest of the world if:
  - a major war broke out in the Middle East
  - China announced it was closing all trade links with the rest of the world
  - the United States responded to a large fall in the exchange value of the dollar by doubling interest rates?

Unemployment and inflation worldwide

Table 13.12 shows unemployment and inflation rates for the UK and a number of other countries.

Table 13.12

Country	Unemployment rate (%) 1995	Inflation rate (%) 1995
Argentina	0.5	18.8
Australia	0.3	8.5
Brazil	6.9	6.2
China	2.8	2.8
France	1.2	11.6
Japan	1.7	3.2
Mexico	20.6	4.7
Poland	15.9	13.1
Spain	2.0	22.9
UK	3.1	8.2
USA	2.3	4.5

Source: The Stationery Office 1999

The difference between the countries is quite marked. Should the UK be concerned about the rates in other countries? Due to internationalisation and globalisation, the answer is increasingly 'yes'.

Rising unemployment in, for example, the US, could lead to other countries finding it more difficult to sell their products because of falling incomes amongst a large number of potential customers. At the same time, the US government may introduce measures to protect its domestic producers from foreign competition and in this way stop unemployment from becoming worse. Many US companies are likely to suffer from falling incomes and profits because of the difficulties they have in selling within their own country. If those profits are a source of finance for developing their overseas plants, then capital investment through US-owned multinationals in the UK and elsewhere will suffer.

A similar analysis can be undertaken with regard to, for example, rising or falling inflation in Japan. Conclusions can then be drawn about the impact on trade, exchange rates, investment and other variables, within and between Japan and the UK. Of course, different countries will be at different stages in their economic cycles and the net result in the UK will depend on the relative importance of the different countries within the international economy and the policies followed in each country to change the inflation or unemployment rates.

The tigers that changed their stripes

The countries of South-East Asia are home to some 500 million people and have a combined GDP of more than $700 billion. Their largely young populations, with large numbers of well-educated and hard-working people, helped to make the region one of the fastest-growing in the world. No one believed that the boom could stop. When it did, the region's self-confidence was shattered. As the value of South-East Asian currencies tumbled, foreigners and locals alike tried to pull their money out, causing fragile financial systems to collapse. Far from being a little local difficulty – a 'few small glitches along the road' as President Clinton initially described it – the trouble spread well beyond South-East Asia, to Russia and the Americas.

In the end the bust proved to be overhyped, just like the boom before it. Last year the region staged a sharp recovery, with an average growth of about 3.4 per cent. But it's not quite business as usual. The crisis, says Mr Goh, Singapore's Prime Minister, has produced 'four positive outcomes': it has speeded up the opening of economies; forced Asians to be more aware of good corporate governance; made the region concentrate on its real competitive strengths; and provided a hard lesson about globalisation.

Source: Adapted from *The Economist,* 17 February 2000

Think about it

- Read the extract 'The tigers that changed their stripes'. (For more on the so-called 'Tiger economies', see also Unit 14 pages 441–442)
- Why and how do you think that Russia and the Americas were affected by the end of the boom in the so-called Tiger economies?
- What hard lessons might the Tiger economies have learned about globalisation?

14 Economic growth and development

Introduction: the objectives of growth

Economic growth is often put forward as something that is in itself desirable, but those who advocate the pursuit of growth actually do so because they perceive a need for the production of more goods and services. We can all think of important areas of shortage:

- deficiencies in the health and education services which could be eliminated if more resources were committed to them
- accommodation for the homeless
- more roads and improved public transport to ease traffic congestion, facilitate travel and improve communication and distribution links.

These and other deficiencies, it is suggested, could be reduced if growth in terms of increased productivity occurred. This is true. They could also be reduced if existing resources were used differently, however. If as a community we spent less on cigarettes, or computer games, or holidays, we could pay for more hospital equipment to be produced. But there is no guarantee that we would.

What people are looking for from economic growth tends to be 'a higher standard of living'. To many individuals, that might be more obvious in the form of a new computer game or more expensive holiday than in the form of a new scanner in a hospital that is of no immediate benefit to themselves.

We begin the unit with an attempt to define economic growth, and take a brief look at how it is measured. We then examine the effects of growth on the standard of living, and the increasing need to balance economic growth with sustainability. This is followed by a look at the sources of economic growth, both short term and long term.

The next main section of the unit focuses on growth and development trends in specific economies: the UK, countries in Central and Eastern Europe, and countries in South-East Asia. This is followed by a look at the problems of growth in developing countries and the policies that have been followed to help mitigate them.

Finally, we return to the concept of sustainable development, this time in the context of globalisation and the problems of overconsumption.

What is economic growth?

Economic growth is often held up as an objective of modern society and a goal of politics. But what exactly do we mean when we talk about 'economic growth'? There is no single definition of, or way of measuring, economic growth, and the drive for economic growth can often lead to problems in other areas, such as employment, the environment or social conditions.

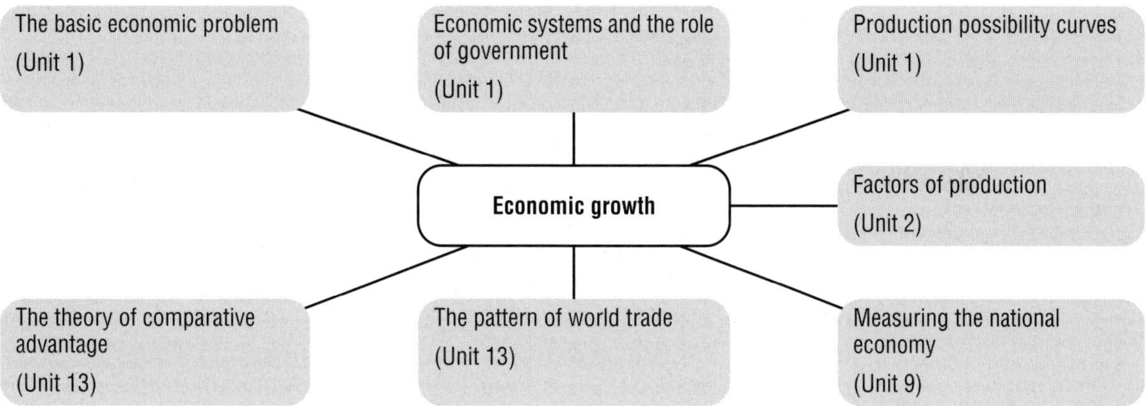

The term 'economic growth' is used in two senses: short term and long term.

- **Short-term growth:** Any increase in the total output of the economy from one year to another is often regarded as evidence of growth. Leaving aside the fact that we need a satisfactory means of measuring such changes, this represents a narrow view of growth.

  In Figure 14.1, growth might be reflected in the move from X to Y between year 1 and year 2. But the output represented by Y (year 2) could have been produced in year 1. It wasn't produced then because for some reason resources were under-employed: this might have been the result of a lack of demand or simply poor organisation. Whatever the reason, the move from X to Y is not the best indicator of economic growth.

Fig. 14.1 Changes in production possibilities

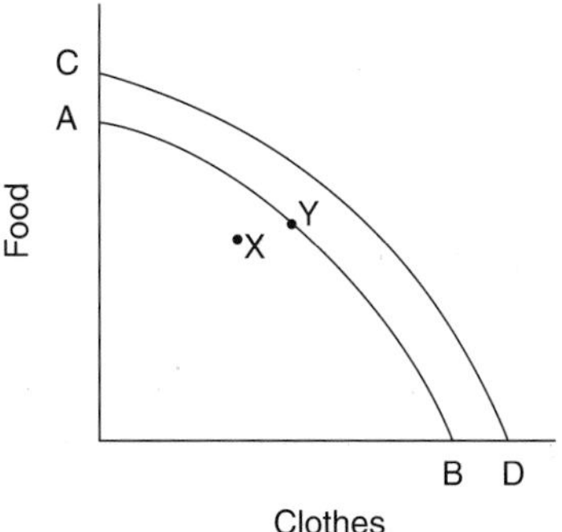

- **Long-term growth:** Because an increase in GDP (a frequently used measure of growth) may occur over a period of two or three years in the manner described above, it is preferable to take a longer view. Then we can measure growth by the increase in the real GDP over a period of perhaps twenty years. This would show the underlying trend – annual fluctuations then becoming less significant.

  Taking a view over a long period itself brings problems (it is important to compare two years in which the level of unemployment, for example, is about the same), but it is more likely to show changes in the *capacity* of the economy to produce goods and services. This is what is meant by growth in this sense. It would be indicated by a move of the production possibility curve to the right – from AB to CD in Figure 14.1.

Measuring growth

The only really convenient method of measuring economic growth is to use national income statistics. It is true that we are trying to assess the underlying capacity of the economy, but it would be confusing to produce an inventory of the supply of factors of production. So when we are measuring the growth of the UK economy we have to concentrate on what is produced in the UK – and it is better to use GDP rather than GNP (see Unit 9). Table 14.1 shows how GDP at constant factor cost has changed over a relatively short period. Values are given at constant prices (in this case 1995 prices) to eliminate the effects of inflation.

Table 14.1

	GDP at market prices (£bn at 1995 prices)
1988	640.6
1989	654.3
1990	658.3
1991	648.6
1992	649
1993	664
1994	693
1995	712.5
1996	730.8
1997	756.1

Something to do

While using GDP figures is a convenient way of measuring economic growth in a country, it cannot be used to measure some factors that might be considered essential elements of any real development in a country's well-being.

- Make a list of any factors you can think of that GDP does not measure.
- Can you think of any statistics that *can* be used to measure those factors?

Economic growth and the standard of living

We have seen that economic growth is measured by changes in the real domestic product. Generally, an increase in the real GDP is taken to indicate an improvement in the standard of living. (We could debate for some time what is meant by 'standard of living', but let us accept for now that a general increase in the availability of goods and services is indicative of an improvement in the standard of living.) If we know that the economy has shown an increase of, say, 3 per cent per year in the real GDP, what considerations need to be taken into account before concluding that there has been a similar increase in living standards?

- The size of the population may increase more rapidly than the domestic product. In this case, GDP per person (per capita GDP) will fall and with it, perhaps, living standards. This is not a problem in the industrial economies, but rapid population growth is an important reason for low living standards in less developed countries.
- What is produced? If most of the extra output consists of plant and machinery, or defence items, it may have little effect on the standard of living, which is more directly affected by the availability of consumer goods. Even if the extra output is mainly in the form of consumer goods, the impact on the standard of living will depend on what consumer goods are produced: extra cigarettes may have a different effect from extra food. Indeed, extra cigarettes may have a perverse effect: not only will their production be recorded as an increase in GDP, but their consumption may lead in future to the employment of more doctors and nurses, recorded as another rise in GDP.
- Do we know that the increase in incomes is shared out fairly? Given that monopoly forces are at work in factor markets, it is unlikely that it will be. If the 3 per cent rise in GDP each year benefits mainly rich people, it is unlikely that the general standard of living will have increased.
- National income statistics record all the goods and services produced. In a sense they could be said to record the benefits of economic activity. If they were to adopt a more neutral stance, they might allow for some of the costs or **disutilities** of economic growth. More motor vehicles mean more pollution of the atmosphere, more serious injuries, more fatalities. These are not easily quantifiable in financial terms, but they need to be considered if we want to make a proper assessment of the change in the standard of living. Some increases in output may have such disadvantages for some citizens as to have a negative effect on the standard of living: the building of an airport or a nuclear power station might come into this category.
- Sometimes the rise in output may be achieved only at the cost of people surrendering more leisure time. This reminds us that the standard of living is not just a matter of the goods produced or the money received: rather it is a matter of the quality of life. It is when economic growth is achieved at the expense of the quality of life that it provokes objections and raises questions. The following examples serve to illustrate this:

- Aerosol cans are a great convenience in many households and could be regarded as improving the standard of living. However, it has become clear that the propellant used in some of them has undesirable effects on the Earth's atmosphere and their net effect may be negative, especially in the long run.
- Agriculture in the UK has become more productive partly by taking out hedgerows, trees and ditches to make large fields. Birds and other wildlife dependent on the hedges for food or accommodation are driven elsewhere or perhaps into extinction. This may be a price worth paying to obtain the extra food, but it is important to be clear about the choice.
- Rapid growth, and the attendant changes, may cause social disruption, for example, the break-up of families and communities; a switch from 'traditional' values to 'consumerist' values.

- A related consideration is the time-scale involved. There are two aspects to this. The first is simply that we can choose to have a higher standard of living now at the expense of the future by encouraging consumption rather than investment. The other point is that the faster the economy grows, the faster we use up non-renewable resources. We can enjoy a higher standard of living today by using North Sea oil and gas. The question really is: to what extent should these resources be consumed in such a way that the benefits are shared out between several generations?

We may conclude that the question as to the extent to which a rise in GDP implies a rise in the standard of living is a difficult one. Not least is the problem of deciding how to measure the standard of living.

How to measure standard of living

The UN human development index (HDI) is one way to measure changes in the standard of living without relying solely on income per person. The HDI combines GNP per person with life expectancy and literacy rates into a single index.

The HDI

- The main advantage of the HDI is that while key criteria associated with the wider concept of development are prominent in the measure, it still recognises the importance of income per person.
- The disadvantages include
  - the fact that the HDI is still an average figure which can hide an uneven distribution of improvements, and
  - the narrow set of criteria on which the index is based.

The ISEW

The index of sustainable economic welfare (ISEW) was devised by the New Economics Foundation and, like the HDI, provides an alternative to GDP for measuring changes in the standard of living. The ISEW is a more complex and wide ranging measure than the HDI, calculating economic performance against over twenty indicators. It incorporates measures included in GDP calculations, such as growth in consumption and investment, but also measures changes in pollution and noise levels, commuting costs and the loss of natural resources. Whilst real GNP per person in the UK has doubled over the past 30 years or so, the ISEW index indicates that economic welfare has only marginally improved.

Economic growth and sustainability

Increasingly, the nations of the world are considering economic growth in terms of its **sustainability** – in other words, can it be maintained not just for the present, but for future generations? For example, oil is a non-renewable resource that is currently used in vast quantities in manufacturing and transporting goods. Much of the economic growth occurring in the world is based on the continued use of oil. But current supplies of oil will not last for ever, and while it is based on the use of oil, therefore, economic growth cannot continue for ever.

However, technological developments mean that alternative forms of fuel may become available in the future, and replace oil. This poses a problem: should we continue using as much oil as we need right now in order to pursue our own objectives of economic growth, hoping (knowing?) that an alternative fuel will become available before our reserves of oil finally run out? Or should we conserve the oil that we have, accepting a lower rate of economic growth until we have an alternative type of fuel to take its place, bearing in mind that if we do this we may be reducing our own level of continued economic growth to enable future generations to enjoy growth as well?

The United Nations Earth Summit was established in Rio de Janeiro in 1992 to debate exactly such questions. Nations are still debating them.

Think about it

- To what extent do you think our priorities should change to take account of the need for sustainability?

Determinants of economic growth

Sources of short-term growth

Short-term growth is likely to be a matter of improving the use of existing resources: either bringing into employment some factors previously lying idle or reorganising the use of those already in employment, thus increasing their productivity. It has already been suggested (see pages 427–428) that gains from this kind of process are limited and are of a short-term nature.

Sources of long-term growth

Increases in the underlying capacity of the economy to produce goods and services imply more significant changes. Long-term economic growth of this kind implies one or both of two things:

- an increase in the quantity of the factors of production available
- an improvement in the quality of the factors of production available.

Labour

The size of the working population is related to the age structure of the population (see Unit 2); thus an increase of the quantity of labour available will normally occur as more people move into the working-age group. Such changes, inevitably, occur slowly. More important in a country such as the UK may be changes in the *quality* of labour. The education system may adapt to the changing requirements of the working world: few children leave school now without a knowledge of new technology and information processing. This may improve the contribution that they can make to the output of their employers. Higher education too might need to gear itself more to the requirements of industry. Concern is often expressed that too small a proportion of UK school-leavers move into colleges of further education and universities. Of those that do, it is said that too few study science and engineering. These, of course, are matters of opinion. What is important, though, is that the economy needs to invest resources in the training of labour.

This need not happen only in the traditional educational system. Structural changes in the economy result in thousands of redundancies each year; in addition, many school-leavers cannot find work. The government, through various agencies, offers a variety of training and retraining schemes to equip such people for employment in changing circumstances. In addition, greater emphasis is being placed on education and training at work, through the development of apprenticeship schemes and qualifications such as NVQs.

Capital

Changes in the use of capital can contribute to economic growth in two ways:

- The amount of existing forms of capital may be increased. An operator may purchase an extra lorry identical to those he is already using, employ an additional driver, and increase output. This is known as **capital widening** – the proportion of capital to labour remains the same.
- The operator may change his existing lorries for the same number of larger vehicles, again increasing output. This is **capital deepening** – an increase in the amount of capital per worker, which increases the worker's productivity.

Technology

Changes in technology may be an important source of economic growth. This does not necessarily mean that extra capital is used, but it does mean that different techniques and processes are employed.

Natural resources

While it may be difficult to increase the amount of land available, it is not impossible. Sometimes, an economy may benefit from the discovery and development of hitherto unknown natural resources. North Sea oil and gas deposits are, of course, important examples. Their existence offers an important source of growth. It is true that capital might be diverted from other uses to exploit the oil and gas, but, in fact, much of the capital has come from outside the UK anyway.

Other factors

The influences so far considered are all measurable, but there must be other factors. Economic growth is not simply a matter of increasing investment in machinery or in people – if it were, all countries could achieve high economic growth by diverting a higher proportion of their resources to investment. While those countries that do invest heavily tend to enjoy reasonable economic growth, there is no indisputable link between the two.

Sociological and political influences are important. The attitudes, training and motivation of management and the flexibility, motivation and mobility of labour affect the performance of a company and of an economy. The degree of political stability is also significant. None of these is easily measured, however, and we cannot be certain how they contribute to economic growth.

Economic development in the UK

By international standards, economic growth in the UK as measured by GDP has tended to be below that in other industrialised countries, although rates of growth have fluctuated considerably (see Figure 14.2). The reasons for this are uncertain, but one aspect that concerns some observers has been the process known as **de-industrialisation** – a term relating to the decline of manufacturing industry. To some extent this has long been a feature of economic change, with labour released from manufacturing being absorbed by service industries.

Fig. 14.2 Growth of real GDP

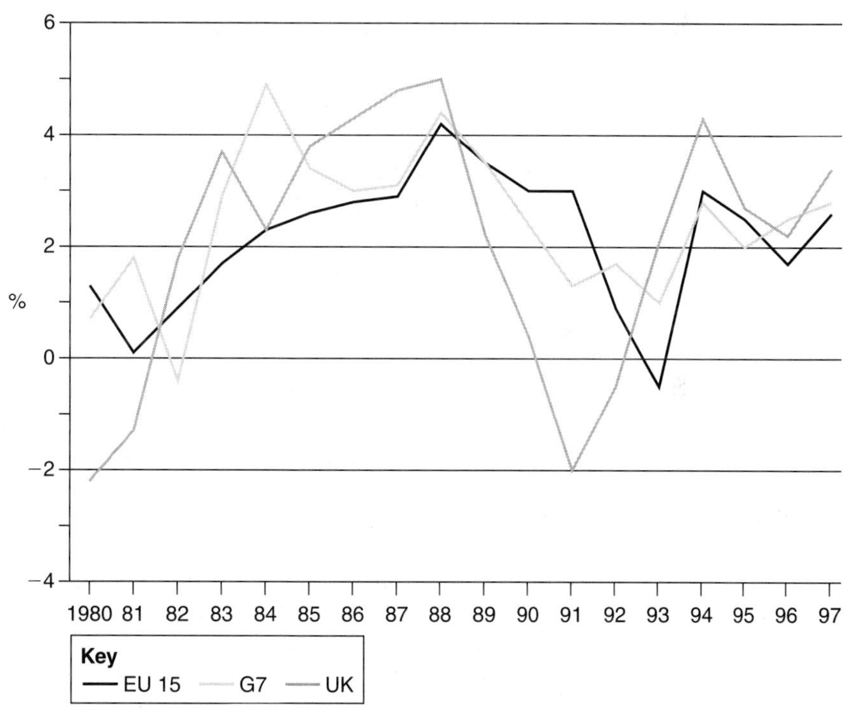

> *Think about it*
>
> We have seen that in order to eliminate as far as possible the effects of inflation, for comparison purposes GDP figures are calculated on the basis of constant prices. This illustrates the difficulties in comparing economic growth statistics over time.
>
> - What other factors influence such statistics and thus make comparison difficult? What can be done to eliminate such difficulties?
> - Consider comparing growth in different countries. What difficulties might be encountered here? How can these be accounted for or eliminated?

Manufacturing output in the UK declined after 1979, and by the mid-1980s the output of many industries had not recovered to its 1970 level – only electrical engineering and chemicals showed any significant growth. Indeed, by the mid-1980s, the UK was for the first time running a deficit on trade in manufactured goods. Since in most countries manufacturing makes an important contribution to economic growth, the process of de-industrialisation raises awkward questions about the future growth of the UK economy.

Trends in the economy

Output

The general aim of economic activity is the production of goods and services. Figure 14.3 shows how GDP and manufacturing output changed year on year between 1980 and 1997. Apart from the fall in GDP in 1980 and 1981, and again in 1991 and 1992, there would seem to have been a steady growth of output. The fall in manufacturing output in the early 1980s was more marked, and manufacturing took longer to recover, although increases in manufacturing production in 1983 and 1988 were higher than overall increases in GDP. It is not that we are buying fewer manufactured goods – more of them are coming from overseas.

Fig. 14.3 Year-on-year changes in GDP and manufacturing output

Since GDP rose by about 15 per cent between 1990 and 1997, and manufacturing output by less than 1 per cent in the same period, we may infer that other forms of output expanded more rapidly. The most notable of these are services, in particular financial services, which rose by almost 21 per cent.

Employment Along with changes in output, there have been changes in the level of employment and unemployment. Unemployment remained high throughout the 1970s and 1980s, falling again in the late 1990s.

The fall in manufacturing output in the early 1980s was, not surprisingly, accompanied by a fall in employment in that sector; but even when production began to increase from 1983 onwards, employment continued to decline and by 1986 it was only three-quarters of its 1980 level. Employment in manufacturing stabilised for a brief period during 1988, declining again between 1989 and 1993, since when it has stabilised once more. Increases in productivity per employee, largely due to developments in technology, have added to the decline in employment in manufacturing.

Service industries were also adversely affected by the recessions of the early 1980s and 1990s. The numbers employed in financial services, particularly banking and insurance, showed a steady increase throughout the period, however, although even here new technology improved productivity and reduced employment. These trends are expected to continue throughout the first decade of the twenty-first century.

Fig. 14.4 Inflation and earnings

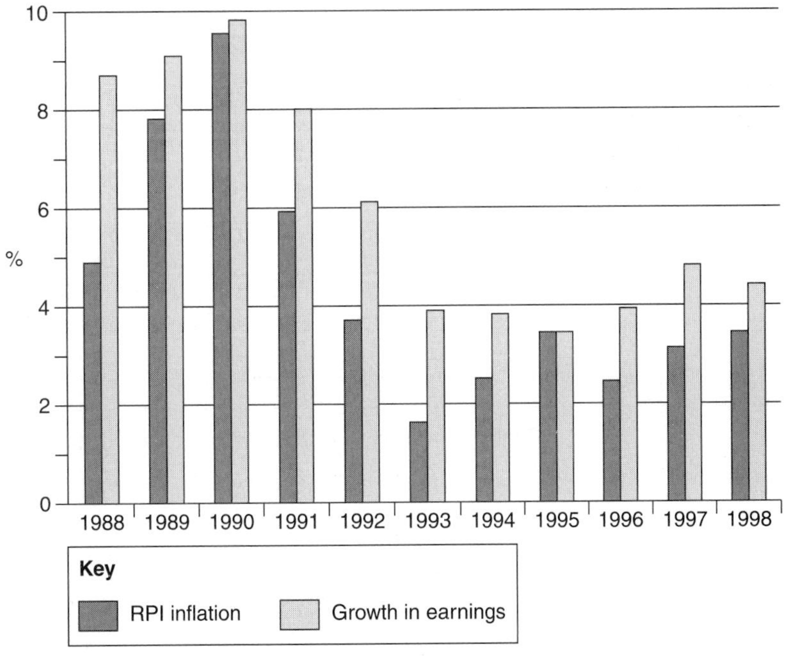

Inflation There was a steady increase in prices and incomes during the ten years 1988–98, as shown in Figure 14.4. Incomes more than kept pace with inflation. Trading profits do not arise solely from the production and sale of British goods, however – indeed, a notable feature of the period was the increase of the importance of consumer durable goods. Rising imports more than balanced the increase in exports resulting from North Sea oil, producing a series of deficits in visible trade (see Figure 14.5).

Fig. 14.5 UK balance of payments (£m)

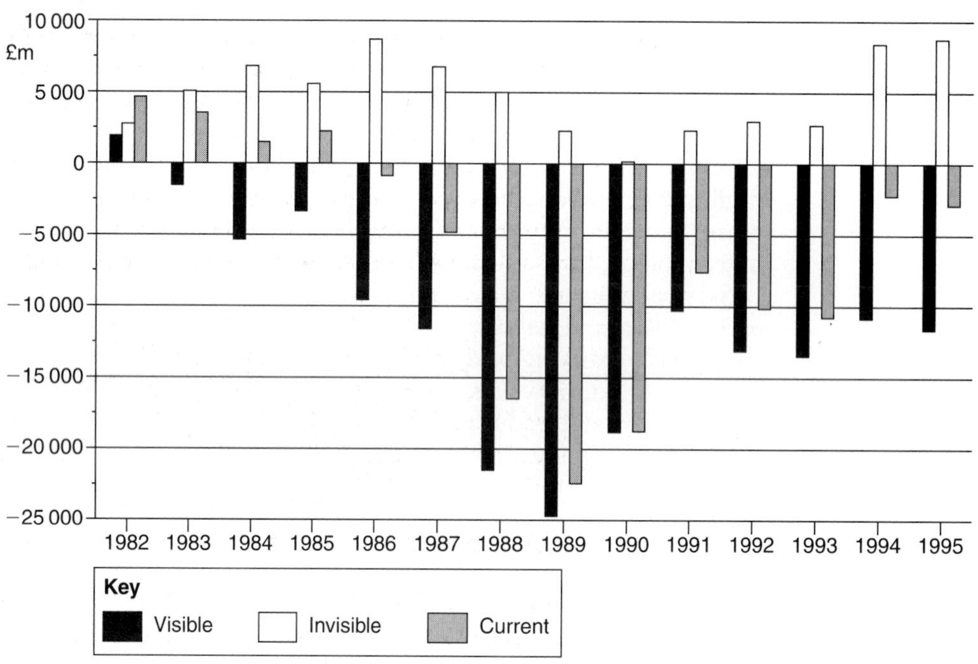

The balance of payments

Until the beginning of the 1980s, the UK's visible trade showed substantial surpluses, mainly because of the effects of North Sea oil. Gradually, though, the decline in manufacturing noted above, together with the increasing demand for consumer durable goods from abroad, eroded the surplus, producing serious deficits by the end of the decade. At the same time, the invisible account showed an annual surplus but, although this tended to increase in the mid-1980s, by 1987 it was more than outweighed by the visible deficit – a trend that has continued.

Pension provision in the current demographic climate

With the rise in living standards that have taken place since 1945 as a result of sustained economic growth, we find that, on average, we are living longer; this, as well as being a positive indicator of advancement, also causes certain problems that governments are keen to address. One such problem is pension provision. A growing proportion of the population is not only retiring earlier (some have no choice in the matter) but also living longer (advances in health care, nutrition, life styes, and so on, have all contributed to this). At the turn of the century there were around two million people in the UK aged over 65 but predictions estimate that by 2031 this figure will have risen to around fourteen million. This has huge implications for the welfare state. In the last two decades governments have attempted to shift the burden of pension provision from the state to individuals. One such example was the rebate system on National Insurance contributions offered to individuals in the 1980s who were willing to 'opt out' of SERPS (the state earnings related pension scheme) and, as an alternative, take out a private pension. The present government is keen to promote the idea of 'stakeholder' pensions – low cost private pension provision aimed at people on low incomes, and available from April 2001. The Government hopes enough people and companies will sign up for these to enable its expenditure on pensions to fall as a proportion of total spending.

Economic growth and social issues

What do the trends examined above tell us about economic growth in the UK? If we look at each trend as a possible measure of economic growth, we can see that during the 1980s and 1990s

- GDP showed a real increase
- the increase in prices (inflation) was more than offset by an increase in earnings.

However, we can also see that

- the UK balance of payments was consistently in deficit from 1986, although this showed a continued reduction after 1989
- by the late 1990s, unemployment had reduced from the high levels of the late 1980s and early 1990s.

In the introduction to Unit 1, we said that while much of the information that economists use is in the form of statistics, perhaps displayed as a table or a chart of some kind, economics itself is concerned with understanding the real situations behind the statistics – the problems society has in meeting the needs and wants of people, and how these are solved by governments, businesses and people themselves. In trying to understand the economic development of a country or group of countries, we are thus faced with a difficulty. While the statistics can show, for example, the growth of GDP over time, most people see the economic growth and development as being reflected in an increase in their material and social well-being. And while an increase in GDP may be easy to quantify, changes in well-being are not so easy to measure.

One possibility is to use per capita GDP (in other words, GDP per person). GDP tells us about the size of an economy. Per capita GDP tells us what each person in the country would get if GDP were shared out equally. Yet even per capita GDP cannot tell us the whole story. The country's income is not shared out equally amongst its citizens: some are unemployed, some are pensioners, some are on other benefits, some are too young to be a part of the labour force. In any case, other factors besides material benefits affect people's well-being, including social and environmental factors. Before we turn to examine ways in which we can measure economic development including these factors, we look at trends in the economies of other countries in the world.

Something to do

- Using the data in this unit as indicators of growth (or otherwise), write an account of economic growth in the UK. Are the data sufficient? If not, what other information do you need?

Economic development in Europe and the rest of the world

Since the 1980s, European economic developments have been dominated by two movements:

- the move towards economic integration in Western Europe
- the move away from communism and central planning in Eastern Europe.

We considered the role of the European Union as a whole in Unit 13. Here we briefly look at the move away from communism and central planning in Eastern Europe before going on to look at two important areas of economic growth and development: the 'Tiger economies' of Eastern Asia, and the problems of growth in developing countries.

Central and Eastern Europe

The political reforms that dismantled communism in Central and Eastern Europe during the 1980s led to profound economic changes. From 1989, control was no longer from Moscow, and the former communist states increasingly moved towards market-based economies.

There were several reasons why the old, controlled economies were not working efficiently:

- Capital and equipment was old and needed replacing, but communist governments had been unwilling to invest.
- Incentives to produce efficiently were poor and ineffective – why should the managers of factories or their workers work hard if they got no benefit from doing so?
- Productivity was therefore low.
- Finance to invest in new and updated capital was raised from Western countries, but due to poor planning and management many projects were unfinished, thus leaving the country with mounting debts in place of the benefits that should have come from the investment.
- Economic decisions about employment, investment and production were made by government bureaucrats, usually resulting in the use of more resources for little return.

As a result, Central and Eastern European countries had lower standards of living than countries in Northern Europe (see Figure 14.6).

Fig. 14.6 Per capita GDP of selected Eastern European countries, 1988/89

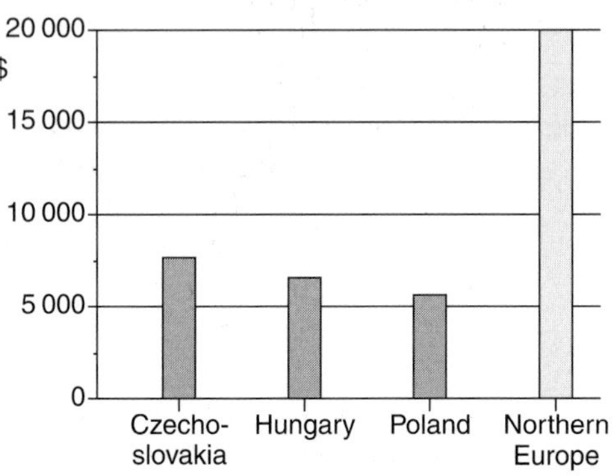

From 1989, however, most Central and Eastern European countries began programmes of economic reform; specifically, reform of production processes and methods of allocating resources (supply-side reform). If their economies were to become efficient in market terms, then the allocation of resources had to be left to the influence of the price mechanism. There were two main reasons for this:

- Artificially low prices did not reflect the true scarcity of some goods or resources. The low prices and inflation figures were meaningless, since producers were unable to purchase resources at the artificially low prices and therefore they were unable to produce the goods that consumers wanted.
- This in turn led to chronic excess demand, as consumers' wants were unsatisfied. The result was queues at bread shops and other shops, even though there was little to buy.

Inevitably, since they had been held artificially low, once restrictions were removed, prices rose dramatically. In Poland, for example, January 1990 saw inflation at 70 per cent – equivalent to an annual figure of some 840 per cent! This was, admittedly, only a temporary situation, although, as can be seen from Figure 14.7, inflation remained high throughout the first half of the 1990s. However, as we saw in Unit 3, such price rises are in effect signals to suppliers to increase production to meet demand.

Fig. 14.7 Inflation (% change per annum)

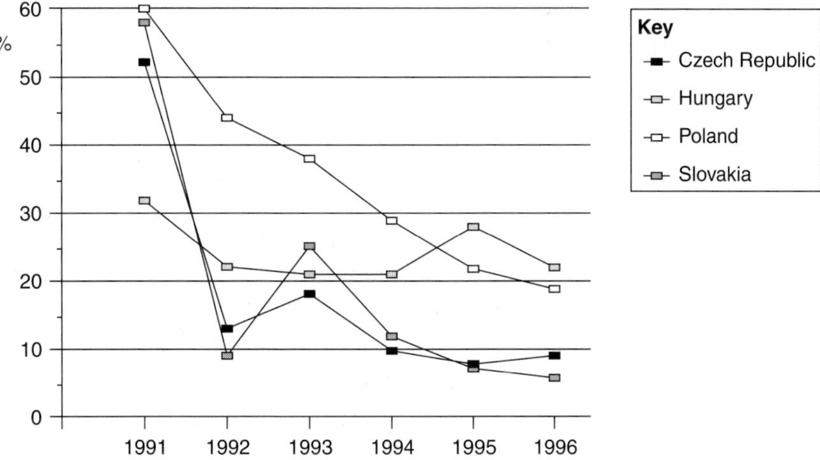

Price rises were not accompanied by matching increases in wages. This meant that increased production led to increased profitability (had wages risen in line with prices, the result would have been continuing rapidly escalating inflation). In fact, real wages fell initially and there was some unemployment. Since unemployment had been kept artificially low under communism, however, this was natural and to be expected. To offset this, standards of living generally rose, since although products cost more, at least they were now being produced and were available for consumers to purchase.

Fig. 14.8 Real output, 1990–96 (% change per annum)

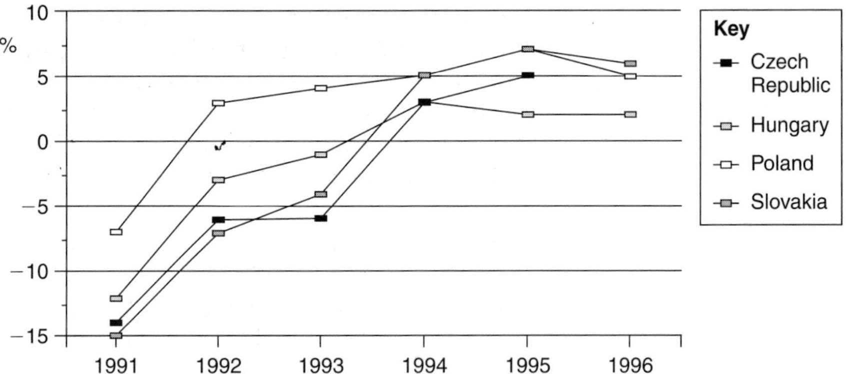

The operation of the price mechanism meant that profitable businesses were encouraged to increase production. In order to further this, many industries were privatised, so that profits were retained by the business rather than going to the government. This enabled businesses to look for ways to improve efficiency and increase production, leading to lower levels of unemployment. Figure 14.8 shows how real output changed between 1990 and 1996.

To find outlets for the increased production, new export markets were needed. Poland, Hungary and the Czech Republic signed agreements with the European Union in 1992, although there was an element of protectionism in the EU's decision not to extend freedom of trade in commodities such as textiles and agricultural products. (In this, the EU actually missed an opportunity to aid the economic growth of its Central and Eastern European neighbours, which could have resulted in cheaper imports and at the same time provided growing markets for its own exports.)

Fig. 14.9 1996 output level (1989 = 100)

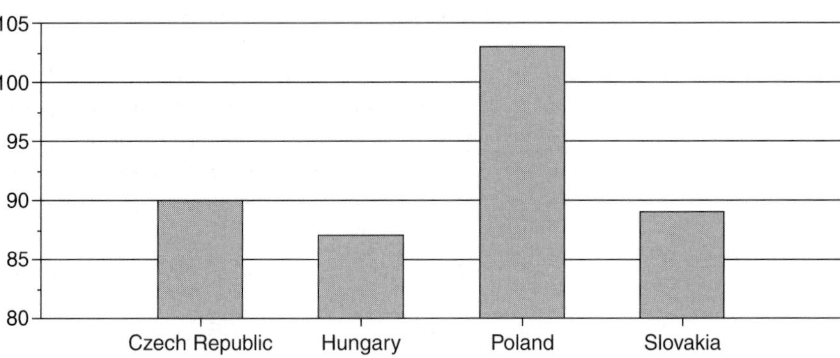

Figure 14.9 shows that, despite reform, production levels in most Central and Eastern European countries fell significantly in the period 1990–96. This, coupled with the high levels of inflation (see Figure 14.7), gave cause for concern about the way reform is being carried out and managed. While the reliability of some statistics is still questionable, the deep recession that occurred, and from which these countries have not yet recovered, cannot just be ascribed to either the statistics themselves or to temporary situations such as high initial inflation.

For one thing, the Soviet Union was the principal export market for most Central and Eastern European countries. Its demise led to the collapse of those markets at a time when larger markets were being sought. Adjusting to such a situation takes time. In addition, Central and Eastern European governments were slow to privatise banks and financial institutions. These institutions, while still under government control, were often reluctant to respond to the needs of the new market economies, continuing to lend money to enterprises – many themselves still in government hands – in order to help them meet production targets or provide employment. Such a course tend to maintain inefficiencies in production and the allocation of resources. What is needed now is for interest rates and exchange rates to find their own equilibrium level, uninfluenced by government.

The 'Tiger economies'

The so-called 'Tiger economies' of the newly industrialised Asian countries faced a different problem from that of the former communist countries in the final years of the twentieth century. Since the 1960s, and until the mid-1990s these countries – which include Singapore, Taiwan, South Korea, Thailand, Indonesia and the Philippines – were looked at by the West as models of economic growth and development. Throughout the 1960s and 1970s, they achieved average growth rates of GNP in excess of 6 per cent, and even higher in the 1980s and early 1990s. Western governments fought for investment in companies from the Tiger economies.

The success of the Tiger economies can be attributed to various factors:

- There is an emphasis on free-market enterprise and the operation of market forces (encouraged by governments).
- Export-led growth, coupled with tying exchange rates to the US dollar, has provided stability for long-term planning.
- Financial markets are deregulated, although some controls are retained, notably in South Korea and Taiwan, and this has encouraged an inflow of foreign capital.
- The lack of natural factors of production has been countered by increased investment in people, notably education, and borrowing (particularly from Japan) in order to finance investment.
- At the same time, labour has been made more flexible, to the extent that wages are low, trade unions have few powers, and there is uncertainty of employment.
- Companies have diversified into markets for new non-traditional products, such as cars and ships.
- Producing goods on a large scale and selling them throughout the world has enabled companies from the Tiger economies to benefit from economies of scale.

It must be said, however, that while Tiger governments have encouraged free enterprise, they have themselves often been accused of social repression. In some Tiger economies, personal savings are encouraged so that savings ratios are almost 40 per cent of GDP – the highest in the world. This provides further funds for investment, and also reduces the need for state welfare provision.

The first sign that all was not well came in July 1997, when the value of the baht, Thailand's currency, fell by 40 per cent against other currencies. This led to panic selling not only of the baht, but of the currencies of Indonesia, the Philippines and Malaysia as well. The South Korean currency, the won, fell 50 per cent against the US dollar. These falls were followed by a series of rescue packages from the IMF.

Problems were not confined to the newer Tiger economies, however. In November 1997, Yamaichi Securities, Japan's fourth largest brokerage house, collapsed amidst rumours of economic crisis. Japan set up measures intended to reflate the economy, but confidence was lost.

While some countries, such as Taiwan and Singapore, were stronger and seemed less affected, other countries, including South Korea and Malaysia, had to find ways of generating cash quickly. In one incident, in Medang, Indonesia, where land was being cleared in order to grow cash crops, a plane crashed, partly as a result of smoke from fires. This smoke also caused widespread pollution that adversely affected the local tourist trade.

In terms of the local economies, the crisis has been catastrophic. Forecast GNP growth rates have been revised downwards from around 7 per cent to a mere 1 per cent or even less. In terms of the global economy, the effect has been critical. The dumping of products from the Tiger economies at low prices on such a large scale in order to generate cash has depressed world demand for other goods. This in turn has led to significant global unemployment.

Something to do

- Write an account comparing the situations of economies in Central and Eastern Europe with the Tiger economies. What lessons can we learn from the experiences of these economies?

The problems of growth in developing countries

We have seen that the result of economic growth is the availability of more goods and services and hopefully a greater level of economic welfare. Nowhere is the need for extra goods and services greater than in the **Third World**, or the developing countries. But because they have the lowest levels of income, these are the countries that are least able to set aside the resources needed to induce growth. There are a number of factors contributing to the difficulties of such countries.

The nature of the problem

World population is growing rapidly. It doubled in the 40 years from 1940 to 1980. It now stands at approximately 6 billion and is increasing at a rate of around 80 million a year. The growth is fastest in Africa, Asia and South America, where falling death rates have been accompanied by high birth rates. The age structure in many of these countries is such that birth rates are likely to remain high. Attempts to induce a reduction in birth rates have so far met with minimal success.

While there is an abundance of labour in many developing countries, there is a shortage of capital. Since national income is low, savings are low. If all income is spent on consumption, nothing is available for investment. Accordingly, the possibility of higher output and better living standards is remote. Sometimes population grows faster than output, so income per head actually falls.

Many developing countries are heavily in debt to the industrialised nations, and much of their income has to be set aside to pay those debts and the interest on them.

The costs and benefits of development

There is debate amongst economists over the extent to which – or, indeed, whether – 'growth' leads to 'development'. Growth may not lead to development if, for example, it is distributed unevenly amongst the population, or if it causes environmental damage, etc. However, let us assume for the moment that economic growth does lead to development (in some way or other) for most countries. What, then, are the costs and benefits of such development?

The benefits

- Generally, the standard of living will rise. We often measure standard of living by calculating income per head, but it is much broader than this: the well-being and welfare of individuals is measured and in this case will increase on average.
- People will have access to more goods and services – for example, consumer items such as cars and telephones – but also to more fundamental items such as health facilities and education opportunities.
- Development should lead to more choice, not simply in terms of more goods, but in opportunities, for example, employment and political participation, particularly for women.
- The greater the development, the more scope there will be for a country to decide on its own objectives (economic and political) instead of having these imposed from outside by the World Bank, the IMF or other global organisations. The country's destiny is, to a greater degree, in its own hands.
- With development usually comes a whole set of statistics favourable to people's well-being: higher life expectancy, better literacy rates, lower child mortality, more doctors and nurses per head of population, and so on.

The costs

- If development is not planned carefully, then depletion of natural resources is likely to follow.
- Irreversible environmental damage can be caused by a 'dash for growth' that takes no account of sensitive ecosystems. Pollution can be one danger, if lax controls and inappropriate technology allow a poisoning of the atmosphere. In the belief that outside investment is the answer, some countries have allowed multinational corporations virtually free reign to exploit resources; this often leads to exploitation of people and natural resources. For example, in Peru, in an attempt to entice American companies to buy up privatised companies, the government has given investing companies 'holidays' from all taxes and environmental controls, leading to much pollution.
- 'Dual economies' can develop within the same country, where one sector thrives whilst another stagnates due to neglect (for example, rural versus urban development).
- There can also be social and cultural conflict. Should a country allow the development of a natural resource such as oil if this means the destruction of a way of life of particular ethnic groups living in that vicinity?

These are all issues that have to be considered if development is going to truly lead to a better way of life.

Kenya

Kenya has altered its agricultural output dramatically in recent decades. It has switched production from potatoes, maize, carrots and cabbages, which local people eat, to the production of flowers and luxury vegetables such as French beans, which are all flown to the more prosperous European market.

This switch in production has meant that horticulture has overtaken coffee and become the country's second largest export commodity after tea. In 1992, Kenya was exporting some 57 000 tons of flowers and luxury vegetables, from which it earned $78 million. By the beginning of 2000, this figure is expected to rise to around $406 million per year.

To be able to do this, much land has been given over to the production of these new high-value goods. In 1991, for example, the army bulldozed 100 acres of tropical forest to make way for Sian Roses. Large quantities of water from Lake Naivasha, the only freshwater lake in the Rift Valley, are pumped to the precious export crop. Ecologists fear that the lake will dry up and warn that massive amounts of pesticides and fertilisers are finding their way into the lake from the nearby rose plantations.

Think about it

- What are the cost and benefits to Kenya of the switch from more traditional crops to the horticultural varieties depicted in the above extract?

Indicators of development in developing countries

What are the indicators of development? Development means much more than growth, as explained by Professor Dudley Seers (The Meaning of Development – Eleventh World Conference of the Society of International Development, 1969). He asserted that:

'The questions to ask about a country's development are therefore: What has happened to poverty? What has been happening to unemployment? What has been happening to inequality? If all three of these have declined from high levels, then beyond doubt this has been a period of development for the country concerned. If one or two of these central problems have been growing worse, especially if all three have, it would be strange to call the result "development" even if per capita income doubled.'

Professor Michael Todaro writes:

'Development in all societies must have at least the following three objectives:

1. *to increase the availability and widen the distribution of basic life sustaining goods such as food, shelter, health;*
2. *to raise levels of living, including, in addition to higher incomes, the provision of more jobs, better education and more attention to cultural and humanistic values;*
3. *to expand the range of economic and social choice to individuals and nations by freeing them from servitude and dependence, not only in relation to other people and nation-states but also to the forces of ignorance and human misery.'*

Source: *Economics For A Developing World*, 1992

Differences between developing countries

It is important to remember that no two countries are the same. Developing countries may have certain characteristics that allow us to group them together and talk about them as a whole, but they also display much diversity and each country has its own particular set of obstacles to overcome in order for it to develop successfully.

- **Geographical factors** 'Developing countries' include states from every part of the globe. We find therefore that there are many different problems and opportunities associated with climate and terrain. The influence of geography can be seen not only in *what* and *how* these countries produce but also in the balance and structure of their economies in terms of the proportion that each sector (primary, secondary, tertiary) contributes to total output (GDP).
- **Historical factors** Some countries have stronger ties to Western economies because of their colonial past, (for example India with the UK). This can often be seen in their internal organisation – their civil service, education system or legal structure, for example.
- **Political structure** also varies enormously. Some countries are relatively new to democracy and many have suffered years of civil war (for example, many African states have had their development held back because of war; Ethiopia and Mozambique illustrate this point). In some countries democracy prevails, as in India; in others, such as China, a one-party state exists.
- **Culture and religion** also have an impact. In Afghanistan, following civil war, the Taliban, an extreme form of Muslim rule, has been imposed, restricting the activity of women and, as a consequence, holding back development.
- Developing countries differ greatly in population and size. China has a population of over 1 billion, whilst Jamaica accommodates some three million. So it is with land mass: China has a total area of 9 600 000 square kilometres which dwarfs Jamaica at 10 991 square kilometres.

We can see from the above that, when looking into the problems of development, we also need to take into account the significant differences that exist between these economies.

Think about it

- The countries below, although all classed as developing, have significant differences which affect their prospects for raising living standards. Find some basic statistics on these countries (such as population size, land mass, climate) and think about the particular problems each country faces. Use the factors outlined above to help you assess the differences between the countries.

China Bangladesh Mozambique Chile

World debt relief

In 1996, the 'Jubilee 2000' campaign was initiated. The main organiser is Christian Aid, supported by non-conformists, Catholics and Anglicans. The campaign is, in effect, an inter-denominational pressure group whose initial aim was to see the new millennium marked by the cancellation of the unpayable debts of the world's poorest countries – the highly indebted low income countries. Drawing on the Old Testament concept of a jubilee as a debt 'amnesty', it called for a once and for all loan write-off to coincide with the new millennium. The campaign began out of the work of some 40 charities (the Debt Crisis Network) whose workers reported that any contact they had with poor countries inevitably led them to be involved with lobbying about debt. It was a fundamental problem that needed to be solved.

The proposal caught the public imagination and has turned the campaign into a much higher profile one – what started as a coalition between churches and development agencies has since been joined by newspapers and celebrities. There have been some successes. In June 1999, at the G7 meeting in Cologne, promises were made to reduce the debt stock of the most severely affected states by $100 bn (£62 bn). In December 1999, Britain announced that it would write off all debts owed to it by the 41 countries which the World Bank and IMF have singled out as being the most in need of debt relief.

Think about it

There are 32 countries classified by the World Bank as severely indebted low income countries (SILICs). They have debt-service-to-gross-national-product ratios of more than 80 per cent, or debt-service-to-export ratios of over 220 per cent. Last year repayments of $16 billion fell due, but they were able to pay less than half this amount, with the rest added to arrears.

Zambia dramatically illustrates the worsening trend. Per capita spending on primary school children is one sixth of the level of a decade ago, and health spending is 30 per cent lower. On the most optimistic budget projections, Zambia will have spent $26 million on primary education in 1995. Its obligations to multinational creditors are around $127 million.

- Discuss how the debt position of Zambia might affect its prospects for development.

The way forward

The policies that have been attempted in response to the problems of the less developed countries fall into two groups:

- those which make extra resources available to those countries – various kinds of economic aid
- those designed to increase the trading opportunities available to them.

Here we confine ourselves to economic aid.

Economic aid

Economic aid (or foreign aid) occurs in various forms, the most obvious of which are as follows:

- **Financial aid** is the provision of foreign currency either by a single donor country (bilateral aid) or by a group of countries (multilateral aid). Bilateral aid is normally 'tied' in that it may be provided on the basis of political allegiance or it may have to be spent on a particular project or projects not contributing greatly to the productive capacity of the recipient and/or spent on purchases from the donor country. There is therefore a tendency to prefer multilateral aid, with financial contributions from many countries being channelled via an international institution such as the **World Bank** (see opposite).
- **Technical aid** may be available in two forms: first, in the supply of skilled personnel to supervise the development of new projects and perhaps manage them until local people take them over; second, in the form of education and training provided by developed countries to the nationals of developing countries. Clearly the latter is important if developing countries are to take full advantage of modern developments in their economies.

The IMF and the World Bank

Although these are two distinct organisations they work closely together. IMF loans are more likely to have political, social or financial reform conditions attached to them, whereas World Bank loans are lent more conventionally at market rates.

The **International Monetary Fund (IMF)** was set up in 1945. Its original purpose was to promote international monetary stability by helping member countries with balance-of-payments problems and supporting exchange rates. Its role has since evolved to restructuring international debts and helping debtor countries develop and implement policies of economic reform and financial stabilisation.

One of the largest international organisations through which money is channelled from the developed countries to less developed countries is the World Bank (whose full name is the **International Bank for Reconstruction and Development** – IBRD).

Members of the World Bank (about 150 countries) pay a subscription to the Bank based roughly on their economic importance. On the security of this capital and on the strength of their reputation, the Bank is able to raise long-term loans on the world financial market at competitive rates of interest. These funds can then be lent to member countries for development projects. Each project will have been subject to careful evaluation by the World Bank to ensure its overall viability and, once approved, is closely supervised by the Bank to ensure the efficient completion of the work.

Although these restrictions may be unwelcome to some recipients, the channelling of aid through the World Bank is important to them for two reasons:

- They could not raise the money independently at such low interest rates.
- The Bank's procedures and technical expertise ensure that both external and local resources are used effectively. It is only in this way that successful development can occur so that living standards in developing countries can be improved.

Even more fundamental though may be the need to reduce the rate of population growth – until this can be achieved, progress will be limited.

Financial aid can also be given via 'unofficial aid', that is, provided by organisations that are not government bodies. Such organisations include the Red Cross, Oxfam and churches. They are known as NGOs – non-governmental organisations. Some of them are international, like the ones mentioned above, and others indigenous to certain countries and regions. The private commercial sector is also a large source of finance via MNCs (multinational corporations). Multinationals are often far bigger, in terms of turnover, than many of the developing countries who need them to invest. There has been a rapid expansion in private direct foreign investment in developing countries in the last 40 years mainly due to MNC activity. These companies bring not just finance, which plugs a vital savings/investment gap, but also technical and managerial expertise. (It should be noted, however, that many commentators believe there is a price to be paid in terms of dependency, environmental damage and exploitation. See also Unit 4, pages 158–160, for the kinds of problems associated with investment by multinational companies.)

- **Commodity aid,** normally in the form of food, may be of the most immediate benefit to recipients by covering a shortfall in local supplies and alleviating the problems of hunger. In the long run it may be the least beneficial in that it discourages local production and may prevent the proper development of agriculture.

Sustainable growth and globalisation

The sustainability of economic growth

In this unit, we have seen that to be of lasting benefit, growth must be sustainable. But is sustainable growth really feasible? Despite major advances in technology and communications that have increased the productivity and availability of factors of production, the basic economic problem remains: people in society have potentially infinite wants, but the resources available to satisfy them are limited. As the world population increases, pressure on these scarce resources increases with it. Figure 14.10 shows the extent to which current global consumption exceeds available resources.

Fig. 14.10 Global over-consumption of environmental space

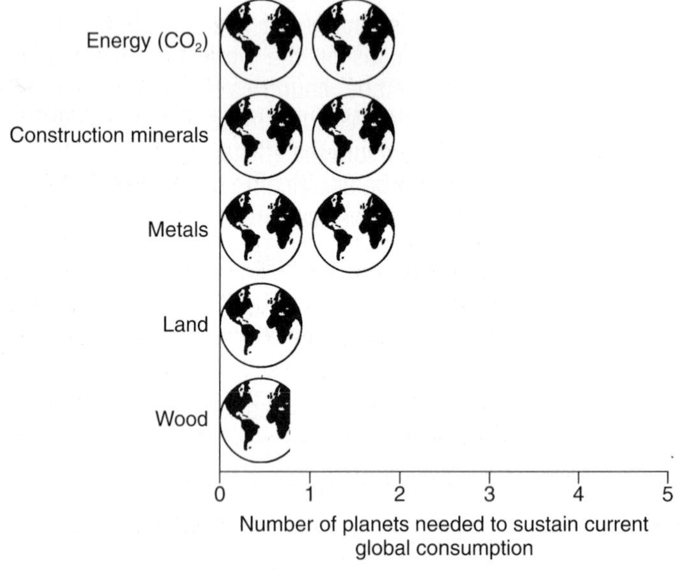

Source: Friends of the Earth, 1998

It is clear that there are limits to the expansion of human activities. Such was the view of Adam Smith in the eighteenth century, though it has to be admitted that – fortunately for those of us who now inhabit the Earth – so far his predictions have not been realised. But what of the future? Can economic growth be sustained at its present – or indeed *any* – level? And how can we tell?

At the third session of the United Nations Commission on Sustainable Development, in April 1995, a working list of 134 indicators of sustainable development were identified for testing by countries throughout the world. These went beyond the commonly used economic indicators of material well-being to include social, environmental and institutional indicators, so as to provide a broader, more complete indication of the development of society.

These indicators, which include measures of factors such as literacy, employment and pollution, are currently being voluntarily tested by countries throughout the world, including major industrial nations such as Germany and the UK as well as developing countries such as Mauritius and Thailand. Such indicators are signposts that can point a way towards sustainable development and help show if we are moving in the right direction. They are intended to provide information on which to base decisions, pointing out trends and relationships. The indicators are still being developed and refined in response to testing. In some countries, the United Nations is also working with national organisations to help promote sustainable development (see below).

Tourism growth, ecological impact and environmental protection measures

Location Mauritius

Responsible Organisation Ministry of the Environment and Quality of Life

Description Concern over damage to the environment as a result of the rapid pace of economic development over the past three decades led to the establishment in 1990 of a Ministry of the Environment and Quality of Life and a number of initiatives designed to enhance cohesion among economic, cultural and economic objectives. Within this framework, tourism has been the subject of intense development based on the attractiveness of the island's natural and cultural resources, readily available air transport, the availability of financial resources and the development of a tourism infrastructure capable of receiving a growing number of visitors. While industry has contributed to the diversification of the island's economy and to the creation of jobs, the growth of the tourism industry has also produced severe environmental impacts, especially along the coastal areas. To address this issue, the Government has put into place a 'Master Tourism Plan' for the northern section of the island as well as a series of legislative measures for the environmental conservation of tourist areas.

Issues Addressed Economic development and diversification, tourism, environmental protection

Results Achieved

- Emphasis on environmental education; the utilisation of urban planning and tourism flow management measures;
- Establishment and implementation of measures for coastal protection, control of beach dune systems, boat anchorages, preservation of coral reefs, and preservation of the island's flora and fauna;
- Establishment of measures for the improvement of environmental sanitation; reduction of air and noise pollution through improvement in automobile maintenance and the use of more environmentally friendly fuels;
- Preparation of environmental impact studies for the location of new tourist projects;
- Utilization of appropriate architectural designs and use of local materials;
- Improvement of water supply and treatment systems for tourist centres;
- Design of tourist facilities with more efficient energy management and conservation systems; introduction of waste management measures.

Lessons Learned Severe environmental impact, mainly along the coast.

Contact Ministry of the Environment and Quality of Life, Government House, Port Louis, Mauritius.

Source: Sustainable Development Success Stories, Copyright © United Nations, Division for Sustainable Development. Comments and suggestions: dsd@un.org (21 April 1999)

The globalisation of economies and business

It is not only the United Nations and individual governments that have to consider sustainability. As more and more giant multinational companies become truly global in size and operation (a phenomenon known as **globalisation**), their influence on the allocation of resources, on levels of employment and on world production, is increasing. While a major global company may have limited impact on the economy of the USA, a decision by such a company to base its African production and distribution operation in Chad, for example, could transform that country's economy. And a decision to move out could bring economic ruin. Indeed, the annual turnover of companies such as Ford and Coca-Cola exceed the GDP of many smaller and developing nations.

Many global companies are finding that as well as addressing the sustainable allocation of resources and manufacturing methods, they are having to develop environmental and social programmes. For example, Nike has made commitments to

- develop, through innovative design and teamwork, a sustaining business – that is, a business that is dedicated to replacing rather than depleting resources
- conserve resources, cut waste and reduce adverse impact on the environment within the context of their business practices
- educate and encourage the participation of their employees, consumers, business partners and competitors in ecological endeavours
- foster responsible outdoor athleticism and stewardship to preserve and restore the planet's outdoor playgrounds.

Such commitments are important to the sustained development of the world's economies and environment. Yet for every company such as Nike, there are hundreds of businesses throughout the world that continue operations without regard to the consequences of their actions. There is still a long way to go in education and testing before we know the extent to which continued economic development is sustainable. But at least there is a growing awareness of the problem and a desire to solve it before it is too late.

Think about it

Globalisation means that companies such as Ford, Coca-Cola, Nike and Microsoft have manufacturing plants and sales outlets in many industrialised and developing countries throughout the world. To a large extent, a developing country may depend on a large multinational company to purchase its raw materials and employ its available working population. By investing in the developing country, a multinational company will not only contribute to that country's economy and level of employment, but may be a major contributor to government income, through tax. This means that the multinational company may be able to influence the government unduly in its favour (for example, regarding taxes, employment subsidies or wages, and purchasing policies). Some multinational companies are able to 'dump' unsuitable products on developing countries, in the knowledge that the country cannot afford to go elsewhere.

- Do you think that the activities of global companies should be controlled? If so, how?

Glossary

absolute advantage an advantage in the production of all goods and services

absolute monopoly a firm that supplies and controls the entire market for its product

accepting house a merchant bank that accepts bills of exchange

accounting cost the cost of something in financial terms

***ad-valorem* tax** a tax based on value, for example, VAT is currently charged at 17.5 per cent of the value of the product

aggregate (monetary) demand the total level of demand for all goods and services in an economy

aggregate supply the total supply of goods and services

allocation problem the problem of how best to allocate scarce resources to the production of the goods and services that will satisfy the wants of society

allocative efficiency the efficiency with which resources are allocated to the production of different goods and services in order to maximise the utility obtained by society from those resources

arithmetic progression a sequence of numbers each of which differs from the preceding one by a constant amount (for example, 2, 4, 6, 8, 10, 12 . . .)

artificial resource a resource that does not occur naturally

asset a long-lasting capital item not used up in the process of production

at call and short notice a loan that is repayable on demand

average cost total cost divided by output

average product the average product of a factor of production is the total product divided by the number of units of that factor employed

balance of payments a summary of a country's financial transactions with the rest of the world during the preceding twelve months

balance of trade a summary of a country's visible imports and exports during the preceding twelve months

balance sheet an accounting statement showing the assets and liabilities of an organisation at a point in time

balancing item an item included to cover errors and omissions and make an account balance

bank bill a bill of exchange that has been accepted by a clearing bank or accepting house

Bank of England the central bank of the United Kingdom, having responsibility for setting interest rates and implementing the government's monetary policies

bank rate originally the rate at which the Bank of England would rediscount bills of exchange; this is now often used to refer to the minimum lending rate

barriers to entry/exit difficulties or obstacles to entering or leaving a particular market, such as the costs of setting up

base year a year chosen as the standard against which other years can be statistically compared

bill of exchange a form of credit whereby the seller of goods or services sets out the amount owed by a purchaser and demands payment on a specified date. The purchaser acknowledges the debt by signing the bill, which may then be discounted for cash by an accepting house

bond fixed interest-bearing securities

branding establishing a recognisable identity for a product normally associated with a brand name

broad money M4 is a measure of money supply that includes notes and coins in circulation plus non-interest bearing retail bank deposits, other interest bearing deposits up to five years original maturity, building society shares and deposits up to five years maturity, all outside the public sector; M5 consists of M4 plus most national savings ordinary accounts plus some money-market items such as treasury bills and bank bills

budget a financial plan setting targets for expenditure and income

building society a financial institution that raises money almost entirely from private citizens and provides loans almost entirely for the purpose of house purchase

capital resources such as land, buildings, machinery and materials that are used for the production of goods and services but are not used up in the production process; *see also* circulating capital, fixed capital

capital cost the cost of capital items required by a business, such as premises, machinery and equipment

capital deepening an increase in the amount of capital per worker in an economy, increasing productivity per worker

capital deficiency the lack of productive capital equipment such as machinery in an economy, which therefore has to rely on the use of less productive labour

capital formation the creation of capital

capital gain the increase in value of a capital item over time

capital market the market for large funds that can be used to purchase capital items

capital widening an increase in an economy's capital where the proportion of capital to labour remains the same

capital-intensive production production using a large amount of machinery and equipment in relation to labour

cartel an association of firms providing the same product for the purposes of controlling the market for that product

cash flow the inflows and outflows of a firm's money

cash reserve ratio a bank's ratio of cash to loans

central bank a financial institution that has a role in implementing government economic policy and acts as banker to commercial banks and the government

centralised economy a government-controlled economy

certificate of deposit a promise issued by a bank in return for a deposit, to repay the amount deposited with interest on a specified date

ceteris paribus a latin term meaning 'all things being equal'

cheque a form instructing a bank to transfer money from the drawer's account to the account of the payee. Cheques can also be used to instruct a bank to pay cash to the payee (who may also be the drawer)

circulating capital resources that are used up in the production of goods and services, sold to customers as finished goods and returned to the business as income from the sale of those goods

classical (theory of) unemployment unemployment due to institutional factors such as a high minimum wage, or trade unions and professional organisations demanding high wages

clearing banks high street banks, sometimes known as commercial or retail banks, forming the link between ordinary citizens and the financial system by providing a channel for money to be deposited and used for credit creation

closed economy a self-sufficient economy that does not have to rely on international trade

closed shop a firm or industry in which employment is open only to those who are members of specified trade unions

coefficient of price elasticity a numerical measure of price elasticity

collective bargaining negotiations over pay and conditions carried out by groups of employers and their employees, who are normally represented by trade unions

commercial bank *see* clearing banks

commercial rent the reward earned by owners of land for the use of their land

commodity agreement an agreement concerning the production, supply and price of a primary good

common agricultural policy (CAP) EU policy covering the level of production, price and subsidy of agriculture and agricultural produce in member states

comparative advantage a relative advantage in the production of some goods or services

competition commission regulatory body set up by the government to ensure that any proposed merger between firms that might affect the competitiveness of the market is in the interests of consumers

competitive demand demand for goods that are substitutes for each other

complementary goods goods that are generally used or consumed in conjunction with other goods, such as pens and ink

conditions of demand factors affecting the level of demand generally or for a specific product

conditions of supply factors affecting the level of supply generally or for a specific product

consumption function the relationship between income and planned aggregate consumption

contestable market a market that is open to competition

cost–benefit analysis method of calculating the non-financial costs and benefits, including externalities, of a project

cost of living a measure of the general level of household expenditure

cost-push inflation a rise in prices due to the costs of production increasing more rapidly than production

costs of production expenditure on items such as raw materials, parts and labour used directly in the production of goods and services, and used up in the production of those goods and services

council tax local tax imposed on households by local authorities

credit creation the use of funds deposited with a financial institution to make loans in excess of the amount deposited

cross elasticity the effect of a change in the price of one product on the demand for or supply of another

current account an account with a financial institution which is used for day-to-day financial transactions

customs union an association of countries aimed at removing barriers to free trade between them, while maintaining barriers to imports from countries outside the customs union

cyclical unemployment unemployment due to a downturn in the business cycle

debenture a preferential long-term loan normally at a fixed rate of interest

deficit an excess of debits over credits (for example, expenditure over income)

deflation a reduction in the level of economic activity

deflationary gap a deficiency of demand below that required to allow for full employment

de-industrialisation the reduction of industry in an economy (for example, the decline in manufacturing in the UK)

demand demand for goods or services is created when people want those goods or services; effective demand is demand supported by the willingness and ability of people to pay for goods and services to be produced or supplied

demand curve a graph showing the relationship between demand and price or other condition of demand

demand-deficiency unemployment unemployment due to insufficient demand leading to a drop in production

demand-pull inflation an increase in prices caused by demand rising more rapidly than production

demand-side factors arising from changes in demand

demerit goods goods that, although demanded by some members of society, are generally considered harmful or undesirable

dependent population that part of the population of a country that relies on others for the satisfaction of its needs, for example, children and state pensioners

deposit account an account with a financial institution used for longer-term deposits on which the institution will pay interest

depreciation the decline in value of an asset over time

deregulation the removal of restrictions on trading, especially concerning competition

derived demand demand for a product or commodity that results from demand for another product or commodity

devaluation a lowering of the value of a currency against other currencies

diminishing marginal utility the tendency for additional units of a commodity eventually to provide less utility

diminishing returns the law of diminishing returns states that if additional units of a variable factor are used in production, eventually the extra output from each additional unit will decrease

direct cost a cost that is incurred directly in the process of production (for example, raw materials)

direct production direct production exists where a unit of society itself produces the goods and services that it needs

direct tax a tax imposed directly on individuals

discount house a financial institution that buys bills of exchange at a discount before they are due

discount market the market for trading in discounted bills of exchange

discriminating monopoly a monopoly that is able to discriminate between different categories of customers, for example by charging different prices

diseconomies of scale disadvantages that accrue from an increase in the size of a business

distribution problem the problem of allocating resources, goods and services to individuals and groups, businesses or other organisations, in a way that most effectively satisfies the needs of people in society

disutility the costs of economic growth, such as pollution

division of labour the principle of dividing the production process into discrete tasks and allocating each task to a specific unit of labour

dumping the sale of goods more cheaply in export markets than in the home market in order to undercut world prices and encourage exports

duopoly a market that is controlled by two firms

dynamic efficiency the changing efficiency of an economy in the face of changing conditions, such as technology

economic aid help provided to less developed nations by more developed nations. Such aid may be financial, in the form of commodities, such as food and medicines, or technical, in the form of equipment, skills or training

economic dependence the dependence of one nation on another for providing goods and services that meet the needs of its society, and that cannot be produced, or cannot be produced with the same economic efficiency, by that nation

economic development an increase in the efficiency of economic activity

economic efficiency a situation in which the goods and services produced in an economy afford the optimum satisfaction to society

economic growth an increase in GDP

economic model a representation of an economic system or part of a system

economic rent the earnings of any factor of production in excess of its cost

economies of scale advantages that accrue from an increase in the size of an organisation

effective demand demand for goods and services that is backed up by the ability and willingness to pay for them

entrepreneur(ship) the acceptance of risks involved in setting up an enterprise

environmental free good goods and resources that are provided freely in nature

equilibrium position the point at which supply exactly equals demand

equilibrium price a price arrived at by the free interaction of supply and demand in the market

equilibrium quantity the amount of a product supplied in response to the free interaction of demand and price

equilibrium rate of interest the level of interest required for the supply of funds to equal demand

equilibrium wage the level of wages at which demand for labour equals its supply

equity a) the ordinary shares of, or risk capital invested in, a firm; b) the fairness of distribution of goods and services between members of society; *see also* horizontal equity, vertical equity

exchange rate the rate at which the currency of one country can be exchanged for that of another

excise duty taxes on goods imposed by customs and excise

expenditure relative a relationship with changes in the level of expenditure

expenditure tax a tax on goods purchased

externalities costs, often social or environmental, associated with the provision of goods and services that are not a direct part of the production system

factor cost the financial cost of factors of production; the cost of a good or service in terms of the cost of its factors of production

factor incomes the revenue earned by factors of production

factor of production land, capital, labour or enterprise involved in the production of a good or service

fiduciary issue the issue by banks of promises to pay that are not covered by the banks' assets

financial (wealth) capital money available to purchase assets

fine bill *see* bank bill

fiscal policy economic policy that relies on government income and expenditure

fixed capital long-lasting items of capital that are not used up in the production process

fixed cost a cost that does not vary with the level of output of a firm (for example, rent)

fixed exchange rate a rate of exchange between currencies that has been set at a specific level

fixed factor of production a factor of production that cannot easily be varied

floating debt that part of the national debt in the form of treasury bills

foreign exchange rate the rate at which a unit of one country's currency exchanges for that of another country

fractionally backed notes bank notes that have a nominal value greater than the value of the bank's assets

free resource resources that are freely available in nature

free-rider a person who enjoys the benefits of a product without paying for it

frictional unemployment unemployment due to people changing jobs

funding the provision of finance for a project

geometric progression a sequence of numbers that increases by a constant ratio (for example, 2, 4, 8, 16, 32, 64 . . .)

Giffen goods basic products such as staple foods, demand for which tends to rise as prices rise

gilt-edged market the market for government bonds

gilt-edged security a government bond

gilt a gilt-edged security

globalisation the trend towards international and worldwide business organisations giving rise to supra-national economic activity

gold standard the system of fixing exchange rates of currencies in terms of the value of gold

goods of ostentation goods that tend to be purchased because they are expensive, often considered status symbols, so that demand for them often increases when their price rises simply because they cost more

government expenditure expenditure by the government on the goods and services it provides

government failure government failure can be said to have taken place when government intervention in markets leads to worse economic problems than if there had been no such intervention

gross domestic product (GDP) the aggregate value of the goods and services produced in one year by factors of production located within a country, even though they may be owned abroad

gross national product (GNP) the value of all goods and services produced in one year by factors of production owned within a country, even though they may be located abroad

horizontal equity the like treatment of identical people in society

hyperinflation a high level of inflation, often giving rise to social disorder

immobility of labour the tendency of labour to have difficulty moving from one industry or location to another

imperfect competition competition that is not entirely free

imports goods produced abroad and brought into a country

imputed rent the value of a service that is provided privately for which no actual payment is made (for example, housework, DIY)

income effect a change in demand that results from a change in the purchasing power of incomes rather than the general level of incomes

income elasticity of demand the degree to which changes in the level of income affects demand

income tax a direct, proportional tax that is levied on an individual's income

incomes policy government policy on controlling the level of income and wage increases

incorporated business a business that has been incorporated as a limited company, and is therefore considered a legal entity

independent demand demand for goods and services that is unrelated to demand for other goods and services

index linked a value linked to the rate of inflation

indifference level the level at which the marginal utility consumers derive from one product exactly equals the marginal utility derived from an alternative

indirect cost a cost that is not incurred directly in the production process (for example, administration expenses)

indirect production where the goods and services that a society needs are produced outside that society and obtained through trade

indirect tax a tax on the activities or products of individuals or firms

individual demand the level of demand of one consumer

individual supply the level of goods or services provided by one supplier

induction the process of drawing a conclusion from a set of premises or circumstances

inferior goods goods that are purchased when incomes are low, but discarded for other, more expensive goods when incomes are higher

inflation a continuing increase in the general level of prices

inflationary gap an excess of demand over that required to produce full employment

injection money coming into an economy (for example, income from exports)

interest revenue earned by money

International Monetary Fund (IMF) an organisation whose objective is to promote international trade by increasing the exchange rate stability of major currencies through a fund from which countries with balance of payment deficits may borrow

investment multiplier the continuing effect of an injection of investment into the economy

invisible transactions income and expenditure for services, investments and other transfers between countries

issuing house a merchant bank authorised to issue shares in companies

joint supply goods that are produced as a by-product of the process of producing other goods

labour-intensive production production using a large amount of labour in relation to machinery and equipment

labour as a factor of production labour is the work or effort provided by people

leakage money going out of an economy (for example, payments for imports)

liability a debt or promise to pay

limited liability a restriction on the liability of the owners of an incorporated business to the amount of their original investment

liquid asset an asset that can be turned into cash quickly

liquidity the ability to quickly turn assets into cash

liquidity preference the desire to hold money rather than spend it

loanable funds money that is available for making loans

Maastricht Treaty treaty signed in Maastricht, Holland, in 1991, which created the European Union out of the existing European Community. It aimed at closer economic, political and social harmonisation and links between member states, including European monetary union

macro-economics that part of economics that looks at wider economic problems such as unemployment and inflation

managed flexibility a system of controlling exchange rates that operated between 1945 and 1973. The values of currencies were set against the dollar, itself tied to the value of gold, with a small margin for fluctuation

marginal cost the increase in total cost when output is increased by one unit

marginal product the increase in total product resulting from the employment of an extra unit of a variable factor

marginal productivity the additional productivity gained from the employment of one additional unit of a factor of production

marginal revenue the increase in total revenue when output is increased by one unit

marginal tax rate the rate of tax you would pay on any increase in income over and above your current income

marginal utility the amount of additional utility provided by one extra unit of a product

market demand the total demand of all consumers for one or more good or service

market economy an economy in which the supply of goods and services is unregulated and left to market forces

market efficiency the effectiveness of a market in producing and distributing goods or services to meet the needs of society

market failure a situation in which a free market fails to adequately provide for the needs of all members of society

market forces those influences on demand, supply and price that are not subject to government or other interference

market mechanism the interaction of the unregulated forces of demand and supply to set the price, quantity demanded and quantity supplied of a product

market price the price of a product resulting from the interaction of the market forces of supply and demand

market supply the total supply of one or more goods and services

merchant bank a private bank normally acting as an accepting house and issuing house

merit goods goods and services that are generally considered too important to be left to the operation of a free market

micro-economics that part of economics that investigates basic economic principles such as demand and supply

minimum lending rate the minimum rate for normal loans made by banks, set from time to time by the Bank of England

minimum wage the lowest wage that can legally be paid

mixed economy an economy that is partly regulated by government and partly left to market forces

mobility of labour the ease with which labour is able to move to different areas or industries

monetary policy policy designed to influence the economy by controlling the money supply

monetary sector financial institutions that come under the auspices of, and have to deposit a proportion of their funds with, the Bank of England

money market the market for short-term funds

money supply the amount of money in the economy

monopoly a firm that supplies at least 25 per cent of the market and is able to control the supply and price of a product

monopoly rent the additional profit that a monopolist is able to make by controlling supply and price of a product

monopsonist an employer in the position of being a sole buyer of labour in an industry or market, and therefore able to set wage rates

multiplier a factor used to show the effect of changing one aspect of the economy

narrow money a measure of money supply (M0) that consists mainly of notes and coins in circulation; sometimes private sector sight deposits at banks are included (M1) and other accounts subject to withdrawal by cheque plus other deposits due to mature within one month (M2)

national accounts statements of national income and expenditure

national debt the accumulated outstanding borrowing by the government

national income income received from all factors of production owned by a country in a year

national product the aggregate production of goods and services by all factors of production owned by a country in a year

nationalisation the transfer of private sector industries into public ownership

natural monopoly an industry in which it would be wasteful or inefficient to have more than one supplier

natural rate of unemployment the rate of unemployment when the labour market is in equilibrium

natural resources resources that are found in nature

negative externality a social cost associated with production

net domestic product gross domestic product adjusted for taxes and depreciation

net national product gross national product adjusted for net property income from abroad, taxes and depreciation

net property income from abroad property income from abroad less property income paid abroad

non price-based competition competition between firms using factors other than price to discriminate between products

non-accelerating inflation rate of unemployment (NAIRU) the level of unemployment that is consistent with zero inflation

non-contestable market a market that is not open to competition

non-excludability the inability to limit the provision of a good or service to specific paying customers

non-renewable resource a resource that cannot be replaced once it has been used up

non-tariff barriers barriers to imports other than tariffs (for example, discriminatory administrative practices)

normal rate of profit the minimum return that will keep a firm in its particular industry after all other factors of production have been paid for

normative economics a type of economic method that uses economic theory as a basis for action or political policy

oligopoly a group of firms that between them control a market

open economy an economy that trades with other economies for goods and services

open market operation transactions that occur in the free market and are subject to normal forces of demand and supply

opportunity cost the cost of something in terms of the next best alternative forgone

optimum population the most appropriate size of population for a country, having regard to its needs and the resources available to satisfy those needs

overdraft an arrangement with a commercial bank whereby a customer is allowed to draw cheques in excess of the amount they have deposited with the bank

pareto efficiency a situation in which nobody in an economy can be made better off without somebody else becoming worse off

perfect competition competition in a market in which there are many customers for and suppliers of identical products, and customers have complete knowledge of suppliers and prices of those products

perfect elasticity of demand a hypothetical price elasticity where at one price demand for a product is zero but if the price falls slightly demand becomes infinite

Phillips curve a graph showing the relationship between inflation and unemployment

positive economics a type of economic thinking confined to showing what is likely to happen in different circumstances, without drawing conclusions about what future course of action should be taken

positive externality a benefit associated with the production of a good or service that affects people not directly involved in its production

poverty trap a situation in which a person is unable to escape poverty since any increase in their personal income would be negated by a reduction in the amount of state benefits they received

precautionary demand for money the demand for money to be held in reserve against unexpected events

price agreements agreements between firms on price levels

price elasticity the extent to which the quantity of a product demanded or supplied is affected by its price

price mechanism the process of setting prices through the free interaction of demand and supply

price relative a relationship with the level of prices

price-based competition competition between firms that is based on offering a product at the most attractive price

primary sector that sector of industry that obtains the raw materials used in manufacturing

private benefit benefits associated with the provision of goods and services that accrue to the producers or consumers of those goods and services

private cost costs associated with the provision of goods and services that accrue to the producers or consumers of those goods and services

private sector that sector of industry owned and operated by private individuals rather than the government

private sector liquidity the ability of firms in the private sector to convert assets into cash in order to cover their liabilities

privatisation the transfer of state-owned industries into private ownership

producer goods goods, such as machinery and office equipment, which is used by businesses in the production of other goods

producer surplus the difference between the amount producers require to induce them to supply additional units of a product, and the amount they actually receive from selling the additional units

production industry an industrial organisation that operates in more than one industrial sector, i.e. obtaining raw materials (primary) and manufacturing goods from them (secondary)

production possibility curve or frontier the maximum combination of the number of units of two types of goods that can be produced using available resources

productive assets assets that are used to produce goods or services

productive or technical efficiency production using the minimum resources required

productivity the volume of output from given resources

progressive taxation a tax that increases with an increase in the value of the item taxed

propensity to consume the predisposition of people in society to spend a proportion of their income rather than save it

propensity to save the predisposition of people in society to save a proportion of their income rather than spend it

proportional taxation a tax system in which all taxpayers hand over the same proportion of their income in tax

public expenditure expenditure by the government on goods and services

public finance the method of raising revenue and principles of public expenditure employed by the government

public goods goods that are supplied by government, since their non-excludability is likely to mean that there would be no incentive to supply them in a free market

public sector businesses and other organisations owned by the state

public sector net cash requirement (PSNCR) the finance needed by government to operate the public sector, taking into consideration the government's anticipated income and expenditure

purchasing power the value of a currency in terms of the goods and services a unit of that currency will purchase

purchasing power parity a comparison of currencies in terms of purchasing power

quango a body established and funded by the government, but which operates independently under its own board of governors

quantity theory of money a theory based on the premise that the general level of prices depends upon the supply of money

quasi or temporary rent payment for a factor of production that is above its transfer earnings, due to a temporary shortage of that factor

quasi-public goods goods that are supplied by the government, but may have some element of excludability

quaternary sector subdivision of the tertiary sector that provides services to business

quota a permitted or prescribed volume or value

rate of discount the rate at which an accepting house will discount (pay less than) the face value of a bill of exchange. The rate of discount will vary according to the source of the bill and its due date

rate of interest the rate at which a financial institution will pay interest on money deposited and charge interest on loans

recession a period of declining economic activity

reflation an increase in economic activity

regional unemployment unemployment in a particular region due to changes in economic activity in that region (such as a declining local industry)

regressive taxation system of taxation under which people with lower incomes pay a higher proportion of their incomes in tax than those with higher incomes

renewable resources natural resources that can be replaced

residual error a small accounting error often attributable to rounding figures up or down, or due to small items that cannot accurately be calculated

restrictive practices court a tribunal set up to ensure that business mergers, trading agreements and other business practices are in the public interest

restrictive practices behaviour aimed at preventing the free operation of a market

retail bank *see* clearing banks

retail price index (RPI) a measure of the change in prices of a range of goods and services, representative of general household expenditure over time

retained profit that part of the profit of a firm that is retained by the firm after all dividends, taxes, etc. have been paid

returns to scale the amount by which costs vary with levels of output

revenue the income received from the sale of goods or services

scarcity the finite nature of all resources

seasonal unemployment unemployment resulting from the seasonal nature of an industry

secondary sector that sector of industry that manufactures goods

securities market the market for government and other bonds

share a stake in the capital of a company

sight deposits money in a bank current account, which may be interest bearing

Single European Market (SEM) unified market comprising the European Union within which the goods and services of member states can be freely exchanged, but which is protected from imports from other countries by common tariffs

social accounting the process of compiling national accounts

social benefit a benefit to society that arises as a by-product of the production of a good or service

social capital items of fixed capital that are provided for the good of society, such as roads and hospitals

social cost a cost to society that arises as a by-product of the production of a good or service

special deposit an amount that clearing banks can be required to deposit with the Bank of England in order to control the money supply

specialisation the concentration on producing specific goods and services, or carrying out discrete activities in the production of those goods and services

specific tax a tax that is levied per unit of a product rather than by value

speculative demand for money demand for money to speculate on the price movements of bonds

standard for deferred payment a commodity that may be accepted in payment for goods and services that can subsequently be exchanged for other goods and services

standard of living the level of material wealth or welfare of a society, or specific sector of a society

static efficiency the efficiency of an economy at a specific point in time under the conditions prevailing at that time

stock appreciation the increase in value of stock over time

structural unemployment unemployment due to the permanent decline in an industry

subsidy financial support provided by the government out of taxation

substitute goods goods that are considered acceptable alternatives, so that if the price of one rises, demand may be switched to the alternative

substitution effect the tendency of consumers to purchase more of a product when the price falls because that product represents better value than substitute products

sunk costs capital costs of a firm not recoverable in the short-term in the event of the firm wanting to exit a market

supply the provision of resources, goods and services

supply-side factors arising from changes in supply

surplus an excess of credits over debits (for example, income over expenditure)

sustainability the ability to maintain economic growth without exhausting natural resources or causing ecological damage

tariff a tax on imports designed to raise their price and so increase demand for home-produced goods

technological unemployment unemployment that arises due to the introduction of new labour-saving technology in an industry

tertiary sector that sector of industry that provides services

third world a collective term for nations with less developed or industrialised economies

time deposit money deposited for a specified time in an interest bearing bank account

trade bill a bill of exchange issued by a commercial organisation

trade creation the 'creation' of trade behind tariffs as consumers are encouraged to buy home-produced goods

trade diversion the diversion of trade from its normal channels as overseas producers lose their traditional markets

trade union an association of workers, normally in a specific trade or industry, whose purpose is to negotiate on behalf of its members on employment matters, including pay and conditions

trading surplus the surplus of income from exports after expenditure on imports

transactions demand for money demand for money to be used for day-to-day expenditure

transfer earnings the amount a factor of production could earn if used in its next best alternative occupation

transfer payments the transfer of money from one source to another without the donor receiving any productive service in return (for example, pensions)

treasury bill bill of exchange issued by the treasury

underwriting the process of guaranteeing a payment by a third party; the guarantee by an issuing house to purchase all shares of a new issue made through that house not otherwise taken up

unincorporated business a business that has not been incorporated as a company, the affairs of which are considered the same as those of the owners of the business

unit labour cost the cost of one unit of labour

unit of account a basic unit of currency or exchange

unit of production an identifiable part of a source of output

unlimited liability the unrestricted liability of the owners of a business for the debts and other affairs of that business

utility the satisfaction obtained from a given amount of a good or service

value added the increase in value of a product at each stage of the production process

value added tax (VAT) a tax on the increase in value of a product at each stage of the production process

variable capital items of capital used in a production process that vary with the level of production

variable cost a cost that varies with the level of production (for example, raw materials)

variable factor of production a factor of production that can easily be increased or reduced

velocity of circulation the average number of times that each unit of money changes hands

vertical equity the discriminatory treatment of different people in society in an attempt to achieve a fair distribution of goods, services and opportunities

wage control government policy on controlling the level of wage increases

wage differentials accepted differences between wage levels for different types or levels of occupation

ways and means advances loans to the government by the Bank of England

weighting giving greater prominence to one factor by increasing its value by a given ratio to other factors

working capital items of capital that are used up in the production process

working population that part of the population of a country that is eligible and available for employment

World Bank (International Bank for Reconstruction and Development) an international co-operative organisation formed to assist economic development, especially of third world countries, through loans guaranteed by the governments of member nations

yield the return on an investment

Bibliography and Internet sources

Books

Bagehot, Walter, *Lombard Street: A Description of the Money Market* (John Wiley and Sons, 1999)

Bannock, Graham et al., *The Penguin Dictionary of Economics* (Penguin Books, 1998)

Beck, Ulrich, *What Is Globalization?* (Polity Press, 1999)

Bernanke, Ben S. et al., *Inflation Targetting* (Princeton University Press, 1998)

Burda, Michael and Wyplosz, Charles, *Macroeconomics: a European Text* (Oxford University Press, 1997)

Chabot, Christian N., *Understanding the Euro* (McGraw-Hill, 1998)

Coase, R. H., *The Firm, the Market and the Law* (University of Chicago Press, 1990)

Coggan, Philip, *The Money Machine* (Penguin Books, 1999)

Curwen, Peter (ed.), *Understanding the UK Economy* (Macmillan, 1997)

Davies, Glen, *A History of Money* (University of Wales Press, 1996)

Dicken, Peter, *Global Shift* (Sage Publications, 1998)

Dornbusch, Rudiger and Fischer, Stanley, *Macroeconomics* (McGraw-Hill, 1997)

Driffill, John, *Economics* (W. W. Norton & Co., 2000)

Edwards, Michael, *Future Positive* (Earthscan, 1999)

Eichengreen, Barry, *Globalizing Capital: A History of the International Monetary System* (Princeton University Press, 1998)

Evans, David and Schmalensee, Richard, *Paying with Plastic* (MIT Press, 1999)

Frank, Robert, *Luxury Fever* (Free Press, 1999)

Friedman, Milton and Friedman, Rose, *Free to Choose* (Harcourt Brace, 1980)

Fujita, Masahisa et al., *The Spacial Economy* (MIT Press, 1999)

Galbraith, John Kenneth, *The New Industrial State* (Penguin Books, 1974)

Galbraith, John Kenneth, *The Affluent Society* (Penguin Books, 1984)

Galbraith, John Kenneth, *A History of Economics* (Penguin Books, 1991)

Gardner, H. Stephen, *Comparative Economic Systems* (Dryden Press, 1998)

Gastells, Manuel, *The Information Age: Economy, Society and Culture* (Blackwell, 1999)

Gates, Jeff, *The Ownership Solution: Towards a Shared Capitalism for the Twenty-first Century* (Penguin Books, 1999)

Gillespie, Andrew, *Advanced Economics through Diagrams* (Oxford University Press, 1998)

Gorringe, Timothy, *Fair Shares: Ethics and the Global Economy* (Thames and Hudson, 2000)

Gray, John, *False Dawn: the Delusions of Global Capitalism* (Granta Books, 1998)

Greider, William, *One World Ready or Not* (Penguin Books, 1998)

Griffiths, Alan and Wall, Stuart (eds), *Applied Economics* (Longman, 1999)

Gustafson, Thane, *Capitalism Russian-style* (Cambridge University Press, 1999)

Heilbronner, Robert L., *The Worldly Philosophers* (Penguin Books, 2000)

Heilbronner, Robert L. and Thurow, Lester, *Economics Explained* (Pocket Books, 1998)

Held, David et al., *Global Transformations* (Polity Press, 1999)

Hirst, Paul and Thompson, Graham, *Globalization in Question* (Polity Press, 1999)

Hobson, Dominic, *The National Wealth: Who Gets What in Britain* (HarperCollins, 1998)

Howells, Peter and Bain, Keith, *The Economics of Money, Banking and Finance* (Longman, 1998)

Hutton, Will, *The State We're In* (Vintage, 1996)

Jehle, Geoffrey A. and Reny, Philip, *Advanced Microeconomic Theory* (Longman, 1998)

Jowsey, Ernie, *100 Essay Plans for Economics* (Oxford University Press, 1998)

Kennedy, Paul, *Preparing for the Twenty-first Century* (Fontana Press, 1994)

Keynes, John Maynard, *The General Theory of Employment, Interest and Money* (Prometheus Books, 1936)

Kindleberger, Charles P., *Manias, Panics and Crashes: a History of Financial Crises* (John Wiley and Sons, 1996)

Korten, David C., *The Post-Corporate World* (Berrett-Koehler, 1999)

Krugman, Paul, *Currencies and Crises* (CIT Press, 1995)

Krugman, Paul, *The Age of Diminished Expectations* (MIT Press, 1997)

Krugman, Paul, *Development, Geography and Economic Theory* (MIT Press, 1997)

Krugman, Paul, *The Accidental Theorist* (Penguin Books, 1999)

Krugman, Paul, *The Return of Depression Economics* (Penguin Books, 2000)
Krugman, Paul and Obstfeld, Maurice, *International Economics* (Longman, 1997)

Lavigne, Marie, *The Economics of Transition* (Macmillan Press, 1999)
Luttwak, Edward, *Turbo Capitalism* (Orion, 1999)

Magretta, Joan (ed.), *Managing the New Economy* (Harvard Business School Press, 1999)
Mallet, Victor, *The Trouble with Tigers* (HarperCollins, 1999)
Mankiw, N. Gregory, *Principles of Economics* (Dryden Press, 1997)
Mankiw, N. Gregory, *Macroeconomics* (Worth Publishers, 1999)
Mas-Colell, Andreu et al., *Microeconomic Theory* (Oxford University Press, 1995)
Mishkin, Frederic S., *The Economics of Money, Banking and Financial Markets* (Addison Wesley Longman, 1998)
Morris, Charles R., *Money, Greed and Risk: Why Financial Crashes Happen* (John Wiley and Sons, 2000)

Nellis, Joe and Parker, David, *The Essence of the Economy* (Prentice Hall, 1996)
Nellis, Joe and Parker, David, *The Essence of Business Economics* (Prentice Hall, 1997)
North, Douglass, *Institutions, Institutional Change and Economic Performance* (Cambridge University Press, 1990)

Obstfeld, Maurice and Rogoff, Kenneth, *Foundations of International Macroeconomics* (MIT Press, 1996)
O'Hara, Maureen, *Market Microstructure Theory* (Blackwell Publishers, 1997)
Olson, Mancur, *The Rise and Decline of Nations: Economic Growth, Stagflation and Social Rigidities* (Yale University Press, 1983)
Ormerod, P., *The Death of Economics* (Faber and Faber, 1995)
Owen, Geoffrey, *From Empire to Europe* (HarperCollins, 1999)

Pentecost, Eric, *Macroeconomics: An Open Economy Approach* (Macmillan Press, 2000)
Polanyi, Karl, *The Great Transformation* (Beacon Press, 1971)
Porter, Michael E., *Competitive Advantage of Nations* (Macmillan Press, 1998)

Ray, Debraj, *Development Economics* (Princeton University Press, 1998)
Remenyi, Joe, *Microfinance and Poverty Alleviation* (Pinter Publishers, 2000)
Ricardo, David, *Principles of Political Economy and Taxation* (Prometheus Books, 1817)
Rodrik, Dani, *The New Global Economy and Developing Countries: Making Openness Work* (Johns Hopkins University Press, 1998)
Romer, David, *Advanced Macroeconomics* (McGraw-Hill, 1995)

Sala-i-Martin, Xavier, *Economic Growth* (MIT Press, 1999)
Samuelson, Paul, *Economics* (McGraw-Hill, 1998)
Sassen, Saskia, *Globalization and its Discontents: Essays on the New Mobility of People and Money* (New Press, 1999)
Schiller, Dan, *Digital Capitalism* (MIT Press, 1999)
Schumpeter, Joseph A., *Capitalism, Socialism and Democracy* (HarperCollins, 1962)
Schiller, Robert J., *Market Volatility* (MIT Press, 1992)
Simon, Carl P. and Blume, Lawrence E., *Mathematics for Economists* (W. W. Norton, 1994)
Sloman, John, *Economics* (Prentice Hall, 1998)
Smith, Adam, *The Money Game* (Vintage Books, 1996)
Solomon, Michael et al., *Consumer Behaviour* (Prentice Hall, 1998)
Soros, George, *The Crisis of Global Capitalism* (Little, Brown & Company, 1998)
Steit, Clara C., *European Capital Markets* (Macmillan Press, 2000)
Studies in the UK Economy Series (Heinemann)

Tapscott, Don, *The Digital Economy* (McGraw-Hill, 1997)
Temperton, Paul, *The Euro* (John Wiley and Sons, 1998)
Thaler, Richard H., *The Winner's Curse: Paradoxes and Anomalies of Economic Life* (Princeton University Press, 1994)
Thurow, Lester, *The Future of Capitalism* (Nicholas Breasley Publishing, 1997)

Valdez, Stephen, *An Introduction to Global Financial Markets* (Macmillan Press, 2000)
Varian, Hal, *Intermediate Micro-economics* (W. W. Norton, 1999)

Walsh, Carl, *Monetary Theory and Policy* (MIT Press, 1998)
Warburton, Peter, *Debt and Delusion* (Allen Lane The Penguin Press, 1999)
Whinston, Andrew B. et al., *The Economics of Electronic Commerce* (Macmillan Press, 1997)

Periodicals

Economist
Economics Review
Economics Today
Teaching Business and Economics: Journal of the Economics and Business Education Association

Internet sources

Bank of England: http://www.bankofengland.co.uk
BBC News: http://www.news.bbc.co.uk
Bized: http://bized.ac.uk

Economist: http://www.economist.co.uk
European Union: http://www.europa.eu.int

Financial Times: http://www.ft.com

Guardian: http://www.guardian.co.uk

HM Treasury: http://www.hm-treasury.gov.uk

Independent: http://www.independent.co.uk
International Monetary Fund: http://www.imf.org

OECD: http://www.oecd.org
Office for National Statistics: http://www.ons.gov.uk

Times: http://www.the-times.co.uk
Tutor2u: http://www.tutor2u.co.uk

United Nations: http://www.un.org
United States Central Intelligence Agency: http://ic.gov

World Bank: http://worldbank.org
World Trade Organisation: http://www.wto.org

Recommended reading

Unit 1

Bannock, Graham et al., *The Penguin Dictionary of Economics* (Penguin Books, 1999)

Galbraith, John Kenneth, *A History of Economics* (Penguin Books, 1991)

Gastells, Manuel, *The Information Age: Economy, Society and Culture* (Blackwell, 1999)

Hobson, Dominic, *The National Wealth: Who Gets What in Britain* (HarperCollins, 1998)

Schumpeter, Joseph A., *Capitalism, Socialism and Democracy* (HarperCollins, 1962)

Sloman, John, *Economics* (Prentice Hall, 1998)

Unit 2

Galbraith, John Kenneth, *The New Industrial State* (Penguin Books, 1967)

Keynes, John Maynard, *The General Theory of Employment, Interest and Money* (Prometheus Books, 1936)

Mankiw, N. Gregory, *Principles of Economics* (Dryden Press, 1997)

Smith, Adam, *The Wealth of Nations* (Penguin Books, 1776)

Unit 3

Begg, David, Fischer, Stanley and Dornbusch, Rudiger *Economics* (McGraw-Hill, 1997)

Galbraith, John Kenneth, *The Affluent Society* (Penguin Books, 1958)

Mas-Colell, Andreu et al., *Microeconomic Theory* (Oxford University Press, 1995)

Solomon, Michael et al., *Consumer Behaviour* (Prentice Hall, 1998)

Varian, Hal, *Intermediate Micro-economics* (W. W. Norton, 1999)

Unit 4

Coase, R. H., *The Firm, the Market and the Law* (University of Chicago Press, 1990)

Galbraith, John Kenneth, *The New Industrial State* (Penguin Books, 1974)

Gates, Jeff, *The Ownership Solution: Towards a Shared Capitalism for the Twenty-first Century* (Penguin Books, 1999)

Hurl, Bryan (series editor), *Studies in the UK Economy: Multinationals* (Heinemann)

Korten, David C., *The Post-Corporate World* (Berrett-Koehler, 1999)

Nellis, Joe and Parker, David, *The Essence of Business Economics* (Prentice Hall, 1997)

Unit 5

Coase, R. H., *The Firm, the Market and the Law* (University of Chicago Press, 1990)

Griffiths, Alan and Wall, Stuart (eds), *Applied Economics* (Longman, 1999)

O'Hara, Maureen, *Market Microstructure Theory* (Blackwell, 1997)

Shiller, Robert J., *Market Volatility* (CIT Press, 1992)

Unit 6

Curwen, Peter (ed.), *Understanding the UK Economy* (Macmillan, 1997)

Gardner, H. Stephen, *Comparative Economic Systems* (Dryden Press, 1998)

Keynes, John Maynard, *The General Theory of Employment, Interest and Money* (Prometheus Books, 1936)

Unit 7

Curwen, Peter (ed.), *Understanding the UK Economy* (Macmillan, 1997)

Friedman, Milton and Friedman, Rose, *Free to Choose* (Harcourt Brace, 1980)

Gardner, H. Stephen, *Comparative Economic Systems* (Dryden Press, 1998)

Hurl, Bryan (series editor), *Studies in the UK Economy: Equity, Efficiency and Market Failure* (Heinemann)

Hurl, Bryan (series editor), *Studies in the UK Economy: Green Economics* (Heinemann)

Unit 8

Bagehot, Walter, *Lombard Street: A Description of the Money Market* (John Wiley and Sons, 1999)

Coggan, Philip, *The Money Machine* (Penguin Books, 1999)

Howells, Peter and Bain, Keith, *The Economics of Money, Banking and Finance* (Longman, 1998)

Mishkin, Frederic S., *The Economics of Money, Banking and Financial Markets* (Addison Wesley Longman, 1998)

Steit, Clara, *European Capital Markets* (Macmillan Press, 2000)

Valdez, Stephen, *An Introduction to Global Financial Markets* (Macmillan Press, 2000)

Unit 9

Curwen, Peter, *Understanding the UK Economy* (Macmillan, 1997)
Dornbusch, Rudiger and Fischer, Stanley, *Macroeconomics* (McGraw-Hill, 1997)
Hurl, Bryan (series editor), *Studies in the UK Economy: The UK Economy* (Heinemann)

Unit 10

Curwen, Peter, *Understanding the UK Economy* (Macmillan, 1997)
Griffiths, Alan and Wall, Stuart (eds), *Applied Economics* (Longman, 1999)
Hurl, Bryan (series editor), *Studies in the UK Economy: Inflation and UK Monetary Policy* (Heinemann)
Hurl, Bryan (series editor), *Studies in the UK Economy: Supply-side Economics* (Heinemann)
Hurl, Bryan (series editor), *Studies in the UK Economy: UK Fiscal Policy* (Heinemann)
Hutton, Will, *The State We're In* (Vintage, 1996)
Margretta, Joan (ed.), *Managing the New Economy* (Harvard Business School Press, 1999)
Ricardo, David, *Principles of Political Economy and Taxation* (Prometheus Books, 1817)
Walsh, Carl, *Monetary Theory and Policy* (MIT Press, 1998)

Unit 11

Curwen, Peter, *Understanding the UK Economy* (Macmillan, 1997)
Griffiths, Alan and Wall, Stuart (eds), *Applied Economics* (Longman, 1999)
Hurl, Bryan (series editor), *Studies in the UK Economy: The UK Labour Market* (Heinemann)
Hurl, Bryan (series editor), *Studies in the UK Economy: UK Unemployment* (Heinemann)
Keynes, John Maynard, *The General Theory of Employment, Interest and Money* (Prometheus Books, 1936)

Unit 12

Bank of England quarterly Report
Bernanke, Ben S. et al., *Inflation Targetting* (Princeton University Press, 1998)
Curwen, Peter, *Understanding the UK Economy* (Macmillan, 1997)
Griffiths, Alan and Wall, Stuart (eds), *Applied Economics* (Longman, 1999)
Hurl, Bryan (series editor), *Studies in the UK Economy: Inflation and UK Monetary Policy* (Heinemann)

Unit 13

Beck, Ulrich, *What is Globalisation?* (Polity Press, 1999)
Dicken, Peter, *Global Shift* (Sage Publications, 1998)
Gorringe, Timothy, *Fair Shares: Ethics and the Global Economy* (Thames and Hudson, 2000)
Greider, William, *One World Ready or Not* (Penguin Books, 1998)
Hurl, Bryan (series editor), *Studies in the UK Economy: The European Union* (Heinemann)
Krugman, Paul and Obstfeld, Maurice, *International Economics* (Longman, 1997)
Temperton, Paul, *The Euro* (John Wiley and Sons, 1998)

Unit 14

Curwen, Peter, *Understanding the UK Economy* (Macmillan, 1997)
Edwards, Michael, *Future Positive* (Earthscan, 1999)
Hurl, Bryan (series editor), *Studies in the UK Economy: Development Economics* (Heinemann)
Krugman, Paul, *Development, Geography and Economic Theory* (MIT Press, 1997)
Ray, Debraj, *Development Economics* (Princeton University Press, 1998)
Sala-i-Martin, Xavier, *Economic Growth* (MIT Press, 1999)

Answers to numerical activities

Unit 1 None

Unit 2 None

Unit 3 Page 98

- Cross elasticity of demand for 35 mm camera = 0.12/0.09 = 1.33
- Cross elasticity of demand for colour films = 0.05/0.09 = 0.56
- Cameras and films are complementary goods.

Page 100

- Income elasticity of demand for theatre tickets = 0.14/0.08 = 1.75
- Conditions of demand for tickets (for example, income levels, taste, etc.) at other theatres may vary.

Unit 4 Page 144

- Average product per worker = 91.67 sandwiches
- Marginal product of additional employee = 75 sandwiches

Unit 5 None

Unit 6 None

Unit 7 None

Unit 8 Page 273

- 11%
- £15 619 500

Page 275

Willowbrook Central Bank			
Assets	**£**	**Liabilities**	**£**
Cash in hand	15 000 000	Customers' deposits	15 000 000

Page 276

Willowbrook Central Bank			
Assets	**£**	**Liabilities**	**£**
Cash in hand	1 650 000	Customers' deposits	15 000 000
Loans to customers (or promises to repay)	13 350 000		
Total	15 000 000	Total	15 000 000

Page 277

Willowbrook Central Bank			
Assets	**£**	**Liabilities**	**£**
Cash	1 640 000	Customers' deposits	14 990 000
Loans to customers (promises to repay)	13 350 000		
Total	14 990 000	Total	14 990 000

Page 278
- 10.94%
- 0.06% = £8010

Unit 9

Page 307
- VAT = £52.5 billion
- Subsidy = £0.2 billion
- Excluding these, GDP = £447.3 billion

Unit 10

Page 323
- 1.47 billion

Page 325
- £469

Unit 11

Page 356
- £4 million

Unit 12

Page 373
- If the velocity of money remains constant, the value of money will half. However, there is nothing to say that the velocity of money *will* remain constant.

Unit 13

None

Unit 14

None

Index

Java, Java, Java!

Object-Oriented Problem Solving

Ralph Morelli
Trinity College

Prentice Hall
Upper Saddle River, New Jersey 07458

To my parents.

Library of Congress Cataloging-in-Publication Data

Morelli, Ralph
Java, Java, Java! / Ralph Morelli.
p. cm.
Includes bibliographical references and index.
ISBN 0–13–011332–8
1. Java, Java, Java! 2. Object-Oriented Problem Solving. I. Title.
TK7867.H345 2000 99–21128
621.381–dc21 CIP

Publisher: *Alan Apt*
Project manager: *Ana Terry*
Editor-in-chief: *Marcia Horton*
Senior marketing manager: *Jennie Burger*
Production manager: *Rose Kernan*
Development editor: *Jerry Ralya*
Managing editor: *David George*
Executive managing editor: *Vince O'Brien*
Cover design: *Heather Scott*
Manufacturing coordinator: *Pat Brown*
Editorial assistant: *Toni Holm*
Composition: *PreTEX, Inc.*

Printed in the United States of America

10 9 8 7 6 5 4 3

ISBN 0-13-011332-8

Prentice-Hall International (UK) Limited, *London*
Prentice-Hall of Australia Pty. Limited, *Sydney*
Prentice-Hall Canada Inc., *Toronto*
Prentice-Hall Hispanoamericana, S.A., *Mexico*
Prentice-Hall of India Private Limited, *New Delhi*
Prentice-Hall of Japan, Inc., *Tokyo*
Prentice-Hall (Singapore) Pte. Ltd., *Singapore*
Editora Prentice-Hall do Brasil, Ltda., *Rio de Janeiro*

Preface

Who Should Use This Book?

The topics covered and the approach taken in this book are suitable for a typical depth-first Introduction to Computer Science (CS1) course or for a slightly more advanced Java as a Second Language course. The book is also useful to professional programmers making the transition to Java and object-oriented programming.

The book takes an "objects first" approach to programming and problem solving. It assumes no previous programming experience and requires no prior knowledge of Java or object-oriented programming.

Why Start with Objects?

Java, Java, Java takes an "objects early" approach to teaching Java, with the assumption that teaching beginners the "big picture" early gives them more time to master the principles of object-oriented programming.

The first time I taught Java in our CS1 course I followed the same approach I had been taking in teaching C and C++ — namely, start with the basic language features and structured programming concepts and then, somewhere around midterm, introduce object orientation. This approach was familiar, for it was one taken in most of the textbooks then available in both Java and C++.

One problem with this approach was that many students failed to get the big picture. They could understand loops, if-else constructs, and arithmetic expressions, but they had difficulty decomposing a programming problem into a well-organized Java program. Also, it seemed that this procedural approach failed to take advantage of the strengths of Java's object orientation. Why teach an object-oriented language if you're going to treat it like C or Pascal?

I was reminded of a similar situation that existed when Pascal was the predominant CS1 language. Back then the main hurdle for beginners was *procedural abstraction* — learning the basic mechanisms of procedure call and parameter passing and learning how to **design** programs as a collection of procedures. *Oh! Pascal!*, my favorite introductory text, was typical of a "procedures early" approach. It covered procedures and parameters in Chapter 2, right after covering the assignment and I/O constructs in Chapter 1. It then covered program design and organization in Chapter 3. It didn't get into loops, if-else, and other structured programming concepts until Chapter 4 and beyond.

Presently, the main hurdle for beginners is *object abstraction*. Beginning programmers must be able to see a program as a collection of interacting objects and must learn how to decompose programming problems into well-designed objects. Object orientation subsumes both procedural abstraction and structured programming concepts from the Pascal days.

Teaching "objects early" takes a top-down approach to these three important concepts. The sooner you begin to introduce objects and classes, the better the chances that students will master the important principles of object orientation.

Object Orientation (OO) is a fundamental problem solving and design concept, not just another language detail that should be relegated to the middle or the end of the book (or course). If OO concepts are introduced late, it is much too easy to skip over them when push comes to shove in the course.

Java is a good language for introducing object orientation. Its object model is better organized than C++. In C++ it is easy to "work around" or completely ignore OO features and treat the language like C. In Java there are good opportunities for motivating the discussion of object orientation. For example, it's almost impossible to discuss applets without discussing inheritance and polymorphism. Thus rather than using contrived examples of OO concepts, instructors can use some of Java's basic features — applets, the class library, GUI components — to motivate these discussions in a natural way.

Key Features

In addition to its objects early approach, this book has several other important features.

- **The `CyberPet` Example.** Throughout the text a `CyberPet` class is used as a running example to motivate and illustrate important concepts. The `CyberPet` is introduced in Chapter 2, as a way of "anthropomorphizing" the basic features of objects. Thus individual `CyberPets` belong to a class (definition), have a certain state (instance variables), and are capable of certain behaviors like eating and sleeping (instance methods). Method calls are used to command the `CyberPets` to eat and sleep. In Chapter 3 the emphasis is on defining and using methods and parameters to promote communication with `Cyberpets`. In subsequent chapters, concepts such as inheritance, randomness, animation, and threads are illustrated in terms of the `CyberPet`. Some of the lab and programming exercises are also centered around extending the behavior and sophistication of the `CyberPet`.
- **Applets and GUIs.** Applets and GUIs are first introduced in Chapter 4 and then used throughout the rest of the text. Clearly, applets are a "turn on" for introductory students and can be used as a good motivating factor. Plus, *event-driven programming* and Graphical User Interfaces (GUIs) are what students ought now to be learning in CS1. We are long past the days when command-line interfaces were the norm in applications programming. Another nice thing about Java applets is that they are fundamentally object oriented. To understand them fully, students need to understand basic OO concepts. That's why applets are not introduced until Chapter 4, where they provide an excellent way to motivate the discussion of inheritance and polymorphism.

- **Companion Web Site.** The text is designed to be used in conjunction with a companion Web site that includes many useful resources, including the Java code and Java documentation (in HTML) for all the examples in the text, additional lab and programming assignments, on-line quizzes that can be scored automatically, and PowerPoint class notes.
- **Problem Solving Approach.** A pedagogical, problem solving approach is taken throughout the text. There are total of 13 fully developed case studies, as well as numerous other examples that illustrate the problem solving process. Marginal notes in the text repeatedly emphasize the basic elements of object-oriented problem solving: What objects do we need? What methods and data do we need? What algorithm should we use? And so on.
- **Self-study Exercises.** The book contains more than 200 self-study exercises, with answers provided at the back of each chapter.
- **End-of-Chapter Exercises.** Over 400 end-of-chapter exercises are provided, including "Challenge" exercises at the end of most sets. The answers are provided in an Instructor's Manual, which is available to adopters.
- **Programming, Debugging and Design Tips.** The book contains nearly 400 separately identified "tips" (Programming Tips, Debugging Tips, Effective Design Principles, and Java Language Rules) that provide useful programming and design information in a nutshell.
- **Laboratory Sections.** Each chapter concludes with a laboratory exercise, so the text can easily be used to support lab-based CS1 courses (such as ours). For CS1 courses that are not lab-based, these sections can still be read as preparation for a programming assignment. For each lab in the text, the companion Web site contains additional resources and handouts, as well as a repository of alternative lab assignments.
- **From the Library Sections.** Each chapter includes a section that introduces one or more of the library classes from the Java API (Application Programming Interface). In the early chapters these sections provide a way of introducing tools, such as I/O classes and methods, needed to write simple programs. In subsequent chapters, some of these sections introduce useful but optional topics, such as the `NumberFormat` class used to format numeric output. Others introduce basic GUI (Graphical User Interface) components that are used in program examples and the laboratory sections.
- **Object-Oriented Design Sections.** Each chapter includes a section on Object-Oriented Design which is used to underscore and amplify important principles such as inheritance, polymorphism, and information hiding.
- **Java Language Summary.** Those chapters that introduce language features contain Java Language Summary sections that summarize the features' essential syntax and semantics.

Organization of the Text

The book is organized into three main parts. The first part (Chapters 0 through 4) introduces the basic concepts of object orientation, including objects, classes, methods, parameter passing, information hiding, inheritance, and polymorphism. Although the primary focus in these chapters is on object orientation, rather than Java language details, each of these chapters has a Java Language Summary section that summarizes the language elements introduced.

In Chapters 1 to 3 students are given the basic building blocks for constructing a Java program from scratch. Although the programs at this stage have limited functionality in terms of control structures and data types, the priority is placed on how objects are constructed and how they interact with each other through method calls and parameter passing.

The second part (Chapters 5 through 8) focuses on the remaining language elements, including data types and operators (Chapter 5), control structures (Chapter 6), strings (Chapter 7), and arrays (Chapter 8). Once the basic structure and framework of an object-oriented program are understood, it is relatively easy to introduce these language features.

Part three (Chapters 9 through 16) covers a variety of advanced topics, including graphical user interfaces (Chapter 9), graphics (Chapter 10), exceptions (Chapter 11), recursion (Chapter 12), threads (Chapter 13), files (Chapter 14), sockets (Chapter 15), and data structures (Chapter 16). Topics from these chapters can be used selectively depending on instructor and student interest.

Table 1 provides an example syllabus from my one-semester CS1 course. Our semester is 13 weeks (plus one reading week during which classes do not meet).

Note that the advanced topic chapters needn't be covered in order. Recursion (Chapter 12) could be introduced at the same time or even before loops (Chapter 6). The recursion chapter includes examples using strings, arrays, and drawing algorithms (fractals), as well as some standard numerical algorithms (factorial). Another way to teach recursion would be to incorporate it into the discussion of strings (Chapter 7), arrays (Chapter 8), and graphics (Chapter 10), thereby treating iteration and recursion in parallel.

Exceptions (Chapter 11) could also be covered earlier. The examples in the first few sections of this chapter use simple arithmetic operations and the basic for loop. If theses language elements are introduced separately, then exceptions could be covered right after Chapter 3.

Some of the examples in the advanced chapters use applets (Chapter 4) and GUIs (Chapter 9), so these chapters should ideally be covered before Chapters 10 (graphics), 13 (threads), 14 (files), and 15 (sockets and networking). However, Chapter 15 (data structures) and sections of the other advanced topic chapters can be covered independently of applets and GUIs. Figure 1 shows the major chapter dependencies in the book.

Table 1.

Weeks	A one-semester course Topics	Chapters
1	Introduction	Chapters 0
	Programming Process	Chapter 1
2–4	Objects and Class Definitions	Chapter 2
	Methods and Parameters	Chapter 3
	Selection structure (if-else)	
5	Applet Programming	Chapter 4
	Inheritance	
6	Data Types and Operators	Chapter 5
7–8	Control Structures (Loops)	Chapter 6
	Structured Programming	
9	String Processing (loops)	Chapter 7
10	Array Processing	Chapter 8
11	Recursion	Chapter 12
12	Advanced Topic (GUIs)	Chapter 9
13	Advanced Topic (Exceptions)	Chapter 11
	Advanced Topic (Threads)	Chapter 13

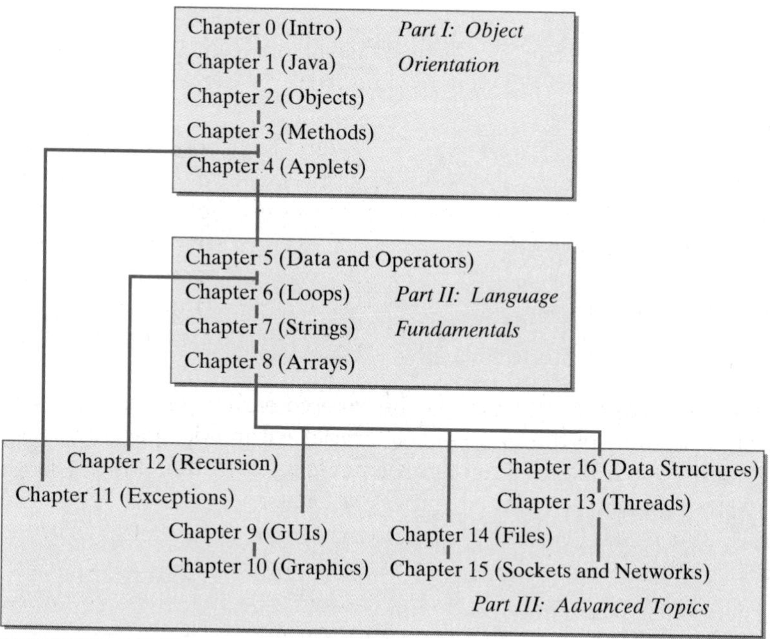

Figure 1 Chapter dependencies. A more detailed chart is available on the companion Web site.

Acknowledgments

First I would like to thank the reviewers and technical reviewers, whose comments often suggested important additions and revisions. These include Pedro Larios (Metrowerks), Laird Dornin (Sun Microsystems), Katherine Lowrie (Trilogy Inc.), Robert Holloway (University of Wisconsin at Madison), Deborah Trytten (University of Oklahoma), Alan Miller (Golden Gate University), Haklin Kimm (University of Tennessee), and Jim Roberts (Carnegie Mellon University).

At Prentice Hall, my appreciation goes to Sandi Hakansan for encouraging me to send the manuscript to PH; to Alan Apt for taking on this project and for being a source of guidance and encouragement throughout; to Ana Arias Terry for her cheerful and professional management of the project; to Rose Kernan for guiding the project through a very tough production phase; Eric Unhjem and Toni Holm for their help and support. I especially want to thank my development editor, Jerry Ralya, whose careful work and many suggestions helped shape and improve the final result in immeasurable ways.

I want to thank a number of Trinity College students who helped track down typos and other errors in earlier drafts of the text. These include Christian Allen, Jeff Green, Ryan Carmody, and Michael Wilson. I especially want to thank Jamie Mazur, whose feedback on the manuscript and enthusiasm for the objects-first approach and whose role in developing the solutions manual were much appreciated.

Thanks to my colleague Joe Palladino in the Engineering Department, who served as the LaTeX meister throughout the project; to Chuck Liang in the Computer Science Department for interesting Java examples; and to my good Hawaii friend and limerick meister, Lanning Lee.

To my Trinity computer science colleagues, Madalene Spezialetti and Ralph Walde, thanks for their generous support and advice, especially during the early stages of this project. They're the ones who pulled me back over the rail when I went overboard with the "objects first" juggernaut. They also helped rescue CyberPet from its germ as a (lame!) horse. With their conjurings and refinements it evolved through a dog, a parrot, and then a "net pet," before settling, rather nicely we think, as CyberPet. They also have my gratitude for being willing to subject our students to earlier (incomplete) drafts of the manuscript in their sections of our intro course. Madalene's suggestion to emphasize basic language features early, led eventually to the book's "Java Language Summary" sections. She also took the first pass at drafting material that appears in Chapter 0 and 1. Although that material has been rewritten (and whatever flaws it has are entirely mine), it still bears the stamp of her influence. Their criticisms and suggestions have improved the text in immeasurable and significant ways, and the gentleness, subtleness, and humor with which they delivered their suggestions has helped sustain our friendship.

Finally, thanks to my wife, Choong Lan How, for her love and encouragement, and for her careful reading of the first three chapters; to my daughter Alicia for her feedback on artistic matters; and to my daughter Meisha for her tremendous help in producing the solutions manual and the online study guide.

Contents

Applets: Programming for the World Wide Web 166

Java Data and Operators 219

Sockets and Networking 816

Data Structures: Lists, Stacks, and Queues 875

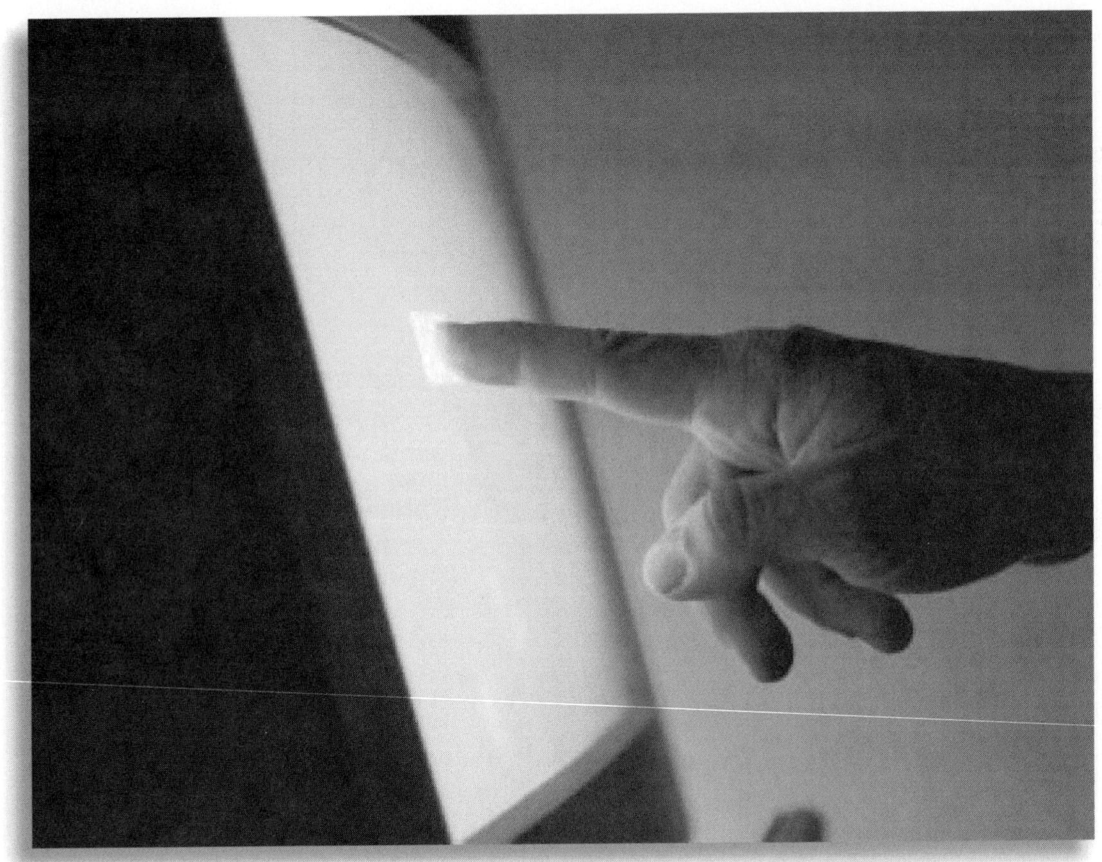

Photograph courtesy of Nick Koudis, PhotoDisc, Inc.

0

Computers, Objects, and Java

OBJECTIVES

After studying this chapter, you will

- Be familiar with the notion of programming.
- Understand why Java is a good introductory programming language.
- Know some of the principles of the object-oriented programming approach.
- Understand basic computer terminology that will be used in the rest of the book.

OUTLINE

0.1 Welcome

Welcome to *Java, Java, Java*. This book introduces you to object-oriented programming using the Java language. Three important questions come to mind: Why study programming? Why study Java? What is object-oriented programming? This first chapter will address these questions and will provide a brief introduction to computers.

0.2 Why Study Programming?

A **computer program** is a set of instructions that directs the computer's behavior. **Computer programming** is the art and science of designing and writing programs. Years ago it was widely believed that entrance into the computer age would require practically everyone to learn how to program. But this is no longer true. Today's computers come with so much easy-to-use software that knowing how to use a computer no longer requires programming skills.

Another reason to study programming might be to gain entry into computer science. However, although programming is one of its primary tools, computer science is a broad and varied discipline, which ranges from engineering subjects, such as processor design, to mathematical subjects such as performance analysis. So there are many computer scientists who do little or no programming as part of their everyday work. If you plan to major or minor in computer science, you will certainly learn to program, but good careers in the computing field are available to programmers and nonprogrammers alike.

One of the best reasons to study programming is because it is a creative and enjoyable problem solving activity. This book will teach you to develop well-designed solutions to a range of interesting problems. One of the best things about programming is that you can actually see and experience your solutions as running programs. As many students have indicated, there's really nothing like the kick you get from seeing your program solving a problem you've been struggling with. Designing and building well-written programs provide a powerful sense of accomplishment and satisfaction. What's more, Java is a language that makes programming even more fun, because once they're finished, many Java programs can be placed on the World Wide Web (WWW) for all the world to see!

0.3 Why Java?

Java is a relatively young programming language. It was initially designed by Sun Microsystems in 1991 as a language for embedding programs into electronic consumer devices, such as microwave ovens and home security systems. However, the tremendous popularity of the **Internet** and the **World Wide Web (WWW)** led Sun to recast Java as a language for embedding programs into Web-based applications. As you probably know, the Internet is a global computer network, and the WWW is that portion of the network that provides multimedia access to a vast range of information. Java is now becoming one of the most important languages for Web and Internet applications.

Java was initially named "Oak" after a tree outside the office of its developer, James Gosling. When it was discovered that there was already a programming language named Oak, the name "Java" was suggested by members of its development team during a visit to a local coffee shop.

Java has also generated significant interest in the business community where it is seen as having commercial potential. In addition to being a useful tool for helping businesses promote their products and services over the Internet, Java is also a good language for distributing software and providing services to employees and clients on private corporate networks or *intranets* .

Because of its original intended role as a language for programming microprocessors embedded in consumer appliances, Java has been designed with a number of interesting features:

- Java is a *simple* language. While it uses many of the same language constructs as C and C++, Java is designed to be simple enough so that fluency in the language should come relatively easily compared to learning C or C++.
- Java is **object-oriented** . Object-oriented languages divide programs into separate modules, called **objects**, that encapsulate the program's various attributes and actions. Thus, Object-Oriented Programming (OOP) and Object-Oriented Design (OOD) refer to a particular way of organizing programs, one which is rapidly emerging as the preferred approach for building complex software systems. Java is much more object-oriented than C++, and it comes with an excellent collection of libraries that can be used to build object-oriented programs.
- Java is *robust*, meaning that errors in Java programs don't cause system crashes as often as errors in other programming languages. Certain features of the language enable many potential errors to be detected before a program is run, and its excellent *exception handling* capability allows it to "catch" errors while a program is running.
- Java is *platform independent* . A platform, in this context, is just a particular kind of computer system, such as a Macintosh or a Windows system. So this means that a Java program can be run without changes on different kinds of computers. This is not true for any other high-level programming language, and this is one reason that Java is suited for WWW applications.
- Java is a *distributed* language, which means that its programs can be designed to run on computer networks. It contains features and code libraries that make it particularly easy to build applications for the Internet and the WWW. This is one of the reasons why Java is so well suited for supporting applications on corporate networks.

- Java is a *secure* language. Designed to be used on networks, Java contains features that protect against *untrusted code* — code that might introduce a virus or corrupt your system in some way. For example, Web-based Java programs are severely constrained in the actions they can take once they are downloaded into your browser.

Despite this list of attractive features, perhaps the best reason for choosing Java as an introductory programming language is its potential for bringing fun and excitement into learning how to program. In what other language can a beginning programmer write a computer game or a graphically based application that can be distributed on a Web page to just about any computer in the world? The simplicity of Java's design, and its easily accessible libraries, bring such accomplishments within reach of the most neophyte programmers.

For example, one of the projects we will work on throughout the text is the CyberPet program, which we begin designing in Chapters 1 and 2. CyberPet starts out as a very simple simulation of a pet that responds to commands like "eat" and "sleep." As we learn more sophisticated programming techniques we gradually build more complexity into the simulation. For example, we learn how to add graphical images to the program in Chapter 4. In Chapter 6 we learn how to animate the CyberPet's eating behavior. In Chapter 8 we add randomness to the CyberPet's behavior so that it disobeys our commands from time to time. Finally in Chapter 13 we learn how to introduce multiple CyberPets of different kinds that behave in a completely autonomous fashion (see Fig 0–1). To get a look at where we're headed you might want to play with CyberPet by visiting the book's companion Web site at
`http://www.prenhall.com/morelli/cyberpet`.

Figure 0–1 An image from the CyberPet applet.

0.4 What Is Object-Oriented Programming?

An object is program module that encapsulates some portion of a program's characteristics and behavior. A Java program is a set of objects that interact with each other by sending and receiving messages among themselves. This notion of objects passing messages around might seem rather strange at first. To most of us, objects are inanimate sorts of things, like sticks and stones, and the idea that these sorts of things can talk to each other is just weird (and possibly confusing).

But objects also include animate things, such as animals, and people. For these kinds of objects the notions of interaction and communication are quite natural. Indeed, one of the main motivations behind our CyberPet is that it is animate and we can communicate with it. As we have done with CyberPet, this tendency to *anthropomorphize* things — make them humanlike — can make the notion of interacting objects more accessible.

Thus, one way to think about things is to imagine that when any kind of object is put into a Java program, it becomes alive and thereby able to act and communicate. Our CyberPet can tell us its name and respond to our commands. A button on the screen can tell us how big it is and whether it is visible or not. A calculator object can be given a number and asked to compute its square root.

As Robert Holloway, one of the early reviewers of this book, has aptly suggested, as programmers we have this ability to bring objects to life. All objects are alive in this sense. However, because you are bringing things to life, you have to know how to control them. Otherwise, like Disney's sorcerer's apprentice, you could end with a disaster on your hands. This is precisely what the object-oriented approach is about: designing objects that work together to carry out a particular task.

This idea of interacting objects is the basic metaphor of object-oriented programming. It is a very natural metaphor that conforms to the way we do things and solve problems in our everyday world.

For example, suppose I want to order a piece of software from the Acme Computer Warehouse catalog. How would I carry out this transaction? First I need to contact the catalog center and place my order. If I contact the catalog center by phone, I would carry on a conversation with a service agent, identifying the catalog number and description of the software I want to purchase. The agent might tell me how much it costs and ask for my credit card information, to which I would reply by providing my credit card number and expiration date.

The action of placing this order takes place between two objects, me and the service representative, and it involves the passing back and forth of certain specific information — the software's part number and description, and my credit card number and expiration date. Moreover, once I tell the service agent to go ahead and process the order, this sets into motion several other transactions that eventually lead to the software being delivered to my home. Each of these transactions involves objects (mostly persons) interacting with each other by exchanging various kinds of information and then processing the information. The sales agent processes my order by passing it on, perhaps on a certain kind of form (another object), to a warehouse clerk (another object). The warehouse clerk uses the form to locate the software in the warehouse and passes it on, along with a delivery from, to a delivery dispatcher (another object). The dispatcher processes the delivery form by making arrangements with a courier (another object), and so on.

This transaction shows several characteristics that are important elements of object-oriented programming.

- **Divide and Conquer Principle .** There is a *division of labor* at work. A very complicated and complex transaction has been divided into smaller, more manageable tasks. This *divide-and-conquer* approach is an important problem solving strategy as well as an important element in designing object-oriented programs. Generally, the first step in designing a program is to divide the overall problem into a set of well-defined subtasks and then to design an object to solve each of the subtasks. Dividing a task up in this way reduces the amount of information that each agent (object) needs to know in order to perform its job. This simplifies each task and increases the chances that it will be performed correctly.
- **Encapsulation Principle .** Each agent involved in this complicated transaction is an expert in one aspect of the overall process. In addition to knowing how to perform the task, each agent knows exactly what information is required for the task, and exactly what information needs to be passed on to the next agent. Another way to say this is that each agent *encapsulates* the expertise needed to perform a certain task. In the same way, the objects in an object-oriented program are designed to be self-contained *modules* that encapsulate specific aspects of the overall task. Each object is defined in terms of what it does, and each object contains the information and the means to perform its given task.
- **Interface Principle .** In order for agents to work cooperatively and efficiently, we have to clarify exactly how they should interact, or interface, with one another. This is called the *interface principle*. For example, the interface to the delivery dispatcher in our transaction might be a particular paper form that must be filled in. Once the form is properly filled in, the dispatcher can perform the task. Similarly, an object's interface limits the way the object can be used. Think of the different interfaces presented by a digital and analog clock. In one case, time is displayed in discrete units, and buttons are used to set the time in hours and minutes. In the other, the time is displayed by hands on a clock face, and time is set by turning a small wheel. In both cases the clock's interface determines how it can be used.
- **Information Hiding Principle .** The work that each agent performs is hidden from the other agents. The sales agent knows what information to pass to the warehouse clerk but does not know exactly what the warehouse clerk does with the information. Warehouse clerks may use spreadsheets or pencil and paper to manage their tasks, but the sales agent needn't know these details. Similarly, in the clock analogy, in

order to use a clock we needn't know how its timekeeping mechanism works. That level of detail is hidden from us. This form of *information hiding* is also employed in the object-oriented approach. While each object in the program presents a certain interface to the other objects, it also shields the details of exactly how it accomplishes its task from the other objects.

- **Generality Principle .** As long as we are designing an object to solve a problem, we might as well do it in a general way so that the object can be used in any situation that requires its expertise. In other words, we design objects not for a particular task, but rather for a particular *kind* of task. We might call this the *generality principle.* For example the dispatcher knows dispatching in general and is able to ship anything for the Acme warehouse, not just customer orders. Similarly, if they are designed well, objects can be used in any number of programs that require their services. The Java class library contains objects that specialize in performing certain kinds of input and output operations. Rather than having to write our own routine to print a message on the console, we can use a library object to handle our printing tasks.
- **Extensibility Principle .** One of the strengths of the object-oriented approach is the *extensibility* of objects. This too has its analogue in the everyday world. Once an agent acquires expertise in a given task, it is not difficult to extend the agent's expertise to accomplish a related task. For example, if Acme needs sales agents who specialize in hardware orders, it would be more economical to extend the skills of some of the current agents instead of training a novice from scratch. In the same way, in the object-oriented approach, an object whose specialty is inputting data might be specialized to handle numeric data. As we will see in Chapter 2, Java's *inheritance* mechanism supports this kind of extensibility.

Taken together, these principles describe object-oriented programming and problem solving. Taken individually, each of the above principles provides a manifestation of the more general principle of *abstraction* . Abstraction is the ability to group large quantities of information together into a single *chunk.* A chunk is a unit of memory. The term was coined by George Miller in his 1956 article "The Magic Number Seven, Plus or Minus Two," in which he claimed that humans have the ability to manage only seven (plus or minus two) pieces of information at one time. Therefore, we manage large quantities of information by forming abstractions. For example, its easier to remember a long string of digits if we chunk the digits. So a phone number gets organized into three chunks (200–990–1179), rather than one chunk consisting of ten digits (2009901179).

Abstraction occurs throughout the above principles. Organizing a complex set of details into a single module, and then dealing with the module as a whole is a form of abstraction. Dividing a problem into its component parts is a form of abstraction, similar in nature to dividing a phone number into its components. Presenting a certain public interface forces the user to deal with an object in terms of the abstractions defined by the interface.

In terms of program design, a good abstraction is extensible and achieves the right degree of generality.

0.5 What Is a Computer?

A **computer** is a machine that performs calculations and processes information. A computer works under the control of a computer program , a set of instructions that tell a computer what to do. **Hardware** refers to the electronic and mechanical components of a computer. **Software** refers to the programs that control the hardware.

A **general-purpose computer** of the sort that we will be programming stores its control programs in its memory and is capable of changing its control program and hence changing what it does. This is in contrast to a **special-purpose computer**, such as the one that resides in your microwave oven or the one that controls your digital watch or calculator. These types of computers contain control programs that are fixed and cannot be changed.

A computer's hardware is organized into several main subsystems or components.

- The **output devices** provide a means by which information held in the computer can be displayed in some human-sensible form. Common output devices include printers, monitors, and audio speakers.
- The **input devices** bring data and information into the computer. Some of the more common input devices are the keyboard, mouse, microphone, and scanner.
- The **primary memory** or **main memory** of a computer is used to store both data and programs. This type of memory is built entirely out of electronic components — integrated circuit chips — which makes it extremely fast. A computer's main memory is *volatile*, which means that any information stored in it is lost when the computer's power is turned off. In a sense, main memory acts as the computer's scratch pad, storing both programs and data temporarily while a program is running.
- The **secondary storage** devices are used for long-term or permanent storage of relatively large amounts of information. These devices include magnetic disks, Compact Disks (CDs), and magnetic tapes. All of these devices are *nonvolatile*, meaning that they retain information when the computer's power is turned off. Compared to a computer's primary memory, these devices are relatively slow, because their access devices all require some form of mechanical motion to retrieve and store data.
- The **central processing unit (CPU)** is the computer's main engine. The CPU is the computer's *microprocessor*, such as the Intel Pentium processor, which serves as the foundation for most Windows PCs, or the PowerPC processor, which serves as the foundation for Macintosh computers. Under the direction of computer programs (software), the CPU issues signals that control the other components that make up the computer system. One portion of the CPU, known as the *arithmetic-logic unit (ALU)*, performs all calculations, such as addition and subtraction, and all logical comparisons, such as when one piece of data is compared to another to determine if they are equal.

The computer's software can be distinguished into two main types:

- **Application software** refers to programs designed to provide a particular task or service, such as word processors, computer games, spreadsheet programs, and Web browsers.
- **System software** includes programs that perform the basic operations that make a computer usable at all. For example, an important piece of system software is the *operating system*, which contains programs that manage the data stored on the computer's disks.

Another important thing that the operating system does is to serve as an interface between the user and the hardware. The operating system determines how the user will interact with the system, or conversely, how the system will look and feel to the user. For example, in *command-line* systems, such as Unix and DOS (short for Disk Operating System), a program is run by typing its name on the command line. By contrast, in graphically based systems, such as Windows and Macintosh, a program is run by clicking on its icon with the mouse. Thus, this "point and click" interface has a totally different "look and feel," but does the same thing.

Processors Then and Now

To give you some idea of how rapidly computer hardware technology has advanced, let's compare the first digital processor with one of today's models.

The *ENIAC* (which stood for Electronic Numerical Integrator and Calculator) was developed in 1946 at the University of Pennsylvania. ENIAC occupied more than 640 square feet of floor space and weighed nearly 30 tons. Instead of the *integrated circuits* used in today's computers, ENIAC's digital technology was based on over 17,000 vacuum tubes. At a speed of 100,000 pulses per second, ENIAC ran more than 500 times faster than other computing machines of that day and age. Its main application was for computing ballistic trajectories for the U.S. Army. It could perform around 300 multiplications in a second. To program the ENIAC, you would have to manipulate hundreds of cables and switches. It took two or three days for a team of several programmers, most of whom were young women, to set up a single program that would then run for a few seconds.

The Pentium III processor is Intel's most advanced and powerful processor for desktop computers. The chip contains 9.5 million transistors and runs at speeds up to 500 MHz (500 million cycles per second). The Pentium processor is small enough to fit completely within the confines of the fingernail on your pinky finger. It executes millions of instructions per second. It supports a huge range of multimedia applications, including three-dimensional graphics, streaming audio and video, and speech recognition applications. To program the Pentium, you can choose from a wide range of high-level programming languages, including the Java language.

Photograph courtesy of Roger Duboisson, The Stock Market

0.6 The Internet and the World Wide Web

Most personal computers contain software that enables them to be connected to *networks* of various sizes. Networks allow many individual users to share costly computer resources, such as a high-speed printer or a large disk drive or *file server* that is used to store and distribute both data and programs to the computers on the network.

File servers are just one example of *client/server computing* , a computing model made possible by networks. According to this model, certain computers on the network are set up as *servers,* which provide certain well-defined services to *client* computers. For example, one computer in a network may be set up as the *mail server* with the responsibility of sending, receiving and storing mail for all users on the network. Users may use client application software, such as Eudora or Pine, to access their mail on the server. Similarly, another server may be set up as a *Web server* with the responsibility of storing Web pages for all the users on the network. Users can run Web browsers, another type of client software, to access Web pages on the server. Java is particularly well suited for these types of networked or distributed applications, where part of the application software resides on a server and part resides on the client computer.

Networks can range in size from *Local Area Networks (LANs),* which connect computers and peripherals over a relatively small area, such as within a lab or a building, through *Wide Area Networks (WANs),* which can span large geographic areas, such as cities and nations.

The *Internet* (with a capital I) is a network of networks whose geographical area covers the entire globe. The *World Wide Web (WWW)* is another example of distributed, client/server computing. The WWW is not a separate physical network. Rather it is a subset of the Internet that uses the **HyperText Transfer Protocol (HTTP)**. A **protocol** is a set of rules and conventions that govern how communication takes place between two computers. HTTP is a multimedia protocol. It supports the transmission of text, graphics, sound, and other forms of information. Certain computers within a network run special software that enables them to play the role of HTTP servers. They store Web documents and are capable of handling requests for documents from client browser applications. The servers and clients can be located anywhere on the Internet.

The documents stored on Web servers are encoded in a special text-based language known as **HyperText Markup Language,** or **HTML** . Web browsers, such as Netscape's Navigator and Microsoft's Internet Explorer, are designed to interpret documents coded in this language. The language itself is very simple. Its basic elements are known as *tags,* which consist of certain keywords or other text contained within angle brackets, < and >. For example, if you wanted to italicize a chunk of text on a Web page you would enclose it between the < *I* > and < /*I* > tags. Thus, the following HTML code

```
<i>Italic font</i> can be used for <i>emphasis</i>.
```

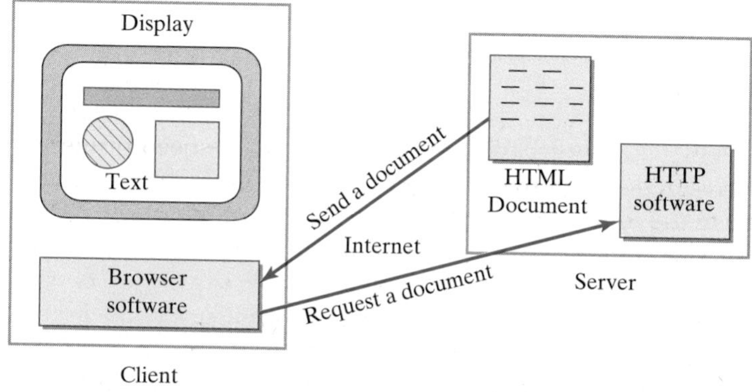

Figure 0–2 WWW: The client's browser requests a page from a Web server. When the HTML document is returned it is interpreted and displayed by the browser.

would be displayed as

Italic font can be used for *emphasis.*

by the Web browser.

When you use a Web browser to surf the Internet, you repeatedly instruct your browser to go to a certain location and retrieve a page that is encoded in HTML. For example, if you typed the following **URL (Uniform Resource Locator)**

```
http://www.prenhall.com/morelli/index.html
```

into your browser, the browser would send a message to the Web server `troy` located in the `prenhall.com` domain — the `prenhall` portion of this address specifies Prentice Hall and the `com` portion specifies the commercial domain of the Internet — requesting that the document named `index.html` in the `morelli` home directory be retrieved and sent back to your computer (Fig 0–2). The beauty of the Web is that it is possible to embed text, sound, video, and graphics within an HTML document, making it possible to download a wide range of multimedia resources through this (relatively) simple mechanism.

The Web has enormous potential to change business, entertainment, commerce, and education. The fact that it is now possible to download computer games and other application software from the Web may completely change the way new software is purchased and distributed. Similarly, as noted earlier, many businesses have begun to organize their information systems into intranets — private networks that have implemented the HTTP protocol. Currently, one of the big areas of development on the Web is commerce. As soon as consumers gain confidence that credit card information can be securely transmitted over the Web (as it can over a telephone), the Web will be poised to explode as a marketing medium as powerful, perhaps, as television is today. Because Java has been designed to support secure, distributed, networked applications, it is ideally suited to be used as the language for these types of applications.

0.7 Programming Languages

Most computer programs today are written in a **high-level language** , such as Java, C, C++, or FORTRAN. A programming language is considered high-level if its statements resemble English language statements. For example, all of the languages just mentioned have some form of an if statement, which says, "if some condition holds, then take some action."

Computer scientists have invented hundreds of high-level programming languages although relatively few of these have been put to practical use. Some of the widely used languages have special features that make them suitable for one type of programming application or another. COBOL (COmmon Business-Oriented Language), for example, is still widely used in commercial applications. FORTRAN (FORmula TRANslator) is still preferred by some engineers and scientists. C and C++ are still the primary languages used by systems programmers.

In addition to having features that make them suitable for certain types of applications, high-level languages use symbols and notation that make them easily readable by humans. For example, arithmetic operations in Java make use of familiar operators such as "+" and "−" and "/", so that arithmetic expressions look more or less the way they do in algebra. So, to take the average of two numbers you might use the expression

```
(a + b) / 2
```

The problem is that computers cannot directly understand such expressions. In order for a computer to run a program, the program must first be translated into its **machine language** , which is the *instruction set* understood by its CPU or microprocessor. Each type of microprocessor has its own particular machine language. That's why typically when you buy a piece of software it runs either on a Macintosh, which uses the PowerPC chip, or on a Windows machine, which uses the Pentium chip, but not on both. The fact that a program can run on just one type of chip is known as *platform dependence* .

In general, machine languages are based on the *binary code*, a two-valued system that is well suited for electronic devices. In a binary representation scheme everything is represented as a sequence of 1's and 0's, which corresponds closely to the computer's electronic "on" and "off" states. For example, the number 13 would be represented as 1101. Similarly, a particular address in the computer's memory might be represented as 01100011, and an instruction in the computer's instruction set might be represented as 001100.

The instructions that make up a computer's machine language are very simple and basic. In most cases, a single instruction carries out a single machine operation. For example, a typical machine language might include instructions for ADD, SUBTRACT, DIVIDE, and MULTIPLY, but it wouldn't contain an instruction for AVERAGE. Therefore the process of averaging two numbers would have to be broken down into two or more steps. A machine language instruction itself might have something similar to the following format, in which an *opcode* is followed by several *operands*, which refer to locations in the computer's primary memory. The following instruction says ADD the number in LOCATION1 to the number in LOCATION2 and store the result in LOCATION3:

Opcode	**Operand 1**	**Operand 2**	**Operand 3**
011110	110110	111100	111101
(ADD)	(LOCATION 1)	(LOCATION 2)	(LOCATION 3)

Given the primitive nature of machine language, an expression like the one above, (a + b)/2, would have to be translated into a sequence of several machine language instructions which, in binary code, might look as follows:

```
011110110110111100111101
000101000100010001001101
001000010001010101111011
```

In the early days of computing, before high-level languages were developed, computers had to be programmed directly in their machine languages, an extremely tedious and error prone process. Imagine how difficult it would be to detect an error that consisted of putting a 0 in the above program where a 1 should occur!

Fortunately we no longer have to worry about machine languages, because special programs can be used to translate a high-level or **source code** program into machine language or **object code** . In general, a program that translates source code to object code is known as a *translator* (Fig 0–3). Thus, with suitable translation software for Java or C++ we can write programs as if the computer could understand Java or C++ directly.

Source code translators come in two varieties. An **interpreter** translates a single line of source code directly into machine language and executes the code — which means runs it on the computer — before going on to the next line of source code. A **compiler** translates the entire source code program into executable object code. The object code can then be run directly without further translation.

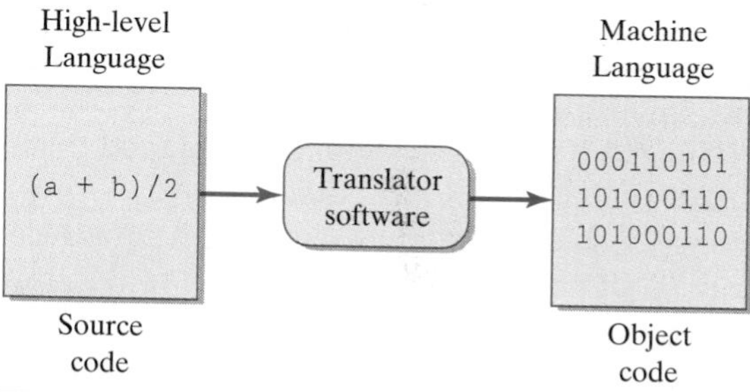

Figure 0–3 Translator software translates high-level *source code* to machine language *object code.*

There are advantages and disadvantages to both approaches. Interpreted programs generally run less efficiently than compiled programs because they must translate and execute each line of the program at the same time. Once compiled, an object program is just executed without any need for further translation. It is also much easier to optimize compiled code to make it run more efficiently. But interpreters are generally easier to write and provide somewhat better error messages when things go wrong. Some languages, such as BASIC, LISP, and PERL, are mostly used in interpreted form, although compilers are also available for these languages. Programs written in COBOL, FORTRAN, C, C++, and PASCAL are compiled. As we will see, Java programs use both compilation and interpretation in their translation process.

CHAPTER SUMMARY

Technical Terms

application software
compiler
computer program
general-purpose computer
high-level language
HyperText Markup Language (HTML)
Internet
machine language
object
object-oriented
software
special-purpose computer
system software
World Wide Web
Central Processing Unit (CPU)
computer
computer programming
hardware
HyperText Transfer Protocol (HTTP)
input device
interpreter
main memory
object code
output device
source code
secondary storage
Uniform Resource Locator (URL)

Summary of Important Points

- A Java program is a set of interacting objects. This is the basic metaphor of *object-oriented programming*. The main principles of the object-oriented programming approach are:
  - Divide and Conquer : Successful problem solving involves breaking a complex problem into small, manageable tasks.
  - Encapsulation and Modularity : Each task should be assigned to an object; the object's function will be to perform that task.
  - Public Interface : Each object should present a clear public interface that determines how other objects will use it.
  - Information Hiding : Each object should shield its users from unnecessary details of how it performs its task.
  - Generality : Objects should be designed to be as general as possible.
  - Extensibility : Objects should be designed so that their functionality can be extended to carry out more specialized tasks.

- *Abstraction* is the ability to group a large quantity of information into a single chunk so it can be managed as a single entity. Abstraction is an overarching principle of the OOP approach.
- A computer system generally consists of input/output devices, primary and secondary memory, and a central processing unit. A computer can only run programs in its own *machine language*, which is based on the *binary code*. Special programs known as *compilers* and *interpreters* translate *source code* programs written in a *high-level language*, such as Java, into machine language *object code* programs.
- *Application software* refers to programs designed to provide a particular task or service; *systems software* assists the user in using application software.
- The *client/server* model is a form of *distributed computing* in which part of the software for a task is stored on a *server* and part on *client* computers.
- Hypertext Markup Language (HTML) is the language used to encode WWW documents.

EXERCISES

1. Fill in the blanks in each of the following statements.

   a. Dividing a problem or a task into parts is an example of the ----- principle.
   b. Designing a class so that it shields certain parts of an object from other objects is an example of the ----- principle.
   c. The fact that Java programs can run without change on wide variety of different kinds of computers is an example of ---------- .
   d. The fact that social security numbers are divided into three parts is an example of the ------- principle.
   e. To say that a program is robust means that ---------- .
   f. An ----- is a separate module that encapsulates a Java program's attributes and actions.

2. Explain the difference between each of the following pairs of concepts.

   a. *hardware* and *software*
   b. *systems* and *application* software
   c. *compiler* and *interpreter*
   d. *machine language* and *high-level language*
   e. *general-purpose* and *special-purpose* computer
   f. *primary* and *secondary* memory
   g. the *CPU* and the *ALU*
   h. the *Internet* and the *WWW*
   i. a *client* and a *server*
   j. *HTTP* and *HTML*
   k. *source* and *object* code

3. Fill in the blanks in each of the following statements.

   a. A _____ is a set of instructions that directs a computer's behavior.
   b. A disk drive would be an example of a __________ device.
   c. A mouse is an example of an _____ device.
   d. A monitor is an example of an _____ device.
   e. The computer's _____ functions like a scratch pad.
   f. Java is an example of a __________ programming language.
   g. The Internet is a network of _____ .
   h. The protocol used by the World Wide Web is the _____ protocol.
   i. Web documents are written in _____ code.
   j. A _____ is a networked computer that is used to store data for other computers on the network.

4. Identify the component of computer hardware that is responsible for the following functions.

   a. The *fetch-execute cycle*
   b. arithmetic operations
   c. executing instructions
   d. storing programs while they are executing
   e. storing programs and data when the computer is off

5. Explain why a typical piece of software, such as a word processor, cannot run on both a Macintosh and a Windows machine.
6. What advantages do you see in platform independence? What disadvantages?
7. In what sense is a person's name an *abstraction*? In what sense is any word of the English language an abstraction?
8. Analyze the process of writing a term paper in terms of the divide-and-conquer and encapsulation principles.
9. Analyze your car in terms of object-oriented design principles. In other words, pick one of your car's systems, such as the braking system, and analyze it in terms of the divide-and-conquer, encapsulation, information-hiding, and interface principles.
10. Suppose your car's radiator is broken. Consider the process of getting it fixed in terms of the object-oriented programming principles. In other words, describe how divide-and-conquer and encapsulation strategies are used in this process. Describe various forms of information hiding and interfacing involved in this process.

Photograph courtesy of Hisham F. Ibrahim, PhotoDisc, Inc.

1

Java Program Development

OBJECTIVES

After studying this chapter, you will

- Know the basic steps involved in the program development process.
- Understand the difference between a Java application and a Java applet.
- Understand how a Java program is translated into machine language.
- Know how to edit, compile, and run Java programs.
- Know how to use simple output operations in a Java program.
- Be able to distinguish between syntax and semantic errors in a program.

OUTLINE

1.1 Introduction

This chapter introduces some of the basic concepts and techniques involved in Java program development. We begin by distinguishing two types of Java programs: applications, which are typical stand-alone programs that you would find in any programming language, and applets, which are unique Java programs that are embedded in a Web browser. We discuss the details of editing, compiling, and running both kinds of programs. Next we provide an overview of the several steps involved in the program development process. The steps are illustrated by designing a program that represents a simple geometric rectangle.

Next we begin to familiarize ourselves with Java's extensive class library by studying its `PrintStream` and `System` classes. These classes contain objects and methods that enable us to print output from a program. By the end of the chapter you will be able to design and write a Java application that "sings" your favorite song. Finally, the lab project for this chapter involves editing, compiling, and running a Java applet. Once you get the applet running, you will perform several experiments designed to illustrate the different kinds of errors that can occur in a program.

1.2 Java Applications and Applets

Java programs come in two varieties. A Java **application** is a stand-alone program such as a computer game or a word processor. A Java **applet** is a program that runs within the context of a Web browser. An application is "standalone" in the sense that it does not depend on a browser for its execution.

Perhaps the simplest example of a Java application program might be the traditional HelloWorld program—"traditional" because practically every introductory programming text begins with it. The HelloWorld program (Fig 1–1) just displays the message "Hello world!" on the console.

As this program illustrates, Java programs are contained within a *class* definition, which consists of a *header* that contains the name of the program plus a *body* which contains a collection of statements enclosed within braces.

Figure 1–1 The `HelloWorld` application program.

```
/**
 * The HelloWorld application program
 */

public class HelloWorld                    // Class header
{                                          // Start of class body

    public static void main(String argv[])   // Main method
    {
        System.out.println("Hello world!");
    } // End of main

} // End of HelloWorld
```

Every Java application must contain a main() method , which is where execution of the program begins when the program is run. A *method* is simply a named section of the program's executable code that can be *called* or *invoked* to perform certain well-defined tasks. The main() method in this case performs the task of saying hello and contains just one executable statement:

```
System.out.println("Hello world!");
```

When the HelloWorld program is run, this statement causes the message "Hello world!" to be displayed on the console or monitor. Text within the program that begins with double slashes (//) is a Java *single-line comment* .

JAVA LANGUAGE RULE **Comments.** Double slashes (//) can be used to turn any line or part of a line into a *single-line comment*, which is ignored by the compiler.

Comments are used to document the program and make it more readable. One good use for comments is to annotate closing braces so it is easier to tell where certain blocks of code begin and end. In this program comments are used to mark the end of the main() method, as well as the end of the HelloWorld class itself.

An **applet** is a Java program that is embedded within a Web page, and executed by a Web browser. Fig 1–2 shows a Java applet named HelloWorld.

This applet does more or less the same thing as the application program: It displays the "HelloWorld" message. As in the case of the application, the program consists of a class definition. It contains a single method, in this case the paint() method, which contains a single executable statement:

```
g.drawString("HelloWorld",10,10);
```

Figure 1–2 The HelloWorld applet program.

```
/**
 * HelloWorld applet program
 */

import java.applet.Applet;     // Import the Applet class
import java.awt.Graphics;      //   and the Graphics class

public class HelloWorld extends Applet           // Class header
{                                                // Start of body

    public void paint(Graphics g)                // The paint method
    {
        g.drawString("HelloWorld",10,10);
    }  // End of paint

}  // End of HelloWorld
```

which displays the "HelloWorld" message. But in this case the message is *painted* on a window within the Web browser.

Because they are intended to run within a Web browser, and because they use a *Graphical User Interface (GUI)*, Java applets are a little more complicated to write than Java applications—at least Java applications, such as the `HelloWorld` application, that don't use a GUI. For example, the `HelloWorld` applet begins with two `import` statements. These statements refer to code from the Java class libraries. The Java class libraries are organized into *packages*, which have names like `java.awt` and `java.applet`. The `java.applet` package contains classes used to create an applet and to enable the applet to communicate with its environment. The `java.awt` package contains classes that define `Buttons`, `TextFields`, and other objects that are used to create graphical interfaces.

Library packages

Because an applet lives within the browser's environment, we have to be able to interact with it the same way we interact with the browser—by clicking on buttons, opening windows, and so on. Fortunately, Java supplies an entire library of classes to support applet and GUI programming.

1.3 Compiling and Executing a Java Program

A Java programming environment typically consists of several programs that perform different tasks required to edit, compile, and run a Java program. The following description will be based on the *Java Development Kit (JDK)*, a collection of software development tools available free from the Sun Microsystems Java web site `http://www.javasoft.com`. Versions of JDK are available for Unix, Windows, and Macintosh computers. (For more details about the JDK, see Appendix B.)

In some cases the individual programs that make up the JDK have been integrated into a single program development environment. For example, Metrowerk's Codewarrior provides an *integrated development environment* for Java for Macintosh, Windows, and Sun Solaris computers.

The process of creating and running a Java program requires three steps: *editing, compiling,* and *running*, as illustrated in Fig 1–3. The discussion that follows here assumes that you are using the JDK as your development environment. If you are using some other environment, it will be necessary to read the documentation provided to determine exactly how to edit, compile, and run Java programs in that environment.

—Step 1. Editing a Program

Any text editor may be used to edit the program, and the process consists merely of typing the program and making corrections as needed. Two popular Unix editors are `vi` and `emacs`. On Macintosh systems, popular editors include `SimpleText` and `BBEdit`. On Windows systems, an editor such as `WinEdit` may be used. The program should be saved in a text file named *ClassName.java* where *ClassName* is the name of the Java class contained in the file.

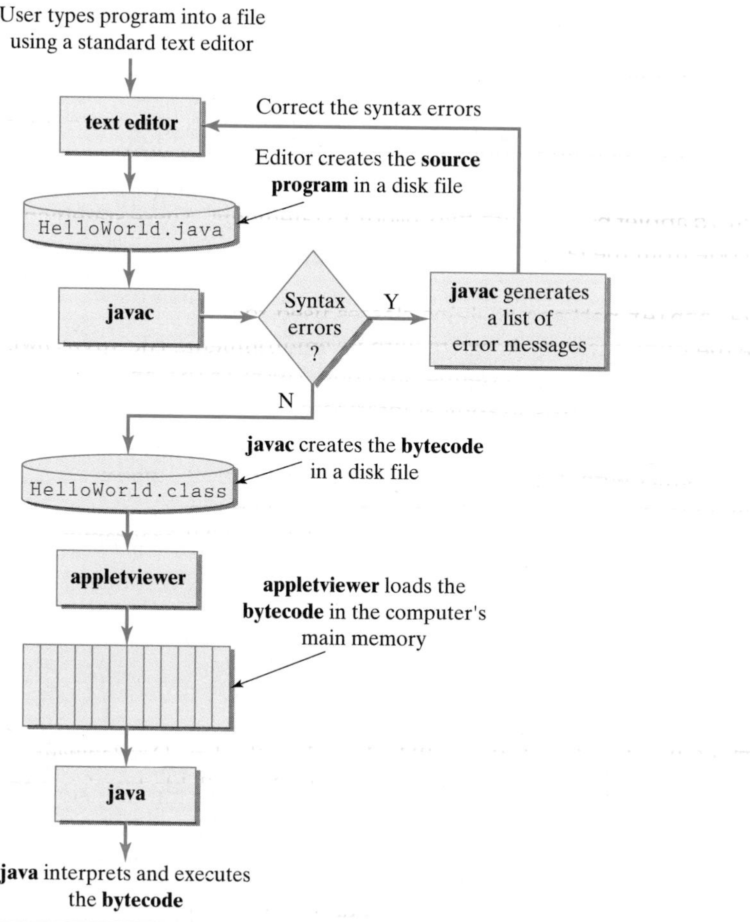

Figure 1–3 Editing, compiling, and running `HelloWorld.java`.

> **JAVA LANGUAGE RULE** **File Names.** If a file contains a `public` class named `ClassName`, then it must be saved in a text file named `ClassName.java`, otherwise an error will result.

For example, in the case of our HelloWorld programs, either the applet or the application, the file must be named `HelloWorld.java`. Also, because Java is *case sensitive*, which means that Java pays attention to whether a letter is typed uppercase or lowercase, it would be an error if the file were named `helloworld.java` or `Helloworld.java`.

> **JAVA LANGUAGE RULE** **Case Sensitivity.** Java is *case sensitive* which means that it treats `helloWorld` and `Helloworld` as different names.

—Step 2. Compiling the Program

Recall that before you can run a Java source program you have to translate it (or compile it) into the computer's machine language. There is no difference between compiling an applet and an application. Compilation translates Java language statements that make up the *source program* into Java *bytecode* , the intermediate code understood by the *Java Virtual Machine (JVM)*. To run a Java program, whether an applet or an application, the JVM is then used to interpret and execute the bytecode.

Platform independence

Java bytecode is said to be *platform independent*, which means that it can run on any hardware or software platform that supports the JVM. All of the major operating systems—Unix, MacOS, Windows—and both of the major browsers—Netscape Navigator, Internet Explorer—have incorporated the JVM into their software and can therefore run Java programs. Applets run within the browser environment while applications run directly within the operating system environment.

The Java Development Kit (JDK) Java compiler is named `javac`. In some environments—such as within Unix or Windows—`HelloWorld.java` would be compiled by keyboarding the following command at the system prompt:

```
javac HelloWorld.java
```

If the `HelloWorld.java` program does not contain errors, the result of this command is the creation of a Java bytecode file named `HelloWorld.class`—a file that has the same prefix as the course file but the suffix `.class`. If `javac` detects errors in the Java code, a list of error messages will be printed.

If you are using some other development environment besides JDK, you would follow the instructions provided for how to compile your program in that environment. If the compilation works, the `.class` file will be created.

—Step 3. Running the Program

In order to run a program on any computer, the program's *executable code* must be loaded into the computer's main memory. For Java environments, this means that the program's `.class` file must be loaded into the computer's memory where it is then interpreted by the Java Virtual Machine. On Solaris and Windows systems, an application program would be run by typing

```
java HelloWorld
```

at the command prompt. This command loads the JVM which will then load and interpret the application's bytecode (`HelloWorld.class`). The "HelloWorld" string will be displayed on the command line.

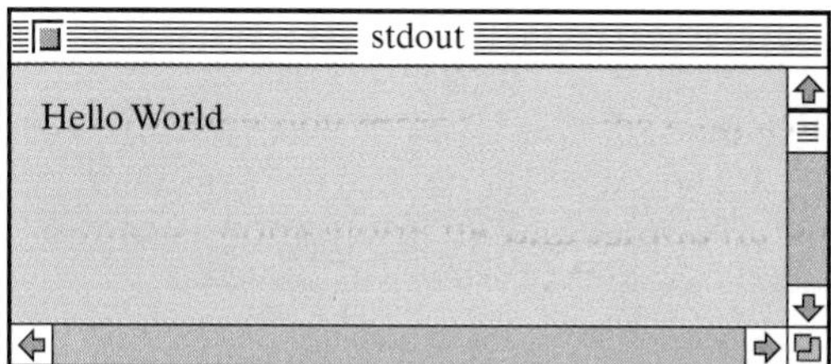

Figure 1–4 Running the `HelloWorld.java` application program.

On Macintosh systems, which do not have a command line, you would select the compile and run commands from a menu. Once the code is compiled, the run command will cause the JVM to be loaded, and the bytecode to be interpreted. The "HelloWorld!" output would appear in a text-based window that automatically pops up on your computer screen. In any case, regardless of the system you use, running the `HelloWorld` application program will cause the "HelloWorld" message to be displayed on some kind of standard output device (Fig 1–4).

In the case of Java applets, the program is loaded into memory either by a Web browser or by the JDK's `appletviewer` program, a kind of stripped down Web browser that loads and runs Java applets. Both the Web browser and appletviewer load the class files (produced by the Java compiler) from an HTML (HyperText Markup Language) document that must contain an `<applet>` tag, as shown in Fig 1–5. (See Appendix B for more details about the appletviewer and the `<applet>` tag.)

The code in Fig 1–5 would be placed in a file named with an `.html` suffix to indicate that it is an HTML file. The name of the file in this case is not important, but let's suppose we give it the name `Hello.html`. What is important is that the `<applet>` tag be specified correctly, designating the name of the Java bytecode that should be executed (`HelloWorld.class`). It is also necessary that the HTML file be stored in the same directory or folder as the class file. (There are ways to get around this, but we'll deal with those later.)

Figure 1–5 An example of an HTML file containing an `<applet>` tag. This specification will run the Java program named `HelloWorld.class`.

```
<html>
...
<applet code="HelloWorld.class" width= 200 height=200 >
</applet>
...
</html>
```

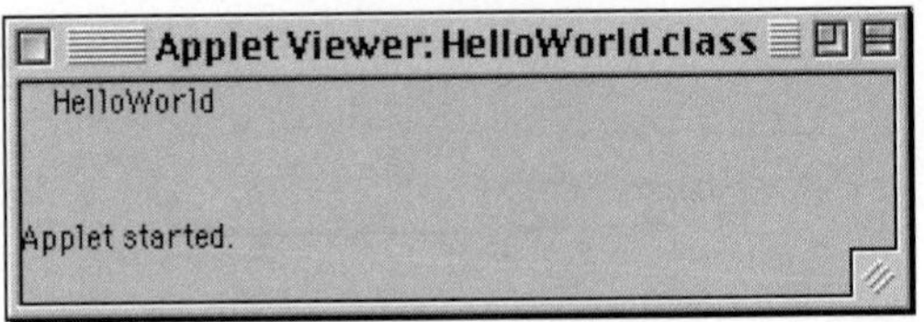

Figure 1–6 Running the `HelloWorld.java` applet.

The `appletviewer` can be used to load and run the applet by typing the following command on the command line:

```
appletviewer Hello.html
```

If you are using a Web browser to run the applet, you would use the browser's menu to load `Hello.html` into the browser, either across the Internet by supplying its *URL (Uniform Resource Locator)* or from your local disk by supplying its file name. In any case, the appletviewer or the browser will load the program's bytecode into the computer's main memory and then verify, interpret, and execute the program. The result, as shown in Fig 1–6, is that the "Hello world!" message will be displayed within the browser or appletviewer window.

1.4 Designing Good Programs

The preceding section described how to edit, compile, and run a Java program. But this is only part of the story. Programming is not simply a question of keyboarding Java code. Rather, it involves a considerable amount of planning and designing. Badly designed programs hardly ever work correctly. Even though it is tempting for novice programmers to start entering code almost immediately, one of the first rules of programming is

> **PROGRAMMING TIP:** The sooner you begin to type code, the longer the program will take to finish. Careful design of the program must precede coding of the program.

In other words, the more thought and care you put into designing a program, the more likely you are to end up with one that works correctly. The following sections provide a brief overview of the program development process.

Program development involves designing, coding, testing, and revising a program. As Fig 1–7 illustrates, design is involved at several stages of the process. Designing an object-oriented program is a matter of designing its classes, its data, its methods, and its algorithms. As we learn more about Java, and as the problems we tackle become more sophisticated, we will learn about each of these stages.

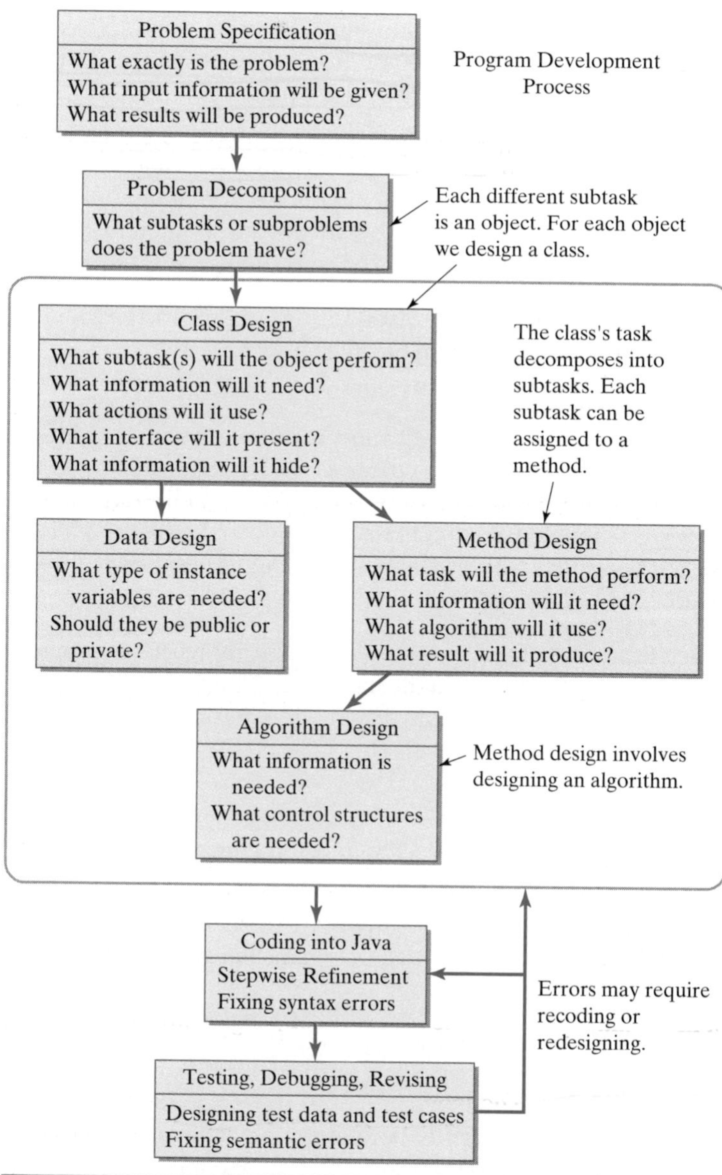

Figure 1–7 An overview of the program development process.

The program development process involves the principles we listed in Chapter 0. For example, the divide-and-conquer principle comes into play as a problem is decomposed into subproblems. Decomposition occurs also during class design, where the class's primary task is divided into subtasks, each one of which may be assigned to a separate method. Deciding how many classes or methods are needed also involves application of the encapsulation and abstraction principles. When should we stop subdividing? How much of a task should be assigned to a single object or a single method? The answers to these and similar questions are not easy.

Good answers require the kind of good judgment that comes through experience. Here again, as we learn more about object-oriented programming, we'll learn more about how to apply these principles.

Problem Specification

The first step in the program development process is making sure you understand the problem. Thus we begin by developing a detailed *problem specification* which should address three basic questions:

- What exactly is the problem to be solved?
- What information will the program be given as input?
- What results will the program be expected to produce?

In the real world, the problem specification is often arrived at through a process of negotiation between the customer and the developer. In an introductory programming course, the specification is usually given in the laboratory or programming assignment itself.

To help make these ideas a little clearer, let's design a solution to a very simple problem.

Problem Specification. Design a class that will represent a simple geometric rectangle with a given length and width. The definition of this class should make it possible to create rectangles of various dimensions and to calculate their areas.

1.4.1 Problem Decomposition

Most programming problems are too big and too complex to be solved in one fell swoop. So the next step in the design process is to divide the problem into parts that make the solution more manageable. This *divide-and-conquer* approach should be applied repeatedly, until the resulting subproblems or subtasks become so small that they are simple to solve. In the object-oriented approach, each of the problem's parts is assigned to a specific object. Each object will handle one specific aspect of the problem. In effect, each object will become an expert or specialist in some subtask of the problem.

Note that there is some ambiguity here about what constitutes a task and a subtask, and about how far we should go in decomposing a given problem. This ambiguity is inherent in the design process. How much we should decompose a problem before its parts become "simple to solve" depends on the problem itself and on the problem solver. For this simple problem, we need just one class, which will provide a representation of the rectangle.

1.4.2 Design Specification

Once we have decomposed a problem into its subproblems or subtasks, designing a Java program is primarily a matter of designing and creating the set of objects that will perform these subtasks. For each object, we must answer the following basic design questions:

- What subtask(s) will the object perform?
- What information will it need to perform its task?
- Which actions will it use to process the information?
- What interface will it present to other objects?
- What information will it hide from other objects?

For our rectangle object, the answers to these questions are shown in Fig 1–8. Note that although we talk about "designing an object," we're really designing a *class of objects*. The following discussion shows how we arrived at these decisions.

What task(s) will the object perform?

The task of the `Rectangle` object is to represent a geometric rectangle. This is its main or primary task. Because a rectangle is defined in terms of its length and width, our `Rectangle` object will need some way to store these two pieces of information. An **instance variable** is a memory location that belongs to an object. Variables are used to the store information that an object needs to carry out its task. Deciding on these variables provides the answer to the question, "What information does the object need to perform its task?"

What information will the object need?

What actions will the object use?

Next we decide what actions a `Rectangle` object will take. As specified in Fig 1–8, each `Rectangle` object should provide some means of setting its dimensions and calculating its area. For this particular problem—representing a rectangle—these are the object's subtasks. These are the actions it will perform or carry out in support of the main task of representing a rectangle. Each of these capabilities or actions will be encapsulated in a Java method.

A **method** is a named section of code that can be invoked or called upon to perform a particular action. In the object-oriented approach, **method invocation** is the means by which interaction occurs among objects. For example, when we want to find out a rectangle's area, we can invoke its "calculate area" method, which will give us this information.

Figure 1–8 Design specification for the `Rectangle` class.

- Class Name: Rectangle
- Task: To represent a geometric rectangle
- Information Needed (variables)
    - Length: A variable to store the rectangle's length (private)
    - Width: A variable to store the rectangle's width (private)
- Manipulations Needed (public methods)
    - Rectangle: A method to set a rectangle's length and width
    - calculateArea: A method to calculate a rectangle's area

What interface will it present, and what information will it hide?

In designing an object, we must decide which methods should be made available to other objects. This is what's involved in deciding what interface the object should present, and what information it should hide from other objects. In general, those methods that will be used to communicate with an object are designated as part of the object's *interface* . Except for its interface, all other information maintained by each rectangle should be kept "hidden" from other objects. For example, it is not necessary for other objects to know how a rectangle represents its length and width and how exactly it calculates the area.

Taken together these various design decisions lead to the specification shown in Fig 1–8. As our discussion has illustrated, we arrived at the decisions by asking and answering the right questions.

1.4.3 Data, Methods, and Algorithms

Once we have developed a specification for the rectangle object, the next step is to design its parts. There are two basic questions involved:

- What type of data will be used to represent the information needed by the rectangle?
- How will each method carry out its appointed task?

What type of data will be used?

Like other programming languages, Java provides a wide range of different types of data, some simple and some complex. So deciding what type of data to use can often require considerable thought, depending on the complexity of the problem at hand. Obviously a rectangle's length and width should be represented by some kind of numeric data. So let's use Java's `double` type, which will enable us to represent real number values such as 15.6 and 12.5.

How will each method carry out its task?

Designing a method is much like designing the class itself. You have to decide what task the method will carry out. In order to carry out its task, a method will need certain information, which it may store in variables. Plus it will have to carry out a sequence of individual actions to perform the task. And finally, you must decide what result the method will produce. Thus, as in designing objects, it is important to ask the right questions:

- What specific task will the method perform?
- What information will it need to perform its task?
- What algorithm will the method use?
- What result will the method produce?

An **algorithm** is a step-by-step description of the solution to a problem. For example, the algorithm for calculating the area of a rectangle consists of a one-step process: "Multiply length times width." Obviously, the only information it needs to perform this task are the two numbers that represent the rectangle's length and the width. Just as obviously, the result that it produces will be the product of length times width—that is, the rectangle's

Figure 1–9 Design specification for the `calculateArea()` method.

- Method Name: calculateArea
- Task: To calculate the area of a rectangle
- Information Needed (variables)
  - Length: A variable to store the rectangle's length (private)
  - Width: A variable to store the rectangle's width (private)
- Algorithm

  1. area = length x width

area. So this is very simple method to design: Given a rectangle's length and width, multiply them together to obtain the rectangle's area. A summary of our design is shown in Fig 1–9.

Not all methods are so simple to design, and not all algorithms are so trivial. Even when programming a simple arithmetic problem, the steps involved in its algorithm will not always be as obvious as they are when doing the calculation by hand. For example, suppose the problem were to calculate the sum of a list of numbers. If we were telling our classmate how to do this problem, we might just say, "add up all the numbers and report their total." But this description is far too vague to be used in a program. By contrast, here's an algorithm that a program could use.

1. Initialize the sum to 0.
2. If there are no more numbers to total, go to step 5.
3. Add the next number to the sum.
4. Go to step 2.
5. Report the sum.

Note that each step in this algorithm is simple and easy to follow. It would be relatively easy to translate it into Java. Because English is somewhat imprecise as an algorithmic language, programmers frequently write algorithms in the programming language itself or in **pseudocode**, a hybrid language that combines English and programming language structures without being too fussy about programming language syntax. For example, the above algorithm might be expressed in pseudocode as follows:

```
sum = 0
while ( more numbers remain )
   add next number to sum
print the sum
```

This pseudocode makes use of the `while` structure, a standard looping structure found in most programming languages. It is therefore even easier to translate into Java.

Of course, it is unlikely that an experienced programmer would take the trouble to write out pseudocode for such a simple algorithm. But many programming problems are quite complex and require careful design to minimize the number of errors that the program contains. In such a situation pseudocode could be useful.

Another important part of designing an algorithm is *tracing* it on some sample data. For example, we might test the list summing algorithm by tracing it on the following list of numbers:

Sum	List of Numbers
0	54 30 20
54	30 20
84	20
104	-

Initially, the sum starts out at 0 and the list of numbers contains 54, 30 and 20. On each iteration through the algorithm the sum increases by the amount of the next number and the list diminishes in size. The algorithm stops with the correct total left under the sum column. While this trace didn't turn up any errors, it is frequently possible to find flaws in an algorithm by tracing it in this way.

1.4.4 Coding into Java

Once a sufficiently detailed design has been developed, it is time to start generating Java code. The wrong way to do this would be to keyboard the entire program and then compile and run it. This generally leads to dozens of errors that can be both demoralizing and difficult to fix.

The right way to code is to use the principle of **stepwise refinement** . The program is coded in small stages, and after each stage the code is compiled and tested. In this way, small errors are caught before moving on to the next stage. This approach will be demonstrated in the laboratory section of this chapter.

The code for the `Rectangle` class is shown in Fig 1–10. Even though we have not yet begun learning the details of the Java language, you can easily pick out the key parts of this program: the instance variables `length` and `width` of type `double`, which are used to store the rectangle's dimensions; the `calculateArea()` method, which computes the rectangle's area; the `public` methods that make up its interface; and the `private` portions that are hidden from other objects. The specific language details needed to understand each of these elements will be covered in the next chapter.

Syntax and Semantics

Writing Java code requires that you know its syntax and semantics. A language's **syntax** is the set of rules that determine whether a particular statement is correctly formulated. For example, the following Java statement contains a *syntax error*:

```
sum = 0
```

Figure 1–10 The `Rectangle` class definition.

```
public class Rectangle
{
    private double length;       // Instance variables
    private double width;

    public Rectangle(double l, double w)    // Constructor method
    {
        length = l;
        width = w;
    } // Rectangle constructor

    public double calculateArea()           // Access method
    {
        return length * width;
    } // calculateArea

} // Rectangle class
```

because it does not end with a semicolon.

Similarly, the programmer must know the **semantics** of the language—that is, the meaning of each statement. In a programming language, a statement's meaning is determined by what effect it will have on the program. For example, in the above algorithm, to initialize the `sum` to 0, an assignment statement is used to store the value 0 into the memory location named `sum`. Thus we say that the statement

```
sum = 0;
```

assigns 0 to the memory location `sum`, where it will be stored until it is needed by some other part of the program.

Learning Java's syntax and semantics is a major part of learning to program. This aspect of learning to program is a lot like learning a foreign language. The more quickly you become fluent in the new language (Java), the better you will be at expressing solutions to interesting programming problems. The longer you struggle with the rules and conventions of Java, the more difficult it will be to talk about problems in a common language. Also, computers are a lot more fussy about correct language than humans, and even the smallest syntax or semantic error can cause tremendous frustration. So, try to be very precise in acquiring an understanding of Java's syntax and semantics.

1.4.5 Testing, Debugging, and Revising

Coding, testing, and revising a program is an iterative process, one that recycles through the different stages as necessary (Fig 1–7). The process should develop in small incremental stages, where the solution becomes more refined at each step. However, no matter how much care you take, things can still go wrong during the coding process.

Any *syntax errors* in the code will be detected by the Java compiler. Syntax errors are relatively easy to fix once you understand the error messages provided by the compiler. As long as a program contains syntax errors, the programmer must correct them and recompile the program (Fig 1–3). If the compiler fails to detect any errors, it will produce an executable version of the program which can then be executed.

When a program is run, the computer carries out the steps specified in the program and produces results. However, just because a program runs does not mean that its actions and results are correct. A running program can contain *semantic errors*, or *logical errors*. A semantic error is caused by an error in the logical design of the program causing it to behave incorrectly, producing incorrect results.

Unlike syntax errors, semantic errors cannot be detected automatically. For example, suppose that a program contains the following statement for calculating the area of a rectangle:

```
return length + width;
```

Because we are adding length and width instead of multiplying them, the resulting area will be incorrect. Because there is nothing syntactically wrong with the expression `length + width`, the compiler won't detect an error in this statement. The error resides in the program's logic and meaning. The programmer should have written `length * width`. Nevertheless, the computer will still execute this statement and compute the incorrect area. But you shouldn't believe the results!

Semantic errors are sometimes very hard to detect, and they can only be discovered by *testing* the program . Because program testing can only detect the presence of errors, not their absence, it is important to do as much testing as possible. The fact that a program *appears* to run correctly might just mean that it has not been adequately tested.

When semantic errors are detected, they must be found and fixed. This phase of programming is known as *debugging* , and when subtle errors occur it can be the most frustrating part of the whole program development process. The various lab exercises presented in this textbook will provide hints and suggestions on how to track down *bugs* in your code. One point to remember when you are debugging the subtlest of bugs is that no matter how convinced you are that your code is correct and that the bug must be caused by some kind of error in the computer, the error is almost certainly caused by your code!

Lanning's Limerick

There are some vain hackers so smug,
They can't see their code has a bug.
They curse the computer,
And some blame the tutor,
When the problem's a hole that they dug.

1.4.6 Writing Readable Programs

Becoming a proficient programmer goes beyond simply writing a program that produces correct output. It also involves developing good *programming style*, which covers, among other things, how readable and understandable your code is, both to yourself and to others. Our goal is to develop a programming style that satisfies the following principles:

- **Readability.** Programs should be easy to read and understand. Comments should be used to document and explain the program's code.
- **Clarity.** Programs should employ well-known constructs and standard conventions and should avoid programming tricks and unnecessarily obscure or convoluted code.
- **Flexibility.** Programs should be designed and written so that they are easy to maintain and change.

Throughout this book care has been taken to adopt good design principles and to follow appropriate style and coding conventions (see Appendix A). We will elaborate further on these style guidelines in the laboratory project for this chapter.

Grace Hopper and the First Computer Bug

Rear Admiral Grace Murray Hopper (1906–1992) was a pioneer computer programmer and one of the original developers of the COBOL programming language, which stands for COmmon Business-Oriented Language. Among her many achievements and distinctions Admiral Hopper also had a role in coining the term "computer bug."

In August 1945, she and a group of other programmers were working on the Mark I, an electro-mechanical computer developed at Harvard that was one of the ancestors of today's electronic computers. After several hours of trying to figure out why the machine was malfunctioning, someone located and removed a two-inch moth from one of the computer's circuits. From then on whenever anything went wrong with a computer, Admiral Hopper and others would say "it had bugs in it." The first bug itself is still taped to Admiral Hopper's 1945 log book, which is now in the collection of the Naval Surface Weapons Center.

In 1991, Admiral Hopper was awarded the National Medal of Technology by President Bush. To commemorate and honor Admiral Hopper's many contributions, the U.S. Navy recently named a warship after her. For more information on Admiral Hopper, see the Web site at `http://www.chips.navy.mil/chips/grace_hopper/`.

Photograph courtesy of Navy Visual News Service

From the Java Library: System and PrintStream

Java programs need to be able to accept input and to display output. For Java applets, input and output, which we abbreviate as I/O, are usually handled through the applet's *Graphical User Interface (GUI)*, which will be covered in Chapter 4. For application programs the type of input and output required can vary. Many applications also handle I/O through a GUI. For some applications, input is accepted from the keyboard and output is displayed on the computer console. For others, input and output might occur across a network connection or might involve files on the disk drive.

In Java, any source or destination for I/O is considered a *stream* of bytes or characters. Even characters entered at a keyboard, if considered as a sequence of keystrokes, can be represented as a stream. There are no I/O statements in the Java language. Instead, I/O is handled through methods that belong to classes contained in the `java.io` package.

We have already used the output method `println()` in our `HelloWorld` application:

```
System.out.println("HelloWorld");
```

This statement prints the message "HelloWorld" on the Java console. Let's now examine this statement more carefully to see how it makes use of the Java I/O classes.

The `java.io.PrintStream` class is Java's printing expert, so to speak. It contains `print()` and `println()` methods that can be used to print all of the various types of data we find in a Java program. A partial definition of `PrintStream` is as follows:

```
public class PrintStream extends FilterOutputStream
{
    ...
    public void print   (String s)  { ... }
    public void print   (boolean b) { ... }
    public void print   (int i )    { ... }
    public void println (String s)  { ... }
    public void println (boolean b) { ... }
    public void println (int i )    { ... }
    ...
}
```

The ellipses (...) in this definition indicate where we have omitted details of its implementation, including additional methods to handle other types of data. The fact that `PrintStream` and its methods are declared `public` means that we can use the methods in our programs, as we have done in `HelloWorld`.

Because the various `print()` and `println()` methods belong to the `PrintStream` class, we can only use them by finding a `PrintStream` object and "telling" it to print data for us. Java's `java.lang.System` class contains three predefined streams, including two `PrintStreams`:

```
public final class System
{
    public void static PrintStream out;  // Standard output stream
    public void static PrintStream err;  // Standard error stream
    public void static InputStream in;   // Standard input stream
}
```

As its name implies, the `System` class is part of the `java.lang` package. This package contains classes fundamental to the design of the Java language.

Both the `System.out` and `System.err` objects can be used to write output to the console. As its name suggests, the `err` stream is used primarily for error messages, whereas the `out` stream is used for other printed output. Similarly, as its name suggests, the `System.in` object can be used to handle input, which will be covered in Chapter 2.

The only difference between the `print()` and `println()` methods is that `println()` will also print a carriage return and line feed after printing its data, thereby allowing subsequent output to be printed on a new line. For example, the following statements:

```
System.out.print("hello");            // Ask out to print "hello"
System.out.println("hello again"); // Ask out to print "hello again"
System.out.println("goodbye");      // Ask out to print "goodbye"
```

would produce the following output:

```
hellohello again
goodbye
```

Now that we know how to use Java's printing expert, let's use it to "sing" a version of *Old MacDonald Had a Farm.* As you might guess, this program will simply consist of a sequence of `System.out.print()` statements each of which prints a line of the verse. The complete Java application program is shown in Fig 1–11.

Figure 1–11 The `OldMacDonald.java` class .

```
public class OldMacDonald
{
    public static void main(String argv[])   // Main method
    {
        System.out.println("Old MacDonald had a farm");
        System.out.println("E I E I O.");
        System.out.println("And on his farm he had a duck.");
        System.out.println("E I E I O.");
        System.out.println("With a quack quack here.");
        System.out.println("And a quack quack there.");
        System.out.println("Here a quack, there a quack,");
        System.out.println("Everywhere a quack quack.");
        System.out.println("Old MacDonald had a farm");
        System.out.println("E I E I O.");
    } // End of main
} // End of OldMacDonald
```

This example illustrates the importance of using the Java class library. If there's a particular task we want to perform, one of the first things we should ask is whether there is already an "expert" in Java's class library that performs that task. If so, we can use methods, provided by the expert, to perform that particular task.

EFFECTIVE DESIGN: Using the Java Library. Learning how to use the Java class library is an important element of object-oriented programming.

SELF-STUDY EXERCISES

EXERCISE 1.1 One good way to learn how to write programs is to modify existing programs. Modify the `OldMacDonald` class to "sing" one more verse of the song.

EXERCISE 1.2 Write a Java class that prints the following design:

```
**********
* **  ** *
*   **   *
* *    * *
*  ****  *
**********
```

1.5 Qualified Names in Java

You may be wondering about the meaning of names such as `java.io.PrintStream` and `System.out.print()`, when they occur in a Java program. These are examples of *qualified names*. They use *dot notation* to clarify or disambiguate the name of something.

Just as in our natural language, the meaning of a name within a Java program depends on the context. For example, the expression `System.out.print()` refers to the `print()` method which belongs to the `System.out` object. If we were using this expression from within `System.out`, you wouldn't need to qualify the name in this way. You could just refer to `print()` and it would be clear from the context which method you meant.

This is no different than using someone's first name ("Kim") when there's only one Kim around, but using a full name ("Kim Smith") when the first name alone would be too vague or ambiguous.

One thing that complicates the use of qualified names is that they are used to refer to different kinds of things within a Java program. But this is no different, really, than in our natural language, where names ("George Washington") can refer to people, bridges, universities, and so on.

Here again, just as in our natural language, Java uses the context to understand the meaning of the name. For example, the expression `java.lang.System` refers to the `System` class in the `java.lang` package, whereas the expression `System.out.print()` refers to a method in the `System.out` object.

How can you tell these apart? Java can tell them apart because the first one occurs as part of an `import` statement, so it must be referring to something that belongs to a package. The second expression would only be valid in a context where a method invocation is allowed. You will have to learn a bit more about the Java language before you'll be able to completely understand these names. But here are some naming rules to get you started.

JAVA LANGUAGE RULE **Library Class Names.** Class names in Java begin with capital letter. When referenced as part of a package, the class name is the last part of the name. For example, `java.lang.System` refers to the `System` class in the `java.lang` package.

JAVA LANGUAGE RULE **Dot Notation.** Names expressed in Java's *dot notation* depend for their meaning on the context in which they are used. In qualified names—that is, names of the form X.Y.Z—the last item in the name (Z) is the referent. The items which precede it (X.Y.) are used to qualify the referent.

The fact that names are context dependent in this way certainly complicates the task of learning what's what in a Java program. Part of learning to use Java's built-in classes is learning where a particular object or method is defined. It is a syntax error if the Java compiler can't find the object or method that you are referencing.

DEBUGGING TIP: Not Found Error. If Java cannot find the item you are referring to, it will report an "X not found" error, where X is the class, method, variable, or package being referred to.

IN THE LABORATORY: EDITING, COMPILING, AND RUNNING AN APPLET

The purpose of this first laboratory project is to give you some hands-on experience editing and compiling a Java program. This will not only familiarize you with the software that will be used in your course but will also elaborate on some of the concepts introduced in this chapter. The objectives of this exercise are

- To familiarize you with the process of editing, compiling, and running a Java applet.
- To introduce the *stepwise refinement* coding style.
- To provide some examples of both syntax and semantic errors.

Don't worry that you won't understand all of the Java code in the applet. We'll eventually get to language details in subsequent chapters.

As shown in Fig 1–12, this applet plays a silly game with the user. Every time the user clicks on the button labeled "Watch How Time Flys!" the applet reports how many milliseconds have been wasted since the applet began running. If you want to try this applet, its URL is

http://www.prenhall.com/morelli/sourcecode/ch01/timerapplet

Program Walkthrough: Program Style and Documentation

`TimerApplet`'s complete source code is shown in Fig 1–13. The program begins with a *comment block* which presents important information about the program, including the name of the file that contains it, the name of the author, and a brief description of what the program does.

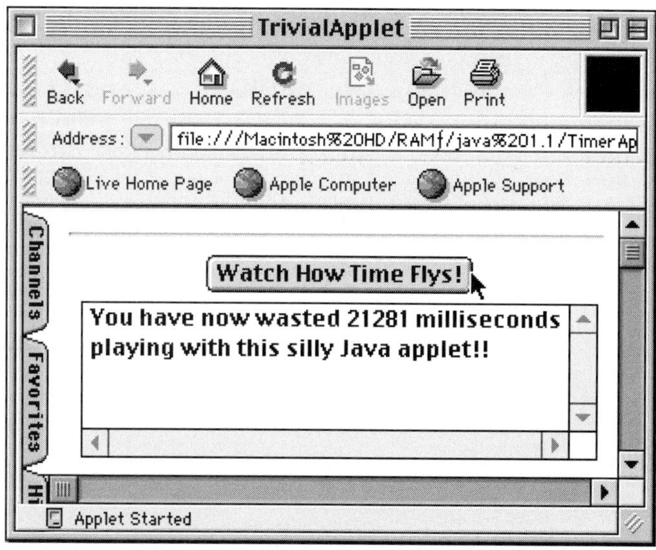

Figure 1–12 An applet that reports elapsed time.

JAVA LANGUAGE RULE **Comments.** A *multiline comment* begins with "/*" and ends with "*/" and may extend over several lines. It is ignored by the compiler. A multiline comment that begins with "/**" and ends with "*/" is called a *documentation comment*. These kinds of comments can be processed by special software provided by Java that will automatically generate documentation for the class.

PROGRAMMING TIP: Use of Comments. A well-written program should begin with a comment block that provides the name of the program, its author, and a description of what the program does.

In addition to the comment block at the beginning of `TimerApplet`, there is also a comment block in front of the `actionPerformed()` method (Fig 1–13). There are also several single-line comments used to clarify the code. Commenting your code in this way is an important part of program development. Appendix A lays out the style and documentation guidelines that are followed in this book. In subsequent laboratory projects, as our programs become more sophisticated, we will introduce additional documentation requirements.

Students invariably hate putting comments in their programs. After all, it seems somewhat anticlimactic, having to go back and document your program after you have finished designing, writing, and testing it. The way to avoid the sense of anticlimax is to "document as you go" rather than leaving it to the end. In many cases, your design document can serve as the basis for the comments in your program. One of the main reasons for commenting code is so that you, or someone else, will be able to understand the code the next time you have to modify it. Students who go on to be professional programmers often write back with reports that

Figure 1–13 `TimerApplet`, a Java applet to calculate elapsed time.

```
/**
 *  File: TimerApplet.java
 *  Author: Chris LaFata, '93
 *  Modified by: Java Java Java
 *  Last Modified: May 1999
 *  Description: This applet reports how many seconds the user
 *  has wasted since the applet started running.
 */

import java.awt.*;
import java.applet.Applet;
import java.awt.event.*;

/*
 *  The TimerApplet class tells the user how much time is wasting.
 *  @author Java Java Java
 */

public class TimerApplet extends Applet implements ActionListener
{
    private Button calculate;                               // The button
    private TextArea display;                               // The display area

    private long startTime;                                 // When the applet starts
    private long currentTime;                               // Time of current click
    private long elapsedTime;                               // Time since it started

    /**
     *  The init() method initializes the applet.
     */
    public void init()
    {
        startTime = System.currentTimeMillis();             // Get the current time
                                                            // Set up the applet interface
        calculate = new Button("Watch How Time Flys!");     // Button
        calculate.addActionListener(this);
        display = new TextArea(4,35);                       // Display area
        add(calculate);
        add(display);
    } // init()

    /**
     *  The actionPerformed() method is called whenever the calculate button is clicked.
     */
    public void actionPerformed (ActionEvent e)
    {
        currentTime = System.currentTimeMillis();
        elapsedTime = currentTime - startTime;              // Compute the time wasted
        display.setText("You have now wasted " + elapsedTime
                        + " milliseconds\n"
                        + "playing with this silly Java applet!!");
    } // actionPerformed()
} // End of TimerApplet
```

they now understand how important program documentation is. As one of my former students told me,

Lanning's Limerick

```
All hard-headed coders say ''Phooey,
Putting comments in code is just hooey!''
But when they are asked,
To reread what they hacked,
They discover their programs are screwy.
```

Program Walkthrough: The `import` Declaration

The next portion of the program contains the three `import` statements:

```
import java.applet.Applet;
import java.awt.*;
import java.awt.event.*;
```

The `import` statement is a convenience that allows you to refer to library classes by their short names rather than by their fully qualified names. For example, the first import statement tells the compiler that in this program we will refer to the `java.applet.Applet` class simply as `Applet`. This allows us to write a statement like

```
public class TimerApplet extends Applet
```

instead of being required to use the full name for the `Applet` class

```
public class TimerApplet extends java.applet.Applet
```

The expression `java.awt.*` uses the asterisk ("*") as a *wildcard character* that matches any public class name in the `java.awt` package. This allows you to refer to all public classes in the `java.awt` package—for example, `java.awt.Button` and `java.awt.TextArea`—by their short names. The third statement matches all the class names in the `java.awt.event` package, which allows the program to refer to `java.awt.event.ActionListener` by its short name.

Program Walkthrough: Class Definition

The next element in the program is the *header* of the class definition:

```
public class TimerApplet extends Applet implements ActionListener
```

which serves the purpose of naming the class `TimerApplet`, designating its accessibility `public`, specifying that it is an `Applet`, and declaring that it implements `ActionListener`, an interface for handling (or listening for) events such as mouse clicks. The header begins the definition of the class, which extends all the way to the last line of the program—the line marked with the `// End of TimerApplet` comment. A **block** is a sequence of statements enclosed within braces. The body of a class definition is a block, as is the body of a method. Note how the statements in the block are indented, and how the braces are aligned and commented. These style conventions serve to make the program more readable.

PROGRAMMING TIP: Use of Indentation . The code within a block should be indented, and the block's opening and closing braces should be aligned. A comment should be used to mark the end of a block of code.

Following the header are several *variable declarations*:

```
private Button calculate;      // The button
private TextArea display;      // The display area

private long startTime;        // When the applet starts
private long currentTime;      // Time of current click
private long elapsedTime;      // Time since it started
```

The first two declarations declare the names of a `Button` object and a `TextArea` object. Both of these objects are visible in the applet's window (Fig 1–12). The next line of declarations declares three integer variables that are used by the applet to store various times. As we will see in more detail in the next chapter, *variables* are memory locations that can store values. For now, just note that the names of these variables, `startTime`, `currentTime`, and `elapsedTime`, have been chosen to be descriptive of their purpose in the program.

PROGRAMMING TIP: Choice of Variable Names . Names chosen for variables, methods, and classes should be descriptive of the element's purpose and should be written in a distinctive style to distinguish them from other elements of the program. For variable and method names, our convention is to start the name with a lowercase letter and use uppercase letters to distinguish words within the name—for example, `elapsedTime`. Class names begin with an uppercase letter (`TimerApplet`).

The first variable will be used to store the time at which the applet started. The second variable will be used to store the current time, and the third variable will be used to store their difference, which is the elapsed time.

Program Walkthrough: Method Definition

The next element of the program is the `init()` method:

```
public void init()
{
    startTime = System.currentTimeMillis();             // Get the current time
                                                        // Set up the applet interface
    calculate = new Button("Watch How Time Flys!");     // Button
    calculate.addActionListener(this);
    display = new TextArea(4,35);                       // Display area
    add(calculate);
    add(display);
} // init()
```

The `init()` method is called once, automatically, whenever an applet is loaded into the Java Virtual Machine. Its purpose is to *initialize* the applet's interface and any variables used in the applet's processing. As the method's comments indicate, the method gets the current time from the `System` object and stores it in the `startTime` variable. It then creates (`new`) a `Button` and a `TextArea` and `adds` them to the applet, which causes them to appear on the screen when the applet is run.

The `actionPerformed()` method is the last element in the program:

```
public void actionPerformed (ActionEvent e)
{
    currentTime = System.currentTimeMillis();
    elapsedTime = currentTime - startTime;              // Compute the time wasted
    display.setText("You have now wasted " + elapsedTime
                    + " milliseconds\n"
                    + "playing with this silly Java applet!!");
} // actionPerformed()
```

This method is called automatically whenever the applet's button is clicked. Its purpose is to "perform action" when a button-click event takes place. In this case the action it takes is to get the current time again from the `System` object. This time it stores it in the `currentTime` variable. It then computes `elapsedTime` as the difference between `currentTime` and `startTime`. It displays the result in the applet's `TextArea`, which is named `display`. Notice that something that looks like an arithmetic expression is used to incorporate the current value of `elapsedTime` into the "You have now wasted" message.

Lab Exercise 1: Editing, Compiling, and Running

Using whatever programming environment you have available in your computing lab, edit, compile, and run the `TimerApplet` program. However, don't just keyboard the whole program and then compile it. Instead, use the stepwise refinement approach as outlined here.

- **Stepwise Refinement: Stage 1.** Begin by keyboarding the entire comment block at the beginning of the program, the `import` statements, and the following class definition:

```
public class TimerApplet extends Applet implements ActionListener
{
    public void actionPerformed (ActionEvent e)
    {
    } // actionPerformed
} // End of TimerApplet
```

This is an example of a stub class. A **stub class** has the basic outline for a class but no real content. In this case the definition must contain a stub definition of the `actionPerformed()` method, which is part of the `ActionListener` interface. After entering this, compile and run the program. It should compile correctly, but it won't do anything because it doesn't contain any executable code.

- **Stepwise Refinement: Stage 2.** Keyboard the declarations given at the beginning of the class definition and the stub method definitions for the `init()` method. A **stub method** contains a correctly defined *method header* but an incomplete *method body*. The idea is that you will fill in the details of the body later. Your program should then contain the following code:

```
public class TimerApplet extends Applet implements ActionListener
{
    private Button calculate;                // The button
    private TextArea display;                // The display area

    private long startTime;                  // When the applet starts
    private long currentTime;                // Time of current click
    private long elapsedTime;                // Time since it started

    public void init()
    {
    } // init()

    public void actionPerformed (ActionEvent e)
    {
    } // actionPerformed
} // End of TimerApplet
```

Recompile the program and run it again. It should compile correctly, but it still won't really do anything. But you've accomplished a lot, because you've now correctly coded the basic structure of the program.

- **Stepwise Refinement: Stage 3.** Complete the coding of the `init()` method by keyboarding all of the executable statements contained within its body. Then recompile and run the program. Now when the program runs you should see a `Button` and a `TextArea` on the applet. Note that if any errors occur as you are coding this portion of the program, you know that they must be located in the `init()` method, because you haven't touched the rest of the program. You've now successfully implemented the applet's user interface.

- **Stepwise Refinement: Stage 4.** Complete the coding of the `actionPerformed()` method by keyboarding all of the statements in its method body. Then recompile and run the applet. It should now have its full functionality. Every time you click on the button, it should report how much time you've wasted since the applet started. Cool, eh!?

Hopefully, going through this exercise has illustrated some of the advantages of the stepwise refinement approach to writing Java code.

PROGRAMMING TIP: Stepwise Refinement. *Stepwise refinement* is a coding and testing strategy that employs the divide-and-conquer principle. Keyboard and test small segments of the program in a step-by-step fashion. In addition to breaking up the task into more manageable subtasks, this approach helps to *localize* any problems that arise.

Lab Exercise 2: Generating Syntax Errors

In this exercise you will make modifications to `TimerApplet` which will introduce syntax errors into your program. The main purpose here is to give you a first look at how your programming environment reports error messages. You'll also learn some of the most fundamental rules of Java syntax.

For each of the items below, make the editing change and then recompile the program. Make note of any error messages that are generated by the compiler. Try to understand what the message is telling you, and try to learn from the error, so it will be less likely to occur next time. After you have finished with that error, restore the code to its original form and move on to the next item.

- **Java Language Rule. Every Java statement must end with a semicolon.** Delete the semicolon at the end of one of the lines in the program. Repeat this experiment for different lines and note the error messages. Are they always the same? Sometimes the compiler can tell that you've forgotten a semicolon, but sometimes a missing semicolon causes the compiler to lose its place.

- **Java Language Rule. Variables must be declared before they can be used.** Turn the line in which the three time variables are declared into a comment by typing double slashes "//" at the beginning of the line. The compiler will now skip that line. Because you haven't removed the line from the source code, you can easily put it back in the program by removing the double slashes.

- **Java Language Rule. Java names are case sensitive.** Change the spelling of `startTime` to `StartTime` in the declaration statement but nowhere else in the program.

Lab Exercise 3: Generating Semantic Errors

Recall that semantic errors cannot be detected by the compiler. They are errors in the logic of the program which cause it to do something it is not really supposed to do. For each of the following errors, try to think about what will happen before you run the program. Then try to describe the logic error that is being committed. Ask yourself what kind of test you might perform to detect the error (if your didn't already know where it was).

- **Button, button, who's got the button?** Comment out the line (by beginning it with double slashes) that contains the `add(calculate);` statement. This is a pretty easy error to detect.
- **Where has the time gone?** Comment out the second statement in the body of the `actionPerformed()` method. How will this affect the program's result?
- **What's the difference?** Change the minus sign (−) to a division sign (/) in the line in the `actionPerformed()` method where the elapsed time is calculated. This error is a little more subtle than the others. How would you detect this error?

That's enough! Feel free to make up your own experiments and play around some more with the program.

CHAPTER SUMMARY

Technical Terms

algorithm	applet	application
block	method	method invocation
pseudocode	stepwise refinement	semantics
stub class	stub method	syntax
variable		

New Java Keywords

`double`	`import`	`private`
`public`	`return`	

Java Library Classes

`ActionListener`	`Applet`	`Button`
`PrintStream`	`System`	`TextArea`

Java Library Methods

`actionPerformed()`	`main()`	`init()`
`paint()`	`print()`	`println()`

Programmer-Defined Classes

`HelloWorld`	`OldMacDonald`	`Rectangle`
`SampleApplet`	`Square`	`TimerApplet`

Programmer-Defined Methods

`calculateArea()` `getName()`

Summary of Important Points

- A Java *applet* is an embedded program that runs within the context of a WWW browser. A Java *application* runs in stand-alone mode. Java applets are identified in HTML documents by using the `applet tag`.
- Java programs are first *compiled* into *bytecode* and then *interpreted* by the *Java Virtual Machine*.
- A Java source program must be stored in a file that has a `.java` extension. A Java bytecode file has the same name as the source file but a `.class` extension. It is an error in Java if the name of the source file is not identical to the name of the public Java *class* defined within the file. Java is *case sensitive*.
- Good program design requires that each *object* and *method* have a well-defined task and clear definition of what information is needed for the task and what results will be produced.
- An *algorithm* is a step-by-step process that solves some problem. *Pseudocode* is a hybrid language that combines English and programming language constructs.
- Coding Java should follow the *stepwise refinement* process and should make ample use of *stub methods*.
- A *syntax error* results when a statement violates one of Java's syntax rules. Syntax errors are detected by the compiler. A *semantic error* or *logic error* is an error in the program's design and cannot be detected by the compiler.
- Testing a program can only reveal the presence of bugs, not their absence. No matter how convinced you are that a bug is not your program's fault, you're almost certainly wrong! Good program design is important; the sooner you start coding, the longer the program will take to finish.
- Good programs should be designed for *readability*, *clarity*, and *flexibility*.
- The expression `System.out.print("hello")` uses Java *dot notation* to invoke the `print()` method of the `System.out` object. Dot notation takes the form, *reference.elementName*.

ANSWERS TO SELF-STUDY EXERCISES

EXERCISE 1.1

```
public class OldMacDonald
{
    public static void main(String argv[])    // Main method
    {
        System.out.println("Old MacDonald had a farm");
        System.out.println("E I E I O.");
        System.out.println("And on his farm he had a duck.");
        System.out.println("E I E I O.");
        System.out.println("With a quack quack here.");
        System.out.println("And a quack quack there.");
        System.out.println("Here a quack, there a quack,");
        System.out.println("Everywhere a quack quack.");
        System.out.println("Old MacDonald had a farm");
        System.out.println("E I E I O.");

        System.out.println("Old MacDonald had a farm");
        System.out.println("E I E I O.");
        System.out.println("And on his farm he had a pig.");
        System.out.println("E I E I O.");
        System.out.println("With a oink oink here.");
        System.out.println("And an oink oink  there.");
        System.out.println("Here a oink, there a oink,");
        System.out.println("Everywhere a oink oink.");
        System.out.println("Old MacDonald had a farm");
        System.out.println("E I E I O.");
    } // End of main
} // End of OldMacDonald
```

EXERCISE 1.2

```
public class Pattern
{
    public static void main(String argv[])    // Main method
    {
        System.out.println("**********");
        System.out.println("* **  ** *");
        System.out.println("*   **   *");
        System.out.println("* *    * *");
        System.out.println("*  ****  *");
        System.out.println("**********");
    } // End of main
} // End of Pattern
```

EXERCISES

1. Fill in the blanks in each of the following statements.

   a. A Java class definition contains an object's _____ and _____ .
   b. A stub class is one which contains a proper _____ but an empty _____.

2. Explain the difference between each of the following pairs of concepts.

   a. *Application* and *applet*.
   b. *Single-line* and *multiline* comment.
   c. *Compiling* and *running* a program.
   d. *Source code* file and *bytecode* file.
   e. *Syntax* and *semantics*.

f. *Syntax error* and *semantic error*.
g. *Data* and *methods*.
h. *Variable* and *method*.
i. *Algorithm* and *method*.
j. *Pseudocode* and *Java code*.
k. *Method definition* and *method invocation*.

3. For each of the following, identify it as either a syntax error or a semantic error. Justify your answers.

   a. You write your class header as `public Class MyClass`.
   b. You define the `init()` header as `public vid init()`.
   c. You print a string of five asterisks by `System.out.println("***");`
   d. You forget the semicolon at the end of a `println()` statement.
   e. You calculate the sum of two numbers as `N - M`.

4. Suppose you have a Java program stored in a file named `Test.java`. Describe how the compilation and execution process for this program, naming any other files that would be created.
5. Suppose *N* is 15. What numbers would be output by the following pseudocode algorithm? Suppose *N* is 6. What would be output by the algorithm in that case?

```
0. Print N.
1. If N equals 1, stop.
2. If N is even, divide it by 2.
3. If N is odd, triple it and add 1.
4. Go to step 0.
```

6. Suppose *N* is 5 and *M* is 3. What value would be reported by the following pseudocode algorithm? In general, what quantity does this algorithm calculate?

```
0. Write 0 on a piece of paper.
1. If M equals 0, report what's on the paper and stop.
2. Add N to the quantity written on the paper.
3. Subtract 1 from M
4. Go to step 1.
```

7. **Puzzle Problem**: You are given two different length strings that have the characteristic that they both take exactly one hour to burn. However, neither string burns at a constant rate. Some sections of the strings burn very fast, other sections burn very slow. All you have to work with is a box of matches and the two strings. Describe an algorithm that uses the strings and the matches to calculate when exactly 45 minutes has elapsed.
8. **Puzzle Problem**: A polar bear that lives right at the North Pole can walk due south for one hour, due east for one hour, and due north for one hour, and end up right back where it started. Is it possible to do this anywhere else on earth? Explain.

9. **Puzzle Problem**: Lewis Carroll, the author of *Alice in Wonderland*, used the following puzzle to entertain his guests: A captive Queen weighing 165 pounds, her son weighing 90 pounds, and her daughter weighing 135 pounds, were trapped in a very high tower. Outside their window was a pulley and rope with a basket fastened on each end. They managed to escape by using the baskets and a 75-pound weight they found in the tower. How did they do it? The problem is anytime the difference in weight between the two baskets is more than 15 pounds, someone might get killed. Describe an algorithm that gets them down safely.
10. **Puzzle Problem**: Here's another Carroll favorite: A farmer needs to cross a river with his fox, goose, and a bag of corn. There's a rowboat that will hold the farmer and one other passenger. The problem is that the fox will eat the goose, if they are left alone, and the goose will eat the corn, if they are left alone. Write an algorithm that describes how he got across without losing any of his possessions.
11. **Puzzle Problem**: Have you heard this one? A farmer lent the mechanic next door a 40-pound weight. Unfortunately the mechanic dropped the weight and it broke into four pieces. The good news is that according to the mechanic, it is still possible to use the four pieces to weigh any quantity between one and 40 pounds on a balance scale. How much did each of the four pieces weigh? (*Hint*: You can weigh a 4-pound object on a balance by putting a 5-pound weight on one side and a 1-pound weight on the other.)
12. Suppose your little sister asks you to help her calculate her homework average in her science course by showing how to use a pocket calculator. Describe an algorithm that she can use to find the average of 10 homework grades.
13. A Caesar cipher is a secret code in which each letter of the alphabet is shifted by *N* letters to the right, with the letters at the end of the alphabet wrapping around to the beginning. For example, if *N* is 1, "daze" would be written as "ebaf." Describe an algorithm that can be used to create a Caesar encoded message with a shift of 5.
14. Suppose you received the message, "sxccohv duh ixq," which you know to be a Caesar cipher. Figure out what it says and then describe an algorithm that will always find what the message said regardless of the size of the shift that was used.
15. Suppose you're talking to your little brother on the phone and he wants you to calculate his homework average. All you have to work with is a piece of chalk and a very small chalkboard—big enough to write one four-digit number. What's more, although your little brother knows how to read numbers, he doesn't know how to count very well so he can't tell you how many grades there are. All he can do is read the numbers to you. Describe an algorithm that will calculate the correct average under these conditions.
16. Write a *header* for a public applet named `SampleApplet`.
17. Write a *header* for a public method named `getName`.
18. Design a class to represent a geometric square with a given length of side, such that it is capable of calculating the area and the perimeter of the square. Use the design specification we created for the `Rectangle` class as a model.
19. Write a *stub definition* for a public class named `Square`.
20. Complete the definition of the `Square` class using the definition of `Rectangle` (Fig 1–10) as a model.
21. Modify the `OldMacDonald` class to "sing" either *Mary Had a Little Lamb* or your favorite nursery rhyme.

22. Define a Java class, called `Patterns`, modeled after `OldMacDonald`, that will print the following patterns of asterisks, one after the other heading down the page:

```
*****     *****   *****
 ****     *   *   * * *
  ***     *   *    * *
   **     *   *   * * *
    *     *****   *****
```

23. Write a Java class that prints your initials as block letters, for example,

```
****** *       *
*    * **     **
*    * * *   * *
****** *  * *  *
**     *   *   *
* *    *       *
*  *   *       *
*   *  *       *
```

24. **Challenge:** Define a class that represents a `Temperature` object. It should store the current temperature in an instance variable of type `double`, and it should have two `public` methods, `setTemp(double t)`, which assigns `t` to the instance variable, and `getTemp()`, which `returns` the value of the instance variable. Use the `Rectangle` class as a model.
25. **Challenge:** Define a class named `TaxWhiz` that computes the sales tax for a purchase. It should store the current tax rate as an instance variable. Following the model of the `Rectangle` class, you can initialize the rate using a `TaxWhiz()` method. This class should have one `public` method, `calcTax(double purchase)`, which `returns` a `double`, whose value is`purchases` times the tax rate. For example, if the tax rate is 4 percent, 0.04, and the purchase is $100, the `calcTax()` should return 4.0.

Objects: Defining, Creating, and Using

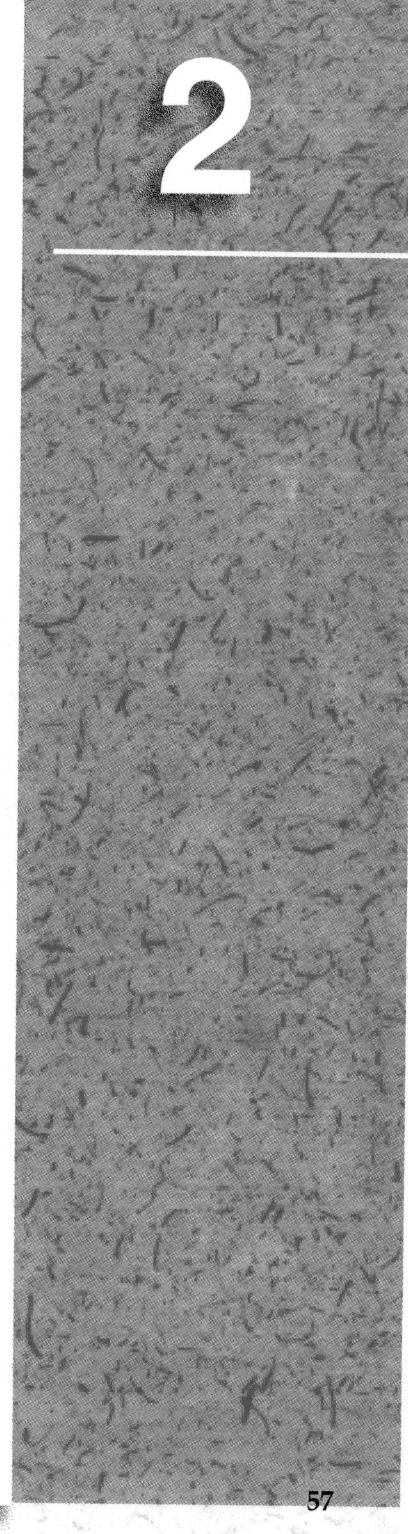

OBJECTIVES

After studying this chapter, you will

- Understand the concept of a class hierarchy.
- Be familiar with the relationship between classes and objects in a Java program.
- Be able to understand and write simple programs in Java.
- Be familiar with some of the basic principles of object-oriented programming.
- Understand some of the basic elements of the Java language, including *keywords, identifiers, primitive data types, variables, expressions, operators,* and *statements.*

OUTLINE

2.1 Introduction

This chapter introduces some of the basic principles of object oriented programming. We begin by revisiting the very core of the object-oriented approach, the objects themselves, by reconsidering the software ordering example from Chapter 0 as a Java applet. Next we provide an overview of a Java program by doing a detailed walkthrough of the `Rectangle` class we designed in Chapter 1. We focus on the basic Java language elements involved. By the end of this section, you should know how to identify the key elements that make up a Java program.

We then present a detailed example of the programming development process by designing `CyberPet`, a Java class that simulates a pet that responds to eat and sleep commands. Finally, the lab project for this chapter involves the design, implementation, and testing of a simple class. By completing the lab project, you will have written a complete Java application program from scratch.

2.2 Interacting Objects

As we discussed in Chapter 0, the basic idea of object-oriented programming is that of *objects* interacting with each other by sending and receiving messages. Recall the example we discussed there of ordering a piece of software from Acme Computer Warehouse. Suppose that Acme has automated this transaction so that customers can now use a Java applet to place their orders (Fig 2–1). The applet provides three `TextFields` for the customer's name, credit card number, and software item number. Once these fields are filled in, the customer can click on the "Submit Order" `Button` to process the order or on the "Cancel" `Button` to clear the form and start over.

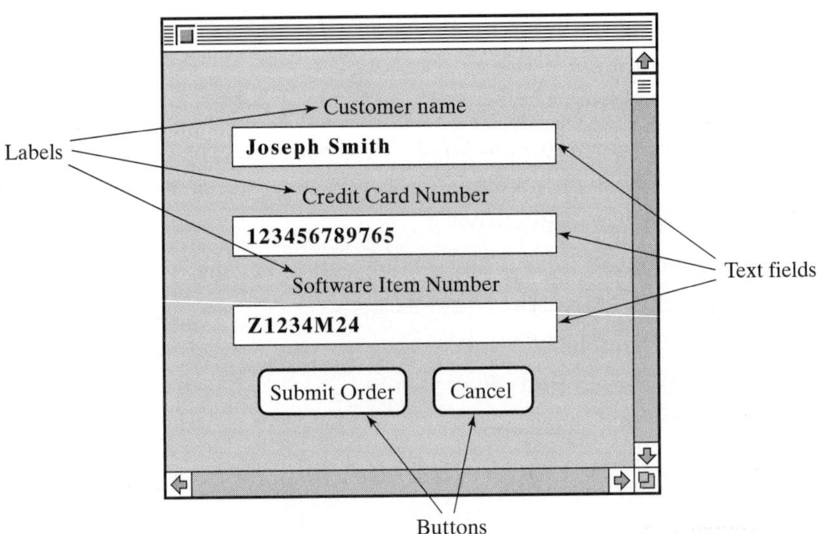

Figure 2–1 A Java-based WWW form for ordering a piece of software.

Interface

This applet involves interactions among several objects. First there is the applet itself, which serves as a visual interface between the user and `orderForm`, an (invisible) object that replaces the clerk in the manual process. An *interface* is something that mediates an interaction between two things. In this case, the applet mediates an interaction between the user, a person, and the order form, an invisible object in the program's memory. In the manual process, the telephone serves as an interface between two people, the customer and the clerk.

Next, the three `TextFields` are objects whose purpose is to store the order information. Finally, the two `Buttons` are objects whose purpose is to enable the user to communicate with the `orderForm` object. When the user clicks on "submit order," the applet asks each of the three `TextFields` for their stored information and then passes it to the `orderForm`. In Java code, communication between the applet, a `TextField` and the `orderForm` would take the following form:

```
orderform.setCustomerName ( customerNameField.getText() );
```

In this chunk of code the applet is getting the customer's name from the `TextField` and passing it to the `orderForm`. At first glance, the code looks complicated. But what it does is like the interaction between the customer and Acme's sales agent:

Just as in the transaction between human agents, each object has its own specialty, its own well-defined task. The successful performance of this computer-based transaction depends on division of labor, and on communication and processing of certain information among the objects involved. The objects encapsulate the expertise and functionality required to carry out the transaction. The information passing among the various objects controls the overall process. This is how object-oriented programming works.

Encapsulation

SELF-STUDY EXERCISES

EXERCISE 2.1 What objects are involved in the transaction of adding an additional course to your schedule? Describe the messages that are passed among them. Make a list of the objects involved in this transaction. Don't forget the registrar!

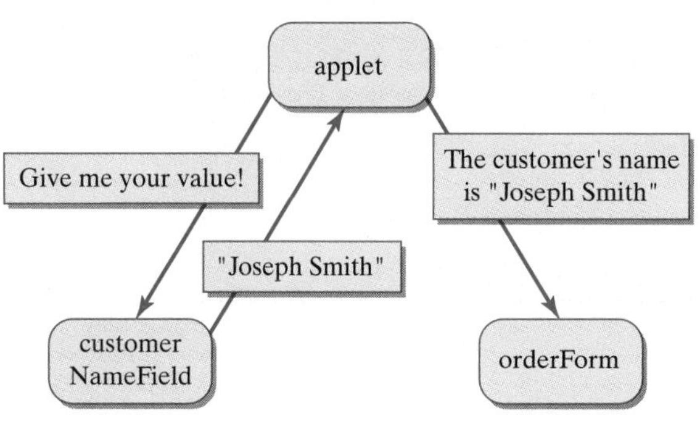

Figure 2–2 A depiction of part of the software ordering transaction: The applet object gets data ("Joseph Smith") from the `customerNameField` object and passes it to the `orderForm` object.

2.3 The Java Class Hierarchy—Classifying Objects

Classifying means grouping things together based on their similarities. The ability to classify is an important element in our thinking, and a natural part of our attempt to understand the world. For example, biologists divide organisms into five major classes including the animal and plant kingdoms. The animal kingdom is divided into the vertebrates and invertebrates, and the vertebrates are broken down into mammals, reptiles, amphibians, fish, and so on (Fig 2–3). In general, classification provides us a natural way of organizing the world so that we can understand it and interact with it.

Superclass/subclass

Fig 2–3 is a *hierarchy chart* that shows the relationships among a collection of classes. The most general class in this hierarchy is the `Animal` class. All the other classes are its **subclasses**, and it is a **superclass** of all other classes. The chart also indicates that the `Mammal` class is a subclass of the `Animal` class and, vice versa, the `Animal` class is a superclass of the `Mammal` class.

Class inheritance

One implication of the subclass relationship is that mammals have all of the characteristics possessed by animals. This is a form of **class inheritance**, whereby members of the subclass **inherit** all of the characteristics of members of the superclass. The subclass relationship extends throughout the hierarchy. So characteristics of a given class are inherited by all the classes that occur below it in the hierarchy. Thus, dogs and cats have all the characteristics of animals.

The objects in Java programs are also organized into classes. The Java hierarchy is rooted in the `Object` class, which is the superclass of all other Java classes (Fig 2–4). Note that the `Component` branch includes the various objects, such as `TextFields` and `Buttons`, that are used to build Graphical User Interfaces (GUIs), such as the one in Fig 2–1.

Java class inheritance

You can see from the hierarchy chart that a `TextField` is a type of `TextComponent`, which is a type of `Component`. In other words, the `TextField` class is a subclass of the `TextComponent` class, which in turn is a subclass of the `Component` class. Just as dogs and cats inherit the characteristics of the animal class, the `TextField` and `Button` classes *inherit* all the characteristics of the `Component` class. Like all other `Components`, `TextFields` and `Buttons` have a size, location, foreground and background color and can be added to an applet.

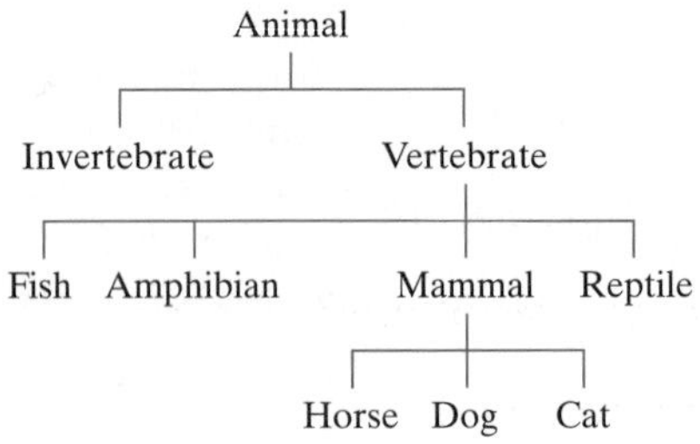

Animal
Invertebrate Vertebrate
Fish Amphibian Mammal Reptile
Horse Dog Cat

Figure 2–3 *Hierarchy chart* showing a classification of objects.

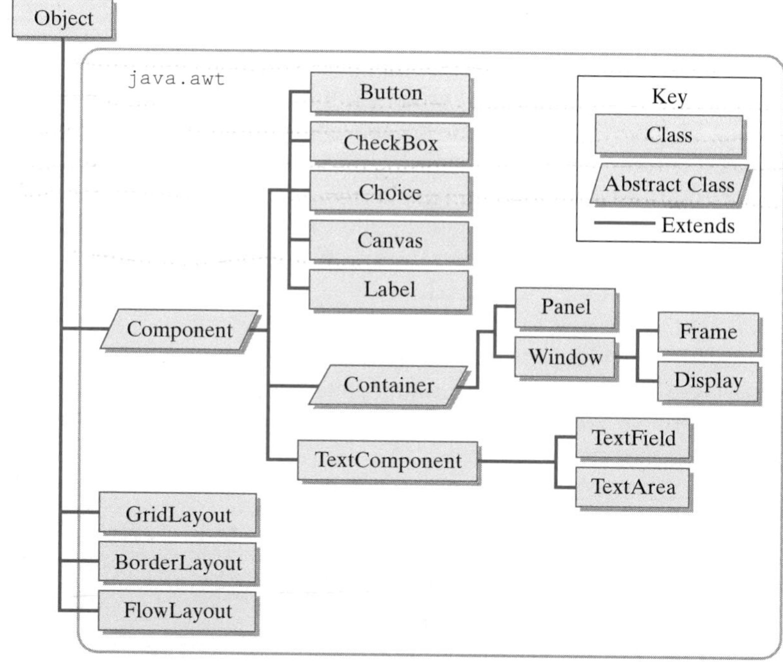

Figure 2–4 Part of Java's class hierarchy rooted at `Object`.

2.4 Class Definition

The class as template

To program in Java the main thing you do is write class definitions for the various objects that will make up the program. A class definition *encapsulates* its objects' data and actions. Once a class has been defined, it serves as a *template*, or blueprint, for creating individual *objects* or **instances** of the class.

Variables and methods

A class definition contains two types of elements: variables and methods. *Variables* are used to store the object's information. *Methods* are used to process the information. To design an object you need to answer five basic questions:

1. What tasks will the object perform?
2. What information will it need to perform its tasks?
3. What methods will it use to process its information?
4. What information will it make public for other objects?
5. What information will it hide from other objects?

2.4.1 The Rectangle Class

Instance variables

Recall our definition of the Rectangle class from Chapter 1 (Fig 2–5). This definition specifies that each Rectangle will have two instance variables, length and width. Each of these variables stores a certain kind of real number known as a double. The class definition also specifies what each method will do. The Rectangle() method assigns initial values (l and w) to its length and width variables. The calculateArea() method calculates and returns a rectangle's area — that is, its length times its width. (Note that in Java the asterisk — "*" — is used as the symbol for multiplication.)

Private vs. public access

The instance variables length and width are designated as private, but the calculateArea() method is designated as public. These designations follow two important object-oriented design conventions:

EFFECTIVE DESIGN: Private Variables. Instance variables are usually declared private. This means they are *hidden* from other objects. The private elements of an object cannot be directly accessed by other objects.

EFFECTIVE DESIGN: Public Methods. An object's public methods can be used by other objects to interact with the object. They make up the object's **interface**.

The reason for these design conventions will become apparent shortly. For now, remember that we determine what is hidden, and what is part of an object's interface simply by labeling an element either private or public in the class definition.

Figure 2–5 The Rectangle class definition.

```
public class Rectangle
{
    private double length;      // Instance variables
    private double width;

    public Rectangle(double l, double w)  // Constructor method
    {
        length = l;
        width = w;
    } // Rectangle constructor

    public double calculateArea()         // Access method
    {
        return length * width;
    } // calculateArea

} // Rectangle class
```

Note also that the `Rectangle` class itself is declared `public`. This lets other classes have access to the class and to its public variables and methods. Java provides mechanisms that determine the accessibility of classes and their elements.

> **JAVA LANGUAGE RULE** **Class Access.** A `public` class is accessible to any other class, if its containing package is accessible. Otherwise, a class is accessible only to the other classes in its package. Whether a package is accessible or not is determined by the Java runtime system.

As this rule suggests, Java classes are organized into *packages*. When you define a class, you can declare what package it belongs to using the statement

```
package MyPackage;
```

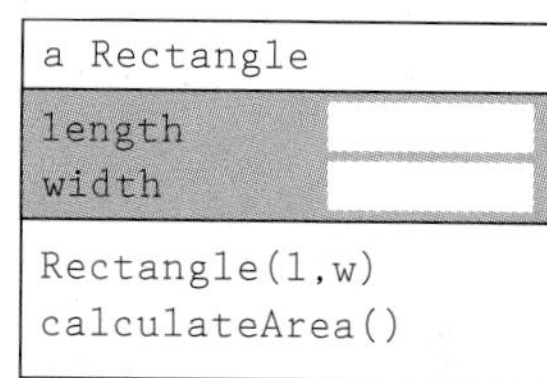

Figure 2–6 A class is a blueprint. It describes an object's form but not its content. Notice that the instance variables, `length` and `width`, have no values.

The package declaration is optional, and if it is omitted, Java will place the class in a default, unnamed package. The class definitions in this book will usually omit the package declaration, which is the usual convention when developing small programs. Java runtime systems are required to have at least one unnamed package that is accessible.

Fig 2–6 gives a conceptual view of the `Rectangle` class. A class is like a blueprint. It has form but no content. Thus a `Rectangle` has a private (shaded) and a public (unshaded) aspect. The class definition specifies the type of information that each individual `Rectangle` contains, but it doesn't contain any actual values. It defines the methods that each `Rectangle` can perform, but it doesn't actually invoke the methods. In short, a class serves as a template , providing a detailed blueprint of the objects (or instances) of that class.

Class as blueprint

2.4.2 The `RectangleUser` Class

Although it is a good representation of a geometric rectangle, the `Rectangle` class is not a complete Java application program, because it does not have a `main()` method. Let's define a second class to serve as an interface with various `Rectangle` objects. `RectangleUser` will contain a `main()` method, in which we will create and interact with some `Rectangle` objects. Its outline takes the following form:

```
public class RectangleUser
{
    public static void main(String argv[])
    {
    }
}
```

By convention, the header of the `main()` method, must be specified exactly as shown here.

2.4.3 Object Instantiation: Creating `Rectangle` Instances

These statements create, or *instantiate* , two *instances* of the `Rectangle` class:

```
Rectangle rectangle1 = new Rectangle(30,10);
Rectangle rectangle2 = new Rectangle(25,20);
```

An object is an instance of a class

The `rectangle1` object is an *instance* of the `Rectangle` class. In this statement it is given 30 and 10 as the initial values of its `length` and `width`, respectively. In the same way, when `rectangle2` is created, it is passed 25 and 20 as its `length` and `width`. Fig 2–7 gives a conceptual view of these two objects. Each object has its own `private` instance variables, which hold its essential data, and its own copies of the methods that were defined in the class definition. Each object can be referred to by a unique name (`rectangle1` and `rectangle2`).

rectangle1		rectangle2	
a Rectangle		a Rectangle	
length	30	length	25
width	10	width	20
Rectangle(l,w)		Rectangle(l,w)	
calculateArea()		calculateArea()	

Figure 2–7 Two rectangles. Notice that their instance variables have different values.

2.4.4 Interacting with `Rectangles`

Once we have created `Rectangle` instances and given them their initial length and width, we can ask each rectangle to calculate and tell us its area:

```
rectangle1.calculateArea()
rectangle2.calculateArea()
```

Method call

These two expressions are examples of *method calls.* A *method* is a named chunk of code, and calling a method is a means of executing its code. The first method call gets the area of `rectangle1`, and the second gets the area of `rectangle2`. Recall that as we defined the `calculateArea()` method, it `returns` a rectangle's `length` times its `width`. So the first of these statements will return 300 (30 * 10). The second statement will return 500 (25 * 20).

DEBUGGING TIP: Method Call versus Method Definition. Don't confuse method calls with method definitions. The definition specifies the method's actions. The method call takes those actions.

If we want to display a rectangle's area, we can embed these method calls within a `println()` statement

```
System.out.println("rectangle1 area" + rectangle1.calculateArea());
System.out.println("rectangle2 area" + rectangle2.calculateArea());
```

The expression within the parentheses of the `println()` method concatenates, or joins together, the string `rectangle1 area` and the value 300 into a single string, which is displayed on the screen. Thus the output produced by these two statements will be:

```
rectangle1 area 300
rectangle2 area 500
```

Fig 2–8 shows the complete definition of the `RectangleUser` class. This is a very simple user interface . It creates two `Rectangle` objects, named `rectangle1` and `rectangle2`. It then asks each object to calculate its area, and it displays the areas on the screen. As in our other examples, note the sense in which the work has been divided here between an object that encapsulates the data and methods of a `Rectangle`, and an object that serves as the user interface. Interaction between `RectangleUser` and `Rectangle` takes place by using the `public` methods provided by `Rectangle`.

2.4.5 Define, Create, Use

As our rectangle example illustrated, once a program's classes have been designed, writing a Java program is a matter of three basic steps:

- Define one or more classes (class definition).
- Create objects as instances of the classes (object instantiation).
- Use the objects to do tasks (object use).

The Java class definition determines what information will be stored in each object and what methods each object will perform. Instantiation creates an instance and associates a name with it in the program. The object's methods can then be called as a way of getting the object to perform certain tasks.

Figure 2–8 The `RectangleUser` class.

```
public class RectangleUser
{
    public static void main(String argv[])
    {
        Rectangle rectangle1 = new Rectangle(30,10);
        Rectangle rectangle2 = new Rectangle(25,20);
        System.out.println("rectangle1 area" +
                           rectangle1.calculateArea());
        System.out.println("rectangle2 area" +
                           rectangle2.calculateArea());
    } // main()
} // RectangleUser
```

SELF-STUDY EXERCISES

EXERCISE 2.2 Identify the following elements in the `Rectangle` class (Fig 2–5):

- The name of the class.
- The names of two instance variables.
- The names of two methods.

EXERCISE 2.3 Identify the following elements in the `RectangleUser` class (Fig 2–8):

- The names of two `Rectangle` instances.
- All six method calls in the program.
- Two examples of qualified names.

2.5 CASE STUDY: Simulating a CyberPet

In this section, we will design and write a complete Java application program. The program will simulate a CyberPet that responds to simple commands. The program will introduce Java programming fundamentals and object-oriented program design. We will focus on some details of the Java language, with the objective being to get you to understand what the program is doing and how it works without necessarily understanding why it works the way it does. We will get to "why" later in the book.

2.5.1 Designing the `CyberPet` Class

Problem Specification

Let's design and write a program that simulates the behavior of a CyberPet. This pet will do two things, eat and sleep, when we tell it to. When we tell it to eat (or sleep), it should simply report that it is eating (or sleeping) by printing a message.

Problem Decomposition

What objects do we need?

Following the design we used in the `Rectangle` example, we need two types of objects: one to represent the CyberPet and one to serve as a user interface. The first type of object will be analogous to the `Rectangle` class — its task will be to represent something — while the second will be analogous to the `RectangleUser` class — its task will be to provide a user interface. The `CyberPet` class will represent whether an individual pet is eating or sleeping and will implement methods to define the eat and sleep commands. The `TestCyberPet` class will create a couple of `CyberPet` instances and get them to eat and sleep on command.

Class Design: CyberPet

As we saw in the Rectangle example, class definitions can usually be broken down into two parts: (1) the information that the object needs, and (2) the actions the object can take. The information stored in an object's instance variables is sometimes referred to as the object's *state*. For example, a Rectangle's state would be its length and width. Taken together, an object's state and its methods form a *representation*, or a *model*, of the object.

A consistent model of a pet's state will ensure that a pet is either sleeping or eating, but it cannot be doing both at the same time. One way to model these two mutually exclusive states is to treat them like light switches that can be either on or off. When the eating light is on, the sleeping light must be off, and vice versa.

What data do we need?

The Java boolean data type provides a close approximation of a light switch. Each boolean variable can have one of two values, true or false, which are good analogues for a switch's on and off state. Suppose that we represent our pet's state using two boolean variables named isEating and isSleeping. Table 2–1 relates the values of these two instance variables to the pet's overall state. A CyberPet is eating when its isEating variable is true and its isSleeping variable is false. Conversely, a CyberPet is sleeping when its isEating variable is false and its isSleeping variable is true.

Table 2.1. Definition of a pet's state

State	isEating	isSleeping
eating	true	false
sleeping	false	true

Method Decomposition

What methods do we need?

How should we divide up (or decompose) the task of representing a CyberPet? Clearly, we need a method, analogous to the Rectangle() method, that will be used to give a CyberPet its initial state. Also, we'll need methods to represent the CyberPet's basic actions: eating and sleeping. Thus, the eat() method will simply put the pet in the eating state, and the sleep() method will put the pet in the sleeping state.

CyberPet *Design Specification*

We're ready to organize our various design decisions into a detailed specification for the CyberPet class (Fig 2–9). Some methods will be made public and will thereby form the pet's interface. These will be the methods that other objects will use to interact with a CyberPet. Similarly, we have followed the convention of designating that an object's instance variables — its state — be kept hidden from other objects, and so we have designated them as private.

Figure 2–9 Specification for the CyberPet class.

- Class Name: CyberPet
- Task: To represent and simulate a CyberPet
- Information Needed (variables)
  - isEating: Set to true when the pet is eating (private)
  - isSleeping: Set to true when the pet is sleeping (private)
- Manipulations Needed (public methods)
  - CyberPet(): A constructor method to initialize the pet
  - sleep(): A method to put the pet to sleep
  - eat(): A method to get the pet to eat

2.5.2 Defining the CyberPet Class

Given our design specification, the next step in building our CyberPet simulation is to write the class definition in Java, so this section will focus on details of the Java language. The definition of the CyberPet class is given in Fig 2–10.

Figure 2–10 Definition of the CyberPet class.

```
public class CyberPet
{

  // Data
   private boolean isEating = true;      // CyberPet's state
   private boolean isSleeping = false;

  // Methods
   public void eat()                     // Start eating
   {
       isEating = true;                  // Change the state
       isSleeping = false;
       System.out.println("Pet is eating");
       return;
   } // eat()

   public void sleep()                   // Start sleeping
   {
       isSleeping = true;                // Change the state
       isEating = false;
       System.out.println("Pet is sleeping");
       return;
   } // sleep()
} // CyberPet class
```

The Class Header

A class definition in Java consists of a class header and a class body. A *class header* gives the class a name and specifies how the class can be used. A *class body* contains all the variables and methods that make up the class:

```
public class CyberPet        // Class header
{                            // Beginning of class body
}                            // End of class body
```

In general, a class header takes the following form:

$$ClassModifiers_{opt} \ \texttt{class} \ ClassName \ Pedigree_{opt}$$

A class header consists of an optional list of *ClassModifiers* , followed by the word `class`, followed by the name that you want to give your class, followed, optionally, by the class's *Pedigree* . As the "opt" subscript indicates, some of these elements, such as the *ClassModifiers* and the *Pedigree*, are optional. If they are omitted the Java compiler will supply *default* values, but for now we won't worry about this complication.

Our definition of `CyberPet` uses the access modifier `public`. An *access modifier* determines whether other objects can have access to the class. By designating `CyberPet` as `public`, we allow it to be accessed by any other object. If this modifier were omitted, Java would restrict access to `CyberPet`. For the most part the classes we define will have `public` access.

`public` *access*

The word `class` is a Java **keyword** , which is a term that has special meaning within Java programs. Java has around 50 such keywords (see the Java Language Summary later in the chapter). The name given to our class, `CyberPet`, is an *identifier*.

> **JAVA LANGUAGE RULE** **Identifiers.** An **identifier** is a name for a variable, method or class. It must begin with a letter of the alphabet, and may consist of any number of letters, digits and the special underscore character (_). An identifier cannot be identical to a Java keyword.

Note that `CyberPet`'s header omits *Pedigree*. A class's *pedigree* describes where it fits in the Java class hierarchy. By default, if the pedigree is not specified, Java considers the class a direct subclass of the `Object` class, as shown in Fig 2–4. (Remember, as a subclass of `Object`, `CyberPet` *inherits* certain methods and variables from `Object`.) Instead of relying on Java's default interpretation, we can make `CyberPet`'s pedigree explicit by changing its header declaration to

Default pedigree

```
public class CyberPet extends Object
```

The `extends` keyword merely specifies that `CyberPet` is a direct subclass of `Object`.

The Class's Instance Variables

Variables and methods

The body of a class follows the header and is contained within curly brackets, {}. As we see both here and in the case of the `Rectangle` class, the body of a class definition generally consists of two parts: the class's state, which is represented by its instance variables, and the class's methods. In general, a class definition will take the form shown in Fig 2–11.

Although Java does not impose any particular order on variable and method declarations, in this book we'll define classes using the style shown in Fig 2–11. The class's instance variables go at the beginning of the class definition, followed by method declarations. In Java, instance variables are known technically as *fields*, and their declarations are called *field declarations*. They should be distinguished from other kinds of variables that may be declared within a class — for example, from *local variables* that are declared within methods.

Fields vs. local variables

A declaration for an instance variable, or a *field declaration*, takes the following form:

$$FieldModifiers_{opt} \quad TypeId \quad VariableId \quad Initializer_{opt}$$

Here are some examples of valid field declarations that we have encountered earlier:

```
private double length;
private double width;
private Button calculate;
private TextArea display;
```

Each of these declarations contains a *FieldModifier* (`private`), a `TypeId` (`double`, `Button`, or `TextArea`), and a *VariableId* (`length`, `width`, and so on). None of these declarations has the optional *Initializer*.

Field declaration

A field declaration is a variable declaration that occurs at the class level. It specifies that a certain memory location within the class's objects will store data of type *TypeId* and will be named or referred to as *VariableId*. The *TypeId* must either be one of Java's primitive types, such as `boolean`, or

Figure 2–11 A template for constructing a Java class definition.

```
public class ClassName
    {
      // Instance variables that make up the object's state
       VariableDeclaration1
       VariableDeclaration2
       ...

      // Methods
       MethodDefinition1
       MethodDefinition2
       ...
    } // End of class
```

must be the name of one of the classes in the Java class hierarchy, including those classes which may be defined by your program. The *VariableId* must be a valid Java identifier.

Public/Private Access

A field declaration can have an optional list of *FieldModifiers*, including *access modifiers*, which determine how the field can be accessed. Access to a field can be `public`, `private`, or `protected`. To determine whether a field is accessible, you must first determine whether its containing class is accessible. If the containing class is accessible, then a field that is declared `private` cannot be accessed outside the class in which it is declared. A field that is declared `protected` can only be accessed by subclasses of the class in which it is declared or by other classes that belong to the same package. A field that is declared `public` can be referenced, and hence modified, by any other class. An object's instance variables should almost never be declared `public`.

`private` *access*

EFFECTIVE DESIGN: Private Instance Variables. As a rule, it is good design to declare instance variables `private`, making them hidden from other objects. This will prevent other objects from being able to directly modify the object's state.

If another object had access to an object's instance variables, it could change the object's state, thereby possibly introducing errors. For example, suppose we declared `CyberPet`'s `isEating` and `isSleeping` as `public` and suppose we have a `CyberPet` named `george`. In that case some other object would be able to execute the following statements:

```
george.isEating = true;   // Access OK if isEating is public
george.isSleeping = true; // Access OK if isSleeping is public
```

In this case both `isEating` and `isSleeping` have been set to `true`, which results in `george` having an inconsistent state, since a pet cannot be both eating and sleeping at the same time. By restricting access to its instance variables, a `CyberPet` can guarantee that its state will always be consistent. It does this by requiring other objects to use the `eat()` and `sleep()` methods to change a `CyberPet`'s state. So the proper way of getting `george` to change his state is to use his `public` methods:

```
george.eat();          // Access OK because eat() is public
```

As long as the `eat()` and `sleep()` methods are designed correctly to preserve the consistency of its state, there is no chance that `george` will end up in an inconsistent state. Thus by controlling which methods are `public` and, hence, accessible outside the class, the class definition defines an *interface* that other objects must use to interact with it.

Defining an object's interface

EFFECTIVE DESIGN: An Object's Interface. An object's interface is defined by designating some elements of an object `private` and other elements `public`. This allows carefully controled access to the object.

Identifier Scope

An identifier's *scope* is simply that portion of the class where it may be used. Fields or instance variables in Java have a scope that extends throughout the entire body of the class definition in which they are declared.

JAVA LANGUAGE RULE **Class Scope.** Fields or instance variables have *class scope*, which means their names can be used anywhere within the class in which they are declared.

Initializer Expressions

Let's now consider the details involved in the field declarations given in the `CyberPet` class:

```
public class CyberPet
{
    private boolean isEating = true;     // CyberPet's state
    private boolean isSleeping = false;

} // CyberPet
```

Default initialization

Note that both declarations include *Initializer* expressions. Whenever a field is declared, the location assigned to that field is given an initial value. If an *Initializer* is omitted from the declaration, the Java compiler supplies a default value. In the case of `boolean` variables, the initial value would be `false`. An *Initializer* can be used to override the default.

JAVA LANGUAGE RULE **Initializer Expression.** An **initializer** expression always takes the form

$$Variable = expression.$$

The expression on the right of the assignment operator (=) is evaluated and its value is assigned to the variable on the left of the (=).

Assignment puts a value into a memory location

The assignment operator (=) means "assign the following value to this location" or "put the following value in this location." It literally takes the value that follows the operator and stores it in that variable's memory location. The value being assigned must have the same type as the variable. It would be a syntax error in Java if we tried to initialize `isEating` to 0, because `isEating` is a `boolean` variable and 0 is an integer value of type `int`. An `int` value just won't fit into a `boolean` memory location; it's too big.

DEBUGGING TIP: Type Error. Assigning a value of one type to a variable of another type will generate a syntax error.

In the CyberPet class, isEating is given an initial value of true, and isSleeping is given an initial value of false. This means that any CyberPet created from this class definition will initially be eating. Assigning initial values to a class's instance variables is one conventional way of setting the initial state of the class's instances.

Initializing an object's state

Fig 2–12 shows the CyberPet class. Recall that a class serves as a template used to define instances of the class. CyberPet contains two fields, isEating and isSleeping, which have been given the initial values specified in the class definition. The fact that they are located in the shaded part of the picture indicates that these are private fields and so are hidden from other objects.

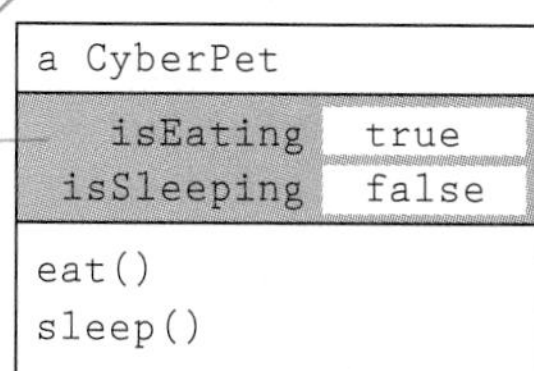

Figure 2–12 A conceptual view of the CyberPet class. Note that its instance variables have been initialized.

To summarize, despite its apparent simplicity, a field declaration actually accomplishes five tasks:

1. It sets aside a portion of the object's memory that can be used to store a certain type of data.
2. It specifies the type of data that can be stored in that location.
3. It associates a name or *variable identifier* with that location.
4. It determines which objects have access to the variable's name.
5. It assigns an initial value to the location.

The Class's Methods

Method definitions are those parts of classes that contain executable statements — that is, statements that perform some kind of action when the program is run. A *method* is a named section of code designed to perform a particular task. By associating a name with the code segment, the program can *call* or *invoke* the method, thereby executing its statements.

Designing and defining methods is a form of abstraction that is sometimes called *procedural abstraction* . By defining a certain sequence of actions (a procedure) as a method, you encapsulate those actions under a single name that can be invoked whenever needed. Instead of having to list the entire sequence again each time you want it performed, you simply call it by name.

Procedural abstraction

A method definition consists of two parts, the method header and the method body. The *method header* declares the name of the method and other general information about the method. The *method body* contains the executable statements that the method performs:

```
public void methodName()      // Method header
{                             // Beginning of method body
}                             // End of method body
```

The Method Header

A method header has the general form shown in the following table. The table also contains several examples of method headers that we have encountered earlier.

MethodModifiers$_{opt}$	*ResultType*	*MethodName*	(*FormalParameterList*)
`public static`	`void`	`main`	`(String argv[])`
`public`	`void`	`paint`	`(Graphics g)`
`public`	`void`	`init`	`()`
		`Rectangle`	`(double l, double w)`
`public`	`double`	`calculateArea`	`()`
`public`	`void`	`eat`	`()`
`public`	`void`	`sleep`	`()`

Thus, a method header consists of an optional list of *MethodModifiers* , followed by the method's *ResultType*, followed by the *MethodName*, followed by the method's *FormalParameterList* (which is enclosed in parentheses). The method body follows the method header.

Let's compare the above template with the method header used in the definition of the `eat()` method in the `CyberPet` class:

```
public void eat()
```

Our definition of the `eat()` method contains the access modifier `public`. The rules on scope and method access are the same as the rules on field access: `private` methods are accessible only within the class itself, `protected` methods are accessible only to subclasses of the class in which the method is defined, and `public` methods are accessible to all other classes. A class's `public` methods make up its *interface*.

EFFECTIVE DESIGN: Object Interface. A class's `public` methods serve as its interface . Choosing and designing appropriate methods to serve as the interface is an important design consideration.

Interface methods vs. helper methods

By controlling which methods are made public, a class definition can control information flow to and from its objects. Generally an object's public methods are those used by other objects to communicate with it. At the same time, methods used only to perform internal operations should be hidden by being declared `private` . These methods are sometimes called *utility methods* or *helper methods*.

EFFECTIVE DESIGN: Public versus Private Methods. If a method is intended to be used to communicate with an object, or if it passes information to or from an object, it should be declared `public`. If a method is intended to be used solely for internal operations within the object, it should be declared `private`.

The `eat()` and `sleep()` methods should clearly be declared `public`, because they are used to the tell a `CyberPet` when to eat or sleep. Similarly, for the `Rectangle` class, the `calculateArea()` method should be `public` because it retrieves a `Rectangle`'s area.

As in the case of a class's fields, the scope of a method's name extends throughout the class in which the method is defined.

> **JAVA LANGUAGE RULE** **Class Scope.** A method has *class scope* , which means it can be called from anywhere within the class in which it is defined.

A method's *ResultType* specifies the type of value (`boolean`, `double`, `Object`) that the method returns. Returning a value is the main way that a method, and hence the object to which it belongs, can pass information back to the object that called the method. However, some methods, such as our `eat()` and `sleep()` methods, do not return a value. In this case, their *ResultType* is specified as `void`. In this chapter we will only use methods that do not return values.

Methods have a result type

> **JAVA LANGUAGE RULE** **Void Methods.** Methods that do not return a value should be declared `void` . A `return` statement is optional for void methods.

The *MethodName* can be any valid Java identifier. The method's name is followed by a *FormalParameterList* enclosed in parentheses. Formal parameters are special variables used to pass information into and out of the method. If no parameters are needed in a particular method, the method's name is just followed by empty parentheses. Because ordering a pet to eat or sleep does not require passing the pet any additional information, `CyberPet`'s `eat()` and `sleep()` methods have an empty parameter list.

Parameters

SELF-STUDY EXERCISES

EXERCISE 2.4 Add a new declaration to `CyberPet` for a `private boolean` variable named `isDreaming`. Assign the variable an initial value of `false`.

EXERCISE 2.5 Add a new definition to `CyberPet` for a `public` method named `dream`. Assume that this is a `void` method that requires no parameters, and that it simply puts the `CyberPet` into the dreaming state.

EXERCISE 2.6 Suppose the `CyberPet` class had a `String` instance variable named `food` and a method named `pickFood()`, which set the value of `food` to either "meat" or "potato." Should this method be declared `public` or `private`?

EXERCISE 2.7 Create a (partial) definition of a `Square` class. Declare appropriate instance variables. Declare stub methods for calculating perimeter and area, and for its constructor. A stub method is a method that has a correctly defined header but an empty body.

The Method Body

Designing a method is an application of the encapsulation principle.

The body of a method definition is a block of Java statements enclosed in braces, {}, which will be executed in sequence when the method is called. This method body is taken from the eat() method:

```
{
    isEating = true;         // Change the state
    isSleeping = false;
    System.out.println("Pet is eating");
    return;
} // eat()
```

The return statement indicates that the method's execution is complete. It causes Java to return control to the object that called the method. When a method does not return any particular result, the return statement may be omitted. If a void method does not contain a return, control will automatically return to the calling object after the last statement of the method has been executed. We'll discuss how method invocation works later in this section.

void *methods*

The eat() and sleep() methods can be used to command a CyberPet to eat and sleep. Recall that according to our design, a CyberPet is eating when its isSleeping field is false and its isEating field is true. The eat() method effects this change in state by executing the following two **assignment statements** :

```
isEating = true;         // Change the state
isSleeping = false;
```

JAVA LANGUAGE RULE **Assignment Statement.** A (simple) **assignment statement,** which takes the form

VariableName = *Expression*,

evaluates the *Expression* on the right of the assignment operator (=) and stores its value in the variable named on left of the operator.

VariableName must be the name of a declared variable. Thus, the first of the above statements stores the value true in the isEating variable, and the second statement stores the value false in the isSleeping variable. This puts CyberPet in the eating state. Similarly, the first two statements in the sleep() method (Fig 2–10) put a CyberPet in the sleeping state by setting isSleeping to true and isEating to false.

The next statement in the eat() method,

```
System.out.println("Pet is eating");
```

displays the message "Pet is eating" on the screen. The purpose of this statement is to give some indication of `CyberPet`'s current state. There are lots of other ways this could be done, including ways that make use of Java's extensive graphics library. However, for now let's keep things simple.

Note the use of the dot (.) notation here. As we saw in Section 1.5, the expression `System.out.println()` invokes the `println()` method which belongs to the `out` object, which is defined in the `System` class.

> **JAVA LANGUAGE RULE** **Qualified Name.** A **qualified name** takes the form *reference.elementName*, where *reference* is a reference to some object, and *elementName* is the name of one of the object's variables or methods. The expression is used to refer to the *elementName* contained in *reference*.

Qualified name

Qualified names are context dependent. In some contexts the *reference* can be a simple reference to an object, such as in `rectangle1.calculateArea()`. In other contexts the reference may refer to a hierarchy of objects, classes, and other entities, such as in `System.out.println()` or `java.awt.Color.red`.

Our `CyberPet` class is finished for now. To summarize, as presently defined, a `CyberPet` can be in one of two states, eating or sleeping. Its state is modeled by two private instance variables, `isEating` and `isSleeping`. These are `boolean` variables whose values can be either `true` or `false`. The `CyberPet`'s interface consists of two methods, `eat()` and `sleep()`, which have the effect of changing the pet's state from sleeping to eating or from eating to sleeping. Whenever a pet's state changes, it will output a message on the screen indicating its present state.

SELF-STUDY EXERCISES

EXERCISE 2.8 Complete the definition of the `Square` class, which you began in the previous exercise, by filling in the bodies of its methods. Model your solution on the `Rectangle` class.

EXERCISE 2.9 Write a `main()` method for the `Square` class, which creates two `Square` instances, setting their sides to 10 and 15, respectively, and then prints their respective perimeters and areas.

2.5.3 Creating `CyberPet` Instances

A class definition is an abstract entity. We now want to use it to create some `CyberPet` objects or instances. Creating an object consists of two steps:

1. Declaring a *reference variable* or a name for the object.
2. Creating an instance of the object.

Declaring a Reference Variable

A reference variable is associated with an object and can be used to refer to the object. We declare a reference variable the same way we declare any other kind of variable. The reference variable's type is the name of the class whose objects it can refer to. Thus declaring a reference to an object takes the following form:

ClassName VariableName;

In other words, to declare a reference to an object, we give the name of the class to which the object belongs, followed by the name of the reference itself, followed by a semicolon. The *ClassName* must be the name of a validly defined class, either a class that is included in Java's class library or one that has been defined by the programmer. The *VariableName* must be a valid Java identifier.

For example, to declare references to `CyberPets`, we can use the following declarations:

```
CyberPet pet1;
CyberPet pet2;
```

Declaring vs. creating

Here both `pet1` and `pet2` are names or references that can be used to refer to `CyberPets`. At this point they don't refer to anything, since we haven't yet created any objects for them to name. That will happen during the second part of object creation when we create instances of the `CyberPet` class.

DEBUGGING TIP: Declaring a Reference Variable. Don't confuse declaring a reference variable with creating an object.

Object Instantiation: Creating a `CyberPet` *Instance*

Declaring a reference variable does not by itself create an instance of an object. To *instantiate* a reference variable — that is, to create an object that the variable will refer to — we use the operator, `new`, in conjunction with a *constructor* method for that object. We saw an example of this when we discussed the `Rectangle` class. In the case of our `CyberPet` class, we can use these statements to instantiate `pet1` and `pet2`:

```
pet1 = new CyberPet();
pet2 = new CyberPet();
```

Constructing a new object

These are assignment statements and work the same way as any other assignment statement. The expression on the right of the assignment operator is evaluated, and its value is assigned to the variable on the left of the operator. However, in this case the term on the right-hand side,

CyberPet(), is an invocation of CyberPet's default *constructor* method. Constructor methods are special methods that are used during object instantiation. If a class does not define a constructor, Java will supply a default, which consists of some very generic code that merely creates an instance of that class. The expression CyberPet() creates an instance of the CyberPet class — an object that has all of the basic features, including the initial state, of a CyberPet.

Allocating memory

The operator, new , allocates a portion of memory for the new object and stores the new object there. It then returns the object's address, so, the value of the expression on the right of the assignment operator in the above statements is the *address* of the object that was created. This address is stored in the reference variable on the left of the assignment operator.

Consider again the statements:

```
CyberPet pet1;
pet1 = new CyberPet();
```

To visualize what happens when an object is created, let's trace through the actions of these statements. The first statement creates a reference variable named pet1 of type CyberPet [Fig 2–13(a)]. Because pet1 does not yet refer to any object, Java assigns it the initial value null, which is shown in the figure as a grounded arrow.

null *reference*

Next, consider the second statement. This assignment statement will evaluate new CyberPet(), the expression on the right of the "=," and will then assign the result to pet1. First, space is allocated for the new class instance. Then a default constructor is called to create a new CyberPet object. In so doing, the declarations of the CyberPet class are executed, setting aside space for the instance variables isEating and isSleeping and assigning initial values to them. The result is the creation of a CyberPet object [See Fig 2–13(b)]. Finally, the address where the new object is stored

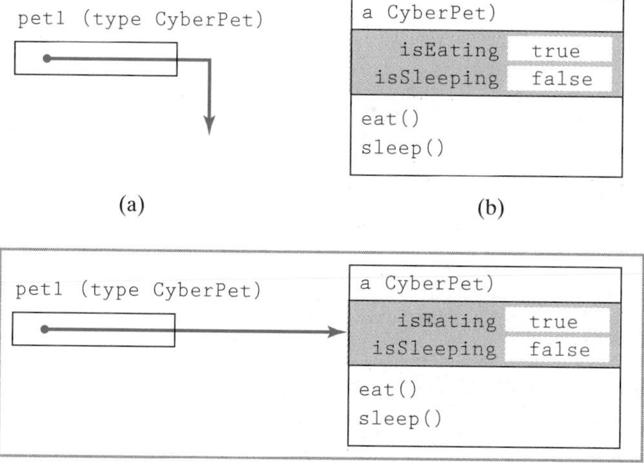

Figure 2–13 Declaring and instantiating a reference to a CyberPet.

is assigned to `pet1` [Fig 2–13(c)]. Because the value returned is an address, we show it as an arrow in the figure. A reference variable *points to* its object.

When a second `CyberPet` object is created, the process is just the same, except that the second instance will be stored at a different memory location. Thus the result of executing the following statements,

```
CyberPet pet1;
CyberPet pet2;
pet1 = new CyberPet();
pet2 = new CyberPet();
```

is shown in Fig 2–14.

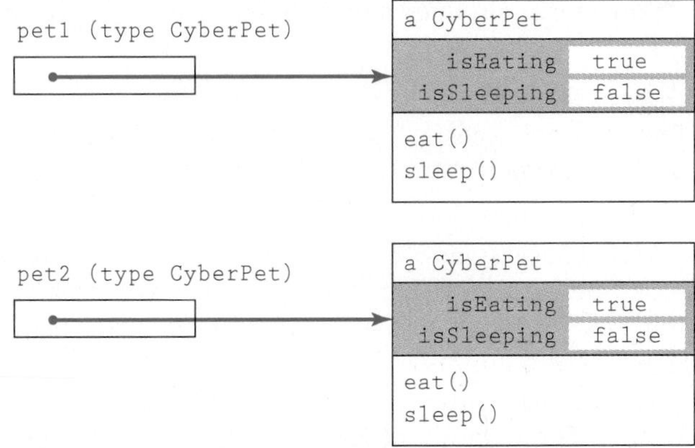

Figure 2–14 A conceptual depiction of two `CyberPet` objects, `pet1` and `pet2`.

JAVA LANGUAGE RULE **Variable versus Object.** Like the relationship between your name and you, a reference variable refers to an object. They are two different things in the program.

Primitive Types and Reference Types

Java data types

In Java there are two categories of types, *primitive types* and *reference types* . So far we have encountered two examples of primitive types: `boolean`, which was used in the `CyberPet` class, and `double`, which was used in the `Rectangle` class. A variable of a primitive type always stores a value of that type and, as we noted, it is an error to try to store some other type of value in that variable. For example, the `isEating` variable can only store the values `true` or `false`.

Reference variables, such as `pet1` and `pet2`, are examples of variables that have reference types. Their types are the classes of the objects to which they can refer. Both `pet1` and `pet2` are of type `CyberPet` because they can refer to instances of the `CyberPet` class.

Rather than storing the object to which it refers, a reference variable actually stores the *address* of the object. Thus, unlike variables of primitive type, which store values of that type, reference variables are said to *refer to* or *point to* their values. If you could open the computer's cabinet and look at what was stored in a primitive variable of type `boolean`, you would see either `true` or `false`. If you opened up the cabinet and looked at the contents of a reference variable you would find an address of some other location in the computer's memory. If you went to that location, you would then find the object that the variable refers to. Because Java takes care of finding the object for you, whenever you want to refer to an object, you can just use its name, just as you would when referring to an object by name in the natural world.

Reference variables point to their objects

For example, in Fig 2–13(c), `pet1` is a reference variable. It stores a reference to a `CyberPet` instance, which is symbolized by the arrow. By contrast, `isEating` and `isSleeping` are primitive variables (within the `CyberPet` object). They simply store their respective values.

2.5.4 Using CyberPets

Now that we have seen how to create instances of the `CyberPet` class, let's use their reference variables to "order" them to eat and sleep. Our objects, you will recall, are named `pet1` and `pet2`. In other words, we can use the terms `pet1` and `pet2` to refer to these objects, just as you would use the term "Mary" to refer to a person named Mary. When we use an object's reference, we needn't worry about the fact that `pet1` is a reference variable and that it stores the object's address. Java handles the details.

Naming an object

To get `pet1` to eat, we want to call its `eat()` method. This is easily done using Java's dot operator:

```
pet1.eat();
```

In order to call an object's method in this way, the method must be *accessible*. In this case, the `eat()` method is accessible because it was declared `public`.

The dot operator can also be used to refer to an object's instance variables, provided they are accessible. For example, we can refer to `isEating` using the dot operator as follows:

```
pet1.isEating = true;    // Access error
```

Although `pet1.isEating` is a valid reference, our use of it here would cause an access error because we declared `isEating` to be `private`. Even though this is a valid reference, the field referenced is inaccessible.

Access error

DEBUGGING TIP: Access Error. An attempt to refer to one of an object's private variables or methods will cause a syntax error.

2.5.5 Testing the CyberPet Class

Now that we know how to create and refer to instances of the `CyberPet` class, let's test that it works properly. There are a number of ways to test the `CyberPet` class. We could design and implement an application program or applet to use CyberPet. Or we could incorporate a main() method right into the definition of CyberPet, thereby turning it into a Java application. Let's explore each of these options.

Class Design: The TestCyberPet *Application*

As a Java application, the TestCyberPet class must contain a main() method. Within main() we will want to create two instances of CyberPet. That way we can test that the class definition serves as a template from which we can create as many instance objects as we wish. Once we have created the instances, we can then write several statements to "command" them to eat and sleep. This will test whether we can successfully use the object's names to refer to their public methods.

The following pseudocode (pseudocode was discussed briefly in Chapter 1) provides an outline for an appropriate main() method:

1. Declare reference variables pet1 and pet2.
2. Instantiate pet1 and pet2 by creating two *new* objects of type CyberPet.
3. Command pet1 to sleep.
4. Command pet1 to eat.
5. Command pet2 to sleep.

Execution starts in main()

We have already discussed how to do each of these steps, so coding them into Java should be easy. This leads to defining TestCyberPet as shown in Fig 2–15. The header for main() is the same as it was in the RectangleUser program earlier in this chapter. Note that we have inserted two println() statements, one at the beginning of main() and one at the end. These will help visualize what's happening when we run the program. Recall that the purpose of having a main() method in an application is to provide a fixed starting point for the program's execution. Execution of an application begins with the first statement in main()'s body. Note also the use of comments to explain what each line of the program is doing. When

Figure 2–15 The TestCyberPet class.

```
public class TestCyberPet
{
    public static void main (String argv[])
    {
                            // Execution starts here
        System.out.println("main() is starting");
        CyberPet pet1;              // Declare two references
        CyberPet pet2;
        pet1 = new CyberPet();      // Instantiate the references
        pet2 = new CyberPet();      //  by creating new objects
        pet1.sleep();               // Tell pet1 to sleep.
        pet1.eat();                 // Tell pet1 to eat.
        pet2.sleep();               // Tell pet2 to sleep.
        System.out.println("main() is finished");
        return;                     // return to the system
    } // main()
} // TestCyberPet
```

we become more conversant with Java, these comments will seem trivial and will no longer be needed, but at this stage they still help to clarify the code and make it more readable.

When it is run, the `TestCyberPet` application will produce the following output:

```
main() is starting
Pet is sleeping
Pet is eating
Pet is sleeping
main() is finished
```

Unfortunately the output doesn't distinguish between `pet1` and `pet2`. That's because the `eat()` and `sleep()` methods just refer to "Pet" and have no way of knowing the pet's name. This is obviously a shortcoming in our design, which we'll have to fix in subsequent versions of `CyberPet`.

Flow of Control: Method Call and Return

It's very important that you understand the **flow of control** involved in this program. A program's flow of control is the order in which its statements are executed. Understanding flow of control in an object-oriented program is especially important, because control passes from one object to another during the program's execution. It's important to have a clear understanding of this process.

In order to understand a Java program, it is necessary to understand the **method call and return** mechanism . We will encounter it repeatedly. A method call causes a program to transfer control to a statement located in another method. Fig 2–16 shows the method call and return structure.

In this example, we have two methods. We make no assumptions about where these methods are in relation to each other. They could be defined in the same class or in different classes. The `method1()` method executes sequentially until it calls `method2()`. This transfers control to the first statement in `method2()`. Execution continues sequentially through the statements in `method2()` until the `return` statement is executed.

JAVA LANGUAGE RULE **return Statement.** The `return` statement causes a method to return control to the *calling statement* — that is, to the statement that called the method in the first place.

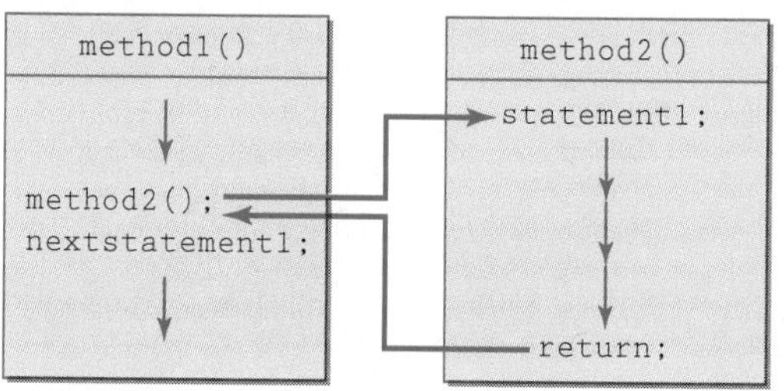

Figure 2–16 The method call and return control structure.

Default returns

Recall that if a `void` method does not contain a `return` statement, then control will automatically return to the calling statement after the invoked method executes its last statement.

Tracing the TestCyberPet *Program*

In order to simplify our trace of `TestCyberPet`, Fig 2–17 shows all of the Java code involved in the program. In addition, it adds line numbers to the program to show the order in which its statements are executed. Keep in mind that there are two source code files involved in this application, `TestCyberPet.java` and `CyberPet.java`. The representation in Fig 2–17, which might make it appear as if all of the code is contained in one file, is for illustrative purposes.

Figure 2–17 A trace showing the order of execution of the `TestCyberPet` program.

```
        public static void main (String argv[])
        {
                                     // Execution starts here
1           System.out.println("main() is starting");
2           CyberPet pet1;               // Declare two references
3           CyberPet pet2;
4           pet1 = new CyberPet();       // Instantiate the references
7           pet2 = new CyberPet();       //  by creating new objects
10          pet1.sleep();                // Tell pet1 to sleep.
15          pet1.eat();                  // Tell pet1 to eat.
20          pet2.sleep();                // Tell pet2 to sleep.
25          System.out.println("main() is finished");
26          return;                      // Return to the system
        } // main()

        public class CyberPet
        {
           // Data
5,8         private boolean isEating = true;  // CyberPet's state
6,9         private boolean isSleeping = false;

           // Methods
            public void eat()             // Start eating
            {
16              isEating = true;          // Change the state
17              isSleeping = false;
18              System.out.println("Pet is eating");
19              return;
            } // eat()

            public void sleep()          // Start sleeping
            {
11,21           isSleeping = true;      // Change the state
12,22           isEating = false;
13,23           System.out.println("Pet is sleeping");
14,24           return;
            } // sleep()

        } // CyberPet class
```

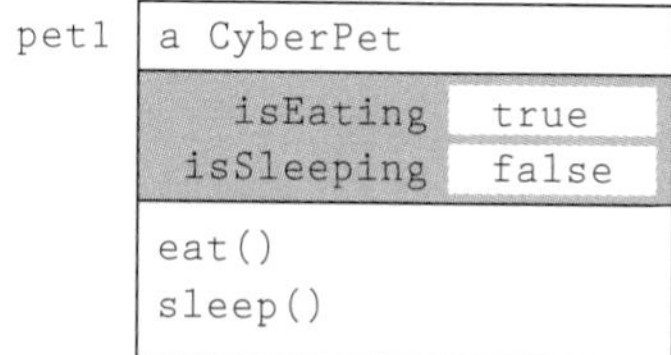

Figure 2–18 The initial state (eating) of `pet1`, a `CyberPet` object.

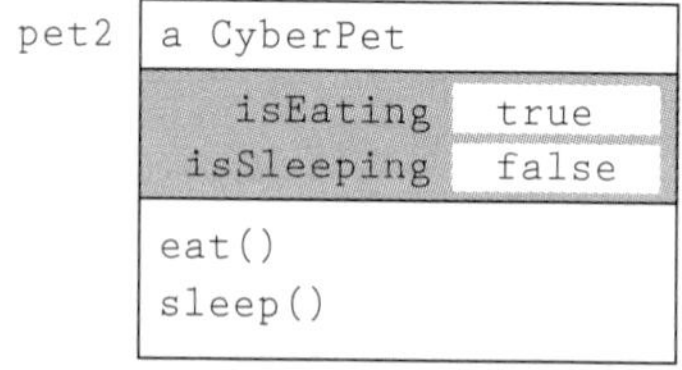

Figure 2–19 The initial state (eating) of `pet2`, a `CyberPet` object.

Execution of the `TestCyberPet` program begins with the `println()` statement on line 1. This has the effect of displaying the message "main() is starting" on the screen. The next two statements, 2 and 3, will create reference variables `pet1` and `pet2` and give them initial values of `null` to indicate that they do not yet refer to any object.

In line 4 the program instantiates `pet1` by creating an instance of the `CyberPet` class and associating it with `pet1`. It does this by transferring to lines 5 and 6, which are contained in the `CyberPet` class. When lines 5 and 6 are executed, `pet1`'s instance variables (`isEating` and `isSleeping`) are created and assigned the initial values `true` and `false`, respectively. Thus, initially `pet1` is eating. When line 6 has finished executing, control is returned to line 4, where the remaining steps involved in creating a new object are completed. The result of executing lines 4 to 6 is that `pet1` refers to a new instance of the `CyberPet` class. This state of affairs is shown in Fig 2–18.

Execution continues with line 7 in `main()`. Lines 7 to 9 have the same basic effect as lines 4 to 6. They create a new instance of a `CyberPet` and initialize its state to eating. However, in this case, the new object is associated with `pet2`. This state of affairs is shown in Fig 2–19.

Class as a template

It's important to understand what's going on when lines 5 to 6 (and 8 to 9) are executed. As Fig 2–17 indicates, these are really just the same lines of code executed twice. But this is exactly what we mean when we say that a class definition serves as a template for creating instances of the class. Lines 5 to 6 (and 8 to 9) are used to create instance variables for each instance of the `CyberPet` class. The first time they are executed (lines 5 to 6), they are used to create and initialize `pet1`'s instance variables. The next time they are executed they are used to create and initialize `pet2`'s instance variables.

Calling a method

After both `pet1` and `pet2` are created, execution continues on line 10. The statement on line 10 tells `pet1` to sleep. When the `sleep()` method is called, control transfers to line 11, the first line in the `sleep()` method. Lines 11 and 12 cause `pet1`'s state to change from eating to sleeping. The effect of these statements is to change the values of `isEating` and `isSleeping` to `false` and `true`, respectively. Thus after lines 11 and 12 are executed, `pet1`'s state will be as shown in Fig 2–20. Line 13 causes the message "Pet is sleeping" to be displayed on the screen, and line 14 returns control to the `main` method.

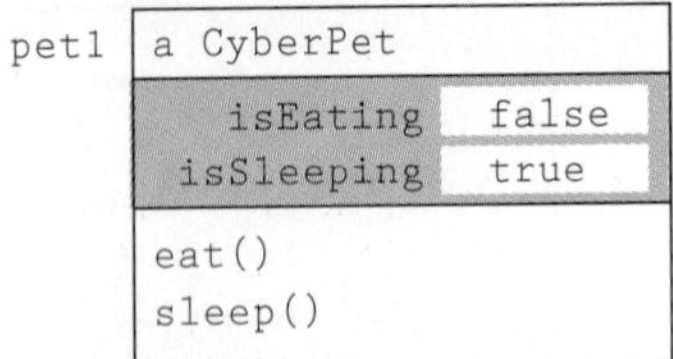

Figure 2–20 pet1 is now sleeping.

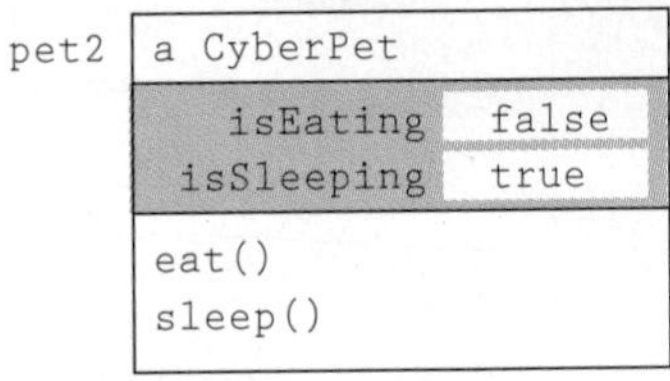

Figure 2–21 pet2 is now sleeping.

Control resumes on line 15 of `main()`, where `pet1`'s `eat()` method is called. This transfers control to line 16, the first line in the `eat()` method. Lines 16 and 17 have the effect of changing `pet1`'s state back to eating, so that after these statements are executed, `pet1` will again have the state shown in Fig 2–18. Line 18 causes the message "Pet is eating" to appear on the screen and line 19 returns control to `main()`.

Control resumes on line 20 of `main()`, where `pet2`'s `sleep()` method is called. This transfers control to line 21, the first line in the `sleep()` method. Lines 21 and 22 have the effect of changing `pet2`'s state from eating to sleeping. After these statements are executed, `pet2` will have the state shown in Fig 2–21. Line 23 causes the message "Pet is sleeping" to be output, and line 24 returns control to the `main()` method.

`pet1` *vs.* `pet2`

It's important to see that lines 11 to 14 are executed twice (once as lines 11 to 14, and the second time as lines 21 to 24). They are executed once as `pet1`'s `sleep()` method and once as `pet2()`'s sleep method. In the first case, the method changes `pet1`'s instance variables, and in the second case it changes `pet2`'s instance variables. Here again we see clearly the sense in which a class definition — in this case a method within a class definition — serves as a template for the class's instance objects.

The final lines of the program are line 25, which causes the message `"main() is finished"` to be output, and line 26, which causes the program to terminate and to give control back to the operating system.

Class Design: The `TestCyberPetApplet`

A Java applet that tests the `CyberPet` class will closely resemble the application. The main difference is that we replace the application's `main()` method, with an `init()` method. Recall that the basic outline for the definition of an applet class is as follows:

```
public class TestCyberPetApplet extends Applet
{
} // TestCyberPetApplet
```

The main change we have to make to this is to incorporate an `init()` method, the method that will be executed as soon as the applet is run. The `init()` method has the following form:

Figure 2–22 The TestCyberPetApplet.

```
import java.applet.*;

public class TestCyberPetApplet extends Applet
{
    public void init()
    {                              // Execution starts here
        System.out.println("init() is starting");
        CyberPet pet1;             // Declare two references
        CyberPet pet2;
        pet1 = new CyberPet();     // Instantiate the references
        pet2 = new CyberPet();     //  by creating new objects
        pet1.sleep();              // Tell pet1 to sleep.
        pet1.eat();                // Tell pet1 to eat.
        pet2.sleep();              // Tell pet2 to sleep.
        System.out.println("init() is finished");
        return;                    // Return to the system
    } // init()
} // TestCyberPetApplet
```

```
public void init()
{
} // init()
```

Let's simply model our `init()` method after the `main()` method from the application program. In other words, let's take all of the statements from within the body of `main()` and encapsulate them in `init()`'s body. The only change we will make is to change the word "main" to "init" in each of the `println` statements (Fig 2–22).

The `TestCyberPetApplet` applet is actually a very rudimentary example of a Java applet. It doesn't use any of the Graphical User Interface (GUI) objects, such as buttons or text fields, that characterize an applet interface. Instead it merely produces text output, just like the application. The output generated by the applet will be almost identical to the output produced by the application:

```
init() is starting
Pet is sleeping
Pet is eating
Pet is sleeping
init() is finished
```

(Note that if you run this applet using a Web browser you may have to use the browser's menu to open the Java console. Otherwise you won't be able to see the output. Most browsers assume, rightly so, that a Java applet will have a GUI interface and will not use the Java console window.)

The trace of the `TestCyberPetApplet` applet is nearly identical to the trace of the application program, so we will not go through it in detail. Suffice it to say that execution begins at the first statement in the `init()` method. The two `CyberPet` instances are created in the same way — by using the `CyberPet` class definition as a template — and have the same ini-

Execution begins in `init()`

Figure 2–23 Including a main() method in the CyberPet class.

```
public class CyberPet {

  // Data
   private boolean isEating = true;  // CyberPet's state
   private boolean isSleeping = false;

  // Methods
   public void eat()           // Start eating
   {
       isEating = true;        // Change the state
       isSleeping = false;
       System.out.println("Pet is eating");
       return;
   } // eat()

   public void sleep()       // Start sleeping
   {
       isSleeping = true;      // Change the state
       isEating = false;
       System.out.println("Pet is sleeping");
       return;
   } // sleep()

   public static void main (String argv[])
   {
       System.out.println("main() is starting");        // Execution starts here
       CyberPet pet1;                 // Declare two references
       CyberPet pet2;
       pet1 = new CyberPet();         // Instantiate the references
       pet2 = new CyberPet();         //  by creating new objects
       pet1.sleep();                  // Tell pet1 to sleep.
       pet1.eat();                    // Tell pet1 to eat.
       pet2.sleep();                  // Tell pet2 to sleep.
       System.out.println("main() is finished");
       return;                        // Return to the system
   } // main()
} // CyberPet class
```

tial state. Whenever pet1's sleep() method is called in init(), control transfers to pet1, and the statements in its sleep() method are executed, and then control returns to init().

Again, although this is an incomplete use of Java's applet class, this example does illustrate that we can use an applet to use and test the CyberPet class.

Class Design: The CyberPet *Application*

A third way of using and testing the CyberPet class is to give it its own main() method. We can use the very same definition of main() from the TestCyberPet application above. The resulting class definition is shown in Fig 2–23. The CyberPet application does exactly the same thing as the TestCyberPet application. Its output and trace are left as exercises.

OBJECT-ORIENTED DESIGN: Basic Principles

This completes our discussion of the CyberPet class. Before we move on, let's briefly review some of the object-oriented design principles that were employed in this example.

- **Encapsulation .** The CyberPet class was designed to encapsulate a certain state and a certain set of actions. It was designed to simulate a pet that could eat, sleep, and respond to the user via the eat and sleep commands. In addition, CyberPet's methods encapsulate the actions that make up their particular tasks.

Alan Kay and the Smalltalk Language

Although *Simula* was the first programming language to use the concept of an object, the first pure object-oriented language was *Smalltalk*. Smalltalk was first started by Alan Kay in the late 1960s. Kay is an innovative thinker who has had a hand in the development of several advances, such as windowing interfaces and laser printing and the client/server model, that are now commonplace in modern PCs.

One of the abiding themes throughout Kay's career has been the idea that computers should be easy enough for kids to use. In the late 1960s, while still in graduate school, Kay designed a computer model that consisted of a notebook-sized portable computer with a keyboard, screen, mouse, and high-quality graphics interface. He had become convinced that graphics and icons were a far better way to communicate with a computer than the command-line interfaces that were prevalent at the time.

In the early 1970s Kay went to work at the Xerox Palo Alto Research Center (PARC), where he developed a prototype of his system known as the *Dynabook*. Smalltalk was the computer language Kay developed for this project. Smalltalk was designed along a biological model, in which individual entities or "objects" communicate with each other by passing messages back and forth. Another goal of Smalltalk was to enable children to invent their own concepts and build programs with them — hence the name "Smalltalk."

Xerox's management was unable to see the potential in Kay's innovations. However during a visit to Xerox in 1979, Steve Jobs, the founder of Apple Computer, was so impressed by Kay's work that he made it the inspiration of the Macintosh computer, which was first released in 1984.

Kay left Xerox in 1983 and became an Apple Fellow in 1984. In addition to working for Apple, Kay spent considerable time teaching kids how to use computers at his Open School in West Hollywood. In 1996 Kay became a Fellow (an "Imagineer") at the Walt Disney Imagineering's Research and Development Organization, where he continues to explore innovative ways to enhance the educational and entertainment value of computers.

- **Information Hiding.** `CyberPet`'s state is represented by a pair of `boolean` variables, `isEating` and `isSleeping`, which are declared `private`, thereby making them inaccessible to other objects. By hiding this aspect of its implementation, we can insure that other objects cannot change their values. This will help insure that the `CyberPet` remains in a valid state — that is, a state in which either `isEating` or `isSleeping`, but not both, is true at the same time.
- **Clearly Designed Interface .** `CyberPet`'s interface is defined in terms of the public methods `eat()` and `sleep()`. These methods constrain the way users can interact with `CyberPets` and preserve the consistency of a `CyberPet`'s state. Those are the main purposes of a good interface.
- **Generality and Extensibility .** There is nothing in our design of `CyberPet` that limits its use and its extensibility. Moreover, as we will see later, we can easily extend its functionality both by adding new functionality to the class definition itself (by extending its state to cover thinking and other behaviors) and by allowing the definition to serve as a superclass in a `CyberPet` hierarchy (by allowing subclasses to be defined for certain types of pets such as dogs and cats).

Java Language Summary

This section provides an overview of the details and rules of the Java language elements that have been used up to this point. As explained in the "In the Laboratory" section from Chapter 1, the *syntax* of a language is the set of rules that define how its words and symbols may be combined to form valid expressions. The *semantics* of a language is the set of rules that determine what its expressions mean. Obviously, learning a new language is a matter of learning both kinds of rules.

As an example of a syntax rule, consider the following two English statements:

```
The rain in Spain falls mainly on the plain.   // Valid english sentence
Spain rain the mainly in on the falls plain.   // Invalid sentence
```

The first sentence follows the rules of English syntax (grammar), and it means that it rains a lot on the Spanish plain. The second sentence does not follow English syntax, and, as a result, it is rendered meaningless. Usually, when you break an English syntax rule, the meaning of a sentence becomes unclear, or the sentence could become completely meaningless if enough rules are broken.

In a programming language, the relationship between syntax and semantics is much stricter. If you break even the lightest syntax rule — for example, if you forget to put a semicolon at the end of a Java statement — the program won't compile at all. It becomes completely meaningless.

Java Language Summary

Java Class Definition

In keeping with Java's object-oriented nature, a program in Java is expressed as a class definition, which is how an object is defined. An application program is an object that contains a `main()` method. Fig 2–24 illustrates the key elements of a class definition.

Figure 2–24 A Java application program is a class definition that contains a `main()` method.

```
public class Example extends Object        // Class header
{                                          // Start of class body
    private double num = 5.0;              // Instance variable

    public void print()                    // Method definition header
    {                                      // Start of method body
        System.out.println(num);           //   Output statement
    } // print()                           // End of print method body

    public static void main(String args[]) // Method definition header
    {                                      // Start of method body
        Example example;                   //   Reference variable declaration
        example = new Example();           //   Object instantiation statement
        example.print();                   //   Method call
    } // main()                            // End of method body
} // Example                               // End of class body
```

Comments

class header

In Fig 2–24 the *single-line comments*, which begin with double slashes, (//), serve to identify the important components of the program. The program consists of a class definition, which has two parts: a *class header* and a *class body*. The purpose of the header is to identify a class's name (`Example`), its accessibility (`public` as opposed to `private`), and its *pedigree*. The `Example` class is a *subclass of* (`extends`) the `Object` class, which is the root class of the entire Java class hierarchy.

Class body

The class's body, which is enclosed within curly brackets ({}), contains the elements that make up the objects of the class. There are generally two kinds of elements: *instance variables* (`num`), which store various kinds of data, and *methods* (`print()`), which represent the object's actions. An `Example` object has only one piece of data, the floating point (`double`) number 5.0, and its only action is to `print()` the numbers' value.

Method Definition

A *method* is a named section of code that can be called on or *invoked* to carry out an action or an operation. A method definition consists of two

Java Language Summary

Defining method parts: the method's header and its body. The method header identifies certain important properties of the method, including its name (`print`), its accessibility (`public` or `private` or `protected`), the type of data it returns as a result (`void`), and its list of *parameters*, which in this case is an empty list, (). By contrast, the `main()` method has a `String` variable in its parameter list. Methods that don't generate a result, such as the methods in this program, have a result type of `void`.

Method header

Method body

The method's body contains the program's executable statements. For example, the `print()` method contains one statement `System.out.println(num)`, which simply prints the object's number. This statement is an example of a *method call statement*. It calls the `println()` method, which is a member of the `System.out` object.

Access Rules

Java provides mechanisms to control access to classes and their fields and methods. When a class, field, or method is defined, you can declare it `public`, `protected`, or `private`. Or you can leave its access unspecified, in which case Java's default accessibility will apply.

Java determines accessibility in a top-down manner. Instance variables and methods are contained in classes, which are contained in packages. To determine whether a field or method is accessible, Java starts by determining whether its containing package is accessible, and then whether its containing class is accessible. Access to packages is controlled by the Java runtime system. Access to classes, fields, and methods is defined according to the rules shown in Table 2–2.

Table 2.2. Java's accessibility rules.

Type	**Declaration**	**Rule**
Package	N/A	Accessibility determined by the system.
Class	`public`	Accessible if its package is accessible.
	by default	Accessible only within its package.
Member (field or method) of an accessible class	`public`	Accessible to all other objects.
	`protected`	Accessible to its subclasses and to other classes in its package.
	`private`	Accessible only within the class.
	by default	Accessible only within the package.

Java Language Summary

Object Instantiation

In order to get a Java program to take any action — print a string, add two numbers, and so on — you define methods containing the particular actions you want to take, and then you call or invoke those methods. Of course, methods can only be contained by objects. So, as we said above, writing a Java program is a matter of defining objects. Once you define an object — in this case an `Example` object — you can create an *instance* of it and then use its methods to perform certain actions. That's what happens in the `main()` method. A *reference variable* (`example`) is declared. The variable serves as the name for the `new` *instance* that is created. And then the instance is used to print a number: `example.print()`.

Creating an object

This example illustrates some of the key elements and key terminology of a Java program. This program consists of just two objects: the `Example` object, named `example`, and the `System.out` object that is used for printing. Most Java programs will consist of many objects, some predefined, such as `System.out`, and some programmer-defined, such as `Example`. Once an object has been designed, the basic steps involved in coding it are: define the object's class, instantiate one or more instances of the object, and use the instances to do the tasks needed for the program.

Program Layout

Java is said to be a *free form* language, which means that white space — blank spaces and blank lines — may occur anywhere in a Java program. Program expressions and statements may occur one per line, several per line or one per several lines. The fact that the rules governing program layout are so lax makes it all the more important that elements of good programming *style* be used to make programs easy to read. As illustrated in the examples we've presented, ample use of spacing between program elements helps to make programs more readable and more attractive.

Keywords

Java has 47 predefined words or *keywords* (Table 2–3). An important restriction on keywords is that they cannot be used as the names of methods, variables and classes.

Identifiers

Identifiers are names for classes, methods and variables, and they have the following syntax:

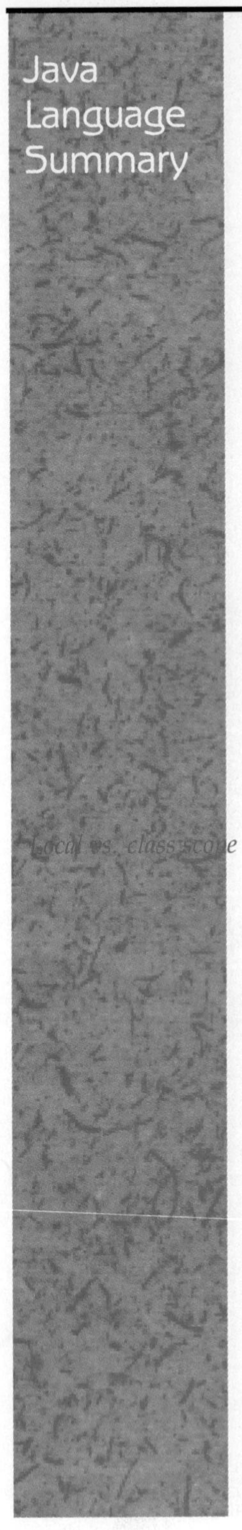

Table 2.3. Java keywords

abstract	default	if	private	throw
boolean	do	implements	protected	throws
break	double	import	public	transient
byte	else	instanceof	return	try
case	extends	int	short	void
catch	final	interface	static	volatile
char	finally	long	super	while
class	float	native	switch	
const	for	new	synchronized	
continue	goto	package	this	

JAVA LANGUAGE RULE **Identifier.** An **identifier** must begin with a letter (A to Z, a to z) and may be followed by any number of letters or digits (0 to 9) or underscores (_). An identifier may not be identical to a Java keyword.

Remember that Java is *case sensitive* so that two distinct identifiers may contain the same letters — for example, `thisVar` and `ThisVar` — with the only difference being the use of capitalized letters.

Identifier Scope

The **scope** of an identifier determines where it may be used in the program. Instance variables (`isEating`) and instance methods (`eat()`) have *class scope* and may be used throughout the class in which they are defined. In contrast, *local variables* — those declared within methods or within a compound statement — have *local scope* and can only be used within the methods or code blocks in which they are declared.

Primitive Data Types

Java is a *strongly typed* language, which means that every piece of data is classified according to its *type*. A datum's type determines how it can be used. For example, because `Example.num` is a `double` variable, it would be a syntax error to assign the `boolean` value `true` to it.

Almost everything in Java is an object. In this and the previous chapter, we defined several classes of objects — `Rectangle`, `CyberPet`, `HelloWorld` — and we mentioned several types of predefined objects — `TextField`, `Button`, `Applet`. Java also defines several data types that are not considered objects. These **primitive types** , which are used to represent numbers, characters and boolean data, are summarized in Table 2–4. Each data type is listed with its keyword and its size in bits. A *bit* is a single binary digit — a 0 or a 1. Thus, you can see from the table that only one bit is required to represent the two boolean values — 0 represents `false` and 1 represents `true`.

Java Language Summary

Table 2.4. Java primitive data types. Except for the `boolean` type, the size of the primitive types is defined in the Java Language Specification.

Type	Keyword	Size in Bits	Examples
boolean	`boolean`	-	`true` or `false`
character	`char`	16	`'A'`, `'5'`, `'+'`
byte	`byte`	8	−128 to + 127
integer	`short`	16	−32768 to + 32767
integer	`int`	32	−2147483648 to + 2147483647
integer	`long`	64	*really big integers*
real number	`float`	32	`21.3, −0.45, 1.67e28`
real number	`double`	64	`21.3, −0.45, 1.67e28`

- **Integers.** An **integer** is a positive or negative whole number, and Java provides several types based on the number of bits in their representation. A `byte` uses 8 bits and can represent integer values in the range −128 to +127. An `int`, which is probably the most widely used integer type, requires 32 bits and can represent integers in the range $-2^{31} \rightarrow +2^{31} - 1$. When an integer **literal** — an actual value — is used in a Java program, it must observe the following formation rule. *Literal values*

> **JAVA LANGUAGE RULE** **Literals.** An *integer literal* may be begin with an optional plus (+) or minus (−) sign followed by one or more digits (0 ...9). A literal of type long must be terminated with an L or l. All other integer literals are treated as type int.

Thus, the following are examples of valid and invalid integer literals:

```
23   -1   0   50000   987612098774L   // Valid integer literals
50,000   5% "55" '6'                  // Invalid integer literals
```

Integer literals cannot include punctuation of any sort (no commas, dollar signs, and so forth) and cannot be enclosed within quotes, which would turn them into either characters ('5') or `Strings` ("56").

- **Real Numbers**. Real numbers, or **floating point numbers**, are numbers that contain a fractional part, such as 0.1274 and 3.14. Java provides two types of reals: `float`, which requires 32 bits, and `double`, which requires 64 bits. Java also allows real numbers to be expressed in *exponential notation*. Thus the number 5.041e4 can be used to represent 5.041×10^4 or 50410. The symbol `e4` represents 10 raised to the power of 4. This notation can be used to avoid having to write

Java Language Summary

literals such as 0.00000000000000003456 or 3456000000000000000 in a Java program. Real literals can also employ a suffix (`F, f, D, d`) to distinguish between `double` and `float`. If the suffix is omitted, the literal is treated as a `double`. The following are examples of valid and invalid real literals:

```
23.7    -1.0    50000.336    .14 -1.314e-10F // Valid real literals
50,000.336    $78.99    1.5% "1.9" '1.9'    // Invalid real literals
```

- **Characters.** Characters in Java are represented by the 16-bit `char` type. Typical characters include letters of the alphabet, (`A to Z`), digits (`0 to 9`), and symbols of various sorts (+ , *). A `char` literal is always represented as a single character enclosed within *single* quotes. Note that a single character enclosed within *double* quotes is a Java `String` ("a"). Java characters can also include certain non-printing characters, such as the newline character (\n) and the tab character (\t). These are called **escape sequences** and may be embedded within strings to add formatting to printed output — for example,

```
"This\tstring\thas\ttabs\tbetween\twords\n\n"
```

The following are examples of valid and invalid character literals:

```
'A'   'a'   '$'   '8'   '\n'          // Valid character literals
'AB'   '692'   "a"                     // Invalid character literals
```

- **Booleans.** Boolean values are used to represent whether something is true or false. The two boolean values, `true` and `false`, are both Java keywords. Note that these values are not enclosed within quotes.

Strings

`Strings` in Java are full-fledged objects and are treated as such. A `String` literal is a sequence of one or more characters (`char`) enclosed within double quotes (quotation marks). The following are valid string literals:

```
"What is your name?"   "There are 3 students"   "F"   "6547"
```

A string composed of digits should not be mistaken for an integer. Thus, the string "6547" is not the same as the integer 6547.

SELF-STUDY EXERCISES

EXERCISE 2.10 Identify the data type of each of the following literal expressions:

```
(a) 44    (b) 65.98     (c) "42" (d) "true"
(e) true  (f) "\$65.98" (g) -42  (h) '6'
```

Wrapper Classes

For each primitive data type, Java supplies a **wrapper class**, which allows primitive data to be represented as objects (Table 2–5). Wrapper classes also serve to encapsulate methods that can be used to perform certain data conversions. For example, one of the most useful methods of the `Integer` class is the `parseInt()` method, which can be used as follows to convert a `String` into an `int`:

```
int intValue = Integer.parseInt( "125"); // Converts "125" to 125
```

As we will see in "From the Java Library" later in the chapter, this type of conversion is necessary to handle numeric input in a program.

Table 2.5. Java *wrapper classes* for the primitive data types

Primitive Type	Wrapper Class
`boolean`	`Boolean`
`char`	`Character`
`byte`	`Byte`
`short`	`Short`
`int`	`Integer`
`long`	`Long`
`float`	`Float`
`double`	`Double`

Variables, Expressions, and Operators

A **variable** is a named storage location that can store a value of a particular type. In the `Example` class, the *instance* variable `num` stores a value of type `double`. In the `CyberPet` class (Fig 2–10), the instance variables `isEating` and `isSleeping` stored values of type `boolean`. In the `TestCyberPet` class (Fig 2–15), the *local* variables `pet1` and `pet2` stored values of type `CyberPet`.

Variables must always store a value; there's no such thing as a memory location with no value in it. The programmer may not know what value is stored in a variable, but that just means the variable's value is *undetermined*.

> **JAVA LANGUAGE RULE** **Variable Initialization.** By default, Java assigns all numeric variables, reals or integers, an initial value of 0, and all `boolean` variables an initial value of `false`. All reference variables, which refer to objects, are given an initial value of `null`.

In general, the only way to set or change the value stored in a variable is by using an *assignment* operator.

Java Language Summary

Expressions and Operators

An *expression* is used to specify or produce a value within a Java program, and all expressions have a type. For example, suppose the `isEating` variable is declared as a `boolean`. Then the following are examples of `boolean` expressions, because they evaluate to either true or false:

```
true                   // A literal boolean value
isEating               // A variable (with a boolean value)
isEating == true       // An equality expression (yields a boolean)
(isEating == false)    // Another equality expression
isEating = true        // An assignment expression (also boolean)
```

The last of these examples is an **assignment** expression, which is somewhat special. All five of these expressions are said to *have a value* or *evaluate to a value*. The assignment expression has a value of `true`, since it is assigning `true` to `isEating`. But the assignment expression also has the effect of *storing* the value `true` in the variable `isEating`. No matter what value was previously stored there, after the assignment expression is evaluated, `isEating` will contain the value `true`.

> **JAVA LANGUAGE RULE** **Equality and Assignment.** Be careful not to confuse = and == . The symbol = is the *assignment operator*. It assigns the value on its right-hand side to the variable on its left hand side. The symbol == is the *equality operator*. It evaluates whether the expressions on its left- and right-hand sides have the same value and returns either `true` or `false`.

A *method invocation* is another kind of expression. For example, the following statements from the `Rectangle` class (Fig 2–5) are method invocations that produce a value of type `double`.

```
rectangle1.calculateArea(); // Produces 300
rectangle2.calculateArea(); // Produces 500
```

The values produced by these expressions can be used in other expressions. For example, the following statement

```
System.out.println( rectangle1.calculateArea() );
```

would output `rectangle1`'s area — for example, 300.

Another type of expression is one that involves one or more of Java's 37 *operators*. For example, the following are examples of integer expressions because they each produce an integer value:

```
25 + 3          // Produces 28
25 * 3          // Produces 75
25 - 3          // Produces 22
25 / 3          // Produces 8
```

Java Language Summary

Type restrictions

Like variables and values, operators are *type dependent*. An arithmetic operator such as (/) produces an integer result (8), with no decimal places, when used to divide two integers (25 / 3). It produces a real result (8.333), which includes the decimal places required for a more exact answer, when used to divide two real numbers (25.0 / 3.0), or when an integer and decimal number are mixed (25.0 / 3 or 25 / 3.0).

To summarize, an expression is one of the following:

- A *literal* value, such as `true`, `55`, `0.5`, 'b', or `"hi"`
- A *variable* of a particular type, such as `isEating`
- A *method invocation*, such as `calculateArea()`
- A syntactically valid combination of literals, variables, method invocations, and operators (`isEating == true` or `calculateArea() + 5`)

Statements

The **flow of control** , or *sequence of execution*, in a Java program is controlled by *statements* . A **block** or a **compound statement** is a sequence of statements contained within braces. Thus, the body of a method definition is considered a block of statements. In general, statements are separated from each other by *separators* or *punctuators*, which include the semicolon (;) and braces ({}).

- **Declaration Statements** A **declaration statement** declares a variable of a particular type. Java distinguishes between **instance variables** or **fields**, which are declared at the class level, and *local variables*, which are declared within method bodies or, more generally, within a statement block. The main difference is that field declarations can contain *Field Modifiers*, whereas local variable declarations cannot. Local variables cannot be declared `public` or `private`.

- **Expression Statements** An *expression statement* is an expression that is used as a statement. For example, a method invocation is an expression statement:

  ```
  System.out.println( "Hello world" );
  ```

  Any expression can be turned into a statement by simply following it with a semicolon. The expression statement is executed by simply evaluating the expression. Thus, even though they are somewhat unusual and of limited use, the following would be valid expression statements:

  ```
  5 + 6 ;                       // Evaluates to 11
  true;                         // Evaluates to true
  rectangle1.calculateArea();   // Evaluates to 300
  ```

Java Language Summary

- **Return statements** The `return` statement is used within a method to return control to the invoker of the method (Fig 2–16). The `return` keyword can be followed by an expression and *must* be followed by an expression of the appropriate type in methods that return values, such as the `calculateArea()` method in the `Rectangle` class. The `return` statement may be omitted in `void` methods.

From the Java Library: `BufferedReader`, `String`, `Integer`

Java has an extensive class library that contains carefully designed and efficiently programmed class definitions that can be applied to a wide variety of tasks. An important principle of object-oriented design is that one should avoid the temptation to "reinvent the wheel." In other words, when presented with a programming task, one of the first questions you should ask is: Is there a library class that handles this task? Chances are that library code is far more efficient and better designed than code you would have time to write yourself.

EFFECTIVE DESIGN: The Code-Reuse Principle. Before designing and writing your own code, search the Java library to see if it contains a class that solves the problem you're trying to solve.

As a way of encouraging this approach to program design, each chapter will include a section that features one or more important classes from the Java library. In addition to describing the library class, these sections will contain a simple example showing how the class can be used.

I/O errors

Accepting input is actually one of the more complicated programming tasks because so many things can go wrong during an input operation. For example, an Internet connection can break while downloading a Web page; or a file that is usually readable can be accidently moved or deleted; or the user can type a letter when asked to type a number. In this section we'll describe how to do simple input of `String` and numeric data from the keyboard.

As we saw in the previous chapter, `System.in` is a predefined `InputStream` that is normally associated with the keyboard. However, one limitation of the `java.io.InputStream` class is that it does not contain methods that can be used for simple input. Fortunately, the `java.io.BufferedReader` class has a `readLine()` method which can be used for simple I/O:

```
public class BufferedReader extends Reader
{
    public BufferedReader(Reader in); // Constructor
    public String readLine();
}
```

As its name implies, the BufferedReader class contains methods that perform buffered input. A *buffer* is portion of memory where input is held until it is needed by the program. Using a buffer between, say, the keyboard and the program, allows you to use a Backspace key to delete a character. When you hit the Enter key, any characters that you deleted will be ignored when the program retrieves characters from the input buffer.

Buffers

Note that BufferedReader's constructor takes a Reader as a parameter. If you want to perform buffered input on the System.in stream, you would pass System.in into the constructor as follows:

```
BufferedReader input = new BufferedReader
   ( new InputStreamReader (System.in) );
```

This code is rather ugly syntactically, but it does enable us to convert System.in into a buffered reader.

Once we have created a BufferedReader, here named input, we can use the readLine() method to read one line of characters from the keyboard and store it in a Java String object. A string is just a sequence of characters, such as "Hello World." However, in addition to storing the characters themselves, a Java String object keeps track of certain properties of the String, such as its length, and includes a number of methods for manipulating Strings. The following statement reads one line from the keyboard buffer and stores it in the String named inputString.

```
String inputString = input.readLine();
```

The readLine() method will read all the characters up to the first Enter keystroke and return a String. Once a line input by the user is stored in a String variable, we can use other library methods to manipulate the input. For example, the following code *prompts* the user for his or her name, grabs the input, stores it in the String variable named inputString, and then prints "Hello" plus whatever the user typed:

```
System.out.print("Hello, input your name please ");
String inputString = input.readLine();
System.out.println("Hello " +  inputString ); // Concatenate and print
```

The "+" sign used here is Java's *string concatenation* operator. Suppose the user typed "Puddintane" for a name. The expression "Hello " + inputString will concatenate "Hello" and "Puddintane" into a single string. Thus the program will print "Hello Puddintane." We could also have produced the same output without using the concatenation operator by first printing "Hello" and then printing inputLine on the same line:

Concatenating strings

```
System.out.print("Hello, input your name please ");
String inputString = input.readLine();
System.out.print("Hello " );
System.out.println( inputString  );
```

I/O exceptions

Because an input operation is subject to all kinds of unpredictable problems, the `readLine` method *throws* or raises an `IOException` if some kind of input error occurs. An *exception* is Java's way of handling errors that occur while a program is running. (Exceptions are covered in Chapter 11.) In order to use `readLine()` in a program, we must either *catch* the exception (handle it) or specify that we are not going to handle it. In the latter case the exception will be handled in some default manner by the Java Virtual Machine. Since the latter option is the simpler one at this point, let's choose not to handle this IOException when using `readLine()`.

The simple program in Fig 2–25 illustrates how this is done. Note that in the declaration of the `main()` method we have specified `throws IOException`, which says that some kind of `IOException` may get thrown and not caught during `main()`'s execution. Should this occur, `main()` will simply throw the exception to the Java Virtual Machine, where it will be handled.

Figure 2–25 Definition of the `Hello` class.

```
import java.io.*;                    // Java I/O classes

public class Hello
{                                    // Performs screen i/o

    public static void main(String argv[]) throws IOException
    {
        BufferedReader input = new BufferedReader
            (new InputStreamReader(System.in));

        System.out.print("Hello, input your name please ");
        String inputString = input.readLine();
        System.out.println("Hello " + inputString);

    } // main()
} // Hello

Hello, input your name please Puddintane
Hello Puddintane
```

Java's I/O code is admittedly complicated compared to other aspects of the language. At this point it is not important that you fully understand the concept of a `BufferedReader` and an `InputStreamReader`. We will deal with these concepts in detail in Chapter 14. At this point you can simply use the code as we have presented it whenever you need to input values from the keyboard.

Reading Numbers from the Keyboard

Converting numeric input

Handling numeric input from the keyboard can also be tricky. One way to handle numeric input is to use `readLine()` to read in one line of data and then to extract the number from the line. For example, the following line will convert `inputString` into an `int`:

```
int number = Integer.parseInt( inputString );
```

Here we are using the `parseInt` method of the `java.lang.Integer` class to convert the `inputString` into an `int`. We must do this conversion if we wish to use the number typed at the keyboard in an arithmetic operation.

The `Integer` class is known as a **wrapper class** (see the "Java Language Summary" in this chapter). Its main function is to convert primitive data of type `int` into an object that can fit into Java's class hierarchy. Wrapper classes also include many useful methods, such as `parseInt()`, which converts one type of data to another.

The `Integer` *wrapper*

To see why this is so useful, consider a program that computes the average of three exam grades (Fig 2–26). This program prompts the user for three numbers. On each input operation the user's input is stored in the `String` variable `inputString`. Then `inputString` is converted into an `int` and stored in one of the three `int` variables (`midterm1`, `midterm2`, `finalExam`). The statement

```
sum = midterm1 + midterm2 + finalExam;
```

computes the sum of the three grades. And the following statement prints the student's average, which is computed by `sum/3` (dividing `sum` by 3):

```
System.out.print("Your average in this course is " );
System.out.println( sum/3 );
```

Figure 2–26 Definition of the `Grader` class.

```
import java.io.*;     // Java I/O classes
public class Grader
{
    public static void main(String argv[]) throws IOException
    {
        BufferedReader input = new BufferedReader
            (new InputStreamReader(System.in));
        String inputString;

        int midterm1, midterm2, finalExam;  // Three exam grades
        float sum;                          // The sum of the 3 grades

        System.out.print("Input your grade on the first midterm: ");
        inputString = input.readLine();
        midterm1 = Integer.parseInt(inputString);
        System.out.println("You input: " + midterm1);
        System.out.print("Input your grade on the second midterm: ");
        inputString = input.readLine();
        midterm2 = Integer.parseInt(inputString);
        System.out.println("You input: " + midterm2);
        System.out.print("Input your grade on the final exam: ");
        inputString = input.readLine();
        finalExam = Integer.parseInt(inputString);
        System.out.println("You input: " + finalExam);
        sum = midterm1 + midterm2 + finalExam;
        System.out.print("Your average in this course is ");
        System.out.println(sum/3);
    } // main()
} // Grader
```

I/O problems are more likely to happen when reading numeric data. In the `Grader` program in Fig 2–26, if the user types 45.9 when Java expects to receive an integer, this will cause an error, because 45.9 contains a decimal point. For example, consider what happens when we type nonnumeric data in the `Grader` program:

```
Input your grade on the first midterm: 65.8
java.lang.NumberFormatException: 65.8
    at java.lang.Integer.parseInt(Integer.java)
    at java.lang.Integer.parseInt(Integer.java)
    at Grader.main(Grader.java:20)
```

Note that the exception that results in this case is a `NumberFormatException`, not an `IOException`. The I/O operation happens without error because "65.8" is a valid `String` and that's what `readLine` is looking for. The error happens when we try to convert "65.8" into an `int` in the following statement:

```
midterm1 = Integer.parseInt( inputString );
```

In Chapter 11 we will learn how to handle this kind of exception more gracefully.

JAVA LANGUAGE RULE **Default Exception Handling.** Java's default exception handling makes it far superior to other languages in the way it handles runtime errors.

SELF-STUDY EXERCISE

EXERCISE 2.11 Suppose that the user of the `Grader` program had typed in 85, 95, and 90 as her three exam grades. If, as we have done in the program, these input values are converted to `int`s and then added together using the expression `midterm1` + `midterm2` + `finalExam`, we would get 270 as their sum. What would we have gotten if we stored the user's input in three separate `String` variables, `s1`, `s2`, `s3`, and then performed the following statement?

```
System.out.println(s1 + s2 + s3);  // Concatenation
```

IN THE LABORATORY: THE `Circle` CLASS

The purpose of this laboratory project is to give you practice designing and implementing a Java class definition. The exercise is patterned after the Java program development described in Chapter 1. The objectives of this project are

- To give practice designing a simple Java class to represent a geometric circle.
- To convert the design into a working Java program.
- To compile, run, and test the Java program.

The following sections provide a step-by-step framework for completing this exercise.

Problem Statement

Design and implement a class to represent a geometric circle, and then test your class definition by implementing a `main()` method that creates `Circle` instances and displays their circumferences and areas. Your program should produce the following output on the screen:

```
The diameter of circle1 is 20.0
The area of circle1 is 314.0
The circumference of circle1 is 62.80
The diameter of circle2 is 30.0
The area of circle2 is 706.5
The circumference of circle2 is 94.2
```

Problem Decomposition

This problem can be divided into one class, the `Circle` class, which will implement the geometric circle. It will contain its own `main()` method so that it can create and test `Circle` instances.

Problem Design

Your design should be closely modeled on that of the `Rectangle` and `Square` classes discussed earlier. Develop a detailed *specification* for the `Circle` class, which identifies the purpose of the class, its *instance variables* and *methods*. Designate which information will be hidden and which parts of the class will make up its *interface*.

Specification

Type the specification using the same text editor you use for typing the program itself. Enclose the specification within a Java comment block and save it in a file named `Circle.java`. This file will be the file you use for defining the `Circle` class. The comment will serve as documentation for the program.

A comment block in Java begins with either "/*" or "/** " and ends with "*/". It can extend over multiple lines. As explained in Appendix A, comments that begin with "/**" are *documentation comments*, which can be automatically turned into documentation for the class using software that comes with the Java Development Kit (JDK). You would use documentation comments to describe a class's specification. Here's an example format that you can use:

Comments

```
/**
 * Class Name: Circle
 *
 * ... ( the rest of your specification )
 *
 */
```

Implementation

Stepwise refinement

Use the *stepwise refinement* approach, described in Chapter 1, to convert your specification into a Java class definition. That is, write the program in small stages, compiling and running the program after each stage is coded. This will enable you to localize any errors that are made. Remember that Java is *case sensitive* and very fussy about the spelling of *identifiers* and *keywords*.

Note: Rather than typing everything from scratch, another way to write this code is to copy and paste an existing program. You can download the `Rectangle` source code from the book's companion web site. Just follow the links on

```
http:www.prenhall.com/morelli/sourcecode/ch02/rectangle
```

You can then modify it using cut, copy, and paste editing.

Reasonable coding stages for this project would be

- Code the header of the `Circle` class but leave its body empty. Code the header and an empty body for the `main` method, which should be coded exactly as shown in the examples in this chapter.
- Code the declarations for the instance variables as well as the *constructor* method. The constructor method should be closely modeled after `Rectangle`'s constructor.
- Create a `Circle` instance in the `main()` method, so that you can use it to test the constructor. This is where you would use the operator `new` plus the constructor method.
- Write one access method at a time, as well as a method call in `main()` that tests the method. Here is where you would use method calls embedded within `println()` expressions to display the circle's area and perimeter. For example, here's a pair a statements that will output `circle1`'s area:

```
System.out.print("The area of circle1 is ");
System.out.println(circle1.calculateArea());
```

- Complete the documentation for your program. Add comments to your code that will make your program more readable. A good rule might be that you should be able to read your program two years from now and still understand what it does. See Appendix A for guidelines about documentation conventions.

CHAPTER SUMMARY

Technical Terms

assignment statement
class scope
escape sequence
flow of control
initializer expression
integer
method call and return
scope
variable
block
compound statement
field
keyword
instance
interface
primitive data type
subclass
void method
class inheritance
declaration statement
floating point number
identifier
instance variable
literal
qualified name
superclass
wrapper class

New Java Keywords

`boolean`
`class`
`false`
`long`
`private`
`return`
`void`
`byte`
`double`
`float`
`new`
`protected`
`short`
`char`
`extends`
`int`
`null`
`public`
`true`

Java Library Classes

`BufferedReader`
`Component`
`Double`
`String`
`TextField`
`Button`
`Container`
`Integer`
`TextField`
`Byte`
`Float`
`Object`
`TextComponent`

Java Library Methods

`init()`
`print()`
`main()`
`println()`
`parseInt()`
`readLine()`

Programmer-Defined Classes

`Circle`
`Grader`
`Rectangle`
`TestCyberPet`
`CyberPet`
`NumberAdder`
`RectangleUser`
`TestCyberPetApplet`
`Example`
`NumberCruncher`
`Square`

Programmer-Defined Methods

`calculateArea`
`eat()`
`CyberPet()`
`sleep()`

Summary of Important Points

- A Java program is a set of interacting objects. Writing a Java program is a matter of defining a Java *class*, which serves as a *template* for instances of the class. Classes typically contain two kinds of elements, *instance variables* and *methods*. Together they represent an object's *state*.
- The Java *class hierarchy* organizes all Java classes into a single hierarchy rooted in the `Object` class. Classes in a hierarchy are related by the *subclass* and *superclass* relationships. The `Object` class is the superclass of all other classes in the Java hierarchy .
- A *class definition* consists of a *header* , which names the class and describes its use and pedigree , and the *body* , which contains its details. A class's *pedigree* describes where it fits in the Java class hierarchy. By default a class is considered a direct subclass of `Object`.
- A class definition *encapsulates* the data and methods needed to carry out the class's task. A well-designed class should have a well-defined purpose, should present a well-articulated interface , should hide its implementation details, and should be as general and extensible as possible.
- A `boolean` variable is a *primitive type* that can have one of two values, `true` or `false`.
- Those class elements that are declared `public` are said to make up the object's *interface*.
- A *keyword* is a term that has special meaning in the Java language.
- An *identifier* must begin with a letter of the alphabet and may consist of any number of letters, digits and the special underscore character (_). An identifier cannot be identical to a Java keyword.
- A class's instance variables are called *fields*. A *field declaration* reserves memory for the field within the object, associates a name and type with the location, and specifies its accessibility.
- A class's instance variables should generally be hidden by declaring them `private` .
- The *scope* of an identifier is that portion of the class in which it may be used. A class's fields and methods have *class scope*, which means they can be used anywhere within the class.
- A *method definition* consists of two parts: a *header* , which names the methods and provides other general information about it, and a *body* which contains its executable statements.
- Methods that have a return type must `return` a value of that type. Methods that don't return a value should be declared `void`.
- A method's *formal parameters* are variables that are used to bring information into the method.
- A *qualified name* is one which involves the *dot operator* (.) and is used to refer to an object's methods and instance variables.

- *Declaring* a *reference variable* creates a name for an object but doesn't create the object itself.
- *Instantiating* a reference variable creates an object and assigns the variable as its name or reference.
- Execution of a Java application begins with the first statement in the body of the `main()` method.

ANSWERS TO SELF-STUDY EXERCISES

EXERCISE 2.1 One way of identifying the objects involved in a transaction or process is to identify the nouns involved in its description. In this case the objects would be (more or less) the student (user), the schedule, the courses, change-of-course form, the registration receipt,and the registrar. For each course, the following objects would be involved: course name, course id, and time of day. The messages required for this transaction would include add-course(course), which would be a message from the student to the registrar, providing the registrar with the course information. Another message would be the passing of a receipt from the registrar to the student.

EXERCISE 2.2 For the `Rectangle` class (Fig 2–5):

- The name of the class: `Rectangle`
- The names of two instance variables: `length`, `width`
- The names of two methods: `Rectangle()`, `calculateArea()`

EXERCISE 2.3 For `RectangleUser` class (Fig 2–8):

- The names of two `Rectangle` instances: `rectangle1`, `rectangle2`
- All six method calls in the program: `Rectangle(30, 10)`, `Rectangle(25, 20)`, `rectangle1.calculateArea()`, `rectangle2.calculateArea()`, and the two `System.out.println()` calls
- Two examples of qualified names: `rectangle1.calculateArea()` and `rectangle2.calculateArea()`

EXERCISE 2.4

```
public class CyberPet
{
   private boolean isDreaming = false;
}
```

EXERCISE 2.5

```
public class CyberPet
{
    public void dream()
    {
        isDreaming = true;
        isEating  = false;
        isSleeping = false;
    }
}
```

EXERCISE 2.6 Should the CyberPet's `pickFood()` method be declared `public` or `private`? It depends. If you wish to allow other objects to tell the `CyberPet` what to eat, it should be `public`. If the `CyberPet` is allowed to decide for itself, it should be declared `private`.

EXERCISE 2.7 Note that in this case the two stub methods return 0. If a method declares a non-void return type, it must contain a proper return statement.

```
public class Square
{
    private double side;
    public Square(double s);
    public double calcPerimeter() { return 0 ; }
    public double calcArea()      { return 0 ; }
}
```

EXERCISE 2.8

```
public class Square
{
    private double side;
    public Square(double s)
    {
        side = s;
    }
    public double calcPerimeter()
    {
        return 4 * side;
    }
    public double calcArea()
    {
        return side * side;
    }
} // Square
```

EXERCISE 2.9

```
public static void main(String argv[])
{
    Square square1;              // Declare reference variables
    Square square2;
    square1 = new Square( 25 );  // Create instances
    square2 = new Square( 15 );
                                 // Statements to test the access methods
    System.out.print("The area of square1 is ");
    System.out.println(square1.calcArea());
    System.out.print("The perimeter of square1 is ");
    System.out.println(square1.calcPerimeter());
    System.out.print("The area of square2 is ");
    System.out.println(square2.calcArea());
    System.out.print("The perimeter of square2 is ");
    System.out.println(square2.calcPerimeter());
} // main()
```

EXERCISE 2.10 (a) `int` (b) `double` (c) `String` (d) `String` (e) `boolean` (f) `String` (g) `int` (h) `char`

EXERCISE 2.11 If we perform string concatenation on the strings, "85," "95," and "90," we would get a string result "859590." The lesson here is that when you use the plus operator, +, on strings, it performs *string concatenation*. When you use it on numbers, it performs addition. Using the same operator for two completely different operations is an example of *operator overloading*, which we will take up in more detail later on.

EXERCISES

1. Consider the transaction of asking your professor for your grade in your computer science course. Identify the objects in this program and the type of messages that would be passed among them.
2. Now suppose the professor in the previous exercise decides to automate the transaction of looking up a student's grade and has asked you to design a program to perform this task. The program should let a student type in his or her name and ID number and should then display his or her grades for the semester, with a final average. Suppose there are five quiz grades, three exams, and two program grades. Identify the objects in this program and the type of messages that would be passed among them. (*Hint*: The grades themselves are just data values, not objects.)
3. Consider the *hierarchy chart* in Fig 2–4. For each of the following pairs of classes, determine if they are related as *subclass/superclass*.
   a. BorderLayout/FlowLayout
   b. TextArea/TextComponent
   c. TextField/Component
   d. Button/Component
   e. Panel/Object
4. Name all the *subclasses* of the `Container` class.
5. Based on the hierarchy chart in Fig 2–4, which of the following statements would be true?
   a. A `Container` is an `Object`.
   b. A `TextComponent` is a `Component`.
   c. A `Button` is a `Component`.
   d. A `Panel` is a `Container`.
   e. A `TextField` is a `Component`.
6. In the `RectangleUser` class (Fig 2–8), give two examples of object instantiation and explain what is being done.
7. Explain the difference between a *method definition* and a *method call*. Give an example of each from the `Rectangle`, `RectangleUser`, `TestCyberPet`, and `CyberPetUser` examples discussed in this chapter.
8. In the `RectangleUser` class (Fig 2–8), identify three examples of method calls and explain what is being done.
9. Describe how the slogan "define, create, manipulate" applies to the `Rectangle` and the `CyberPet` examples.
10. An *identifier* is the name for a _____, _____, or a _____.
11. Which of the following would be valid *identifiers*?

```
int  74ElmStreet  Big_N    L$&%#  boolean  Boolean  _number
Int  public       Private  Joe    j1       2*K      big numb
```

12. Explain what is meant by *class scope* in terms of the variables and methods of the `CyberPet` class.
13. Identify the syntax error (if any) in each declaration. Remember that some parts of a field declaration are optional.

```
(a)   public boolean isEven ;
(b)   Private boolean isEven ;
(c)   private boolean isOdd
(d)   public boolean is Odd ;
(e)   string S ;
(f)   public String boolean ;
(g)   private boolean even = 0;
(h)   private String s = helloWorld ;
(i)   private int payRate = 5.0 ;
(j)   private double wageRate = 10 ;
```

14. Write declarations for each of the following instance variables.

```
(a) A private boolean variable named bool that has
an initial value of true.
(b) A public string variable named str has an initial
value of "hello."
(c) A private double variable named payrate that is
not assigned an initial value.
```

15. For each of the following data types, identify what default value Java will give a instance variable of that type if no initializer expression is used when it is declared: `boolean`, `int`, `String`, `double`, `CyberPet`.
16. Identify the syntax error (if any) in each method header:

```
(a)   public String boolean()
(b)   private void String ()
(c)   private void myMethod
(d)   private myMethod()
(e)   public static void Main (String argv[])
```

17. Identify the syntax error (if any) in each assignment statement. Assume that the following variables have been declared:

```
      public int m;
      public double d;
      public boolean b;
      public String s;
(a)     m = 86.5 ;
(b)     d = 86 ;
(c)     d = true ;
(d)     s = 1295 ;
(e)     s = "1295.98" ;
(f)     b = "true" ;
(g)     b = false
```

18. Given the definition of the `NumberAdder` class, add statements to its `main()` method to create two instances of this class, named `adder1` and `adder2`. Then add statements to set `adder1`'s numbers to 10 and 15, and `adder2`'s numbers to 100 and 200. Then add statements to print their respective sums.

```
public class NumberAdder
{
    private double num1;
    private double num2;
    public void setNums(double n1, double n2)
    {
        num1 = n1;
        num2 = n2;
    }
    public double getSum()
    {
        return num1 + num2 ;
    }
    public static void main(String args[])
    {
    }
}
```

19. For the `NumberAdder` class in the previous exercise, what are the names of its instance variables and instance methods? Identify three expressions that occur in the program and explain what they do. Identify two assignment statements and explain what they do.
20. Explain the difference between each of the following pairs of concepts.

    a. A *method definition* and a *method invocation*.
    b. Declaring a reference variable and creating an instance.
    c. Defining a variable and instantiating an object.

21. Look at the following Java program, which uses the `CyberPet` class defined in Fig 2–10. What would the program output be?

```
public class TestCyberPet
{
    public static void main(String argv[])
    {
        CyberPet pet1;
        pet1 = new CyberPet();
        pet1.eat();
        pet1.sleep();
        CyberPet pet2;
        pet2 = new CyberPet();
        pet2.sleep();
        pet2.eat();
        pet1.eat();
    } // main()
} // TestCyberPet
```

22. Write a `main` method that creates two `CyberPets` named `lilly` and `billy` and then asks each of them to sleep and then eat.
23. Modify `CyberPet` to have a `String` instance variable, `name`. Give `name` an initial value and add a public method `tellMeYourName()` that prints the pet's name. Test your method by invoking it from `main()`.

24. Define a Java class named `NumberCruncher` which has a single `double` value as its only instance variable. Then define methods that perform the following operations on its number: get, double, triple, square, and cube. Set the initial value of the number by following the way the `length` and `width` variables are set in the `Rectangle` class.
25. Write a `main()` method and add it to the `NumberCruncher` class defined in the previous problem. Use it to create a `NumberCruncher` instance, with a certain initial value, and then get it to report its double, triple, square, and cube.
26. **Challenge:** Modify your solution to the previous exercise so that it lets the user input the number to be crunched. Follow the example shown in this chapter's "From the Java Library" section.
27. Write a Java class definition for a `Cube` object. The object should be capable of reporting its surface area and volume. The surface area of a cube is six times the area of any side. The volume is calculated by cubing the side.
28. Write a Java class definition for a `CubeUser` object that will use the `Cube` object defined in the previous exercise. This class should create three `Cube` instances, each with a different side, and then report their respective surface areas and volumes.
29. **Challenge:** Modify your solution to the previous exercise so that it lets the user input the side of the cube. Follow the example shown in this chapter's "From the Java Library" section.
30. **Challenge:** Define a Java class that represents an address book entry, `Entry`, which consists of a name, address, and phone number, all represented as `String`s. For the class's interface, define methods to set and get the values of each of its instance variables. Thus, for the `name` variable, it should have a `setName()` and a `getName()` method.
31. **Challenge:** Write a Java class definition for a `Temperature` object that is capable of reporting its temperature in either Fahrenheit or Celsius. This class should have one instance variable called `temperature` and two public methods, one called `getFahrenheit`, which returns the temperature in Fahrenheit, and one called `getCelsius()`, which returns the temperature in Celsius. This method has to convert the stored temperature to Celsius before returning it. An expression for converting Fahrenheit to Celsius is $(5 \times (F - 32)/9)$, where F is the temperature in Fahrenheit.

Photograph courtesy of New Zealand National Archives

Methods: Communicating with Objects

3

OBJECTIVES

After studying this chapter, you will

- Understand the role that methods play in an object-oriented program.
- Know how to use parameters and arguments to pass data to an object.
- Understand how constructor methods are used to instantiate objects.
- Know the difference between passing a value and passing a reference to an object.
- Be able to design your own methods.
- Know how to use the selection control structure.

OUTLINE

3.1 Introduction

In this chapter we take a look at Java methods and parameters. Methods and parameters are the primary mechanisms for passing information into and out of an object. We will once again focus on the `CyberPet` simulation that we designed in the previous chapter. In that version a `CyberPet`'s state is represented by two boolean variables, `isEating` and `isSleeping`, and its repertoire of activity consists of responding to two commands, `eat()` and `sleep()` (Fig 2–10).

This version of `CyberPet` was sufficient to introduce us to Java objects and classes, but it wasn't much of a simulated pet. For one thing, a `CyberPet` had no name, no color, and so on. And, although our `CyberPet` had a state, there was no way for it to communicate its state to the rest of the world — we had no means of simply asking a `CyberPet`, "What are you doing?"

In this chapter we want to expand `CyberPet` to make our simulation more realistic. We begin by learning how to pass information to an object. That will enable us to give our `CyberPet`s names. We then consider special methods, constructors, that are used to initialize an object's state when it is created. We also learn how to retrieve information from an object. That will enable us to ask a `CyberPet` what its name is and what it is doing. Finally, in the lab project for this chapter you will design and implement methods that extend the `CyberPet`'s behavior even more.

3.2 Passing Information to an Object

What data does the object need?

Let's begin by expanding `CyberPet` to include a variable that can store the `CyberPet`'s name. Let's name the variable `name` because that is descriptive of its purpose. The question now is, how should we initialize this variable? If we give it some name as an initial value, say "Socrates," then every `CyberPet` instance will have the name "Socrates." That's not a very good design. Instead, let's initialize `name` to "no name," meaning that the `CyberPet` has yet to be assigned a name. So, we will add the following declaration to the `CyberPet` class:

```
private String name = "no name";
```

We declared `name` to be `private`, thereby preventing other objects from accessing it directly. This is in keeping with the convention that instance variables should be hidden.

What actions will the class perform?

Now that we have added `name` to our class, we will need methods to access it. One convention of object-oriented programming is to provide `public` methods to *set* and *get* the value of some of its `private` instance variables. The set method would assign a value to the variable, and the get method would retrieve the variable's value. It is up to the designer of the class to determine which private variables require access methods. If you were designing a `BankAccount` class, you might want a `getAccountNumber` method, but you would probably not want a `getAccountPassword` method.

EFFECTIVE DESIGN: Access Methods. An **access method** is a public method used to provide controlled access to an object's instance variables. Such methods are often named *setVariable()* and *getVariable()*, where *Variable* is the name of the variable that's being accessed.

In the case of setting and getting the `name` variable, we would name our access methods `setName()` and `getName()`. The `setName()` method would be used by other objects to pass a name string to a particular `CyberPet`. The `getName()` method would be used by other objects to retrieve a particular `CyberPet`'s name.

Access methods

Consider the following definition for the `setName()` method:

```
public void setName ( String str )
{
    name = str;
}
```

Assume that the above method has been added to the `CyberPet` class definition, along with the declaration and initialization of the `name` instance variable (Fig 3–1).

Recall from Chapter 2 that the general form for a method definition in Java is

MethodModifiers$_{opt}$ *ResultType* *MethodName* (*FormalParameterList*)
MethodBody

Figure 3–1 The `CyberPet` class with the `setName()` method added.

```
public class CyberPet
{
  // Data
   private boolean isEating = true;     // CyberPet's state
   private boolean isSleeping = false;
   private String name = "no name";     // CyberPet's name

  // Methods
   public void setName(String str)
   {
       name = str;
   } // setName()

   public void eat()                    // Start eating
   {
       isEating = true;                 // Change the state
       isSleeping = false;
       System.out.println(name + " is eating");
       return;
   } // eat()

   public void sleep()                  // Start sleeping
   {
       isSleeping = true;               // Change the state
       isEating = false;
       System.out.println(name + " is sleeping");
       return;
   } // sleep()
} // CyberPet
```

Parameters

In particular, note the method's *FormalParameterList* that follows the method's name. Formal parameters are used to pass information into a method when the method is invoked. Because neither the `eat()` nor `sleep()` method was passed any information, their parameter lists were empty. In both of those cases, simply calling the method was sufficient to tell the `CyberPet` to eat or sleep. No other information was necessary.

Passing information to an object

In the case of the `setName()` method, the situation is quite different. The purpose of this method is to set a `CyberPet`'s `name`. In order to do this, `setName()` must be given (or passed) a `String` that represents a pet's name. It will then take that string and assign it to its `name` instance variable, thereby setting the `CyberPet`'s name to the string it was passed. The formal parameter is used to hold the string that it is passed while the method is executing.

JAVA LANGUAGE RULE **Formal Parameter.** A **formal parameter** is a variable that serves as a storage location for information that is being passed to a method. To specify a formal parameter, you must provide a type identifier followed by variable identifier, and you must place this declaration inside the parentheses that follow the method's name.

If a method uses more than one formal parameter, use a comma to separate the individual parameter declarations. For example, if we had a method that required both a first and last name, its parameter list would contain two `String` declarations:

```
(String first, String last )
```

Parameter Scope

Local scope

Recall that a variable's or a method's **scope** defines where it can be used in a program. A parameter's scope is limited to the method in which it is declared. In contrast to instance variables, which have class scope, parameters have **local scope** . The reason for this distinction is that parameters have a relatively short life span. Once the flow of execution leaves a method, its parameters cease to exist. This means that we can only refer to the `setName()`'s `str` parameter from within the `setName()` method. For example, it would be a syntax error if we tried to use the `str` variable within the `eat()` or `sleep()` methods.

JAVA LANGUAGE RULE **Scope.** Instance variables have **class scope** , which extends throughout the class. Parameters have **local scope**, which is confined to the method in which they are declared.

```
public class CyberPet
{
  //DATA
  private boolean isEating = true; //CyberPet's state
  private boolean isSleeping = false;
  private String name = "no name"; //CyberPet's name

  //METHODS

  public void setName(String str)
  {
    name = str;
  }//setName()

  public void eat()       //start eating
  {
    isEating = true;      //change the state
    isSleeping = false;
     System.out.println(Pet is eating");
     return;
  }//eat()

  public void sleep()     //start sleeping
  {
    isSleeping = true;    //change the state
    isEating = false;
     System.out.println("Pet is sleeping");
     return;
  }//sleep()

}//end of CyberPet class
```


Figure 3–2 Class scope extends through a class whereas local scope is confined to individual methods.

Class scope vs. local scope

One way to visualize the difference between local and class scope is to draw boxes around portions of a program to indicate an identifier's scope (Fig 3–2). For class scope you would draw a box around the entire class. An instance variable or method can be used anywhere within that box. Similarly, draw boxes around each of the methods in the class. The scope of a method's parameters, if it has any, would be confined within these smaller boxes. From within a smaller box you can refer to an instance variable, because the smaller box is completely contained within the class's box. But from within one small box, you cannot refer to anything within one of the other small boxes. This is yet another sense in which both a method and a class encapsulate their elements.

DEBUGGING TIP: Scope Error. It would be a syntax error to refer to a method's parameters from outside the method.

3.2.1 Arguments and Parameters

Now that we have incorporated the new method and instance variable into `CyberPet`, let's create a `CyberPet` instance and use these new features. Suppose then we have the following statement in a Java program:

```
CyberPet pet1 = new CyberPet();
```

If we want to set `pet1`'s name to "Socrates," we need to pass the string "Socrates" to the `setName()` method. Then `setName()` will do its task, which is to assign "Socrates" to `pet1`'s `name` variable. In order to effect this action for `pet1`, we would use the following method call:

```
pet1.setName("Socrates");
```

Because the definition of `setName()` now includes a single `String` parameter, when we invoke it we must supply a single `String` value (such as "Socrates"). When `setName()` is invoked, its formal parameter (`str`) will be set to the value we supply — (to "Socrates"). The value we supply can be any `String`. It needn't be a literal string such as "Socrates." It can also be a `String` variable, as shown in the following example:

```
String s = "Hal";
pet1.setName(s);
```

In this case, the value being passed to `setName()` is "Hal," the value that `s` has at the time the method call is made.

It would be an error to try to pass a value that was not a `String` to `getName()`. For example, each of the following invocations of `setName()` would cause an error:

```
pet1.setName();             // no String supplied
pet1.setName(Socrates) ; // Socrates is not a String
pet1.setName(10);           // 10 is not a String
```

Parameter vs. argument

The value that is passed to a method when a method is called is known as an **argument** . Even though the terms *argument* and *parameter* are sometimes used interchangeably, it will be useful to observe a distinction. We will use the term **parameter** to refer to the formal parameter — the place holder — that occurs in the method declaration. We use the term **argument** to refer to the actual value that is supplied when the method is invoked.

DEBUGGING TIP: Type Error. It would be a syntax error to use an argument whose type doesn't match the type of its corresponding parameter.

Hopefully the distinction between parameter and argument will help drive home the difference between *defining* a method and *invoking* a method. Beginning programmers easily confuse the two. Defining a method is a matter of writing a method definition, such as

Defining vs. calling a method

```
public void printStr(String s)
{
  System.out.println(s);
}
```

This method definition defines a method that takes a single `String` parameter, `s`, and simply prints the value of its parameter.

On the other hand, invoking a method is a matter of writing a method call statement, such as

```
printStr("HelloWorld");
```

This statement calls the `printStr` method and passes it the string "HelloWorld." You might wonder why this method call does not use the dot operator, as have most of our other examples. The rule in Java is that references to methods (or variables) within the same class do not require qualified names (the dot operator) but just the method (or variable) name itself. Thus, if both the above definition and method call occurred in the same class, this would be valid.

Simple vs. qualified names

JAVA LANGUAGE RULE **Qualified Names.** Within a class, references to methods or variables are made in terms of a simple name. Qualified names are used to refer to methods or variables that belong to other classes.

3.2.2 Passing a String to `CyberPet`

To get a clearer picture of the interaction that takes place when we invoke `setName()` and pass it a string, let's write a simple test program to use our new version of `CyberPet`. As in the previous chapter, we'll call it `TestCyberPet`. Our first version of this program is shown in Fig 3–3.

Figure 3–3 A program to test the `CyberPet` class.

```
public class TestCyberPet
{
    public static void main (String argv[])
    {
        CyberPet pet1;                 // Declare a CyberPet
        pet1 = new CyberPet();         // Instantiate the references
        pet1.setName("Socrates");      // Set the pet's name
        return;                        // Return to the system
    } // main()
} // TestCyberPet
```

The TestCyberPet program simply creates an instance that is referenced by pet1 and then invokes the setName() method to set pet1's name to "Socrates":

```
pet1.setName("Socrates");  // set the pet's name
```

We know in general that invoking the setName() method, as shown here, will cause the string "Socrates" to be stored in pet1's name variable. But let's trace through the transaction and see how it works. We want to see how information is passed from one object (TestCyberPet) to another object (CyberPet).

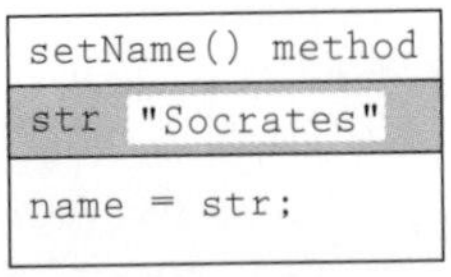

```
setName() method
str "Socrates"
name = str;
```

Figure 3–4 Conceptually, when the setName("Socrates") method is called, the str parameter contains the string "Socrates."

When we make a call to the setName() method,

```
pet1.setName("Socrates");
```

the formal parameter of setName(), str, gains access to the value "Socrates" and can use it within the method. Strings are full-fledged objects in Java, and so the parameter str is a reference variable (rather than a primitive variable). As we explained in Chapter 2, a reference variable stores a reference to an object rather than the object itself. Nevertheless, whenever you use str you will be referring to the String "Socrates." Conceptually, you can think of str as containing the String "Socrates," as shown in Fig 3–4.

Primitive vs. reference variable

Now let's imagine that we have called the setName() method and passed the string "Socrates" to it. At this point the variable str has the value "Socrates." Let's pick up the flow of control from that point. Inside the setName() method, there is only a single assignment statement

```
name = str ;
```

which assigns the value stored in the parameter str into the name instance variable. Thus after executing this assignment statement, pet1's name variable will have been set to "Socrates."

Information flow

To review the flow of information here, we called the setName() method with the argument "Socrates," which was passed to the setName() formal parameter, str. Within the method itself, the value of str ("Socrates") was then assigned to the name instance variable of pet1. Each of these individual steps leads to the name variable in pet1 being assigned the value "Socrates." After completion of this process, pet1 will have the state shown in Fig 3–5.

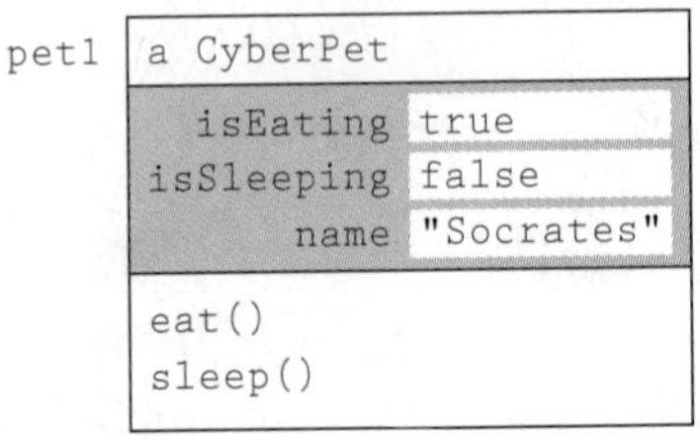

```
pet1  a CyberPet
        isEating  true
      isSleeping  false
            name  "Socrates"
      eat()
      sleep()
```

Figure 3–5 pet1's state after setting its name to "Socrates."

Figure 3–6 A program to test the CyberPet class.

```
public class TestCyberPet
{
    public static void main (String argv[])
    {
        CyberPet pet1;              // Declare CyberPet variables
        CyberPet pet2;
        pet1 = new CyberPet();      // Instantiate the references
        pet1.setName("Socrates"); // Set the pet's name
        pet2 = new CyberPet();
        pet2.setName("Plato");
        pet1.eat();                 // Tell pet1 to eat
        pet2.sleep();               // Tell pet2 to sleep
        pet1.sleep();               // Tell pet1 to sleep
        return;                     // Return to the system
    } // main()
} // TestCyberPet
```

3.2.3 Parameters and the Generality Principle

One of the nice parts about methods with parameters is that they allow us to design more general methods. To illustrate this, consider the following badly designed method:

```
public void setNameSocrates()      // Bad bad method!
{
    name = "Socrates" ; // Set pet's name to "Socrates"
}
```

Like our `setName()` method, this method could be used to set the name of `pet1` to "Socrates." But it's too narrow in its design. It can't be used to set the pet's name to "Plato" or "Guinevere." In contrast, because it uses a parameter, the `setName()` method can be used to set a pet's name to anything we like. Thus, using parameters enables us to design methods that are more general in what they do, which is an important principle of object-oriented design.

Generalizing a method

To complete this section, let's modify our `TestCyberpet` application so that it creates two pets with two different names (Fig 3–6). The revised program will have `pet1` named "Socrates" and `pet2` named "Plato." The situation that results is shown in Fig 3–7.

Recall that output generated by our `CyberPet` class in Chapter 2 couldn't distinguish one pet from another. When we commanded `pet1` to eat, the

Figure 3–7 TestCyberPet creates two CyberPets, one named "Socrates" and one named "Plato."

program would output "Pet is eating." When we commanded pet2 to eat, it would still display "Pet is eating." Now that our CyberPets have individual names, it is relatively simple to fix this problem. Consider the following revised versions of println() statements in eat() and sleep():

```
System.out.println( name + " is eating");
System.out.println( name + " is sleeping");
```

These modifications have been incorporated into the revised version of the CyberPet class shown in Fig 3–1. If we now run the test program shown in Fig 3–6, the following (improved) output will be generated:

```
main is starting
Socrates is eating
Plato is sleeping
Socrates is sleeping
main is finished
```

SELF-STUDY EXERCISES

EXERCISE 3.1 Explain the difference between a *method declaration* and a *method invocation.*

EXERCISE 3.2 Explain the difference between a *formal parameter* and an *argument*.

EXERCISE 3.3 Show how you would add an instance variable of type String to the CyberPet class to keep track of what kind of pet this is — for example, "dog," "cat." Write a method named setKind() that sets the pet's kind to a certain value (for example, "mouse").

EXERCISE 3.4 Write a method call statement to set pet1's kind to "mouse" and pet2's kind to "cat."

3.3 Constructor Methods

In the example just finished, we saw how we could define an access method, setName(), that assigns a value to a private instance variable. For some instance variables, it would be convenient to be able to set the initial values of these variables each time an object is created.

Constructor names

A **constructor** method is used to create an instance object for a class. A constructor declaration looks just like a method definition except it must have the same name as the class, and it cannot declare a result type. Unlike a class's fields and methods, constructors are not considered members of the class. Therefore they are not inherited by a class's subclasses. Access to constructors is governed by the access modifiers public and private. Here is a simple constructor for our CyberPet class:

```
public CyberPet()
{
    isSleeping = false;
    isEating = true;
}
```

Constructing an object

This constructor merely sets the initial values of the instance variables, `isSleeping` and `isEating`. In our current version of `CyberPet` these variables are given initial values by using initializer statements when they are first declared:

```
private boolean isSleeping = false;
private boolean isEating = true;
```

So we now have two ways to initialize a class's instance variables. In the `CyberPet` class it doesn't really matter which way we do it. However, the constructor provides more flexibility because it allows the pet's state to be initialized at runtime. Of course, it would be somewhat redundant (though permissible) to initialize the same variable twice, once when it is declared and again in the constructor, so we should choose one or the other way to do this. For now, let's stick with initializing the instance variables when they are declared. Later we'll see some other initialization tasks a constructor can do.

EFFECTIVE DESIGN: Constructors. Constructors provide a flexible way to initialize an object's instance variables when the object iscreated.

Constructors can't return a value

A constructor cannot return a value, and therefore its declaration cannot include a return type. Because they cannot return values, constructors cannot be invoked by a regular method invocation. Instead, constructors are invoked as part of an *instance creation expression* when instance objects are created. An instance creation expression involves the keyword `new` followed by the constructor invocation:

```
CyberPet pet1 = new CyberPet(); // Declare and instantiate pet1
CyberPet pet2 = new CyberPet(); // Declare and instantiate pet2
```

Note here that we have combined variable declaration and instantiation into a single statement, whereas in previous examples we used separate declaration and instantiation statements. Either way is acceptable.

JAVA LANGUAGE RULE Constructors. Constructors cannot return a value. Therefore no return type should be declared when the constructor is defined.

DEBUGGING TIP: When to Use return. All method definitions except constructors must declare a return type.

State initialization

Constructors should be used to perform the necessary initialization operations during object creation. In the case of a CyberPet object, what initializations should be performed? One initialization that would seem appropriate is to initialize the pet's name. In order to do this we would need a constructor with a single String parameter:

```
public CyberPet(String str)
{
    name = str;
}
```

Now that we have this constructor we can use it when we create instances of CyberPet:

```
CyberPet pet1 = new CyberPet("Socrates");
CyberPet pet2 = new CyberPet("Plato");
```

The effect of these two statements is the same as if we had used the setName() method to set the names of pet1 and pet2. The difference is that we can now set a pet's name when we create it instead of using the setName() method.

Redundancy and flexibility

Should we keep the above constructor and get rid of the setName() method? No. Let's keep both in our class definition. The constructor can only be invoked as part of a new statement when the object is created. The setName() method can be called anytime we want. If we ever want to change a CyberPet's name, we will need to use setName(). So let's keep it in our class definition along with the above constructor.

EFFECTIVE DESIGN: Using Redundancy. Incorporating some redundancy into a class, such as providing more than one way to set the value of an instance variable, makes the class more widely usable.

SELF-STUDY EXERCISES

EXERCISE 3.5 What's wrong with the following constructor definition?

```
public void CyberPet(String s)
{
    name = str;
}
```

EXERCISE 3.6 Change the CyberPet(String) constructor so that it uses the setName() method to set the pet's name.

3.3.1 Default Constructors

As we noted in Chapter 2, when a class does not contain a constructor, Java automatically provides a *default constructor*.

JAVA LANGUAGE RULE Default Constructor. If a class contains no constructor declarations, Java will automatically supply a default constructor . The default constructor takes no parameters. If the class is public, the default constructor will also be public and hence accessible to other objects.

The default constructor's role is simply to create an instance (an object) of that class. It takes no parameters. In terms of what it does, the default constructor for Cyberpet would be equivalent to a public constructor method with an empty body:

```
public CyberPet() { }
```

This explains why the statement

```
CyberPet socrates = new CyberPet();
```

is valid regardless of whether a constructor was explicitly declared in the CyberPet class.

3.3.2 Constructor Overloading and Method Signatures

Flexible design

It is often quite useful to have more than one constructor for a given class. For example, consider the following two CyberPet constructors:

```
public CyberPet() {}                // Constructor #1

public CyberPet(String str)         // Constructor #2
{
    name = str;
}
```

The first is an explicit representation of the default constructor. The second is the constructor we defined earlier to initialize a pet's name.

Method overloading

In Java, as in some other programming languages, when two different methods have the same name, it is known as **method overloading**. In this case, CyberPet is used as the name for two distinct constructor methods. What distinguishes one constructor from another is its **signature**, which consists of its name together with the number and types of formal parameters it takes. Thus, our CyberPet constructors have the following distinct signatures:

```
CyberPet()
CyberPet(String)
```

Both have the same name, but the first takes no parameters whereas the second takes a single String parameter.

Methods are known by their signatures

The same point applies to methods in general. Two methods can have the same name as long as they have distinct signatures. A **method signature** consists of its name, return type, and the number and types of its formal parameters. A class may not contain two methods with the same signature, but it may contain several methods with the same name, provided each has a distinct signature.

> **JAVA LANGUAGE RULE** **Method Signature.** A **method signature** consists of the method's name, plus its return type, plus the number and type of formal parameters. A class may not contain two methods with the same signature.

There is no limit to the amount of overloading that can be done in designing constructors and methods. The only restriction is that each method have a distinct signature. For example, suppose in addition to the two constructors we have already defined, we want a constructor that would let us set a pet's name and what kind of animal it is. To solve this problem, assume that we declare a `String` instance variable named `kind`. Given this new variable, the following constructor will do what we want:

```
private String kind;      // What kind of pet?

public CyberPet(String nStr, String kStr)
{
    name = nStr;           // Initialize pet's name
    kind = kStr;           // Initialize pet's kind
}
```

This constructor takes two `String` parameters. The first is `nStr`, which is meant to be passed a string representing the pet's name. The second is `kStr`, which is meant to be passed a string representing its kind. In the method itself, the first string is assigned to `name` and the second to `kind`. When we call this constructor, we will have to take care to pass a name as the value of the first argument and a kind as the value of the second argument:

```
CyberPet pet3 = new CyberPet("Buddy", "dog");
CyberPet pet4 = new CyberPet("Petunia", "pig");
```

Passing values

When passing values to a method, Java passes the first argument to the first parameter, the second argument to the second parameter, and so forth. If we mistakenly reversed "Buddy" and "dog" in the first of these statements, we would end up with a `CyberPet` named "dog" whose kind was "Buddy."

We have now defined three constructor methods for the `CyberPet` class. Each constructor has the name `CyberPet`, but each has a distinct signature:

```
CyberPet()
CyberPet(String)
CyberPet(String, String)
```

3.3.3 Constructor Invocation

A constructor is invoked once to create an object

A constructor method is invoked only once, as part of a `new` statement, when an instance object is first created. Each of these is a valid invocation of a `CyberPet` constructor:

```
CyberPet pet1 = new CyberPet() ;                // Default constructor
pet1.setName("Pet1");                           // So use setName()
CyberPet pet2 = new CyberPet("Pet2");           // Sets the pet's name
CyberPet pet3 = new CyberPet("Pet3", "dog");    // Sets name and kind
```

As the comments indicate, the first constructor is the default constructor, which doesn't set either the name or kind. So we need to call `setName()` (in line 2) to set the name of `pet1`. The constructor used for `pet2` sets its name, and the constructor used for `pet3` sets both name and kind.

These constructor invocations are invalid for the reason given in the comments:

```
CyberPet pet4 = new CyberPet(true) ;            // No matching constructors
CyberPet pet5 = new CyberPet("Pet2" , "dog", "sleeping") ;
```

In the first case, there is no constructor method that takes a `boolean` parameter, so there's no matching constructor. In the second case there is no constructor that takes three `String` arguments. In both cases, the Java compiler would complain that there is no constructor method that matches the invocation.

DEBUGGING TIP: Method Call. A method call must exactly match the name and parameter types of the method definition.

3.4 Retrieving Information from an Object

The modifications we've made to the `CyberPet` class allow us to set a `CyberPet`'s name, but there is no way for us to retrieve a `CyberPet`'s name. We declared `CyberPet`'s `name` field as `private`, so we cannot access it directly. Therefore, we will need an access method to *get* a `CyberPet`'s name. Consider the following method definition:

```
public String getName()
{
    return name;
}
```

Recall again that the general form of a method declaration is

MethodModifiers$_{opt}$ *ResultType* *MethodName* (*FormalParameterList*)
MethodBody

and note that a method's *ResultType* is specified just in front of the *MethodName*. The `eat()`, `sleep()`, and `setName()` methods did not return a value. So in each case their result types were declared as `void` (see Fig 3–1). In this case we want `getName()` to return a `String` that represents the `CyberPet`'s name. Therefore, its result type is declared `String`.

Note that in this definition of getName() it has an empty parameter list. Because we will not be passing it any information, it does not need formal parameters. This is not to say that a method that returns a value cannot have a parameter list. For example, consider the following method, which returns the average of its two int parameters:

```
public double average (int n1, int n2)
{
    return (n1 + n2) / 2;   // return the average of n1 and n2
}
```

Note that this method requires both a formal parameter list and a nonvoid return value.

3.4.1 Invoking a Method That Returns a Value

Retrieving information

When we invoke a method that returns a value, the invocation expression takes on, or becomes, the value that is returned. For example, if we execute the following statements

```
pet1.setName("Socrates");
pet1.getName();
```

the expression pet1.getName() will take on the value "Socrates" after the getName() method is finished executing. We can manipulate this value the same way we manipulate any other String in a Java program. We can use System.out.println() method to output "Socrates" on the Java console:

```
System.out.println(pet1.getName()) ; // prints "Socrates"
```

Nested expressions

This is an example of a *nested method call*, in which pet1.getName() is *nested* inside the expression System.out.println(). To evaluate expressions such as these, you always proceed from the inside out — that is, from the innermost nested parentheses. In this case, the method call pet1.getName() is being passed as an argument to the System.out.println() method. Because the value of pet1.getName() is "Socrates," this is the same as if println() were being passed the argument "Socrates." Before an argument can be passed to a method, it must first be evaluated. In this case the argument, pet1.getName(), is evaluated by invoking pet1's getName() method, which returns the value "Socrates." Thus the value that gets passed to println() is "Socrates."

Another way that we can use the value produced by the method call pet1.getName() is to assign it to another String variable:

```
String myString ;
myString = pet1.getName();  // Stores "Socrates" in myString
```

The result of these two statements is that myString would now have "Socrates" as its value. Thus when you invoke a method that returns a value, the method invocation expression — pet1.getName() — becomes the value that is returned. So pet1.getName() becomes "Socrates" and can be manipulated in the same way that any other String can be manipulated.

Evaluating a method call

> **JAVA LANGUAGE RULE** **Evaluating Method Calls.** A method call is an expression that has a value. Nonvoid methods return a value of a particular type. Calling a nonvoid method replaces the method call with its value.

Let's revise the CyberPet definition again to incorporate the getName() method and the constructor that we discussed (Fig 3–8). Let's also modify

Figure 3–8 The CyberPet class with the CyberPet(String) constructor and getName() methods added.

```
public class CyberPet
{
   // Data
    private boolean isEating = true;    // CyberPet's state
    private boolean isSleeping = false;
    private String name = "no name";    // CyberPet's name

   // Methods
    public CyberPet() {}              // Explicit default constructor

    public CyberPet(String str)       // Constructor method
    {
        name = str;
    }

    public void setName(String str) // Access method
    {
        name = str;
    } // setName()

    public String getName()           // Access method
    {
        return name;                  // Return CyberPet's name
    } // getName()

    public void eat()                 // Start eating
    {
        isEating = true;              // Change the state
        isSleeping = false;
        System.out.println(name + " is eating");
        return;
    } // eat()

    public void sleep()               // Start sleeping
    {
        isSleeping = true;            // Change the state
        isEating = false;
        System.out.println(name + " is sleeping");
        return;
    } // sleep()
} // CyberPet
```

Figure 3–9 TestCyberPet now contains statements to get a pet's name.

```
public class TestCyberPet
{
    public static void main (String argv[])
    {
        CyberPet pet1;                          // Declare CyberPet variables
        CyberPet pet2;
        pet1 = new CyberPet("Socrates");        // Create pet1 named "Socrates"
        System.out.println("pet1's name is ");
        System.out.println(pet1.getName());     // Print pet1's name
        pet2 = new CyberPet("Plato");           // Create pet2 named "Plato"
        System.out.println("pet2's name is ");
        System.out.println(pet2.getName());     // Print pet1's name
        pet1.eat();                             // Tell pet1 to eat
        pet2.sleep();                           // Tell pet2 to sleep
        return;                                 // Return to the system
    } // main()
} // TestCyberPet
```

TestCyberPet to make use of the getName() method, as shown in Fig 3–9. Our new version of TestCyberPet now contains the following sequence of statements in its main() method:

```
pet1 = new CyberPet("Socrates");        // Create pet1 named "Socrates"
System.out.print("pet1's name is ");
System.out.println(pet1.getName());     // Print pet1's name
pet2 = new CyberPet("Plato");           // Create pet2 named "Plato"
System.out.print("pet2's name is ");
System.out.println(pet2.getName());     // Print pet2's name
```

The first statement sets pet1's name to "Socrates." The second statement produces the message "pet1's name is" on the standard output device. The third statement calls the getName() method to retrieve pet1's name ("Socrates") and then displays it on the screen. Similarly, the next three statements set, retrieve, and output pet2's name. The result of these six statements is that the following output would be printed on the screen:

```
pet1's name is Socrates
pet2's name is Plato
```

SELF-STUDY EXERCISES

EXERCISE 3.7 What would these segments of Java code display on the screen?

```
CyberPet myPet = new CyberPet("Fido");
System.out.println(myPet.getName());

CyberPet myPet2 = new CyberPet("Trigger");
System.out.println(myPet2.getName());
```

EXERCISE 3.8 Write a Java method for the `CyberPet` class to *get* a `CyberPet`'s kind where `kind` is an instance variable of type `String`.

EXERCISE 3.9 Write a method to return a description of a `CyberPet` — for example, "Fido is a dog."

3.5 Passing a Value and Passing a Reference

How the value "Socrates" is passed to the `CyberPet.setName()` method is actually somewhat more complicated than we let on. In fact, the effect of passing arguments to a method differs slightly depending on whether you are passing a **primitive** value or a **reference** value (see Section 2.5.5.) When an argument of primitive type is passed to a method, a copy of the argument is passed to the formal parameter. For example, consider the `PrimitiveCall` class, shown in Fig 3–10. Note that we have an `int` variable `k`, which is currently storing the value 5, and a method `myMethod()`, which takes an `int` parameter `n`. In this case, when we invoke `myMethod(k)`, `k`'s value (5) is copied into `n` and stored there during the method.

Passing a primitive value

One implication of passing a primitive value to a method is that the original value of `k` cannot be altered from inside the method. For example, the output generated by `PrimitiveCall` would be

```
main: k= 5
myMethod: n= 5
myMethod: n= 100
main: k= 5
```

Note that in `main()` `k`'s value is printed both before and after `myMethod()` is called, but that its value remains unaffected even though `n`'s value is changed within the method.

Figure 3–10 Passing a primitive value to a method.

```
public class PrimitiveCall
{
    public static void myMethod(int n)
    {
        System.out.println("myMethod: n= " + n);
        n = 100;
        System.out.println("myMethod: n= " + n);
    } // myMethod()
    public static void main(String argv[])
    {
        int k = 5;
        System.out.println("main: k= " + k);
        myMethod(k);
        System.out.println("main: k= " + k);
    } // main()
} // PrimitiveCall
```

JAVA LANGUAGE RULE **Passing a Value.** When a value of a primitive type — `boolean, int` — is passed to a method, its original value remains unchanged outside the method, even if it is changed inside the method.

Passing a reference value

In contrast to this, when an argument of reference type is passed to a method, a copy of the reference is passed to the parameter. Because `String`s are objects, in the case of a `String` parameter, the method is passed a reference to the `String` rather than the `String` object itself. Similarly, if a method took a `CyberPet` parameter, it would be passed a reference to the actual `CyberPet` object, rather than the object itself. It would just be too inefficient to pass an entire object, with all of its instance variables and its method.

However, because a reference is really a pointer to an object, the method has access to the object and can make changes to the object from within the method. For example, consider the `ReferenceCall` class (Fig 3–11).

In this case, `myMethod()` takes a parameter `p` of type `CyberPet`. Because `CyberPet` is an object, `p` is a reference variable. So when `myMethod(pet)` is invoked in `main()`, a reference to `pet` is passed to `myMethod()`. Note that in `myMethod()`, we use `CyberPet.setName()` to change the name of `p` from "Harry" to "Mary," and that this change persists even after the method is exited. The reason is that during the method's execution, both `pet` and `p` refer to the exact same object. The output generated by `ReferenceCall` would be

```
main: pet name is Harry
myMethod: pet name is Harry
myMethod: pet name is Mary
main: pet name is Mary
```

Figure 3–11 Passing a reference value to a method.

```
public class ReferenceCall
{
    public static void myMethod(CyberPet p)
    {
        System.out.println("myMethod: pet name is " + p.getName());
        p.setName("Mary");
        System.out.println("myMethod: pet name is " + p.getName());
    } // myMethod()

    public static void main(String argv[])
    {
        CyberPet pet = new CyberPet();
        pet.setName("Harry");
        System.out.println("main: pet name is " + pet.getName());
        myMethod(pet);
        System.out.println("main: pet name is " + pet.getName());
    }// main()
} // ReferenceCall
```

This illustrates that when passing a reference variable to a method, it is possible for the method to change the state of the object associated with the reference variable. In subsequent chapters we will see ways to make use of this feature of reference parameters.

JAVA LANGUAGE RULE **Passing a Reference.** When a reference to an object is passed to a method, any changes made to the object inside the method will persist when the method is done.

DEBUGGING TIP: Side Effects. A unintended change to an object is called a **side effect**. Care should be taken in designing methods that the method does not produce unwanted side effects in objects passed as reference parameters.

3.6 Flow of Control: Selection Control Structures

We've seen how to write methods that return information from an object. What other information besides its name should a `CyberPet` object be able to provide when asked? If the `CyberPet` object is going to be of any use in a simulation, we would want to know its state at any given time, so let's write a method that reports a `CyberPet`'s state.

What information should the method receive and return?

Like the `getName()` method, the `getState()` method should return a `String` that describes the `CyberPet`'s state. When `CyberPet` is sleeping, `getState()` should return "Sleeping," and when the `CyberPet` is eating, `getState()` should return "Eating." Because there is no need to pass the `CyberPet` any information in this case, this method does not require any formal parameters. Following these design decisions, we can devise a preliminary implementation of `getState()`:

```
public String getState()
{
    return "Error in State";
}
```

Stepwise refinement

Recall from the lab exercise in Chapter 1 that a **stub method** consists of a complete header and an incomplete body. If this version of `getState()` were added to the `CyberPet` class in this form, it would always return "Error in State" when invoked. Note that the following definition would not be a correct stub for the `getState()` method, because it does not return a `String`:

```
public String getState() {}
```

The Java compiler would flag this as an error. The rule is that any method that has a nonvoid result type must contain a `return` statement.

JAVA LANGUAGE RULE **Method Return.** A nonvoid method must contain a `return` statement, and the method's algorithm must ensure that the `return` statement will, in fact, be executed.

DEBUGGING TIP: Nonvoid Stub Methods. For nonvoid methods, a *stub method* must `return` a value of the appropriate type.

3.6.1 The Simple If Statement

Algorithm design

Let's now use stepwise refinement to complete the body of this method. In this case, we want `getState()` to return 'Sleeping" when `CyberPet` is sleeping (that is, when `isSleeping` is `true`) and "Eating" when the `CyberPet` is eating (when `isEating` is `true`). Consider the definition of `getState()`:

```
public String getState()
{
    if (isEating)
        return "Eating";        // Exit the method
    if (isSleeping)
        return "Sleeping";      // Exit the method
    return "Error in State";    // Exit the method
}
```

The `getState()` method makes use of two *if statements* to select between alternative results ("Eating" or "Sleeping"). The first if statement tests whether `isEating` is `true`, and if so returns the `String` "Eating" and exits the method. If this path is taken, then the rest of the statements in the method are not executed. Control returns immediately to the calling method because the `return` statement is executed.

If `isEating` is `false`, the `return` statement is not executed and control drops down to the second if statement, which tests whether `isSleeping` is `true`. If so, it returns the `String` "Sleeping" and exits the method. If not, control drops down to the last statement in the method, and the `String` "Error in State" is returned. Notice that if neither `isEating` nor `isSleeping` is `true`, then this indeed constitutes an error in the `CyberPet`'s state, because one or the other (but not both) of these variables must be true in order for the `CyberPet` model to be in a consistent state.

Selecting a path

The if statement is an example of the **selection** control structure, because it allows the program to select one or the other of two alternative paths of execution.

JAVA LANGUAGE RULE **If Statement.** The *if statement* takes the following form:

if (*booleanexpression*)
  statement ;

The statement contained in the if statement can be any valid Java statement, including a compound statement. A boolean expression is an expression that is either `true` or `false`. As we saw in the previous chapter, the simplest possible `boolean` expression is the `boolean` literal `true` or `false`. Similarly, a `boolean` variable, such as `isSleeping`, which has a value of either `true` or `false`, is another example of a boolean expression. A third example of a boolean expression would be the equality expression `isSleeping == false`.

JAVA LANGUAGE RULE **Equality Operator.** The == is Java's equality operator, and the expression `isSleeping == false` says "isSleeping equals false," a statement which itself is either true or false.

We will see more complex examples of boolean expressions in Chapter 5.

DEBUGGING TIP: Equals versus Assigns. A common semantic error is to use the assignment operator (=) where the equality operator is intended. Because `isSleeping = false` is syntactically valid, such an error won't be caught by the compiler.

Given this description of if statement syntax, the following are examples of valid if statements:

```
if (true) System.out.println("Hello");
if (isSleeping == false) System.out.println("not sleeping");
```

For readability, we usually write an if statement with its statement indented on the next line:

```
if (true)
    System.out.println("Hello");
if (isSleeping == false)
    System.out.println("not sleeping");
```

The following are all examples of syntax errors involving the if statement:

```
if true                              // Parentheses are missing
    System.out.println("Hello"); //  around the boolean expression

if (isSleeping) return               // Semicolon missing at end

if ("true") return;                  // "true" is a String not a boolean

if (true) "Hello";                   // "Hello" is a value not a statement
```

Figure 3–12 Flowchart of the if statement. Diamond-shaped symbols at the branch points contain boolean expressions. Rectangular symbols can only contain executable statements. Circles act simply as connectors, to connect two or more paths.

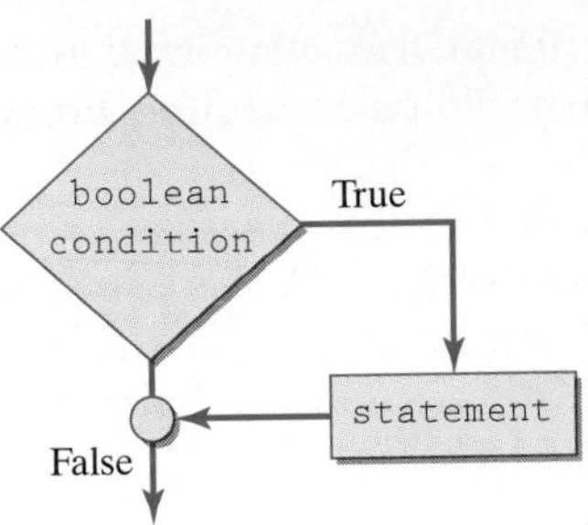

If statement semantics

Semantically, the if statement has the following interpretation: First, the **boolean expression** or *boolean condition* is evaluated. If it is true, then the contained *statement* is executed; if it is false, then the contained *statement* is not executed. This is shown in Fig 3–12. The flowchart clearly shows that program flow will take one or the other of the alternative paths coming out of the diamond-shaped boolean condition box. The branch through the rectangular statement box will be taken when the boolean condition is true; otherwise the statement will be skipped.

The flowchart in Fig 3–13 shows the program flow of the entire `getState()` method. It is important to note that when a `return` statement is executed in a method, control is returned immediately to the calling method. Thus, if `isEating` is true, the string "Eating" is returned to the calling method and the `getState()` method exits at this point. If it is false, then `isSleeping` should be true (if we have a consistent state) and the string "Sleeping" should be returned and the method exited. Thus if we have a consistent state — that is, if the pet is either eating or sleeping — then the third `return` statement should never be reached.

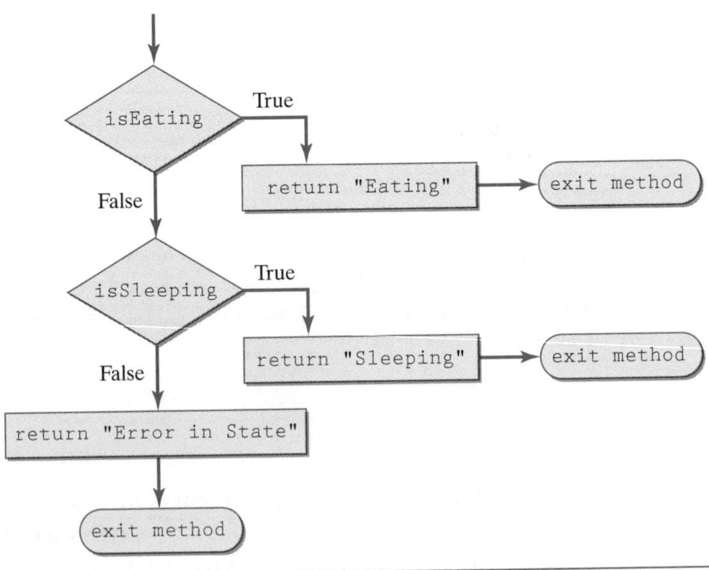

Figure 3–13 Flowchart of the `getState()` method.

As the following example shows, the statement contained in an if statement can be a compound statement:

Compound statement

```
if (isSleeping)
{
    String s = "sleeping";
    System.out.print (name);
    System.out.println (" is sleeping ");
    return s;
}
```

If `isSleeping` is true, then all four statements in the contained compound statement will be executed. Note here that we are declaring the local variable s in this block. Its scope would extend to the end of the block. Note also that when we use a compound statement, the compound statement itself is not followed by a semicolon because it is already enclosed in braces.

A common programming error is to forget the braces around the compound statement. Merely indenting the statements following the if clause doesn't alter the logic of the if statement. For example, the following if statement still has only one statement in its if clause:

```
if (condition1)
    System.out.println("One");
    System.out.println("Two");  // Not part of if's scope
```

This segment will always print "Two" because the second `println()` falls outside the scope of the if statement. To include it in the scope, you must use braces:

```
if (condition1)
{
    System.out.println("One");
    System.out.println("Two");  // Part of if's scope
}
```

DEBUGGING TIP: Indentation. Indentation can improve the readability of a program but doesn't affect its logic. Braces must be used to group statements in the if clause.

3.6.2 The `if-else` Statement

A second version of the if statement incorporates an *else clause* into the structure. This allows us to execute either of two separate statements (simple or compound) as the result of one boolean expression. For example, the statement

```
if (isEating)
    System.out.println("Is Eating");
else
    System.out.println("Is NOT Eating");
```

will print "Is Eating" if `isEating` is true. Otherwise, it will print "Is NOT Eating."

> **JAVA LANGUAGE RULE** **if-else Statement.** The *if-else statement* has the following syntax:
>
> `if` (*boolean expression*)
>   *statement1* ;
> `else`
>   *statement2* ;

If-else syntax

As in the case of the simple if statement, the keyword `if` is followed by a parenthesized *boolean expression*, which is followed by *statement1*, which may be either simple or compound. If *statement1* is a simple statement, then it is followed by a semicolon. The *else clause* follows immediately after *statement1*. It begins with the keyword `else`, which is followed by *statement2*, which can also be either a simple or compound statement.

If-else semantics

Semantically, the if-else statement has the following interpretation: If the *boolean expression* is true, execute *statement1*; otherwise execute *statement2*. This interpretation is shown in Fig 3–14.

3.6.3 Flow of Control: Multiway Selection

Multiple alternatives

The statements that one inserts in place of *statement1* and *statement2* in the if-else statement can be any executable statement, including another if statement or if-else statement. In other words, it is possible to embed one or more if-else statements inside another if-else statement, thereby creating a *nested* control structure. As with most things, making a control structure too complex isn't a good idea, but there is a standard nested if-else control

Figure 3–14 Flowchart of the `if-else` statement.

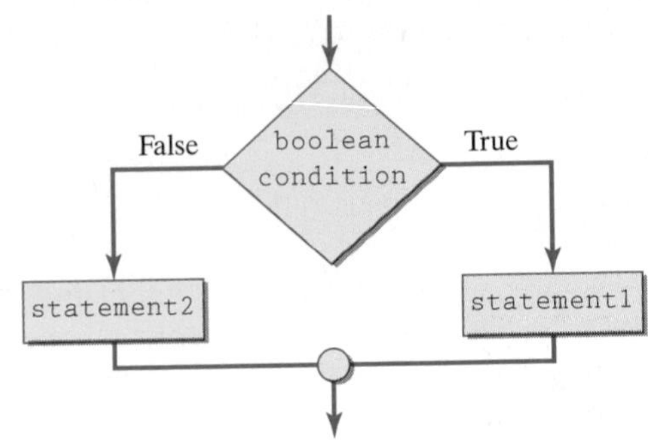

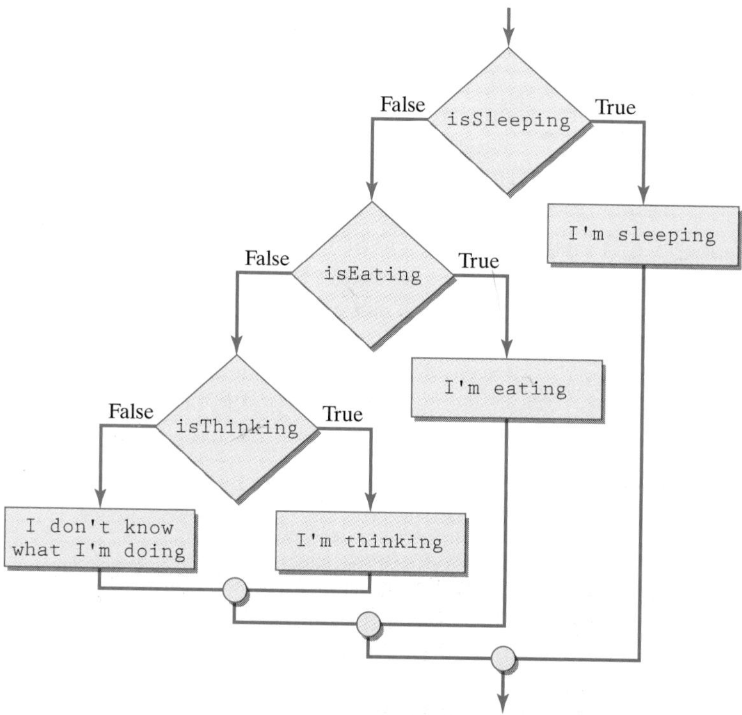

Figure 3–15 Flowchart of a nested if-else statement.

structure that is very useful. It is known as **multiway selection**. As shown in Fig 3–15, the multiway structure is used when you want to select one and only one option from several alternatives.

Suppose we have a CyberPet that can be in one of three states: eating, sleeping, or thinking. In the example shown in Fig 3–15 there are three alternatives plus an error state. Here is the Java code for this example:

```
if (isSleeping)
    System.out.println("I'm sleeping");
else if (isEating)
    System.out.println("I'm eating");
else if (isThinking)
    System.out.println("I'm thinking");
else
    System.out.println("Error: I don't know what I'm doing");
```

Note that the multiway structure has a single entry point and that only one of the four possible alternatives is executed. The CyberPet will print either that it is sleeping, eating, thinking, or that it doesn't know what it is doing.

We will have many occasions to use the if-else structure. Although it does not represent a significant change, we can rewrite our `getState()` method to make use of the if-else instead of the simple if statement, as follows:

```
public String getState()
{
    if (isEating)
        return "Eating" ;          // Exit the method
    else
        return "Sleeping" ;        // Exit the method
}
```

In some respects this version of getState() is simpler. It has only one boolean condition to test, and because isEating must be either true or false, one or the other of "Eating" or "Sleeping" will be returned as the result. There's no longer a need for a return "Error" statement at the end of the method, because it would be never be reached (isEating has to be either true or false). The flowchart for this version of getState() is left as an exercise.

3.6.4 The Dangling Else Problem

Dangling else

One of the traditional problems associated with the if-else statement is the **dangling else** problem. This is a syntax problem primarily for the programmer, not the compiler. Consider the following nested if-else statement:

```
if (condition1)
    if (condition2)
        System.out.println("One");
else
    System.out.println("Two");
```

From the way this statement is laid out and indented, it looks as if the else clause goes with the first if statement, such that if condition1 were false, then "Two" would be printed. However, this is *not* what happens. The rule in Java is this:

> **JAVA LANGUAGE RULE** **Nested if-else.** Within a nested if-else statement, an else clause matches with the closest previous unmatched if clause.

According to this rule, the second else clause is matched with the second if clause (condition2). So if condition1 were false, nothing would be printed. The flowchart in Fig 3–16 illustrates the proper interpretation of this statement. The proper indentation for this statement should help to clarify its syntactic and semantic structure:

Indentation

```
if (condition1)
    if (condition2)
        System.out.println("One");
    else
        System.out.println("Two");
```

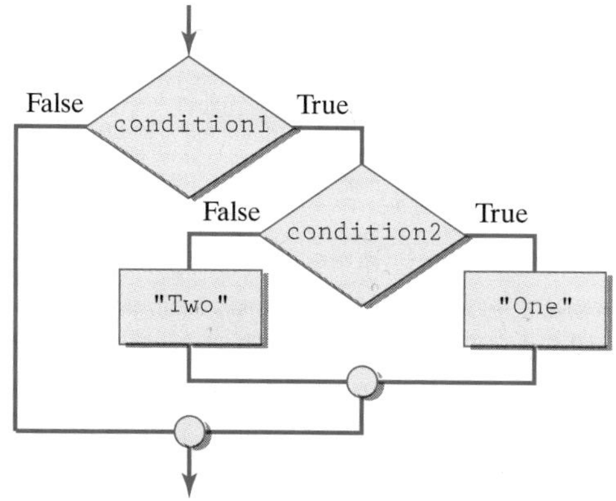

Figure 3–16 Proper interpretation of a dangling else statement.

In this case, the else clause is properly aligned under its matching if clause. Of course, because Java is a free-form language, indentation is simply ignored by the compiler and has no effect on the syntax of a statement. So although indentation makes the code more readable, it doesn't change the way the code is interpreted.

DEBUGGING TIP: Indentation. Indentation can improve the readability of a program but doesn't affect its logic.

Using indentation and brackets

What if we want "Two" to be printed when `condition1` is false? In that case, we would have to use braces to associate the else clause with the first if clause:

```
if (condition1)
{
    if (condition2)
        System.out.println("One");
}
else
    System.out.println("Two");
```

In this case, the statement associated with `condition2` does not contain an else clause; the braces turn it into a simple if statement. Therefore, the else clause now matches the first if clause, which is now the closest previous unmatched if clause.

Whenever there is a chance of ambiguity, it is always best to use braces to clarify the if-else structure. Similarly, take care to use proper indentation when coding if-else statements. Else clauses should be aligned with their corresponding if clauses as in the examples we have discussed. These practices will make the code more readable, and may help to avoid subtle semantic errors.

PROGRAMMING TIP: If-else Statements. Take care when coding if-else statements to make sure that else clauses are aligned with their corresponding if clauses. Braces may be necessary to achieve the proper logical relationship.

SELF-STUDY EXERCISES

Flowchart symbols

EXERCISE 3.10 Draw a flowchart for the if-else version of the `getState()` method. Use the figures in this section as a guide. Each if-else structure should be drawn exactly as shown in Fig 3–14. It should have a single entry point that leads directly to the top of a diamond-shaped box which contains a boolean condition. There should be two branches coming out of the condition box. The one going to the right is the true case, and the one going to the left is the false case. Each of these branches should contain one rectangular box, which contains the statements that would be executed in that case. The left and right branches should be connected by a circular symbol which is aligned directly under the diamond box whose conditions its connects. There should be a single exit arrow pointing directly down.

EXERCISE 3.11 Identify the error in the following statements:

```
if (isEating == true)
    System.out.println("Eating");
else ;
    System.out.println("Sleeping");

if (isEating == true)
    System.out.println("Eating")
else
    System.out.println("Sleeping");
```

EXERCISE 3.12 Suppose we had a pet model with three possible states, eating, sleeping, and playing, represented by three boolean variables, `isEating`, `isSleeping`, and `isPlaying`. Write a `getState()` method that returns a `String` spelling out the state for this version of the pet model.

EXERCISE 3.13 How does a *value parameter* differ from a *reference parameter*?

3.7 The Improved CyberPet

Stepwise refinement

The final version (for this chapter) of the `CyberPet` class is shown in Fig 3–17. It has grown in an incremental fashion from a very simple program into one that does quite a few things. Compared to our first version (in Chapter 2), this version of `CyberPet` presents an interface (to other objects) that is easy and convenient to use. The access methods, `getName()`, `setName()`, and `getState()`, provide convenient means to find out the `CyberPet`'s name and state and to set or reset its name. The constructor method provides an easy way to initialize `CyberPet` instances. At the

Figure 3–17 The CyberPet class, including the getState() method.

```
public class CyberPet
{
    private boolean isEating = true;     // CyberPet's state
    private boolean isSleeping = false;
    private String name = "no name";     // CyberPet's name

    public CyberPet (String str)         // Constructor method
    {
        name = str;
    }

    public void setName (String str)     // Access method
    {
        name = str;
    } // setName()

    public String getName()
    {
        return name;             // Return CyberPet's name
    } // getName()

    public void eat()            // Start eating
    {
        isEating = true;         // Change the state
        isSleeping = false;
        return;
    } // eat()

    public void sleep()          // Start sleeping
    {
        isSleeping = true;       // Change the state
        isEating = false;
        return;
    } // sleep()

    public String getState ()
    {
        if (isEating)
            return "Eating";     // Exit the method
        if (isSleeping)
            return "Sleeping";   // Exit the method
        return "Error in State"; // Exit the method
    } // getState()
} // CyberPet
```

same time, our use of private instance variables prevents other objects from tampering with a CyberPet's state.

Note that we have deleted the statements that output the pet's state in the eat() and sleep() methods. Because CyberPet() now has a getState() method, we can print the pet's state in the main() method, as shown in the revised version of TestCyberPet (Fig 3–18). Note that a single println() statement can be used to print both the pet's name and its state by concatenating the results of the calls to the getName() and getState() methods:

Figure 3–18 TestCyberPet now contains statements to get a pet's name.

```
public class TestCyberPet
{
    public static void main (String argv[])
    {
        CyberPet pet1;                      // Declare CyberPet variables
        CyberPet pet2;
        pet1 = new CyberPet("Socrates");    // Create pet1 named "Socrates"
        pet2 = new CyberPet("Plato");       // Create pet2 named "Plato"

                                            // Print the pets' names and states
        System.out.println(pet1.getName() + " is " + pet1.getState());
        System.out.println(pet2.getName() + " is " + pet2.getState());
        pet1.eat();                         // Tell pet1 to eat
        pet2.sleep();                       // Tell pet2 to sleep

                                            // Print the pets' names and states
        System.out.println(pet1.getName() + " is " + pet1.getState());
        System.out.println(pet2.getName() + " is " + pet2.getState());
        return;                             // Return to the system
    } // main()
} // TestCyberPet
```

```
System.out.println(pet1.getName() + " is " + pet1.getState());
```

Information hiding

Equally important, our design of the `CyberPet` class makes appropriate use of Java's access modifiers, `private` and `public`, to control access to the individual `CyberPet` objects. By making the `CyberPet`'s instance variables `private`, we ensure that other objects cannot corrupt its state, thus ensuring its integrity. At the same time, by making the access methods `public`, we allow other objects to interact with `CyberPets` in ways that make sense and preserve their integrity. Taken together, the public access methods provide other objects with an *interface* that they can use to communicate with individual `CyberPet` objects.

EFFECTIVE DESIGN: Interfaces. Well-designed objects provide a useful interface and protect the object's private elements from other objects.

To reiterate a point made at the outset, object-oriented programming is a process of constructing objects that will interact with each other. Object-oriented programs must ensure that the objects themselves are well designed in terms of their ability to carry out their designated functions. Good design in this sense requires careful selection of instance variables, and careful design of methods to ensure that the object can carry out its assigned tasks. However, equal care must be taken to ensure that the interactions that take place among objects are constrained in ways that make sense for that particular program. This aspect of designing objects comes into play in designing the methods — both constructor and access methods — that make up the object's interface.

From the Java Library: `Object`

Inheritance

The most general class in Java's class hierarchy is the `java.lang.Object` class. It is the superclass of all classes that occur in Java programs. By default, it is the direct superclass of any class which does not explicitly specify its pedigree in its class definition.

The `public` and `protected` methods contained in `Object` are *inherited* by all of its subclasses — which means by all classes, because every class is a subclass of `Object`. In this section, let's look briefly at how we can use an inherited method, and also at how we can *override* it, if it doesn't exactly suit our purposes.

One of the most useful method's in the `Object` class is the `toString()` method:

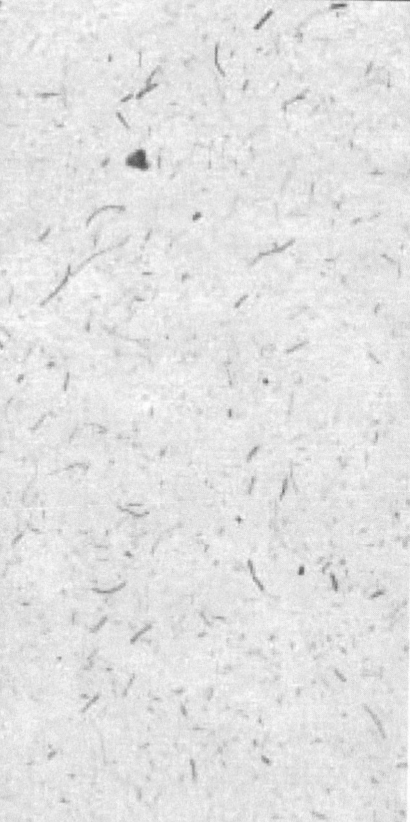

Intelligent Agents

Wouldn't it be nice if we had a CyberPet that could schedule appointments for us, remind us of meetings and commitments, find information for us on the WWW, and manage our e-mail messages for us? Wouldn't it be nice to have a personal assistant CyberPet?

Actually such programs are called *intelligent agents* and intelligent agent technology is becoming an important research area in computer science. An intelligent agent is a program that is capable of acting autonomously to carry out certain tasks. Most agent programs incorporate some kind of machine learning capability, so that their performance improves over time.

As a typical agent activity, suppose I was able to tell my CyberPet to buy me a copy of a certain book that I just heard about. Given a command like, "buy me a copy of X," the agent would perform a search of on-line book sellers and come up with the best deal. Once it had found the best buy, the agent would communicate with a computer-based agent representing the book seller. My agent would make the order and pay for it (assuming I gave it authority to do so), and the book seller's agent would process the order.

As far fetched as the capability may now seem, this is the direction that research in this area is headed. Researchers are developing agent languages, and describing protocols that agents can use to exchange information in a reliable and trustworthy environment. Obviously, you wouldn't want your agent to give your money to a fraudulent book seller, so there are significant problems to solve in this area that go well beyond the problem of simply exchanging information between two agents.

The best way to learn more about this research area is to do a Web search using the search string "Intelligent Agent." There are numerous research groups and companies that provide on-line descriptions and demos of their products.

```
public class Object
{
    public String toString() ;
}
```

The toString() method returns a String representation of the Object. For example, o1.toString() will return a String that in some sense describes o1.

To illustrate the default behavior of toString(), let's use it with a CyberPet instance:

```
CyberPet p1 = new CyberPet("Ernie");
CyberPet p2 = new CyberPet("Bert");
System.out.println( p1.toString() );
System.out.println( p2.toString() );
```

This code segment creates two CyberPets, one named "Ernie" and the other named "Bert." The toString() method is then invoked on each CyberPet, which produces the following output:

```
    CyberPet@1dc6077b
    CyberPet@1dc60776
```

Default toString()

What this experiment shows is that the default definition of toString() returns some kind of internal representation of the object. It looks as if it returns the name of the object's class concatenated with its memory address. This may be useful for some applications. But for most objects we will want to *override* the default definition to make the toString() method return a string that is a bit more descriptive.

Method Design: toString()

Overriding a method

What String should the CyberPet.toString() method return? Let's have it return a String that reports the CyberPet's name and current state. To override a method, you simply define a method with the exact same signature in the subclass. Thus, the CyberPet.toString() will have the following signature:

```
public String toString();
```

If we were just returning CyberPet's name, the body for this method would consist of a single statement:

```
return name;
```

However, we also want to return the CyberPet's state. Since the state is represented by a boolean variable, one way to do this is to use a multiway if-else statement to distinguish between the CyberPet's possible states. Using this approach, the toString() algorithm will resemble the algorithm we used in the getState() method (Fig 3–17). For any given state, we concatenate an appropriate String, representing the state, to the CyberPet's name and return the result:

Algorithm design

```
public String toString()
{
    if (isEating)
        return name + " is eating";
    else if (isSleeping)
        return name + " is sleeping";
    return "error";
}
```

If our CyberPet had more than these two possible states, we would simply add more else clauses to the if-else statement.

An even better way to design this algorithm is simply to invoke the getState() method in the toString() method. There's no need to test what state CyberPet is in, since this is what getState() does:

```
public String toString()
{
    return name + " is " + getState();
}
```

We've thus reduced the body of toString() to one statement, a much simpler design that reuses code we've already written. Plus, this version makes CyberPet easier to extend and maintain. If we decide to add more states to CyberPet, we would only need to change the getState() method. With the other design, we would have to change both getState() and toString().

Simplicity, extensibility, and maintainability

EFFECTIVE DESIGN: Method Abstraction. Instead of duplicating code at several different places within a program, it is better to encapsulate the code in a method and call the method wherever the code is needed. A method is easier to maintain and extend, and the resulting program will be shorter and better structured.

If we add the toString() method to CyberPet and then run the program shown in Fig 3–19, we get the following output:

```
Ernie is Eating
Bert is Sleeping
```

Figure 3–19 An application to test the overridden `toString()` method.

```
public class TestPetToString
{
    public static void main(String argv[])
    {
        CyberPet pet1 = new CyberPet("Ernie");
        CyberPet pet2 = new CyberPet("Bert");
        pet2.sleep();
        System.out.println(pet1.toString());
        System.out.println(pet2.toString());
    }//main
} //TestPetToString
```

OBJECT-ORIENTED DESIGN: Class Inheritance

Inheritance

This use of `Object`'s `toString()` method provides our first look at Java's inheritance mechanism, and how it promotes the generality and extensibility of the object-oriented approach. As a subclass of `Object`, our `CyberPet` class automatically inherits `toString()` and any other `public` or `protected` methods defined in `Object`. We can simply use these methods as is, in so far as they are useful to us. As we saw in this case, the default version of `toString()` wasn't very useful. In that case, we can override the method, by defining a method in our class with the exact same method signature. The new version of `toString()` can be customized to do exactly what is most appropriate for the subclass.

One of the great benefits of the object-oriented approach is the ability to define a task, such as `toString()`, at a very high level in the class hierarchy, and let the inheritance mechanism spread that task throughout the rest of the hierarchy. Because `toString()` is defined in `Object`, you can invoke this method for any Java object. Moreover, if you override `toString()` in classes you define, you will be contributing to its usefulness. One of the important lessons we can gain from this example is

EFFECTIVE DESIGN: Inheritance. The higher up in the class hierarchy that a method is defined, the more widespread its use can be.

Obviously there is much more that needs to be explained about Java's inheritance mechanism. Therefore, we will be revisiting this topic again on numerous occasions in subsequent chapters.

IN THE LABORATORY: FEEDING `CyberPet`

The purpose of the lab exercise is to familiarize you with Java methods and parameters. You will make several modifications to extend the functionality of the `CyberPet` class. The objectives of the lab are

- To give practice writing Java methods from scratch.
- To give practice using parameters to pass information to a method.
- To give practice using return values to pass information back from a method.

Problem Statement

Modify the CyberPet and TestCyberPet classes to create a simulation in which pets can eat different kinds of food. The completed program should be capable of producing the following output:

Problem specification

```
pet1's name is Socrates
Socrates is eating an apple
Socrates is sleeping
pet2's name is Cleopatra
Cleopatra is eating beans
Cleopatra is sleeping
...
```

Lab Exercise 1: Editing, Compiling, and Running

Download the `CyberPet.java` and the `TestCyberPet.java` source files from the companion Web site at `http://www.prenhall.com/morelli/`. Compile and run the program, which corresponds to the program shown in Figures 3–17 and 3–18.

For each of the items below, make the editing change and then recompile the program. Make note of any error messages that are generated by the compiler. Try to understand what the message is telling you, and try to learn from the error, so it will be less likely to occur next time. After you have finished with that error, restore the code to its original form and move on to the next item.

- **Java is case sensitive.** Change the assignment statement in `setName()` to `Name = str` with an uppercase "N."
- **Strings require double quotes.** Leave off one of the double quote marks around "Socrates" in the `main()` method in `TestCyberPet`.
- **Methods that return a value require a `return` statement.** Comment out the `return` statement in the `getName()` method. That is, turn the `return` statement into a comment line by adding double slashes (//) at the beginning of the line.
- **String concatenation requires an operator.** Delete the plus sign (+) in the `System.out.println()` expressions in `eat()`.
- **Objects must be instantiated.** Comment out the line beginning `pet1 = new Pet("Socrates")` in `main()`.

Lab Exercise 2: Modifying the CyberPet class.

Method design

Write a void access method named eat() which takes a single String parameter that represents a type of food — "spinach," "ice cream," and so on. The method should take the food string that is passed to it and assign it to an instance variable named food. It should also do everything that the other version of eat() does.

Note that this new method will have the same name as an existing method in CyberPet. How will these two methods be distinguished from one another?

Modify the TestCyberPet application program so that it will conduct appropriate tests to make sure your new eat() method is working properly. When you are finished, the output should match the output shown above in the problem statement. Your test algorithm should tell your CyberPet to eat certain foods.

Be sure to make appropriate use of private and public in your revisions to the CyberPet class.

Lab Exercise 3: Order of Execution

Modify your TestCyberPet program so that it produces the following output:

```
pet1 name is Socrates
Socrates is sleeping
Socrates is eating an apple
Socrates is eating a Macintosh
Socrates is eating a Windows/PC
```

Lab Exercise 4: Generating a Trace

Testing and debugging

Add System.out.println() statements to your eat(String) method in order to generate a visible trace of the method call and return mechanism. Use println() to display eat()'s parameter, and the food instance variable both before and after the assignment statement. Try to generate the following output:

```
starting the eat method
str parameter = bananas
food instance variable = no food
str parameter = bananas
food instance variable = bananas
exiting the eat method
```

Using println() statements to display the values of variables and to trace program control is a good debugging technique. You will want to use this technique to locate bugs when things go wrong.

Java Language Summary

Method Declaration

The general form for a method definition is

MethodModifiers$_{opt}$ *ResultType* *MethodName* (*FormalParameterList*) *MethodBody*

where *MethodModifiers* may be one of `public`, `private`, or `protected`. Methods declared `private` are only accessible from within the class; `protected` methods are accessible only in subclasses and within classes contained in the same package; and `public` methods are accessible to all other objects. If a method's accessibility is not explicitly declared, Java's default is to make the method accessible only to other classes in the same package.

Methods with a non `void` *ResultType* must contain a `return` statement of the form *return(value)*, where *value* is the same type as *ResultType*; `void` methods may omit the `return` statement.

A method's *FormalParameterList* is a list of zero or more parameter declarations, each of which takes the following form:

TypeId1 ParameterId2, TypeId2 ParameterId2, . . .

Method Call and Return

A method is invoked (or called) by using its name and by providing arguments for each of its formal parameters. For example, if a method has the signature,

```
public void myMethod(String s, int n);
```

it would be invoked by calling

```
myMethod("hello", 5);
```

The arguments must match the type and order of the parameters. Thus "hello" is a `String` and 5 is an `int`, and they must be provided in that order.

Passing values to a method

When a method is called, the arguments are passed to their corresponding formal parameters. Control is then transferred to the first statement in the method's body. When the method is done executing, control is returned to the calling statement. See Fig 2–16 for an illustration of this.

The program in Fig 3–20 will print "hello," "goodbye," and then "hello friend" on three separate lines. The flow of control follows the sequence given in the program's comments. In the first two method calls, when the method is done executing, it may seem as if control returns to the

Figure 3–20 A program illustrating method call and return structures.

```
public class MethodCalls
{
    public void method1(String s)
    {
        System.out.println(s);            // 2, 4
    }

    public String method2()
    {
        return "hello";                   // 6
    }

    public static void main(String args[])
    {
        MethodCalls obj = new MethodCalls();
        obj.method1("hello");                              // 1
        obj.method1("goodbye");                            // 3
        System.out.println(obj.method2() + " friend"); // 5
    } // main()
} // MethodCalls
```

statement following the calling statement (rather than to the calling statement itself, as we have said). Thus, `method1()` is called on line 1. Control passes to line 2. When the method is done, it looks as if control returns to line 3. However, this is somewhat illusory, even though in this case it makes no practical difference to say that control returns to the statement on line 3.

Returning a value from a method

But don't forget that some methods return a value. That value is used in the calling statement *before* control passes to the next statement. Thus, in the method call on line 5, control passes to line 6. The value "hello" is returned to the statement on line 5, where it is conjoined with "friend" and printed. This clearly illustrates that control always returns to the calling statement of a method call. If there's nothing left for the calling statement to do, control then passes on to the next statement.

The If and If-Else Statements

The *if statement* and *if-else statement* take the following forms:

`if` (*boolean expression*)
    statement ;

`if` (*boolean expression*)
    statement1 ;
`else`
    statement2 ;

CHAPTER SUMMARY

Technical Terms

access method	argument	boolean expression
class scope	constructor	dangling else
local scope	method definition	method invocation
method overloading	method signature	multiway selection
parameter	primitive type	reference type
scope	selection structure	side effect
stub method		

New Java Keywords

`boolean`	`else`	`false`
`if`	`int`	`private`
`protected`	`public`	`return`
`true`	`void`	

Java Library Classes

`Object`	`String`

Java Library Methods

`main()`	`println()`	`toString()`

Programmer-Defined Classes

`CyberPet`	`OldMacdonald`	`PrimitiveCall`
`ReferenceCall`	`TestCyberPet`	`TestPetToString`

Programmer-Defined Methods

`CyberPet()`	`eat()`	`eieio()`
`getName()`	`getState()`	`hadAnX()`
`myMethod()`	`setKind()`	`setName()`
`toString()`	`withA()`	

Summary of Important Points

- A *formal parameter* is a place holder in a method declaration and it always consists of a type followed by variable identifier. An *argument* is a value that is passed to a method via a formal parameter when the method is invoked. A method's *parameters* constrain the type of information that can be passed to a method.
- **Parameter Passing.** When an argument of primitive type is passed to a method, it cannot be modified within the method. When an argument of reference type is passed to a method, the object it refers to can be modified within the method.

- Except for `void` methods, a *method invocation* or *method call* is an expression which has a a value of a certain type. For example, `pet1.getName()` might have the `String` value "Socrates."
- The *signature* of a method consists of its name, its return type, and the number and type of its formal parameters. A class may not contain more than one method with the same signature.
- A *constructor* is a method that is invoked when an instance object is created. If a class does not contain a constructor method, the Java compiler supplies a *default constructor*.
- Restricting access to certain portions of a class is a form of *information hiding*. Generally, instance variables are hidden by declaring them `private`. The class's `public` methods make up its interface.
- The *if statement* executes a statement only if its boolean condition is true. The *if-else statement* statement executes one or the other of its statements depending on the value of its boolean condition. *Multiway selection* allows one and only one of several choices to be selected depending on the value of its boolean condition.

ANSWERS TO SELF-STUDY EXERCISES

EXERCISE 3.1 A *method declaration* defines the method by specifying its name, qualifiers, return type, formal parameters, and its algorithm, thereby associating a name with a segment of executable code. A *method invocation* calls or uses a defined method.

EXERCISE 3.2 A *formal parameter* is a place holder in the method declaration, whose purpose is to store the method's arguments while the method is running. An *argument* is a value that is passed to a method in place of a formal parameter.

EXERCISE 3.3

```
String kind = "no kind";
public void setKind(String str)
{
    kind = str;
}
```

EXERCISE 3.4

```
pet1.setKind("mouse");
pet2.setKind("cat");
```

EXERCISE 3.5 A constructor cannot have a return type, such as void.

EXERCISE 3.6

```
private String kind = "no kind";

public CyberPet(String str)
{
    setName(str);
}
```

EXERCISE 3.7

```
Fido
Trigger
```

EXERCISE 3.8

```
public String getKind()
{
    return kind;
}
```

EXERCISE 3.9

```
public String getKind()
{
    return name + " is a " + kind;
}
```

EXERCISE 3.10 See Fig 3–21.

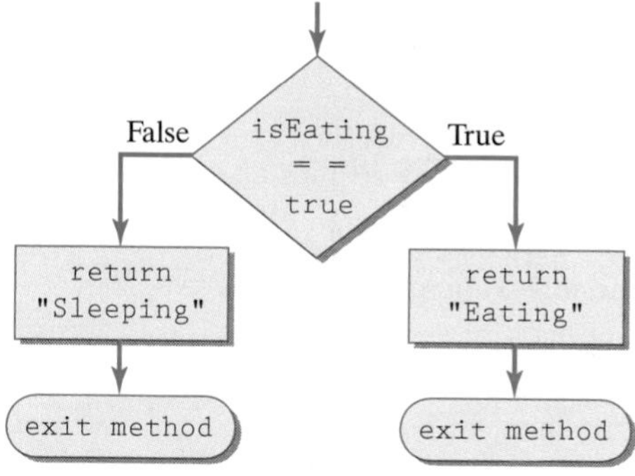

Figure 3–21 Flowchart of the if-else version of the `getState()` method.

EXERCISE 3.11

```
if (isEating == true)
    System.out.println("Eating") ;
else ;                              // Error (no semicolon here)
    System.out.println("Sleeping");
if (isEating == true)
    System.out.println("Eating")  // Error (missing semicolon here)
else
    System.out.println("Sleeping");
```

EXERCISE 3.12

```
public String getState()
{
    if (isEating == true)
        return "Eating";
    else if (isSleeping == true)
        return "Sleeping";
    else if (isPlaying == true)
        return "Playing";
    else
        return "Error in state";
}
```

EXERCISE 3.13 A *value parameter* is used when a primitive value is passed to a method. A *reference parameter* is used when an object is passed to a method.

EXERCISES

1. Fill in the blanks in each of the following sentences:

    a. When two different methods have the same name, this is an example of ______.
    b. Methods with the same name are distinguished by their ______.
    c. A method that is invoked when an object is created is known as a ______ method.
    d. A method whose purpose is to provide access to an object's instance variables is known as an ______ method.
    e. A `boolean` value is an example of a ______ type.
    f. A `CyberPet` variable is an example of a ______ type.
    g. A method's parameters have ______ scope.
    h. A class's instance variables have ______ scope.
    i. Generally, a class's instance variables should have ______ access.
    j. The methods that make up an object's interface should have ______ access.
    k. A method that returns no value should be declared ______.
    l. Java's if statement and if-else statement are both examples of ______ control structures.
    m. An expression that evaluates to either `true` or `false` is known as a ______.
    n. In an if-else statement, an else clause matches ______.
    o. The ability to use a superclass method in a subclass is due to Java's ______ mechanism.
    p. The process of redefining a superclass method in a subclass is known as ______ the method.

2. Explain the difference between the following pairs of concepts:

    a. *Parameter* and *argument*.
    b. *Method definition* and *method invocation*.
    c. *Local scope* and *class scope*.
    d. *Primitive type* and *reference type*.
    e. *Access method* and *constructor method*.

3. Translate each of the following into Java code.

a.
```
If b1 is true then print "one" otherwise print "two".
```

b.
```
If b1 is false then if b2 is true  then print "one" otherwise print "two".
```

c.
```
If b1 is false and if b2 is true  then print "one"
otherwise print "two" otherwise print "three."
```

4. Identify and fix the syntax errors in each of the following.

a.
```
if ( isWalking == true ) ;
   System.out.println("Walking");
else
   System.out.println("Not walking");
```

b.
```
if (isWalking)
    System.out.println("Walking")
else
    System.out.println("Not walking");
```

c.
```
if (isWalking)
    System.out.println("Walking");
else
    System.out.println("Not walking")
```

d.
```
if (isWalking = false)
    System.out.println("Walking");
else
    System.out.println("Not walking");
```

5. For each of the following, suppose that `isWalking` is `true` and `isTalking` is `false`. First draw a flowchart for each statement and then determine what would be printed by each statement.

a.
```
if (isWalking == false)
    System.out.println("One");
    System.out.println("Two");
```

b.
```
if (isWalking == true)
    System.out.println("One");
    System.out.println("Two");
```

c.
```
if (isWalking == false)
{
    System.out.println("One");
    System.out.println("Two");
}
```

d.
```
if (isWalking == false)
    if (isTalking == true)
        System.out.println("One");
    else
        System.out.println("Two");
else
    System.out.println("Three");
```

6. Show what would be output if the following version of `main()` method were executed.

```
public static void main(String argv[])  //  Execution starts here
{
    System.out.println("main() is starting");
    CyberPet pet1;
    pet1  = new CyberPet();
    CyberPet pet2;
    pet2 = new CyberPet();
    pet1.setName("Mary");          // Set pet1's name
    pet2.setName("Peter");         // Set pet2's name
    pet1.eat();                    // Tell pet1 to eat
    pet1.sleep();                  // Tell pet1 to sleep
    pet2.sleep();                  // Tell pet2 to sleep
    pet2.eat();                    // Tell pet2 to eat
    System.out.println("main() is finished");
    return;                        // Return to the system
}
```

7. **Dangling else**. For each of these unindented statements, first draw a flowchart of the statement and then determine its output assuming that `isWalking` is true and `isTalking` is false. Then rewrite the statements using proper indentation techniques. Recall that according to the syntax of the if-else statement an `else` matches the closest previous unmatched `if`.

a.
```
if (isWalking == true)
if (isTalking == true)
System.out.println("One");
else
System.out.println("Two");
System.out.println("Three");
```

b.
```
if (isWalking == true)
if (isTalking == true)
System.out.println("One");
else {
System.out.println("Two");
System.out.println("Three");
}
```

c.
```
if (isWalking == true) {
if (isTalking == true)
System.out.println("One");
}
else {
System.out.println("Two");
System.out.println("Three");
}
```

d.

```
if (isWalking == true)
if (isTalking == true)
System.out.println("One");
else
System.out.println("Two");
else
System.out.println("Three");
```

8. Determine the output of the following program.

```
public class Mystery
{
    public String myMethod(String s)
    {
        return("Hello" + s);
    }
    public static void main(String argv[])
    {
        Mystery mystery = new Mystery();
        System.out.println( mystery.myMethod(" dolly");
    }
}
```

9. Suppose you have the following method which contains a boolean parameter and a `CyberPet` parameter, where `CyberPet` is defined as shown in Fig 3–17:

```
public void myMethod(CyberPet p, boolean b)
{
    b = false;
    p.sleep();
}
```

What output would be produced by the following statements? Recall the distinction between *pass by value* and *pass by reference*.

```
CyberPet pet1 = new CyberPet("Socrates");
boolean isSocrates = true;
System.out.println(pet1.getState());
myMethod(pet1, isSocrates);
if (isSocrates == true)
    System.out.println(" Socrates");
else
    System.out.println(" NOT Socrates");
System.out.println(socrates.getState());
```

10. Write a `boolean` method—a method that returns a `boolean`—that takes an `int` parameter and converts the integers 0 and 1 into `false` and `true`, respectively.
11. Define an `int` method that takes a `boolean` parameter. If the parameter's value is `false`, the method should return 0; otherwise it should return 1.
12. Define a `void` method named `hello` that takes a single `boolean` parameter. The method should print "Hello" if its parameter is true; otherwise it should print "Goodbye."

13. Define a method named `hello` that takes a single `boolean` parameter. The method should return "Hello" if its parameter is true; otherwise it should return "Goodbye." Note the difference between this method and the one in the previous exercise. This one returns a `String`. That one was a `void` method.
14. Write a method named `hello` that takes a single `String` parameter. The method should return a `String` that consists of the word "Hello" concatenated with the value of its parameter. For example, if you call this method with the expression `hello(" dolly")`, it should return "hello dolly." If you call it with `hello(" young lovers wherever you are")`, it should return "hello young lovers wherever you are."
15. Define a void method named `day1` that prints "a partridge in a pear tree."
16. Write a Java application program called `TwelveDays` that prints the Christmas carol "Twelve Days of Christmas." For this version, write a void method name `intro()` that takes a single `String` parameter that gives the day of the verse and prints the intro to the song. For example, `intro("first")`, should print, "On the first day of Christmas my true love gave to me." Then write methods `day1()`, `day2()`, and so on, each of which prints its version of the verse. Then write a `main()` method that calls the other methods to print the whole song.
17. Define a `void` method named `verse` that takes two `String` parameters and returns a verse of the Christmas carol, "Twelve Days of Christmas." For example, if you call this method with `verse("first", "a partridge in a pear tree")`, it should return, "On the first day of Christmas my true love gave to me, a partridge in a pear tree."
18. Define a `void` method named `permute`, which takes three `String` parameters and prints out all possible arrangements of the three strings. For example, if you called `permute("a", "b", "c")`, it would produce the following output: abc, acb, bac, bca, cab, cba, with each permutation on a separate line.
19. Design a method that can produce limericks given a bunch of rhyming words. For example, if you call

```
limerick("Jones","stones","rained","pained","bones");
```

your method might print (something better than)

```
There once a person named Jones
Who had a great liking for stones,
But whenever it rained,
Jones' expression was pained,
Because stones weren't good for the bones.
```

20. Write a constructor method that can be used to set both the name and initial state of a `CyberPet`.
21. Write a constructor method that can be used to set a pet's initial state to something besides its default state. (Hint: Use boolean variables.)
22. Extend the definition of `CyberPet` so that a pet's state can have three possible values: eating, sleeping, and thinking. Modify any existing methods that need to be changed, and add the appropriate access methods for the new state.
23. **Challenge.** Add a *size* instance variable to `CyberPet`, making certain it can be set to either "big" or "small" through a constructor or an access method. Then write an `encounter(CyberPet)` method that allows one `CyberPet` to encounter another. Note that the method should take a `CyberPet` parameter. Depending on the size of the pet, the small pet should be chased by the larger pet or the two should befriend each other. This encounter should be described

with a returned `String`. For example, if you create two pets such that `pet1` is big and `pet2` is small, and then you invoke `pet1.encounter(pet2)`, it should return something like "I'm going to eat you."

For each of the following exercises, write a complete Java application program.

24. Define a class named `Donor` that takes has two instance variables, the donor's name and rating, both `Strings`. The name can be any string, but the rating should be one of the following values: "high," "medium," or "none." Write the following methods for this class: a constructor, `Donor(String,String)`, that allows you to set both the donor's name and rating; and access methods to set and get both the name and rating of a donor.
25. **Challenge.** Define a `CopyMonitor` class that solves the following problem. A company needs a monitor program to keep track of when a particular copy machine needs service. The device has two important (boolean) variables: its toner level (too low or not) and whether it has printed more than 100,000 pages since its last servicing (it either has or has not). The servicing rule that the company uses is that service is needed when either 100,000 pages have been printed or the toner is too low. Your program should contain a method that reports either "service needed" or "service not needed" based on the machine's state. (Pretend that the machine has other methods that keep track of toner level and page count.)
26. **Challenge.** Design and write an `OldMacdonald` class that sings several verses of "Old MacDonald Had a Farm." Use methods to generalize the verses. For example, write a method named `eieio()` to "sing" the "E I E I O" part of the verse. Write another method with the signature `hadAnX(String s)`, which sings the "had a duck" part of the verse, and a method `withA(String sound)` to sing the "with a quack quack here" part of the verse. Test your class by writing a `main()` method.

4

Applets: Programming for the World Wide Web

OBJECTIVES

After studying this chapter, you will

- Be able to design and implement a Java applet.
- Understand Java's event handling model.
- Be able to handle button clicks in your programs.
- Have a better appreciation of inheritance and polymorphism.
- Know how to design a simple Graphical User Interface (GUI).

OUTLINE

4.1 Introduction

An **applet** is a Java program embedded within a Web page and run by a *Web browser* such as Netscape Navigator or Internet Explorer. In Lab Exercise 1 (in Chapter 1), we compiled and executed `TimerApplet`, a playful applet that displayed how much time we wasted playing with the applet.

GUIs

As we saw in that example, one of the most attractive features of an applet is its **graphical user interface (GUI)**. Java applet programming makes it easy to build programs that use graphical components, like windows, menus, and control buttons, to interact with the user. You interact with a Java applet in much the same way as you interact with a Web browser — by using pull-down menus, clicking buttons, and entering text into text fields. And just as with the browser itself, Java applets can handle *multimedia* resources — sound, graphics, and video.

Java applets derive much of their power from two key features of object oriented programming: *class inheritance* and *method polymorphism*. In this chapter we will look at these mechanisms.

event-driven programming

Java applet programming is also *event-driven programming*. A Java applet reacts to events, such as mouse clicks and key presses, that occur in the browser interface. We will therefore take a look at Java's *event model* and learn how to write programs that can handle simple events.

This chapter introduces the basics of Java applet programming. We begin by studying a very simple applet, `SimpleApplet`, which introduces the basic elements of applet programming. We then design and build `CyberPetApplet`, an applet that provides a GUI interface for our `CyberPet` simulation. The interface will contain *eat* and *sleep* buttons corresponding to each of the `CyberPet`'s commands and a text field that display's the `CyberPet`'s name and state.

This chapter introduces no new statements, control structures, or types of data. Instead, it seeks to provide a good grounding in fundamentals of event-driven GUI programming.

4.2 The `Applet` Class

The `java.applet.Applet` class is part of Java's class library or **Application Programming Interface (API)**. A partial definition of `Applet` is shown in Fig 4–1. Because applets run within the context of a browser, most of the `Applet`'s public methods serve to define an interface between the applet and its browser environment. There are methods that get the applet's URL [`getDocumentBase()`], methods that enable the applet to play audio files and load images [`play()`, `getImage()`], and methods that control the applet's execution [`init()`, `start()`, and `stop()`].

4.2.1 Java's GUI Components

AWT and Swing components

Java's API contains two complete sets of buttons, menus, text fields, checkboxes, and other GUI components: the *Abstract Windowing Toolkit (AWT)* and the *Swing component set*. The AWT has been part of Java since version 1.0. The Swing component set was introduced in version 1.2. Because

Figure 4–1 Partial definition of the Applet class.

```
public class Applet extends Panel
{
  // Public instance methods
    public URL getDocumentBase();              // Get the applet's URL
    public String getParameter(String name); // Get an applet parameter

    public Image getImage(URL url, String name); // Load an image
    public AudioClip getAudioClip(URL url);      // Load an audio file
    public void play(URL url);                   // Play an audio clip

    public void init();                        // Initialize the applet
    public void start();                       // Begin execution
    public void stop();                        // Stop execution
}
```

the AWT model is somewhat simpler than Swing, we will introduce the AWT components in this chapter. However, the Swing components provide greater functionality and address some of the limitations of the AWT. Therefore, in Chapter 9 we'll give a full treatment of the Swing components.

The components in the AWT package (`java.awt`) are organized into a class hierarchy , part of which is shown in Fig 4–2. As the hierarchy illustrates, an `Applet` *is a* type of `Panel`, which *is a* type of `Container`. As you might expect, a `Container` is a `Component` that can contain other `Components`, so an `Applet` can contain `Buttons`, `TextFields` and other types of `Components`. Note that the `Component` class is a subclass of `Object` and that the `Button`, `Label`, `Container`, and `TextField` classes are all subclasses of the `Component` class.

4.2.2 Class Inheritance

Inheritance

Inheritance is the mechanism by which a class of objects can acquire the methods and variables of its superclasses. An object of a subclass is said to inherit the functionality of all of its superclasses. On page 152 we showed how all classes in the Java hierarchy inherit the `toString()` method from the `Object` class. The lesson there was that an object in a subclass can use (or override) any `public` method defined in any of its superclasses. In this chapter we want to look at other ways to employ inheritance. In particular, we show that a new class can be defined by *extending* an existing class.

We noted in Chapter 2 that if a class's *pedigree* is not specified in the class definition, the class is assumed to be a direct subclass of `Object`. This would apply to our definition of `CyberPet`. We can make `CyberPet`'s pedigree explicit by changing its header declaration to

```
public class CyberPet extends Object { ... }
```

The `extends` keyword specifies explicitly that `CyberPet` is a direct subclass of `Object`.

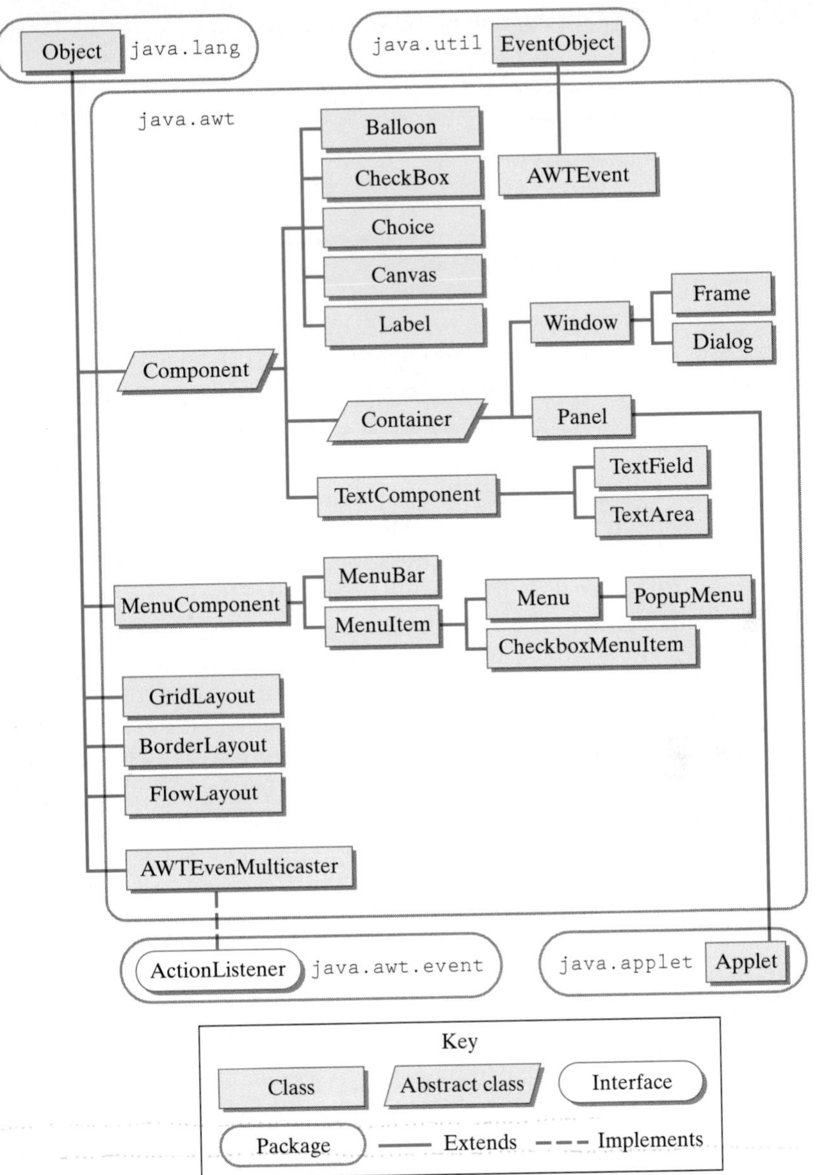

Figure 4–2 Part of Java's *Abstract Windowing Toolkit (AWT)* hierarchy.

The `extends` keyword is used to specify the subclass/superclass relationships that hold in the Java class hierarchy. It is used to define the *is a* relationship among objects in a class hierarchy. Thus, since `Applet` *is a* subclass of `Panel`, its class definition takes the following form:

```
public class Applet extends Panel { ... }
```

Similarly, the definitions of the Panel, Container, and Button classes would take the following forms

```
public class Panel extends Container { ... }
public class Container extends Component { ... }
public class Button extends Component { ... }
```

to reflect their places in the class hierarchy.

Extending a class in this way enables us to create a new class by specializing an existing class. Recall that in our software ordering example from Chapter 1, we talked about a sales agent as an expert in helping a customer order something from Acme's catalog. Suppose now that Acme grows so large it needs to have some sales agents who are experts in software and some who are experts in hardware. To acquire these kinds of experts, it would be good company policy to train some of the existing agents to acquire these new specialties, rather than to train a new person entirely from scratch.

Specialization

In the same way, if SalesAgent were an existing Java class, we could use it as the basis for definitions of SoftwareSalesAgent and HardwareSalesAgent:

```
public class SoftwareSalesAgent extends SalesAgent { ... }
public class HardwareSalesAgent extends SalesAgent { ... }
```

As subclasses of SalesAgent, these new classes would inherit its public and protected elements. So if SalesAgent had a getCreditCardNumber() method, they could make use of this method. But they could also be given new elements (methods and variables) that would support their new specialties. The SoftwareSalesAgent might be given a new method displaySoftwareList() to help it describe software products to a customer.

4.2.3 The Square Class

To see better how inheritance works in Java, let's define a Square as an extension of the Rectangle class we defined in Chapter 2. Before we can do that however, we must revise Rectangle so that its instance variables are protected. This will make them accessible to the Square class. Given this modification of Rectangle we can define a Square as shown in Fig 4–3.

protected *elements*

JAVA LANGUAGE RULE **Inheritance.** Only protected and public elements can be inherited. Elements declared private are not inherited by the subclass.

Since Square inherits length, width, and calculateArea() from Rectangle, all we really need to define is a Square() constructor method. The only new Java language introduced here is the keyword super, which we use in Square() to invoke Rectangle's constructor. The expression

```
super(side, side);
```

super keyword

invokes the superclass's constructor method, passing it side as both its length and width parameters. This is equivalent to invoking Rectangle(side,side) which has the effect of setting both length and width to side. Thus, according to this definition, a square is a rectangle whose length and width are equal.

> **JAVA LANGUAGE RULE** **super.** The super keyword is used to invoke an object's superclass constructor. You can think of it as shorthand for the name of the superclass.

The TestSquare class shown in Fig 4–4 illustrates how we can use Square. We instantiate Square by calling its constructor and passing it 100 as the length of its side. When we subsequently invoke square.calculateArea(), it will calculate its area as 100 x 100, as the following output shows:

```
square's area is 10000.0
```

Thus, we have used Java's inheritance mechanism to define an entirely new class, Square, by extending an existing class, Rectangle.

SELF-STUDY EXERCISES

EXERCISE 4.1 Given the definitions of Rectangle and Square (Fig 4–3), write a public method named calcPerimeter() for the Rectangle class.

Figure 4–3 The Rectangle and Square classes. Note that Square is a subclass of Rectangle.

```
public class Rectangle
{
    protected double length;     // Instance variables
    protected double width;

    public Rectangle(double l, double w)  // Constructor method
    {
        length = l;
        width = w;
    } // Rectangle constructor

    public double calculateArea()         // Access method
    {
        return length * width;
    } // calculateArea

} // Rectangle class

public class Square extends Rectangle // Subclass of Rectangle
{
    public Square(double side)
    {
        super(side,side);        // Call Rectangle's Constructor
    }
} // Square
```

Figure 4–4 The `TestSquare` class.

```
public class TestSquare
{
    public static void main(String argv[])
    {
        Square square = new Square ( 100 );
        System.out.println( "square's area is " + square.calculateArea() );
    }
} // TestSquare
```

It should take no parameters and should return a `double` representing the rectangle's perimeter — the sum of its four sides.

EXERCISE 4.2 Given the definition of the `calcPerimeter()` method from the previous exercise, write Java code that would be added to the `main()` method in `TestSquare` (Fig 4–4) that prints out `square`'s perimeter.

EXERCISE 4.3 Explain how the inheritance mechanism works in the example from the previous exercise.

4.3 Applet Subclasses

Instantiating vs. extending

Some classes in the Java hierarchy are designed to be *extended* rather than *instantiated* directly. In other words, some classes are designed to be used as the basis for defining subclasses (extended), whereas others are designed to be used as the basis for creating instance objects (instantiated). For example, `CyberPet` and `Rectangle` were designed to be directly instantiated:

Instantiating a `CyberPet`

```
CyberPet pet1 = new CyberPet();        // Create an instance
Rectangle rect1 = new Rectangle();
```

These declarations create `pet1` and `rect1` as objects (or instances) of the `Cyberpet` and `Rectangle` class, respectively. Similarly, classes such as `Button` and `TextField` are also designed to be directly instantiated:

Instantiating a `Button`

```
Button b1 = new Button();              // Create an instance
TextField field1 = new TextField();
```

In contrast to these examples, applets are not directly instantiated. In other words, you will never see a declaration such as the following:

```
Applet a = new Applet(); // Not the way to do it!
```

in which we directly create an instance of the `Applet` class.

Instead, applets are made by first defining a subclass of `Applet` and then creating an instance of the subclass. In general outline at least, writing Java applets takes the following form:

Extending the `Applet` *class*

```
public class AppletSubclass extends Applet { ... } // Define a subclass
AppletSubclass myApplet = new AppletSubclass();    // and instantiate it
```

Thus we first define the `AppletSubclass` as a subclass of `Applet` and then use it as the basis for creating instances.

> **JAVA LANGUAGE RULE** **Creating an Applet.** A Java applet is an object that is created by first defining a subclass of `Applet` and then creating an instance of the subclass.

Embedded programs

The reason for doing things this way is somewhat complicated, which is why we have delayed discussing it until now. It has to do with an applet's special status as an *embedded program* — that is, a program that runs within the context of a Web browser. Applets have to be constructed in such a way that they can be instantiated and executed by the browser . *Class inheritance* and *method polymorphism* make this possible. This will become clearer in the next sections.

4.4 A Simple Applet

Let's create a simple applet and examine how it works. The applet shown in Fig 4–5 consists of a button which is initially labeled "The machine is off." Each time the button is clicked, its label changes from "The machine is off" to "The machine is on," and vice versa.

Java library packages

The Java code for this applet is shown in Fig 4–6. The first three lines of the program `import` from the `java.applet`, `java.awt`, and `java.awt.event` packages.

```
import java.applet.*;
import java.awt.*;
import java.awt.event.*;
```

The first package , `java.applet`, contains the definition of the `Applet` class. The second package, `java.awt`, contains the definition of the `Button` class. The third package, `java.awt.event`, contains the definition of the `ActionListener` interface. (A Java interface is like a class but contains only methods, not instance variables.) Class definitions from these packages are used whenever the compiler comes to a term, such as `Button` or `Applet`, which is neither a Java keyword nor a class defined within the `SimpleApplet` program itself.

For example, the following declaration occurs at the beginning of the `SimpleApplet` definition:

```
private Button toggle;
```

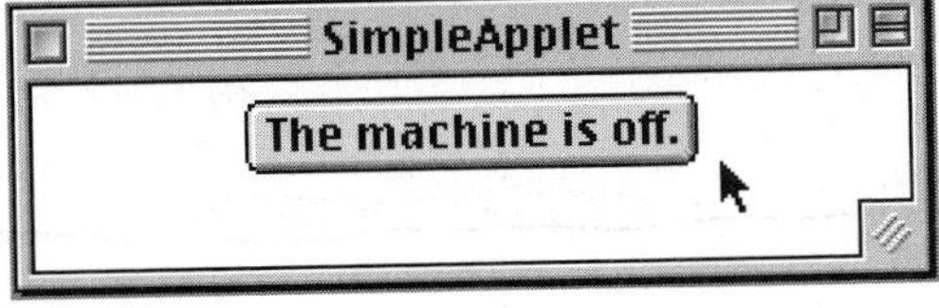

Figure 4–5 A simple Java applet. Each time the user clicks on the button, its label changes from "The machine is on" to "The machine is off."

Figure 4–6 Defining a simple applet.

```
import java.applet.*;
import java.awt.*;
import java.awt.event.*;

public class SimpleApplet extends Applet implements ActionListener
{
    private Button toggle;          // From java.awt.*

    public void init()
    {
        toggle = new Button ("The machine is off");
        toggle.addActionListener(this);
        add(toggle);
    } // init()

    public void actionPerformed(ActionEvent e)
    {
        String str = toggle.getLabel();   // Get the toggle Button's label
        if (str.equals("The machine is on"))      // and change it
            toggle.setLabel("The machine is off");
        else                                      // or
            toggle.setLabel("The machine is on"); // change it back
    } // actionPerformed()
} // SimpleApplet
```

In this statement, when the Java compiler encounters the identifier `Button`, it will search the imported packages for its definition. The wildcard asterisk in the package names (*) tells the compiler to look for undefined names in all the class definitions contained in the `java.applet`, `java.awt`, or `java.awt.event` packages. For beginning programmers it is better to use the wild card, because that way all the classes in a package can be used by the compiler. This will lead to fewer "undefined identifier" errors.

JAVA LANGUAGE RULE **Import Statement.** The `import` statement is used to import names and definitions for library classes and methods used in the program. Its general form is *import packagename.classname*. The wild card character (*) can be used in place of *classname* to include all the classes in a package.

DEBUGGING TIP:Not Found Error. A class or method not found error will occur if you use a library class or method without importing its definition.

4.4.1 Inheriting Functionality

The next line in the program is the header of the class definition:

```
public class SimpleApplet extends Applet implements ActionListener
```

Explicit pedigree

Unlike the other examples we have seen, this class header provides an explicit description of `SimpleApplet`'s *pedigree*:

```
extends Applet implements ActionListener
```

The `extends` keyword here defines `SimpleApplet` as a subclass of `Applet`.This means `SimpleApplet` inherits the functionality defined in `Applet`. Whatever an `Applet` can do, a `SimpleApplet` can do.

Similarly, the significance of the `implements` keyword here is to define `SimpleApplet` as an implementor of one or more methods inherited from the `ActionListener` interface.

Inheritance mechanisms: Extending and implementing

Both `extends` and `implements` are inheritance mechanisms in Java. Together they provide the chief means by which Java programs (applets and applications) can make use of the predefined functionality contained in the Java API. Let's take a careful look at each of these mechanisms.

Extending a Superclass

By *extending* `Applet`, `SimpleApplet` acquires several public methods that define its interface with the Web browser, including the `play()` method, which can be used to play audio clips:

```
public void play(URL url)
```

As its signature indicates, `play()` takes an audio file's `URL` (or address specification) and plays the sounds defined in the file. Obviously, if we had to write the Java code needed to play an audio file, it would be very complicated. The fact that `Applet` has already defined `play()` means that our `SimpleApplet` can play an audio file by simply calling this method and passing it the file's URL:

```
play("Hello.au");
```

Inheriting functionality

This is an example of *inheriting functionality*. `SimpleApplet` inherits all of `Applet`'s functionality and is able to use any of `Applet`'s `public` and `protected` methods *as if they were its own.*

It's important to note that this inheritance mechanism extends all the way up the Java object hierarchy. Thus, `SimpleApplet` inherits functionality from all of its superclasses — from `Applet`, `Panel`, `Container`, `Component`, and `Object` (Fig 4–7). Thus, the `add()` method, which is defined in the `Container` class, is used to add a `Component` to a `Container`:

```
public Component add(Component comp)
```

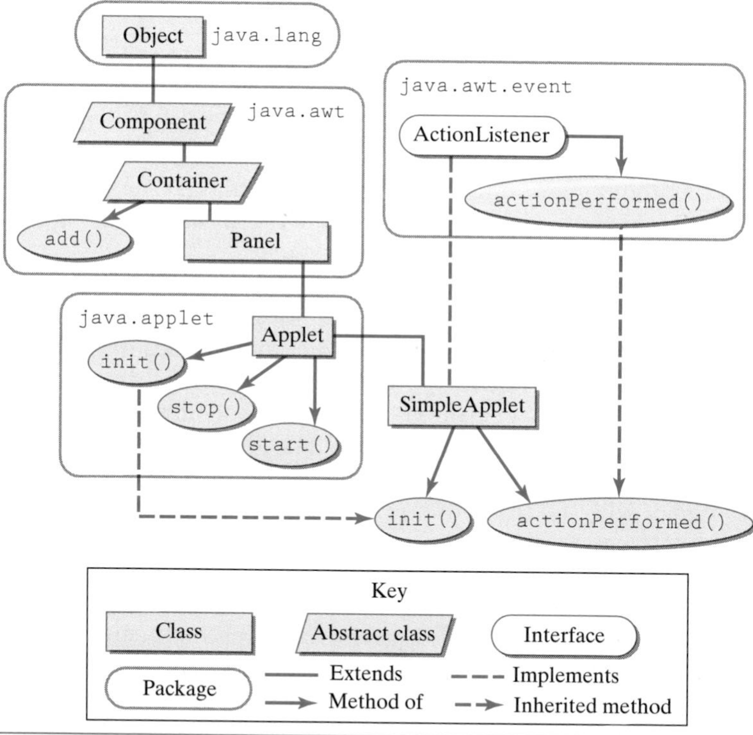

Figure 4–7 Hierarchy showing the position of the SimpleApplet in the Java class hierarchy . Note that both of its methods are inherited (dashed arrows).

The `Component` is passed as the value of its parameter. Because a `SimpleApplet` is a `Container`, it can use `add()` to add components to itself.

For example, in `SimpleApplet`'s `init()` method, the following code adds the `toggle` `Button` to the applet:

```
public void init()
{
    toggle = new Button ("The machine is off");
    ... // Code omitted here
    add(toggle);
} // init()
```

Components that are added to an applet will be displayed when the applet itself is executed (Fig 4–5).

EFFECTIVE DESIGN: The Inheritance Principle. An object of a particular subclass can use the `public` and `protected` methods and variables of any of its superclasses. The object *inherits* the functionality contained in its superclasses.

4.4.2 Implementing an Interface

Java interfaces

A Java **interface** is like a class but it contains only methods and constants (`final` variables). It cannot contain instance variables. The designer of an interface specifies what methods are supported by the classes that *implement* the interface. In the interface definition, the methods are defined abstractly — without specifying the body of the method. The method's body — its implementation — is defined within those classes that implement the method.

The idea of an `interface` corresponds to what we've been saying all along about the role that methods play in defining an object's interface. Methods in a Java class are like the buttons on your clothes dryer; they define the dryer's actions or behavior. If you want to tell the dryer to use the permanent press cycle, you press the "Permanent Press" button. If your dryer doesn't contain a "Spin Only" button, then there's no way to tell it to spin the clothes without heat. The dryer's buttons constrain the way you interact with the dryer in much the way that a class's methods constrain the way you interact with its objects.

Interfaces vs. classes

One use of an `interface` is to define methods that can extend the functionality of a variety of different classes. Defining a class that implements an interface, allows the class to attach the methods contained in the interface. This would be something like installing a "Spin Only" button on your dryer. By wiring it up in the correct way, you can add this new functionality to a dryer which previously lacked the ability to spin clothes with the heat turned off.

Java's `ActionListener` interface is an example of this kind of extension to a class. It adds `actionPerformed()`, a method that enables objects to perform actions in response to events, such as mouse clicks, that happen during the running of the program:

```
public abstract interface ActionListener extends EventListener
{
    // Public Instance Methods
    public abstract void actionPerformed(ActionEvent e);
}
```

Abstract methods

Note that instead of using the keyword `class` in its definition, `ActionListener` uses the keyword `interface` to indicate that it is an interface. The definition also designates `ActionListener` as an `abstract` interface, which means that it contains *abstract* methods — methods that do not have method bodies. For example, `ActionListener` contains only a single method definition:

```
// Public Instance Methods
public abstract void actionPerformed(ActionEvent e);
```

Declaring this method as `abstract` means that it lacks a method body and that its implementation will be left to the class that *implements* it. Its signature specifies what the method should do. In this case, `actionPer-`

formed() should take an ActionEvent object named *e* and perform some kind of action. Of course, the details of the action performed are left to the implementor.

SimpleApplet provides the following implementation of actionPerformed:

```
public void actionPerformed(ActionEvent e)
{
    String str = toggle.getLabel();            // Get the toggle Button's label
    if (str.equals("The machine is on"))       // and change it
        toggle.setLabel("The machine is off");
    else                                       // or
        toggle.setLabel("The machine is on");  // change it back
} // actionPerformed()
```

Note that the header in this definition has exactly the same declaration as the abstract definition given in the ActionListener interface. All we have added to the method is its body, the list of executable statements that specifies, for this program, what action should be performed when a button is clicked. We have thus implemented the actionPerformed() method in a way that is appropriate to SimpleApplet.

Implementing an abstract method

JAVA LANGUAGE RULE **Implementing an Interface.** Implementing an interface means filling in the details in the method body for each abstract method defined in the interface.

4.4.3 Extending Functionality

In addition to inheriting functionality from its superclasses and interfaces, a subclass, such as SimpleApplet, also extends the functionality of its superclasses and interfaces.

An Applet is an executable object that can be run from within a Web browser. Therefore it contains methods that the browser can invoke to init(), start(), and stop() applets. These methods, which are are defined in Applet, are meant to be *overridden* or *redefined* in its subclasses:

Stub methods

```
public class Applet extends Panel  // Partial definition
{   ...
    public void init() { }    // Stub methods, trivial bodies
    public void start() { }
    public void stop() { }
    ...
}
```

To *override* a stub predefined method, a method with the exact same signature must be defined in the subclass, as in this example of init():

```
public void init ()
{
    toggle = new Button ("The machine is off");
    toggle.addActionListener(this);
    add(toggle);
} // init()
```

The role of the `init()` method is to *initialize* the applet, which usually consists of initializing its instance variables, creating and initializing its various components, and adding them to the applet. For this program, the only instance variable is `toggle`, a `Button` which is created and then added to the applet.

The first statement in `init()` creates a `Button` labeled "The machine is off." The second statement registers the `toggle` with the object that will respond to its clicks. (We'll explain more about this later.) The third statement adds `toggle` to the applet. These are the only initialization steps necessary for `SimpleApplet`.

The `init()` method is called to start the applet

The `init()` method is an example of a method you will never invoke in your program. Instead, `init()` is called automatically *by the browser* when the applet is executed. When you run a Java applet from within a browser (or appletviewer), the browser creates an instance of the applet and begins its execution by calling the applet's `init()` method. For example, suppose the browser uses names such as `applet1`, `applet2`, and so on to name the applets it creates. Then the following code segment illustrates how the browser would begin execution of `SimpleApplet`:

```
SimpleApplet applet1 = new SimpleApplet(); // Create an instance
applet1.init();                            //  and initialize it
```

The first statement in this example creates an instance of `SimpleApplet`. The second calls `applet1`'s `init()` method, which creates a `Button` named `toggle` and adds it to `applet1`.

EFFECTIVE DESIGN: The Extensibility Principle. A class definition extends the functionality of its superclass by *overriding* or *redefining* its methods.

The `actionPerformed()` method is called to handle action events

A similar mechanism is at work in the case of the `actionPerformed()` method. `SimpleApplet` implements this method by defining its method body. But `actionPerformed()` is another example of a method you will never directly invoke in your programs. Instead, Java automatically invokes `actionPerformed()` whenever a `Button` is clicked. By just implementing `actionPerformed()` with statements that pertain to `toggle`, we can get `SimpleApplet` to take appropriate action whenever `toggle` is clicked.

4.4.4 Using the Inheritance Hierarchy

Java's default behavior

What if we had forgotten to override the `init()` method? When `applet1.init()` is called by the browser, Java first tries to find it in `SimpleApplet`—that is, in the class to which `applet1` belongs. If Java doesn't find it there, it looks in `SimpleApplet`'s parent class, which is `Applet`. What Java finds in `Applet` is the stub version of `init()`, which it then executes. Of course, because this version of `init()` is a stub method that does nothing, no components would be created and nothing would be added to the applet. Thus Java uses an object's **inheritance hierarchy** to determine which method to run when a method associated with the object is invoked.

To see this mechanism at work again, consider what happens when the `add()` method is invoked in `SimpleApplet`'s `init()` method:

```
add(toggle);
```

This method invocation does not include a receiving object, and so it is assumed to pertain to *this* object — that is, to `applet1`, the `SimpleApplet`. Thus Java will look in `SimpleApplet`'s class definition for an `add()` method. Not finding one there, Java will look in `SimpleApplet`'s parent class, `Applet`. Not finding one there either, Java will continue up `SimpleApplet`'s inheritance hierarchy until it finds an `add()` method. According to Fig 4–7, the `add()` method is defined in the `Container` class. So Java will use the method definition given there, which describes how to add a `Component` (in this case `toggle`) to a `Container` (in this case `applet1`). Thus, in this case, `applet1` uses functionality inherited from the `Container` class to perform the task of adding a component to itself.

JAVA LANGUAGE RULE **Inheritance.** Java uses an object's *inheritance hierarchy* to resolve method invocations associated with the object. It searches up the object's hierarchy until the method is found.

What if we had forgotten to implement the `actionPerformed()` method? In this case, `SimpleApplet` won't compile successfully. It is a syntax error to declare that a class `implements` some interface without providing an implementation for *all* the methods defined in that interface . Thus in `SimpleApplet`, we must provide a full definition of the `actionPerformed()` method.

JAVA LANGUAGE RULE **interface.** An `interface` is like a class but it contains only instance methods and constant fields — that is, `public static final` fields. It cannot contain instance variables. If a class `implements` an interface, all the methods from the interface must be implemented in the class.

Stub vs. abstract methods

This also points up the difference between a *stub method* , such as `init()`, and an **abstract method** , such as `actionPerformed()`. A stub method *has* an implementation, but the implementation is trivial — one that will "work" with any of a class's subclasses. By contrast, an abstract method has *no* implementation. Any class which implements such a method must therefore define its body or the program simply won't compile.

4.4.5 Polymorphism and Extensibility

One question that might occur to you is why we bother to define the `init()` method in the `Applet` class if we're just going to override it in its subclasses. The answer holds the key to understanding how applets work.

Extensible systems

Java applets are an excellent example of an *extensible* system — a system that is designed to work on objects that have yet to be defined. Because any applet — any object that belongs to a subclass of the `Applet` class — has `init()`, `start()`, and `stop()` methods, it can be executed by a Web browser. If the applet redefines these inherited methods, it can customize its performance to suit its purposes. If it fails to redefine these methods, then stub methods, defined in its superclasses, will be used when the browser invokes `applet1.init()` or `applet1.start()`. In either case, the applet will run successfully within the browser's context. If the applet does not redefine inherited methods, then its functionality will be trivial — that is, it won't really do anything. However, if the methods are overridden, the applet can significantly extend what its superclasses do.

By thus designing a system that will process generic `Applets` — applets that do nothing — we also have a system that will process `SimpleApplets` and all other subclasses of `Applet`. Java's applet system is *extensible*. By designing certain functionality into the superclass, we can extend a system to its subclasses — indeed, to subclasses that are not yet defined.

EFFECTIVE DESIGN: The Extensibility Mechanism. Generic functionality designed into a superclass can be extended to its subclasses by *overriding* its stub methods.

Method polymorphism

Methods such as `init()` are known as *polymorphic* methods. The term **polymorphism** is from the Greek roots *poly-*, which means many, and *morph-*, which means forms. So literally the term means *having multiple forms*. Obviously, because `init()` is intended to be overridden in every subclass of `Applet`, it will have many forms. Thus we have a single method that is called whenever an applet is started, but one which has many forms depending on how it is redefined in each subclass. Any method that performs some sort of operation — such as initialization of an applet — on different types of objects — such as on different subclasses of `Applet` — is said to be polymorphic. By redefining `init()` in every `Applet` subclass, we end up with a method that performs the same operation (initialize) on many different types of objects.

Object-oriented design

In later chapters we'll see other examples of inheritance and polymorphism. When used with objects and classes, both inheritance and polymorphism are important principles of object-oriented design. They can be used to design systems of objects that can be extended to accommodate new objects without ever needing revision or recompilation. In this way class libraries, such as the applet package, can be created once and used to build a whole range of objects that inherit and extend the generic features of their superclasses.

EFFECTIVE DESIGN: Object-Oriented Design *Class inheritance* and *polymorphism* can be used to design *extensible* systems — that is, systems that inherit and extend the functionality of their superclasses.

SELF-STUDY EXERCISES

EXERCISE 4.4 The HTML files that contain applets can have tags that supply information to the applet. These are called parameters. The `Applet` class contains a method named `getParameter()` (Fig 4–1) that enables the applet to get a parameter that's defined by name in the applet's HTML file. For example, suppose that `SimpleApplet` (Fig 4–6) had an HTML file containing the following HTML code:

```
<html>
 <head><title>Simple Applet</title></head>
 <body>
  <applet code="SimpleApplet.class" width=200 height=200>
    <parameter name="author" value="Java Java Java">
    <parameter name="date" value="February 1999">
  </applet>
 </body>
</html>
```

Add statements to `SimpleApplet`'s `init()` method to print the values of the `"author"` and `"date"` parameters. Just use `System.out.println()`.

EXERCISE 4.5 Define an applet named `SmallApplet` that simply displays a `Button` with the label "Click me!" Don't worry about the applet's `actionPerformed()` method.

EXERCISE 4.6 Add a statement to the applet you defined in the previous problem to print your button's label in the `init()` method.

EXERCISE 4.7 Java's + operator is also polymorphic. Explain.

4.5 Event-Driven Programming

Java applets run under an **event-driven** execution model (Fig 4–8). According to this model, anything that happens while the computer is running is classified as an event. Every keystroke and mouse click, every time a disk is inserted into a disk drive, every time you close a window on the screen, an event is generated. The computer hardware is designed to encode and classify these events so that they can be handled by the system software — either the operating system (such as Windows, Unix, MacOS) or the browser (such as Navigator, Explorer).

Events drive the program

When a regular application program is running, including a Java application, events generated by the hardware are first passed up to the operating system. The operating system handles those events for which it is responsible and passes any events that it doesn't handle to the application program.

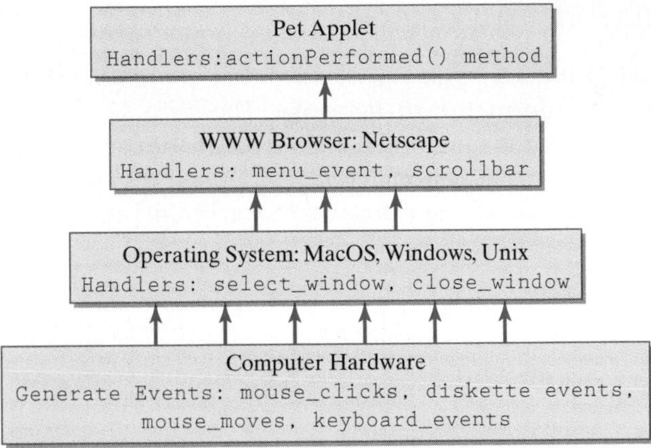

Figure 4–8 Java's event model.

Mouse events

For example, if you are running a word processor, whenever you click the mouse on an object that's outside of the word processor's window, that event will be handled by the operating system. Thus, the event generated by clicking in the window of another application (an E-mail program, say) will cause the operating system to transfer control from the word processor to the E-mail program.

Key events

On the other hand, if you then type a character in the word processor window, that event will be passed up through the operating system to the word processing application, where it is handled appropriately. In modern windowing environments, such as MacOS and Windows, all applications are event-driven, which means that all applications are designed to handle those events that fall under their responsibility.

Handling events

The same sort of thing happens with a Java applet, except that with applets, the browser becomes another level of software residing between your applet and the computer hardware (Fig 4–8). Events generated by the hardware are passed up through the operating system to the browser, which handles those events that apply to the browser itself. Events that apply to the applet are passed on to it. When the applet receives an event, it must handle the event in an appropriate way. If you click on your browser's menu bar or on its *reload* button, that event will be handled by the browser itself. If you click on an applet's button, for example, the `toggle` button in `SimpleApplet`, that event will be handled by the applet.

4.5.1 The Java Event Model

Java's event hierarchy

In Java, all events are represented by a subclass of the `java.util.EventObject` class. Events that happen as part of an applet's interface, AWT events, are defined as subclasses of `java.awt.AWTEvent`, which is a subclass of `EventObject`. For example, a `Button` can be the source of `ActionEvents` and `MouseEvents`, both of which are generated whenever the user clicks on the `Button`. Similarly, a `TextField` object can be the source of `ActionEvents`, `KeyEvents` and `TextEvents`, all of which are generated whenever the user types a key inside the `TextField`.

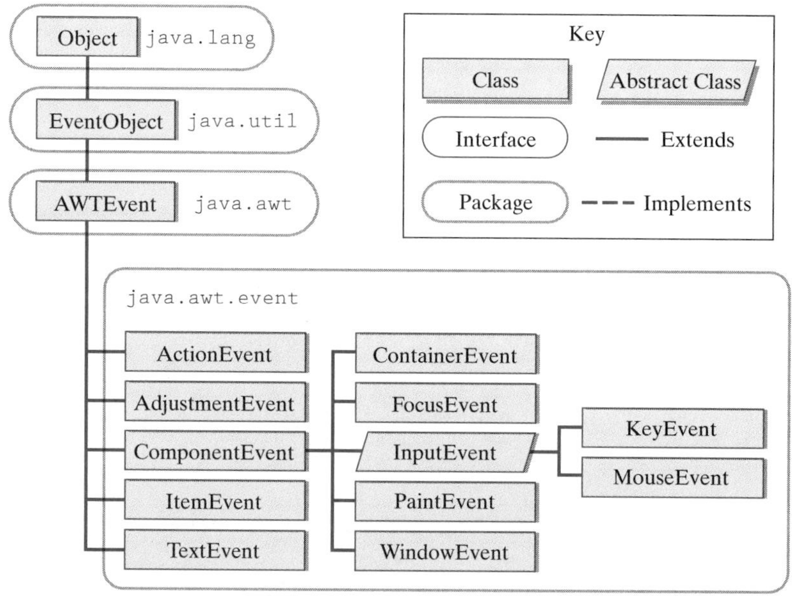

Figure 4–9 Java's event hierarchy.

Fig 4–9 shows Java's `EventObject` hierarchy. Each time an event occurs, some type of `EventObject` is created to represent the event. Among other things the `EventObject` records the *source* of the event — the object in which the event happened — the time and location of the event, and so on. For example, when the user types a key on the keyboard, a KEY_PRESS event and KEY_RELEASE event are generated in quick succession. The `KeyEvent` objects created in these two cases would record when the event happened, what key was pressed and released, and whether any special keys, such as the SHIFT key, were also pressed at the same time.

Similarly, when the user moves the mouse in the applet's window, a MOUSE_MOVE event is generated to indicate that the mouse has been moved, and a `MouseEvent` object is created to keep track of the mouse's horizontal and vertical window coordinates.

Multiple events

If you point the mouse at a button on the applet and then click it, this indicates to Java that you wish to take whatever action is associated with the button. The `ActionEvent` object created for this event will record the source of the mouse click — which button was clicked. A single mouse click on a `Button` will generate both mouse events and action events. It is possible to handle one or the other or both of these types of events, depending on what the applet is supposed to do. In `SimpleApplet`, we handle the action event and simply ignore mouse events. When we study drawing programs later in the book, we'll learn how to handle the lower-level mouse events.

Tracing a button click

Let's trace what happens when the user clicks on the `toggle Button` in `SimpleApplet`. When the user clicks on `toggle`, this generates an ACTION_EVENT. Java will automatically create a new `ActionEvent` object with appropriate information about this particular event — what object was

was clicked, and so on — and pass it to the `actionPerformed()` method in the object designated as `toggle`'s `ActionListener`. As its name suggests, an `ActionListener` is an object that listens for action events. It is the object that you designate in the program to handle that particular type of event. Let's see how we tell Java which object will serve as the action listener.

Button actions

Whenever we create a `Button`, we must tell Java which object will handle its actions. We do that in the `init()` method by designating an `ActionListener` for `toggle`:

```
toggle.addActionListener(this);
```

The `addActionListener()` method is defined in `Button` and has the following signature:

```
public void addActionListener(ActionListener l);
```

An `addActionLister()` takes a single parameter of type `ActionListener`. An `ActionListener` is any object whose class implements the `ActionListener` interface. Because `SimpleApplet` is such a class, *this* instantiation of it counts as an `ActionListener` and can be designated as the listener for clicks on `toggle`. Note that `this` is a Java keyword that refers to the current object — the object which executes the `this` statement.

JAVA LANGUAGE RULE **this.** The `this` keyword is self-referential. It refers to whichever object uses the term. It is similar to saying "me" or "I."

Event objects are passed to listener objects

So any clicks on `toggle` will generate an `ActionEvent` that will be passed to the `actionPerformed()` method implemented in `SimpleApplet`. Let's look at the details of that method:

```
public void actionPerformed(ActionEvent e)
{
    String str = toggle.getLabel();              // Get the toggle Button's label
    if (str.equals("The machine is on"))         // and change it
        toggle.setLabel("The machine is off");
    else                                         // or
        toggle.setLabel("The machine is on");    // change it back
} // actionPerformed()
```

The event handler

So `actionPerformed()` begins by getting `toggle`'s label and assigns it to the `String` variable `str`. It then checks whether `str` equals "The machine is on" or "The machine is off" and changes it to its opposite value using the `setLabel()` method. Recall here that `setLabel()` and `getLabel()` are methods defined in the `Button` class.

In this case, because `toggle` is the only object in `SimpleApplet` that generates `ActionEvents`, we know that it must have been clicked in order for `actionPerformed()` to have been invoked by the browser. Therefore we can proceed directly to toggling its label from "The machine is off" to "The machine is on," or vice versa. (As we will see, in other cases `actionPerformed()` may be handling events for several different buttons, in which case we would have to determine which button was clicked before taking action.)

The action taken whenever `toggle` is clicked is very simple. However, the Java code required to effect this action is somewhat complicated, and it is important that you understand how it works. Thus to create a `Button` on an applet and handle its actions appropriately, the following steps must be taken:

Creating and handling a button

1. Declare a subclass of `Applet` that implements the `ActionListener` interface.
2. Declare a `Button` instance variable in the applet.
3. Create a `Button` object in the applet's `init()` method.
4. Use `addActionListener()` to designate in the `init()` method that `this` applet is the listener for the `Button`.
5. Use the `add()` method to add the `Button` to the applet (in `init()`).
6. Implement an `actionPerformed()` method in the applet with the particular actions that you want performed each time the `Button` is clicked.

As our applets get more sophisticated in their design and behavior we will add steps to this process, but the overall outline of the code will remain more or less as described here.

4.5.2 Tracing an Applet

As we have said, as long as `SimpleApplet` is running, any events that happen within its window will be passed to it. If the event is an `ACTION\_EVENT`, such as a click on the `toggle` button, it will be passed to its `actionPerformed()` method, where appropriate action will be taken. In effect, after the applet is initialized, it will do nothing until it is passed an `ActionEvent` that indicates that the user has clicked on `toggle`, in which case it will spring into action and change `toggle`'s label. This behavior will continue until the applet is destroyed.

Fig 4–10 uses pseudocode to show what happens when `SimpleApplet` is run. As shown there, the browser first creates an instance of `SimpleApplet` named `applet1`. The browser first initializes `applet1` by calling its `init()` method. Then, after performing some other startup tasks, the browser repeatedly checks whether an `ACTION\_EVENT` occurred, and if so passes the event to `applet1`'s `actionPerformed()` method.

Browser/applet relationship

Figure 4–10 A summary of what happens when a Java applet is run within a browser.

```
SimpleApplet applet1 = new SimpleApplet()  ; // Create an applet instance,
applet1.init() ;                             //  and call its init()
...                                          // Handle other tasks

repeat  until applet_is_stopped {
...                                          // Handle other tasks
    if (ACTION_EVENT)                        // If an action occurs,
        applet1.actionPerformed(anActionEvent);    //  pass it to the applet
    if (user_quits_browser)                  // If the user quits session,
        applet1.destroy();                         //  kill the applet
}
```

Let's wrap up this section by providing a trace showing the order of execution of SimpleApplet for a couple of simple events. Recall from Chapter 1 that an applet is run when the browser opens an HTML document that contains an applet tag specifying the applet's class:

```
<html>
 <head><title>Simple Applet</title></head>
 <body>
  <applet code="SimpleApplet.class" width=200 height=200>
    <parameter name="author" value="Java Java Java">
    <parameter name="date" value="February 1999">
  </applet>
 </body>
</html>
```

Tracing SimpleApplet

The applet tag tells the browser which java class to instantiate and load into memory. The order of execution of the statements in SimpleApplet is shown in Fig 4–11. Note that the statements in init() are the first to be executed. If an applet contains an init() method — and not all applets do — then its statements will be executed first. Their effect is to create the toggle button with the label "The machine is off." Once the applet is initialized, the browser waits for events to happen, passing all clicks on the toggle button to the actionPerformed() method. The first time toggle is clicked, statements numbered 4 through 6 will be executed, and its label will be changed to "The machine is on." The second time it is clicked statements 7 through 9 will be executed, and its label is changed back to "The machine is off." Execution will continue in this way until the applet is destroyed.

4.5.3 Interacting Objects

Reflect for a moment on how this simple applet example conforms to the basic object-oriented programming principle of *interacting objects*. Let's identify the different objects involved here and describe their various tasks.

First there is the applet itself, which we've named applet1. As we have seen, the browser or appletviewer will run applet1 by calling its init() and start() methods.

Figure 4–11 A trace of `SimpleApplet` showing the order of execution that would result in two consecutive clicks on its `toggle` button.

```
import java.applet.*;
import java.awt.*;
import java.awt.event.*;

public class SimpleApplet extends Applet implements ActionListener
{
    private Button toggle;        // From java.awt.*

    public void init ()
    {
1       toggle = new Button ("The machine is off");
2       toggle.addActionListener(this);
3       add(toggle);
    } // init()

    public void actionPerformed(ActionEvent e)
    {
4,7     String str = toggle.getLabel();           // Get the toggle Button's
5,8     if (str.equals("The machine is on"))      // label and change it
  9         toggle.setLabel("The machine is off");
        else                                      // or
6           toggle.setLabel("The machine is on"); // change it back
    } // actionPerformed()
} // SimpleApplet
```

Next, `applet1` contains a `Button` named `toggle`. The purpose of `toggle` is to perform some action when it is clicked. It has a label, initially set to "The machine is off," which is another object, whose task is simply to display some text on the `Button`. The label's value can be gotten by asking `toggle` to `getLabel()`. This is a form of communication or interaction between `applet1` and `toggle`.

Interacting objects

Within the `actionPerformed()` method, we create a temporary `String` object named `str` to store `toggle`'s label. We can ask `str` if it equals "The machine is on" and it will tell us yes or no (`true` or `false`). This again is a form of communication between `applet1` and `str`. Here again public methods are used to carry out the communication.

Finally, whenever `toggle` is clicked, an `ActionEvent` object is created and passed to the `actionPerformed()` method. This is a form of communication between Java and `applet1`, because it is Java's runtime environment that takes care of directing events to their appropriate listeners.

Interacting objects

Thus, despite its name, `SimpleApplet` actually carries a quite sophisticated "conversation" among a number of different objects. Each object is an expert at carrying out some particular task, and each uses methods to communicate with other objects.

SELF-STUDY EXERCISES

EXERCISE 4.8 A `TextField` is a component into which the user can type text. Whenever the user types the Enter key in a `TextField`, an `ActionEvent` is generated. Using the `toggle Button` example as a guide, describe how an applet would be programmed to handle this event.

EXERCISE 4.9 What would happen if the line labeled 2 in Fig 4–11 were deleted?

EXERCISE 4.10 What would happen if the line labeled 3 in Fig 4–11 were deleted?

4.6 Case Study: The `CyberPetApplet`

Our CyberPet simulation program from previous chapters represented a CyberPet as an object whose entire state could be specified by its name and by whether it was eating or sleeping. The `CyberPet` class supplied two commands that allowed us to change a `CyberPet`'s state: `eat()`, which put the `CyberPet` in the eating state, and `sleep()`, which put the `CyberPet` in the sleeping state.

Let's now build a Graphical User Interface (GUI) that will support this simulation. The interface should enable us to interact with a single CyberPet object. It should display the CyberPet's state at all times, including its name and whether it is eating or sleeping. The interface should also make it possible for the user to issue "eat" and "sleep" commands, and it should display the CyberPet's new state after each action.

4.6.1 Specifying the Interface

What objects do we need?

As in designing any other Java program, the first question we need to ask is *what objects are needed to perform the program's task?*

One technique used in decomposing a problem is to analyze the problem statement to identify the objects that will make up a solution to the problem. A good general rule to follow is that the nouns in the problem statement are likely candidates for distinct objects in the problem solution.

EFFECTIVE DESIGN: Problem Decomposition. In order to decompose a problem into its constituents, identify the nouns in the problem statement as likely candidates for objects in the problem solution.

The nouns mentioned in describing our present problem (at the start of Section 4.6) include CyberPet, GUI, commands (eat and sleep), state, and name. Obviously our solution will involve a `CyberPet` object. The GUI is best handled by some kind of applet object. So we will define a subclass of `Applet`. The commands required in our solution suggest that we use `Buttons` to allow the user to issue commands, and the pet's state and name should perhaps be displayed in a `TextField`. Fortunately, most of the objects needed for our solution are defined in the Java API.

Problem decomposition

Our plan, then, for designing this solution is as follows. The `CyberPet` will represent the pet and simulate its eating and sleeping. The applet will serve as an interface between the user and the `CyberPet`, as shown in Fig 4–12. It will allow the user to issue commands, such as "eat" and "sleep" and it will pass these along to the `CyberPet`. Of course, the applet itself will contain several other objects — such as `Buttons` and `TextFields` — to help it carry out its tasks. An applet implementation, as we saw in

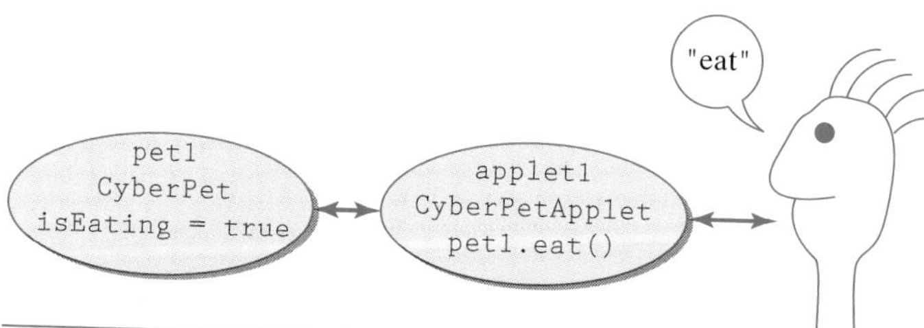

Figure 4–12 Relationship between the user, the CyberPetApplet object, and a CyberPet object.

the previous example, will generate a number of other objects — such as ActionEvents — to help effect the applet's behavior.

Interacting objects

The interface in Fig 4–13 contains four GUI objects. It has a TextField, which is used to display the CyberPet's current state. It has a Label, which is used to display the CyberPet's name. It has two Buttons, which are used to give the CyberPet commands that will change its state. Whenever the user clicks on the "Eat" Button, the applet should display CyberPet's new state in the TextField.

4.6.2 Designing CyberPetApplet

The CyberPetApplet will provide an interface between the user and the latest version of CyberPet (Fig 3–17). CyberPet contains public methods eat() and sleep(), which the applet can use to carry out user commands, and it has public methods getName() and getState(), which can be used by the applet to get the CyberPet's name and state. The applet can then display the pet's name and state on the applet.

Class design

Designing an applet is the same as designing any other Java class. We must decide on the applet's overall task, on what information it will need to represent and what methods it will need to carry out its task. Fig 4–14 provides a summary of these design issues.

4.6.3 Defining CyberPetApplet

The definition of the CyberPetApplet class begins with a header that extends the Applet class and implements ActionListener:

```
import java.awt.*;
import java.applet.*;
import java.awt.event.*;

public class CyberPetApplet extends Applet implements ActionListener
{
} // CyberPetApplet
```

Figure 4–13 A GUI design for the pet simulation.

Figure 4–14 Design specifications for the CyberPetApplet class.

- Class Name: CyberPetApplet
- Task: To provide a user interface for the CyberPet simulation.
- Information (instance variables)
  - pet: A reference to a CyberPet
  - nameLabel: A Label for the pet's name.
  - stateField: A TextField for the pet's state.
  - eatButton: A Button for the eat command.
  - sleepButton: A Button for the sleep command.
- Manipulations Needed (public methods)
  - init: A method to create the GUI components and initialize the applet.
  - actionPerformed: A method to handle clicks on the applet's Buttons.

As in the definition of SimpleApplet, the keyword extends signifies that CyberPetApplet is a subclass of Applet. Similarly, the keyword implements signifies that CyberPetApplet will implement the methods defined in the ActionListener interface. Given this definition, the class hierarchy for our program would look something like the hierarchy shown in

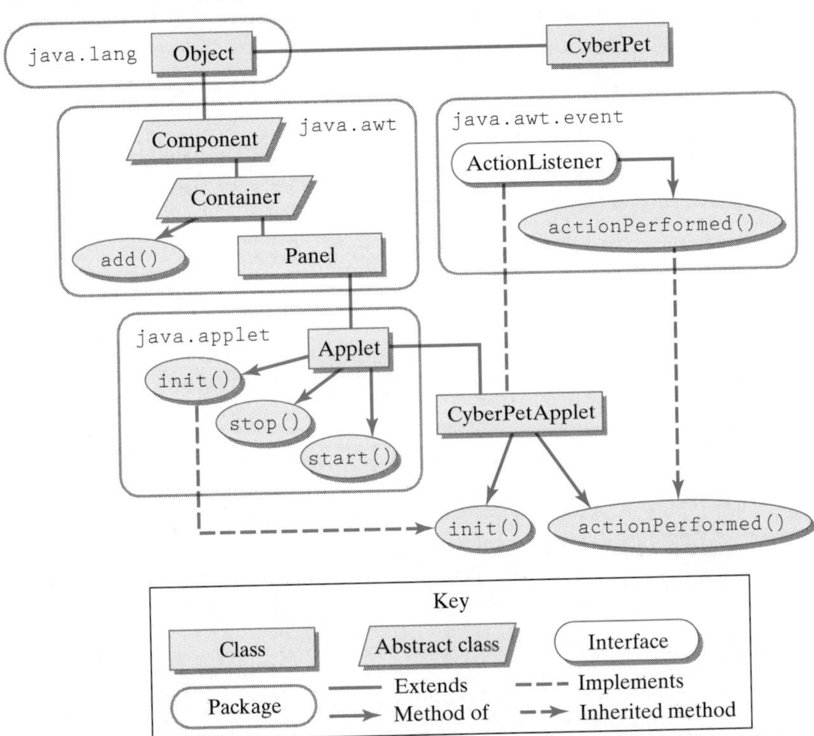

Figure 4–15 Hierarchy showing the position of the CyberPet and CyberPetApplet classes.

Fig 4–15. As this hierarchy shows, the CyberPet class is a direct descendant of the Object class, whereas CyberPetApplet is a subclass of Applet.

What data do we need?

The next step in defining CyberPetApplet is to define its instance variables. There are two ways to do this. The identifiers for the instance variables can be declared and instantiated in the global portion of the class, immediately after the header (Fig 4–16 top). Alternatively, the identifiers for the instance variables can be declared in the global portion of the class definition, and their instantiation can be done in the init() method (Fig 4–16 bottom).

Declaring vs. instantiating

For this applet there is no practical difference between these approaches. Let's adopt the latter method, because it makes clearer the distinction between declaring a variable and instantiating the object that becomes the reference of the variable. Note that all of the instance variables used in this example are declared private, which means they can only be accessed from within the CyberPetApplet class. This is an appropriate design, as there is no obvious need for these variables to be accessible outside of the applet itself.

What instance variables do we need?

The instance variables used in CyberPetApplet are of two varieties. First there is a CyberPet variable named pet1. This variable is instantiated by invoking the constructor method we defined in the previous chapter:

Figure 4–16 Two ways of declaring and instantiating an applet's instance variables: (1) Declare and instantiate in the global portion of the class; (2) Declare in the global portion and instantiate in the init() method.

```
public class CyberPetApplet extends Applet                // Top (1)
{
  // Declare and instantiate the instance variables.
   private CyberPet pet1 = new CyberPet("Socrates"); // The CyberPet
   private Label nameLabel = new Label("Name:");       // A Label
   private TextField stateField = new TextField(12); // A TextField
   private Button eatButton = new Button("Eat!");      // Two Buttons
   private Button sleepButton = new Button("Sleep!");
} // CyberPetApplet

public class CyberPetApplet extends Applet                // Bottom (2)
{
  // Declare instance variables.
   private CyberPet pet1;                       // The CyberPet
   private Label nameLabel;                     // Label
   private TextField stateField;                // TextField
   private Button eatButton, sleepButton;       // Buttons

   public void init()
   {
     // Instantiate the instance variables
      pet1 = new CyberPet("Socrates");          // The CyberPet
      nameLabel = new Label("Hi! My name is " + pet1.getName() +
                        " and currently I am : ");
      stateField = new TextField(12);           // TextField
      eatButton = new Button("Eat!");           // Buttons
      eatButton.addActionListener(this);
      sleepButton = new Button("Sleep!");
      sleepButton.addActionListener(this);
   } // init
} // CyberPetApplet
```

```
CyberPet( "Socrates" )
```

which has the effect of initializing pet1's state and giving pet1 the name "Socrates." Recall from previous chapters that CyberPet is initially in the eating state.

Object instantiation

In addition to the CyberPet variable, there are several *GUI* objects. These objects are instantiated by invoking their respective constructor methods. Because all of these objects are defined in Java class libraries, such as java.awt, we have to consult the documentation of these libraries to determine the signatures of the various constructor methods. We will provide a more detailed discussion of each of these component classes in Chapter 9, but for now, let's just consider the following three constructor methods:

```
Label(String)    // Set Label's text to String
Button(String)   // Set Button's label to String
TextField(int)   // Create a TextField of int characters in length
```

Each of the Label , Button , and TextField classes has several different constructors, but we limit ourselves in this example to one constructor for each type of object.

Labels

A Label is a component that displays a single line of uneditable text in the applet's window. Typically, a Label is used to label a portion of the applet. In CyberPetApplet we use a Label to greet the user and display the pet's name. The constructor used in this case takes a single String parameter, whose value is used to set the label's text:

```
nameLabel = new Label("Hi! My name is " + pet1.getName() +
                      " and currently I am : ");
```

Note the use of string concatenation together with getName() to incorporate pet1's name into the label. The method is used to get the name from pet1.

Buttons

As we saw in Chapter 2, a Button is a labeled component that is used to trigger some form of action when it is clicked. The Button constructor in this case takes a single String parameter, whose value is used to set the initial value its label. In this example, we have two buttons, which are instantiated as follows:

```
eatButton = new Button("Eat!");
sleepButton = new Button("Sleep!");
```

As their labels suggest, the user will click on the "Eat!" button to tell the pet to eat and on the "Sleep!" button to tell the pet to sleep.

Algorithm: Handling action events

After we instantiate a Button, we need to register it with an Action Listener as in the following statements:

```
eatButton.addActionListener(this);
sleepButton.addActionListener(this);
```

Note that both buttons will use the same listener, which means we'll have to distinguish which button was actually clicked within the actionPerformed() method.

A TextField is a component that displays a single line of editable text. The constructor used in this case takes a single int parameter whose value is used to set the width of the text field — that is, how many characters it can display:

TextField

```
stateField = new TextField(12);
```

The TextField used in this program will display up to 12 characters, which seems sufficient to display strings such as "eating" and "sleeping." Because stateField is being used to display information and not to input information, we will make it *uneditable,* which will prevent the user from typing in it. We will also display pet1's initial state as its initial value. The following statements will effect these changes:

```
// Initialize the text fields.
stateField.setEditable(false);
stateField.setText(pet1.getState());
```

The setEditable() method is defined in TextComponent, which is the superclass of TextField.

Note that in the second statement the applet gets pet1's state using its getState() method, and passes it to stateField using its setText() method. Here we have three objects interacting: The applet, let's call it applet1, is in control of the activity and mediates the interaction between pet1 and stateField. In more anthropomorphic terms, the applet asks pet1, "What is your state?" and pet1 answers "sleeping." The applet then tells stateField "Use 'sleeping' as your value." Fig 4–17 shows this relationship.

Interacting objects

Once the GUI components have been instantiated and initialized they must be added to the applet. Because an Applet is a Container we use the add() method to add its Components. This should be done within the applet's init() method, which is shown in Fig 4–18.

Algorithm: Adding components to the applet

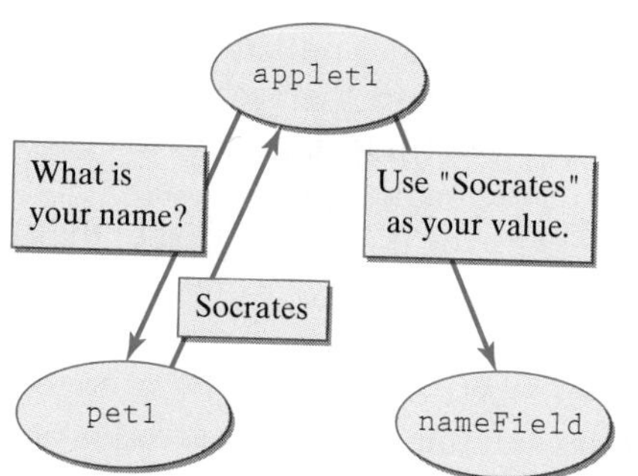

Figure 4–17 Pet1, applet1, and nameField interacting

Figure 4–18 The `init()` method.

```
public void init()
{
    /* Instantiate the instance variables.  This
     * creates both the CyberPet, pet1, and the
     * GUI elements that are displayed on the applet
     */
    pet1 = new CyberPet("Socrates");        // CyberPet

     /* Create the GUI components */

    nameLabel = new Label("Hi! My name is " + pet1.getName() +
                          " and currently I am : ");
    stateField = new TextField(12);
    eatButton = new Button("Eat!");         // Buttons
    eatButton.addActionListener(this);      // Assign the listeners
    sleepButton = new Button("Sleep!");
    sleepButton.addActionListener(this);

   /* Initialize the TextField  */

     stateField.setText(pet1.getState());
     stateField.setEditable(false);

   /* Add the components to the applet  */

     add(nameLabel);
     add(stateField);
     add(eatButton);
     add(sleepButton);

     setSize(300,150);          // Set the applet's size to 300 x 150 pixels
 } // init
```

DEBUGGING TIP: Adding Components to an Applet. If you forget to *add* a component to the applet, it will not appear in the applet's window.

The abstraction principle

What does it mean to *add* components to an applet? After all, an applet is an abstract thing, not a physical container. It's not really like dropping marbles into a cup. A `Container` in the Java class library is an *abstraction*, or a *model* of a real container. To model the idea of containment, each container maintains a list of its contents. Each time a component is added to a container, a new entry is made and added to the container's list. The entries on the list refer to the individual components themselves. Thus it is possible for a container to display all of its components, or to tell each of its components to display themselves. Adding the above components to `CyberPetApplet` means that `CyberPetApplet` maintains a list of these four components, which it manipulates in various ways as necessary to display the components on the screen.

Default `FlowLayout`

This leads to another question. How will these components be arranged on the screen? Obviously screen layout is an important consideration in

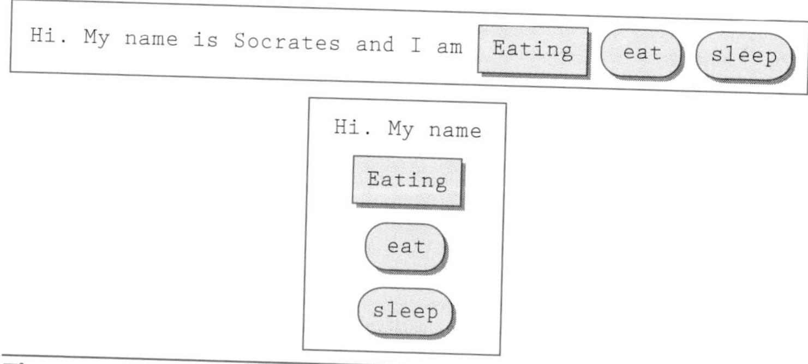

Figure 4–19 Possible flowlayout of CyberPetApplet in wide window and narrow windows.

designing a GUI interface. The geometric relationships between the components can affect the program's usability. By default, components added to a container are arranged in what is known as a FlowLayout — one component after another arranged horizontally across the window starting at the top of the applet's window. If the window is wide enough or too narrow, FlowLayout could lead to one or the other of the layouts shown in Fig 4–19.

The actual layout that results from FlowLayout depends on the browser and is quite arbitrary. In Chapter 9 we will learn how to gain more control over applet layout. For now, however, we can use the WIDTH and HEIGHT attributes in the APPLET tag to specify the applet's dimensions:

```
<html>
 <head><title>CyberPet Applet</title></head>
 <body>
  <applet code="CyberPetApplet.class" width=300 height=150>
  </applet>
 </body>
</html>
```

For most browsers, the values used here will produce the layout shown in Fig 4–13. Another way to control the applet's window size is to use the setSize(int w, int h) method to set the applet's width (w) and height (h). This is a method that's defined in the Component class and inherited by the applet. You would place a call to this method in the applet's init() method, as shown in Fig 4–18.

4.6.4 Handling CyberPetApplet Actions

Handling user actions

In order to handle events when the user clicks on either eatButton or sleepButton, we must implement the actionPerformed() method , which will be invoked when either button is clicked. Therefore, that method must be able to distinguish when the eatButton is clicked and when the sleepButton is clicked, as in the following implementation:

```
public void actionPerformed(ActionEvent e)
{
    if (e.getSource() == eatButton)        // If eat button clicked,
        pet1.eat();                        //  tell the pet to eat
    else if (e.getSource() == sleepButton) // If sleep button clicked,
        pet1.sleep();                      //  tell the pet to sleep

    stateField.setText(pet1.getState());   // Display the pet's state
} // actionPerformed()
```

Which control structure?

An if-else statement is used in this case to choose between two alternatives. If the `eatButton` is clicked — `e.getSource() == eatButton` — then the pet is told to eat — `pet1.eat()`. Otherwise, if the `sleepButton` is clicked — `e.getSource() == sleepButton` — then the pet is told to sleep — `pet1.sleep()`. Following one or the other of these actions, the pet's new state is displayed in the applet's state field using the same statement that we used in `init()`:

```
stateField.setText( pet1.getState() ); // Display new state
```

There are a number points to note about this implementation of `actionPerformed()`. Most importantly, because it must be able to distinguish between clicks on both the `eatButton` and `sleepButton`, we need to use an if-else statement. This approach can be easily generalized to handle as many buttons as we have in an applet:

```
if (e.getSource() == firstButton)
  // Do firstButton's action
else if (e.getSource() == secondButton)
  // Do secondButton's action
else if (e.getSource() == thirdButton)
  // Do thirdButton's action
.
.
.
```

Which object caused the event?

Another important point is that we use the `ActionEvent`'s `getSource()` method to determine which button was clicked. Recall that when a button is clicked, Java will create an `ActionEvent` containing information about the event, including its `source` — that is, the object which generated the event. The entire `ActionEvent` object is then passed to `actionPerformed()`, where it is referred to as `e`. As our applets become more sophisticated we will get other information from `e`, but in this case we need only use `getSource()` to determine which button the user clicked.

4.6.5 Running `CyberPetApplet`

Testing and debugging

The complete listing of the `CyberPetApplet.java` class is shown in 4–20. The line numbers indicate the order in which statements are executed.

Figure 4–20 Definition of the CyberPetApplet class.

```
import java.applet.*;
import java.awt.*;
import java.awt.event.*;

public class CyberPetApplet extends Applet implements ActionListener
{
   // Declare instance variables
    private CyberPet pet1;                      // The CyberPet
    private Label nameLabel;                    // A Label
    private TextField stateField;               // A TextField
    private Button eatButton, sleepButton;      // Two Buttons

    public void init()
    {
        /*
         * Instantiate the instance variables.  This creates both the
         * CyberPet, pet1, and the GUI elements that are displayed on the applet.
         */
        pet1 = new CyberPet("Socrates");    // CyberPet

        // Create the GUI components

        nameLabel = new Label("Hi! My name is " + pet1.getName() +
                              " and currently I am : ");
        stateField = new TextField(12);
        eatButton = new Button("Eat!");       // Buttons
        eatButton.addActionListener(this);     // Assign the listeners.
        sleepButton = new Button("Sleep!");
        sleepButton.addActionListener(this);

        // Initialize the TextField

        stateField.setText(pet1.getState());
        stateField.setEditable(false);

        // Add the components to the applet.

        add(nameLabel);
        add(stateField);
        add(eatButton);
        add(sleepButton);

        setSize(300,150);            // Set the applet's size to 300 x 150 pixels
    } // init

    /*
     * The actionPerformed() method is the method that gets called
     * when one of the buttons is pressed
     */
    public void actionPerformed( ActionEvent e)
    {
        if (e.getSource() == eatButton)
            pet1.eat();
        else if (e.getSource() == sleepButton)
            pet1.sleep();

        stateField.setText(pet1.getState());
    }//actionPerformed

} // CyberPetApplet
```

No line numbers are shown for the `actionPerformed()` method, because the order of execution there depends on what particular events take place during the program's execution.

Because so much happens automatically when a Java applet is run, it will be useful to trace `CyberPetApplet`'s execution. As we saw in the `SimpleApplet` example, when you run an applet within your browser, the applet's class definition is used to create an instance of the applet. The first thing that happens is that the browser calls the applet's `init()` method to perform any initialization that may be necessary.

Following the call to `init()`, the browser starts the applet, which continues to run until it is stopped. [The browser uses `Applet`'s `start()` and `stop()` methods for these tasks.] Once an applet is running, the browser will repeatedly pass applet-related events to listener objects. In our example, we have designated the applet itself as the `ActionListener` for its two buttons. If either of these buttons is clicked, the applet invokes one of `pet1`'s methods to change the pet's state.

Tim Berners-Lee, Creator of the WWW

It's hard to believe that the World Wide Web (WWW) was invented by one man. Given the great wealth that the WWW has generated, it's even harder to believe that its inventor has not made any effort to use his invention to enrich himself personally.

In 1989, Tim Berners-Lee was a Fellow at CERN, the European Particle Physics Laboratory, when he conceived of the idea of a multimedia system that could be used by researchers to exchange data, text, images, sounds, and other forms of information that they use in their research.

With a background in system design, real-time communications, and text processing, Berners-Lee wrote the first Web server and the first Web browser, which was called "WorldWideWeb" (no spaces). He later changed the browser's name to "Nexus" to distinguish it from the rapidly emerging multimedia network known as the World Wide Web. His browser was released (for free) on the Internet in 1991, where it was, more or less, an immediate hit. Its success led to the development of other servers and browsers, and the rest, as they say, is history.

Throughout the rapid expansion of the Web, Berners-Lee has devoted himself to trying to preserve the open and public nature of the Web. Between 1991 and 1993, Berners-Lee developed initial specifications for HTTP and HTML, which were refined and discussed in larger public circles as the Web technology spread. In 1994, Berners-Lee joined the Laboratory for Computer Science (LCS) at the Massachusetts Institute of Technology (MIT), where he serves as Director of the W3 Consortium. The Consortium's goal is to lead the Web to its full potential, ensuring its stability through rapid evolution and revolutionary transformations of its usage. The Consortium can be found at http://www.w3.org/.

OBJECT-ORIENTED DESIGN: Inheritance and Polymorphism

Extending a class

The ability to extend an existing class is one of the most powerful features of object-oriented programming. It allows objects to reuse code defined in the superclasses without having to redefine or recompile the code. Thus `CyberPetApplet` uses the `public` methods defined for `Applets`, `Panels`, `Containers`, `Components`, and `Objects` simply by invoking them with a standard method call. By the same token, it can use all of the `public` and `protected` instance variables and constants defined in these classes by simply referring to them in its own code. It inherits all of this functionality by virtue of its location in Java's class hierarchy.

If the preexisting code doesn't exactly suit its purposes, `CyberPetApplet` can override (redefine) existing methods or define new methods, as we have done with `init()` and `actionPerformed()`.

Problem decomposition

`CyberPetApplet` provides one illustration of how inheritance can be used to effect a particular action — such as toggling the label of a `Button`. However, from a design perspective, our previous example is perhaps not the best way to toggle a button's label. A more object-oriented design would be to define `ToggleButton` as a `Button` subclass that automatically toggles its label whenever it is clicked in addition to carrying out some kind of associated action.

`ToggleButton` class

A light switch is a `ToggleButton` in this sense. Whenever you flick a switch, it changes its label from "on" to "off," but it also turns the lights on or off. The action associated with the switch is something that might change from switch to switch — the hall light or the bedroom light — but every light switch toggles its label each time it is clicked. So let's design a `ToggleButton` that behaves like a light switch.

Using existing functionality

To begin with a `ToggleButton` is a `Button` and we want it to act as its own `ActionListener` so that it can toggle its own label whenever it is clicked. Therefore it must `extend Button` and `implement ActionListener`. The rest of its definition is shown in Fig 4–21. A `ToggleButton` needs two `String` variables to store its two labels, which are named simply `label1` and `label2`. We can provide it with a a constructor method that allows its labels to be set during instantiation:

```
public ToggleButton(String l1, String l2) // Constructor method
{
    super(l1);   // Call Button's constructor to set the label
    label1 = l1;              // Set my two labels
    label2 = l2;
    addActionListener(this); // Act as my ActionListener
}
```

`super`

Recall that `Button` has a constructor method with the signature `Button(String)`, which allows us to set a `Button`'s label during instantiation. We need to do the same thing with one of `ToggleButton`'s two labels. That is, when we create a `ToggleButton`, we want to initialize its label to one of its two alternative labels (here, "On" or "Off"). Fortunately, Java supplies the `super` keyword for just this purpose. `super` refers to a class's

Figure 4–21 Definition of the ToggleButton class.

```
import java.awt.*;
import java.awt.event.*;

public class ToggleButton extends Button implements ActionListener
{
    private String label1;   // Two Labels to toggle between
    private String label2;

    public ToggleButton(String l1, String l2) // Constructor method
    {
        super(l1);                    // Use l1 as the default label
        label1 = l1;
        label2 = l2;
        addActionListener(this);
    }

    public void actionPerformed(ActionEvent e)
    {
        String tempS = label1;  // Swap the labels
        label1 = label2;
        label2 = tempS;
        ToggleButton.this.setLabel(label1);
    } // actionPerformed()
} // ToggleButton
```

superclass, so when used in `super(l1)`, this is equivalent to calling `Button(l1)` — that is, it is equivalent to calling `Button`'s constructor method. The only restriction on doing this is that we must call `Button`'s constructor as the very first statement in `ToggleButton()`. By passing it `l1` we are making the first string that the user gives us the default label for our `ToggleButton`. This will be the label that appears on the button when it is first displayed in the applet.

Note also that the constructor designates itself as its own `ActionListener`, so whenever it is clicked, its `actionPerformed()` method will be invoked.

Swapping algorithm

```
public void actionPerformed(ActionEvent e)
{         // Swap the labels of label1 and label2
                            //   tempS label1 label2
    String tempS = label1;  // 1 off   off    on
    label1 = label2;        // 2 off   on     on
    label2 = tempS;         // 3 off   on     off
    setLabel(label1);       // 4 off-->on or vice versa
} // actionPerformed()
```

The `actionPerformed()` method exchanges the button's current label for its other label. Swapping two values in memory is a standard programming practice used in lots of different algorithms. In order to do it properly, you must use a third variable to temporarily store one of the two values you are swapping. The comments in `actionPerformed()` provide a step-by-step trace of the values of the three variables involved.

PROGRAMMING TIP: Swapping Values. It is necessary to use a temporary variable whenever you are swapping two values, of any type, in memory. The temporary variable holds the first value while you overwrite it with the second value.

Swapping values requires a temporary variable

The first statement in `actionPerformed()` creates a temporary `String` variable named `tempS` and assigns it the value of `label1`. Recall that `label1` was the button's initial label. To make this example easier to follow, let's suppose that initially `label1` is "off" and that `label2` is "on." So after line 1 is executed, both `tempS` and `label1` contain "off" as their value. Line 2 then assigns `label2`'s value to `label1`. So now both `label1` and `label2` store "on" as their values. In line 3 we assign `tempS`'s value to `label2`. Now `label2` stores "off" and `label1` stores "on," and we have effectively swapped their original values.

Note that the next time we invoke `actionPerformed()` `label1` and `label2` will have their opposite values initially. So swapping them a second time will assign them their initial values again. We can continue toggling their values in this way indefinitely. To complete the method, the last statement in `actionPerformed()` assigns `label1`'s current value as the new `ToggleButton`'s label.

Multiple event handlers

So a `ToggleButton` toggles its label between two values. But what about performing an associated action? For this we have to look at `ToggleTest`, an applet that *uses* a `ToggleButton` (Fig 4–22). In its overall structure, this applet is the same as the other applets we have studied in this chapter. It extends the `Applet` class and implements the `ActionListener` interface. In this example we use a `ToggleButton` to simulate a light switch. Note that we assign this applet as an `ActionListener` for the `lightSwitch`, so that `lightSwitch` has two listeners that will respond to its events: the `ToggleButton` itself, as a result of the `actionPerformed()` method in

Figure 4–22 Definition of the `ToggleTest` class.

```
import java.applet.*;
import java.awt.*;
import java.awt.event.*;

public class ToggleTest extends Applet implements ActionListener
{
    private ToggleButton lightSwitch;

    public void init()
    {
        lightSwitch = new ToggleButton ("off","on");
        add(lightSwitch);
        lightSwitch.addActionListener(this);
    } // init()

    public void actionPerformed(ActionEvent e)
    {
        showStatus("The light is " + lightSwitch.getLabel());
    } // actionPerformed()
} // ToggleTest
```

Figure 4–23 The `ToggleTest` applet. The button's action is to display "The light is on" or "The light is off" in the applet's status bar.

its class, and the `ToggleTest` applet, as a result of `actionPerformed()` method in this class.

The particular action taken by the applet when `lightSwitch` is clicked is to display the message "The light is on" or "The light is off" in the applet's status bar (Fig 4–23). But this suffices to illustrate that a `ToggleButton` both toggles its own label *and* carries out some associated action.

Object-oriented design

The design of `ToggleButton` satisfies several of the key design principles of object-oriented programming. It encapsulates `ToggleButton`'s essential behavior within the `ToggleButton` class itself, and it hides the mechanism by which a `ToggleButton` manages its labels. It uses inheritance to extend the functionality of the predefined `Button` class.

EFFECTIVE DESIGN: Inheritance. Inheritance enables you to specialize an object's behavior. A `ToggleButton` does everything that a `Button` does, plus it can toggle its own label.

SELF-STUDY EXERCISES

EXERCISE 4.11 Write a code segment (not a whole method) to swap two boolean variables, `b1` and `b2`.

EXERCISE 4.12 Suppose you are designing an applet that plays a card game, and you want a single button that can be used both to deal the cards and collect the cards. Write a code segment that creates this type of button, adds it to the applet, and designates the applet as its `ActionListener`.

From the Java Library: `Image`

Java's AWT makes it especially easy to add images to an applet. As we've seen, the `Applet` class contains the public `getImage()` method, which can be used to load an image into a program given its URL (Uniform Resource Locator). The `java.awt.Image` class is an abstract class that cannot be directly instantiated through a constructor. Instead, an `Image` object is obtained by using a method such as `Applet.getImage()`. The `Image` class has the following declaration:

```
public abstract class Image extends Object
{
  ... // Details omitted
}
```

Note the use of the `abstract` qualifier in the heading. This means that some of the methods defined in the `Image` class are abstract methods—that is, methods whose implementations (bodies) have not yet been defined.

Abstract class

EFFECTIVE DESIGN: Abstract Class. An **abstract class** is one that contains one or more abstract methods. An abstract class cannot be directly instantiated and is intended to be subclassed.

Consider the applet definition in Fig 4–24. It declares two `private` instance variables of type `Image` to store the two images that are loaded when the applet runs. The images themselves are in files named `lighton.gif` and `lightoff.gif`, which are stored in the same directory as the applet itself. The images are loaded into the applet using its `getImage()` method:

```
lightOn = getImage(getCodeBase(),"lighton.gif");
lightOff = getImage(getCodeBase(),"lightoff.gif");
```

The `getCodeBase()` method returns the applet's URL (location), which is used as the first argument in `getImage()`. The second argument in `getImage()` is the name of the image's GIF file.

Figure 4–24 Definition of the `Lights` class.

```
import java.applet.*;
import java.awt.*;

public class Lights extends Applet
{
    private Image lightOn, lightOff;  // Declare two Image variables

    public void init()
    {
        lightOn = getImage(getCodeBase(),"lighton.gif");
        lightOff = getImage(getCodeBase(),"lightoff.gif");
    } // init()

    public void paint (Graphics g)
    {
        g.drawImage(lightOn, 10, 10, this);
        g.drawImage(lightOff, 70, 10, this);
    } // paint()
} // Lights
```

The remaining code in this applet is the `paint()` method, which is defined in `java.awt.Component`. Applets that display images or do graphics must override `paint()`, as shown here. Recall that we also overrode `paint()` in our very first example of `HelloWorld()`. The `drawImage()` method used to display the images is taken from the `Graphics` class. It has the following signature:

```
drawImage(Image img, int x, int y, ImageObserver observer)
```

The parameters required here are first the image to be displayed, followed by the image's coordinates on the applet, followed by the object that "observes" the image. In our case that is the applet itself, which is referred to simply as `this`. When the applet runs, it appears as shown in Fig 4–25.

Figure 4–25 The `Lights` applet illustrates how to use `Images` in an applet.

IN THE LABORATORY: CyberPetApplet

The purpose of this lab exercise is to familiarize you with Java applets. You will make several modifications to extend the functionality of the `CyberPetApplet` class. The objectives of the lab are

- To introduce the principles of writing a Java applet.
- To introduce some of the basic GUI Components.
- To give additional practice using the *if* and *if-else* control structures.
- To introduce a simple graphical object: Image. (optional)

Problem Description

Problem specification

Extend the `CyberPet` and `CyberPetApplet` classes by adding a third state to the pet simulation — for example, thinking. The applet GUI should continue to display the CyberPet's name and current state as well as an image that depicts the pet's current state. It should also include command buttons for each of `CyberPet`'s states.

Lab Exercise 1: Getting Set Up

Download the CyberPet.java and the CyberPetApplet source files from the companion Web site at http://www.prenhall.com/morelli/labs/ directory. These files correspond to the programs shown in Figures 4–20 and 3–17. Place both of these files into the same directory.

Compile and run CyberPetApplet to make sure it runs properly. If you are using JDK, you can compile both CyberPetApplet.java and CyberPet.java by simply typing

```
javac CyberPetApplet.java
```

at the command line. The compiler will look for CyberPet.java in the same directory and will compile it automatically. To run the applet with JDK you will need an HTML file which contains the following applet tag:

```
<APPLET CODE="CyberPetApplet.class" WIDTH=325 HEIGHT=75>
</APPLET>
```

Assuming the HTML file is named CyberPetApplet.html, you can run it with the appletviewer by typing

```
appletviewer CyberPetApplet.html
```

Lab Exercise 2: Resizing the Applet Window

Controlling the size of the applet's window is important because in this version of the program the applet's components appear in what's called a FlowLayout. Under this layout, components are just placed in the applet, one after another, in a row from left to right until there's no more room in the row. Then a new row is started.

The applet tag in PetApplet.html should contain WIDTH and HEIGHT parameters, which control the initial size of the applet. By carefully setting these values, you can exert some control over the applet's layout. Try changing both of these values, one at a time, and observing the effect it has on the appearance of the applet. Through trial and error find appropriate values for the applet's size.

Lab Exercise 3: Paying Attention to Java Syntax

Make each of the following changes to CyberPetApplet.java, one at a time, then recompile it and note the syntax error that results. Copy the syntax error into your write-up for this lab with a brief note of what caused the error.

- Comment out the first import statement in the program.
- Delete the semicolon after pet1.eat() in the actionPerformed() method.
- Change the spelling of TextField to Textfield in one of the lines in init().

Lab Exercise 4: Tracing the Applet

`CyberPetApplet` inherits a number of methods from its superclasses. The main ones are

- `start()` is called once when the applet is started by the browser or appletviewer. This method calls `init()` and `paint()` automatically and then calls `run()` to get the applet running.
- `run()` is called by the `start()` method. It starts the applet running.
- `stop()` is called by the browser or appletviewer when the applet is quit.
- `init()` is called once when an applet starts up to perform any required initializations.
- `paint()` paints the graphics on the applet. It is called once when the applet starts and then it can be called by `repaint()` whenever the applet's appearance is changed. This is where you should place any drawing commands.

In addition to the above methods, which are inherited from `Applet`, our applets implement the `ActionListener` interface, so they also inherit the following method, which must be redefined in the applet.

- `actionPerformed()` is called automatically whenever one of the `Buttons` is clicked. It is passed information about the `ActionEvent`. This is where you should place commands that handle the applet's button clicks.

Of these methods, `CyberPetApplet` redefines `init()` and implements `actionPerformed()`. Definitions for the other methods don't appear in `CyberPetApplet`.

Place a `System.out.println("In method X")` statement, where *X* is the name of the method, in each method of both the `CyberPetApplet` and `CyberPet` classes. Run the program and note the output that it produces. Write down the order of execution of the statements in `CyberPetApplet` and `CyberPet` for various actions, such as clicking on the eat button or the sleep button.

Lab Exercise 5: Paying Attention to Runtime Errors

Make each of the following changes, one at a time, to your program and then rerun it. Make a note of the semantic errors that occur and try to explain each error.

- Comment out the line beginning `eatButton = new ...` in the `init()` method. This is a very common mistake: Declaring a variable for an object but failing to create an instance of the object.
- Comment out the statement in `init()` that adds the `eatButton` to the applet.
- Delete one of the double quote marks from any pair of quote marks.
- Comment out the last statement in the `actionPerformed()` method.
- Add the following statement to the beginning of the `init()` method: Button b1 = new Button ("Local");

Figure 4–26 A subtle semantic error occurs in this program because the instance Button b1 is never instantiated.

```
import java.awt.*;
import java.applet.*;
import java.awt.event.*;

public class SemanticError extends Applet implements ActionListener
{
    private Button b1;    // This b1 has class scope but is not instantiated

    public void init()
    {                       // Declare and instantiate a local b1
        Button b1 = new Button ("Local"); // This b1 has local scope
        add(b1);                       // The local b1 is added to the applet
        b1.addActionListener(this);
    } // init()

    public void actionPerformed(ActionEvent e)
    {
        b1.setLabel("Global");       // This refers to the uninstantiated b1.
    } // actionPerformed()
} // SemanticError
```

Local scope error

This last semantic error is a very subtle one and is worth additional comment. Consider the example in Fig 4–26. The semantic error in this case is a *scoping* error. There are two variables with the same identifier. The first is the instance variable, whose scope extends throughout the class. It has *class scope* . The second is the local variable declared within the init() method, the scope of which is limited to that method. Once the init() completes its execution, the local variable ceases to exist. Outside of the init() method, any references to b1 will refer to the instance variable. The problem here is that the instance variable was never instantiated. So there is no actual button associated with its name. In the actionPerformed() method, the reference to b1 is a reference to the instance variable, but there is no button on the applet that corresponds to this variable, because in the init() method, the local variable's button was added to the applet.

DEBUGGING TIP: Scope Error. Don't declare a component variable in the init() method. You won't be able to refer to it in the rest of the program.

Lab Exercise 6: Adding a New State to CyberPet

Add a third state to the CyberPet class and make the appropriate changes in the CyberPetApplet. Let's suppose you are adding a *thinking* state. You will need to create an instance variable for isThinking and a think() method, plus you need to revise the other access methods. All of these revisions would occur in the CyberPet.java file. In the CyberPetApplet.java file, you would need to add a third button to the applet. If you add a third button, you would need to revise the actionPerformed() method to handle clicks on the new button.

Lab Exercise 7: Adding Images to CyberPetApplet (optional)

Download the image files provided for this lab. There are three images: spidereat.gif, spidersleep.gif, and spiderthink.gif. Place them in the same directory as your source code (*.java) files.

Add images to the applet that correspond to CyberPet's three states. Follow the example shown in Section 4.6. There are two modifications that must be made to that example. First, the paint() method should draw the image that corresponds to CyberPet's current state:

```
public void paint(Graphics g)
{
    String petState = pet1.getState();          // Get pet1's state
    if (petState.equals("Eating"))              // Draw the appropriate image
        g.drawImage(eatImage, 20, 100, this);
    else if ( petState.equals("Sleeping"))
        g.drawImage(sleepImage, 20, 100, this);
    else if ( petState.equals("Thinking"))
        g.drawImage(sleepImage, 20, 100, this);
}
```

Finally, it is necessary to repaint() the applet after each button click. To do this you would add the following statement at the end of your actionPerformed() method:

```
repaint(); // Call the paint() method
```

The repaint() method just calls the applet's paint() method. The reason that paint(Graphics) is not called directly here is because it requires a Graphics parameter, which is not directly available to the actionPerformed() method. The repaint() method takes care of getting the applet's Graphics object and passing it to paint(), so the images can be displayed on it.

Java Language Summary

Keywords: extends, super, import, this

extends

- The extends keyword is used in a class definition in order to define a subclass of a class. It causes the subclass to *inherit* the superclass's public and protected instance variables and instance methods. For example, the following definition defines a Square as a subclass of Rectangle:

```
public class Square extends Rectangle // Subclass of Rectangle
{
    public Square(double side)
    {
        super(side,side);        // Call Rectangle's Constructor
    }
} // Square
```

Java Language Summary

- The `super` keyword refers to an object's superclass. It can be used in an object's constructor to invoke the superclass constructor. When so used, it should be the first statement in the constructor. For example, note in the code segment just preceding this item, how the `Rectangle()` constructor is invoked in the `Square()` constructor by using `super`. super
- The `import` declaration allows classes declared in other (usually library) packages to be referred to by a simple name rather than by their fully qualified name. It takes the form `import` *package.class*, where *package* is the name of library package containing the `class`. For example, if your program declares `import java.applet.Applet`, it will be able to refer to this class simply as `Applet`. The wildcard character, *, may be used to import all the class definitions in a particular package. For example, the following statement imports definitions of all of the public class names in the Abstract Windowing Toolkit (AWT) package: import

```
import java.awt.*;
```

- The `this` keyword is self-referential. Just as "I" refers to the person who utters it, `this` refers to whatever object uses it. For example, in the following `init()` method, this

```
public class MyApplet extends Applet implements ActionListener
{
    private Button button = new Button("click me!");
    public void init()
    {
        this.add(button);
        button.addActionListener(this);
    } // init()
} MyApplet
```

`this` refers to whichever `MyApplet` object executes the statement. That object becomes the listener for `button`'s action events.

Keywords: `abstract, interface, protected`

- An `abstract` class is one that contains one or more `abstract` methods. An `abstract` method is one which lacks a method body. It consists entirely of the method header. Classes that extend an abstract class should implement the abstract methods. abstract
- An `interface` is, essentially, a class that contains only instance methods and constants. It cannot contain instance variables. A class that `implements` an interface commits itself to defining all the methods contained in the interface. This is a second form of *inheritance*, similar to extending a superclass. For example, applets that need to handle button clicks should implement the `ActionListener` interface, which consists of one method, the `actionPerformed()` method. Here's an example: interface

Java Language Summary

```
public class MyClass extends Applet implements ActionListener
{
    // Code deleted here

    public void actionPerformed(ActionEvent e)
    {
        // Code to handle button clicks goes here
    } // actionPerformed()
}
```

protected

- Instance variables and instance methods that are declared `protected` are inherited by subclasses (as well as its `public` elements). Unlike `public` elements, `protected` elements are not accessible by other objects.

CHAPTER SUMMARY

Technical Terms

abstract class
applet
event-driven
inheritance
interface
abstract method
Application Programming Interface (API)
Graphical User Interface (GUI)
inheritance hierarchy
polymorphism

New Java Keywords

`abstract`	`class`	`double`
`extends`	`implements`	`import`
`interface`	`protected`	`super`
`this`		

Java Library Classes

`ActionEvent`	`ActionListener`	`Applet`
`Button`	`Component`	`Container`
`EventObject`	`Event`	`FlowLayout`
`Graphics`	`Image`	`Label`
`MouseEvent`	`Object`	`Panel`
`String`	`TextComponent`	`TextField`

Java Library Methods

`actionPerformed`	`add()`	`drawImage()`
`getCodeBase()`	`getImage()`	`getLabel()`
`getParameter()`	`init()`	`main()`
`paint()`	`play()`	`repaint()`
`run()`	`setEditable()`	`setLabel()`
`setText()`	`start()`	`stop()`
`toString()`		

Programmer-Defined Classes

`CyberPet`	`CyberPetApplet`	`Rectangle`
`SimpleApplet`	`SmallApplet`	`Square`
`TestSquare`	`ToggleButton`	`ToggleTest`

Programmer-Defined Methods

`calcPerimeter()`	`getName()`	`getState()`

Summary of Important Points

- An *applet* is an embedded program that runs within the context of a Web browser.
- The Java *Application Programming Interface (API)* is a set of predefined classes that can be used to write programs.
- A *Graphical User Interface (GUI)* enables the user to interact with a program via graphical elements such as windows, button, menus and so on. Java's GUI components are defined in the *Abstract Windowing Toolkit (AWT)* package. The `import` statement is used to import definitions of predefined classes into a Java program.
- The `extend` keyword is used to define a class's *pedigree*—that is, its place within the Java class hierarchy. A class that *extends* another class is said to be a *subclass* of that class which is its *superclass.* A subclass *inherits* the `public` and `protected` methods and fields (instance variables) of its superclasses.
- Methods defined in a class's superclasses can be *overridden* in the subclass by defining a method with the same signature — that is, with the same name, return type, and the same number and type of formal parameters.
- Any method that performs some type of operation on different types of objects is said to be *polymorphic*. An applet's `init()` method is an example, since it is redefined in all of `Applet` subclasses.
- Java applets are *event-driven* which means they are programmed to react to certain events. An `Event` is an object that records specific information about a particular event, such as a mouse click or a key press. Clicking on a `Button` in an applet generates an ACTION_EVENT which should be handled by an `actionPerformed()` method.
- A `Label` is a GUI component that displays a single line of uneditable text on the applet. A `Button` is a labeled GUI component that is used to trigger some kind of action when clicked. A `TextField` is a GUI component that displays a single line of editable text. The `setText()` and `getText()` methods can be used to set a `Button`'s label or a `TextField`'s text.
- The default layout pattern for Java applets is the `FlowLayout`.

ANSWERS TO SELF-STUDY EXERCISES

EXERCISE 4.1

```
public double calcPerimeter()
{
    return 2 * length + 2 * width;
}
```

EXERCISE 4.2 The following code should be added to `main()` in `TestSquare` (Fig 4–4):

```
System.out.println("square's perimeter is " + square.calcPerimeter());
```

EXERCISE 4.3 Because `Square` is a subclass of `Rectangle`, it inherits the `calcPerimeter()` method, so it can use it in the statement `square.calcPerimeter`, just as if it were defined in the `Square` class.

EXERCISE 4.4 The following code should be added to `init()`:

```
System.out.println("The author of this applet is" + getParameter("author"));
System.out.println("The date of this applet is " + getParameter("date"));
```

EXERCISE 4.5

```
import java.awt.*;
public class SmallApplet extends Applet
{
    private Button clickme;                    // Declare a variable

    public void init()
    {
        clickme = new Button("Click me!");  // Create the button
        add(clickme);                       // Add it to the applet
    } //init()
} //SmallApplet
```

EXERCISE 4.6 The following statement should be added to `init()` after the `clickme Button` has been instantiated:

```
System.out.println( clickme.getLabel() );
```

EXERCISE 4.7 The + operator is used to add numbers and to concatenate strings. Thus, it is overloaded. It performs different operations on different types of data.

EXERCISE 4.8 You would declare your applet to implement the `ActionListener` interface and would create a `TextField` instance in your program. In the `init()` method, you would use `addActionListener()` to designate the `TextField` as the listener for its own action events. Then you would implement the `actionPerformed()` method, giving it instructions on what to do when the user types the Enter key.

EXERCISE 4.9 The applet would ignore the user's clicks on the `toggleButton`, because no listener was assigned to handle them.

EXERCISE 4.10 The `toggleButton` would not show up on the screen.

EXERCISE 4.11

```
boolean temp = b1;  // Save b1's value
b1 = b2;            // Change b1 to b2
b2 = temp;          // Change b2 to b1's original value
```

EXERCISE 4.12

```
private ToggleButton dealer = new ToggleButton("deal","collect");
add( dealer );
dealer.addActionListener( this );
```

EXERCISES

1. Fill in the blanks in each of the following sentences:

   a. An ______ is an embedded Java program.
   b. A method that lacks a body is an _____ method.
   c. An ______ is like a class except that it contains only instance methods, no instance variables.
   d. Two ways for a class to inherit something in Java is to ______ a class and ______ an interface.
   e. Classes and methods not defined in a program must be ______ from the Java class library.
   f. Instance variables and instance methods that are declared ______ or ______ are inherited by the subclasses.
   g. An object can refer to itself by using the ______ keyword.
   h. The `Button`, `TextField` and `Component` classes are defined in the ______ package.
   i. Java applets utilize a form of control known as ______ programming.
   j. When the user clicks on an applet's `Button`, an ______ will automatically be generated.
   k. Two kinds of objects that generate `ActionEvents` ______ and ______.
   l. `Buttons`, `TextFields`, `Containers`, and `Labels` are all subclasses of ______.
   m. The `Applet` class is a subclass of ______.
   n. If an applet intends to handle `ActionEvents`, it must implement the ______ interface.
   o. An applet's `init()` method is an example of a ______ method, because it does different things depending upon the object that invokes it.
   p. When an applet is started, its ______ method is called automatically.

2. Explain the difference between the following pairs of concepts:

   a. *Class* and *interface.*
   b. *Stub method* and *abstract method.*
   c. *Extending a class* and *instantiating an object.*
   d. *Defining a method* and *implementing a method.*
   e. A `protected` method and a `public` method.
   f. A `protected` method and a `private` method.
   g. An `ActionEvent` and an `ActionListener` method.

3. Draw a hierarchy chart to represent the following situation. There are lots of languages in the world. English, French, Chinese and Korean are examples of natural languages. Java, C, and C++ are examples of formal languages. French and Italian are considered Romance languages, while Greek and Latin are considered classical languages.
4. Arrange the Java library classes listed in the Chapter Summary into their proper hierarchy, using the `Object` class as the root of the hierarchy.
5. Look up the documentation for the `Button` class on the Sun's Web site (http://java.sun.com), and list the names of all the methods that are inherited by its `ToggleButton` subclass.
6. Suppose we want to set the text in our applet's `TextField`. What method should we use and where is this method defined? (*Hint*: Look up the documentation for `TextField`. If no appropriate method is defined there, see if it is inherited from a superclass.)
7. Does an `Applet` have an `init()` method? Explain.
8. Does a `Applet` have an `add()` method? Explain.
9. Does a `Button` have an `init()` method? Explain.
10. Does a `Button` have an `add()` method? Explain.
11. Suppose you type the URL for a "Hello World" applet into your browser. Describe what happens — that is, describe the processing that takes place in order for the applet to display "Hello World" in your browser.
12. Suppose you have an applet containing a `Button` named `button`. Describe what happens, in terms of Java's event handling model, when the user clicks on the button.
13. Java's `Object` class contains a public method, `toString()`, which returns a string that represents this object. Because every class is a subclass of `Object`, the `toString()` method can be used by any object. Show how you would invoke this method for a `Button` object named `button`.
14. The following applet contains a semantic error in its `init()` method. The error will cause the `actionPerformed()` method never to display "Clicked" even though the user clicks on the button in the applet. Why? (*Hint*: Think scope!)

```
public class SomeApplet extends Applet implements ActionListener
{
    // Declare instance variables
    private Button button;

    public void init()
    {   // Instantiate the instance variable
        Button button = new Button("Click me");
        add(button);
        button.addActionListener(this);
    } // init()

    public void actionPerformed(ActionEvent e)
    {
        if (e.getSource() == button)
           System.out.println("Clicked");
    } // actionPerformed()
} // SomeApplet
```

15. What would be output by the following applet?

```
public class SomeApplet extends Applet
{
    // Declare instance variables
    private Button button;
    private TextField field;

    public void init()
    {   // Instantiate instance variables
        button = new Button("Click me");
        add(button);
        field = new TextField("Field me");
        add(field);
        System.out.println(field.getText() + button.getText());
    } // init()
} // SomeApplet
```

16. Modify the `ToggleTest` applet so that it displays an image of a light bulb in the "on" or "off" state on alternate clicks of its `lightSwitch`.

17. Write a simple Java applet that creates a `Button`, a `TextField`, and a `Label`. Add statements to the `init()` method that use the `toString()` method to display each object's string representation.

18. Modify the `SimpleApplet` program so that it contains a second button labeled initially "The Doctor is in." Modify the `actionPerformed()` method so that every time the user clicks on a button, its label is toggled. The label on the second button should toggle to "The Doctor is out."

19. Modify the `SimpleApplet` program so that it contains two `Buttons`, initially labeled "Me first!" and "Me next!" Modify the `actionPerformed()` method so that every time the user clicks on either one of the buttons, the labels on both buttons are exchanged. (*Hint*: You don't need an if-else statement for this problem.)

20. Modify the `SimpleApplet` program so that it contains three `Buttons`, initially labeled "First," "Second," and "Third." Modify the `actionPerformed()` method so that every time the user clicks on one of the buttons, the labels on the buttons are rotated. Second should get first's label, third should get second's, and first should get third's label.

21. Modify the `SimpleApplet` program so that it contains a `TextField` and two `Buttons`, initially labeled "Left" and "Right." Modify the `actionPerformed()` method so that every time the user clicks on a button, its label is displayed in the `TextField`.

22. You can change the size of an applet by using the `setSize(int h, int v)` method, where *h* and *v* give the horizontal and vertical dimensions of the applet's window in pixels. Write an applet that contains two `Buttons`, labeled "Big" and "Small." Whenever the user clicks on small, set the applets dimensions to 200 x 100, and whenever the user clicks on big, set the dimensions to 300 x 200.

23. Rewrite the size-adjusting applet in the previous exercise so that it uses a single button, whose label is toggled appropriately each time it is clicked. Obviously, when the `Button` is labeled "Big," clicking it should give the applet its big dimensions.

24. **Challenge:** Design and write an applet that allows the user to change the applet's background color to one of three choices, indicated by buttons. Like all other Java `Components`, applet's have an associated background color, which can be set by the following commands:

```
setBackground( Color.red );
setBackground( Color.yellow );
```

    The `setBackground()` method is defined in the `Component` class, and 13 primary colors—`black, blue, cyan, darkGray, gray, green, lightGray, magenta, orange, pink, red, white, yellow` — are defined in the `java.awt.Color` class.
25. **Challenge:** Modify `CyberPet` and `CyberPetApplet` so that `CyberPet` can eat two different things — for example, a fly or a beetle. Your interface design should allow the user to set the `CyberPet`'s food type. Whenever the `CyberPet` is eating, its state should be reported as "Socrates is eating a fly."

Photograph courtesy of Craig Brewer, PhotoDisc, Inc.

Java Data and Operators

5

OBJECTIVES

After studying this chapter, you will

- Understand the role that data plays in effective program design.
- Be able to use all of Java's primitive types and their operators.
- Appreciate the importance of information hiding.
- Be able to use class constants and class methods in a program.
- Know how to use Java's `Math` and `NumberFormat` classes.
- Be able to perform various kinds of data conversions.

OUTLINE

5.1 Introduction

This chapter has two primary goals. One is to elaborate upon Java's *primitive data types*, which were first introduced in Chapter 2. We will cover boolean, integer, character, and real number data types, including the various operations that you can perform on these types. For each type of data we will provide examples of its typical uses.

Our second goal is to introduce various object-oriented design principles, such as information hiding and scalability, and to illustrate the idea that programming is a matter of choosing an appropriate way to represent a problem as well as choosing an appropriate sequence of actions to solve the problem.

To illustrate these principles we will develop two different implementations of the `CyberPet` class, one based on `boolean` data, as we did in Chapter 2, and the other based on integer (`int`) data. Each *model* or *representation* will be designed in such a way that it will function properly with `CyberPetApplet`, the interface we designed in Chapter 4. In other words, we will change the underlying implementation of the `CyberPet` class, without changing the interface to it in any way.

5.2 Programming = Representation + Action

Programming is a form of problem solving. Problem solving can be viewed as a two part process: *representation* and *action*.

Representation means finding a way to look at the problem. This might involve seeing the problem as an example of a known problem or as closely related to a known problem. It might involve seeing that parts of the problem can be broken up into smaller problems that you already know how to solve. In terms of programming problems, representation often means choosing the right kinds of objects and structures.

Action is the process of taking well-defined steps to solve a problem. Given a particular way of representing the problem, what steps must we take to arrive at its solution?

Choosing an appropriate representation is often the key to solving a problem. For example, consider this problem: Can a chessboard, with its top-left and bottom-right squares removed, be completely tiled by dominoes that cover two squares at a time?

One way to solve this problem might be to represent the chessboard and dominoes as shown in Figure 5–1. If we represent the board in this way, then the actions needed to arrive at a solution involve searching for a tiling that completely covers the board. In other words, we can try one way of placing the dominoes on the board. If that doesn't work, we try another way. And so on. This process will be very time consuming, because there are 31! (= 55,937,677,919,577,706,243,031,040,000,000) ways of placing the 31 dominoes on the board.

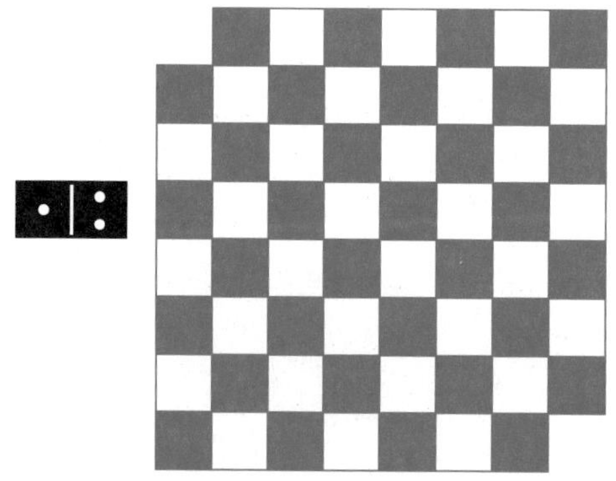

Figure 5–1 Can the chessboard be tiled with dominoes?

An alternative way to represent this problem comes from seeing that the top-left and bottom-right squares of the board are both white. If you remove them, you'll have a board with 62 squares, 32 black and 30 white. To cover the board you'll need 31 dominoes, and each domino must cover one white and one black square. But you can't cover 32 black squares and 30 white squares with 31 dominoes, so the board cannot be tiled.

Thus by representing the problem as the total number of black and white squares, the actions required to solve it involve a very simple reasoning process. This representation makes it almost trivial to find the solution. On the other hand, the *brute force* representation presented first — trying all possible combinations — made it almost impossible to solve the problem.

In the remainder of this chapter we consider two different representations for a `CyberPet` — `boolean` and `int` — and discuss which of the representations provide the best solution to the problem of simulating a CyberPet.

5.3 Boolean Data and Operators

The `boolean` type is a one of Java's primitive types. In the `boolean` type, there are only two possible values, `true` and `false`. The `boolean` type is derived from the work of George Boole , a British mathematician, who in the 1850s developed a type of algebra to process logical expressions such as *p and q*. Such *boolean expressions* produce a value that is either *true* or *false*. Every modern programming language provides some means of representing boolean expressions.

George Boole

The `boolean` type has several important uses. As we have seen in the `CyberPet` example, a `boolean` variable can be used to represent the presence or absence of a particular characteristic — sleeping or not sleeping. The `boolean` type is also used to represent the condition in the if statement:

Conditional statement

```
if (boolean expression)
    statement;
```

Boolean flag

For this reason, boolean expressions are also called *conditions*. Along these same lines, a `boolean` variable can be used as a *flag* or a *signal* to "remember" whether or not a certain condition holds. For example, in the following code fragment, we use `isDone` to mark when a particular process is completed:

```
boolean isDone = false; // Initialize the flag
...                     // Do some processing task
isDone = true;          // Set the flag when the task is done
...                     // Do some other stuff
if (isDone)             // Check whether we finished the task
...                     //  If so do something
else
...                     //  Otherwise, do something else
```

5.3.1 Boolean (or Logical) Operations

Data and operations

Like all the other simple data types, the `boolean` type consists of certain data — the values `true` and `false` — and certain actions or operations that can be performed on those data. For the boolean type there are four basic operations, AND (&&), OR (||), EXCLUSIVE-OR (∧), and NOT (!). The effect of these operations can be defined by the *truth table* shown in Table 5–1.

Binary operator

The boolean AND operation is a **binary** operation — that is, it requires two operands, *o1* and *o2* (column 3 of Table 5–1). If both *o1* and *o2* are true, then *(o1 && o2)* is true. If either *o1* or *o2* or both *o1* and *o2* are false, then the expression *(o1 && o2)* is false. The only case in which *(o1 && o2)* is true is when both *o1* and *o2* are true.

The boolean OR operation (column 4 of Table 5–1) is also a binary operation. If both *o1* and *o2* are false, then (*o*1 || *o*2) is false. If either *o1* or *o2* or both *o1* and *o2* are true, then the expression (*o*1 || *o*2) is true. Thus the only case in which (*o*1 || *o*2) is false is when both *o1* and *o2* are false.

The boolean EXCLUSIVE-OR operation (column 5 of Table 5–1) is a binary operation, which differs from the OR operator in that it is true when either *o1* or *o2* is true, but it is false when both *o1* and *o2* are true.

Table 5.1. Truth-table definitions of the boolean operators: AND (&&), OR (||), EXCLUSIVE-OR (∧), and NOT (!)

o1	o2	o1 && o2	o1 || o2	o1 ∧ o2	!o1
true	true	true	true	false	false
true	false	false	true	true	false
false	true	false	true	true	true
false	false	false	false	false	true

The NOT operation (the last column of Table 5–1) is a **unary operator** — it takes only one operand — and it simply reverses the truth value of its operand. Thus, if *o1* is true, *!o1* is false, and vice versa.

Unary operator

5.3.2 Precedence, Associativity, and Commutativity

In order to evaluate complex boolean expressions, it is necessary to understand the order in which boolean operations are carried out by the computer. For example, what is the value of the following expression?

```
true || true && false
```

The value of this expression depends on whether we evaluate the || first or the && first. If we evaluate the || first, the expression's value will be false; if we evaluate the && first, the expression's value will be true. In the following example, we use parentheses to force one operation to be done before the other:

```
EXPRESSION                    EVALUATION
----------                    ----------
( true || true ) && false     ==> true && false ==> false
true || ( true && false )     ==> true || false ==> true
```

As these evaluations show, we can use parentheses to force one operator or the other to be evaluated first. However, in Java, the && operator has higher precedence than the || operator. Therefore the second alternative corresponds to the default interpretation that Java would apply to the unparenthesized expression. In other words, given the expression *true || true && false*, the AND operation would be evaluated before the OR operation even though the OR operator occurs first (i.e., to the left) in the unparenthesized expression.

Parentheses supersede

As this example illustrates, the boolean operators have a built-in **precedence order** which is used to determine how boolean expressions are to be evaluated (Table 5–2). A simple method for evaluating an expression is to

Table 5.2. Precedence order of the boolean operators

Precedence Order	Operator	Operation
1	( )	Parentheses
2	!	NOT
3	&&	AND
4	^	EXCLUSIVE-OR
5	||	OR

parenthesize the expression and then evaluate it. For example, to evaluate the complex expression

```
true || !false ^ false && true
```

we would first parenthesize it according to the precedence rules set out in Table 5–2, which gives the following expression:

```
true || ((!false) ^ (false && true))
```

We can then evaluate this fully parenthesized expression, step by step, starting at the innermost parentheses:

```
Step 1. true || (true ^ (false && true))
Step 2. true || (true ^ false)
Step 3. true || true
Step 4. true
```

PROGRAMMING TIP: Parentheses. Parentheses can (and should) be used to clarify any expression that appears ambiguous, or to override Java's default precedence rules.

In addition to operator precedence, it is necessary to know about an operator's *associativity* in order to evaluate boolean expressions of the form (*op*1 || *op*2 || *op*3). Should this expression be evaluated as ((*op*1 || *op*2) || *op*3) or as (*op*1 || (*op*2 || *op*3))? The binary boolean operators all associate from left to right. Thus the following expressions

```
true ^ true ^ true         // Same as: (true ^ true) ^ true
true && true && true       // Same as: (true && true) && true
true || true || true       // Same as: (true || true) || true
```

would be evaluated as follows:

```
EXPRESSION                      EVALUATION
----------------                -----------------
(true ^ true)  ^ true           ==> false ^ true ==> true
(true && true)  && true         ==> true  && true ==> true
(true || true)  || true         ==> true  || true ==> true
```

Finally, all of the binary boolean operators are *commutative*, that is *p op q* is equivalent to *q op p* where *op* is any one of the binary boolean operators.

SELF-STUDY EXERCISES

EXERCISE 5.1 Suppose the following variable declarations are made:

```
boolean A = true, B = true, C = true;
boolean X = false, Y = false, Z = false;
```

Given these declarations, evaluate each of the following expressions. Don't forget to take operator precedence and associativity into account.

a. `A | B & Z`
b. `A ^ X & Z`
c. `A ^ X | C`
d. `!A & !B`
e. `A & B & X & Y`
f. `(!X ^ A) & (B ^ !Y)`

5.4 The Boolean-based CyberPet Model

The `CyberPet` class we designed in Chapters 2 to 4 (see Figure 3–17) is based on a boolean representation of the pet's state. A `CyberPet` 's state is represented by two private `boolean` variables: `isEating` and `isSleeping`. And changing the pet's state from one mode to the other requires that we assign `true` to one of these variables and `false` to the other.

```
private boolean isEating;          // CyberPet's state
private boolean isSleeping;
...
public CyberPet ()                 // Constructor method
{
    isEating = true;
    isSleeping = false;
}
```

This representation is simple and easy to understand, but it is somewhat unwieldy and hard to modify. One problem is that each time we wish to add another value to `CyberPet`'s state, we have to add another `boolean` variable and we have to add assignment statements to each of the methods that affect the state. For example, suppose we want to extend our model to allow for a `CyberPet` that can also think as well as eat and sleep. Let's suppose that thinking, eating, and sleeping are mutually exclusive for our simple minded pets.

To add a thinking state to our `CyberPet` class, we would have to add a new boolean variable:

```
boolean isThinking;
```

and we would have to add a `think()` method to the class:

```
public void think()  // Change the pet's state to thinking
{
    isSleeping = false;
    isEating = false;
    isThinking = true;
}
```

In addition, we would have to modify several of the existing methods to account for the fact that the value of this new state variable must be set each time the state changes. For example, the default constructor method would have to be modified to

```
public CyberPet()                // Constructor method
{
    isSleeping = false;
    isEating = true;
    isThinking = false;
}
```

and the eat() method would have to be modified to

```
public void eat()
{
    isSleeping = false;      // Change the state
    isEating = true;
    isThinking = false;
}
```

Thus, to add a thinking state to `CyberPet`, we have to modify every method in the class.

Lack of scalability

Obviously, using boolean variables to represent a CyberPet's state is not very practical. While the initial model was simple, it is not easily *extensible* . The model is based on the idea that each component of an object's state is represented by a separate `boolean` variable. This is like adding a new light switch that must be turned on or off each time we wish to extend the model by one new value. If a CyberPet's state is eventually going to have 20 possible values, we would need 20 boolean variables. That's a lot of light switches to manage! We might say that one problem with this representation is that it doesn't scale. It is not easy to extend the functionality of our model.

EFFECTIVE DESIGN: Scalability Principle. A well-designed model or representation should be easily extensible. It should be easy to add new functionality to the model.

Another problem with the boolean representation is that each change in the state requires modifications in every method in the class. A good design will minimize this ripple effect. Ideally, we want a representation that allows us to add new instance variables and methods without having to modify existing methods. The boolean representation forces us to create methods (that is, modules) that are not complete and self-contained. This is a violation of the modularity principle .

Lack of modularity

Are We Computers?

George Boole published his seminal work, *An Investigation of the Laws of Thought*, in 1854. His achievement was in developing an algebra for logic— that is, a purely abstract and symbolic system for representing the laws of logic. Boole's was not the first attempt to explore the relationship between the human mind and an abstract system of computation. Back in 1655 Thomas Hobbes had already claimed that all thought was computation.

It is estimated that the human brain contains ($10^{12} = 10{,}000{,}000{,}000{,}000$) *neurons*. And each neuron contains something like 10,000 *dendrites*, the fibers that connect one neuron to another. Together the neurons and dendrites make up a web of enormous complexity. Since the 1840s it's been known that the brain is primarily electrical, and by the 1940s scientists had developed a pretty good model of the electrical interactions among neurons. According to this model, neurons emit short bursts of electricity along their *axons*, which function like output channels. The bursts leap over the gap separating axons and dendrites, which function like the neurons' input channels.

In 1943, just before the first digital computers were developed, Warren McCulloch, a nuerophysiologist, and Walter Pitts, a mathematician, published a paper titled "A Logical Calculus of the Ideas Imminent in Nervous Activity." In this paper they showed that all of the boolean operators — AND, OR, NOT, and EXCLUSIVE-OR — could be represented by the behavior of small sets of neurons. For example, they showed that three neurons could be connected together in such a way that the third neuron fired if and only if both of the other two neurons fired. This is exactly analogous to the definition of the boolean AND operator.

A few years later, when the first computers were built, many scientists and philosophers were struck by the similarity between the logic gates and flip-flops that made up the computer's circuits, and the neuronal models that McCulloch and Pitts had developed.

The area of neural networks, a branch of artificial intelligence, one of the applied areas of computer science, is based on this insight by McCulloch and Pitts. Researchers in this exciting and rapidly advancing field, develop neural network models of various kinds of human thinking and perception.

EFFECTIVE DESIGN: Modularity Principle. A well-designed representation will allow us to design methods that do not require modification each time the model is extended.

Given these limitations to the boolean version of `CyberPet`, we will develop an alternative model based on an integer representation.

5.5 Numeric Data and Operators

Java has two kinds of numeric data: integers, which have no fractional part, and real numbers or floating point numbers, which contain a fractional component. Java has four different kinds of integers, `byte` , `short` , `int` , and `long` , which are distinguished by the the number of *bits* used to represent them. Java has two different kinds of real numbers, `float` and `double` , which are also distinguished by the number of bits used to represent them. See Table 5–3.

One bit can represent two possible values, 1 and 0, which can be used to stand for true and false, respectively. Two bits can represent four possible values: 00, 01, 10, and 11; three bits can represent eight possible values: 000, 001, 010, 100, 101, 110, 011, 111. And in general, an n-bit quantity can represent 2^n different values.

As illustrated in Table 5–3, an integer is a positive or negative whole number. Perhaps the most commonly used integer type in Java is the `int` type, which is represented in 32 bits. This means that Java can represent 2^{32} different `int` values, which range from −2,147,483,648 to 2,147,483,647 — that is, from -2^{31} to $(2^{31} - 1)$. Similarly, an 8-bit integer, a `byte`, can represent 2^8 or 256 different values, ranging from −128 to +127. A 16-bit integer, a `short`, can represent 2^{16} different values, which range from −32768 to 32767. And a 64-bit integer, a `long`, can represent whole number values ranging from -2^{63} to $2^{63} - 1$.

For floating point numbers, a 32-bit `float` type can represent 2^{32} different real numbers and a 64-bit `double` value can represent 2^{64} different real numbers.

Table 5.3. Java's numeric types

Type	Bits	Range of Values
byte	8	−128 to +127
short	16	−32768 to 32767
int	32	−2147483648 to 2147483647
long	64	-2^{63} to $2^{63} - 1$
float	32	$-3.40292347E+38$ to $+3.40292347E+38$
double	64	$-1.79769313486231570E+308$ to $+1.79769313486231570E+308$

EFFECTIVE DESIGN: Platform Independence. In Java a data type's size (number of bits) is part of its definition and therefore remains consistent across all platforms. In C and C++ the size of a data type is dependent on the compiler.

Data types are abstractions

It is worth noting that Java's numeric types are representations or models of whole numbers and real numbers in just the same way as our `CyberPet` class is a representation or model of a real pet. In all these cases, the representation is an abstraction, which has certain built-in limitations. In designing Java's data types, various trade-offs have been made in order to come up with a practical implementation.

Representation trade-offs

One trade-off is that the set of integers is infinite, but Java's `int` type can only represent a finite number of values. Similarly, Java cannot represent the infinite number of values that occur between, say, 1.111 and 1.112. So, certain real numbers cannot be represented at all. For example, one number that cannot be represented exactly is $\frac{1}{10}$. This can cause problems in trying represent dollars and cents accurately in a program. One possible solution is to use a penny as the basic unit of measurement so that dollar amounts can be represented as whole numbers.

Round-off error

DEBUGGING TIP: Roundoff Error. A *round-off error* is the inability to represent certain numeric values exactly.

Another source of problems in dealing with numeric data is due to limits in their *precision*. For example, a decimal number represented as a `double` value can have at most 17 *significant digits*, and a `float` can have at most 8. If you tried to store values such as 12345.6789 or 0.123456789 in a `float` variable, they would be rounded off to 12345.679 and 0.12345679, respectively, causing a possible error.

DEBUGGING TIP: Significant Digits. In using numeric data be sure the data type you choose has enough precision to represent the values your program need.

SELF-STUDY EXERCISES

EXERCISE 5.2 List all of the binary values that can be represented in 4 bits — that is, all values in the range 0000 to 1111.

EXERCISE 5.3 If a 6-bit representation were used for an integer type, how many different integers could be represented?

EXERCISE 5.4 Give an example of how the size of a data type affects platform dependence.

EXERCISE 5.5 If you were writing a program to process scientific data that had to be accurate to at least 12 significant (decimal) digits, what type of data would you use?

Table 5.4. The standard arithmetic operators in Java

Operation	Operator	Java	Algebra
Addition	+	$x + 2$	$x + 2$
Subtraction	-	$m - 2$	$m - 2$
Multiplication	*	$m * 2$	$2m$ *or* $2 \times m$
Division	/	x/y	$x \div y$ *or* $\frac{x}{y}$
Modulus	%	$x\%y$	*x modulo y (for integers x and y)*

5.5.1 Numeric Operations

Numeric operators

The operations that can be done on numeric data include the standard algebraic operations: *addition* (+), *subtraction* (−), *multiplication* (*), *division* (/), as well as the *modulus* (%) operator. Note that in Java, the multiplication symbol is * and not the ×. The arithmetic operators are binary operators, meaning that they each take two operands. Table 5–4 compares expressions involving the Java operators with their standard algebraic counterparts:

Although these operations should seem familiar, there are some important differences between their use in algebra and their use in a Java program. Consider the following list of expressions:

```
3 / 2        ==>  value 1     An integer result
3.0 / 2.0    ==>  value 1.5   A floating point result
3 / 2.0      ==>  value 1.5   A floating point result
3.0 / 2      ==>  value 1.5   A floating point result
```

Integer division gives integer result

In each of these cases we are dividing the quantity 3 by the quantity 2. However, different results are obtained depending on the *type* of the operands involved. When both operands are integers, as in (3/2), the result must also be an integer . Hence (3/2) has the value 1, an integer. Because integers cannot have a fractional part, the 0.5 is simply discarded. Integer division (/) always gives an integer result. Thus the value of (6/2) is 3 and the value of (7/2) is also 3. Because 3.5 is not an integer, the result of dividing 7 by 2 cannot be 3.5. Integer division cannot yield a result that has a fractional part.

DEBUGGING TIP: Integer Division. A common source of error among beginning programmers is forgetting that integer division always gives an integer result.

On the other hand, when either operand is a real number, as in the last three cases, the result is a real number. Thus, while the same symbol (/) is used for dividing integers and real numbers, there are really two different operations involved here: *integer division* and *floating-point division* . This use of the same symbol (/) for different operations is called **operator overloading**. It is similar to *method overloading* , which was discussed in Chapter 3.

What if you want to keep the remainder of an integer division? Java provides the modulus operator (%) which takes two integer operands. The expression (7%5) gives the remainder after dividing 7 by 5 — 2 in this case. In general the expression ($m\%n$) (read m mod n) gives the remainder after m is divided by n. For example:

Modular arithmetic

```
6 % 4    ==> 6 mod 4 equals 2
4 % 6    ==> 4 mod 6 equals 4
6 % 3    ==> 6 mod 3 equals 0
3 % 6    ==> 3 mod 6 equals 3
```

Numeric Promotion Rules

Because Java is a *strongly typed* language, expressions such as (3/2) have a type associated with them. In cases where one arithmetic operand is an integer and one is a floating point number, Java *promotes* the integer into a floating point value and performs a floating point operation.

Expressions have a type

Promotion is a matter of converting one type to another type. For example, in the expression (5 + 4.0) the value 5 must be promoted to 5.0 before floating point addition can be performed on (5.0 + 4.0). Generally speaking, automatic promotions such as these are allowed in Java whenever it is possible to perform the promotion *without loss of information*. Because an integer (5) does not have a fractional component, no information will be lost in promoting it to a real number (5.0). On the other hand, you cannot automatically convert a real (5.4) to an integer (5) because that might lead to loss of information. This leads to the following rule:

> **JAVA LANGUAGE RULE** **Integer Promotion.** In expressions that contain both integer and floating point operands, the integers are *promoted* to floating point values *before* the expression is evaluated.

This rule is actually an instance of a more general rule, for whenever an expression involves operands of different types, some operands must be converted before the expression can be evaluated. Consider the following example:

```
byte n = 125, short m = 32000;
n * m;
```

In this case *(n * m)* involves two different integer types, `byte` and `short`. Before evaluating this expression Java must first promote the `byte` to a `short` and carry out the operation as the multiplication of two `short`s. Conversion of `short` to `byte` would not be possible because there's no way to represent the value 32000 as a `byte`.

It is important to note that this conversion rule applies regardless of the actual values of the operands. In applying the rule Java looks at the operand's type, not its value. So even if m were assigned a value that could be represented as a byte (for example, 100), the promotion would still go from smaller to larger type. This leads to the general rule:

Promotion is automatic

JAVA LANGUAGE RULE **Type Promotion** In general, when two different types are involved in an expression, the smaller type — the one with fewer bits — is converted to the larger type before the expression is evaluated. To do otherwise would risk losing information.

Table 5–5 summarizes the actual promotion rules used by Java in evaluating expressions involving mixed operands. Note that the last rule implies that integer expressions involving `byte` or `short` or `int` are performed as `int`. This explains why integer *literals* — such as 56 or −108 — are represented as `int` types in Java.

Table 5.5. Java promotion rules for mixed arithmetic operators

If either operand is	The other is promoted to
`double`	`double`
`float`	`float`
`long`	`long`
`byte` *or* `short`	`int`

SELF-STUDY EXERCISES

EXERCISE 5.6 Evaluate each of the following integer expressions:

a. `8 / 2`
b. `9 / 2`
c. `6 / 8`
d. `9 % 2`
e. `8 % 6`
f. `6 % 8`
g. `8 % 4`
h. `4 % 8`

EXERCISE 5.7 Evaluate each of the following expressions, paying special attention to the *type* of the result in each case

a. `8 / 2.0`
b. `9 / 2.0`
c. `6 / 8`
d. `0.0 / 2`
e. `8.0 / 6.0`

EXERCISE 5.8 Suppose that the following variable declarations are made:

```
byte m = 3, short n = 4, int p = 5, long q = 6, double r = 7.0;
```

Use type promotion rules to determine the type of the expression and then evaluate each of the following expressions.

a. `m + n`
b. `p * q`
c. `m + n + r`
d. `p * q * m`
e. `r - m`

Table 5.6. Precedence order of the arithmetic operators

Precedence Order	Operator	Operation
1	( )	*Parentheses*
2	* / %	*Multiplication, Division, Modulus*
3	+ −	*Addition, Subtraction*

5.5.2 Operator Precedence

The built-in precedence order for arithmetic operators is shown in Table 5–6. Parenthesized expressions have highest precedence and are evaluated first. Next come the multiplication, division, and modulus operators, followed by addition and subtraction. When we have an unparenthesized expression that involves both multiplication and addition, the multiplication would be done first, even if it occurs to the right of the plus sign. Operators at the same level in the precedence hierarchy are evaluated from left to right. For example, consider the following expression:

```
9 + 6 - 3 * 6 / 2
```

In this case the first operation to be applied will be the multiplication (*), followed by division (/), followed by addition (+), and then finally the subtraction (−). We can use parentheses to clarify the order of evaluation. A parenthesized expression is evaluated outward from the innermost set of parentheses:

```
Step 1.  ( (9 + 6) - ((3 * 6) / 2 ) )
Step 2.  ( (9 + 6) - (18 / 2 ) )
Step 3.  ( (9 + 6) - 9 )
Step 4.  ( 15 - 9 )
Step 5.  6
```

Parentheses can (and should) always be used to clarify the order of operations in an expression. For example, addition will be performed before multiplication in the following expression:

```
(a + b) * c
```

Another reason to use parentheses is that Java's precedence rules will sometimes cause expressions that look fine to contain subtle syntax errors. For example, consider the following expressions:

```
18.0 / 6 % 5          // This expression has a syntax error
18.0 + 6 % 5          // This valid expression equals 19.0
```

The first expression contains a syntax error. Because the division operation would be done first and since (18.0 / 6) yields a floating point result, the left-hand operand of the % operator is not an integer, which causes a syntax error. In the second expression, because the % operation is performed first, there is no syntax error, as both operands of the % operator are integers. You must be aware of these kinds of issues when evaluating expressions in your programs.

PROGRAMMING TIP: Parenthesize! To avoid subtle bugs caused by Java's precedence rules, use parentheses to specify the order of evaluation in an expression.

SELF-STUDY EXERCISES

EXERCISE 5.9 Parenthesize and then evaluate each of the following expressions taking care to observe operator precedence rules. Watch for subtle syntax errors.

a. `4 + 5.0 * 6`
b. `(4 + 5) * 6`
c. `4 + 5 / 6`
d. `(4 + 5) / 6`
e. `4 + 5 % 3`
f. `(4 + 5) % 3`
g. `9 % 2 * 7 / 3`
h. `5.0 / 2 * 3 % 2`

5.5.3 Increment and Decrement Operators

Java provides a number of unary operators that are used to increment or decrement an integer variable. For example, the expression *k*++ uses the *increment operator* ++ to increment the value of the integer variable *k*. The expression *k*++ is equivalent to the following Java statements:

```
int k;
k = k + 1 ;  // Add 1 to k and assign the result back to k
```

Preincrement and postincrement

The *unary* ++ operator applies to a single integer operand, in this case to the variable *k*. It increments *k*'s value by 1 and assigns the result back to *k*. It may be used either as a *preincrement* or a *postincrement* operator. In the expression *k*++ the operator *follows* the operand, indicating that it is being used as a *postincrement* operator. This means that the increment operation is done *after* the operand's value is used.

Contrast that with the expression ++*k* in which the ++ operator *precedes* its operand. In this case it is used as a *preincrement* operator, which means that the increment operation is done *before* the operand's value is used.

When used in isolation, there is no practical difference between *k*++ and ++*k*. Both are equivalent to $k = k + 1$. However, when used in conjunction with other operators, there is a significant difference between preincrement and postincrement. For example, in the following code segment,

```
int j = 0, k = 0;    // Initially both j and k are 0
j = ++k;             // Final values of both j and k are 1
```

the variable k is incremented *before* its value is assigned to j. After execution of the assignment statement, j will equal 1 and k will equal 1. The above sequence is equivalent to

Precedence order

```
int j = 0, k = 0;    // Initially both j and k are 0
k = k + 1;
j = k;               // Final values of both j and k are 1
```

However, in the following example,

```
int i = 0, k = 0; // Initially both i and k are 0
i = k++;          // Final value of i is 0 and k is 1
```

the variable k is incremented *after* its value is assigned to i. After execution of the assignment statement, i will have the value 0 and k will have the value 1. The above sequence is equivalent to

```
int i = 0, k = 0;    // Initially both i and k are 0
i = k;
k = k + 1;           // Final value of i is 0 and k is 1
```

In addition to the increment operator, Java also supplies the *decrement* operator $--$, which can also be used in the predecrement and postdecrement forms. The expression $--k$ will first decrement k's value by one and then use k in any expression in which it is embedded. The expression $k--$ will use the current value of k in the expression in which k is contained and then it will decrement k's value by 1. Table 5–7 summarizes the increment and decrement operators. The unary increment and decrement operators have higher precedence than any of the binary arithmetic operators.

Predecrement and postdecrement

Table 5.7. Java's increment and decrement operators

Expression	Operation	Interpretation
$j = ++k$	*preincrement*	$k = k + 1;\ j = k;$
$j = k++$	*postincrement*	$j = k;\ k = k + 1;$
$j = --k$	*predecrement*	$k = k - 1;\ j = k;$
$j = k--$	*postdecrement*	$j = k;\ k = k - 1;$

JAVA LANGUAGE RULE **Pre- and Postincrement/Decrement.** If an expression like $++k$ or $--k$ occurs in an expression, k is incremented or decremented *before* its value is used in the rest of the expression. If an expression like $k++$ or $k--$ occurs in an expression, k is incremented or decremented *after* its value is used in the rest of the expression.

PROGRAMMING TIP: Increment and Decrement Operators. Because of their subtle behavior, be careful in how you use the unary increment and decrement operators. They are most appropriate and useful for incrementing and decrementing loop variables, as we'll see later.

SELF-STUDY EXERCISES

EXERCISE 5.10 What value will *j* and *k* have after each of the following calculations? Assume that *k* has the value 0 and *j* has the value 5 before each operation is done.

a. `k = j;`
b. `k = j++;`
c. `k = ++j;`
d. `k = j--;`
e. `k = --j;`

5.5.4 Assignment Operators

In addition to the simple assignment operator (=), which was covered in Section 2.5, Java supplies a number of shortcut assignment operators that allow you to combine an arithmetic operation and an assignment in one operation. These operations can be used with either integer or floating point operands. For example the += operator allows you to combine addition and assignment into one expression. The statement

```
k += 3;
```

is equivalent to the statement

```
k = k + 3;
```

Similarly, the statement

```
r += 3.5 + 2.0 * 9.3 ;
```

is equivalent to

```
r = r + (3.5 + 2.0 * 9.3);   // i.e., r = r + 19.1;
```

As these examples illustrate, when using the += operator, the expression on its right-hand side is first evaluated and then *added* to the current value of the variable on its left-hand side.

Table 5–8 lists the other assignment operators that can be used in combination with the arithmetic operators. For each of these operations, the interpretation is the same: Evaluate the expression on the right-hand side of the operator and then perform the arithmetic operation (such as addition or multiplication) to the current value of the variable on the left of the operator.

Table 5.8. Java's assignment operators

Operator	Operation	Example	Interpretation
=	*Simple assignment*	$m = n;$	$m = n;$
+=	*Addition then assignment*	m += 3;	$m = m + 3;$
−=	*Subtraction then assignment*	m −= 3;	$m = m - 3;$
∗=	*Multiplication then assignment*	m ∗= 3;	$m = m * 3;$
/=	*Division then assignment*	m /= 3;	$m = m/3;$
%=	*Remainder then assignment*	m %= 3;	$m = m\%3;$

SELF-STUDY EXERCISES

EXERCISE 5.11 What value will j and k have after each of the following calculations? Assume that k has the value 10 and that j has the value 5 before each operation is done.

a. `k += j;`
b. `k -= j++;`
c. `k *= ++j * 2;`
d. `k /= 25 * j--;`
e. `k %= j - 3;`

EXERCISE 5.12 Write four different statements that add 1 to the integer k.

5.5.5 Relational Operators

There are several *relational* operations that can be performed on integers: <, >, <=, >=, ==, !=. These correspond to the algebraic operators: $<$, $>$, $\leq$, $\geq$, $=$, and $\neq$. Each of these operators takes two operands (integer or real) and returns a boolean result. They are defined in Table 5–9.

Note that several of these relational operators require two symbols in Java. Thus the familiar equal sign (=) is replaced in Java by ==. This is so the equality operator can be distinguished from the assignment operator. Also, less than or equal to (<=), greater than or equal to (>=), and not equal to (!=) each require two symbols, instead of the familiar $\leq$, $\geq$, and $\neq$ from algebra. In each case the two symbols should be consecutive. It is an error in Java for a space to appear between the < and = in <=.

Equals vs. assigns

Table 5.9. Relational operators

Operator	Operation	Java Expression
<	*less than*	5 < 10
>	*greater than*	10 > 5
<=	*less than or equal to*	5 <= 10
>=	*greater than or equal to*	10 >= 5
==	*equal to*	5 == 5
!=	*not equal to*	5 != 4

DEBUGGING TIP: Equality and Assignment. A common semantic error among beginning programmers is to use the assignment operator (=) when the equality operator (==) is intended.

Among the relational operators, the inequalities (<, >, <=, and >=) have higher precedence than the equality operators (== and !=). In an expression that involves both kinds of operators the inequalities would be evaluated first. Otherwise the expression is evaluated from left to right.

Taken as a group the relational operators have lower precedence than the arithmetic operators. Therefore, in evaluating an expression that involves both arithmetic and relational operators, the arithmetic operations are done first. Table 5–10 includes all of the numeric operators introduced so far.

To take an example, let us evaluate the following complex expression:

```
9 + 6 <= 25 * 4 + 2
```

To clarify the implicit operator precedence, we first parenthesize the expression

```
( 9 + 6 ) <= ( (25 * 4 ) + 2 )
```

and then evaluate it step by step

```
Step 1. ( 9 + 6 ) <= ( (25 * 4 ) + 2 )
Step 2. ( 9 + 6 ) <= ( 100+ 2 )
Step 3. 15 <= 102
Step 4. true
```

The following expression is an example of an ill-formed expression:

```
9 + 6 <= 25 * 4 = 2
```

Table 5.10. Numeric operator precedence including relations

Precedence Order	Operator	Operation
1	( )	*Parentheses*
2	++ --	*Increment, Decrement*
3	* / %	*Multiplication, Division, Modulus*
4	+ -	*Addition, Subtraction*
5	< > <= >=	*Relational Operators*
6	== !=	*Equality Operators*

which becomes obvious if we parenthesize it and then attempt to evaluate it:

```
Step 1. ( ( 9 + 6 )  <= ( 25 * 4 ) ) == 2
Step 2. ( 15  <= 100 ) == 2
Step 3. true == 2                // Syntax error results here
```

The problem here is that the expression `true == 2` is an attempt to compare an `int` and a `boolean` value, which can't be done. As with any other binary operator, the == operator requires that both of its operands be of the same type. This is another example of Java's strong type checking.

Strong typing

SELF-STUDY EXERCISES

EXERCISE 5.13 For each of these questions, what is the value of m? Assume that k equals 2, j equals 3, and m equals 10, before each question. Don't forget about precedence.

```
a. m = j++ + k ;                 d. m *= j++ + k++;
b. m = ++j + k;                  e. m *= ++j + ++k;
c. m += j + k;
```

EXERCISE 5.14 Evaluate each of the following expressions taking care to observe operator precedence rules. If an expression is illegal, mark it illegal and explain why.

```
a. 4 + 5 ==  6 * 2               e. 4 + 5 % 3 != 7 - 2
b. (4 + 5) <= 6 / 3              f. (4 + 5) % 3 = 10 -4
c. 4 + 5 / 6 >= 10 % 2           g. 9 % 2 * 7 / 3 > 17
d. (4 = 5) / 6
```

5.6 CASE STUDY: Converting Fahrenheit to Celsius

To illustrate some of the issues that arise in using numeric data, let's design an applet that performs temperature conversions from Fahrenheit to Celsius and vice versa.

5.6.1 Problem Decomposition

This problem requires two classes, a `Temperature` class and a `TemperatureTest` class. The `Temperature` class will perform the temperature conversions, and `TemperatureTest` will serve as the user interface (Figure 5–2).

What objects do we need?

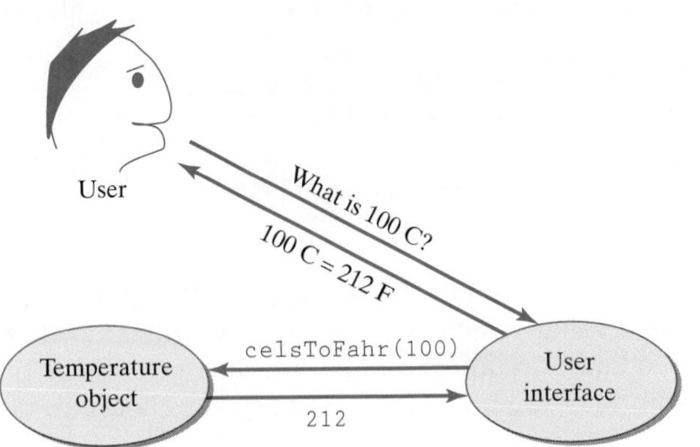

Figure 5–2 Interaction objects: The user interacts with the interface, which interacts with the Temperature object.

5.6.2 Class Design: Temperature

What data do we need?

The whole purpose of the Temperature class is to perform the temperature conversions. In order to do this, it doesn't really need to store any data. When we give it a Celsius value, it will just return the equivalent Fahrenheit value, and vice versa. So this class doesn't need any instance variables. It doesn't have an internal state to represent.

What methods do we need?

To perform its tasks, the Temperature class will need two public methods: one to convert from Fahrenheit to Celsius and one to convert from Celsius to Fahrenheit. These methods will use the standard conversion formulas: $F = \frac{9}{5}C + 32$ and $C = \frac{5}{9}(F - 32)$.

What type of data do we need?

Because we want to be able to handle temperatures that aren't whole numbers (98.6), we should use real number data for these methods. The double type is more widely used than float, because Java represents real literals as double. Using double variables, therefore, cuts down on the number of implicit data conversions that the program has to perform. So both methods should take a double parameter and return a double result.

PROGRAMMING TIP: Numeric Types. Java uses the int type for integer literals and double for real number literals. Unless you have some reason to prefer some other type, using these types for your variables and parameters reduces the number of implicit conversions your program would perform.

These considerations lead to the following design specification:

```
// Design Specification for the Temperature class
public Temperature();                        // Constructor
public double fahrToCels(double temp);       // Public instance methods
public double celsToFahr(double temp);
```

Implementation

The implementation of the Temperature class is shown in Figure 5–3. Note that because celsToFahr() uses the double value temp in its calculation, it uses floating point literals (9.0, 5.0, and 32.0) in its conversion expression:

```
private double celsToFahr( double temp )
{
    return (9.0 * temp / 5.0 + 32.0);
}
```

Figure 5–3 The `Temperature` class.

```
public class Temperature
{
    public Temperature() {}

    public double fahrToCels( double temp )
    {
        return (5.0 * (temp - 32.0) / 9.0);
    }
    public double celsToFahr( double temp )
    {
        return (9.0 * temp / 5.0 + 32.0);
    }
} // Temperature
```

This helps to reduce the reliance on Java's built-in promotion rules, which can lead to subtle errors. For example, suppose we had written what looks like an equivalent expression using integer literals:

```
return (9 / 5 * temp + 32);  // Error: equivalent to (tempt + 32)
```

Because 9 divided 5 gives the integer result 1, this expression is always equivalent to `temp + 32`, which is not the correct conversion formula. This kind of subtle *semantic* error can be avoided if you avoid mixing types wherever possible.

Semantic error

PROGRAMMING TIP: Don't Mix Types. You can reduce the incidence of semantic errors caused by implicit type conversions if, whenever possible, you explicitly change all the literals in an expression to the same type.

Testing and Debugging

Testing strategy

How should this program be tested? As always, you should test the program in a stepwise fashion. As each method is coded, you should test it both in isolation, and in combination with the other methods, if appropriate.

Designing test data

Also, you should develop appropriate *test data*. It is not enough to just plug in any values. The values you use should test for certain potential problems. For this program, the following tests are appropriate:

- Test converting 0 degrees C to 32 degrees F.
- Test converting 100 degrees C to 212 degrees F.
- Test converting 212 degrees F to 100 degrees C.
- Test converting 32 degrees F to 0 degrees C.

The first two tests use the `celsToFahr()` method to test the freezing point and boiling point temperatures, two boundary values for this problem. The second pair of tests perform similar checks with the `fahrToCels()` method. One advantage of using these particular values is that we know their outcomes.

EFFECTIVE DESIGN: Test Data. Developing appropriate test data is an important part of program design. One type of test data should check the boundaries of the particular calculations you are making.

DEBUGGING TIP: Test, Test, Test! The fact that your program runs correctly on some data is no guarantee of its correctness. The more testing, and the more careful the testing you do, the better.

5.6.3 The `TemperatureTest` Class

The purpose of the `TemperatureTest` class is to serve as a user interface. It will accept a Fahrenheit or Celsius temperature from the user and convert it using the public methods of the `Temperature` class. Its implementation is shown in Figure 5–4.

Algorithm design

The `TemperatureTest` program follows an **input-process-output** model for its main algorithm. The user will enter a temperature at the keyboard. The program will convert the temperature from Fahrenheit to Celsius. And the program will output the result:

```
Prompt the user and input a value.
Process the input.
Report the result.
```

User-interface design

Note how the program begins with a *prompt* that explains its purpose to the user. It also prompts the user for each input value. A well-designed user interface should provide appropriate prompts to guide the user's actions.

EFFECTIVE DESIGN: User Interface. Prompts should be used to explain a program's purpose to the user and to guide the user's actions, especially when inputting data.

To read the user's keyboard input, the program uses a `BufferedReader` object, which was covered in the "From the Java Library" section of Chapter 2. This object has a `readLine()`, which can be use to read the user's input into a `String` variable. The `BufferedReader` can be instantiated right in the `main()` method, but because the `readLine()` method can cause an `IOException`, `main()` must declare that it `throws` the exception:

```
public static void main(String argv[]) throws IOException
{
%    BufferedReader input = new BufferedReader    // Handles console input
        (new InputStreamReader (System.in));
    String inputString;                          //  inputString stores the input

    // Code deleted from here

    System.out.print("Input a temperature in Fahrenheit > ");
    inputString = input.readLine();
}
```

Figure 5–4 The TemperatureTest class.

```
import java.io.*;                    // Import the Java I/O classes

public class TemperatureTest
{
    public static double convertStringTodouble(String s)
    {
        Double doubleObject = Double.valueOf(s);
        return doubleObject.doubleValue();
    }

    public static void main(String argv[]) throws IOException
    {
        BufferedReader input = new BufferedReader    // Handles console input
            (new InputStreamReader(System.in));
        String inputString;                          // inputString stores the input

        Temperature temperature = new Temperature(); // Create a Temperature object
        double tempIn, tempResult;

        System.out.println("This program will convert Fahrenheit to Celsius and vice versa.");

                   // Convert Fahrenheit to Celsius

        System.out.print("Input a temperature in Fahrenheit > ");   // Prompt for Celsius
        inputString = input.readLine();                             // Get user input
        tempIn = convertStringTodouble(inputString);                // Convert to double
        tempResult = temperature.fahrToCels(tempIn);                // Convert to Celsius
        System.out.println(tempIn + " F = " + tempResult + " C ");  // Report the result

                   // Convert Celsius to Fahrenheit

        System.out.print("Input a temperature in Celsius > ");      // Prompt for Celsius
        inputString = input.readLine();                             // Get user input
        tempIn = convertStringTodouble(inputString);                // Convert to double
        tempResult = temperature.celsToFahr(tempIn);                // Convert to Fahrenheit
        System.out.println(tempIn + " C = " + tempResult + " F ");  // Report the result
    } // main()
} // TemperatureTest
```

5.6.4 Algorithm Design: Data Conversion

One subproblem that this program faces is that the user's input will be in the form of `String` data, but the temperature conversions require `double` data. Therefore, the program has to convert `Strings` such as "85.5" into `doubles` such as `85.5`.

Recall that Java supplies the `java.lang.Double` *wrapper class* for just this purpose (Chapter 2 Java Language Summary on page 97). Unfortunately, `Double` does not contain a method that directly converts `String` to `double`. However, it does provide the following two methods which can be used together to perform the desired conversion:

```
public static Double valueOf(String);  // Converts String to Double
public static double doubleValue();    // Converts Double to double
```

The `valueOf()` method can be used to convert a `String` into a `Double` object, and the `doubleValue()` method can be used to convert a `Double` object into its corresponding primitive `double` value:

```
double d = Double.valueOf(inputString).doubleValue(); // Ugly conversion
```

Method composition

Note here how the dot operator is used to *compose* two method calls. **Method composition** is the process of following one method call with another. The output from the first is used as the input to the second. The subexpression `Double.valueOf(inputString)` returns a `Double` object, to which we then apply the `doubleValue()` method.

Hide the ugly details!

Although it works fine, the syntax of this expression is pretty ugly and may be confusing to beginning programmers. To make the program more readable, let's break the conversion into two steps. Also, because we'll need to make this conversion every time we take user input, let's encapsulate it in a method:

```
public static double convertStringTodouble( String s )
{
    Double doubleObject = Double.valueOf(s); // String to Double
    return doubleObject.doubleValue();       // Double to double
}
```

Given the `convertStringTodouble()` method, we can now perform all the conversions needed by our program in one (relatively easy) step:

```
double userTemp = convertStringTodouble(inputString);
```

We just pass `inputString` to our method and it gives us back a `double` value.

Note that using a method for this operation has several important advantages. It hides the details of a complex and messy conversion from the rest of the program. By making the conversion into a method, we localize it. This helps to reduce and manage errors. If there's an error in the conversion expression, we just have to change the one method. If we didn't use a method, we'd have to change every occurrence of the conversion in the program. Once we get the method right, we can forget the messy details and just remember the name of the method!

Information hiding

Maintainability

Finally, using a method is self-documenting. It helps to raise the level of abstraction in the program. The method's name is descriptive of the operation it performs. In this case, when we call the method, it is clear that we're converting a `String` to a `double`. This is not at all obvious in the messy expression we used to do the actual conversion.

Method abstraction

EFFECTIVE DESIGN: Method Abstraction. Encapsulating complex operations in a method reduces the chances for error, and makes the program more readable and maintainable. Using methods tends to raise the level of abstraction in the program.

Given the `convertStringTodouble()` method, the algorithm in the main program is now straightforward:

```
System.out.print("Input a temperature in Celsius > ");      // Prompt for Celsius
inputString = input.readLine();                              // Get user input
tempIn = convertStringTodouble(inputString);                 // Convert to double
tempResult = temperature.celsToFahr(tempIn);                 // Convert to Fahrenheit
System.out.println(tempIn + " C = " + tempResult + " F ");   // Print the result
```

5.6.5 The `TemperatureApplet` class

Let's now design an applet interface to perform temperature conversions. The `TemperatureApplet` accepts a Fahrenheit or Celsius temperature from the user and converts it using the methods of the `Temperature` class. It will then display the result.

Problem Decomposition

In addition to the `Temperature` object, which will perform the conversions, the applet uses several GUI components to handle the interface tasks (Figure 5–5). As in `CyberPetApplet` (Chapter 4), `Buttons` are used to let the user control the program: one to convert from Fahrenheit to Celsius, and one to convert in the other direction.

What objects do we need?

A `TextField` is used to input temperatures from the user. As you know, a `TextField` displays one line of editable text. It has the following access methods:

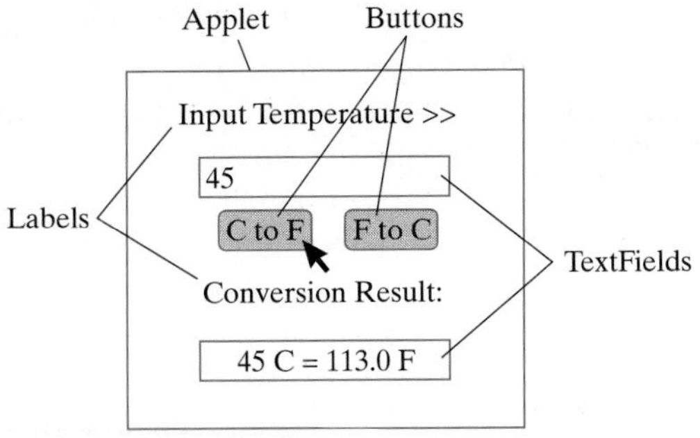

Figure 5–5 GUI layout for the TemperatureApplet.

```
TextField(int size);              // Create a TextField of size characters
public String getText();          // Extract the text from a TextField
public void setText(String s);    // Put a String into a TextField
```

When the user clicks one of the control buttons, we'll use the `getText()` method to read the input into the program.

Although it would be possible to use the same `TextField` for both input and output, it would be better to use two different `TextFields`, one for input and one for output. We'll use the `getText()` method to get the user's input from one, and we'll use the `setText()` method to display the result in the other. We'll use `Labels` to indicate which field is which.

What variables and methods do we need?

The applet will use an *input-process-output algorithm*. Depending on which button was clicked, it will get the user's input from the input `TextField`, process it, and display the result in the output `TextField`. The applet's `init()` method will instantiate all the GUI components and initialize the applet. The `actionPerformed()` method will handle the `Button` actions. Because this program must also convert from `String` to `double`, we'll use the `convertStringTodouble()` method that we developed earlier. Taken together these design decisions lead to the following specification:

```
// Design specification of the TemperatureApplet class
 private Temperature temperature;              // Temperature object
 private TextField inField;                    // GUI components
 private TextField resultField;                // GUI components
 private Button celsToFahr;
 private Button fahrToCels;
 public void init();                             // Initialization method
 public void actionPerformed(ActionEvent e);     // Event handling method
 private double convertStringTodouble(String s); // Conversion method
```

Implementation

The `TemperatureApplet` class is shown in Figure 5–6. Like our other applet examples, this one `extends Applet` and `implements ActionListener`. Note that all of the instance variables are declared `private` and instantiated in the global section of the class.

Figure 5–6 The `TemperatureApplet` class .

```
import java.applet.*;
import java.awt.*;
import java.awt.event.*;

public class TemperatureApplet extends Applet implements ActionListener
{
    private TextField inField = new TextField(15);      // GUI components
    private TextField resultField = new TextField(15);
    private Label prompt1 = new Label("Input Temperature >>");
    private Label prompt2 = new Label("Conversion Result:");
    private Button celsToFahr = new Button("C to F");
    private Button fahrToCels = new Button("F to C");

    private Temperature temperature = new Temperature();  // The temperature object

    public void init()
    {                       // Set up the user interface
        add(prompt1);         // Input elements
        add(inField);
        add(celsToFahr);      // Control buttons
        add(fahrToCels);
        add(prompt2);         // Output elements
        add(resultField);
        celsToFahr.addActionListener(this);  // Register buttons with listeners
        fahrToCels.addActionListener(this);
        setSize(175,200);
    } // init()

    public void actionPerformed(ActionEvent e)
    {
        String inputStr = inField.getText();                // Get user's input
        double userInput = convertStringTodouble (inputStr); // Convert it to double
        double result = 0;

        if (e.getSource() == celsToFahr) {                  // Process and report
            result = temperature.celsToFahr(userInput);
            resultField.setText(inputStr + " C = " + result  + " F \n");
        } else {
            result = temperature.fahrToCels(userInput);
            resultField.setText(inputStr + " F = " +  result  + " C \n");
        }
    } // actionPerformed()

    private double convertStringTodouble(String s)
    {
        return Double.valueOf(s).doubleValue();
    }
} // end of TemperatureApplet
```

Instantiation of each `TextField` object requires that we specify the number of characters that it will hold. This determines how big the `TextField` will be in the applet. We must also remember to `add()` it to the applet in the `init()` method:

```
TextField inField = new TextField(15);   // Declare and instantiate
add(tempField);                          // Add to applet -- in init()
```

Instantiation of each `Button` requires that we set the button's label, add it into the applet, and designate its `ActionListener`, which handles its button clicks:

```
private Button celsToFahr = new Button("C to F"); // Declare and instantiate
add(celsToFahr);                                  // Add to applet -- in init()
celsToFahr.addActionListener(this);               // Add its listener -- in init()
```

What control structures should be used?

The applet's `actionPerformed()` method implements the input-process-output algorithm. It uses an if-else statement to distinguish between the Celsius to Fahrenheit and Fahrenheit to Celsius cases:

```
public void actionPerformed(ActionEvent e)
{
    String inputStr = inField.getText();                       // Get user's input
    double userInput = convertStringTodouble(inputStr);  // Convert it to double
    double result = 0;

    if (e.getSource() == celsToFahr) {                    // Process and report
        result = temperature.celsToFahr(userInput);
        resultField.setText(inputStr + " C = " + result  + " F \n");
    } else {
        result = temperature.fahrToCels(userInput);
        resultField.setText(inputStr + " F = " +  result   + " C \n");
    }
} // actionPerformed
```

Interacting objects

It is here that we can easily see the interaction between the various objects involved in this program (Figure 5–2). The applet, through its `action-Performed()` method , is serving as an interface between the user and the `Temperature` object. It takes the user's input from the `TextField`, converts it, and passes it to the `Temperature` object. It gets a result from the `Temperature` object and displays it for the user in the `TextField` object. Figure 5–7 shows the applet's final appearance.

Note the use of the three local variables, `inputStr`, `userInput`, and `result`, to help break the computation into separate steps. The variables serve to carry values over from one step to the next. We use a temporary variable (of the correct type) to store a value produced in one statement and then use that value in the next statement.

PROGRAMMING TIP: Use of Variables. Use temporary variables within methods to store intermediate values produced during a calculation. These variables have local scope.

PROGRAMMING TIP: Divide and Conquer. Use temporary variables to divide a complicated computation into smaller steps.

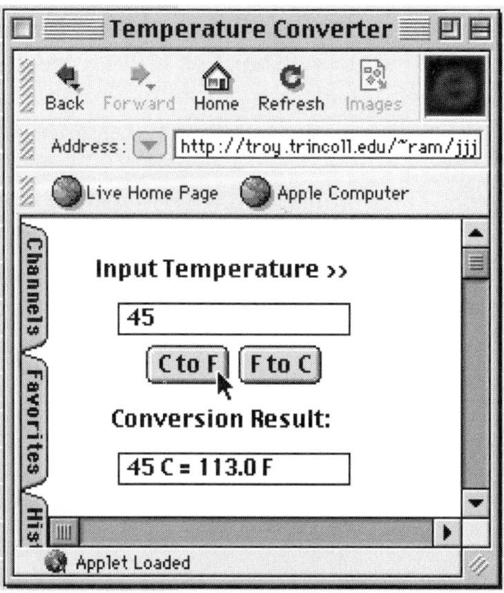

Figure 5–7 GUI layout for the `TemperatureApplet`.

5.7 An Integer-based CyberPet Model

Now that we have introduced the `int` type, let's use it to simplify our representation of the `CyberPet` class. Recall that the boolean representation forced us to introduce a new `boolean` variable for each possible value of the CyberPet's state. This caused all kinds of difficulties when we tried to add new states to the class. Many of these problems will go away if we use an integer variable to represent `CyberPet`'s state.

Suppose we declare the CyberPet's state as the following `int` variable:

```
private int petState;
```

We can now use integer values — for example, `0, 1, 2, ...` — to represent the different `CyberPet` states — 0 for eating, 1 for sleeping, 2 for thinking.

5.7.1 Class Constants

Class constants

Instead of using *integer literals* — 0, 1, 2 — Java provides a way of creating *named constants* that give names to the state values:

```
public static final int EATING = 0;
public static final int SLEEPING = 1;
public static final int THINKING = 2;
```

A **class constant** is a `final static` variable that is associated with the class, rather than with its instances.

static keyword

If a variable is declared `static`, there is exactly one instance of that variable created no matter how many times its class is instantiated. Even if the class has no instances — even if no individual `CyberPet` objects are created — the class itself will keep a single copy of its static variables. Because static variables do not depend on the creation of objects (instances), they are called **class variables** .

Class variables

final keyword

The `final` keyword is used to declare a variable that has a constant value throughout the duration of the program. Variables declared `final` must have an initializer — for example, `EATING = 0`. Once a `final` variable has been initialized, any attempt to change its value will cause a syntax error.

Finally, by declaring these constants as `public`, we make them accessible to objects that use the `CyberPet` class. There are two ways to reference class constants. They can be accessed through any `CyberPet` instance, in the same way that we access an instance variable or instance method. Or they can be accessed through the class itself:

Using the class as a reference

```
CyberPet socrates = new CyberPet();      // Create an instance
System.out.println(socrates.EATING);     // Refer to a constant

System.out.println(CyberPet.EATING);     // No instance needed
```

Both `socrates.EATING` and `CyberPet.EATING` refer to the same value (0).

Being able to refer to class constants before creating an instance allows us to use them in the constructor to set the pet's initial state. For example, our new version of `CyberPet` (Figure 5–8) provides four constructor methods, including one with a new signature: `CyberPet(String,int)`. The second parameter here requires an integer that represents the initial value of `CyberPet`'s `petState` variable. This is one place where we can use a class constant:

```
CyberPet pet3 = new CyberPet ( "Ernie", CyberPet.SLEEPING );
```

The Advantage of Class Constants

The notion of associating a constant with a class makes perfect sense. Clearly the proper place for constants such as EATING and SLEEPING is with the class itself and not with any particular `CyberPet` object, because their values don't depend on the state of any particular `CyberPet` instance.

Class constants are used extensively in the Java class library. For example, the various built-in colors are represented as constants of the `java.awt` `Color` class — `Color.blue` and `Color.red`. The `java.awt.Label` uses `int` constants to specify how a label's text should be aligned: `Label.CENTER`.

Maintainability

Using constants, whether `static` or not, makes it much easier to modify and maintain a program. As the new version of `CyberPet` illustrates (Figure 5–8), constants, such as `EATING`, are declared at the beginning of

Figure 5–8 An integer-based CyberPet model.

```
public class CyberPet
{
    public static final int EATING = 0;   // Class constants
    public static final int SLEEPING = 1;
    public static final int THINKING = 2;

    private int petState;   // Instance variables
    private String name;

    public CyberPet() {             // Constructor #1
        name = "no name";
        petState = EATING;
    }
    public CyberPet(String str) {  // Constructor #2
        name = str;
        petState = EATING;
    }
    public CyberPet(String str, int inState) { // Constructor #3
        name = str;
        petState = inState;
    }
    public CyberPet(String str, boolean sleeping) {  // Constructor #4
        name = str;
        if (sleeping == true)
            petState = SLEEPING;
        else
            petState = EATING;
    }
    public void   setName(String str) { name = str; } // setName()
    public String getName()  { return name;         } // getName()
    public void   eat()      { petState = EATING;   } // eat()
    public void   sleep()    { petState = SLEEPING; } // sleep()
    public void   think()    { petState = THINKING; } // think()
    public String toString() { return "I am a CyberPet named " + name;  }

    public String getState() {
        if (petState == EATING)
            return "Eating";          // Exit the method
        if (petState == SLEEPING)
            return "Sleeping";        // Exit the method
        if (petState == THINKING)
            return "Thinking";
        return "Error in State";      // Exit the method
    } // getState()
} // CyberPet
```

the class definition and then used throughout the program instead of literal integer values. If it becomes necessary to change a constant's value, we need only change its initializer. For literals, on the other hand, we'd have to change every occurrence of the literal, which could easily lead to errors. So using constants makes program maintenance easier and less prone to error.

EFFECTIVE DESIGN: Maintainability. Constants should be used instead of literal values in a program. This will make the program easier to modify and maintain .

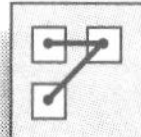

Programming Style

Note that we have used uppercase characters for the names of the four constants. This is a stylistic convention intended to make our program more readable. It has no effect on the compiler, which only cares about the constant's `static final` qualifiers. Using uppercase makes constants easily identifiable and easily distinguishable from genuine variables.

PROGRAMMING TIP: Readability. To make your programs more readable, use uppercase font for constant identifiers.

5.7.2 The Revised `CyberPet` Class

Given our new representation for a CyberPet's state, we have to make corresponding changes to its methods (Figure 5–8). The good news is that several of the methods remained unchanged, including the `setName()`, `getName()`, and `toString()` methods. More good news is that several of the other methods actually became simpler to implement. For example the constructor methods now require a single assignment statement to set the initial state of a `CyberPet`:

```
petState = EATING;
```

And several of the access methods are now so short they can be written on a single line:

```
public String getName()  { return name;        }    // getName()
public void   eat()      { petState = EATING;  }    // eat()
```

The most significant change required in the integer model occurs in the constructor method, `CyberPet(String,boolean)`. In that case we have to change the method definition as follows:

```
          Old version
----------------------------------------
CyberPet(String str, boolean sleeping) {
    name = str;
    isSleeping = sleeping;
    isEating = !isSleeping;
}

         New Version
-----------------------------------
CyberPet(String str, int inState) {
    name = str;
    petState = inState;
}
```

Since we have changed our state representation from boolean to int, we have to change the second parameter in this method from boolean to int.

However, unlike the other changes, this change has implications that extend beyond CyberPet itself. Any program that was using the CyberPet(String, boolean) constructor — for example, pet1 = new CyberPet("pete", true) — will no longer compile and run, if we remove it from our definition. This is not good. In general, if we make changes to a class, such as CyberPet, we don't want to break the programs that were using that old version of the class. Can anything be done to prevent this situation?

The answer is that instead of removing CyberPet(String,boolean), we should reimplement it as follows:

```
public CyberPet(String str, boolean sleeping) { // Constructor #4
    name = str;
    if (sleeping == true)
        petState = SLEEPING;
    else
        petState = EATING;
}
```

This reimplementation of CyberPet(String,boolean) is compatible with our new state representation, but it can still be used by those programs that were using the old version of CyberPet. It allows the integer-based version of CyberPet to be *backward compatible* with the previous version.

EFFECTIVE DESIGN: Backward Compatibility. Modifications to a class should try to preserve its compatibility with other classes that use it.

Backward compatibility

The problem of backward compatibility is ever present in the software industry, where products are continually revised and upgraded. This goes for the Java language itself, which has gone through versions 1.0, 1.1, and 1.2 within the space of a few years. New classes have been added and existing classes have changed. Sun Microsystems warns users when a *deprecated* method or class is being used in a program — that is, one that has been superseded in the new version. But in an effort to maintain compatibility with older versions of Java, it still supports the deprecated element, much as we have done in our modification to CyberPet 1.0!

5.7.3 Advantages of the Integer-based CyberPet

Simplicity

Our new CyberPet is a big improvement over the previous version. For one thing it uses a much simpler state representation. Maintaining a single integer variable is much simpler than maintaining several boolean variables. Also, the methods used to change the state are much simpler, requiring just a single assignment statement to do their respective tasks.

Extensibility

Moreover, because its methods are more self-contained, our new model is more extensible. For example, note how CyberPet was extended to cover the state of thinking. A class constant was defined:

```
public static final int THINKING = 2;
```

A (thinking) access method was defined:

```
public void think() {
    petState = THINKING;
}
```

And a third if statement was added to the getState() method:

```
if (petState == THINKING)
    return "Thinking";
```

Modularity

These are the only required changes. Most importantly, because of the improved modularity in its method design, a change in one method does not ripple through the entire class, as it did in the boolean version.

Generality

The integer representation can also be used to model other aspects of a CyberPet's state. For example the pet's kind could be incorporated into the model:

```
private int kind;                          // Instance variable

public static final int DOG = 0;           // Class constants
public static final int CAT = 1;
public static final int PARAKEET = 2;
public static final int GERBIL = 3;
                                          // Access methods
public void setKind(int inKind) { kind = inKind; }
public int  getKind()           { return kind;   }
```

In sum, the integer version of CyberPet is much superior to the boolean-based model. Not only does it adopt a simpler state representation, but it also makes the model more extensible. Moreover, the model is general enough to be easily extended without sacrificing backwards compatibility. All of these are important design considerations when deciding on an appropriate model for representing a program's objects.

SELF-STUDY EXERCISES

EXERCISE 5.15 To confirm that either the boolean-based CyberPet or the integer-based CyberPet will work the same way, run both models using the CyberPetApplet interface you developed in Chapter 4. What does the success of this experiment signify for object-oriented design?

OBJECT-ORIENTED DESIGN: Information Hiding

The fact that the integer-based version of CyberPet is *backward compatible* with the previous version is due in large part to the way we have divided up its public and private elements. Because the new version of CyberPet still presents the same *public interface*, an object such as CyberPetApplet can continue to use CyberPet without changing a single line of its own code.

Preserving the public interface

Although we have completely changed the underlying representation of CyberPet, the implementation details — its data and algorithms — are hidden from other objects. As long as CyberPet's public interface remains compatible with the old version, changes to its private elements won't cause any inconvenience to those objects that were dependent on the old version. This ability to change the underlying implementation without affecting the outward functionality of a class is one of the great benefits of the information hiding principle.

Information hiding

This modification in the CyberPet class is analogous to the Acme Computer Warehouse (Chapter 1) changing its internal procedures for processing catalog orders. As long as the internal changes don't affect the user interface, Acme's customers can continue to be served effectively.

The lesson to be learned here is that the public parts of a class should be restricted to just those parts that must be accessible to other objects. Everything else should be private. Things work better, in Java programming and in the real world, when objects are designed with the principle of information hiding in mind.

EFFECTIVE DESIGN: Information Hiding. In designing a class, other objects should be given access just to the information they need and nothing more.

5.8 Character Data and Operators

Another primitive data type in Java is the character type, `char` . A character in Java is represented by a 16-bit unsigned integer. This means that a total of 2^{16} or 65536 different Unicode characters can be represented, corresponding to the integer values 0 to 65535. The *Unicode* character set is an international standard that has been developed to enable computer languages to represent characters in a wide variety of languages, not just English. Detailed information about this encoding can be obtained at `http://www.unicode.org`.

Unicode

It is customary in programming languages to use unsigned integers to represent characters. This means that all the digits (0, . . . , 9), alphabetic letters ($a, \ldots, z, A, \ldots, Z$), punctuation symbols (such as . ; , " " ! _ -), and nonprinting control characters (LINE_FEED, ESCAPE, CARRIAGE_RETURN, . . .) that make up the computer's character set are represented in the computer's memory by integers. A more traditional set of

Table 5.11. ASCII codes for selected characters

Code	32	33	34	35	36	37	38	39	40	41	42	43	44	45	46	47
Char	SP	!	"	#	$	%	&	'	(	)	*	+	,	-	.	/

Code	48	49	50	51	52	53	54	55	56	57
Char	0	1	2	3	4	5	6	7	8	9

Code	58	59	60	61	62	63	64
Char	:	;	<	=	>	?	@

Code	65	66	67	68	69	70	71	72	73	74	75	76	77
Char	A	B	C	D	E	F	G	H	I	J	K	L	M

Code	78	79	80	81	82	83	84	85	86	87	88	89	90
Char	N	O	P	Q	R	S	T	U	V	W	X	Y	Z

Code	91	92	93	94	95	96
Char	[	\	]	^	_	‘

Code	97	98	99	100	101	102	103	104	105	106	107	108	109
Char	a	b	c	d	e	f	g	h	i	j	k	l	m

Code	110	111	112	113	114	115	116	117	118	119	120	121	122
Char	n	o	p	q	r	s	t	u	v	w	x	y	z

<table>
<tr><th>Code</th><th>123</th><th>124</th><th>125</th><th>126</th></tr>
<tr><td>Char</td><td>{</td><td>|</td><td>}</td><td>~</td></tr>
</table>

ASCII code

characters is the *ASCII (American Standard Code for Information Interchange)* character set. ASCII is based on a 7-bit code and therefore defines 2^7 or 128 different characters, corresponding to the integer values 0 to 127. In order to make Unicode backward compatible with ASCII systems, the first 128 Unicode characters are identical to the ASCII characters. Thus in both the ASCII and Unicode encoding, the printable characters have the integer values shown in Table 5–11.

5.8.1 Character to Integer Conversions

Is 'A' a character or an integer? The fact that character data are stored as integers in the computer's memory, can cause some confusion about whether a given piece of data is a character or an integer. In other words when is a character, say 'A,' treated as the integer (65) instead of as the character 'A'? The rule in Java is that a character literal — 'a' or 'A' or '0' or '?' — is always treated as a character, unless we explicitly tell Java to treat it as an integer. So if we display a literal's value

```
System.out.println('a');
```

the letter 'a' will be displayed. Similarly, if we assign 'a' to a `char` variable and then display the variable's value,

```
char ch = 'a';
System.out.println(ch);          // Displays 'a'
```

the letter 'a' will be shown. If on the other hand we wish to output a character's integer value, we must use an explicit *cast* operator as follows:

```
System.out.println((int)'a') ;   // Displays 97
```

A **cast operation** [(int)] converts one type of data ('a') into another (97). This is known as a **type conversion** . Similarly, if we wish to store a character's integer value in a variable, we can *cast* the char into an int as follows:

```
int k = (int)'a';        // Converts 'a' to 97
System.out.println(k);  // Displays 97
```

The cast operator

As these examples show, a *cast* is a type conversion operator. Java allows a wide variety of both explicit and implicit type conversions. Certain conversions (for example, promotions) take place when methods are invoked, when assignment statements are executed, when expressions are evaluated, and so on.

Type conversion in Java is governed by several rules and exceptions. In some cases Java allows the programmer to make implicit cast conversions. For example in the following assignment a char is converted to an int even though no explicit cast operator is used:

```
char ch;
int k;
k = ch; // convert a char into an int
```

Implicit type conversion

Java permits this conversion because no information will be lost. A character char is represented in 16 bits whereas an int is represented in 32 bits. This is like trying to put a small object into a large box. Space will be left over, but the object will fit inside without being damaged. Similarly, storing a 16-bit char in a 32-bit int will leave the extra 16 bits unused. This *widening primitive conversion* changes one primitive type (char) into a wider one (int), where a type's *width* is the number of bits used in its representation.

Widening conversion

On the other hand, trying to assign an int value to a char variable leads to a syntax error:

```
char ch;
int k;
ch = k;    // Syntax error: can't assign int to char
```

Trying to assign a 32-bit int to 16-bit char is like trying to fit a big object into an undersized box. The object won't fit unless we shrink it in some way. Java will allow us to assign an int value to a char variable, but only if we perform an explicit cast on it:

```
ch = (char)k; // Explicit cast of int k into char ch
```

The (char) cast operation performs a careful "shrinking" of the int by lopping off the last 16 bits of the int. This can be done without loss of information provided that *k*'s value is in the range 0 to 65535 — that is, in the range of values that fit into a char variable. This *narrowing primitive conversion* changes a wider type (32-bit int) to a narrower type (16-bit char). Because of the potential here for information loss, it is up to the programmer to determine that the cast can be performed safely.

Narrowing conversion

JAVA LANGUAGE RULE **Type Conversion.** Java permits *implicit* type conversions from a narrower type to a wider type. A *cast* operator must be used when converting a wider type into a narrower type.

The cast operator can be used with any primitive type. It applies to the variable or expression that immediately follows it. Thus, parentheses must be used to cast the expression $m + n$ into a char:

```
char ch = (char)(m + n);
```

The following statement would cause a syntax error because the cast operator would only be applied to m:

```
char ch = (char)m + n;    // Syntax error: right hand side is an int
```

In the expression on the right-hand side, the character produced by (char)m will be promoted to an int because it is part of an integer operation whose result will still be an int. Therefore it cannot be assigned to a char without an explicit cast.

SELF-STUDY EXERCISES

EXERCISE 5.16 Suppose that *m* and *n* are integer variables of type int and that *ch1* and *ch2* are character variables of type char. Determine in each of the following cases whether the assignment statements are valid. If not, modify the statement to make it valid.

a. `m = n;`
b. `m = ch1;`
c. `ch2 = n;`
d. `ch1 = ch2;`
e. `ch1 = m - n;`

5.8.2 Lexical Ordering

Although the actual integer values assigned to the individual characters by ASCII and UNICODE encoding seem somewhat arbitrary, there are a number of important encoding regularities. For example, note that various sequences of digits, `'0'...'9'`, and letters, `'a'...'z'` and `'A'...'Z'`, are represented by sequences of integers (Table 5.11). This makes it possible to represent the concept of *lexical order* among characters in terms of the *less than* relationship among integers. The fact that 'a' comes before 'f' in alphabetical order is represented by the fact that 97 (the integer code for 'a') is less than 102 (the integer code for 'f'). Similarly, the digit '5' comes before the digit '9' in an alphabetical sequence because 53 (the integer code for '5') is less than 57 (the integer code for '9').

This ordering relationship extends throughout the character set. Thus it is also the case that 'A' comes before 'a' in the lexical ordering because 65 (the integer code for 'A') is less than 97 (the integer code for 'a'). Similarly, the character '[' comes before '}' because its integer code (91) is less than 125, the integer code for '}.'

5.8.3 Relational Operators

`char` *relations*

Given the lexical ordering of the `char` type, the following relational operators can be defined: <, >, <=, >=, ==, !=. Given any two characters, *ch1* and *ch2*, the expression *ch1 < ch2* is true if and only if the integer value of *ch1* is less than the integer value of *ch2*. In this case we say that *ch1 precedes ch2* in lexical order. Similarly, the expression *ch1 > ch2* is true if and only if the integer value of *ch1* is greater than the integer value of *ch2*. In this case we say that *ch1 follows ch2*. And so on for the other relational operators. This means that we can perform comparison operations on any two character operands (Table 5–12).

Table 5.12. Relational operations on characters

Operation	Operator	Java	True Expression
precedes	<	*ch1 < ch2*	*'a' <' b'*
follows	>	*ch1 > ch2*	*'c' >' a'*
precedes or equals	<=	*ch1 <= ch2*	*'a' <=' a'*
follows or equals	>=	*ch2 >= ch1*	*'a' >=' a'*
equal to	==	*ch1 == ch2*	*'a' ==' a'*
not equal to	!=	*ch1 != ch2*	*'a' != 'b'*

5.9 Example: Character Conversions

Lowercase to uppercase

Another interesting implication of representing the characters as integers is that we can represent various character operations in terms of integer operations. For example, suppose we want to capitalize a lowercase letter. Table 5–11 shows that the entire sequence of lowercase letters (`'a,' ..., 'z'`) is displaced by 32 from the sequence of uppercase letters (`'A,'..., 'Z'`), so we can convert any lowercase letter into its corresponding uppercase letter by subtracting 32 from its integer value, provided we perform an explicit cast on the result. When we perform the cast `(char) ('a' - 32 )` the resulting value is `'A'`, as the following example shows:

```
(char)('a' - 32)              ==>  'A'
```

Recall that in evaluating `'a' - 32` Java will promote 'a' to an `int` and then perform the subtraction. Thus a step-by-step evaluation of the expression would go as follows:

```
Step 1. (char)((int)'a' - 32)  // Promote 'a' to int
Step 2. (char)(97 - 32)        // Subtract
Step 3. (char) (65)            // Cast result to a char
Step 4. 'A'                    // Giving 'A'
```

Uppercase to lowercase

Similarly, we can convert an uppercase letter into the corresponding lowercase letter by simply adding 32 to its integer code and casting the result back to a char:

```
(char)('J' + 32)              ==>  'j'
```

We can group these ideas into a method that performs conversion from lowercase to uppercase:

```
char toUpperCase(char ch) {
    if ((ch >= 'a') && (ch <= 'z'))
        return ch - 32 ;             // Syntax error: can't return an int
    return ch;
}
```

Type error

This method takes a single `char` parameter and returns a `char` value. It begins by checking if *ch* is a lowercase letter — that is, if *ch* falls between 'a' and 'z' inclusive. If so, it returns the result of subtracting 32 from *ch*. If not, it returns *ch* unchanged. However, the method contains a syntax error which becomes apparent if we trace through its steps. If we invoke it with the expression `toUpperCase('b')`, then since *'b'* is between *'a'* and *'z'*, the method will return *'b' - 32*. Because the integer value of *'b'* is 98, it will return *98 - 32* or 66, which is the integer code for the character *'B'*. However, the method is supposed to return a `char` so this last statement will generate the following syntax error:

```
Incompatible type for return. An explicit cast needed to convert int to char.
>>    return ch - 32 ;
>>    ^
```

In order to avoid this error, the result must be converted back to `char` before it can be returned:

```
char toUpperCase (char ch) {
    if ((ch >= 'a') && (ch <= 'z'))
        return (char)(ch - 32);     // Explicit cast required
    return ch;
}
```

Another common type of conversion is to convert a digit to its corresponding integer value. For example, we convert the character '9' to the integer 9 by making use of the fact that the digit '9' is 9 characters beyond the digit '0' in the lexical order. Therefore, subtracting '0' from '9' gives integer 9 as a result:

Digit to integer

```
('9' - '0')  ==> (57 - 48) ==>   9
```

More generally, the expression *ch - '0'* will convert any digit, *ch*, to its integer value. We can encapsulate these ideas into a method that converts any digit into its corresponding integer value:

```
int digitToInteger(char ch) {
    if ((ch >= '0') && (ch <= '9'))
        return ch - '0';
    return -1 ;
}
```

This method takes a single `char` parameter and returns an `int`. It first checks that *ch* is a valid digit, and if so, it subtracts the character '0' from it. If not, the method just returns −1, which indicates that method received an invalid input parameter. Obviously, when an object invokes this method, it should first make sure that the value it passes is in fact a digit.

The Java application program shown in Figure 5–9 illustrates several of the ideas discussed in this section.

5.9.1 Static Methods

Note that the public methods in the `Test` class (Figure 5–9) are declared `static` . This is due to a restriction in Java applications that prevents `static` methods, such as `main()`, from using nonstatic methods or instance variables. Recall that the modifier `static` means that exactly one copy of the variable or method is created, whether or not the class in which is occurs is instantiated.

Figure 5–9 A Java program illustrating character conversions.

```
public class Test {
    public static void main(String argv[]) {
        char ch = 'a';                 // Local variables
        int k = (int)'b';

        System.out.println(ch);
        System.out.println(k);
                                      // ch = k erroneous assignment
        ch = (char)k;                 // so we use an explicit cast
        System.out.println(ch);
        System.out.println(toUpperCase('a'));
        System.out.println(toUpperCase(ch));
        System.out.println(digitToInteger('7'));
    }

    public static char toUpperCase(char ch) {
        if ((ch >= 'a') && (ch <= 'z'))
            return (char)(ch - 32);
        return ch;
    }

    public static int digitToInteger(char ch) {
        if ((ch >= '0') && (ch <= '9'))
            return ch - '0';
        return -1 ;
    }
} // Test
       ************************************************************
       The output produced by this program on the Java console

       a
       98
       b
       A
       B
       7
       ************************************************************
```

Static methods

The fact that `main()` is `static` means that there is exactly one instance of it no matter how many instances (including none) of its class exist. In order for `main()` to be valid in all cases — even when its class is not instantiated — the methods and variables it uses must also be `static`, so they will exist even if their class is not instantiated.

> **JAVA LANGUAGE RULE** **Static Methods.** Static elements — methods, variables, constants – are associated with the class itself, not with its instances, and may only be used with other static elements.

Methods declared `static` are **class methods**, and they can be invoked through the class (as well as through any instances of the class). For example, the `Test.digitToInteger()` method can be invoked, even if there are no instances of the `Test` class. We have seen several examples of `static` methods already, including those found in the wrapper classes: `Integer.parseInt()`, `Boolean.valueOf()`, `Double.doubleValue()`.

From the Java Library: The Math Class

The `java.lang.Math` class provides many common mathematical functions that will prove useful in performing numerical computations. As an element of the `java.lang` package, it is included implicitly in all Java programs. Table 5–13 lists some of the most commonly used Math class methods.

All `Math` methods are `static` *class methods* and are therefore invoked through the class name. For example, we would calculate 2^4 as `Math.pow (2,4)`, which evaluates to 16. Similarly, we compute the square root of 225.0 as `Math.sqrt(225.0)`, which evaluates to 15.0.

Java's `Math` class cannot be instantiated and cannot be subclassed. Its basic definition is

```
public final class Math {      // A final class cannot be subclassed
    private Math() {}           // A private constructor cannot be invoked
    ...
    public static native double sqrt(double a)
           throws ArithmeticException;
}
```

Table 5.13. A selection of `Math` class methods

Method	Description	Examples
abs(int x) *abs(long x)* *abs(float x)*	*absolute value of x*	*if x >= 0 abs(x) is x* *if x < 0 abs(x) is -x*
ceil(double x)	*rounds x to the smallest integer not less than x*	*ceil(8.3) is 9* *ceil(−8.3) is −8*
floor(double x)	*rounds x to the largest integer not greater than x*	*floor (8.9) is 8* *floor(−8.9) is −9*
log(double x)	*natural logarithm of x*	*log (2.718282) is 1*
pow(double x, double y)	*x raised to the y power* (x^y)	*pow(3, 4) is 81* *pow(16.0 , 0.5) is 4.0*
double random()	*generates a pseudorandom number in the interval [0,1)*	*random() is 0.5551* *random() is 0.8712*
round(double x)	*rounds x to an integer*	*round(26.51) is 27* *round (26.499) is 26*
sqrt(double x)	*square root of x*	*sqrt(4.0) is 2*

By declaring the Math class public final, we indicate that it can be accessed (public) but it cannot be extended or subclassed (final). By declaring its default constructor to be private, we prevent this class from being instantiated. The idea of a class that cannot be subclassed and cannot be instantiated may seem a little strange at first. The justification for it here is that it provides a way to introduce helpful math functions into the Java language.

Defining the Math class in this way makes it easy to use, because you don't have to create an instance of it. It is also a very efficient design. Because its methods are static elements of the java.lang package, they are loaded into memory at the beginning of your program's execution, and they persist in memory throughout your program's lifetime. Because Math class methods do not have to be loaded into memory each time they are invoked, their execution time will improve dramatically.

Rounding to Two Decimal Places

When dealing with applications that involve monetary values — dollars and cents — it is often necessary to round a calculated result to two decimal places. For example, suppose a program computes the value of a Certificate of Deposit (CD) to be 75.19999. Before we output this result we would want to round it to two decimal places — to 75.20. The following algorithm can be used to accomplish this:

Algorithm design

```
1. Multiply the number by 100, giving 7519.9999.
2. Add 0.5 to the number giving 7520.4999.
3. Drop the fraction part giving 7520
4. Divide the result by 100, giving 75.20
```

Step 3 of this algorithm can be done using the Math.floor() method. If the number to be rounded is stored in the double variable *R*, then the following expression will round R to two decimal places:

```
R = Math.floor(R * 100.0 + 0.5) / 100.0;
```

Alternatively, we could use the Math.round() method (Table 5–13). This method rounds a floating point value to the nearest integer. For example, Math.round(65.3333) rounds to 65 and Math.round(65.6666) rounds to 66. The following expression uses it to round to two decimal places:

```
R = Math.round(100.0 * R) / 100.0;
```

It's important here to divide by 100.0 and not by 100. Otherwise the division will give an integer result and we'll lose the two decimal places.

DEBUGGING TIP: Division. Using the correct type of literal in division operations is necessary to ensure that you get the correct type of result.

From the Java Library: The Number Format Class

Although the Math.round() method is useful for rounding number, it is not suitable for business applications. Even for rounded values, Java will drop trailing zeroes. So a value such as $10,000.00 would be output as $10000.0. This wouldn't be acceptable for a business report.

Fortunately, Java supplies the java.text.NumberFormat class precisely for the task of representing numbers as dollar amounts, percentages, and other formats.

```
public abstract class NumberFormat extends Format {
    // Class methods
    public static final NumberFormat getInstance();
    public static final NumberFormat getCurrencyInstance();
    public static final NumberFormat getPercentInstance();

    // Public instance methods
    public final String format(double number);
    public final String format(long number);
    public int getMaximumFractionDigits();
    public int getMaximumIntegerDigits();
    public void setMaximumFractionDigits(int newValue);
    public void setMaximumIntegerDigits(int newValue);
}
```

The NumberFormat class is an abstract class, which means it cannot be directly instantiated. Instead you would use its getInstance() methods to create an instance which can then be used for the desired formatting tasks.

Once a NumberFormat instance has been created, the format() method can be used to put a number into a particular format. Methods such as setMaximumFractionDigits() and setMaximumIntegerDigits() can be used to control the number of digits before and after the decimal point.

For example, the following statements might be used to format a decimal number as a currency string in dollars and cents:

```
NumberFormat dollars = NumberFormat.getCurrencyInstance();
System.out.println( dollars.format(10962.555));
```

These statements would cause the value 10962.555 to be shown as $10,962.56. Similarly, the following statements,

```
NumberFormat percent = NumberFormat.getPercentInstance();
percent.setMaximumFractionDigits(2);
System.out.println( percent.format(6.55));
```

would display the value 6.55 as 6.55%.

5.10 Example: Calculating Compound Interest

To illustrate how we might use the methods of the `Math` and `NumberFormat` classes, let's write an application that compares the difference between daily and annual compounding of interest as it applies to a Certificate of Deposit (CD). How much better will daily compounding be for a given principal, interest and maturity period?

The formula for compounding interest is shown in Table 5–14. It assumes that interest in compounded annually. For daily compounding, the annual rate must be divided by 365, and the compounding period must be multiplied by 365, giving: $a = p(1 + r/365)^{365n}$

Problem statement

Our program should input a certain principal, interest and period (in years). It should output the CD's value at the end of the period under both annual and daily compounding.

What objects do we need?

Because this is such a simple calculation, let's use a single class for this problem, the `CDInterest` class. This class will handle its own I/O.

Class Design: `CDInterest`

What data and methods do we need?

This is a straightforward input-process-output algorithm. We can make use of `double` variables to represent the data needed in the interest calculation, all of which would be declared as `private` instance variables:

```
private double principal;       // The CD's initial principal
private double rate;            // CD's interest rate
private double years;           // Number of years to maturity
private double cdAnnual;        // Accumulated principal with annual compounding
private double cdDaily;         // Accumulated principal with daily compounding
```

Code reuse

We can use a `BufferedReader` object to handle keyboard input from the user. Similarly, we can use our `convertStringTodouble()` method again to handle the task of converting the user's `String` input into `double` data. Finally, we can use the `Math.pow()` method to translate the compounding formulas into Java:

```
cdAnnual = principal * Math.pow(1 + rate, years);          // Calculate interest
cdDaily = principal * Math.pow(1 + rate/365, years*365);
```

Task decomposition

In addition to using these methods, let's divide the program's task into two tasks: (1) inputting the data, and (2) calculating and reporting the results. If we tried to handle the entire task in one method, the method

Table 5.14. Formula for calculating compound interest

$a = p(1 + r)^n$ where

- a is the CD's value at the end of the nth year
- p is the principal or original investment amount
- r is the annual interest rate
- n is the number of years or the compounding period

would be too long. A method is like a paragraph. If you make it too long, it begins to lose its focus. So it's a good idea to avoid trying to do too much in a single method.

EFFECTIVE DESIGN: Method Length. Methods should be focused on a single task. If you find your method becoming more than 20 or 30 lines of code, try to divide it into separate methods.

Given these decisions, our program's `main()` method would be very simple:

```
public static void main( String args[] ) throws IOException {
    CDInterest cd = new CDInterest();    // Create an instance
    cd.getInput();                       // Get user's inputs
    cd.calcAndReportResult();            // Calculate and report results
 } // main()
```

The `CDInterest` program is shown in Figure 5–10. There are several points to note about this program. First, both `main()` and `getInput()` must declare that they `throw` an `IOException`. The `getInput()` method uses the `BufferedReader.readLine()` method, which could throw an `IOException`, and `main()` calls `getInput()`. (Exceptions and the details behind this requirement will be covered in Chapter 11.)

Second, note how the number formatting is done within the `calcAndReportResult()` method. The method begins by creating to `NumberFormat` objects, one for currency amount and one for the interest rate:

```
NumberFormat dollars = NumberFormat.getCurrencyInstance(); // Set up formats
NumberFormat percent = NumberFormat.getPercentInstance();
percent.setMaximumFractionDigits(2);
```

Then when the output is printed, we simply call on these objects to produce the output in the format. For example, a currency amount is output as follows:

```
System.out.println("The original principal is " + dollars.format(principal));
```

The output produced by this program is as follows:

```
*********************************** OUTPUT **********************
This program compares daily and annual compounding for a CD.
   Input the CD's initial principal, e.g.  1000.55 > 10000
   Input the CD's interest rate, e.g.  6.5 > 7.768
   Input the number of years to maturity, e.g., 10.5 > 10
The original principal is $10,000.00
The resulting principal compounded daily at 7.77% is $21,743.23
The resulting principal compounded yearly at 7.77% is $21,129.94
*********************************** OUTPUT **********************
```

Figure 5–10 Java application to calculate compound interest .

```
import java.io.*;                  // Import the Java I/O Classes
import java.text.NumberFormat;     // For formatting as $nn.dd or n%

public class CDInterest {
%    private BufferedReader input = new BufferedReader    // Handles console input
              (new InputStreamReader(System.in));
    private String inputString;                    // Stores the input
    private double principal;                      // The CD's initial principal
    private double rate;                           // CD's interest rate
    private double years;                          // Number of years to maturity
    private double cdAnnual;          // Accumulated principal with annual compounding
    private double cdDaily;           // Accumulated principal with daily compounding
    private double convertStringTodouble(String s) {
        Double doubleObject = Double.valueOf(s) ;
        return doubleObject.doubleValue();
    }

    private void getInput() throws IOException {
                                           // Prompt the user and get the input
        System.out.println("This program compares daily and annual compounding for a CD.");

        System.out.print("     Input the CD's initial principal, e.g.  1000.55 > ");
        inputString = input.readLine();
        principal = convertStringTodouble(inputString);

        System.out.print("     Input the CD's interest rate, e.g.  6.5 > ");
        inputString = input.readLine();
        rate = (convertStringTodouble(inputString)) / 100.0;

        System.out.print("     Input the number of years to maturity, e.g., 10.5 > ");
        inputString = input.readLine();
        years = convertStringTodouble(inputString);
    } //getInput()

    private void calcAndReportResult() {
                                           // Calculate and output the result
        NumberFormat dollars = NumberFormat.getCurrencyInstance(); // Set up formats
        NumberFormat percent = NumberFormat.getPercentInstance();
        percent.setMaximumFractionDigits(2);

        cdAnnual = principal * Math.pow(1 + rate, years);        // Calculate interest
        cdDaily = principal * Math.pow(1 + rate/365, years*365);
                                                                 // Print the results
        System.out.println("The original principal is " + dollars.format(principal));
        System.out.println("The resulting principal compounded daily at " +
                    percent.format(rate) + " is " + dollars.format(cdDaily));
        System.out.println("The resulting principal compounded yearly at " +
                    percent.format(rate) + " is " + dollars.format(cdAnnual));
    } // calcAndReportResult()

    public static void main( String args[] ) throws IOException {
        CDInterest cd = new CDInterest();
        cd.getInput();
        cd.calcAndReportResult();
    } // main()
} // Interest
```

Thus, our tasks of calculating interest and formatting the output have been greatly simplified by using the appropriate classes from the Java class library.

EFFECTIVE DESIGN: Code Reuse. Often the best way to solve a programming task is to find the appropriate methods in the Java class library.

5.11 Problem Solving = Representation + Action

Designing classes involves a careful interplay between representation (data) and action (methods). As our comparison of the `boolean` and `int` versions of `CyberPet` shows, the data used to represent an object's state can either complicate or simplify the design of the methods needed to solve a problem.

In writing object-oriented programs, choosing an appropriate data representation is just as important as choosing the correct algorithm. The concept of an object allows us to encapsulate representation and action into a single entity. It is a very natural way to approach problem solving.

If you look closely enough at any problem, you will find this close relationship between representation and action. For example, compare the task of performing multiplication using Arabic numerals — 65 * 12 = 380 — and the same task using Roman numerals — LXV * XII = DCCLXXX. It's doubtful that our science and technology would be where it is today if our civilization had to rely forever on the Roman way of representing numbers!

EFFECTIVE DESIGN: Representation and Action. Representation (data) and action (methods) are equally important parts of the problem solving process.

IN THE LABORATORY: THE LEAP YEAR PROBLEM

The purpose of this lab is to emphasize the object-oriented design principles discussed in this and previous chapters and to use some of Java's basic language structures, such as if-else, assignment, and arithmetic expressions. The objectives of this project are

- To give practice designing and writing a simple Java program.
- To give practice using if-else and assignment statements.
- To give practice using basic arithmetic and relational operators.

Problem Description

A year is a *leap year* if it is evenly divisible by 4 but not evenly divisible by 100 unless it is also evenly divisible by 400. So 1996 was a leap year. But 1900 was not a leap year because, although it is divisible by 4, it is also divisible by 100 and not by 400. 2000 is a leap year because it is divisible by 400.

Design and write a Java applet that allows the user to enter a year (as an integer) and reports whether the year entered is a leap year or not.

Problem Decomposition

One way to decompose this problem is to divide it into two classes, the `LeapYearApplet` class, which implements the user interface, and the `Year` class, which contains the expertise needed to decide whether a given value is a leap year or not. `LeapYearApplet` should get the input from the user (in a `TextField`), pass it to `Year`, converting it to whatever form `Year` requires, and then display the result that `Year` returns.

Problem Design: `Year`

The `Year` class is very simple. Its whole purpose in life is just to wait until it is passed a value and then to determine if that value is a leap year or not. One design we could use here is that of the `Temperature` class. In that case public methods were used to convert from Fahrenheit to Celsius.

Another design that would be appropriate here is to model `Year` after the `Math` class — that is, as a utility class that provides a useful method, but which is not designed to be instantiated at all. Since this latter design is simpler, let's adopt it.

- Purpose: To determine if a year is a leap year
- Modifiers: Final, so it cannot be extended
- Constructor: Private, so no instantiation is possible
- Instance Variables: None (no need to store anything)
- Public Instance Methods: None (no need to have instances)
- Public Static Methods: isLeapYear(int) tests whether its parameter is a leap year using the rule described above.

The `isLeapYear()` method should be a `public` method that takes a single `int` parameter and returns the `boolean` value `true` if its parameter is a leap year and `false` otherwise. In terms of its algorithm, this method should use an if-else control structure to test whether a year is divisible by 400, by 100, and so on. To determine if an integer is *divisible* by another integer, you can use the mod operator (%). For example, if *N % 100* equals 0, then *N* is divisible by 100. That is, *N* is divisible by 100 if dividing it by 100 leaves a remainder of 0:

Figure 5–11 The `LeapYearApplet`.

```
if (N % 100 == 0) ...
```

You may find it helpful to draw a flowchart for the `isLeapYear()`. See Chapter 3 to review the guidelines for drawing flowcharts.

Problem Design: `LeapYearApplet`

The design of the `LeapYearApplet` should be similar to that of other applets we've built. It should contain a `TextField` for user input and a `Label` for prompting the user. Its interface is shown in Figure 5–11. Note that the interface does not contain a `Button`. With no button to click, how does the user tell the applet to test whether a year is a leap year or not? The answer is that a `TextField` generates an action event whenever the user types the Enter key in it. As with button clicks, these events can be handled by an `ActionListener`. Therefore, after instantiating a `TextField`, you can simply register it with an appropriate `ActionListener`:

```
inputField = new TextField(10);      // Create a TextField
inputField.addActionListener(this); // Register it with a Listener
```

In this case, the applet's `actionPerformed()` method would handle the `TextField`'s action events just as if it were a `Button`.

The `LeapYearApplet` should implement the `ActionListener.actionPerformed()` method to handle `TextField` actions. When the user types Enter, `actionPerformed()` should get the input from the `TextField` and convert it from `String` to `int`. Recall that the `parseInt()` method in the `Integer` class can be used for this purpose:

```
int num = Integer.parseInt(yearField.getText());
```

Here it is assumed that the user's input is in a text field named `yearField`. The integer should then be passed to `Year.isLeapYear()`, which will return a `boolean`. The applet should then report the result.

How should this applet handle the reporting of the result? Perhaps the easiest way is to override `Applet`'s `paint()` method, which was the approach we took in the `HelloWorld` applet in Chapter 1. Recall that `paint()` uses the following kind of statement to display a `String` on an applet:

```
g.drawString("HelloWorld", 10, 50);
```

The *g* in this expression is a reference to paint()'s Graphics object, which controls any drawing or painting on the applet. The two numbers in the expression are the horizontal and vertical coordinates that specify where "HelloWorld" will be painted on the applet. You will have do some planning and experimenting to determine what values to use for these coordinates.

One important question remains: How will paint() know whether to report that the year is or is not a leap year? Perhaps the best way to handle this is to have actionPerformed() invoke the Year.isLeapYear() method and store its result in an instance variable. Suppose this boolean variable is named yearIsLeapYear. Then paint() could check its value and print the appropriate message:

```
if (yearIsLeapYear)
    g.drawString("That year is a leap year", 10, 50);
```

As members of LeapYearApplet, both actionPerformed() and paint() will have access to yearIsLeapYear.

Recall also, that since we have patterned Year after the Math class (and Integer class), there is no need to instantiate it in order to use its static methods. So to test whether a given number is a leap year, we could simply say

```
if (Year.isLeapYear(num)) ...
```

The isLeapYear() method is a *class method* — that is, a static method that is associated with the class itself.

Implementation

The implementation of this program is left to you as a lab (or programming) exercise.

Java Language Summary

Operator Precedence Order

Java operators are evaluated according to the precedence hierarchy shown in Table 5–15. The lower the precedence number, the earlier an operator is evaluated. So the operators at the top of the table are evaluated before operators that occur below them in the table. Operators at the same precedence level are evaluated according to their *association*, either left to right (L to R) or right to left (R to L).

Table 5.15. Java operator precedence and associativity table

<table>
<tr><th>Order</th><th>Operator</th><th>Operation</th><th>Association</th></tr>
<tr><td>0</td><td>( )</td><td>Parentheses</td><td></td></tr>
<tr><td>1</td><td>++ -- .</td><td>Postincrement, Postdecrement, DotOperator</td><td>L to R</td></tr>
<tr><td>2</td><td>++ -- + - !</td><td>Preincrement, Predecrement</td><td>R to L</td></tr>
<tr><td></td><td>@</td><td>Unary plus, Unary minus, Boolean NOT</td><td></td></tr>
<tr><td>3</td><td>(type) new</td><td>Type Cast, Object instantiation</td><td>R to L</td></tr>
<tr><td>4</td><td>* / %</td><td>Multiplication, Division, Modulus</td><td>L to R</td></tr>
<tr><td>5</td><td>+ - +</td><td>Addition, Subtraction, String Concatenation</td><td>L to R</td></tr>
<tr><td>6</td><td>< > <= >=</td><td>Relational Operators</td><td>L to R</td></tr>
<tr><td>7</td><td>== !=</td><td>Equality Operators</td><td>L to R</td></tr>
<tr><td>8</td><td>∧</td><td>Boolean XOR</td><td>L to R</td></tr>
<tr><td>9</td><td>&&</td><td>Boolean AND</td><td>L to R</td></tr>
<tr><td>10</td><td>||</td><td>Boolean OR</td><td>L to R</td></tr>
<tr><td>11</td><td>= += -= *= /= %=</td><td>Assignment Operators</td><td>R to L</td></tr>
</table>

Operator Promotion and Casting

Java is a *strongly typed* language, which means that operations are type dependent. All expressions have an associated type. In numeric expressions containing values (operands) of different types, Java will generally *promote* the smaller type to a larger type according to Table 5–16.

Java's promotion rules represent an implicit form of type *casting* — that is, converting one type of data to another. The *cast operator* — *(type)* — is a unary operator that converts the value that follows it to the specified type. In this example, the floating point (`double`) value, 95.6, is converted into an `int` before being assigned to *k*:

```
int k = (int)95.6;
```

Table 5.16. Java promotion rules for mixed arithmetic operators.

If either operand is	The other is promoted to
`double`	`double`
`float`	`float`
`long`	`long`
`byte` or `short`	`int`

Java Language Summary

Table 5.17. Java operators showing operator overloading

Data Types	Operators
Floating Point Types `double float`	`+ - * / = += -= *= /=` `< > <= >= == !=`

Integer Types
`int long`
`byte short`
	Same as floating point types plus
	`% ++ --`

`char`	*Same as integer types*
`boolean`	`&& || ^ ! == !=`
`String`	`+`

Operator Overloading

Operator symbols are *overloaded* in Java, meaning they may be used for more than one type-dependent operation. For example, the plus sign (+) is used for addition and string concatenation. Table 5–17 lists the operators that apply to each type of data.

Keywords: `static` and `final`

Class elements

- Within a class definition, elements that are declared `static` are called *class elements* — class methods or class variables — and are associated with the class itself, not with its instances. Such elements exist even if no objects of that class exist. They are referenced by qualifying their name with the name of the class. For example, to use the square root method in the `java.lang.Math`, you would refer to it as `Math.sqrt()`.

Constants

- Within a class definition, any variables that are declared `final` are called *constants*. They must be given an initial value, which cannot be changed by the program. Constants are frequently declared `static` as well as `final`, since then one copy of the constant can be shared by all instances of the class. The following is an example of a *class constant* declaration:

```
public class MyClass {
    public static final int MAXWIDTH = 500;
}
```

As with other class elements, the class name is used as a qualifier in referring to a class constant — `MyClass.MAXWIDTH`.

CHAPTER SUMMARY

Technical Terms

action
binary operator
cast operation
class constant
class method
class variable
helper method
method composition
operator overloading
precedence order
promotion
representation
type conversion
unary operator

New Java Keywords

`boolean` `byte` `char` `double` `final` `float` `int` `long` `private` `public` `short` `static` `throws`

Java Library Classes

`ActionListener` `Applet` `BufferedReader` `Button` `Color` `Double` `IOException` `Math` `NumberFormat` `String` `TextComponent` `TextField`

Java Library Methods

`actionPerformed()` `doubleValue()` `round()` `format()` `getInstance()` `valueOf()` `main()` `readLine()` `setMaximumIntegerDigits()` `floor()` `init()`

Programmer-Defined Classes

`CDInterest` `CyberPet` `HelloWorld` `Interest` `LeapYearApplet` `Temperature` `TemperatureApplet` `TemperatureTest` `Test` `Year`

Programmer-Defined Methods

`calcCDInnterest()` `celsToFahr()` `convertStringTodouble()` `fahrToCels()` `getInput()` `isLeapYear()` `setFahrenheit()` `think()` `toUpperCase()`

Summary of Important Points

- The way we approach a problem can often help or hinder us in our ability to it. Choosing an appropriate *representation* for a problem is often the key to solving it.

- Choosing the wrong type of data to represent a problem can constrain the extensibility of the model. The *scalability principle* states that a well-designed model or representation should be easily *extensible* . The *modularity principle* states that a well-designed model or representation will contain methods that do not have to be modified each time we extend the model.

- In order to evaluate complex expressions, it is necessary to understand the *precedence order* and *associativity* of the operators involved. Parentheses can always be used to override an operator's built-in precedence.

- Java provides several types of integer data, including the 8-bit `byte`, 16-bit `short`, 32-bit `int`, and 64-bit `long` types. Integer literals are represented as `int` data in a Java program.

- Java provides two types of floating point data, the 32-bit `float` type and the 64-bit `double` type. Floating point literals are represented as `float` data.

- In general, if a data type uses n bits in its representation, then it can represent 2^n different values.

- The fact that Java's primitive types are defined in terms of a specific number of bits is one way that Java promotes *platform independence*.

- It is necessary to distinguish integer operations from floating point operations even though the same symbols are used. (7/2) is 3, while (7.0/2) is 3.0.

- When revising a class that is used by other classes, it is a good idea to make it *backward compatible*. In revising a class that is used by other classes it is important to preserve as much of the class's *interface* as possible.

- In Java, character data are based on the Unicode character set, which provides 2^{16} = 65,536 different character codes. To provide backwards compatibility with the ASCII code, the first 128 characters are the ASCII coded characters.

ANSWERS TO SELF-STUDY EXERCISES

EXERCISE 5.1 a. true b. true c. true d. true e. false f. false

EXERCISE 5.2 0000, 0001, 0010, 0011, 0100, 0101, 0110, 0111, 1000, 1001, 1010, 1011, 1100, 1101, 1110, 1111

EXERCISE 5.3 In 6 bits, you can represent $2^6 = 64$ different values.

EXERCISE 5.4 Suppose you write a program on a system that uses 32 bits to represent the `int` type, and your program uses numbers like 2,000,000,000. This number cannot be represented properly in 16 bits, so you can't run your program on systems where the `int` type is represented as 16 bits.

EXERCISE 5.5 If you have to represent up to 12 significant digits, you should use `double`, which goes up to 17 digits.

EXERCISE 5.6 a. 4 b. 4 c. 0 d. 1 e. 2 f. 6 g. 0 h. 4

EXERCISE 5.7 a. 4.0 b. 4.5 c. 0 d. 0.0 e. 1.25

EXERCISE 5.8 a. 7 (`int` b. 30 `long` c. 14.0 `double` d. 90 `long` e. 4.0 `double`

EXERCISE 5.9 a. 34.0 b. 54 c. 4 d. 1 e. 6 f. 0 g. 2 h. error

EXERCISE 5.10 a. k==5, j==5 b. k==5, j==6 c. k==6, j==6 d. k==5,j==4 e. k==4,j==4

EXERCISE 5.11 a. k==15, j==5 b. k==4, j==6 c. k==120, j==6 d. k==0,j==4 e. k==0,j==5

EXERCISE 5.12

```
int k;
k = k + 1;
k += 1;
k++;
++k;
```

EXERCISE 5.13 a. m = 5 b. m = 6 c. m = 15 d. m = 25 e. m = 35

EXERCISE 5.14 a. false b. false c. true d. illegal e. true f. illegal g. false

EXERCISE 5.15 In the `CyberPet` experiment, the implementation of `CyberPet` is hidden from the user, who interacts only with the `CyberPet` applet interface. Therefore it doesn't matter to the user *how* we design `CyberPet`, as long as it works correctly. Of course, as programmers, it does matter to us how `CyberPet` is designed.

EXERCISE 5.16 a. valid b. valid c. ch2 = (char)n; d. valid e. ch1 = (char)(m+n);

EXERCISES

1. Explain the difference between the following pairs of terms.

    1. *Representation* and *action*.
    2. *Binary operator* and *unary operation*.
    3. *Class constant* and *class variable*.
    4. *Helper method* and *class method*.
    5. *Operator overloading* and *method overloading*.
    6. *Method call* and *method composition*.
    7. *Type conversion* and *type promotion*.

2. Arrange the Java library classes listed in the chapter summary into a hierarchy rooted at the `Object` class.
3. For each of the following data types, list how many bits are used in its representation and how many values can be represented:

    a. `int`
    b. `char`
    c. `byte`
    d. `long`
    e. `double`

4. Fill in the blank.

    1. Methods and variables that are associated with a class rather than with its instances must be declared ______.
    2. When an expression involves values of two different types, one value must be ______ before the expression can be evaluated.
    3. Constants should be declared ______.
    4. Variables that take `true` and `false` as their possible values are known as ______.

5. Arrange the following data types into a *promotion* hierarchy: `double`, `float`, `int`, `short`, `long`.
6. Assuming that *o1* is true, *o2* is false, and *o3* is false, evaluate each of the following expressions:

    a. `o1 || o2 && o3`
    b. `o1 ^ o2`
    c. `!o1 && !o2`

7. Arrange the following operators in precedence order:

```
+ - () * / % < ==
```

8. Arrange the following operators into a precedence hierarchy:

```
*,++, %, ==
```

9. Parenthesize and evaluate each of the following expressions. If an expression is invalid, mark it as such.

   a. `11 / 3 % 2 == 1`
   b. `11 / 2 % 2 > 0`
   c. `15 % 3 >= 21 %`
   d. `12.0 / 4.0 >= 12 / 3`
   e. `15 / 3 == true`

10. What value would *m* have after each of the following statements is executed? Assume that *m, k, j* are reinitialized before each statement.

```
int m = 5, k = 0, j = 1;
```

   a. `m = ++k + j;`
   b. `m += ++k * j;`
   c. `m %= ++k + ++j;`
   d. `m = m - k - j;`
   e. `m = ++m;`

11. What value would *b* have after each of the following statements is executed? Assume that *m, k, j* are reinitialized before each statement. It may help to parenthesize the right-hand side of the statements before evaluating them.

```
boolean b;
int m = 5, k = 0, j = 1;
```

   a. `b = m > k + j;`
   b. `b = m * m != m * j;`
   c. `b = m <= 5 && m % 2 == 1;`
   d. `b = m < k || k < j;`
   e. `b = --m == 2 * ++j;`

12. For each of the following expressions, if it is valid, determine the value of the variable on the left-hand side. If not, change it to a valid expression.

```
char c = 'a' ;
int  m = 95;
```

   a. `c = c + 5;`
   b. `c = 'A' + 'B';`
   c. `m = c + 5;`
   d. `c = (char) m + 1;`
   e. `m = 'a' - 32;`

13. Translate each of the following expressions into Java.

   a. Area equals *pi* times the radius squared.
   b. Area is assigned *pi* times the radius squared.
   c. Volume is assigned *pi* times radius cubed divide by *h*.
   d. If *m* and *n* are equal then *m* is incremented by one, otherwise *n* is.
   e. If *m* is greater than *n* times 5 then square *m* and double *n* otherwise square *n* and double *m*.

14. What would be output by the following code segment?

```
int m = 0, n = 0, j = 0, k = 0;
m = 2 * n++;
System.out.println("m= " + m + " n= " + n);
j += ( --k * 2 );
System.out.println("j= " + j + " k= " + k);
```

Each of the following problems asks you to write a method. Of course, as you are developing the method in a stepwise fashion, you should test it. Here's a simple application program that you can use for this purpose. Just replace the `square()` method with your method. Note that you must declare your method `static` if you want to call it directly from `main()` as we do here.

```
public class MethodTester {
    public static int square(int n) {
        return n * n;
    }

    public static void main(String args[]) {
        System.out.println("5 squared = " + square(5));
    }
}
```

15. Write a method to calculate the sales tax for a sale item. The method should take two `double` parameters, one for the sales price and the other for the tax rate. It should return a `double`. For example, `calcTax(20.0, 0.05)` should return 1.0.
16. **Challenge:** Suppose you're writing a program that tells what day of the week someone's birthday falls on this year. Write a method that takes an `int` parameter, representing what day of the year it is, and returns a `String` like "Monday." For example, for 1999, the first day of the year was on Friday. The thirty-second day of the year (February 1, 1999) was a Monday, so `getDayOfWeek(1)` should return "Friday" and `getDayOfWeek(32)` should return "Monday." (*Hint*: If you divide the day of the year by 7, the remainder will always be a number between 0 and 6, which can be made to correspond to days of the week.)
17. **Challenge:** As part of the same program you'll want a method that takes the month and the day as parameters, and returns what day of the year it is. For example, `getDay(1,1)` should return 1; `getDay(2,1)` should return 32; and `getDay(12,31)` should return 365. (*Hint*: If the month is 3, and the day is 5, you have to add the number of days in January plus the number of days in February to 5 to get the result: 31 + 28 + 5 = 64.)
18. Write a Java method that converts a `char` to lowercase. For example, `toLowerCase('A')` should return 'a.' Make sure you guard against method calls like `toLowerCase('a')`.
19. **Challenge:** Write a Java method that shifts a `char` by *n* places in the alphabet, wrapping around to the start of the alphabet, if necessary. For example, `shift('a', 2)` should return 'c'; `shift('y', 2)` should return

'a.' This method can be used to create a Caesar cipher, in which every letter in a message is shifted by *n* places — hfu ju?

20. Write a method that converts its `boolean` parameter to a `String`. For example, `boolToString(true)` should return "true."
21. Write a Java application that prompts the user for three numbers, which represent the sides of a rectangular cube, and then computes and outputs the volume and the surface area of the cube.
22. Write a Java application that prompts the user for three numbers, and then outputs the three numbers in increasing order.
23. Write a Java application that inputs two integers and then determines whether the first is divisible by the second. (*Hint*: Use the modulus operator.)
24. Write a Java application that prints the following table:

```
N  SQUARE   CUBE
1  1        1
2  4        8
3  9        27
4  16       64
5  25       125
```

25. Design and write a Java applet that converts kilometers to miles and vice versa. Use a `TextField` for I/O and `Buttons` for the various conversion actions.
26. Design and write an (applet) GUI that allows a user to calculate the maturity value of a CD. The user should enter the principal, interest rate, and period, and the applet should then display the maturity value. Make use of the `CDInterest` program covered in this chapter. Use separate `TextFields` for the user's inputs and a separate `TextField` for the result.
27. Design and write an (applet) GUI that lets the user input a birth date (month and day), and reports what day of the week it falls on. Use the `getDayOfWeek()` and `getDay()` methods that you developed in previous exercises.
28. Design and write an (applet) GUI that allows the users to input their exam grades for a course and computes their average and probable letter grade. The applet should contain a single `TextField` for inputting a grade and a single `TextField` for displaying the average and letter grade. The program should keep track internally of how many grades the student has entered. Each time a new grade is entered, it should display the current average and probable letter grade.

6

Control Structures

OBJECTIVES

After studying this chapter, you will

- Be able to solve problems involving repetition.
- Understand the difference among various loop structures.
- Know the principles used to design effective loops.
- Improve your algorithm design skills.
- Understand the goals and principles of structured programming.

OUTLINE

6.1 Introduction

Suppose you want to write a method that prints the word "Hello" 100 times. One way to code this would be to write 100 `println()` statements into the method body:

```
public void hello100() {
    System.out.println("Hello");
    System.out.println("Hello");
    System.out.println("Hello");
    System.out.println("Hello");
    ...
    System.out.println("Hello");
}
```

This approach is tedious and would be completely impractical if we wanted to print "Hello" 65,535 times or a million times. Another way to handle this problem is illustrated in the following method:

```
public void hello100() {
    for (int k = 0; k < 100; k++)       // For 100 times
        System.out.println("Hello");    //  Print "Hello"
}
```

In this example, `println("Hello")` is executed 100 times by the for statement, a built-in loop control statement.

This chapter introduces Java's looping *control structures*, including the *for*, *while* and *do-while* statements, all of which are used for repetition. We begin by introducing the idea of a *counting loop*, which is used for performing repetitive tasks when you know beforehand exactly how many iterations are necessary. This type of loop is most often implemented using a `for` statement.

We then distinguish two kinds of *conditional loops*, which are used for performing repetitive tasks where the number of repetitions depends on some kind of noncounting *bound*. These kind of loops are usually implemented using Java's `while` and `do-while` statements. We give examples of several different kinds of loop bounds, and use them to identify several useful principles of loop design. Finally, we introduce some of the key principles of the *structured programming* approach, a disciplined design approach that preceded the object-oriented approach.

6.2 Flow-of-Control: Repetition Structures

A **repetition structure** is a control structure that repeats a statement or sequence of statements. Many programming tasks require a repetition structure. Consider some examples.

- You're working for the National Security Agency trying to decipher secret messages intercepted from foreign spys, and you want to count the number of times a certain letter, 'a' say, occurs in a document containing *N* characters. In this case you would want to employ something like the following (pseudocode) algorithm:

```
initialize totalAs to 0
for each character in the document
    if the character is an 'a'
        add 1 to totalAs
return totalAs as the result
```

- You're working for a caterer who wants to number the invitations to a client's wedding, so you need to print all of the numbers between 1 and 5000 on the invitation cards (it's a big wedding)! In this case you want to go through each number, 1 to 5000 and simply print it out.

```
for each number, N, from 1 to 5000
    print N on the invitation card
```

- The caterer decides it would be a cute gimmick to give every hundredth guest a door prize, so she wants you to print a special annotation on every hundredth invitation. You decide that every time you come to a number that is divisible by 100, you will also print a special symbol on that card. In this case you want to go through each number, 1 to 5000, test if it is divisible by 100 and, if so, print the special mark on it.

```
for each number, N, from  1 to 5000
    print N on the card
    if (N % 100 == 0)
        print a special symbol on the card
```

- You are helping the Forest Service in Alaska keep track of the number of black bear sightings, and you want to compute the average number of sightings per month. Suppose the user enters each month's count at the keyboard, and uses a special number, say 9999, to signify the end of the sequence. 9999 should not be figured into the average. This example differs a bit from the preceding ones because here you don't know exactly how many numbers the user will input:

```
initialize sumOfBears to 0
initialize numOfMonths to 0
repeat the following steps
    read a number from the keyboard
    if the number is NOT 9999
        add it to the sumOfBears
        add 1 to numOfMonths
until the number read is 9999
divide sumOfBears by numOfMonths giving average
return average as the result
```

We repeat the process of reading numbers and adding them to a running total "until the number read is 9999."

- Student records are stored in a file and you want to calculate Erika Wilson's current GPA. Here we need to perform a repetitive process — searching through the file for Erika Wilson's record — but again we don't know exactly how many times to repeat the process:

```
repeat the following steps
    read a record from the file
until Erika Wilson's record is read
compute Erika Wilson's GPA
return gpa as the result
```

As these examples suggest, two types of loops are used: counting loops and noncounting loops. Counting loops are used whenever you know in advance exactly how many times an action must be performed. Noncounting loops are used when the number of repetitions depends on some condition — for example, the number of data items input from the keyboard, or the input of a particular record from a file.

6.3 Counting Loops

The type of loop structure used in the `hello100` example, and in the first three examples above, is a **counting loop** or a *counter-controlled loop*. The exact number of times the loop repeats is known beforehand and can be made dependent on the value of a counter.

```
for (int k = 0; k < 100; k++)
    System.out.println("Hello");
```

Zero indexing

In this case the counter is the variable *k*, which counts from 0 through 99 — that is, it counts 100 times. Note that we start counting from 0, instead of 1. This is a common programming convention for counting loops. Although it doesn't really make any practical difference in this case, later on we will use loops to process structures, such as strings and arrays, which use **zero indexing**. It's easier to process these structures if our loop counter also starts at 0.

Loop counter

The variable *k* is called a *counter variable* or a *loop counter* . Although it is certainly possible to name the counter variable anything we like, it is customary to use single letters like *i, j,* and *k* as loop counters. The fundamental feature of a counting loop is that we must know beforehand exactly how many iterations the loop will take.

EFFECTIVE DESIGN: Loop Design. A *counting loop* can be used whenever you know exactly how many times a process must be repeated.

6.3.1 The For Structure

Although there are many ways to code a counting loop, Java's *for statement* is ideally suited for this purpose. The for statement has the following syntax:

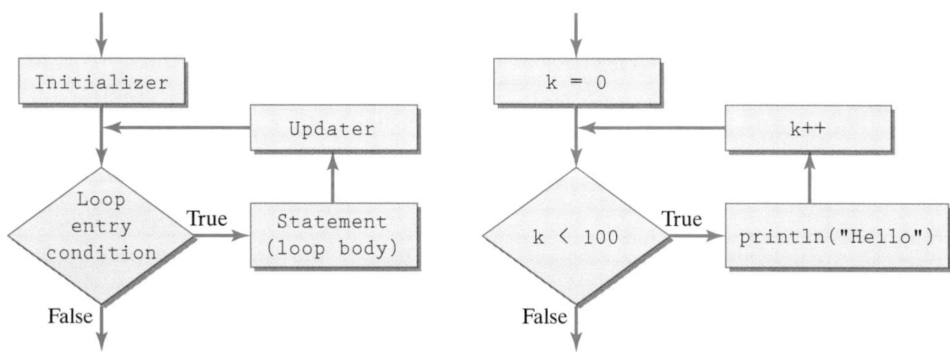

Figure 6–1 Flowchart of the for statement.

for (*initializer* ; *loop entry condition* ; *updater*)
for loop body ;

The for statement begins with the keyword `for`, which is followed by a parenthesized list of three expressions separated by semicolons: an **initializer**, a **loop entry condition**, and an **updater**. Following the parenthesized list is the **for loop body**, which is either a single statement or a sequence of statements contained in curly brackets, `{...}`.

Figure 6–1 shows how the for statement works. First the initializer is evaluated. In this example, the initializer sets the integer variable *k* to 0. Then the loop entry condition, which must be a boolean expression, is evaluated. If it is true, the body of the loop is executed; if it is false, the body of the loop is skipped and control passes to the next statement following the for statement. The updater is evaluated after the loop body is executed. After completion of the updater, the loop entry condition is reevaluated and the loop body is either executed again or not, depending on the truth value of the loop entry condition. This process is repeated until the loop entry condition becomes false.

Tracing the order in which the for loop components are evaluated gives this sequence:

```
evaluate initializer
evaluate loop entry condition ==> True
execute for loop body;
evaluate updater
evaluate loop entry condition ==> True
execute for loop body;
evaluate updater
evaluate loop entry condition ==> True
execute for loop body;
evaluate updater
.
.
.
evaluate loop entry condition ==> False
```

As this trace shows, the loop entry condition controls entry to the body of the loop and will therefore be the last thing done before the loop terminates.

Loop variable scope

We have followed the standard convention of declaring the counter variable in the header of the for statement. This restricts the variable's *scope* to for statement itself. It would be a syntax error to use *k* outside the scope of the for loop, as in this example:

```
for (int k = 0; k < 100; k++)
    System.out.println("Hello");
 System.out.println("k = " + k);    // Syntax error, k is undeclared
```

For some problems it may be necessary to use the loop variable outside the scope of the for statement, in which case the variable should be declared before the for statement:

```
int k = 0;                         // Declare the loop variable here
for (k = 0; k < 100; k++)
    System.out.println("Hello");
System.out.println("k = " + k);  // So it can be used here
```

6.3.2 Loop Bounds

Loop bound

A counting loop starts at some initial value and counts 0 or more iterations until its **loop bound** is reached. In a counting loop, the *loop entry condition* should be a boolean expression that tests whether the loop's bound has been reached. Similarly, in a counting loop, the *updater* should modify the loop counter so that it makes progress toward reaching its bound. Counting loops often increment or decrement their counter by 1, depending on whether the loop is counting forwards or backwards. The following method contains a countdown loop, which prints `10 9 8 7 6 5 4 3 2 1 BLASTOFF`. In this case progress toward the loop bound is made by decrementing the loop counter:

```
public void countdown() {
    for (int k = 10; k > 0; k--)
        System.out.print(k + " ");
    System.out.println("BLASTOFF");
} // countdown()
```

Unit indexing

Note in this case that we are using *unit indexing* instead of *zero indexing*, because countdowns iterate from 10 down to 1, not from 10 down to 0.

6.3.3 Infinite Loops

If the loop bound is never reached, the loop entry condition will never become false and the loop will repeat forever. This is known as an

infinite loop. Each of the following for statements will result in an infinite loop. Can you see why?

Infinite loop

```
for (int k = 0; k < 100 ; k--)          // Infinite loop
    System.out.println("Hello");

for (int k = 1; k != 100 ; k+=2)        // Infinite loop
    System.out.println("Hello");

for (int k = 98; k < 100 ; k = k / 2) // Infinite loop
    System.out.println("Hello");
```

In the first example, *k* starts out at 0 and is decremented on each iteration, taking on values −1, −2, −3, and so on, so *k* will never reach its loop bound.

In the second example, *k* starts out at 1 and is incremented by 2 on each iteration, taking on the values 3, 5, 7, and so on. Because all these values are odd, *k* will never equal 100. A much safer loop bound in this case would be *k <= 100*.

In the third example, *k* starts out at 98 and is halved on each iteration, taking on the values 49, 24, 12, 6, 3, 1, 0, 0, and so on, forever. Thus it too will be stuck in an infinite loop.

Encountering an unintended infinite loop when developing a program can be very frustrating. If the program is stuck in a loop that generates output, it will be obvious that it's looping, but if no output is being generated, the computer will appear to "freeze," no longer responding to your keyboard or mouse commands. Some programming environments allow you to break out of a looping program by typing a special keyboard command such as `CONTROL-C` or `CTRL-ALT-DELETE` or `CONTROL-APPLE-ESCAPE`, but if that doesn't work you will have to reboot the computer, possibly causing loss of data. The best way to avoid infinite loops is to determine that the loop's updater expression will eventually reach the loop bound.

6.3.4 Loop Indentation

Note how indentation is used to distinguish the loop body from the heading and from the statement that follows the loop:

```
for (int k = 10 ; k > 0 ; k--)          // Loop heading
    System.out.print (k + " ");         //  Indent the body
System.out.println( "BLASTOFF" );       // After the loop
```

Indenting the loop body is a stylistic convention intended to make the code more readable. However, the indentation itself has no effect on how the code is interpreted by Java. Each of the following code segments would still produce the exact same countdown:

```
for (int k = 10 ; k > 0 ; k--)
System.out.print (k + " ");
System.out.println("BLASTOFF");

for (int k = 10 ; k > 0 ; k--) System.out.print(k + " ");
System.out.println("BLASTOFF");

for
(int k = 10 ; k > 0 ; k--)
System.out.print (k + " ");
System.out.println("BLASTOFF");
```

In each case the statement, `System.out.println("BLASTOFF")`, is not part of the for loop body and is executed only once when the loop terminates.

PROGRAMMING TIP: Loop Indentation . To make loops more readable, indent the loop body to set it off from the heading and to highlight which statement(s) will be repeated.

DEBUGGING TIP: Loop Indentation . Loop indentation has no effect on how Java interprets the loop. The loop body is determined entirely by the syntax of the for statement.

Note that so far, the loop body has consisted of a single statement, which may be either a simple statement, such as a `println()`, or a compound statement. Consider the following examples. The first example prints the sequence 0, 5, 10, 15, . . . , 95. Its loop body consists of a single if statement:

```
for (int k = 0; k < 100; k++)          // Print 0 5 10 15 ... 95
    if (k % 5 == 0)                    // Loop body is a single if statement
        System.out.println("k= " + k);
```

The next example prints the lowercase letters of the alphabet. In this case the loop counter is of type `char`, and it counts the letters of the alphabet. The loop body consists of a single `print()` statement:

```
for (char k = 'a' ; k <= 'z'; k++)     // Print 'a' 'b' 'c' ... 'z'
    System.out.print (k + " ");        // Loop body is a single print()
```

The next example prints the sequence 5, 10, 15, . . ., 50, but it uses several statements within the loop body:

```
for (int k = 1 ; k <= 10; k++) {     // Print 5 10 15 20 ... 50
    int m = k * 5;                   // Begin body
    System.out.print (m + " ");
}                                    // End body
```

The scope of the local variable m, declared within the loop body, is limited to the loop body and cannot used outside of that scope.

JAVA LANGUAGE RULE **Loop Body .** The body of a for statement consists of the statement that immediately follows the for loop heading. This statement can be either a simple statement or a **compound statement** — a sequence of statements enclosed within braces, {...}.

Of course, braces can be used in the loop statement even when the loop body consists of a single statement. And some coding styles recommend that braces should always be used for the body of a loop statement. For example, it's always correct to code the for loop as

```
for (int k = 1 ; k <= 10; k++) {    // Print 1 2 ... 10
    System.out.print (k + " ");     // Begin body
}                                   // End body
```

Another advantage of this coding style is that you can easily place additional statements in the loop body by placing them within the braces.

DEBUGGING TIP: Missing Braces. A common programming error for novices is to forget to use braces to group the statements they intend to put in the loop body. The result will be that only the first statement after the loop heading will be iterated.

SELF-STUDY EXERCISES

EXERCISE 6.1 Identify the syntax error in the following for loop statements:

a.
```
for (int k = 5, k < 100, k++)
  System.out.println(k);
```

b.
```
for (int k = 0; k < 12 ; k--;)
  System.out.println(k);
```

EXERCISE 6.2 Identify those statements that result in infinite loops:

a.
```
for (int k = 0; k < 100; k = k )
  System.out.println(k);
```

b.
```
for (int k = 1; k == 100; k = k + 2 )
  System.out.println(k);
```

c.
```
for (int k = 1; k >= 100; k = k - 2 )
  System.out.println(k);
```

EXERCISE 6.3 Suppose you're helping your little sister learn to count by fours. Write a for loop that prints the following sequence of numbers: 1, 5, 9, 13, 17, 21, 25.

EXERCISE 6.4 What value will *j* have when the following loop terminates?

```
for (int i = 0; i < 10 ; i++) {
    int j;
    j = j + 1;
}
```

6.3.5 Nested Loops

It's possible for the for loop body to contain a **nested** for loop. For example, suppose you are working for Giant Auto Industries, and they want you to print a table that can be used by their buyers to figure the cost of buying multiple quantities of a certain part. The cost of individual parts ranges from $1 to $9. The cost of *N* items is simply the unit price times the quantity.

Thus, you'll want to print something like the following table of numbers:

```
1  2  3  4  5  6  7  8  9
2  4  6  8  10 12 14 16 18
3  6  9  12 15 18 21 24 27
4  8  12 16 20 24 28 32 36
```

To produce this multiplication table, we could use the following nested for loops:

```
for (int row = 1; row <= 4 ; row++) {         // For each of 4 rows          (1)
    for (int col = 1; col <= 9; col++)        // For each of 9 columns       (2)
        System.out.print(col * row + "\t" ); //  Print a number and a tab (3)
    System.out.println();                     // Start a new row             (4)
} // for row
```

Inner and outer loop

Note how indenting is used here to distinguish the levels of nesting and to make the code more readable . In this example the *outer loop* controls the number of rows in the table, hence our choice of `row` as its loop counter. The `println()` statement is executed after the *inner loop* is done iterating, which allows us to print a new row on each iteration of the outer loop. The inner loop prints the nine values in each row by printing the expression *col*row*. Obviously, the value of this expression depends on both loop variables.

Let's dissect this example a bit. How many times is the for statement on line 2 executed? The inner loop is executed once for each iteration of the outer loop. Thus it is executed 4 times, which is the same number of times that line 4 is executed. How many times is the statement on line 3 executed? The body of the inner loop is executed 36 times — 9 times for each execution of line 2.

Sometimes it is useful to use the loop variable of the outer loop as the bound for the inner loop. For example, consider the following pattern:

Algorithm design

```
# # # # #
# # # #
# # #
# #
#
```

Note that the number of # symbols in each row varies inversely with the row number. In row 1, we have five symbols; in row 2 we have four; and so on down to row 5, where we have one #.

To produce this kind of two-dimensional pattern, we need two counters: one to count the row number, and one to count the number of # symbols in each row. Because we have to print each row's symbols before moving on to the next row, the outer loop will count row numbers, and the inner loop will count the symbols in each row. But note that the inner loop's bound will depend on the row number. Thus, in row 1 we want five symbols; in row 2 we want four symbols; and so on. If we let `row` be the row number, then in each row we want to print $6 - row$ symbols. The following table shows the relationship we want:

```
Row   Bound (6-row)     Number of # Symbols
---   -------------     -------------------
 1         6-1                  5
 2         6-2                  4
 3         6-3                  3
 4         6-4                  2
 5         6-5                  1
```

If we let j be the counter for the inner loop, then j will be bound by the expression $6 - row$. This leads to the following nested loop structure:

```
for (int row = 1; row <= 5; row++) {      // For each row
    for (int j = 1; j <= 6 - row; j++)   //  Print the row
        System.out.print('#');
     System.out.println();                //  And a new row
} // for row
```

Note that the bound of the inner loop varies according to the value of *row*, the loop counter for the outer loop.

6.4 Example: Car Loan

Recall the program from Chapter 5 that calculated the value of a CD (a) given its initial principle (p), interest rate (r) and number of years (n), using the formula $a = p(1 + r)^n$. The same formula can be used to figure out how much a car loan will cost for various interest rates, over various time periods.

Problem Description

For example, suppose you're planning on buying a car that cost $20,000. You find that you can get a car loan ranging anywhere from 8 to 11 percent, and you can have the loan for periods as short as two years, and as long as eight years. Let's use our loop constructs to create a table, showing what the car will actually cost you, including financing. In this case, *a* will represent the total cost of the car, including the financing, and *p* will represent the price tag on the car ($20,000).

```
              8%          9%         10%         11%
Year 2  $23,469.81  $23,943.82  $24,427.39  $24,920.71
Year 3  $25,424.31  $26,198.42  $26,996.07  $27,817.98
Year 4  $27,541.59  $28,665.32  $29,834.86  $31,052.09
Year 5  $29,835.19  $31,364.50  $32,972.17  $34,662.19
Year 6  $32,319.79  $34,317.85  $36,439.38  $38,692.00
Year 7  $35,011.30  $37,549.30  $40,271.19  $43,190.31
Year 8  $37,926.96  $41,085.02  $44,505.94  $48,211.60
```

Algorithm Design

Nested loop design

The key element in this program is the nested for loop that generates the table. Because the table contains seven rows, the outer loop should iterate seven times, through the values 2, 3, . . . 8:

```
for ( int years = 2; years <= 8; years++ )      // For years 2 through 8
```

The inner loop should iterate through each of the interest rates, 8 through 11:

```
for (int years = 2; years <= 8; years++) {      // For years 2 through 8
    for (int rate = 8; rate <= 11; rate++ ) {
    } // for rate
} // for years
```

The financing calculation should be placed in the body of the inner loop together with a statement to print one cell (not row) of the table. Suppose the variable we use for *a* in the above formula is `carPriceWithLoan`, and the variable we use for the actual price of the car is `carPrice`. Then our inner loop body is

```
carPriceWithLoan = carPrice * Math.pow(1 + rate / 100.0 / 365.0, years * 365.0);
System.out.print(dollars.format(carPriceWithLoan)  + "\t");
```

Note that the rate is divided by both 100.0 (to make it a percentage) and by 365.0 (for daily compounding), and the year is multiplied by 365.0 before these values are passed to the `Math.pow()` method. It's important here to use 100.0 and not 100 so that the resulting value is a `double` and not the `int` 0.

Figure 6–2 The CarLoan application.

```
import java.text.NumberFormat;    // For formatting $nn.dd or n%

public class CarLoan {

    public static void main(String args[]) {
        double carPrice = 20000;  // Car's actual price
        double carPriceWithLoan;  // Total cost of the car plus financing

        NumberFormat dollars = NumberFormat.getCurrencyInstance(); // Number formatting
        NumberFormat percent = NumberFormat.getPercentInstance();
        percent.setMaximumFractionDigits(2);
                                                   // Print the table
        for (int rate = 8; rate <= 11; rate++)         // Print the column heading
            System.out.print("\t" + percent.format(rate/100.0) + "\t" );
        System.out.println();

        for (int years = 2; years <= 8; years++) {     // For years 2 through 8
            System.out.print("Year " + years + "\t");    // Print row heading
            for (int rate = 8; rate <= 11; rate++) {     // Calc and print CD value
                carPriceWithLoan = carPrice * Math.pow(1 + rate / 100.0 / 365.0, years * 365.0);
                System.out.print( dollars.format(carPriceWithLoan)  + "\t");
            } // for rate
            System.out.println();                        // Start a new row
        } // for years
    } // main()
} // CarLoan
```

Implementation

The program must also contain statements to print the row and column headings. Printing the row headings should be done within the (outer) loop, because it must be done for each row. Printing the column headings should be done before the outer loop is entered. Finally, our program should contain code to format the dollar and cents values properly. For this we use the `java.util.NumberFormat` class, as described in Chapter 5 . The complete program is shown in Figure 6–2.

Formatting output

SELF-STUDY EXERCISES

EXERCISE 6.5 As the engineer hired to design ski jumps write a nested for loop to print the following pattern:

```
#
# #
# # #
# # # #
# # # # #
```

6.5 Conditional Loops

Unlike the problems in the previous section, not all loops can be coded as counting loops. Here's a problem that can't be solved by a counting loop.

Mathematicians, especially number theorists, have found that certain operations on numbers lead to interesting sequences. For example, the *3N + 1 problem* is a theorem in number theory which says that if *N* is any positive integer, then the sequence generated by the following rules will always terminate at 1.

```
Case           Operation
----           ---------
N is odd       N = 3 * N + 1
N is even      N = N / 2
```

In other words, start with any positive integer, *N*. If *N* is odd, multiply it by 3 and add 1. If *N* is even, divide it by 2. In either case assign the result back to *N*. The theorem states that *N* will eventually equal 1. For example, if *N* is initially 26, then the sequence generated is 26, 13, 40, 20, 10, 5, 16, 8, 4, 2, 1.

The 3*N*+1 problem is an example of non-counting loop. Because for any given *N* we don't know how long the 3*N*+1 sequence will be, we need a loop that terminates when the loop variable reaches a *sentinel* value — when *N* equals 1. This is an example of a loop that is terminated by a **sentinel bound**. With the exception of infinite loops, all loops are bounded by some condition, which is why they are sometimes refered to as **conditional loop** structures. The count and sentinel bounds are just special cases of the conditional loop structure.

6.5.1 The While Structure

Consider the following pseudocode algorithm for the 3*N* +1 problem:

```
Algorithm for computing the 3N+1 sequence
    While N is not equal to 1, do: {
        Print N.
        If N is even, divide it by 2.
        If N is odd, multiply N by 3 and add 1.
    }
    Print N
```

In this structure, the body of the loop prints *N*, and then updates *N*'s value, using the 3*N* + 1 rules. Suppose *N* equals 5 when this code segment begins. It will print the following sequence: 5, 16, 8, 4, 2, 1. Note that the loop body is entered as long as *N* is not equal to 1. So the loop entry condition in this case is *N != 1*. Conversely, the loop will terminate when *N* equals 1. Also, note that in this code segment the loop bound is tested *before* the body of the loop is executed.

We can implement this algorithm using Java's *while statement*:

```
while (N != 1) {                   // While N is not equal to 1
    System.out.print(N + " ");     // Print N
    if (N % 2 == 0)                // If N is even
        N = N / 2;                 //   divide it by 2
    else                           // If N is odd
        N = 3 * N + 1;             //   multiply N by 3 and add 1
}
System.out.println(N);             // Print N
```

The **while statement** is a loop statement in which the loop entry condition occurs before the loop body. It has the following general form:

`while` (*loop entry condition*) *loop body* ;

Note that unlike the for statement, the while statement does not contain syntax for the initializer and the updater. These must be coded separately.

Let's make a distinction between a *loop statement* , which is part of the language, and a *loop structure*, which is built by the programmer using the language. For example, the `while` statement is a construct of the Java language. But as we have seen, it lacks syntax for the initializer and updater, which are important elements of the while loop structure. If we make this distinction, then we can state the following loop-design principle:

EFFECTIVE DESIGN: Loop structure. A properly designed *loop structure* must include an *initializer*, a *boundary condition*, and an *updater*. The updater should guarantee that the boundary condition is eventually satisfied, thereby allowing the loop to terminate.

In pseudocode, the *while structure* would take the following form:

```
InitializerStatements;            // Initializer
while (loop entry condition) {    // Bound test
    Statements;                   // Loop body
    UpdaterStatements;            // Updater
}
```

As its form suggests, the while structure is designed so that on some conditions the loop body will never be executed. Because it tests for the loop bound *before* the loop body, it is possible that the loop body is never executed. We might say that it is designed to perform 0 or more interations.

For example, going back to the 3*N* +1 problem, what if *N* equals 1 initially? In that case, the loop body will be skipped, because the loop entry condition is false to begin with. No interations will be performed, and the algorithm will simply print the value 1.

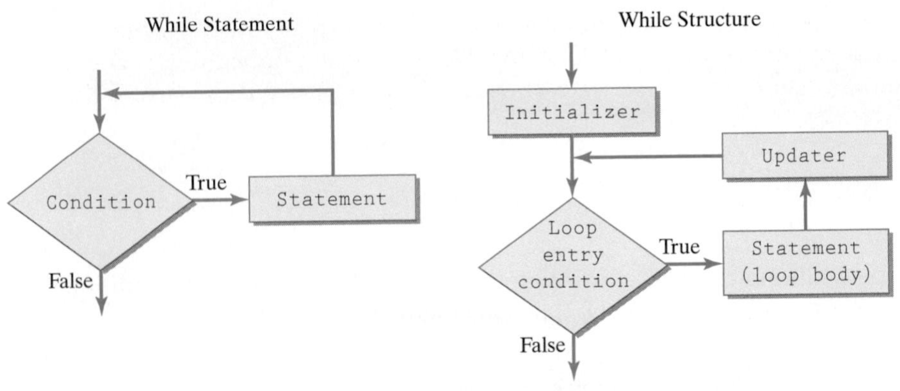

Figure 6–3 Flowchart of the while statement and while structure.

Note also that in the while statement the bound test is preceded by initializer statements, and the loop body contains updater statements. The semantics of the while structure is shown in Figure 6–3.

The while structure would be an appropriate control structure for the following type of problem:

```
write the homework assignment on the assignment sheet    // Initializer
while there are homework problems on the assignment sheet // Bound test
    do a problem                                          // Loop body
    cross it off the assignment sheet                     // Updater
```

It is possible that the assignment sheet contains no homework problems to begin with. In that case, there's no work for the body of the loop to do and it should be skipped.

SELF-STUDY EXERCISES

EXERCISE 6.6 Here's another number theory problem. Start with any positive integer, *N*. If *N* is even, divide it by 2. If *N* is odd, subtract 1 and then divide it by 2. This will generate a sequence that is guaranteed to terminate at 0. For example, if *N* is initially 15, then you get the sequence: 15, 7, 3, 1, 0. Write a method that implements this sequence. Use a while statement.

6.5.2 The Do-While Structure

Problem description

Here's another problem that can't be solved with a counting loop. Your father has been fretting about the bare spots on the front lawn and is considering hiring the ChemSure Lawn Service to fertilize. However, your scientifically minded younger sister wants to reassure him that at the rate the grass is dying, there will be enough to last through the summer. Using techniques she learned in biology, your sister estimates that the grass is dying at the rate of 2 percent per day. How many weeks will it take for half the lawn to disappear?

One way to solve this problem would be to keep subtracting 2 percent from the current amount of grass until the amount dipped below 50 percent, all the while counting the number of iterations required. Consider the following pseudocode algorithm:

Algorithm design

```
Algorithm for calculating grass loss
    Repeat the following statements {
        Initialize amtGrass to 100.0
        Initialize nDays to 0
        Repeat the following statements
            amtGrass -= amtGrass * 0.02;
            ++nDays;
        As long as amtGrass > 50.0
    }
    Print nDays / 7
```

We begin by initializing `amtGrass` to 100.0, representing 100 percent. And we initialize our counter, `nDays` to 0. Then we repeatedly subtract 2 percent of the amount and increment the counter until the amount drops below 50 percent. In other words, in this case, we repeat the loop body as long as the amount of grass remains above 50 percent of the original. When the loop finishes, we report the number of weeks it took by dividing the number of days by 7.

The loop bound in this case is known as a **limit bound**. The loop will terminate when a certain limit has been reached — in this case, when the amount of grass dips below 50 percent of the original amount. Note that in this case the loop bound is tested *after* the loop body. This is appropriate for this problem, because we know in advance that the loop will iterate at least once.

Limit bound

We can implement this algorithm using Java's *do-while statement*:

```
public int losingGrass(double perCentGrass) {
    double amtGrass = 100.0;                // Initialize amount of grass
    int nDays = 0;                          // Initialize day counter
    do {                                    // Repeat
        amtGrass -= amtGrass * LOSSRATE; //   Update amount of grass
        ++nDays;                            //   Increment the counter
    } while ( amtGrass > perCentGrass ); // As long as enough grass remains
    return nDays / 7;                       // Return the number of weeks
} // losingGrass()
```

The **do-while statement** is a loop statement in which the loop entry condition occurs after the loop body. It has the following general form:

`do` *loop body* `while (` *loop entry condition* `);`

Note, again, that unlike the for statement, the do-while statement does not contain syntax for the initializer and the updater. These must be coded separately.

If we distinguish again between a loop statement and a loop structure, then the *do-while structure* takes the following form:

```
InitializerStatements1;           // Initializer
do {                              // Beginning of loop body
    InitializerStatements2;       //    Another place for initializer
    Statements;                   //    Loop body
    UpdaterStatements             //    Updater
} while (loop entry condition);   // End of body and Bound test
```

Note that initializer statements may be placed before the loop body, at the very beginning of the loop body, or in both places, depending on the particular problem. Like the other loop structures, updater statements occur within the body of the loop. A flowchart of the do-while structure is shown in Figure 6–4.

The do-while structure would be an appropriate control structure for the following type of problem:

```
do
    dial your friend's telephone number  // Initializer
    if you get a busy signal
        hang up                          // Updater
while there's a busy signal              // Bound test
```

In this case you want to perform the actions in the body of the loop at least once and possibly more than once (if you continue to receive a busy signal).

EFFECTIVE DESIGN: Do-While Loops. The *do-while loop* is designed for solving problems in which at least one iteration must occur.

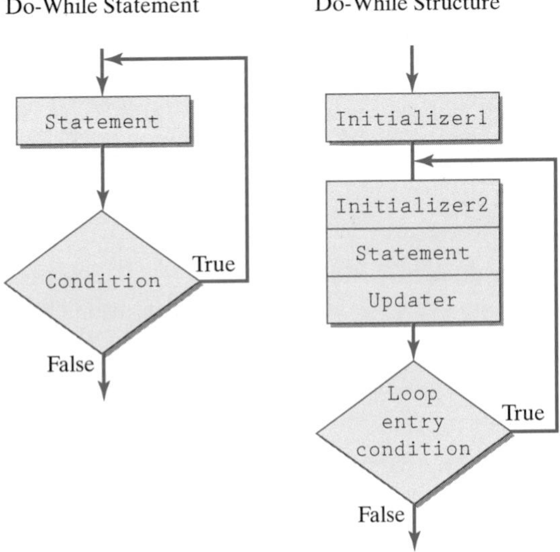

Figure 6–4 Flowchart of the do-while statement and do-while structure.

EFFECTIVE DESIGN: While versus Do-While Structures. For problems where a non-counting loop is required, the *while loop structure* is more general and therefore preferable to the *do-while structure*. Use *do-while* only when at least one iteration must occur.

SELF-STUDY EXERCISES

EXERCISE 6.7 For each of the following problems, decide whether a counting loop structure, a while-structure, or a do-while structure should be used, and write a pseudocode algorithm.

- Print the names of all visitors to your Web site.
- Validate that a number input by the user is positive.
- Change all the backslashes (\) in a Windows Web page address to the slashes (/) used in a Unix Web page address.
- Find the car with the best MPG ratio among the cars in the *Consumer Reports* database.
- Generate the sequence, guaranteed to terminate at 0, using the following rules: Start with an N greater than or equal to 0. If N is even, divide it by 2. If N is odd, subtract 1 and then divide it by 2.

6.6 Example: Computing Averages

Algorithm design: what kind of loop?

Suppose you want to compute the average of your exam grades in a course. Grades, represented as real numbers, will be input from the keyboard. To signify the end of the list, we will use a *sentinel value* — 9999 or −1 or some other value that won't be confused with a legitimate grade. Because we do not know exactly how many grades will be entered, we will use a noncounting loop in this algorithm. Also, because it's always possible that there will be no grades to average, we will use a while structure. That makes it possible to skip the loop entirely in case there are no grades to average.

Algorithm design

The algorithm should add each grade to a running total, keeping track of the number of grades entered. Thus, this algorithm requires two variables: one to keep track of the running total, and the other to keep track of the count. Both should be initialized to 0. After the last grade has been entered, the total should be divided by the count to give the average. In pseudocode the algorithm for this problem is as follows:

```
initialize runningTotal to 0             // Initialize
initialize count to 0
prompt and read the first grade          // Priming read
while the grade entered is not 9999 {    // Sentinel bound test
    add it to the runningTotal
    add 1 to the count
    prompt and read the next grade       // Update
}
if (count > 0)                           // Guard against dividing by 0
    divide runningTotal by count
output the average as the result
```

Priming read

Note that in this problem our loop variable, grade, is read before the loop test is made. This is known as a **priming read**. It is necessary in this case, because the loop test depends on the value that is read. Within the body the updater reads the next value for grade. This is a standard convention for coding while structures that involve input, as this problem does. Note also that we must make sure that count is not 0 before we attempt to compute the average. Otherwise we would create a divide-by-zero error.

Translating the pseudocode algorithm into Java raises several issues. Suppose we store the grades in a double variable named grade. The loop will terminate when grade equals 9999, so its entry condition will be (grade != 9999). Because this condition uses grade, it is crucial that the grade variable be initialized before the bound test is made. This requires a priming read. However, in Java, keyboard input is read as a String, so we will need a second variable, inputString, to store the input, which we must then convert to a double. We can use the converStringTodouble() method to perform this subtask. This design insures that the loop will be skipped, if the user happens to enter the sentinel (9999) on the very first prompt.

Initialization step

```
System.out.print("Input a grade (e.g., 85.3) ");
System.out.print("or 9999 to indicate the end of the list >> ");
inputString = input.readLine();                    // Initialize: Priming read
read grade = convertStringTodouble(inputString);
```

In addition to this initialization, we must initialize the variables used for the running total and the counter.

Within the body of loop we must add the grade to the running total and increment the counter. Since these variables are not tested in the loop entry condition, they will not affect the loop control. Our loop updater in this case must read the next value from the user, convert it to a double, and assign it to grade. Placing the updater statement at the end of the loop body will ensure that the loop terminates immediately after the user enters the sentinel value.

Updater step

```
while (grade != 9999) {                                 // Sentinel test
    System.out.println("You input " + grade + "\n");
    runningTotal += grade;
    count++;
                                                        // Update: get the next grade
    System.out.print("Input a grade (e.g., 85.3) ");
    System.out.print("or 9999 to indicate the end of the list >> ");
    inputString = input.readLine();
    grade = convertStringTodouble(inputString);
} // while
```

Modularity

It's somewhat redundant to repeat the same four statements needed to do the initialization and the updating of the grade variable. A better design would be to encapsulate these into a method and then call the method both before and within the loop. The method should take of prompting the user, reading the input, converting it to double, and returning the input value. The method doesn't require a parameter:

```
private double getInput() throws IOException {
    System.out.print("Input a grade (e.g., 85.3) ");
    System.out.print("or 9999 to indicate the end of the list >> ");
    String inputString  = input.readLine();
    double grade = convertStringTodouble(inputString);
    System.out.println("You input " + grade + "\n");  // Confirm user input
    return grade;
}
```

Note that we've declared this as a `private` method. It will be used to help us perform our task but won't be available to other objects. Also, note that because this method performs I/O, it must declare an `IOException`.

This is a much more modular design. In addition to cutting down on redundancy, it makes the program easier to maintain—for example, there's only one method to change if we decide to change the prompt message—and easier to debug—input errors are now localized to the `getInput()` method.

EFFECTIVE DESIGN: Modularity. Encapsulating code in a method is a good way to avoid redundancy in a program.

DEBUGGING TIP: Localization. Encapsulating code in a method removes the need to have the same exact code at several locations in a program. By localizing the code in this way, you make it easier to modify and debug.

Another advantage of encapsulating the input task in a separate method is that it simplifies the task of calculating the average. This task should also be organized into a separate method:

```
public double inputAndAverageGrades() throws IOException {
    grade = getInput();                   // Initialize: priming input
    while (grade != 9999) {               // Loop test: sentinel
        runningTotal += grade;
        count++;
        grade = getInput();               // Update: get next input
    } // while

    if (count > 0)                        // Guard against divide-by-zero
        return runningTotal / count;      // Return the average
    else
        return 0;                         // Special (error) return value
}
```

Note that we have declared this as a `public` method. This will be the method you call to calculate your course average. Also, because this method calls `getInput()`, which throws an `IOException`, this method must also declare the exception.

Method decomposition

Because we have decomposed the problem into its subtasks, each subtask is short and simple, making it easier to read and understand.

EFFECTIVE DESIGN: Method Decomposition. Methods should be designed to have a clear focus. If you find a method becoming too long, you should break its algorithm into subtasks and define a separate method for the subtask.

The complete `Average.java` application shown in Figure 6–5. Its overall design is similar to application programs we designed in previous chapters. The only instance variable it uses is the `BufferedInput` variable. The other variables are declared locally, within the methods. In this case, declaring them locally makes the algorithms easier to read.

One final point about this program is to note the care taken in the design of the user interface to explain the program to the user, to prompt the user before a value is input, and to confirm the user's input after the program has read it.

EFFECTIVE DESIGN: User Interface. Whenever you're asking a user for input, the user should know *why* you are asking and *what* you are asking for. Prompts should be used for this purpose. It's also a good idea to confirm that the program has received the correct input.

SELF-STUDY EXERCISES

EXERCISE 6.8 Identify the syntax error in the following while structures:

a.
```
int k = 5;
  while (k < 100) {
      System.out.println( k );
      k++
  }
```

b.
```
int k = 0;
  while (k < 12 ;) {
      System.out.println( k );
      k++;
  }
```

EXERCISE 6.9 Determine the output and/or identify the error in each of the following while structures:

a.
```
 int k = 0;
while (k < 100)
    System.out.println( k );
```

b.
```
while ( k < 100 ) {
    System.out.println(k);
    k++;
}
```

EXERCISE 6.10 Your younger sister is now learning how to count by sixes. Write a while loop that prints the following sequence of numbers: 0, 6, 12, 18, 24, 30, 36.

Figure 6–5 A program to compute average grade using a `while` structure.

```
import java.io.*;
public class Average {

    private BufferedReader input = new BufferedReader  // Handles console input
        (new InputStreamReader(System.in));

    private double convertStringTodouble(String s) {
        Double doubleObject = Double.valueOf(s);
        return doubleObject.doubleValue();
    }

    private double getInput() throws IOException  {
        System.out.print("Input a grade (e.g., 85.3) ");
        System.out.print("or 9999 to indicate the end of the list >> ");
        String inputString  = input.readLine();
        double grade = convertStringTodouble(inputString);
        System.out.println("You input " + grade + "\n");  // Confirm user input
        return grade;
    }

    public double inputAndAverageGrades() throws IOException {
        double runningTotal = 0;
        int count = 0;
        double grade = getInput();                  // Initialize: priming input
        while (grade != 9999) {                     // Loop test: sentinel
            runningTotal += grade;
            count++;
            grade = getInput();                     // Update: get next input
        } // while

        if (count > 0)                              // Guard against divide-by-zero
            return runningTotal / count;            // Return the average
        else
            return 0;                               // Special (error) return value
    }

    public static void main(String argv[]) throws IOException {
        System.out.println("This program calculates average grade."); // Explain program
        Average avg = new Average();
        double average = avg.inputAndAverageGrades();
        if (average == 0)                                              // Error case
            System.out.println("You didn't enter any grades.");
        else
            System.out.println("Your average is " + average);
    } // main()
} // Average
```

6.7 Example: Data Validation

One frequent programming task is *data validation* . This task can take different forms depending on the nature of the program. One use for data validation occurs when accepting input from the user.

In the previous program, suppose the user types −10 by mistake when asked to input an exam grade. Obviously this is not a valid exam grade and should not be added to the running total. How should a program handle this task?

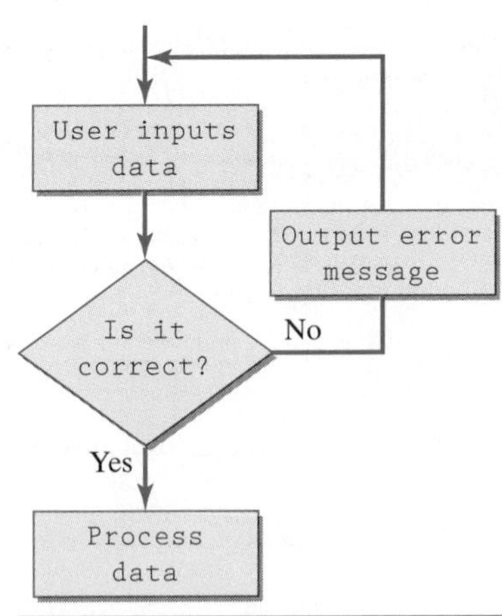

Figure 6–6 Because the user must input at least one value *before* you can check if it is valid, data validation is a good task for a do-while structure.

Algorithm Design

Algorithm design

Because it is possible that the user may take one or more attempts before getting the input correct, we should use a do-while structure for this problem (Figure 6–6). The program should first input a number from the user. The number should then be checked for validity. If it is valid, the loop should exit and the program should continue on computing average grade. If it is not valid, the program should print an error message and input the number again. For example, suppose only numbers between 0 and 100 are considered valid. The data validation algorithm would be as follows:

```
do
    Get the next grade                               // Initialize: priming input
    if the grade < 0 or grade > 100 and grade != 9999    // Error case
        print an error message
while the grade < 0 or grade > 100 and grade != 9999    // Sentinel test
                                                     // Continue on to compute the average
```

Initialization and update step

Note here that initialization and updating of the loop variable are performed by the same statement. This is acceptable because we must update the value of `grade` on each iteration *before* checking its validity. Note also that for this problem the loop-entry condition is coded twice: once in the if statement, so that an appropriate error message can be displayed, and once as the bound test. It is the second occurrence of the condition that will control the loop's behavior.

Let's incorporate the data validation code into the `getInput()` method we designed in the previous section (Figure 6–5):

```
private double getAndValidateGrade() throws IOException {
    double grade = 0;
    do {
        System.out.print("Input a grade (e.g., 85.3) ");
        System.out.print("or 9999 to indicate the end of the list >> ");
        String inputString  = input.readLine();
        grade = convertStringTodouble(inputString) ;
        if ((grade != 9999) && ((grade < 0) || (grade > 100)))
            System.out.println("Error: grade must be between 0 and 100\n");  // Input error
        else
            System.out.println("You input " + grade + "\n");                 // OK input
    } while ((grade != 9999) && ((grade < 0) || (grade > 100)));
    return grade;
} // getAndValidateGrade()
```

We've changed the name of the method to suggest that it takes care of the entire input and validation task, returning a number between 0 and 100 to the calling method. It therefore has a return type of `double`. The only other change we need to make in the `Average` program (Figure 6–5) is to revise the method calls to reflect the new name we have given our input method:

```
grade = getAndValidateGrade();
```

The revised application, which we've renamed `Validate`, is shown in Figure 6–7.

SELF-STUDY EXERCISES

EXERCISE 6.11 Identify the syntax error in the following do-while structures:

a.
```
 int k = 0;
do while (k < 100)
     System.out.println( k );
     k++
}
```

b.
```
 int k = 0;
do {
    System.out.println( k );
    k++;
} while (k < 12)
```

EXERCISE 6.12 Your sister has moved on to counting by sevens. So write a do-while loop that prints the following sequence of numbers: 1, 8, 15, 22, 29, 36, 43.

EXERCISE 6.13 As the owner of Pizza Heaven, every night at the close of business you quickly enter the price of every pizza ordered that day. You take the data from the servers' receipts. Pizzas cost $8, $10, or (the Heavenly Special) $15. You enter the data without dollar signs, and use 99 to indicate you're finished for the day. Write a Java method to input and validate a single Pizza data item. If an incorrect price is entered, the program should print an error message, and prompt for corrected input. Correct input is used to compute a daily total.

Figure 6–7 A program to compute average grade using a `while` structure. This version validates the user's input.

```
import java.io.*;

public class Validate {
    private BufferedReader input = new BufferedReader  // Handles console input
        (new InputStreamReader(System.in));

    private double convertStringTodouble(String s) {
        Double doubleObject = Double.valueOf(s);
        return doubleObject.doubleValue();
    }

    private double getAndValidateGrade() throws IOException {
        double grade = 0;
        do {
            System.out.print("Input a grade (e.g., 85.3) ");
            System.out.print("or 9999 to indicate the end of the list >> ");
            String inputString  = input.readLine();
            grade = convertStringTodouble(inputString) ;
            if ((grade != 9999) && ((grade < 0) || (grade > 100)))
                System.out.println("Error: grade must be between 0 and 100\n");  // Input error
            else
                System.out.println("You input " + grade + "\n");                  // OK input
        } while ((grade != 9999) && ((grade < 0) || (grade > 100)));
        return grade;
    } // getAndValidateGrade()

    public double inputAndAverageGrades() throws IOException {
        double runningTotal = 0;
        int count = 0;
        double grade = getAndValidateGrade();   // Initialize: priming input
        while (grade != 9999) {                 // Loop test: sentinel
            runningTotal += grade;
            count++;
            grade = getAndValidateGrade();      // Update: get next grade
        } // while
        if (count > 0)                          // Guard against divide-by-zero
            return runningTotal / count;            // Return the average
        else
            return 0;                               // Special (error) return value
    } // inputAndAverageGrades()

    public static void main( String argv[] ) throws IOException {
        System.out.println("This program calculates average grade."); // Explain program
        Validate avg = new Validate();
        double average = avg.inputAndAverageGrades();
        if (average == 0)                                        // Error case
            System.out.println("You didn't enter any grades.");
        else
            System.out.println("Your average is " + average );
    } // main()
} // Validate
```

EXERCISE 6.14 Because the pizza prices in the previous exercise are fixed, change the method so you can save time on keyboarding. Instead of entering the price, you'll enter codes of 1, 2, or 3 (corresponding to the \$8, \$10, and \$15 pizzas), and 0 to indicate that you're finished. Validate that the data value entered is correct, and then convert it to the corresponding price, before returning it.

6.8 CASE STUDY: Animated CyberPet

One thing that loops are good for is to create animations. You might remember creating animations as a kid by drawing images on several pieces of paper, and then rapidly flipping between the pages to create the illusion of motion. This is the classical motion picture animation technique, still used. A similar effect can be achieved in a computer program. In computer animation the idea is to switch rapidly between two or more images displayed on the screen. In the "From the Library" section of Chapter 4 we learned how to incorporate images into an applet. Now let's use our new found expertise with loops to animate these images.

6.8.1 Problem Description and Specification

In a previous version of `CyberPetApplet`, described in the lab exercise in Chapter 4, we learned how to load and display images in an applet. In that version, the image we used to represent the eating state was just a static image of the pet with its mouth open, about to gobble a fly [Figure 6–8(a)]. One way to use animation here is to have the spider chew its prey, and then flash a nice smile when its done. We can do this by using two additional images, one to represent the spider with its mouth closed [Figure 6–8(b)], and the other to represent the happy spider [Figure 6–8(c)]. The animation effect can be achieved by rapidly switching between images *a* and *b* in Figure 6–8. So we want to modify `CyberPetApplet` to incorporate this animation behavior.

6.8.2 Class Design: `CyberPetApplet`

To accomplish this task we must incorporate several additional variables and methods into the `CyberPetApplet` class. Because the proposed changes do not affect the `CyberPet` itself, just our representation of it in the user interface, we don't have to make any changes to the `CyberPet` definition.

What variables do we need?

We will need one variable for each image that will be used in the program. Let's suppose that we have a two-state version of `CyberPet` — one that

(a)

(b)

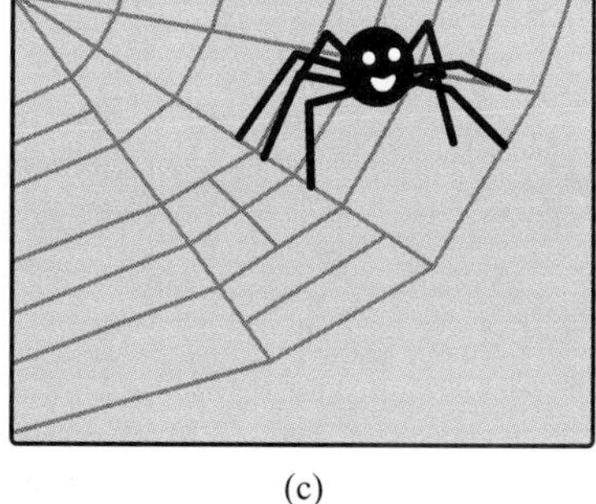

(c)

Figure 6–8 Animation can be created by alternating rapidly between images (a) and (b), with image (c) being used to represent the pet's state after the fly is eaten.

alternates between eating and sleeping. We therefore need four Image variables:

```
private Image eatImg, eat2Img, sleepImg, happyImg;
```

The names we've chosen reflect the images' purposes in the animation. The images themselves must be loaded into the applet during the initialization phase. Thus, the following statements should be added to the init() method:

```
eatImg = getImage(getCodeBase(), "eatImage.gif");
eat2Img = getImage(getCodeBase(), "eat2Image.gif");
sleepImg = getImage(getCodeBase(), "sleepImage.gif");
happyImg = getImage(getCodeBase(), "happyImage.gif");
```

What methods do we need?

In order to process the animation, we will need several new methods. First, the images must be *painted* onto the applet after each action. To paint the image itself, we can use the awt.Graphics.drawImage() method. But we have to paint the right image at the right time. When the pet is sleeping, we have to paint the sleeping image, and when the pet is eating, we have to do the eating animation. In order to coordinate the applet with the pet's state, we must ask the CyberPet to tell us its state:

```
public void paint(Graphics g) {
    String petState = pet1.getState();      // Get the pet's state
   if (petState.equals("Eating"))           // Display appropriate image
       doEatAnimation(g);
   else if (petState.equals("Sleeping"))
       g.drawImage(sleepImg, 20, 100, this);
} // paint()
```

Note how we use the String.equals() method to determine what state the CyberPet is in. Note also how we have encapsulated the animation task itself into a separate method, doEatAnimation(). Because this method will also draw images, it must be passed a reference to the Graphics object, *g*.

6.8.3 Algorithm Design: doEatAnimation()

The algorithm for the doEatAnimation() method will implement the idea we just described: It will rapidly alternate between the eatImg and eat2Img. By doing this several times, the applet will give the illusion of the pet chewing its fly:

```
// Pseudocode for the animation algorithm
 For several iterations
     Display the opened mouth image (eatImg)
     Delay for an instant.
     Display the closed mouth image (eat2Img)
     Delay for an instant.
```

Note that we have incorporated two delays into the algorithm. If we don't do this, the computer will display the images so rapidly that they will go by in one big blur. Therefore, we have to slow down the alternation between the two images.

Algorithm Design: `busyWaiting()` *Algorithm*

Let's design a method that we can call after displaying an image to cause the computer to delay for an instant. One way to do this is to employ a looping technique known as **busy waiting**. In busy waiting the computer just sits in a loop and does nothing:

```
for ( int k = 0; k < N; k++ ) ;  // Empty body --- does nothing
```

If we simply place a semicolon after the for loop heading, we create a for loop with an empty body. It will still iterate from 0 to $N - 1$, but it won't do anything. This leads to the following method definition:

```
private void busyWait(int N) {
    for (int k = 0; k < N; k++) ;    // Empty for body --- does nothing
}
```

Busy waiting is a rather old fashioned way of getting an algorithm to delay. A loop that does nothing is actually wasteful of the computer's time. A more modern technique would make use of separate `threads` to implement the pause, a technique that we will learn in Chapter 13.

DEBUGGING TIP: Null Loop Statement. A for loop with no body is said to contain a *null statement*. When done unintentionally, by mistakenly putting a semicolon after the loop condition, this code will cause a hard-to-find semantic error. When done intentionally, it should be well documented.

6.8.4 Implementation

The complete implementation of the `AnimatedCyberPet` applet is shown in Figure 6–9. In addition to the various design issues we've discussed, there are several implementation details worth noting about this applet. First, note the use of the named constant, PAUSE, to represent the length of the delay between alternating images. A **named constant** is a `final` variable whose values remains constant throughout the program. Using PAUSE makes the program easier to read and easier to maintain. When we see PAUSE in the program, we immediately know what its purpose is. Also, if we decide to change the PAUSE to, say, 100000, we need only change one line of the program. If we had used a literal, we would have to find and change every occurrence of it in the program.

Named constant

Figure 6–9 The AnimatedCyberPet applet.

```
import java.applet.*;
import java.awt.*;
import java.awt.event.*;

public class AnimatedCyberPet extends Applet implements ActionListener {
    private final int PAUSE = 2000000;                    // Named constant
                                                          // Instance variables.
    private CyberPet pet1 = new CyberPet("Socrates");     // CyberPet
    private Label nameLabel = new Label("Hi! My name is "  // Label
            + pet1.getName() + " and currently I am : ");
    private TextField stateField = new TextField(12);     // A TextField
    private Button eatButton = new Button("Eat!");        // Two Buttons
    private Button sleepButton = new Button("Sleep!");
    private Image eatImg, eat2Img, sleepImg, happyImg;    // Images for animation

    public void init() {
        eatButton.addActionListener(this);      // Assign the listeners to the buttons.
        sleepButton.addActionListener(this);
        stateField.setText( pet1.getState() ); // Initialize the TextField
        stateField.setEditable(false);
        add(nameLabel);                         // Add the components to the applet.
        add(stateField);
        add(eatButton);
        add(sleepButton);
        eatImg = getImage(getCodeBase(), "eatImage.gif");     // Load the images
        eat2Img = getImage(getCodeBase(), "eat2Image.gif");
        sleepImg = getImage(getCodeBase(), "sleepImage.gif");
        happyImg = getImage(getCodeBase(), "happyImage.gif");
        setSize(300,300);                                     // Set the applet's size
    } // init()

    public void paint(Graphics g) {
        String petState = pet1.getState();
        if (petState.equals("Eating"))
            doEatAnimation(g);
        else if (petState.equals("Sleeping"))
            g.drawImage(sleepImg, 20, 100, this);
    } // paint()

    private void doEatAnimation(Graphics g) {
        for (int k = 0; k < 5; k++) {
            g.drawImage( eatImg ,20, 100, this);
            busyWait(PAUSE);
            g.drawImage(eat2Img, 20, 100, this);
            busyWait(PAUSE);
        }
        g.drawImage(happyImg, 20, 100, this);
    } // doEatAnimation()

    private void busyWait(int N) {
        for (int k = 0; k < N; k++) ;    // Empty for body --- does nothing
    } // busyWait()

    public void actionPerformed(ActionEvent e) {
        if (e.getSource() == eatButton)
            pet1.eat();
        else if (e.getSource() == sleepButton)
            pet1.sleep();
        stateField.setText(pet1.getState());
        repaint();
    } // actionPerformed()
} // AnimatedCyberPet
```

PROGRAMMING TIP: Named Constants. Avoid using literal values in your programs. Using named constants instead of literal values makes a program much more self-documenting, and makes it easier to revise and maintain.

Second, note the use of the `repaint()` method in `actionPerformed()`. This is the conventional way of invoking the `paint()` method, which is never called directly within a program. The `paint()` method is another example of a polymorphic method. By overriding its definition in an applet, you enable the system to invoke a `paint()` method that is appropriate for that particular context. By designing it to work this way, Java can pass it the correct referent to the applet's `Graphics` context. So the method inherits functionality but allows for extensibility.

Polymorphism

Finally, look at the implementation of the `doEatAnimation()` method. It alternately displays the two eating images, with pauses in between, and when the loop is exited, it displays an image of the happy spider. This implementation is highly platform dependent, because the actual length of the wait depends heavily on the processor's speed. It may be necessary to experiment with how big to make N in order to create an realistic animation. We will remedy this shortcoming when we discuss threads in Chapter 13.

6.9 Principles of Loop Design

Before moving on, it will be useful to summarize the main principles involved in correctly constructing a loop.

- A *counting loop* can be used whenever you know in advance exactly how many iterations are needed. Java's *for statement* is an appropriate structure for coding a counting loop.
- A *while structure* should be used when the problem suggests that the loop body may be skipped entirely. Java's *while statement* is specially designed for the while structure.
- A *do-while structure* should be used only when a loop requires one or more iterations. Java's *do-while-statement* is specially designed for the do-while structure.
- The *loop variable* is used to specify the *loop entry condition*. It must be initialized to an appropriate initial value and it must be updated on each iteration of the loop.
- A loop's *bound* may be a *count*, a *sentinel*, or, more generally, a *conditional bound*. It must be correctly specified in the loop-entry expression, and progress toward the bound must be made in the *updater*.
- An *infinite loop* may result if either the initializer, loop-entry expression, or updater expression is not correctly specified.

The loop types are also summarized in Table 6–1.

Table 6.1. A summary of the design decisions required when coding a loop

Use	If	Java Statement
Counting loop	*Number of iterations known in advance*	*for*
While structure	*Number of iterations not known* *Loop may not be entered at all*	*while*
Do-while structure	*Number of iterations not known* *Loop must be entered at least once*	*do-while*

OBJECT-ORIENTED DESIGN: Structured Programming

Structured programming is the practice of writing programs that are built up from a small set of predefined control structures. As an overall approach to programming, structured programming has largely been superseded by the object-oriented approach. Nevertheless its design principles are still relevant to the design of the algorithms and methods that make up a program's objects.

The principles of structured programming seem so obvious today that it may be difficult to appreciate their importance. In the 1960s and 1970s, one of the main controls used in programs was the infamous *go to* statement, which could be used to transfer control of a program to any arbitrary location within it, and from there to any other arbitrary location, and so on. This led to incredibly complex and ill-formed programs — so called "spaghetti code" — that were almost impossible to understand and modify.

Structured programming evolved in reaction to the unstructured software development practices of the 1960s, which were fraught with budget overruns, costly delays, and failed products. One of the classic research results of that era was a 1966 paper by Boehm and Jacopini that showed that any program using go to's could be represented by an equivalent program that used a sequence of two types of controls: if/else and while structures. Another influential paper by Edgar Dikjstra ("GoTo Statement Considered Harmful") pointed out the various ways in which the go to statement could lead to impossibly complex programs.

The Pascal language, introduced by Nicklaus Wirth in 1971, was designed to promote structured programming techniques and became the language of choice within academic institutions because of its suitability as a teaching language. In Pascal the go to was replaced with the four structures that control the flow of execution in a program (Figure 6–10) :

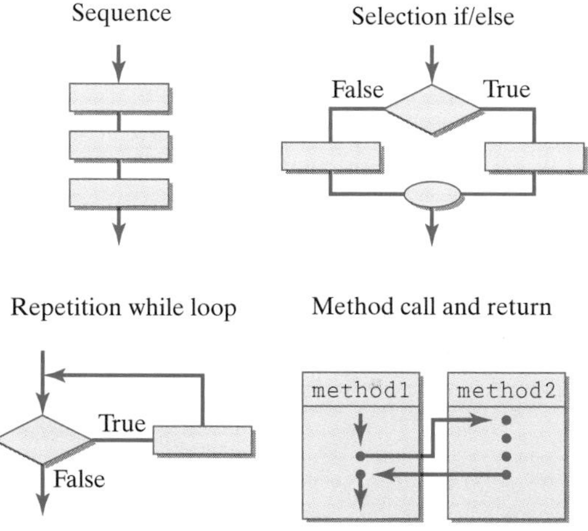

Figure 6–10 Flowcharts of the four types of control structures. Each small rectangle represents a single executable statement.

- *Sequence* — The statements in a program are executed in sequential order unless their flow is interrupted by one of the following control structures.
- *Selection* — The `if`, `if/else`, and `switch` statements are *branching* statements that allow choice through the forking of the control path into two or more alternatives.
- *Repetition* — The `for`, `while`, and `do-while` statements are *looping* statements that allow the program to repeat a sequence of statements.
- *Method Call* — Invoking a method transfers control temporarily to a named method. Control returns to the point of invocation when the method is completed.

No matter how large or small a program you write, its flow of control can be constructed as a combination of these four basic types of structures.

Preconditions and Postconditions

The Java language supplies us with a good collection of control structures, and its syntax constrains the way we can use them. One of the features of the four control structures is that each has a single entry point and exit (Figure 6–10). This is an extremely important property. To grasp its importance, consider the following debugging problem:

```
k = 0;                              // 1. Unstructured code
System.out.println("k= " + k);      // 2. k should equal 0 here
goto label1;                        // 3.
label2:
System.out.println("k= " + k);      // 4. k should equal 1 here
```

Suppose we're trying to determine how *k* has acquired an erroneous value, and that its value is correct in line 2 of this sequence. Given the go to statement on line 3, there's no guarantee that control will ever return to the `println()` statement on line 4. Thus, in unstructured code it is very difficult to narrow the scope of an error to a fixed segment of code. Because the go to statement can transfer control anywhere in the program, with no guarantee of return, any segment of code can have multiple entry points and multiple exits.

Now contrast the above code with the following well-structured code:

```
k = 0;                          // 1. Structured code
System.out.println("k= " + k);  // 2. k should equal 0 here
someMethod();                   // 3.
System.out.println("k= " + k);  // 4. k should equal 1 here
```

In this case we can be certain that control will eventually return to line 4. If *k's* value is erroneous on line 4, we can trace through `someMethod()` to find the error. Because any segment of a structured program has a single entry and exit, we can use a pair of `println()` statements in this way to converge on the location of the program bug.

An important implication of the single-entry/single-exit property is that we can use **preconditions** and **postconditions** to help us design and debug our code. The previous example provided a simple example: The precondition is that *k* should equal 0 on line 2, and the postcondition is that *k* should equal 1 on line 4. Figure 6–11 shows some additional examples.

In the first example, we use pre- and postconditions to define the semantics of an assignment statement. No matter what value *k* has before the assignment, the execution of the assignment (`k = 5`) will make the postcondition (`k == 5`) true.

In the second example, the postcondition follows from the semantics of the while loop. Because the loop-entry condition is `k < 100`, when the loop exits the postcondition (`k >= 100`) must be true.

The third example shows how pre- and postconditions can be used to design and document methods. The *factorial(n)* is defined for $n \geq 0$ as follows:

```
factorial(n) is 1, if n == 0
factorial(n) is n * n-1 * n-2 * ... * 1, n > 0
```

In other words, the factorial of *N* is defined as the cumulative produce of multiplying 1 times 2, times 3, and so on up to *N*. For example, if *N* is 5, then `factorial(5)` is 1 * 2 * 3 * 4 * 5 = 120.

Note how the factorial computation is done in the method. The variable *f*, which is used to accumulate the product, is initialized to 1. Then on each iteration of the for loop, *f* is multiplied by *k* and the product is assigned back to *f*. This is similar to the way we accumulate a sum, except in this case we are accumulating a product.

Figure 6–11 Using pre- and postconditions to document code.

- ```
  int k = 0;    // Precondition: k == 0
  k = 5;        // Assignment to k
                // Postcondition: k == 5
  ```
- ```
  int k = 0;              // Precondition: k == 0
  while (k < 100) {       // While loop
      k = 2 * k + 2;
  }
                          // Postcondition: k >= 100
  ```
- ```
  /**
   * factorial(n) -- factorial(n) is 1 if n is 0
   *                 factorial(n) is n * n-1 * n-2 * ... * 1 if n > 0
   * Precondition:  n >= 0
   * Postcondition: factorial(n) = 1 if n = 0
   *                             = n * n-1 * n-2 * ... * 1 if n > 0
   */
  public int factorial(int n) {
      if (n == 0)
          return 1;
      else {
          int f = 1;                          // Init a temporary variable
          for (int k = n; k >= 1; k--)        // For n down to 1
              f = f * k;                      //     Accumulate the product
          return f;                           // Return the factorial
      }
  } // factorial()
  ```

The precondition on the `factorial()` method represents the condition that must be true in order for the method to work correctly. Factorial is undefined for $n < 0$, so it is important that n be greater than or equal to 0 whenever this method is called. Given that the precondition holds, the postcondition gives a precise specification of what must be true when the method is finished.

Design: Defensive Programming

The pre- and postconditions for a method can be used to design defensive code — that is, code that guards against errors. For example, what action should `factorial()` take if its precondition fails to hold? One rather radical approach would be to terminate the program when a precondition fails:

```
public int factorial(int n) {
    if (n < 0) {                              // Precondition failure
        System.out.println("Error in factorial(), n = " + n);
        System.exit( 0 );
    }
    if (n == 0)
        return 1;
    else {
        int f = 1;                            // Init a temporary variable
        for (int k = n; k >= 1; k--)          // For n down to 1
            f = f * k;                        //     Accumulate the product
        return f;                             // Return the factorial
    }
} // factorial()
```
```

The `System.exit()` method can be used to terminate the program in an orderly fashion. Note that an error message is printed before exiting.

This error handling strategy would guard against an erroneous value being propagated throughout the program by the `factorial()` method. The failure of the precondition in `factorial()` points to a problem elsewhere in the program, because it is doubtful that the program deliberately passed a negative value to `factorial()`. The discovery of this error should lead to modifications in that part of the program where `factorial()` was invoked — perhaps to some validation of the user's input:

```
int num = Integer.parseInt(textIn.getText());
if (num >= 0)                        // If factorial() precondition is valid
    factNum = factorial(num);        //   Compute the factorial
else
    System.out.println("Error");     //   Report error in user input
```

This would be the traditional way to handle this kind of error. It incorporates error checking and error handling code right into the program's algorithm. As we will see in Chapter 11, Java's built-in *exception handling* mechanism provides a much more systematic way to handle erroneous or exceptional conditions.

Using Pre- and Postconditions

The use of preconditions and postconditions in the ways we've described can help improve a program's design at several distinct stages of its development:

- Design stage: Using pre- and postconditions in design helps to clarify the design and provides a precise measure of correctness.
- Implementation and testing stage: Test data can be designed to demonstrate that the preconditions and postconditions hold for any method or code segment.
- Documentation stage: Using pre- and postconditions to document the program makes the program more readable and easier to modify and maintain.
- Debugging stage: Using the pre- and postconditions provides precise criteria that can be used to isolate and locate bugs. A method is incorrect if its precondition is true and its postcondition is false. A method is improperly invoked if its precondition is false.

Like other programming skills and techniques, learning how to use pre- and postconditions effectively requires practice. The lab exercise for this chapter and subsequent chapters will require that you provide additional documentation in your programs to identify the pre- and postconditions for each method and for each loop.

Appendix A provides guidelines on how to incorporate pre- and postconditions into your program's documentation. However, it would be a mistake to get in the habit of leaving the identification of pre- and postconditions to the documentation stage. They should identified during the design stage and should play a role in all aspects of program development.

Effective Program Design

What we're really saying here is that using pre- and postconditions forces you to analyze your program's logic. It is not enough to know that a single isolated statement within a program works correctly at the present time. You have to ask yourself: Will it continue to work if you change some other part of the program? Will other parts of the program continue to work if you revise it? No matter how clever you are, it is not possible to keep an entire model of a good-sized program in your head at one time. It is always necessary to focus on a few essential details and leave aside certain others. Ideally, what you hope is that the details you've left aside for the moment aren't the cause of the current bug you're trying to fix. Using pre- and postconditions can help you determine the correctness of the details you choose to set aside.

EFFECTIVE DESIGN: Pre- and Postconditions. Pre- and postconditions are an effective way of analyzing the logic of your program's loops and methods. They should be identified at the earliest stages of design and development. They should play a role in the testing and debugging of the program. Finally, they should be included, in a systematic way, in the program's documentation.

PROGRAMMING TIP: Develop your program's documentation at the same time that you develop its code, and include the pre- and postconditions in the documentation.

As the programs you write become longer and more complex, the chances that they contain serious errors increase dramatically. There's no real way to avoid this complexity. The only hope is to try to manage it. In addition to analyzing your program's structure, another important aspect of program design is the attempt to reduce its complexity.

EFFECTIVE DESIGN: Reducing Complexity. Design your programs with an aim toward reducing their complexity.

Perhaps the best way to reduce complexity is to build your programs using a small collection of standard structures and techniques. The basic control structures (Figure 6–10) help reduce the potential complexity of a program by constraining the kinds of branching and looping structures that can be built. The control structures help to manage the complexity of your program's algorithms. In the same way, the following practices can help reduce and manage the complexity in a program.

PROGRAMMING TIP: Standard Techniques. Acquire and use standard programming techniques for standard programming problems. For example, using a temporary variable to swap the values of two variables is a standard technique.

PROGRAMMING TIP: Encapsulation. Use methods wherever appropriate in your own code to encapsulate important sections of code and thereby reduce complexity.

PROGRAMMING TIP: Code Reuse. Instead of reinventing the wheel, use library classes and methods whenever possible. These have been carefully designed by experienced programmers. Library code has been subjected to extensive testing.

Lanning's Limerick

Bad hackers will say without blinking,
That analysis hampers their thinking.
But a task very complex
That's coded by reflex,
Very often will end up just stinking.

What Can Be Computed?

Did you ever wonder whether there are problems that cannot be solved by a computer, no matter what kind of control structures are used? Well, back in 1939, in his seminal paper titled "On Computable Numbers," Alan Turing proved that indeed there are an infinite number of unsolvable problems. Prior to this, mathematicians and logicians thought all problems could be solved. So Turing's proof was quite a blow!

To help him prove this point Turing defined an abstract computer, which has come to be known as a Turing machine. A Turing machine has an alphabet of symbols; a read/write head; an infinitely long tape, on which the read/write head can write symbols, and from which it can also read symbols; and a control unit, which controls the movement and action of the read/write head. Note that the Turing machine elements correspond to key components of a real computer—although Turing invented this concept a decade before the first computers were developed. The read/write head corresponds to a computer's Central Processing Unit (CPU). The tape corresponds to the computer's memory. And the control unit corresponds to the computer program.

A Turing machine represents a purely abstract concept of computation. It represents the pure idea of an algorithmic solution to a problem. Equipped with this concept, Turing was able to prove that there are unsolvable problems — that is, problems for which no algorithm can arrive at a solution.

One such problem is the *halting problem.* This problem asks whether an algorithm can be devised to determine whether an arbitrary program will eventually halt. If there were such an algorithm, it could be used to detect programs that contain infinite loops, a service that might be really helpful in an introductory computing lab, among other places! But, alas, there can be no such algorithm.

Here's a sketch of a proof by contradiction that the halting problem is unsolvable. (This particular version of the proof was suggested by J. Glenn Brookshear in *Computer Science: An Overview*, Benjamin-Cummings, 1985.)

Suppose you had a program, *P*, that solves the halting problem. That is, whenever *P* is given a self-halting program, suppose it sets a variable *isTerminating* to *true*, and otherwise it sets *isTerminating* to false. Now let's create a new version of *P*, named *P′*, which is identical to *P* except that right after where *P* sets *isTerminating* to true or false, *P′* contains the following loop:

```
while (isTerminating == true);  // Infinite loop if isTerminating is true
```

In other words, if the input to *P′* is a self-terminating program, then *P′* will enter an infinite loop and it won't terminate. Otherwise, if a non self-terminating program is input to *P′*, *P′* will skip the loop and will terminate.

Now what if we give a representation of *P′* to itself. Will it halt? The answer generates a contradiction: If *P′* is a self-terminating program, then when it is input to itself, it will not terminate. And if *P′* is not self-terminating, when it is input to itself, it will terminate. Because our assumption that P solves the halting problem has led to a contradiction, we have to conclude that it wasn't a very good assumption in the first place. Therefore, there is no program that can solve the halting problem.

The topic of computability is a fundamental part of the computer science curriculum, usually taught in a sophomore or junior level course on the theory of computation.

SELF-STUDY EXERCISES

EXERCISE 6.15 Identify the pre- and postconditions on *j* and *k* where indicated in the following code segment:

```
int j = 0; k = 5;
do {
    if (k % 5 == 0)  {
                           // Precondition
        j += k;
        k--;
    }
    else k *= k;
} while (j <= k);
                         // Postcondition
```

EXERCISE 6.16 Identify the pre- and postconditions for the following method, which computes $x^n \; for \; n \geq 0$.

```
public double power(double x, int n) {
    double pow = 1;
    for (int k = 1; k <= n; k++)
        pow = pow * x;
    return pow;
} // power()
```

From the Java Library: The TextArea Class

A `java.awt.TextArea` is an AWT component for storing and manipulating multiple lines of text (whereas a `TextField` allows just a single line of text to be input or output). The main features of the `TextArea` class are

```
public class TextArea extends TextComponent {
   // Constructors
    public TextArea();
    public TextArea(String s, int rows, int cols);
  // Instance methods
    public synchronized void append(String s);
    public int getColumns();
    public int getRows();
    public void setColumns(int cols);
    public void setRows(int rows);
}
```

In addition to these methods, a `TextArea` inherits several important methods from `TextComponent`, including the following, which are also inherited by `TextField`:

```
public class TextComponent extends Component {
   // No constructors
   // Editing Methods
    public synchronized String getText();
    public boolean isEditable();
    public synchronized void setEditable(boolean b);
    public synchronized setText (String s);
}
```

To create a `TextArea` you can use one of the following constructors:

```
TextArea()
TextArea(String s, int rows, int cols)
```

The first creates an empty `TextArea` of default size. The second creates a `TextArea` containing the text *s* as its initial value and the specified number of rows and columns:

```
TextArea myText = new TextArea("hello", 5, 60);
```

To use a `TextArea` for output only, we want it to be uneditable:

```
myText.setEditable(false);
```

To write text into a `TextArea`, you can use either the `setText()` or `append()` methods:

```
myText.setText("Hello again!\n");
myText.append("Welcome back!\n");
```

The `setText()` method will replace whatever text was in the `TextArea` with "Hello again!" whereas `append()` will append "Welcome back!" to the end of the text that was already in the `TextArea`. To extract text from a `TextArea`, you would use `getText()`, which is inherited from `TextComponent`:

```
String str = myText.getText();
```

Figure 6–12 A Graphical User Interface (GUI) for simple IO operations.

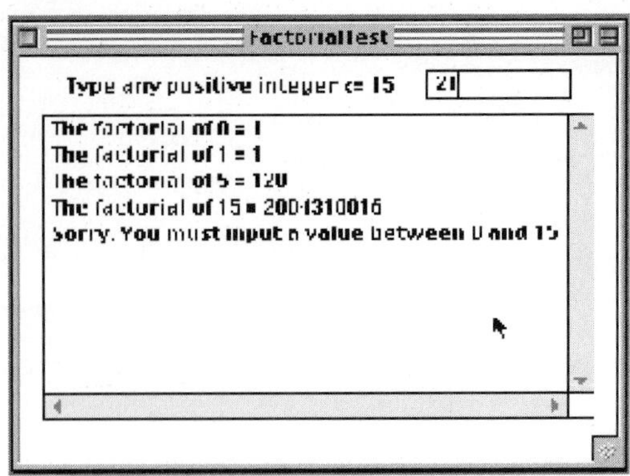

GUI design

Using a `TextArea` as an output device is very simple. The program in Figure 6–12 provides an example of how to set up a simple Graphical User Interface (GUI) for performing I/O operations. A `TextField` is used as an input device, and a `Label` is used to prompt the user. A `TextArea` is used as an output device — where the program's results are displayed. In this example, the GUI is used to test the `factorial()` method we defined earlier (Figure 6–11). Each time the user types a number into the `TextField`, the applet checks whether the number is in the appropriate range and then displays its factorial in the `TextArea`. This combined use of a `Label`, a `TextField`, and a `TextArea` is very general and can be used as the basic design for a wide variety of GUIs.

The `FactorialTest` program is shown in Figure 6–13. It instantiates the three components visible in Figure 6–12. These are added to the applet in its `init()` method. Note that the `TextField` must be registered with an `ActionListener` so that the applet can handle the user's input actions. Also, the `TextArea` is made *uneditable*, which means for this program, it will only be used to display output. Java will just ignore any typing that takes place within it.

There are several other important points worth making about this example. First, note here again we use named constant, `BOUND`, instead of using the *literal* value 15 throughout the program. As always, this makes the program easier to read and easier to maintain.

Also, note how the error handling is done in this program. In the `actionPerformed()` method, we check that the user's input is between 0 and `BOUND` before calling the `factorial()` method. This validates the user's input and prevents the violation of `factorial()`'s precondition.

Finally, note how we have simplified the algorithm for `factorial()`. In the previous version of this method (Figure 6–11) we explicitly tested for the case of $n == 0$ and simply returned 1 as the method's value in that case. However, this case is not strictly necessary. If we initialize our result f to 1 and then iterate from n down to 1, the method will still return 1 in the case where $n == 0$. In that case, the loop body is skipped entirely because its loop entry condition is false to begin with.

Figure 6–13 Definition of the `FactorialTest` class.

```
import java.awt.*;
import java.awt.event.*;
import java.applet.*;

public class FactorialTest extends Applet implements ActionListener {

    private final int BOUND = 15;                    // Named constant

    private Label prompt = new Label("Type any positive integer <= " + BOUND);
    private TextField input = new TextField(10);    // Input device
    private TextArea display = new TextArea(10,40); // Output device

    /**
     * Pre:  n >= 0
     * Post: factorial(n) = 1 if n = 0
     *                    = n * n-1 * n-2 * ... * 1, if n > 0
     */
    private int factorial(int n) {
        int f = 1;
        for(int k = n; k >= 1; k--)
            f = f * k;
        return f;
    } // factorial()

    public void init() {
        input.addActionListener(this);       // Register with a Listener
        display.setEditable(false);          // Make TextArea read only
        add(prompt);
        add(input);
        add(display);
    } // init()

    public void actionPerformed(ActionEvent e) {
        int num = Integer.parseInt(input.getText());
        if (num >= 0 && num <= BOUND)
        display.append("The factorial of" + num + " = " + factorial(num) + "\n");
    } // actionPerformed()
} // FactorialTest
```

IN THE LABORATORY: FINDING PRIME NUMBERS

The purpose of this lab is to provide practice using loop control structures in designing and implementing solutions to programming problems. The objectives are

- To give practice using simple looping constructs.
- To introduce the `TextArea` component for use in outputting multiple lines of text.

Problem Statement

Suppose that Atlas Computer Security has contacted you about consulting for them to develop public key encryption software. One thing you're going to need in this software is a method that can test whether a number is a prime or not. To help demonstrate your prime number tester, the company wants you to write a Java applet that prompts the user for a positive integer and then displays all of the prime numbers less than or equal to the user's integer. If they like your demo, they will probably give you the contract for the encryption software.

GUI Specifications

The Graphical User Interface (GUI) for this applet needs a component to handle the user's input, and another component to display the prime numbers. A `TextField` would be an appropriate input component, because the user needs to input a single integer value. The `TextField` can also serve as the means by which the user indicates that an action should be taken. Whenever the user types a Return or Enter in the `TextField`, the program should test the `TextField`'s current value for primality.

Cryptography

Cryptography is the study of secret writing — the study of *encrypting* and *decrypting* secret messages. It is an ancient art and science that's been used throughout history. For example, Caesar used what's come to be known as the *Caesar cipher* to encrypt messages to his generals during the Gaulic campaigns. In a Caesar cipher, a simple integer between 1 and 25, is used as a *secret key*, and a message is encrypted by shifting each letter by the number of letters specified in the key, wrapping around the end of the alphabet, if necessary. For example, if we use a key of 1, then "hello" would be encrypted as "ifmmp." (We will study the Caesar cipher itself in Chapter 7.)

Up until very recently, the best and strongest encryption schemes were owned by the military and government agencies. Today, however, there's a form of *public key encryption* that anybody can use. For example, the popular PGP (Pretty Good Privacy) program is freely distributed on the Web (http://web.mit.edu/network/pgp.html). This approach is based on the idea of breaking up a person's key into a private and public half. Anybody can send secret messages to Alice, by using her public key, but only Alice can decrypt the message using her private key.

The effectiveness of public key encryption depends on the use of very large prime numbers. A *prime number* is a positive integer that is divisible only by itself and 1. A *composite* number is a number that is not prime. Any composite number can be represented as the product of prime numbers. For example, 20 = 2 * 2 * 5, and 65 = 5 * 13. What protects a PGP-encrypted message is the inability of eavesdroppers to factor the large composite numbers that make up the person's key. So, prime numbers play a critical role in the development of effective encryption software.

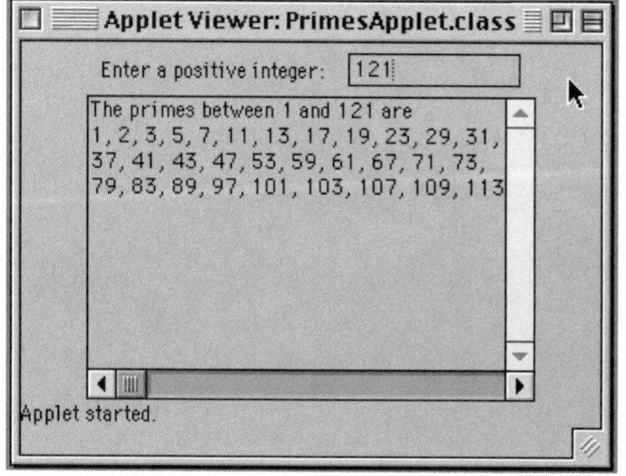

Figure 6–14 The user interface for `PrimesApplet`.

The output component should allow the program's output to extend over several lines. This is a perfect job for a `TextArea`. In addition to these components, we'll need a `Label` to prompt the user as to what kind of input is expected. Figure 6–14 provides a summary of the GUI.

Problem Decomposition

There are two tasks involved in the demo program. One is to provide a user interface, a GUI. The other is to provide the expertise needed to determine whether a number is prime. This suggests that we should break this problem up into two objects: a `PrimesApplet` object, which will manage the interface, and a `Primes` object, which will contain methods to determine whether a number is prime and to find prime numbers within a certain range.

Problem Design: The PrimesApplet Class

What variables and methods are needed?

The design of `PrimesApplet` should be similar to that of other applets we've built. Of course, the applet must create an instance of the `Primes` class. This is the object it will call upon to test whether numbers are prime.

In terms of its GUI elements, the applet should contain a `TextField` for user input and a `Label` for prompting the user. These components should be instantiated in the applet and added to the applet in the `init()` method. Because it will generate user actions, whenever the user types the Enter key, the `TextField` should be given an `ActionListener`. This should also be done in the `init()` method. (See "In the Laboratory" project in Chapter 5).

Event-driven algorithm

The algorithm used by `PrimesApplet` is event driven. In the `init()` method, the applet should be registered as the listener for `ActionEvents` that occur in the `TextField`. Then, whenever such an event occurs, Java will call the applet's `actionPerformed()` method, where the event should be handled. The `actionPerformed()` method should get the input from the `TextField`, convert it to an integer, and then display all of the prime numbers less than the user's number:

```
1. Get the user's input from the TextField.
2. Convert the input String into an int.
3. Display in the TextArea all the prime numbers less than
   the user's number.
```

Step 2 of this algorithm will require us to use the `Integer.parseInt()` method to convert a `String` into an `int`:

```
int num = Integer.parseInt("564"); // Converts "564" to 564
```

Step 3 of this algorithm will require a loop, and it is here where the applet must call on the expertise of the `Primes` object. Because this step will be somewhat complex, it should be encapsulated into a separate method.

Taken together, these design decisions lead to the following specification for the `PrimesApplet` class:

- Purpose: To provide a GUI interface for computing primes.
- Private instance variables: `TextArea`, `TextField`, `Label`
- Public instance methods: `init()`, `actionPerformed()`
- Private instance method: `findPrimes(int)` displays in the `TextArea` all of the primes between 1 and its `int` parameter.

Note that the `findPrimes()` method will be a `private` method. This is appropriate, since it is not intended to be used outside of this class.

Problem Design: The `Primes` Class

As our design of the `PrimesApplet` class suggested, the `Primes` class should have a public method that can be used to test whether a number is prime. A *prime* is any positive integer that is divisible only by itself and 1. Let's call this method `isPrime()`. This should be a `boolean` method that should return true when its `int` parameter is a prime number. Otherwise it should return false.

What variables are needed?

The `Primes` class does not have any kind of internal state that would be represented in the form of instance variables. Any variables that it may need to determine if a number is prime can be declared within the `isPrime()` method. Thus, its specification is very simple:

- Purpose: To determine if a number is prime.
- Public instance method: `isPrime(int)` returns `true` if its parameter is a prime number

The `findPrimes()` Algorithm

The `findPrimes()` method takes a single `int` parameter, *N*, and will display all of the prime numbers, less than or equal to *N*, in the applet's `TextArea`. Its algorithm should use a loop to test the numbers between 1 and *N* and display all the prime numbers in that range. Obviously, this is a counting loop, because you know exactly how many iterations it must make before entering the loop. Also, the task of determining whether an integer is prime or not will be farmed out to the `Primes` object. Thus, this gives us the following algorithm:

Counting loop or conditional loop?

```
Display "The following are the primes between 1 and N" in TextArea
for each integer, k, in the range 1 to N
    if k is prime
        display k in the TextArea
```

The `isPrime()` Algorithm

The `isPrime()` method should employ a loop to find whether its parameter, N, is a prime. The algorithm in this case should make use of the definition of a prime number — that is, a number divisible only by itself and 1. It could try dividing N by K, where K is 2, 3, 4, 5 . . . and so on up to $N-1$. If any of these numbers is a divisor of N, then N is not a prime number. If none is a divisor of N, then N is a prime number. Because the number of iterations required for this loop is not known beforehand, it will require a noncounting loop structure.

To test whether N is prime it is necessary to have an entry condition that is the conjunction of two conditions. The loop should iterate while K is less than N, *and* while none of the preceding values of K were divisors of N. In other words, the loop should terminate when a value K is found that evenly divides N. One way to handle this task is to use a local boolean variable as a **flag** that will be raised when a value K is found that divides N:

While or do-while loop?

```
Initialize notDivisibleYet to true
Initialize K to 2
while (notDivisibleYet AND K < N)  {
    if N is divisible by K
        set notDivisibleYet to false
    increment K;
}
```

This is an example of a complex loop bound . It involves the conjunction of both a count bound and a *flag bound* and it will terminate when *either* bound is reached. Thus the loop terminates when *either* K equals N *or when* N is divisible by some value of $K < N$. If it terminates with K equal to N, that indicates that N is prime.

Note that for the conjunction *notDivisibleYet AND* $K < N$ to be true, both halves of it must be true. However, for it to be false, either half may be false; it is not necessary that both halves be false. In this case *either* `notDivisibleYet` will be false *or* $K \geq N$ will be false. This is an instance of the logic rule known as *DeMorgan's Law* , which can be stated as follows:

```
!(P && Q) == !P || !Q
```

where P and Q are simple `boolean` conditions.

Implementation

The implementation of this program is left to you as a lab (or programming) exercise, but here are some hints and suggestions:

- **Stepwise refinement.** A good first step for writing this program would be to create the `TextField` and a `TextArea` components and implement the `init()` and `actionPerformed()` methods. The first version of the applet should merely display in the `TextArea` whatever number the user types into the `TextField`, without testing for primality.

  Once you have successfully written and tested a simple interface, define the `Primes` class and write and test the `isPrime()` method. In order to write this method, you will have to complete the development of the algorithm described in the previous section. Use pseudocode to help you lay out the algorithm. You can use your interface to help you test the method. Have the user input an integer, and then just test whether that integer is prime.

  Once you have a correct `isPrime()` method, write and test the `findPrimes()` methods. This last step should be very simple.

- **Preconditions and Postconditions.** Use pre-and postconditions in your specification and documentation of the `isPrime()` and `findPrimes()` methods. Then use the conditions to help design appropriate test data to verify that your code is correct.

- **Null pointer error.** Beware of "null pointer" errors which result when you forget to instantiate (create) an object before using it. A null pointer error occurs when you attempt to refer to an object using a reference that has a value of `null`. When you declare a reference variable, it is given a default value of `null`. If you forget to instantiate it, you'll get this error. The typical sequence is declare, create, and use, although these don't always happen in the same place in the program. For example, the `TextArea display` can be declared in the global portion of the program, instantiated in `init()` and used in `actionPerformed()`:

```
TextArea display;                  // Declare a variable
.
.
display = new TextArea();          // Create an instance (init() )
.
.
display.appendText ("blah") ;      // Use it (actionPerformed() )
```

  If you forget to instantiate in `init()` the use of `display` in `actionPerformed()` will cause a null pointer exception.

Optional Refinement

As we described, public key encryption involves the use of composite numbers as well as prime numbers. A challenging extension to this lab would be to let the user type in a composite number and display its prime factorization. Design a method that takes an integer parameter and displays its prime factors in the `TextArea`. For example, if the user inputs 40, your method should display $40 = 2 * 2 * 2 * 5$.

Java Language Summary

Repetition Control Structures

Java provides three repetition statements: the `for` statement, used primarily for counting loops, the `while` statement, used for conditional loops, and the `do-while` statement, used for conditional loops that must iterate at least once.

All loop structures must have three elements: an *initializer*, which sets the initial value of the *loop variable*; a *loop entry condition* or *loop boundary condition*, which controls entry (and exit) to (and from) the *loop body*; and an *updater*, a statement that updates the loop variable before the next iteration.

When designing a loop, it is important to analyze the loop structure to make sure that the loop bound will eventually be satisfied. Table 6–2 summarizes the types of loop bound that we have identified. A loop that fails to satisfy its bound will repeat forever and is therefore known as an *infinite loop*.

The For Loop

The for statement has the following syntax:

for (*initializer* ; *loop entry condition* ; *updater*)
for loop body ;

Execution of the for loop begins by executing the initializer statement. This is usually used to set the initial value of the *loop variable*. Next, the loop entry condition is tested. If it is true, the loop body is executed. If it is false, the loop body is skipped, and control passes beyond the for statement. After each iteration of the loop body, the updater statement is executed, and then the loop entry condition is retested.

Table 6.2. A summary of various loop bounds

Bound	Example
Counting	$k < 100$
Sentinel	*input* != 9999
Flag	*done* != *true*
Limit	*amount* < 0.5

Java Language Summary

The following for loop prints the values from 1 to 100.

```
for(int k = 1;  k <= 100; k++ )
   System.out.println( k );
```

The While Loop

The while statement takes the following form:

while (*loop entry condition*) *loop body* ;

Note that unlike the for statement, the while statement does not contain syntax for the initializer and the updater. These must be coded separately. As in the for loop, the loop body can be either a simple statement or a set of statements enclosed within braces.

When a while statement is executed, its loop entry condition is tested *before* the loop body is entered. If it is true, the loop body is executed; otherwise it is skipped and control passes to the next statement beyond the while statement. The loop entry condition is retested after each iteration of the loop body.

The following while loop prints the numbers from 1 to 100:

```
int k = 1;                    // Initializer
while( k < 100 ) {
    System.out.println( k );
    k++;                      // Updater
}
                              // Postcondition: k >= 100
```

The Do-While Loop

The do-while statement has the following general form:

do *loop body* while (*loop entry condition*) ;

Note, again, that the initializer and the updater statements must be coded separately in the do-while structure.

When a do-while statement is executed, its loop body is executed first. Then its loop entry condition is tested. If it is true, the loop body is executed again. Otherwise control passes to the next statement following the while statement. The do-while statement should be used primarily for loops that require at least one iteration.

Here's an example of a do-while loop to print the numbers between 1 and 100. Note the subtle differences between the postcondition of this example and the while loop example.

```
int k = 1;                    // Initializer
do {
    System.out.println( k );
    k++;                      // Updater
} while ( k <= 100 );         // Loop entry condition
                              // Postcondition: k > 100
```

CHAPTER SUMMARY

Technical Terms

busy waiting
counting loop
infinite loop
loop body
nested loop
priming read
named constant
unit indexing
compound statement
do-while statement
initializer
loop bound
null pointer error
repetition
updater
zero indexing
conditional loop
flag bound
limit bound
loop entry condition
null statement
sentinel bound
while statement

New Java Keywords

`boolean`
`do`
`private`
`char`
`for`
`public`
`count`
`null`
`while`

Java Library Classes

`ActionListener`
`IOException`
`ItemListener`
`TextArea`
`Choice`
`IOException`
`Label`
`TextComponent`
`Graphics`
`Image`
`java.util.NumberFormat`
`TextField`

Java Library Methods

`String.equals()`
`awt.Graphics.drawImage()`
`paint()`
`print()`
`setText()`
`System.exit()`
`getText()`
`Integer.parseInt()`
`println()`
`actionPerformed()`
`init()`
`Math.pow()`
`repaint()`

Programmer-Defined Classes

`AnimatedCyberPet`
`CyberPetApplet`
`PrimesApplet`
`Average`
`CyberPet`
`Primes`
`CarLoan`
`FactorialTest`
`Validate`

Programmer-Defined Methods

`busyWait()`
`factorial()`
`getAndValidateGrade()`
`isPrime()`
`convertStringTodouble()`
`fibonacci(N)`
`getInput()`
`losingGrass()`
`doEatAnimation()`
`findPrimes()`
`inputAndAverageGrades()`
`main`

Summary of Important Points

- A *repetition structure* is a control structure that allows a statement or sequence of statements to be repeated.
- All loop structures involve three elements — an *initializer*, a *loop entry condition* or a *loop boundary condition*, and an *updater*.
- *Structured programming* is the practice of writing programs that are built up from a small set of predefined control structures — the *sequence*, *selection*, *repetition* and *method-call* structures. An important feature of these structures is that each has a single entry and exit.
- A *precondition* is a condition that must be true before a certain code segment executes. A *postcondition* is a condition that must be true when a certain code segment is finished. Preconditions and postconditions should be used in the design, coding, documentation, and debugging of algorithms and methods.
- The `System.exit(int)` method can be used to terminate a program in an orderly fashion in case a serious error is detected.

ANSWERS TO SELF-STUDY EXERCISES

EXERCISE 6.1 Identify the syntax error in the following for loop statements:

a.
```
Commas are used instead of semicolons in the header.
 for ( int k = 5; k < 100; k++ )
   System.out.println( k );
```

b.
```
There shouldn't be 3 semicolons in the header
 for ( int k = 0; k < 12 ; k--  )
   System.out.println( k );
```

EXERCISE 6.2 Identify those statements that result in infinite loops:

a.
```
Infinite loop because k is never incremented.
```

b.
```
Infinite loop because k is always odd and thus never equal to 100.
```

EXERCISE 6.3 Your sister is learning to count by fours. Write a for loop that prints the following sequence of numbers: 1, 5, 9, 13, 17, 21, 25.

```
for (int k = 1; k <= 25; k = k +4)
   System.out.print( k + " ");
```

EXERCISE 6.4 What value will *j* have when the following loop terminates? *Answer*: *j* will be undefined when the loop terminates. It is a local variable whose scope is limited to the loop body.

```
for (int i = 0; i < 10 ; i++ )
{
  int j;
  j = j + 1;
}
```

EXERCISE 6.5 Write a nested for loop to print the following geometric pattern:

```
#
# #
# # #
# # # #
# # # # #

for (int row = 1; row <= 5; row++)  {      // For each row
    for (int col = 1; col <= row; col++) // Number of columns per row
        System.out.print('#');
    System.out.println();                // New line
} // row
```

EXERCISE 6.6 If *N* is even, divide it by 2. If *N* is odd, subtract 1 and then divide it by 2. This will generate a sequence that is guaranteed to terminate at 0. For example, if *N* is initially 15, then you get the sequence 15, 7, 3, 1, 0. Write a method that implements this sequence. Use a while statement.

```
public static void sub1Div2(int N) {
    while(N != 0) {
        System.out.print(N + " ");
        if (N % 2 == 0)
            N = N / 2;
        else
            N = (N - 1) / 2;
    }
    System.out.println( N );
} // sub1Div2()
```

EXERCISE 6.7 For each of the following problems, decide whether a counting loop structure, a while structure or a do-while structure should be used, and write a pseudocode algorithm.

- Printing the names of all the visitors to a Web site could use a counting loop since the exact number of visitors is known.

```
for each name in the visitor's log
    print the name
```

- Validating that a user has entered a positive number requires a `do-while` structure in which you repeatedly read a number and validate it.

```
do
    read a number
    if number is invalid, print error message
while number is invalid
```

- Change all the backslashes (\) in a Windows Web page address, to the slashes (/) used in a Unix Web page address.

```
for each character in the Web page address
    if it is a backslash replace it with slash
```

- Finding the largest in a list of numbers requires a `while` loop to guard against a empty list.

```
initialize maxMPG to smallest possible number
while there are more cars in the database
    if current car's MPG is greater than maxMPG
        replace maxMPG with it
```

- If N is even, divide it by 2. If N is odd, subtract 1 and then divide it by 2. This will generate a sequence that is guaranteed to terminate at 0. This problem is best solved with a while structure. If N is initially 0, the loop should be skipped entirely.

EXERCISE 6.8 Identify the syntax error in the following while structures:

a.

```
int k = 5;
while (k < 100) {
    System.out.println(k);
    k++                          << Missing semicolon
}
```

b.

```
int k = 0;
while (k < 12;) {           << Extra semicolon
    System.out.println(k);
    k++;
}
```

EXERCISE 6.9 Determine the output and/or identify the error in each of the following while structures.

a.

```
    int k = 0;
   while (k < 100)
       System.out.println(k);  << Missing the updater in loop body
Output: infinite loop prints 0 0 0 0 0...
    while (k < 100) {           << Missing initializer
       System.out.println(k);
       k++;
   }
Output: unpredictable since k's initial value is not known
```

EXERCISE 6.10 Your younger sister is now learning how to count by sixes. Write a while loop that prints the following sequence of numbers: 0, 6, 12, 18, 24, 30, 36.

```
int k = 0;                  // Initializer
while (k <= 36) {           // Loop-entry condition
    System.out.println(k);
    k += 6;                   // Updater
}
```

EXERCISE 6.11 Identify the syntax error in the following do-while structures:

a.

```
 int k = 0;
do while (k < 100) << Misplaced condition
{
     System.out.println(k);
     k++
}                     << Belongs here
```

b.
```
    int k = 0;
do {
    System.out.println(k);
    k++;
} while (k < 12) << Missing semicolon
```

EXERCISE 6.12 Your sister has moved on to counting by sevens. Write a do-while loop that prints the following sequence of numbers: 1, 8, 15, 22, 29, 36, 43.

```
n = 1;                              // Initializer
do {
    System.out.print ( n + " " );
    n += 7;                         // Updater
} while (n <= 43);                  // Loop entry condition
```

EXERCISE 6.13 Write a method to input and validate pizza sales.

```
public int getAndValidatePizzaPrice() {
    int pizza = 0;
    do {
        System.out.print("Input a pizza price (e.g., 8, 10, or 15) ");
        System.out.print("or 99 to indicate the end of the list >> ");
        String inputString  = input.readLine();
        pizza = Integer.parseInt(inputString) ;
        if ((pizza != 99) && (pizza != 8) && (pizza != 10) && (pizza != 15))
            System.out.println("Error: you've entered an invalid pizza price\n"); // Error input
        else
            System.out.println("You input " + pizza + "\n");                  // OK input
    } while ((pizza != 99) && (pizza != 8) && (pizza != 10) && (pizza != 15));
    return pizza;
} // getAndValidatePizzaPrice()
```

EXERCISE 6.14 Write a method to input and validate pizza sales using the numbers 1, 2, and 3 to represent different priced pizzas.

```
public int getAndValidatePizzaPrice() {
    int pizza = 0;
    do {
        System.out.print("Input a 1,2 or 3 to indicate pizza price ( 1($8), 2($10), or 3($15) ) ");
        System.out.print("or 0 to indicate the end of the list >> ");
        String inputString  = input.readLine();
        pizza = Integer.parseInt(inputString);
       if ((pizza < 0) || (pizza > 3))
           System.out.println("Error: you've entered an invalid value\n"); // Error input
       else
           System.out.println("You input " + pizza + "\n");             // OK input
    } while ( (pizza < 0) || (pizza > 3) );
    if (pizza == 1)
        return 8;
    else if (pizza == 2)
        return 10;
    else if (pizza == 3)
        return 15;
    else
        return 0;
} // getAndValidatePizzaPrice()
```

EXERCISE 6.15 Identify the pre- and postconditions on j and k where indicated in the following code segment:

```
int j = 0; k = 5;
do {
    if ( k % 5 == 0 ) {
                    // Precondition: j <= k
        j += k;
        k--;
    }
    else k *= k;
} while ( j <= k );
                    // Postcondition: j > k
```

EXERCISE 6.16 Identify the pre- and postconditions for the following method, which computes x^n for $n \geq 0$.

```
// Precondition: N >= 0
// Postcondition: power(x,n) == x^n
public double power(double x, int n ) {
    double pow = 1;
    for (int k = 1; k <= n; k++)
        pow = pow * x;
    return pow;
} // power()
```

EXERCISES

1. Explain the difference between the following pairs of terms.

    a. *Counting loop* and *conditional loop*.
    b. *For statement* and *while statement*.
    c. *While statement* and *do-while statement*.
    d. *Zero indexing* and *unit indexing*.
    e. *Sentinel bound* and *limit bound*.
    f. *Counting bound* and *flag bound*.
    g. Loop *initializer* and *updater*.
    h. *Named constant* and *literal*.
    i. *Compound statement* and *null statement*.

2. Fill in the blank:

    a. The process of reading a data item before entering a loop is known as a _____.
    b. A loop that does nothing except iterate is an example of _____ .
    c. A loop that contains no body is an example of a _____ statement.
    d. A loop whose entry condition is stated as ($k < 100 \mid\mid k \geq 0$) would be an example of an _____ loop.
    e. A loop that should iterate until the user types in a special value should use a _____ bound.
    f. A loop that should iterate until its variable goes from 5 to 100 should use a _____ bound.
    g. A loop that should iterate until the difference between two values is less than 0.005 is an example of a _____ bound.

3. Identify the syntax errors in each of the following:

a.
```
for (int k = 0; k < 100; k++)
  System.out.println( k )
```

b.
```
for (int k = 0; k < 100; k++);
  System.out.println( k );
```

c.
```
 int k = 0
while  k < 100
{
   System.out.println( k );  k++;
}
```

d.
```
 int k = 0;
do
{
   System.out.println( k );  k++;
}
while  k < 100 ;
```

4. Determine the output and/or identify the error in each of the following code segments:

a.
```
for (int k = 1; k == 100; k += 2)
  System.out.println( k );
```

b.
```
 int k = 0;
while ( k < 100 )
   System.out.println( k );
   k++;
```

c.
```
for (int k = 0; k < 100; k++) ;
  System.out.println( k );
```

5. Write pseudocode algorithms for the following activities, paying particular attention to the *initializer*, *updater*, and *boundary condition* in each case.

a. `a softball game`
b. `a five-question quiz`
c. `looking up a name in the phone book`

6. Identify the pre- and post-conditions for each of the following statements. Assume that all variables are `int` and have been properly declared.

a.
```
int result = x / y;
```

b.
```
int result = x % y;
```

c.
```
 int x = 95;
do
  x /= 2;
while( x >= 0 );
```

7. Write three different loops — a for loop, a while loop, and a do-while loop — to print all the multiples of 10, including 0, up to and including 1,000.
8. Write three different loops — a for loop, a while loop, and a do-while loop — to print the following sequence of numbers: 45, 36, 27, 18, 9, 0, −9, −18, −27, −36, −45.

9. Write three different loops — a for loop, a while loop, and a do-while loop — to print the following ski-jump design:

```
#
# #
# # #
# # # #
# # # # #
# # # # # #
# # # # # # #
```

10. The Straight Downhill Ski Lodge in Gravel Crest, Vermont, gets lots of college students on breaks. The lodge likes to keep track of repeat visitors. Straight Downhill's database includes an integer variable, *visit*, which gives the number of times a guest has stayed at the lodge (1 or more). Write the pseudocode to catch those visitors who have stayed at the lodge at least twice and to send them a special promotional package (pseudocode = send promo). (*Note:* The largest number of stays recorded is eight. The number nine is used as an end-of-data flag.)
11. Modify your pseudocode in the previous exercise. In addition to every guest who has stayed at least twice at the lodge receiving a promotional package, any guest with three or more stays should also get a $40 coupon good for lodging, lifts, or food.
12. Write a method that is passed a single parameter, *N*, and displays all the even numbers between 1 and *N*.
13. Write a method that is passed a single parameter, *N*, that prints all the odd numbers between 1 and *N*.
14. Write a method that is passed a single parameter, *N*, that prints all the numbers divisible by 10 from *N* down to 1.
15. Write a method that is passed two parameters — a `char` *Ch* and an `int` *N*, and prints a string of *N Chs*.
16. Write a method that uses a nested for loop to print the following multiplication table:

```
   1  2  3  4  5  6  7  8  9
1  1
2  2  4
3  3  6  9
4  4  8 12 16
5  5 10 15 20 25
6  6 12 18 24 30 36
7  7 14 21 28 35 42 48
8  8 16 24 32 40 48 56 64
9  9 18 27 36 45 54 63 72 81
```

17. Write a method that uses nested for loops to print the following patterns. Your method should use the following statement to print the patterns: `System.out.print('#')`.

```
# # # # # # # #     # # # # # # # #   # # # # # # # #   # # # # # # # #
  # # # # # # #     # # # # # # #       #         #                 #
    # # # # # #     # # # # # #           #     #                 #
      # # # # #     # # # # #               # #                 #
        # # # #     # # # #                 # #               #
          # # #     # # #                 #     #           #
            # #     # #                 #         #       #
              #     #                 # # # # # # # #   # # # # # # # #
```

18. Write a program which asks the user for the number of rows and the number of columns in a box of asterisks. Then use nested loops to generate the box.
19. Write a Java application that lets the user input a sequence of consecutive numbers. In other words, the program should let the user keep entering numbers as long as the current number is one greater than the previous number.
20. Write a Java application that lets the user input a sequence of integers terminated by any negative value. The program should then report the largest and smallest values that were entered.
21. How many guesses does it take to guess a secret number between 1 and *N*? For example, I'm thinking of a number between 1 and 100. I'll tell you whether your guess is too high or too low. Obviously, an intelligent first guess would be 50. If that's too low, an intelligent second guess would be 75. And so on. If we continue to divide the range in half, we'll eventually get down to one number. Because you can divide 100 seven times (50,25,12,6,3,1,0), it will take at most seven guesses to guess a number between 1 and 100. Write a Java applet that lets the user input a positive integer, *N*, and then reports how many guesses it would take to guess a number between 1 and *N*.
22. Suppose you determine that the fire extinguisher in your kitchen loses *X* percent of its foam every day. How long before it drops below a certain threshold (*Y* percent), at which point it is no longer serviceable? Write a Java applet that lets the user input the values *X* and *Y*, and then reports how many weeks the fire extinguisher will last?
23. Leibnitz's method for computing π is based on the following convergent series: $\frac{\pi}{4} = 1 - \frac{1}{3} + \frac{1}{5} - \frac{1}{7} + \cdots$
    How many iterations does it take to compute π using this series? Write a Java program to find out.
24. Newton's method for calculating the square root of *N* starts by making a (non zero) guess at the square root. It then uses the original guess to calculate a new guess, according to the following formula:

```
guess = (( N / guess) + guess) / 2;
```

    No matter how wild the original guess is, if we repeat this calculation, the algorithm will eventually find the square root. Write a square root method based on this algorithm. Then write a program to determine how many guesses are required to find the square roots of different numbers. Uses `Math.sqrt()` to determine when to terminate the guessing.
25. Your employer is developing encryption software and wants you to develop a Java applet that will display all of the factorials less than *N*, where *N* is a number to be entered by the user. In addition to displaying the factorials themselves, provide a count of how many there are. Use the method that was developed in this chapter's "Object Oriented Design" section.
26. Your little sister asks you to help her with her multiplication and you decide to write a Java application that tests her skills. The program will let her input a starting number, such as 5. It will generate multiplication problems ranging from from 5×1 to 5×12. For each problem she will be prompted to enter the correct answer. The program should check her answer and should not let her advance to the next question until the correct answer is given to the current question.

27. Write an application that prompts the user for four values and draws corresponding bar graphs using an ASCII character. For example, if the user entered 15, 12, 9, and 4, the program would draw

```
******************

************

*********

****
```

28. Revise the application in the previous problem so that the bar charts are displayed vertically. For example, if the user inputs 5, 2, 3, and 4, the program should display

```
 **
 **          **
 **      **  **
 **  **  **  **
 **  **  **  **
-------------
```

29. The Fibonacci sequence (named after the Italian mathematician Leonardo of Pisa, ca.1200) consists of the numbers 0, 1, 1, 2, 3, 5, 8, 13, . . . in which each number (except for the first two) is the sum of the two preceding numbers. Write a method `fibonacci(N)` that prints the first *N* Fibonacci numbers.
30. The Nuclear Regulatory Agency wants you to write a program that will help them determine how long certain radioactive substances will take to decay. The program should let the user input two values: a string giving the substance's name, and its half-life in years. (A substance's half-life is the number of years required for the disintegration of half of its atoms.) The program should report how many years it will take before there is less than 2 percent of the original number of atoms remaining.
31. Modify the `CarLoan` program so that it calculates a user's car payments for loans of different interest rates and different loan periods. Let the user input the amount of the loan. Have the program output a table of monthly payment schedules.

The next chapter also contains a number of loop exercises.

Photograph courtesy of Lawrence Lawry, PhotoDisc, Inc.

Strings and String Processing

7

OBJECTIVES

After studying this chapter, you will

- Be more familiar with the string data structure.
- Know how to solve problems that involve manipulating strings.
- Be able to use loops in designing string processing algorithms.
- Have a better understanding of how inheritance can be used in program design.

OUTLINE

7.1 Introduction

Inyay isthay apterchay eway illway udystay owhay otay useyay ingsstray andyay igpay atinlay!

Translation: In this chapter we will study how to use strings and pig latin.

Remember those Pig Latin games from grade school? In this chapter we will study how to manipulate strings and how to translate normal English words into Pig Latin. To translate "string" into "ingstray," we first divide it into the prefix "str" and the suffix "ing." We then concatenate these in reverse order, "ing" + "str," and add the new suffix "ay" to the result. This gives "ing" + "str" + "ay," or "ingstray."

A **data structure** is a collection of data that is organized (structured) in some way. A **string** is a collection of character (`char`) data. Strings are important data structures in a programming language, and they are used to represent a wide variety of data.

Programmers often have to work with strings. Think of some of the tasks performed by a typical word processor, such as cut, paste, copy, and insert. When you cut and paste text from one part of the document to another, the program has to move one string of text, the cut, from one location in the document, and insert it in another.

As we have seen throughout the first few chapters, `String`s are used extensively in Java interfaces as the contents of `TextField`s and other text components, as the value of `Label`s, as the labels for `Button`s, and so on. Moreover, all sorts of I/O operations involve `String`s, such as inputting a number either through a `TextField` or directly from the keyboard.

`String`s are also used as a standard way of presenting or displaying objects. One of the key conventions of the Java class hierarchy is that every class inherits the `Object.toString()` method, which can be used to provide a string representation of any object. For example, `Integer.toString()` converts an `int` to a `String`, so that it can be used in `TextField`s or `Label`s.

The main purpose of this chapter is to introduce the details of Java's string classes, including the `String`, `StringBuffer`, and `StringTokenizer` classes. These are the important classes for writing string processing applications. Our goal is to introduce the important `String` methods and illustrate common string processing algorithms. We'll learn how to build strings from scratch and from other data types. We'll learn how to find characters and substrings inside bigger strings. We'll learn how to take strings apart and how to rearrange their parts. Finally, we'll learn how to apply these string processing skills to an interesting encryption problem.

7.2 String Basics

Are strings objects?

In Java, Strings are considered full-fledged objects. A java.lang.String object is a sequence of characters plus a collection of methods for manipulating strings. Like other object variables, String variables serve as *references* to their respective objects. However, unlike other Java objects, Strings have certain characteristics in common with the primitive data types. For example, strings can have literals. A String literal is a sequence of zero or more characters contained in double quotes — for example, "Socrates" and "" (**empty string**). Similarly, unlike other Java objects, Strings can be used in assignment statements:

```
String s = "hello";
```

7.2.1 Constructing Strings

The String class has many constructors, including the following:

```
public String();                       // Creates an empty string
public String(String initial_value);   // Creates a copy of a string
```

When we create an object using the first constructor, as in

```
String name = new String();
```

Java will create a String object and make name the reference to it (Figure 7–1). Note that in addition to its literal value, a String object stores a count of how many characters it contains; plus, as for all other objects, a String object contains a bunch of instance methods.

String literals

When Java encounters a new literal string in a program, it constructs an object for it. For example, if your program contained the literal "Socrates," Java would create an object for it and treat the literal itself as a reference to the object (Figure 7–2).

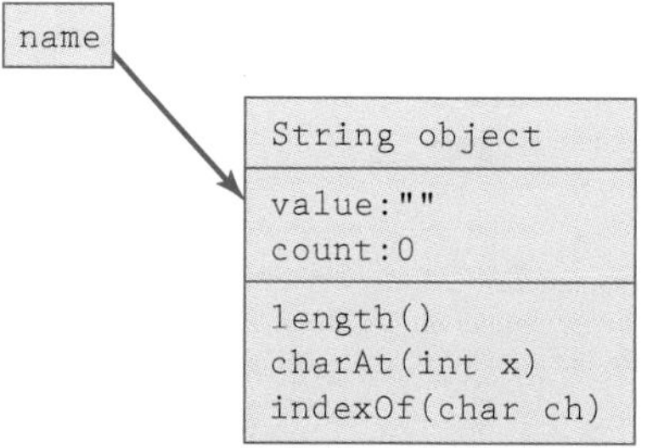

Figure 7–1 An empty string is a String object with value "" and count 0.

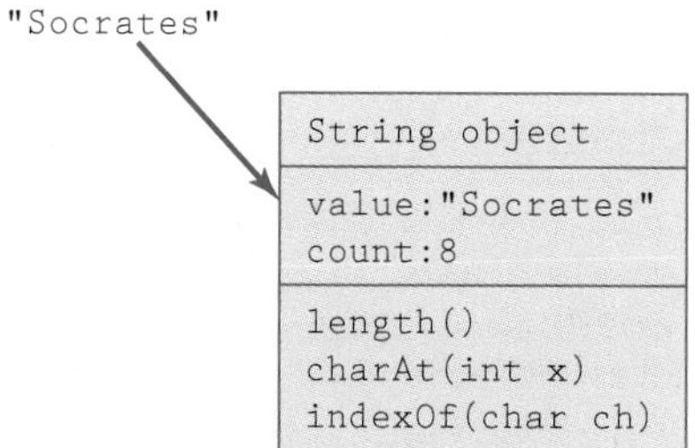

Figure 7–2 The literal String "Socrates."

String literals are often used to assign a value to a String variable:

```
String s;                  // The value of s is initially null
s = "Socrates";            // s now refers to the "Socrates" object
```

Default value

In this case, the reference variable *s* is initially null — that is, it has no referent. However, after the assignment statement *s* would refer to the literal object "Socrates" that we created in Figure 7–2. Given these two statements together with the preceding declarations, we still have only one object. But now we have two references to it: the literal string "Socrates," and the reference variable *s*.

Assignment statements can also be used as initializers when declaring a String variable:

```
String name1 = "";             // Reference to the empty string
String name2 = "Socrates";     // References to "Socrates"
String name3 = "Socrates";
```

String literals

In this case, Java does not construct new String objects. Instead, it simply makes the variables, name1, name2, name3, serve as references to the same objects that are referred to by the literal strings "" and "Socrates." This is a direct consequence of Java's policy of creating only one object to serve as the referent of a literal string, no matter how many occurrences there are of that literal. Thus, these declarations result in no new objects, just new references to existing objects (Figure 7–3).

Finally, consider the following declarations, which do invoke the String constructors:

```
String name4 = new String();              // Creates an object
String name5 = new String("Socrates");
String name6 = name4;
```

In this case, Java creates two new objects and sets name4 to refer to the first and name5 to refer to the second. It gives name4 the empty string as its value, and it gives name5 "Socrates" as its value. But these two objects must be distinguished from the objects corresponding to the literals ("" and "Socrates") themselves (Figure 7–4). The declaration of name6 just creates a second reference to the object referred to by name4.

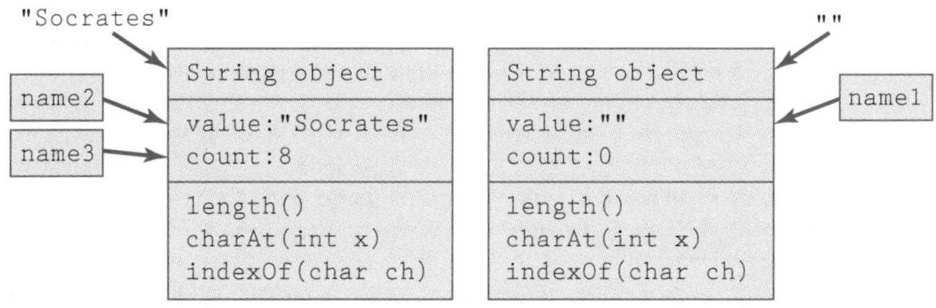

Figure 7–3 The variables name1, name2, name3 serve as references to the literal String objects "Socrates" and "".

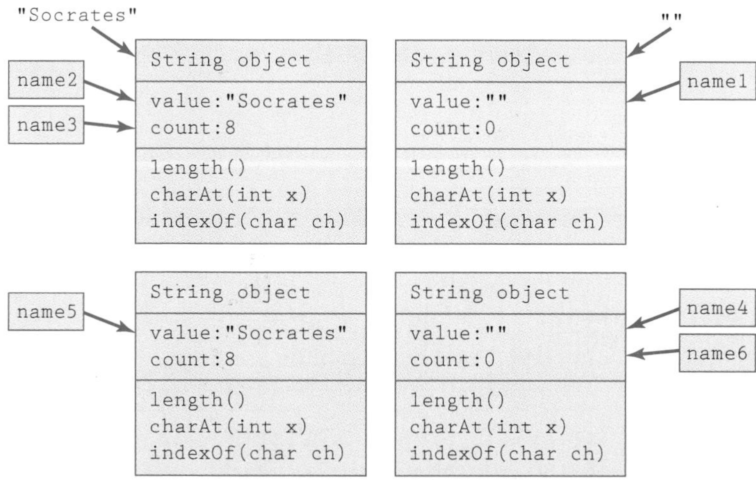

Figure 7–4 Four different `String` objects with eight different references to them, including the literals "Socrates" and "".

JAVA LANGUAGE RULE **Strings.** Java `String`s are full-fledged objects, but they have some properties in common with primitive types. They can have literal values and they can be used in assignment statements.

JAVA LANGUAGE RULE **String Declaration and Instantiation.** Unless a `String()` constructor is called explicitly, no new `String` object is created, when declaring a `String` variable and assigning it an initial value.

7.2.2 Concatenating `Strings`

Another way to build a `String` object is to concatenate two other strings:

```
String lastName = "Onassis";
String jackie = new String("Jacqueline " + "Kennedy " + lastName);
```

String concatenation

The second of these statements uses the *concatenation operator*, +, to create the `String` "Jacqueline Kennedy Onassis."

JAVA LANGUAGE RULE **String Concatenation.** When surrounded on either side by a `String`, the + symbol is used as a binary **concatenation** operator. It has the effect of joining two strings together to form a single string, as in `string1 + string2 ==> string3`.

Using the + symbol as the string concatenation operator is another example of *operator overloading* — using the same operator for two or more different operations.

Note that primitive types are automatically promoted to Strings when they are mixed with concatenation operators. Thus the following statement

```
System.out.println("The square root of 25 = " + 5);
```

will print the string "The square root of 25 = 5." The int literal 5 will automatically be converted to "5" before the concatenation is done.

SELF-STUDY EXERCISES

EXERCISE 7.1 What will be printed by each of the following segments of code?

a. `String s1 = "silly"; System.out.println(s1);`
b. `String s2 = s1; System.out.println(s2);`
c. `String s3 = new String (s1 + " stuff"); System.out.println(s3);`

EXERCISE 7.2 Write a String declaration that satisfies each of the following descriptions.

a. Initialize a String variable, str, to the empty string.
b. Instantiate a String object, str2, and initialize it to the word "stop".
c. Initialize a String variable, str, to the concatenation of str1 and str2.

EXERCISE 7.3 Evaluate the following expressions.

```
int M = 5, N = 10;
String s1 = "51", s2 = "75";
```

a. `M + N`
b. `M + s1`
c. `s1 + s2`

EXERCISE 7.4 Draw a picture, similar to Figure 7–14, showing the objects and references that are created by the following declarations.

```
String s1, s2 = "Hello", s3 = "Hello";
String s4 = "hello";
String s5 = new String("Hello");
String s6 = s5;
String s7 = s3;
```

7.2.3 Indexing Strings

String length

The number of characters in a string is called its *length*. The String instance method, length(), returns an integer that gives the String's length. For example, consider the following String declarations and the corresponding values of the length() method for each case:

```
String string1 = "";                        string1.length()  ==> 0
String string2 = "Hello";                   string2.length()  ==> 5
String string3 = "World";                   string3.length()  ==> 5;
String string4 = string2 + " " + string3;   string4.length()  ==> 11;
```

String index

The position of a particular character in a string is called its **index**. All Strings in Java are **zero indexed** — that is, the index of the first character is zero. For example, in "Socrates," the letter 'S' occurs at index 0, the letter 'o' occurs at index 1, 'r' occurs at index 3, and so on. Thus, the String "Socrates" contains eight characters indexed from 0 to 7 (Figure 7–5). Zero indexing is customary in programming languages. We will see other examples of this when we talk about arrays and vectors.

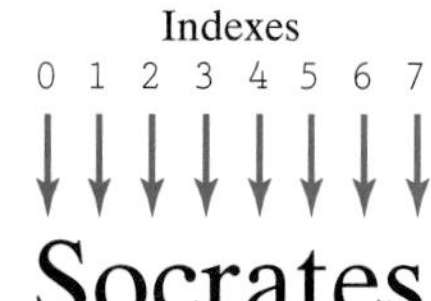

Figure 7–5 The string "Socrates" has eight characters, indexed from 0 to 7. This is an example of *zero indexing*.

JAVA LANGUAGE RULE **String Indexing.** Strings are indexed starting at 0. The first character in a string is at position 0. However the String length() method is **unit indexed** — that is, it starts counting at 1.

DEBUGGING TIP: Zero versus Unit Indexing. Syntax and semantic errors will result if you forget that strings are zero indexed. In a string of N characters, the first character occurs at index 0 and the last at index $N - 1$. In contrast, a string's length is unit indexed.

7.2.4 Converting Data to String

The String.valueOf() method is a *class method* that is used to convert a value of some primitive type into a String object. For example, the expression, String.valueOf(128) converts its int argument to the String "128."

There are different versions of the valueOf(), each of which has the following type of signature:

```
static public String valueOf(Type);
```

where Type stands for any primitive data type, including boolean, char, int, double, and so on.

The valueOf() method is most useful for initializing Strings. Because valueOf() is a class method, it can be used as follows to instantiate new String objects:

```
String number = new String (String.valueOf(128));  // Creates "128"
String truth = new String (String.valueOf(true));  // Creates "true"
String bee = new String (String.valueOf('B'));     // Creates "B"
String pi = new String(String.valueOf(Math.PI));   // Creates "3.14159"
```

SELF-STUDY EXERCISES

EXERCISE 7.5 Evaluate each of the following expressions.

a. String.valueOf (45)
b. String.valueOf (128 - 7)
c. String.valueOf ('X')

EXERCISE 7.6 Write an expression to satisfy each of the following descriptions:

a. Convert the integer value 100 to the string "100."
b. Convert the character 'V' to the string "V."
c. Initialize a new String object to X times Y.

7.3 Finding Things within a String

The indexOf() and lastIndexof() methods are instance methods that can be used to find the index position of a character or a substring within a String. There are several versions of each:

```
public int indexOf(int character);
public int indexOf(int character, int startingIndex);
public int indexOf(String string);
public int indexOf(String string, int startingIndex);

public int lastIndexOf(int character);
public int lastIndexOf(int character, int startingIndex);
public int lastIndexOf(String string);
public int lastIndexOf(String string, int startingIndex);
```

The indexOf() method searches from left to right within a String for either a character or a substring. The lastIndexOf() method searches from right to left for a character or substring. To illustrate, suppose we have declared the following Strings:

```
String string1 = "";
String string2 = "Hello";
String string3 = "World";
String string4 = string2 + " " + string3;
```

Recalling that Strings are indexed starting at 0, searching for 'o' in the various strings gives the following results:

```
string1.indexOf('o')  ==> -1
string2.indexOf('o')  ==> 4
string3.indexOf('o')  ==> 1
string4.indexOf('o')  ==> 4

string1.lastIndexOf('o')  ==> -1
string2.lastIndexOf('o')  ==> 4
string3.lastIndexOf('o')  ==> 1
string4.lastIndexOf('o')  ==> 7
```

Sentinel return value

Because string1 is the empty string, "", it does not contain the letter 'o.' Therefore indexOf() returns −1—a value that cannot be a valid index for a String. This convention is followed in indexOf() and lastIndexOf(). Because string2 and string3 each contain only one occurrence of the letter 'o,' both indexOf() and lastIndexOf() return the same value when used on these Strings. Because string4 contains two occurrences of 'o,' indexOf() and lastIndexOf() return different values in this case.

As Figure 7–6 shows, the first 'o' in "Hello World" occurs at index 4, the value returned by indexOf(). The second 'o' occurs at index 7, which is the value returned by lastIndexOf().

By default, the single-parameter versions of indexOf() and lastIndexOf() start their searches at their respective (left or right) ends of the string. The two-parameter versions of these methods allow you to specify both the direction and starting point of the search. The second parameter specifies the starting index. Consider these examples:

```
string4.indexOf('o', 5)     ==> 7
string4.lastIndexOf('o', 5) ==> 4
```

If we start searching in both cases at index 5, then indexOf() will miss the 'o' that occurs at index 4. The first 'o' it finds will be the one at index 7. Similarly, lastIndexOf() will miss the 'o' that occurs at index 7 and will find the 'o' that occurs at index 4.

The indexOf() and lastIndexOf() methods can also be used to find substrings:

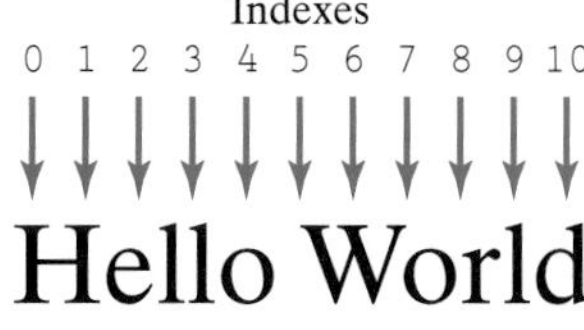

Figure 7–6 The indexing of the "Hello World" string.

```
string1.indexOf("or")  ==> -1
string2.indexOf("or")  ==> -1
string3.indexOf("or")  ==> 1
string4.indexOf("or")  ==> 7

string1.lastIndexOf("or") ==> -1
string2.lastIndexOf("or") ==> -1
string3.lastIndexOf("or") ==> 1
string4.lastIndexOf("or") ==> 7
```

The substring "or" does not occur in either `string1` or `string2`. It does occur beginning at location 1 in `string3` and beginning at location 7 in `string4`. For this collection of examples, it doesn't matter whether we search from left to right or right to left.

SELF-STUDY EXERCISES

EXERCISE 7.7 Suppose the `String` variable `s` has been initialized to "mom." Evaluate each of the following expressions:

a. `s.indexOf("m");`
b. `s.indexOf("o");`
c. `s.indexOf("M");`

EXERCISE 7.8 Suppose you have the following declaration:

```
String s1 = "Java, Java, Java";
```

Evaluate each of the following expressions:

a. `s1.length()`
b. `String.valueOf(s1.length())`
c. `s1.indexOf('a')`
d. `s1.lastIndexOf('a')`
e. `s1.indexOf("av")`
f. `s1.lastIndexOf("av")`
g. `s1.indexOf('a', 5)`
h. `s1.lastIndexOf('a', 5)`
i. `s1.indexOf("av", s1.length() - 10)`
j. `s1.lastIndexOf("av", s1.length() - 4)`
k. `s1.indexOf("a", s1.indexOf("va"))`

EXERCISE 7.9 Evaluate the following expression:

```
String tricky = "abcdefg01234567";
tricky.indexOf( String.valueOf( tricky.indexOf("c")));
```

7.4 Example: Keyword Search

One of the most widely used Web browser functions is the search utility. You probably know how it works. You type in a keyword and click on a button, and it returns with a list of Web pages that contain the keyword.

Suppose you were writing a browser in Java. How would you implement this function? Of course, we don't know yet how to read files or Web pages, and we won't cover that until Chapter 14. But, for now, we can write a method that will search a string for all occurrences of a given keyword. That's at least part of the task that the browser's search engine would have to do.

Method design

So we want a method, `keywordSearch()`, that takes two `String` parameters, one for the string that's being searched, and the other representing the keyword. Let's have the method return a `String` that lists the number of occurrences of the keyword, followed by the index of each occurrence. For example, if we asked this method to find all occurrences of "is" in "This is a test," it should return the string "2: 2 5" because there are two occurrences of "is," one starting at index 2 and the other at index 5 in the string.

Algorithm design

The algorithm for this method will require a loop, because we want to know the location of every occurrence of the keyword in the string. One way to do this would be to use the `indexOf()` method to search for the location of substrings in the string. If it finds the keyword at index N, it should record that location and then continue searching for more occurrences starting at index $N+1$ in the string. It should continue in this way until there are no more occurrences.

```
Suppose S is our string and K is the keyword.
Initialize a counter variable and result string.
Set P to the indexOf() the first occurrence of K in S.
While ( P != -1 )
    Increment the counter
    Insert P into the result string
    Set P to the next location of the keyword in S
Insert the count into the result string
Return the result string as a String
```

Implementation

As this pseudocode shows, the algorithm uses a while loop with a *sentinel bound*. The algorithm terminates when the `indexOf()` method returns a -1, indicating that there are no more occurrences of the keyword in the string.

Translating the pseudocode into Java gives us the method shown in Figure 7–7. Note how string concatenation is used to build the `resultStr`. Each time an occurrence is found, its location (`ptr`) is concatenated to the right-hand side of the `resultStr`. When the loop terminates, the number of occurrences (`count`) is concatenated to the left-hand side of the `resultStr`.

Figure 7–7 The keywordSearch() method.

```
/**
 * Pre:  s and keyword are any Strings
 * Post: keywordSearch() returns a String containing the
 *  number of occurrences of keyword in s, followed
 *  by the starting location of each occurrence
 */
public String keywordSearch(String s, String keyword) {
    String resultStr = "";
    int count = 0;
    int ptr = s.indexOf(keyword);
    while (ptr != -1) {
        ++count;
        resultStr = resultStr + ptr + " ";
        ptr = s.indexOf(keyword, ptr + 1);    // Find next occurrence
    }
    resultStr = count + ": " + resultStr;     // Insert the count
    return resultStr;                         // Return as a String
} // keywordSearch()
```

Testing and Debugging

What test data do we need?

What test data should we use for the keywordSearch() method? One important consideration in this case is to test that the method works on strings that contain keyword occurrences at the beginning, middle, and end of the string. These will help verify that the loop will terminate properly. We should also test the method with a string that doesn't contain the keyword. Given these considerations, the following tests were made:

Test Performed	Expected Result
`keywordSearch( "this is a test","is")`	2: 2
`keywordSearch( "able was i ere i saw elba","a")`	4: 0 6 18 24
`keywordSearch( "this is a test","taste")`	0:

Given this set of tests, the method did produce the expected outcomes. While these tests do not guarantee its correctness, they provide considerable evidence that the algorithm works correctly.

EFFECTIVE DESIGN: Test Data. In designing test data to check the correctness of a string searching algorithm, it's important to use data that test all possible outcomes.

From the Java Library: `StringBuffer`

One problem with the `keywordSearch()` method is that it is not very efficient. The problem is that a `String` in Java is a **read-only** object. This means that once it has been instantiated, a `String` cannot be changed. You can't insert new characters or delete existing characters from it.

> **JAVA LANGUAGE RULE** **Strings Are Unalterable.** Once instantiated, a Java `String` cannot be altered in any way.

Strings can't be changed

Given this fact, how are we able to build the `resultStr` in the `keywordSearch()` method? The answer is that every time we assign a new value to `resultStr`, Java has to create a new `String` object. Thus, given the following statement

```
resultStr = resultStr + ptr + " ";
```

Java will evaluate the right-hand side, creating a new `String` object, whose value would be the concatenation of `resultStr + ptr + " "` [Figure 7–8(a)]. It would then assign the new object as the referent of `resultStr` [Figure 7–8(b)]. This turns the previous referent of `resultStr` into an *orphan* — that is, into an object that no longer has any references to it .

Built-in garbage collection

The fact that this assignment statement occurs within a loop means that several new objects are created and later garbage collected. Because object creation is a relatively time consuming and memory consuming operation, this algorithm is somewhat wasteful of Java's resources.

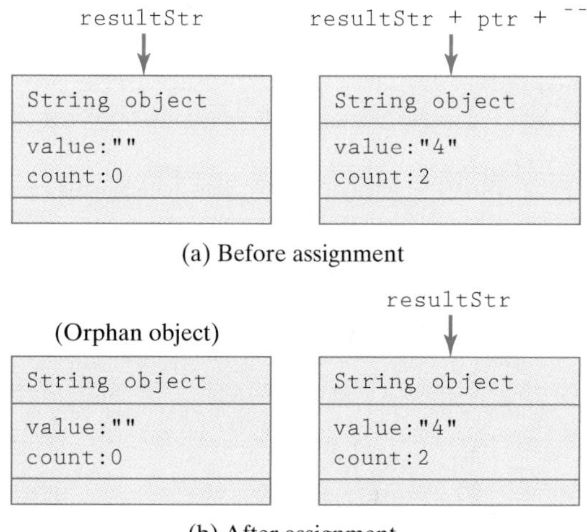

Figure 7–8 Suppose that `ptr` equals 4. Then (a) shows the situation before the assignment statement is completed, and (b) shows the situation after the assignment is made. In (b) the original `resultStr` has become an orphan, because there are no more references to it. It will be garbage collected.

Of course, except for the inefficiency of doing it this way, Java's garbage collector will automatically reclaim the memory used by the orphaned object, so no real harm is done.

> **JAVA LANGUAGE RULE** **Automatic Garbage Collection.** An object that has no reference to it can no longer be used in a program. Therefore, Java will automatically get rid of it. This is known as *garbage collection*.

Choosing the appropriate data structure

A more efficient way to write the `keywordSearch()` method would make use of a `StringBuffer` to store and construct the `resultStr`. The `java.lang.StringBuffer` class represents a string of characters. However, unlike the `String` class, a `StringBuffer` can be modified, and it can grow and shrink in length as necessary. Most string processing algorithms use `StringBuffer`s instead of `String`s as their preferred data structure.

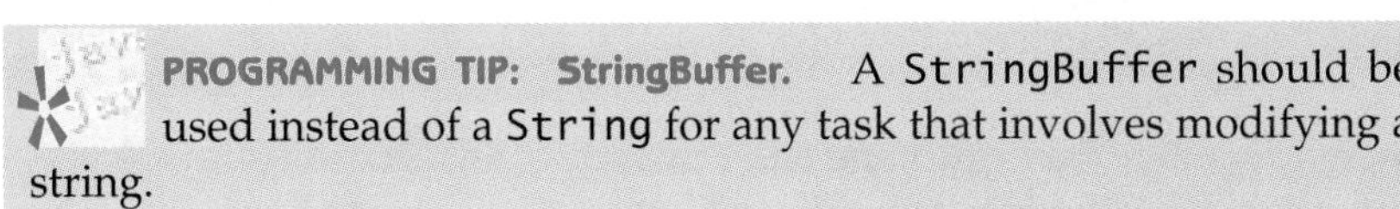
PROGRAMMING TIP: StringBuffer. A `StringBuffer` should be used instead of a `String` for any task that involves modifying a string.

The `StringBuffer` class provides several methods that are useful for string processing. Some of the main ones are

```
// Constructors
 public StringBuffer(String s);
// Public instance methods
 public StringBuffer append(Type t);  // Type may be int, long,float,double
                                      //  boolean, char, Object, String
 public StringBuffer insert(int offset, Type t); // Same Types as append()
 public String toString();
```

The constructor method, `StringBuffer(String)`, makes it easy to convert a `String` into a `StringBuffer`. Similarly, once you are done processing the buffer, the `toString()` method makes it easy to convert a `StringBuffer` back into a `String`.

The typical way to use a `StringBuffer` is shown in the following revised version of the `keywordSearch()` method:

```
public String keywordSearch(String s, String keyword) {
    StringBuffer resultStr = new StringBuffer(); // Create a StringBuffer
    int count = 0;
    int ptr = s.indexOf(keyword);
    while (ptr != -1) {
        ++count;
        resultStr.append(ptr + " ");          // Insert letters into it
        ptr = s.indexOf(keyword, ptr + 1);
    }
    resultStr.insert(0, count + ": ");
    return resultStr.toString();             // Convert buffer back to a String
} // keywordSearch()
```

We declare `resultStr` as a `StringBuffer` instead of a `String`. Then, for each occurrence of a keyword, instead of concatenating the `ptr` and reassigning the `resultStr`, we `append()` the `ptr` to the `resultStr`. Similarly, after the loop exits, we `insert()` the `count` at the front (index 0) of the `resultStr`. Finally, we convert `resultStr` into a `String` by using the `toString()` method before returning the method's result.

One advantage of the `StringBuffer` class is that there several versions of its `insert()` and `append()` methods. These make it possible to insert any type of data — `int`, `double`, `Object`, and so on — into a `StringBuffer`. The method itself takes care of the type conversion for us.

7.5 Retrieving Parts of Strings

The `charAt(int index)` method is a `String` instance method that can be used to retrieve the character stored at a certain index. The several varieties of the `substring()` method can be used to retrieve a substring of characters from a `String`. These methods are defined as follows:

```
public char charAt(int index)
public String substring(int startIndex)
public String substring(int startIndex, int endIndex)
```

The `charAt()` method returns the character located at the index supplied as its parameter. Thus, `str.charAt(0)` retrieves the first character in `str`, while `str.charAt(str.length()-1)` retrieves the last character.

The `substring()` methods work in a similar way, except that you need to specify both the starting and the ending index of the substring you wish to retrieve. The first version of `substring(int startindex)` takes a single parameter and returns a `String` consisting of all the characters beginning with `startindex` and continuing up to the end of the `String`. For example, if the `str` is "HelloWorld," then `str.substring(5)` would return "World" and `str.substring(3)` would return "loWorld":

```
String str = "HelloWorld";
str.substring(5)                ==> "World"
str.substring(3)                ==> "loWorld";
```

The `substring(int, int)` version requires that you specify both the starting and ending index of the substring. Note that the second index always points to the character that is 1 beyond the last character in the `String` you want to retrieve. For example,

```
//             0123456789
String str = "HelloWorld";
str.substring(5,7)              ==> "Wo"
str.substring(0,5)              ==> "Hello";
str.substring(5, str.length())  ==> "World"
```

Note here that when we want to retrieve "Wo" form `str`, we specify its substring as indexes 5 and 7; the 7 points to the character just beyond "Wo." Similarly, `substring(0,5)`, picks out the first five characters ("Hello"). Note that in the third example the `length()` method is used to specify the substring beginning at index 5 and extending to the end of the string. This is equivalent to `str.substring(5)`:

```
//              0123456789
String str = "HelloWorld";
str.substring(5, str.length())    ==> "World"
str.substring(5)                  ==> "World"
```

Delimited strings

The fact that the second parameter in `substring()` refers to the character one beyond the desired substring may seem a bit confusing at first, but it is actually a very useful way to designate a substring. For example, many string processing problems have to do with retrieving substrings from a *delimited string* of the form "substring1:substring2." In this case the *delimiter* is the `':'`. The following code can be used to retrieve the substring preceding the delimiter:

```
String str = "substring1:substring2";
int n = str.indexOf(':');
str.substring(0,n)                ==> "substring1"
```

Thus by making the second index of `substring()` refer to the character one beyond the last character in the desired substring, we can use `indexOf()` and `substring()` together to process delimited strings. Note that it is not necessary to use a temporary variable *n* to store the index of the delimiter, because the two method calls can be nested:

```
String str = "substring1:substring2";
str.substring(0,str.indexOf(':'))      ==> "substring1"
```

DEBUGGING TIP: `substring(int p1, int p2)`. Don't forget that the second parameter in the `substring()` methods refers to the character just past the last character in the substring. Forgetting this fact can cause of an off-by-one error.

SELF-STUDY EXERCISES

EXERCISE 7.10 Suppose the following declaration is made:

```
    String s = "abcdefghijklmnopqrstuvwxyz";
```

Evaluate each of the following expressions:

a. `s.substring(20)`
b. `s.substring(1, 5)`
c. `s.substring(23)`
d. `s.substring(23, 25)`
e. `s.substring(s.indexOf('x'))`

EXERCISE 7.11 Given the above declaration of `s` evaluate each of the following expressions:

a. `s.substring(20, s.length())`
b. `s.substring(s.indexOf('b'), s.indexOf('f'))`
c. `s.substring(s.indexOf( "xy" ))`
d. `s.substring(s.indexOf(s.charAt(23)))`
e. `s.substring(s.length() - 3)`

7.6 Example: Processing Names and Passwords

Many computer systems stores users' names and passwords as delimited strings, such as

```
smith:bg1s5xxx
mccarthy:2ffo900ssi
cho:biff4534ddee4w
```

Obviously, if the system is going to process passwords, it needs some way to take apart these name-password pairs.

Let's write methods to help perform this task. The first method will be passed a name-password pair and will return the name. The second method will be passed a name-password pair and will return the password. In both cases, the method takes a single `String` parameter, and returns a `String` result:

Algorithm design

```
String getName(String str);
String getPassword(String str);
```

To solve this problem we can make use of two `String` methods. We use the `indexOf()` method to find the location of the *delimiter* — which is the ':' — in the name-password pair and then we use `substring()` to take the substring occurring before or after the delimiter. It may be easier to see this if we take a particular example:

```
          10
0123456789012345
jones:b34rdffg12    // (1)
cho:rtf546          // (2)
```

In the first case, the delimiter occurs at index position 5 in the string. Therefore to take the name substring, we would use `substring(0,5)`. To take the password substring, we would use `substring(6)`. Of course, in the general case, we would use variables to indicate the position of the delimiter, as in the following methods:

```
public static String getName(String str) {
    int posColon = str.indexOf(':');              // Find the delimiter
    String result = str.substring(0, posColon); // Extract the name
    return result;
}

public static String getPassword(String str) {
    int posColon = str.indexOf(':');               // Find the delimiter
    String result = str.substring(posColon + 1); // Extract the password
    return result;
}
```

Note in both these cases we have used local variables, `posColon` and `result`, to store the intermediate results of the computation — that is, the index of the ':' and the name or password substring.

An alternative way to code these operations would be to use nested method calls to reduce the code to a single line:

```
return str.substring(0, str.indexOf(':'));
```

In this line, the result of `str.indexOf(':')` is passed immediately as the second argument to `str.substring()`. This version dispenses with the need for additional variables. And the result in this case is not unreasonably complicated. But whenever you are faced with a trade-off of this sort — nesting versus additional variables — you should opt for the style that will be easier to read and understand.

EFFECTIVE DESIGN: Nested Method Calls. Nested method calls are fine as long as there are not too many levels of nesting. The goal should be to produce code that is easy to read and understand.

7.7 Processing Each Character in a `String`

Many string processing applications require you to process each character in a string. For example, to encrypt the string "hello" into "jgnnq," we have to go through each letter of the string and change each character to its substitute.

Algorithm: Counting loop

These type of algorithms usually involve a counting loop bounded by the length of the string. Recall that the `length()` method determines the number of characters in a String, and that strings are zero indexed. This means that the first character is at index 0, and the character is at index length()-1. Here is an example that prints all of the characters in a String:

```
// Precondition:  str is not null
// Postcondition: the letters in str will have been printed
public void printLetters(String str) {
    for (int k = 0; k < str.length(); k++)    // For each character
        System.out.println( str.charAt(k));  //  Print it
}
```

Note that our loop bound is k < str.length(), since the index of the last character of any String is length()-1. Note also the use of str.charAt(k) to retrieve the *k*th character in str on each iteration of the loop.

Counting bound

Note the use of pre- and postconditions in the method's documentation. The precondition states that str has been properly initialized — that is, it is not null. The postcondition merely states the expected behavior of the method.

7.7.1 Off-by-One Error

A frequent error in coding counter-controlled loops is known as the **off-by-one error**, which can occur in many different ways. For example, if we had coded the loop boundary condition as k <= str.length(), this would cause an off-by-one error, because the last character in str is at location length()-1. This would lead to a Java IndexOutOfBoundsException, which would be reported as soon as the program executed this statement.

Off-by-one error

The only way to avoid off-by-one errors is to check your loop bounds whenever you code a loop. Always make sure you have the loop counter's initial and final values correct.

DEBUGGING TIP: Off-by-One Errors. Loops should be carefully checked to make sure they don't commit an off-by-one error. During program testing, test data should be developed to test the loop bound's initial and final values.

7.7.2 Example: Counting Characters

As another example of an algorithm that processes each character in a string, consider the problem of computing the frequency of the letters in a given document. Certain text analysis programs perform this type of function.

Figure 7–9 A method to count the occurrence of a particular character in a string.

```
// Precondition: Neither str nor ch are null
// Postcondition: countchar() == the number of ch in str
public int countChar(String str, char ch) {
    int counter = 0;                             // Initialize a counter
    for (int k = 0; k < str.length(); k++)  // For each character
        if (str.charAt(k) == ch)             //  If it's a ch
            counter++;                           //    count it
    return counter;                              // Return the result
}
```

Method design

The `countChar()` method will count the number of occurrences of any particular character in a `String` (Figure 7–9). This method takes two parameters: a `String` parameter that stores the string being searched, and a `char` parameter that stores the character being counted.

Algorithm design

It begins by initializing the local variable, `counter`, to 0. As in the previous example, the for loop here will iterate through each character of the `String` — from 0 to `length()-1`. On each iteration a check is made to see if the character in the *k*th position (`str.charAt(k)`) is the character being counted. If so, `counter` is incremented. The method ends by returning `counter` which, when the method completes, will store an integer representing the number of blanks in `str`.

7.8 CASE STUDY: Silly `CyberPet` String Tricks

Many string processing tasks involve iterating through each character of the string and converting it in some way. We'll use our CyberPet to illustrate these kinds algorithms.

The last time we left our CyberPet it was just eating and sleeping, although its eating was becoming quite animated! Suppose now we want to give the pet some clever `String` tricks to perform. These are like card tricks, but they use `Strings` instead of cards. What they all have in common is that they change the original string into a different string. You might think of these as CyberPet's attempt at a pun!

Problem decomposition

One way to give our CyberPet this new capability is to create a `StringTricks` class. We'll define a bunch of different string tricks and let the CyberPet pull one out of the bag each time the user asks for one. By encapsulating all the tricks in `StringTricks`, we not only organize them into a single, well-focused class, but we also avoid cluttering up the `CyberPet` class with too many additional methods.

7.8.1 Class Design: `StringTricks`

What data and methods do we need?

For starters, let's put three tricks (methods) into `StringTricks`: a method to reverse a string, a method to change each letter of a string to UPPERCASE, and a method to change every other letter to UpPeRcAsE. Each of these methods will take a `String` parameter and return a `String` result.

In addition to the tricks themselves, let's write a method to get one of the tricks from the repertoire. The getNextTrick() method will decide which trick to perform and then simply invoke it. To help with this task, let's give the StringTricks class a nextTrick variable, which will keep track of the next trick to perform.

Give these considerations, we get the following design for the StringTricks class:

```
public class StringTricks {
    private final int NTRICKS = 3;           // Number of tricks
    private int nextTrick = 0;               // Next trick to perform

    public String getNextTrick(String s); // Perform the next trick
    public String reverse(String s);       // Reverse s
    public String toUpperCase(String s);   // Change s to UPPERCASE
    public String toEveryOther(String s); // Change s to EvErYoThEr
} // StringTricks
```

7.8.2 Method Design: getNextTrick()

The getNextTrick() method should take its String parameter and simply pass it to the method whose turn it is, getting back a result string that will be returned to CyberPet. It must also update the nextTrick variable. The algorithm for this method uses a multiway selection structure to choose among the available tricks:

What control structure do we need?

```
/**
 * Pre:  s is any non null string
 * Post: A trick is picked and s is transformed and returned
 *       The nextTrick variable is incremented modulo NTRICKS
 */
public String getNextTrick(String s) {
    String result = new String();           // Stores the result
    if (nextTrick == 0)                     // Do the next trick
        result = reverse(s);
    else if (nextTrick == 1)
        result = toEveryOther(s);
    else
        result = toUpperCase(s);
    nextTrick = (nextTrick + 1) % NTRICKS; // Update for next time
    return result;
} // getNextTrick()
```

Note how modular arithmetic is used here to increment the nextTrick variable. If NTRICKS is 3, then once nextTrick reaches 2, the expression (nextTrick + 1) % NTRICKS will wrap around to 0. This allows nextTrick to cycle between the values 0, 1, ..., NTRICKS-1, which are the numbers of the available tricks.

Modular arithmetic

7.8.3 Method Design: reverse()

The reverse() method should use a simple counting loop to reverse the letters in its String parameter. If the loop iterates from the last character to

Algorithm design

the first, then we can just append each character, left to right, in the result string. As in the other string manipulation algorithms — for example, `keywordSearch()` — we should us a `StringBuffer` to store the method's result:

```
/**
 * Pre:  s is any non null string
 * Post: s is returned in reverse order
 */
public String reverse(String s) {
    StringBuffer result = new StringBuffer();
    for (int k = s.length() -1; k >= 0; k--) {
        result.append(s.charAt(k));
    } //for
    return result.toString();
} // reverse()
```

Note how the `result StringBuffer` is declared at the beginning of the method and then converted back into a `String` at the end of the method.

PROGRAMMING TIP: Changing Each Character in a String. Algorithms that require you to alter a string should use a `StringBuffer` to store the result.

7.8.4 Method Design: `toUpperCase()`

Algorithm design

The `toUpperCase()` method should use a simple counting loop algorithm to change each letter in the `String` parameter to uppercase.

The `toUpperCase()` method illustrates how this kind of algorithm is designed. Like the `reverse()` method, it should use a `StringBuffer` for its result. It should iterate from 0 to `s.length()-1`, using the `charAt()` method to extract each character from the string. If the character is a lowercase letter, 'a' to 'z,' it should be converted to uppercase. Recall that we can convert lowercase to uppercase by subtracting 32 from letter's integer representation.

```
(char)(s.charAt(k) - 32)
```

Data conversion

Note that it is necessary to cast the result of this operation back to a `char`. Of course, we would only do this on letters that fall in the 'a' to 'z' range:

```
/**
 * Pre:  s is any non NULL string
 * Post: Each letter in s is converted to UPPERCASE
 */
public String toUpperCase(String s) {
    StringBuffer result = new StringBuffer();
    for (int k = 0; k < s.length(); k++) {
        if ((s.charAt(k) >= 'a') && (s.charAt(k) <= 'z'))// If lowercase
            result.append((char)(s.charAt(k) - 32));     // Convert to uppercase
        else
        result.append((char)s.charAt(k));
    } //for
    return result.toString();
} // toUpperCase()
```

7.8.5 Method Design: `toEveryOther()`

The algorithm for the `toEveryOther()` method is similar to the `toUpperCase()` algorithm. In this case, however, we only change every other letter. This task is made simpler if we first convert the string to uppercase. Then we can iterate though it changing every other letter in the range 'A' to 'Z' to lowercase. We can use modular arithmetic to convert all the odd indexed letters and leave the even indexed letters alone.

Algorithm design

```
/**
 * Pre:  s is any non null string
 * Post: s is returned with every other letter UpPeRcAsE
 */
public String toEveryOther(String s) {
    StringBuffer result = new StringBuffer();
    s = toUpperCase(s);                          // Change to all UPPERCASE

    for (int k = 0; k < s.length(); k++) {       // Convert every other letter
        if ((k % 2 != 0) && (s.charAt(k) >= 'A') && (s.charAt(k) <= 'Z'))
            result.append((char)(s.charAt(k) + 32));        // to lowercase
        else
            result.append((char)s.charAt(k));
    } //for
    return result.toString();
} // toEveryOther()
```

The complete implementation of the `StringTricks` class is shown in Figure 7–10.

SELF-STUDY EXERCISES

EXERCISE 7.12 Show the changes necessary to incorporate `StringTricks` into the CyberPet's repertoire. Start by add a `TRICKING` state and a `trick(String)` method. Then add an instance variable for the pet's bag of tricks.

EXERCISE 7.13 Given the changes to `CyberPet` in the previous exercise, modify the `AnimatedCyberPet` applet (Figure 6–9) so that the user can ask it to do a string trick. Use a `TextField`, with its own `ActionListener`, to input the user's string and to show the altered string.

EXERCISE 7.14 Add a method to the `StringTricks` class that will remove any blanks from a string. It should take a `String` parameter and should return a `String` result.

7.8.6 Miscellaneous `String` Methods

In addition to the several `String` class methods we have discussed — `valueOf()`, `equals()`, `indexOf()`, `lastIndexOf()`, `charAt()`, `substring()` — Table 7–1 shows some of the other useful methods in the `String` class. Note that because of what we said about the read-only nature of `Strings`, methods such as `toUpperCase()`, `toLowerCase()`, and `trim()`, do not change their string. Instead they produce a new string. If you want to use one of these methods to convert a string, you must reassign its result back to the original string:

Figure 7–10 Definition of the `StringTricks` class.

```
public class StringTricks {

    public static final int NTRICKS = 3;
    public static int nextTrick = 0;

    /**
     * Pre:  s is any non null string
     * Post: A trick is picked and s is transformed and returned
     *       The nextTrick variable is incremented modulo NTRICKS
     */
    public String getNextTrick(String s) {
        String result = new String();           // Stores the result
        if (nextTrick == 0)                     // Do the next trick
            result = reverse(s);
        else if (nextTrick == 1)
            result = toEveryOther(s);
        else
            result = toUpperCase(s);
        nextTrick = (nextTrick + 1) % NTRICKS; // Update for next time
        return result;
    } // getNextTrick()

    /**
     * Pre:  s is any non null string
     * Post: s is returned in reverse order
     */
    public String reverse(String s) {
        StringBuffer result = new StringBuffer();
        for (int k = s.length() -1; k >= 0; k--) {
            result.append(s.charAt(k));
        } //for
        return result.toString();
    } // reverse()

    /**
     * Pre:  s is any non null string
     * Post: s is returned with every other letter UpPeRcAsE
     */
    public String toEveryOther(String s) {
        StringBuffer result = new StringBuffer();
        s = toUpperCase(s);                          // Change to all UPPERCASE

        for (int k = 0; k < s.length(); k++) {     // Convert every other letter
            if ((k % 2 != 0) && (s.charAt(k) >= 'A') && (s.charAt(k) <= 'Z'))
                result.append((char)(s.charAt(k) + 32));          // to lowercase
            else
                result.append((char)s.charAt(k));
        } //for
        return result.toString();
    } // toEveryOther()

    /**
     * Pre:  s is any non NULL string
     * Post: Each letter in s is converted to UPPERCASE
     */
    public String toUpperCase(String s) {
        StringBuffer result = new StringBuffer();
        for (int k = 0; k < s.length(); k++) {
            if ((s.charAt(k) >= 'a') && (s.charAt(k) <= 'z'))  // If lowercase
                result.append((char)(s.charAt(k) - 32));  // Convert to uppercase
            else
            result.append((char)s.charAt(k));
        } //for
        return result.toString();
    } // toUpperCase()
} // StringTricks
```

```
String s = new String("hello world");
s = s.toUpperCase();                    // s now equals "HELLO WORLD"
```

Table 7.1. Some useful String methods. The examples assume that the String str has been assigned the value "Perfection" including the leading and trailing blanks.

Method Signature	Example
boolean endsWith(String suffix)	"Perfection".endsWith("tion") ⇒ true
boolean startsWith(String prefix)	"Perfection".startsWith("Per") ⇒ true
boolean startsWith(String prefix, int offset)	"Perfection".startsWith("fect",3) ⇒ true
String toUpperCase()	"Perfection".toUpperCase() ⇒ "PERFECTION"
String toLowerCase()	"Perfection".toLowerCase() ⇒ "perfection"
String trim()	"Perfection".trim() ⇒ "Perfection"

7.9 Comparing Strings

Strings are compared according to the their lexicographic order. For the letters of the alphabet, lexicographic order just means alphabetical order. Thus 'a' comes before 'b' and 'd' comes after 'c.' The string "hello" comes before "jello" because 'h' comes before 'j' in the alphabet.

For Java and other programming languages, the definition of lexicographic order is extended to cover all the characters that make up the character set. We know, for example, that in Java's Unicode character set the uppercase letters come before the lowercase letters (Table 5–11). Therefore the letter 'H' comes before the letter 'h' and the letter 'Z' comes before the letter 'a.'

H precedes h

Lexicographic order can be extended to include strings of characters. Thus "Hello" precedes "hello" in lexicographic order because its first letter, 'H,' precedes the first letter, 'h,' in "hello." Similarly, the string "Zero" comes before "aardvark," because 'Z' comes before 'a.' To determine lexicographic order for strings, we must perform a character by character comparison, starting at the first character and proceeding left to right. As an example, the following strings are arranged in lexicographic order:

```
" " "!" "0" "A" "Andy" "Z" "Zero" "a" "an" "and" "andy" "candy" "zero"
```

We can define **lexicographic order** for strings as follows.

JAVA LANGUAGE RULE **Lexicographic Order.** For strings *s1* and *s2*, *s1* precedes *s2* in lexicographic order if its first character precedes the first character of *s2*. If their first characters are equal, then *s1* precedes *s2* if its second character precedes the second character of *s2*, and so on. Finally, the empty string is handled as a special case, preceding all other strings.

Perhaps a more precise way to define lexicographic order is to define a Java method:

```
public boolean precedes(String s1, String s2) {
    int minlen = Math.min(s1.length(), s2.length()); // Pick shorter length
    int k = 0;                                        // Start at the first character
    while (k < minlen) {                              // While there are more characters
        if (s1.charAt(k) < s2.charAt(k))              // If kth char in s1 < kth char in s2
            return true;                              //    then s1 precedes s2
        else if (s2.charAt(k) < s1.charAt(k))         // If kth char in s2 < kth char in s1
            return false;                             //    then s1 does not precede s2
        else                                          // If neither case
            k++;                                      //    go on to the next character
    } // while
    return s1.length() < s2.length();                 // If all characters so far are equal
} // precedes()                                     //  then s1 < s2 if it is shorter than s2
```

Algorithm: Loop bound

This method does a character by character comparison of the two strings, proceeding left to right, starting at the first character in both strings. Its while loop uses a counting bound, which starts at *k* equal to zero and counts up to the length of the shorter string. This is an important point in designing this algorithm. If you don't stop iterating when you get past the last character in a string, your program will generate an `StringIndexOutOfBounds` exception. To prevent this error, we need to use the shorter length as the loop bound.

Note that the loop will terminate early if it finds that the respective characters from *s1* and *s2* are unequal. In that case either *s1* precedes *s2* or vice versa. If the loop terminates normally, that means that all the characters compared were equal. In that case the shorter string precedes the longer. For example if the two strings were "alpha" and "alphabet," then the method would return true, because "alpha" is shorter than "alphabet."

SELF-STUDY EXERCISES

EXERCISE 7.15 Arrange the following strings in lexicographic order:

```
zero bath bin alpha Alpha Zero Zeroes a A z Z
```

EXERCISE 7.16 Modify the `precedes()` method so that it will also return true when *s1* and *s2* are the equal — for example, when *s1* and *s2* are both "hello."

7.9.1 Object Identity versus Object Equality

Java provides several methods for comparing `Strings`:

```
public boolean equals(Object anObject);      // Overrides Object.equals()
public boolean equalsIgnoreCase(String  anotherString)
public int compareTo(String  anotherString)
```

The first comparison method, `equals()`, overrides the `Object.equals()` method. Two `Stringss` are equal if they have the exact same letters in the exact same order. Thus for the following declarations,

```
String s1 = "hello";
String s2 = "Hello";
```

`s1.equals( s2 )` is `false`, but `s1.equals("hello")` is `true`.

Equality vs. identity

You have to be careful when using Java's `equals()` method. According to the default definition of `equals()`, defined in the `Object` class, "equals" means "identical." Two `Objects` are equal only if their names are references to the same object.

This is like the old story of the morning star and the evening star, which were thought to be different objects before it was discovered that both were just the planet Venus. After the discovery, it was clear that "the morning star" and "the evening star" and "Venus" were just three different references to one and the same object (Figure 7–11).

We can create an analogous situation in Java by using the following `Button` definitions:

```
Button b1 = new Button("a");
Button b2 = new Button("a");
Button b3 = b2;
```

Given these three declarations, `b1.equals(b2)` and `b1.equals(b3)` would be `false`, but `b2.equals(b3)` would be `true` because *b2* and *b3* are just two names for the same object (Figure 7–12).

Object identity

Moreover, in Java the equality operator (==) is interpreted in the same way as the default `Object.equals()` method. So it really means object identity. Thus `b1 == b2` and `b1 == b3` would be `false` and `b2 == b3` would be `true`. These points are illustrated in the program shown in Figure 7–13.

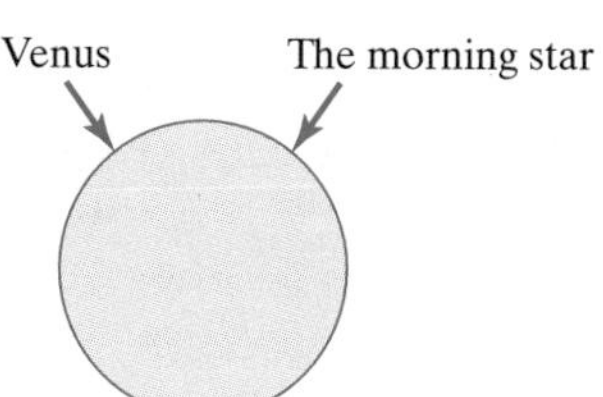

Figure 7–11 Venus is the morning star, so "Venus" and "the morning star" are two references to the same object.

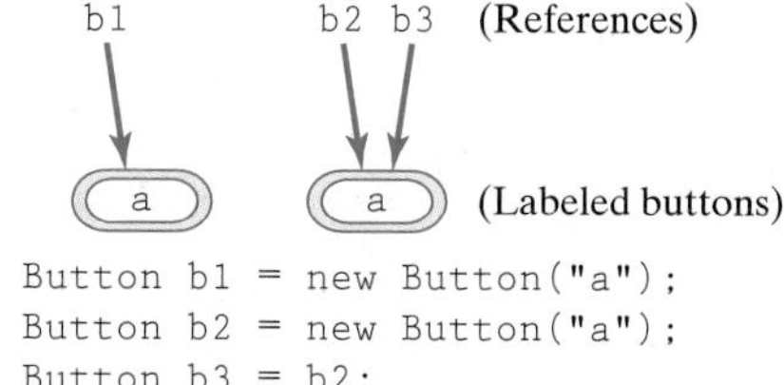

Figure 7–12 For most objects, equality means identity. Buttons b2 and b3 are identical (and hence equal), but Buttons b1 and b2 are not identical (and hence unequal).

Figure 7–13 The TestEquals program tests Java's default equals() method, which is defined in the Object class
.

```
import java.awt.*;

public class TestEquals {
    static Button b1 = new Button ("a");
    static Button b2 = new Button ("b");
    static Button b3 = b2;

    private static void isEqual(Object o1, Object o2) {
        if (o1.equals(o2))
            System.out.println(o1.toString() + " equals " + o2.toString());
        else
            System.out.println(o1.toString() + " does NOT equal " + o2.toString());
    } // isEqual()

    private static void isIdentical( Object o1, Object o2 ) {
        if (o1 == o2)
            System.out.println(o1.toString() + " is identical to " + o2.toString());
        else
            System.out.println(o1.toString() + " is NOT identical to " + o2.toString());
    } // isIdentical()

    public static void main(String argv[]) {
        isEqual(b1, b2);          // not equal
        isEqual(b1, b3);          // not equal
        isEqual(b2, b3);          // equal

        isIdentical(b1, b2);      // not identical
        isIdentical(b1, b3);      // not identical
        isIdentical(b2, b3);      // identical
    } // main()
} // TestEquals
```

The program uses methods isEquals() and isIdentical() to perform the comparisons and print the results. Its output is as follows:

```
java.awt.Button[button0,0,0,0x0,invalid,label=a]
        does NOT equal java.awt.Button[button1,0,0,0x0,invalid,label=b]
java.awt.Button[button0,0,0,0x0,invalid,label=a]
        does NOT equal java.awt.Button[button1,0,0,0x0,invalid,label=b]
java.awt.Button[button1,0,0,0x0,invalid,label=b]
        equals java.awt.Button[button1,0,0,0x0,invalid,label=b]
java.awt.Button[button0,0,0,0x0,invalid,label=a]
        is NOT identical to java.awt.Button[button1,0,0,0x0,invalid,label=b]
java.awt.Button[button0,0,0,0x0,invalid,label=a]
        is NOT identical to java.awt.Button[button1,0,0,0x0,invalid,label=b]
java.awt.Button[button1,0,0,0x0,invalid,label=b]
        is identical to java.awt.Button[button1,0,0,0x0,invalid,label=b]
```

7.9.2 String Identity versus String Equality

Equality vs. identity

In comparing Java Strings we must be careful to distinguish between object identity and string equality. Thus consider the following declarations, which create the situation shown in Figure 7–14.

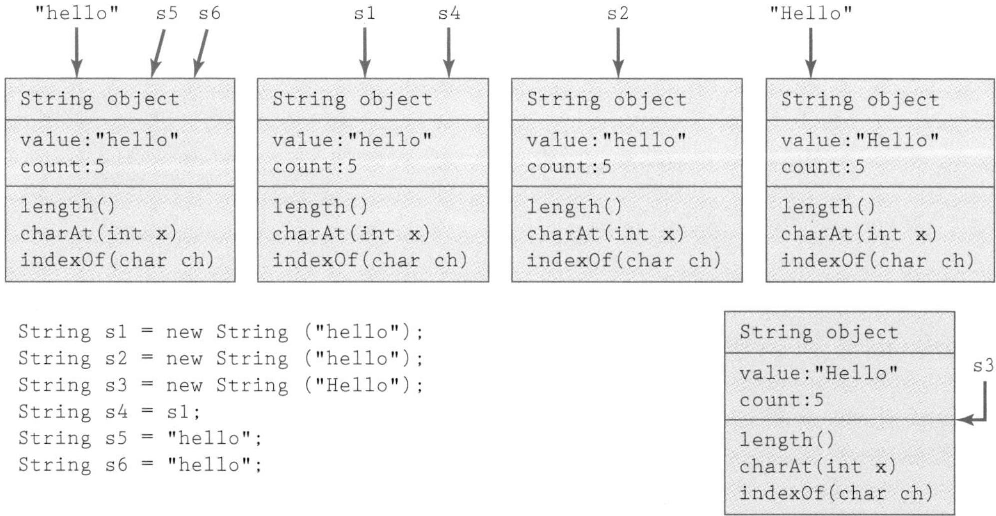

Figure 7–14 For String objects, equality and identity are different. Two distinct (non-identical) String objects are equal if they store the same string value. So s1, s2, s4, s5 and s6 are equal. Strings s1 and s4 are identical, and so are strings s5 and s6.

```
String s1 = new String("hello");
String s2 = new String("hello");
String s3 = new String("Hello");
String s4 = s1;                    // s1 and s4 are now identical
String s5 = "hello";
String s6 = "hello";
```

Given these declarations, we would get the following results if we compare the equality of the Strings:

```
s1.equals(s2)              ==> true
s1.equals(s3)              ==> false
s1.equalsIgnoreCase(s3)    ==> true
s1.equals(s4)              ==> true
s1.equals(s5)              ==> true
s1.equals(s6)              ==> true
```

and the following results if we compare their identity:

```
s1 == s2                   ==> false
s1 == s3                   ==> false
s1 == s4                   ==> true
s1 == s5                   ==> false
s5 == s6                   ==> true
```

Figure 7–15 Program illustrating the difference between string equality and identity.

```
import java.awt.*;

public class TestStringEquals {
    static String s1 = new String("hello"); // s1 and s2 are equal, not identical
    static String s2 = new String("hello");
    static String s3 = new String("Hello"); // s1 and s3 are not equal
    static String s4 = s1;                  // s1 and s4 are identical
    static String s5 = "hello";             // s1 and s5 are not identical
    static String s6 = "hello";             // s5 and s6 are identical

    private static void testEqual(String str1, String str2) {
        if (str1.equals(str2))
            System.out.println(str1 + " equals " + str2);
        else
            System.out.println(str1 + " does not equal " + str2);
    } // testEqual()

    private static void testIdentical( String str1, String str2 ) {
        if (str1 == str2)
            System.out.println(str1 + " is identical to " + str2);
        else
            System.out.println(str1 + " is not identical to " + str2);
    } // testIdentical()

    public static void main(String argv[]) {
        testEqual(s1, s2);          // equal
        testEqual(s1, s3);          // not equal
        testEqual(s1, s4);          // equal
        testEqual(s1, s5);          // equal
        testEqual(s5, s6);          // equal

        testIdentical(s1, s2);      // not identical
        testIdentical(s1, s3);      // not identical
        testIdentical(s1, s4);      // identical
        testIdentical(s1, s5);      // not identical
        testIdentical(s5, s6);      // identical
    } // main()
}// TestStringEquals
```

The only true identities among these `Strings` are *s1* and *s4*, and *s5* and *s6*. In the case of *s5* and *s6*, both are just references to the literal string, "hello," as we described in Section 7.2. The program in Figure 7–15 illustrates these points. Its output is

```
PROGRAM OUTPUT : ::::::::::::::::::::::::::::
   hello equals hello
   hello does not equal Hello
   hello equals hello
   hello equals hello
   hello equals hello
   hello is not identical to hello
   hello is not identical to Hello
   hello is identical to hello
   hello is not identical to hello
   hello is identical to hello
END OUTPUT : ::::::::::::::::::::::::::::::
```

SELF-STUDY EXERCISES

EXERCISE 7.17 Given the following String declarations,

```
String s1 = "java", s2 = "java", s3 = "Java";
String s4 = new String(s2);
String s5 = new String("java");
```

evaluate the following expressions:

a. `s1 == s2`
b. `s1.equals(s2)`
c. `s1 == s3`
d. `s1.equals(s3)`
e. `s2 == s3`
f. `s2.equals(s4)`
g. `s2 == s4`
h. `s1 == s5`
i. `s4 == s5`

EXERCISE 7.18 Why are the variables in `TestStringEquals` declared `static`?

EXERCISE 7.19 Given the following declarations:

```
String s1 = "abcdefghijklmnopqrstuvwxyz";
String s2 = "hello world";
```

write Java expressions to carry out each of the following operations:

a. `swap the front and back half of s1 giving a new string.`
b. `swap "world" and "hello" in s2 giving a new string.`
c. `combine parts of s1 and s2 to create a new string "hello abc".`

From the Java Library: `StringTokenizer`

One of the most widespread string processing tasks is that of breaking up a string into its components or **tokens**. For example, when processing a sentence, you may need to break the sentence into its constituent words. When processing a name/password string, such as "boyd:14irXp," you may need to break it into a name and a password.

Java's `java.util.StringTokenizer` class is specially designed for breaking strings into their tokens:

```
public class StringTokenizer extends Object implements Enumeration {
   // Public constructors
    public StringTokenizer( String str, String delim );
    public StringTokenizer( String str );
   // Public instance methods
    public int countTokens();
    public boolean hasMoreTokens();
    public String nextToken();
    public String nextToken( String delim );
   // Methods of the Enumeration interface
    public boolean hasMoreElements();
    public String nextElement();
}
```

Delimited strings

When instantiated with a String, a StringTokenizer breaks the string into tokens separated by any of the characters specified in the delim parameter. If no *delimiter* is specified, StringTokenizer assumes that the string is delimited by white space — that is, by tabs, blanks, and line feeds.

For example, if we instantiated a StringTokenizer as follows:

```
StringTokenizer sTokenizer
    = new StringTokenizer("This is an English sentence.");
```

it would break the string into the following tokens, which would be stored internally in the StringTokenizer in the following order:

```
This
is
an
English
sentence.
```

Note that the period is part of the last token ("sentence."). This is because punctuation marks are not considered delimiters by default. If you wanted to include punctuation symbols as delimiters, you could use the following instantiation:

```
StringTokenizer sTokenizer
    = new StringTokenizer("This is an English sentence.", "\b\t\n,;.!");
```

In this case, the second parameter provides a string of those characters that should be used as delimiters. Note the use of the escape sequences to specify blanks, tabs, and newlines.

The hasMoreTokens() and nextToken() methods can be used to process a delimited string, one token at a time. The first method returns true as long as more tokens remain; the second gets the next token in the list. For example, here's a code segment that will break a standard URL into its constituent parts:

```
String url = "http://troy.trincoll.edu/jjj/index.html";
StringTokenizer sTokenizer = new StringTokenizer( url,":/" );
while (sTokenizer.hasMoreTokens()) {
    System.out.println(sTokenizer.nextToken());
}
```

This code segment will produce the following output:

```
http
troy.trincoll.edu
jjj
index.html
```

The only delimiters used in this case were the ':' and '/' symbols. And note that nextToken() does not return the empty string between ':' and '/' as a token.

Historical Cryptography

Cryptography , the study of secret writing, has had a long and interesting history. Modern day cryptographic techniques employ sophisticated mathematics to *encrypt* and *decrypt* messages. Today's most secure encryption schemes are safe from attack by even the most powerful computers. Given our widespread dependence on computers and the Internet, secure encryption has become an important application area within computer science. The cryptographic techniques used up through World War II are too simple to serve as the basis for modern day encryption schemes, but they provide an interesting and accessible introduction to this important area of computer science.

One of the earliest and simplest *ciphers* is the Caesar cipher, used by Julius Caesar during the Gallic wars. According to this scheme, letters of the alphabet are *shifted* by three letters, wrapping around at the end of the alphabet:

```
PlainText:     abcdefghijklmnopqrstuvwxyz
CaesarShifted: defghijklmnopqrstuvwxyzabc
```

When encrypting a message, you take each letter of the message and replace it with its corresponding letter from the shifted alphabet. To decrypt a secret message, you perform the operation in reverse — that is, you take the letter from the shifted alphabet and replace it with the corresponding letter from the **plaintext** alphabet . Thus "hello" would be Caesar encrypted as "khoor."

Substitution cipher

The Caesar cipher is a **substitution cipher** , because each letter in the plaintext message is replaced with a substitute letter from the **ciphertext** alphabet . A more general form of a substitution cipher uses a *keyword* to create a ciphertext alphabet:

```
PlainText:  abcdefghijklmnopqrstuvwxyz
Ciphertext: xylophneabcdfgijkmqrstuvwz
```

In this example, the keyword "xylophone," (with the second 'o' removed) is used to set up a substitution alphabet. According to this cipher the word "hello" would be encrypted as "epddi." Substitution ciphers of this form are found frequently in cryptogram puzzles in the newspapers.

Transposition cipher

Another type of cipher is known as a **transposition** cipher. In this type of cipher, instead of replacing the letters in a message with substitutes, we rearrange the letters in some methodical way. A simple example would be if we reversed the letters in each word so that "hello" became "olleh." Another technique might rotate the letters of the word, by a fixed number of characters, wrapping around to the beginning if necessary. Thus "hello" would become "lohel," if we shifted each character within the word two places to the right.

OBJECT-ORIENTED DESIGN: The abstract Cipher Class

Using Inheritance to Define Ciphers

Suppose we wish to design a collection of cipher classes, including a Caesar cipher and a transposition cipher. Because the basic operations used in all forms of encryption are the same, both the `Caesar` class and the `Transpose` class will have methods to `encrypt()` and `decrypt()` messages. These methods will take a `String` of words, and translate each word using the encoding method that is appropriate for that cipher. Therefore, in addition to `encrypt()` and `decrypt()`, each cipher class will need `encode()` and `decode()` methods, which take a single word and encode or decode it according to the rules of that particular cipher.

From a design perspective the `encrypt()` and `decrypt()` methods will be the same for every class: They simply break the message into words and encode or decode each word. However, the `encode()` and `decode()` methods will be different for each different cipher. The `Caesar.encode()` method should replace each letter of a word with its substitute, whereas the `Transpose.encode()` method should rearrange the letters of the word. Given these considerations, how should we design this set of classes?

Problem decomposition

Because all of the various ciphers will have the same methods, it will be helpful to define a common `Cipher` superclass (Figure 7–16). `Cipher` will encapsulate those features that the individual cipher classes have in common — the `encrypt()`, `decrypt()`, `encode()`, and `decode()` methods.

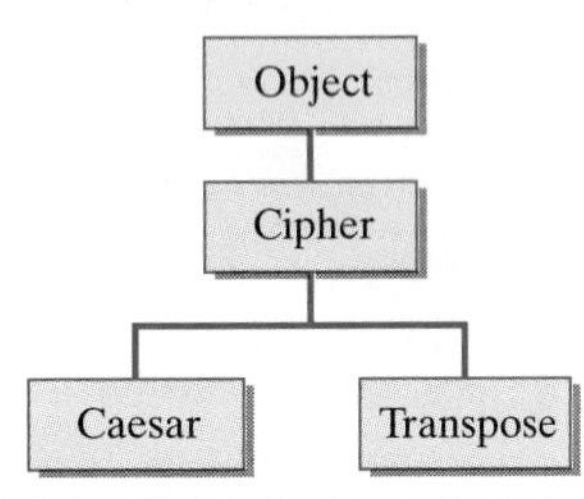

Figure 7–16 A hierarchy of cipher classes. The `Cipher` class implements operations common to all ciphers. The `Caesar` and `Transpose` classes implement functions unique to those kinds of ciphers.

Some of these methods can be implemented in the `Cipher` class itself. For example, the `encrypt()` method should take a message in a `String` parameter, encode each word in the message, and return a `String` result. The following method definition will work for any cipher:

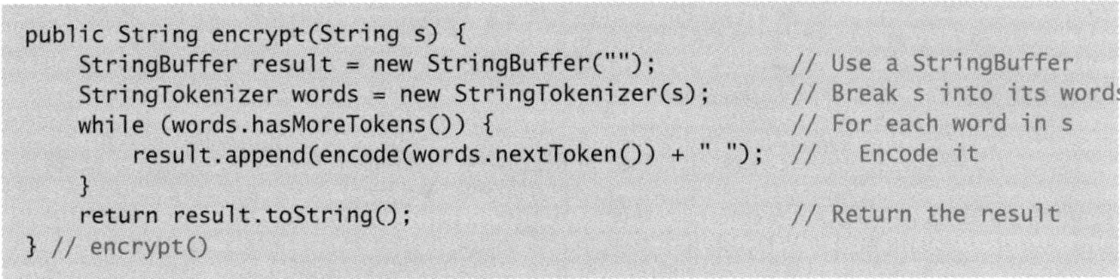

```
public String encrypt(String s) {
    StringBuffer result = new StringBuffer("");            // Use a StringBuffer
    StringTokenizer words = new StringTokenizer(s);        // Break s into its words
    while (words.hasMoreTokens()) {                        // For each word in s
        result.append(encode(words.nextToken()) + " ");    //   Encode it
    }
    return result.toString();                              // Return the result
} // encrypt()
```

This method creates a local `StringBuffer` variable, `result`, and uses `StringTokenizer` to break the original `String` into its component words. It uses the `encode()` method to encode the word, appending the result into `result`. The result is converted back into a `String` and returned as the encrypted translation of *s*, the original message.

Inheritance

If we define `encrypt()` in the superclass, it will be inherited by all of `Cipher`'s subclasses. Thus if we define `Caesar` and `Transpose` as

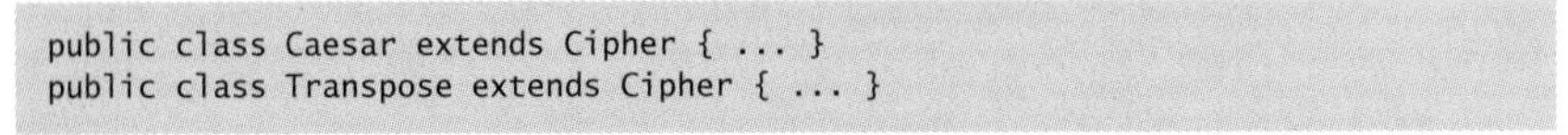

```
public class Caesar extends Cipher { ... }
public class Transpose extends Cipher { ... }
```

instances of these classes will be able to use the encrypt() method.

Abstract method

On the other hand, the encode() method cannot be implemented within Cipher. This is because unlike the encrypt() method, which is the same for every Cipher subclass, the encode() method will be different for every subclass. Fortunately Java allows us to define a method without implementing it by declaring the method abstract. An abstract method has no body. It is defined by providing its signature followed by a semicolon. Thus, within the Cipher class, we would define encode() and decode() as follows:

```
public abstract String encode(String word); // Abstract method
public abstract String decode(String word); // Abstract method
```

Note here that the semicolon replaces the method's body. This declaration, within the Cipher class, tells the compiler that this method will be implemented within Cipher's subclasses. By defining it as abstract, encode() can be used within the Cipher class, as it was within the encrypt() method above.

Rules for Abstract Methods and Classes

Java has the following rules on using abstract methods and classes :

- Any class containing an abstract method must be declared an abstract class.
- An abstract class cannot be instantiated. It must be subclassed.
- A subclass of an abstract class may be instantiated only if it implements *all* of the superclass's abstract methods. A subclass that implements only some of the abstract methods must itself be declared abstract.
- A class may be declared abstract even it contains no abstract methods. It could, for example, contain instances variables that are common to all its subclasses. An abstract class cannot be instantiated.

We've seen other examples of abstract classes and interfaces. The ActionListener interface, introduced in Chapter 4, is an example of an abstract interface. It defines but does not implement the actionPerformed() method, which must be implemented in any class that implements the interface. The Image class (see "From the Java Library" in Chapter 4) is an example of an abstract class.

Class Design: Caesar

Figure 7–17 provides the full definition of the Cipher class. The encode() and decode() methods are declared abstract. They are intended to be implemented by Cipher's subclasses.

Figure 7–17 The abstract `Cipher` class

```
import java.util.*;

public abstract class Cipher {

    public String encrypt(String s) {
        StringBuffer result = new StringBuffer("");          // Use a StringBuffer
        StringTokenizer words = new StringTokenizer(s);      // Break s into its words
        while (words.hasMoreTokens()) {                      // For each word in s
            result.append(encode(words.nextToken()) + " "); //   Encode it
        }
        return result.toString();                            // Return the result
    } // encrypt()

    public String decrypt(String s) {
        StringBuffer result = new StringBuffer("");          // Use a StringBuffer
        StringTokenizer words = new StringTokenizer(s);      // Break s into words
        while (words.hasMoreTokens()) {                      // For each word in s
            result.append(decode(words.nextToken()) + " "); //  Decode it
        }
        return result.toString();                            // Return the decryption
    } // decrypt()

    public abstract String encode(String word);              // Abstract methods
    public abstract String decode(String word);
} // Cipher
```

encode() and decode() are polymorphic

Note that `encrypt()` and `decrypt()`, which are implemented in `Cipher`, invoke `encode()` and `decode()`, respectively, which are declared in `Cipher` but implemented in `Cipher`'s subclasses. The compiler will take care of invoking the appropriate implementation of `encode()` or `decode()`, depending on what type of object is involved. For example, if `caesar` and `transpose` are `Caesar` and `Transpose` objects, respectively, then the following calls to `encrypt()` will cause their respective `encode()` methods to be invoked:

```
caesar.encrypt("hello world");     // Invokes caesar.encode()
transpose.encrypt("hello world");  // Invokes transpose.encode()
```

Method polymorphism

When `caesar.encrypt()` is called, it will in turn invoke `caesar.encode()` — that is, it will call the `encode()` method implemented in the `Caesar` class. When `transpose.encrypt()` is invoked, it will in turn invoke `transpose.encode()`. In this way each object can perform the encoding algorithm appropriate for its type of cipher.

Algorithm Design: Shifting Characters

The `Caesar` class is defined as an extension of `Cipher` (Figure 7–18). The only methods implemented in `Caesar` are `encode()` and `decode()`. The `encode()` method takes a `String` parameter and returns a `String` result. It takes each character of its parameter (`word.charAt(k)`) and performs a Caesar shift on the character. Note how the shift is done:

Figure 7–18 The Caesar class

```
public class Caesar extends Cipher {
    /**
     * encode(String word) --- iteratively performs a Caesar shift
     *  on word where the shift is fixed at 3.
     *  Pre:  word != NULL
     *  Post: each letter in word has been shifted 3
     */
    public String encode(String word) {
        StringBuffer result = new StringBuffer();       // Initialize a string buffer
        for (int k = 0; k < word.length(); k++) {       // For each character in word
            char ch = word.charAt(k);                   //  Get the character
            ch = (char)('a' + (ch -'a'+ 3) % 26);       //  Perform caesar shift
            result.append(ch);                          //  Append it to new string
        }
        return result.toString();                       // Return the result as a string
    } // encode()

     /**
      * decode(String word) ---  performs a reverse Caesar
      *  shift on word where the shift is fixed at 3.
      * Pre:  word != NULL
      * Post: each letter in word has been shifted by 26-3
      */
     public String decode(String word) {
         StringBuffer result = new StringBuffer();      // Initialize a string buffer
         for (int k = 0; k < word.length(); k++) {      // For each character in word
             char ch = word.charAt(k);                  //  Get the character
             ch = (char)('a' + (ch - 'a' + 23) % 26);   //  Perform reverse caesar shift
             result.append(ch);                         //  Append it to new string
         }
         return result.toString();                      // Return the result as a string
     } // decode()
} // Caesar
```

```
ch = (char)('a' + (ch -'a'+ 3) % 26);  //  Perform Caesar shift
```

Recall from Chapter 5 that `char` data in Java are represented as 16-bit integers. This enables us to manipulate characters as numbers. Thus to shift a character by 3, we simply add 3 to its integer representation.

Character conversions

For example, suppose that the character (`ch`) is 'h,' which has an ASCII code of 104 (ee Table 5–11.) We want to shift it by 3, giving 'k,' which has a code of 107. In this case we could simply add 3 to 104 to get the desired result. However, suppose that `ch` was the character 'y,' which has an ASCII code of 121. If we simply add 3 in this case, we get 124, a code which corresponds to the symbol '|,' which is not our desired result. Instead, we want the shift in this case to "wrap around" to the beginning of the alphabet, so that 'y' gets shifted into 'b.' In order to accomplish this we need to do some modular arithmetic.

Let's suppose the 26 characters 'a' to 'z' were numbered 0 through 25, so that 'a' corresponds to 0, 'b' to 1, and so on up to 'z' to 25. If we take any number *N* and divide it (modulo 26), we would get a number between 0 and 25. Suppose, for example, 'y' were numbered 24. Then shifting it by 3 would give us 27, and `27 % 26` would give us 1, which corresponds to 'b.' So, if the 'a' to 'z' were numbered 0 through 25, then we can shift any character within that range using the formula:

```
(ch + 3) % 26          // Shift by 3 with wraparound
```

To map a character in the range 'a' to 'z' onto the integers 0 to 25, we can simply subtract 'a' from it:

```
'a' - 'a' = 0
'b' - 'a' = 1
'c' - 'a' = 2
...
'z' - 'a' = 25
```

Finally, to complete the shift operation we simply map the number 0 through 25 back to the characters 'a' to 'z':

```
(char)('a' + 0) = 'a'
(char)('a' + 1) = 'b'
(char)('a' + 2) = 'c'
...
(char)('a' + 25) = 'z'
```

Note the use here of the cast operator `(char)` to covert an integer into a `char`.

Modular arithmetic

To summarize, we can shift any character by 3 if we map it into the range 0 to 25, then add 3 to it mod 26, then map that result back into the range 'a' to 'z.' Thus shifting 'y' would go as follows:

```
(char)('a' + (ch -'a'+ 3) % 26)     // Perform Caesar shift
(char)('a' + ('y' - 'a' +3) % 26)   //  on 'y'
(char)(97 + (121 - 97 + 3) % 26)    // Map 'y' to 0..25
(char)(97 + (27 % 26))              // Shift by 3, wrapping around
(char)(97 + 1)                      // Map result back to 'a' to 'z'
(char)(98)                          // Convert from int to char
'b'
```

Note that in `decode()` a reverse Caesar shift is done by shifting by 23, which is 26 – 3. If the original shift is 3, we can reverse that by shifting an additional 23. Together this gives a shift of 26, which will give us back our original string.

Class Design: `Transpose`

The `Transpose` (Figure 7–19) class is structured the same as the `Caesar` class. It implements both the `encode()` and `decode()` methods. The key element here is the transpose operation, which in this case is a simple reversal of the letters in the word. Thus "hello" becomes "olleh." This

Figure 7–19 The Transpose class

```
public class Transpose extends Cipher {
    /**
     * encode(String word) --- reverses the letters in word
     * Pre:  word != NULL
     * Post: the letters in word have been reversed
     */
    public String encode(String word) {
        StringBuffer result = new StringBuffer(word);// Initialize a string buffer
        return result.reverse().toString();         // Reverse and return it
    } // encode()

    /**
     * decode(String word) --- reverses the letters in word by
     *  by just calling encode
     * Pre:  word != NULL
     * Post: the letters in word have been reversed
     */
    public String decode(String word) {
        return encode(word);                     // Just call encode
    } // decode
} // Transpose
```

is very easy to do, using the `StringBuffer.reverse()` method. The `decode()` method is even simpler, so all you need to do in this case is call `encode()`. Reversing the reverse of a string gives you back the original string.

Testing and Debugging

Figure 7–20 provides a simple test program for testing `Cipher` and its subclasses. It creates a `Caesar` cipher and a `Transpose` cipher and then encrypts and decrypts the same sentence using each cipher. If you run this program, it will produce the following output:

Figure 7–20 The TestEncrypt class

```
public class TestEncrypt {
    public static void main(String argv[]) {
        Caesar caesar = new Caesar();
        String plain = "this is the secret message";   // Here's the message
        String secret = caesar.encrypt(plain);          // Encrypt the message
        System.out.println(" ********* Caesar Cipher Encryption *********");
        System.out.println("PlainText: " + plain);    // Display the results
        System.out.println("Encrypted: " + secret);
        System.out.println("Decrypted: " + caesar.decrypt(secret)); // Decrypt

        Transpose transpose = new Transpose();
        secret = transpose.encrypt(plain);
        System.out.println("\n ********* Transpose Cipher Encryption *********");
        System.out.println("PlainText: " + plain);    // Display the results
        System.out.println("Encrypted: " + secret);
        System.out.println("Decrypted: " + transpose.decrypt(secret)); // Decrypt
    } // main()
} // end TestEncrypt
```

```
 ********* Caesar Cipher Encryption *********
PlainText: this is the secret message
Encrypted: wklv lv wkh vhfuhw phvvdjh
Decrypted: this is the secret message

 ********* Transpose Cipher Encryption *********
PlainText: this is the secret message
Encrypted: siht si eht terces egassem
Decrypted: this is the secret message
```

SELF-STUDY EXERCISES

EXERCISE 7.20 Modify the `Caesar` class so that it will allow various sized shifts to be used. (*Hint*: Use an instance variable to represent the shift.)

EXERCISE 7.21 Modify `Transpose.encode()` so that it uses a rotation instead of a reversal. That is, a word like "hello" should be encoded as "ohell" with a rotation of one character.

IN THE LABORATORY: PIG LATIN TRANSLATION

The purpose of this lab is to use some of the methods of the `String` class and to employ basic looping structures in solving a programming problem.

- To introduce the `String` class methods.
- To give practice using simple looping constructs.

Problem Description

Write a Java applet that translates an English sentence or expression into Pig Latin . The rules of Pig Latin are

- If the word begins with a consonant — such as "string," "Latin" — divide the word at the first vowel, swapping the front and back halves and append "ay" to the word — "ingstray," "atinLay."
- If the word begins with a vowel — such as "am," "are," "i" — append "yay" to the word — "amyay," "areyay," "iyay."
- If the word has no vowels (other than 'y') — such as "my," "thy" — append "yay" to it — "myyay," "thyyay."

GUI Specifications

The Graphical User Interface (GUI) for this applet should contain an input `TextField` and an output `TextArea`. The user should be prompted to type a phrase into the `TextField` and the applet should convert the phrase to PigLatin and display the result in the `TextArea`. See Figure 7–21.

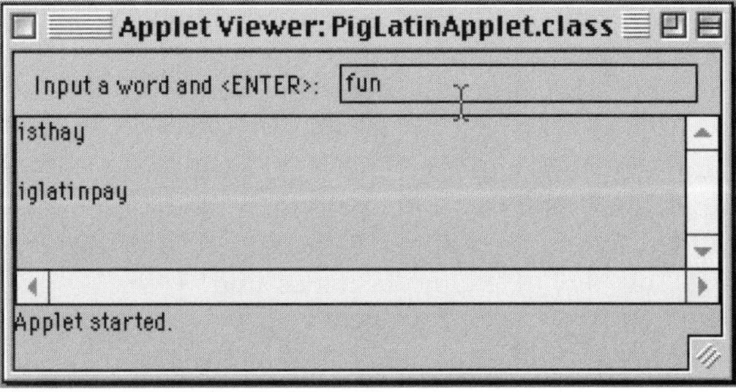

Figure 7–21 The user interface for the Pig Latin applet.

Problem Decomposition

One way to decompose this problem is to divide it into two classes: `PigLatinApplet`, which implements the user interface, and `PigLatin`, which contains the expertise needed to translate English into Pig Latin. `PigLatinApplet` should get the input from the user (in a `TextField`), pass it to `PigLatin`, which will translate it into Pig Latin, and then display the result in the `TextArea`.

The Algorithm

The algorithm for this lab will solve the following problem: Given an English sentence or expression — a string of words separated by blanks — translate the string word by word into Pig Latin. For the sake of simplicity, let's leave off all punctuation symbols. The algorithm should go through the string word by word, and for each word, it should translate it into Pig Latin and concatenate it to the result string. As we know, in order to translate a word into Pig Latin, we must find the location of its first vowel and then follow the above translation rules. This suggests the following algorithm, which could be encapsulated into the `translate()` method:

```
Initialize a result string
For each word in the input string      // String tokenizer task
    translate it into Pig Latin        // translateWord task
    Append it to the result string     // String concatenation task
Return the result string
```

As the comments suggest, this algorithm can be broken up into subtasks. The first subtask is to get each word out of the input string. This is a perfect job for the `StringTokenizer` class discussed earlier. The second subtask is to translate a single word into Pig Latin. This task is substantial enough to be encapsulated into a separate method, the `translateWord()` method. Lastly, string concatenization is easily done by using the "+" operator.

The `translateWord()` Method. To translate a word into Pig Latin, you must find the location of its first vowel ('a,' 'e,' 'i,' 'o,' or 'u') and then apply the above rules. If the word begins with a vowel (or doesn't contain a vowel) you simply append "yay" to the end of the word — "able" becomes "ableyay" and "my" becomes "myyay." Otherwise you divide the word into substrings with the first vowel becoming the first letter of the Pig Latin word and any letters preceding it being appended to the end of the word and followed by "ay" — "string" becomes "ing" + "str" + "ay" or "ingstray."

The `findFirstVowel()` Method. The task of finding the first vowel in a string is also a good candidate for encapsulation into a separate method. It takes an English word as its `String` parameter and returns an `int` giving the index location of the first vowel.

If the word does not contain a vowel — for example, "my" — the method should return 0. For example, `findFirstVowel("hello")` should return 1 as the location of 'e,' and `findFirstVowel("able")` should return 0, and `findFirstVowel("my")` should also return 0. The reason for having it return 0 in two different cases is that in both cases you handle the translation in the same way — "able" becomes "ableyay" and "my" becomes "myyay." In other words, according to the Pig Latin rules, there's no difference between a word that begins with a vowel and one that doesn't contain a vowel.

Problem Design: The PigLatin Class

The above analysis leads to the following specification for the `PigLatin` class. Its main role is to translate English expressions into Pig Latin. One design we could use here is to model `PigLatin` after the `Math` class — that is, as a utility class which provides a useful method, but which is not designed to be instantiated at all.

- Purpose: To translate an English expression into Pig Latin.
- Modifiers: `final`, so it cannot be extended.
- Constructor: `private`, so no instantiation is possible.
- Instance variables: None (no need to store anything).
- Public instance methods: None (no need to have instances).
- Public static method: `translate(String)` translates its `String` parameter into Pig Latin.
- Private static method: `translateWord(String)` translates a single word into PigLatin.
- Private static method: `findFirstVowel(String)` returns the location of the first vowel in its `String` parameter.

As this design suggests, the `PigLatin` class will have only one `public` method but will utilize the `private` methods described above to help perform its task.

Problem Design: PigLatinApplet

The design of `PigLatinApplet` should be similar to that of other applets we've built. It should contain a `TextField` for user input and a `Label` for prompting the user. Note that its interface (Figure 7–21) does not contain a `Button`, so the applet's action events will be generated when the user types the Enter key in the `TextField`. (See the "In the Laboratory" section in Chapter 5.)

`PigLatinApplet` should implement the `ActionListener.actionPerformed()` method to handle `TextField` actions. When the user types Enter, `actionPerformed()` should get the input from the `TextField` and pass it to `PigLatin.translate()`, which will return a (Pig Latin) string. The applet should then append the result to the `TextArea`.

Recall that since we have patterned `PigLatin` after the `Math` class (and `Integer` class), there is no need to instantiate it in order to use its `static` methods. So to translate "Hello World" into Pig Latin we could simply write

```
System.out.println(PigLatin.translate("Hello World"));
```

The `translate()` method is a *class method* — a `static` method that is associated with the class itself.

Implementation

The implementation of this program is left to you as a lab (or programming) exercise. Remember to use stepwise refinement as you develop your program. Also, develop and use appropriate preconditions and postconditions for each of the methods in your program. These will be helpful during design, coding, and testing of your algorithms. For example, the `findFirstVowel()` method would have the following conditions:

```
// findFirstVowel(String s)
// PRE:  s != NULL
// POST: findFirstVowel(s) == 0 If s contains no vowels
//       findFirstVowel(s) == n IF s.charAt(n) is first vowel
```

Optional Refinement

Because it's redundant in Pig Latin to have words like "myyay" that contain "yy," revise your program so that it converts "my" and "why" into "myay" and "whyay" instead of "myyay" and "whyyay." To do this, you could treat English words that end in "y" as a special case in your `translate()` method. Think about what sort of Java expression you would use to determine if a word's last letter is 'y'? What `String` method(s) will you need to form this expression?

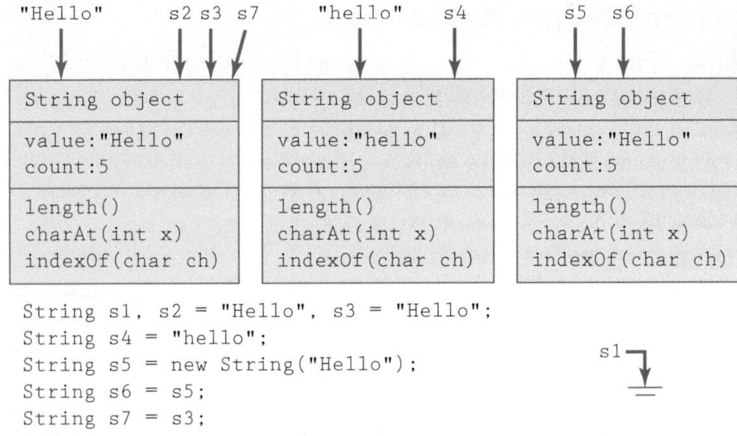

Figure 7–22 Note that *s1* is `null`, because it has not been instantiated and has not been assigned a literal value.

Java Language Summary

New `String` objects can only be created in two ways. First, a `String` object is created automatically by Java the first time it encounters a *literal string*, such as "Socrates," in a program. Subsequent occurrences of the literal do not cause additional objects to be instantiated. Instead, every occurrence of the literal "Socrates" refers to the same object.

Second, a `String` object is created whenever the `new` operator is used in conjunction with a `String()` constructor — for example, `new String("hello")`. Figures 7–4 and 7–22 provide an illustration of this point.

CHAPTER SUMMARY

Technical Terms

ciphertext	concatenation	cryptography
data structure	off-by-one error	orphaned object
plaintext	read only	string literal
substitution cipher	token	transposition cipher
unit indexed	zero indexed	

New Java Keywords

`abstract`	`char`	`final`

Java Library Classes

`ActionEvent`	`ActionListener`	`Button`
`Choice`	`Image`	`IndexOutOfBoundException`
`Integer`	`Math`	`Object`
`StringBuffer`	`StringTokenizer`	`String`
`TextArea`	`TextField`	

Java Library Methods

actionPerformed()	add()	equals()
append()	charAt()	getState()
getCodeBase()	indexOf()	init()
hasMoreTokens()	paint()	length()
insert()	toLowerCase()	repaint()
nextToken()	toUpperCase()	trim()
substring()	addItem()	valueOf()
toString()		

Programmer-Defined Classes

Caesar	Cipher	CyberPetApplet
CyberPet	PetTricksApplet	PigLatinApplet
PigLatin	StringTricks	TestEncrypt
TestEquals	TestStringEquals	Transpose

Programmer-Defined Methods

countChar()	decode()	encode()
encrypt()	findFirstVowel()	isEquals()
getName()	getPassword()	precedes()
isIdentical()	keywordSearch()	reverse()
remove()	removeBlanks()	translate()
toEveryOther()	toUpperCase()	
translateWord()	transpose	

Summary of Important Points

- A `String` literal is a sequence of 0 or more characters enclosed within double quote marks. A `String` object is a sequence of 0 or more characters, plus a variety of class and instance methods and variables.
- The `String` concatenation operator is the overloaded + symbol; it is used to combine two `strings` into a single `String`: "hello" + "world" ==> "helloworld."
- `Strings` are indexed starting at 0. The `indexOf()` and `lastIndexOf()` methods are used for finding the first or last occurrence of a character or substring within a `String`. The `valueOf()` methods are used to convert a nonstring into a `String`. The `length()` method is used to determine the number of characters in a `String`. The `charAt()` method is used to return the single character at a particular index position. The various `substring()` methods are used to return the substring at particular index positions in a `String`.
- The overloaded `equals()` method returns true if two `Strings` contain the same exact sequence of characters. The == operator, when used on `Strings`, returns true if two references designate the same `String`.

- A `StringTokenizer` is an object that can be used to break a `String` into a collection of *tokens* separated by *delimiters*. The whitespace characters, — tabs, blanks, and newlines — are the default delimiters.
- An `abstract` class is one that contains one or more `abstract` methods, which are methods that lack a method body or an implementation. An `abstract` class can be subclassed by not instantiated.

ANSWERS TO SELF-STUDY EXERCISES

EXERCISE 7.1 a. silly b. silly c. silly stuff

EXERCISE 7.2 a. `String str1 = "";` b. `String str2 = new String("stop");` c. `String str3 = str1 + str2;`

EXERCISE 7.3 a. 15 b. "551" c. "5175"

EXERCISE 7.4 See Figure 7–22.

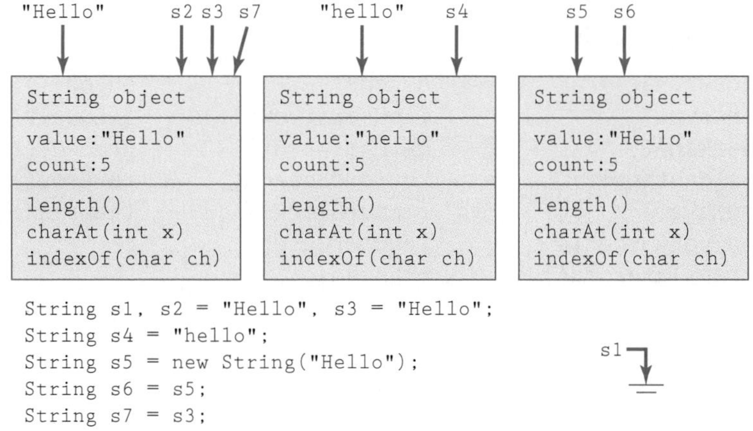

Figure 7–22 Answer to Exercise 7.4. Note that *s1* is `null`, because it has not been instantiated and has not been assigned a literal value.

EXERCISE 7.5 a. "45" b. "121" c. "X"

EXERCISE 7.6 a. `String.valueOf(100)` b. `String.valueOf( 'V' );` c. `String s = new String( String.valueOf( X * Y ));`

EXERCISE 7.7 a. 0 b. 1 c. −1

EXERCISE 7.8 a. 16 b. "16" c. 1 d. 15 e. 1 f. 13 g. 7 h. 3 i. 7 j. 8 k. 3

EXERCISE 7.9 Evaluate the following expression:

```
String tricky = "abcdefg01234567";
tricky.indexOf( String.valueOf( tricky.indexOf("c")));
tricky.indexOf( String.valueOf( 2 ));
tricky.indexOf( "2");
Answer: 9
```

EXERCISE 7.10 a. "uvwxyz" b. "bcdef" c. "xyz" d. "xyz" e. "xyz"

EXERCISE 7.11 a. "uvwxyz" b. "bcde" c. "xyz" d. "xyz" e. "xyz"

EXERCISE 7.12 Changes necessary to `CyberPet` class

```
public static final int TRICKING = 2;              // New state
private StringTricks tricks = new StringTricks(); // New bag of tricks

public String trick(String s) {                   // New instance method
    petState = TRICKING;
    return tricks.getNextTrick(s);
} // trick()

public String getState() {              // Revised method
    if (petState == EATING)
        return "Eating";
    else if (petState == SLEEPING)
        return "Sleeping";
    else if (petState == TRICKING)      // Here
        return "Tricking";
    else
        return "Error in State";
} // getState()
```

EXERCISE 7.13 Changes required in `AnimatedCyberPet` applet:

```
private Label nameLabel = new Label(
      "Hi! Type a string into the text field and "
      + "I'll do a trick with it.");                // Revised prompt
private TextField field = new TextField(30);        // New component

// Changes in init() method
  add(field);                                   // Add the new TextField
  field.addActionListener(this);                // Give it an ActionListener

// Modified ActionPerformed() Method
public void actionPerformed( ActionEvent e ) {
    if (e.getSource() == eat)
        pet.eat();
    else if (e.getSource() == sleep)
        pet.sleep();
    else if (e.getSource() == field) {            // Perform a trick
        String s = pet.trick(field.getText());    // With the string in the TextField
        field.setText(s);                         // Show the result in the TextField
    }
}
```

EXERCISE 7.14 Method to remove all blanks from a string:

```
// Pre: s is a non null string
// Post: s is returned with all its blanks removed
public String removeBlanks( String s ) {
  StringBuffer result = new StringBuffer();
  for ( int k = 0; k < s.length();  k++ )
    if (s.charAt(k) != ' ')            // If this is not a blank
      result.append( s.charAt(k) ); //  append it to result
  return result.toString();
}
```

EXERCISE 7.15 A Alpha a alpha bath bin Z Zero Zeroes z zero

EXERCISE 7.16 To modify `precedes` so that it also returns true when its two string arguments are equal, just change the first character comparison to:

```
if (s1.charAt(k) <= s2.charAt(k) )
  return true;
```

EXERCISE 7.17 a. true b. true c. false d. false e. false f. true g. false h. false i. false

EXERCISE 7.18 The variables in `TestStringEquals` are declared `static` because they are used in `static` methods. Whenever you call a method directly from `main()` it must be `static` because `main()` is static. Remember that `static` elements are associated with the class, not with its instances. So `main()` can only use static elements, because they don't depend on the existence of instances.

EXERCISE 7.19

```
a. String s3 = s1.substring( s1.indexOf('n'))
              + s1.substring(0,s1.indexOf('m'));
b. String s4 = s2.substring( 6 ) + " " + s2.substring(0,4);
c. String s5 = s2.substring( 0,4 ) + s1.substring(0,2);
```

EXERCISE 7.20 Modify the `Caesar` class so that it will allow various sized shifts to be used.

```
private int Shift;                                    // Caesar shift
public void setShift( int n ) { Shift = n;    }
public int getShift()         { return Shift; }
// Modification to encode():
ch = (char)( 'a' + (ch -'a'+ Shift) % 26 );         //  Perform caesar shift
// Modification to decode():
ch = (char)( 'a' + (ch -'a'+ (26-Shift)) % 26 ); //  perform caesar shift
```

EXERCISE 7.21 Modify `Transpose.encode()` so that it uses a rotation instead of a reversal. The operation here is very similar to the shift operation in the Caesar cipher. Use modular arithmetic with k and the length of the word:

```
// Modification to encode():
result = result + word.charAt((k+2)%len);  // Rotate the word by 2
```

EXERCISES

1. Explain the difference between the following pairs of terms.
   a. *Ciphertext* and *plaintext*.
   b. *Unit indexing* and *zero indexing*.
   c. *Substitution cipher* and *transposition cipher*.
   d. *Data structure* and *data type*.
   e. `StringBuffer` and `String`.
   f. `String` and `StringTokenizer`.
   g. *Declaring a variable* and *instantiating a* `String`.
   h. *Abstract method* and *stub method*.

2. Fill in the blanks.

   a. The fact that the first character in a string has index 0 is known as _______.
   b. A method that contains no body — no implementation — is known as an _______ method.
   c. If a class contains methods that have no bodies, the class must be declared _______.
   d. A bunch of characters enclosed within quotes is known as a _______.
   e. A Caesar cipher is an example of a _______ cipher.

3. Given the `String` *str* with the value "to be or not to be that is the question," write Java expressions to extract each of the following substrings. Provide two sets of answers. One that uses the actual index numbers of the substrings — for example, the first "to" goes from 0 to 2 — and the second that will retrieve the same substring from the following string "it is easy to become what you want to become." (*Hint*: In the second case, use `length()` and `indexOf()` along with `substring()` in your expressions. If necessary, you may use local variables to store intermediate results. The answer to (a) is provided as an example.)

   a. `the first "to" in the string`

   ```
   ANSI: str.substring(0, 2)
   ANS2: (str.indexOf("to"),
          str.indexOf("to") + 2)
   ```

   b. `the last "to" in the string`
   c. `the first "be" in the string`
   d. `the last "be" in the string`
   e. `the first four characters in the string`
   f. `the last four characters in the string`

4. Identify the syntax errors in each of the following: Assume that the `String s` equals "exercise."

   a. `s.charAt("hello")`
   b. `s.indexOf(10)`
   c. `s.substring("er")`
   d. `s.lastIndexOf(er)`
   e. `s.length`

5. Evaluate each of the following expressions assuming that the `String s` equals "exercise."

   a. `s.charAt(5)`
   b. `s.indexOf("er")`
   c. `s.substring(5)`
   d. `s.lastIndexOf('e')`
   e. `s.length()`

6. Write your own `equalsIgnoreCase()` method using only other `String` methods.
7. Write your own `String` equality method without using `String.equals()`. (*Hint*: Modify the `precedes()` method.)
8. Write a method for the `StringTricks` class that takes a `String` argument and returns a `String` result which is the lowercase version of the original string.

9. Implement a method that uses the following variation of the Caesar cipher. The method should take two parameters, a `String` and an `int` N. The result should be a `String` in which the first letter is shifted by N, the second by $N+1$, the third by $N+2$, and so on. For example, given the string "Hello", and an initial shift of 1, your method should return "Igopt".
10. **Challenge:** Imagine a Caesar cipher that uses the letters of a keyword to determine the shift of each letter in the plaintext. For example, suppose we choose the word "ace" as the keyword. You could also think of "ace" in terms of how many places each of its letters is shifted from the letter 'a.' Thus 'a' is shifted by 0, 'c' is shifted by 2, and 'e' is shifted by 4. So given this keyword, the first letter of the plaintext would be shifted by 0, the second by 2, the third by 4, the fourth by 0, and so on. For example,

```
key:        acea ce a ceacea ceaceac
plaintext:  this is a secret message
shift:      0240 24 0 240240 2402402
ciphertext: tjms jw a uictit oisuegg
```

Write a method to implement this cipher. The method should take two `String` arguments: the string to be encrypted and the keyword.
11. One way to make it more difficult to decipher a secret message is to destroy the word boundaries. For example, consider the following two versions of the same sentence:

```
Plaintext:    This is how we would ordinarily write a sentence.
Blocked text: Thisi showw ewoul dordi naril ywrit easen tence.
```

Write a method that converts its `String` parameter so that letters are written in blocks five characters long.
12. Design and implement an applet that lets the user type a document into a `TextArea`, and then provides the following analysis of the document: The number of words in the document, the number of characters in the document, and the percentage of words that have more than six letters.
13. Design and write an applet that searches for single-digit numbers in a text and changes them to their corresponding words. For example, the string "4 score and 7 years ago" would be converted into "four score and seven years ago."
14. A palindrome is a string that is spelled the same way backwards and forwards. For example, *mom, dad, radar, 727* and *able was i ere i saw elba* are all examples of palindromes. Write a Java applet that lets the user type in a word or phrase, and then determines whether the string is a palindrome.
15. Suppose you're writing a maze program and are using a string to store a representation of the maze. For example, consider the following string and the corresponding maze:

```
String: XX_XXXXXXXX__XXX_XXXX_XX___XXX_XX_XX_XXX___XXXXXXXXX_X

Maze:
    XX XXXXXXX
    X  XXX XXX
    X XX    XX
    X XX XX XX
    X   X
    XXXXXXXX X
```

Write a method that accepts such a string as a parameter and prints a two-dimensional representation of the maze.

16. Write a method that takes a delimited string, which stores a name and address, and prints a mailing label. For example, if the string contains "Sam Penn:14 Bridge St.:Hoboken:NJ:01881", the method should print

```
Sam Penn
14 Bridge St.
Hoboken, NJ 01881
```

17. Design and implement a `Cipher` subclass to implement the following substitution cipher: each letter in the alphabet is replaced with a letter from the opposite end of the alphabet: 'a' is replaced with 'z,' 'b' with 'y,' and so forth.
18. One way to design a substitution alphabet for a cipher is to use keyword to construct the alphabet. For example, suppose the keyword is "zebra." You place the keyword at the beginning of the alphabet, and then fill out the other 21 slots with remaining letters, giving the following alphabet:

```
Cipher alphabet:   zebracdfghijklmnopqstuvwxy
Plain alphabet:    abcdefghijklmnopqrstuvwxyz
```

Design and implement an `Alphabet` class for constructing these kinds of substitution alphabets. It should have a single public method that takes a keyword `String` as an argument and returns an alphabet string. Note that an alphabet cannot contain duplicate letters, so repeated letters would have to be removed a keyword like "xylophone".

19. Design and write a `Cipher` subclass for a substitution cipher that uses an alphabet from the `Alphabet` class created in the previous exercise.
20. Design and implement an applet that plays Time Bomb with the user. Here's how the game works. The computer picks a secret word and then prints one asterisk for each letter in the word: * * * * *. The user guesses at the letters in the word. For every correct guess, an asterisk is replaced by a letter: * e * * *. For every incorrect guess, the time bomb's fuse grows shorter. When the fuse disappears, after say six incorrect guesses, the bomb explodes. Store the secret words in a delimited string and invent your own representation for the time bomb.
21. **Challenge:** A common string processing algorithm is the global replace function found in every word processor. Write a method that takes three `String` arguments: a document, a target string, and a replacement string. The method should replace every occurrence of the target string in the document with the replacement string. For example, if the document is "To be or not to be, that is the question" and the target string is "be" and the replacement string is "see," the result should be "To see or not to see, that is the question."
22. **Challenge:** Design and implement an applet that plays the following game with the user. Let the user pick a letter between 'A' and 'Z.' Then let the computer guess the secret letter. For every guess the player has to tell the computer whether it's too high or too low. The computer should be able to guess the letter within five guesses. Do you see why?
23. **Challenge:** Find a partner and concoct your own encryption scheme. Then work separately with one partner writing `encode()` and the other writing `decode()`. Test to see that a message can be encoded and then decoded to yield the original message.

24. **Challenge:** A *list* is a sequential data structure. Design a List class which uses a comma-delimited String — such as, "a,b,c,d,12,dog" — to implement a list. Implement the following methods for this class:

```
void addItem( Object o );        // Use Object.toString()
String getItem(int position);
String toString();
void deleteItem(int position);
void deleteItem(String item);
int getPosition(String item);
String getHead();                    // First element
List getTail();                      // All but the first element
int length();                        // Number of items
```

25. **Challenge:** Use a delimited string to create a PhoneList class with an instance method to insert names and phone numbers, and a method to look up a phone number given a person's name. Since your class will take care of looking things up, you don't have to worry about keeping the list in alphabetical order. For example, the following string could be used as such a directory:

```
mom:860-192-9876::bill g:654-0987-1234::mary lancelot:123-842-1100
```

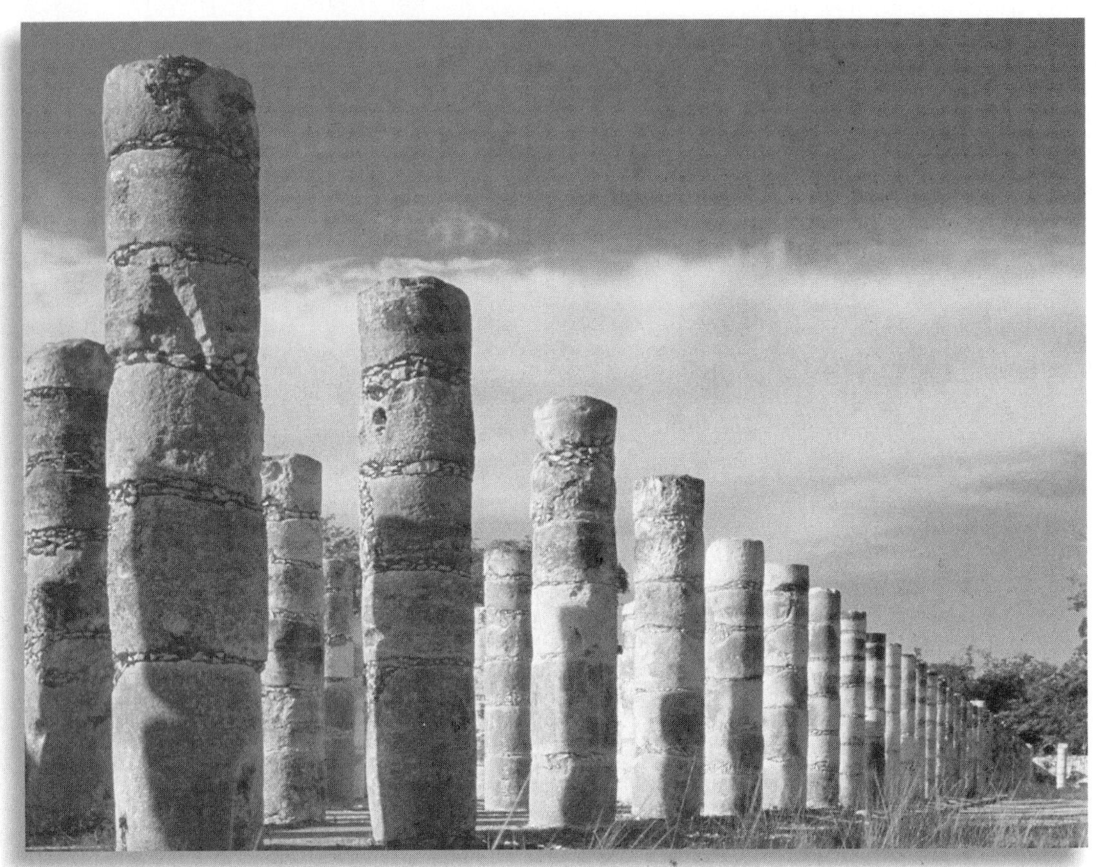

Photograph courtesy of Adalberto Rios, PhotoDisc, Inc.

Arrays and Array Processing

8

CHAPTER OBJECTIVES

After studying this chapter, you will

- Know how to use array data structures.
- Be able to solve problems that require collections of data.
- Know how to sort an array of data.
- Be familiar with sequential and binary search algorithms.
- Have a better understanding of inheritance and polymorphism.

OUTLINE

8.1 Introduction

In this chapter we'll learn about arrays. An **array** is a named collection of contiguous storage locations — storage locations that are next to each other — that contain data items of the same type.

Arrays offer a more streamlined way to store data than using individual data items for each variable. You can also work with data stored in arrays more efficiently than with individual variables.

Let's see why. Suppose you want to animate CyberPet. The usual way to do this is to create a sequence of images, each of which shows the pet in a slightly different position. These images can then be loaded into memory. We can give the illusion of motion by displaying each image in turn, with a short delay between one image and the next. The delay should be long enough to allow each separate image to be seen, but short enough to blur the transition between one image and the next.

If the number of images is large, it would be inconvenient to create separate variables for each image, because each storage location would require a unique identifier. For example, if our animation used ten images, we would need ten identifiers:

```
Image image1;
Image image2;
.
.
.
Image image10;
```

and to load each image into memory we would need ten `getImage()` statements:

```
image1 = getImage(getDocumentBase(), "image1.gif");
image2 = getImage(getDocumentBase(), "image2.gif");
.
.
.
image10 = getImage(getDocumentBase(), "image10.gif");
```

To display each image for a brief instant, we would need ten `drawImage()` statements. And we would need ten `wait(DELAY)` statements to create a brief delay before the next image is displayed.

```
g.drawImage(image1, 1, 1, this);  wait(DELAY);
g.drawImage(image2, 1, 1, this);  wait(DELAY);
.
.
.
g.drawImage(image10, 1, 1, this);  wait(DELAY);
```

This approach is tedious. Think how much harder it would be if our animation consisted of 100 images or a 1000.

What we need is some way use a loop to load and display the images, using a loop counter, *k*, to refer to the *k*th image on each iteration of the loop. The *array* data structure lets us do that.

Our discussions of arrays begins by showing how to store and retrieve data from one-, two- and three-dimensional arrays. Among the array processing algorithms we study are sorting and searching algorithms. Finally, we illustrate how arrays can be used in a variety of applications, including an animation problem, a sorting class, and a card playing program.

8.2 One-Dimensional Arrays

The array data structure

An array is a named collection of contiguous storage locations that contain data items of the same type. Each element of the array is referred to by its position within the array. If the array is named `arr`, then the elements are named `arr[0], arr[1], arr[2], ..., arr[n-1]`, where *n* gives the number of elements in the array. In Java, as in C, C++, and some other programming languages, the first element of an array has index 0. (This is the same convention we used for `Strings`.)

Zero indexing

Figure 8–1 shows an array named `arr` which contains 15 `int` elements. The syntax for referring to elements of an array is

arrayname [*subscript*]

where *arrayname* is the name of the array — any valid identifier will do — and **subscript** is the position of the element within the array. As Figure 8–1 shows, the first element in the array has subscript 0, the second has subscript 1, and so on.

Subscript expressions

An array subscript must be either an integer value or an integer expression. For example, suppose that *j* and *k* are integer variables equaling 5 and 7, respectively. Each of the following then would be valid references to elements of the array *arr*:

```
arr[4]          Refers to 16
arr[j]          Is arr[5] which refers to 20
arr[j + k]      Is arr[5+7] which is arr[12] which refers to 45
arr[k % j]      Is arr[7%5] which is arr[2] which refers to -1
```

As these examples show, when an expression is used as a subscript, it is evaluated before the reference is made.

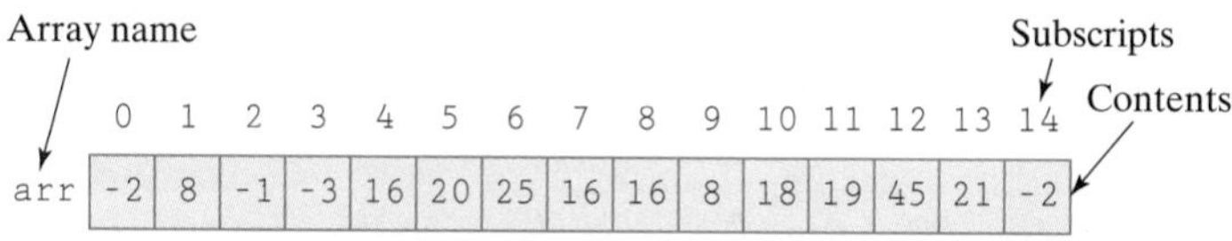

Figure 8–1 An array of 15 integers named `arr`.

It is a syntax error to use a noninteger type as an array subscript. Each of the following expressions would be invalid:

```
arr[5.0]        // 5.0 is a float and can't be an array subscript
arr['5']        // '5' is a character not an integer
arr["5"]        // "5" is a string not an integer
```

For a given array, a valid array subscript must be in the range `0 ... N-1`, where `N` is the number of elements in the array. It is a semantic error to use a subscript whose value is not in this range. This is a runtime error — that is, an error that occurs when the program is running — rather than a syntax error which can be detected when the program is compiled. For the array `arr`, each of the following would lead to runtime errors:

```
arr[-1]         // Arrays cannot have negative subscripts
arr[15]         // The last element of arr has subscript 14
arr[j*k]        // Since j*k equals 35
```

Each of these references would lead to an `IndexOutOfBoundsException`, which means that the subscript in each case refers to an element that is not within the *bounds* of the array. (*Exceptions* are covered in detail in Chapter 11.)

JAVA LANGUAGE RULE **Array Subscripts.** Array subscripts must be integer values in the range `0...(N-1)`, where *N* is the number of elements in the array.

DEBUGGING TIP: Array Subscripts. In developing array algorithms it's important to design test data that show that array subscripts do not cause runtime errors.

8.2.1 Declaring and Creating Arrays

Are arrays objects?

In Java, arrays are (mostly) treated as objects. They are instantiated with the `new` operator. They have instance variables (for example, `length`). Array variables are *reference* variables. When arrays are used as parameters, a reference to the array is passed rather than the entire array. The primary difference between arrays and full-fledged objects is that arrays don't belong to an `Array` class. There is no such thing. Thus arrays don't fit neatly into Java's `Object` hierarchy. They don't inherit any properties from `Object` and they can't be subclassed.

An array contains a number of variables. An *empty* array is one that contains zero variables. As we've seen, the variables contained in an array object are not referenced by name but by their relative position in the array. The variables are called *components*. If an array object has *N* components, then we say that the **length** of the array is *N*. Each of the components of the array has the same type, which is called the array's *component type*.

A **one-dimensional** array has components that are called the array's **elements** . Their type is the array's **element type**. An array's elements may be of any type, including primitive and reference types. So you can have arrays of `int, char, boolean, String, Object, Image, TextField, CyberPet` and so on.

Components and elements

When declaring a one-dimensional array, you have to indicate both the array's element type and its length. Just as in declaring and creating other kinds of objects, creating an array object requires that we create both a name for the array and then the array itself. The following statements create the array shown in Figure 8–1:

```
int arr[];              // Declare a name for the array
arr = new int[15];      // Create the array itself
```

These two steps can be combined into a single statement as follows:

```
int arr[] = new int[15];
```

In this example, the array's element type is `int` and its `length` is 15. This means that the array contains 15 variables of type `int`, which will be referred to as `arr[0], arr[1], ..., arr[14]`.

8.2.2 Array Allocation

Creating an array, in this case, means allocating 15 storage locations that can store integers. Note that one difference between declaring an array and declaring some other kind of object is that square brackets (`[]`) are used to indicate that an array type is being declared. The brackets can be attached either to the array's name or to its type as in the following examples:

```
int arr[];             // The brackets may follow the array's name
int[] arr;             // The brackets may follow the array's type
```

The following example creates an array of five `Strings` and then uses a for loop to assign the strings `"hello1", "hello2", "hello3", "hello4"` and `"hello5"` to the five array locations.

```
String strarr[];                              // Declare a name for the array
strarr = new String[5];                       // Create the array itself
                                              // Assign strings to the array
for (int k = 0; k < strarr.length; k++)       // For each array element
    strarr[k] = new String("hello" + k + 1); //  Assign it a new string
```

Note that the expression `k < strarr.length` is used to specify the loop bound. Each array has a `length` instance variable which refers to the number of elements contained in the array. Arrays, like `Strings`, are zero indexed, so the last element of the array is always given by its `length - 1`. However, unlike for `Strings`, where `length()` is an instance method, for arrays, `length` is an instance variable. It would be a syntax error in this example to refer to `strarr.length()`.

`length` *vs.* `length()`

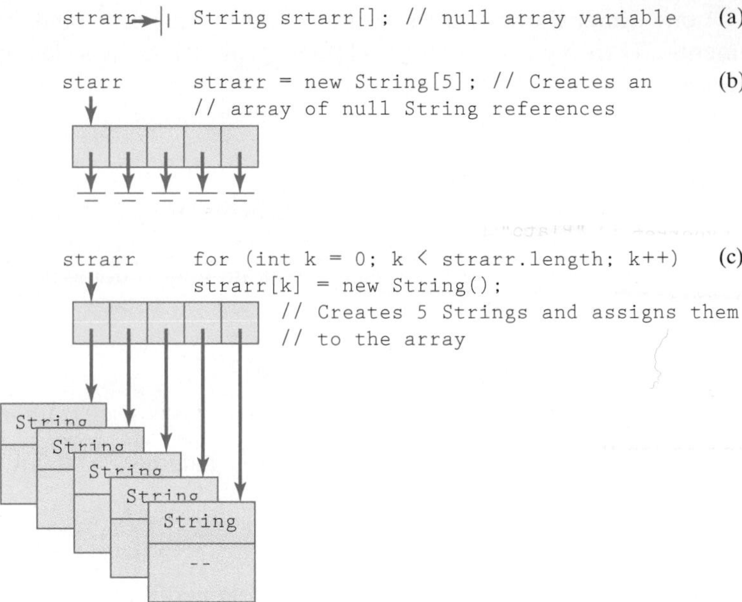

Figure 8–2 Creating an array of five `Strings` involves six objects, because the array itself is a separate object. In (a), the array variable is declared. In (b) the array is instantiated, creating an array of five `null` references. In (c), the five `Strings` are created and assigned to the array.

DEBUGGING TIP: Array Length. A common syntax error involves forgetting that for arrays, `length` is an instance variable, not an instance method, as it is for `Strings`.

In this example, once the array `strarr` is created, a `String` constructor is used to create the five `Strings` that are stored in the array. It is important to realize that creating an array to store five `Objects` (as opposed to five primitive data elements) does not also create the `Objects` themselves that will be stored in the array.

Arrays of objects

When an `array` of objects is created, the array's elements are references to those objects (Figure 8–2). Their initial values, like all reference variables, are `null`. So to create and *initialize* the array `strarr`, we need to create *six* objects — the array itself, which is like a container, and then the five `Strings` that are stored in `strarr`.

One more example will help underscore this point. The following statements create four *new* `Objects`, an array to store three `CyberPets` plus the three `CyberPets` themselves:

```
CyberPet pethouse[] = new CyberPet[3];   // Create an array of 3 CyberPets
pethouse[0] = new CyberPet("Socrates");  // Create the first CyberPet
pethouse[1] = new CyberPet("Plato");     // Create the second CyberPet
pethouse[2] = new CyberPet("Aristotle"); // Create the third CyberPet
```

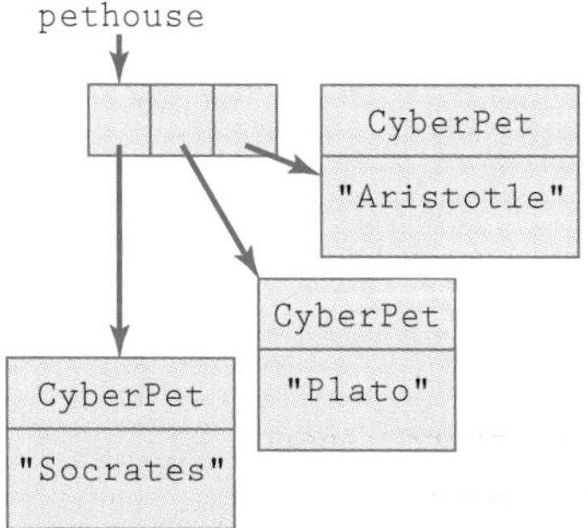

Figure 8–3 An array of CyberPets.

The first statement creates an array named `pethouse` to store three `CyberPets`, and the next three statements create the individual `CyberPets` and assign them to the array (Figure 8–3). Thus creating the array and initializing its elements requires four `new` statements.

DEBUGGING TIP: Array Instantiation. Creating a new `array` does not also create the objects that are stored in the array. They must be instantiated separately. It is a semantic error to refer to an uninstantiated (`null`) array element.

Now that we've assigned the three `CyberPets` to the array, we can refer to them by means of subscripted references. A reference to the `CyberPet` named "Socrates" is now `pethouse[0]`, and a reference to the `CyberPet` named "Plato" is `pethouse[1]`. In other words, to refer to the three individual pets we must refer to their locations within `pethouse`. Of course, we can also use variables, such as loop counters, to refer to a `CyberPet`'s location within `pethouse`. The following for loop invokes each `CyberPet`'s `getState()` method to print out its current state:

```
for (int k = 0; k < pethouse.length; k++)
    System.out.println(pethouse[k].getState());
```

What if the three `CyberPets` already existed before the array was created? In that case we could just assign their references to the array elements, as in the following example:

```
CyberPet pet1 = new CyberPet("Socrates"); // Existing CyberPets
CyberPet pet2 = new CyberPet("Plato");
CyberPet pet3 = new CyberPet("Aristotle");
CyberPet pets = new CyberPet[3];                   // Array
pets[0] = pet1;
pets[1] = pet2;
pets[2] = pet3;
```

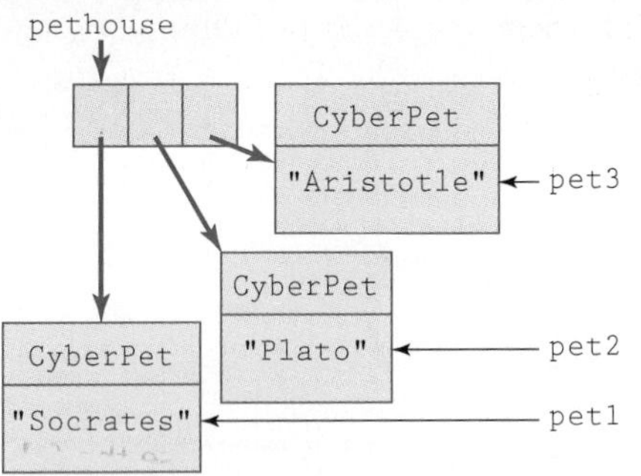

Figure 8–4 Arrays of objects store references to the objects, not the objects themselves.

In this case, each of the three `CyberPet` objects can be referenced by two different references — its variable identifier (such as `pet1`) and its array location (such as `pets[0]`). For arrays of objects, Java stores just the reference to the object in the array itself, rather than the entire object. This conserves memory, since references require only 4 bytes each whereas each object may require hundreds of bytes (Figure 8–4).

How much memory?

Thus, when an array of *N* elements is created, the compiler *allocates* storage for *N* variables of the element's type. In the case of `intarr`, above, the compiler would allocate storage for 15 `ints` — 60 contiguous bytes of storage, because each `int` requires 4 bytes (32 bits) of storage. If we declare an array of 20 `doubles`,

```
double arr[] = new double[20];
```

the compiler will allocate 160 bytes of storage — 20 variables of 8 bytes (64 bits) each. In the case of the `CyberPet` examples and `String` examples, because these are objects (not primitive types) the compiler will allocate space for *N* addresses, where *N* is the length of the array.

SELF-STUDY EXERCISES

EXERCISE 8.1 How much space (in bytes) would be allocated for each of the following?

```
(a) int a[] = new int[5];
(b) double b[] = new double[10];
(c) char c[] = new char[30];
(d) String s[] = new String[10];
(e) CyberPet p[] = new CyberPet[5];
```

8.2.3 Initializing Arrays

Array elements are automatically initialized to default values that depend on the element type: Boolean elements are initialized to `false`. Integer and real types are initialized to 0. Reference types — that is, arrays of objects — are initialized to `null`.

Arrays can also be assigned initial values when they are created, although this is feasible only for relatively small arrays. An **array initializer** is written as a list of expressions separated by commas and enclosed by braces. For example, we can declare and initialize the array shown in Figure 8–1 with the following statement:

```
int arr[] = {-2,8,-1,-3,16,20,25,16,16,8,18,19,45,21,-2};
```

Similarly, to create and initialize an array of `Strings` we can use the following statement:

```
String strings[] = {"hello", "world", "goodbye", "love"};
```

This example creates and stores four `Strings` in the array. Subsequently, to refer to "hello," we would use the reference `strings[0]` and to refer to "love," we would use the reference `strings[3]`. Note in these examples that when an array declaration contains an initializer, it is not necessary to use `new` and it is not necessary to specify the number of elements in the array. The number of elements is determined from the number of values in the initializer list.

8.2.4 Assigning and Using Array Values

Array assignment

Array elements can be used in the same way as other variables. The only difference, of course, is that references to the elements are subscripted. For example, the following assignment statements assign values to the elements of two arrays, `arr` and `strings`:

```
arr[0] = 5;
arr[5] = 10;
arr[2] = 3;
strings[0] = "who";
strings[1] = "what";
strings[2] = strings[3] = "where";
```

The following loop assigns the first 15 squares — `1, 4, 9` ... — to the array `arr`:

```
for (int k = 0; k < arr.length; k++)
    arr[k] = (k+1) * (k+1);
```

The following loop prints the values of the array `arr`:

```
for (int k = 0; k < arr.length; k++)
    System.out.println(arr[k]);
```

SELF-STUDY EXERCISES

EXERCISE 8.2 Declare an array named `farr` that contains ten `floats` initialized to the values `1.0, 2.0, ..., 10.0`.

EXERCISE 8.3 Write an expression that prints the first element of `farr`.

EXERCISE 8.4 Write an assignment statement that assigns 100.0 to the last element in `farr`.

EXERCISE 8.5 Write a loop to print all of the elements of `farr`.

8.3 Simple Array Examples

Maintainability Principle

The program in Figure 8–5 creates two arrays of ten elements each and displays their values on the Java console. In this example the elements of `intArr` have not been given initial values whereas the elements of `realArr` have been initialized. Note the use of the integer constant `ARRSIZE` to store the arrays' size. By using the constant in this way we do not have to use the literal value `10` anywhere in the program, thereby making it easier to modify the program. If we want to change the size of the array that the program handles, we can just change the value of `ARRSIZE`. This is an example of the Maintainability Principle .

Figure 8–5 A program that displays two arrays.

```
public class PrintArrays {
    static final int ARRSIZE = 10;                       // The array's size

    static int intArr[] = new int[ARRSIZE];              // Create the int array
    static double realArr[] = { 1.1, 2.2, 3.3, 4.4,
         5.5, 6.6, 7.7, 8.8, 9.9, 10.10 };               // And a double array

    public static void main(String args[]) {
        System.out.println("Ints \t Reals");     // Print a heading
        for (int k = 0; k < intArr.length; k++) // For each int and float element
            System.out.println( intArr[k] + " \t " + realArr[k]); // Print them
    } // main()
} // PrintArrays

                &&&&&&&&& PROGRAM OUTPUT &&&&&&&&&
                 Ints           Reals
                 0               1.1
                 0               2.2
                 0               3.3
                 0               4.4
                 0               5.5
                 0               6.6
                 0               7.7
                 0               8.8
                 0               9.9
                 0               10.1
                &&&&&&&&&&&&&&&&&&&&&&&&&&&&&&&&&&&
```

For large arrays, it is not always feasible to initialize them in an initializer statement. Consider the problem of initializing an array with the squares of the first 100 integers. Not only would it be tedious to set these values in an initializer statement, it would also be error prone, since it is relatively easy to type in the wrong value for one or more of the squares.

Array initializers

DEBUGGING TIP: Array Initialization. Initializer statements should be used only for relatively small arrays.

The example in Figure 8–6 creates an array of 100 integers and then fills the elements with the values 1, 4, 9, 16, and so on. It then prints the entire array.

This example illustrates a couple of important points about the use of array variables. The array's elements are individual storage locations. In this example, `intArr` has 100 storage locations. Storing a value in one of these variables is done by an assignment statement:

```
intArr[k] = (k+1) * (k+1);
```

Figure 8–6 A array which stores the squares of the first 100 integers.

```
public class Squares {
    static final int ARRSIZE = 100;              // The array's size
    static int intArr[] = new int[ARRSIZE];      // Create an int array

    public static void main(String args[]) {
        for (int k = 0; k < intArr.length; k++)  // Initialize the array
            intArr[k] = (k+1) * (k+1);

        System.out.print("The first 100 squares are"); // Print a heading
        for (int k = 0; k < intArr.length; k++) {      // Print the array
            if (k % 10 == 0)
                System.out.println(" ");               // 10 elements per row
            System.out.print( intArr[k] + " ");
        } // for
    } // main()
} // Squares

          &&&&&&&&&&&&&&&&&&&&& PROGRAM OUTPUT &&&&&&&&&&&&&&&&&&&
           The first 100 squares are
           1 4 9 16 25 36 49 64 81 100
           121 144 169 196 225 256 289 324 361 400
           441 484 529 576 625 676 729 784 841 900
           961 1024 1089 1156 1225 1296 1369 1444 1521 1600
           1681 1764 1849 1936 2025 2116 2209 2304 2401 2500
           2601 2704 2809 2916 3025 3136 3249 3364 3481 3600
           3721 3844 3969 4096 4225 4356 4489 4624 4761 4900
           5041 5184 5329 5476 5625 5776 5929 6084 6241 6400
           6561 6724 6889 7056 7225 7396 7569 7744 7921 8100
           8281 8464 8649 8836 9025 9216 9409 9604 9801 10000
          &&&&&&&&&&&&&&&&&&&&&&&&&&&&&&&&&&&&&&&&&&&&&&&&&&&&&&
```

Zero vs. unit indexing

The use of the variable *k* in this assignment statement allows us to vary the location that is assigned on each iteration of the for loop. Note that in this example *k* occurs as the array index on the left-hand side of this expression, while *k+1* occurs on the right-hand side as the value to be squared. The reason for this is that arrays are indexed starting at 0 but we want our table of squares to begin with the square of 1. So the square of some number *n+1* will always be stored in the array whose index is one less that the number itself — that is, *n*.

An array's `length` variable can always be used as a loop bound when iterating through all elements of the array:

```
for (int k = 0; k < intArr.length; k++)
    intArr[k] = (k+1) * (k+1);
```

Off-by-One error

However, it is important to note that the last element in the array is always at location `length-1`. Attempting to refer to `intArr[length]` would cause an `IndexOutOfBoundsException` because no such element exists.

DEBUGGING TIP: Off-by-One Error. Because of zero indexing, the last element in an array is always `length-1`. Forgetting this fact can cause an off-by-one error.

SELF-STUDY EXERCISES

EXERCISE 8.6 Declare an array of 100 `double`s and write a loop to assign the first 100 square roots to its elements. [Use `Math.sqrt(double)`.]

8.4 Example: Testing a Die

Suppose you're writing a computer game that uses the roll of a six-side die to determine (randomly) which player goes next. Of course, you want the die to be fair. If there are six players, then each player should get a turn approximately one-sixth of the time. If you were using a real die, rather than a computer simulation, this is the behavior you would expect.

8.4.1 Generating Random Numbers

In computer games a special method, called a **random number generator**, is used to generate random numbers, which can then be used to simulate things such as a die or a coin toss. Java's `Math.random()` method is such a method. Each time you call this method, it will generate a random value in the range [0, 1) that is, from 0 to 0.99999999. The value 1.0 is not included in the range. Within this range the numbers are fairly evenly distributed: If we generated 1000 values, there would be roughly the same number of values occurring in the interval 0 to 0.1 as in the interval 0.2 to 0.3.

Actually, the numbers generated by `Math.random()` are not truly random. Given the same first number—the same *seed* value—`Math.random()` will generate the same sequence of numbers every time. Like truly random numbers, pseudorandom numbers have certain desirable characteristics, such as being uniformly distributed over their given range, but they are generated in a nonrandom way. That's why, strictly speaking, these numbers are called **pseudorandom numbers**. However, as long as you understand that these numbers are not truly random, we'll refer to them, in most contexts, simply as random numbers.

Pseudorandom numbers

Random number generators are used in a variety of applications, including simulations and games. For example, a flight simulator would use random numbers to simulate events that occur during flight. Epidemiologists use random numbers to study the spread of a disease. In computer games, random numbers are used to simulate the rolling of dice, flipping of a coin, and a variety of other random or chance events.

`Math.random()` is a method that takes no parameters and generates a `double` value in the range [0.0,1.0):

```
0.0 <= Math.random() < 1.0
```

To illustrate its use, let's use `Math.random()` to simulate a fair coin flip. One way to do this is to multiply `Math.random()` by 2 and convert the result to an `int`:

```
int coinFlip = (int)(Math.random() * 2);    // Heads or tails
```

Multiplying `Math.random()` by 2 will produce a value in the range [0,1.99999). Examples of possible values include 0.0, 0.111, 0.999, 1.001, 1.504, and 1.998. If we convert these values to `int`, we will get 0, 0, 0, 1, 1, 1 — that is, three 0s and three 1's. If we let the 0's represent heads and the 1's represent tails, these numbers can be used to represent a coin flip . Thus, assuming that `Math.random()` generates numbers evenly distributed over the range [0,1), we can expect that our "coin flip" will come up heads approximately half the time.

The process of multiplying `Math.random()` by 2 is known as **scaling** and takes the following general form:

Scaling factor

```
(int)(Math.random() * N)
```

In general, the above expression will produce *N* integer values in the range `[0, N-1]`. *N* is called the *scaling factor*. In the fair coin example, the scaling factor was 2 and two integer values were produced in the range [0,1].

To simulate rolling a die , we would need six values in the range 1 to 6. The following expression will generate six values in the range 0 to 5:

```
int die = (int)(Math.random() * 6);
```

Note the placement of the parentheses in this expression. The entire expression (Math.random() *6) must be cast into an int, so it is necessary to surround it with parentheses.

Scaling and shifting

If we want to *shift* the values into the range 1 to 6, we can simply add 1 to this expression:

```
int die = 1 + (int)(Math.random() * 6);
```

The variable die now has an equal chance of being set to one of the values 1, 2, 3, 4, 5, or 6, thus simulating the tossing of a fair die. In general, then, the Java expression we use for generating a set of N random integer values in the range M to $M + N - 1$ is

```
M + (int)(Math.random() * N)
```

SELF-STUDY EXERCISES

EXERCISE 8.7 Write a Java expression that generates random integers in the range 0 through 10.

EXERCISE 8.8 Write a Java expression that generates random integers in the range 2 through 12.

EXERCISE 8.9 Suppose you are simulating a card game in which you represent cards by two integer values, a suit and a rank. For example, the 2 of clubs has clubs as its suit and 2 as its rank. The ace of diamonds has diamonds as its suit and 14 as its rank. Write Java statements to assign random values to suit and rank.

EXERCISE 8.10 Let's give our CyberPet a mind of its own. Modify CyberPet.eat() and CyberPet.sleep() so that a CyberPet will eat and sleep on command only half the time. [*Hint*: Test the value that random() gives you. If it's above 0.5, have the pet obey the command. Otherwise, have the petulant pet just ignore the command (see Figure 5–8.)]

8.4.2 The Die Testing Experiment

Problem statement

Now that we understand how to use Math.random(), let's conduct an experiment to test how good it is — that is, to test how random its values are. To do so, let's create a simple die tossing simulation that will use Math.random() to simulate a die with six faces. We will repeatedly "toss" the die and count the number of times it comes up 1, 2, 3, 4, 5, and 6. If it's a fair die — if the random number generator produces nicely distributed values — we would expect to get roughly the same number of 1's, 2's,

3's, 4's, 5's, and 6's over a period of 1000 or 10,000 die tosses. That is, the frequencies of the six outcomes should be roughly equal to one-sixth.

In order to keep track of the six frequencies, we will need six distinct counters. To represent the counters, let's use a six-element `int` array. The elements will store the frequencies of the die rolls. Initially we will need to set each counter to 0. We can declare, create, and initialize our counters with the following statement:

What data do we need?

```
int counter[] = {0,0,0,0,0,0} ;
```

Note that it is not necessary to initialize the contents of the array. Java will automatically initialize all numeric elements to zero when the array is created with `new`. We do it in this case to show how initialization can be done, and also to make the program somewhat more readable.

Readability

After each die toss, the appropriate counter will incremented. Because the value of the die will be in the range 1 to 6, we can use the following statement, where `die` represents the die roll, to increment the counter that corresponds to the die's face value:

```
++counter[die - 1];
```

The reason we use the expression `die-1` as the array subscript here is that die's values will range from 1 to 6, but the `counter`'s subscripts range from 0 to 5. In general, the frequency of a die toss of n, where n is between 1 and 6, will be stored in `counter[n-1]`.

Our experiment should simply toss the die a given number of times, keeping track of the frequencies. It should then report the respective frequencies. Let's break this up into two methods: one to perform the die tosses, and the other to report the results.

What methods do we need?

Design: The `testDie()` *Method*

The `testDie()` method should take a single `int` parameter, giving the number of trials to run. It should then run through the trials, keeping track of the frequencies. Let's assume that the array of counters has already been properly initialized. We can then use a simple counting loop to iterate through the trials, generating a random number from 1 to 6 on each trial, and updating the appropriate counter:

Algorithm: counting loop

```
/**
 * Pre: counter[] array has been initialized
 *      and nTrials, the number of trials, is >= 0.
 * Post: the frequencies of nTrials die rolls will be recorded in counter[]
 */
public void testDie(int nTrials) {
    int die;                                    // Represents the die
    for (int k = 0; k < nTrials; k++) {         // For each trial
        die = 1 + (int)(Math.random() * NFACES); // Toss the die
        ++counter[die - 1];                     // Update the appropriate counter
    } // for
} //testDie()
```

This method assumes that the array of counters is an instance variable of the class. Therefore, there's no need to pass it as a parameter.

Method Design: The `printResults()` *Method*

Algorithm: counting loop

After we have run our experiment for a given number of trials, we can print the result by printing the values of each of the six `counters`. The `printResults()` method uses a simple for loop to print the count of each counter:

```
/**
 * Pre: counter[] array has been initialized and nTrials >= 0
 * Post: the value of each counter is printed
 */
public void printResults(int nTrials) {
    System.out.println("Out of " + nTrials + " die rolls, there were: ");
    for (int k = 1; k <= NFACES; k++)
        System.out.println("    " + counter[k-1] + " " + k + "s");
} // printResults()
```

Zero vs. unit indexing

Note that we have given this method an `nTrials` parameter, so that it can report the number of die rolls in the experiment. Note here again the array subscript we use is `k-1`, because we want to print the value of each die as 1 to 6, but our counters are indexed from 0 to 5. The complete source code for this simulation is shown in Figure 8–7. One run of this program on 6000 trials generated the following output:

```
Out of 6000 die rolls, there were:
    981 1s     998 2s     1024 3s     956 4s     1008 5s     1033 6s
```

As you can see, the results are fairly evenly distributed, with each face coming up approximately one-sixth of the time.

The problem of keeping track of the frequencies of die rolls turns out to be a perfect use for an array. Overall the use of arrays in this example makes the code compact and easy to read and understand. Imagine how difficult this problem would be if we could not use arrays. In that case we would need six distinct `int` counters and we have would to refer to each one by name rather than by index, and we would have to use individual assignment statements rather than a for loop to update them. That would surely lead to some tedious code.

EFFECTIVE DESIGN: Representation+Action. Arrays can be processed effectively with counting loops to solve a wide range of problems.

SELF-STUDY EXERCISES

EXERCISE 8.11 It might be argued that one shortcoming with the design of the `TestRandom` class is that it uses a class constant, `NFACES`, to specify the number of faces on the die, but it doesn't use this value to instantiate

Figure 8–7 Using arrays to store frequencies of die tosses.

```
public class TestRandom {
    public static final int NTRIALS = 6000;      // Number of experimental trials
    private final int NFACES = 6;                // Number of faces on the die
    private int counter[] = { 0,0,0,0,0,0 } ;    // The six counters

    /**
     * Pre: counter[] array has been initialized
     *      and nTrials, the number of trials, is >= 0.
     * Post: the frequencies of nTrials die rolls will be recorded in counter[]
     */
    public void testDie(int nTrials) {
        int die;                                         // Represents the die
        for (int k = 0; k < nTrials; k++) {              // For each trial
            die = 1 + (int)(Math.random() * NFACES);     // Toss the die
            ++counter[die - 1];                          // Update the appropriate counter
        } // for
    } //testDie()

    /**
     * Pre: counter[] array has been initialized and nTrials >= 0
     * Post: the value of each counter is printed
     */
    public void printResults(int nTrials) {
        System.out.println("Out of " + nTrials + " die rolls, there were: ");
        for (int k = 1; k <= NFACES; k++)
            System.out.println("    " + counter[k-1] + " " + k + "s");
    } // printResults()

    public static void main(String args[]) {
        TestRandom tester = new TestRandom();
        tester.testDie(NTRIALS);
        tester.printResults(NTRIALS);
    } // main()
} // TestRandom
```

the array. So you couldn't run this experiment on a 12-sided die, unless you change not only `NFACES` but also the way the array is initialized. Let's remedy this shortcoming. Use `NFACES` in the instantiation of `counters[]` and write a separate method to be added to `TestRandom` that can be used to initialize the array of counters no matter how many faces the die has.

8.5 CASE STUDY: `CyberPet` Animation

Let's return to the problem of making CyberPet move. In this case, we need an array to store the images that will be used in the animation.

What data do we need?

```
Image image[] = new Image[NIMAGES]; // Create the array
```

Note again that the above statement creates an array to store `Images`, but it does *not* create the images themselves. In order to create an `Image` object for each array location, we use a simple for loop:

```
for (int k = 0; k < image.length; k++)  // Create the images
    image[k] = new Image();              // And store in the array
```

In this example, `Image`'s default constructor is used to create an `Image` for each array element. A *GIF* file is a common type of graphics file format, widely used to represent images on the WWW. (See the section on *Data Compression* for more on GIF files.) Another way to create images for the array would be to read them from gif files using the `java.applet.Applet.getImage()` method:

GIF files

```
for (int k = 0; k < image.length; k++)
    image[k] = getImage(getCodeBase(), "image" + k + ".gif");
```

`getImage()` takes two arguments: the location of the applet (the code base) and the name of the file containing the image. In this example the file name is constructed by concatenating a base file name (`"image"`) with a number (*k*) and the `".gif"` suffix. This will generate file names such as `"image1.gif"` and `"image2.gif."` Assuming these files are stored in the same directory as the applet (the code base), the images will be loaded into the program and stored in the `image` array.

Constructing file names

PROGRAMMING TIP: Image Loading. Depending on the number and size of the images, the process of loading images may take considerable time. It is good interface design to inform the user whenever this delay will be noticeable.

Algorithm Design: Animation

Once the images are stored in the array, they can be displayed using Java's `Graphics.drawImage()` method:

```
for (int k = 0; k < image.length; k++) {
    g.drawImage(image[k], 1, 1, this);
    wait(DELAY);
}
```

Drawing images

The `drawImage()` method takes four arguments. The first is a reference to the image, which in our example is a reference to the *k*th array element. The second and third arguments give the horizontal and vertical coordinates at which the image will be displayed. The last argument provides a reference to the applet in which the image will be displayed.

To illustrate these principles, let's create a simple animation of our `CyberPet`. The animation will cycle through the five images shown in Figure 8–8, which are named "spider1.gif" through "spider5.gif" and stored in the same directory as the applet. The applet loads these images into an array and then repeatedly cycles through the array until the user quits the applet.

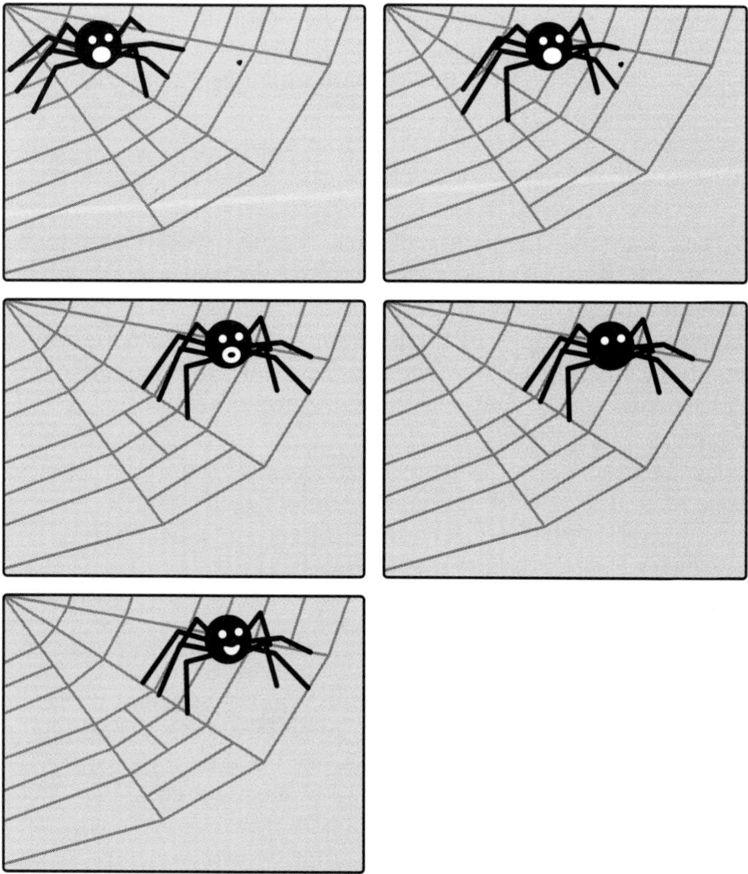

Figure 8–8 The five images used to animate Spidey.

The `init()` method loads the image files into the `image` array:

```
public void init() {
    showStatus("Loading image files.  Please wait.");
    for (int k = 0; k < image.length; k++) // Read each image from file to array
        image[k] = getImage(getDocumentBase(), "spider" + k + ".gif");
} // init()
```

The `paint()` method repeatedly displays an image and then delays for 200 milliseconds. This delay is necessary to prevent the images from flashing by so quickly that the illusion of motion is lost.

```
public void paint(Graphics g) {
    g.drawImage(image[imageN], 1, 1, this);  // Draw an image
    imageN = (imageN + 1) % NIMAGES;         // Select the next image
    delay(MILLISECS);                        // Delay for a while
    repaint();                               // Then do it all over again
} // paint()
```

It begins by drawing one of the images from the `image` array. The variable `imageN` is set to current image. It then updates `imageN` to the value of the next image to be displayed. Note the use of modular arithmetic here:

```
imageN = (imageN + 1) % NIMAGES;
```

Because `NIMAGES` is 5, this statement will cause `imageN` to take on the values 0 through 4. When `imageN` equals 4, adding 1 modulo 5 will give 0, thereby causing `imageN` to wrap around to 0.

Repainting the applet

Recall that the `paint()` method is called automatically when the applet begins execution. Note the call to `repaint()` on the last line of `paint()`. This will cause the cycle of drawing and delaying to be repeated indefinitely.

Delaying the animation

The `delay()` method is a private method that causes the applet to pause for *n* milliseconds. It causes the applet to sleep for *n* milliseconds. We will discuss how it works when we talk about threads in Chapter 13. The complete `Animate.java` program is shown in Figure 8–9.

Data Compression

The *Graphical Interchange Format (GIF)* was developed by CompuServe, the commercial online service provider, as a way for transferring digital images over networked computers. GIF files transfer 8-bit digital images — that is images in which 8 bits are used to represent each pixel. This means that it is limited to images that contain at most $256 = 2^8$ colors.

LZW algorithm

GIF files are compressed using an algorithm known as Lempel-Ziv-Welch compression, or LZW for short. This is an algorithm that recognizes common string patterns. Instead of representing each separate character in a file, LZW encoding represents each string pattern as a bit pattern. For example, suppose the file consisted of the following sentence, which we depict here as an array of characters, with the array indexes of the first ten characters written above the string:

```
0123456789              // Indexes
the theory is that...   // String to compress
```

This sentence can be also represented as follows:

```
the [0,3]ory[3,1]is[3,1][0,2]a[0,1]
```

The first four characters contain no repeats so they are listed verbatim. However, the string "the" repeats the three letters that started at index 0. Instead of repeating "the," we insert the notation [0,3], which means "insert the three characters starting at index 0." The other bracketed expressions perform similar insertions.

Even though this example did not achieve any real compression, significant compression would result if we had a longer file. On average a typical text file is reduced by 50 percent by LZW compression. It is used in common commercial compression programs, such as Stuffit and Zipit.

Figure 8–9 The Animate applet.

```
import java.applet.Applet;                    // Import the applet library
import java.awt.*;                            // Import the GUI components

public class Animate extends Applet {
    private static int NIMAGES = 5;
    private static int MILLISECS = 200;

    private Image image[] = new Image[NIMAGES];
    private int imageN = 0;

    public void init() {
        showStatus("Loading image files.  Please wait.");
        for (int k = 0; k < image.length; k++)      // Read each image from file to array
            image[k] = getImage(getDocumentBase(), "spider" + k + ".gif");
    } // init()

    public void paint(Graphics g) {
        g.drawImage(image[imageN], 1, 1, this);  // Draw an image
        imageN = (imageN + 1) % NIMAGES;         // Select the next image
        delay(MILLISECS);                        // Delay for a while
        repaint();                               // Then do it all over again
    } // paint()

    private void delay(int n) {      // Private helper method
        try {
            Thread.sleep( n );                 // Pause the applet for n milliseconds
        } catch (InterruptedException e) {
            System.out.println(e.toString());
        }
    } // delay()
} // Animate
```

8.6 Array Algorithms: Sorting

Sorting an array is the process of arranging its elements in ascending or descending order. Sorting algorithms are among the most widely used algorithms. Any time large amounts of data are maintained, there is some need to arrange them in a particular order. For example, the telephone company needs to arrange its accounts by the last name of the account holder as well as by phone number.

8.6.1 Bubble Sort

The first sorting algorithm we'll look at is known as **bubble sort**, so named because on each pass through the array the algorithm causes the largest element to "bubble up" toward the "top" of the array, much as the bubbles in a carbonated drink. A second sorting, **selection sort** is covered in Section 8.6.3.

Bubble sort requires repeated passes over the unsorted array, but it sorts the elements *in place*, which means that it doesn't require any additional memory to store the sorted elements. In pseudocode, bubble sort can be represented as follows:

```
Bubble sort an array of N elements into ascending order
1. For each of the N-1 passes over the entire array
2.   For each of the N-1 pairs of adjacent elements in the array
3.     If the lower indexed element is greater than the higher indexed element
4.        Swap the two elements
```

To see how this works, consider an integer array containing the ages of five friends:

```
21  20  27  24  19
```

For this five-element array, bubble sort will make four passes, comparing each pair of adjacent elements (step 3), swapping elements that are out of order (step 4). Because 21 and 20 are out of order, they are swapped, leading to the following arrangement of the array. The brackets are used to highlight where we are in the trace:

```
[20  21]  27  24  19
```

The next pair of elements, 21 and 27, are in the correct order so the array will remain unchanged. The next pair of elements, 27 and 24, are swapped, giving

```
20  21  [24  27]  19
```

The last pair, 27 and 19, will be swapped, giving

```
20  21  24  [19  27]
```

The result of the first pass over the array is that the largest element, 27, has "bubbled up" to the top of the array. After the second pass through the array, the second largest element, 24, will bubble up to its proper place in the array, giving

```
20  21  19 | 24  27
```

In effect, the numbers to the right of the vertical line are in their proper locations. On the next pass the third largest element will find its proper location giving

```
20  19 | 21  24  27
```

Finally, on the fourth pass, the fourth and fifth largest elements will be arranged in their proper locations. When the algorithm terminates, all of the array elements will have been placed in their proper locations:

```
| 19  20  21  24  27
```

Figure 8–10 The `Sort` class contains the `bubbleSort()` method. Note how the method is passed an integer array, which is declared in the `main()` method.

```
public class Sort {

    /**
     * Goal: Sort the values in arr into ascending order
     * Pre: arr is not null.
     * Post: The values arr[0]...arr[arr.length-1] will be
     *  arranged in ascending order.
     */
    public void bubbleSort(int arr[]) {
        int temp;                              // Temporary variable for swap
        for (int pass = 1; pass < arr.length; pass++)      // For each pass
            for (int pair = 1; pair < arr.length; pair++)  // For each pair
                if (arr[pair-1] > arr[pair]) {             //   Compare
                    temp = arr[pair-1];                    //   and swap
                    arr[pair-1] = arr[pair];
                    arr[pair] = temp;
                } // if
    } // bubbleSort()

    public void print(int arr[]) {
        for (int k = 0; k < arr.length; k++)       // For each integer
            System.out.print( arr[k] + " \t ");    //  Print it
        System.out.println();
    } // print()

    public static void main(String args[]) {
        int intArr[] = { 21, 20, 27, 24, 19 };
        Sort sorter = new Sort();
        sorter.print(intArr);
        sorter.bubbleSort(intArr);
        sorter.print(intArr);
    } // main()
} //Sort
```

Note that for a five-element array, each pass requires that we compare 4 pairs of adjacent elements. In general, for an N element array, we would have to compare $N - 1$ pairs of adjacent elements on each pass through the array. Also on each pass one array element will bubble up to its proper location in the sorted array. Thus to sort an N element array, bubble sort will make $N - 1$ passes, comparing $N - 1$ adjacent elements on each pass.

$N - 1$ passes

Figure 8–10 translates the above pseudocode into a Java method. Because it takes an `int` array as a parameter, the `bubbleSort()` method will sort any array of integers, regardless of the array's length. Note how bracket notation (`[]`) is used to declare an array parameter . If the brackets were omitted, then `arr` would be indistinguishable form an ordinary `int` parameter. Using the brackets indicates that this method takes an array of integers as its parameter.

Array parameters

DEBUGGING TIP: Array Parameter. When declaring an array parameter, it is necessary to use brackets after the array name; otherwise Java will think you're passing a simple data value rather than an array of values.

8.6.2 Algorithm: Swapping Memory Elements

Swapping blunder

A second important feature of this method is its use of the `int` variable `temp` to store one of the two array elements that are being swapped. The need for this variable is a subtlety that beginning programmers frequently overlook, but consider what would happen if `temp` were not used. Suppose that `arr[pair-1]` refers to 4 and `arr[pair]` refers to 2 in the following array:

```
1 4 2 8
```

and suppose in an attempt to swap 4 and 2 we execute the following two assignment statements:

```
arr[pair-1] = arr[pair];
arr[pair] = arr[pair-1];
```

Because the first assignment statement places 2 in the location that was holding 4, both locations will now be holding 2. The 4 will be overwritten and will no longer be available in the second assignment statement. Thus the result of these two statements is

```
1 2 2 8
```

Swapping algorithm

The proper way to swap the two elements is to use a temporary variable to store the first element while its location is overwritten and then retrieve the stored value from the temporary variable and assign it to the second element:

```
temp = arr[pair-1];      // Save first element in temp
arr[pair-1] = arr[pair]; // Overwrite first with second
arr[pair] = temp;        // Overwrite second from temp (i.e.,first)
```

This code will lead to the result we want—that is, to 4 and 2 being swapped in the array:

```
1 2 4 8
```

In general, the following method implements the swap algorithm for two elements, *el1* and *el2* of an `int` array.

```
/**
 * Goal: Swap el1 and el2 in the int array, arr
 * Pre: arr is not null and el1 and el2 refer to indexes
 *  between 0 and arr.length - 1
 * Post: The values arr[el1] and arr[el2] will be swapped.
 */
void swap(int arr[], int el1, int el2) {
    int temp = arr[el1];  //  Assign the first element to temp
    arr[el1] = arr[el2];  //  Overwrite first with second
    arr[el2] = temp;      //  Overwrite second with temp (i.e., first)
} // swap()
```

PROGRAMMING TIP: Swapping Variables. Whenever you are swapping two memory elements, a temporary variable must be used to store one of the elements while its memory location is being overwritten.

8.6.3 Selection Sort

To illustrate the *selection sort* algorithm, suppose you want to sort a deck of 52 cards. Cards are arranged in order of face value, 2 through 10, jack, queen, king, ace. And suits are arranged according to clubs, diamonds, hearts, and spades, so the first card in the deck will be the two of clubs, and the last card will be the ace of spades.

Selection sort algorithm

Lay the 52 cards out on a table, face up, one card next to the other. Then starting with the first card, look through the deck and find the smallest card (the two of clubs), and exchange it with the card in the first location. Then go through the deck again starting at the second card, find the next smallest card (the three of clubs) and exchange it with the card in the second location. Repeat this process 51 times.

Translating this strategy into pseudocode gives the following algorithm:

```
Selection sort of a deck of 52 cards from small to large
1. For count assigned 1 to 51                         // Outer loop
2.   smallestCard = count
3.   For currentCard assigned count+1 to 52           // Inner loop
4.     If deck[currentCard] < deck[smallestCard]
5.        smallestCard = currentCard
6.   If smallestCard != count                         // You need to swap
7       Swap deck[count] and deck[smallestCard]
```

For a deck of 52 cards, you need to repeat the outer-loop 51 times. In other words, you must select the smallest card and insert it in its proper location 51 times. The inner loop takes care of finding the smallest remaining card.

On each iteration of this outer loop, the algorithm assumes that the card specified by the outer loop variable, `count`, is the smallest card (line 2). (It usually won't be, of course, but we have to start somewhere.)

The inner loop then iterates through the remaining cards (from `count+1` to 52) and compares each one with the card that is currently the smallest (lines 4 and 5). Whenever it finds a card that is smaller than the smallest card, it designates it as the smallest card so far (line 5). In effect the `smallestCard` variable is used to remember where the smallest card is in the deck.

Finally, when the inner loop is finished, the algorithm swaps the smallest card with the card in the location designated by `count`. Don't forget that in order to swap to memory elements (line 6), you need to use a temporary variable.

The implementation of the selection sort method, as part of the `Deck` class, is left as a lab exercise or programming assignment.

SELF-STUDY EXERCISES

EXERCISE 8.12 Sort the array, 24 18 90 1 0 85 34 18, by hand using bubble sort. Show the order of the elements after each iteration of the outer loop.

EXERCISE 8.13 Sort the array, 24 18 90 1 0 85 34 18, by hand using selection sort. Show the order of the elements after each iteration of the outer loop.

EXERCISE 8.14 Write a Java code segment to swap two `CyberPets`, `pet1` and `pet2`.

EXERCISE 8.15 The `bubbleSort()` in this section will keep passing over the array even if it's already sorted. Modify the algorithm so that it stops when the array is sorted. (*Hint*: Use a `boolean` variable to keep track of whether a swap was made inside the loop, and check this variable in the loop entry condition.)

8.6.4 Passing Array Parameters

When an array is passed to a method, as in `bubbleSort()`, only the name of the array should be specified in the method call statement. For example, suppose we have declared an array of integers as follows:

```
int arr[] = { 21, 13, 5, 10, 14, 6, 2 };
```

To sort this array we would use the following method call:

```
bubbleSort(arr); // Correct way to pass an array to a method
```

It would be incorrect to use the following statement as a method call:

```
bubbleSort(arr[]); // Syntax error --- brackets aren't allowed
```

DEBUGGING TIP: Passing an Array Argument. A common syntax error is to use brackets when passing an array argument. In passing an array to a method, just use the name of the array. Brackets are only used in the method definition, not in the method call.

Pass by Value and Pass by Reference

Recall from Section 3.5 that when an `Object` is passed to a method, a copy of the reference to the `Object` is passed. Because an array is an `Object`, a reference to the array is passed to `bubbleSort()` rather than the whole array itself. This is in contrast to how a value of a primitive type is passed. In that case a copy of the actual value is passed.

JAVA LANGUAGE RULE **Primitive versus Object Parameters.** In Java, when a value of a primitive data type — `int, double, char, boolean` — is passed as a parameter , a copy of the value itself is passed; when a reference to an `Object` is passed, a copy of the reference is passed.

One implication of this distinction is that when the argument is a primitive type, the original argument cannot be changed within the method, because the method just has a copy of its value. For example, the following method takes a single `int` parameter *n*, which is incremented within the method:

```
public void add1(int n) {
    System.out.println("n = " + n);
    n = n + 1;
    System.out.println("n = " + n);
}
```

Passing a primitive value

But because *n* is a parameter of primitive type, incrementing it within the method has no effect on its associated argument. Thus in the following segment the value of *Num*—*n*'s associated argument—will not be affected by what goes on inside the `add()` method:

```
int Num = 5;
System.out.println("Num = " + Num);
add1(Num);
System.out.println("Num = " + Num);
```

and the output generated by this code segment would be:

```
Num = 5
n = 5
n = 6
Num = 5
```

Passing an object

Note that while *n*'s value has changed, *Num*'s value remains unaffected.

The case is much different when we pass a reference to an object. In that case, the method *can* manipulate the object itself. The `bubbleSort()` method is a good illustration. In the following code segment, the array `anArr` is printed, then sorted, and then printed again:

```
int anArr[] = { 5, 10, 16, -2, 4, 6, 1 };  // Initialize

for (int k = 0; k < an_arr.length; k++)    // Print
    System.out.print(an_arr[k] + " ");

System.out.println("");
bubbleSort(an_arr);                         // Sort

for (int k = 0; k < an_arr.length; k++)    // Print again
    System.out.print(an_arr[k] + " ");
```

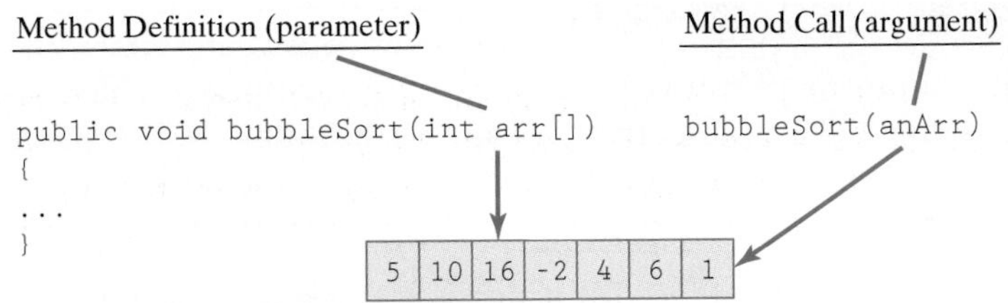

Figure 8–11 When an array is passed to a method as an argument, both the array reference itself and the corresponding method parameter are references to the same object.

The output generated by this code would be the following:

```
5 10 16 -2 4 6 1
-2 1 4 5 6 10 16
```

which illustrates that changes within `bubbleSort` to the array referenced by `arr` are actually being made to `anArr` itself. If fact, because `bubbleSort()` is passed a copy of the reference variable `anArr`, both `arr` and `anArr` are references to the very same object — that is, to the same array (Figure 8–11).

Method call overhead

The justification for passing a reference to an object rather than the entire object itself is a matter of efficiency. A reference uses just 4 bytes of data, whereas an object may use thousands of bytes. It would just be too inefficient to copy hundreds of bytes each time an object is passed to a method. Instead, the method is passed a reference to the object, thereby giving it access to the object without incurring the expense of copying large amounts of data.

SELF-STUDY EXERCISES

EXERCISE 8.16 What values will be stored in `myArr` and `k` AFTER you invoke `mystery(myArr, k)`, where `myArr`, `k` and `mystery()` are declared as follows:

```
int myArr[] = {1,2,3,4,5};
int k = 3;
void mystery(int a[], int m) {
    ++a[m];
    --m;
}
```

8.7 Array Algorithms: Searching

Suppose we have a large array and we need to find one of its elements. We need an algorithm to search the array for a particular value, usually called the *key*. If the elements of the array are not arranged in any particular order, the only way we can be sure to find the key, assuming it is in the array, is to search every element, beginning at the first element, until we find it.

8.7.1 Sequential Search

This approach is known as **sequential search**, because each element of the array will be examined in sequence until the key is found (or the end of the array is reached). A pseudocode description of this algorithm is as follows:

```
For each element of the array
    If the element equals the key
        Return the element's index
If the key is not found in the array
    Return -1 (to indicate failure)
```

This algorithm can easily be implemented in a method that searches an integer array, which is passed as the method's parameter. If the key is found in the array, its location is returned. If it is not found, then −1 is returned to indicate failure.

Figure 8–12 shows the Java implementation of the `sequentialSearch()` method. The method takes two parameters: the array to be searched and the key to be searched for. It uses a for statement to examine each element of the array, checking whether it equals the key or not. If an element that equals the key is found, the method immediately returns that element's index. Note that the last statement in the method will only be reached if no element matching the key is found.

EFFECTIVE DESIGN: Sentinel Return Value. Like Java's `indexOf()` method, the `sequentialSearch()` returns a sentinel value (−1) to indicate that the key was not found. This is a common design for search methods.

8.7.2 Binary Search

If the elements of an array have been sorted into ascending or descending order, it is not necessary to search sequentially through each element of the array in order to find or not find the key. Instead, the search algorithm can make use of the knowledge that the array is ordered, and perform what's known as a **binary search**, a divide-and-conquer algorithm that divides the array in half on each iteration and limits its search to just that half that could contain the key.

To illustrate the binary search, recall the familiar guessing game in which you try to guess a secret number between 1 and 100, being told "too high" or "too low" or "just right" on each guess. A good first guess should be 50. If this is too high, the next guess should be 25, because if 50 is too high the number must be between 1 and 49. If 50 was too low, the next guess should be 75. And so on. After each wrong guess, a good guesser should pick the midpoint of the sublist that would contain the secret number.

Figure 8–12 The `Search` class contains both a `sequentialSearch()` and a `binarySearch()`.

```
public class Search {

    /**
     * Performs a sequential search of an integer array
     * @param arr is the array of integers
     * @param key is the element being searched for
     * @return the key's index is returned if the key is
     *  found otherwise -1 is returned
     * Pre:  arr is not null
     * Post: either -1 or the key's index is returned
     */
    public int sequentialSearch(int arr[], int key) {
        for (int k = 0; k < arr.length; k++)
            if (arr[k] == key)
                return k;
        return -1;              // Failure if this is reached
    } // sequentialSearch()

    /**
     * Performs a binary search of an integer array
     * @param arr is the array of integers
     * @param key is the element being searched for
     * @return the key's index is returned if the key is
     *  found otherwise -1 is returned
     * Pre: arr is an array of int in ascending order
     * Post: -1 or arr[k] where arr[k] == key
     */
    public int binarySearch(int arr[], int key) {
        int low = 0;                             // Initialize bounds
        int high = arr.length - 1;
        while (low <= high) {                    // While not done
            int mid = (low + high) / 2;
            if (arr[mid] == key)
                return mid;                      // Success
            else if (arr[mid] < key)
                low = mid + 1;                   // Search top half
            else
                high = mid - 1;                  // Search bottom half
        } // while
        return -1;    // Post condition: low > high implies search failed
    } // binarySearch()
}//Search
```

How many guesses?

Proceeding in this way, the correct number can be guessed in at most $\log_2 N$ guesses, because the base–2 logarithm of N is the number of times you can divide N in half. For a list of 100 items, the search should take no more than seven guesses ($2^7 = 128 > 100$). For a list of 1000 items, a binary search would take at most ten guesses ($2^{10} = 1024 > 1000$).

So a binary search is a much more efficient way to search, provided the array's elements are in order. Note that "order" here needn't be numeric order. We could use binary search to look up a word in a dictionary or a name in a phone book.

A pseudocode representation of the binary search is given as follows:

```
TO SEARCH AN ARRAY OF N ELEMENTS IN ASCENDING ORDER

Assign 0 low and assign N-1 to high initially
As long as low is not greater than high
    Assign (low + high) / 2 to mid
    If the element at mid equals the key
        then return its index
    Else if the element at mid is less than the key
        then assign mid + 1 to low
    Else assign mid - 1 to high
If this is reached return -1 to indicate failure
```

Just as with the sequential search algorithm, this algorithm can easily be implemented in a method that searches an integer array which is passed as the method's parameter (Figure 8–12). If the key is found in the array, its location is returned. If it is not found, then −1 is returned to indicate failure. The method takes two parameters: an integer array to be searched and an integer key to be found. In addition, the local variables `low` and `high` are used as *pointers* to the current low and high ends of the array, respectively. Note the loop-entry condition: `low <= high`. If `low` ever becomes greater than `high`, this indicates that `key` is not contained in the array. In that case the algorithm returns −1.

Note that as the search progresses, the array is repeatedly cut in half and `low` and `high` will be used to point to the low and high index values in that portion of the array that is still being searched. The local variable `mid` is used to point to the approximate midpoint of the unsearched portion of the array. If the key is determined to be past the midpoint, then `low` is adjusted to `mid+1`; if the key occurs before the midpoint, then `high` is set to `mid-1`. The updated values of `low` and `high` limit the search to the unsearched portion of the original array.

Unlike sequential search, binary search does not have to examine every location in the array to determine that the key is not in the array. The reason, of course, is that the algorithm searches only that part of the array which could contain the key. An example will make this clearer. Suppose the array we are searching is declared as follows:

```
int sortArr[] = { 1,2,3,4,5,6,7,8,9,10,11,12,13,14,15,16,17,18,19,20};
```

And suppose we search for the key −5. Since this key is smaller than any element of the array, the algorithm will repeatedly divide the low end of the array in half until the condition `low > high` becomes true. We can see this by tracing the values that low, mid, and high will take during the search:

Key	Iteration	Low	High	Mid
-5	0	0	19	9
-5	1	0	8	4
-5	2	0	3	1
-5	3	0	0	0
-5	4	0	-1	Failure

As this trace shows, in order to determine that −5 is not in the array, the algorithm need only examine locations 9, 4, 1, and 0. After checking location 0, the new value for `high` will become −1 which makes the condition `low <= high` false. So the search loop will terminate.

Figure 8–13 shows a test program that can be used to test two search methods. It creates an integer array, whose values are in ascending order. It then uses the `getInput()` method to input an integer from the keyboard, and then performs both a `sequentialSearch()` and a `binarySearch()` for the number.

SELF-STUDY EXERCISES

EXERCISE 8.17 For the same array as in the previous example, draw a trace showing which elements are examined if you search for 21.

Figure 8–13 The `TestSearch` class.

```
import java.io.*;

public class TestSearch {

    /**
     * Goal: read an integer from the keyboard and return it
     * @return the the integer read
     * Pre: none
     * Post: the input integer is returned
     */
    public static int getInput() throws IOException {
        BufferedReader input =
            new BufferedReader (new InputStreamReader(System.in));
        String inputString = new String();
        System.out.println("This program searches for values in an array.");
        System.out.print("Input any positive integer (or any negative to quit) : ");
        inputString = input.readLine();
       return Integer.parseInt(inputString);
    } // getInput()

    public static void main(String args[]) throws IOException {
        int intArr[] = { 2,4,6,8,10,12,14,16,18,22,24,26,28};
        Search searcher = new Search();
        int key = 0, keyAt = 0;
        key = getInput();
        while (key >= 0) {
            keyAt = searcher.sequentialSearch( intArr, key );
            if (keyAt != -1)
                System.out.println("  Sequential: " + key + " is at intArr[" + keyAt + "]");
            else
                System.out.println("  Sequential: " + key + " is not contained in intArr[]");
            keyAt = searcher.binarySearch(intArr, key);
            if (keyAt != -1)
                System.out.println("  Binary: " + key + " is at intArr[" + keyAt + "]");
            else
                System.out.println("  Binary: " + key + " is not contained in intArr[]");
            key = getInput();
        } // while
    } // main()
} // TestSearch
```

8.8 Two-Dimensional Arrays

A *two-dimensional array*, an array whose components are themselves arrays, is necessary or useful for certain kinds of problems. For example, suppose you are doing a scientific study in which you have to track the amount of precipitation for every day of the year.

One way to organize these data would be to create a one-dimensional array, consisting of 365 elements:

```
double rainfall[] = new double[365];
```

However, this representation would have a major limitation: It would make it very difficult to calculate the average monthly rainfall, which happens to be an important part of your study.

What data do we need?

Therefore a better representation for this problem would be to use a two-dimensional array, one dimension for the months and one for the days. The following statement declares the array variable `rainfall`, and creates a 12 by 31 array object as its reference:

```
double rainfall[][] = new double[12][31];
```

Thus, `rainfall` is an *array of arrays*. You can think of the first array as the 12 months required for the problem. And you can think of each month as an array of 31 days. The months will be indexed from 0 to 12, and the days will be indexed from 0 to 31.

Choosing an appropriate representation

The problem with this representation is that when we want to refer to the rainfall for January 5, we would have to use `rainfall[0][4]`. This is awkward and misleading. The problem is that dates — 1/5/1999 — are unit indexed, while arrays are zero indexed. Because it will be difficult to remember this fact, our representation of the rainfall data may cause us to make errors when we start writing our algorithms.

We can easily remedy this problem by just defining our array to have an extra month and an extra day each month:

```
double rainfall[][] = new double[13][32];
```

This representation creates an array with 13 months, indexed from 0 to 12, with 32 days per month, indexed from 0 to 31. However, we can simply ignore the 0 month and 0 days by using unit indexing in all of the algorithms that process the array. In other words, if we view this array as a two-dimensional table, consisting of 13 rows and 32 columns, we can leave row 0 and column 0 unused (Figure 8–14).

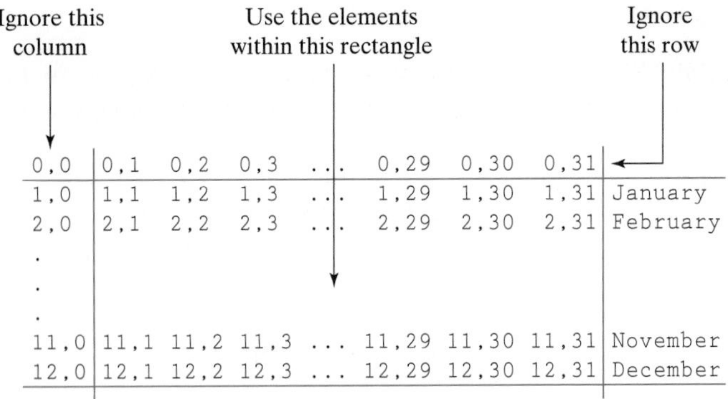

Figure 8–14 A two-dimensional array with 13 rows and 32 columns. To represent 12 months of the year, we can simply ignore row 0 and column 0.

As Figure 8–14 shows, the very first element of this 416-element array has subscripts (0,0) while the last location has subscripts (12,31). The main advantages of this representation is that the program as a whole will be much easier to read and understand, and much less prone to error.

EFFECTIVE DESIGN: Readability. For some array problems, it is preferable to use unit indexing. This can be done by declaring extra array elements and ignoring those with index 0. This should be done only when it will improve the program's overall readability and robustness.

Referring to Elements in a Two-Dimensional Array

In order to refer to an element in a two-dimensional array, you need to use two subscripts. For the `rainfall` array, the first subscript will specify the *month* and the second will specify the *day* within the month. Thus, the following statements assign 1.15 to the `rainfall` element representing January 5, and then print its value:

```
rainfall[1][5] = 1.15;                    // Rainfall for January 5
System.out.println( rainfall[1][5] );
```

Just as in the case of one-dimensional arrays, it is an error to attempt to reference an element that is not in the array. Each of the following examples would cause Java to raise an `IndexOutOfBoundsException`:

```
rainfall[13][32] = 0.15 ;  // No such element
rainfall[11][33] = 1.3;    // No such column
rainfall[14][30] = 0.74;   // No such row
```

SELF-STUDY EXERCISES

EXERCISE 8.18 Declare a two-dimensional array of `int` named `int2d` that contains five rows, each of which contains ten integers.

EXERCISE 8.19 Write a statement that prints the last integer in the third row of the array you created in the previous exercise. Then write an assignment statement that assigns 100 to the last element in the `int2d` array.

Initializing a Two-Dimensional Array

If the initial values of an array's elements are supposed to be zero, there is no need to initialize the elements. Java will do it automatically when you create the array with `new`. However, for many array problems it is necessary to initialize the array elements to some other value. For a two-dimensional array, this would require a nested loop. To illustrate this algorithm, let's use a nested for loop to initialize each element of the `rainfall` array to 0:

```
// Note that both loops are unit indexed.
for (int month = 1; month < rainfall.length; month++)
    for (int day = 1; day < rainfall[month].length; day++)
        rainfall[month][day] = 0.0;
```

Note that both for loops use unit indexing. This is in keeping with our decision to leave month 0 and day 0 unused.

Nested for loops

Remember that when you have a nested for loop, the inner loop iterates faster than the outer loop. Thus for each month, the inner loop will iterate over 31 days. This is equivalent to processing the array as if you were going across each row, and then down to the next row, in the representation shown in Figure 8–14.

Note that for a two-dimensional array, both dimensions have an associated `length` variable, which is used in this example to specify the upper bound of each for loop. For the `rainfall` array, the first dimension (months) has a length of 13 and the second dimension (days) has a length of 32.

Another way to view the `rainfall` array is to remember that it is an *array of arrays*. The length of the first array, which corresponds to the number (13) of months, is given by `rainfall.length`. The length of each month's array, which corresponds to the number of days (32) in a month, is given by `rainfall[month].length`.

The outer loop of the nested for loop iterates through each month of the array. And the inner for loop iterates through each day in each month. In this way, all $416 = 13 \times 32$ elements of the array are set to 0.0. In Table 8–1) the bold-face numbers along the top represent the day subscripts, while the bold-face numbers along the left represent the month subscripts.

Table 8.1. The initialized `rainfall` array. The unused array elements are shown as dashes.

	0	1	2	3	...	30	31
0	–	–	–	–	...	–	–
1	–	0.0	0.0	0.0	...	0.0	0.0
2	–	0.0	0.0	0.0	...	0.0	0.0
⋮	⋮	⋮	⋮	⋮	⋮	⋮	⋮
10	–	0.0	0.0	0.0	...	0.0	0.0
11	–	0.0	0.0	0.0	...	0.0	0.0
12	–	0.0	0.0	0.0	...	0.0	0.0

SELF-STUDY EXERCISES

EXERCISE 8.20 Write a loop to print all of the elements of `int2d`, which you declared in the exercises in the previous section. Print one row per line with a space between each element on a line.

8.8.1 Two-Dimensional Array Methods

Now that we have figured out how to represent the data for our scientific experiment, let's develop methods to calculate some results. First, we want a method to initialize the array. This method will simply incorporate the nested loop algorithm we developed above:

```
/**
 * Initializes the rainfall array
 * @param rain is a 2D-array of rainfalls
 * Pre:  rain is non null
 * Post: rain[x][y] == 0 for all x,y in the array
 * Note that the loops use unit indexing.
 */
public void initRain(double rain[][]) {
    for (int month = 1; month < rain.length; month++)
        for (int day = 1; day < rain[month].length; day++)
            rain[month][day] = 0.0;
} // initRain()
```

Array parameters

Note how we declare the parameter for a multidimensional array. In addition to the element type (`double`), and the name of the parameter (`rain`), we must also include a set of brackets for *each* dimension of the array.

Note, also, that we use the parameter name within the method to refer to the array. As with one-dimensional arrays, the parameter is a reference to the array, which means that any changes made to the array within the method, will persist when the method is exited.

Method: `avgDailyRain()`

Algorithm design

One result that our experiment needs is the average daily (high) rainfall. To calculate this result, we would add up all of the rainfalls stored in the

12 × 31 array, and divide by 365. Of course, the array itself contains more than 365 elements. It zcontains 416 elements, but we're not using the first month of the array, and within some months — those with fewer than 31 days — we're not using some of the day elements. For example, there's no such day as `rainfall[2][30]`, which would represent February 30. However, because we initialized all of the array's elements to 0, the rainfall recorded for the nondays will be 0, which won't affect our overall average.

Method design

The method for calculating average daily rainfall should take our two-dimensional array of `double` as a parameter, and it should return a `double`. Its algorithm will use a nested for loop to iterate through the elements of the array, adding each element to a running total. When the loops exits, the total will be divided by 365 and returned:

```
/**
 * Computes average daily rainfall
 * @param rain is a 2D-array of rainfalls
 * @return The sum of rain[x][y] / 356
 * Pre:  rain is non null
 * Post: The sum of rain / 365 is calculated
 * Note that the loops are unit indexed
 */
public double avgDailyRain(double rain[][]) {
    double total = 0;
    for (int month = 1; month < rain.length; month++)
        for (int day = 1; day < rain[month].length; day++)
            total += rain[month][day];
    return total/365;
} // avgDailyRain()
```

Method: `avgRainForMonth()`

Algorithm design

One reason we used a two-dimensional array for this problem is so we could calculate the average high rainfall for a given month. Let's write a method to solve this problem. The algorithm for this method will not require a nested for loop, because we will just iterate through the 31 elements of a given month. So the month subscript will not vary. For example, suppose we are calculating the average for January, which is represented in our array as month 1:

```
double total = 0;
for (int day = 1; day < rainfall[1].length; day++)
    total = total + rainfall[1][day];
```

Method design

Thus, the month subscript is held constant (at 1) while the day subscript iterates from 1 to 31. Of course in our method, we would use a parameter to represent the month, thereby allowing us to calculate the average monthly rainfall for any given month.

Method design: What data do we need?

Another problem that our method has to deal with is that months don't all have 31 days, so we can't always divide by 31 to compute the monthly average. There are various ways to solve this problem, but perhaps the easiest is to let the number of days for that month to be specified as a third parameter. That way the month itself, and the number of days for the month are supplied by the user of the method:

```
/**
 * Computes average monthly rainfall
 * @param rain is a 2D-array of rainfalls
 * @param month is the month of the year, 1 ... 12
 * @param nDays is the number of days in month, 1 ... 31
 * @return The sum of rain[month] / nDays
 * Pre:  1 <= month <= 12 and 1 <= nDays <= 31
 * Post: The sum of rain[month] / nDays is calculated
 */
public double avgRainForMonth(double rain[][], int month, int nDays) {
    double total = 0;
    for (int day = 1; day < rain[month].length; day++)
        total = total + rain[month][day];
    return total/nDays;
} // avgRainForMonth()
```

Given this definition, we can call this method as follows to calculate and print the average monthly rainfall for March:

```
System.out.println("March: " + avgRainForMonth(rainfall,3,31));
```

Note that when passing the entire two-dimensional array to the method, we just use the name of the array. We do not follow the name with subscripts.

8.8.2 Passing Part of an Array to a Method

Method design: What data?

Instead of passing the entire rainfall array to the `avgRainForMonth()` method, we could redesign this method so that it is only passed the particular month that's being averaged. Remember that a two-dimensional array is an array of arrays, so if we pass the month of January, we are passing an array of 32 days. If we use this approach, we need only two parameters: the month, which is array of days, and the number of days in that month:

```
/**
 * Computes average monthly rainfall for a given month
 * @param monthRain is a 1D-array of rainfalls
 * @param nDays is the number of days in monthRain
 * @return The sum of monthRain / nDays
 * Pre:  1 <= nDays <= 31
 * Post: The sum of monthRain / nDays is calculated
 */
public double avgRainForMonth(double monthRain[], int nDays) {
    double total = 0;
    for (int day = 1; day < monthRain.length; day++)
        total = total + monthRain[day];
    return total/nDays;
} // avgRainForMonth()
```

Given this definition, we can call it as follows to calculate and print the average monthly rainfall for March:

```
System.out.println("March: " + avgRainForMonth(rainfall[3],31));
```

In this case, we're passing an array of `double` to the method, but in order to reference it, we have to pull it out of the two-dimensional array by giving its *row* subscript as well. Thus, `rainfall[3]` refers to one month of data in the two-dimensional array. It refers to the month of March. But `rainfall[3]` is itself a one-dimensional array. Figure 8–15 helps to clarify this point.

Specifying an argument

It's important to note that deciding whether to use brackets when passing data to a method is not just a matter of whether you are passing an array. It is a matter of what type of data the method parameter specifies. So, whenever you call a method that involves a parameter, you have to look at the method definition to see what kind of data that parameter specifies. Then you must supply an argument that refers to that type of data.

For our two-dimensional `rainfall` array, we can refer to the entire array as `rainfall`. We can refer to one of its months as `rainfall[j]`, where *j* is any integer between 1 and 12. And we can refer to any of its elements as `rainfall[j][k]`, where *j* is any integer between 1 and 12, and *k* is any integer between 1 and 31.

JAVA LANGUAGE RULE **Arguments and Parameters.** The argument in a method call must match the data type in the method definition. This applies to all parameters, including array parameters.

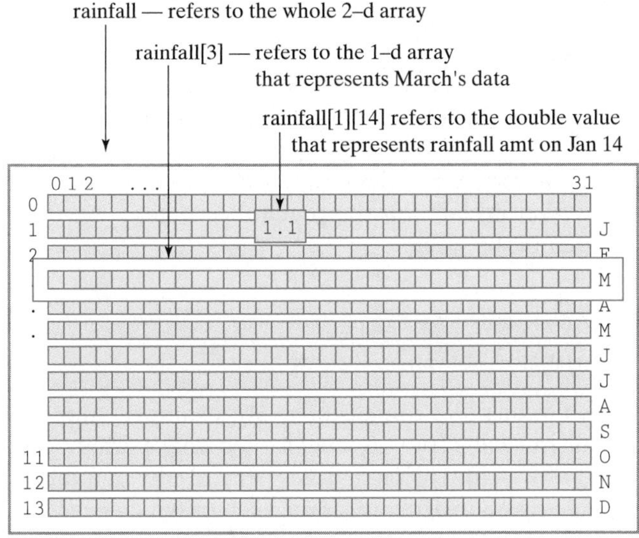

Figure 8–15 Referencing individual elements and array elements in a two-dimensional array.

The Rainfall class (Figure 8–16) shows how we can test our array algorithms. It creates the rainfall array in the main() method. It then initializes the array, and prints out average daily rainfall and average daily rainfall for the month of March. However, note that we have made a slight modification to the initRain() method. Instead of just assigning 0 to each element, we assign a random value between 0 and 2.0:

```
rain[month][day] = Math.random() * 2.0;
```

Generating test data

Using the Math.random() method in this way provides a handy way to generate some realistic test data. In this case, we have scaled the data so that the daily rainfall is between 0 and 2 inches. (Rainfall like this would probably be appropriate for an Amazonian rain forest!) Testing our algorithms with these data provides some indication that our methods are in fact working properly.

EFFECTIVE DESIGN: Generating Test Data. The Math.random() method can be used to generate numeric test data, when large amounts of data are required. The data can be scaled to fit within the range that the actual data are expected to have.

SELF-STUDY EXERCISES

EXERCISE 8.21 Suppose you're going to keep track of the daily newspaper sales at the local kiosk. Declare a 52 × 7 two-dimensional array of int and initialize each of its elements to 0.

EXERCISE 8.22 Write a method to calculate the average newspapers sold per week, using the array you declared in the previous exercise.

EXERCISE 8.23 Write a method to calculate the total newspapers sold per Sunday, using the array you declared in the previous exercise. Assume that Sunday is the last day of the week.

8.9 Multidimensional Arrays

Java doesn't limit arrays to just two dimensions. For example, suppose we decide to extend our rainfall survey to cover a ten year period. For each year we now need a two-dimensional array. This results in a three-dimensional array consisting of an array of years, each of which contains an array of months, each of which contains an array of days:

Figure 8–16 Definition of the Rainfall class.

```
public class Rainfall {

    /**
     * Initializes the rainfall array
     * @param rain is a 2D-array of rainfalls
     * Pre:  rain is non null
     * Post: rain[x][y] == 0 for all x,y in the array
     * Note that the loops use unit indexing.
     */
    public void initRain(double rain[][]) {
        for (int month = 1; month < rain.length; month++)
            for (int day = 1; day < rain[month].length; day++)
                rain[month][day] = Math.random() * 2.0;
    } // initRain()

    /**
     * Computes average daily rainfall
     * @param rain is a 2D-array of rainfalls
     * @return The sum of rain[x][y] / 356
     * Pre:  rain is non null
     * Post: The sum of rain / 365 is calculated
     * Note that the loops are unit indexed
     */
    public double avgDailyRain(double rain[][]) {
        double total = 0;
        for (int month = 1; month < rain.length; month++)
            for (int day = 1; day < rain[month].length; day++)
                total += rain[month][day];
        return total/365;
    } // avgDailyRain()

    /**
     * Computes average monthly rainfall for a given month
     * @param monthRain is a 1D-array of rainfalls
     * @param nDays is the number of days in monthRain
     * @return The sum of monthRain / nDays
     * Pre:  1 <= nDays <= 31
     * Post: The sum of monthRain / nDays is calculated
     */
    public double avgRainForMonth(double monthRain[], int nDays) {
        double total = 0;
        for (int day = 1; day < monthRain.length; day++)
            total = total + monthRain[day];
        return total/nDays;
    } // avgRainForMonth()

    public static void main(String args[]) {
        double rainfall[][] = new double[13][32];

        Rainfall data = new Rainfall();
        data.initRain(rainfall);
        System.out.println("The average daily rainfall = " +  data.avgDailyRain(rainfall));
        System.out.println("The average daily rainfall for March = " +  data.avgRainForMonth(rainfall[3],31));
    } // main()
}//Rainfall
```

```
final int NYEARS = 10;
final int NMONTHS = 13;
final int NDAYS = 32;
double rainfail[][][] = new double[NYEARS][NMONTHS][NDAYS];
```

Following the design convention of not using the 0 month and 0 days, we end up with a 10 × 13 × 32 array. Note the use of `final` variables to represent the size of each dimension of the array. This helps to make the program more readable.

In Figure 8–17 each year of the rainfall data is represented as a separate page, and on each page there is a two-dimensional table, consisting of 12 rows (1 per month) and 31 columns (1 per day).

You might imagine that our study could be extended to cover rainfall data from a number of different cities. That would result in a four-dimensional array, with the first dimension now being the city. Of course, for this to work, cities would have to be represented by integers, because array subscripts must integers.

As you might expect, algorithms for processing each element in a three-dimensional table would require a three-level nested loop. For example, the following algorithm would be used to initialize all elements of our three-dimensional rainfall array:

```
for (int year = 0; year < rainfall.length; year++)
    for (int month = 0; month < rainfall[year].length; month++)
        for (int day = 0; day < rainfall[year][month].length; day++)
            rain[month][day] = 0.0;
```

Note again the proper use of the `length` attribute for each of the three dimensions of the array. In the outer loop, `rainfall.length`, we're refer-

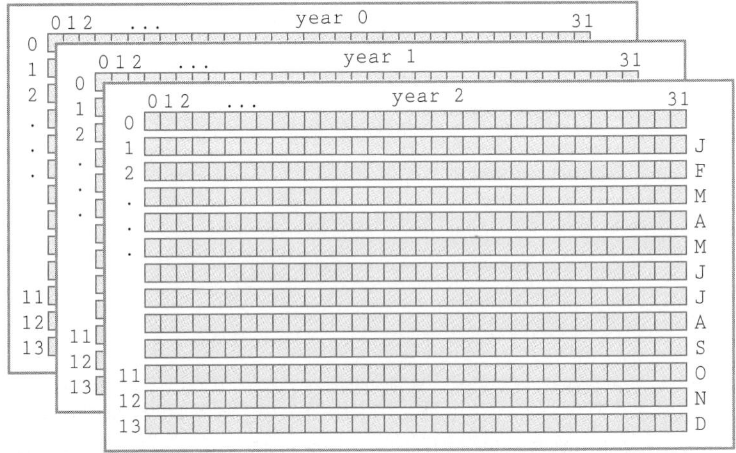

Figure 8–17 Three-dimensional data might be viewed as a collection of pages, each of which contains a two-dimensional table.

ring to the number of years. In the middle loop, `rainfall[year].length`, we're referring to number of months within a given year. In the inner loop, `rainfall[year][month].length`, we're referring to the number of days within a month.

If we added a fourth dimension to our array, and wanted to extend this algorithm to initialize it, we would simply embed the three-level loop within another for loop that would iterate over each city.

8.9.1 Array Initializers

It is possible to use an initializer with a multidimensional array . For example, the following examples create several small arrays and initialize their elements:

```
int a[][] = { {1,2,3}, {4,5,6} } ;
char c[][] = { {'a','b'}, {'c','d'} } ;
double d[][][] = { {1.0,2.0,3.0}, {4.0,5.0}, {6.0,7.0,8.0,9.0} } ;
```

The first of these declarations creates a 2×3 array of integers. The second example creates a 2×2 array of characters, and the third example creates an array of `double` consisting of three rows, each of which has a different number of elements. The first row contains three elements, the second contains two elements and the last row contains four elements. As this last example shows, the rows in a multidimensional array don't all have to have the same length. Java differs from C, C++, and other high-level languages in this regard.

Using initializers, as in these examples, is feasible only for relatively small arrays. To see why, just imagine what the initializer expression would be for our three-dimensional `rainfall` array. It would require $4160 = 10 \times 13 \times 32$ zeroes, separated by commas!

> **PROGRAMMING TIP: Array Initializers.** Initializer (assignment) expressions can be used to assign initial values to relatively small arrays. For larger arrays, an intializer method should be designed.

OBJECT-ORIENTED DESIGN: Polymorphic Sorting

One limitation of the sort routines developed so far is that they only work on one particular type of data. If you've written a bubble sort to sort `int`s, you can't use it to sort `double`s. What would be far more desirable is a **polymorphic** sort method — that is, one method that could sort any kind of data. This is easily done if we apply object-oriented design principles to develop the hierarchy of classes shown in Figure 8–18.

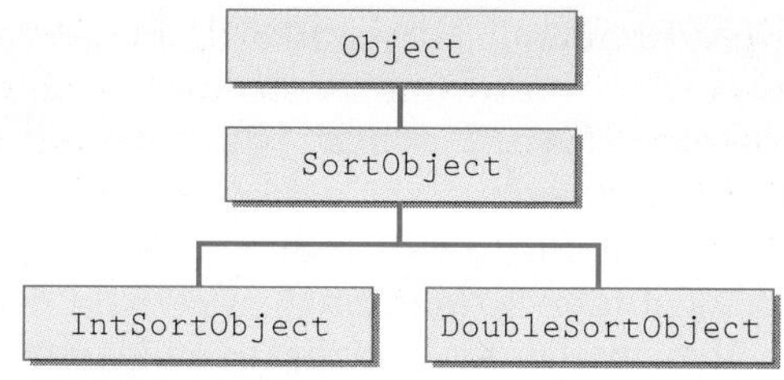

Figure 8–18 Class hierarchy for polymorphic sorting.

Consider the following version of bubble sort:

```
// Polymorphic sort method designed by Chuck Liang
public static void sort(SortObject[] arr) {
    SortObject temp;                                    // Temporary variable for swap
    for (int pass = 1; pass < arr.length; pass++)       // For each pass
        for (int pair = 1; pair < arr.length ; pair++ ) // For each pair
            if (!arr[pair].inOrder(arr[pair-1])) {      //   Compare
                temp = arr[pair-1];                     //   and swap
                arr[pair-1] = arr[pair];
                arr[pair] = temp;
            } // if
} // sort()
```

The primary change we've made is that we've defined its parameter as an array of `SortObject` object. Also, we've modified the statement in which adjacent objects are compared to perform the following comparison:

```
!arr[pair].inOrder(arr[pair-1])
```

In other words, we invoke the `inOrder()` method, defined in the `SortObject` class, to compare array elements. Note that our algorithm no longer refers to `int`s, although we can surely use it to sort integers.

Class design

Our next task is to define the `SortObject` class. This should be an `abstract` class so that we can create a wide variety of `SortObject` subclasses, each of which can be sorted by the polymorphic `sort()` method. We saw a previous example of using an abstract class in this way in Chapter 7 where an `abstract Cipher` class was defined as a way to implement a wide variety of different ciphers, all of which shared certain inherited characteristics. In this case we define `SortObject` as follows:

```
public abstract class SortObject {

    Object datum;               // Object is the most general type of data
    public SortObject(Object newObj) {
        datum = newObj;
    }

    abstract void print();                        // Each object prints itself
    abstract boolean inOrder(SortObject o);  // Order depends on the subclass
} // SortObject
```

Note that SortObject has a single instance variable of type Object. This is the most general type of object in the Java hierarchy. If it can be sorted, then any object can be sorted. SortObject has two abstract methods: print() and inOrder(). Both are intended to be defined by subclasses of SortObject.

For example, consider the following Integer subclass of SortObject:

```
public class IntSortObject extends SortObject {

    public IntSortObject(Integer newInt) {
        super(newInt);
    }

    public void print() {                    // Each object prints itself
        System.out.print( ((Integer) datum).intValue() );
    }

    public boolean inOrder(SortObject o) {    // Defines an order for Integers
        return  ((Integer) datum).intValue() <= ((Integer)o.datum).intValue() ;
    }
} // IntSortObject
```

The constructor method takes an Integer and assigns it to datum, the class's inherited instance variable, by invoking super. Recall that this is a Java keyword used for invoking a superclass's constructor method. Note also how the inOrder() method is defined. The syntax is somewhat complicated:

Invoking super

```
return  ((Integer) datum).intValue() <= ((Integer)o.datum).intValue();
```

It compares the integer values of two Integers. The messy syntax is required because it is necessary to cast datum, which is an Object, into an Integer, so that the intValue() method can be used. The result, however, is that inOrder performs an Integer comparison which can be used by the sort() method described above. If we want to be able to sort Doubles, we can create a DoubleSortObject class with the following implementation of inOrder():

Object conversion

```
public boolean inOrder(SortObject o)  { // Defines an order for Doubles
    return  ((Double) datum).doubleValue() <= ((Double)o.datum).doubleValue() ;
}
```

In this case we must convert datum into a Double so that a Double comparison can be performed. Thus the only real difference among the various subclasses of SortObject will be syntactical differences in the way each subclass defines the inOrder() and print() methods.

Once we have defined IntSortObject and DoubleSortObject we can create arrays of them and sort them using the same method. An example for the IntSortObject class is as follows:

```
public static void main(String args[]) {
    IntSortObject anArr[] = new IntSortObject[20]; // The array to sort

    for (int k = 0; k < anArr.length; k++)     // Initialize with random values
        anArr[k] = new IntSortObject(new Integer((int)(Math.random() * 10000)));

    sort(anArr);                                 // Sort the array

    for (int k = 0; k < anArr.length; k++) {    // Print the array
        if (k % 10 == 0)
            System.out.println();                // New row
        anArr[k].print();
        System.out.print("\t");
    } // for
    System.out.println();
} // main()
```

From the Java Library: `Vector`

The `java.util.Vector` class implements an array of objects that can grow in size as needed. One limitation of regular arrays is that their lengths remain fixed. Once the array is full — once every element is used — you can't allocate additional elements.

The `Vector` class contains methods for storing and retrieving objects, and for accessing objects by their index position within the `Vector`:

```
public class Vector {
   // Constructors
    public Vector(int size);      // Create with an initial size
    public Vector();              // Create empty
   // Public Instance Methods
    public void addElement(Object obj);      // Add obj to next slot
    public Object elementAt(int index);      // Retrieve an element
    public void insertElementAt(Object o, int index); // Add at an index
    public int indexOf(Object obj);          // Find an object's index
    public int lastIndexof(Object obj);
    public void removeElementAt(int index); // Remove an element
    public int size();                       // How many elements
}
```

One use for a `Vector` would be when a program needs to store items, input from the user or a file, without knowing in advance how many items there are. Using a `Vector` is less efficient than an array in terms of processing speed, but it gives you the flexibility of growing the data structure, as necessary, to meet the storage requirements.

As an illustration of this idea, the program in Figure 8–19 creates a random number of integers and then stores them in a `Vector`. The `Vector`, which is declared and instantiated in `main()`, is initially empty. Integers from 0 to the random `bound` are then inserted into the `Vector`. In this case, insertions are done with the `addElement()` method, which causes the `Vector` object to insert the element at the next available location, increasing its size, if necessary.

Figure 8–19 Demonstration of the `Vector` class. (See also the In the Laboratory section of Chapter 11 for another example that uses a `Vector`.)

```
import java.util.Vector;

public class VectorDemo {

    public static void printVector(Vector v) {
        for (int k=0; k < v.size(); k++)
            System.out.println(v.elementAt(k).toString());
    } // printVector()

    public static void main(String args[]) {
        Vector vector = new Vector();              // An empty vector

        int bound = (int)(Math.random() * 20);
        for (int k = 0; k < bound; k++ )           // Insert a random
            vector.addElement(new Integer(k));     //  number of Integers
        printVector(vector);                       // Print the elements
    } // main()
}// VectorDemo
```

Once all the integers have been inserted, the `printVector()` method is called. Note that it uses the `size()` method to determine how many elements the `Vector` contains. This is similar to using the `length()` method to determine the number of characters in a `String`.

Vectors store objects

Finally, note that a `Vector` stores objects. It cannot be used to store primitive data values. You cannot store an `int` in a `Vector`. Therefore, we need to use the `Integer` wrapper class to convert `int`s into `Integer`s before they can be inserted into the `Vector`. Because you can't just print an `Integer`, or any other `Object`, the `toString()` method is used to print the string representation of the object.

By defining `Vector` to store `Object`s, Java's designers have made it as general as it can be, and therefore as widely useful as can be. See the "In the Laboratory" section of Chapter 11 for some additional comparisons between `Vector`s and arrays.

EFFECTIVE DESIGN: Generality. Defining a data collection, such as an array or a `Vector`, in terms of the `Object` class makes it capable of storing, and hence processing, any type of value, including values of the primitive data types. This is because the `Object` class is the root of the Java class hierarchy.

8.10 CASE STUDY: Simulating a Card Deck

Many computer games — Bridge, Solitaire, BlackJack — require a computerized deck of cards, which is an excellent application for an array (Figure 8–20). A card deck can be represented as a simple array of 52 cards:

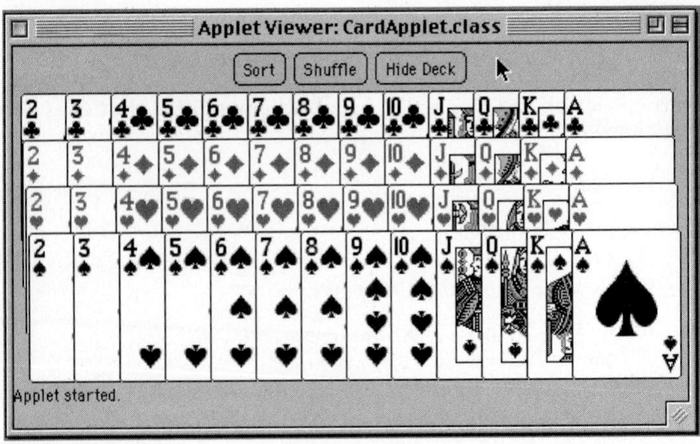

Figure 8–20 A deck of cards can be represented as an array of 52 cards.

```
Card deck[] = new Card[52];  // 52 cards in a deck
```

Problem decomposition

where Card is an object that represents an individual playing card. However, given the specialized tasks associated with a card deck, such as shuffling and dealing, a well-designed card playing application would want to use a Deck class to encapsulate these specialized functions. In that case the array of Cards that make up the deck would become a private instance variable within the Deck object. Among other benefits, this design would make it easier to have a program that uses multiple decks at one time.

8.10.1 Designing a Card Class

Data representation

First, let's design the Card class . Each card must have a *suit* — clubs, diamonds, heart, spades — and a *value* — 2 through 10, jack, queen, king, and ace. We will represent both suit and value as a function of a Card's *rank*, where rank is an int between 0 and 51. This will enable us to place the cards in rank order, which is the order found in a new deck of cards:

```
2C 3C ... TC JC QC KC AC 2D 3D ... TD ... AD 2H 3H ... AH 2S ...AS
```

In this representation, C, D, H, and S stand for clubs, diamonds, hearts and spades, respectively, and T, J, Q, K, A stand for ten, jack, queen, king, and ace.

Given its rank, a card's suit and value can be computed as

```
suit = rank / 13;          // Gives a number between 0..3
value = 2 + rank % 13;     // Gives a number between 2..14
```

Thus a Card's suit will be represented as 0 (clubs), 1 (diamonds), 2 (hearts), and 3 (spades), and a Card's value will be a number between 2 and 14, where the numbers from 2 through 9 represent the card with that numeric face value and those with values 10 through 14 represent ten, jack, queen, king, and ace, respectively.

Graphical representation

In addition to these basic representational issues, each Card will be associated with two graphical images, one for its back and one for its face. Moreover, it's important that the Card's state be able to keep track of whether it is face up or face down. Therefore we will use a boolean variable to record this state.

In terms of a Card's functionality, it will require public methods to display itself, to turn itself face up or face down, as well as various access methods to set and get its value or its image. These design specifications are summarized in the following partial class definition:

```
public class Card {
    public int rank;              // Between 0..51
    public int value;             // Card's numerical 2,3,4,...11(jack)....14(ace)
    public int suit;              // 0=club,1=diamond,2=heart,3=spade

    private Image faceImg;        // Card's face-up image

    private boolean faceUp;       // True when card is face-up

    public Card (int rank) { } // Constructor

    public void showCard(boolean up) { }    // Turn card face up
    public void setImage (Image img) { }    // Assign card's face image
    public Image toImage() {  }             // Represent as an image
    public String toString() {}             // Represent as a string
} // Card
```

The complete implementation of Card is shown in Figure 8–21. Note how we have defined the constructor method. When a new Card is made, the constructor is passed its rank, which it uses to initialize the Card's suit and value:

```
public Card(int rank) {
    this.rank = rank;
    suit = rank / 13;           // Gives a number between 0 and 3
    value = 2 + rank % 13;      // Gives a number between 2 and 14
    faceUp = true;
} // Card()
```

Thus, rank can be used with simple arithmetic operators to figure out the card's suit and face value. The suit and value are used to figure out the card's representation, but its rank is used to figure out its order within the deck. Having the card's rank will make it easy to sort the deck, so, in this case, it's convenient to have both representations available.

Figure 8–21 The `Card` class.

```
import java.awt.*;

public class Card {
    // The following string literals store letters that are used to
    // construct a String representation of the card.

    private final String suitStr = "CDHS";  // C=club,D=diamond,H=heart,S=spade
    private final String valueStr = "??23456789TJQKA";  // two through ace

    public int rank;     // 0..51
    public int value;    // face value 2,3,,,10,11(jack),14(ace)
    public int suit;     // 0=club,1=diamond,2=heart,3=spade

    private Image faceImg;        // Face-up image

    private boolean faceUp;       // True when face-up

    public Card (int rank) {
        this.rank = rank;
        suit = rank / 13;          // Gives a number between 0..3
        value = 2 + rank % 13;     // Gives a number between 2..14
        faceUp = true;
    } // Card()

    public void showCard( boolean up ) {
        faceUp = up;
    } // showCard

    public void setImage (Image img) {
        faceImg = img;
    } // setImage

    public Image toImage() {
        if (faceUp)
            return faceImg;
        else
            return null;
    }

    /**
     *  Goal: Return a 2 character representation of the card. For
     *    example, "2c" means 2 of clubs, "jd" is jack of diamonds.
     * Algorithm: the instance variables, suit, and value,
     *  are used as indexes into strings that store the correct letters
     */
    public String toString() {
        return "" +  valueStr.charAt(value) + suitStr.charAt(suit);
    } // toString

} // Card
```

Algorithm design

Note the implementation of the `toString()` method. This method returns a two-character string that represents a card's suit and value. For example, the two of clubs would be represented as "2C," and the ace of hearts would be "AH." The algorithm that's used here makes use of two string literals that store the letters used to represent the card's suit and value:

```
private final String suitStr = "CDHS";              // C=club,D=diamond,H=heart,S=spade
private final String valueStr = "??23456789TJQKA"; // Two through ace
```

The positions of the letters in the strings correspond to the numeric values of the card's suit and face value, so we can use the instance variables, `suit` and `value`, to extract the correct character representation and concatenate them to form the card's representation. This gives the following definition for `toString()`:

```
public String toString() {
    return "" +  valueStr.charAt(value) + suitStr.charAt(suit);
} // toString
```

For example, the 5 of spades would have `suit` equal to 3 and `value` equal to 5. When used in the above expression, "5S" would be extracted as the card's string representation. Note the use of the empty string in the concatenation expression. This causes Java to convert the entire expression into a `String`.

The `toImage()` method is used to present the `Image()` associated with the `Card`. Note that if the `Card` is face down, this method returns `null`. In that case, the `Deck` will display its card back image.

8.10.2 Designing a Deck Class

Let's now turn to designing the `Deck` class. This class will need an array to store 52 `Cards`. To minimize the amount of manipulation of the array, let's use an `int` variable to represent the `top` of the deck. This will always be a value between 0 and 51. As cards are dealt, the `top` can be incremented to point to the next card in the array, wrapping around if necessary.

```
top = (top + 1) % NCARDS;    // Wrap around to 0 when top == 52
```

In terms of the `Deck`'s functionality, it will need methods to deal a card, shuffle the deck, and sort the deck (into its "new deck" order). This leads to the following design specification:

```
public class Deck   {
    public static final int NCARDS = 52;            // Class constant

   private Card deck[] = new Card [NCARDS];      // 52 Card array
   private int top = 0;                          // Current top card

   private Image cardBack;                       // Deck's image

   public Deck(Applet a, Image img) {}           // Constructor
   public Card dealOneCard(boolean faceUp) { } // Deal a card
   public Image getImage() {                    // Display card's back
       return cardBack;
   }
   public void shuffleDeck() { }                // Shuffle
   public void sortDeck() {}                    // Sort
} // Deck
```

Note that the Deck() constructor takes an Applet as a parameter. The reason for this is to simplify the task of loading Images to use as the card faces when the Deck is created. As we saw earlier, an easy way to load an Image is to use the Applet.getImage():

```
Image img = getImage( getDocumentBase(), "img.gif");
```

However, the Deck object won't be able to utilize getImage() unless it has a reference to its associated applet. When the applet creates a Deck, it simply passes a reference to itself:

```
Deck deck = new Deck( this );
```

This leads to the following implementation of the Deck() constructor:

```
public Deck(Applet a) {
    cardBack = a.getImage( a.getDocumentBase(), "back.gif");

    for (int k = 0; k < deck.length; k++) {  // make the cards
        deck[k] = new Card( k );
        deck[k].setImage(a.getImage(a.getDocumentBase(),
                                 deck[k].toString() + ".gif"));
    } // for
} // Deck()
```

Dot notation

Note how dot notation is used to construct a reference to the applet's methods — for example, a.getImage(). The first Image loaded, which represents the back of the deck, is assigned to Deck.cardBack. Then a for loop is used to create 52 Cards, assigning each one its proper rank. Note that each Card must be instantiated with new. Finally, note how the constructor assigns each Card its appropriate Image. To invoke a method or instance variable of an array component, it is necessary to apply the dot operator *after* the array subscript.

```
deck[k].setImage()
deck[k].toString()
```

The reason, of course, is that deck[k] is a reference to a Card.

Let's now turn to dealing the top Card from the Deck. This method is complicated by the fact that cards may be dealt either face up or face down depending on the game situation. Therefore, dealOneCard() requires a boolean parameter to represent face up or face down. The method should then simply return the top Card and update its value for top, since dealing a card will produce a new top card:

```
public Card dealOneCard(boolean faceUp) {
    Card topCard = deck[top];            // Get the top card
    topCard.showCard(faceUp);            // Turn the card up or down
    top = (top + 1) % NCARDS;            // Top is the new top card
    return topCard;                      // Deal the top card
} // dealOneCard()
```

The boolean variable faceUp will cause showCard() to turn the card up or down depending on whether it is true (up) or false (down). Note the use of a local Card variable here, which is assigned its value from the array, deck[top].

The rest of the implementation of the Deck class is left as laboratory exercise.

IN THE LABORATORY: A CARD-GAME APPLET

The purpose of this lab is to complete a card playing program using the Card and Deck classes just described. The objectives of this lab are

- To give practice using arrays and array algorithms.
- To give practice using Images.
- To introduce a program that requires manipulation of three separate programmer-defined classes: Card, Deck, and CardApplet.

Problem Description

Write an applet that lets the user shuffle, sort, and display a deck of playing cards. The cards will be represented by the Card class, and the deck of cards will be represented by the Deck class. In its completed form the applet will display cards from a set of 53 Images.

However, since it will be too time consuming to load this many images each time you wish to test your program, Card.toString() will be used to represent cards during program development — for example, "2C" (2 of clubs), "JD" (jack of diamonds). After all other methods are developed and tested, the 53 Images will be incorporated into the applet.

GUI Specifications

The Graphical User Interface (GUI) for this applet should contain buttons labeled *Shuffle*, *Sort*, and *Show/Hide Deck*. Shuffling a deck is a matter of rearranging its cards. Sorting a deck will involve putting the deck into its original order, as specified below.

Showing and Hiding the deck should work like a toggle button. If the deck is currently displayed face up, the button should be labeled "Hide Deck," and when it is clicked, it should redisplay the deck face down, and it should toggle its label to "Show Deck." Similarly, if the deck is currently face down, the button should be labeled "Show Deck," and when it is clicked, it should redisplay the deck face up and toggle the button's label to "Hide Deck." (You may wish to use an instance of the ToggleButton class for this button. See Section 4.6.)

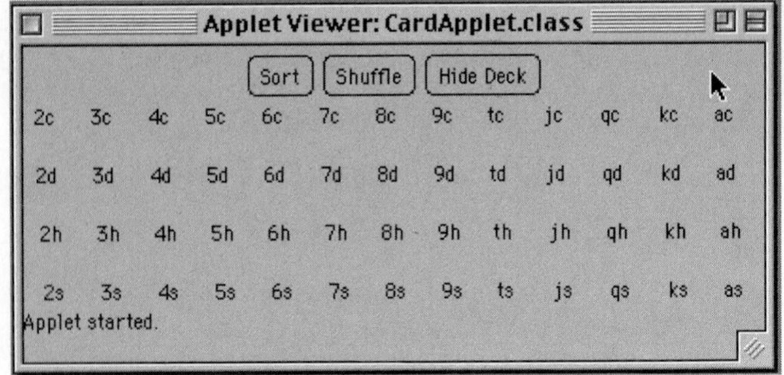

Figure 8–22 The string-based user interface for `CardDeckApplet`.

During program development, the deck should be displayed by painting the `String` representation of each card on the applet (Figure 8–22).

You needn't implement the layout shown here, but your layout should be able to display all 52 cards of the deck in some coherent way. To help with this task, the `Card.toString()` method returns a string representation of the card as "2C" (2 of clubs) or "AS" (ace of spaces). The applet code may have to break this string apart in order to display the card properly.

Problem Decomposition

The problem should be divided into three separate classes: the `Card` class, which was completely implemented earlier, the `Deck` class, which was partially implemented earlier, and the `CardApplet` class , which we will design and implement from scratch.

Problem Design: The Deck Class

To complete the `Deck` class you must implement the `shuffleDeck()` and `sortDeck()` methods, which were outlined in the specification given in Section 8.10.2. The algorithms for shuffling and sorting the deck are discussed below.

Problem Design: The `CardApplet` Class

`CardApplet` requires instance variables for the three `Buttons` and the `Deck`. In addition it will be useful to have a `private` instance variable to keep track of whether the deck is currently face up or face down. This variable can be re-set each time the Show/Hide button is clicked.

`CardApplet` must implement three methods: an `init()` method, where the applet's components are instantiated and added to the applet's interface, a `paint()` method, which handles the painting of the deck, and an `actionPerformed()` method, which handles clicks on the three buttons.

- `init()`: The `init()` method should simply instantiate the objects used by the applet, including the `Deck` object.

- `actionPerformed()`: The `actionPerformed()` method can simply invoke the appropriate `Deck` method to sort or shuffle the deck. To toggle between showing and hiding the deck will require the applet to remember what state the deck is in and will require that the `Button`'s label be toggled each time it is clicked. (*Hint*: Here's the place for that `boolean` variable unless you implement a special `ToggleButton`.)
- `paint()`: The entire deck should be repainted or redealt each time the user selects one of the three actions. To display the deck you can repeatedly call `Deck.dealOneCard()`, which returns the top card on the deck. Once you have a `Card`, stored in a local variable perhaps, you can invoke either its `toString()` or `toImage()` method within the `paint()` method:

```
g.drawString( tmpCard.toString(), hRef,vRef);
g.drawImage( tmpCard.toImage(), hRef,vRef,this);
```

  Note the use of the variables `hRef` and `vRef` here to control horizontal and vertical placement of the `Card`'s image or string on the applet.

Algorithm Design: Shuffling the Deck

Shuffling a deck can be simulated by repeatedly swapping two random cards in the deck, as described in the following pseudocode:

```
For some number of swaps // 26 swaps or so
    Pick random card1     // Pick two random cards
    Pick random card2
    Swap card1 and card2  // Swap their locations in the deck
```

Algorithm Design: Sorting the Deck

The task of sorting the deck can use a variation of either the `bubbleSort()` or the `selectionSort()` algorithms that were described in Section 8.6. Of course these algorithms must be adapted to work on `Card` objects.

In order to sort an array of `Card` objects, it's important to remember that when comparing two `Cards`, you must compare their respective `ranks`. But when swapping two `Cards`, you must exchange the `Cards` themselves in the array. The syntax for comparing two cards would be something like this:

```
if (deck[currentCard].rank < deck[smallestCard].rank) ...
```

You must use dot notation to refer the the `Card`'s `rank`, which is a `public` instance variable. On the other hand, when you swap two `Cards`, you must swap the entire object, not just its rank. This means you will need a temporary `Card` variable, and you would use it to swap `deck[currentCard]` and `deck[smallestCard]`.

Figure 8–23 The user interface for `CardDeckApplet`.

Adding Images to the Applet

After you have completed the implementation of `CardApplet` using `Strings` to display the cards, you may wish to utilize the card images provided for this lab (Figure 8–23). The card images were originally downloaded (with permission) from

```
http://www.waste.org/oxymoron/
```

They can retrieved from the companion CD or downloaded from the companion Web site

```
http://www.prenhall.com/morelli/labs
```

using a Web browser. They should be stored in the same folder as your applet's class files. Once you have downloaded the images, you must implement code in the applet to display the `Card`'s image instead of its `String` representation. You must also implement the code in the `Deck()` constructor that assigns the image to each individual `Card`. But beware: Loading 53 card images may take a few seconds!

Optional Exercise

Extend your program to play a hand of *Acey-Deucy*. In this game two cards are dealt face up. The player decides either to "hit me!" or "pass!" If the player takes a hit, a third card is dealt. If it falls between the other two cards, the player wins. If not, the player loses. For example, if an ace and a deuce are dealt, and the player draws an ace, the player loses.

You can implement the applet portion of this game with two additional buttons. The first button, call it "Deal," deals a new hand off the top of the deck each time it is clicked. The second button, call it "Hit Me," deals the third card. To implement scorekeeping for this game, it will be necessary to design a method which decides for a given card, whether it falls between two other cards. One way to do this might be to design a `Card` method that takes two `Card` parameters and returns a `boolean`:

```
public boolean isBetween(Card c1, Card c2){}
```

Java Language Summary

An **array** is a named collection of contiguous storage locations, each of which stores a data item of the same data type. Each element of an array is referred to by *subscript* — that is, by its position in the array. If the array contains *N* elements, then its length is *N* and its indexes are `0, 1, ..., N`. Array elements are referred to using the following subscript notation:

```
arrayname[subscript]
```

where *arrayname* is any valid identifier, and *subscript* is an integer value in the range 0 to `arrayname.length - 1`. The array's `length` instance variable can be used as a bound for loops that process the array.

An *array declaration* provides the name and type of the array. An array instantiation uses the keyword `new` and causes the compiler to allocate memory for the array's elements:

```
int arr[];                  // Declare a one-dimensional array variable
arr = new int[15];          // Allocate 15 int locations for it
```

Multidimensional arrays have arrays as their components:

```
int twoDarr[][];            // Declare a two-dimensional array variable
twoDarr = new int[10][15]; // Allocate 150 int locations
```

CHAPTER SUMMARY

Technical Terms

array
binary search
element type
polymorphic method
scaling
sorting
array initializer
bubble sort
multidimensional array
pseudorandom number
selection sort
subscript
array length
element
one-dimensional array
random number
sequential search

New Java Keywords

`abstract`
`false`
`new`
`boolean`
`final`
`null`
`double`
`float`
`private`

Java Library Classes

`Button`	`String`	`Vector`
`IndexOutOfBounds Exception`	`Double`	`Image`
	`Integer`	`Object`

Java Library Methods

`actionPerformed()`	`add()`	`addElement()`
`drawImage()`	`elementAt()`	`insertElementAt()`
`init()`	`paint()`	`print()`
`Math.random()`	`repaint()`	`Math.sqrt(double)`
`size()`	`Vector()`	

Programmer-Defined Classes

`Animate`	`CardApplet`	`Card`
`CyberPet`	`Deck()`	`SortObject`
`TestTwoDArrays`		

Programmer-Defined Methods

`avgDailyRain()`	`avgRainForMonth()`	`bubbleSort()`
`delay()`	`getImage()`	`inOrder()`
`printResults()`	`shuffleDeck()`	`sortDeck()`
`sort()`	`testDie()`	`toImage()`
`toString()`	`wait()`	

Summary of Important Points

- An array's values must be initialized by assigning values to each array location. An *initializer* expression may be included as part of the array declaration.
- The `Math.random()` method is used to generate *pseudorandom* numbers, which are useful for simulating chance events such as coin tosses.
- Bubble sort and selection sort are examples of array sorting algorithms. Both algorithms require making several passes over the array.
- When an array is passed as a parameter, a reference to the array is passed rather than the entire array itself.
- Swapping two elements of an array, or any two locations in memory, requires the use of a temporary variable.
- Sequential search and binary search are examples of array searching algorithms. Binary search requires that the array be sorted.
- For multidimensional arrays, each dimension of the array has its own `length` variable.

ANSWERS TO SELF-STUDY EXERCISES

EXERCISE 8.1 How much space (in bytes) would be allocated for each of the following?

a. `int a[] = new int[5];            // 5 * 4 = 20 bytes`
b. `double b[] = new double[20];     // 20 * 64 = 1280 bytes`
c. `char c[] = new char[30];         // 30 * 2  = 60 bytes`
d. `String s[] = new String[10];     // 10 * 4 (reference) = 40 bytes`
e. `CyberPet p[] = new CyberPet[5];// 5 * 4 (reference) = 20 bytes`

EXERCISE 8.2 Declare an array named `farr` that contains 10 `floats` initialized to the values `1.0, 2.0, ..., 10.0`.

```
float farr[] = {1.0,2.0,3.0,4.0,5.0,6.0,7.0,8.0,9.0,10.0};
```

EXERCISE 8.4 Write an expression that prints the first element of `farr`.

```
System.out.println(farr[0]);
```

Write an assignment statement that assigns 100.0 to the last element in `farr`.

```
farr[farr.length-1] = 100.0;
```

EXERCISE 8.5 Write a loop to print all of the elements of `farr`.

```
for (int j = 0; j < farr.length; j++)
    System.out.println(farr[j]);
```

EXERCISE 8.6 Declare an array of 100 `doubles` and write a loop to assign the first 100 square roots to its elements. [Use `Math.sqrt(double)`.]

```
double doubarr[] = new double[100];
for (int k = 0; k < doubarr.length; k++)
    doubarr[k] = Math.sqrt(k+1);
```

EXERCISE 8.7 `(int)(Math.random() * 11)`

EXERCISE 8.8 `2 + (int)(Math.random() * 11)`

EXERCISE 8.9

```
int suit = (int)(Math.random() * 4);       // 4 suits: 0,1,2,3
int rank = 2 + (int)(Math.random() * 13); // 13 cards per suit
```

EXERCISE 8.10

```
public void eat() {
    if (Math.random() > 0.5) // Approximately half the time
        petState = EATING;
}
public void sleep() {
    if (Math.random() > 0.5) // Approximately half the time
        petState = SLEEPING;
}
```

EXERCISE 8.11 The following changes would be made to the `TestRandom` class:

```
private int counter[] = new int[NFACES];  // Declare the array
public void initCounters() {              // Initialize the array
    for (int k = 0; k < counter.length; k++)
        counter[k] = 0;
}
```

EXERCISE 8.12 Sort the array, 24 18 90 1 0 85 34 18, by hand using bubble sort. Show the order of the elements after each iteration of the outer loop.

```
24 18 90 1  0  85 34 18 // Initial
18 24 1  0  85 34 18 90 // Pass 1
18 1  0  24 34 18 85 90 // Pass 2
1  0  18 24 18 34 85 90 // Pass 3
0  1  18 18 24 34 85 90 // Pass 4
0  1  18 18 24 34 85 90 // Pass 5
0  1  18 18 24 34 85 90 // Pass 6
0  1  18 18 24 34 85 90 // Pass 7
```

EXERCISE 8.13 Sort the array, 24 18 90 1 0 85 34 18, by hand using selection sort. Show the order of the elements after each iteration of the outer loop.

```
24 18 90 1   0   85 34 18 // Initial
0  18 90 1   24  85 34 18 // Pass 1
0  1  90 18  24  85 34 18 // Pass 2
0  1  18 90  24  85 34 18 // Pass 3
0  1  18 18  24  85 34 90 // Pass 4
0  1  18 18  24  85 34 90 // Pass 5
0  1  18 18  24  34 85 90 // Pass 6
0  1  18 18  24  34 85 90 // Pass 7
```

EXERCISE 8.14 Write a Java code segment to swap two CyberPets, pet1 and pet2.

```
CyberPet tempPet = pet1;
pet1 = pet2;
pet2 = tempPet;
```

EXERCISE 8.15 The above version of Bubblesort will keep passing over the array even if it's already sorted. Modify the algorithm so that it stops when the array is sorted. (*Hint*: Use a boolean variable to keep track of whether a swap was made inside the loop. And check this variable in the loop entry condition.)

```
public void bubbleSort(int arr[]) {
    int temp;                          // Temporary variable for swap
    boolean sorted = false;            // Initially, assume array is not sorted
    for (int pass = 1; !sorted && pass < arr.length; pass++)  { For each pass
        sorted = true;                                  // Assume it's sorted
        for (int pair = 1; pair < arr.length ; pair++ ) // For each pair
            if (arr[pair-1] > arr[pair]) {              //   Compare
                temp = arr[pair-1];                     //   And swap
                arr[pair-1] = arr[pair];
                arr[pair] = temp;
                sorted = false;                         // It can't be sorted
            } // if
    } // for pass
} // bubbleSort()
```

EXERCISE 8.16 myArr will store 1,2,3,5,5 and *k* will store 3.

EXERCISE 8.17 The following trace will result if you search for 21 in 2, 4, 6, 8, 10, 12, 14, 16, 18, 22, 24, 26, 28.;

```
key  iteration  low   high   mid
---------------------------------
21   0          0     19     9
21   1          10    19     14
21   2          15    19     17
21   3          18    19     18
21   4          19    19     19
21   5          20    19     failure
```

EXERCISE 8.18 Declare a two-dimensional array of int named int2d that contains five rows, each of which contains ten integers.

```
int int2d[] = new int[5][10];
```

EXERCISE 8.19 Write a statement that prints the last integer in the third row of the array you created in the previous exercise. Then write an assignment statement that assigns 100 to the last element in the `int2d`

```
System.out.println( int2d[2][9]);
int2d[4][9] = 100;
```

EXERCISE 8.20 Write a loop to print all of the elements of `int2d`, which you declared in the exercises in the previous section. Print one row per line with a space between each element on a line.

```
for (int k = 0; k < int2d.length; k++) {
     for (int j = 0; j < int2d[k].length; j++)
         System.out.print( int2d[k][j] + " ");
     System.out.println();                       // new line
}
```

EXERCISE 8.21 Declare a 52 × 7 two-dimensional array of `int` and initialize each of its elements to 0.

```
int sales[][] = new int[52][7];
for (int k = 0; k < sales.length; k++)
    for (int j= 0; j < sales[k].length; j++)
        sales[k][j] = 0;
```

EXERCISE 8.22 Write a method to calculate the average newspapers sold per week

```
double avgWeeklySales(int arr[][]) {
    double total = 0;
    for (int k = 0; k < arr.length; k++)
        for (int j= 0; j < arr[k].length; j++)
            total += sales[k][j];
    return total/52;
}
```

EXERCISE 8.23 Write a method to calculate the average newspapers sold per Sunday, where Sunday is the last day of the week.

```
double avgSundaySales( int arr[][] ) {
    double total = 0;
    for (int k = 0; k < sales.length; k++)
        total += sales[k][6];
    return total/52;
}
```

EXERCISES

EXERCISE 8.1 Explain the difference between the following pairs of terms.

a. An *element* and an element *type*.
b. A *subscript* and an *array element*.
c. A *random* number and *pseudorandom* number.
d. A *one-dimensional* array and *two-dimensional* array.
e. An *array* and a *vector*.
f. A *bubble sort* and a *selection sort*.
g. A *binary search* and a *sequential search*.

EXERCISE 8.2 Fill in the blank:

a. The process of arranging an array's elements into a particular order is known as _______.
b. One of the preconditions of the binary search method is that the array has to be _______.
c. An _______ is an object that can store a collection of elements of the same type.
d. An _______ is like an array except that it can grow.
e. For an array, its _______ is represented by an instance variable.
f. An expression that can be used during array instantiation to assign values to the array is known as an _______.
g. A _______ is an array of arrays.
h. A sort method that be used to sort different types of data is known as a _______ method.
i. To instantiate an array you have to use the _______ operator.
j. An array of objects stores _______ to the objects.

EXERCISE 8.3 Make each of the following array declarations.

a. A 4×4 array of `doubles`.
b. A 20×5 array of `Strings`.
c. A 3×4 array of `char` initialized to '*';
d. A $2 \times 3 \times 2$ array of `boolean` initialized to true.
e. A 3×3 array of `CyberPets`.
f. A 2×3 array of `Strings` initialized to "one," "two," and so on.

EXERCISE 8.4 Identify and correct the syntax error in each of the following.

a. `int arr = new int[15];`
b. `int arr[] = new int(15);`
c. `float arr[] = new [3];`
d. `float arr[] = new float {1.0,2.0,3.0};`
e. `int arr[] = {1.1,2.2,3.3};`
f. `int arr[][] = new double[5][4];`
g. `int arr[][] = { {1.1,2.2}, {3.3, 1} };`

EXERCISE 8.5 Evaluate each of the following expressions, some of which may be erroneous.

```
int arr[] = { 2,4,6,8,10 };
```

a. `arr[4]`
b. `arr[ arr.length ]`
c. `arr[ arr[0] ]`
d. `arr[ arr.length / 2 ]`
e. `arr[ arr[1] ]`
f. `arr[ 5 % 2 ]`
g. `arr[ arr[ arr[0] ] ]`
h. `arr[ 5 / 2.0 ]`
i. `arr[ 1 + (int) Math.random()`
j. `arr[ arr[3] / 2 ]`

EXERCISE 8.6 Evaluate each of the following expressions, some of which may be erroneous.

```
int arr[][] = { {2,4,6},{8,10} };
```

a. `arr.length`
b. `arr[1].length`
c. `arr[3][0]`
d. `++arr[0][0]`
e. `arr[0] * arr.length`
f. `arr[0][1]`
g. `arr[arr.length -1 ][0]`
h. `arr[0][3]`
i. `arr[0][1] * arr.length`
j. `arr[ arr[0][0] ][1]`

EXERCISE 8.7 What would be printed by the following code segment?

```
int arr[] = { 24, 0, 19, 21, 6, -5, 10, 16};
for (int k = 0; k < arr.length; k += 2)
  System.out.println( arr[k] );
```

EXERCISE 8.8 What would be printed by the following code segment?

```
int arr[][] = { {24, 0, 19}, {21, 6, -5}, {10, 16, 3}, {1, -1, 0} };
for (int j = 0; j < arr.length; j++)
  for (int k = 0; k < arr[j].length; k++)
    System.out.println( arr[j][k] );
```

EXERCISE 8.9 What would be printed by the following code segment?

```
int arr[][] = { {24, 0, 19}, {21, 6, -5}, {10, 16, 3}, {1, -1, 0} };
for (int j = 0; j < arr[0].length; j++)
    for (int k = 0; k < arr.length; k++)
        System.out.println(arr[k][j]);
```

EXERCISE 8.10 What's wrong with the following code segment, which is supposed to swap the values of the `int` variables, *n1* and *n2*?

```
int temp = n1;
n2 = n1;
n1 = temp;
```

EXERCISE 8.11 What's wrong with the following method, which is supposed to swap the values of its two parameters?

```
public void swapEm(int n1, int n2) {
    int temp = n1;
    n1 = n2;
    n2 = temp;
}
```

EXERCISE 8.12 Declare and initialize an array to store the following two-dimensional table of values:

```
1  2  3  4
5  6  7  8
9 10 11 12
```

EXERCISE 8.13 For the two-dimensional array you created in the previous exercise, write a nested for loop to print the values in the following order: 1 5 9 2 6 10 3 7 11 4 8 12. That is, print the values going down the columns instead of going across the rows.

EXERCISE 8.14 Define an array that would be suitable for storing the following values:

a. The GPAs of 2000 students.
b. The lengths and widths of 100 rectangles.
c. A week's worth of hourly temperature measurements, stored so that it is easy to calculate the average daily temperature.
d. A board for a tic-tac-toe game.
e. The names and capitals of the 50 states.

EXERCISE 8.15 Write code segment that will compute the sum of all the elements of an array of `int`.

EXERCISE 8.16 Write a code segment that will compute the sum of the elements a two-dimensional array of `int`.

EXERCISE 8.17 Write a method that will compute the average of all the elements of a two-dimensional array of `float`.

EXERCISE 8.18 Write a method that takes two parameters, an `int` array and an integer, and returns the location of the last element of the array which is greater than or equal to the second parameter.

EXERCISE 8.19 Write a program that tests whether a 3×3 array, input by the user, is a *magic square*. A Magic square is an $N \times N$ matrix of numbers in which every number from 1 to N^2 must appear just once and every row, column and diagonal must add up to the same total — for example,

```
6 7 2
1 5 9
8 3 4
```

EXERCISE 8.20 Revise the program in the previous exercise so that it allows the user to input the dimensions of the array, up to 4 × 4.

EXERCISE 8.21 Although most dice are 6-sided, they also come in other sizes. Write a Java expression that generates random integers for a 12-sided die. The die contains the numbers 1 to 12 on its faces.

EXERCISE 8.22 Revise the `TestRandom()` program to test the "fairness" of the 12-sided die from the previous exercise.

EXERCISE 8.23 Suppose the 12-sided die from the previous exercise has the numbers 3 through 14 on its faces. Write a Java expression that generates random integers for this die.

EXERCISE 8.24 A *cryptogram* is a message written in secret writing. Suppose you are developing a program to help solve cryptograms. One of the important bits of evidence is to compute the frequencies of the letters in the cryptogram. Write a program that takes a bunch of text as input and displays the relative frequencies of all 26 letters, 'a' to 'z.' (In English, the 'e' is the most frequent letter, with a relative frequency of around 12 percent.

EXERCISE 8.25 Modify the program from the previous exercise to that it can display the relative frequencies of the 10 most frequent and 10 least frequent letters. Use your program to help you distinguish between messages that were created using a substitution cipher and those that were created using a transposition cipher. What differences in letter frequencies would you expect between transposition and substitution?

EXERCISE 8.26 The *merge sort* algorithm takes two collections of data that have been sorted and merges them together. Write a program that takes two 25-element `int` arrays, sorts them, and then merges them, in order, into one 50-element array.

EXERCISE 8.27 **Challenge:** Design and implement a `BigInteger` class that can add and subtract integers with up to 25 digits. Your class should also include methods for input and output of the numbers. If you're really ambitious, include methods for multiplication and division.

EXERCISE 8.28 **Challenge:** Design a data structure for this problem: As manager of Computer Warehouse, you want to keep track of the dollar amount of purchases made by those clients that have regular accounts. The accounts are numbered from `0, 1, ..., N`. The problem is that you don't know in advance how many purchases each account will have. Some may have one or two purchases. Others may have 50 purchases.

EXERCISE 8.29 An *anagram* is a word made by rearranging the letters of another word. For example, "act" is an anagram of "cat", and "aegllry" is an anagram of "allergy." Write a Java program that accepts two words as input and determines if they are anagrams.

EXERCISE 8.30 **Challenge:** An *anagram dictionary* is a dictionary that organizes words together with their anagrams. Write a program that lets the user enter up to 100 words (in a `TextField`, say). After each word is entered, the program should display (in another `TextField` perhaps) the complete anagram dictionary for the words entered. Use the following sample format for the dictionary. Here the words entered by the user were: felt, left, cat, act, opt, pot, top.

```
act:  act cat
eflt:  felt left
opt:   opt pot top
```

EXERCISE 8.31 The Acme Trucking company has hired you to write software to help dispatch its trucks. One important element of this software is knowing the distance between any two cities that it services. Design and implement a `Distance` class that stores the distances between cities in a two-dimensional array. This class will need some way to map a city name, "Boise," into an integer that can be used as an array subscript. The class should also contain methods that would make it useful for looking up the distance between two cities. Another useful method would tell the user the closest city to a given city.

EXERCISE 8.32 Write a `SlideShowApplet` that displays an endless slide show. Use GIF files to store the images that make up the show. Load the images into an array and then repeatedly display an image from the array each time the user clicks on a control button. One modification to this program might be to show the slides in random order. That would make it less boring!

EXERCISE 8.33 Revise `CyberPet` (Figure 5–8) so that approximately half the time when commanded to eat or sleep it goes into a NOTHUNGRY or NOTSLEEPY state instead.

Photograph courtesy of Michal Heron, Pearson Education/PH College

9

Graphical User Interfaces

OBJECTIVES

After studying this chapter, you will

- Acquire a familiarity with the Swing component set.
- Understand the relationship between the AWT and Swing.
- Have a better understanding of Java's event model.
- Be able to design and build simple Graphical User Interfaces (GUI)s.
- Appreciate how object-oriented design principles were used to extend Java's GUI capabilities.

OUTLINE

9.1 Introduction

As we have seen, a *Graphical User Interface (GUI)* creates a certain way of interacting with a program. It is what gives a program its *look and feel*. A GUI is created from a set of basic components, such as buttons, text fields, labels, and text areas.

In the preceding chapters we used GUI components from Java's Abstract Windowing Toolkit (AWT). In this chapter we introduce the Swing component set, which extends the AWT in interesting and powerful ways. The Java Foundation Classes (JFC), of which the Swing set is a part, gives software developers the capability to build sophisticated and efficient software written entirely in Java's windowing system, rather than relying on the platform's windowing system. Prior to the release of the JFC, this was not possible.

Our focus throughout the chapter will be on designing and building simple GUIs using the Swing classes. The Swing library is so large we will concentrate on a relatively small handful of the basic Swing components. We will try to identify design principles that can be applied to the design of more advanced interfaces.

Because Java's GUI classes provide an excellent example of object oriented design, we will also try to call attention to some of the important design decisions and principles that have influenced the development of Java's GUI classes in both the AWT and Swing.

From the Java Library: AWT to Swing

With the release of Java2, also known as Java Development Kit (JDK) 1.2, Java now has two distinct libraries of GUI components. The *Abstract Windowing Toolkit (AWT)* has been part of Java since JDK 1.0. The *Java Foundation Classes (JFC)*, including the *Swing component set*, were originally released with JDK 1.1. Both are included in JDK 1.2 (now renamed Java2).

A Brief History

Although the original version of the AWT was suitable for developing Java applets, it wasn't powerful enough to support full-fledged application development. Programs such as word processors and spreadsheets have GUI requirements that were just too much for the original AWT.

AWT 1.1, which was released with JDK 1.1, improved upon the original version. It was faster, and it provided a better way of handling events. However, despite these improvements, the AWT still did not contain a rich enough set of GUI components to support full-fledged application development. Also, it was still highly dependent on non-Java, native code, so application programs that used the AWT weren't very portable.

Because of these shortcomings, some software developers built their own sets of GUI components. Netscape's *Internet Foundation Classes (IFC)*, which were built upon AWT 1.0 classes, were a vast improvement over the AWT 1.1 classes. Most importantly, the IFC classes were written entirely in Java, which made them much more portable than the AWT classes.

In 1997 Netscape and Sun (JavaSoft) joined forces on the so-called Swing project, whose goal was to develop a sophisticated set of GUI classes written entirely in Java. The results of this effort, the *Java Foundation Classes (JFC)*, including the `Swing` component set, were released with JDK 2.0.

Like their AWT counterparts, Swing components are GUI controls, such as buttons, frames, and textfields. Because they are rendered entirely by Java code, Swing components make it possible to design GUIs that are truly platform independent. A program that uses Swing components will have the same look and feel on a Mac, Windows, or Unix platform.

The *100% Pure Java* initiative is a widespread industry effort to develop a truly platform independent programming environment. Such an environment would make it possible to develop programs that could run on all computers. In the present environment, software developers have to spend millions of dollars developing different versions of their products for each different platform.

Heavyweight versus Lightweight Components

The AWT peer model

AWT components are based on the **peer model**. Every AWT component has a corresponding peer class written in the native system's code. For example, the `java.awt.Button` class has a peer named `java.awt.peer.Button`. The peer class serves as the interface between the Java code and the native windowing system. The methods in the peer class are written in native code. Therefore, AWT components are inherently platform dependent.

AWT components are considered *heavyweight* because they depend on the native (peer) system for their drawing and rendering. Every AWT component has an associated component in the native windowing system. This is why a Java button on a Windows platform looks just like a Windows button. In effect, the Java button, via its peer, creates and uses a Windows button. When you change the Java button's label, it must call a method in the peer class that changes the label of the peer button. This interaction between Java and the native windowing system requires a good deal of overhead, thereby affecting the overall efficiency of the system.

Lightweight components

A **lightweight component** is one that is written in pure Java. Instead of depending on a native component for its rendering, a lightweight component is drawn and rendered entirely by Java code. One way to build a lightweight component is to extend the abstract `java.awt.Component` class and then override its `paint()` method:

```
public class LightWeightButton extends Component {

    public void paint(Graphics g) {
       /* Java code goes here */
    }
}
```

The comment indicates where you would put the commands to draw and paint the button. Because they don't depend on peers in the native

Figure 9–1 Swing classes, part 1: Relationship between the AWT and the top-level Swing windows.

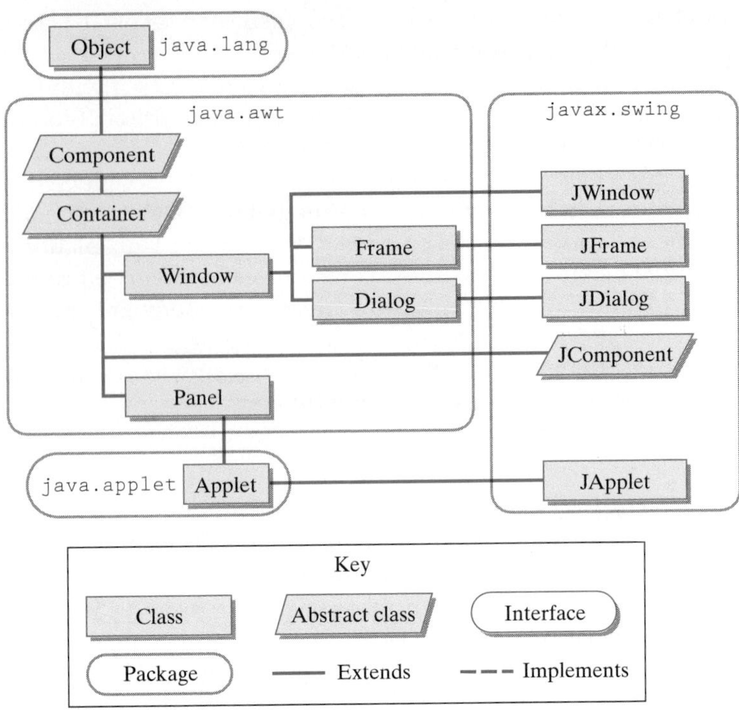

windowing system, lightweight components are much more efficient than the regular AWT components.

All Swing components except for the four top-level window classes — the `JApplet`, `JDialog`, `JFrame`, and `JWindow` — are lightweight components. As you can see, Swing components that have corresponding AWT components have names that begin with "J." Figure 9–1 shows the relationship between the AWT `Container` and `Component` classes and the top-level Swing classes.

Because these four classes are derived from heavyweight components, they themselves are dependent on the native windowing system. However, note that the abstract `JComponent` class is derived directly from the `Container` class. Therefore it, and all of its Swing subclasses, are lightweight components (Figure 9–2).

The Future of the AWT

What's going to happen to the AWT in the future? It is somewhat of a misconception to assume that now that the Swing component set is available, the AWT package will be dropped. However, even if an application or applet uses Swing components (and no AWT component), that will still not break the dependence on the AWT. So despite the introduction of the Swing component set, it is clear that the AWT will remain an essential part of GUI development in Java.

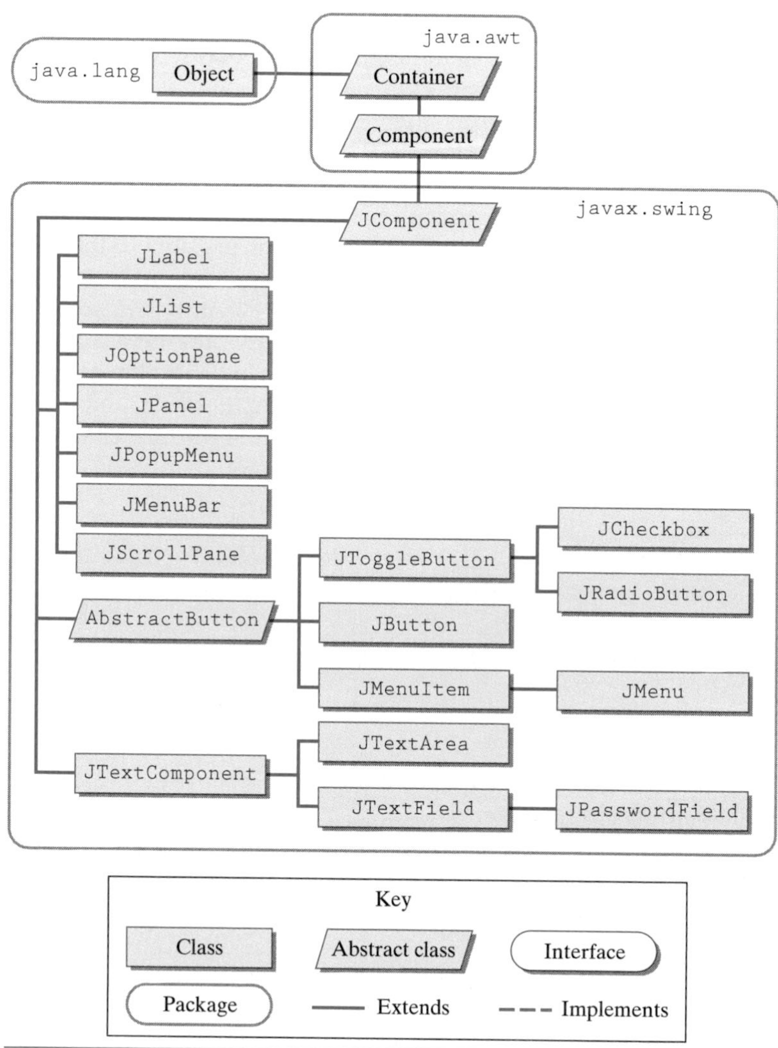

Figure 9–2 Swing classes, part 2: Swing components derived from `JComponent` are lightweight.

First, Swing's top-level window classes — `JApplet`, `JDialog`, `JFrame`, and `JWindow` — are defined as extensions to their AWT counterparts. This means that Swing-based GUIs are still dependent on the AWT. Java programs need to have some way to map their windows to the windowing system used on the native (Windows, Solaris, or MacOS) platform. The AWT's top-level windows — `Window`, `Frame`, `Dialog`, and `Panel` — provide that mapping.

Second, the `JComponent` class, which is the basis for all Swing components, is derived from `java.awt.Container`. And there are many more such dependencies. So Swing components are fundamentally based on the AWT.

Finally, all GUI applications and applets use layout managers (`java.awt.FlowLayout`), fonts (`java.awt.Font`), colors (`java.awt.Color`), and other (noncomponent) classes that are defined in the AWT. So there is no way to design a GUI without using AWT classes.

The programs presented in this chapter will use Swing components instead of AWT components. But they will also use layouts and other elements from the AWT. In terms of GUI components alone, Swing provides a replacement for every AWT component, as well as many new components that have no counterpart in the AWT. Although it is possible to mix and match AWT and Swing components in the same application, this is not advisable. Both sets of components use the same event model, so there are no problems on that score. But, if you are developing new software in Java, you should use the Swing components. This will allow you to take advantage of the new GUI features that come with Swing, and it will also place your programs squarely on the road to the future. That's the approach we will take in this and subsequent chapters.

PROGRAMMING TIP: Swing Documentation. Complete documentation of the Swing classes is available for downloading or browsing on Sun's Web site at:

```
http://java.sun.com/products/jdk/1.2/docs/guide/swing/index.html
```

SELF-STUDY EXERCISES

EXERCISE 9.1 What would have to be done to make a Swing-based GUI completely platform independent?

EXERCISE 9.2 Why are abstract classes, such as the `Container` and `Component` classes, not dependent on peers in the native windowing system?

9.2 The Swing Component Set

Java's Swing components are defined in a collection of packages named `javax.swing.*`, which is assumed by the code shown in this and subsequent chapters. (In JDK 1.1, these packages were named `com.sun.java.swing.*`, so if you are using JDK 1.1, you will have to change the package names in the programs that follow.) Some of the packages included under Swing include the following:

```
javax.swing.event.*
javax.swing.plaf.*
javax.swing.text.*
```

The `javax.swing.event` package defines the various Swing events and their listeners. (In the AWT, the AWT events and listeners were defined in `java.awt.event`.)

The `javax.swing.text` package contains the classes for `JTextField` and `JTextComponent`, the Swing classes that replace the AWT's `TextField` and `TextArea` classes. The Swing text components are more complex than their AWT counterparts. For example, one of their important features is the ability to undo changes made to the text they contain. This feature is crucial for building sophisticated word processing applications.

The `javax.plaf` package contains Swing's look-and-feel classes. The term *plaf* is an acronym for **pluggable look and feel**. It refers to the fact that changing an application's look and feel is a simple matter of "plugging in" a different plaf model. Changing how a program looks does not change what it does.

Swing's platform independent look and feel is achieved by placing all the code responsible for drawing a component in a separate class from the component itself. For example, in addition to `JButton`, the class which defines the button control, there will be a separate class responsible for drawing the button on the screen. The drawing class will control the button's color, shape, and other characteristics of its appearance.

There are several look-and-feel packages built into Swing. For example the `javax.swing.plaf.motif` package contains the classes that implement the Motif interface, a common Unix-based interface. These classes know how to draw each component, and how to react to mouse, keyboard and other events associated with these components. The `javax.swing.plaf.windows` package takes the same responsibility for a Windows 95 style interface.

OBJECT-ORIENTED DESIGN: Model-View-Controller Architecture

Java's Swing components have been implemented using an object-oriented design known as the **model-view-controller (MVC)** model. Any Swing component can be viewed in terms of three independent aspects: what state it's in (its model), how it looks (its view), and what it does (its controller).

For example, a button's role is to appear on the interface waiting to be clicked. When it is clicked, the button's appearance changes. It looks pushed in or it changes color briefly and then it changes back to its original (unclicked) appearance. In the MVC model, this aspect of the button is its **view**. If you were designing an interface for a button, you would need visual representations for both the clicked and the unclicked button (as well as other possible states).

When you click a button, its internal state changes from pressed to unpressed. You've also probably seen buttons that were disabled — that is, in a state where they just ignore your clicks. Whether a button is enabled or disabled, and whether it is pressed or not, are properties of its internal state. All such properties, taken together, constitute the button's **model**. Of course, a button's view — how it looks — depends on its model. When a button is pressed, it has one appearance, and when it is disabled, it has another.

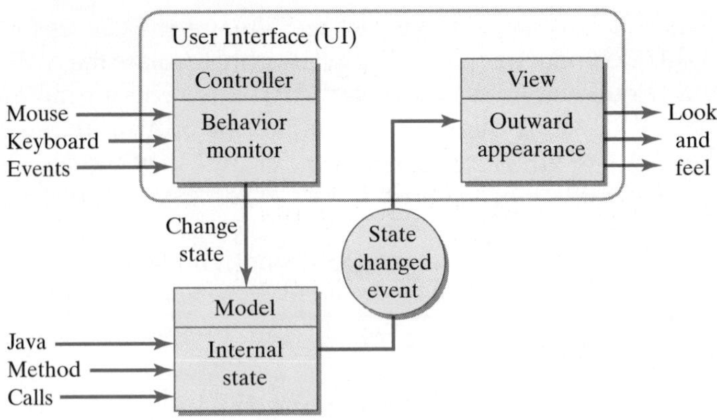

Figure 9–3 The model-view-controller architecture.

Because a button's state will change when it is clicked or when it is enabled by the program, some object needs to keep track of these changes. That part of the component is its **controller**.

Figure 9–3 shows how the button's model, view, and controller interact with each other. Suppose the user clicks on the button. This action is detected by the controller. Whenever the mouse button is pressed, the controller tells the model to change into the pressed state. The model, in turn, generates an event that is passed to the view. The event tells the view that the button needs to be redrawn to reflect its change in state.

When the mouse button is released, a similar sequence of events occurs. The model is told to change to the unpressed state. It in turn generates an event, handled by the view, which changes the button's appearance.

A change in the button's appearance does not necessarily depend on direct action by the user. For example, the program itself could call a method that disables the button. In this case, the program issues a command directly to the model, which in turn generates an event that causes the view to change the object's appearance.

For some Swing components, such as the text components, this three-part model is implemented almost exactly as we just described. For others, such as the `JButton`, one class is used to implement both the view and the controller. The `JButton` model is defined in the `DefaultButtonModel` class, and its view and controller are defined in the `BasicButtonUI` class. The `UI` acronym stands for User Interface. The point is that for some components, Swing has organized the view and control — the look and the feel — into a single class.

Pluggable Look and Feel

The MVC model uses a clear division of labor to implement a GUI component. The main advantage of this design is the independence between the model, the view, and the controller. If you want to give a button a different look and feel, you can redefine its view and its controller.

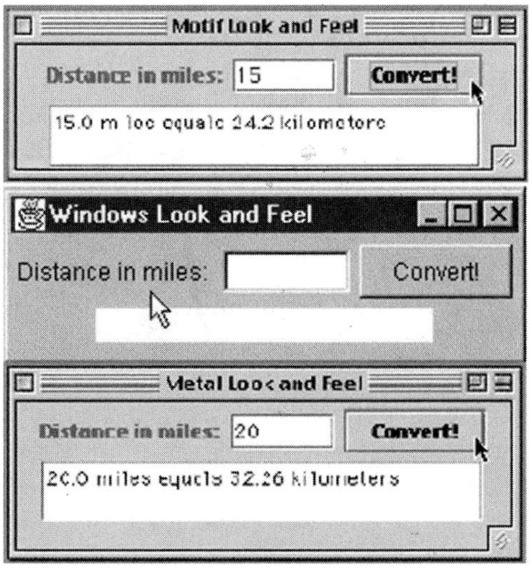

Figure 9–4 The same Java application using the Motif, Windows, and Metal look-and-feel.

model, the view, and the controller. If you want to give a button a different look and feel, you can redefine its view and its controller.

By combining the view and controller into a single class, Swing makes it even easier to change a component's look and feel. For example, to design your own look and feel for a `JButton`, you would define a class that implemented all of the methods in the `BasicButtonUI`. Of course, this is a job for an experienced software developer.

To set the look and feel within a program, you can use the `UIManager.setLookAndFeel()` method:

```
public static void main (String args[]{
    try{
        UIManager.setLookAndFeel(
            "javax.swing.plaf.metal.MetalLookAndFeel");
    }catch (Exception e) {}
}//main()
```

The *Metal* look-and-feel is one designed specifically for Java applications, and it is the default. For a Windows look you can use the following argument: `"com.sun.java.swing.plaf.windows.WindowsLookAndFeel"`. Figure 9–4 shows how the same simple application would appear under the three different look-and-feel styles.

SELF-STUDY EXERCISES

EXERCISE 9.3 The MVC architecture is a model of object-oriented design. But if a `JButton` is really composed of three separate parts, how can we still call it a component? Isn't it really three things?

9.3 The Java Event Model

Back in Chapter 4, we took a brief look at Java's **event model** as it applied to applets. According to this model , anything that happens while the computer is running is classified as an event. Every keystroke and mouse click, every time a disk is inserted into a disk drive, an event is generated.

When a Java program is running, events generated by the hardware are passed up through the operating system (and through the browser, for applets) to the program. Those events that belong to the program must be handled by the program (refer back to Figure 4–8). For example, if you click on your browser's menu bar, that event will be handled by the browser itself. If you click on a button contained in an applet, that event should be handled by the applet.

9.3.1 Events and Listeners

In Java, whenever something happens within a GUI component, whether an AWT or a Swing component, an event object is generated and passed to the *event listener* that has been registered to handle that component's events. You've seen numerous examples of this process in earlier chapters, but it will be useful to review the details here in terms of a Swing example.

Suppose you create a `JButton` in an applet:

```
private JButton clickme = new JButton("ClickMe");
```

Whenever the user clicks on the `JButton`, an `ActionEvent` will be generated. In order to handle these events, the applet must register the `JButton` with a listener object that listens for action events. This is usually done in the applet's `init()` method:

```
public void init() {
    add(clickme);                      // Add clickme to the applet
    clickme.addActionListener(this); // Register it with a listener
}
```

In this case, we have designated the applet itself (`this`) as an `ActionListener` for `clickme`. A **listener** is any object that implements a *listener interface*, which is one of the interfaces derived from `java.util.EventListener`. An `ActionListener` is an object that listens for and receives `ActionEvents`.

Figure 9–5 An applet that handles action events on a `JButton`.

```
import javax.swing.*;
import java.awt.*;
import java.awt.event.*;
import java.applet.*;

public class MyApplet extends JApplet implements ActionListener {
    private JButton clickme = new JButton("ClickMe");

    public void init() {
        getContentPane().add(clickme);    // Add clickme to the applet
        clickme.addActionListener(this); // Register it with a listener
    } // init()

    public void actionPerformed(ActionEvent e) {
        if (e.getSource() == clickme) {
            showStatus("clickme was clicked");
            System.out.println( e.toString() );
        }
    } // actionPerformed()
} // MyApplet
```

In order to complete the event handling code, the applet must implement the `ActionListener` interface. As Figure 9–5 shows, implementing an interface is a matter of declaring the interface in the class heading, and implementing the methods contained in the interface, in this case the `actionPerformed()` method.

Now that we have implemented the code in Figure 9–5, whenever the user clicks on `clickme`, that action is encapsulated within an `ActionEvent` object and passed to the applet's `actionPerformed()` method. This method contains Java code that will handle the user's action in an appropriate way. For this example, it just prints a message in the applet's status bar and displays a string representation of the event.

The methods used to handle the `ActionEvent` are derived from the `java.util.EventObject` class, the root class for all events:

```
public class EventObject {
    public EventObject(Object source);
    public Object getSource();
    public String toString();
}
```

Our example (Figure 9–5) uses the `getSource()` method to get a reference to the object that generated the event. It also uses the `toString()` method to get a string representation of the event that was generated. Here's what it displays:

```
java.awt.event.ActionEvent[ACTION_PERFORMED,cmd=ClickMe]
  on javax.swing.JButton[,58,5,83x27,
  layout=javax.swing.OverlayLayout]
```

As you can see, the event generated was an `ACTION_PERFORMED` event, in response to the `ClickMe` command. The source of the event was the `JButton`.

9.3.2 Event Classes

Although the event model is the same for both AWT and Swing classes, the Swing package introduces many additional events. Table 9–1 lists the events that are generated by both AWT and Swing components. In the preceding chapters we've written applets that handled `ActionEvents` for `Buttons` and `TextFields`. These same events are generated for the Swing counterparts to these components: `JButton` and `JTextField`.

In viewing Table 9–1, it's important to remember that the classes listed there are arranged in a hierarchy. This will affect the events that a particular object can generate. For example, a `JButton` is `JComponent` (Figure 9–2), so in addition to generating `ActionEvents` when the user clicks on it, it can also generate `MouseEvents` when the user moves the mouse over it. Similarly, because a `JTextField` is also a `JComponent`, it can generate `KeyEvents` as well as `ActionEvents`.

Note that the more generic events, such as those that involve moving, focusing, or resizing a component, are associated with the more generic components. For example, the `JComponent` class contains methods that are

Table 9.1. Java's `AWTEvents` for each `Component` type (Original source: David Flanagan, *Java in a Nutshell*, 2d ed., O'Reilly Associates, 1997. Modified for Swing components.)

Components	Events	Description
`Button, JButton`	`ActionEvent`	User clicked button
`CheckBox, JCheckBox`	`ItemEvent`	User toggled a checkbox
`CheckboxMenuItem, JCheckboxMenuItem`	`ItemEvent`	User toggled a checkbox
`Choice, JPopupMenu`	`ItemEvent`	User selected a choice
`Component, JComponent`	`ComponentEvent`	Component was moved or resized
	`FocusEvent`	Component acquired or lost focus
	`KeyEvent`	User typed a key
	`MouseEvent`	User manipulated the mouse
`Container, JContainer`	`ContainerEvent`	Component added/removed from container
`List, JList`	`ActionEvent`	User double-clicked a list item
	`ItemEvent`	User clicked a list item
`Menu, JMenu`	`ActionEvent`	User selected menu item
`Scrollbar, JScrollbar`	`AdjustmentEvent`	User moved scrollbar
`TextComponent, JTextComponent`	`TextEvent`	User edited text
`TextField, JTextField`	`ActionEvent`	User typed Enter key
`Window, JWindow`	`WindowEvent`	User manipulated window

used to manage ComponentEvents. Because they are subclasses of JComponent, JButtons and JTextFields can also use these methods. Defining the more generic methods in the JComponent superclass is another example of the effective use of inheritance.

EFFECTIVE DESIGN: Inheritance. The higher a method is defined in the inheritance hierarchy, the broader its use.

Table 9–2 lists events that are new with the Swing classes. Some of the events apply to new components. For example, JTable and JTree do not have AWT counterparts. Other events provide Swing components with capabilities that are not available in their AWT counterparts. For example, a CaretEvent allows the programmer to have control over mouse clicks that occur within a text component.

SELF-STUDY EXERCISES

EXERCISE 9.4 Is it possible to register a component with more than one listener?

EXERCISE 9.5 Is it possible for a component to have two different kinds of listeners?

Table 9.2. Some of the events that are newly defined in the Swing library.

Component	Events	Description
JPopupMenu	PopupMenuEvent	User selected a choice
JComponent	AncestorEvent	An event occurred in an ancestor
JList	ListSelectionEvent	User double-clicked a list item
	ListDataEvent	List's contents were changed
JMenu	MenuEvent	User selected menu item
JTextComponent	CaretEvent	Mouse clicked in text
	UndoableEditEvent	An undoable edit has occurred
JTable	TableModelEvent	Items added/removed from table
	TableColumnModelEvent	A table column was moved
JTree	TreeModelEvent	Items added/removed from tree
	TreeSelectionEvent	User selected a tree node
	TreeExpansionEvent	User expanded or collapsed a tree node
JWindow	WindowEvent	User manipulated window

9.4 Case Study: Designing a Basic GUI:

What elements make up a basic user interface? If you think about all of the various interfaces you've encountered — and don't just limit yourself to computers — they all have the following elements:

- Some way to provide help/guidance to the user.
- Some way to allow input of information.
- Some way to allow output of information.
- Some way to control the interaction between the user and the device.

Think about the interface on a beverage machine. Printed text on the machine will tell you what choices you have, where to put your money, and what to do if something goes wrong. The coin slot is used to input money. There's often some kind of display to tell you how much money you've inserted. And there's usually a bunch of buttons and levers that let you control the interaction with the machine.

These same kinds of elements make up the basic computer interface. Designing a graphical user interface is primarily a process of choosing components that can effectively perform the tasks of input, output, control, and guidance.

EFFECTIVE DESIGN: User Interface. A user interface must effectively perform the tasks of input, output, control, and guidance.

In the programs we designed in the earlier chapters, we used two different kinds of interfaces. In the *command-line* interface, we used printed prompts to inform the user, typed commands for data entry and user control, and printed output to report results. Our applet interfaces used `Label`s to guide and prompt the user, `TextField`s and `TextArea`s as basic input and output devices, and either `Button`s or `TextFields`s for user control.

Up to this point, all of our GUIs have taken the form of Java applets. So let's begin by building a basic GUI in the form of a Java application. To keep the example as close as possible to the applet interfaces we've used, we'll build it out of the following Swing components: `JLabel`, `JTextField`, `JTextArea`, and `JButton`.

9.4.1 The Metric Converter Application

Suppose the coach of the cross country team asks you to write a Java application that can be used to convert miles to kilometers. The program should let the user input a distance in miles, and it should report the equivalent distance in kilometers.

Before we design the interface for this, let's first define a `MetricConverter` class that can be used to perform the conversions. For now at least, this class's only task will be to convert miles to kilometers, for which it will use the formula that 1 kilometer equals 0.62 miles:

```
public class MetricConverter {

    public static double milesToKm(double miles) {
        return miles / 0.62;
    }
}
```

Note that the method takes a `double` as input and returns a `double`. Also, by declaring the method `static`, we make it a class method, so it can be invoked simply by

```
MetricConverter.milesToKm(10);
```

Choosing the Components

Let's now design a GUI to handle the interaction with the user. First, let's choose Swing components for each of the four interface tasks of input, output, control and guidance. For each component, it may be useful to refer back to Figure 9–2 to note its location in the Swing hierarchy.

Which components do we need?

- A `JLabel` is a display area for a short string of text, an image, or both. Its AWT counterpart, the `Label`, cannot display images. A `JLabel` does not react to input. Therefore it is used primarily to display a graphic or small amounts of static text. It is perfectly suited to serve as a prompt, which is what we will use it for in this interface.
- A `JTextField` is a component that allows editing of a single line of text. It is also identical to its AWT counterpart, the `TextField`. By using its `getText()` and `setText()` methods, a `JTextField` can be used for either input or output, or both. For this problem, we'll use it to perform the interface's input task.
- A `JTextArea` is a multiline text area that can be used for either input or output. It is almost identical to the AWT `TextArea` component. One difference, however, is that a `JTextArea` does not contain scrollbars by default. For this program, we'll use the `JTextArea` for displaying the results of conversions. Because it is used solely for output, we'll make it *uneditable* to prevent the user from typing in it.
- Let's use a `JButton` as our main control for this interface. By implementing the `ActionListener` interface we will handle the user's action events.

Choosing the Top-level Window

The next issue we must decide is what kind of top-level window to use for this interface. For applet interfaces the top-level component would be a `JApplet`. For Java applications, you would typically use a `JFrame` as the top-level window. Both of these classes are subclasses of `Container`, so they are suitable for holding the components that make up the interface (Figure 9–1).

What top-level window should we use?

Also, as we noted earlier, JApplets and JFrames are both examples of heavyweight components, so they both have windows associated with them. To display a JFrame we just have to give it a size and make it visible. Because a frame runs as a stand-alone window, not within a browser context, it should also be able to exit the application when the user closes the frame.

Designing a Layout

How should the components be arranged?

The next step in designing the interface is deciding how to arrange the components so that they will be visually appealing and comprehensible, as well as easy to use.

Figure 9–6 shows a design for the layout. It has the output text area, as the largest component, occupying the center of the JFrame. The prompt, input text field, and control button are arranged in a row above the text area. This is a simple and straightforward layout.

Figure 9–6 also provides a **containment hierarchy**, or a **widget hierarchy**, showing the containment relationships among the various components. Although it may not seem so for this simple layout, the containment hierarchy plays an important role in showing how the various components are grouped together in the interface. For this design, we have a relatively simple hierarchy, with only one level of containment. All of the components are contained directly in the JFrame.

Figure 9–7 shows the implementation of the Converter class. Let's compare its features to those of a comparable applet. Instead of extending the JApplet class, this program extends the JFrame class. As we just mentioned, a JFrame is a top-level window that can contain GUI components. Also, our program implements the ActionListener interface. This will enable it to handle action events. The actionPerformed() method is exactly the same as it would be for an applet, which underscores the fact that the event model is the same for Swing as it was for the AWT.

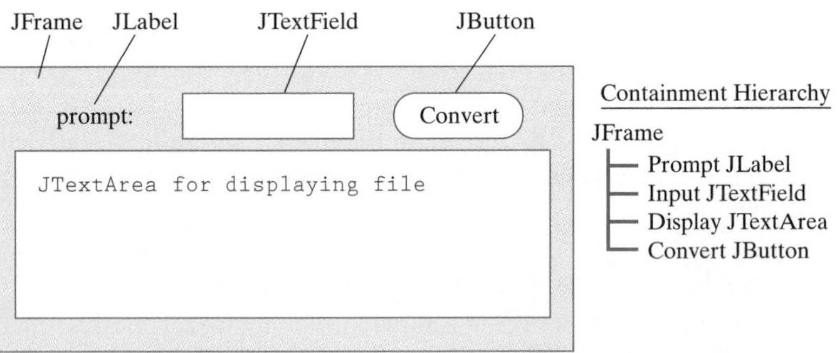

Figure 9–6 A design and layout for the Metric Converter GUI. The *containment hierarchy* (also called a *widget hierarchy*) shows the containment relationships among the components.

Figure 9–7 The `Converter` class implements a simple GUI interface.

```
import javax.swing.*;                 // Packages used
import java.awt.*;
import java.awt.event.*;

public class Converter extends JFrame implements ActionListener{

    private JLabel prompt = new JLabel("Distance in miles: ");
    private JTextField input = new JTextField(6);
    private JTextArea display = new JTextArea(10,20);
    private JButton convert = new JButton("Convert!");

    public Converter() {
        getContentPane().setLayout(new FlowLayout());
        getContentPane().add(prompt);
        getContentPane().add(input);
        getContentPane().add(convert);

        getContentPane().add(display);

        display.setLineWrap(true);
        display.setEditable(false);

        convert.addActionListener(this);
    } // Converter()

    public void actionPerformed( ActionEvent e ) {
        double miles = Double.valueOf(input.getText()).doubleValue();
        double km = MetricConverter.milesToKm(miles);
        display.append(miles + " miles equals " + km + " kilometers\n");
    } // actionPerformed()

    public static void main(String args[]) {
        Converter f = new Converter();
        f.setSize(400, 300);
        f.setVisible(true);
        f.addWindowListener(new WindowAdapter() {      // Quit the application
            public void windowClosing(WindowEvent e) {
                System.exit(0);
            }
        });
    } // main()
} // Converter
```

Note the three packages that are imported. The first contains definitions of the Swing classes, and the other two contain definitions of AWT events and layout managers that are used in the program.

Instead of performing initializations in the `init()` method as we would for an applet, we do all initializing in the constructor. There are two important points to notice about the constructor. First, note that we have set the `JFrame`'s layout to `FlowLayout`. A **layout manager** is the object that is responsible for sizing and arranging the components in a container. A flow layout is the simplest arrangement: The components are arranged left to right in the window, wrapping around to the next "row" if necessary.

Second, note the statements used to set the layout and to add components directly to the JFrame. Instead of adding components directly to the JFrame, we must add them to its content pane:

```
getContentPane().add(input);
```

A **content pane** is a JPanel that serves as the working area of the JFrame. It contains all of the frame's components. Java will raise an exception if you attempt to add a component directly to a JFrame.

DEBUGGING TIP: A JFrame cannot directly contain GUI elements. Instead they must be added to its content pane, which can be retrieved using the getContentPane() method.

Unlike their AWT counterparts, JFrame and all the other top-level Swing windows have an internal structure made up of several distinct objects that can be manipulated by the program. Because of this structure, GUI elements can be organized into different layers within the window, making possible all sorts of sophisticated layouts. Also, one layer of the structure makes it possible to associate a menu with the frame. Thus, the use of a content pane represents a major advance beyond the functionality available with java.awt.Frame.

Finally, note how the Converter frame is instantiated, made visible, and eventually exited in the application's main() method:

```
public static void main(String args[]) {
    Converter f = new Converter();
    f.setSize(400, 300);
    f.setVisible(true);
    f.addWindowListener(new WindowAdapter() {      // Quit the application
        public void windowClosing(WindowEvent e) {
            System.exit(0);
        }
    });
} // main()
```

It is necessary to set both the size and visibility of the frame, since these are not set by default. Because we are using a FlowLayout, it's especially important to give the frame an appropriate size. Failure to do so may cause the components to be arranged is a confusing way and may even cause some components to not show up at all in the window. These are limitations we will fix when we learn how to use some of the other layout managers.

9.4.2 Inner Classes and Adapter Classes

Inner classes

Note also the code that's used to quit the Converter application. The program provides a listener that listens for window closing events. When such an event occurs, it exits the application by calling System.exit().

This syntax used here is an example of an *anonymous inner class*, a language feature that was introduced with JDK 1.1. An inner class is a class defined within another class. The syntax is kind of ugly, because it places the class definition right where a reference to a window listener object would go. In effect what the code is doing is defining a subclass of `WindowAdapter` and creating an instance of it to serve as a listener for window closed events.

Anonymous inner classes provide a useful way of creating classes and objects on the fly to handle just this kind of listener task. The syntax used actually enables us to write one expression that both defines a class and creates an instance of it to listen for window closing events. The new subclass has local scope limited here to the `main()` method. It is anonymous, meaning we aren't even giving it a name, so you can't create other instances of it in the program. Note that the body of the class definition is placed right after the `new` keyword, which takes the place of the argument to the `addWindowListener()` method. For more details on the inner and anonymous classes, see Appendix F.

Adapter class

An *adapter class* is a wrapper class that implements trivial versions of the abstract methods that make up a particular interface. The `WindowAdapter` class implements the methods of the `WindowListener` interface. When you implement an interface, such as `ActionListener`, you must implement all the abstract methods defined in the interface. For `ActionListener`, there's just one method, the `actionPerformed()` method, so we can just implement it as part of our applet or frame class. However, the `WindowListener` interface contains seven methods. But we only want to use the `windowClosed()` method in this program, which is the method implemented in the anonymous inner class:

```
public void windowClosing(WindowEvent e) {
    System.exit(0);
}
```

The `WindowAdapter` is defined simply as

```
public abstract class WindowAdapter implements WindowListener {
    public void windowActivated(WindowEvent e) {}
    public void windowClosed(WindowEvent e) {}
    ...
    // Five other window listener methods
}
```

Note that each method is given a trivial implementation (`{}`). To create a subclass of `WindowAdapter`, you must implement at least one of its abstract methods.

> **JAVA LANGUAGE RULE** **Inner Class.** An inner class is a class defined within another class. Inner classes are mostly used to handle a task that supports the work of the containing class.

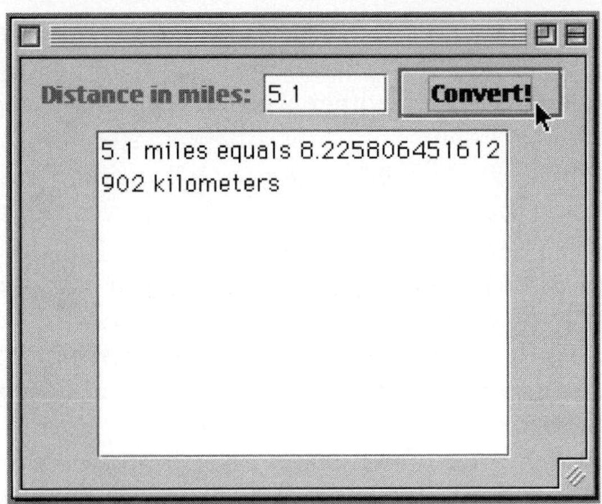

Figure 9–8 The first version of the metric converter GUI.

EFFECTIVE DESIGN: Anonymous Adapter Classes. Anonymous adapter classes provide a useful way of creating an object to handle one particular kind of event within a program.

9.4.3 GUI Design Critique

Figure 9–8 shows the converter interface. Although our basic GUI design satisfies the demands of input, output, control, and guidance, it has a couple of significant design flaws.

First, it forces the user to manually clear the input field after each conversion. Unless it is important that the user's input value remain displayed until another value is to be input, this is just an inconvenience to the user. In this case the user's input value is displayed along with the result in the `JTextArea`, so there's no reason not to clear the input text field:

```
input.setText("");  // Clear the input field
```

EFFECTIVE DESIGN: Reduce the User's Burden. A GUI should aim to minimize the responsibility placed on the user. In general, the program should do any task that it can do, unless, of course, there is a compelling reason that the user should do the task.

A second problem with our design is that it forces the user to switch between the keyboard (for input) and the mouse (for control). Experienced users will find this annoying. An easy way to fix this problem is to make both the `JTextField` and the `JButton` serve as controls. That way, to get the program to do the conversion, the user can just press the Enter key after typing a number into the text field.

To give the interface this type of control, we need only add an `ActionListener` to the `JTextField` during the initialization step:

```
input.addActionListener(this);
```

Like its `TextField` counterpart, a `JTextField` generates an `ActionEvent` whenever the Enter key is pressed inside it. We don't even need to modify the `actionPerformed()` method, since both controls will generate the same action event. This will make it possible for users who prefer the keyboard to carry out all their interactions with the program using just the keyboard.

EFFECTIVE DESIGN: User Interface. A GUI should aim to minimize the number of different input devices (mouse, keyboard) that the user has to manipulate in order to perform a particular task.

Given that the user can now interact with the interface using just the keyboard, a question arises over whether we should keep the button at all. In this case, it seems justifiable to keep both the button and the text field controls. Some users dislike typing and prefer to use the mouse. Also, having two independent sets of controls is a desirable form of redundancy. You see it frequently in menu-based systems that allow menu items to be selected either by mouse or by special control keys.

EFFECTIVE DESIGN: Desirable Redundancy. Certain forms of redundancy in an interface, such as two sets of independent controls (mouse and keyboard), make it more flexible or more widely usable.

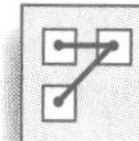

SELF-STUDY EXERCISES

EXERCISE 9.6 Another deficiency in the converter interface is that it doesn't round off its result, leading sometimes to numbers with 20 or so digits. Develop Java code to fix this problem.

EXERCISE 9.7 Give an example of desirable redundancy in the design of your car.

9.4.4 Extending the Basic GUI: Button Array

Suppose the coach likes our program but complains that some of the folks in the office are terrible typists and would prefer not to have to use the keyboard at all. Is there some way we could modify the interface to accommodate these users?

What components do we need?

This gets back to the point we were just making about incorporating redundancy into the interface. One way to satisfy this requirement would be to implement a numeric keypad for input, similar to a calculator keypad. Regular `JButtons` can be used as the keypad's keys. As keypad button's are clicked, their face values — 0 through 9 — are inserted into the text field. The keypad will also need a button to clear the text field and one to serve as a decimal point.

How should the components be organized?

This new feature will add 12 new `JButton` components to our interface. Instead of inserting them into the `JFrame` individually, it will be better to organize them into a separate panel, and to insert the entire panel into the frame as a single unit. This will help reduce the complexity of the display, especially if the keypad buttons can be grouped together visually. Instead of having to deal with 16 separate components, the user will see the keypad as a single unit with a unified function. This is an example of the *abstraction principle*, similar to the way we break long strings of numbers (1–888–889–1999) into subgroups to make them easier to remember.

EFFECTIVE DESIGN: Reducing Complexity. Organizing elements into distinct groups by function, helps to reduce the GUI's complexity.

Figure 9–9 shows the revised design for the converter interface. The containment hierarchy shows that the 12 keypad are contained within a `JPanel`. In the frame's layout, the entire panel is inserted just after the text area.

The `JPanel`

Incorporating the keypad into the interface will require several changes in the program's design. A `JPanel` is generic container. It is a subclass of `Container` via the `JComponent` class (Figure 9–2). Its main purpose is to contain and organize components that appear together on an interface.

In this case, we will use a `JPanel` to hold the keypad buttons. As you might expect, to add elements to a `JPanel`, you use the `add()` method, which is inherited from `Container`, just as we did when adding elements to an applet. (Recall that an `Applet` is also a subclass a `Container` via the `Panel` class.)

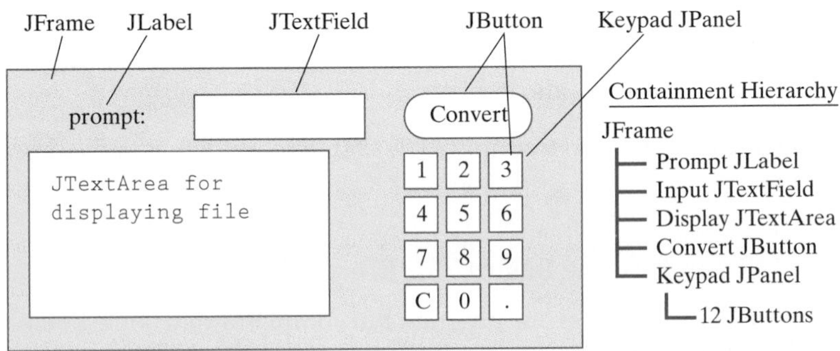

Figure 9–9 A widget hierarchy showing the containment relationships among the components.

What data do we need?

The JPanel will take care of holding and organizing the JButtons within the visual display. We also need some way to organize and manage the 12 keypad buttons within the program's memory. Clearly this is a good job for an array. Actually, two arrays would be even better, one for the buttons and one for their labels:

```
private JButton keyPad[];              // An array of buttons
private String label[] =               // An array of button labels
            { "1","2","3",
              "4","5","6",
              "7","8","9",
              "C","0","." };
```

Algorithm design

The label array stores the strings that we will use as the buttons' labels. The main advantage of the array is that we can use a loop to instantiate the buttons:

```
/**
 * Task: initKeyPad() initializes the keypadPanel and keyPad array
 * Pre: keypadPanel is an JPanel, keyPad is an JButton array,
 *   label is a pre-initialized String array
 * Post: NBUTTONS JButtons are created and stored in the array.
 *   They are also inserted into the JPanel
 */
public void initKeyPad() {
    keyPad = new JButton[NBUTTONS];                 // Create the array itself
    for(int k = 0; k < keyPad.length; k++) {        // For each button
        keyPad[k] = new JButton(label[k]);          //  Create a labeled button
        keyPad[k].addActionListener(this);          //  and a listener
        keypadPanel.add(keyPad[k]);                 //  and add it to the panel
    } // for
} // initKeyPad()
```

The initKeyPad() method would be called from the constructor *before* we add the keypad itself to the application's frame. It begins by instantiating the array itself. It then uses a for loop, bounded by the size of the array, to instantiate each individual button and insert it into the array. Note how the loop variable here, *k*, plays a dual role. It serves as the index into both the button array (keyPad) and the array of strings that serves as the buttons' labels (label). In that way the labels are assigned to the appropriate buttons.

Note also how each button is assigned an ActionListener and added to the keypad panel:

```
keyPad[k].addActionListener(this);     // Add a listener
keypadPanel.add(keyPad[k]);            // add keyPad to the panel
```

Event handling

The final step in completing this revision is to modify the actionPerformed() method so it can handle the actions on the new buttons. The idea here is to distinguish when the user's action applies to the keypad rather than to the actions associated with the text field or the convert button. An if-else statement can be used to distinguish between a conversion action (on the button or text field) and an input action (on the buttons in the keypad):

```
/**
 * Task: actionPerformed() handles all action events in the frame
 * Pre:  convert is an JButton, input is an JTextField
 * Post: the appropriate action is performed
 */
public void actionPerformed(ActionEvent e) {
    if (e.getSource() == convert || e.getSource() == input) {
        double miles = Double.valueOf(input.getText()).doubleValue();
        double km = MetricConverter.milesToKm(miles);
        display.append(miles + " miles equals " + km + " kilometers\n");
        input.setText("");
    } else {                                    // A keypad button was pressed
        JButton b = (JButton)e.getSource();
        if (b.getText().equals("C"))
            input.setText("");
        else
            input.setText( input.getText() + b.getText() );
    }
} // actionPerformed()
```

The `getSource()` method is used to determine whether either the `convert` button or the `input` text field generated the event. If neither of them was the source of the event, then it must have been generated by one of the keypad buttons.

Default logic

The structure of this if-else statement is significant. We are using the else clause as a "catch all" condition to catch and handle the events generated by any one of the 12 buttons in the keypad. This particular logic saves us from having to use a loop to go through the array of keypad buttons testing whether each one generated the event.

PROGRAMMING TIP: If-else Logic. The last else clause in an if-else statement can be used as default clause or a "catch-all" clause to implicitly cover all the cases that weren't explicitly covered in the preceding clauses.

The same kind of "catch-all" logic is used in the second if-else statement, which is nested within the else clause of the first if-else statement. This statement is used to determine whether or not the user has clicked the clear key, whose label equals "C." If so, the input text field is cleared, by setting its text to the empty string. Otherwise, the user must have clicked one of the other keypad buttons, so its label is simply appended to the text already stored in the text field:

```
input.setText( input.getText() + b.getText() );
```

In this way, the user's input will be appended to the text field until the user hits the Enter key or the convert button.

The complete implementation of this revised version of the interface is shown if Figure 9–10. The appearance of the interface itself is shown in Figure 9–11.

Figure 9–10 The second version of the `Converter` class, which implements the GUI shown in Figure 9–11.

```
import javax.swing.*;       // Packages used
import java.awt.*;
import java.awt.event.*;

public class Converter extends JFrame implements ActionListener{ // Version 2

    private final static int NBUTTONS = 12;

    private JLabel prompt = new JLabel("Distance in miles: ");
    private JTextField input = new JTextField(6);
    private JTextArea display = new JTextArea(10,20);
    private JButton convert = new JButton("Convert!");
    private JPanel keypadPanel = new JPanel();

    private JButton keyPad[];                 // An array of buttons
    private String label[] =                  // An array of button labels
            { "1","2","3",
              "4","5","6",
              "7","8","9",
              "C","0","." };

    public Converter () {
        getContentPane().setLayout( new FlowLayout() );
        initKeyPad();
        getContentPane().add(prompt);
        getContentPane().add(input);
        getContentPane().add(convert);
        getContentPane().add(display);
        getContentPane().add(keypadPanel);
        display.setLineWrap( true );
        display.setEditable( false );

        convert.addActionListener(this);
        input.addActionListener(this);
    } // Converter()

    public void initKeyPad() {
        keyPad = new JButton[NBUTTONS];              // Create the array itself
        for(int k = 0; k < keyPad.length; k++) {     // For each button
            keyPad[k] = new JButton(label[k]);       //  Create a labeled button
            keyPad[k].addActionListener(this);       //  and a listener
            keypadPanel.add(keyPad[k]);              //  and add it to the panel
        } // for
    } // initKeyPad()

    public void actionPerformed(ActionEvent e) {
        if (e.getSource() == convert || e.getSource() == input) {
            double miles = Double.valueOf(input.getText()).doubleValue();
            double km = MetricConverter.milesToKm(miles);
            display.append(miles + " miles equals " + km + " kilometers\n");
            input.setText("");
        } else {                                // A keypad button was pressed
            JButton b = (JButton)e.getSource();
            if (b.getText().equals("C"))
                input.setText("");
            else
                input.setText( input.getText() + b.getText() );
        }
    } // actionPerformed()
```

Figure 9–10 *Continued*

```
    public static void main(String args[]) {
        Converter f = new Converter();
        f.setSize(400, 300);
        f.setVisible(true);
        f.addWindowListener(new WindowAdapter() {      // Quit the application
            public void windowClosing(WindowEvent e) {
                System.exit(0);
            }
        });
    } // main()
} // Converter
```

9.4.5 GUI Design Critique

As Figure 9–11 shows, despite our efforts to group the keypad into a `JPanel`, it doesn't appear as single entity in the interface itself. This is a layout problem. The default layout for a `JPanel` is `FlowLayout`. But a numeric keypad should be arranged into a two-dimensional grid pattern, which is the kind of layout our design called for (Figure 9–9).

Fortunately, this flaw can easily be fixed by using a appropriate layout manager from the AWT, as we will do in the next version of the program. Indeed, the `java.awt.GridLayout` is perfectly suited for a two-dimensional keypad layout (Section 9.5.2).

The lesson to be learned from this example is that screen layout is an important element of an effective GUI. If not done well, it can undermine the GUI's effort to guide the user toward the appointed tasks. If done poorly enough, it can even keep the user from doing the task at all.

EFFECTIVE DESIGN: Layout Design. The appropriate layout and management of GUI elements is an important part of interface design. It contributes to the interface's ability to guide the user's action toward the interface's goals.

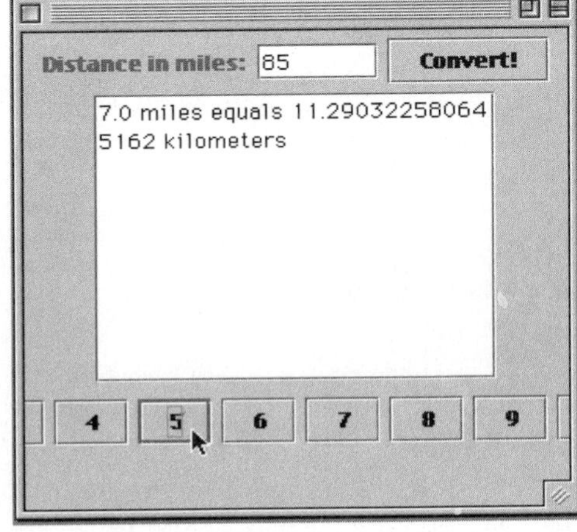

Figure 9–11 The second version of the metric converter GUI uses a set of keypad buttons for input, but they are not properly arranged.

9.5 Containers and Layout Managers

A `Container` is a component that can contain other components. Because containers can contain other containers, it is possible to create a hierarchical arrangement of components, as we did in the second version of our `Converter` interface. In its present form, the hierarchy for `Converter` consists of a `JFrame` as the top-level container (Figure 9–9). Contained within the frame is a `JPanel`, which contains 12 `JButtons`. Most GUIs will have a similar kind of containment hierarchy.

A `Container` is a relatively simple object whose main task is primarily to hold its components in a particular order. It has methods to add and remove components:

```
public Component add(Component comp);
public Component add(Component comp, int index);
public void remove(int index);
public void remove(Component comp);
public void removeAll();
```

As you can see from these methods, a container keeps track of the order of its elements, and it is possible to refer to a component by its index order.

9.5.1 Layout Managers

The real hard work of organizing and managing the elements within a container is the task of the layout manager. A *layout manager* is an object that manages the layout and organization of its container. Among the tasks it performs are

- To determine the overall size of the container.
- To determine the size of each element in the container.
- To determine the spacing between elements.
- To determine the positioning of the elements.

Although it is possible to manage your own layouts, it is not easy to do. For most applications you are much better off by learning to use one of the AWT's built-in layouts. Table 9–3 gives a brief summary of the available layouts. We will show examples of `FlowLayout`, `GridLayout`, and `BorderLayout`.

Some of the widely used Swing containers have a default layout manager assigned to them (Table 9–4). Note that unlike its `Applet` counterpart, which had a default `FlowLayout`, a `JApplet` has a `BorderLayout`. This can cause problems if you are converting an AWT-based applet to a Swing-based `JApplet`. In such cases it is necessary to override `JApplet`'s default layout by using the `setLayout()` method.

Table 9.3. Some of Java's AWT and Swing Layout Managers

Manager	Description
`java.awt.BorderLayout`	Arranges elements along the north, south, east, west, and in the center of the container.
`java.swing.BoxLayout`	Arranges elements in a single row or single column.
`java.awt.CardLayout`	Arranges elements like a stack of cards, with one visible at a time.
`java.awt.FlowLayout`	Arranges elements left to right across the container.
`java.awt.GridBagLayout`	Arranges elements in a grid of variable sized cells (complicated).
`java.awt.GridLayout`	Arranges elements into a two-dimensional grid of equally sized cells.
`java.swing.OverlayLayout`	Arranges elements on top of each other.

To override the default layout for any of the `JApplet`, `JDialog`, `JFrame`, and `JWindow` containers, you must remember to use the `getContentPane()`. The correct statement is

```
getContentPane().setLayout(new FlowLayout());
```

PROGRAMMING TIP: Default Layouts. When converting an AWT applet to Swing applet, it is necessary to override the default layout associated with the `JApplet`'s content pane.

DEBUGGING TIP: Content Pane. Attempting to add a component directly to a `JApplet` or a `JFrame` will cause an exception. For these top-level containers, components must be added to their content panes.

Table 9.4. Default layouts for some of the common Swing containers

Container	Layout Manager
`JApplet`	`BorderLayout` (on its content pane)
`JBox`	`BoxLayout`
`JDialog`	`BorderLayout` (on its content pane)
`JFrame`	`BorderLayout` (on its content pane)
`JPanel`	`FlowLayout`
`JWindow`	`BorderLayout` (on its content pane)

9.5.2 The GridLayout Manager

It is simple to remedy the layout problem that affected the keypad panel in the most recent version of the Converter program. The problem was caused by the fact that the keypad's JPanel uses a default FlowLayout, which causes the keypad's buttons to be arranged in a row. A more appropriate layout for a numeric keypad would be a two-dimensional grid, which is exactly the kind of layout supplied by the java.awt.GridLayout. Therefore, to fix this problem, we need only set the layout of the keypadPanel to a GridLayout. This takes a single statement, which should be added to the beginning of the initKeyPad() method:

```
keypadPanel.setLayout( new GridLayout(4,3,1,1) ); // Arrange in a grid
```

This statement creates a GridLayout object and assigns it as the layout manager for the keypadPanel. It will insure that the keypad will have four rows and three columns of buttons (Figure 9–12). The last two arguments in the constructor affect the relative spacing between the rows and the columns. The higher the number, the larger the spacing. As components are added to the keypad, they will automatically be arranged by the manager into a 4×3 grid.

Note that for a JPanel, the setLayout() method applies to the panel itself. Unlike the top-level containers, such as JFrame, other containers don't have content panes. The same point would apply when adding components to a JPanel: They are added directly to the panel, not to a content pane. Confusion over this point could be the source of bugs in your programs.

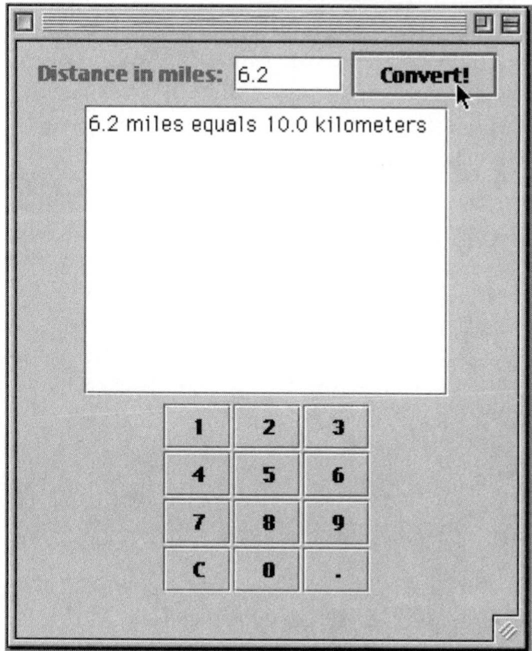

Figure 9–12 This version of the metric converter GUI uses a keypad for mouse-based input. It has an attractive overall layout.

DEBUGGING TIP: Content Pane. Top-level containers, such as `JFrame`, are the only ones that use a content pane. For other containers, such as `JPanel`, components are added directly to the container itself.

As its name suggests, the `GridLayout` layout manager arranges components in a two-dimensional grid. When components are added to the container, the layout manager starts inserting elements into the grid at the first cell in the first row and continues left to right across row 1, then row 2, and so on. If there are not enough components to fill all cells of the grid, the remaining cells are left blank. If an attempt is made to add too many components to the grid, the layout manager will try to extend the grid in some reasonable way in order to accommodate the components. However, despite its effort in such cases, it usually fails to achieve a completely appropriate layout.

PROGRAMMING TIP: Grid Layouts. Make sure the number of components added to a `GridLayout` is equal to the number rows times the number of columns.

9.5.3 GUI Design Critique

The layout in Figure 9–12 is much improved. However, there are still some deficiencies. One problem is that the `convert` button seems to be misplaced. It would seem to make more sense if it were grouped together with the keypad, rather than with the input text field.

A more serious problem results from the fact that we are still using a `FlowLayout` for the program's main window, the `JFrame`. Among all of Java's layouts, `FlowLayout` gives you the least amount of control over the arrangement of the components. Also, `FlowLayout` is most sensitive to changes in the size and shape of its container.

9.5.4 The `BorderLayout` Manager

One way to fix these problems is to use a `BorderLayout` to divide the frame into five areas: north, south, east, west, and center, as shown in Figure 9–13. The areas are arranged along the north, south, east, and west edges of the container and at its center. The `BorderLayout` class contains two constructors:

```
public BorderLayout();
public BorderLayout(int hgap, int vgap);
```

The two parameters in the second version of the constructor allow you to put some spacing between the respective areas.

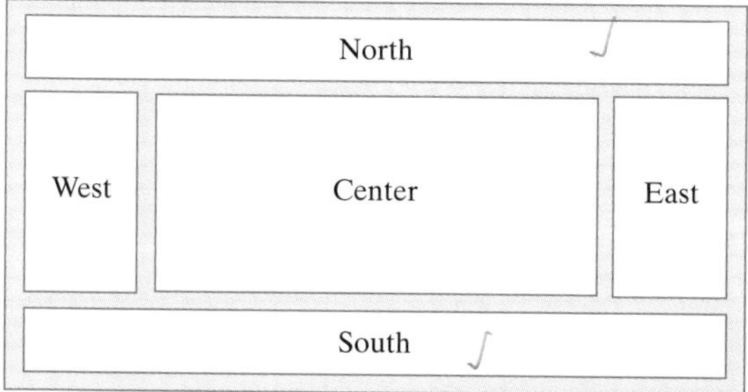

Figure 9–13 Arrangement of components in a border layout. The relative size of the areas will vary.

Components are added to a `BorderLayout` by using the `add (Component,String)` method found in the `Container` class. For example, to set the application window to a border layout and to add the `keypadPanel` to its east area, we would use the following statements:

```
getContentPane().setLayout(new BorderLayout(2, 2));
getContentPane().add(keypadPanel,"East");
```

In this version of the `add()` method the second parameter must be a capitalized `String` with one of the names, "North," "South," "East," "West," or "Center." The order in which components are added does not matter.

Containment hierarchy

One limitation of the `BorderLayout` is that only one component can be added to each area. That means that if you want to add several components to an area, you must first enclose them within a `JPanel` and then add the entire panel to the area. For example, let's create a panel to contain the prompt and the text field and place it at the north edge of the frame:

```
JPanel inputPanel = new JPanel();          // Create the panel
inputPanel.add(prompt);                    // Add the label
inputPanel.add(input);                     // and the text field
getContentPane().add(inputPanel,"North"); // Add the panel to the frame
```

The same point would apply if we want group the keypad together with the convert button and place them at the east edge. There are several ways these elements could be grouped. In this example, we give the panel a border layout, and put the keypad in the center and the convert button at the south edge:

```
JPanel controlPanel = new JPanel(new BorderLayout(0, 0));
controlPanel.add( keypadPanel,"Center" );
controlPanel.add( convert, "South");
getContentPane.add(controlPanel,"East"); // Add the panel to the frame
```

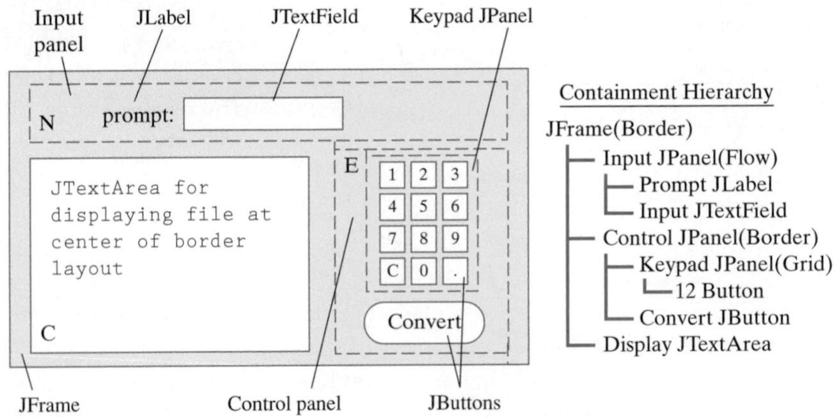

Figure 9–14 A border layout design for the metric converter program. The dotted lines show the panels.

Given these details about the `BorderLayout`, a more appropriate design for the converter application is shown in Figure 9–14. Notice that border layout for the top-level `JFrame` uses only the center, north and east areas. Similarly, the border layout for the control panel uses just the center and south areas.

In a `BorderLayout`, when one (or more) border area is not used, then one or more of the other areas will be extended to fill the unused area. For example, if `West` is not used, then `North, South`, and `Center` will extend to the left edge of the `Container`. If `North` is not used, then `West, East,` and `Center` will extend to the top edge. This is true for all areas except `Center`. If `Center` is unused, it is left blank.

Figure 9–15 shows the results we get when we incorporate these changes into the program. The only changes to the program itself occur in the constructor method, which in its revised form is defined as follows:

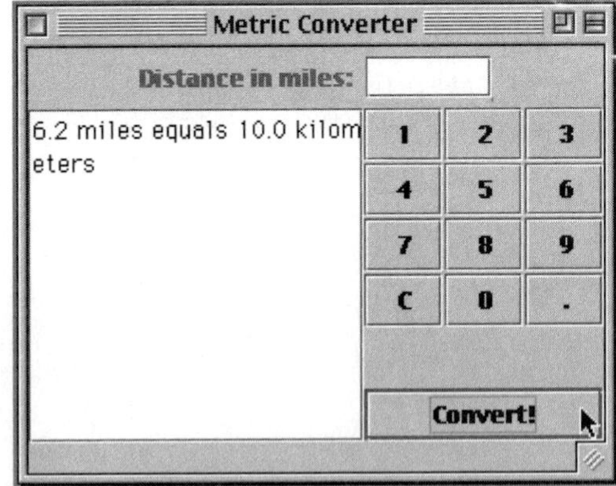

Figure 9–15 The metric converter, showing its appearance when a border design is used.

```
public Converter() {
    getContentPane().setLayout(new BorderLayout());
    initKeyPad();

    JPanel inputPanel = new JPanel();          // Input panel
    inputPanel.add(prompt);
    inputPanel.add(input);
    getContentPane().add(inputPanel,"North");

    JPanel controlPanel = new JPanel(new BorderLayout(0, 0)); // Control panel
    controlPanel.add(keypadPanel, "Center");
    controlPanel.add(convert, "South");
    getContentPane().add(controlPanel, "East");

    getContentPane().add(display,"Center");  // Output display
    display.setLineWrap(true);
    display.setEditable(false);

    convert.addActionListener(this);
    input.addActionListener(this);
} // Converter()
```

This layout divides the interface into three main panels, an input panel, display panel, and control panel, and gives each panel its own layout. In addition, the control panel contains the keypad panel within it. Thus, the containment hierarchy for this design is much more complex than for our original design.

SELF-STUDY EXERCISES

EXERCISE 9.8 The border layout for the top window uses the north, center, and east regions. What other combinations of areas might be used for these three components?

EXERCISE 9.9 Why wouldn't a flow layout be appropriate for the control panel?

9.6 Checkboxes, Radio Buttons, and Borders

Problem statement

Suppose you are the software developer for your own software business specializing in computer games. You want to develop an applet-based order form that can be used for ordering software over the Web. At the moment you have three software titles — a chess game, a checkers game, and a crossword puzzle game. The assumption is that the user will choose one or more of these titles from some kind of menu. The user must also indicate a payment option — either E-cash, credit card, or debit card. These options are mutually exclusive — the user can choose one and only one.

Interface design

Let's design an applet interface for this program. Unlike the previous problem where the input was a numeric value, in this problem the input will be the user's selection from some kind of menu. The result will be the creation of an order. Let's suppose that this part of the task happens behind the scenes — that is, we don't have to worry about creating an actual order. The output the user sees will simply be an acknowledgment that the order was successfully submitted.

What components do we need?

There are several kinds of controls needed for this interface. First, a conventional way to have the users indicate their decisions to make a purchase is to have them click on a Submit button. They should also have the option to Cancel the transaction at any time.

In addition to these button controls, a couple of menus must be presented, one for the software titles, and one for the payment options. Swing and AWT libraries provide many options for building menus.

One key requirement for this interface is the mutually exclusive payment options. A conventional way to handle this kind of selection is with a `JRadioButton`—a button that belongs to a group of mutually exclusive alternatives. Only one button from the group may be selected at one time. The selection of software titles could be handled by a collection of checkboxes. A `JCheckbox` is a button that can be selected and deselected and which always displays its current state to the user. Using a checkbox will make it obvious to the user exactly what software has been selected.

To complete the design, let's use a `JTextArea` again to serve as something of a printed order form. It will confirm the user's order and display other messages needed during the transaction.

Given these decisions, we arrive at the design shown in Figure 9–16. In this case our design uses a main `JPanel` as the main container, instead of using the top window itself. The reason for this decision is that we want to use Swing `Borders` around the various `JPanels` to enhance the overall visual appeal of the design. The borders will have titles that help explain the purpose of the various panels.

What top-level windows do we use?

Note that the top-level window in this case is a `JApplet`. By default it will have a border layout. For the main `JPanel` we are using a 3×1 `GridLayout`. The components in the main panel are the `JTextArea` and two other `JPanels`. The `GridLayout` will take care of sizing these so they are all of equal size.

Component layout

Containment hierarchy

The center panel, which uses a flow layout, contain panels for the checkboxes and the radio buttons. These elements are grouped within their own panels. Again, we can put a border around them in the final implementation (Figure 9–17). The button panels use a `BoxLayout`, which we will discuss below. This design leads to the most complex containment hierarchy thus far.

9.6.1 Checkbox and Radio Button Arrays

What data structures do we need?

Because we will need three checkboxes, one for each title, and three radio buttons, one for each payment option, it will be useful again to use arrays to store both the buttons and their titles:

```
private ButtonGroup optGroup = new ButtonGroup();
private JCheckBox titles[] = new JCheckBox[NTITLES];
private JRadioButton options[] = new JRadioButton[NOPTIONS];
private String titleLabels[] =
    {"Chess Master - $59.95", "Checkers Pro - $39.95","Crossword Maker - $19.95"};
private String optionLabels[] = {"Credit Card", "Debit Card", "E-cash"};
```

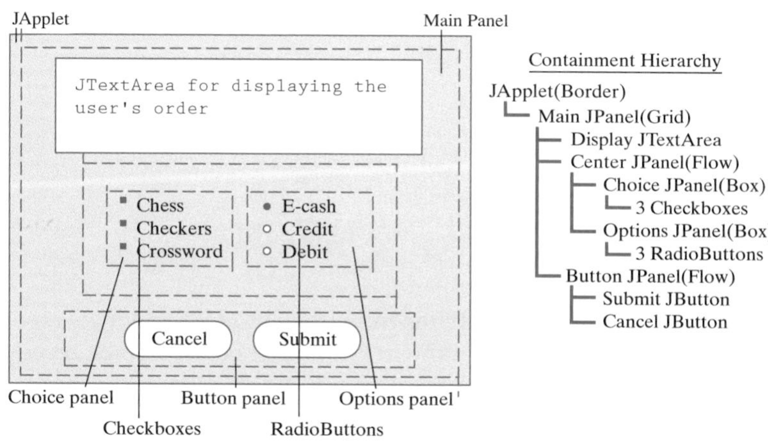

Figure 9–16 A design for an on-line order form interface.

Again, the advantage of this design is that it simplifies the instantiation and initialization of the buttons:

```
for(int k = 0; k < titles.length; k++) {
    titles[k] = new JCheckBox(titleLabels[k]);
    titles[k].addItemListener(this);
    choicePanel.add(titles[k]);
}
```

The only difference between this array of checkboxes and the keypad array of buttons that we used in the `Converter` program is that checkboxes generate `ItemEvents` instead `ActionEvents`. Therefore, each checkbox must be registered with an `ItemListener` (and of course the applet itself must implement the `ItemListener` interface). We'll show how `ItemEvents` are handled below.

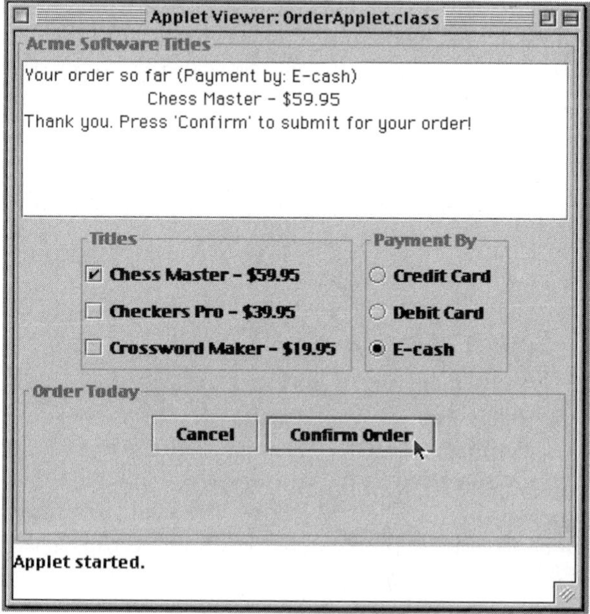

Figure 9–17 Borders around containers help make them stand out more.

The code for instantiating and initializing the radio buttons is almost the same:

```
for(int k = 0; k < options.length; k++) {
    options[k] = new JRadioButton(optionLabels[k]);
    options[k].addItemListener(this);
    optionPanel.add(options[k]);
    optGroup.add(options[k] );
}
options[0].setSelected(true);    // Set the first button on
```

Radio buttons also generate `ItemEvents`, so they too must be registered with an `ItemListener`. Note that the first button is set on, which represents a default payment option for the user.

The difference between checkboxes and radio buttons is that radio buttons must be added to a `ButtonGroup` — here named `optGroup` — in order to enforce mutual exclusion among them. A `ButtonGroup` is an object whose sole task is to enforce mutual exclusion among its members. Whenever you click on one radio button, the `ButtonGroup` will automatically be notified of this event and will turn off whatever other button was turned on.

Divide and conquer

Note the effective division of labor that's used in Java's design of the various objects that a radio button belongs to. The `optionPanel` is a GUI component (a `JPanel`) that contains the button within the visual interface. Its role is to help manage the graphical aspects of the button's behavior. The `ButtonGroup` is just an `Object`, not a GUI component. Its task is to monitor the button's relationship to the other buttons in the group. Each object has a clearly delineated task.

This division of labor is a key feature of object-oriented design. It is clearly preferable to giving one object too broad a responsibility. For example, a less effective design might have given the task of managing a group of buttons to the `JPanel` that contains them. However, this would lead to all kinds of problems, not least of which is the fact that not everything in the container belongs to the same button group. So a clear division of labor is a much preferable design.

EFFECTIVE DESIGN: Division of Labor. In good object-oriented design, objects are specialists (experts) for very narrow, clearly defined tasks. If there's a new task that needs doing, design a new object to do it.

9.6.2 Swing Borders

The Swing `Border` and `BorderFactory` classes can be used to put borders around virtually any GUI element. Using borders is an effective way to make the grouping of components more apparent. Borders can have titles, which enhance the GUI's ability to guide and inform the user. They can also have a wide range of styles and colors, thereby helping to improve the GUI's overall appearance.

A border occupies some space around the edge of a JComponent. For the Acme interface, we place titled borders around four of the panels (Figure 9–17). The border on the main panel serves to identify the company again. The one around the button panel serves to group to two control buttons. The borders around both the checkbox and the radio button menus help to set them apart from other elements of the display, and help identify the purpose of the buttons.

Attaching a titled border to a component — in this case to a JPanel — is very simple. It takes one statement:

```
choicePanel.setBorder(BorderFactory.createTitledBorder("Titles"));
```

The setBorder() method is defined in JComponent and inherited by all Swing components. It takes a Border argument. In this case, we use the BorderFactory class to create a border and assign it a title. There are several versions of the static createTitledBorder() method. This version lets us specify the border's title. It uses default values for type of border (etched), the title's position (sitting on the top line), justification (left), and for type and color of the font.

As you would expect, the Border and BorderFactory classes contain methods that let you exert significant control over the border's look and feel. You can even design and create your own custom borders.

9.6.3 The BoxLayout Manager

Another simple layout to use is the BoxLayout. This can be associated with any container, and it comes as the default with the Swing Box container. We use it in this example to arrange the checkboxes and radio buttons (Figure 9–16).

A BoxLayout is like a one-dimensional grid layout. It allows multiple components to be arranged either vertically or horizontally in a row. The layout will not wrap around, as does the FlowLayout. Unlike the GridLayout, the BoxLayout does not force all its components to be the same size. Instead it trys to use each component's preferred width (or height) in arranging them horizontally (or vertically). (Every Swing component has a preferred size that is used by the various layout managers in determining the component's actual size in the interface.) The BoxLayout manager also tries to align its components' heights (for horizontal layouts) or widths (for vertical layouts).

Once again, to set the layout manager for a container you use of the setLayout() method:

```
choicePanel.setLayout(new BoxLayout(choicePanel,BoxLayout.Y_AXIS));
```

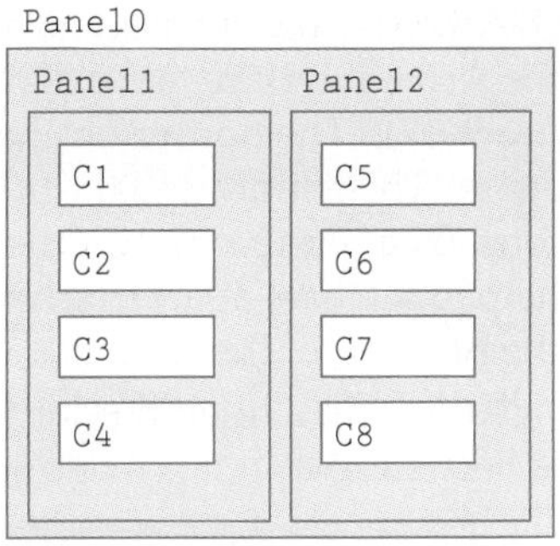

```
Panel0
 Panel1        Panel2
 C1            C5
 C2            C6
 C3            C7
 C4            C8
```

Figure 9–18 Complex layouts can be achieved by nesting containers that use the BoxLayout.

The `BoxLayout()` constructor has two parameters. The first is a reference to the container that's being managed, and the second is a constant that determines whether horizontal (*x*-axis) or vertical (*y*-axis) alignment is used.

One very nice feature of the `BoxLayout` is that it can be used in combinations to imitate the look of the very complicated `GridBoxLayout`. For example, Figure 9–18 shows an example with two panels (Panel1 and Panel2) arranged horizontally within an outer box (Panel0), each containing four components arranged vertically. The three panels all use the `BoxLayout`.

9.6.4 The `ItemListener` Interface

`ItemEvents` are associated with items that make up menus, including `java.awt.Choice` boxes, `JPopupMenus`, `JCheckboxes`, `RadioButtons`, and other types of menus. Item events are handled by the `ItemListener` interface, which consists of a single method, the `itemStateChanged()` method:

```
public void itemStateChanged(ItemEvent e) {
    display.setText("Your order so far (Payment by: ");
    for (int k = 0; k < options.length; k++ )
        if (options[k].isSelected())
            display.append(options[k].getText() + ")\n");
    for (int k = 0; k < titles.length; k++ )
        if (titles[k].isSelected())
            display.append("\t" + titles[k].getText() + "\n");
} // itemStateChanged()
```

This version of the method handles item changes for both the checkbox menu and the radio buttons menu. Two for loops are used. The first iterates through the `options` menu (radio buttons) to determine what payment option the user has selected. Since only one option can be selected, only one title will be appended to the display. The second loop iterates through the titles menu (checkboxes) and appends each title the user selected to the display. In this way, after every selection, the complete status of the user's order is displayed. The `isSelected()` method is used to determine if a checkbox or radio button is selected or not.

In this example, we have no real need to identify the item that caused the event. No matter what item the user selected, we want to display the entire state of the order. However, like the `ActionEvent` class, the `ItemEvent` class contains methods that can be used to retrieve the item that caused the event:

```
getItem();                  // Returns a menu item within a menu
```

The `getItem()` method is an alternative to the `ActionEvent.getSource()` method. It enables you to obtain the object that generated the event but returns a representation of the item that was selected or deselected.

9.6.5 The `OrderApplet`

Figure 9–19 shows the complete implementation of the `OrderApplet`. There are several important points to make about this program. First, five `JPanels` are used to organize the components into logical and visual groupings. This conforms to the design shown in Figure 9–16.

Figure 9–19 The `OrderApplet` class.

```
import javax.swing.*;
import javax.swing.border.*;
import java.awt.*;
import java.awt.event.*;

public class OrderApplet extends JApplet implements ItemListener, ActionListener {

    private final int NTITLES = 3, NOPTIONS = 3;

    private JPanel mainPanel = new JPanel(),
                   centerPanel = new JPanel(),
                   choicePanel = new JPanel(),
                   optionPanel = new JPanel(),
                   buttonPanel = new JPanel();

    private ButtonGroup optGroup = new ButtonGroup();
    private JCheckBox titles[] = new JCheckBox[NTITLES];
    private JRadioButton options[] = new JRadioButton[NOPTIONS];
    private String titleLabels[] =
        {"Chess Master - $59.95", "Checkers Pro - $39.95","Crossword Maker - $19.95"};
    private String optionLabels[] = {"Credit Card", "Debit Card", "E-cash"};

    private JTextArea display = new JTextArea(7, 25);
    private JButton submit = new JButton("Submit Order"),
                    cancel = new JButton("Cancel");
```

Figure 9–19 *Continued*

```
    public void init() {
        mainPanel.setBorder(BorderFactory.createTitledBorder("Acme Software Titles"));
        mainPanel.setLayout(new GridLayout(3, 1, 1, 1));
        cancel.addActionListener(this);
        submit.addActionListener(this);
        initChoices();
        initOptions();
        buttonPanel.setBorder( BorderFactory.createTitledBorder("Order Today"));
        buttonPanel.add(cancel);
        buttonPanel.add(submit);
        centerPanel.add(choicePanel);
        centerPanel.add(optionPanel);

        mainPanel.add( display);
        mainPanel.add(centerPanel);
        mainPanel.add( buttonPanel);
        getContentPane().add(mainPanel);
        setSize(400,400);
    } // init()

    private void initChoices() {
        choicePanel.setBorder(BorderFactory.createTitledBorder("Titles"));
        choicePanel.setLayout(new BoxLayout(choicePanel, BoxLayout.Y_AXIS));

        for (int k = 0; k < titles.length; k++) {
            titles[k] = new JCheckBox(titleLabels[k]);
            titles[k].addItemListener(this);
            choicePanel.add(titles[k]);
        }
    } // initChoices()

    private void initOptions() {
        optionPanel.setBorder(BorderFactory.createTitledBorder("Payment By"));
        optionPanel.setLayout(new BoxLayout(optionPanel, BoxLayout.Y_AXIS));

        for (int k = 0; k < options.length; k++) {
            options[k] = new JRadioButton(optionLabels[k]);
            options[k].addItemListener(this);
            optionPanel.add(options[k]);
            optGroup.add(options[k]);
        }
        options[0].setSelected(true);
    } // initOptions()

    public void itemStateChanged(ItemEvent e) {
        display.setText("Your order so far (Payment by: ");
        for (int k = 0; k < options.length; k++ )
            if (options[k].isSelected())
                display.append(options[k].getText() + ")\n");
        for (int k = 0; k < titles.length; k++ )
            if (titles[k].isSelected())
                display.append("\t" + titles[k].getText() + "\n");
    } // itemStateChanged()

    public void actionPerformed(ActionEvent e){
        String label = submit.getText();
        if (e.getSource() == submit) {
            if (label.equals("Submit Order")) {
                display.append("Thank you. Press 'Confirm' to submit for your order!\n");
                submit.setText("Confirm Order");
            } else {
                display.append("Thank you. You will receive your order tomorrow!\n");
                submit.setText("Submit Order");
            }
        } else
            display.setText("Thank you. Maybe we can serve you next time!\n");
    } // actionPerformed()
} // OrderApplet
```

Second, note the use of titled borders around the four internal panels. These help reinforce visually that the components within the border are related by function.

As in other applets, the `init()` method is used to initialize the interface. This involves setting the layouts for the various containers, and filling the containers with their components. Because their initializations are relatively long, the checkboxes and radio buttons are initialized in separate methods, the `initChoices()` and `initOptions()` methods, respectively.

Finally, note how the `actionPerformed()` method creates a mock order form in the display area. This allows the user to review the order before it is submitted. Also, note that the algorithm used for submittal requires the user to confirm an order before it is actually submitted. The first time the user clicks on the submit button, the button's label is changed to "Confirm Order," and the user is prompted in the display area to click the confirm button to submit the order. This design allows the interface to catch inadvertent button clicks.

A user interface should anticipate potential errors by the user. When an action involves an action that can't be undone — such as placing the order — the program should make sure the user really wants to take that action before carrying it out.

EFFECTIVE DESIGN: Anticipate the User. A well-designed interface should make it difficult for the user to make errors and should make it easy to recover from mistakes when they do happen.

SELF-STUDY EXERCISES

EXERCISE 9.10 What's your favorite interface horror story? The interface needn't be a computer interface.

9.7 Menus and Scroll Panes

Pop-up and pull-down menus allow an application or applet to grow in complexity and functionality without cluttering its interface. Menus are hierarchical in nature. A particular menu is divided into a number of menu items, which can themselves be further subdivided. Menus are very simple to implement in Java.

A `JMenuBar` is an implementation of a menu bar — a horizontal list of names that appears at the top of a window (Figure 9–20). Almost all applications have a menu bar. To construct a menu, you add `JMenu` objects to a `JMenuBar`. A `JMenu` is essentially a clickable area on a menu bar that is associated with a `JPopupMenu`, a small window that pops up and displays the menu's `JMenuItems`. A menu can also contain `JSeparators`, which are dividers that can be placed between menu items to organize them into logical groupings.

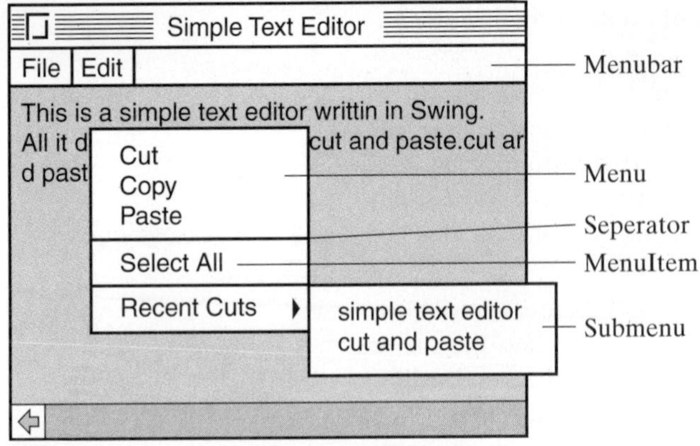

Figure 9–20 An application with a menu bar.

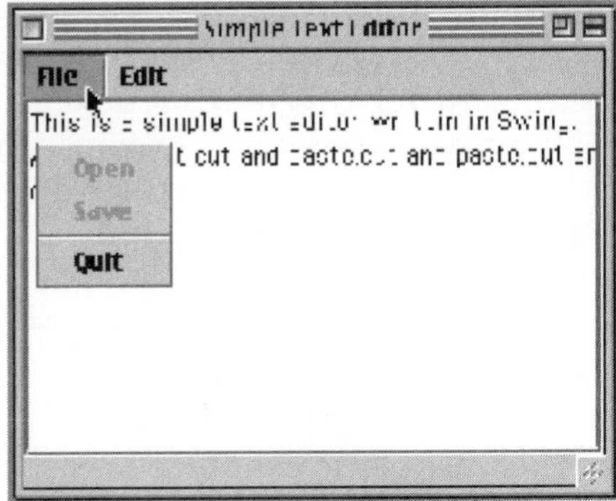

Figure 9–21 The file menu for a simple text editor written in Swing.

9.7.1 Adding a Menu Bar to an Application

It is easy to create menus in Swing The process involves three steps, although they needn't be performed in exactly this order:

1. Create the individual `JMenuItems`.
2. Create a `JMenu` and add the `JMenuItems` to it.
3. Create a `JMenuBar` and add the `JMenus` to it.

For example, suppose you're building the interface for a text editor. A text editor typically contains at least two standard menus. The file menu is used to create new documents, open and close files, save your document, and so on. The edit menu is used to cut and paste selected text from the document. This is essentially the application shown in Figure 9–21.

Here's how you would create the file menu for this program. First you create a menu bar and make it the menu bar for the application's `JFrame` or for the `JApplet`. This is usually done in the application's constructor or in the applet's `init()` method:

```
JMenuBar mBar = new JMenuBar();  // Create the menu bar
this.setMenuBar(mBar);           // Set menu bar for this application
```

The next step involves creating and adding menus and menu items to the menu bar. This is also usually done in the constructor or the `init()` method. If the menu is large, you should break this task up into subtasks and define a method for each subtask.

EFFECTIVE DESIGN: Method Size. A method that gets longer than 20 to 25 lines is probably trying to do too much and should be divided into separate methods, each with a clearly defined subtask.

Here's the definition of the file menu for our simple text editor.

```
private void initFileMenu() {
    fileMenu = new JMenu("File");        // Create the file menu
    mBar.add(fileMenu);                  //  and add it to the menu bar

    openItem = new JMenuItem("Open");    // Open item
    openItem.addActionListener( this );
    openItem.setEnabled(false);
    fileMenu.add(openItem);

    saveItem = new JMenuItem("Save");    // Save item
    saveItem.addActionListener(this);
    saveItem.setEnabled(false);
    fileMenu.add(saveItem);
    fileMenu.addSeparator();             // Logical separator

    quitItem = new JMenuItem("Quit");    // Quit item
    quitItem.addActionListener(this);
    fileMenu.add(quitItem);
} // initFileMenu()
```

The first two statements in the method create the file menu and add it to the menu bar. The rest of the statements create the individual menu items that make up the file menu. Note the use of a *separator* item after the save item. This has the effect of grouping the file handling items (open and save) into one logical category and distinguishing them from the quit item. A separator is represented as a line in the menu (Figure 9–20).

EFFECTIVE DESIGN: Logical Design. In designing interfaces, an effort should be made to use visual cues, such as menu item separators and borders, to group items that are logically related. This will help to orient the user.

Note that that each menu item is given an `ActionListener`. As we'll see shortly, action events for menu items are handled the same way as action events for buttons. Finally, note how the `setEnabled()` method is used to disable both the open and save menu items. We don't know how to open and close files yet, so we can't implement these actions now, a deficiency that will be remedied in Chapter 14.

9.7.2 Menu Hierarchies

Menus can be added to other menus to create a hierarchy. For example, the edit menu will include the standard cut, copy, and paste menu items. Some edit menus also contain an "Undo" item, which can be used to undo the last editing operation that was performed. Most editors seem to allow just a single undo. In other words, if you cut a piece of text, you can undo that operation and get that cut back. But if you cut two pieces of text, the first piece is lost forever. That can be a pain, especially if you didn't mean to do the second cut.

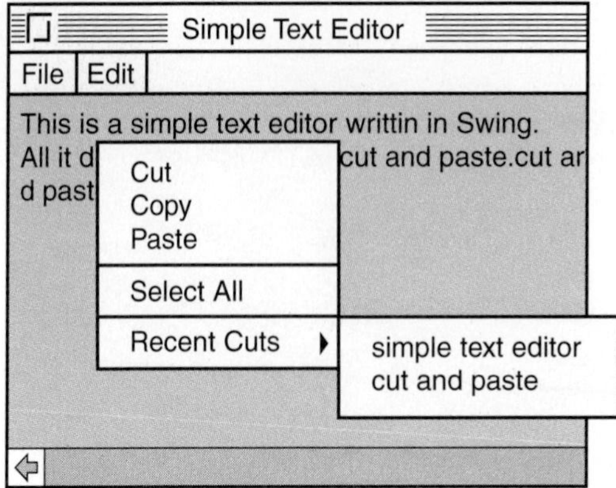

Figure 9–22 A cascading drop-down menu to keep track of the user's cuts.

So let's add a feature to our editor that will keep track of cuts by storing them in a `Vector`. This function will be like an "Unlimited Undo" operation for cuts. For this example, we won't place any limit on the size of the vector. Every cut the user makes will be inserted at the beginning of the vector. To go along with this feature we need a menu that can grow dynamically during the program. Each time the user makes a cut, the string that was cut will be added to the menu.

This kind of menu should occur within the edit menu, but it will have its own items. So this is a menu within a menu (Figure 9–22). This is an example of a *cascading* drop-down menu. The edit menu itself drops down from the menu bar, and the recent cuts menu drops down and to the right of where its arrow points. The following method was used to create the edit menu:

```
private void initEditMenu() {
    editMenu = new JMenu("Edit");      // Create the edit menu
    mBar.add(editMenu);                //  and add it to menu bar

    cutItem = new JMenuItem ("Cut");           // Cut item
    cutItem.addActionListener(this);
    editMenu.add(cutItem);
    copyItem = new JMenuItem("Copy");          // Copy item
    copyItem.addActionListener(this);
    editMenu.add(copyItem);
    pasteItem = new JMenuItem("Paste");        // Paste item
    pasteItem.addActionListener(this);
    editMenu.add(pasteItem);
    editMenu.addSeparator();
    selectItem = new JMenuItem("Select All"); // Select item
    selectItem.addActionListener(this);
    editMenu.add(selectItem);
    editMenu.addSeparator();
    cutsMenu = new JMenu("Recent Cuts");       // Recent cuts submenu
    editMenu.add(cutsMenu);
} // initEditMenu()
```

The main difference between this method and the one used to create the file menu is that here we insert an entire submenu as one of the items in the edit menu. The `cutsMenu` will be used to hold the strings that are cut from the document. Initially it will be empty.

9.7.3 Handling Menu Actions

Handling JMenuItem actions is no different from handling JButton actions. Whenever the user makes a menu selection, an ActionEvent is generated. Programs that use menus must implement the actionPerformed() method of the ActionListener interface. In the text editor example, there are a total of six enabled menu items, including the recent cuts menu. This translates into a large if-else structure, with each clause handling a single menu item. The following actionPerformed() method is used to handle the menu selections for the text editor:

```
public void actionPerformed(ActionEvent e) {
    JMenuItem m  = (JMenuItem)e.getSource();     // Get the selected menu item
    if ( m == quitItem ) {                        // Quit
        dispose();
    } else if (m == cutItem) {                    // Cut the selected text
        scratchPad = display.getSelectedText(); // Copy the text to the scratchpad
        display.replaceRange("",                  //  and delete
            display.getSelectionStart(),          //  from the start of the selection
            display.getSelectionEnd());           //  to the end
        addRecentCut(scratchPad);                 // Add the cut text to the cuts menu
    } else if (m == copyItem)                     // Copy the selected text to the scratchpad
        scratchPad = display.getSelectedText();
    } else if (m == pasteItem) {                  // Paste the scratchpad to the document
        display.insert(scratchPad, display.getCaretPosition());    // at the caret position
    } else if ( m == selectItem ) {
        display.selectAll();                      // Select the entire document
    } else {
        JMenuItem item = (JMenuItem)e.getSource();  // Default case is the cutsMenu
        scratchPad = item.getActionCommand();       // Put the cut back in the scratchpad
    }
} // actionPerformed()
```

The method begins by getting the source of the ActionEvent and casting it into a JMenuItem. It then checks each case of the if-else structure. Because the actions taken by this program are fairly short, they are mostly coded within the actionPerformed() method itself. However, for most programs it will be necessary to write a separate method corresponding to each menu item and then call the methods from actionPerformed().

Our text editor's main task is to implement the cut/copy/paste functions. These are very simple to do in Java. The text that's being edited is stored in JTextArea, which contains instance methods that make it very easy to select, insert, and replace text. To copy a piece of text, the program need only get the text from the JTextArea (getSelectedText()) and assign it to the scratchpad, which is represented as a String. To paste a piece of text, the program inserts the contents of the scratchpad into the JTextArea at the location marked by the *caret*, a cursor-like character in the document that marks the next insertion point.

Default logic

Note how the default case of the if-else is designed. All of the other menu items can be referred to by name. However, the menu items in the cutsMenu are just snippets of a string that the user has previously cut from the text, so they can't referenced by name. Luckily, we don't really need to. For any JMenuItem, the getActionCommand() method returns its text, which in this case is the previously cut text. So we just assign the cut text from the menu to the scratchpad.

PROGRAMMING TIP: Default Cases. Although the order of the clauses in an if-else structure is usually not important, the default clause can sometimes be used to handle cases that can't be referenced by name.

Handling Previously Cut Text

Algorithm design

The most difficult function in our program is the cut operation. Not only must the selected text be removed from the document and stored in the `scratchpad`, it must also be inserted into the vector that is storing all the previous cuts. The `addRecentCut()` method takes care of this last task. The basic idea here is to take the cut string and insert it at the beginning of the vector, so that cuts will be maintained in a last-in-first-out order. Then the `cutsMenu` must be completely rebuilt by reading its entries out of the vector, from first to last. That way the most recent cut will appear first in the menu:

```
private void addRecentCut(String cut) {
    recentCuts.insertElementAt(cut,0);
    cutsMenu.removeAll();
    for (int k = 0; k < recentCuts.size(); k++) {
        JMenuItem item = new JMenuItem((String)recentCuts.elementAt(k));
        cutsMenu.add( item );
        item.addActionListener(this);
    }
} // addRecentCut()
```

The `recentCuts Vector` stores the cut strings. Note the use the `insertElementAt()` method to insert strings into the vector, and the `elementAt()` method to get strings from the vector. (You may find it helpful to review the section on vectors in Chapter 8.)

Note also how menu items are removed and inserted in menus. The `cutsMenu` is reinitialized, using the `removeAll()` method. Then the for loop iterates through the strings stored in the vector, making new menu items from them, which are then inserted into the `cutsMenu`. In this way, the `cutsMenu` is changed dynamically each time the user cuts a piece of text from the document.

9.7.4 Adding Scrollbars to a Text Area

Scrollbars

The complete listing for the `SimpleTextEditor` program is shown in Figure 9–23. It uses a `BorderLayout`, with the `JTextArea` placed at the center. Note how simple it is to add scrollbars to the textarea:

```
this.getContentPane().add(new JScrollPane(display));
```

Figure 9–23 A menu-based SimpleTextEditor application.

```
import javax.swing.*;
import java.awt.*;
import java.awt.event.*;
import java.util.Vector;

public class SimpleTextEditor extends JFrame implements ActionListener{
    private JMenuBar mBar = new JMenuBar();               // Create the menu bar
    private JMenu fileMenu, editMenu, cutsMenu;           // Menu references
    private JMenuItem cutItem, copyItem, pasteItem, selectItem,recentcutItem; // Edit items
    private JMenuItem quitItem, openItem, saveItem;       // File items
    private JTextArea display = new JTextArea();          // Here's where the editing occurs
    private String scratchPad = "";                       // Scratch pad for cut/paste
    private Vector recentCuts = new Vector();

    public SimpleTextEditor() {
        super("Simple Text Editor");     // Set the window title
        this.getContentPane().setLayout(new BorderLayout());
        this.getContentPane().add("Center", display);
        this.getContentPane().add(new JScrollPane(display));
        display.setLineWrap(true);
        this.setJMenuBar(mBar);         // Set this program's menu bar
        initFileMenu();                 // Create the menus
        initEditMenu();
    } // SimpleTextEditer()

    private void initEditMenu() {
        editMenu = new JMenu("Edit");      // Create the edit menu
        mBar.add(editMenu);                //  and add it to menu bar
        cutItem = new JMenuItem ("Cut");           // Cut item
        cutItem.addActionListener(this);
        editMenu.add(cutItem);
        copyItem = new JMenuItem("Copy");          // Copy item
        copyItem.addActionListener(this);
        editMenu.add(copyItem);
        pasteItem = new JMenuItem("Paste");        // Paste item
        pasteItem.addActionListener(this);
        editMenu.add(pasteItem);
        editMenu.addSeparator();
        selectItem = new JMenuItem("Select All"); // Select item
        selectItem.addActionListener(this);
        editMenu.add(selectItem);
        editMenu.addSeparator();
        cutsMenu = new JMenu("Recent Cuts");       // Recent cuts submenu
        editMenu.add(cutsMenu);
    } // initEditMenu()

    private void initFileMenu() {
        fileMenu = new JMenu("File");       // Create the file menu
        mBar.add(fileMenu);                 //  and add it to the menu bar
        openItem = new JMenuItem("Open");   // Open item
        openItem.addActionListener( this );
        openItem.setEnabled(false);
        fileMenu.add(openItem);
        saveItem = new JMenuItem("Save");   // Save item
        saveItem.addActionListener(this);
        saveItem.setEnabled(false);
        fileMenu.add(saveItem);
        fileMenu.addSeparator();            // Logical separator
        quitItem = new JMenuItem("Quit");   // Quit item
        quitItem.addActionListener(this);
        fileMenu.add(quitItem);
    } // initFileMenu()
```

Figure 9–23 *Continued*

```
    public void actionPerformed(ActionEvent e) {
        JMenuItem m  = (JMenuItem)e.getSource();    // Get the selected menu item
        if ( m == quitItem ) {                      // Quit
            dispose();
        } else if (m == cutItem) {                  // Cut the selected text
            scratchPad = display.getSelectedText(); // Copy the text to the scratchpad
            display.replaceRange("",                //  and delete
                display.getSelectionStart(),        //  from the start of the selection
                display.getSelectionEnd());         //  to the end
            addRecentCut(scratchPad);               // Add the cut text to the cuts menu
        } else if (m == copyItem) {                 // Copy the selected text to the scratchpad
            scratchPad = display.getSelectedText();
        } else if (m == pasteItem) {                // Paste the scratchpad to the document
            display.insert(scratchPad, display.getCaretPosition());   // at the caret position
        } else if ( m == selectItem ) {
            display.selectAll();                    // Select the entire document
        } else {
            JMenuItem item = (JMenuItem)e.getSource();  // Default case is the cutsMenu
            scratchPad = item.getActionCommand();       // Put the cut back in the scratchpad
        }
    } // actionPerformed()

    private void addRecentCut(String cut) {
        recentCuts.insertElementAt(cut,0);
        cutsMenu.removeAll();
        for (int k = 0; k < recentCuts.size(); k++) {
            JMenuItem item = new JMenuItem((String)recentCuts.elementAt(k));
            cutsMenu.add( item );
            item.addActionListener(this);
        }
    } // addRecentCut()

    public static void main(String args[]) {
        SimpleTextEditor f = new SimpleTextEditor();
        f.setSize(300, 200);
        f.setVisible(true);
        f.addWindowListener(new WindowAdapter() {      // Quit the application
            public void windowClosing(WindowEvent e) {
                System.exit(0);
            }
        });
    } // main()
} // SimpleTextEditor
```

This statement creates a `JScrollPane` and adds it to the application's container. A `JScrollPane` is one of Swing's scrollbar classes. Its function is to manage the viewing and scrolling of a scrollable component, such as a `JTextArea`. A `JScrollPane` is actually a container. That's why it takes the `display` as an argument. The `display` is being added to the `JScrollPane`.

Figure 9–24 shows the key elements in a scroll pane. In this case the `JTextArea` is the scrollable client. The scroll pane provides a *viewport* into the text area. Horizontal and vertical scrollbars allow the user to scroll the viewport through the document.

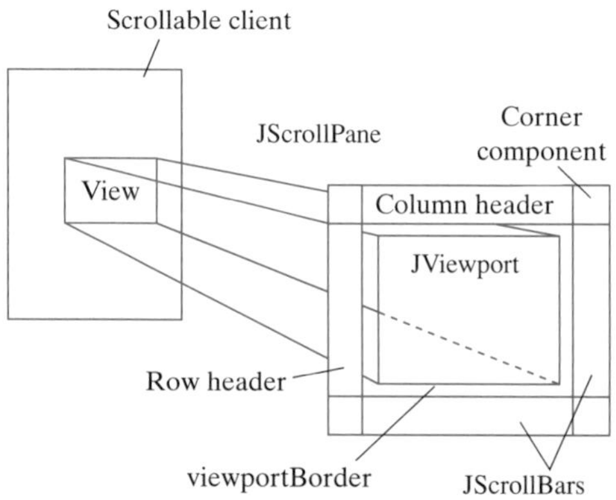

Figure 9–24 The parts of a scroll pane. (Source: http://java.sun.com/products/jdk/1.2/docs/api/javax/swing/JScrollPane.html.)

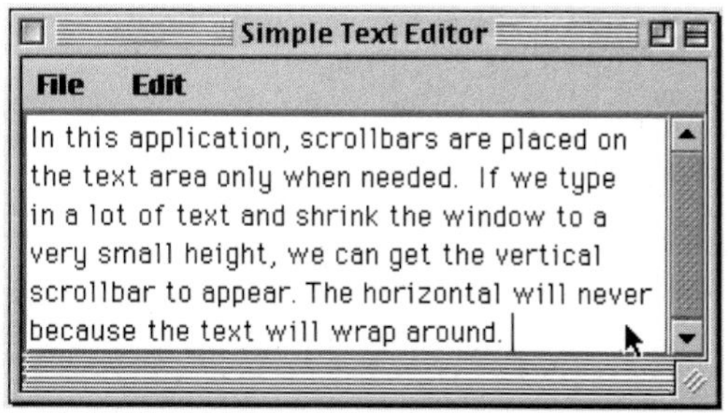

Figure 9–25 The scrollbars appear on the text area only when they are needed. In this case only a vertical scrollbar is necessary.

A `JScrollPane` can be attached to just about any component. Once a scroll pane is attached to a component, it will completely manage the scrolling functions by itself. The default constructor used in this example takes a single `Component` parameter. This refers to the scrollable component, in this case to the `JTextArea`. Another constructor that you might use takes the following form:

```
public JScrollPane(Component comp, int vsbPolicy, int hsbPolicy);
```

The two integers refer to the vertical and horizontal scrolling policies. These cover properties such as whether the scrollbars are always present or just as needed. The default is to attach scrollbars to the component only when needed. Thus, to see the scrollbars in the `SimpleTextEditor`, you would have to shrink the window to the point where all of the text cannot be viewed (Figure 9–25). Because the text area in this example is wrapping the text, the horizontal scrollbar will never be needed.

SELF-STUDY EXERCISES

EXERCISE 9.11 Modify the `addRecentCut()` method so it limits the cuts stored in the vector to the last ten cuts.

EXERCISE 9.12 Modify the `addRecentCut()` method so that it doesn't duplicate cuts already stored in the vector. (*Hint*: Use the vector's `indexOf(String)` method.)

IN THE LABORATORY: THE ATM MACHINE

The purpose of this lab is use Java GUI components and layouts to design and implement an interface for a bank Automatic Teller Machine (ATM). The interface, and eventually the completed application, should be designed so that it may be implemented either as an applet or an application. The objectives are

- To develop from scratch an `AtmMachine` class that simulates an ATM interface.
- To develop a flexible interface design that will work with either an applet or an application.
- To gain additional practice using arrays.
- To gain additional practice using AWT components and layouts.

Problem Description

Design and implement a Java class that simulates an ATM interface. Your solution should implement the class, `AtmMachine`, as an ATM interface, as shown in Figure 9–26. It is not necessary to build a complete ATM machine functionality into the applet beyond that which is described below — just implement the interface. If you wish, you may design your own layout for the interface, as long as it has the components required in the specification.

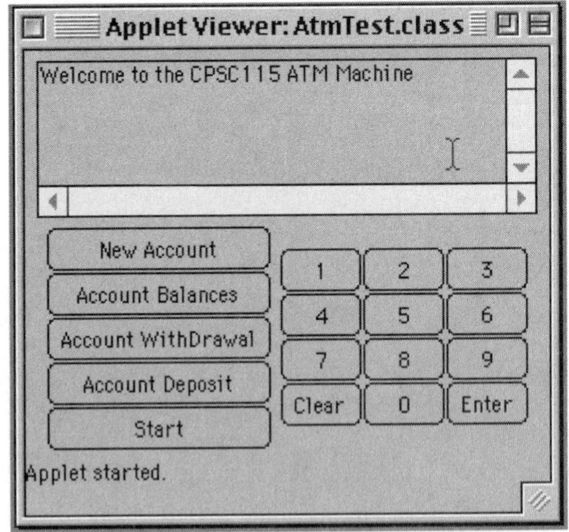

Figure 9–26 The user interface for `AtmMachine`.

Are Computers Intelligent?

Contemporary computer interfaces are largely visual and graphical, and many things we use a computer for, such as word processing, still require us to type. Will there come a day when instead of typing a letter or E-mail message, we'll be able to dictate it to our computer? Will computers eventually have the same kind of interface we have — that is, will we someday be able to carry on conversations with our computers? Clearly, a "conversational interface" would require substantial intelligence on the part of the computer. Do computers have any chance of acquiring such intelligence?

The question of machine intelligence or *Artificial Intelligence (AI)* has been the subject of controversy since the very first computers were developed. In 1950, in an article in the journal *Mind*, Alan Turing proposed the following test to settle the question of whether computers could be intelligent. Suppose you put a person and a computer in another room, and you let a human interrogate both with any kind of question whatsoever. The interrogator could ask them to parse a Shakespearian sonnet, or solve an arithmetic problem, or tell a joke. The computer's task would be to try and fool the interrogator into thinking that it was the human. And the (hidden) human's task would be to try to help the interrogator see that he or she was the human.

Turing argued that someday computers would be able to play this game so well that interrogators would have no better than a 50/50 chance of telling which was which. When that day came, he argued, we would have to conclude that computers were intelligent.

This so-called Turing test has been the subject of controversy ever since. Many of the founders of AI and many of its current practitioners believe that computation and human thinking are basically the same kind of process and that eventually computers will develop enough capability that we'll have to call them intelligent. Skeptics argue that even if computers could mimic our intelligence, there's no way they will be self-conscious and therefore they can never be truly intelligent. According to the skeptics, merely executing programs, no matter how clever the programs are, will never add up to intelligence.

Computers have made some dramatic strides lately. In 1997, an IBM computer named Deep Blue beat world chess champion Gary Kasparov in a seven-game chess match. In 1998, a computer at Los Alamos National Laboratory proved a mathematical theorem that some of the best mathematicians were unable to prove for the past 40 years.

However, despite these achievements, most observers would agree that computers are not yet capable of passing the Turing test. One area where computers fall short is in natural language understanding. Although computers are good at understanding Java and other computer languages, human languages are still too complex and require too much commonsense knowledge for computers to understand them perfectly. Another area where computers still fall somewhat short is in speech recognition. However, just recently an American company demonstrated a telephone that could translate between English and German (as well as some other languages) in real time. The device's only limitation was that its discourse was limited to the travel domain. As computer processing speeds improve, this limitation is expected to be only temporary. Thus, we may be closer than we think to having our "conversational user interface."

Natural language understanding, speech recognition, learning, perception, chess playing, and problem solving are the kinds of problems addressed in AI, one of the major applied areas of computer science. Almost every major research group in AI has a Web site that describes their work. To find some of these, just do a search for "artificial intelligence" and then browse through the links that are found.

GUI Specifications

The Graphical User Interface (GUI) should contain a numeric *keyPad* — a 4 x 3 array of buttons — and a *commandPad*, a collection of buttons for the various functions that one finds on an ATM machine. It should contain a `JTextArea` which displays the result of clicking one of the buttons. Feel free to design your own layout of these components!

Designing the ATM Layout

The demo applet consists of a `JTextArea` that is used as the ATM's display screen. It displays all I/O during an ATM session. The only other interface components are the 12 key pad and 5 function `JButtons`. The demo uses several `JPanels` to achieve its overall layout (Figure 9–27). First there

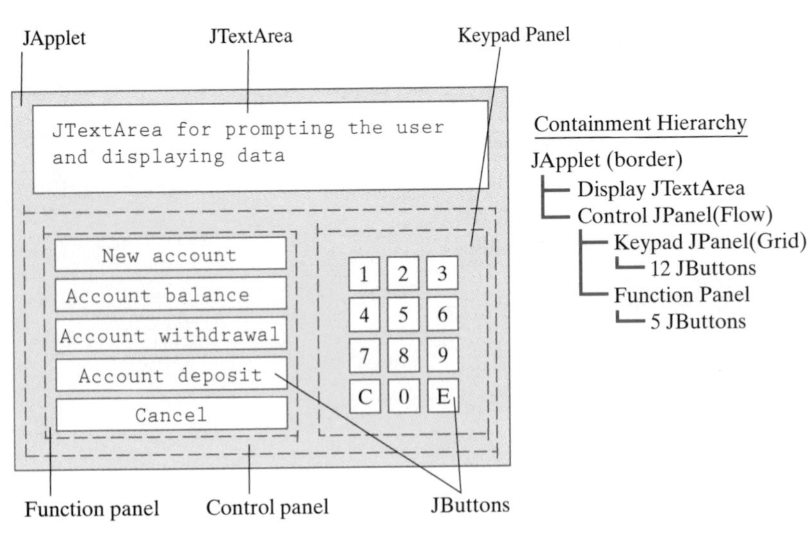

Figure 9–27 The containment hierarchy for the components used in the ATM machine GUI.

is a main panel that contains all of the interface components. It uses a BorderLayout with the machine's display in the center and the keypad and function pad at the south edge. The function pad and keypad are organized into separate panels and arranged as GridLayouts. Finally, a fourth panel is used to group the two collections of buttons so that they may be added to the south area of the main panel.

Problem Decomposition

One goal of this lab is to develop an ATM interface that can be used as either an applet or a stand-alone application. This suggests that the interface itself should be defined as a separate class that gets instantiated either in an application or an applet. Let's call this the AtmMachine class.

The AtmMachine class can use a JPanel as the main container for its components. However, a JPanel cannot stand by itself. It must be added to either a JFrame or a JApplet. If AtmMachine is to be used with an applet, it can simply add its main panel to the applet itself. However, if it is to be used with an application, it will need to add its main panel to the application's JFrame. This suggest that AtmMachine will need two constructors, one to be used with an application and one with an applet:

```
public AtmMachine(JFrame f) {    // Application constructor from a frame
    atmPanel = createInterface();
    f.getContentPane().add(atmPanel);
    f.pack();
    f.show();
}

public AtmMachine(JApplet app)  { // Applet constructor from an applet
    atmPanel = createInterface();
    app.getContentPane().add(atmPanel);
}
```

Note that each constructor leaves the main task of creating the interface to the createInterface() method, which has the following signature:

```
private JPanel createInterface();
```

It takes no parameters but returns a reference to a JPanel, which is assigned in the constructor to the main atmPanel. The applet constructor adds atmPanel to the applet, which is passed as its parameter. The application constructor adds atmPanel to the application's JFrame, which is passed as its parameter. In this way we achieve a flexible AtmMachine class that can be used as the basis for either an applet or an application.

To use AtmMachine as an applet, we need only create an AtmMachine in the init() method. Thus the entire applet definition is

```
import javax.swing.*;
import java.awt.*;
import java.applet.Applet;

public class AtmTest extends JApplet {
    AtmMachine atm;                         // Declare AtmMachine

    public void init() {
        setSize(500,300);
        atm = new AtmMachine(this);  // Create a new atm
    } // init()
} // AtmTest
```

Invoking AtmMachine's constructor in init() will effectively pass control to the new AtmMachine. Note that the applet does not handle any actions directly. All actions are handled by its atm object.

To create an application that uses AtmMachine is equally simple:

```
import javax.swing.*;
import java.awt.*;

public class AtmApplication extends JFrame {
    public static void main(String args[]) {
        AtmApplication f = new AtmApplication();
        f.setSize(300,500);
        AtmMachine atm = new AtmMachine( f );
    }
}
```

In this case we create a AtmApplication (a subclass of JFrame) for the AtmMachine in main() and pass a reference to it to the AtmMachine constructor. This effectively passes control to atm, which will handle all of the application's action events.

Problem Design: The AtmMachine Class

The design of AtmMachine is straightforward. It will require the following GUI components: 12 keypad JButtons, 5 function pad JButtons, and one JTextArea to serve as the main display area. These should be declared as instance variables and instantiated in the createInterface() method or in one of its submethods. Of course, if AtmMachine() is going to handle the ActionEvents generated by its various buttons, it must implement the ActionListener interface.

The keypad buttons are too numerous to implement as 12 distinct instance variables, so an array should be used to store each JButton as in the MetricConverter example in Figure 9–7. It may be useful to define a separate method to handle the subtask of creating the keypad panel. Like the createInterface() method, it should return a JPanel, which contains all of the keypad buttons. The result of the method could then be assigned to the AtmMachine's fnPanel:

```
fnPanel = createKeypadPanel();  // Create the whole functionpad
```

Like the calculator example, the keypad should utilize a GridLayout. Of course, each JButton should invoke the addActionListener() method to register the AtmMachine as its ActionListener. Any object that implements the ActionListener interface can serve as an ActionListener.

The function buttons may also be implemented as an array. Like createKeypadPanel(), this subtask might also be defined as a separate method which returns a JPanel.

The actionPerformed() method should handle the various ActionEvents that will be generated. It should use an if-else structure, similar to the algorithm we used in the SimpleTextEditor example (Figure 9–23). The method should begin by getting the *source* of the event. Because getSource() returns an Object, its result must be cast into a JButton. It will also be useful to get the button's label, since this can be used to determine which Button generated the event:

```
public void actionPerformed(ActionEvent e) {
    Button b = (Button)e.getsource(); // Get the button that was pressed
    String label = b.getText();      //  and its label
    if (b == newAcc)
        newAccount();                 // New account
    else if (b == accBal)
        accountBalance();             // Check balance
    else if (b == accDP)
        accountDeposit();             // Make deposit
    else if (b == accWD)
        accountWithdrawal();          // Withdrawal
    else if (b == cancel)
        cancel();                     // Cancel transaction
    else
        processKeyPad(label);         // Process the 12 key pad
} // actionPerformed()
```

The control structure used in this method is an if-else *multiway selection* structure.

Note that each of the function keys is associated with its own method. This is a flexible design that will allow us to "grow" the application. As more functionality is added, changes can be made directly to these methods without altering the overall structure of the program. This is a good use of *stepwise refinement* in our design.

Finally, note that all of the keypad functions are handled by a single method processKeyPad(), which takes the Button's label as its parameter. This also will enable us to "grow" the application's functionality without changing its overall structure.

The Algorithm

Although AtmMachine will not be fully implemented, it can only be properly tested if it has some degree of functionality. Therefore let's design an algorithm that will at least demonstrate that it has the proper structure for a full-fledged implementation.

As you know, the first thing you do when using an ATM is enter your personal ID number (PIN). If you enter it correctly, you are then allowed to enter one or more transactions. If not, you are given an error message and allowed to reenter it. Once your PIN has been validated, you are allowed to perform one or more transactions — withdrawal, deposit, and so forth. When you are finished, you press the "Cancel" key to end the session.

For this partial implementation, the various transactions can be implemented by simply printing a message on the ATM's display. For example, a withdrawal could be handled as

```
if (state == GO_STATE)
  display.appendText("How much do you want to withdraw?\n");
```

Note that this transaction depends on the machine being in the GO_STATE. If the machine is not in the proper state, clicks on the withdrawal button should just be ignored.

Our partial implementation should be able to distinguish the various phases of the user's interaction with the AtmMachine. One way to implement this is by using a *state* variable whose values represent the phases of an ATM transaction. One design might be the following:

```
private static final int INIT_STATE = 0;  // State constants
private static final int PIN_STATE = 1;
private static final int GO_STATE = 2;

private int state = 0;          // State of the atm machine
```

In this design the machine can be in one of three states: an INIT_STATE, which lasts until the user clicks on the Start Button; a PIN_STATE, which lasts until the user enters a correct PIN; and a GO_STATE, which lasts until the user cancels the session.

Obviously, the methods that carry out the various transactions must check and update the state depending on the user's input. For example, the cancel Button on the function pad could be used both to start and cancel a transaction, depending on the ATM's state:

```
private void cancel() {
    if (state == INIT_STATE) {
        cancel.setText("Cancel");
        display.appendText("Please enter your PIN and click on ENTER.\n");
        state = PIN_STATE;
    } else if (state == GO_STATE || state == PIN_STATE)
        state = INIT_STATE;
    cancel.setText("Start");
} // cancel()
```

Initially the `cancel` `Button` is labeled "Start." If the ATM is in the initial state when it is clicked, then its label is changed to "Cancel" and the user is prompted to enter a PIN. In all other states, `cancel` will be labeled "Cancel." In those cases, if it is clicked, the user wishes to cancel an operation or quit the session, so the method should set the machine back to its initial state.

Optional Exercise

The most difficult state transition occurs between the `PIN_STATE` and the `GO_STATE`, because it is here that the user's PIN must be checked for validity. What complicates this task is that the keypad must be used to enter the PIN. Therefore the `processKeyPad()` method must check the machine's state in order to know how to process the number keys. There are three possible states, whose actions can be identified by the following table:

State	Key Press	Action
`INIT_STATE`	Any key	Ignore it
`PIN_STATE`	Enter	Validate the User's PIN
	A digit key	Mask key and append to PIN
`GO_STATE`	Enter	Display the key's label
	Digit key	Display the key's label

Thus when the machine is in its initial state, all key presses on the keypad are ignored. If the user is in the process of entering a PIN (`PIN_STATE`), then if the Enter key is pressed, this signals that the user has finished entering the PIN, which should then be validated. If it is valid, the machine should switch into the `GO_STATE`. Otherwise an error message should be displayed. If a digit key is pressed while the user is entering a PIN, then that digit should be appended to the PIN and displayed as a (*) — that is, masked — in the display. Finally, when the machine is in `GO_STATE`, all key presses on the keypad should simply be echoed in the display. Of course, in a full-fledged implementation these key presses would have to be handled in an appropriate, context-sensitive manner. This would require that we expand the number of states to include things like `WITHDRAWAL_STATE`, and so on.

To process the user's PIN, the `AtmMachine` should maintain an instance variable of type `String`, which is initially set to the empty string. As the user enters a PIN, the individual digits can be appended to the `String`, which can be validated by a separate method when the user types the Enter key. For testing purposes, it will suffice to develop a simple validity test — for example, the PIN must contain a value between 1111 and 9999.

CHAPTER SUMMARY

Technical Terms

content pane
layout manager
model
view
controller
lightweight component
Model-View-Controller (MVC)
widget hierarchy
event model
listener
peer model

New Java Keywords

`super`
`this`

Java Library Classes

`ActionEvent`	`ActionListener`	`Applet`
`BasicButtonUI`	`BorderFactory`	`BorderLayout`
`Border`	`BoxLayout`	`Box`
`ButtonGroup`	`Button`	`CaretEvent`
`Choice`	`Component`	`Container`
`DefaultButtonModel`	`FlowLayout`	`FocusEvent`
`Frame`	`GridLayout`	`ItemEvent`
`ItemListener`	`JApplet`	`JBox`
`JButton`	`JComponent`	`JDialog`
`JFrame`	`JLabel`	`JList`
`JMenuBar`	`JMenuItem`	`JMenu`
`JPanel`	`JPopupMenu`	`JRadioButton`
`JScrollPane`	`JTable`	`JTextArea`
`JTextField`	`JTree`	`JWindow`
`KeyEvent`	`Label`	`ListDataEvent`
`MouseEvent`	`Object`	`String`
`TableColumnModelEvent`	`TextArea`	`TextComponent`
`TextField`	`TreeExpansionEvent`	`TreeSelectionEvent`
`UndoableEditEvent`	`Vector`	

Java Library Methods

`actionPerformed()`	`add()`	`addActionListener()`
`createTitledBorder()`	`elementAt()`	`getActionCommand()`
`getContentPane()`	`getItem()`	`getSelectedText()`
`getSource()`	`init()`	`insertElementAt()`
`isSelected()`	`main()`	`removeAll()`
`setBorder()`	`setLayout()`	

Programmer-Defined Classes

`AtmApplication`	`AtmMachine`	`Calculator`
`Converter`	`MetricConverter`	`OrderApplet`
`ReplaceText`	`SimpleTextEditor`	

Programmer-Defined Methods

`addRecentCut()`	`createInterface()`	`createKeypadPanel()`
`initChoices()`	`initKeyPad()`	`initOptions()`
`processKeyPad()`		

Summary of Important Points

- Java now provides two sets of Graphical User Interface (GUI) components, the Abstract Windowing Toolkit (AWT), which was part of Java 1.0 and modified in Java 1.1, and the Swing component set, the GUI part of the Java Foundation Classes (JFC), introduced in JDK 1.1 and now available in JDK 1.2 (which is also known as Java 2).
- Unlike their AWT counterparts, Swing components are written entirely in Java. This allows programs written in Swing to have a platform-independent look and feel. There are three built-in look-and-feel packages in Swing: a Windows 95 style, a Unix-like Motif style, and a purely Java Metal style.
- Swing components are based on the *Model-View-Controller (MVC)* architecture, in which the component is divided into three separate objects: how it looks (*view*), what state it's in (*model*), and what it does (*controller*). The view and controller parts are sometimes combined into a single *user interface* class, which can be changed to create a customized look-and-feel.
- AWT components are based on the *peer model*, in which every AWT component has a peer in the native windowing system. This model is less efficient and more platform dependent than the MVC model.
- Java's *event model* is based on *event listeners*. When a GUI component is created it is registered with an appropriate event listener, which takes responsibility for handling the component's events.
- A user interface combines four functions: guidance of the user, input, output and control.
- The components in a GUI are organized into a *containment hierarchy* rooted at the top-level window. `JPanel`s and other `Container`s may be used to organize the components into a hierarchy according to function or some other criterion.
- The top-level Swing classes — `JApplet`, `JDialog`, `JFrame`, and `JWindow` — use a *content pane* as their component container.

- A GUI should minimize the number of input devices the user needs to manipulate, as well as the complexity the user needs to deal with. Certain forms of redundancy — such as two independent but complete sets of controls — are desirable because they make the interface more flexible and more widely applicable.
- A *layout manager* is an object that manages the size and arrangement of the components in a container. The AWT and Swing provide a number of built-in layouts, including flow, border, grid and box layouts.
- A *radio button* is a toggle button that belongs to a group such that only one button from the group may be selected at the same time. A *checkbox* is a toggle button that always displays its state.
- A well-designed interface should reduce the chance of user error and should make it as easy as possible to recover from errors when they do occur.

ANSWERS TO SELF-STUDY EXERCISES

EXERCISE 9.1 The top-level containers — the `JApplet`, `JDialog`, `JFrame`, and `JWindow` — would have to be implemented completely in Java, thereby breaking their dependence on peer windows in the native windowing environment.

EXERCISE 9.2 Abstract classes cannot be instantiated. They can only be subclassed. Therefore by definition they cannot have a peer instance. That's what makes them suitable as the foundation for lightweight components.

EXERCISE 9.3 How can a button still be considered a component under the MVC model? This is a good question. The `JButton` class acts as an wrapper class and hides the model-view-controller details. When you instantiate a `JButton`, you still get a single instance. Think of it this way. Your body consists of several systems that interact (internally) among themselves, but it's still one body that other bodies interact with as a single object.

EXERCISE 9.4 A component can indeed be registered with more than one listener. For example, the `ToggleButton` that we defined in Section 4.6 has two listeners. The first is the button itself, which takes care of toggling the button's label. The second is the applet in which the button is used, which takes care of handling whatever the button is associated with.

EXERCISE 9.5 Some components can have two different kinds of listeners. For example, imagine a "sticky button" that works like this. When you click and release the button, it causes some action to take place, just like a normal button. When you click and hold the mouse button down, the button "sticks" to the cursor and you can then move it to a new location. This button would need listeners for `ActionEvents`, `MouseEvents`, and `MouseMotionEvents`.

EXERCISE 9.6 To round a double you could use the `Math.round()` method. For example, suppose the number you want to round is `d`. Then the expression `Math.round(100 * d)/100.0` will round it to two decimal places. Alternatively you could use the `java.text.NumberFormat` class. Both of these approaches were covered in Chapter 5.

EXERCISE 9.7 Many cars today have cruise control as a alternative way to the accelerator. Push buttons, usually located on the steering wheel, are used to speed up and slow down, so you can drive with your foot or your hand.

EXERCISE 9.8 As an alternative border layout for the top-level window in the `Converter` north-west-center might work. So might center-south-east, and center-south-west. What makes these possible is the fact that the layout manager will use up space in any edge area that is not assigned a component.

EXERCISE 9.9 A flow layout would not be appropriate for the control panel because you would have little control of where the `convert` button would be placed relative to the keypad.

EXERCISE 9.10 Interface design disaster: My car uses the same kind of on/off switch for the headlights and the windshield wipers. One is a stem on the left side of the steering wheel, and the other is on a stem on the right side of the steering wheel. On more than one occasion, I've managed to turn off the headlights when I intended to turn on the wipers.

EXERCISE 9.11 Modify the `addRecentCut()` method so it limits the cuts stored in the vector to the last ten cuts. Solution: check the size of the vector after inserting the cut. If it exceeds ten, remove the last element in the vector.

```
private void addRecentCut(String cut) {
    recentCuts.insertElementAt(cut, 0);
    if (recentCuts.size() > 10) {          // If more than 10 cuts
        recentCuts.removeElementAt(10);  // remove the oldest one
    }
    cutsMenu.removeAll();
    for (int k = 0; k < recentCuts.size(); k++) {
        JMenuItem item = new JMenuItem((String) recentCuts.elementAt(k));
        cutsMenu.add(item);
        item.addActionListener(this);
    }
} // addRecentCut()
```

EXERCISE 9.12 Modify the `addRecentCut()` method so that it doesn't duplicate cuts stored in the vector. Solution: Use the `indexOf()` method to search for the cut in the vector. If it's already there, don't insert the cut.

```
private void addRecentCut(String cut) {
    if (recentCuts.indexOf(cut) == -1) {     // If not already cut
        recentCuts.insertElementAt(cut,0);
        if (recentCuts.size() > 10) {          // If more than 10 cuts
            recentCuts.removeElementAt(10);  // remove the oldest one
        }
        cutsMenu.removeAll();
        for (int k = 0; k < recentCuts.size(); k++) {
            JMenuItem item = new JMenuItem((String) recentCuts.elementAt(k));
            cutsMenu.add(item);
            item.addActionListener(this);
        }
    } // if not already cut
} // addRecentCut()
```

EXERCISES

1. Explain the difference between the following pairs of terms.

   a. A *model* and a *view*.
   b. A *view* and a *controller*.
   c. A *lightweight* and *heavyweight* component.
   d. A `JButton` and a `Button`.
   e. A *layout manager* and a *container*
   f. A *containment hierarchy* and an *inheritance hierarchy*.
   g. A *content pane* and a `JFrame`.

2. Fill in the blank:

   a. The GUI component that is written entirely in Java is known as a _______ component.
   b. The AWT is not platform independent because it uses the _______ model to implement its GUI components.
   c. The visual elements of a GUI are arranged in a _______.
   d. A _______ is an object that takes responsibility for arranging the components in a container.
   e. The default layout manager for a `JLabel` is _______.
   f. The default layout manager for a `JApplet` is _______.

3. Describe in general terms what you would have to do to change the standard look and feel of a Swing `JButton`.
4. Explain the differences between the model-view-controller design of a `JButton` and the design of an AWT `Button`. Why is MVC superior?
5. Suppose you have an applet that contains a `JButton` and a `JLabel`. Each time the button is clicked the applet rearranges the letters in the label. Using Java's event model as a basis, explain the sequence of events that happens in order for this action to take place.
6. Draw a containment hierarchy for the most recent version of the `CyberPetApplet` program.
7. Create a GUI design, similar to the one shown in Figure 9–16, for a program that would be used to buy tickets on-line for a rock concert.
8. Create a GUI design, similar to the one shown in Figure 9–16, for an on-line program that would be used to play musical recordings.
9. Design and implement a GUI for the `CDInterest` program (Figure 5–10). This program should let the user input the interest rate, principal, and period, and should accumulate the value of the investment.
10. Design and implement a GUI for the `Temperature` class (Figure 5–3). One challenge of this design is to find a good way for the user to indicate whether a Fahrenheit or Celsius value is being input. This should also determine the order of the conversion: F to C, or C to F.

11. Convert the CyberPetApplet to a Swing-based version. The top-level window should be a JApplet.

12. The TextField class has a setEchoChar() method. When the echo character is set, that's the character that will will be displayed in the text field as the user types. If it is unset, the text field will just echo the character that the user types. Setting the echo character to '*' is one way to hide sensitive input—for example, while entering a password. Design and implement a PasswordField class that *always* hides the user's input. This should be a subclass of TextField.

13. Design an interface for a 16-button integer calculator that supports addition, subtraction, multiplication, and division. Implement the interface so that the label of the button is displayed in the calculator's display — that is, it doesn't actually do the math.

14. **Challenge:** Design and implement a Calculator class to go along with the interface you developed in the previous exercise. It should function the same way as a hand calculator except it only handles integers.

15. Modify the Converter application so that it can convert in either direction: from miles to kilometers, or from kilometers to miles. Use radio buttons in your design to let the user select one or the other alternative.

16. Here's a design problem for you. A biologist needs an interactive program that calculates the average of some field data represented as real numbers. Any real number could be a data value, so you can't use a sentinel value, such as 9999, to indicate the end of the input. Design and implement a suitable interface for this problem.

17. **Challenge:** A dialog box is a window associated with an application that appears only when needed. Dialog boxes have many uses. An error dialog is used to report an error message. A file dialog is used to help the user search for and open a file. Creating a basic error dialog is very simple in Swing. The JOptionPane class has class methods that can be used to create the kind of dialog shown in Figure 9–28. Such a dialog box can be created with a single statement:

```
JOptionPane.showMessageDialog(this, "Sorry, your number is out of range.");
```

Convert the Average program (Figure 6–7) to a GUI interface and use the JOptionPane dialog to report errors.

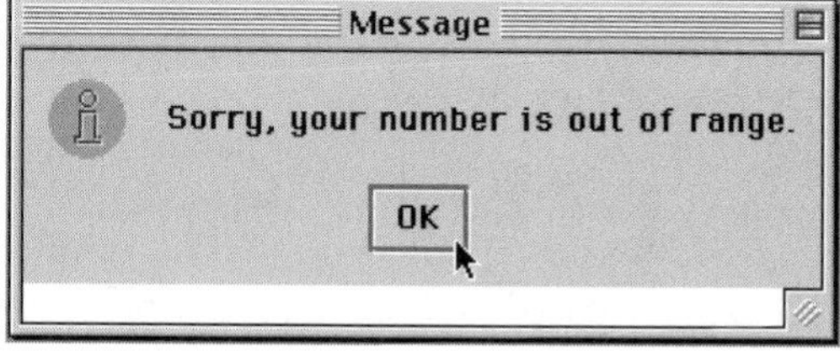

Figure 9–28 A basic JOptionPane error dialog.

18. **Challenge:** Design and implement a version of the game *Memory*. In this game you are given a two-dimensional grid of boxes that pairs of matching images or strings. The object is to find the matching pairs. When you click on a box, its contents are revealed. You then click on another box. If its contents match the first one, their contents are left visible. If not, the boxes are closed up again. The user should be able to play multiple games without getting the same arrangement every time.

10

Graphics and Drawing

OBJECTIVES

After studying this chapter, you will

- Know how to use Java's drawing classes and methods.
- Understand the concept of a graphics context.
- Be able to design scalable drawings.
- Know how to design and implement interfaces.
- Be familiar with handling mouse events.

OUTLINE

10.1 Introduction

Instead of using predrawn images to display a visual representation of our `CyberPet`, we could also use Java's drawing and painting methods. In some ways, drawing our own images within the program gives us more flexibility and control. For example, we can scale the drawing to give the impression of movement toward and away from the viewer.

In this chapter we continue our discussion of Java's GUI elements, this time focusing on its drawing, painting, and mouse-handling functions. All of these elements are part of the Java's Abstract Windowing Toolkit (AWT). Most of our attention will be directed toward the `java.awt.Graphics` class. Except for the issue of choosing an appropriate component class to use as a drawing surface, the Swing component set has had little effect one the way drawing is done in Java.

An important design theme of this chapter is the use of parameters to develop very general methods. An example is in the design of **scalable** drawings — that is, drawings that can easily be made larger or smaller. Another example of using parameters with general methods is drawing scalable text displays that work with different fonts.

After introducing essential details of the relevant AWT classes, we will provide several case studies that illustrate how they can be used effectively.

10.2 The Drawing Surface

What to draw on?

In order to draw and paint in a Java program, you need something to draw and paint on. In the Abstract Windowing Toolkit (AWT), a `Canvas` component is the usual drawing surface. However, Swing does not contain a direct counterpart for this class. Instead, in Swing programs you can either draw directly on the top-level windows — `JApplet`, `JFrame` — or on a `JPanel`. `JPanel` is a direct subclass of `JComponent`.

Transparent or opaque?

In order to draw on a `JPanel`, you have to make a subclass of it. Another possible choice for a drawing surface is to make a subclass of `JComponent`. The difference between these two alternatives boils down to whether you want a *transparent* or *opaque* drawing surface. A `JComponent` is always transparent. It will always let its container show through. A `JPanel`, on the other hand, is transparent by default, but it can be made opaque. We'll see an example of this in the next section.

PROGRAMMING TIP: Drawing Surface. In Swing applications, use a subclass of `JComponent` if you want a transparent drawing surface. Otherwise use a subclass of `JPanel`.

10.3 The `Graphics` Context

What to draw with?

Every Java component, including Swing components, has an associated **graphics context**, represented by an object of the `java.awt.Graphics` class. This is the object you use whenever you want to draw or paint in a

Figure 10–1 Using a JPanel's graphics context to draw "Hello World" and a rectangle.

```
import javax.swing.*;
import java.awt.*;
import java.awt.event.*;

public class DrawingPanel extends JPanel {

public void paintComponent(Graphics g) {
    super.paintComponent(g);              // Make the panel opaque
    g.setColor(getForeground());          // Set g's drawing color
    g.drawString("Hello World", 10, 50);
    g.fillRect(10, 55, 80, 20);
}

public static void main(String args[]) {
    JFrame frame = new JFrame("Drawing Panel");
    DrawingPanel panel = new DrawingPanel();
    frame.getContentPane().add(panel);
    frame.setSize(200, 100);
    frame.setVisible(true);
    frame.addWindowListener(new WindowAdapter() {        // Quit the application
        public void windowClosing(WindowEvent e) {
            System.exit(0);
        }
    });
} // main()
} // DrawingPanel
```

program. It contains the drawing methods. However, the Graphics class is abstract, so you can't create a Graphics object directly. You have to get one from a component, such as a JPanel or any subclass of JComponent.

Figure 10–1 illustrates how this done for a JPanel. This program draws "Hello World" and paints an 80 × 20 rectangle at location (10,55) of the panel (Figure 10–2).

The main difference between this Swing program and an AWT drawing program is that for Swing components you override the paintComponent() method, whereas in an AWT program, you override the paint() method. In both cases, Swing and AWT, the graphics object, *g*, is used for both drawing and painting (or filling). It might be useful to compare this program with the HelloWorld applet from Chapter 1 (Figure 1–2).

Figure 10–2 Using the JFrame's graphics context to draw "Hello World."

PROGRAMMING TIP: Graphics Object. When drawing on AWT components, you override the paint() method. When drawing on Swing components, you override the paintComponent() method.

The main() method creates a JFrame as the top-level window and then adds an instance of the DrawingPanel to it (Figure 10–1). Recall that for a top-level Swing container (such as a JFrame) components are added to its *content pane* (getContentPane()) rather than to the container itself.

The content pane

DEBUGGING TIP: Content Pane. It is a semantic error to try to add a component to a top-level Swing window, such as a `JApplet` or `JFrame`. Instead you add the component to the window's content pane.

Let's look at the `paintComponent()` method (Figure 10–1). This method overrides the `JPanel.paintComponent()` method. This is the method that will be called automatically whenever its component needs to be repainted.

The first two lines of the method are used to give the panel a background color (rather than leave it transparent) and to set the drawing color of the `Graphics` object. The first line calls the superclass (`JPanel`) method, whose only task is to draw its background.

Opaque `JPanel`

If you leave these two statements out, the panel will remain transparent, and anything you draw on it will appear on its enclosing frame — on the `JFrame`. The actual appearance of the panel will depend on the program's look and feel default. In the Window's look and feel, putting these statements in or leaving them out won't make any difference, because the `JFrame` and the `JPanel` have the same background color. Of course, whether to make the panel transparent or opaque depends on how you are planning to use it in your application.

PROGRAMMING TIP: Transparent or Opaque. To make a `JPanel` opaque, you must call the default `paintComponent()` method. Otherwise the panel will be transparent by default.

A possible source of frustration could occur if you make the panel opaque (line 1) but forget to set the color of the `Graphics` object to the panel's default foreground color (line 2). In that case, nothing will appear on the panel, because the `Panel.paintComponent()` method will have set the color of the the `Graphics` object to the component's *background* color. If you draw on the gray background with a gray pen, nothing will show up. So, if you make the panel opaque, you must always set the color of the `Graphics` object to something besides the component's background color.

DEBUGGING TIP: Setting the Graphics Color. For opaque `JPanels` — those that invoke `JPanel.paintComponent()` — you must set the color of `Graphics` object. Otherwise it will be set to the component's background color.

10.3.1 Graphics Color and Component Color

Another possible source of confusion is the difference between the component's colors (foreground and background) and the `Graphics` color. The

Graphics object has one color, which is the color it uses for drawing and painting.

One helpful way to think about this is to imagine that the graphics object has a pen for drawing and a paintbrush for painting. When you use the g.setColor() method, as we did in the DrawingPanel program, you set the color of both the pen and the paintbrush. Any subsequent drawing or painting by that graphics object will take place in that color.

What color is the pen and paintbrush?

PROGRAMMING TIP: Drawing and Painting. Drawing refers to making a line drawing. In general, methods named *drawX* [drawRect()] are for drawing. Painting refers to filling a bounded object with color. Methods named *fillX* [fillRect()] are for painting. All painting and drawing is done by a Graphics object in its current pen and paintbrush color.

By contrast, every component has two colors associated with it: a *foreground* and a *background* color. For some components the difference between foreground and background is clear. For a JButton, the button's label is drawn in the foreground color on the button's background color. For a JTextField, the text is drawn in the foreground color, and the text field itself is rendered in the background color. Other components, such as a JPanel, don't use a foreground color. They consist entirely of a background color.

What color is the component?

For any component, the following access methods, which are defined in Component, can be used to get and set its colors:

```
public Color getBackground();
public Color getForeground();
public void setBackground(Color c);
public void setForeground(Color c);
```

DEBUGGING TIP: Setting Colors. A common mistake is to forget that foreground and background apply to the component, not to its associated graphics object.

10.3.2 The Graphics Coordinate System

The graphics context uses a simple coordinate system in which each picture element (**pixel**) is represented by its x and y coordinates. The **origin** of the coordinate system — the point with coordinates (0,0) — is located at the top-left corner of the component. The *x coordinate* represents the *horizontal* displacement of a point from the origin, and the *y coordinate* represents its *vertical* displacement. The x coordinate increases from left to right, and the y coordinate increases from top to bottom (Figure 10–3).

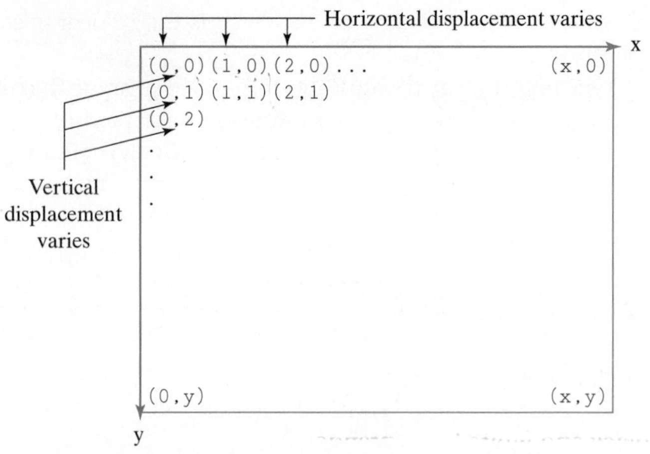

Figure 10–3 Java's coordinate system.

10.3.3 Properties of the Graphics Context

The graphics state

A `Graphics` object has an internal state that consists of several properties that remain fixed during drawing and painting operations (Table 10–1). One of these is its color, which we have already discussed. Another is the current *font* that is used for drawing text. The *origin* is the point with coordinates (0,0). By default this is set to the component's top-left corner, but it can be *translated* (moved) to any point in the component's coordinate system. The **clip region** is that area of the component where drawing is permitted. By default, the clip region is set to the entire component, but this can be changed.

Default drawing mode

The default **drawing mode** is to just paint over pixels. For example, if the background is white and the drawing color is black, then in normal mode drawing a pixel will turn it black. However, this too can be changed. One alternative mode is **XORmode**, or *bitwise exclusive or* mode, so named because it matches the logic of the boolean exclusive or operator. In XOR-mode, an exclusive or is performed on the background and foreground pixels, where the foreground pixel is determined by the pen's color. For black and white drawing, the following table defines what happens:

Background Color	Pen Color	Color of Result
White	Black	Black
Black	Black	White

XORmode drawing

In other words, if the drawing pen is black, then wherever the background is white, the drawing will be black. On the other hand, wherever the background is already black, the drawing will be white. Thus XOR mode,

Table 10.1. Properties of the graphics context

Property	Description	Default Value
Color	Current drawing color	The JComponent's foreground color
Font	Current text font	The JComponent's font
Drawing mode	Controls the pixel color	New pixels replace old pixels in the same location
Clip region	The drawing region	The entire JComponent
Origin	The point with coordinate (0,0)	Top-left pixel of the JComponent

in this case, will reverse the color of the background. Of course, on a colored background, while a similar effect is obtained, the results aren't so black and white (pun intended!).

The java.awt.Graphics class contains access methods that allow you to alter the default values of these properties. Examples in the following sections will illustrate how these methods are used:

```
public class Graphics extends Object {
   // Property access methods
     public abstract Shape getClip();
     public abstract Rectangle getClipBounds();
     public abstract Color getColor();
     public abstract Font getFont();
     public abstract FontMetrics getFontMetrics();
     public abstract void setClip(int x, int y, int width, int height);
     public abstract void setClip(Shape clip);
     public abstract void setColor(Color c);
     public abstract void setFont(Font f);
     public abstract void setPaintMode();
     public abstract void setXORMode(Color c);
     public abstract void translate(int x, int y); // Move the origin
}
```

SELF-STUDY EXERCISES

EXERCISE 10.1 For Figure 10–3, suppose the screen is 200 × 200. What are the coordinates for the pixel in the bottom-right corner of the screen?

EXERCISE 10.2 Suppose we define the clip region of window with g.setClip(0,0,100,100), and we follow that with a g.drawString("Hello World",150,150). What do you suppose will happen?

EXERCISE 10.3 Describe a problem for which drawing in XOR mode would be useful.

10.4 The Color Class

RGB colors

Java colors are created from an **RGB value**, which is a collection of three numbers that specify the amount of red, green, and blue that are mixed together to form the color. The Color class provides three constructors, each of which uses a different way of representing a color's RGB value:

```
public Color(int r, int g, int b);
public Color(int rgb);
public Color(float r, float g, float b);
```

In the first constructor, an RGB value is represented as three separate `ints`, one for red, green and blue, respectively. In this case each integer represents a value between 0 and 255. The second constructor specifies the RGB value as a single integer which is constructed as follows:

```
RGB = 65536 * R + 256 * G + B
```

This is the form in which the RGB is actually stored by the `Color` object. The third constructor takes the R, G, and B specifications as three `float` values in the range 0.0 to 1.0 respectively. The closer an R, G, or B value is to 1.0, the more of that hue is mixed into the color.

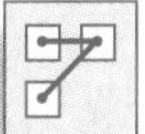

EFFECTIVE DESIGN: Colors. Care must be taken in designing programs that use color, because color representation is inherently system dependent. In theory, it is possible to specify 256 × 256 × 256 = 16,777,216 different colors. In practice, however, the number of different colors that can actually be displayed depends on the quality of your system's monitor.

PROGRAMMING TIP: Color Processing. If your monitor uses only 8 bits to represent each pixel, then it can represent at most $2^8 = 256$ colors. In that case, the operating system decides which 256 (out of 16,277,216) colors to make available. If your program requests a color that is not one of the 256 available colors, the system will choose the closest available color.

In addition to the three constructors, described above, the `Color` class defines the following standard colors as class constants:

```
public static final Color black;       // 0,0,0
public static final Color blue;        // 0,0,255
public static final Color cyan;        // 0,255,255
public static final Color darkGray;    // 140,140,140
public static final Color gray;        // 128,128,128
public static final Color green;       // 0,255,0
public static final Color lightGray;   // 192,192,192
public static final Color magenta;     // 255,0,255
public static final Color orange;
public static final Color pink;
public static final Color red;         // 255,0,0
public static final Color white;       // 255,255,255
public static final Color yellow;      // 255,255,0
```

These can be used directly to define new `Color` objects as follows:

```
Color color1 = Color.red;
Color color2 = Color.magenta;
```

If you wish to define a custom color, you can specify the individual R, G, and B components of your color.

PROGRAMMING TIP: Creating Custom Colors. The primary colors — red, green, and blue — are represented by giving two of the other three R, G, B, components a value of zero. A color whose green and blue components are both 0 will be some shade of red.

PROGRAMMING TIP: Creating Shades of Gray. The RGB mixture (255,255,255) can be used to create pure white, while (0,0,0) is used to specify black. Shades of gray are colors whose RGB components have equal values. Thus (128,128,128) is the specification for `Color.gray`, while (192,192,192) represents a lighter shade and (140,140,140) a darker shade of gray.

The `Color` class also provides several instance methods for modifying colors:

```
public Color brighter();
public Color darker();
public boolean equals(Object o); // Overrides Object.equals()
public int getBlue();
public int getGreen();
public int getRGB();
public int getRed();
public String toString();    // Overrides Object.toString()
```

The various `get()` methods enable you to retrieve a `Color`'s individual RGB value. The `brighter()` and `darker()` methods enable you to start with a standard color and darken or lighten it:

```
Color red = Color.red;                 // Pure red
Color brightRed = red.brighter();      // Brighter red
Color darkRed = red.darker();          // Darker red
```

Try.

SELF-STUDY EXERCISES

EXERCISE 10.4 Describe what will happen if you pick a color in Java that can't be displayed on your monitor.

EXERCISE 10.5 Design question: Why are the built-in colors defined as class constants?

EXERCISE 10.6 Although technically millions of colors are possible, most are minor shade or brightness variants indistinguishable by the human eye. Which three colors do color monitors "mix" to make all the rest, whether dozens or "millions"?

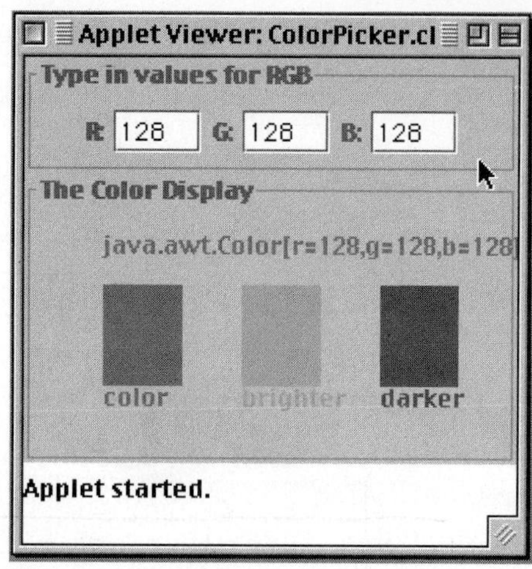

Figure 10–4 Output from the `ColorPicker` program.

10.4.1 Example: The `ColorPicker` Applet

To illustrate how to use the methods of the `Color` class, consider the `ColorPicker` applet, whose interface is shown in Figure 10–4. This applet lets you experiment with the various RGB ratios. It provides three labeled `JTextFields` for the R, G, and B values that make up a color. When a return is typed in any text field, a new `Color` object is made with the three input values and then displayed on a separate `JPanel` located in the center of the applet.

The new color is displayed in various formats. First, it is displayed using the `Color.toString()` method, which just displays the integer values of the color's RGB components. Next the color is used to paint a colored rectangle and draw a colored string. Finally the color is brightened and darkened, and these new colors are displayed as both a rectangle and a string.

The applet's border interface is divided into two separate panels: a `controls JPanel`, which contains the input text fields, and a `canvas JPanel`, which is responsible for all the drawing and painting (Figure 10–5). Although it is possible to draw directly on a `JApplet`, a more flexible interface can be created by using a separate `JPanel`, within the applet window, for drawing. That's the purpose of the `Canvas` class, which is described below.

EFFECTIVE DESIGN: Drawing Interface Design. If a drawing program uses controls and other components, it is best to use a separate panel for the drawing area. That way the program's layout can be managed by a layout manager.

Figure 10–5 The `ColorPicker` program allows you to experiment with the RGB ratios of the various colors.

```
import javax.swing.*;
import java.awt.*;
import java.awt.event.*;

public class ColorPicker extends JApplet implements ActionListener {
    private JTextField redIn, greenIn, blueIn;
    private JLabel R = new JLabel("R:"),
                   G = new JLabel("G:"),
                   B = new JLabel("B:");
    private JPanel controls = new JPanel();
    private Canvas canvas = new Canvas();

    public void init() {
        initControls();
        getContentPane().add(controls, "North");
        getContentPane().add(canvas, "Center");
        canvas.setBorder(BorderFactory.createTitledBorder("The Color Display"));
        getContentPane().setBackground(Color.white);
        setSize(250,150);
    } // init()

    private void initControls() {
        redIn = new JTextField("128", 4);      // Create 3 input textfields
        greenIn = new JTextField("128", 4);
        blueIn = new JTextField("128", 4);
        redIn.addActionListener(this);         // Give them listeners
        greenIn.addActionListener(this);
        blueIn.addActionListener(this);
        controls.setLayout( new FlowLayout());
        controls.setBorder(BorderFactory.createTitledBorder("Type in values for RGB"));
        controls.add(R);
        controls.add(redIn);     // Add prompts and textfields
        controls.add(G);
        controls.add(greenIn);
        controls.add(B);
        controls.add(blueIn);
    } // initControls()

    public void actionPerformed(ActionEvent e) {
        int r = Integer.parseInt(redIn.getText());      // Get user's inputs
        int g = Integer.parseInt(greenIn.getText());
        int b = Integer.parseInt(blueIn.getText());
        canvas.setColor(new Color(r, g, b));            // Reset the canvas's color
        repaint();                                      // Repaint the applet
    } // actionPerformed()
} // ColorPicker
```

Note how the applet's layout is created in the `init()` and `initControls()` methods. Once again, because a `JApplet` is a top-level Swing container, the panels must be added to its content pane. Note how the `BorderFactory` class is used to create borders around each of the panels. This helps to improve the applet's overall appearance, while dividing the interface into logical regions at the same time.

Each time the user types a return in one of the `JTextFields`, the `actionPerformed()` method retrieves the three RGB values from the `JTextFields` and uses them to create a new `Color`. It uses the color to set the `canvas`'s color.

Figure 10–6 The Canvas class is a JPanel subclass that can be used for drawing on an applet.

```
import javax.swing.*;
import java.awt.*;

public class Canvas extends JPanel {
    private final int HREF = 40, VREF = 55;      // Reference points
    private final int WIDTH = 40, HEIGHT = 50;  // Rectangle dimensions
    private final int HGAP = 70,  VGAP = 60;    // Spacing constants

    private Color color = Color.gray;
    public void setColor(Color c) {
        color = c;
    }

    public void paintComponent(Graphics g) {
        super.paintComponent(g);                          // Make the panel opaque
        g.setColor(color);                                // Set the pen's color
        g.drawString(color.toString(), HREF, VREF-15 ); // Draw the color's RGB's
        g.fillRect(HREF, VREF, WIDTH, HEIGHT);            // Color a rectangle
        g.drawString("color", HREF, VREF + VGAP);
        g.setColor(color.brighter());                     // Brighten the color
        g.fillRect(HREF + HGAP, VREF, WIDTH, HEIGHT);
        g.drawString("brighter", HREF + HGAP, VREF + VGAP);
        g.setColor(color.darker());                       // Darken the color
        g.fillRect(HREF + HGAP * 2, VREF, WIDTH, HEIGHT);
        g.drawString("darker", HREF + HGAP * 2, VREF + VGAP);
    } // paintComponent()
} // Canvas
```

The canvas JPanel takes care of all the drawing (Figure 10–6). This class has the same basic design as the DrawingFrame class we defined earlier. It extends JPanel and overrides the paintComponent() method, which is the method where all the drawing takes place.

10.4.2 Painting Components

Repainting rules

It's important to understand how Java's event handling works in this program. As you know, an applet is repainted automatically whenever it is moved, or resized, or made visible again after being hidden. This is done by calling the applet's paint() method. A program can also force an applet to repaint itself by explicitly calling repaint(), as we have done in this case. But this applet doesn't contain a paint() method.

Repainting protocol

So how is this applet painted? The answer is that it is repainted as part of Java's default event handling. The reason the applet does not contain a paint() method is because it doesn't do any painting of its own. That task is handled by the canvas object. However, as a subclass of Container, a JApplet invokes Container.paint() method. The default behavior of this method is to paint all the components contained in the container. It does this by calling their respective paint methods.

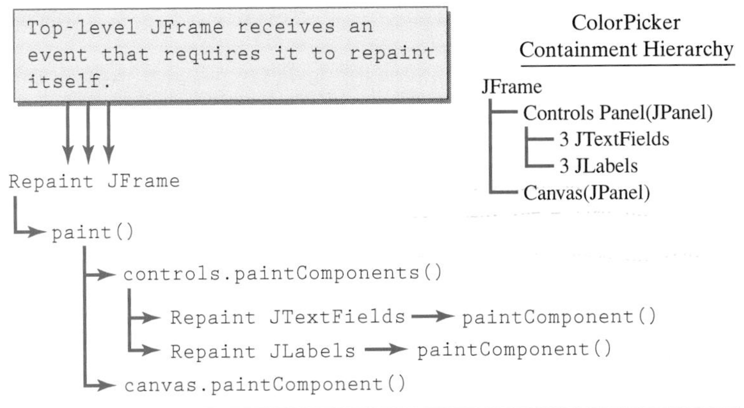

Figure 10–7 Output from the `ColorPicker` program.

Figure 10–7 illustrates how this process works for the `ColorPicker` applet. Whenever the applet is repainted, all of the text fields and labels are repainted, and the `canvas` is repainted. Because the `canvas` is a `JPanel`, it is repainted by calling its `paintComponent()` method. Thus, every time the user types a return key in one of the text fields, the `actionPerformed()` method repaints the `JApplet`, which in turn repaints all of the components that it contains. If the components are containers themselves, then all of their components will be repainted.

> **PROGRAMMING TIP: Automatic Repainting.** Whenever a container, such as an a `JApplet`, `JFrame`, or `JPanel`, is repainted, all of its contained components are repainted.

SELF-STUDY EXERCISES

EXERCISE 10.7 For each of the following expressions, predict what color would be produced:

```
(a)  new Color(255,10,10)    (b) new Color(0,255,20)    (c) new Color(10,15,255)
```

EXERCISE 10.8 Explain what would happen if you remove the `repaint()` method call from the `ColorPicker`'s `actionPerformed()` method.

EXERCISE 10.9 What's the difference between the `JApplet`'s `paint()` method and the `JPanel`'s `paintComponent` method?

OBJECT-ORIENTED DESIGN: Reference Constants

Note how the constants — the `final int` variables — are used in the `Canvas` class to simplify the layout of the drawing area (Figure 10–6). `HREF` and `VREF` serve as reference points. All of the drawing takes place relative to these two values. Also, the horizontal and vertical spacing are defined in terms of the `HGAP` and `VGAP` constants. This enables you to develop simple formulas for aligning and spacing the output. For example, the following three strings

```
color        brighter       darker
```

are printed, horizontally spaced, on the same line, by using the following three statements:

```
g.drawString("color", HREF, VREF + VGAP);
...
g.drawString("brighter", HREF + HGAP, VREF + VGAP);
...
g.drawString("darker", HREF + HGAP * 2, VREF + VGAP);
```

Note the use of the formula `HREF + HGAP * k` (where *k* ranges from 0 to 2) to produce the desired spacing. Similarly, note the use of the `WIDTH` and `HEIGHT` constants to specify the size of the colored rectangles:

```
g.fillRect(HREF, VREF, WIDTH, HEIGHT);
...
g.fillRect(HREF + HGAP, VREF, WIDTH, HEIGHT);
...
g.fillRect(HREF + HGAP * 2, VREF, WIDTH, HEIGHT);
```

Here again `HREF, VREF,` and `HGAP` are used to control the spacing of the rectangles.

Symbolic constants

The main advantage of using constants in this way is that the program is easier to develop and maintain. By using symbolic constants in the code, you can easily try different values until you get the right layout. To change the size of horizontal spacing of the elements, you need only edit one value in the program — the constant definition — no matter how often that value is used. Also, it is easy to incorporate new elements into the scheme, making the program easier to maintain over time. In this case, because the reference points and sizes of the components don't change, we are able to use constants. In subsequent examples we will use variables and method parameters to achieve results that are even more general.

EFFECTIVE DESIGN: Use symbolic constants — that is, `final` variables — in place of literal values to make your code more general. It will be easier both to develop and to maintain.

SELF-STUDY EXERCISES

EXERCISE 10.10 Write a method to display a sequence of 20 small 3 × 3 rectangles horizontally across the screen starting at XREF, VREF, with a space of HGAP between each pair of rectangles. This should be a void method and should take a Graphics parameter.

EXERCISE 10.11 Write a method to display a sequence of 20 small 3 × 3 rectangles diagonally across the screen starting at XREF, VREF, with a horizontal and vertical space of HGAP and VGAP between each pair of rectangles. This should be a void method and should take a Graphics parameter.

From the Java Library: Points and Dimensions

The java.awt.Point class represents a point the the Graphics coordinate system:

```
public class Point extends Object {
   // Constructors
     public Point();
     public Point(Point p);          // Copy another point
     public Point(int x, int y);
   // Public instance variables
     public int x;
     public int y;
   // Public instance methods
     public boolean equals(Object obj); // Overrides Object.equals()
     public Point getLocation();
     public Point setLocation(Point p);
     public Point setLocation(int x, int y);
}
```

As you can see, the Point class makes it possible to manipulate *x*- and *y*-coordinates as a single entity. It also makes it possible to break a point up into its *x*- and *y*-coordinates. Note that a Point's *x*- and *y*-coordinates are defined as public instance variables. This makes it possible to refer to them using the following convenient syntax:

```
Point p = new Point(100, 50);
System.out.println("x = " + p.x + " y = " + p.y);
```

The main justification for making *x* and *y* public is that it is more efficient to access them directly than being forced to use getX() and getY() methods. Method calls require more processing overhead than direct access and efficiency is an important factor in drawing three-dimensional graphics.

EFFECTIVE DESIGN: Public Instance Variables. Although instance variables should usually be declared private, there are situations, such as when efficiency is of paramount importance, when you are justified making them public.

The `java.awt.Dimension` class represents the size (width and height) of a component:

```
public class Dimension {
  // Constructors
   public Dimension();
   public Dimension(Dimension d);          // Copy another dimension
   public Dimension(int width, int height);
  // Instance variables
   public int height;
   public int width;
  // Instance methods
   public boolean equals(Object o);       // Overrides Object.equals()
   public Dimension getSize();
   public void setSize(Dimension d);
   public void setSize(int width, int height);
   public String toString();              // Overrides Object.toString()
}
```

A `Dimension` makes it possible to manipulate an object's width and height as a single entity. Because `height` and `width` are public instance variables, the following syntax can be used to refer to a component's dimensions:

```
Dimension d = new Dimension(100, 50);
System.out.println("width = " + d.width + " height = " + d.height);
```

Note the redundancy built into the `Dimension` class. For example, in addition to being able to set a `Dimension`'s instance variables directly, public access methods are provided. Also, by defining more than one version of some access methods, the class achieves a higher level of flexibility. The same can be said for providing several different constructors, including a copy constructor. Finally, note how it overrides the `equals()` and `toString()` methods. These are all examples of good object-oriented design.

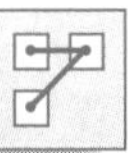

EFFECTIVE DESIGN: Redundancy. Redundancy is often a desirable characteristic of object design. It makes the object easier to use and more widely applicable.

EFFECTIVE DESIGN: Overriding Generic Methods. All classes that are designed for widespread use, especially library classes, should override the `Object` class's `toString()` and `equals()` methods.

SELF-STUDY EXERCISES

EXERCISE 10.12 Write a method that takes two parameters, a `Graphics` object and a `Point p`, and draws a sequence of 20 small 3 × 3 rectangles horizontally across the screen starting at `p.x, p.y`, with a space of `HGAP` between each pair of rectangles.

EXERCISE 10.13 Suppose you have a `JPanel` whose dimensions are represented by `Dimension d`. Write an expression to calculate its area.

10.5 Painting and Drawing Lines and Shapes

In addition to the `fillRect()` method, which we used in the `ColorPicker` program, Java's `java.awt.Graphics` class contains a good assortment of methods that are used for drawing and painting lines and shapes:

```
// Drawing methods
public void draw3DRect(int x, int y, int w, int h, boolean raised);
public abstract void drawArc(int x, int y, int w, int h, int startAngle, int arcAngle);
public abstract void drawLine(int x1, int y1, int x2, int y2);
public abstract void drawOval(int x, int y, int w, int h);
public abstract void drawPolygon(int[] xPoints, int[] yPoints, int nPoints);
public void drawPolygon(Polygon p);
public abstract void drawPolyline(int[] xPoints, int[] yPoints, int nPoints);
public void drawRect(int x, int y, int w, int h);
public abstract void drawRoundRect(int x, int y, int w, int h, int arcW, int arcH);

// Filling methods
public abstract void clearRect(int x, int y, int w, int h);
public void fill3DRect((int x, int y, int w, int h, boolean raised);
public abstract void fillArc(int x, int y, int w, int h, int startAngle, int arcAngle);
public abstract void fillOval(int x, int y, int w, int h);
public abstract void fillPolygon(int[] xPoints, int[] yPoints, int nPoints);
public void fillPolygon(Polygon p);
public abstract void fillRect(int x, int y, int w, int h);
public abstract void fillRoundRect(int x, int y, int w, int h, int arcW, int arcH);
```

Drawing and painting shapes

The methods categorized as drawing methods are used to draw lines, arcs, and various kinds shapes, including ovals, rectangles, and n-sided polygons. The methods categorized as filling methods are used to fill bounded regions, such as ovals, rectangles, and polygons with a color.

As we've seen, the conventional way to draw or paint in color is first to set the context's color and then to use one of these methods. For example, the following statements will draw a red rectangle and a red oval:

```
g.setColor(Color.red  );        // Set the drawing color to red
g.drawRect(10, 50, 100, 50);  // A 100 x 50 rectangle at location 10,50
g.drawOval(150, 50, 100, 50); // An oval inscribed in a 100 x 50 rectangle
```

Both `drawRect()` and `drawOval()` take the same parameters, the x- and y-coordinates where the shape should be located, and the shape's *length* and *width*. In the case of `drawRect()`, the coordinates refer to the rectangle's top-left corner. In the case of `drawOval()`, they refer to the top-left corner and the length and width of an invisible rectangle within which the oval is inscribed. You can also use these methods to draw squares and circles, which are just special cases of rectangle and oval.

In both cases the outline of the shapes would be red. The inside of the shapes would be transparent — that is, they would have the color of the container's background. The following statements draw the same shapes, but fill the shapes with color:

```
g.setColor(Color.red);          // Set the drawing color to red
g.fillRect(10, 50, 100, 50);  // A 100 x 50 rectangle at location 10,50
g.fillOval(150, 50, 100, 50); // An oval inscribed in a 100 x 50 rectangle
```

SELF-STUDY EXERCISES

EXERCISE 10.14 Use `drawRect()` to draw an 80 × 40 rectangle, and place the top left of the rectangle at coordinates (0,20).

EXERCISE 10.15 Write the Java code to inscribe a yellow oval in the rectangle you drew in the previous exercise.

10.6 Example: The ShapeDemo Applet

The `ShapeDemo` applet (Figure 10–8) illustrates the use of the various drawing and painting commands. The program shows two kinds of shapes: drawn shapes (top) and filled shapes (bottom). It shows examples of ovals, 3-D rectangles, and rounded rectangles.

Problem decomposition

Note how this program (Figure 10–9) is designed. Unlike the `Colorpicker` applet, this applet does not contain components, such as text fields or buttons. It just does drawing. Therefore the drawing can be done directly on the its top-level container — the `JApplet`. This means that the drawing will be done by the `paint()` method, rather than the `paintComponent()` method. The `paintComponent()` method only applies to subclasses of `JComponent`. (You may want to review the Swing hierarchy diagram in Figure 9–1).

DEBUGGING TIP: Painting AWT and Swing Components. A possible source of confusion concerns which paint method to use for a component. Swing `JComponents` use `paintComponent()`. AWT components and top-level Swing windows, `JApplet` and `JFrame`, which are subclasses of `java.awt.Component`, use the `paint()` method.

The `drawLine()` method is used to draw a line separating the two types of shapes (Figure 10–9). Note again how symbolic constants are used to specify the locations, spacing, and sizes of the shapes. Even the size of the applet screen is calculated as a function of these constant values:

Setting a container's size

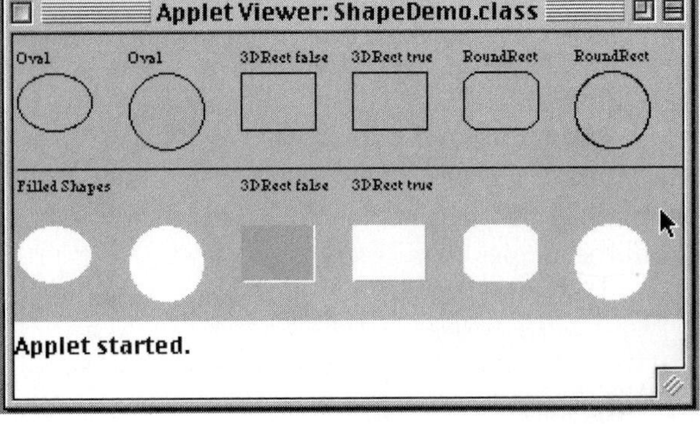

Figure 10–8 Output from the ShapeDemo program. A "RoundRect" is a rectangle with rounded corners. Note that if you set the parameters right, you can make it into a circle. A "3DRect" is a rectangle that has a 3D appearance. Two examples are shown.

Figure 10–9 The ShapeDemo Class illustrates the use of the `Graphics` class's basic drawing and painting methods.

```
import java.awt.*;
import javax.swing.*;

public class ShapeDemo extends JApplet {
    public final int NFIGS = 5;         // Number of shapes
    public final int HREF = 2;          // Horizontal reference
    public final int VREF = 20;         // Vertical reference
    public final int WIDTH = 40;        // Width of figure
    public final int HGT = 20;          // Height of figure
    public final int HGAP = 20;         // H gap between figures
    public final int VGAP = 20;         // V gap between figures

    public void paint( Graphics g ) {
        setSize((NFIGS +1) * (WIDTH + HGAP), 3 * (HGT + HGAP));
        setBackground(Color.lightGray);
        g.setFont(new Font("Serif", Font.PLAIN, 9));
        int fontHgt = g.getFontMetrics().getHeight();
        g.drawString("Oval", HREF, VREF - 5 );
        g.drawOval(HREF, VREF, WIDTH, HGT);
        g.drawString("Oval", HREF + (WIDTH + HGAP), VREF - 5);
        g.drawOval(HREF + (WIDTH + HGAP), VREF, WIDTH, WIDTH);
        g.drawString("3DRect false", HREF + 2 * (WIDTH + HGAP), VREF - 5);
        g.draw3DRect(HREF + 2 * (WIDTH + HGAP), VREF, WIDTH, HGT, false);
        g.drawString("3DRect true", HREF + 3 * (WIDTH + HGAP), VREF - 5);
        g.draw3DRect(HREF + 3 * (WIDTH + HGAP), VREF, WIDTH, HGT, true);
        g.drawString("RoundRect", HREF + 4 * (WIDTH + HGAP), VREF - 5);
        g.drawRoundRect(HREF + 4 * (WIDTH + HGAP), VREF, WIDTH, HGT, WIDTH/2, HGT/2);
        g.drawString("RoundRect", HREF +5 * (WIDTH + HGAP), VREF - 5);
        g.drawRoundRect(HREF + 5 * (WIDTH + HGAP), VREF, WIDTH, WIDTH, WIDTH, WIDTH);

        g.drawLine(HREF, VREF + HGT + VGAP, HREF + (NFIGS + 1) * (WIDTH + HGAP ), VREF + HGT + VGAP);

        g.drawString("Filled Objects", HREF, VREF + HGT + VGAP + fontHgt );
        g.drawString("3DRect false", HREF + 2 * (WIDTH + HGAP), VREF + HGT + VGAP + fontHgt);
        g.drawString("3DRect true", HREF + 3 * (WIDTH + HGAP),  VREF + HGT + VGAP + fontHgt);
        g.setColor(Color.white);
        g.fillOval(HREF ,VREF + 2 *  HGT + VGAP, WIDTH, HGT);
        g.fillOval(HREF + (WIDTH + HGAP), VREF + 2 *  HGT + VGAP, WIDTH, WIDTH);
        g.fill3DRect(HREF + 2 * (WIDTH + HGAP), VREF + 2 * HGT + VGAP, WIDTH, HGT, false);
        g.fill3DRect(HREF + 3 * (WIDTH + HGAP), VREF + 2 * HGT + VGAP, WIDTH, HGT, true);
        g.fillRoundRect(HREF + 4 * (WIDTH + HGAP), VREF + 2 * HGT + VGAP, WIDTH, HGT, WIDTH/2, HGT/2);
        g.fillRoundRect(HREF + 5 * (WIDTH + HGAP), VREF + 2 * HGT + VGAP, WIDTH, WIDTH, WIDTH, WIDTH);
    } // init()
} // ShapeDemo
```

```
setSize((NFIGS +1) * (WIDTH + HGAP), 3 * (HGT + VGAP));
```

This formula says that the horizontal dimension of the screen is calculated by assuming that each shape is given a horizontal space equal to its `WIDTH` plus the horizontal gap between shapes, `HGAP`. The horizontal dimension of the screen is then calculated as the number of shapes, `NFIGS +1`, times each shape's allotted horizontal space. The "+1" adds a little extra space. The vertical dimension of the screen is calculated as three times the sum of the height of each shape, `HGT`, plus the vertical spacing between each shape, `VGAP`.

Algorithm design

The program's output (Figure 10–8) shows the difference between drawn and filled shapes of the same dimensions. The drawn shapes are transparent, while the filled shapes are colored (white). The 3D shapes were drawn by the following commands:

```
g.draw3DRect(HREF + 2 * (WIDTH + HGAP), VREF, WIDTH, HGT, false);
g.draw3DRect(HREF + 3 * (WIDTH + HGAP), VREF, WIDTH, HGT, true);
g.fill3DRect(HREF + 2 * (WIDTH + HGAP), VREF + 2 * HGT + VGAP, WIDTH, HGT, false);
g.fill3DRect(HREF + 3 * (WIDTH + HGAP), VREF + 2 * HGT + VGAP, WIDTH, HGT, true);
```

The `boolean` argument in these methods determines the rectangle's color scheme. When false, the main part of the rectangle is drawn in the current pen color, and the outline (bottom, right sides) consist of an alternate color. When false, these colors are reversed.

? tme

Note also the use of the rounded rectangle shapes, which can be used to draw shapes ranging from a circle to a rectangle with rounded corners. The statements used to produce these shapes are

```
g.drawRoundRect(HREF + 4 * (WIDTH + HGAP), VREF, WIDTH, HGT, WIDTH/2, HGT/2);
g.drawRoundRect(HREF + 5 * (WIDTH + HGAP), VREF, WIDTH, WIDTH, WIDTH, WIDTH);
g.fillRoundRect(HREF + 4 * (WIDTH + HGAP), VREF + 2 * HGT + VGAP, WIDTH, HGT, WIDTH/2, HGT/2);
g.fillRoundRect(HREF + 5 * (WIDTH + HGAP), VREF + 2 * HGT + VGAP, WIDTH, WIDTH, WIDTH, WIDTH);
```

Rounded rectangles

The last two parameters in each of these methods are used to specify the width and the height of the arc that defines the shape's corners. As the program illustrates, the larger the arc, the more rounded the corners. When using these kinds of shapes in your program, the best strategy is to experiment with different values until you get the desired appearance. Again, however, the use of symbolic constants, instead of literal values, makes the program easier to develop and modify. In this case it also helps to clarify the relationship between the arcs and the dimensions of the enclosing rectangles.

SELF-STUDY EXERCISES

EXERCISE 10.16 What kind of shape would be drawn by the following statement?

```
g.drawRoundRect(XREF, VREF, 50, 50, 50, 50);
```

EXERCISE 10.17 Write a statement using the `drawRoundRect()` method to draw a circle with diameter `D`, inside of the rectangle located at `XREF`, `YREF`.

10.7 Graphing Equations

No discussion of graphics would be complete without an illustration of how to use the drawing commands to graph equations. For mathematical and scientific graphs, it is necessary to use the **Cartesian coordinate system**. As you know, in Cartesian coordinates, the origin (0,0) is located in the center of the graph and is intersected by the x- and y-axes. Obviously, graphing lines and equations on the Cartesian plane would be made much easier if we could move the drawing frame's origin to the center of the frame. Fortunately, this is very simple to do using the `Graphics.translate()` method.

Translating the origin

For example, assuming the size of the frame is 400 × 400, we can place the origin at the center with the following statement:

```
g.translate(200, 200); // Move origin to the center
```

This statement will move the origin 200 pixels to the right and 200 pixels down from its present (top-left corner) location. Of course, this will not, by itself, give us a Cartesian coordinate system, because the vertical coordinates will still grow from small to large as you move downward from the origin. In Cartesian coordinates, the y coordinates decrease as you move downward, so, in graphing equations, we will have to make this adjustment in our programs.

DEBUGGING TIP: Moving the Origin. The parameters in the `translate()` method specify the horizontal and vertical displacement by which the origin should be moved. They do not specify the coordinates of the new location.

DEBUGGING TIP: Your graphs will come out upside down if you forget to reorient them to account for the fact that in Java's coordinate system, the y-axis grows in the downward direction.

Once you translate the origin, any subsequent references to coordinates will now assume that the origin is at (200,200). For example, the following statement,

```
g.fillOval(0, 0, 2, 2);
```

will draw an oval inscribed within a 2×2 rectangle whose upper-left corner is at the very center of the screen.

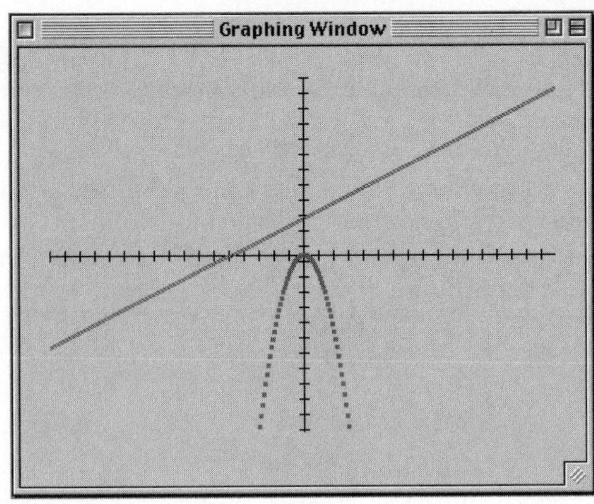

Figure 10–10 Graphing mathematical or scientific equations.

SELF-STUDY EXERCISES

EXERCISE 10.18 Suppose you have a 200 × 200 `JPanel`. Relative to its default origin, in which (0,0) is at the top-left corner of the panel, where would the origin be after the following statements are executed?

```
g.translate(50, 200);
g.translate(-10, -150);
```

10.7.1 Example: The `Graph` Program

Translating the origin in this way makes it very simple to develop programs to draw mathematical or scientific graphs (Figure 10–10).

Problem decomposition

The `Graph` application (Figure 10–11) provides an illustration of the basic techniques. First, note how the application is designed. It defines the `Graph` class as a subclass of `JPanel`. This means that all the drawing for this application will be done in the `paintComponent()` method. The `main()` method creates a top-level window for the application `JFrame` and then adds the `Graph` to the window. The `Graph`'s initial size is set in its constructor. Note that `Graph`'s class constants, `WIDTH` and `HEIGHT`, are used to set the initial size of the top-level window.

Figure 10–11 The `Graph` application illustrates how to draw mathematical and scientific graphs.

```
import java.awt.*;
import javax.swing.*;

public class Graph extends JPanel {

    private final int WIDTH = 400, HEIGHT = 400; // Default width and height

    public Graph () {
        setSize(WIDTH,HEIGHT);
    }
```

Figure 10–11 *Continued*

```
    public void paintComponent(Graphics g) {
        Dimension size = this.getSize();
        g.setColor(getBackground());                         // Clear the drawing area
        g.setClip(0, 0, size.width, size.height);
        g.fillRect(0, 0, size.width, size.height);
        g.setClip(20, 20, size.width - 40, size.height - 40); // Reset the clip region
        g.translate(size.width / 2, size.height / 2);        // Place origin at middle
        g.setColor(Color.black);
        drawXYAxes(g);                                       // Draw the X and Y axes
        graphLine(g, 0.5, 25.2);                             // Graph y = 0.5x + 25.2
        graphQuadratic(g, -0.125, 0, 0 );                    // Graph 4y = -x2
    } // paintComponent()

    private void drawXYAxes(Graphics g) {
        Dimension size = this.getSize();                 // Get the panel's size
        int hBound = size.width / 2;                     // Use it to set the bounds
        int vBound = size.height / 2;
        int tic = size.width / 100;

        g.drawLine(-hBound,0,hBound,0);                  // Draw X-axis
        for (int k = -hBound; k <= hBound; k+=10)
            g.drawLine(k, tic, k, -tic);
        g.drawLine(0, vBound, 0, -vBound);               // Draw Y-axis
        for (int k = -vBound; k <= vBound; k+=10)
            g.drawLine(-tic, k, +tic, k);
    } // drawXYAxes()

    private void graphLine(Graphics g, double m, double b) {
        Dimension size = this.getSize();                // Get the panel's size
        int hBound = size.width / 2;                    // Use it to set the bounds
        g.setColor( Color.red );
        for (int x = -hBound; x <= hBound; x++) {       // For each pixel on x axis
            int y = (int)(m * x + b );
            y = -y;                                     // Reverse y coordinate (Cartesian)
            g.drawLine(x, y, x+1, y+1);                 // Draw a point
        }
    } // graphLine()

    private void graphQuadratic( Graphics g, double a, double b, double c ) {
        Dimension size = this.getSize();              // Get the panel's size
        int hBound = size.width/2;                    // Use it to set the bounds
        g.setColor(Color.red);
        for (int x = -hBound; x <= hBound; x++) { // For each pixel on x axis
            int y = (int)(a * x * x + b * x + c);
            y = -y;                                   // Reverse y coordinate (cartesian)
            g.fillOval(x-1, y-1, 3, 3);               // Draw a point
        }
    } // graphQuadratic()

    public static void main(String args[]) {
        JFrame f = new JFrame("Graphing Window");
        Graph graph = new Graph();
        f.getContentPane().add(graph);
        f.setSize(graph.getSize().width, graph.getSize().height);
        f.setVisible(true);
        f.addWindowListener(new WindowAdapter() {       // Quit the application
            public void windowClosing(WindowEvent e) {
                System.exit(0);
            }
        });
    } // main()
}// Graph
```

Algorithm design

All of the drawing in the application is handled by the `paintComponent()` method. Remember that this method will be called automatically each time the application's window is resized, so we want to design an algorithm that will produce an appropriately sized graph, no matter how big the window is.

What data do we need?

To accomplish this goal, we will make the location and size of the graph dependent on the size of its panel. The `paintComponent()` method begins by getting the `JPanel`'s current size and stores it in a local `Dimension` variable:

```
/**
 * paintComponent() is invoked automatically to repaint the JPanel
 *  whenever necessary.  It clears the panel, then redraws the x and
 *  y axes and then draws two sample graphs, a line and a curve.
 */
public void paintComponent(Graphics g) {
    Dimension size = this.getSize();
    g.setColor(getBackground());                    // Clear the drawing area
    g.setClip(0, 0, size.width, size.height);
    g.fillRect(0, 0, size.width, size.height);
    g.setClip(20, 20, size.width - 40, size.height - 40);  // Reset the clip region
    g.translate(size.width / 2, size.height / 2);   // Place origin at middle
    g.setColor(Color.black);
    drawXYAxes(g);                                  // Draw the X and Y axes
    graphLine(g, 0.5, 25.2);                        // Graph y = 0.5x + 25.2
    graphQuadratic(g, -0.125, 0, 0 );               // Graph 4y = -x2
} // paintComponent()
```

Centering the origin

The `size` is used to calculate the clip region, and to calculate the location of the panel's center, which is used by `translate()` method to relocate the origin:

```
g.translate(size.width / 2, size.height / 2);         // Place origin at middle
```

Clearing the panel

Thus, no matter what size the window is, the graph's origin will be located at the center. Note that it is necessary to clear the panel each time `paint-Component()` is called. Otherwise, the old version of the graph would remain visible in the resized panel. This is another possible source of confusion between drawing on AWT and Swing components. When an AWT method is updated, because it's been resized or moved, its background is cleared. When a Swing `JComponents` is updated, its background is not cleared. This is an appropriate design, because `JComponents` can be transparent.

DEBUGGING TIP: Clearing a Component. AWT components have their backgrounds cleared whenever they are updated, but Swing `JComponents` are not automatically cleared.

In order to improve the appearance of the graph, the panel's clip region is set to an area 20 pixels inside of its borders:

```
g.setClip(20, 20, size.width - 40, size.height - 40); // Reset the clip region
```

This will prevent the drawing commands from drawing right up to the panel's edges. In this case, it is important that the clip region be set *before* moving the origin, because it's much easier to specify the clip region when the top-left corner (the default origin) is used as a reference point.

Clipping the drawing

Given now that the origin is at the center of the frame, it is very easy to define a method to draw the graph's axes:

```
/** drawXYAxes() --- draws tic-marked X and Y axes for the graph,
 *  using the JPanel's size to determine the bounds of the graph.
 */
private void drawXYAxes(Graphics g) {
    Dimension size = this.getSize();          // Get the panel's size
    int hBound = size.width / 2;              // Use it to set the bounds
    int vBound = size.height / 2;
    int tic = size.width / 100;

    g.drawLine(-hBound,0,hBound,0);            // Draw X-axis
    for (int k = -hBound; k <= hBound; k+=10)
        g.drawLine(k, tic, k, -tic);
    g.drawLine(0, vBound, 0, -vBound);         // Draw Y-axis
    for (int k = -vBound; k <= vBound; k+=10)
        g.drawLine(-tic, k, +tic, k);
} // drawXYAxes()
```

Note again how the `JPanel`'s size is used to calculate the horizontal and vertical bounds of the axes and the size of their tic marks. The axes themselves are just lines [`g.drawLine(-hBound,0,hBound,0)`], but a for loop is used to draw their tic marks (Figure 10–10). The tic marks are placed every 10 pixels (no matter what size the window is). However, note that the `tic` variable is defined as `size.width/100`, so that it will always be proportional to the size of the graph itself. You should experiment to test how well it scales when you resize its window.

Drawing the axes

Finally, given the ability to place the origin at the center of the frame, it is quite simple to design methods to graph equations. Two examples are shown in Figure 10–11.

```
/** graphLine() graphs a linear equation represented in slope-
 *  intercept form: y = mx + b, where m represents the slop and
 *  b represents the y intercept.
 */
private void graphLine(Graphics g, double m, double b) {
    Dimension size = this.getSize();          // Get the panel's size
    int hBound = size.width / 2;              // Use it to set the bounds
    g.setColor( Color.red );
    for (int x = -hBound; x <= hBound; x++) { // For each pixel on x axis
        int y = (int)(m * x + b );
        y = -y;                               // Reverse y coordinate (Cartesian)
        g.drawLine(x, y, x+1, y+1);           // Draw a point
    }
} // graphLine()
```

The graphLine() method graphs a linear equation, given its **slope-intercept** representation. In slope-intercept form, the equation of a line is given by:

$$y = mx + b$$

Graphing a line

where m represents the line's slope and b represents its y intercept. The graphLine() method takes m and b as parameters and then uses the above equation to determine the line's coordinates. A for loop is used to calculate the y-coordinate for each x on the graph. Note the statement used to reverse y's sign to translate the graph for the Cartesian plane. Note again the use of the panel's size to determine the bounds of the graph.

Similarly, the following method graphs a quadratic equation using the same basic approach:

```
/** graphQuadratic() graphs a quadratic equation represented in the
 *  form: y = ax2 + bx + c.
 */
private void graphQuadratic( Graphics g, double a, double b, double c ) {
    Dimension size = this.getSize();           // Get the panel's size
    int hBound = size.width/2;                 // Use it to set the bounds
    g.setColor(Color.red);
    for (int x = -hBound; x <= hBound; x++) { // For each pixel on x axis
        int y = (int)(a * x * x + b * x + c);
        y = -y;                                // Reverse y coordinate (cartesian)
        g.fillOval(x-1, y-1, 3, 3);           // Draw a point
    }
} // graphQuadratic()
```

A quadratic equation takes the following form:

$$y = ax^2 + bx + c$$

Graphing a parabola

The method takes the coefficient's a, b, and c as parameters. It uses a for loop to calculate the curve's coordinates. As you can see from Figure 10–10, the equation used in the sample program yields a parabola.

EFFECTIVE DESIGN: Relative Locations. Graphing equations is simplified by making the graph's origin be the origin of the graphics context. Then all points can be plotted relative to the origin.

SELF-STUDY EXERCISES

EXERCISE 10.19 What would be the consequences of forgetting to set the Graph object's size in its constructor method?

10.8 Drawing Bar Charts and Pie Charts

The origin of the Graphics context can be relocated repeatedly. This is particularly handy if you want to draw more than one graph on the frame. To illustrate this, let's design a bar chart and a pie chart and place them on the same drawing panel.

Suppose you want to display your company's sales data for the most recent quarter. There are five sellers and your boss wants a bar chart comparing each seller's sales for the past two quarters. She also wants a pie chart of this quarter's sales, broken up by each seller's percentage of total sales. And, she wants it all in dazzling shades of gray!

Suppose that the data for this program are stored in arrays:

```
private double quarter1[] = {1099.85, 2105.86, 3105.25, 987.20, 5000.45};
private double quarter2[] = {2199.85, 3105.86, 2805.25, 1500.20, 6250.95};
```

The bar chart should compare `quarter1` and `quarter2` sales for each seller, and the pie chart should compare each seller's `quarter2` sales.

10.8.1 Scaling the Bar Chart

A bar chart, or **histogram**, consists of plain old rectangles of a fixed width, but of varying heights. The rectangle's height illustrates the *relative* size of the quantity being graphed. In this case, the height of a bar will represent the seller's total sales for the quarter. You can't use the actual quantity because it might be greater than the size of the window. For example, the sales quantities might be numbers like 5000, but we don't have 5000 pixels on the screen. Therefore, the height of each bar must be *scaled* to guarantee that it fits within the screen.

Scaling a shape

One way to scale the bars would be to base their size on a predetermined maximum sales amount. For example, suppose we know that the maximum sales for a quarter will be no more than $10,000. We can then decide to represent this quantity by a certain size bar. For example, let's say a bar that is 75 percent of the frame's height will represent $10,000. If the frame is 400 pixels in height, then the maximum sales amount will be presented by a rectangle of 300 pixels. Amounts smaller than the maximum will be represented proportionally (Figure 10–12). This analysis suggests that we want to declare the following constants:

```
public static final int WIDTH = 400, HEIGHT = 300; // Initial Width and Height
private final int NSELLERS = 5;
private final int MAXSALES = 6000;  // Max quarter sales amount
private final double SCALE = 0.75;  // % of height used for max sales amount
```

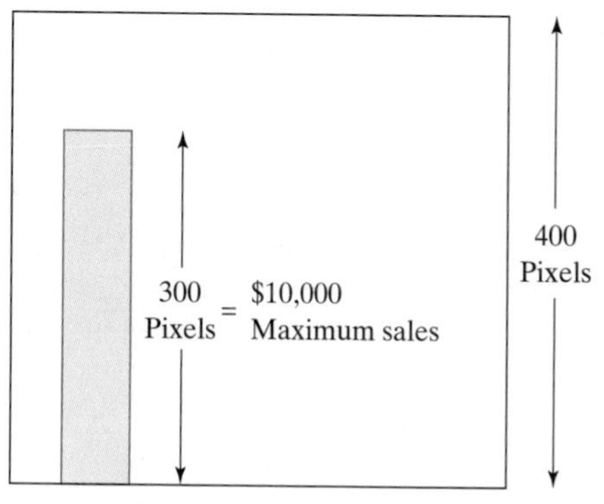

Figure 10–12 Scaling a bar in a histogram.

The WIDTH and HEIGHT are used to set the panel's initial size (Figure 10–13). The other constants are used to control the size of the bar chart.

Figure 10–13 ChartDemo illustrates how to draw bar charts and pie charts.

```
import java.awt.*;
import javax.swing.*;
public class ChartDemo extends JPanel {

    public static final int WIDTH = 400, HEIGHT = 300; // Initial Width and Height
    private final int NSELLERS = 5;
    private final int MAXSALES = 6000;             // Max quarter sales amount
    private final double SCALE = 0.75;             // % of height used for maximum sales

    private double quarter1[] = {1099.85, 2105.86, 3105.25, 987.20, 5000.45};
    private double quarter2[] = {2199.85, 3105.86, 2805.25, 1500.20, 6250.95};

    public ChartDemo() {
        setSize(WIDTH, HEIGHT);
    }

    public void paintComponent( Graphics g ) {
        Dimension size = this.getSize();
        g.setColor(getBackground());
        g.fillRect(0, 0, size.width, size.height);                    // Clear the panel
        g.translate(size.height / 20, size.height - size.height / 20); // Move origin to bottom left of frame
        drawBarChart(g);
        int pieSize = Math.min(size.width, size.height) / 3;
        int barWidth = size.width / 40;
        g.translate(NSELLERS * 4 * barWidth, -pieSize);             // Move origin to the right and up
        drawPieChart(g, pieSize);
    } // paintComponent()

    public void drawBarChart(Graphics g) {
        Dimension size = this.getSize();
        int maxBar = (int)(SCALE * size.height);               // Size of tallest bar in histogram
        int barWidth = size.width / 40;                        // Width of bars
        int hGap = size.width / 60;                            // Gap between bars
        g.drawLine(0, 0, NSELLERS * (2 * barWidth + hGap), 0); // Draw the x-axis

        int href = 0;
        for (int k = 0; k < NSELLERS; k++ ) {                  // For each seller
            int hgt = (int)(maxBar * quarter1[k] / MAXSALES);  // Height of quarter1 sales
            g.setColor(Color.black);
            g.drawString( k+1 + "", href + 5, 13);             // Label the chart
            g.fillRect(href, -hgt, barWidth, hgt);
            hgt = (int)(maxBar * quarter2[k] / MAXSALES);     // Height of quarter2 sales
            href += barWidth;                                 // Move reference point
            g.setColor(Color.darkGray);                       // Use 2nd color
            g.fillRect(href, -hgt, barWidth, hgt);
            href += barWidth  + hGap;                         // Move reference pt
        } // for
    } // drawBarChart()

    private double total(double sales[]) {
        double sum = 0;
        for (int k = 0; k < NSELLERS; k++)
            sum += sales[k];
        return sum;
    } // total()
```

Figure 10–13 *Continued*

```
    public void drawPieChart(Graphics g, int pieSize) {
        double sumq2 = (int)total(quarter2);              // Compute total sales for qtr
        int rgb = 0;
        Color color = null;
        int startAngle = 0;
        for (int k = 0; k < NSELLERS; k++) {                          // For each seller
            color = new Color(rgb, rgb, rgb);                         // For grays r = g = b
            g.setColor(color);
            rgb += 32;                                                // Lighten the color
            double percent = quarter2[k] / sumq2;                     // Percentage sales
            int currAngle = (int)Math.round(360 * percent);           // Scale to 360 degrees
            g.fillArc(0, 0, pieSize, pieSize, startAngle, currAngle); // Draw pie slice
            startAngle += currAngle;                                  // Advance start angle
        } //for
    } // drawPieChart()

    public static void main(String args[]) {
        JFrame f = new JFrame("Chart Window");
        ChartDemo chart = new ChartDemo();
        f.getContentPane().add(chart);
        f.setSize( chart.WIDTH, chart.HEIGHT );
        f.setVisible(true);
        f.addWindowListener(new WindowAdapter() {        // Quit the application
            public void windowClosing(WindowEvent e) {
                System.exit(0);
            }
        });
    } //main()
} // ChartDemo
```

Given these quantities, each rectangle in the bar chart can be drawn relative to the size of the panel:

```
int maxBar = (int)(SCALE * size.height);               // Size of biggest bar in histogram
int barWidth = size.width / 40;                        // Width of bar
int hgt = (int)(maxBar * quarter1[k] / MAXSALES);     // Height of quarter1 sales
g.fillRect(href, -hgt, barWidth, hgt);                 // Draw the bar
```

This example calculates the rectangle's height for the quarter 1 sales of the *k*th seller. The height of the rectangle is proportional to the seller's quarterly sales as they compare to MAXSALES.

The drawBarChart() method, from the ChartDemo program (Figure 10–13), draws the entire bar chart. There are several points worth noting about this method. First, the method assumes that the bar chart's origin is at its lower-left corner. The method begins by recalculating the chart's dimensions — the maxBar, barWidth, and hGap. It then draws a single horizontal line to represent the chart's *x*-axis.

Algorithm design

The drawing of the bar chart itself is handled by a for loop, which iterates through NSELLERS. For each seller, it displays a black rectangle for the quarter1 sales, and a darkGray rectangle for the quarter2 sales. Note how the color is changed within the loop, and note also how the horizontal reference point for the rectangle's location, href, is recalculated after each rectangle is drawn. Here is where we use the constant and variable quantities that we described above. Finally, note the statement used to paint the rectangle itself:

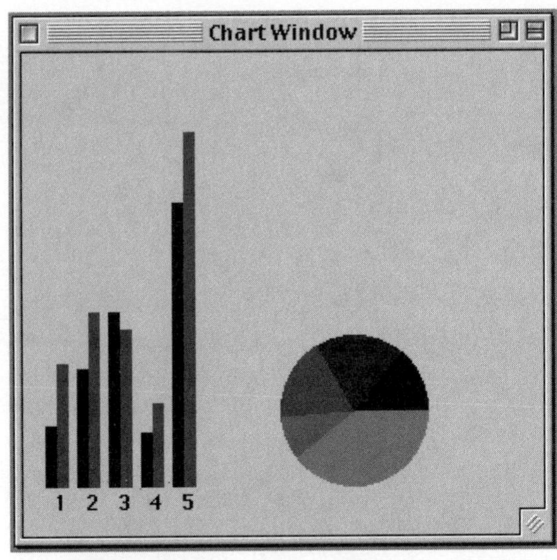

Figure 10–14 Output from the ChartDemo program. Resizing the frame will resize the charts themselves.

```
g.fillRect(href, -hgt, barWidth, hgt);
```

Given the relocated origin, the value `(href,-hgt)` gives the coordinates for the rectangle's top-left corner, and `barWidth` and `hgt` represent the rectangle's width and height, respectively. Figure 10–14 shows how the bar chart would appear when you run the `ChartDemo` program.

EFFECTIVE DESIGN: Scalability. Variables representing its location and dimensions should be used to generalize a figure's design. In addition to making the figure itself *scalable*, this strategy helps to simplify both its development and its maintainability.

10.8.2 Drawing Arcs

To draw a pie chart we will use the `fillArc()` method, which takes the following parameters:

```
fillArc(int x, int y, int width, int hgt, int startAngle, int arcAngle );
```

Like many other shapes, arcs are drawn within a bounding rectangle, whose top-left corner is specified by *x* and *y*, and whose width and height are specified by *width* and *hgt*. The arc itself is drawn starting at the `startAngle` and turning through `arcAngle` degrees.

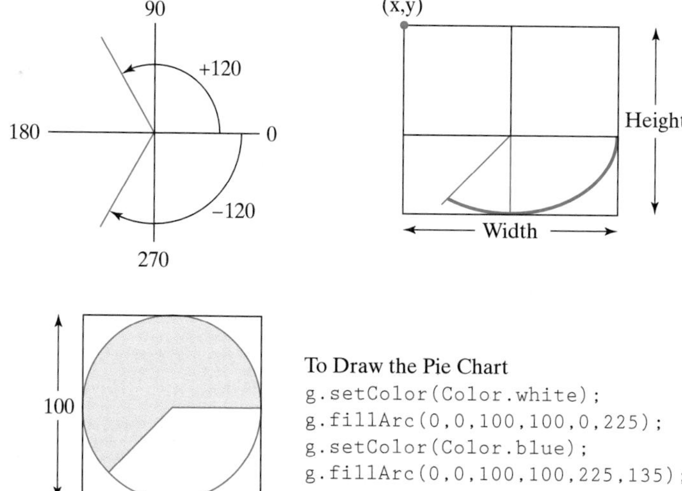

Figure 10–15 To draw or fill an arc, you must specify its bounding rectangle plus the starting angle of the arc and its size in degrees.

The angles used by arcs are measured in degrees and use the coordinate system shown in Figure 10–15. Positive arcs sweep in a counterclockwise direction. Negative arcs sweep in a clockwise direction. The sample pie chart shown in Figure 10–15 was drawn with the following statements:

```
g.setColor(Color.black );
g.fillArc(0, 0, 100, 100, 0, 225);
g.setColor(Color.darkGray);
g.fillArc(0, 0, 100, 100, 225, 135);
```

Starting and reference angle

The first pie segment has a starting angle of 0 and an arc of 225 degrees. The second segments starts where the first one left off (225 degrees) and has an arc of 135 degrees. These two segments take the entire 360 degrees of the pie (225 + 135 = 360).

Note that because the entire pie chart is contained within a bounding rectangle, the first four parameters are the same for every segment in the chart. The segments of the pie chart depend only on the values of the `startAngle` and `arcAngle` parameter. By adjusting these two parameters, we can draw all the segments of the pie chart, going in a counterclockwise direction.

PROGRAMMING TIP: Drawing Arcs. When using `fillArc(x,y,w, h,startAngle,arcAngle)` to draw pie chart segments, the `startAngle` for each new pie segment is calculated as the sum of the previous `startAngle` plus the previous `arcAngle`. By using variables to represent these two angles, you can use a loop to draw any pie chart.

Drawing a Pie Chart

Algorithm design

Given this background, let's design our pie chart. Again, we want to design it so that its size is proportional to the frame's size. Since a pie chart is round, we'll want an enclosing rectangle that is square — one that has the same width and height. Let's use the frame's smaller dimension to calculate the size of the pie chart:

```
int pieSize = Math.min(width, height) / 3;
```

According to this formula, the pie chart will always be approximately one-third the size of the smaller of the panel's two dimensions. Now let's position the pie chart on the frame by once again moving the origin. This time we want to move it to the right of the bar chart. Of course, the distance we move it depends on the size of the bar chart, which can be calculated as `NSELLERS * 4 * barWidth`:

```
g.translate(NSELLERS * 4 * barWidth,-pieSize); // Move origin to the right and up
```

The reason we have to move the origin up by `-pieSize` is because the arcs we draw will be contained within a rectangle specified by its top-left corner.

Pie chart algorithm

We want to draw a pie chart showing each seller's proportion of the total `quarter2` sales. If one seller sold one-third of total sales, his or her section should represent one-third of the pie chart, or 120 degrees. In order to represent a seller's percentage of total sales, we must calculate total sales for the entire quarter. This is done by the `total()` method. So to calculate each segment of the pie, we have to calculate the seller's percentage of total sales and then scale that value to 360 degrees. This will represent the size of the angle of that pie segment:

```
double sumq2 = (int)total(quarter2);                         // Compute total sales for qtr
double percent = quarter2[k] / sumq2;                        // Percentage sales
int currAngle = (int)Math.round(360 * percent);              // Scale to 360 degrees
g.fillArc(0, 0, pieSize, pieSize, startAngle, currAngle); // Draw pie slice
```

Note that this algorithm uses the `quarter2` sales for the *k*th seller. Thus we can use a for loop to draw one pie segment for each seller. On each iteration of the for loop two things must change: the starting angle and the color of the pie segment. Assuming that the starting angle starts at 0, we can update it as follows on each iteration of the loop:

```
startAngle += currAngle;           // Advance the start angle
```

That is, on each iteration the starting angle simply advances in the counterclockwise direction.

To modify the drawing color for each pie segment, we can make use of the fact that all shades of gray have equal values for their red, green, and blue components, so, one way to manage the pie chart's colors is to start with black and then increase the RGB values by a constant amount on each iteration of the loop. Thus assuming that `rgb` is initialized to 0, we use the following statements within the loop:

Color iterations

```
color = new Color(rgb, rgb, rgb); // For grays r = g = b
g.setColor(color);                // Set the drawing color
rgb += 32;                        // Lighten the color for next time
```

Because R = G = B, we can use one variable for all three color components, and we can simply increase its value on each iteration of the loop. The remaining details of the `drawPieChart()` method, are shown in the listing of `ChartDemo` in Figure 10–13.

PROGRAMMING TIP: Extensibility. By using constants and variables to serve as reference points, simple algorithms can be developed to create a more general and more extensible program.

SELF-STUDY EXERCISES

EXERCISE 10.20 What do you suppose would happen if you reversed the order of the `setSize()` and `setVisible()` statements in the `main()` method in `ChartDemo`?

EXERCISE 10.21 What purpose does the empty string serve in this expression: `g.drawString(k+1 + "", href+5, 13)`?

10.9 Handling Text in a Graphics Context

In order to create attractive interfaces, it is often necessary to be able to select and control the font that is used. Even a simple drawing task, such as being able to center a component's label, requires that we know the font's dimensions and be able to manipulate them. In this section we learn how to work with Java's fonts and font control methods.

Each graphics context has an associated `Font` and `FontMetrics` object, and the `Graphics` class provides the following methods to access them:

```
public abstract Font getFont();
public FontMetrics getFontMetrics();
public abstract FontMetrics getFontMetrics();
public abstract void setFont(Font c);
```

A FontMetrics is an object that encapsulates important data about a font, such as its height and width. Java assigns a default font to each Graphics object. This is the font used by the drawString() method. The particular font used is system dependent but to override the default one can simply invoke the setFont() method:

```
g.setFont(new Font("TimesRoman", Font.ITALIC, 12));
```

In this case the Font() constructor is used to specify a 12-point, italicized, *TimesRoman* font. Once the font is set, it will be used in all subsequent drawings.

10.9.1 The Font and FontMetrics Classes

The Font class provides a platform-independent representation of an individual font. A font is distinguished by its name, size, and style, and the Font class includes protected instance variables for these properties, as well as a constructor method which allows these three characteristics to be specified:

```
public class Font extends Object implements Serializable  {
    // Class constants
     public static final int BOLD;
     public static final int ITALIC;
     public static final int PLAIN;

    // Instance variables
     protected String name;
     protected int size;
     protected int style;

// Constructor
     public Font(String name, int style, int size);
}
```

In Java 1.1 and later versions, the supported font names include "Serif," "SansSerif," "Monospaced," "Dialog," and "DialogInput." And the supported styles include PLAIN, BOLD, ITALIC, and BOLD+ITALIC. These names and styles are platform independent. When used in a program, they are mapped to real fonts available in the host system. If the host system does not have an exact match for the specified font, it will supply a substitute. For example, if you specify a 48-point, italic, Monospaced font,

```
Font myFont = new Font("Monospaced", Font.ITALIC, 48);
```

the system may map this to a 24-point, italic Courier font, if that's the largest fixed-spaced font available.

Figure 10–16 The FontNames applet.

```
import java.awt.*;
import javax.swing.*;

public class FontNames extends JApplet {

    public void paint(Graphics g) {

        // Get the font names available in this graphics environment
        GraphicsEnvironment ge = GraphicsEnvironment.getLocalGraphicsEnvironment();
        String[] fonts = ge.getAvailableFontFamilyNames();

        // Display hello world and font's name in the first 10 fonts
        int vRef = 30;
        int vGap = 15;
        g.drawString("The first 10 fonts on this system are: ", 30, vRef);
        for (int k = 0; k < 10; k++) {
            vRef += vGap;
            g.setFont(new Font(fonts[k], Font.PLAIN, 12));
            g.drawString("Hello World! (" + fonts[k] + ")", 30, vRef);
        }
    } // paint()
} // FontNames
```

10.9.2 Example: The FontNames Applet

The FontNames applet (Figure 10–16) demonstrates the use of Font class methods. The applet consists of a paint() method, which uses java.awt.GraphicsEnvironment's getAvailableFontFamilyNames() method to retrieve an array of the names of the fonts available on this system. It then draws "Hello World" plus the font's name for the first ten fonts (Figure 10–17). Each font is displayed in PLAIN style and 12-point size. Note that this list begins with the standard Java fonts. However, the list doesn't specify what sizes and styles are available in each of these fonts. Even if a host system has the SansSerif font, it may not have the particular size requested. In that case, the system will supply a substitute.

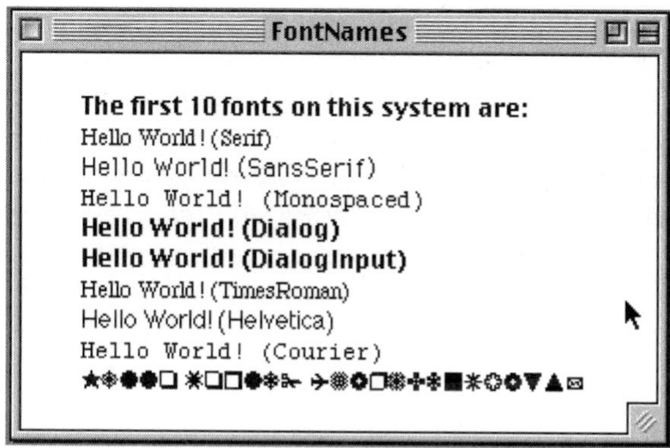

Figure 10–17 The names and appearance of the first ten fonts on my Macintosh. The first line is the system font. Note that some fonts with different names appear to be the same.

The `Font()` constructor used in this example is designed to work with any set of arguments. Thus if you supply the name of a font that is not available, the system will supply a default font as a substitute. For example, on my system, specifying a nonexistent font named "Random,"

```
g.setFont(new Font("Random", Font.ITALIC, 12) );
g.drawString("Hello World! (random, italic, 12)", 30, 45);
```

produces the same font used as the mapping for "Dialog" and "DialogInput."

EFFECTIVE DESIGN: Font Portability. The fact that `Font()` will produce a font for virtually any set of arguments is important in ensuring that a Java program will run on any platform. This is another example of how Java has been designed for portability.

The `FontNames` example uses the `setFont()` method to set the font associated with the graphics context. All AWT and JFC components have an associated font, which can be accessed using the `Component.setFont()` and `Component.getFont()` methods. For example, the following code could be used to override a `Button`'s font:

```
Button b = new Button("Label");
b.setFont(new Font("Times", Font.ITALIC, 14));
```

If 14-point, italic, Times font is not available on the host system, a substitute will be supplied.

SELF-STUDY EXERCISES

EXERCISE 10.22 In the `FontNames` applet, why is the `paint()` method used instead of the `paintComponent()` method?

10.9.3 Font Metrics

Problem statement

To illustrate how to use the `FontMetrics` class, let's write a "Hello World" applet that centers its message both horizontally and vertically in the applet window. The message should be centered regardless of the size of the applet window. Thus, we will have to position the text relative to the window size, which is something we learned in positioning geometric shapes. The message should also be centered no matter what font is used. This will require us to know certain characteristics of the font itself, such as the height and width of its characters, whether the characters have a fixed or variable width, and so on. In order to get access to these properties, we will use the `FontMetrics` class.

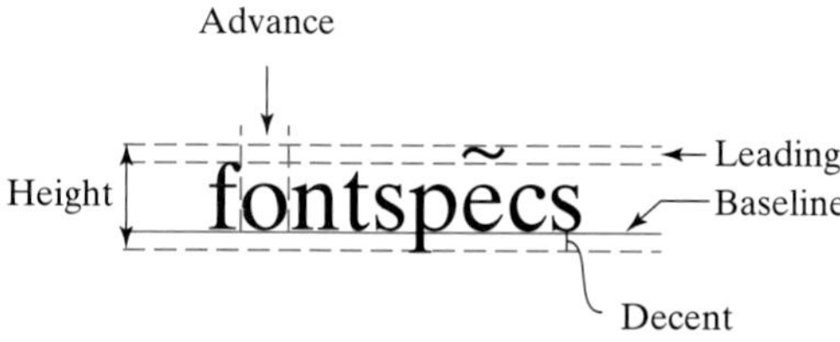

Figure 10–18 An illustration of the various font measurements.

Figure 10–18 illustrates the various properties that are associated with a font. The **baseline** of a font refers to the line on which the bottom of most characters occurs. When drawing a string, the *x*- and *y*-coordinates determine the baseline of the string's first character. Thus, in

```
g.drawString("Hello World", 10, 40);
```

the bottom left of the *H* in "Hello World" would be located at (10, 40).

All characters ascend some distance above the baseline. This is known as the character's **ascent**. Some characters, such as *y*, may extend below the baseline, into what's known as the *descent*. Each font has a *maximum descent*. Similarly, some characters, such as accent characters, may extend above the *maximum ascent* into a space known as the *leading*.

The *height* of a font is defined as the sum (in pixels) of the ascent, descent and leading values. The height is a property of the font itself, rather than of any individual character. Except for fixed-width fonts, in which the width of all characters are the same, the characters that make up a font have varying widths. The width of an individual character is known as its *advance*.

The `FontMetrics` class provides methods for accessing a font's properties. These can be useful to control the layout of text on a GUI:

```
public class FontMetrics extends Object implements Serializable {
    protected FontMetrics(Font font);
    protected Font font;
    public int charWidth(int ch);
    public int charWidth(char ch);
    public int charsWidth(char[] chars, int off, int len);
    public int getAscent();
    public int getDescent();
    public Font getFont();
    public int getHeight();
    public int getLeading();
    public int getMaxAdvance();
    public int getMaxDescent();
    public int stringWidth();
}
```

For example, when drawing multiple lines of text, the `getHeight()` method is useful for determining how much space should be left between lines. When drawing character by character, the `charWidth()` method can be used to determine how much space must be left between characters. Alternatively, the `stringWidth()` method can be used to determine the number of pixels required to draw the entire string.

10.9.4 Example: Centering a Line of Text

Algorithm design: Generality

Given this background, let's take on the task of centering a message in an applet window. In order for this applet to work for any font, we must take care not to base its design on characteristics of the particular font that we happen to be using. To underscore this point, let's design it to work for a font named "Random" which, as we noted earlier, will be mapped to some font by the system on which the applet is run. In other words we will let the system pick a font for this applet's message. An interesting experiment would be to run the applet on different platforms to see what fonts are chosen.

The only method we need for this applet is the `paint()` method. Let's begin by setting the font used by the graphics context to a random font. To get the characteristics of this font, we create a `FontMetrics` object and get the font metrics for the font we just created:

```
g.setFont(new Font("Random", Font.BOLD, 24));
FontMetrics metrics = g.getFontMetrics();
```

The next step is to determine the applet's dimensions using the `getSize()` method, and then to use its width and height to calculate the x- and y-coordinates for the string.

Centering text

In order to center the string horizontally, we need to know its width, which is supplied by the `metrics` object. If the applet is `d.width` pixels wide, then the following expression subtracts the width of the string from the width of the applet and then divides the left over space in half:

```
int x = (d.width - metrics.stringWidth(str)) / 2; // Calculate coordinates
```

Similarly, the following expression subtracts the height of the string from the height of the applet and divides the left over space in half:

```
int y = (d.height + metrics.getHeight()) / 2;
```

Taken together, these calculations give the coordinates for the lower left pixel of the first character in "Hello World!" The only remaining task is to draw the string (Figure 10–19).

Figure 10–19 The `CenterText` applet.

```
import java.awt.*;
import javax.swing.*;

public class CenterText extends JApplet {
                              // Print hello world! in center of applet
public void paint(Graphics g) {
    String str = "Hello World!";
    g.setFont(new Font("Random", Font.PLAIN, 24));     // Create a random font
    FontMetrics metrics = g.getFontMetrics();           //  And get its metrics

    Dimension d = getSize();                            // Get the applet's size
    int x = (d.width - metrics.stringWidth(str)) / 2;  // Calculate coordinates
    int y = (d.height + metrics.getHeight()) / 2;

    g.drawString( str, x, y );                          // Draw the string
} // paint()
} // CenterText
```

Since the `paint()` method is called automatically whenever the applet is resized, this applet, whose output is shown in Figure 10–20, will recenter its message whenever it is resized by the user.

PROGRAMMING TIP: Generality. By using a component's size and font as the determining factors, you can center text on virtually any component. These values are available via the component's `getFont()` and `getSize()` methods.

SELF-STUDY EXERCISES

EXERCISE 10.23 Modify the `FontNames` applet so that for each of the first ten fonts, a random font size is chosen between 10 and 24 point. Use the `FontMetrics.height` value to provide the appropriate spacing for each line of output. Also, modify the algorithm so that each line of output is horizontally centered.

Figure 10–20 The `CenterText` applet keeps its message centered no matter how the applet window is resized.

10.10 CASE STUDY: Interactive Drawing

In all of our drawing examples so far, the drawing has been done by the program. What if we want to enable the user to draw? In order to support drawing by the user, or interactive drawing, we need to learn how to control the mouse. As you would expect, mouse control is exerted by handling the various kinds of mouse related events that can occur.

10.10.1 Handling Mouse Events

There are two types of mouse events: **mouse events** and **mouse motion events**. Each type is handled by its own listener interface. The `MouseMotionListener` handles mouse events that involve motion:

```
public abstract interface MouseMotionListener extends EventListener {
    public abstract void mouseDragged(MouseEvent e);
    public abstract void mouseMoved(MouseEvent e);
}
```

The mouse is said to be "dragged" if it is moved while one of its buttons is held down. It is "moved" when it is moved without holding any buttons down. The `MouseListener` interface handles mouse events:

```
public abstract interface MouseListener extends EventListener {
    public abstract void mouseClicked(MouseEvent e);
    public abstract void mouseEntered(MouseEvent e);
    public abstract void mouseExited(MouseEvent e);
    public abstract void mousePressed(MouseEvent e);
    public abstract void mouseReleased(MouseEvent e);
}
```

As the names of the methods suggest, mouse events occur when the mouse is clicked and when the mouse enters or exits a GUI component. The `mousePressed()` and `mouseReleased()` methods are called when the user has pressed and released one of the mouse buttons. The `mouse Clicked()` method is called when the user has pressed and released a mouse button without any intervening mouse drag — that is, the pressing and releasing of the button occurred while the mouse was at the same location.

Obviously, a mouse clicked and mouse released event can be generated by the same user action. We will see examples that help us decide which event is significant within a given context.

10.10.2 An Interactive Painting Program

Problem statement

To illustrate how both interfaces are used, let's develop a simple interactive painting application. You've probably used this type of program. It lets the user draw letters or pictures by dragging the mouse within a drawing area. Our simple version will let the user (1) draw within a drawing region by dragging the mouse, and (2) clear the drawing area by clicking within a certain area of the screen.

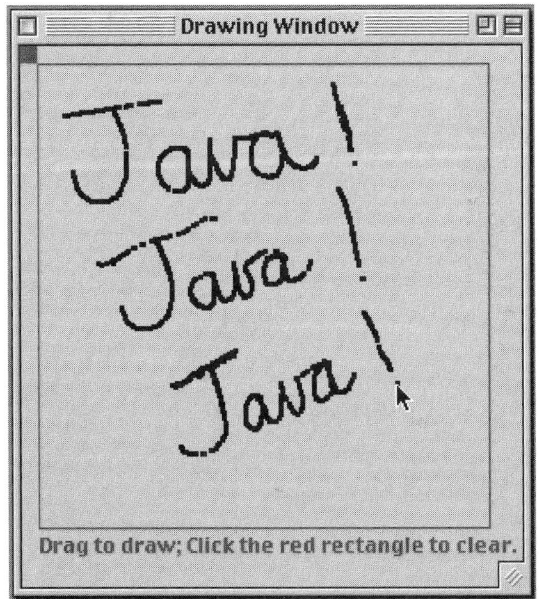

Figure 10–21 GUI design for the drawing program. Clicking on the small colored rectangle in the top left corner will clear the drawing.

10.10.3 GUI Design

In order to define the drawing area, we can draw a large red square on the screen. When the user drags the mouse within this area, the program will paint a dot at the mouse's current location. In order to make the drawing area stand out from the rest of the screen, let's indent it by 10 or 20 pixels from the edge of the applet's screen.

Mouse-based user control

One way to indicate the "clear screen" action is to have the user click within a rectangular area that's located in the frame's top-left corner. To help define this area, let's fill this rectangle with red. Finally, to help orient the user, let's draw a string at the very bottom of the screen, outside the drawing area, which gives some simple directions. Figure 10–21 shows the details of this GUI design.

10.10.4 Problem Decomposition: The `MousePaint` Class

What classes do we need?

This program is simple enough to implement with a single class, the `MousePaint` class. As in our other application, this class should be a subclass of `JPanel`. An instance of this class will be added to the application's top-level `JFrame`. Because it will handle mouse events, this class must implement both the `MouseListener` and `MouseMotionListener` interfaces. In fact, designing these interface methods will be one of the main challenges in developing this program.

What data do we need?

The main thing we'll have to keep track of in this program is the location of the mouse. That's how we'll decide what the user wants to do. If the user clicks on the mouse while it is at the top left of the rectangle, the applet should clear the drawing area. If the user drags the mouse within the drawing area, the applet should draw. We'll need a `Point` object to keep track of the mouse's coordinates.

There are a couple of things that won't change during this program. One constant is the color of the rectangles that define the drawing area and the clear area. A second constant is the color used for drawing. These should be defined as `final` variables and placed at the beginning of the program, so that they can easily be changed if you decide to change the color scheme. Another thing that won't change is the location of the clear rectangle. Therefore, let's use constants to define its location. Even if the user changes the applet's size, the location of this rectangle will remain fixed.

The problem decomposition considerations we just made lead to the following initial definition of `MousePaint`:

```
import javax.swing.*;
import java.awt.*;
import java.awt.event.*;

public class MousePaint extends JPanel implements MouseListener,
                                           MouseMotionListener {

    private static final int WIDTH = 300, HEIGHT = 300; // Initial size
    private static final int LEFT = 10;                 // Reference points
    private static final int TOP = 10;
    private static final int BORDER = 30;

    private static final Color backColor = Color.gray;  // Background color
    private static final Color lineColor = Color.red;   // Outline color

    private Point mouse = new Point();                  // Mouse's current location

    public void paintComponent (Graphics g) { }

    public static void main(String args[]) {
        JFrame f = new JFrame("Drawing Window");  // Create the top-level window
        MousePaint mp = new MousePaint();         // And give it a drawing panel
        f.getContentPane().add(mp);
        f.setSize(mp.WIDTH, mp.HEIGHT);
        f.setVisible(true);
    }
} // MousePaint
```

10.10.5 Algorithm: Handling Mouse Events

Because this applet implements both the `MouseListener` and `MouseMotionListener` interfaces, it must implement a total of seven methods. However, most of the methods won't really be used, so their bodies can be left empty. Which methods are these?

What methods do we need?

First, with respect to the mouse's motion, we only care about when the user drags the mouse, so we only need to implement the `mouseDragged()` method from the `MouseMotionListener` interface. Second, with respect to the other mouse actions, we only care about when the user clicks within the "clear" rectangle. To handle this event, we only need to implement the `mouseClicked()` method from the `MouseListener` interface. That means we can leave the bodies empty for the following five methods:

```
public void mouseEntered(MouseEvent e) { } // These five interface methods are not used
public void mouseExited(MouseEvent e)  { } //  but must be defined anyway
public void mousePressed(MouseEvent e) { }
public void mouseReleased(MouseEvent e){ }
public void mouseMoved(MouseEvent e)   { }
```

Method design?

Let's now design the `mouseClicked()` and `mouseDragged()` methods. What should these methods do? Actually, their tasks are quite simple. All they need to do is keep track of the mouse's location and repaint the screen every time one of these events occurs. The `paint()` method can handle the decision as to where the mouse was clicked and dragged. If it was clicked within the "clear" rectangle, then the drawing area should be cleared. If it was dragged within the drawing area, the drawing should be shown.

The mouse's coordinates are stored as part of the `MouseEvent` whenever an event occurs. The `getPoint()` method can be used to retrieve them:

```
public void mouseDragged(MouseEvent e) {   // When the mouse is dragged
    mouse = e.getPoint();                    //  get its coordinates
    repaint();
}

public void mouseClicked(MouseEvent e) {   // When mouse is clicked
    mouse = e.getPoint();                    //  get its coordinates
    repaint();
}
```

As you can see, the implementations for both of these methods are the same: Just record the mouse's location and repaint the applet.

10.10.6 Algorithm: The `paintComponent()` Method

The `paintComponent()` method creates the layout for the user interface and handles all of the drawing and clearing actions. First, `paintComponent()` gets the `JPanel`'s dimensions. It then uses these values to draw the interface, including the instructions to the user:

```
Dimension d = getSize();
g.setColor(lineColor);
g.fillRect(0, 0, LEFT, TOP);                                  // The clear rectangle
g.drawRect(LEFT, TOP, d.width - BORDER, d.height - BORDER); // The drawing area
g.drawString("Drag to draw; Click the red rectangle to clear.", LEFT, d.height - 5);
g.setColor(Color.black);                                      // Set drawing color
```

Note that the "clear" rectangle is located at the top left of the screen. Its location is not dependent on the panel's size. However, the drawing area rectangle, and the instructions at the very bottom of the screen, are based on the panel's dimensions. Note that a fixed `BORDER` is used around the drawing area.

Once the fixed part of the interface is drawn, the `paintComponent()` method can handle any drawing or clearing that needs to be done:

```
if ((mouse.x > LEFT) && (mouse.x < LEFT + d.width - BORDER)
                     && (mouse.y > TOP) && (mouse.y < TOP + d.height - BORDER))
    g.fillRect(mouse.x, mouse.y, 3, 3);

                     // If clicked at top left clear the drawing
if ((mouse.x < LEFT) && (mouse.y < TOP))
    g.clearRect(LEFT + 1, TOP + 1, d.width - BORDER - 1, d.height - BORDER - 1);
```

The mouse's location determines the program's action

Note the expressions used in these conditions. They depend on the panel's dimensions, as stored in `d.width` and `d.height`, as well as the mouse's current coordinates, as stored in `mouse.x` and `mouse.y`. The first if statement checks whether the mouse is in the drawing area. If so, it draws a small, 3×3 rectangle at the current location. This is the drawing action. It takes place when the user drags the mouse.

The second if statement checks whether the mouse is in the "clear" rectangle. If so, it clears a rectangular area that is 1 pixel smaller all around than the drawing area itself. The complete implementation of `MousePaint` is shown in Figure 10–22.

DEBUGGING TIP: Swing versus AWT If a `JApplet` or `JFrame` is used as a drawing canvas, it would be necessary to override Java' default definition of the `update()` method Because `JApplet` and `JFrame` are subclasses of AWT `Component` class, the `update()` method would be called automatically after each mouse event, and it would clear the window. The following implementation will do the trick: `public void update(){}`.

Figure 10–22 The `MousePaint` application.

```
import javax.swing.*;
import java.awt.*;
import java.awt.event.*;

public class MousePaint extends JPanel implements MouseListener,
                                                  MouseMotionListener {

    private static final int WIDTH = 300, HEIGHT = 300; // Initial size
    private static final int LEFT = 10;                 // Reference points
    private static final int TOP = 10;
    private static final int BORDER = 30;

    private static final Color backColor = Color.gray;  // Background color
    private static final Color lineColor = Color.red;   // Outline color

    private Point mouse = new Point();                  // Mouse's current location
    public MousePaint() {
        addMouseMotionListener(this);    // Add mouse and mouse motion listeners
        addMouseListener(this);
        setSize(WIDTH, HEIGHT);
    } // MousePaint()
```

Figure 10–22 *Continued*

```
    public void paintComponent(Graphics g) {
        Dimension d = getSize();
        g.setColor(lineColor);
        g.fillRect(0, 0, LEFT, TOP);                                 // The clear rectangle
        g.drawRect(LEFT, TOP, d.width - BORDER, d.height - BORDER); // The drawing area
        g.drawString("Drag to draw; Click the red rectangle to clear.", LEFT, d.height - 5);
        g.setColor(Color.black);                                     // Set drawing color

                // If the mouse is within the drawing area, draw a dot
        if ((mouse.x > LEFT) && (mouse.x < LEFT + d.width - BORDER)
                    && (mouse.y > TOP) && (mouse.y < TOP + d.height - BORDER))
            g.fillRect(mouse.x, mouse.y, 3, 3);

                // If the mouse is clicked at top left corner clear the drawing
        if ((mouse.x < LEFT) && (mouse.y < TOP))
            g.clearRect(LEFT + 1, TOP + 1, d.width - BORDER - 1, d.height - BORDER - 1);
    } // paintComponent()

  /* Mouse Handling Interfaces:   MouseMotionListener and MouseListener */

    public void mouseDragged(MouseEvent e) {   // When the mouse is dragged (mouse motion listener)
        mouse = e.getPoint();                  //  get its coordinates
        repaint();
    }

    public void mouseClicked(MouseEvent e) {   // When mouse is clicked (mouse listener)
        mouse = e.getPoint();                  //  get its coordinates
        repaint();
    }
    public void mouseEntered(MouseEvent e) { } // These five interface methods are not used
    public void mouseExited(MouseEvent e)  { } //  but must be defined.
    public void mousePressed(MouseEvent e) { }
    public void mouseReleased(MouseEvent e){ }
    public void mouseMoved(MouseEvent e)   { }

    public static void main(String args[]) {
        JFrame f = new JFrame("Drawing Window");  // Create the top-level window
        MousePaint mp = new MousePaint();         // And give it a drawing panel
        f.getContentPane().add(mp);
        f.setSize(mp.WIDTH, mp.HEIGHT);
        f.setVisible(true);
        f.addWindowListener(new WindowAdapter() {     // Quit the application
            public void windowClosing(WindowEvent e) {
                System.exit(0);
            }
        });
    } // main()
} // MousePaint
```

OBJECT-ORIENTED DESIGN: The Scalable CyberPet

The various drawing examples that we have looked at have illustrated the importance of using reference points and reference values to orient and organize the drawing. Thus, in the ColorPicker and ShapeDemo examples we used constants and variables to serve as the reference points and dimensions of the various objects that were displayed. In Graph and ChartDemo programs, in addition to using constants and variables to design the layout, we changed the location of the origin to help simplify the calculation of the graphs and charts. Also, by making the layout dependent on the dimensions of the main screen, we were able to scale the size of the graphs and charts to the size of the screen.

These examples illustrate an important principle that applies not only to designing drawings, but more broadly to designing any object or method:

EFFECTIVE DESIGN: Generality and extensibility. Objects and methods should be designed to be as general and as extensible as possible.

To underscore this point, let's design a version of our `CyberPet` that permits members of its subclasses to be drawn in a variety of ways at a wide range of scales. In other words, we want a design that will easily allow a CyberDog or a CyberCat to be drawn. Moreover, we want to draw the object, not just display a canned image of the object.

Programmer-defined interfaces

As we have seen in studying the Java class hierarchy, one of the best ways to design extensible objects is to use interfaces. An **interface** defines the methods that a class of objects can perform. Thus, the listener interfaces define the various kinds of events that an object can handle. If we follow this approach, then the best way design a `CyberPet` that can be drawn and scaled in an endless variety of ways is to define interfaces for these drawing and scaling actions. `CyberPet` subclasses can then implement the interfaces to suit their unique circumstances.

An interface is more appropriate here than an abstract class, which we used in designing the `Cipher` classes in Chapter 7. An abstract class is appropriate when there's a certain amount of basic behavior that should be inherited by its subclasses. Thus the `Caesar` and `Transpose` subclasses of `Cipher` both implemented the abstract `encode()` and `decode()` methods, but inherited the `encrypt()` and `decrypt()` methods from `Cipher`. In this case however, there's no way to inherit drawing behavior. Each type of pet will have to have its own drawing and scaling routines. That's why we want to use an interface.

EFFECTIVE DESIGN: Interfaces versus Abstract Classes. An interface should be used to implement a set of well-defined behaviors. An abstract superclass should be used when its subclasses must all inherit some shared behavior or state.

Thus, to define a `CyberPet` that can be drawn, we'll define a `Drawable` interface. To define a `CyberPet` that can change size, we'll define a `Scalable` interface. Once we define these interfaces, they can be attached (implemented by) any class of objects. For example, if we needed a button that would change its size depending on the size of its frame, we could define a scalable button as

```
public class ScalableButton extends Button implements Scalable ;
```

A Drawable Interface

What methods do we need?

In some sense, defining a Drawable interface is a matter of defining what it means to draw an object. The Drawable interface must define, but not implement, those methods that would be used to draw an object. Most of the shapes that we have drawn have used either draw or fill methods to represent the object. For example, we used drawRect(), fillRect(), drawOval(), and fillOval(). Therefore, let's conclude that in order to draw any object, you must implement either a draw method, a fill method, or both. This gives us the following definition for Drawable:

```
import java.awt.*;

/**
 *  The Drawable interface defines two methods used for drawing
 *   graphical objects, the draw() and fill() methods.
 */
public interface Drawable {
    public abstract void draw(Graphics g);
    public abstract void fill(Graphics g);
} // Drawable
```

Note that both methods take a reference to a graphics context, which will usually be the context of the applet or application within which the drawing is done. Note also that no coordinates are supplied as parameters. This assumes that an object that implements this interface knows its own location, so, when a drawable CyberPet is created, we will have to give it location variables.

A Scalable Interface

The Scalable interface is just as simple to define. By "scalable" we mean that an object can be enlarged or reduced in size without affecting its overall proportions. Thus if the CyberPet's head is approximately one-third the height of its whole body, it should retain these proportions when it is enlarged or reduced.

What methods do we need?

We could have a method to enlarge and a method to reduce. Both of these methods would require some kind of parameter to indicate the amount of enlargement or reduction. For example, we might want to enlarge by doubling or tripling the size, or reduce by halving the size. A good candidate for the type of this parameter would be double, as that would provide the most flexibility in terms of scaling an object.

If we define both enlarge and reduce, what will be meant by enlarge (0.5) and enlarge(1.5)? Or by reduce(0.5) or reduce(1.5)? These seem somewhat confusing, because enlarging by 0.5 suggests reducing the size of the object. Therefore let's dispense with these method names and just use a single method, scale(), to either reduce or enlarge an object:

```
/**
 *  The Scalable interface defines the scale() method, which
 *   is used to resize graphical objects.
 */
import java.awt.*;

public interface Scalable {
    public abstract void scale(double ratio);
}//Scalable
```

Thus, `scale(0.5)` will mean to cut the size in half, and `scale(1.5)` will mean to increase the size by 50 percent.

The `DrawableCyberPet` Class

To create a drawable, scalable CyberPet, we will define a subclass of the `CyberPet` class defined in Figure 5–8. You may want to consult that definition now. This class will implement both the `Drawable` and `Scalable` interfaces. Also, as we noted, the drawable pet will need to have a location and a size. This leads to the following preliminary definition:

```
public class DrawablePet extends CyberPet implements Drawable, Scalable {

    protected int size = 30;           // Default size = vertical radius of head
    protected Point location;           // Top left corner of head

    public DrawablePet(String s, int radius,  Point loc) {
        super(s);
        size = radius;
        location = loc;
    }

    public void setLocation(Point p) {
        location = p;
    }
    public Point getLocation() {
        return location;
    }

    public void draw(Graphics g) { }
    public void fill(Graphics g) { }
    public void scale(double ratio) { }
} // DrawablePet
```

What's missing from this definition are the actual definitions of the drawing and scaling methods which, for now, have been left as stubs. Note that the class's instance variables, `size` and `location`, are declared `protected`. This makes it possible for subclasses of `DrawablePet` to inherit them.

The `size` variable refers to the vertical radius of the head. All of the other dimensions of the pet's body will be defined as a factor of this one variable. In addition to the instance variables, we've defined a constructor method and two public access methods for getting and setting the pet's location.

EFFECTIVE DESIGN: Multiple Inheritance. Java interfaces provide a limited and controlled form of **multiple inheritance**. A class that extends a superclass and implements one or more interfaces inherits methods from all of those sources. Because interfaces cannot contain instance variables, they cannot conflict with any of the superclass's state variables.

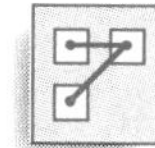

Multiple inheritance

Multiple inheritance is a mechanism that allows a class to inherit elements from two or more unrelated superclasses. For example, if class A and class B are not related — neither is a subclass of the other — multiple inheritance would occur if class C could extend both A and B. Languages such as C++ support full-fledged multiple inheritance. In C++, unlike in Java, a subclass can inherit not only methods but also instance variables from two or more unrelated superclasses. This can sometimes cause problems if the instance variables conflict in some way. For example, suppose both A and B have an instance variable named `size`. This could pose all kinds of potential problems for class C. Java avoids these kinds of problems by only allowing multiple inheritance of methods (via interfaces). Many language designers think that this restricted form of multiple inheritance is a good feature of the language.

Drawing the `CyberPet`

Let's now design an image that looks something like a spider. Before you can write methods to draw a figure, you need to do some planning. Figure 10–23 shows our plan for the drawing.

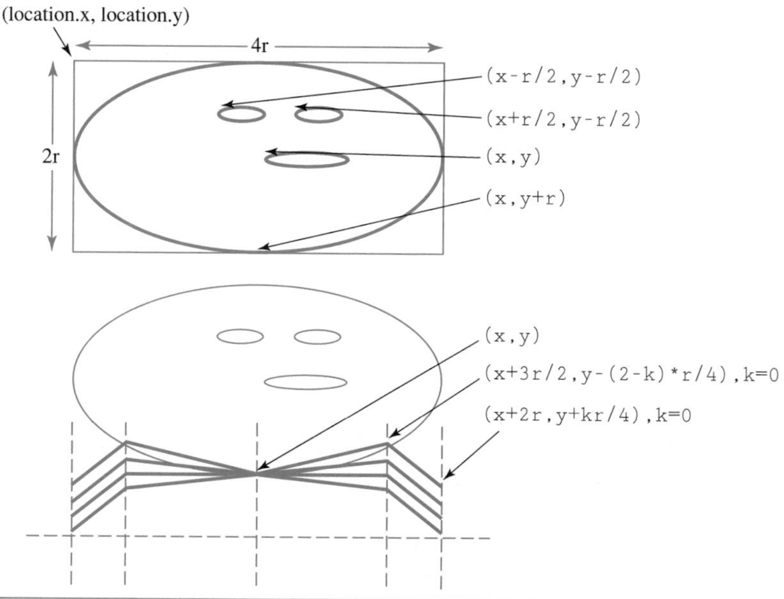

Figure 10–23 A plan for the drawing of the spider. The variable `r` in this plan corresponds to the `size` variable in the program.

The spider's head is an oval whose width is four times the `size` variable and whose height is twice the `size` variable. The `location` variable defines the top-left corner of its enclosing rectangle. This is the point that will be used to draw the outline of the head.

Design: Find a good reference point

To draw the spider's face, it will be easier if we use the center of the oval, *(x,y)*, as a reference point. It is easier to position the eyes at certain displacement above and to the left and right of *(x,y)* than it would be with respect to `location`. Also, it is important that the size and location of the eyes be computed as a factor of the `size` variable rather than as some absolute value. This will enable the `CyberPet`'s face to scale properly when it is resized. Because all the facial components are determined relative to *(x,y)*, we can easily design a `drawFace(x,y)`, where `(x,y)` is the location of the center of the face.

Design: Pick a suitable reference point

Similarly, note how the legs are designed. All eight legs start at a common point located at `(location.x + 2r, location.y + 2r)`—relative to the spider's overall location. However, rather than use the `location` variable as their reference point, the legs will be much easier to draw if we use their common starting point as the reference. Let's call this point *(x,y)*, but note that it is not the same *(x,y)* that we used as the reference point for the face. We can do this because we will use separate methods, each with their local *(x,y)* reference point, to draw the face and the legs. Thus, we can define a method, `drawJointedLegs(x,y)`, where `(x,y)` defines the starting point of all eight legs. Everything within the method will be measured relative to this point.

Each leg contains a knee joint, so we will need two `drawLine()` statements of the following form to draw each leg:

```
g.drawLine(x, y, x1, y1);
g.drawLine(x1, y1, x2, y2);
```

Use symmetry to simplify things

How can we calculate the three points, (x,y), (x1,y1), and (x2,y2)? Let's break this problem up into two parts: the horizontal (x) and the vertical (y) coordinates for each leg. Because the left and right sets of legs are symmetrical, we'll limit our discussion to the right set.

For the horizontal coordinates, note in Figure 10–23 that all the knee joints have the same x-coordinate, and all the leg ends have the same x-coordinate. The joints are displaced by $\frac{3}{2}$ of a radius to the right of the reference point, *(x,y)*, and the leg ends are displaced by two radii to the right of the reference point. If r represents the radius, we get the following equations for the x-coordinates of the right legs:

```
x1 = x + 3r/2
x2 = x + 2r
```

Look for regularities

For the vertical coordinates, we want to find a similar regularity. Notice that the y-coordinates of the legs are evenly spaced. Thus we can represent the y coordinates by some proportion of r from the reference point, *(x,y)*. If you measure the distance between the legs, you'll find that they are separated by $r/4$. However, notice that the knee joint for the first leg is above the reference point by *r/4*, while the end of its leg is below the reference point by *r/4*. This suggests the following table of values for displacements of the *y*-coordinates from the reference point *(x,y)*:

Leg	Knee joint	End of Leg
1	-r/4	r/4
2	0	2r/4
3	r/4	3r/4
4	r/2	r

So, the *y*-coordinate of the first leg's knee joint will be *y - r/4* and the *y*-coordinate of the end of that leg will be *y + r/4*. Note that as you move down the rows of the table, you are just adding *r/4* to the value in the previous row.

Assuming that *k* is the leg number, the above table of values leads to the following formulas for the *y*-coordinates of the knee joint and end of leg.

```
y2 =  y - (2 - k) * size / 4  // Knee joint
y3 =  y + k       * size / 4  // End of leg
```

Because we can easily express these formulas in terms of *k*, we will be able to use a for loop to draw the legs.

EFFECTIVE DESIGN: Exploiting Regularities. To simplify drawing of complex figures, it is helpful to look for symmetries and other regularities that can be incorporated into the design. These serve to make the design more general and more extensible.

The Drawing Methods

Our design considerations translate easily into the drawing methods shown in Figure 10–24. There are several points to note about the program. Recall

Figure 10–24 The `DrawablePet` class.

```
import java.awt.*;

public class DrawablePet extends CyberPet implements Drawable, Scalable {

    protected int size = 30;      // Default size = vertical radius of head
    protected Point location;     // Top-left corner of head
    protected Color color;

    public DrawablePet(String s, int radius, Point loc, Color c) {
        super(s);
        size = radius;
        location = loc;
        color = c;
    } // DrawablePet
```

Figure 10–24 *Continued*

```
    public void setLocation(Point p) {
        location = p;
    }
    public Point getLocation() {
        return location;
    }

    public void draw( Graphics g ){
        g.drawOval(location.x, location.y, 4 * size, 2 * size);          // Draw the head
        drawFace(g, location.x + 2 * size, location.y + size);
        drawJointedLegs(g, location.x + 2 * size, location.y + 2 * size, size / 12);
    } // draw()

   // x,y gives center of the head

    private void drawFace(Graphics g, int x, int y ) {
        g.drawOval(x, y, size, size / 2);                               //Mouth
        g.drawOval(x - size / 2, y - size / 2, size / 2, size / 3); //Eye
        g.drawOval(x + size / 2, y - size / 2, size / 2, size / 3); //Eye
    } // drawFace()

    private void drawJointedLegs(Graphics g, int x, int y, int lineWidth) {
        int x1 = x - 2 * size;
        int x2 = x - 3 * size / 2;
        int x3 = x + 3 * size / 2;
        int x4 = x + 2 * size;
        for (int j = 0; j < lineWidth; j++) {   // Loop to control width of legs
            for (int k = 1; k <= 4; k++) {      // Draw 4 left, right pairs of legs
                int y2 = y - (2 - k) * size / 4;
                int y3 = y + k * size / 4;
                g.drawLine(x, y, x2, y2);             //Left leg
                g.drawLine(x2, y2, x1, y3);
                g.drawLine(x, y, x3, y2);             //Right leg
                g.drawLine(x3, y2, x4, y3);
            }
            y++;                                  // Redraw line 1 pixel off to give width
        }
    } // drawJointedLegs()

    public void fill(Graphics g){
        g.setColor( color );
        g.fillOval(location.x, location.y, 4 * size, 2 * size);
        fillFace(g, location.x + 2 * size, location.y + size);
    } // fill()

    private void fillFace(Graphics g, int x, int y ) {
        g.setColor(Color.white);
        g.fillOval(x, y, size, size / 2);                               //Mouth
        g.fillOval(x - size / 2, y - size / 2, size / 2, size / 3); //Eye
        g.fillOval(x + size / 2, y - size / 2, size / 2, size / 3); //Eye
        g.setColor(Color.black);
    } // fillFace()

    public void scale( double ratio ){
        size = (int) (size * ratio);
    } // scale()
} // DrawablePet
```

that in order to implement the `Drawable` interface, we just implement the `draw()` method. If you look at that method, you will see that the drawing task has been broken down into three subtasks: drawing the head, drawing the face, and drawing the legs. The first subtask is handled by simply drawing an oval for the outline of the head at `(location.x,location.y)`. The second is encapsulated in the `drawFace()` method, which uses the center of the head as its reference point. The third is encapsulated in the `drawJointedLegs()` method, which uses the base of the legs as its reference point. We saw above how the use of reference points simplifies the design of the drawing. In the same way, the use of parameters simplifies the design of the corresponding methods.

Method decomposition

In terms of the details of the methods, the `drawFace()` method simply draws three ovals for the mouth and the two eyes. The mouth is one-half the `size` variable, whereas the eyes are one-third of `size`. So all of the facial features are proportional to `size`.

As we described above, the `drawJointedLegs()` method uses the reference point *(x,y)* and the `size` to position and proportion the legs. Note the use of the for loop to draw the four legs. The only new feature added here is that a second for loop is used to give some width to the legs. Instead of using a single, one-pixel line for each leg, we draw several lines for each leg, each one displaced by one pixel in its *y*-coordinate:

Loops can exploit regularities

```
for (int j = 0; j < lineWidth; j++) {   // Loop to control width of legs
     ...            // Draw the four legs
     y++;           // Move the y-coordinate down by 1 pixel
}
```

As all other dimensions of our drawing, the width of the legs must also be made proportional to the size of the figure. Thus when we call the `drawJointedLegs()` method, we pass it `size/12` as the `lineWidth` argument. The smaller the spider, the skinnier its legs will be!

The implementation of the `fill()` method and the corresponding `fillFace()` method are nearly identical to `draw()` and `drawFace()`. The major difference is that the fill methods use the `fillOval()` method instead of `drawOval()`. They also set the graphic context's color, based on the pet's color scheme.

Finally, in order to implement the `Scalable` interface, we must implement the `scale()` method. Given the way we've designed our drawing methods, this method need only change the pet's `size` variable by the desired ratio:

```
public void scale( double ratio ){
    size = (int)(size * ratio);
}
```

Figure 10–25 An applet to display the scalable CyberPet.

```
import java.awt.*;
import javax.swing.*;

public class DrawablePetApplet extends JApplet {

    private DrawablePet pet;

    public void init() {
        setSize(400,400);
    }

    public void paint(Graphics g) {
        pet = new DrawablePet("Spidey", 60, new Point(50,10), Color.green);
        pet.sleep();
        pet.setLocation( new Point(50, 10 ) );
        pet.draw(g);
        pet.fill(g);
        pet.scale( 0.5 );
        pet.eat();
        pet.setLocation( new Point(100, 200 ) );
        pet.draw(g);
        pet.scale( 0.5 );
        pet.setLocation( new Point(300, 200 ) );
        pet.draw(g);
    }
} // DrawablePetApplet.java
```

EFFECTIVE DESIGN: Scalability. A scalable object is one whose dimensions are defined relative to one or more variables. By changing the value of the variables, you change the dimensions of the the object.

Testing the `DrawablePet`

To test `DrawablePet` we need only draw several images at different locations and different scales which is what the applet in Figure 10–25 does. The program's output can be seen if Figure 10–26.

One important feature of the applet is that a new `DrawablePet` is created in the `paint()` method, rather than in `init()`. This leads to a better visual effect when the applet's window is repainted. Unless you create a new pet each time, the drawings will be reduced each time — because of the `pet.scale(0.5)` statements — until they are too small to see. That's the bad news. The good news is that no matter how small they get, `DrawablePet`s maintain their proportions!

SELF-STUDY EXERCISES

EXERCISE 10.24 Modify the `DrawablePet.drawFace()` method so that the spider's eyes are closed a bit more when it is sleeping.

Figure 10–26 Output from the DrawablePet program.

IN THE LABORATORY: THE SelfPortrait CLASS

The purpose of this lab is to gain some hands-on experience with the design and drawing techniques discussed in this chapter. Your main task will be to design and draw a self-portrait. The objectives of the lab are

- To design a portrait of yourself which uses reference points in the same way they were used in the DrawablePet example.
- To define a SelfPortrait class that implements the Drawable and Scalable interfaces and draws your self-portrait.

Problem Description

Design a portrait of yourself that contains at least the following elements: a head, a face with eyes, nose, and mouth, a hat, some hair, and a torso wearing a sweater with your school's letter on it. A sample figure is shown in Figure 10–27. Your design for the portrait should make careful use of reference points, the way we did in the DrawablePet example. Once you have developed a satisfactory design, define a SelfPortrait class and implement the Drawable and Scalable interfaces for it.

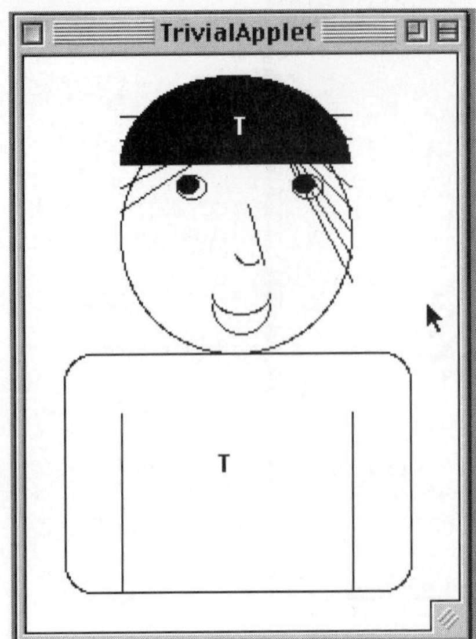

Figure 10–27 Self portrait of the author.

Problem Decomposition

This problem breaks down into four classes and interfaces.

- The `SelfPortrait` class will contain the implementation of the `Drawable` and `Scalable` interfaces. It will be responsible for drawing the portrait.
- The `Drawable` interface was defined earlier and should be incorporated into your project.
- The `Scalable` interface was defined earlier and should be incorporated into your project.
- The `PortraitApplet` or `PortraitFrame` is the main program. It should create instances of `SelfPortrait` and test that they work correctly.

The `SelfPortrait` Class

As in the `DrawablePet` example, this class will need instance variables to define its size, color, and any other features that make up its internal state. There should be an appropriate collection of `public` access methods for these variables — for example, the `getSize()` and `setSize()` methods.

In addition to the `draw()`, `fill`, and `scale()` methods, this class should contain methods to draw the major features of your portrait — for example, the face, the torso, the hat, and so on. Each of these methods should take a set of *x* and *y* parameters which serve as a *reference point* for that particular portion of the drawing.

Algorithm Development and Testing

Because the "correctness" of this program depends on how it looks, it is very important to develop it in a stepwise fashion. Even the most careful design on paper may not look the way you want it to when you incorporate it into your program. Also, if you get just one coordinate wrong in the program, its very easy to end up with a completely indecipherable mess.

Therefore, test each method, line by line and statement by statement, as you develop it. For example, in drawing the face, write the code needed to draw the outline and test it. Write the code needed to draw the mouth and test it. And so on. As you add each new facial feature, run your code and see whether it looks the way you had planned it.

Documentation

Be sure to provide appropriate documentation of your final program according to the document specifications described in Appendix A.

CHAPTER SUMMARY

Technical Terms

RGB value	ascent	baseline
Cartesian coordinates	clip region	drawing mode
graphics context	histogram	interface
mouse events	mouse motion events	multiple inheritance
origin	pixel	scalable
slope-intercept form		XORmode

New Java Keywords

final	protected

Java Classes

`Applet`	`Button`	`Choice`
`Dimension`	`Color`	`Font`
`FontMetrics`	`Graphics`	`ItemListener`
`JApplet`	`JFrame`	`JPanel`
`JTextfield`	`MouseEvent`	`MouseListener`
`MouseMotionListener`	`Point`	`String`

Java Library Methods

`charWidth()`	`drawLine()`	`drawOval()`
`drawRect()`	`drawString()`	`fillArc()`
`fillOval()`	`fillRect()`	`setColor()`
`getColor()`	`getFont()`	`getHeight()`
`getPoint()`	`getSize()`	`itemStateChanged()`
`getAvailableFontFamilyNames()`	`mouseClicked()`	`mouseDragged()`
	`mouseReleased()`	`paintComponent()`
`mousePressed()`	`translate()`	`update()`
`setClip()`		

Programmer-Defined Classes

`CenterText`	`ChartDemo`	`ColorPicker`
`CyberPet`	`DrawAble`	`DrawablePet`
`FontNames`	`Graph`	`MousePaint`
`Scalable`	`SelfPortrait`	`ShapeDemo`

Programmer-Defined Methods

`draw()`	`drawBarChart()`	`drawBoxes()`
`drawFace()`	`drawGasket()`	`drawJointedLegs()`
`fill()`	`fillFace()`	`graphLine()`
`graphQuadratic()`	`scale()`	

Summary of Important Points

- Every Java component has an associated *graphics context*, an instance of the `Graphics` class, which provides the drawing methods used on that object.
- In Java's coordinate system, the *origin*, (0,0), is located in the top left corner. Each *pixel* of the screen has an *x*- and *y-coordinate*. The *x*-coordinates increase in value from left to right and the *y*-coordinates increase in value from top to bottom. This is different from the *Cartesian coordinate* system, which you used in mathematics.
- Every graphics context has certain properties that remain fixed during drawing. These are the context's *origin*, *color*, *font*, *drawing mode*, and *clip region*. The `Graphics` object has methods that can be used to change these properties.
- `Colors` in Java are represented as a combination of the three primary colors, red, green, and blue (RGB). The *RGB value* for a color can be specified in its constructor. There are 13 predefined colors in the `Color` class, which also contains methods to brighten and darken a given color.
- A *symbolic constant* is a variable specified as `final` so its value cannot be changed during a program. Constants should be used to define reference points and dimensions whose values are not expected to change during drawing or painting. This is an example of the *generality principle*.
- Drawn shapes are transparent while filled shapes are colored in the current color of the graphics context. The `Graphics` class contains methods for drawing and filling a variety of shapes, including arcs, ovals, rectangles, lines, and polygons.
- Graphing equations is made easier by translating the default origin of the graphics context to the graph's origin, using the `Graphics.translate()` method, and then drawing the graph relative to the origin. Remember however that the *y*-axis is reversed in Java's coordinate system.
- The `fillArc()` method is useful for creating pie charts, which are also made simpler by translating the origin to the reference point needed for the `fillArc()` method.

- In order to make your drawings *scalable*, it is important to define all locations and dimensions in the drawing relative to some fixed reference point. A good way to do this is to make the reference point a parameter of the drawing method.
- The `FontMetrics` class is used to obtain the specific dimensions of the the various `Fonts`. It is useful when you wish to center text. `Fonts` are inherently platform dependent. For maximum portability, it is best to use default fonts.
- You can make your drawings scalable within a frame by designing their dimensions relative to the frame size.
- The `MouseListener` and `MouseMotionListener` interfaces must be implemented in any class that purports to handle mouse events. The former interface handles mouse clicks, while the latter handles mouse motion, including dragging.

ANSWERS TO SELF-STUDY EXERCISES

EXERCISE 10.1 The bottom-right corner would have coordinates (199,199).

EXERCISE 10.2 If the clip region is defined from (0,0) to (100,100) and the drawing is done starting at (150,150), nothing will show up because it is outside the clip region.

EXERCISE 10.3 One use of XORmode is when you want to draw a string that will span two differently colored backgrounds, for example, imagine two adjacent areas, one black and one white. If you draw a black string across both areas in XORmode, it will show up white on black and black on white.

EXERCISE 10.4 If you pick a color not supported by your monitor, Java will pick the closest color that your monitor can display.

EXERCISE 10.5 The built-in colors are defined as class constants so they can be used even when no `Color` instance is defined.

EXERCISE 10.6 All colors are made by mixing red, green, and blue.

EXERCISE 10.7 Each of the three color expression is dominated by one of the three RGB values, so the resulting colors will be a shade of the primary color in each case: a shade of red (a), a shade of green (b), and a shade of blue (c).

EXERCISE 10.8 If you remove the `repaint()` method call from `ColorPicker`'s `actionPerformed()` method, the `canvas` panel will never change in response to the user's actions.

EXERCISE 10.9 The `JApplet`'s `paint()` method is called automatically to paint AWT components and their subclasses, of which `JApplet` is one. The `paintComponent()` method is called automatically to paint Swing `JComponents` and members of its subclasses.

EXERCISE 10.10

```
// A method to draw 20 3 x 3 horizontal
//  rectangles starting at HREF,VREF:

public void drawHRects(Graphics g) {
    int href = HREF;
    for (int k = 0; k < 20; k++) {
        g.drawRect(href, VREF, 3, 3);
        href += HGAP;
    }
}
```

EXERCISE 10.11

```
// A method to draw 20 3 x 3 diagonally
//  rectangles starting at HREF,VREF:

public void drawDiagonalRects(Graphics g) {
    int href = HREF;
    int vref = VREF;
    for (int k = 0; k < 20; k++) {
        g.drawRect(href, vref, 3, 3);
        href += HGAP;
        vref += VGAP;
    }
}
```

EXERCISE 10.12

```
// A method to draw 20 3 x 3 rectangles horizontal
//  starting at point p with a gap of HGAP.
public void drawHRects(Graphics g, Point p) {
    int href = p.x;
    for (int k = 0; k < 20; k++) {
        g.drawRect(href, p.y, 3, 3);
        href += HGAP;
    }
}
```

EXERCISE 10.13 The area of a `JPanel` with `Dimension d` is given by `d.width * d.height`.

EXERCISE 10.14 An 80 × 40 rectangle at (0,20): `g.drawRect(0,20,80,40);`.

EXERCISE 10.15 To inscribe a yellow oval inside an 80 × 40 rectangle at (0,20): `g.fillOval(0,20,80,40);`.

EXERCISE 10.16 The shape drawn by `g.drawRoundRect(XREF,VREF,50,50,50,50);` would turn out to be a circle with diameter 50.

EXERCISE 10.17 A circle with diameter D, inside a rectangle located at XREF, YREF, can be drawn by g.drawRoundRect(XREF,VREF,D,D,D,D);.

EXERCISE 10.18 After translating the origin from (0,0) by first (50,200) and then by (−10, −150), would place it finally at (40,50) relative to the default origin.

EXERCISE 10.19 If you forget to set the Graph object's size in the constructor, this will affect the size of the top-level window, which by default will be 0.

EXERCISE 10.20 If you reverse the setSize() and setVisible() statements in ChartDemo.main() the window will not be properly sized. It should be sized before it is made visible.

EXERCISE 10.21 In the expression g.drawString(k+1 + "", href+5, 13) the empty string forces the + operator to be interpreted as string concatenation rather than addition. It forces k+1 to be promoted to a String.

EXERCISE 10.22 The paint() method is used in FontNames because the drawing is done on a JApplet, which is not a subclass of JComponent.

EXERCISE 10.23 The algorithm for varying the vertical line space according to the height of the font is as follows:

```
public void paint( Graphics g ) {
    String[] fonts = Toolkit.getDefaultToolkit().getFontList();
    FontMetrics metric = g.getFontMetrics();
    int fontHgt = metric.getHeight();
    int vRef = 30;
    int vGap = 2;
    g.drawString("The first 10 fonts on this system are: ", 30, vRef);
    for (int k = 0; k < 10; k++) {
        vRef += fontHgt + vGap;                          // Use font hgt to set vertical ref
        int fontSize = (int)(10 +  Math.random() * 15);
        g.setFont( new Font (fonts[k], Font.PLAIN, fontSize) );
        g.drawString( "Hello World! (" + fonts[k] + ")", 30, vRef );
        metric = g.getFontMetrics();                               // Get font's metrics
        fontHgt = metric.getHeight();                              // And its height
    }
}
```

EXERCISE 10.24

```
private void drawFace(Graphics g, int x, int y ) {
    if (state != SLEEPING) {
        g.drawOval(x, y, size, size / 2);                              //mouth
        g.drawOval(x - size / 2, y - size / 2, size / 2, size / 3); //eye
        g.drawOval(x + size / 2, y - size / 2, size / 2, size / 3); //eye
    } else {
        g.drawOval(x, y, size, size / 8);                              //mouth
        g.drawOval(x - size / 2, y - size / 2, size / 2, size / 8); //eye
        g.drawOval(x + size / 2, y - size / 2, size / 2, size / 8); //eye
    }
}
```

EXERCISES

1. Explain the difference between the following pairs of terms.

   a. *Drawing* and *painting*.
   b. *Cartesian coordinates* and *Java coordinates*.
   c. An *RGB value* and a *color*.
   d. A *graphics context* and a *component*.
   e. *Background* and *foreground* colors.
   f. An *interface* and a *class*.
   g. *XORmode* and *normal mode* drawing.
   h. The `paint()` and `paintComponent()` methods.
   i. A *mouse event* and a *mouse motion event*.
   j. A `public` and a `protected` element.
   k. A `private` and a `protected` element.
   l. A `Font` and a `Fontmetrics` object.
   m. A `Dimension` and a `Point` object.

2. As we have discussed, when a window is reopened or resized, it is necessary to repaint it. Explain how Java uses knowledge of the window's *containment hierarchy* to repaint the window.
3. Java interfaces give Java a limited form of *multiple inheritance*. Explain.
4. Fill in the blank:

   a. Components that are subclassed from `JComponent` should use the _______ method to do their drawing.
   b. A `JApplet` or `JFrame` should use the _______ method to do its drawing.
   c. When a _______ component is updated, its background is not automatically cleared.
   d. When a _______ component is updated, its background is automatically cleared.
   e. When the mouse is clicked, this event should be handled by methods of the _______ interface.
   f. When the mouse is dragged, this event should be handled by methods of the _______ interface.

5. Write Java statements to implement the following tasks. Where necessary, use *g* as a reference to the graphics context.

   a. Move the default origin to a point that's displaced 50 pixels to the right and 100 pixels above the origin's current location.
   b. Draw a 50×100 blue rectangle at location (10,10).
   c. Paint a 50×100 magenta oval at location (100,10).
   d. Paint a red circle with diameter 100 at location (200,10).
   e. Draw a 50×100 3D yellow rectangle at location (10,200).
   f. Paint a white 50×100 rounded rectangle at location (100,200).
   g. Paint an black 50×100 rounded rectangle at location (100,200).
   h. Set a `JPanel`'s size to 400×300.
   i. Set a `JPanel`'s foreground color to yellow and its background color to blue.

6. Write a method that takes an array of `Points` and paints a 3×3 rectangle at each point. This should be a `void` method and should also take a `Graphics` parameter.

7. One `Graphics` method that was not demonstrated in the chapter was the `drawPolygon()` method. For parameters this method takes two `int` arrays representing the x and y coordinates of the polygon's points. A third `int` parameter gives the number of points in the polygon. Here's an example of how this can be used:

```
int xcoords[] = {100, 50, 70, 130, 100};
int ycoords[] = {100, 150, 200, 200, 100};
g.drawPolygon(xcoords, ycoords, xcoords.length);
```

   Use graph paper and pencil to design a hexagon (six-sided figure) and an octagon (eight-sided figure). Then use `drawPolygon()` to draw their shapes in an application.
8. Use the `drawPolygon()` and corresponding `fillPolygon()` method to draw the three-dimensional object shown in Figure 10–28. (*Hint*: Each face can be viewed as a polygon or a rectangle.)
9. Write a method to draw a bullseye. This method can make good use of `g.setXORMode(Color.black)`. Here's how the method should work. Draw the outer circle of the bullseye. Then draw a slightly smaller circle within it, then a slightly smaller circle within that. And so on. The method should take a `Graphics` parameter as well as parameters for the bullseye's location and diameter.
10. Write a method that takes an array of `Points` and draws a line between each pair of consecutive points. This should be a `void` method and should also take a `Graphics` parameter.
11. Design and implement a Java applet or application that draws a colored pie chart representing the relative numbers of As, Bs, Cs, Ds, and Fs in a fictitious computer science course. Allow the numbers of each grade to be input by the user.
12. Design and implement an applet or application that draws a histogram representing the relative numbers of As, Bs, Cs, Ds, and Fs in a fictitious computer science course. Allow the numbers of each grade to be input by the user.
13. Design and implement an applet or application that displays a multiline message in various fonts and sizes input by the user. Let the user choose from among a fixed selection of fonts, sizes, and styles.
14. Modify the `Graph` program so the user can enter the coordinates of the linear or quadratic equations to be graphed.
15. Design and implement a Java applet or application that draws and paints a scalable logo for a fictitious company.
16. Design and implement an applet or application that plays the following game with the user. Draw a shape or an image on the screen and invite the user to click on it. Every time the user clicks on it, move the shape to an new random location.
17. Modify the program in the previous exercise so that the shape moves whenever the user moves the mouse to within a certain distance of the shape.
18. **Challenge:** Design and implement an applet or application that plays the following game with the user. Place a puck at a random location on the screen and paint a goal in some other location. Invite the user to move the puck into the goal. Have the user's mouse-controlled stick exert a repulsive force on the image. The puck always moves away from the stick on an imaginary line originating at the stick and intersecting the puck. When the user gets the puck in the goal, draw a happy face on the screen.

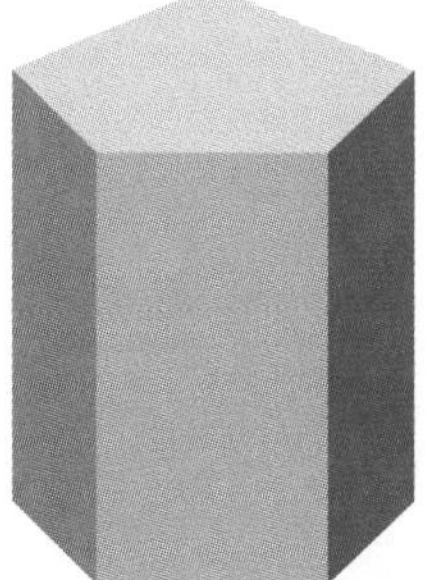

Figure 10–28 Use polygons to draw this figure.

19. Create a DrawableRectangle subclass of the Rectangle class (defined in Chapter 1) that implements the Drawable and Scalable interfaces.
20. **Challenge:** Add the ability to handle mouse operations to the DrawableRectangle class defined in the previous exercise. In other words, it should implement MouseListener and MouseMotionListener. These handlers should enable a user to pick up and move a rectangle to a new location.
21. **Challenge:** Design and implement your own Polygon class, using an array of Point as the primary data structure. Use the Drawable interface.
22. **Challenge:** Design and implement a class that creates and renders three-dimensional cubes, of varying size. The class should contain a constructor that takes three parameters: length, width, and height. It should contain access methods for the cube's location, size, and color. Use the Drawable and Scalable interfaces in your design.

Photograph courtesy of Adam Crowley, PhotoDisc, Inc.

11

Exceptions: When Things Go Wrong

OBJECTIVES

After studying this chapter, you will

- Understand Java's exception handling mechanisms.
- Be able to use the Java `try/catch` statement.
- Know how to design effective exception handlers.
- Be able to design your own `Exception` subclasses.
- Appreciate the importance that exception handling plays in program design.
- Understand the computational overhead of exception handling.

OUTLINE

11.1 Introduction

Mistakes happen. Making mistakes is the norm rather than the exception. This is not to say that we make mistakes more often than we get it right. It is to say that (almost) nothing we do or build is ever perfectly correct, least of all computer software.

No matter how well designed a program is, there is always the chance that some kind of error will arise during its execution. A software designer forgets to guard against a certain type of unexpected input value that crashes the program when it is run. A programmer is unaware of a certain subtlety in Java's promotion rules that causes a computation to produce an erroneous value. Another programmer typed a '*' where a '+' was intended, thereby causing a computational error. A user misunderstood what the program was asking for and typed in an erroneous input. The list of ways that mistakes could happen when developing software is endless.

A well-designed program should include code to handle errors and other exceptional conditions when they arise. This code should be incorporated into the program from the very first stages of its development. That way it can help identify problems during development. In Java, the preferred way of handling such situations is to use *exception handling*, a divide-and-conquer approach that separates a program's normal code from its error handling code.

This chapter describes Java's exception handling features. We begin by contrasting the traditional way of handling errors within a program with Java's exception handling mechanism. We show how exceptions are raised (thrown) and handled (caught) within a program and identify the rules that apply to different kinds of exceptions. We then focus on some of the key design issues that govern when, where, and how to use exceptions in your programs. As a lesson in when not to use exceptions, the lab project for this chapter focuses on the computational costs of exception handling. It shows that because exceptions require a relatively high computational overhead, they should not be used to handle routine processing tasks. Instead they should be used to deal with truly exceptional circumstances.

11.2 Handling Exceptional Conditions

Figure 11–1 shows a method that computes the integer average of the first *N* elements of an integer array `arr[]`. Taking an integer average is, admittedly, somewhat of a contrived example. We use it mainly to introduce the basic syntax and semantics of exception handling.

As its precondition suggests, the `intAverage()` method expects that *N* will be greater than 0. If *N* happens to be 0, an error will occur in the expression `avg/N`, because you cannot divide an integer by 0.

11.2.1 Traditional Error Handling

Divide-by-zero error

Obviously, this method should not simply ignore the possibility that N might be 0. Figure 11–2 shows a revised version of the method, which includes code that takes action if the method's precondition fails. Because

Figure 11–1 Bad design. No attempt is made to guard against a divide-by-zero error.

```
/**
 * Precondition:  N > 0
 * Postcondition: intAverage() equals the integer average of the
 *   array's first N (N > 0) elements
 */
public int intAverage(int arr[], int N) {
    int avg = 0;
    for (int k = 0; k < N; k++)
        avg += arr[k];
    avg = avg / N;                  // WHAT IF N is 0 ??
    return avg;
} // intAverage()
```

there is no way to compute an average of 0 elements, the revised method decides to abort the program. This appears to be a better alternative than returning 0 or some other default value (like −1) as the method's result and thereby allowing an erroneous value to propagate throughout the program. That would just compound the error.

Of course, this policy assumes that this is the kind of program that can be aborted. If this were a library method, or a method in a nuclear power plant monitor, then it would not be appropriate to abort it. But let's assume that this is an "abortable" program — one that can be terminated abnormally without causing major problems.

EFFECTIVE DESIGN: Unfixable Error. If an unfixable error is detected, it is far better to terminate the program abnormally than to allow the error to propagate throughout the program.

Figure 11–2 One way to handle a divide-by-zero error might be to terminate the program, assuming it's the kind of program that can be safely aborted. This version does not use exceptions.

```
/**
 * Precondition:  N > 0
 * Postcondition: intAverage() equals the integer average of the
 *   array's first N (N > 0) elements
 */
public int intAverage( int arr[], int N ) {
    int avg = 0;
    if (N <= 0) {
        System.out.println("ERROR intAverage: Can't average 0 items");
        System.out.println("ERROR intAverage: Program terminating abnormally");
        System.exit(0);
    }
    for (int k = 0; k < N; k++)
        avg += arr[k];
    avg = avg / N;                  // At this point,  N > 0
    return avg;
} // intAverage()
```

The revised `intAverage()` method takes the traditional approach to error handling: Error handling code is built right into the algorithm. If *N* happens to be 0 when `intAverage()` is called, the following output will be generated:

```
ERROR intAverage: Can't average 0 items
ERROR intAverage: Program terminating abnormally
```

11.2.2 Trying, Throwing, and Catching an Exception

Pulling the program's fire alarm

In Java, errors and other abnormal conditions are handled by throwing and catching exceptions. When an error or an exceptional condition is detected, you can **throw an exception** as a way of signaling the abnormal condition. This is like pulling the fire alarm. When an exception is thrown, an **exception handler** will **catch** the exception and deal with it.

The typical way of handling this error in Java would be to *throw* an exception in the `intAverage()` method and *catch* it in the calling method. In this way the detection of the error is separated from its handling. This division of labor opens up a wide range of possibilities. For example, a program could dedicate a single object to serve as the handler for all its exceptions. The object would be sort of like the program's fire department.

To illustrate Java's `try/throw/catch` mechanism, let's modify the `intAverage()` method. The version shown in Figure 11–3 uses Java syntax to mimic the traditional way of handling the error — that is, it detects and handles the error right in the `intAverage()` method. This version doesn't really improve the program's error handling ability, but we'll get to a better design after we get the syntax and semantics out of the way.

Figure 11–3 This version of `intAverage()` replaces the traditional syntax with Java's `try/throw/catch` statement. Caution: Exiting the program from within a method like this is not a particularly good way to handle the error.

```
/**
 * Precondition:  N > 0
 * Postcondition: intAverage() equals the integer average of the
 *   array's first N (N > 0) elements
 */
public int intAverage( int arr[], int N ) {
    int avg = 0;
    try {                           // Try block: exception thrower
        if (N <= 0)
            throw new Exception("ERROR: Can't average 0 items \nTerminating abnormally");
        for (int k = 0; k < N; k++)
            avg += arr[k];
        avg = avg / N;              // We can assert that n > 0
    } catch (Exception e) {         // Catch block: exception handler
        System.out.println(e.getMessage());
        System.exit(0);
    } finally {                     // Optional finally block
        return avg;                 // The method must return an int
    }
} // intAverage()
```

The first thing to notice is that when the divide-by-zero error is detected, the method throws an exception:

```
if (N <= 0)
    throw new Exception("ERROR: Can't average 0 items \nTerminating abnormally");
```

Note the syntax of the throw statement. It creates a new Exception object and passes it a message that describes the error.

The try block

A try block begins with the keyword try followed by a block of code enclosed within curly braces. A try block can contain other statements besides the throw statement. In fact, the conventional practice is not to place every throw statement within its own try block. That would make the program difficult to read:

PROGRAMMING TIP: Coding a Try Block. Placing each throw statement within its own try block will make your code cluttered and unreadable. If a try block is going to be used in a method, it's better to place as many statements as possible within the block.

Responding to the fire alarm

As we said, throwing an exception is like raising an alarm. The "fire department" in this case is the code contained in the catch clause that immediately follows the try block. This is the exception handler for this particular exception.

The catch block

A *catch clause* or **catch block** consists of the keyword catch, followed by a parameter declaration which identifies the type of Exception being caught, followed by a collection of statements enclosed within curly braces. These are the statements that handle the exception by taking appropriate action.

In this example, the first thing the exception handler does is to get the error message from the Exception object, e. The message it retrieves is the same message that was passed to the object when it was created in the throw statement. There's a game of catch going on here: The try block throws an Exception object and the catch block catches it and handles it. Here is what would be printed when this exception handler is executed:

```
ERROR: Can't average 0 items
Terminating abnormally
```

Once an exception is thrown, control is transferred out of the try block to an appropriate catch block. Control does not return to the try block.

JAVA LANGUAGE RULE **Try Block Control.** If an exception is thrown, the try block is exited and control does not return to it.

In this particular example, the language rule that control does not return to the try block poses a dilemma because it conflicts with another rule — namely, that every nonvoid method must return a value. The `intAverage()` method must return an `int`. However, we cannot put the `return` statement at the end of the try block. The compiler will detect that the `return` statement might never be executed (because an exception might be thrown) and will issue a syntax error.

The finally block

There are two ways to resolve this dilemma. One way is to place the `return` statement within the optional **finally block**, as we have done in this example. A finally block can optionally follow the catch block. When it is present, statements in the finally block are executed regardless of whether an exception is thrown or not. Of course, if the program terminates in the `catch` clause, then the finally block will not be executed.

A second alternative is to place the `return` statement outside the `try` statement altogether:

```
try {
    // Possibly throw an exception
} catch (Exception e)
    // Handle an exception
}
return value;
```

This is the preferred way to code the `return` statement. It makes it clear that the method's last act is to execute the return.

JAVA LANGUAGE RULE **Return Statement.** For a nonvoid method the last statement executed *must* be a return statement.

Design flaws

As we said, this version of `intAverage()` merely uses the `try/catch` syntax to implement a traditional way of handling the divide-by-zero error (Figure 11–3). However, this is a flawed method because it really shouldn't be left up to this method to abort the program. As we'll see, Java's exception handling mechanism is more general and more principled than this particular example indicates.

11.2.3 Syntax and Semantics of Try/Throw/Catch

As the preceding example illustrates, Java's approach to handling exceptions is based on the `try/throw/catch/finally` combination, which is outlined in Figure 11–4.

The try block is meant to include a statement or statements that might throw an exception. The catch blocks — there can be one or more — are meant to handle exceptions that are thrown in the try block. A catch block will handle any exception that matches its parameter class, including subclasses of that class. The finally block is optional. It will always be executed whether an exception is thrown or not.

Figure 11–4 Java's try/throw/catch/finally mechanism.

```
try {
     // Block of statements
     // At least one of which may throw an exception

     if ( /* Some condition obtains */ )
         throw new ExceptionName();

} catch (ExceptionName ParameterName) {
    // Block of statements to be executed
    // If the ExceptionName exception is thrown in try
}
...  // Possibly other catch clauses
}  catch (ExceptionName2 ParameterName) {
    // Block of statements to be executed
    // If the ExceptionName2 exception is thrown in try
} finally {
    // Optional block of statements that is executed
    // Whether an exception is thrown or not
}
```

The statements in the try block are part of the program's normal flow of execution. By encapsulating a group of statements within a try block you thereby indicate that one or more exceptions may be thrown by those statements, and that you intend to catch them. In effect, you are *trying* a block of code with the possibility that something might go wrong.

Normal flow of execution

If an exception is thrown within a try block, Java exits the block and transfers control to the first `catch` block that matches the particular kind of exception that was thrown. Exceptions are thrown by using the `throw` statement, which takes the following general form:

Exceptional flow of execution

```
throw new ExceptionClassName(OptionalMessageString);
```

The keyword `throw` is followed by the instantiation of an object of the `ExceptionClassName` class. This is done the same way we instantiate any object in Java: by using the `new` operator and invoking one of the exception's constructor methods. Some of the constructors take an `OptionalMessageString`, which is the message that gets returned by the exception's `getMessage()` method.

A `catch` block has the following general form:

```
catch (ExceptionClassName ParameterName) {
    // Exception handling statements
}
```

A `catch` block is very much like a method definition. It contains a parameter, which specifies the class of exception that is handled by that block. The *ParameterName* can be any valid identifier, but it is customary to use `e` as the `catch` block parameter. The parameter's scope is limited to the catch block, and it is used to refer to the caught exception.

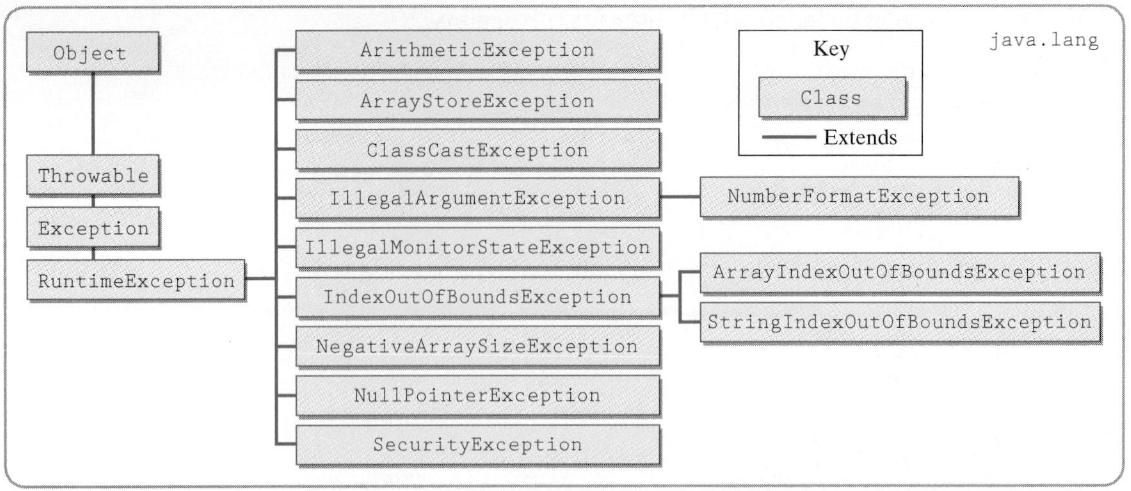

Figure 11–5 Part of Java's exception hierarchy. All subclasses of `RuntimeException` are known as *unchecked* exceptions. Java programs are not required to catch these exceptions.

Exceptions are objects

The *ExceptionClassName* must be one of the classes in Java's exception hierarchy, which is rooted at the `Exception` class (see Figure 11–5). A thrown exception will match any parameter of its own class or any of its superclasses. For example, if an `ArithmeticException` is thrown, it will match both an `ArithmeticException` parameter and an `Exception` parameter, because `ArithmeticException` is a subclass of `Exception`.

Restrictions on the `try/catch/finally` *Statement*

There are several important restrictions that apply to Java's exception handling mechanism. We'll describe these in more detail later.

- A try block must be immediately followed by one or more catch clauses and a catch clause may only follow a try block.
- A `throw` statement is used to throw both **checked** and **unchecked** exceptions, where unchecked exceptions are those belonging to `RuntimeException` or its subclasses. Unchecked exceptions need not be caught by the program.
- A `throw` statement must be contained within the dynamic scope of a try block, and the type of `Exception` thrown must match at least one of the try block's catch clauses. Or, the `throw` statement must be contained within a method or constructor that has a `throws` clause for the type of thrown `Exception`.

> **JAVA LANGUAGE RULE** **Try/catch Syntax.** A try block must be followed immediately—with no intervening code—by one or more catch blocks. A catch block can only be preceded by a try block or by another catch block. You may not place intervening code between catch blocks.

Figure 11–6 The `CalcAverage` class places the `catch` clauses in the `main()` method.

```
public class CalcAverage {

    public int intAverage(int arr[], int N) {
        int avg = 0;
        if (N <= 0)
            throw new ArithmeticException("ERROR: can't average 0 elements");
        for (int k = 0; k < N; k++)
            avg += arr[k];
        avg = avg / N;
        return avg;
    } // intAverage()

    public static void main(String args[]) {
        int numbers[] = {10, 20, 30, 30, 20, 10};
        try {
            CalcAverage ca = new CalcAverage();
            System.out.println( "AVG + " + ca.intAverage(numbers, 0));
        } catch (ArithmeticException e) {
            System.out.println( e.getMessage() );
            e.printStackTrace();
            System.exit(0);
        }
    } // main()
} // CalcAverage
```

11.2.4 Separating Error Checking from Error Handling

Divide and conquer

An important difference between Java's exception handling and more traditional approaches is that it is not necessary that the error handling code be incorporated right into the `intAverage()` method itself. It could be located elsewhere in the program, as shown in Figure 11–6. In that case the `intAverage()` method consists entirely of the normal code for calculating an average. It still *checks* for the error and it still `throws` an exception if *N* does not satisfy the method's precondition. But it does not contain a try block and it does not contain code for handling the exception. Note also that in this version we `throw` an `ArithmeticException`, which is another one of Java's built-in exceptions.

Look now at the program's `main()` method, which does contain a `try` block and a `catch` clause for handling an `ArithmeticException`. This is the `catch` clause that will be executed if the `ArithmeticException` is thrown in `intAverage()`. In this case, we have added one additional element to our exception handling: The `e.printStackTrace()` method will print a trace of all the methods that were called leading up to the method that threw the exception. Thus, the following output will be generated whenever the exception is thrown in `intAverage()`:

The method stack trace

```
ERROR: can't average 0 elements
java.lang.ArithmeticException: ERROR: can't average 0 elements
        at CalcAverage.intAverage(CalcAverage.java:11)
        at CalcAverage.main(CalcAverage.java:22)
        at com.mw.Exec.run(JavaAppRunner.java:47)
```

This program creates a clear separation between the normal algorithm and the exception handling code. One advantage of this design is the normal algorithm is uncluttered by error-handling code and therefore easier to read.

Another advantage is that the program's response to errors has been organized into one central location. By locating the exception handler in `main()` rather than in the method where the exception was raised, one exception handler can be used to handle other errors of that type. For example, this catch clause could handle *all* `ArithmeticExceptions` that get thrown in the program. Its use of `printStackTrace()` will identify exactly where the exception occurred.

EFFECTIVE DESIGN: Normal versus Exceptional Code. A key element of Java's exception handling mechanism is that the exception handler — the catch block — is distinct from the code that throws the exception — the try block. The try block contains the normal algorithm. The catch block contains code for handling exceptional conditions.

11.2.5 Dynamic versus Static Scoping

How does Java know that it should execute the `catch` clause in `main()` when an exception is thrown in `intAverage()`? Also, doesn't the latest version of `intAverage()` (Figure 11–6) violate the restriction that a `throw` statement must occur within a try block?

An exception can only be thrown within a *dynamically enclosing* try block. This means that the `throw` statement must fall within the **dynamic scope** of an enclosing try block. Let's see what this means.

Dynamic scope

Dynamic scoping refers to the way a program is executed. For example, in the `CalcAverage` program (Figure 11–6), the `intAverage()` method is called from within the try block located in the `main()` method. Thus, it falls within the dynamic scope of that try block.

Static scope

Dynamic scoping must be contrasted with **static scoping**, which we've used previously to define the scope of parameters and local variables (Figure 11–7). Static scoping refers to the way a program is written. A statement or variable occurs within the scope of a block if its text is actually written within that block. For example, consider the definition of `MyClass` (Figure 11–8). The variable `X` occurs within the (static) scope of `method1()`, and the variable `Y` occurs within the (static) scope of `method2()`:

A method's parameters and local variables occur within its static scope. Also, in the `MyClass` definition, the `System.out.println()` statements occur within the static scope of `method1()` and `method2()`, respectively. In general, static scoping refers to where a variable is declared or where a statement is located. Static scoping can be completely determined by just reading the program.

Dynamic scoping can only be determined by running the program. You can't necessarily determine it by reading the program. For example, in `MyClass` the order in which its statements are executed depends on the result of `Math.random()`. Suppose that when `random()` is executed it

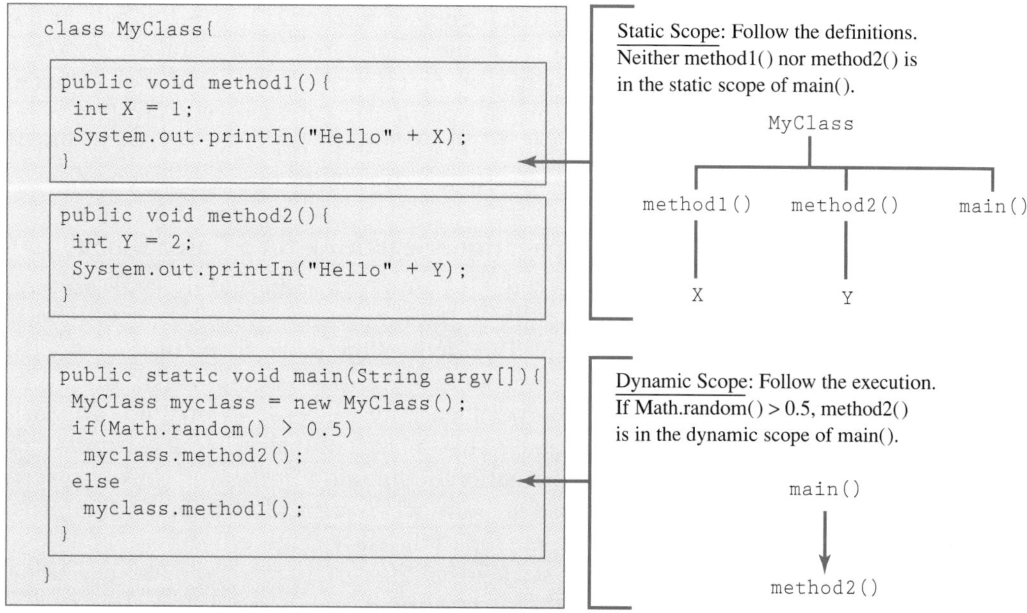

Figure 11–7 Dynamic versus static scoping. Static scoping refers to how the program is written. Look at its definitions. Dynamic scope refers to how the program executes. Look at what it actually does.

returns the value 0.99. In that case, `main()` will call `method2()`, which will call `System.out.println()`, which will print "Hello2." In that case the statement `System.out.println(''Hello'' + Y)` has the following dynamic scope:

```
main()
    method2()
        System.out.println("Hello" + Y);
```

Figure 11–8 An example of dynamic versus static scoping.

```
public class MyClass {
    public void method1() {
        int X = 1;
        System.out.println("Hello" + X);
    }
    public void method2() {
        int Y = 2;
        System.out.println("Hello" + Y);
    }
    public static void main( String argv[] ) {
        MyClass myclass = new MyClass();
        if (Math.random() > 0.5)
            myclass.method2();
        else
            myclass.method1();
    }
} // MyClass
```

It occurs within the (dynamic) scope of `method2()`, which is within the (dynamic) scope of `main()`. On the other hand, if the result of `random()` had been 0.10, that statement wouldn't have been executed at all. Thus to determine the dynamic scope of a particular statement, you must trace the program's execution. In fact, this is what the `printStackTrace()` method does. It prints a trace of a statement's dynamic scope.

11.2.6 Exception Propagation: Searching for a Catch Block

The method call stack

When an exception is thrown, Java uses both static and dynamic scoping to find a catch clause to handle it. Java knows how the program is defined — after all it compiled it. This defines the static scope of its methods. Java also keeps track of every method call the program makes during its execution. It uses a method call stack for this task. A **method call stack** is a data structure that behaves like a stack of dishes in the cafeteria. For each method call, a representation of the call, a *method call block*, is placed on top of the stack (like a dish), and when particular method call returns, its block is removed from the top of the stack (Figure 11–9).

Method stack trace

The nice thing about a stack is that the current method that is executing is always represented by the top block on the method call stack. If an exception happens during that method call, you can trace backwards through the method calls, if necessary, to find an exception handler for that exception. In Figure 11–9, you can visualize this back trace as a matter of reversing the direction of the curved arrows.

In order to find a matching catch block for an exception, Java uses its knowledge of the program's static and dynamic scope. The basic idea is

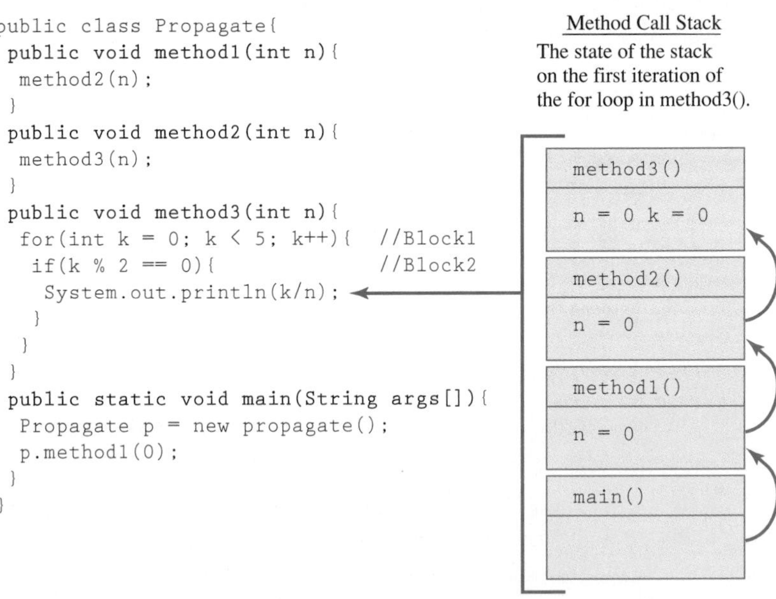
public class Propagate{
public void method1(int n){
method2(n);
}
public void method2(int n){
method3(n);
}
public void method3(int n){
for(int k = 0; k < 5; k++){ //Block1
if(k % 2 == 0){ //Block2
System.out.println(k/n);
}
}
}
public static void main(String args[]){
Propagate p = new propagate();
p.method1(0);
}
}
Method Call Stack
The state of the stack on the first iteration of the for loop in method3().
method3()
n = 0 k = 0
method2()
n = 0
method1()
n = 0
main()

Figure 11–9 The method call stack for the `Propagate` program. The curved arrows give a trace of the method calls leading to the program's present state.

that Java traces backwards through the program until it finds an appropriate catch clause. The trace begins within the block that threw the exception. Of course, one block can be nested (statically) within another block. If the exception is not caught by the block in which it is thrown, Java searches the enclosing block. This is static scoping. If it is not caught within the enclosing block, Java searches the next higher enclosing block, and so on. This is still static scoping.

If the exception is not caught at all within the method in which it was thrown, Java uses the method call stack (Figure 11–9) to search backwards through the method calls that were made leading up to the exception. This is dynamic scoping. In the last `intAverage()` example, Java would search backwards to the `main()` method, which is where `intAverage()` was called, and it would find the `catch` clause there for handling `ArithmeticExceptions`. It would therefore execute that clause.

SELF-STUDY EXERCISES

EXERCISE 11.1 In the following program, suppose that the first time `random()` is called it returns 0.98, and the second time it is called it returns 0.44. What output would be printed by the program?

```
class MyClass2 {
    public void method1(double X) {
        if (X > 0.95)
            throw new ArithmeticException(X + " is out of range");
        System.out.println("Hello " + X);
    }
    public void method2(double Y) {
        if (Y > 0.5)
             throw new ArithmeticException(Y + " is out of range");
        System.out.println("Hello " + Y);
    }
    public static void main(String argv[]) {
        MyClass2 myclass = new MyClass2();
        try {
            myclass.method1( Math.random() );
            myclass.method2( Math.random() );
        } catch (ArithmeticException e) {
            System.out.println(e.getMessage());
        }
    } // main()
} // MyClass2
```

EXERCISE 11.2 For the values returned by `random()` in the previous exercise, show what would be output if `printStackTrace()` were called in addition to printing an error message.

EXERCISE 11.3 In the `MyClass2` program, suppose that the first time `random()` is called it returns 0.44, and the second time it is called it returns 0.98. What output would be printed by the program?

EXERCISE 11.4 For the values returned by `random()` in the previous exercise, show what would be output if `printStackTrace()` were called instead of printing an error message.

Figure 11–10 In this program an exception will be thrown because of the divide-by-zero error in `method3()`. See Figure 11–9 to trace how this exception propagates through the program.

```
public class Propagate {
    public void method1(int n) {
        method2(n);
    }
    public void method2(int n) {
        method3(n);
    }
    public void method3(int n) {
        for (int k = 0; k < 5; k++) {      // Block1
            if (k % 2 == 0) {              // Block2
                System.out.println( k / n );
            }
        }
    }
    public static void main(String args[]) {
        Propagate p = new Propagate();
        p.method1(0);
    }
} // Propagate
```

11.2.7 A Propagation Example

To illustrate how Java searches for a matching `catch` block, let's reconsider the `Propagate` program that was pictured in Figure 11–9. This program (Figure 11–10) will throw an `ArithmeticException` because of the divide-by-zero error in `method3()`.

Let's trace the program's execution. First, `method1()` is called with an argument of 0, which is passed to `method2()` and then to `method3()`, where it is used as the denominator in an integer division. Because you cannot divide by zero, this will cause an `ArithmeticException` to be thrown. Note that the statement which causes the exception is embedded within Block2, which is contained by Block1, which is contained within `method3()`.

Static scope

To process this exception, Java will search upward through Block2 and Block1. In this phase, it is searching through the program's static scope hierarchy (Figure 11–11). Note that `method3()` contains the for statement within its scope, and the for statement contains the if statement within its scope.

Dynamic scope

Because Java does not find a matching catch clause by searching (statically) within `method3()`, it will then search backward (dynamically) through the history of the method calls that led to `method3()` (Figure 11–9). Thus it will search in `method2()` and then in `method1()` before ending up in `main()`, at which point it will generate the following output and exit the program:

```
java.lang.ArithmeticException: divide by zero
    at Propagate.method3(Propagate.java:19)
    at Propagate.method2(Propagate.java:13)
    at Propagate.method1(Propagate.java:9)
    at Propagate.main(Propagate.java:26)
    at com.mw.Exec.run(JavaAppRunner.java:47)
```

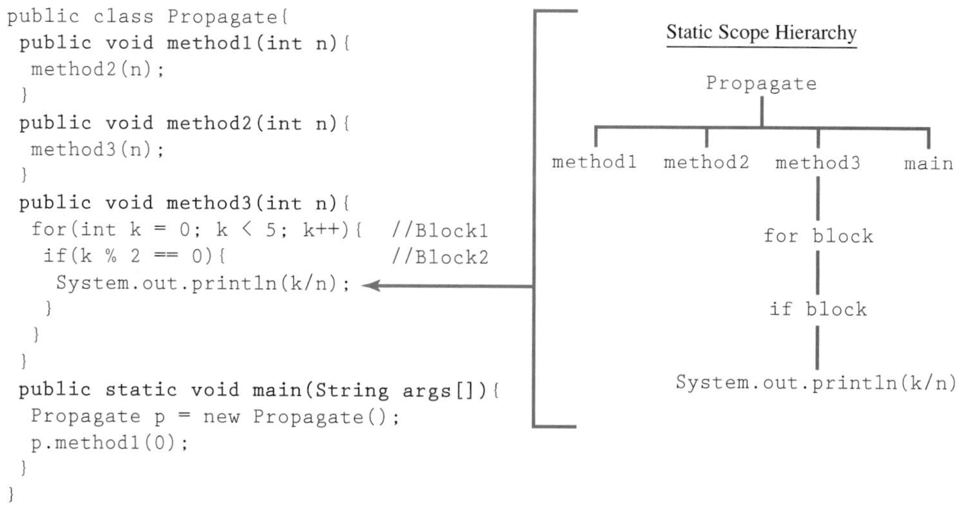
public class Propagate{
public void method1(int n){
method2(n);
}
public void method2(int n){
method3(n);
}
public void method3(int n){
for(int k = 0; k < 5; k++){ //Block1
if(k % 2 == 0){ //Block2
System.out.println(k/n);
}
}
}
public static void main(String args[]){
Propagate p = new Propagate();
p.method1(0);
}
}
Static Scope Hierarchy
Propagate
method1
method2
method3
main
for block
if block
System.out.println(k/n)

Figure 11–11 A program's static scoping relationships can be represented by a hierarchy chart. To find a catch clause for the exception raised by the `println()` statement, Java would search upwards on the `method3()` branch of the hierarchy.

Method stack trace

The message identifies the exception and then displays the history of the method calls that led to the exception, in reverse order. This is known as the **method stack trace**, which is exactly what we did in the divide-by-zero example when we called the `printStackTrace()` method. The fact that it provides the line numbers of the method calls makes it easy to find the code which caused the exception to be thrown.

SELF-STUDY EXERCISES

EXERCISE 11.5 Find the divide-by-zero error in the following program and then show what stack trace would be printed by the program.

```
public class BadDivide {
    public void method1 (int n) {
        method2(100, n);
    }

    public void method2 (int n, int d) {
         System.out.println(n / d);
    }

    public static void main(String args[]) {
        BadDivide bd = new BadDivide();
        for (int k = 0; k < 5; k++)
            bd.method1(k);
    }
}
```

EXERCISE 11.6 Modify `method2()` so that it handles the divide-by-zero exception itself, instead of letting Java handle it. Have it print an error message and a stack trace.

EXERCISE 11.7 Modify `CalcAverage` (Figure 11–6) so that it guards against the `NullPointerException` if the array parameter in `intAverage()` happens to be `null`. It is a good idea to use exceptions in this way to check that parameters satisfy their pre-conditions.

11.2.8 Java's Default Exception Handling

Java's default

In general, then, when an exception is thrown, it propagates upward through the program's *block hierarchy* and backward through its *method-call history*, until it is handled by some `catch` clause. But what happens if no matching `catch` clause is found? In that case Java will handle the exception itself by printing an error message and a trace of the method calls that led to the exception. If the program is a command-line program — that is, one that lacks a GUI interface — Java will also terminate the program.

In `CalcAverage`, we can create this situation by simply omitting the `try/catch` statement from `main()` altogether:

```
public static void main(String args[]) {
    int numbers[] = {10, 20, 30, 30, 20, 10};
    CalcAverage ca = new CalcAverage();
    System.out.println( "AVG + " + ca.intAverage(numbers, 0));
} // main()
```

In this case, when the exception is thrown in `intAverage()`, Java will handle the exception itself, producing the following output:

```
java.lang.ArithmeticException: ERROR: can't average 0 elements
    at CalcAverage.intAverage(CalcAverage.java:9)
    at CalcAverage.main(CalcAverage.java:20)
    at com.mw.Exec.run(JavaAppRunner.java:47)
```

Java's built-in handling of the exception produces pretty much the same output as our code. In such cases it may be better simply to let Java handle the exception.

EFFECTIVE DESIGN: Using an Exception. Unless your program's handling of an exception is significantly different from Java's default handling of it, the program should just rely on the default.

11.2.9 Java's Default Exception Throwing

Java's creators incorporated exception handling throughout its code. For the divide-by-zero error, Java will handle the whole situation for us, including the detection, throwing, and catching of the error.

Java's default

For example, if we remove all exception handling code from the `CalcAverage` program (Figure 11–12), Java will generate the following message if *N* happens to be 0 when `intAverage()` is called:

Figure 11–12 This version of CalcAverage leaves the exception handling completely up to Java.

```
public class CalcAverage {

    public int intAverage(int arr[], int N) {
        int avg = 0;
        for (int k = 0; k < N; k++)
            avg += arr[k];
        avg = avg / N;
        return avg;
    } // intAverage()

    public static void main(String args[]) {
        int numbers[] = {10, 20, 30, 30, 20, 10};
        CalcAverage ca = new CalcAverage();
        System.out.println( "AVG + " + ca.intAverage(numbers, 0));
    } // main()
} // CalcAverage
```

```
java.lang.ArithmeticException: divide by zero
    at CalcAverage.intAverage(CalcAverage.java:12)
    at CalcAverage.main(CalcAverage.java:20)
    at com.mw.Exec.run(JavaAppRunner.java:47)
```

What this tells us is that within the Java Virtual Machine, the routine that performs integer division throws an `ArithmeticException` when the denominator is 0. Java's designers coded the integer division operation so that it checks for divide-by-zero. This exception is caught and handled by the JVM itself.

SELF-STUDY EXERCISES

EXERCISE 11.8 What would be printed by the following code segment if `someValue` equals 1000?

```
int M = someValue;
try {
    System.out.println("Entering try block");
    if (M > 100)
        throw new Exception(M + " is too large");
    System.out.println("Exiting try block");
} catch (Exception e) {
    System.out.println("ERROR: " + e.getMessage());
}
```

EXERCISE 11.9 What would be printed by the code segment in the preceding question if `someValue` equals 50?

EXERCISE 11.10 Write a `try/catch` block which throws an `Exception` if the value of variable `X` is less than zero. The exception should be an instance of `Exception` and when it is caught, the message returned by `getMessage()` should be "ERROR: Negative value in X coordinate."

11.3 Java's Exception Hierarchy

Exception hierarchy

Figure 11–5 provides a partial summary of Java's exception hierarchy. The root class of the hierarchy, `java.lang.Exception`, is located in the `java.lang` package, but not all `Exception` subclasses are contained in this package. Some of the various `IOException` classes are contained in the `java.io` package, while others are contained in the `java.net` package. In general, exception classes are placed in the package that contains the methods that throw those exceptions.

Each of the classes in Figure 11–5 identifies a particular type of exception, and each is a subclass of the `Exception` class, which serves as the root of the hierarchy. Obviously a subclass defines a more specific exception than its superclass. Thus both `ArrayIndexOutOfBoundsException` and `StringIndexOutOfBoundsException` are more specific than `IndexOutOfBoundsException`. Table 11–1 gives a brief summary of some of the most important exceptions.

You've undoubtedly encountered some of the exceptions listed in Table 11–1, because they are raised by methods we have used repeatedly in programming examples. Table 11–2 summarizes the exceptions raised by some of the methods we've used most frequently.

SELF-STUDY EXERCISES

EXERCISE 11.11 Suppose a program throws a `ArrayIndexOutOfBoundsException`. Using the exception hierarchy in Figure 11–5, determine which of the following catch clauses could handle that exception.

a. `catch (RunTimeException e)`
b. `catch (StringIndexOutOfBoundsException e)`
c. `catch (IndexOutOfBoundsException e)`
d. `catch (Exception e)`
e. `catch (ArrayStoreException e)`

Table 11.1. Some of Java's important exceptions

Class	**Description**
`ArithmeticException`	Division by zero or some other kind of arithmetic problem
`ArrayIndexOutOfBoundsException`	An array index is less than zero or greater than or equal to the array's length
`FileNotFoundException`	Reference to a file that cannot be found
`IllegalArgumentException`	Calling a method with an improper argument
`IndexOutOfBoundsException`	An array or string index is out of bounds
`NullPointerException`	Reference to an object which has not been instantiated
`NumberFormatException`	Use of an illegal number format, such as when calling a method
`StringIndexOutOfBoundsException`	A `String` index is less than zero or greater than or equal to the `String`'s length

Table 11.2. Some of Java's important exceptions by method

Class	Method	Exception Raised	Description
Double	valueOf(String)	NumberFormatException	The String is not a double
Integer	parseInt(String)	NumberFormatException	The String is not a int
String	String(String)	NullPointerException	The String is null
	indexOf(String)	NullPointerException	The String is null
	lastIndexOf(String)	NullPointerException	The String is null
	charAt(int)	StringIndexOutOfBoundsException	The int is not a valid index
	substring(int)	StringIndexOutOfBoundsException	The int is not a valid index
	substring(int,int)	StringIndexOutOfBoundsException	An int is not a valid index

EXERCISE 11.12 What type of exception would be thrown for the following statements?

a. `Integer.parseInt("26.2");`
b. `String s; s.indexOf('a');`
c. `String s = "hello"; s.charAt(5);`

11.3.1 Checked and Unchecked Exceptions

Checked exceptions

Java's exception hierarchy is divided into two types of exceptions. A **checked exception** is one that *must* either be caught within the method where it is thrown or at least declared within that method. Checked exceptions are those that can be analyzed by the compiler. When the compiler encounters a statement that may throw a checked exception, it checks to see whether its containing method either handles or declares the exception. Compile-time checking for these exceptions is designed to reduce the number of exceptions that are not properly handled within a program.

The IOException, which we encountered in Chapter 5, is a checked exception. If you look back at Figure 5–4, you will see that its main() method called the BufferedInput (readLine()) method, which is a method that can throw an IOException:

```
public static void main(String argv[]) throws IOException {

    BufferedReader input = new BufferedReader
            (new InputStreamReader(System.in));

    String inputString = input.readLine();    // May throw IOException
}
```

Because main() does not catch the IOException, it must declare it, by adding a throws IOException clause to main()'s header. The compiler knows that readLine() is a method that can throw an IOException. It would generate a syntax error if the throws clause were omitted.

Throwing an exception

In general, any method that contains a statement that may throw an uncaught exception, must declare the exception. Moreover, if a dynamically enclosing method does not catch a checked exception, it too must declare it in a `throws` clause. For example, consider the following program, which contains an uncaught `IOException`:

```
import java.io.*;

public class Example {
    BufferedReader input = new BufferedReader
            (new InputStreamReader(System.in));

    public void doRead() throws IOException {
        String inputString = input.readLine();    // May throw IOException
    }

    public static void main(String argv[]) throws IOException {
        Example ex = new Example();
        ex.doRead();
    }
}
```

The `IOException` might be thrown by the `readLine()` in the `doRead()` method. Because neither `doRead()` nor `main()` catches the exception, both methods need a `throws IOException` clause. The uncaught exception propagates from `doRead()` to `main()` and is caught in neither place.

Unchecked Exceptions

An **unchecked exception** is any exception belonging to a subclass of `RuntimeException`. Unchecked exceptions are not checked by the compiler. The possibility that some statement or expression will lead to a `ArithmeticException` or `NullPointerException` is extremely difficult to detect at compile time. The designers of Java decided that forcing programmers to declare such exceptions would not significantly improve the correctness of Java programs.

Runtime (unchecked) exceptions

Therefore, unchecked exceptions do not have to be handled within a program. And, they do not have to be mentioned in a `throws` clause if they are not caught within a method. For these exceptions, you can either choose to handle them within your program, or not. If they are left uncaught, they will be handled by Java's default exception handlers. As we'll see in Section 11.4, in many cases this may be the best course of action.

JAVA LANGUAGE RULE **Unchecked versus Checked Exceptions.** An unchecked exception — one belonging to some subclass of `RunTimeException` — does not have to be caught within your program. A checked exception must be either caught within the method in which it is thrown or the method must declare that it throws the exception.

11.3.2 The `Exception` class

The `java.lang.Exception` class itself, which serves as the root of the hierarchy, is very simple, consisting of just two constructor methods:

```
public class Exception extends Throwable {
    public Exception();
    public Exception(String message);
}
```

The `Throwable` class, from which `Exception` is inherited, is the root class of Java's exception and error hierarchy. This is where the `getMessage()` and `printStackTrace()` methods are defined.

Arranging `catch` *clauses*

As we have seen, a thrown exception will be caught by the first `catch` clause it matches. Therefore, `catch` clauses should be arranged in order from most specific to most general. If a more general catch clause precedes a more specific one, it will prevent the more specific one from executing. In effect, the more specific clause will be hidden by the more general one. You might as well just not have the more specific clause at all.

To illustrate how to arrange catch clauses, suppose an `ArithmeticException` is thrown in the following `try/catch` statement:

```
try {
    // Suppose an ArithmeticException is thrown here
} catch (ArithmeticException e) {
    System.out.println("ERROR: " + e.getMessage() );
    e.printStackTrace();
    System.exit(1);
} catch (Exception e) {
    System.out.println("ERROR: " + e.getMessage() );
}
```

Which handler to use?

In this case the exception would be handled by the more specific `ArithmeticException` block. On the other hand, if some other kind of exception is raised, it will be caught by the second catch clause. The `Exception` class will match any exception that is thrown. Therefore, it should always occur last in a sequence of `catch` clauses.

PROGRAMMING TIP: Arranging Catch Clauses. Catch clauses should be arranged from most specific to most general. The `Exception` clause should always be the last in the sequence.

SELF-STUDY EXERCISES

EXERCISE 11.13 Which of the following are examples of *unchecked* exceptions?

a. IOException
b. IndexOutOfBoundsException
c. NullPointerException
d. ClassNotFoundException
e. NumberFormatException

11.4 Error Handling and Robust Program Design

Let Java do it?

An important element of program design is to develop appropriate ways of handling erroneous and exceptional conditions. As we have seen, the Java interpreter will catch any exceptions that are not caught by the program itself. For your own (private) programs, the best design may simply be to use Java's default exception handling. The program will terminate when an exception is thrown, and then you can debug the error and recompile the program.

On the other hand, this strategy would be inappropriate for commercial software, which cannot be fixed by its users. A well-designed commercial program should contain exception handlers for those truly exceptional conditions that may arise.

What action should we take?

In general there are three ways to handle an exceptional condition that isn't already handled by Java (Table 11–3). If the exceptional condition cannot be fixed, the program should be terminated, with an appropriate error message. Second, if the exceptional condition can be fixed without invalidating the program, then it should be remedied and the program's normal execution should be resumed. Third, if the exception cannot be fixed, but the program cannot be terminated, the exceptional condition should be reported or logged in some way, and the program should be resumed.

EFFECTIVE DESIGN: Handling Exceptions. There are three general ways to handle exceptions: (1) Report the exception and terminate the program; (2) fix the exceptional condition and resume normal execution; and (3) report the exception to a log and resume execution.

11.4.1 Print a Message and Terminate

Program development

Our divide-by-zero example is a clear case where the exception is best handled by terminating the program. In fact this particular error is best left to Java's default exception handling. There is simply no way to satisfy the postcondition of the `intAverage()` method when the array contains 0 elements. This type of error often calls attention to a design flaw in the program's logic that should be caught during program development. The raising of the exception, helps identify the design flaw.

Table 11.3. Exception handling strategies

Kind of Exception	Kind of Program	Action to be Taken
Caught by Java		Let Java handle it
Fixable condition		Fix the error and resume execution
Unfixable condition	Stoppable	Report the error and terminate the program
Unfixable condition	Not stoppable	Report the error and resume processing

EFFECTIVE DESIGN: Exceptions and Program Development. Java's built-in exception handling helps identify design flaws during program development. Your own use of exceptions should follow this approach.

Similar problems can (and often do) arise in connection with errors that are not caught by Java. For example, suppose your program receives an erroneous input value, whose use would invalidate the calculation it is making. This won't be caught by Java. But it should be caught by your program, and an appropriate alternative here is to report the error and terminate the program. Fixing this type of error may involve adding routines to validate the input data before they are used in the calculation.

Don't spread bad data!

In short, rather than allowing an erroneous result to propagate throughout the program, it is best to terminate the program.

EFFECTIVE DESIGN: Report and Terminate. If an exceptional condition is serious enough to affect the correctness or integrity of the program, then unless the error can be fixed or unless the program cannot reasonably be terminated, it is better to report the error and terminate the program rather than allowing the program to continue running with an erroneous value.

11.4.2 Log the Error and Resume

Of course, the advice to stop the program assumes that the program can *be* terminated reasonably. Some programs — such as programs that monitor the space shuttle or programs that control a Nuclear Magnetic Resonance (NMR) machine — cannot (and should not) be terminated because of such an error.

Such *failsafe* programs are designed to run without termination. For these programs, the exception should be reported in whatever manner is most appropriate, but the program should continue running. If the exceptional condition invalidates the program's computations, then the exception handler should make it clear that the results are tainted.

Failsafe programs

Other programs — such as programs that analyze a large transaction database — should be designed to continue processing after catching such errors. For example, suppose the program is one that a large airline runs, once a day, to analyze the ticketing transactions that took place. This kind of program might use exceptions to identify erroneous transactions, or transactions that involve invalid data of some sort. Clearly, there's no question here of fixing the error. And because there are bound to be many errors of this kind in the database, it is not reasonable to stop the program. This kind of program shouldn't stop until it has finished processing all of the exceptions. So an appropriate action for this kind of program is to log the exceptions into some kind of file and continue processing the transactions.

Programs that can't be stopped

Suppose a divide-by-zero error happened in one of these programs. In that case you would override Java's default exception handling to ensure that the program is *not* terminated. More generally, it's important that these types of programs be designed to catch and report such exceptions. This type of exception handling should be built right into the program's design.

EFFECTIVE DESIGN: Report and Resume. If an unfixable exception arises in a program that cannot be terminated reasonably, the exception should be reported and the program should continue executing.

11.4.3 Fix the Error and Resume

Problem statement

As an example of a problem that can be fixed, consider the task of inputting an integer into a text field. As you have probably experienced, if the program is expecting an integer and you attempt to input something beside an integer, this will generate a `NumberFormatException` and the program will terminate. For example, if you attempt to input "$55" when prompted to input an integer dollar amount, this will generate an exception when the `Integer.parseInt()` method is invoked. The input string cannot be parsed into a valid `int`. However, this is the kind of error that can be fixed.

Problem decomposition

Let's design a special `IntField` that functions like a normal text field but accepts only integers. If the user enters a value that generates a `NumberFormatException`, an error message should be printed and the user should be invited to try again. We want this special field to be a subclass of `JTextField` and to inherit the basic `JTextField` functionality. It should have the same kind of constructors that a normal `JTextField` has. This suggests the definition shown in Figure 11–13.

What constructors do we need?

Note that the constructor methods use `super` to call the `JTextField` constructor. For now, these two constructors should suffice. However, below we will introduce a third constructor that allows us to associate a bound with the `IntField`.

What methods do we need?

Our `IntField` class needs a method that can return its contents. This method should work like `JTextField.getText()`, but it should return a valid integer. The `getInt()` method takes no parameters and will return an `int`, assuming that a valid integer is typed into the `IntField`. If the users types "55," a `NumberFormatException` will be thrown by the `Integer.parseInt()` method. Note that `getInt()` declares that it throws this exception. This is not necessary, but it makes the code clearer.

Where and how should this exception be handled? The exception cannot easily be handled within the `getInt()` method. This method has to return an integer value. If the user types in a noninteger, there's no way to return a valid value. Therefore it's better to just throw the exception to the calling method, where it can be handled more easily.

Figure 11–13 `IntField.getInt()` guards against `NumberFormatExceptions`.

```
import javax.swing.*;

public class IntField extends JTextField {

    public IntField () {
        super();
    }
    public IntField (int size) {
        super(size);
    }

    public int getInt() throws NumberFormatException {
        return Integer.parseInt(getText());
    } // getInt()

} // IntField
```

In a GUI application or applet, the calling method is likely to be an `actionPerformed()` method, such as the following:

```
public void actionPerformed(ActionEvent e) {
    try {
        userInt = intField.getInt();
        message = "You input " + userInt + " Thank you.";
    } catch (NumberFormatException ex) {
        JOptionPane.showMessageDialog(this,
            "The input must be an integer.  Please reenter.");
    } finally {
        repaint();
    }
} // actionPerformed()
```

The call to `getInt()` is embedded in a `try/catch` block. If the user inputs a valid integer, the program will report a message that displays the value. A more real-world example would do something more interesting with the value. On the other hand, if the user types an erroneous value, the program will pop up the dialog box shown in Figure 11–14. (See the "From the Library" section of this chapter for more on dialog boxes.) When the user clicks the "OK" button, the program will resume normal execution, so when an exception is raised, the input value is not used, and no harm is done by an erroneous value. The user can try again to input a valid integer. Note that the finally clause repaints the GUI. In this case repainting would display the appropriate message on the applet or application.

This is an example of defensive design. We anticipate a possible input error and take steps to insure that a bad value is not propagated throughout the program.

Defensive design: Anticipating an exception

EFFECTIVE DESIGN: Defensive Design. Well-designed code should anticipate potential problems, especially potential input problems. Effective use of exceptions can help with this task.

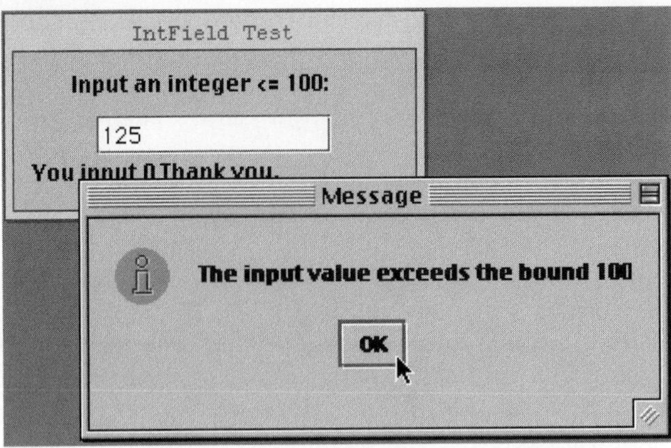

Figure 11–14 This exception handler opens a dialog box to display an error message.

Admittedly, the sense in which the error here is "fixed" is simply that the user's original input is ignored and reentered. This is a legitimate and simple course of action for this particular situation. It is far preferable to not handling the exception. If the program does not handle this exeption itself, Java will catch it and will print a stack trace and terminate the program. That would not be a very user-friendly interface!

Anticipating exceptions

Clearly this is the type of exceptional condition that should be anticipated during program design. If this happens to be a program designed exclusively for your own use, then clearly this type of exception handling may be unnecessary. But if the program is meant to be used by others, it is important that the program be able to handle user input without crashing.

EFFECTIVE DESIGN: Fixing an Exception. If a method can handle an exception effectively, it should handle it locally. This is both clearer and more efficient.

EFFECTIVE DESIGN: Library Exception Handling. Many of Java's library classes do not handle their own exceptions. The thinking behind this design is that the user of the class is in a better position to handle the exception in a way that's appropriate to the application.

11.4.4 To Fix or Not to Fix

Let's now consider a problem where it is less clear whether an exception can be successfully fixed "on the fly." Suppose you have a program that contains an array of `Strings`, which is initially created with just two elements.

```
String list[] = new String[2];
```

If an attempt is made to add more than two elements to the array, an `ArrayIndexOutOfBoundsException` will be raised. This exception can be handled by extending the size of the array and inserting the element. Then the program's normal execution can be resumed.

Problem statement

Let's design a method that will insert a string into the array. Suppose that this is intended to be a `private` method that will only be used within the program. Also, let's suppose that the program maintains a variable, `count`, that keeps track of how many values have been stored in the array. Therefore, it will not be necessary to pass the array as a parameter. So, this will be a `void` method with one parameter, the `String` to be inserted:

```
private void insertString(String str) {
    list[count] = str;    // Might throw ArrayIndexOutOfBoundsException
    ++count;
}
```

The comment notes where an exception might be thrown.

Algorithm design

Can we handle this exception? When this exception is raised, we could create a new array with one more element than the current array. We could copy the old array into the new array, and then insert the `String` in the new location. Finally, we could set the variable `list`, the array reference, so that it points to the new array. Thus we could use the following `try/catch` block to handle this exception:

```
private void insertString(String str) {
    try {
        list[count] = str;
    } catch (ArrayIndexOutOfBoundsException e) {
        String newList[] = new String[ list.length + 1 ];// Create a new array
        for (int k = 0; k < list.length ; k++)          // Copy old to new
            newList[k] = list[k];
            newList[count] = str;                        // Insert item into new
            list = newList;                             // Make old point to new
    } finally {                                // Since the exception is now fixed
        count++;                               // Increase the count
    }
} // insertString()
```

The effect of the `catch` clause is to create a new array, still referred to as `list`, but containing one more element than the original array.

Note the use of the `finally` clause here. For this problem it's important that we increment `count` in the `finally` clause. This is the only way to guarantee that `count` is incremented exactly once whenever an element is assigned to the array.

The `FixArrayBound` class in Figure 11–15 provides a simple GUI interface that enables you to test the `insertString()` method. This program has a standard Swing interface. A `JFrame` is used as the top-level window. The program's components are contained within a `JPanel` that's added to the `JFrame` in the `main()` method.

Figure 11–15 FixArrayBound increases the size of the array when a ArrayIndexOutOfBoundsException is raised.

```
import java.awt.*;
import java.awt.event.*;
import javax.swing.*;

public class FixArrayBound extends JPanel implements ActionListener  {
    public static final int WIDTH = 350, HEIGHT = 100;

    private JTextField inField = new JTextField(10);
    private JLabel prompt = new JLabel("Input a word and type <ENTER>: ");
    private String list[] = new String[2];      // Initially list has 2 elements
    private int count = 0;

    public  FixArrayBound() {
        inField.addActionListener(this);
        add(prompt);
        add(inField);
        setSize(WIDTH, HEIGHT);
    } // FixArrayBound()

    public void paintComponent(Graphics g) {
        g.setColor(getBackground());                // Clear the background
        g.fillRect(0, 0, WIDTH, HEIGHT);
        g.setColor(getForeground());
        String tempS = "";
        for (int k = 0; k < list.length; k++)
            tempS = tempS +  list[k] + " ";
        g.drawString(tempS, 10, 50);
    } // paintComponent

    private void insertString(String str) {
        try {
            list[count] = str;
        } catch (ArrayIndexOutOfBoundsException e) {
            String newList[] = new String[ list.length + 1 ];// Create a new array
            for (int k = 0; k < list.length ; k++)          // Copy old to new
                newList[k] = list[k];
                newList[count] = str;                           // Insert item into new
                list = newList;                                 // Make old point to new
        } finally {                                 // Since the exception is now fixed
            count++;                                // Increase the count
        }
    } // insertString()

    public void actionPerformed(ActionEvent evt) {
        insertString(inField.getText());
        inField.setText("");
        repaint();
    } // actionPerformed()

    public static void main( String args[] ) {
        JFrame f = new JFrame("Array Fixer");
        FixArrayBound panel = new FixArrayBound();
        f.getContentPane().add(panel);
        f.setSize(panel.WIDTH, panel.HEIGHT);
        f.setVisible(true);
        f.addWindowListener(new WindowAdapter() {       // Quit the application
            public void windowClosing(WindowEvent e) {
                System.exit(0);
            }
        });
    } // main()
} // FixArrayBound
```

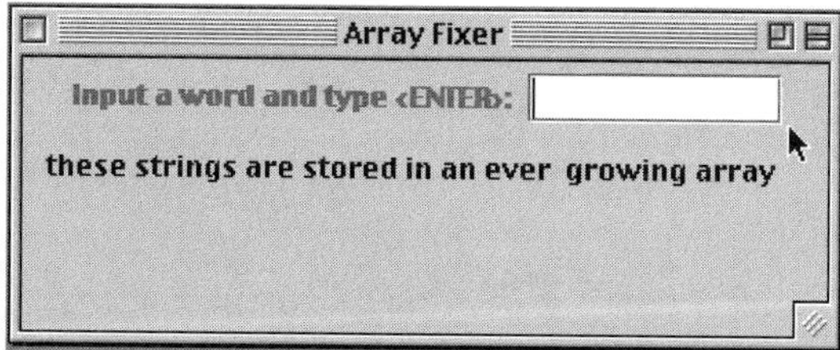

Figure 11–16 The strings displayed are stored in an array that is extended each time a new string is entered.

Each time the user types a string into the text field, the `actionPerformed()` method calls the `insertString()` method to add the string to the array. On each user action, the `JPanel` is repainted. The `paintComponent()` method simply clears the panel, and then displays the array's elements (Figure 11–16).

DEBUGGING TIP: Clearing the JPanel. Swing components, such as `JPanel`, do not automatically clear their backgrounds, so this must be done explicitly in the `paintComponent()` method.

This example illustrates how an exception *can* be handled successfully and the program's normal flow of control resumed. However, the question is whether such an exception *should* be handled this way.

Poor program design

Unfortunately, this is not a well-designed program. The array's initial size is way too small for the program's intended use. Therefore, the fact that these exceptions arise at all is the result of poor design. In general, exceptions should *not* be used as a remedy for poor design.

EFFECTIVE DESIGN: Truly Exceptional Conditions. A well-designed program should use exception handling to deal with truly exceptional conditions, not to process conditions that arise under normal or expected circumstances.

Proper array usage

For a program that uses an array, the size of the array should be chosen so that it can store all the objects required by the program. If the program is some kind of failsafe program, which cannot afford to crash, then something like the above approach might be justified, provided this type of exception occurs very rarely. Even in that case it would be better to generate a message that alerts the program's user that this condition has occurred. The alert will indicate a need to modify the program's memory requirements and restart the program.

Choosing the correct data structure

If it is not known in advance how many objects will be stored in an array, a better design would be to make use of the `java.util.Vector` class (see From the Java Library in Chapter 8). Vectors are designed to grow as necessary as new objects are inserted. In some ways the exception handling code in our example mimics the behavior of a vector. However, the `Vector` class makes use of efficient algorithms for extending its size. By contrast, exception handling code is very inefficient. Because exceptions force the system into an abnormal mode of execution, it takes considerably longer to handle an exception than it would to use a `Vector` for this type of application. (See In the Laboratory in this chapter.)

EFFECTIVE DESIGN: Appropriate Data Structure. A major component of problem solving is choosing the best way to represent the data. A vector should be used as an array structure whenever the size of the array will grow and shrink dynamically during the program's execution.

SELF-STUDY EXERCISES

EXERCISE 11.14 For each of the following exceptions, determine whether it can be handled in such a way that the program can be resumed or whether the program should be terminated.

a. A computer game program detects a problem with one of its GUI elements and throws a `NullPointerException`.
b. A factory assembly line control program determines that an important control value has become negative and generates an `ArithmeticException`.
c. A company's Web-based order form detects that its user has entered an invalid `String` and throws a `SecurityException`.

11.5 Creating and Throwing Your Own Exceptions

Like other Java classes, the `Exception` class can be extended to handle cases that are not already covered by Java's built-in exceptions. Exceptions that you define will be handled the same way by the Java interpreter, but you will have to `throw` them yourself.

For example, let's define an exception that can be used for validating that an integer is less than or equal to a certain maximum value:

```
/**
 *  IntOutOfRangeException reports an exception when an
 *    integer exceeds its bound.
 */
public class IntOutOfRangeException extends Exception {

    public IntOutOfRangeException (int Bound) {
        super("The input value exceeds the bound " + Bound);
    }
}
```

The class extends Exception and consists entirely of a constructor method that merely calls the superclass constructor. The argument passed to the superclass constructor is the message that will be returned by getMessage() when an instance of this exception is created.

Inheriting functionality

Now let's consider an example where this new exception will be thrown. Suppose we wish to constrain the IntField class that we developed above (Figure 11–13) so that it will only accept numbers that are less than a certain bound. First, let's modify IntField so that its bound can be set when an instance is created.

Algorithm design

Thus, we want its bound to be an instance variable, with some initial value, and we want to provide a constructor that can be used to override the default. This leads to the following revision of IntField:

```
public class IntField extends JTextField {
    private int bound = Integer.MAX_VALUE;

    public IntField(int size, int max) {
        super(size);
        bound = max;
    }

   // The rest of the class is unchanged for now

} // IntField
```

Our new constructor has the signature, IntField(int,int), which doesn't duplicate any of JTextField's constructors. This is good. In extending a class, we want to be careful about the effect our definitions have on the original methods in the superclass. Superclass methods should be overridden by design, not by accident. If a method is redefined inadvertently, it may not function as expected by users of the subclass.

EFFECTIVE DESIGN: Extending a Class. When extending a class, care must taken to insure that the superclass's methods are not inadvertently overridden. A superclass method should only be overridden by design, not by accident.

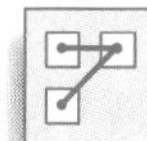

Note how we have handled the problem of setting the default value of the bound. Integer.MAX_VALUE is a class constant that sets the maximum value for the int type. It's an appropriate value to use, because any valid int that the user types, should be less than or equal to MAX_VALUE. Given these changes to IntField, let's now incorporate our new exception into its getInt() method (Figure 11–17).

This new version of getInt() throws an exception if the integer input by the user is greater than the IntField's bound. Here again, it is difficult to handle this exception appropriately in this method. The method would either have to return an erroneous value — because it must return something — or it must terminate. Neither is an acceptable alternative. It is far better to throw the exception to the calling method.

Figure 11–17 The revised IntField class containing the revised getInt() method.

```
import javax.swing.*;

public class IntField extends JTextField {
    private int bound = Integer.MAX_VALUE;

    public IntField (int size) {
        super(size);
    }

    public IntField(int size, int max) {
        super(size);
        bound = max;
    }

    public int getInt() throws NumberFormatException,
                               IntOutOfRangeException {
        int num = Integer.parseInt(getText());
        if (num > bound)
            throw new IntOutOfRangeException(bound);
        return num;
    } // getInt()

} // IntField
```

The IntFieldTester class (Figure 11–18) provides a simple GUI interface to test the IntField class. It prompts the user to type in an integer that is less than 100, and then it echoes the user's input. Note how the exception is handled in the actionPerformed() method. If an exception is thrown in IntField.getInt(), the actionPerformed() method pops up an error dialog. The erroneous input is not used. Instead the user is given another chance to enter a valid integer.

SELF-STUDY EXERCISES

EXERCISE 11.15 Define a new Exception named FieldIsEmptyException which is meant to be thrown if the user forgets to enter a value into a IntField.

EXERCISE 11.16 Modify the IntField.getInt() named so that it throws and catches the FieldIsEmptyException.

From the Java Library: JOptionPane

A **dialog box** is a window that can be opened by a program to communicate in some way with the user. Dialog boxes come in many varieties and have many uses in a GUI environment. You've undoubtedly encountered them when using your own computer.

For example, a *file dialog* is opened whenever you want to open or save a file. It provides an interface that lets you name the file and helps you search through the computer's directory structure to find a file.

Figure 11–18 An application that uses an `IntField` object to input integers.

```
import java.awt.*;
import java.awt.event.*;
import javax.swing.*;

public class IntFieldTester extends JPanel implements ActionListener  {
    public static final int WIDTH = 300, HEIGHT = 300;

    private JLabel prompt = new JLabel("Input an integer <= 100: ");
    private IntField intField = new IntField(12, 100);
    private int userInt;
    private String message = "Hello";

    public IntFieldTester() {
        add(prompt);
        intField.addActionListener(this);
        add(intField);
        setSize(WIDTH, HEIGHT);
    } // IntFieldTester()

    public void paintComponent( Graphics g ) {
        g.setColor(getBackground());             // Clear the panel
        g.fillRect(0, 0, WIDTH, HEIGHT);
        g.setColor(getForeground());
        g.drawString(message, 10, 70);
    } // paintComponent()

    public void actionPerformed(ActionEvent evt) {
        try {
            userInt = intField.getInt();
            message = "You input " + userInt + " Thank you.";
        } catch (NumberFormatException e) {
            JOptionPane.showMessageDialog(this,
               "The input must be an integer.  Please reenter.");
        } catch (IntOutOfRangeException e) {
            JOptionPane.showMessageDialog(this, e.getMessage());
        } finally {
            repaint();
        }
    } // actionPerformed()

    public static void main(String args[]) {
        JFrame f = new JFrame("IntField Tester");
        IntFieldTester panel = new IntFieldTester();
        f.getContentPane().add(panel);
        f.setSize(panel.WIDTH, panel.HEIGHT);
        f.setVisible(true);
        f.addWindowListener(new WindowAdapter() {      // Quit the application
            public void windowClosing(WindowEvent e) {
                System.exit(0);
            }
        });
    } // main()
} // IntFieldTester
```

A *warning dialog* or **error dialog** is opened whenever a program needs to notify or warn you that some kind of error occurred. It usually presents an error message and an "OK" button that you click to dismiss the dialog.

Dialogs are easy to create and use in Java. The Swing component set provides several different kinds of basic dialogs that can be incorporated into your program with one or two lines of code. For example, the IntFieldTester class makes use of a simple message dialog to report an input error to the user. This dialog was created by the following code segment in the program (see Figure 11–18):

```
catch (NumberFormatException e) {
    JOptionPane.showMessageDialog(this,
        "The input must be an integer.  Please reenter.");
}
```

This method call displays the window shown in Figure 11–14. It contains the error message and an "OK" button that is used to close the window. The showMessageDialog() method is a static method of the javax.swing.JOptionPane class. This class provides a collection of similar methods for creating and displaying basic dialog boxes.

A dialog differs from other kinds of top-level windows — such as JApplet and JFrame — in that it is associated with another window. The first parameter in this version of the showMessageDialog() method is a reference to the dialog's parent window. The second parameter is a String representing the message.

Modal dialogs

The basic message dialog used in this example is known as a **modal dialog**. This means that once it's been displayed, you can't do anything else until you click the "OK" button and dismiss the dialog. It's also possible to create **nonmodal** dialogs. These can stay around on the screen while you move on to other tasks.

Note that the dialog box also contains an *icon* that symbolizes the purpose of the message (Figure 11–14). The icon is representative of the dialog's message type. Among the basic types available in JOptionPane are the following:

```
JOptionPane.PLAIN_MESSAGE
JOptionPane.INFORMATIONAL_MESSAGE      // Default
JOptionPane.WARNING_MESSAGE
JOptionPane.QUESTION_MESSAGE
JOptionPane.ERROR_MESSAGE
```

To set the dialog to anything other than the default (informational) type, you can use the following version of showMessageDialog():

```
showMessageDialog(Component comp, Object message, String title, int msgType);
```

The first parameter is a reference to the parent window. The second is the message string. The third is a string used as the dialog window's title, and the fourth is one of the five dialog types. For example, we can change our dialog to an error dialog with the following statement:

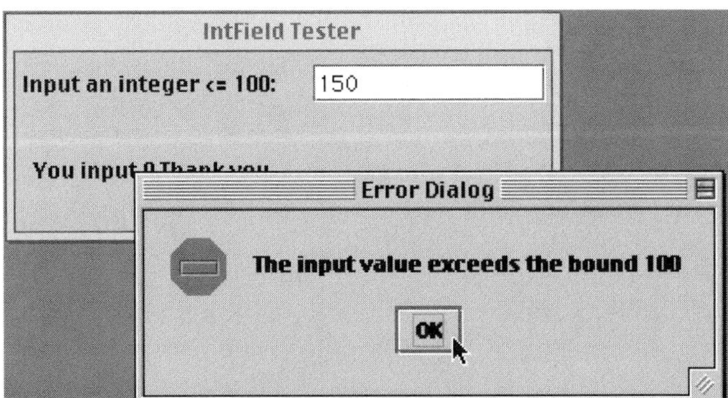

Figure 11–19 An error dialog.

```
catch (IntOutOfRangeException e) {
    JOptionPane.showMessageDialog(this,
            e.getMessage(),
            "Error dialog",
            JOptionPane.ERROR_MESSAGE);
}
```

This would produce the dialog shown in Figure 11–19.

The other kinds of basic dialogs provided by the `JOptionPane` class are listed in Table 11–4. All of the dialogs listed there can be created with a line or two of code. In addition to these, it's also possible to create sophisticated dialogs that can be as customized as any other GUI interface you can build in Java.

Basic Swing dialogs

Table 11.4. Basic dialogs provided by `JOptionPane`

Dialog	Description
Message Dialog	Presents a simple error or informational message
Confirm Dialog	Prompts the user to confirm a particular action
Option Dialog	Lets the user choose from a couple of options
Input Dialog	Prompts and inputs a string

IN THE LABORATORY: MEASURING EXCEPTION OVERHEAD

The purpose of this lab is to design an experiment to measure the amount of computational overhead required by Java's exception handling mechanism. The lesson of this experiment will be that exceptions should only be used to handle truly exceptional situations, not as a means of solving the problem at hand. The objectives of this lab are

The Y2K Exception?

By the time you read this, we'll either be looking back at the Year 2000 Problem (Y2K) as a technological tempest in a teapot, or we'll be suffering its consequences. Would we have had the Y2K problem, if Java were around 30 years ago?

That's an interesting question. Clearly Java's exception handling mechanism could be used to detect values such as "00" that could cause computational problems, but would merely detecting the problem have done any good? That's the real question.

The Y2K problem was caused by the way dates were represented in programs written in the 1960s and 1970s. Many of these programs were written in COBOL (Common Business Oriented Language). In COBOL a date would typically be represented in MM-DD-YY format, where each of M, D, and Y would be decimal digits in the range 0 to 9. The reason for using YY instead of YYYY was to save two digits worth of memory. When this formatting was first begun in the 1960s, the YYs were values like 69, and no one anticipated that the programs would still be around 30 years later, so saving two digits of memory seemed entirely justified.

It's easy to see why this representation would cause problems in the year 2000. If you were born in 1982, then right through 1999, your age could be computed as $99 - 82 = 17$. But in the year 2000 this formulation would yield $0 - 82 = -82$. You can imagine similar kinds of problems for other calculations.

Would Java exceptions help avoid this problem? Clearly we could throw a Java exception when the value in a YY field is 0:

```
if (YY == 0)
    throw new Year2000Exception(YY);
```

The problem, however, is not merely in detecting the error, but in fixing it. If this code were written in 1970, then a value of 0 in a YY field might have indicated an input or data error. In that case, throwing a Java exception would have been helpful. But in 2000, a 0 in a YY field would most likely indicate that the program itself was erroneous.

What kind of catch clause could you write to repair this kind of error? Unfortunately, there's little you can do besides reporting the problem and exiting the program. There are just too many ways a date could be used in a calculation to write catch clauses to handle them all. So, even if there were something like a Year2000Exception in COBOL, it's unlikely that it would have helped much. For the Y2K problem, there's no real alternative but to rewrite all the code segments that contain YY in a calculation!

As long as the code is rewritten we might as well use a Java `short` integer to represent the year value in a date. Then programmers won't have to worry about this problem again until the year 32,768!

- To implement `try/catch` statements.
- To develop and test appropriate design strategies for handling `Exceptions`.
- To demonstrate the inefficiency of using exception handling as a means of normal program control.

Introduction

Each time an exception is thrown, the Java Virtual Machine must suspend normal execution of the program and search for and execute an exception handler. All of this takes time. How much overhead does Java exception handling expend? That's the question you will be addressing in this lab.

Exception processing overhead

Suppose you are writing an application that must store a variable number of objects in memory. You don't know for certain how many objects will be stored. You want to test three different ways of solving this problem. One way will use an array of 0 (initial) elements and will grow the array each time a new element is to be inserted. This approach will use the algorithm designed in the `FixArrayBound` program to expand the array as needed. Therefore, this approach will generate one exception on each insertion.

The second way will utilize an array with *N* (initial) elements. No exceptions should be thrown for this approach, because the array is always the correct size.

The third approach will use a vector to store the objects. The `java.util.Vector` class is specifically designed for the problem of storing objects in an array that can expand in size as needed.

Problem Description

Write a Java application that will test the relative efficiency of the three approaches just described. The application should prompt the user to input the number, *N*, of objects to be stored in the array. It should then insert *N* objects into each of the three structures described — a 0-element array, an *N*-element array, and a `Vector` — and it should measure how long each approach takes.

Problem specification

Once you have correctly implemented and tested your application program, perform at least 10 trials, using different values for *N*. Obtain data for the following three situations:

1. Milliseconds required to insert *N* items into a vector.
2. Milliseconds required to insert *N* items into an array of *N* elements.
3. Milliseconds required to insert *N* items into an array of 0 elements.

You should observe a considerable difference between these three times. Note that the third case represents the situation in which *N* exceptions will be generated, one for each insertion.

Create a table and a graph of your results, and try to calculate the amount of *overhead* time, in milliseconds, that the system uses to process a single exception in this case. The overhead is the amount of time the system requires in order to process the exception. By comparing cases two and three, you should be able to get a pretty good estimate for this value.

Analyzing the results

You should also see a significant difference between the time required to store the objects in a `Vector` and the time required to store the objects in an array of *N* elements. Use this difference to estimate the amount of overhead required to implement a Java `Vector`. As you might expect, it is more efficient to store values in an array that is large enough to hold values than it is to store them in a vector which must dynamically change its size on each insertion.

Problem Decomposition

What classes should we use?

An appropriate design for this problem should make use of some of the classes we designed in this chapter. The `IntField` class will be useful for inputting *N*, the number of objects used in each run of the experiment. The `IntOutOfRangeException` class is used by `IntField.getInt()`, so it should be included in your project. Finally, the main class, call it `ExceptionExperiment`, should be a frame-based application. It should present a simple GUI and be responsible for running the various experiments. This leads to the following breakdown:

1. `ExceptionExperiment` — a subclass of `Frame` that serves as the main program for this application.
2. `IntField` — a subclass of `JTextField` that serves as the main input element for this application (Figure 11–17).
3. `IntOutOfRangeException` — a subclass of `Extension`, this class was developed and tested above.

GUI Design

The GUI for this application should be kept simple. It uses a `JFrame` as the main container. Remember that the default layout for `JFrame`s is `BorderLayout`. Along the north border, you should place a control panel that consists of a simple prompt and the `IntField`. In the center of the frame you should place a `JTextArea` that will be used to display the results of the experiments.

The application should run the experiments each time the user inputs a valid number in the `IntField`. Remember that `IntField.getInt()` returns 0 if the user types a value that is out of range. The output from each experiment should look something like the following:

```
100 Integers were inserted into
    Vector in 4 milliseconds
    array of 0 elements in 53 milliseconds
    array of 100 elements in 1 milliseconds
1000 Integers were inserted into
    Vector in 37 milliseconds
    array of 0 elements in 1225 milliseconds
    array of 1000 elements in 8 milliseconds
```

As you can see from these results, which were taken from an actual run, there is a significant time difference among the three approaches.

Importing from the Java Library

This project will require several classes from the Java class library, including the `java.util.Vector` class and the `java.awt.*` and `java.awt.event.*` packages.

Designing the `ExceptionTester` Class

What data structures do we need?

`ExceptionTester` should contain two `private` instance variables, a `Vector` and an `array`. In terms of this experiment's objectives, it doesn't matter what types of objects are stored in these fields. However, the same type of object should be stored in both structures. `Integer` objects would be a good choice, because it is easy to generate `N` different `Integer` objects using a `for` loop. For example, the following statement can be used to generate *N* integers for a `Vector`:

```
vector = new Vector(0);
for (int k = 0; k < N; k++)
    vector.addElement(new Integer(k));
```

The `Vector` and the `array` can be instantiated anew for each experiment. An example of this will be given below. All other variables can be declared, as needed, within the class's methods.

Algorithm Design

The algorithm for this program can be decomposed into the following methods:

- `actionPerformed()` — This method will get the value of *N* from the `intField()` and then run the three experiments.
- `testVector(int N)` — This method will perform *N* insertions into the `Vector` and will report the number of milliseconds required. The code required to insert *N* `Integer`s into a `Vector`, *vector*, is as follows:

```
vector = new Vector(0);                    // Instantiate the Vector, vector
for (int k = 0; k < N; k++)                // For n iterations
    vector.addElement(new Integer(k));     // Insert a new integer into vector
```

- `testArray(int N)` — This method will perform *N* insertions into

```
list = new Integer[0];
```

In this case, we are using an array of `Integer`s. This is the method in which the `ArrayIndexOutOfBoundsException`s will be thrown.

- testBigEnoughArray(int N) — This method will perform *N* insertions into an array of *N* elements and will report the number of milliseconds required. The difference between this method and the previous one is that in this case the array is instantiated with an initial size of *N*, so that no exceptions will be generated as the *N* items are inserted.

- insertAt(int k) — This method will be called by both testBigEnoughArray() and testArray() to insert an item into the array at index *k*. It should be a simple variant of the insertString() method that was designed in Section 11.4.4.

  It is important for the experiment that the same method be used to do the insertions in both arrays. That way the only difference in the time taken will be due to the exceptions raised.

  One modification that you'll want to make to the insertString() method is that you can drop its finally clause. The variable k will be passed into the method as a parameter and will be incremented by the calling method. A loop such as the following can be used in both testArray() and testBigEnoughArray():

```
for (int k = 0; k < N; k++)
    insertAt(k);
```

- main() — Finally, the main() method for this application will simply create an instance of the application:

```
public static void main(String args[]) {
    ExceptionTester et = new ExceptionTester();
    et.show();
} // main()
```

Timing an Operation

Timing an operation in Java is easy. You may recall that we used a timing algorithm in the very first applet we worked on in Chapter 1. To time an operation you can just call the System.currentTimeMillis() before and after the operation and then compute the difference in the two values:

```
long startTime = System.currentTimeMillis();
for (k = 0; k < size; k++)
    insertAt(k);
long currentTime = System.currentTimeMillis();
System.out.println("Elapsed time = " + (currentTime - startTime));
```

In this case we are computing the time it takes to insert *size* items into the array.

Testing Your Algorithm

When testing your program, it is important to make sure that it is successfully inserting the elements into the appropriate structures. Therefore, during program development, you want to use a `for` loop to display the array and the `Vector` after the items have been inserted. For example, something like the following code should be used to verify that the objects are actually installed in the array:

```
// Display the array contents
for (int j = 0; j < size; j++)
    System.out.println(list[j]);
```

This part of the program should be deleted or commented out during the running of the experiments themselves.

Reporting Your Results

Use your experimental results to answer the following questions:

1. On average, how many milliseconds does it take to handle a thrown exception on your system?
2. On average, how much longer does it take to insert an element into a vector as opposed to a (suitably sized) array?
3. Why does it take longer to insert something into a vector than into an array?
4. Because a `Vector` requires more overhead than an array, why would you ever use a `Vector`? That is, describe an application problem where you can't use a "big enough" array.

Optional Exercise

Java would not use a loop to copy one array into another as we have done in the `FixArrayBound` program. Instead it would use the `java.lang.System.arraycopy()` method:

```
public static void arraycopy(Object src, int srcP, Object dest, int destP, int len);
```

For example, to copy all the elements of `array1` into `array2` you could use the following statement:

```
arraycopy(array1, 0, array2, 0, array1.length);
```

Modify your experiment to make use of this method, which is the method used by the `Vector` class when it needs to resize. This will give a measure of the overhead caused by exception throwing.

Java Language Summary

The `try/catch/finally` statement has the following syntax:

```
try {
   // Block of statements
   // At least one of which may throw an exception

   if ( /* Some condition obtains */ )
      throw new ExceptionName();
} catch (ExceptionName ParameterName) {
   // Block of statements to be executed
   // If the ExceptionName exception is thrown in try
}
..
} catch (ExceptionName2 ParameterName) {
   // Block of statements to be executed
   // If the ExceptionName2 exception is thrown in try
} finally {
   // Optional block of statements that is executed
   // Whether an exception is thrown or not
}
```

The try block is meant to include a statement or statements that might throw an exception. The catch blocks — there can be one or more — are meant to handle exceptions that are thrown in the try block. A catch block will handle any exception that matches its parameter class, including subclasses of that class. The finally block is optional. It will be executed whether an exception is thrown or not. If an exception is thrown in the try block, the try block is exited permanently.

The `throw` statement inside the try block is there to illustrate how `throw` can be used. You will usually not see a `throw` statement in a try block, because most throws are done from within Java library methods, which are called from a `try` block.

CHAPTER SUMMARY

Technical Terms

catch block	catch an exception	checked exception
dialog box	dynamic scope	error dialog
exception	exception handler	finally block
method stack trace	static scope	throw an exception
try block	unchecked exception	

New Java Keywords

`catch`	`finally`	`super`
`throws`	`throw`	`try`

Java Classes

ArithmeticException	ArrayIndexOutOfBoundsException
BorderLayout	Exception
FieldIsEmptyException	FileNotFoundException
IOException	IllegalArgumentException
IndexOutOfBoundsException	Integer
JFrame	JOptionPane
JPanel	JTextArea
JTextField	NullPointerException
NumberFormatException	RunTimeException
StringIndexOutOfBoundsException	String
Vector	

Java Library Methods

actionPerformed()	getMessage()	insertAt()
lastIndexOf()	main()	paintComponent()
printStackTrace()	random()	readLine()
showMessageDialog()		

Programmer-Defined Classes

BadDivide	CalcAverage	MyClass
ExceptionTester	FixArrayBound	ExceptionExperiment
IntField	IntOutOfRange Exception	IntFieldTester
MyClass2		InvalidPasswordException

Programmer-Defined Methods

insertString()	intAverage()	getInt()
intField()	method1()	method2()
method3()	testArray()	testBigEnoughArray()
testVector()		

Important Points

- In Java, when an error or exceptional condition occurs, you `throw` an `Exception` which is caught by special code known as an *exception handler*. A `throw` statement — `throw new Exception()` — is used to throw an exception.
- A *try block* is block of statements containing one or more statements that may throw an exception. Embedding a statement in a try block indicates your awareness that it might throw an exception and your intention to handle the exception.
- Java distinguishes between *checked* and *unchecked* exceptions. Checked exceptions must either be caught by the method in which they occur or you must declare that the method containing that statement `throws` the exception.

- The unchecked exceptions are those that belong to subclasses of `RuntimeException`. If they are left uncaught, they will be handled by Java's default exception handlers.
- A *catch block* is a block of statements that handles the exceptions that match its parameter. A catch block can only follow a try block, and there may be more than one catch block for each try block.
- The `try/catch` syntax allows you to separate the normal parts of an algorithm from special code meant to handle errors and exceptional conditions.
- A *method stack trace* is a trace of the method calls that have led to the execution of a particular statement in the program. The `Exception.printStackTrace()` method can be called by exception handlers to print a trace of exactly how the program reached the statement that threw the exception.
- *Static scoping* refers to how the text of the program is arranged. If a variable is declared within a method or a block, its static scope is confined to that method or block.
- *Dynamic scoping* refers to how the program is executed. A statement is within the dynamic scope of a method or block, if it is called from that method or block, or if it is called by some other method that was called from that method or block.
- When searching for a catch block to handle an exception thrown by a statement, Java searches upward through the statement's static scope, and backward through its dynamic scope, until it finds a matching catch block. If none is found, the Java Virtual Machine will handle the exception itself by printing an error message and a method stack trace.
- Many Java library methods throw exceptions when an error occurs. These `throw` statements do not appear in the program. For example, Java's integer division operator will throw an `ArithmeticException` if an attempt is made to divide by zero.
- Generally, there are four ways to handle an exception: (1) Let Java handle it; (2) Fix the problem that led to the exception and resume the program; (3) Report the problem and resume the program; and (4) Print an error message and terminate the program. Most erroneous conditions reported by exceptions are difficult or impossible to fix.
- A `finally` statement is an optional part of a `try/catch` block. Statements contained in a finally-block will be executed whether an exception is raised or not.
- A well-designed program should use exception handling to deal with truly exceptional conditions, not as a means of normal program control.
- User-defined exceptions can be defined by extending the `Exception` class or one of its subclasses.

ANSWERS TO SELF-STUDY EXERCISES

EXERCISE 11.1 If `Math.random()` in `MyClass2` returns 0.98 and then 0.44, the program will generate the following output. Note that because the out-of-range error occurs in `method1()`, `method2()` is not called at all.

```
0.98 is out of range
```

EXERCISE 11.2 If `Math.random()` in `MyClass2` returns 0.98 and then 0.44, the following stack trace would be printed:

```
java.lang.ArithmeticException: 0.98 is out of range
    at MyClass2.method1(MyClass2.java:3)
    at MyClass2.main(MyClass2.java:15)
```

EXERCISE 11.3 If `Math.random()` in `MyClass2` returns 0.44 and then 0.98, the program will generate the following output:

```
Hello 0.44
0.98 is out of range
```

EXERCISE 11.4 If `Math.random()` in `MyClass2` returns 0.44 and then 0.98, the following stack trace would be printed:

```
java.lang.ArithmeticException: 0.98 is out of range
    at MyClass2.method2(MyClass2.java:8)
    at MyClass2.main(MyClass2.java:16)
```

EXERCISE 11.5 The divide-by-zero error in `BadDivide` occurs in the expression `n/d` in `Method2()`. It would generate the following stack trace:

```
java.lang.ArithmeticException: divide by zero
    at BadDivide.method2(BadDivide.java:7)
    at BadDivide.method1(BadDivide.java:3)
    at BadDivide.main(BadDivide.java:13)
```

EXERCISE 11.6 The following version of `BadDivide.method2()` will handle the divide-by-zero error itself:

```
public void method2 (int n, int d) {
    try {
        System.out.println(n / d);
    } catch (ArithmeticException e) {
        System.out.println(e.getMessage());
        e.printStackTrace();
        System.exit(0);
    }
}
```

EXERCISE 11.7 The following revised version of CalcAverage guards against both NullPointerException and ArithmeticException.

```
public class CalcAverage {

    public int intAverage(int arr[], int N) {
        int avg = 0;
        if (arr == null)
            throw new NullPointerException("ERROR: array is empty");
        if (N <= 0)
            throw new ArithmeticException("ERROR: can't average 0 elements");
        for (int k = 0; k < N; k++)
            avg += arr[k];
        avg = avg / N;
        return avg;
    } // intAverage()

    public static void main(String args[]) {
        int numbers[] = {10, 20, 30, 30, 20, 10};
        int numbers2[] = null;
        try {
            CalcAverage ca = new CalcAverage();
            System.out.println( "AVG + " + ca.intAverage(numbers2, 1));
        } catch (NullPointerException e) {
            System.out.println( e.getMessage() );
            e.printStackTrace();
            System.exit(0);
        } catch (ArithmeticException e) {
            System.out.println( e.getMessage() );
            e.printStackTrace();
            System.exit(0);
        }
    } // main()
} // CalcAverage
```

EXERCISE 11.8 If someValue equals 1000, the code segment will print

```
Entering try block
ERROR: 1000 is too large
```

EXERCISE 11.9 If someValue equals 50, the code segment will print

```
Entering try block
Exiting try block
```

EXERCISE 11.10

```
try {
    if (X < 0)
        throw new Exception"ERROR: Negative value in X coordinate");
} catch (Exception e) {
    System.out.println( e.getMessage() );
}
```

EXERCISE 11.11 A ArrayIndexOutOfBoundsException could be handled by the handlers in a, c, or d, because their classes are all superclasses of ArrayIndexOutOfBoundsException.

EXERCISE 11.12

a. `Integer.parseInt("26.2");` ==> `NumberFormatException`
b. `String s; s.indexOf('a');` ==> `NullPointerException`
c. `String s = "hello"; s.charAt(5);` ==> `StringIndexOutOfBoundsException`

EXERCISE 11.13 The unchecked exceptions are IndexOutOfBoundsException, NumberFormatException, NullPointerException, because these are subclasses of RuntimeException. The others are checked exceptions.

EXERCISE 11.14

a. It depends. This is a computer game, so one way to handle this problem would be to generate a message into a log file and resume the game. If the GUI element is crucial to the game, it's hard to see how it could be successfully handled.
b. It depends. You would have to decide whether it would be more harmful or dangerous to continue production or not.
c. The program could report the security violation to the user and to the system manager and then keep accepting user input.

EXERCISE 11.15

```
public class FieldIsEmptyException extends Exception {

    public FieldIsEmptyException () {
        super("The input field is empty ");
    }
}
```

EXERCISE 11.16

```
public int getInt() {
    int num = 0;
    try {
        String data = getText();
        if (data.equals(""))
            throw new FieldIsEmptyException();
        num = Integer.parseInt( getText() );
        if (num > bound)
            throw new IntOutOfRangeException(bound);
    } catch (FieldIsEmptyException e) {
        System.out.println("Error: " + e.getMessage() );
    } catch (NumberFormatException e) {
        System.out.println("Error: You must input an integer.  Please try again.");
    } catch (IntOutOfRangeException e) {
        System.out.println(e.getMessage());
        return 0;
    }
    return num;
}
```

EXERCISES

1. Explain the difference between the following pairs of terms.

   a. *Throwing an exception* and *catching an exception*.
   b. *Try block* and *catch block*.
   c. *Catch block* and *finally block*.
   d. *Try block* and *finally block*.
   e. *Dynamic scope* and *static scope*.
   f. *Dialog box* and *top-level window*.
   g. *Checked* and *unchecked* exception.
   h. *Method stack* and *method call*.

2. Fill in the blank:

   a. ----- an exception is Java's way of signaling that some kind of abnormal situation has occurred.
   b. The only place that an exception can be thrown in a Java program is within a -----.
   c. The block of statements placed within a catch block are generally known as an ----- .
   d. To determine a statement's ----- scope, you have to trace the program's execution.
   e. To determine a statement's ----- scope, you can just read its definition.
   f. When a method is called, a representation of the method call is place on the -----.
   g. The root of Java's exception hierarchy is the ----- class.
   h. A ----- exception must be either caught or declared within the method in which it might be thrown.
   i. An ----- exception may be left up to Java to handle.

3. Compare and contrast the four different ways of handling exceptions within a program.
4. Suppose you have a program that asks the user to input a string of no more than five letters. Describe the steps you'd need to take in order to design a `StringTooLongException` to handle cases where the user types in too many characters.
5. Exceptions require more computational overhead than normal processing. Explain.
6. Suppose the following `ExerciseExample` program is currently executing the if statement in `method2()`. Draw a picture of the `method call stack` that represents this situation.

```
public class ExerciseExample {
    public void method1(int M) {
        try {
            System.out.println("Entering try block");
            method2( M );
            System.out.println("Exiting try block");
        } catch (Exception e) {
            System.out.println("ERROR: " + e.getMessage());
        }
    } // method1()

    public void method2(int M) {
        if (M > 100)
            throw new ArithmeticException(M + " is too large");
    }

    public static void main(String argv[]) {
        ExerciseExample ex = new ExerciseExample();
        ex.method1(500);
    }
} // ExerciseExample
```

7. Repeat the previous exercise for the situation where the program is currently executing the second `println()` statement in `method1()`.
8. Draw a hierarchy chart that represents the static scoping relationships among the elements of the `ExerciseExample` program.
9. What would be printed by the `ExerciseExample` program when it is run?
10. What would be printed by the `ExerciseExample` program, if the statement in its main method were changed to `ex.method1( 5 )`?
11. Consider again the `ExerciseExample` program. If the exception thrown were `Exception` rather than `ArithmeticException`, explain why we would get the following error message: `java.lang.Exception must be caught, or it must be declared....`
12. Write a `try/catch` block which throws an `Exception` if the value of variable X is less than zero. The exception should be an instance of `Exception` and when it is caught, the message returned by `getMessage()` should be "ERROR: Negative value in X coordinate."
13. Look at the `IntFieldTester` program (Figure 11–18) and the `IntField` class definition (Figure 11–17). Suppose the user inputs a value that's greater than 100. Show what the method call stack would look like when the `IntField.getInt()` method is executing the `num > bound` expression.
14. As a continuation of the previous exercise, show what the program's output would be if the user input a value greater than 100.
15. As a continuation of the previous exercise, modify the `IntOutOfRangeException` handler so that it prints the message call stack. Then show what it would print.
16. Define a subclass of `RuntimeException` named `InvalidPasswordException`, which contains two constructors. The first constructor takes no parameters and an exception thrown with this constructor should return "ERROR: invalid password" when its `getMessage()` is invoked. The second constructor takes a single `String` parameter. Exceptions thrown with this constructor should return the constructor's argument when `getMessage()` is invoked.
17. Extend the `IntField` class so that it will constrain the integer `JTextField` to an `int` between both a lower and upper bound. In other words, it should throw an exception if the user types in a value lower than the lower bound or greater than the upper bound.

18. Modify the ColorPicker program presented in the last chapter so that its JTextFields will restrict user inputs to values between 0 and 255. Use the extended IntField class that you defined in the previous exercise.
19. Design Issue: One of the preconditions for the bubbleSort() method (Figure 8–10) is that its array parameter not be null. Of course this precondition would fail if the array were passed a null array reference. In that case Java would throw a NullPointerException and terminate the program. Is this an appropriate way to handle that exception?
20. With respect to the previous exercise, suppose you decide that it is more appropriate to handle the NullPointerException by presenting error dialog. Modify the method to accommodate this behavior.
21. Design Issue: Another possible way to design the sequentialSearch() method (Figure 8–12) would be to have it throw an exception when its key is not found in the array. Is this a good design? Explain.
22. **CyberPet Problem:** One of the CyberPet constructors takes an integer parameter to specify the CyberPet's state. If an erroneous value (for example, −1 or 100) is passed to the constructor, that will invalidate the CyberPet's state, which will cause all kinds of problems for the simulation. Design an appropriate Exception and a handler to fix this problem, and incorporate it into the CyberPet class.
23. **CyberPet Challenge:** One of the problems with the animated CyberPet applet (Figure 8–9) is that if the image files are missing from the applet's directory, the applet will continue to run but no images will show up. First, convert the applet from an AWT program to a Swing program. Then design and implement a way to use exceptions to handle this problem. What kind of exception will you throw? Where and how will you detect it? If an exeption is thrown, open an error dialog and inform the user.

Photograph courtesy of Jim Wehtje, PhotoDisc, Inc.

12

Recursive Problem Solving

OBJECTIVES

After studying this chapter, you will

- Understand the concept of recursion.
- Know how to use recursive programming techniques.
- Have a better appreciation of recursion as a problem solving technique.

OUTLINE

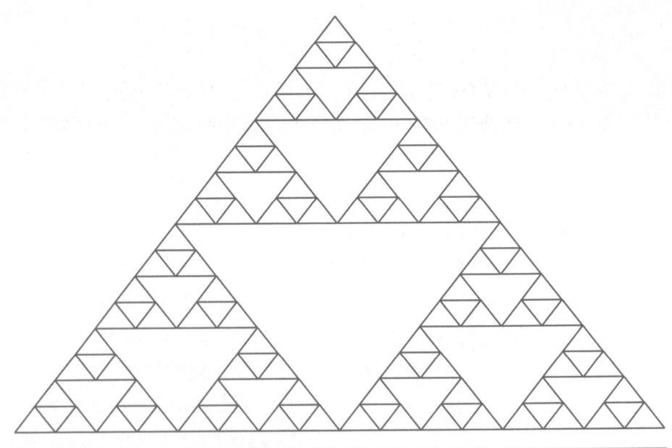

Figure 12–1 The Sierpinski gasket.

12.1 Introduction

The pattern in Figure 12–1 is known as the Sierpinski gasket. Its overall shape is that of an equilateral triangle. But notice how inside the outer triangle, there are three smaller triangles that are similar to the overall pattern. And inside each of those are three even smaller triangles, and so on. The Sierpinski gasket is known as a *fractal* because when you divide it up, you end up with a smaller version of the overall pattern. The overall gasket pattern is repeated over and over, at smaller and smaller scales, throughout the figure.

How would you draw this pattern? If you try to use some kind of nested loop structure, you'll find that it is very challenging. It can be done using loops but it isn't easy. On the other hand, if you use an approach know as *recursion*, this problem is much easier to solve. It's a little bit like the representation issue we discussed in Chapter 5. Your ability to solve a problem often depends on how you represent the problem. Recursion gives you another way to approach problems that involve repetition, such as the problem of drawing the Sierpinski gasket.

The main goal of this chapter is to introduce recursion as both a problem solving technique and as alternative to loops (Chapter 6) for implementing repetition. We begin with the notion of a *recursive definition*, a concept used widely in mathematics and computer science. We then introduce the idea of a *recursive method*, which is the way recursion is used in a program. These ideas are illustrated by means of a number of examples.

Recursion is a topic that is taken up in considerable detail in upper-level computer science courses, so our goal here is mainly to introduce the concept and give you some idea of its power as a problem solving approach. Because our discussion is introductory, the examples we've chosen are very simple. One risk in using simple examples is that you might be tempted to think that recursion is only good for "toy problems." Nothing could be further from the truth. Recursion is often used for some of the most difficult algorithms. Some of the exercises at the end of the chapter provide examples of challenging problems.

12.1.1 Recursion as Repetition

A **recursive method** is a method that calls itself. An **iterative method** is a method that uses a loop to repeat an action. In one sense, *recursion* is an alternative to the iterative (looping) control structures we studied in Chapter 6. In this sense, recursion is just another way to repeat an action.

Iterative method

For example, consider the following iterative method for saying "hello" *N* times:

```
public void hello(int N)  {
    for (int k = 0; k < N; k++)
        System.out.println("Hello");
} // hello()
```

Recursive method

A recursive version of this method would be defined as follows:

```
public void helloI(int N)  {
    System.out.println("Hello");
        if (N > 0)
            hello(N - 1);                      // Recursive call
} // hello()
```

This method is recursive because it calls itself, when *N* is greater than 0. However note that when it calls itself, it passes $N - 1$ as the value for its parameter. If this method is initially called with *N* equal to 5, here's a trace of what happens. Indentation is used to indicate each time the method calls itself:

```
hello(5)
    Print "Hello"
    hello(4)
        Print "Hello"
        hello(3)
            Print "Hello"
            hello(2)
                Print "Hello"
                hello(1)
                    Print "Hello"
```

Thus "Hello" will be printed five times, just as it would be in the iterative version of this method.

So, in one sense, recursion is just an alternative to iteration. In fact, there are some programming languages, such as the original versions of LISP and PROLOG, that do not have loop structures. In these languages, *all* repetition is done by recursion. On the other hand, if a language contains loop structures, it can do without recursion. Anything that can be done iteratively can be done recursively, and vice versa.

Computational overhead

Moreover, it is much less efficient to call a method five times than to repeat a for loop five times. Method calls take up more memory than loops, and involve more **computational overhead** — for such tasks as passing parameters, allocating storage for the method's local variables, and returning the method's results. Therefore, because of its reliance on repeated method calls, recursion is usually less efficient than iteration as a way to code a particular algorithm.

EFFECTIVE DESIGN: Efficiency. Iterative algorithms and methods are generally more efficient than recursive algorithms that do the same thing.

SELF-STUDY EXERCISES

EXERCISE 12.1 What would be printed if we call the following method with the expression `mystery(0)`? What about `mystery(100)`?

```
public void mystery(int N) {
    System.out.println(N);
        if (N <= 5)
            mystery(N + 1);
} // mystery()
```

EXERCISE 12.2 What would be printed if we call the following method with the expression `mystery(5)`?

```
public void mystery(int N) {
    System.out.println(N);
        if (N <= 5)
            mystery(N - 1);
} // mystery()
```

DEBUGGING TIP: Recursive Bound. Just as for iterative (loop) algorithms, an infinite recursion will result if the recursion is not successfully bounded.

12.1.2 Recursion as a Problem Solving Approach

Given that recursion is not really necessary (if a programming language has loops) and not more efficient than loops, why is it so important? The answer is that, in a broader sense, recursion is an effective approach to problem solving. It is a way of viewing a problem. And it is mostly in this sense that we want to study recursion.

Recursion is based on two key problem-solving concepts: *divide and conquer* and **self-similarity** . In recursive problem solving we use the divide-and-conquer strategy repeatedly to break a big problem into a sequence of smaller and smaller problems until we arrive at a problem that is practically trivial to solve.

Subproblems

What allows us to create this series of subproblems is that each subproblem is similar to the original problem — that is, each subproblem is just a smaller version of the original problem. Look again at the task of saying "Hello" N times. Solving this task involves solving the similar task of saying "Hello" $N-1$ times, which can be divided into the similar task of saying "Hello" $N-2$ times. And so on.

Self-similarity

The ability to see a problem as being composed of smaller, self-similar problems is at the heart of the recursive approach. And although you may not have thought about this before, a surprising number of programming problems have this self-similarity characteristic. Let's illustrate these ideas with some simple examples.

PROGRAMMING TIP: Divide and Conquer. Many programming problems can be solved by dividing them into smaller, simpler problems. For recursive solutions, finding the key to the subproblem often holds the solution to the original problem.

12.2 Recursive Definition

One place you may have already seen recursion is in mathematics. A *recursive definition* in mathematics is one that defines the nth case of a concept in terms of the $(n-1)$st case plus some kind of boundary condition.

12.2.1 Factorial: $N!$

For example, consider the problem of calculating the factorial of n — that is, $n!$ for $n \geq 0$. As you may recall, $n!$ is calculated as follows:

```
n! = n * (n-1) * (n-2) * ... * 1, for n > 0
```

In addition, 0! is defined as 1. Let's now look at some examples for different values of n:

```
4! = 4 * 3 * 2 * 1 = 12
3! = 3 * 2 * 1 = 6
2! = 2 * 1 = 2
1! = 1
0! = 1
```

As these examples suggest, $n!$ can always be calculated in terms of $(n-1)!$ This relationship may be clearer if we rewrite the above calculations as follows:

```
4! = 4 * 3 * 2 * 1 = 4 * 3! = 12
3! = 3 * 2 * 1     = 3 * 2! = 6
2! = 2 * 1         = 2 * 1! = 2
1!                 = 1 * 0! = 1
0!                 = 1
```

The only case in which we can't calculate $n!$ in terms of $(n-1)!$ is when n is 0. Otherwise, in each case we see that

```
n! = n * (n-1)!
```

This leads to the following recursive definition:

```
n! = 1           if n = 0    // Boundary (or base) case
n! = n * (n-1)! if n > 0    // Recursive case
```

A **recursive definition** consists of two parts: a recursive part in which the *n*th value is defined in terms of the *(n–1)*st value, and a nonrecursive, boundary case, which defines a limiting condition. Note that if we had omitted the base case, the recursion would have continued to $(-1)!$ and $(-2)!$ and so on.

DEBUGGING TIP: Bounding the Repetition. An infinite repetition will result if a recursive definition is not properly bounded.

The recursive case uses divide and conquer to break the problem into a smaller problem, but the smaller problem is just a smaller version of the original problem. This combination of self-similarity and divide and conquer is what characterizes recursion. The base case is used to stop or limit the recursion.

EFFECTIVE DESIGN: Recursive Definition. For recursive algorithms and definitions, the **base case** serves as the bound for the algorithm. The **recursive case** defines the *n*th case in terms of the *n–1*st case.

12.2.2 Drawing a Nested Pattern

Self-similarity

As another example, consider the problem of drawing the nested boxes pattern in Figure 12–2. The self-similarity occurs in the fact that no matter how you divide the pattern, its parts resemble the whole. The basic shape involved is a square, which is repeated over and over at an ever smaller scale. A recursive definition for this pattern would be

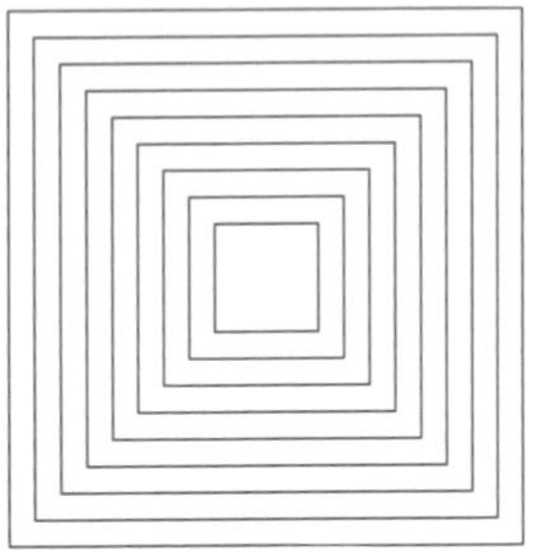

Figure 12–2 The nested squares pattern.

```
Base case:      if side < 5 do nothing
Recursive case: if side >= 5
                   draw a square
                   decrease the side and draw a smaller pattern inside the square
```

Smaller subpattern

This definition uses the length of the square's side to help define the pattern. If the length of the side is greater than or equal to 5, draw a square with dimensions $side \times side$. Then decrease the length of the side and draw a smaller version of the pattern inside that square. In this case, the *side* variable will decrease at each level of the drawing. When the length of the side becomes less than 5, the recursion stops. Thus, the length of the side serves as the limit or bound for this algorithm.

The side as a parameter

You should note that the length of the side functions here like a parameter in a method definition: It provides essential information for the definition, just as a method parameter provides essential data to the method. Indeed, this is exactly the role that parameters play in recursive methods. They provide essential information that determines the method's behavior.

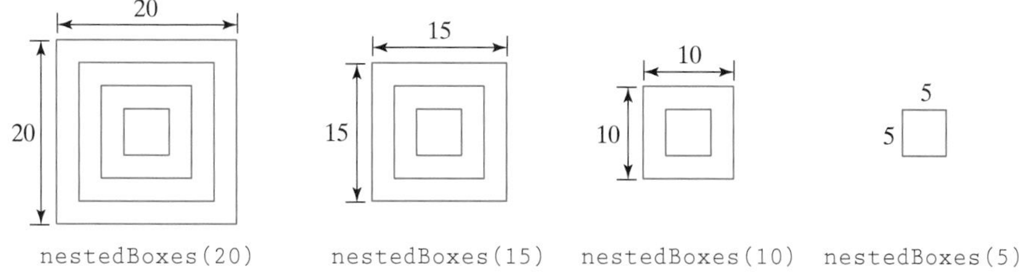

Figure 12–3 A trace of the nested boxes definition starting with a side of 20 and decreasing the side by 5 each time.

Figure 12–3 illustrates how we would apply the definition. Suppose the side starts out at 20 and decreases by 5 at each level of recursion. Note that as you move from left to right across the four patterns, that the pattern to the right is contained within the pattern to its left. So a `nestedBoxes(20)` can be drawn by drawing a 20×20 square and then drawing a `nestedBoxes(15)` pattern inside it. Similarly, a `nestedBoxes(15)` can be drawn by drawing a 15×15 square, and then drawing a `nestedBoxes(10)` pattern inside it. And so on.

Recursive vs. iterative bound

These examples illustrate the power of recursion as a problem solving technique for problems that involve repetition. Like the iterative (looping) control structures we studied in Chapter 6, recursion is used to implement repetition within a bound. For recursive algorithms the bound is defined by the base case, whereas for loops, the bound is defined by the loop's entry condition. In either case, repetition stops when the bound is reached.

DEBUGGING TIP: Infinite Recursion. An unbounded or incorrectly bounded recursive algorithm will lead to infinite repetition. Care must be taken to get the bound right.

SELF-STUDY EXERCISES

EXERCISE 12.3 You can calculate 2^n by multiplying 2 by itself n times. For example, 2^3 is $2 \times 2 \times 2$. Note also that $2^0 = 1$. Given theses facts, write a recursive definition for 2^n, for $n \geq 0$.

EXERCISE 12.4 Generalize your solution to the previous exercise by giving a recursive definition for x^n, where x and n are both integers ≥ 0.

EXERCISE 12.5 Is the recursive definition give earlier for the nested boxes equivalent to the following recursive definition? Explain.

```
Draw a square.          // in every case
If side > 5
    draw a smaller nested boxes inside the square
```

In this case the base case ($side \leq 5$) is implicit.

EXERCISE 12.6 Write a recursive definition for the recursive pattern shown in Figure 12–4.

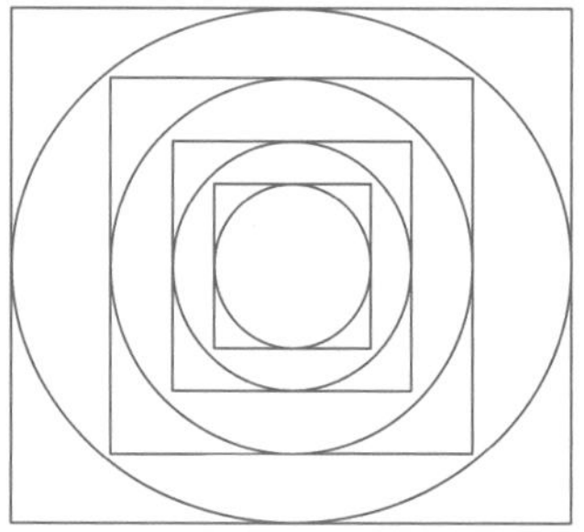

Figure 12–4 Write a recursive definition for this pattern.

12.3 Recursive String Methods

A **recursive method** is a method that calls itself. Like recursive definitions, recursive methods are designed around the divide-and-conquer and self-similarity principles. Defining a recursive method involves very much the same kind of analysis we used in designing recursive definitions. We identify a self-similar subproblem of the original problem plus one or more limiting cases.

How can a method call itself?

The idea of a method calling itself seems a bit strange at first. It's perhaps best understood in terms of a clone or a copy. When a method calls itself, it really calls a copy of itself, one which has a slightly different internal state. Usually the difference in state is the result of a difference in the invoked method's parameters.

12.3.1 Printing a String

To illustrate the concept of a recursive method, let's define a recursive method for printing a string. This is not intended to be a practical method — we already have the `println()` method for printing strings. But pretend for a moment that you only have a version of `println()` that works for characters, and your task is to write a version that can be used to print an entire string of characters.

Head and tail algorithm

A little terminology will help us describe the algorithm. Let's call the first letter of a string the **head** of the string, and let's refer to all the remaining letters in the string as the **tail** of the string. Then the problem of printing a string can be divided into two parts: printing the head of the string, and printing its tail. The limiting case here is when a string has no characters in it. It's trivial to print the empty string — just don't do anything! This leads to the method definition shown in Figure 12–5.

The base case here provides a limit, and bounds the recursion when the length of *s* is 0 — that is, when the string is empty. The recursive case solves the problem of printing *s* by solving the smaller, self-similar problem of printing a substring of *s*. Note that the recursive case makes progress toward the limit. On each recursion, the tail will get smaller and smaller until it becomes the empty string.

Figure 12–5 The recursive `printString()` method.

```
/**
 * printString() prints each character of the string s
 * Pre: s is initialized (non-null)
 * Post: none
 */
public void printString(String s) {
    if (s.length() == 0)
        return;                             // Base case: do nothing
    else {
        System.out.print(s.charAt(0));  // Recursive case: print head
        printString(s.substring(1));    // Print tail of the string
    }
} // printString()
```

EFFECTIVE DESIGN: Recursive Progress. In a recursive algorithm, each recursive call must make progress toward the bound, or base case.

Recursive call

Let's now revisit the notion of a method calling itself. Obviously this is what happens in the recursive case, but what does it mean — what actions does this lead to in the program? Each recursive call to a method is really a call to a *copy* of that method, and each copy has a slightly different internal state. We can define `printString()`'s internal state completely in terms of its recursion parameter, *s*, the string that's being printed. A **recursion parameter** is a parameter whose value is used to control the progress of the recursion. In this case, if *s* differs in each copy, then so will `s.substring(1)` and `s.charAt(0)`.

EFFECTIVE DESIGN: Recursion and Parameters. Recursive methods use a *recursion parameter* to distinguish between self-similar instances of the method call. The parameter controls the progress of the recursion toward its bound.

Self-similar instances

Figure 12–6 illustrates the sequence of recursive method calls and the output that results when `printString("hello")` is invoked. Each box represents a separate instance of the `printString()` method, with its own internal state. In this illustration its state is represented by its parameter, `s`. Because each instance has a different parameter, the behavior of each will be slightly different, so each box also shows the character that will be printed by that instance (`s.charAt(0)`), and the string that will be passed on to the next instance (`s.substring(1)`).

DEBUGGING TIP: Off-by-One Error. The expressions `s.charAt(0)` and `s.substring(1)` will generate exceptions if *s* is the empty string.

The arrows represent the method calls and returns. Note that the first `return` that's executed is the one in the base case. Each instance must wait for the instance it called to return before it can return. That's why the instances "pile up" in a cascadelike structure. The arrowless lines trace the order in which the output is produced.

Each instance of `printString()` is similar to the next in that each will print a character and pass on a substring, but each performs its duties on a different string. Note how the string, the recursion parameter in this case, gets smaller in each instance of `printString()`. This represents progress toward the method's base case `s.length() == 0`. When the empty string is passed as an argument, the recursion will stop. If the method does not make progress toward its bound in this way, the result will be an infinite recursion.

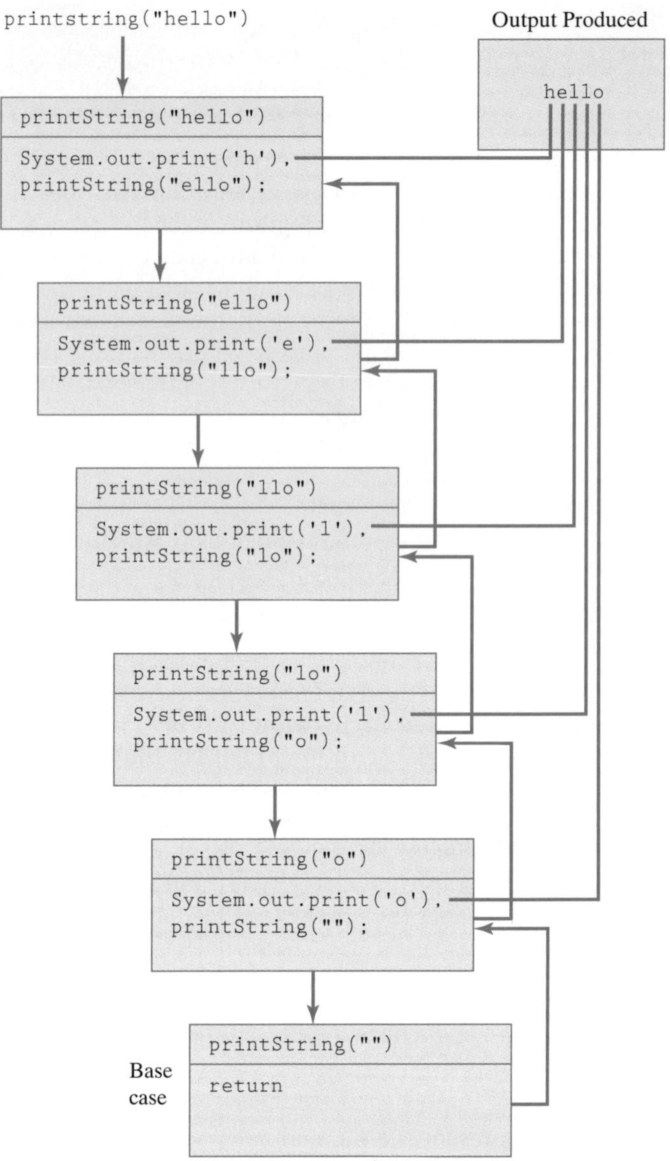

Figure 12–6 A recursive method call invokes a copy of the method, each with a slightly different internal state. As this is done repeatedly, a stack of method calls is created.

EFFECTIVE DESIGN: Bounding the Recursion. For recursive algorithms, the *recursion parameter* is used to express the algorithm's bound, or *base case.* In order for the algorithm to terminate, each recursive call should make progress toward the bound.

Note also the order in which things are done in this method. First `s.charAt(0)` is printed, and then `s.substring(1)` is passed to `printString()` in the recursion. This is a typical structure for a *head/tail algorithm*. What makes this work is that the tail is a smaller, self-similar version of the original structure.

Self-similarity

EFFECTIVE DESIGN: Head/Tail Algorithm. Many recursive solutions involve breaking a sequential structure, such as a string or an array, into its *head* and *tail*. An operation is performed on the head, and the algorithm recurses on the tail.

SELF-STUDY EXERCISES

EXERCISE 12.7 What would be printed by the following version of the `printString2()` method, if it is called with `printString2("hello")`?

```
public void printString2(String s) {
    if (s.length() == 1)
        System.out.print(s.charAt(0));                 // Base case:
    else {
        System.out.print(s.charAt(s.length() - 1));    // Print last char
        printString2(s.substring(0, s.length() - 1)); // Print rest of string
    }
} // printString2()
```

12.3.2 Printing the String Backwards

What do you suppose would happen if we reversed the order of the statements in the `printString()` method? That is, what if the recursive call came before `s.charAt(0)` is printed, as in the following method:

```
/**
 * printReverse() prints each character s in reverse order
 * Pre: s is initialized (non-null)
 * Post: none
 */
public void printReverse(String s) {
    if (s.length() > 0) {                 // Recursive case:
        printReverse(s.substring(1));     //  Print tail of the string
        System.out.print(s.charAt(0));    // Then print the first char
    }
} // printReverse()
```

As its name suggests, this method will print the string in reverse order. The trace in Figure 12–7 shows how this works. Before `printReverse("hello")` can print 'h,' it calls `printReverse("ello")` and must wait for that call to complete its execution and return. But `printReverse("ello")` calls `printReverse("llo")` and so must wait for that call to complete its execution and return.

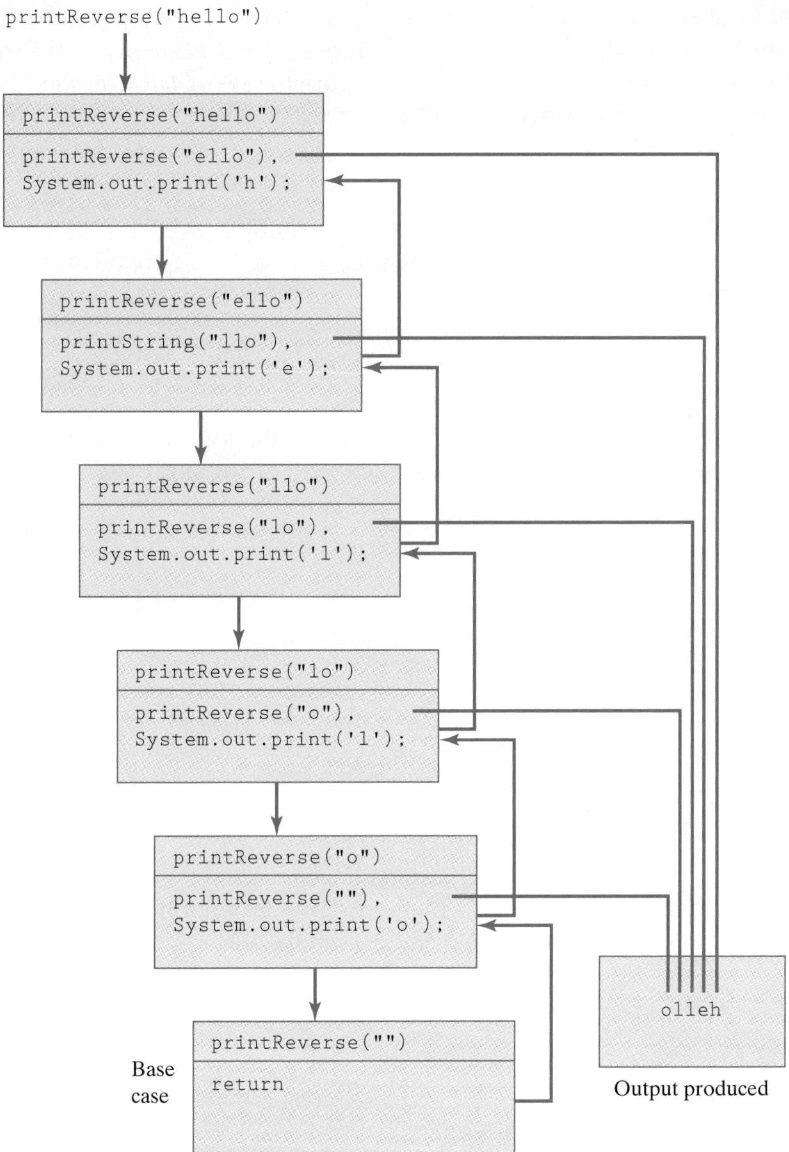

Figure 12–7 A trace of `printReverse(s)`, which prints its string argument in reverse order.

This process continues until `printReverse("")` is called. While the base case is executing, the other five instances of `printReverse()` must each wait for the instance that they called to complete its execution. It is only after the base case returns, that `printReverse("o")` can print its first character and return. So the letter 'o' will be printed first. After `printReverse("o")` has returned, then `printReverse("lo")` can print its first character. So the letter 'l' will be printed next, and so on until the original call to `printReverse("hello")` is completed and returns. Thus, the string will get printed in reverse order.

Note that the method call and return structure in this example follows a **Last-In-First-Out (LIFO) protocol**. That is, the last method called is always the first method to return. This is the protocol used by all method calls, recursive or otherwise.

Last-in-first-out protocol

> **JAVA LANGUAGE RULE** **LIFO.** Procedure call and return in Java, and all other programming languages, uses a last-in-first-out protocol.

Method call stack

For example, compare the order in which things happen in Figure 12–7 with the method stack trace in Figure 11–9. The only real difference between the two figures is that here the method stack is represented as growing downward, whereas in Figure 11–9 it grows upward. As each method call is made, a representation of the method call is placed on the **method call stack**. When a method returns, its block is removed from the top of the stack. The only difference between recursive and nonrecursive method calls is that recursive methods call instances of the same method definition. Of course, as we've seen, the instances are all slightly different from each other.

SELF-STUDY EXERCISES

EXERCISE 12.8 Write a recursive method called `countDown()` that takes a single `int` parameter, $N \geq 0$, and prints a countdown, such as "5, 4, 3, 2, 1, blastoff." In this case the method would be called with `blastOff(5)`.

EXERCISE 12.9 Revise the method in previous exercise so that when it's called with `blastOff(10)`, it will print "10 8 6 4 2 blastoff"; if its called with `blastOff(9)` it prints "9 7 5 3 1 blastoff."

12.3.3 Counting Characters in a String

Problem statement

Suppose you're writing an encryption program and you need to count the frequencies of the letters of the alphabet. Let's write a recursive method for this task.

This method will have two parameters: a `String` to store the string that will be processed, and a `char` to store the target character — the one we want to count. The method should return an `int`, representing the number of occurrences of the target character in the string.

```
// Goal: count the occurrences of ch in s
public int countChar( String s, char ch ) {
    int count = 0;
    ...
}
```

Base case

Here again our analysis must identify a recursive step that breaks the problem into smaller, self-similar versions of itself, plus a base case or limiting case that defines the end of the recursive process. Because the empty string will contain no target characters, we can use it as our base case. So, if the method is passed the empty string, the `countChar()` should just return 0 as its result.

Figure 12–8 The recursive `countChar()` method.

```
/**
 * Pre:  s is a non-null String, ch is any character
 * Post: countblanks() == the number of occurrences of ch in str
 */
public int countChar(String s, char ch) {
    if (s.length() == 0)                              // Base case: empty string
        return 0;
    else if (s.charAt(0) == ch)                       // Recursive case 1
        return 1 + countChar(s.substring(1), ch);    // Head equals ch
    else                                              // Recursive case 2
        return 0 + countChar(s.substring(1), ch);    // Head is not the ch
} // countChar()
```

Recursive case

For the recursive case we can divide the string into its head and tail. If the head is the target character, then the number of occurrences in the string is (1 + the number of occurrences in its tail). If the head of the string is not the target character, then the number of occurrences is (0 + the number of blanks in its tail). Of course, we'll use recursion to calculate the number of blanks in the tail.

This analysis leads to the recursive method shown in Figure 12–8. Note that for both recursive cases the same recursive call is used. In both cases we pass the tail of the original string, plus the target character. Note, also, how the return statement is evaluated:

```
return 1 + countChar(s.substring(1),ch);    // Head equals ch
```

Evaluation order is crucial

Before the method can return a value, it must receive the result of calling `countChar(s.substring(1),ch)` and add it to 1. Only then can a result be returned to the calling method. This leads to the following evaluation sequence for `countChar("dad",'d')`:

```
countChar("dad",'d');
1 + countChar("ad",'d');
1 + 0 + countChar("d",'d');
1 + 0 + 1 + countChar("",'d');
1 + 0 + 1 + 0 = 2              // Final result
```

In this way, the final result of calling `countChar("dad",'d')` is built up recursively by adding together the partial results from each separate instance of `countChar()`. The evaluation process is also shown graphically in Figure 12–9.

DEBUGGING TIP: Return Type. A common error with nonvoid recursive algorithms is forgetting to make sure that those return statements that contain a recursive call yield the correct data type.

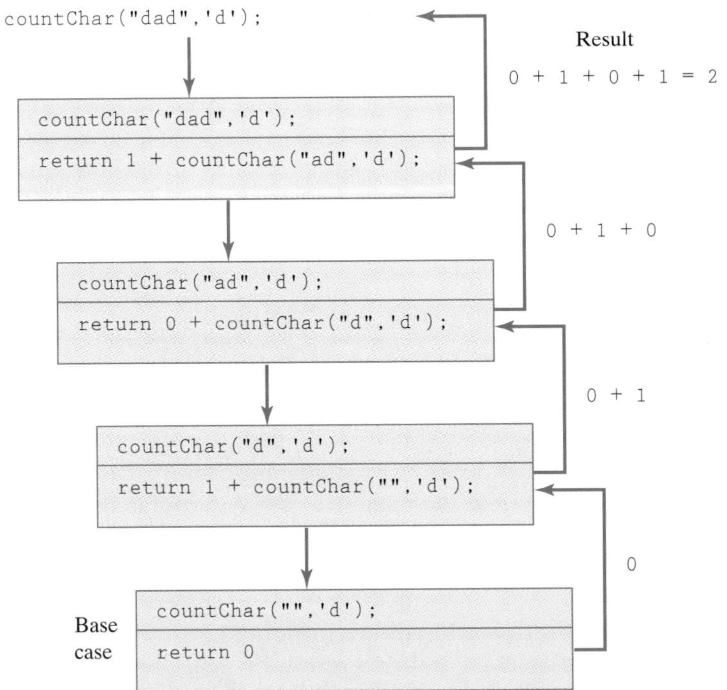
countChar("dad",'d');
Result
0 + 1 + 0 + 1 = 2
countChar("dad",'d');
return 1 + countChar("ad",'d');
0 + 1 + 0
countChar("ad",'d');
return 0 + countChar("d",'d');
0 + 1
countChar("d",'d');
return 1 + countChar("",'d');
0
Base case
countChar("",'d');
return 0

Figure 12–9 A trace of countChar("dad",'d'), which returns the value 2.

SELF-STUDY EXERCISES

EXERCISE 12.10 Here's a numerical problem. Write a recursive method to compute the sum of 1 to N, given N as a parameter.

12.3.4 Translating a String

Problem statement

A widely used string processing task is to convert one string into another string by replacing one character with a substitute throughout the string. For example, suppose we want to convert a Unix path name, which uses the forward slash '/' to separate one part of the path from another, into a Windows path name, which uses the backslash character '\' as a separator. For example, we want a method that can translate the following two strings into one another:

```
/unix_system/myfolder/java
\Windows_system\myfolder\java
```

Method design

Thus, we want a method that takes three parameters: a `String`, on which the conversion will be performed, and two `char` variables, the first being the original character in the string and the second being its substitute. The precondition for this method is simply that each of the these three parameters has been properly initialized with a value. The postcondition is that all occurrences of the first character have been replaced by the second character.

Figure 12–10 The `convert()` method replaces one character with another in a string.

```
/**
 * Pre:  str, ch1, ch2 have been initialized
 * Post: the result contains a ch2 everywhere that ch1 had occurred
 *       in str
 */
public static String convert(String str, char ch1, char ch2) {
    if (str.length() == 0)          // Base case: empty string
        return str;
    else if (str.charAt(0) == ch1)    // Recursive 1: ch1 at head
        return ch2 + convert(str.substring(1), ch1, ch2); // Replace it
    else                              // Recursive 2: ch1 not at head
        return str.charAt(0) + convert(str.substring(1), ch1, ch2);
} // convert()
```

Head/Tail Algorithm

As in our previous string processing methods, the limiting case in this problem is the empty string, and the recursive case will divide the string into its head and its tail. If the head is the character we want to replace, we concatenate its substitute with the result we obtain by recursively converting its tail.

This analysis leads to the definition shown in Figure 12–10. This method has more or less the same head and tail structure as the preceding example. The difference is that here the operation we perform on the head of the string is concatenation rather than addition.

The base case is still the case in which `str` is the empty string. The first recursive case occurs when the character being replaced is the head of `str`. In that case its substitute (`ch2`) is concatenated with the result of converting the rest of the string and returned as the result. The second recursive case occurs when the head of the string is *not* the character being replaced. In this case the head of the string is simply concatenated with the result of converting the rest of the string. Figure 12–11 shows an example of its execution.

SELF-STUDY EXERCISES

EXERCISE 12.11 Write a recursive method that changes each blank within a string into two consecutive blanks, leaving the rest of the string unchanged.

12.4 Recursive Array Processing

Like strings, arrays also have a recursive structure. Just as each substring of a string is similar to the string as a whole, each portion of an array is similar to the array as a whole. Similarly, just as a string can be divided into a head and a tail, an array can be divided into its *head*, the first element, and its *tail*, the rest of its elements (Figure 12–12). Because the tail of an array is itself an array, it satisfies the self-similarity principle. Therefore arrays have all the appropriate characteristics that make them excellent candidates for recursive processing.

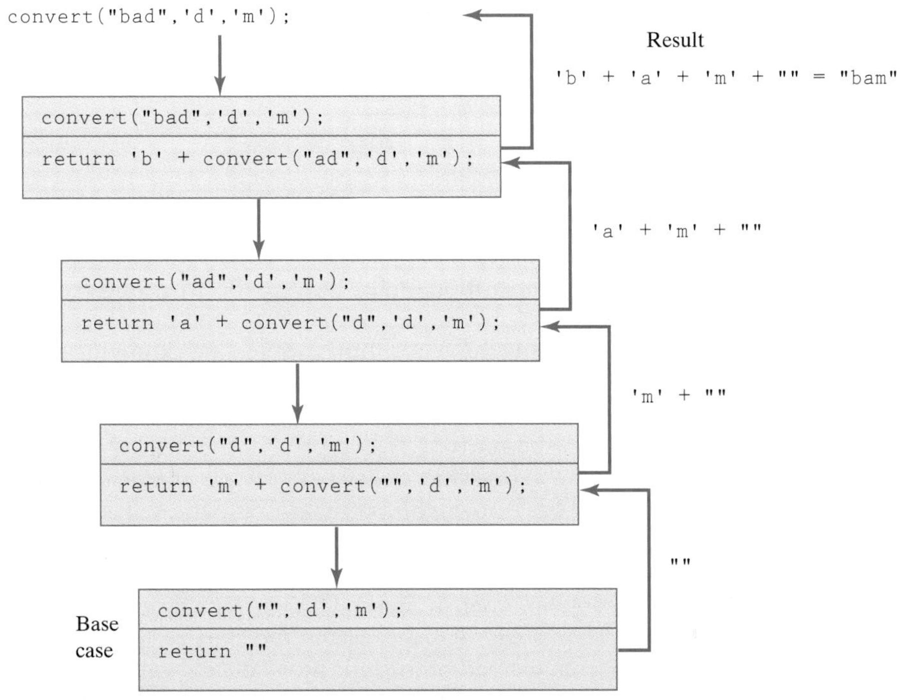

Figure 12–11 A trace of convert("bad",'d','m'), which returns "bam."

12.4.1 Recursive Sequential Search

Let's start by developing a recursive version of the sequential search algorithm that we discussed in Chapter 8. Recall that the sequential search method takes two parameters: the array being searched and the *key*, or target value, being searched for. If the key is found in the array, the method returns its index. If the key is not found, the method returns −1, thereby indicating that the key was not contained in the array. So the iterative version of this method has the following general form:

Method design

```
/**
 * Performs a sequential search of an integer array
 * @param arr is the array of integers
 * @param key is the element being searched for
 * @return the key's index is returned if the key is
 *  found otherwise -1 is returned
 * Pre:  arr is not null
 * Post: either -1 or the key's index is returned
 */
public int sequentialSearch(int arr[], int key) {
    return -1;          // failure if this is reached
}
```

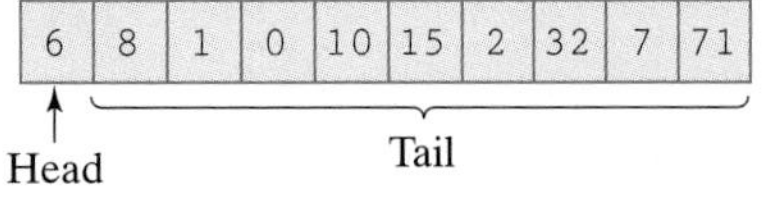

Figure 12–12 An array of int is a recursive structure whose tail is similar to the array as a whole.

If we divide the array into its head and tail, then one way to describe a recursive search algorithm is as follows:

```
If the array is empty, return -1
If the head of the array matches the key, return its index
If the head of the array doesn't match the key,
    return the result of searching the tail of the array
```

This algorithm clearly resembles the approach we used in recursive string processing: Perform some operation on the head of the array and recurse on the tail of the array.

How do we represent head/tail?

The challenge in developing this algorithm is not so much knowing what to do, but knowing how to represent concepts like the head and tail of the array. For strings, we had methods such as `s.charAt(0)` to represent the head of the string and `s.substring(1)` to represent the string's tail. For an array named `arr`, the expression `arr[0]` represents the head of the array. Unfortunately, we have no method comparable to the `substring()` method for strings that let's us represent the tail of the array.

Here's where we can use a parameter to help us out of this dilemma. Let's let the `int` parameter, *head*, represent the current head of the array (Figure 12–13). Then $head + 1$ represents the start of the tail, and `arr.length-1` represents the end of the tail. If we let *head* vary from 0 to `arr.length`, this will let us recurse through the array in head/tail fashion, searching for the key. When `head = arr.length`, we will know that we have gone all the way through the array, and we can stop searching. Our method will always be passed the whole array, but it will restrict the search to the portion of the array starting at *head*.

> **PROGRAMMING TIP: Subarray Parameter.** For methods that take an array argument, an `int` parameter can be used to designate the portion of the array that should be processed in the method.

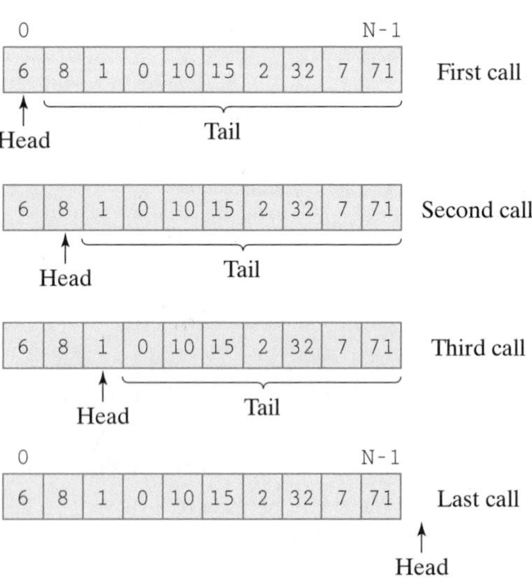

Figure 12–13 A parameter, *head*, can represent the head of some portion of the array.

Figure 12–14 The recursive search method takes three parameters. The *head* parameter points to the beginning of that portion of the array that is being searched.

```
/**
 * rSearch(arr,head,key) --- Recursively search arr for key
 *  starting at head
 * Pre:  arr != null and 0 <= head <= arr.length
 * Post: if arr[k] == key for some k,  0 <= k < arr.length, return k
 *       else return -1
 */
private int rSearch(int arr[], int head, int key)  {
    if (head == arr.length)      // Base case: empty list - failure
        return -1;
    else if (arr[head] == key)  // Base case: key found --- success
        return head;
    else                          // Recursive case: search the tail
        return rSearch(arr, head + 1, key);
}
```

This leads to the definition for recursive search shown in Figure 12–14. Note that the recursive search method takes three parameters: the array to be searched, `arr`, the `key` being sought, and an integer `head` that gives the starting location for the search. The algorithm is bounded when `head = arr.length`. In effect, this is like saying the recursion should stop when we have reached a tail that contains 0 elements. This underscores the point we made earlier about the importance of parameters in designing recursive methods. Here the *head* parameter serves as the **recursion parameter**. It controls the progress of the recursion.

The recursion parameter

Note also, that for the search algorithm we need two base cases. One represents the successful case, where the key is found in the array. The other represents the unsuccessful case, which comes about after we have looked at every possible head in the array and not found the key. This case will arise through exhaustion — that is, when we have exhausted all possible locations for the key.

DEBUGGING TIP: Recursive Search. For the recursive search method to work properly, it must be called with the correct value for the *head* parameter.

12.4.2 Information Hiding

Note that in order to use the `rSearch()` method, you would have to know that you must supply a value of 0 as the argument for the *head* parameter. This is not only awkward, but it is also impractical. After all, if we want to search an array, we just want to pass two arguments, the array and the key we're searching for. It's unreasonable to expect users of a method to know that they also have to pass 0 as the head in order to get the recursion started. This design is also prone to error, because it's quite easy for a mistake to be made when the method is called.

Design issue

For this reason, it is customary to provide a nonrecursive interface to the recursive method. The interface hides the fact that a recursive algorithm is being used, but this is exactly the kind of implementation detail that should be hidden from the user. A more appropriate design would make the recursive method a `private` method that's called by the public method, as shown in the `Searcher` class (Figure 12–15).

Hide implementation details

EFFECTIVE DESIGN: Information Hiding. Unnecessary implementation details, such as whether a method uses a recursive or iterative algorithm, should be hidden within the class. Users of a class or method should be shown only those details that they need to know.

Figure 12–15 The `Searcher` class illustrates the principle of information hiding. Its `public` `search()` method calls its private `rSearch()` to perform the search. It thus hides the fact that it is using a recursive algorithm.

```
public class Searcher {

    /**
     *  search(arr,key) -- searches arr for key.
     * Pre:  arr != null and 0 <= head <= arr.length
     * Post: if arr[k] == key for some k,  0 <= k < arr.length, return k
     *       else return -1
     */
    public int search(int arr[], int key) {
        return rSearch(arr, 0, key);        // Call rSearch to do the work
    }

    /**
     * rSearch(arr, head, key) -- Recursively search arr for key
     *  starting at head
     * Pre:  arr != null and 0 <= head <= arr.length
     * Post: if arr[k] == key for some k,  0 <= k < arr.length, return k
     *       else return -1
     */
    private int rSearch(int arr[], int head, int key)  {
        if (head == arr.length)      // Base case: empty list - failure
            return -1;
        else if (arr[head] == key)   // Base case: key found -- success
            return head;
        else                             // Recursive case: search the tail
            return rSearch(arr, head + 1, key);
    } // rSearch()

    public static void main(String args[]) {
        int numbers[] = {0, 2, 4, 6, 8, 10, 12, 14, 16, 18};
        Searcher searcher = new Searcher();
        for (int k = 0; k <= 20; k++) {
            int result = searcher.search(numbers, k);
            if (result != -1)
                System.out.println(k + " found at " + result);
            else
                System.out.println(k + " is not in the array ");
        } // for
    } // main()
} // Searcher
```

SELF-STUDY EXERCISES

EXERCISE 12.12 Write a `main()` method for the `Searcher` class to conduct the following test of `rSearch()`. Create an `int` array of ten elements, initialize its elements to the even numbers between 0 and 18, and then use a for loop to search the array for each of the numbers between 0 and 20.

12.4.3 Recursive Selection Sort

The *selection sort* algorithm was described in Chapter 8. It goes as follows. Suppose you have a deck of 52 cards. Lay them out on a table, face up, one card next to the other. Then starting at the last card, look through the deck, from last to first, find the largest card, and exchange it with the last card. Then go through the deck again starting at the next to the last card, find the next largest card, and exchange it with the next to the last card. Then go to the next card, and so on. If you repeat this process 51 times, the deck will be completely sorted.

Sorting a deck of cards

DEBUGGING TIP: Off-by-One Error. Sorting algorithms are particularly susceptible to an off-by-one error. To sort an array with N elements, you generally need to make $N-1$ passes.

Let's design a recursive version of this algorithm. The algorithm we just described is like a head/tail algorithm in reverse, where the *last* card in the deck is like the head, and the cards before it are like the tail. After each pass or recursion, the last card will be in its proper location, and the cards before it will represent the unsorted portion of the deck. If we use parameter to represent *last*, then at each level of the recursion, it will be moved one card to the left.

Figure 12–16 illustrates this process for an array of integer. The base case is reached when the *last* parameter is pointing to the first element in the

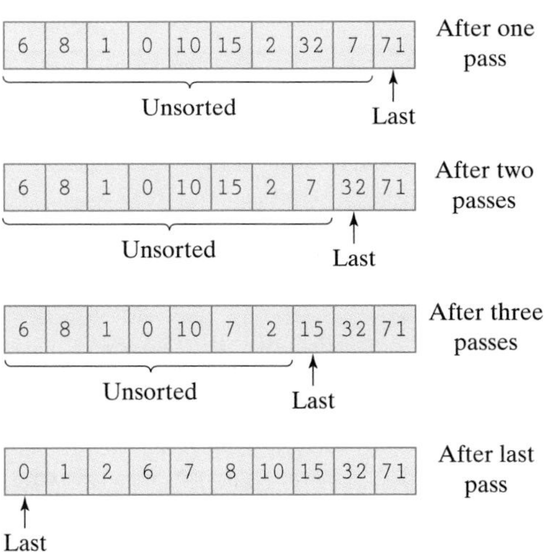

Figure 12–16 Selection sort: Using a head/tail algorithm in reverse to sort an integer array.

Figure 12–17 The `selectionSort()` method uses the `findMax()` and `swap()` methods to help it sort an array.

```
/**
 * selectionSort(arr,last) -- Recursively sort arr starting at last
 * Pre:  arr != null and 0 <= last < arr.length
 * Post: arr will be arranged so that arr[j] <= arr[k], for any j < k
 */
private void selectionSort(int arr[], int last) {
    if (last > 0) {
        int maxLoc = findMax (arr, last);    // Find the largest
        swap(arr, last, maxLoc);             // Swap it with last
        selectionSort(arr, last - 1);        // Move down the array
    }
} // selectionSort()
```

array. An array with one element in it is sorted. It needs no rearranging. The recursive case involves searching an ever smaller portion of the array. This is represented in our design, by moving *last* down one element to the left.

Figure 12–17 provides a partial implementation of selection sort for an array of `int`. In this definition, the array is one parameter. The second parameter, `int last`, defines that portion of the array, from right to left, that is yet to be sorted. On the first call to this method, *last* will be `arr.length-1`. On the second, it will be `arr.length-2`, and so on. When *last* gets to be 0, the array will be sorted. Thus, in terms of the card deck analogy, *last* represents the last card in the unsorted portion of the deck.

Task decomposition

Note how simply the `selectionSort()` method can be coded. Of course, this is because we have used separate methods to handle the tasks of finding the largest element and swapping the last element and the largest. This not only makes sense in terms of the divide-and-conquer principle, but we also already defined a `swap()` method in Chapter 8. So this is a good example of reusing code:

```
/**
 * swap(arr0, el1 el2) swaps el1 and el2 in the arrary, arr
 * Pre: arr is non null, 0 <= el1 < arr.length, 0 <= el2 < arr.length
 * Post: el1 is located where el2 was located in arr and vice versa
 */
private void swap(int arr[], int el1, int el2)  {
    int temp = arr[el1]; //  Assign the first element to temp
    arr[el1] = arr[el2]; //  Overwrite first with second
    arr[el2] = temp;     //  Overwrite second with temp (i.e., first)
} // swap()
```

The definition of the `findMax()` method is left as a self-study exercise.

PROGRAMMING TIP: Method Decomposition. A task can be simplified by breaking it up into simpler subtasks, especially if you already have methods for solving one or more of the subtasks.

SELF-STUDY EXERCISES

EXERCISE 12.13 As in the case of the `rSearch()` method, we need to provide a public interface to the recursive `selectionSort()` method, so that the user can just sort an array by calling `sort(arr)`, where `arr` is the name of the array to be sorted. Define the `sort()` method.

EXERCISE 12.14 Define an iterative version of the `findMax(arr,N)` method that is used in `selectionSort()`. Its goal is to return the location (index) of the largest integer between `arr[0]` and `arr[N]`.

12.5 Example: Drawing (Recursive) Fractals

Fractals

A *fractal* is a geometric shape that exhibits a recursive structure. When it is divided into parts, each part is a smaller version of the whole. Fractal patterns occur throughout nature. If you look at a graph of the Dow Jones Industrial Average (DJIA) over the past year, the graph for each day is similar to the graph of each month, which is similar to the graph of each year, and so on. Each part is a reduced-scale version of the whole. If you look at a coastline from an airplane, the shape of each part of the coastline, no matter how small the scale, resembles the shape of the whole coastline. If you look at a tree, each branch of the tree is similar in shape to the whole tree.

So, fractal patterns are all around us. Because of their self-similarity and divisibility, fractals are well suited for recursive programming. Drawing recursive patterns is also an excellent way to illustrate how to use parameters to create generality in method design. In this section we will develop two simple patterns and incorporate them into an applet.

12.5.1 Nested Squares

Earlier in this chapter, we developed a recursive definition for drawing a nested squares pattern (Figure 12–2). Now let's develop a recursive method that actually draws the pattern. For this pattern, the base case is the drawing of the square. The recursive case, if more divisions are desired, is the drawing of smaller patterns within the square:

```
Draw a square.
If more divisions are desired
    draw a smaller version of the pattern within the square.
```

How should we represent the problem?

An important consideration for this algorithm is to specify precisely what we mean by "if more divisions are desired." In other words, how exactly do we control the recursion? In our earlier definition of the pattern, we used the length of the side to control the algorithm. When $side \geq 5$, we recursed.

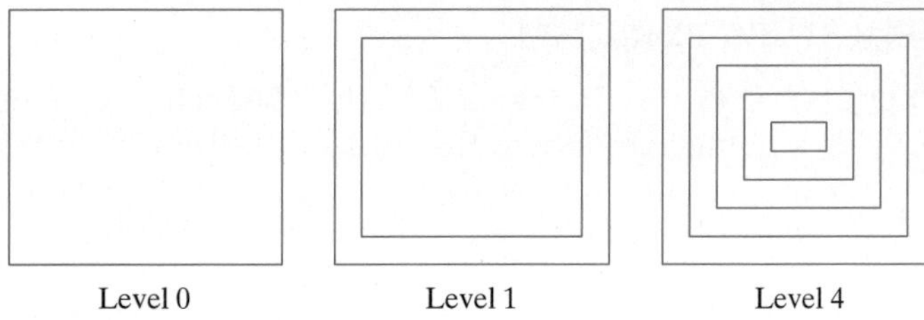

Figure 12–18 Levels 0, 1, and 4 of the nested squares pattern.

Levels of recursion

Another more general way to do this is to describe the fractal structure in terms of its *levels*. For nested squares, the level-zero pattern would be just the basic square shape (Figure 12–18). A level-one pattern would be the basic square shape plus an inner square, and so on. The higher the level, the more subdividing we do. Therefore, one way to control the recursion is to use a *level* parameter as the *recursion parameter* — as the parameter that controls the recursion.

```
Draw a square.
If the level is greater than 0,
    draw a smaller version of the pattern within the square.
```

What other parameters will we need for this method? If we're going to draw a rectangle, we'll need parameters for its *x*- and *y*-coordinates. This is a perfect job for a `Point` object. We'll also need a parameter for the length of sides of the square. Another issue we need to decide is how much the length of the sides should change at each level. Should length change by a fixed amount, by a fixed ratio, or by some other factor? In order to allow this kind of flexibility, let's use another parameter for this value.

These design considerations suggest the method shown in Figure 12–19. Note that we must also provide a `Graphics` parameter so the method can use the `drawRect()` method to draw the square. As we decided, the `level` parameter controls the recursion. Note that its value is decreased by 1 in the recursive call. This will insure that `level` will eventually reach 0, and recursion will stop.

Figure 12–19 The `drawBoxes()` method.

```
/**
 * drawBoxes() --- recursively draws a pattern of nested squares
 *  with loc as the top left corner of outer square and side
 *  being the length square's side.
 * level (>= 0) is the recursion paramenter (base case: level  0)
 * delta is used to adjust the length of the side.
 */
private void drawBoxes(Graphics g, int level, Point loc, int side, int delta) {
    g.drawRect(loc.x, loc.y, side, side );
    if (level > 0) {
        Point newLoc = new Point( loc.x + delta, loc.y + delta);
        drawBoxes(g, level - 1, newLoc, side - 2 * delta, delta);
    }
} // drawBoxes()
```

Finally, note the use of the `delta` parameter. In this case it is used to change the length of the sides by a fixed amount, `2 * delta`, at each level. It is also used to calculate the x- and y-coordinates for the location of the next level of boxes, *(loc.x + delta, loc.y + delta)*. But `delta`'s value remains constant through all the levels. This will lead to a pattern where the "gap" between nested squares is constant.

EFFECTIVE DESIGN: Levels of Recursion. Many recursive algorithms use a *level* parameter as the recursion parameter.

SELF-STUDY EXERCISES

EXERCISE 12.15 Trace through the `drawBoxes()` method and draw the level four and level five versions of the nested boxes pattern. Assume that the initial values for `side` and `delta` are 100 and 5, respectively, and the initial coordinates for `loc` are (20,20).

EXERCISE 12.16 The pattern shown in Figure 12–20 can be drawn by using `delta` as a fixed ratio of the length of the side, for example, 10 percent. Modify the `drawBoxes()` method to use `delta` in this way.

EXERCISE 12.17 Write an iterative version of the `drawBoxes()` method. (*Hint*: on each iteration, you must change the x- and y-coordinates of the square's location and the length of its side.)

12.5.2 The Sierpinski Gasket

Let's return now to the *Sierpinski gasket* pattern that we introduced at the start of this chapter. This is a much more interesting fractal pattern (Figure 12–21). The overall shape of the pattern is that of a triangle, but notice how the outer triangle is divided into three smaller triangles. Then each of those triangles are divided into three smaller triangles. If you continue this process of dividing and shrinking, you get the level-seven pattern shown here.

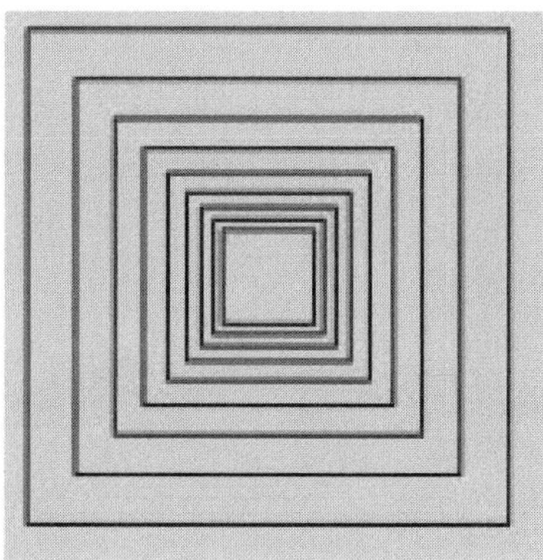

Figure 12–20 This version of nested boxes can be drawn by using `delta` as a fixed percentage of the length of the side.

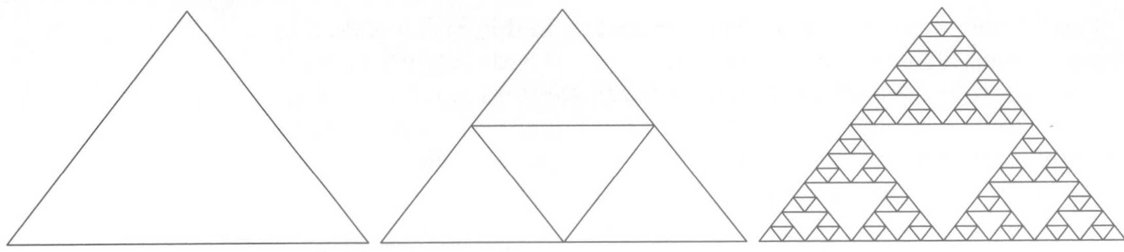

Figure 12–21 Levels 0, 1, and 7 of the Sierpinski gasket fractal pattern.

Let's develop a recursive method to draw this pattern. If we follow the same strategy we used in the nested squares example, we get the following algorithm:

```
Base case:        draw a triangle.
Recursive Case:   if more divisions are desired,
                      draw three smaller gaskets within the triangle.
```

For this pattern the base case is the drawing of the basic triangle. The recursive cases, if more divisions are desired, are the drawing of smaller gaskets within the triangle. Again we will use a `level` pattern to control the depth of the recursion. The higher the level, the more divisions will be drawn.

What other parameters do we need?

If we're going to draw a triangle shape, we need the coordinates of its three vertices — that is, an *x*- and *y*-coordinate for each vertex. This is a perfect job for a `Point` object. Taken together these design considerations suggest the method definition shown in Figure 12–22.

Levels of recursion

As we described earlier, we use the `level` parameter as the recursion parameter for this method. It controls the recursion. Note that each of the three recursive calls decreases the `level` by 1. This will insure that eventually `level` will equal 0, and recursion will stop.

Figure 12–22 The `drawGasket()` method.

```
/**
 * drawGasket() --- recursively draws the Sierpinski gasket
 *  pattern, with points p1, p2, p3, representing the vertices
 *  of its enclosing triangle.
 * level (>= 0) is the recursion paramenter (base case: level  0)
 */
private void drawGasket(Graphics g, int lev, Point p1, Point p2, Point p3) {
    g.drawLine(p1.x, p1.y, p2.x, p2.y);              // Draw a triangle
    g.drawLine(p2.x, p2.y, p3.x, p3.y);
    g.drawLine(p3.x, p3.y, p1.x, p1.y);
    if (lev > 0) {            // If more divisions desired, draw 3 smaller gaskets
        Point midP1P2 = new Point( (p1.x + p2.x) / 2, (p1.y + p2.y) / 2 );
        Point midP1P3 = new Point( (p1.x + p3.x) / 2, (p1.y + p3.y) / 2 );
        Point midP2P3 = new Point( (p2.x + p3.x) / 2, (p2.y + p3.y) / 2 );
        drawGasket(g, lev - 1, p1, midP1P2, midP1P3);
        drawGasket(g, lev - 1, p2, midP1P2, midP2P3);
        drawGasket(g, lev - 1, p3, midP1P3, midP2P3);
    }
} // drawGasket()
```

Note also how the three pairs of coordinates are used. Drawing a triangle is simple. Just draw three lines, from `(p1.x,p1.y)` to `(p2.x,p2.y)`, from `(p2.x,p2.y)` to `(p3.x,p3.y)`, and from `(p3.x,p3.y)` back to `(p1.x, p1.y)`. The most complicated part of the method is calculating the vertices for the three inner gaskets. If you look at Figure 12–21 again, you'll notice that each of the inner triangles uses one of the vertices of the main triangle, plus the *midpoints* of the two adjacent sides. Thus, the triangle on the "left" uses the left vertex `(p1.x,p1.y)`, and the midpoints of the other two lines: from `(p1.x,p1.y)` to `(p2.x,p2.y)` and from `(p1.x,p1.y)` to `(p3.x,p3.y)`. As you may remember from high school math, the formula for computing the midpoint of the line segment $(x1, y1)$ to $(x2, y2)$ is:

Midpoint of a line

```
( (x1 + x2) / 2, (y1 + y2) / 2 )
```

This formula is used repeatedly to calculate the vertices of the three smaller gaskets.

OBJECT-ORIENTED DESIGN: Tail Recursion

Although the `drawBoxes()` method is relatively simple to convert into an iterative version, the same cannot be said for the `drawGasket()` method. It is clearly a case where the recursive approach makes the problem easier to solve.

One difference between `drawBoxes()` and `drawGasket()` is that `drawBoxes()` is an example of a tail recursive method. A method is **tail recursive** if all of its recursive calls occur as the last action performed in the method. You have to be a bit careful about this definition. The recursive call in a tail recursive method has to be the last *executed* statement. It needn't be the last statement appearing in the method's definition.

Tail recursion

For example, the following method will print "Hello" *N* times. This method is tail recursive even though its last statement is not a recursive call:

```
public void printHello(int N) {
    if (N > 1) {
        System.out.println("Hello");
            printHello(N - 1);      // This will be the last executed statement
    } else
        System.out.println("Hello");
} // printHello()
```

This method is tail recursive because the last statement that will be executed, in its recursive cases, is the recursive call.

A tail recursive method is relatively easy to convert into an iterative method. The basic idea is to make the recursion parameter into a loop variable, taking care to make sure the bounds are equivalent. Thus, the following iterative method will print "Hello" *N* times:

```
public void printHelloIterative(int N) {
    for (int k = N; k > 0; k--)
        System.out.println("Hello");
}
```

In this case, we use the paramenter *N* to set the initial value of the loop variable, *k*, and we decrement *k* on each iteration. This is equivalent to what happens when we decrement the recursion parameter in the recursive call.

EFFECTIVE DESIGN: Tail Recursion. Tail recursive algorithms are relatively simple to convert into iterative algorithms that do the same thing.

As you can see, recursive methods that are not tail recursive are much more complex. Just compare the `drawGasket()` and `drawBoxes()` methods. Yet it is precisely for these nontail recursive algorithms that recursion turns out to be most useful. As you might expect, if you can't give a simple tail recursive solution to a problem, the problem probably doesn't have a simple iterative solution either. Thus, the problems where we most need recursion are those where we can't give a simple tail recursive or a simple iterative solution. And there are a lot of such problems, especially when you get into nonlinear data structures such as trees and graphs.

To gain some appreciation for this complexity, consider how difficult it would be to draw the Sierpinski gasket using an iterative approach. We could start by developing an outer for loop to account for the different levels in the pattern:

```
for (int k = level; k > 0; k--) {
    drawGasket(g, lev - 1, p1, midP1P2, midP1P3);
    drawGasket(g, lev - 1, p2, midP1P2, midP2P3);
    drawGasket(g, lev - 1, p3, midP1P3, midP2P3);
}
```

But now each of the method calls within the body of this loop would have to be replaced by very complex loops. That would be a daunting task. So the lesson to be draw from this observation is that recursion is most useful as a problem solving technique, for problems that don't yield to a simple iterative solution.

EFFECTIVE DESIGN: Recursion or Iteration. If you have difficulty designing an iterative solution to a problem, try developing a recursive solution to it.

SELF-STUDY EXERCISES

EXERCISE 12.18 Trace the `drawGasket()` method for a levels two and three. Pick your own values for the three vertices.

EXERCISE 12.19 Is the `printReverse()` method, discussed earlier, tail recursive? Explain.

EXERCISE 12.20 Is the `countChar()` method, discussed earlier, tail recursive? Explain.

OBJECT-ORIENTED DESIGN: Recursion or Iteration

As we mentioned at the outset of this chapter, recursive algorithms require more computational overhead than iterative algorithms. We're now in a good position, perhaps, to appreciate why this is so.

A recursive algorithm incurs two kinds of overhead that are not incurred by an iterative algorithm: memory and CPU time. Both of these are direct results of the fact that recursive algorithms do a lot of method calling.

Method call overhead

As we saw in our various traces, each time a method is called, a representation of the method call is placed on the *method call stack*. These representations often take the form of a *block* of memory locations, which can be quite large. The block must contain space for the method's local variables, including its parameters. Also, unless the method is `void`, the block must contain space for the method's return value. In addition it must contain a reference to the calling method, so it will know where to go when it is done. Figure 12–23 shows what the method call block would look like for the `rSearch()` method.

Memory overhead

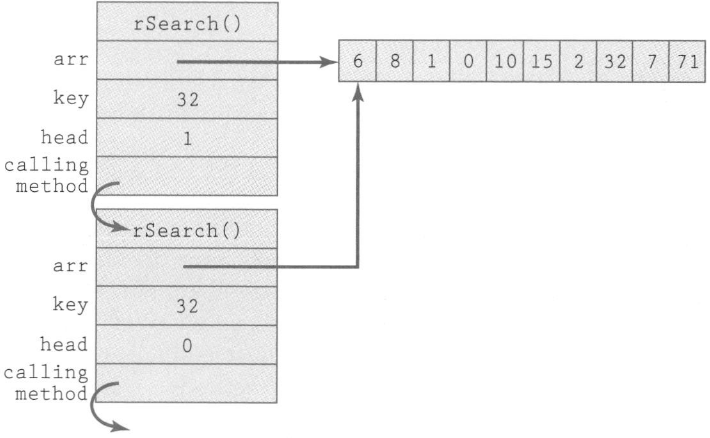

Figure 12–23 A more detailed picture of the method call stack, showing two method blocks for `rSearch()` after two levels of recursion.

CPU overhead

In addition to the memory required, a method call also requires extra CPU time. Each time a method is called, Java must create a method call block, copy the method call arguments to the parameters in the block, create initial values for any local variables that are used by the method, and fill in the return address of the calling method. All of this takes time, and in the case of a recursive method, these steps are repeated at each level of the recursion.

Compare these memory and CPU requirements with what normally transpires for an iterative algorithm — an algorithm involving a loop. The loop structure usually occurs entirely within a method, so it doesn't incur either the memory or CPU overhead involved in recursion. Therefore, iterative algorithms are generally more efficient than recursive algorithms. One useful guideline, then, is when runtime performance and efficiency are of prime importance, you should use iteration instead of recursion.

EFFECTIVE DESIGN: Iteration or Recursion. Use an iterative algorithm instead of a recursive algorithm whenever efficiency and memory usage are important design factors.

On the other hand, for many problems, recursive algorithms are much easier to design than the corresponding iterative algorithms. We tried to illustrate this point in our development of the Sierpinski gasket algorithm, but there are many other examples that we could have used. Given that programmer and designer time is the most expensive resource involved in software development, a recursive solution may be easier to develop and maintain than a corresponding iterative solution. And given the great cost of software development, a less efficient solution that is easier to develop, easier to understand, and easier to maintain may be preferable to an highly efficient algorithm that's difficult to understand. For some problems then, such as the Sierpinski gasket, a recursive algorithm may provide the best solution.

Efficiency of development

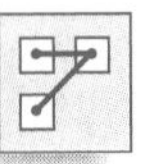

EFFECTIVE DESIGN: Keep It Simple. When all other factors are equal, choose the algorithm (recursive or iterative) that is easiest to understand, develop, and maintain.

One final point that's worth making is that some *optimizing* compilers are able to convert recursive methods into interative methods when they compile the program. The algorithms for doing this are well known. They are often subjects for study in a data structures course, so we won't go into them here. The resulting runtime programs will be just as efficient, in CPU time and memory, as if you had written iterative methods. The point is that if you have such a compiler, you really get the best of both worlds. You get the advantage of using recursion as a problem solving and software development approach, and the compiler takes care of producing an efficient object program.

Optimizing compiler

12.6 Flow of Control: The switch Multiway Selection Structure

The if and if-else selection structures were covered in Chapter 3. Another selection structure to add to our repertoire is the switch structure. It is meant to provide a shorthand way of coding the following type of multiway selection structure:

```
if (integralVar == integralValue1)
    // some statements
else if (integralVar == integralValue2)
    // some statements
else if (integralVar == integralValue3)
    // some statements
else
    // some statements
```

Note that each of the conditions in this case involves the equality of an integral variable and an integral value. This type of structure occurs so frequently in programs that most languages contain statements specially designed to handle it. In Java, we use a combination of the switch and break statements to implement multiway selection.

Exploring the Mandelbrot Set

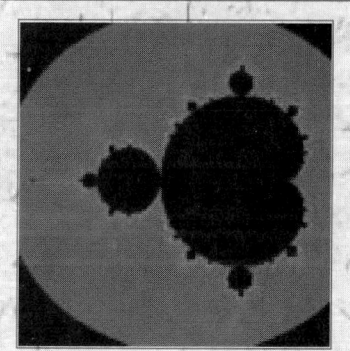

The Mandelbrot set is one of the most fascinating fractals. It is named after its discover, Benoit Mandelbrot, an IBM mathematician. The Mandelbrot set itself is the black, heart-shaped image in the picture. What makes the Mandelbrot set so interesting is that with the help of a Java applet you can explore the set as if you were taking a trip through outer space.

The most interesting regions to explore are those just along the boundary of the set. For example, notice that the boundary contains numerous circular shapes, each of which is itself studded with circular shapes. This is an example of the scaled self-similarity that we found to be so prevalent in recursive structures. By continually expanding the regions around the boundary, you'll find an infinite recursion of fascinating images and shapes. In some regions of the set you'll even find miniature replications of the set itself.

The Mandelbrot set is generated by an *iterated function system*. The mathematics underlying this fascinating object is quite accessible, and there are a number of on-line tutorials that explain how the set is generated and how the pictures are produced. Many of the Mandelbrot and fractal Web sites contain excellent Java applets that let you explore the Mandelbrot set, as well related sets.

An excellent place to start your exploration would be David Joyce's award winning Web site

(http://aleph0.clarku.edu/djoyce/julia/wwwrefs.html),

which contains references to a number other good sites. For a tutorial on how the various Java programs work, see

http://storm.shodor.org/mteach/.

The `switch` is designed to select one of several actions depending on the value of some integral expression:

```
switch (integralExpression)  {
    case integralValue1:
        some statements
    case integralValue2:
        some statements
    case integralValue3:
        some statements
    default:
        some statements
}
```

Integral expression

The *integralExpression* must evaluate to a primitive integral value — that is, a `byte`, `short`, `int`, `char`, `long`, or `boolean`. It may not be a `float`, `double`, or a class type. The *integralValues* must be literals or `final` variables. They serve as labels in the one or more case clauses that make up the `switch` statement body. The `default` clause is optional, but it is a good idea to include it.

A `switch` statement is executed according to the following rules:

a. The *integralExpression* is evaluated.
b. Control passes to the statements following the `case` label whose value equals the *integralExpression* or, if no cases apply, to the `default` clause.
c. Beginning at the selected label or at the default all of the statements up to the end of the `switch` are executed.

Consider the following example:

```
int m = 2;
switch (m)  {
case 1:
    System.out.println("m = 1");
case 2:
    System.out.println("m = 2");
case 3:
    System.out.println("m = 3");
default:
    System.out.println("default case");
}
```

In this case, because m equals 2, the following output would be produced:

```
m = 2
m = 3
default case
```

Obviously, this output does not match the following if-else multiway-selection structure , which would output, simply, `m = 2`:

```
int m = 2;
if (m == 1)
    System.out.println("m = 1");
else if (m == 2)
    System.out.println("m = 2");
else if (m == 3)
    System.out.println("m = 3");
else
    System.out.println("default case");
```

The reason for this disparity is that the `switch` executes *all* statements following the label which matches the value of the *integralExpression* (see again Step 3 above). In order to use the switch as a multiway selection, you must force it to `break` out of the case clause after executing that clause's statements:

```
int m = 2;
switch (m) {
case 1:
    System.out.println("m = 1");
    break;
case 2:
    System.out.println("m = 2");
    break;
case 3:
    System.out.println("m = 3");
    break;
default:
    System.out.println("default case");
}
```

In this example, the `break` statement causes control to pass to the end of the `switch`, with the effect being that one and only one case will be executed within the `switch`. Thus, the output of this code segment will be, simply, `m = 2`, matching exactly the behavior of the multiway if/else selection structure (Figure 12–24).

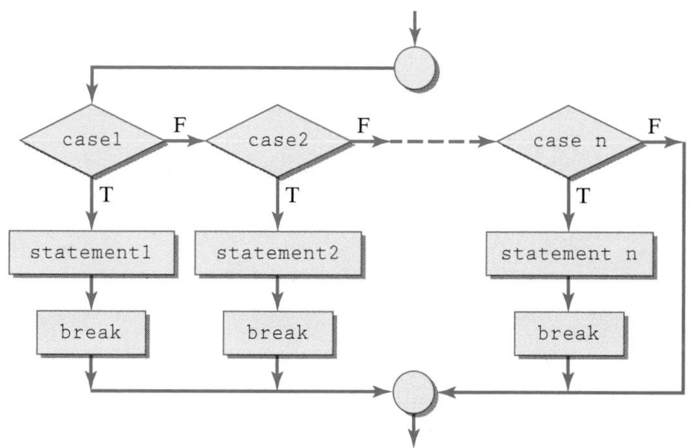

Figure 12–24 Flowchart of the multiway switch structure. Note that because of the `break` statement, one and only one case is executed.

PROGRAMMING TIP: Multiway Selection. A typical use for the `switch` statement is to use it together with `break` to code a multiway selection structure.

JAVA LANGUAGE RULE `break`. The `break` statement transfers control out of its enclosing *block*, where a block is any sequence of statements contained within curly brackets, { and }.

DEBUGGING TIP: Switch without `break`. A common error in coding the switch-based multiway selection is forgetting to put a `break` statement at the end of each clause. This may cause more than one case to be executed.

SELF-STUDY EXERCISES

EXERCISE 12.21 Identify any errors in the following switch structures. If there is no error, specify the output.

```
(a) int k = 0;
   switch (k)
   case 0:
       System.out.println("zero");
       break;
   case 1:
       System.out.println("one");
       break;
   default:
       System.out.println("default");
       break;
(b) int k = 0;
   switch (k + 1) {
   case 0:
       System.out.println("zero");
       break;
   case 1:
       System.out.println("one");
       break;
   default:
       System.out.println("default");
       break;
   }
(c) int k = 6;
   switch (k / 3.0) {
   case 2:
       System.out.println("zero");
       break;
   case 3:
       System.out.println("one");
       break;
   default:
       System.out.println("default");
       break;
   }
```

EXERCISE 12.22 Flavors of ice cream are represented as integers where 0 is vanilla, 1 is chocolate, and 2 is strawberry. Write a `switch` statement that checks an integer variable `flavor` and prints out the name of the ice cream flavor or prints "Error" in the default case.

From the Java Library: `JComboBox`

One of the most common uses for the `switch/break` structure is in implementing menus. The basic idea is that the user selects one option from among several alternatives. The alternatives can serve as the individual cases in the `switch/break` structure. For each case, the program takes the appropriate action. To illustrate this technique for GUI interfaces, we introduce the `JComboBox` component.

A `JComboBox` is a Swing component that combines a text field and a drop-down list. It lets the user either type in a selection or choose a selection from a list that appears when the user requests it. (A `JComboBox`'s drop-down behavior is somewhat similar to a `java.awt.Choice` box.)

Drop-down menu

A `JComboBox` can be used to represent a *drop-down menu*. When the user clicks on a `JComboBox`, a list of options drops down, and the user can select a particular option which is stored in the box's internal state (Figure 12–25). The list of options associated with a `JComboBox` can be built beforehand and inserted into the component in a constructor, or items can be inserted one at a time by repeatedly using its `addItem()` method.

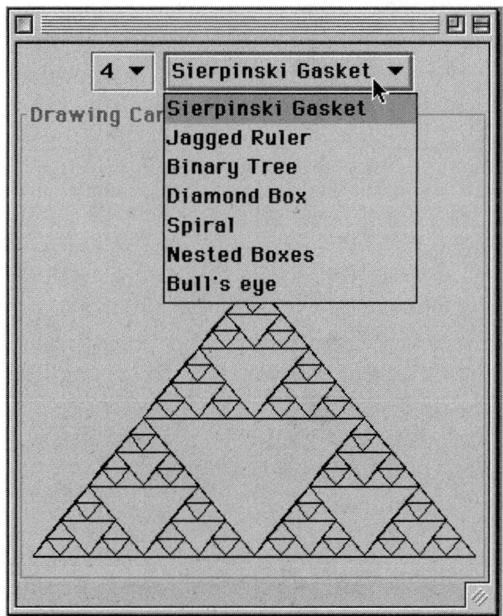

Figure 12–25 Using a `JComboBox` box.

Figure 12–26 The `java.swing.JComboBox` class.

```
public class JComboBox extends JComponent implements ItemSelectable {
   // Constructors
    public JComboBox();
    public JComboBox(Object items[]);
    public JComboBox(Vector items);
   // Public instance methods
    public void   addActionListener(ActionListener l);
    public void   addItem(Object item); // Add an object
    public void   addItemListener(ItemListener l);
    public Object getItemAt(int index); // Get by index
    public int    getSelectedIndex();   // Get selected's position
    public Object getSelectedItem();    // Get selected's name
    public void   setSelectedIndex(int index);    // Select by position
    public void   setSelectedItem(Object item);    // Select by item
}
```

As Figure 12–26 shows, either an array or a vector of items can be passed to a constructor method to initialize the box's menu. The items stored in a `JComboBox` box are references to `Objects`, most commonly `Strings` that represent the name of the menu item. They are stored in the (zero indexed) order in which they are added. The `addItem()` method is used to add an individual `Object` to a `JComboBox`. By default, the first item added to a `JComboBox` will be the *selected* item until the user selects another item.

When the user makes a selection in a `JComboBox`, the item selected can be gotten either by its reference (`getSelectedItem()`) or by its position within the menu (`getSelectedIndex()`). There are also methods to `setSelectedItem()` and `setSelectedIndex()` that let you select an individual item either by its reference or its position. The `addItemListener()` method is used to designate some object as the listener for the `ItemEvents` that are generated whenever the user selects a menu option. Alternatively, the `addActionListener()` method let's you handle action events, such as when the user types a value into the box.

A `JComboBox` Example

Problem statement

As a simple example, let's design an applet interface that can be used to display the fractal patterns we developed earlier. This program will also be used in this chapter's lab, where you will develop some additional fractal drawings. We want an interface that lets the user select from among the available patterns — we'll use the Sierpinski gasket and nested boxes for starters. In addition, the user should also be able to select different levels for the drawings, from 0 to 9. We want to present these options in two menus, with one `JComboBox` for each menu.

The first step is to declare and instantiate the `JComboBoxes` as instance variables:

```
private String items[] = {"Sierpinski Gasket","Nested Boxes"};
private JComboBox patterns = new JComboBox(items);
private JComboBox levels = new JComboBox();
```

Note that in this case we pass the constructor for the patterns menu an entire array of items. If we hadn't done it this way, we would add individual items to the combo box in the applet's init() method. In fact that's how we'll initialize the levels menu:

```
for (int k=0; k < 10; k++)          // Add 10 levels
    levels.addItem(k + "" );
levels.setSelectedItem("4");        // Select level 4 as default
```

This loop would be placed in the applet's init() method. It adds strings representing levels 0 to 9 to the menu and initializes the box so that level 4 is the showing as the default option.

Our next step is to designate the applet as the ItemListener for both menus—that is, the applet is named as the object that will handle the events that occur in the JComboBoxes. Then we add the JComboBox component to the applet's window:

```
controls.add(levels);                        // Control panel for menus
controls.add(patterns);
getContentPane().add(controls, "North"); // Add the controls
getContentPane().add(canvas, "Center");  // And the drawing panel
levels.addItemListener(this);                // Register the menus with a listener
patterns.addItemListener(this);
```

Note that we use a separate controls panel (a JPanel) for the two menus and a canvas panel (another JPanel) for the drawings.

The next step is to implement the itemStateChanged() method to handle the user's selections. Whenever the user selects an item from a JComboBox menu, an ItemEvent is generated. In order to handle these events, the applet must implement the ItemListener interface , which consists of the single method itemStateChanged(). This method is invoked automatically whenever the user selects an item from one of the JComboBoxes:

```
public void itemStateChanged(ItemEvent e) {
    canvas.setPattern(patterns.getSelectedIndex(), levels.getSelectedIndex());
    repaint();
}
```

The itemStateChanged() method has the same general form as the actionPerformed() method, except that its parameter is an ItemEvent. For this example, the program uses the getSelectedIndex() method to get the selected pattern and the selected level by their respective item numbers within the menus. It then passes these values along to the canvas object, which takes care of the drawing. Finally, the method invokes the repaint() method. Because the applet is a container, this will cause all of the its components to be repainted as well. The complete implementation for the applet is given in Figure 12–27.

Figure 12–27 The RecursivePatterns applet.

```
import java.awt.*;
import javax.swing.*;
import java.awt.event.*;

public class RecursivePatterns extends JApplet implements ItemListener  {
    private String choices[] = {"Sierpinski Gasket", "Nested Boxes"};
    private JComboBox patterns = new JComboBox(choices);     // Pattern choices
    private JComboBox levels = new JComboBox();               // Level choices
    private Canvas canvas = new Canvas();                     // Drawing panel
    private JPanel controls = new JPanel();

    public void init() {
        for (int k=0; k < 10; k++)                      // Add 10 levels
            levels.addItem(k + "" );
        patterns.setSelectedItem(choices[0]);          // Initialize the menus
        levels.setSelectedItem("4");

        canvas.setBorder(BorderFactory.createTitledBorder("Drawing Canvas"));
        controls.add(levels);                          // Control panel for menus
        controls.add(patterns);
        getContentPane().add(controls,"North");     // Add the controls
        getContentPane().add(canvas,"Center");      // And the drawing panel
        levels.addItemListener( this );    // Register the menus with a listener
        patterns.addItemListener( this );
        setSize(canvas.WIDTH,canvas.HEIGHT+controls.getSize().width);
    } // init()

    public void itemStateChanged(ItemEvent e) {
        canvas.setPattern(patterns.getSelectedIndex(), levels.getSelectedIndex());
        repaint();                                        // Repaint the applet
    } // itemStateChanged()
} // RecursivePatterns
```

The actual drawing of the fractal patterns is handled by the canvas JPanel component (Figure 12–28). All of the drawing is done in the paintComponent() method. Because the canvas is contained within the applet, the paintComponent() method is called automatically whenever the applet repaints itself. Notice how the switch statement uses the pattern that the user chose, to call the corresponding drawing method. You can see from this switch statement that a JComboBox's items are *zero indexed.*

Zero indexing

Figure 12–28 The Canvas class is a drawing panel.

```
import javax.swing.*;
import java.awt.*;

public class Canvas extends JPanel {
    public static final int WIDTH=400, HEIGHT=400;
    private final int HBOX=10, VBOX=50, BOXSIDE=200, BOXDELTA=10;
    private final Point gasketP1 = new Point(10, 280);   // Initial gasket points
    private final Point gasketP2 = new Point(290, 280);
    private final Point gasketP3 = new Point(150, 110);
    private int pattern = 0 ;                          // Current pattern
    private int level = 4;                             // Current level
```

Figure 12–28 *Continued*

```
    public Canvas() {
        setSize(WIDTH, HEIGHT);
    }

    public void setPattern(int pat, int lev) {
        pattern = pat;
        level = lev;
    }

    public void paintComponent(Graphics g) {
        g.setColor(getBackground());      // Redraw the panel's background
        g.drawRect(0, 0, WIDTH, HEIGHT);
        g.setColor(getForeground());
        switch (pattern) {
        case 0:
            drawGasket(g, level, gasketP1, gasketP2, gasketP3 );
            break;
        case 1:
            drawBoxes(g, level, new Point(HBOX, VBOX), BOXSIDE, BOXDELTA );
            break;
        } // switch
    } // paintComponent()

    /**
     * drawGasket() --- recursively draws the Sierpinski gasket
     *  pattern, with points p1, p2, p3, representing the vertices
     *  of its enclosing triangle.
     * level (>= 0) is the recursion paramenter (base case: level  0)
     */
    private void drawGasket(Graphics g, int lev, Point p1, Point p2, Point p3) {
        g.drawLine(p1.x, p1.y, p2.x, p2.y);             // Draw a triangle
        g.drawLine(p2.x, p2.y, p3.x, p3.y);
        g.drawLine(p3.x, p3.y, p1.x, p1.y);
        if (lev > 0) {            // If more divisions desired, draw 3 smaller gaskets
            Point midP1P2 = new Point( (p1.x + p2.x) / 2, (p1.y + p2.y) / 2 );
            Point midP1P3 = new Point( (p1.x + p3.x) / 2, (p1.y + p3.y) / 2 );
            Point midP2P3 = new Point( (p2.x + p3.x) / 2, (p2.y + p3.y) / 2 );
            drawGasket(g, lev - 1, p1, midP1P2, midP1P3);
            drawGasket(g, lev - 1, p2, midP1P2, midP2P3);
            drawGasket(g, lev - 1, p3, midP1P3, midP2P3);
        }
    } // drawGasket()

    /**
     * drawBoxes() --- recursively draws a pattern of nested squares
     *  with loc as the top left corner of outer square and side
     *  being the length square's side.
     * level (>= 0) is the recursion paramenter (base case: level  0)
     * delta is used to adjust the length of the side.
     */
    private void drawBoxes(Graphics g, int level, Point loc, int side, int delta) {
        g.drawRect(loc.x, loc.y, side, side );
        if (level > 0) {
            Point newLoc = new Point( loc.x + delta, loc.y + delta);
            drawBoxes(g, level - 1, newLoc, side - 2 * delta, delta);
        }
    } // drawBoxes()
} // Canvas
```

IN THE LABORATORY: THE RecursivePatterns APPLET

The purpose of this lab is to gain some some hands-on experience with designing and implementing recursive algorithms. You will develop an applet that draws fractal patterns, similar to the nested boxes and Sierpinski graphics patterns developed earlier in the chapter. The objectives of this lab are

- To design and implement recursive graphics algorithms.
- To build a menu-driven applet interface that uses a `JComboBox`.
- To gain an appreciation for the importance of recursion as a problem solving technique.

Problem Description

Develop methods to draw the fractal patterns shown in Figure 12–29. Each pattern should be developed as a separate recursive method. Here are some design suggestions.

- **DiamondBoxes.** Like the Sierpinski gasket, the nested diamond pattern uses the midpoints of the line segments at one level to determine the vertices of the diamond pattern at the next level. The diamond shape can be drawn using `g.drawLine()`. Unlike Sierpinski gasket, however, it is tail recursive.
- **SquareSpiral.** The challenge in this pattern is to identify the basic pattern that gets repeated, on a smaller scale, at each level. The pattern itself can be drawn using only the `g.drawLine()` method.
- **Bull's-eye.** The bull's-eye pattern is an excellent place to use *XORmode.* If you paint a large circle, and then paint a smaller one inside it in XORmode, the inside circle will be in the opposite color.

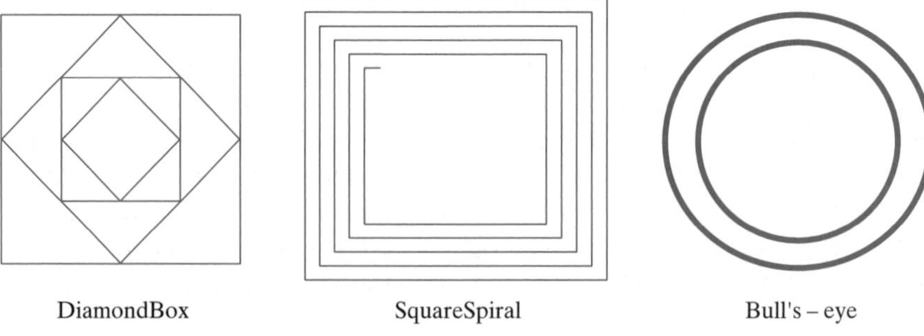

Figure 12–29 All three patterns are shown at level 4.

GUI Design

You can adapt the RecursivePatterns and Canvas classes for use in this project. The drawing methods themselves should be added to the Canvas class. As you incorporate each new pattern into the program, you must add an item for it in the patterns menu in RecursivePatterns. You must also add a case for it to the switch statement in the Canvas.paintComponent() method.

Note the utility of the menus for this program. One lists the available patterns, and the other lists the available drawing levels. This is a convenient way for the user to indicate which pattern to draw. It also constrains the number of levels that can be drawn. This helps prevent the creation of a "runaway algorithm" in case the user enters a large value for the level. If the user accidentally typed in 100, for example, the program would either crash or run for a very long time.

EFFECTIVE DESIGN: Menus. Because they constrain the user's choices to a fixed set of options, the use of menus for certain kinds of input reduces the chance of input errors.

Java Language Summary

The switch/break combination is an alternative to the nested if-else statement for coding multiway selection. It is particularly well suited for handling menu options. It takes the following form:

```
switch (integralExpression)  {
case integralValue1:
    // some statements
    break;
case integralValue2:
    // some statements
    break;
case integralValue3:
    // some statements
    break;
default:
    some statements
}
```

An *integralExpression* is one whose type is either byte, short, int, char, long, or boolean. The values used as case values must be constants—either literals or final variables.

The switch statement evaluates its *integralExpression* and then branches to the *case* whose value equals the expression's value. If no such case exists, it branches to the (optional) default case. Once control passes to a case clause, statements are executed in sequence up to the end of the switch statement or until a break is encountered. A break statement transfers control out of its enclosing block. It is used in this structure to transfer control out of the switch statement after one and only one case is executed.

CHAPTER SUMMARY

Technical Terms

base case	computational overhead	head
iterative method	Last-In-First-Out (LIFO)	method call stack
recursion parameter	recursive method	recursive definition
self-similarity	tail	tail recursive

New Java Keywords

`break`	`case`	`default`
`switch`	`void`	

Java Library Classes

`Choice`	`Graphics`	`ItemEvent`
`ItemListener`	`JComboBox`	`Object`
`Point`	`String`	

Java Library Methods

`actionPerformed()`	`addActionListener()`	`addItem()`
`drawRect()`	`getSelectedIndex()`	`init()`
`itemStateChanged()`	`paintComponent()`	`println()`
`setSelectedIndex()`	`substring()`	

Programmer-Defined Classes

`Canvas`	`RecursivePatterns`	`Searcher`

Programmer-Defined Methods

`convert()`	`countChar()`	`drawGasket()`
`countDown()`	`drawBoxes()`	`printString()`
`findMax()`	`printReverse()`	`swap()`
`rSearch()`	`selectionSort()`	

Summary of Important Points

- A *recursive definition* is one which defines the nth case of a concept in terms of the $(n - 1)$st case plus a limiting condition. It is based on the idea of breaking a problem up into smaller, self-similar problems.
- A *recursive method* is one which calls itself. It is usually defined in terms of a *base case* or limiting case, which stops the recursive process, and a recursive case, which breaks the method into a smaller, self-similar copy of itself. A *recursion parameter* is generally used to to control the recursion.
- An iterative algorithm is one that uses some kind of loop as its control structure. Any algorithm that can be done iteratively can also be done recursively, and vice versa.

- Because method calling is relatively costly both in terms of memory used and CPU time involved, a recursive algorithm is generally less efficient than an iterative one that does the same thing.
- In designing recursive algorithms, the *base case* defines a limit. Each level of recursion should make progress toward the limit, and the algorithm should eventually reach the limit. The limit is usually expressed in terms of the *recursion parameter*.
- A recursive method is *tail recursive* if and only if each of its recursive calls is the last action executed by the method.
- The `switch` statement, in conjunction with the `break` statement, is used for coding multiway selection structures.
- A Swing `JComboBox` component is used to represent a GUI dropdown menu.

ANSWERS TO SELF-STUDY EXERCISES

EXERCISE 12.1 The output produced by `mystery(0)` would be 0 1 2 3 4 5 6. The output produced by `mystery(100)` would be 100.

EXERCISE 12.2 The output produced by `mystery(5)` would be: 5 4 3, and so on. In other words, this is an infinite recursion. The base case, $N > 5$, is never satisfied.

EXERCISE 12.3

```
Definition: twoToN(N), N >= 0
  1, if N == 0                    // base case
  2 * twoToN(N - 1),  N > 0       // recursive case
```

EXERCISE 12.4 The function x^n is known as the power function:

```
Definition: power(X,N), N >= 0
  1, if N == 0                     // base case
  X * power(X, N - 1),  N > 0      // recursive case
```

EXERCISE 12.5 Yes, the two definitions for nested boxes are equivalent. Suppose the square starts out with a side of 20. The definition given in the exercise will also draw squares with sides 20, 15, 10, 5.

EXERCISE 12.6 A recursive definition for the pattern in Figure 12–4:

```
    Draw a square with side, s.
    Inscribe a circle with diameter, s.
    If s > 5,
        Draw a smaller version of the same pattern.  // Recursive case
```

EXERCISE 12.7 The `printString2("hello")` method will print: "olleh."

EXERCISE 12.8 A definition for `countDown()`:

```
/** countDown(N) recursively prints a countdown beginning at N
 *  and ending at 1
 * @param N >= 1
 * Base case: N == 0
 */
void countDown(int N) {
    if (N == 0)                              // Base case
        System.out.println("blastoff");
    else {
        System.out.print(N + ", ");          // Recursive case
        countDown(N - 1);
    }
} // countDown()
```

EXERCISE 12.9 A revised definition for `countDown()`:

```
/** countDown(N) recursively prints a countdown beginning at N,
 *  counting every other number, 10 8 6 ... and ending at "blastoff"
 * @param N >= 1
 * Base case: N <= 0
 */
void countDown(int N) {
    if (N <= 0)                                // Base case
        System.out.println("blastoff");
    else {
        System.out.print(N + ", ");  // Recursive case
        countDown(N - 2 );
    }
} // countDown()
```

EXERCISE 12.10 A method to sum the numbers from 1 to N.

```
int sum(int N) {
    if (N == 0)
        return 0;
    else
        return N + sum(N-1);
}
```

EXERCISE 12.11 A method to change each blank within a string to two blanks.

```
String addBlanks(String s) {
    if (s.length() == 0)
        return "";
    else if (s.charAt(0) == ' ')
        return ' ' + s.charAt(0) + addBlanks(s.substring(1));
    else
        return s.charAt(0) + addBlanks(s.substring(1));
}
```

EXERCISE 12.12

```
public static void main(String args[]) {
    int numbers[] = {0, 2, 4, 6, 8, 10, 12, 14, 16, 18};
    Searcher searcher = new Searcher();
    for (int k = 0; k <= 20; k++) {
        int result = searcher.search(numbers, k);
        if (result != -1)
            System.out.println(k + " found at " + result);
        else
            System.out.println(k + " is not in the array ");
    }
} // main()
```

EXERCISE 12.13 The `sort()` method is used as a public interface to the recursive `selectionSort()` method:

```
    /** sort(arr) sorts the int array, arr
     *  Pre: arr is not null
     *  Post: arr will be arranged so that arr[j] <= arr[k] for any j < k
     */
    public void sort(int arr[]) {
        selectionSort(arr, arr.length - 1);  // Just call the recursive method
    }
```

EXERCISE 12.14 An iterative version of `findMax()`:

```
/** findMax (arr,N) returns the index of the largest
 *  value between arr[0] and arr[N], N >= 0.
 *  Pre: 0 <= N <= arr.length -1
 *  Post: arr[findMax()] >= arr[k] for any k between 0 and N.
 */
private int findMax(int arr[], int N) {
    int maxSoFar = 0;
    for (int k = 0; k <= N; k++)
        if (arr[k] > arr[maxSoFar])
            maxSoFar = k;
    return maxSoFar;
} // findMax()
```

EXERCISE 12.15 Levels 4 and 5 of the nested boxes pattern are shown in Figure 12–30.

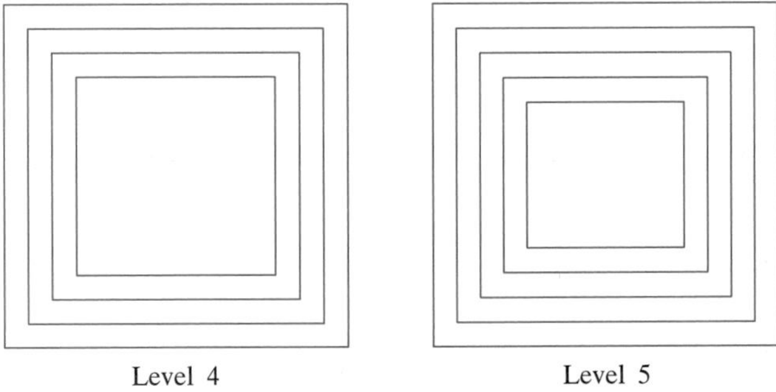

Figure 12–30 Levels 4 and 5 of the nested boxes pattern.

EXERCISE 12.16 The following method will reduce the length of the side by `delta` per cent at each level of recursion. The spacing between the boxes will vary by a constantly decreasing amount.

```
private void  drawBoxes(Graphics g, int level, Point loc, int side, int delta) {
    g.drawRect(loc.x, loc.y, side, side );
    if (level > 0) {
        int deltaside = side * delta / 100;       // Treat delta as a percent
        Point newLoc = new Point(loc.x + deltaside, loc.y + deltaside);
        drawBoxes(g, level - 1, newLoc, side - 2 * deltaside, delta);
    }
} // drawBoxes()
```

EXERCISE 12.17

```
private void drawBoxesIterative(Graphics g, int level, Point loc, int side, int delta) {
   for (int k = level; k >= 0; k--) {
       g.drawRect(loc.x, loc.y, side, side );  // Draw a square
       loc.x += delta;                          // Calculate new location
       loc.y += delta;
       side -= 2 * delta;                       // Calculate new side length
   }
} // drawBoxes()
```

EXERCISE 12.18 The level 2 and 3 gaskets are shown in Figure 12–31.

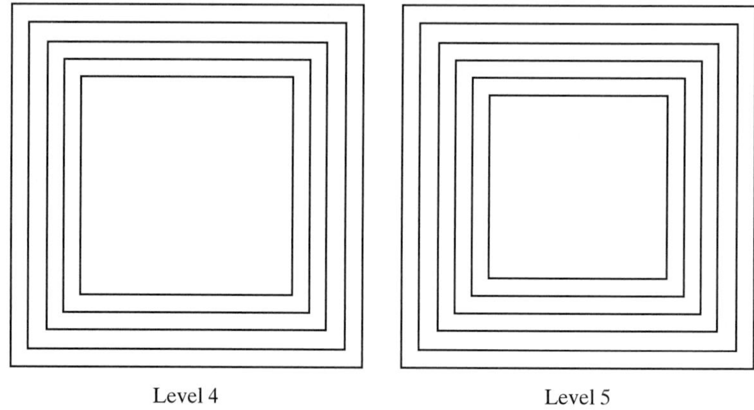

Figure 12–31 Levels 2 and 3 of the Sierpinski gasket.

EXERCISE 12.19 The `printReverse()` method is not tail recursive, because in that method the recursive call is not the last statement executed.

EXERCISE 12.20 The `countChar()` method is tail recursive. The recursive calls are not the last statements in the method definition. However, each of the recursive calls would be the last statement executed by the method.

EXERCISE 12.21 Identify any errors in the following switch structures. If there is no error, specify the output.

```
(a) int k = 0;
   switch (k)             // Syntax error: missing braces
   case 0:
       System.out.println("zero");
       break;
   case 1:
       System.out.println("one");
       break;
   default:
       System.out.println("default");
       break;
(b) int k = 0;
   switch (k + 1) {
   case 0:
       System.out.println("zero");
       break;
   case 1:
       System.out.println("one"); // Output 1
       break;
   default:
       System.out.println("default");
       break;
   }
(c) int k = 6;
   switch (k / 3.0) {    // Syntax error: k/3.0 is not integral value
   case 2:
       System.out.println("zero");
       break;
   case 3:
       System.out.println("one");
       break;
   default:
       System.out.println("default");
       break;
   }
```

EXERCISE 12.22 A `switch` statement to print ice cream flavors:

```
switch (flavor) {
case 1:
    System.out.println("Vanilla");
    break;
case 2:
    System.out.println("Chocolate");
    break;
case 3:
    System.out.println("Strawberry");
    break;
default:
    System.out.println("Error");
}
```

EXERCISES

1. Explain the difference between the following pairs of terms:

    a. *Iteration* and *recursion.*
    b. *Recursive method* and *recursive definition.*
    c. *Base case* and *recursive case.*
    d. *Head* and *tail.*
    e. *Tail* and *nontail* recursive.

2. Describe how the *method call stack* is used during a method call and return.
3. Why is a recursive algorithm generally less efficient than an iterative algorithm?
4. A tree, such as a maple tree or pine tree, has a recursive structure. Describe how a tree's structure displays *self-similarity* and *divisibility*.
5. Write a recursive method to print each element of an array of `double`.
6. Write a recursive method to print each element of an array of `double`, from the last to the first element.
7. Write a recursive method that will concatenate the elements of an array of `String` into a single `String` delimited by blanks.
8. Write a recursive method that is passed a single `int` parameter, $N \geq 0$, and prints all the odd numbers between 1 and N.
9. Write a recursive method that takes a single `int` parameter $N \geq 0$ and prints the sequence of even numbers between N down to 0.
10. Write a recursive method that takes a single `int` parameter $N \geq 0$ and prints the multiples of 10 between 0 and N.
11. Write a recursive method to print the following geometric pattern:

```
#
# #
# # #
# # # #
# # # # #
```

12. Write recursive methods to print each of the following patterns.

```
# # # # # # # #    # # # # # # # #
  # # # # # # #    # # # # # # #
    # # # # # #    # # # # # #
      # # # # #    # # # # #
        # # # #    # # # #
          # # #    # # #
            # #    # #
              #    #
```

13. Write a recursive method to print all multiples of M up to $M * N$.
14. Write a recursive method to compute the sume of grades stored in an array.
15. Write a recursive method to count the occurrences of a substring within a string.
16. Write a recursive method to remove the HTML tags from a string.
17. Implement a recursive version of the `Caesar.decode()` method.
18. The Fibonacci sequence (named after the Italian mathematician Leonardo of Pisa, ca. 1200) consists of the numbers `0,1,1,2,3,5,8,13,...` in which each number (except for the first two) is the sum of the two preceding numbers. Write a recursive method `fibonacci(N)` that prints the first N Fibonacci numbers.
19. Write a recursive method to rotate a `String` by N characters to the right. For example, `rotateR("hello", 3)` should return "llohe."
20. Write a recursive method to rotate a `String` by N characters to the left. For example, `rotateL("hello", 3)` should return "lohel."
21. Write a recursive method to convert a `String` representing a binary number to its decimal equivalent. For example, `binTodecimal("101011")` should return the `int` value 43.
22. A palindrome is a string that is equal to its reverse — "mom," "i," "radar" and "able was i ere i saw elba." Write a recursive `boolean` method that determines whether its `String` parameter is a palindrome.

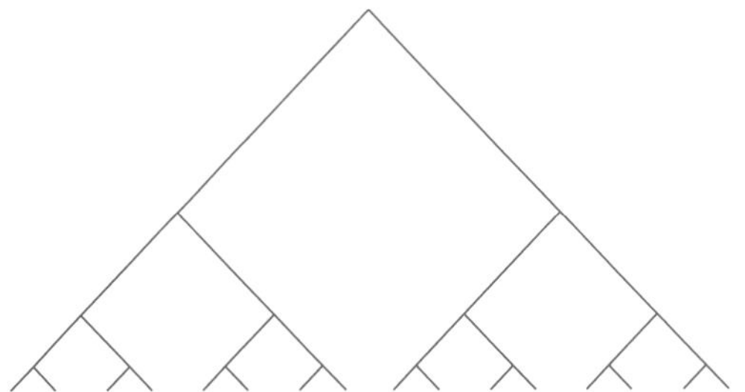

Figure 12–32 A level-4 binary tree pattern.

23. **Challenge:** Incorporate a `drawBinaryTree()` method into the `RecursivePatterns` program. A level–1 binary tree has two branches. At each subsequent level, two smaller branches are grown from the endpoints of every existing branch. The geometry is easier if you use 45 degree angles for the branches. Figure 12–32 shows a level–4 binary tree drawn upside down.
24. **Challenge: Towers of Hanoi.** According to legend, some Buddhist monks were given the task of moving 64 golden disks from one diamond needle to another needle, using a third needle as a backup. To begin with, the disks were stacked one on top of the other, from largest to smallest (Figure 12–32). The rules were that only one disk can be moved at a time, and that a larger disk can never go on top of a smaller one. The end of the world was supposed to occur when the monks finished the task!

    Write a recursive method, `move(int N, char A, char B, char C)`, that will print out directions the monks can use to solve the Towers of Hanoi problem. For example, here's what it should output for the three-disk case, `move(3, "A", "B", "C"`:

```
Move 1 disk from A to B.
Move 1 disk from A to C.
Move 1 disk from B to C.
Move 1 disk from A to B.
Move 1 disk from C to A.
Move 1 disk from C to B.
Move 1 disk from A to B.
```

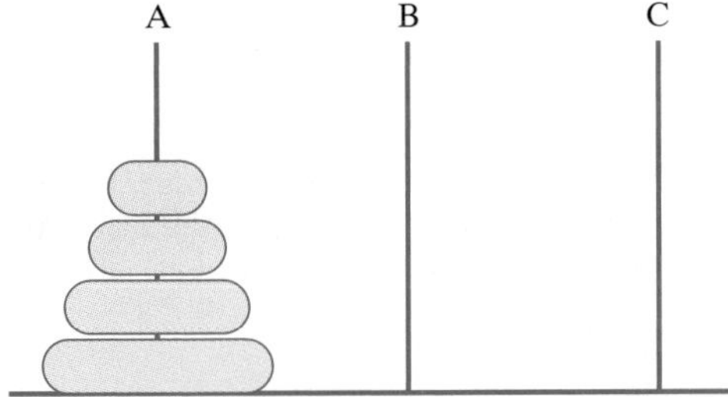

Figure 12–33 The Towers of Hanoi problem. Move all the disks from needle A to needle C. Only one disk can be moved at a time, and a larger disk can never go on top of a smaller one.

Photograph courtesy of Nell Deer, PhotoDisc, Inc.

13

Threads and Concurrent Programming

OBJECTIVES

After studying this chapter, you will

- Understand the concept of a thread.
- Know how to design and write multithreaded programs.
- Be able to use the `Thread` class and the `Runnable` interface.
- Understand the life-cycle of a thread.
- Know how to synchronize threads.
- Appreciate the use of inheritance in threaded applications.

OUTLINE

13.1 Introduction

This chapter concerns doing more than one thing at a time. Doing more than one thing at once is commonplace in our everyday lives. For example, let's say your breakfast today consists of cereal, toast, and a cup of java. You have to do three things at once to have breakfast: eat cereal, eat toast, and drink coffee.

Actually, you do these things "at the same time" by alternating among them: You take a spoonful of cereal, then a bite of toast, and then sip some coffee. Then you have another bite of toast, or another spoonful of cereal, more coffee, and so on, until breakfast is finished. If the phone rings while you're having breakfast, you will probably answer it — and continue to have breakfast, or at least to sip the coffee. This means you're doing even more "at the same time."

Everyday life is full of examples where we do more than one task at the same time.

The computer programs we have written so far have performed one task at a time. But there are plenty of applications where a program needs to do several things at once, or **concurrently**. For example, if you wrote an Internet chat program, it would let several users take part in a discussion group. The program would have to read messages from several users at the same time and broadcast them to the other participants in the group. The reading and broadcasting tasks would have to take place concurrently.

In Java, concurrent programming is handled by threads, as we will now see.

13.2 What Is a Thread?

A **thread** (or a *thread of execution* or a *thread of control*) is a single sequence of executable statements within a program. For Java applications, the flow of control begins at the first statement in `main()` and continues sequentially through the statements of the program. For Java applets, the flow of control begins with the first statement in `init()`. Loops within a program cause a certain block of statements to be repeated. If/else structures cause certain statements to be selected and others to be skipped. Method calls cause the flow of execution to jump to another part of the program, from which it returns after the method's statements are executed. Thus, within a single thread, you can trace the sequential flow of execution from one statement to the next.

Visualizing a thread

One way to visualize a thread is to imagine that you could make a list of the program's statements as they were executed by the CPU. Thus, for a particular execution of a program with loops, method calls, and selection statements, you could list each instruction that was executed, beginning at the first, and continuing until the program stopped, as a single sequence of executed statements. That's a thread!

Now imagine that we break a program up into two or more independent threads. Each thread will have its own sequence of instructions. Within a single thread, the statements are executed one after the other, as usual. However, by alternately executing the statements from one thread and another, the computer can run several threads *concurrently*. Even though the CPU executes one instruction at at time, it can run multiple threads concurrently by rapidly alternating among them. This is the same way you ate toast and cereal and drank coffee in our earlier breakfast example. From our perspective, it might look as if the computer had several CPUs working in parallel, but that's just the illusion created by an effective scheduling of the threads.

> JAVA LANGUAGE RULE **JVM Threads.** The Java Virtual Machine (JVM) is itself an example of a multithreaded program. JVM threads perform tasks that are essential to the successful execution of Java programs.

> JAVA LANGUAGE RULE **Garbage Collector Thread.** One of the JVM threads, the *garbage collector thread*, automatically reclaims memory taken up by objects that are not used in your programs. This happens at the same time that the JVM is interpreting your program.

13.2.1 Concurrent Execution of Threads

Multitasking

The technique of concurrently executing several tasks within a program is known as **multitasking**. It requires the use of a separate thread for each of the tasks. The methods available in the Java `Thread` class make it possible (and quite simple) to implement **multithreaded** programs.

Most computers, including personal computers, are *sequential* machines that consist of a single *Central Processing Unit (CPU)*, which is capable of executing one machine instruction at a time. In contrast, *parallel computers* are made up of multiple CPU's working in tandem.

Today's personal computers, running at clock speeds of over 500 megahertz — 1 *megahertz* equals 1 million cycles per second — are capable of executing millions of machine instructions per second. Despite its great speed, however, a single CPU can process only one instruction at a time.

Since CPUs can execute only one instruction at a time, multithreaded programs are made possible by dividing up the CPU's time and sharing it among the threads. The CPU's schedule is managed by a *scheduling algorithm* that is under the control of the operating system and the Java Virtual Machine (JVM). The choice of a scheduling algorithm is dependent on the platform, with thread scheduling handled differently on Unix, Windows, and Macintosh systems.

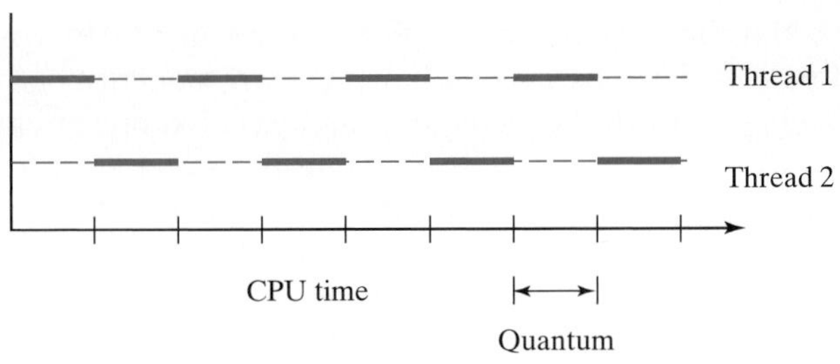

Figure 13–1 Each thread gets a slice of the CPU's time.

CPUs are sequential

One common scheduling technique is known as **time slicing**, in which each thread alternatively gets a slice of the CPU's time. For example, suppose we have a program that consists of two threads. Using this technique, the system would give each thread a small **quantum** of CPU time — say, one thousandth of a second (one *millisecond*) — to execute its instructions. When its quantum expired, the thread would be *preempted* and the other thread would be given a chance to run. The algorithm would then alternate in this **round-robin** fashion between one thread and the other (Figure 13–1). During each millisecond on a 300 megahertz CPU, a thread can execute 300,000 machine instructions. Thus, within each second of real time, each thread will receive 500 time slices and will be able to execute something like 150 million machine instructions.

Time slicing

Priority scheduling

Under **priority scheduling**, threads of higher priority are allowed to run to completion before lower priority threads are given a chance. The only way a high priority thread can be preempted is if a thread of still higher priority becomes available to run. In many cases, higher priority threads are those that can complete their task within a couple of milliseconds, so they can be allowed to run to completion without starving the lower priority threads.

JAVA LANGUAGE RULE **Thread Support.** Depending on the hardware platform, Java threads may be supported by assigning different threads to different processors, by time slicing a single processor, or by time slicing many hardware processors.

13.2.2 Multithreaded Numbers

Let's consider a simple example of a threaded program. Suppose we give each individual thread a unique ID number, and each time it runs, it just repeatedly prints its ID. For example, when the thread with ID 1 runs, the output produced would just be a sequence of 1's: 111111.

A `Thread` subclass

In the following definition, the `NumberThread` class is defined as a subclass of `Thread`:

```
public class NumberThread extends Thread {

    int num;

    public NumberThread(int n) {
        num = n;
    }

    public void run() {
        for (int k=0; k < 10; k++) {
            System.out.print(num);
        } //for
    } // run()
} // NumberThread
```

The constructor takes a single parameter that is used to set the thread's ID number. In the `run()` method, the thread simply executes a loop that prints its own number ten times.

Now let's define another class whose task will be to create a bunch of `NumberThreads` and get them all running at the same time. For each `NumberThread` we want to call its constructor and then `start()` it:

```
public class Numbers {

    public static void main(String args[]) {

        NumberThread number1, number2, number3, number4, number5; // 5 threads

        number1 = new NumberThread(1); number1.start(); // Create and start each thread
        number2 = new NumberThread(2); number2.start();
        number3 = new NumberThread(3); number3.start();
        number4 = new NumberThread(4); number4.start();
        number5 = new NumberThread(5); number5.start();
    } // main()
} // Numbers
```

Starting a thread

When a thread is `start()`ed, it automatically calls its `run()` method. The output generated by this version of the `Numbers` application is as follows:

```
11111111112222222222333333333344444444445555555555
```

From this output, it appears that the individual threads were run in the order in which they were created. As it turned out in this case, each thread was able to run to completion before the next thread started running.

What if we increase the number of iterations that each thread performs? Will each thread still run to completion? The following output was generated for 200 iterations per thread:

```
111111111111111111111111111111111111111111111111111111111111
111111111111111111111111111111111111111111111111111111111111
111111111111111111111111111111111111111111111111111112222222
222222222222222222222222222222222222222222222222222222222222
222222222222222222222222222222222222222222222222222222222222
222222222222222222222222222222222222223333333333333333333333
333333333333333333333333333333333333333333333333333333333333
333333333333333333333334444444444444444444444444444444444444
444444444444444444444444444444444444444444444444444444444444
444444444555555555555555555555555555555555555555555555555555
555555555555555555555555555555555555555555555555555552222222
222233333333333333333333333333333333333333333333333333333333
333333333333444444444444444444444444555555555555555555555555
555555555555555555555555555555555555555555555544444444444444
444444444444444444444444444444
```

Note that in this case only thread 1 managed to run to completion. Threads 2, 3, 4, and 5 did not. As this example illustrates, the order and timing of a thread's execution is highly unpredictable.

> **JAVA LANGUAGE RULE** **Thread Creation.** One way to create a thread in Java is to define a subclass of `Thread` and override the default `run()` method.

From the Java Library: The `Thread` class

The `java.lang.Thread` class contains the following public methods (a partial list):

```
public class Thread extends Object implements Runnable {
    // Constructors
     public Thread();
     public Thread(Runnable target);
     public Thread( String name );

    // Class methods
     public static native void sleep(long ms) throws InterruptedException;
     public static native void yield();

    // Instance methods
     public final String getName();
     public final int getPriority();
     public void run();              // Inherited from runnable
     public final void setName();
     public final void setPriority();
     public synchronized native void start();
     public final void stop();
}
```

Note that `Thread` implements the `Runnable` interface, which consists of the `run()` method:

```
public abstract interface Runnable {
  public abstract void run();
}
```

The Runnable interface

Another way to create a thread is to create a Thread instance and pass it a Runnable object which will become its body. A Runnable object is any object that implements the Runnable interface — that is, any object that implements the run() method. The following example provides an alternative way to implement the NumberThread program:

```
public class NumberPrinter implements Runnable {
    int num;

    public NumberPrinter(int n) {
        num = n;
    }

    public void run() {
        for (int k=0; k < 10; k++)
            System.out.print(num);
    } // run()
} // NumberPrinter
```

Given this definition, we would then pass instances of this class to the individual threads as we create them:

```
public class Numbers {

    public static void main(String args[]) {

        Thread number1, number2, number3, number4, number5; // 5 threads

        number1 = new Thread(new NumberPrinter(1)); number1.start(); // Create and start each thread
        number2 = new Thread(new NumberPrinter(2)); number2.start();
        number3 = new Thread(new NumberPrinter(3)); number3.start();
        number4 = new Thread(new NumberPrinter(4)); number4.start();
        number5 = new Thread(new NumberPrinter(5)); number5.start();
    } // main()
} // Numbers
```

The NumberPrinter class implements Runnable by defining exactly the same run() that was used previously in the NumberThread class. We then pass instances of NumberPrinter when we create the individual threads. Doing things this way gives exactly the same output as above.

JAVA LANGUAGE RULE **Thread Creation.** A thread can be created by passing a Runnable object to a new Thread instance. The object's run() method will be invoked automatically as soon as the thread's start() method is called.

EFFECTIVE DESIGN: Converting a Class to a Thread. Using the Runnable interface to create threads enables you to turn an existing class into a thread. For most applications, using the Runnable interface is preferable to redefining the class as a Thread subclass.

SELF-STUDY EXERCISES

EXERCISE 13.1 Use the Runnable interface to convert the following class into a thread. You want the thread to print all the odd numbers up to its bound:

```
public class PrintOdds {
    private int bound;
    public PrintOdds(int b) {
        bound = b;
    }

    public void print() {
        if (int k = 1; k < bound; k+=2)
            System.out.println(k);
    }
} // PrintOdds
```

Thread Control

Controlling threads

The various methods in the Thread class can be used to exert some control over a thread's execution. The start() and stop() methods play the obvious roles of starting and stopping a thread. These methods will sometimes be called automatically. For example, an applet is treated as a thread by the browser, or appletviewer, which is responsible for starting and stopping it.

As we saw in the NumberThread example, the run() method encapsulates the thread's basic algorithm. It is usually not called directly. Instead, it is called by the thread's start() method, which handles any system-dependent initialization tasks before calling run().

Thread Priority

The setPriority(int) method lets you set a thread's priority to an integer value between Thread.MIN_PRIORITY and Thread.MAX_PRIORITY, the bounds defined as constants in the Thread class. Using setPriority() gives you some control over a thread's execution. In general, higher priority threads get to run before, and longer than, lower priority threads.

JAVA LANGUAGE RULE **Preemption.** A higher priority thread that wants to run will *preempt* any threads of lower priority.

To see how setPriority() works, suppose we change NumberThread's constructor to the following:

```
public NumberThread(int n) {
    num = n;
    setPriority(n);
}
```

In this case, each thread sets its priority to its ID number. So, thread five will have priority five, a higher priority than all the other threads. Suppose we now run two million iterations of each of these threads. Because two million iterations will take a long time if we print the thread's ID on each iteration, let's modify the `run()` method, so that the ID is printed every one million iterations:

Thread priority

```
for (int k = 0; k < 10; k++)
    if (k % 1000000 == 0)
        System.out.print(num);
```

Given this modification, we get the following output when we run `Numbers`:

```
5544332211
```

It appears from this output that the threads ran to completion in priority order. Thus thread five completed two million iterations before thread four started to run, and so on. This shows that, on my system at least, the Java Virtual Machine (JVM) supports priority scheduling.

PROGRAMMING TIP: Platform Dependence. Thread implementation in Java is platform dependent. Adequate testing is necessary to ensure that a program will perform correctly on a given platform.

EFFECTIVE DESIGN: Thread Coordination. One way to coordinate the behavior of two threads is to give one thread higher priority than another.

DEBUGGING TIP: Starvation. A high-priority thread that never gives up the CPU can starve lower-priority threads.

Forcing Threads to Sleep

The `Thread.sleep()` and `Thread.yield()` methods also provide some control over a thread's behavior. When executed by a thread, the `yield()` method causes the thread to yield the CPU, allowing the thread scheduler to choose another thread. The `sleep()` method causes the thread to yield and not to be scheduled until a certain amount of real time has passed.

Sleep vs. yield

JAVA LANGUAGE RULE Sleep versus Yield. Both the `yield()` and `sleep()` methods yield the CPU, but the `sleep()` method keeps the thread from being rescheduled for a fixed amount of real time.

The `sleep()` method can halt a running thread for a given number of milliseconds, allowing other waiting threads to run. The `sleep()` method throws an `InterruptedException`, which is a checked exception. This means that the `sleep()` call must be embedded within a `try/catch` block or the method it's in must throw an `InterruptedException`. Try/catch blocks were covered in Chapter 11.

```
try {
    sleep(100);
} catch (InterruptedException e) {
    System.out.println(e.getMessage());
}
```

For example, consider the following version of the `NumberPrinter.run()`:

```
public void run() {
    for (int k=0; k < 10; k++) {
        try {
            Thread.sleep((long)(Math.random() * 1000));
        } catch (InterruptedException e) {
            System.out.println(e.getMessage());
        }
        System.out.print(num);
    } // for
} // run()
```

In this example, each thread is forced to sleep for a random number of milliseconds between 0 and 1000. When a thread sleeps, it gives up the CPU, which allows one of the other waiting threads to run. As you would expect, the output we get from this example will reflect the randomness in the amount of time that each thread sleeps:

```
14522314532143154232152423541243235415523113435451
```

As we will see, the `sleep()` method provides a rudimentary form of thread synchronization, in which one thread yields control to another.

SELF-STUDY EXERCISES

EXERCISE 13.2 What happens if you run five `NumberThreads` of equal priority through two million iterations each? Run this experiment and note the output. Don't print after every iteration! What sort of scheduling algorithm (round-robin, priority scheduling, something else) was used to schedule threads of equal priority on your system?

EXERCISE 13.3 Try the following experiment and note the output. Let each thread sleep for 50 milliseconds (rather than a random number of milliseconds). How does this affect the scheduling of the threads? To make things easier to see, print each thread's ID after every 100,000 iterations.

EXERCISE 13.4 The purpose of the Java garbage collector is to recapture memory that was used by objects that are no longer being used by your program. Should its thread have higher or lower priority than your program?

The Asynchronous Nature of Threaded Programs

Threads are **asynchronous**. This means that the order of execution and the timing of a set of threads is sporadic and unpredictable. Threads are executed under the control of the scheduling algorithm used by the operating system and the Java Virtual Machine. In general, unless threads are explicitly synchronized, it is impossible to predict when and for how long an individual thread will run. In some systems, under some circumstances, a thread may run to completion before any other thread can run. In other systems, or under different circumstances, a thread may run for a short time and then be suspended while another thread runs.

Thread preemptions are unpredictable

One implication of a thread's asynchronicity is that it is not generally possible to determine where in its source code an individual thread might be preempted. You can't even assume that a thread will be able to complete a Java arithmetic operation once it has started it. For example, suppose a thread had to execute the following operation:

```
int N = 5 + 3;
```

This operation computes the sum of 5 and 3 and assigns the result to N. It would be tempting to think that once the thread started this operation, it would be able to complete it, but that is not necessarily so. You have to remember that Java code is compiled into a rudimentary bytecode, which is translated still further into the computer's machine language. In machine language, this operation would break down into something like the following three steps:

An arithmetic operation can be interrupted

```
Fetch 5 from memory and store it in register A.
Add 3 to register A.
Assign the value in register A to N.
```

Although none of the individual machine instructions can be preempted, the thread could be preempted between any two machine instructions. The point is that Java language instructions cannot be assumed to be uninterruptible. Therefore, it is impossible to make any assumptions about when a particular thread will run and when it will give up the CPU. This suggests the following important principle of multithreaded programs:

Threads are asynchronous

> **JAVA LANGUAGE RULE** **Asynchronous Thread Principle.** Unless they are explicitly prioritized or synchronized, threads behave in a completely *asynchronous* fashion.

> **PROGRAMMING TIP: Thread Timing.** Unless they are explicitly synchronized, your program cannot make any assumptions about when, or in what order, individual threads will execute, or where a thread might be interrupted or preempted during its execution.

As we will see, this principle plays a large role in the design of multi-threaded programs.

13.3 Using Threads to Improve Interface Responsiveness

One good use for a *multithreaded* program is to help make a more responsive user interface. In a single-threaded program, if the program is executing statements in a long (perhaps even infinite) loop, it will remain unresponsive to the user's actions until the loop is exited. Any action events that take place while the program is looping will be postponed until the loop is finished. Thus the user will experience a noticeable and sometimes frustrating delay between the time an action is initiated and the time it is actually handled by the program.

It's always a good idea that the interface be responsive to user input, but sometimes it is crucial to an application. For example, suppose a program is being used in a psychometric experiment that measures how quickly the user responds to a certain stimulus presented by the program. Obviously, for this kind of application, the program should take action as soon as the user clicks on a button to indicate a response to the stimulus.

Problem Statement

Problem specification

A psychologist is conducting a psychometric experiment to measure user response to a visual cue and asks you to create the following program. The program should have two buttons. When the "Draw" button is clicked, the program begins drawing thousands of black dots at random locations within a rectangular region of the screen. After a random time interval, the program begins drawing red dots. This change corresponds to the presentation of the stimulus. As soon as the stimulus is presented the user is supposed to click on a "Clear" button, which clears the drawing area (Figure 13–2). To provide a measure of the user's reaction time, the program should report how many red dots were drawn before the user clicked the "Clear" button.

Problem Decomposition

Interface class and drawing class

This program should be decomposed into two classes, an applet to handle the user interface and a drawing class to manage the drawing, which leads to the following design:

- `RandomDotApplet` Class: This class manages the user interface, responding to user actions by calling methods of the `Dotty` class.
- `Dotty` Class: This class contains `draw()` and `clear()` methods for drawing on the applet's drawing panel.

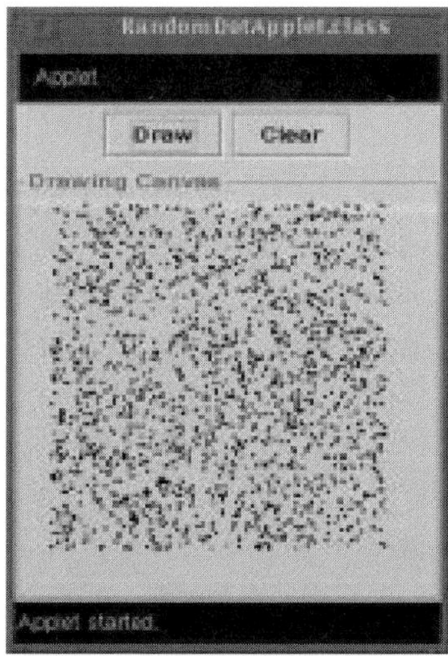

Figure 13–2 Random dots are drawn until the user clicks the "Clear" button.

The RandomDotApplet *Class*

GUI design

Figure 13–3 shows a GUI design for this program's applet interface. It contains a control `JPanel` that contains the two `JButtons`. The dots are drawn on a `JPanel`, which is positioned in the center of a `BorderLayout` design.

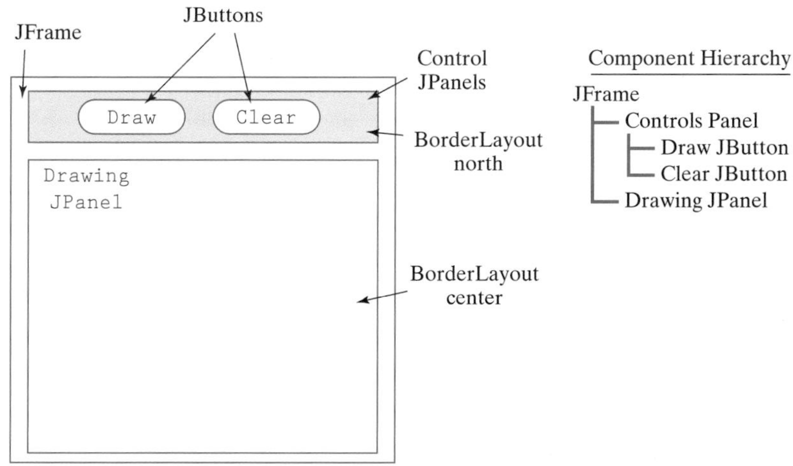

Figure 13–3 GUI design for an applet that draws random dots within a rectangle.

Figure 13–4 The RandomDotApplet class.

```
import java.awt.*;
import javax.swing.*;        // Import Swing classes
import java.awt.event.*;

public class RandomDotApplet extends JApplet implements ActionListener  {
    public final int NDOTS = 10000;

    private Dotty dotty;                              // The drawing class
    private JPanel controls = new JPanel();
    private JPanel canvas = new JPanel();
    private JButton draw = new JButton("Draw");
    private JButton clear = new JButton("Clear");

    public void init() {
        getContentPane().setLayout(new BorderLayout());
        draw.addActionListener(this);
        clear.addActionListener(this);
        controls.add(draw);
        controls.add(clear);
        canvas.setBorder(BorderFactory.createTitledBorder("Drawing Canvas"));
        getContentPane().add("North", controls);
        getContentPane().add("Center", canvas);
        getContentPane().setSize(400, 400);
    } // init()

    public void actionPerformed(ActionEvent e) {
        if (e.getSource() == draw) {
            dotty = new Dotty(canvas, NDOTS);
            dotty.draw();
        } else {
            dotty.clear();
        }
    } // actionPerformed()
} // RandomDotApplet
```

The `RandomDotApplet` (Figure 13–4) arranges the control and drawing panels in a `BorderLayout` and listens for action events on its `JButtons`. When the user clicks the "Draw" button, the applet's `actionPerformed()` method will create a new `Dotty` instance and call its `draw()` method:

```
dotty = new Dotty(canvas, NDOTS);
dotty.draw();
```

Note that `Dotty` is passed a reference to the drawing `canvas` as well as the number of dots to be drawn. When the user clicks the "Clear" button, the applet should call the `dotty.clear()` method. Of course, the important question is, how responsive will the applet be to the user's action?

The `Dotty` *Class*

What data do we need?

The purpose of the `Dotty` class will be to draw the dots and to report how many red dots were drawn before the canvas was cleared. Because it will be passed a reference to the drawing panel and the number of dots to draw, it will need instance variables to store these two values. It will also need a variable to keep track of how many dots were drawn. Finally, since it will be drawing within a fixed rectangle on the panel, the reference coordinates and dimensions of the drawing area should be declared as class constants:

```
private static final int HREF = 20, VREF = 20, LEN = 200; // Coordinates

private JPanel canvas;
private int nDots;            // Number of dots to draw
private int nDrawn;           // Number of dots drawn
private int firstRed = 0;     // Number of the first red dot
private boolean isCleared;    // Set to true when the user clears panel
```

The Dotty() constructor method will be passed a reference to a drawing panel as well as the number of dots to be drawn and will merely assign these parameters to its instance variables. In addition to its constructor method, the Dotty class will have public draw() and clear() methods, which will be called from the applet. The draw() method will use a loop to draw random dots. The clear() will clear the canvas and report the number of dots drawn.

Referring to the applet

The complete implementation of Dotty is shown in Figure 13–5. Note how its draw() method is designed:

```
public void draw() {
    Graphics g = canvas.getGraphics();
    for (nDrawn = 0; nDrawn < nDots; nDrawn++) {
        int x = HREF + (int)(Math.random() * LEN);
        int y = VREF + (int)(Math.random() * LEN);
        g.fillOval(x, y, 3, 3);                    // Draw a dot

       if (Math.random() < 0.001 && firstRed == 0) {
           g.setColor(Color.red);                  // Change color to red
           firstRed = nDrawn;
       }
    } //for
} // draw()
```

The drawing loop is bounded by the number of dots to be drawn. On each iteration the draw() method picks a random location within the rectangle defined by the coordinates, (HREF,VREF) and (HREF+LEN, VREF+LEN), and draws a dot there. On each iteration it also generates a random number. If the random number is less than 0.001, it changes the drawing color to red and keeps track of the number of dots drawn up to that point.

Drawing algorithm

The problem with this design is that as long as the draw() method is executing, the program will be unable to respond to the applet's "Clear" button. In a single-threaded design, both the applet and dotty are combined into a single thread of execution (Figure 13–6). When the user clicks on

Single-threaded design: Waiting for the loop to end

Figure 13–5 The Dotty class.

```
import java.awt.*;
import javax.swing.*;    // Import Swing classes

public class Dotty {
    private static final int HREF = 20, VREF = 20, LEN = 200; // Coordinates

    private JPanel canvas;
    private int nDots;          // Number of dots to draw
    private int nDrawn;         // Number of dots drawn
    private int firstRed = 0;   // Number of the first red dot

    public Dotty(JPanel canv, int dots) {
        canvas = canv;
        nDots = dots;
    }

    public void draw() {
        Graphics g = canvas.getGraphics();
        for (nDrawn = 0; nDrawn < nDots; nDrawn++) {
            int x = HREF + (int)(Math.random() * LEN);
            int y = VREF + (int)(Math.random() * LEN);
            g.fillOval(x, y, 3, 3);                   // Draw a dot

            if ((Math.random() < 0.001) && (firstRed == 0)) {
                g.setColor(Color.red);                // Change color to red
                firstRed = nDrawn;
            }
        } //for
    } // draw()

    public void clear() {                    // Clear screen and report result
        Graphics g = canvas.getGraphics();
        g.setColor(canvas.getBackground());
        g.fillRect(HREF, VREF, LEN + 3, LEN + 3);
        System.out.println("Number of dots drawn since first red = " + (nDrawn-firstRed));
    } // clear()
} // Dotty
```

the "Draw" button, the applet's `actionPerformed()` method is invoked. It then invokes `Dotty`'s `draw()` method, which must run to completion before anything else can be done. If the user clicks on the "Clear" button, while the dots are being drawn, the applet won't be able to get to this until all the dots are drawn.

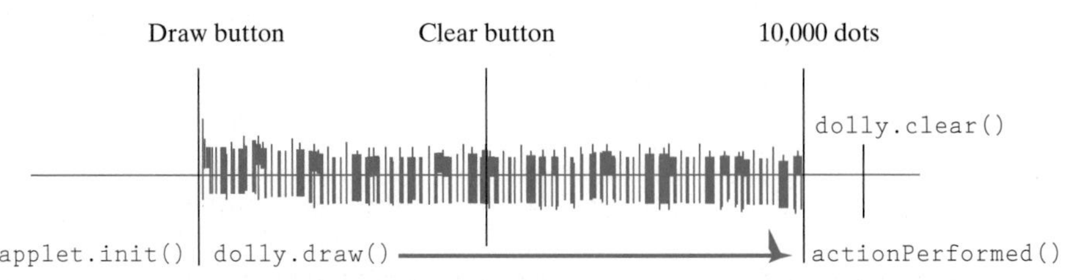

Figure 13–6 A single-threaded execution of random dot drawing.

If you run this program with `nDots` set to 10,000, the program will not clear the drawing panel until all 10,000 dots are drawn, no matter when the "Clear" button is pressed. Therefore, the values reported for the user's reaction time will be wrong. Obviously, since it is so unresponsive to user input, this design completely fails to satisfy the program's specifications.

JAVA LANGUAGE RULE **Single-Threaded Loop.** In a single-threaded design, a loop that requires lots of iterations will completely dominate the CPU during its execution, forcing other tasks, including user I/O tasks, to wait.

SELF-STUDY EXERCISES

EXERCISE 13.5 Suppose the Java Virtual Machine (JVM) was single-threaded, and your program got stuck in an infinite loop. Would you be able to break out of the loop by typing some special command (such as Control-C) from the keyboard?

13.3.1 Multithreaded Drawing: The `Dotty` Thread

One way to remedy this problem is to create a second thread (in addition to the applet itself) to do the drawing. The drawing thread will be responsible just for drawing, while the applet thread will be responsible for handling user actions in the interface. The trick to making the user interface more responsive will be to interrupt the drawing thread periodically so that the applet thread has a chance to handle any events that have taken place.

Multithreaded design: Interrupt the drawing loop

The easiest way to convert `Dotty` into a thread is to have it implement the `Runnable` interface:

```
public class Dotty implements Runnable {

    // Everything else remains the same

    public void run() {
        draw();
    }
}
```

This version of `Dotty` will perform the same task as before except that it will now run as a separate thread of execution. Note that its `run()` method just calls the `draw()` method that we defined in the previous version. When the `Dotty` thread is started by the `RandomDotApplet`, we will have a multithreaded program.

However, just because this program has two threads doesn't necessarily mean that it will be any more responsive to the user. There's no guarantee that the drawing thread will stop as soon as the "Clear" button is clicked. On most systems, if both threads have equal priority, the applet thread won't run until the drawing thread finishes drawing all *N* dots.

Thread control

DEBUGGING TIP: Thread Control. Just breaking a program into two separate threads won't necessarily give you the desired performance. It may be necessary to *coordinate* the threads.

Therefore, we have to modify our design in order to guarantee that the applet thread will get a chance to handle the user's actions. One good way to do this is to have `Dotty` sleep for a short instance after it draws each dot. When a thread sleeps, any other threads that are waiting their turn will get a chance to run. If the applet thread is waiting to handle the user's click on "Clear," it will now be able to call `Dotty`'s `clear()` method.

Using `sleep()` to interrupt the drawing

The new version of `draw()` is shown in Figure 13–7. In this version of `draw()`, the thread sleeps for 1 millisecond on each iteration of the loop. This will make it possible for the applet to run on every iteration, so it will handle user actions immediately.

Another necessary change is that once the `clear()` method is called, the `Dotty` thread should stop running (drawing). The correct way to stop a thread is to use some variable whose value will cause the run loop (or in this case the drawing loop) to exit, so the new version of `Dotty` uses the `boolean` variable `isCleared` to control when drawing is stopped. Note that the variable is initialized to `false` and then set to `true` in the `clear()` method. The for loop in `draw()` will exit when `isCleared` becomes `true`. This causes the `draw()` method to return, which causes the `run()` method to return, which causes the thread to stop in an orderly fashion.

EFFECTIVE DESIGN: Threaded Applets. Designing a multithreaded applet involves creating a secondary thread that will run concurrently with the applet thread. The applet thread handles the user interface, while the secondary thread performs CPU-intensive calculations.

PROGRAMMING TIP: Threading an Applet. To create a second thread within an applet requires three steps: (1) Define the secondary thread as a `Thread` subclass using `extend`, (2) override its `run()` method, and (3) incorporate some mechanism, such as a `sleep()` state, into the thread's run algorithm so that the applet thread will have a chance to run periodically.

Modifications to `RandomDotApplet`

We don't need to make many changes in `RandomDotApplet` to get it to work with the new version of `Dotty`. The primary change comes in the `actionPerformed()` method. In the original version of this method, each time the "Draw" button was clicked, we created a `dotty` instance and then called its `draw()` method. In the revised version we must create a new `Thread` and pass it an instance of `Dotty`, which will then run as a separate thread.

Starting the drawing thread

Figure 13–7 This version of Dotty implements the Runnable interface.

```
import java.awt.*;
import javax.swing.*;      // Import Swing classes

public class Dotty implements Runnable {
    private static final int HREF = 20, VREF = 20, LEN = 200; // Coordinates

    private JPanel canvas;
    private int nDots;                 // Number of dots to draw
    private int nDrawn;                // Number of dots drawn
    private int firstRed = 0;          // Number of the first red dot
    private boolean isCleared = false; // The panel has been cleared

    public void run() {
        draw();
    }

    public Dotty(JPanel canv, int dots) {
        canvas = canv;
        nDots = dots;
    }

    public void draw() {
        Graphics g = canvas.getGraphics();

        for (nDrawn = 0; !isCleared && nDrawn < nDots; nDrawn++) {
            int x = HREF + (int)(Math.random() * LEN);
            int y = VREF + (int)(Math.random() * LEN);
            g.fillOval(x, y, 3, 3);                     // Draw a dot

           if (Math.random() < 0.001 && firstRed == 0) {
               g.setColor(Color.red);                   // Change color to red
               firstRed = nDrawn;
           }

           try {
               Thread.sleep(1) ;                     // Sleep for an instant
           } catch (InterruptedException e) {
               System.out.println(e.getMessage());
           }

        } //for
    } // draw()

    public void clear() {
        isCleared = true;
        Graphics g = canvas.getGraphics();
        g.setColor( canvas.getBackground() );
        g.fillRect(HREF,VREF,LEN+3,LEN+3);
        System.out.println("Number of dots drawn since first red = " + (nDrawn-firstRed) );
    } // clear()
} // Dotty
```

```
public void actionPerformed(ActionEvent e) {
    if (e.getSource() == draw) {
        dotty = new Dotty( canvas, NDOTS );
        dottyThread = new Thread(dotty);
        dottyThread.start();
    } else {
        dotty.clear();
    }
} // actionPerformed()
```

Note that in addition to a reference to `dotty` we also have a reference to a `Thread` named `dottyThread`. This additional variable must be declared within the applet.

Recall that when you call the `start()` method, it automatically calls the thread's `run()` method. When `dottyThread` starts to run, it will immediately call the `draw()` method and start drawing dots. After each dot is drawn, `dottyThread` will sleep for an instant.

Notice how the applet stops the drawing thread. Recall that in the new version, `Dotty.clear()` will set the `isCleared` variable, which will cause the drawing loop to terminate. Once again, this is the proper way to stop a thread. Thus, as soon as the user clicks the "Clear" button, the `Dotty` thread will stop drawing and report its result.

DEBUGGING TIP: Stopping a Thread. The best way to stop a thread is to use a `boolean` control variable whose value can be set to true or false to exit the `run()` loop.

13.3.2 Advantages of Multithreaded Design

By creating a separate thread for `Dotty`, we have turned a single-threaded program into a multithreaded program. One thread, the applet, handles the user interface. The second thread handles the drawing task. By forcing the drawing to sleep on each iteration, we guarantee that the applet thread will remain responsive to the user's actions. Figure 13–8 illustrates the difference between the single- and multithreaded designs. Note that the applet thread starts and stops the drawing thread, and the applet thread executes `dotty.clear()`. The drawing thread simply executes its `draw()` method. In the single-threaded version, all of these actions are done by one thread.

Divide and conquer!

The tradeoff involved in this design is that it will take somewhat longer to draw N random dots, since `dottyThread.draw()` will sleep for an instant on each iteration. But the extra time is hardly noticeable. Thus by

Tradeoff: speed vs. responsiveness

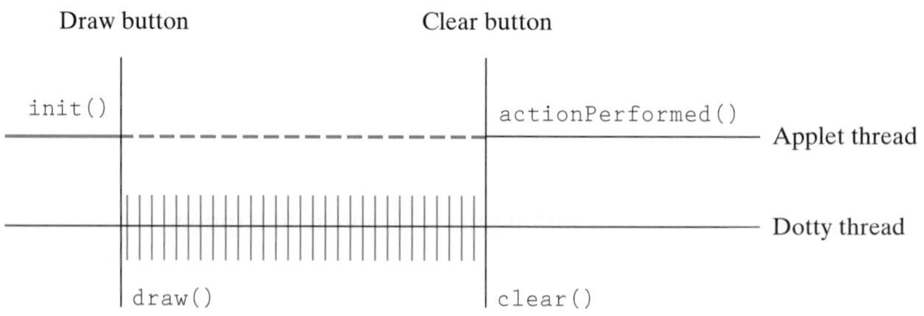

Figure 13–8 Two independent threads: one for drawing, the other for the GUI.

breaking the program into two separate threads of control, one to handle the drawing task and one to handle the user interface, the result is a much more responsive program.

EFFECTIVE DESIGN: Responsive Interfaces. In order to give a program a more responsive user interface, divide it into separate threads of control. Let one thread handle interactive tasks, such as user input, and let the second thread handle CPU-intensive computations.

SELF-STUDY EXERCISES

EXERCISE 13.6 Someone might argue that because the Java Virtual Machine uses a round-robin scheduling algorithm, it's redundant to use the `sleep()` method, since the applet thread will get its chance to run. What's wrong with this argument in terms of interface responsiveness?

EXERCISE 13.7 Instead of sleeping on each iteration, another way to make the interface more responsive would be to set the threaded `Dotty`'s priority to a low number, such as 1. Make this change, and experiment with its effect on the program's responsiveness. Is it more or less responsive than sleeping on each iteration? Why?

13.4 Thread States and Life Cycle

Ready, running, and sleeping

Each thread has a **life cycle** that consists of several different states, which are summarized in the Table 13–1. Much of a thread's life cycle is under the control of the operating system and the Java Virtual Machine. When first created a thread is in the ready state, which means that it is ready to run. In the ready state, a thread is waiting, perhaps with other threads, in the **ready queue**, for its turn on the CPU. A **queue** is like a waiting line. When the CPU becomes available, the first thread in the ready queue will be **dispatched** — that is, it will be given the CPU. It will then be in the running state.

The ready queue

Table 13.1. A summary of the different thread states

State	Description
Ready	The thread is ready to run and waiting for the CPU.
Running	The thread is executing on the CPU.
Waiting	The thread is waiting for some event to happen.
Sleeping	The thread has been told to sleep for a time.
Blocked	The thread is waiting for I/O to finish.
Dead	The thread is terminated.

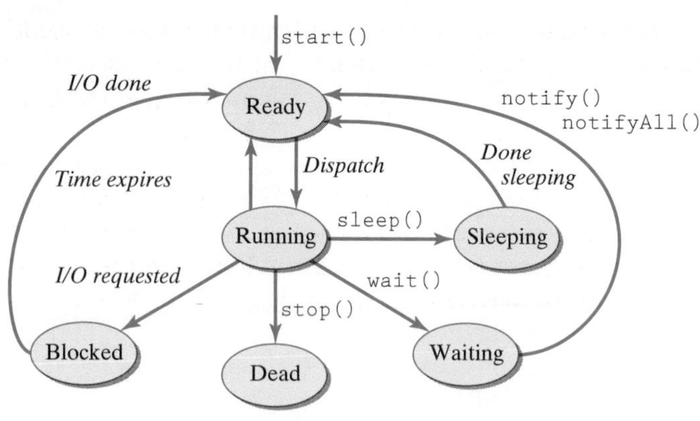

Figure 13–9 A depiction of a thread's life cycle.

CPU Scheduler

Transitions between the ready and running states happen under the control of the CPU scheduler, a fundamental part of the Java runtime system. The job of scheduling a bunch of threads in a fair and efficient manner is a little like sharing a single bicycle among several children. Children who are ready to ride the bike wait in line for their turn. The grown up (scheduler) lets the first child (thread) ride for a period of time, before the bike is taken away and given to the next child in line. In round-robin scheduling, each child (thread) gets an equal amount of time on the bike (CPU).

Controlling a thread

The main states in the *life cycle* of a thread are shown in Figure 13–9. Thread states are represented by labeled ovals, and the transitions between states are represented by labeled arrows. Those transitions represented by method names — such as `start()`, `stop()`, `wait()`, `sleep()`, `notify()` — can be controlled by the program. Of these methods, the `stop()` method has been deprecated in JDK 1.2 because it is inherently unsafe to stop a thread in the middle of its execution. That's why we used a variable to cause the `Dotty` thread to exit in a normal fashion.

EFFECTIVE DESIGN: Stopping a Thread. A thread loop should be controlled by an internal control variable. It is unsafe for one thread to stop another in the middle of its execution.

Transitions whose labels are italicized — such as *dispatch, IO request, IO done, time expired, done sleeping* — are under the control of the CPU scheduler.

When a thread calls the `sleep()` method, it voluntarily gives up the CPU, and when the sleep period is over, it goes back into the ready queue. This would be like one of the children deciding to rest for a moment during his or her turn. When the rest was over, the child would get back in line.

Threads can give up the CPU

When a thread calls the `wait()` method, it voluntarily gives up the CPU, but this time it won't be ready to run again until it is notified by some other thread. This would be like one child giving his or her turn to another child. When the second child's turn is up, it would notify the first child, who would then get back in line.

The system also manages transitions between the **blocked** and ready states. A thread is put into a blocked state when it does some kind of I/O operation. I/O devices, such as disk drives, modems, and keyboards, are very slow compared to the CPU. Therefore, I/O operations are handled by separate processors known as *controllers*. For example, when a thread wants to read data from a disk drive, the system will give this task to the disk controller, telling it where to place the data. Because the thread can't do anything until the data are read, it is blocked, and another thread is allowed to run. When the disk controller completes the I/O operation, the blocked thread is unblocked and placed back in the ready queue.

Threads block on I/O operations

In terms of the bicycle analogy, blocking a thread would be like giving the bicycle to another child when the rider has to stop to tie his or her shoe. Instead of letting the bicycle just sit there, we let another child ride it. When the shoe is tied, the child is ready to ride again and goes back into the ready line. Letting other threads run while one thread is waiting for an I/O operation to complete improves the overall utilization of the CPU.

SELF-STUDY EXERCISES

EXERCISE 13.8 Round-robin scheduling isn't always the best idea. Sometimes *priority scheduling* leads to a better system. Can you think of ways that priority scheduling — higher priority threads go to the head of the line — can be used to improve the responsiveness of an interactive program?

13.5 CASE STUDY: Cooperating Threads

For some applications it is necessary to synchronize and coordinate the behavior of threads to enable them to carry out a cooperative task. Many cooperative applications are based on the **producer/consumer model**. According to this model, two threads cooperate at producing and consuming a particular resource or piece of data. The producer thread creates some message or result, and the consumer thread reads or uses the result. Obviously, the consumer has to wait for a result to be produced, and the producer has to take care not to overwrite a result that hasn't yet been consumed.

One application for this model would be to control the display of data that is read by your browser. As information arrives from the Internet, it is written to a buffer by the producer thread. A separate consumer thread reads information from the buffer and displays it in your browser window. Obviously the two threads must be carefully synchronized. There are many other coordination problems that would fit into the producer/consumer model.

Producer and consumer threads

13.5.1 Problem Statement

Simulating a waiting line

To illustrate how to address the sorts of problems that can arise when you try to synchronize threads, let's consider a simple application in which several threads use a shared resource. You're familiar with those take-a-number devices that are used in bakeries to manage a waiting line. Customers take a number when they arrive, and the clerk announces who's next by looking at the device. As customers are called, the clerk increments the "next customer" counter by one.

Obviously, there are potential coordination problems here. The device must keep proper count and can't skip customers. Nor can it give the same number to two different customers. Nor can it allow the clerk to serve nonexistent customers.

Our task is to build a multithreaded simulation that uses a model of a take-a-number device to coordinate the behavior of customers and a (single) clerk in a bakery waiting line. To help illustrate the various issues involved in trying to coordinate threads, we will develop more than one version of the program.

Problem Decomposition

What classes do we need?

This simulation will use four classes of objects. The `TakeANumber` class will serve as a model of a take-a-number device. This is the resource that will be shared by the threads. It is not a thread itself. The `Customer` class, a subclass of `Thread`, will model the behavior of a customer who arrives on line and takes a number from the `TakeANumber` device. There will be several `Customer` threads created that then compete for a space in line. The `Clerk` thread, which simulates the behavior of the store clerk, should use the `TakeANumber` device to determine who the next customer is and should serve that customer. Finally, there will be a main program which will have the task of creating and starting the various threads. Let's call this the `Bakery` class. This gives us the following list of classes.

- `Bakery` — responsible for creating the threads and starting the simulation.
- `TakeANumber` — represents the gadget that keeps track of the next customer to be served.
- `Clerk` — will use the `TakeANumber` to determine the next customer and will serve the customer.
- `Customer` — represents the customers who will use the `TakeANumber` to take their place in line.

13.5.2 Design: The `TakeANumber` Class

What methods do we need?

The `TakeANumber` class must keep track of two things: which customer will be served next, and which waiting number the next customer will be given. This suggests that it should have at least two public methods: `nextNumber()`, which will be used by customers to get their waiting number, and `nextCustomer()`, which will be used by the clerk to determine who should be served. Each of these methods will simply retrieve the

Figure 13–10 Definition of the TakeANumber class, version 1.

```
class TakeANumber {
    private int next = 0;      // Next place in line
    private int serving = 0;   // Next customer to serve

    public synchronized int nextNumber() {
        next = next + 1;
        return next;
    } // nextNumber()

    public int nextCustomer() {
        ++serving;
        return serving;
    } // nextCustomer()

} // TakeANumber
```

values of the instance variables, `next` and `serving`, which keep track of these two values. As part of the object's state, these variables should be `private`.

How should we make this `TakeANumber` object accessible to all of the other objects — that is, to all of the customers and to the clerk? The easiest way to do that is to have the main program pass a reference to the `TakeANumber` when it constructs the `Customers` and the `Clerk`. They can each store the reference as an instance variable. In this way, all the objects in the simulation can share a `TakeANumber` object as a common resource. Our design considerations lead to the definition of the `TakeANumber` class shown in Figure 13–10.

Passing a reference to a shared object

Note that the `nextNumber()` method is declared `synchronized`. As we will discuss in more detail, this ensures that only one customer at a time can take a number. Once a thread begins executing a `synchronized` method, no other thread can execute that method until the first thread finishes. This is important because otherwise several `Customers` could call the `nextNumber` method at the same time. It's important that the customer threads have mutually exclusive access to the `TakeANumber` object. This form of **mutual exclusion** is important for the correctness of the simulation.

Synchronized methods

SELF-STUDY EXERCISES

EXERCISE 13.9 What is the analogue to mutual exclusion in the real-world example of the bakery situation?

13.5.3 Java Monitors and Mutual Exclusion

An object that contains `synchronized` methods has a **monitor** associated with it. A monitor is a widely used synchronization mechanism that ensures that only one thread at a time can execute a `synchronized` method. When a `synchronized` method is called, a **lock** is acquired on that object. For example, if one of the `Customer` threads calls `nextNumber()`, a lock will be placed on that `TakeANumber` object. While an object is *locked*, no other `synchronized` method can run in that object. Other threads must

The monitor concept

wait for the lock to be released before they can execute a `synchronized` method.

While one `Customer` is executing `nextNumber()`, all other `Customers` will be forced to wait until the first `Customer` is finished. When the `synchronized` method is exited, the lock on the object is released, allowing other `Customer` threads to access its `synchronized` methods. In effect, a `synchronized` method can be used to guarantee mutually exclusive access to the `TakeANumber` object among the competing customers.

Mutually exclusive access to a shared object

JAVA LANGUAGE RULE `synchronized`. Once a thread begins to execute a `synchronized` method in an object, the object is *locked* so that no other thread can gain access to that object's synchronized methods.

EFFECTIVE DESIGN: Synchronization. In order to restrict access to a method or set of methods to one object at at time (*mutual exclusion*), declare the methods `synchronized`.

One cautionary note here is that although a synchronized method blocks access to other synchronized methods, it does not block access to nonsynchronized methods. This could cause potential problems. We will return to this issue in the next case study when we discuss the testing of our program.

13.5.4 The `Customer` Class

Simulating the customer

A `Customer` thread should model the behavior of taking a number from the `TakeANumber` gadget. For the sake of this simulation, let's suppose that after taking a number, the customer just prints it out. This will serve as a simple model of "waiting on line." What about the `Customer`'s state? To help distinguish one customer from another, let's give each customer a unique ID number starting at 10001, which will be set in the constructor method. Also, as we noted earlier, each `Customer` needs a reference to the `TakeANumber` object, which is passed as a constructor parameter. This leads to the definition of `Customer` shown in Figure 13–11. Note that before taking a number, the customer sleeps for a random interval of up to 1000 milliseconds. This will introduce a bit of randomness into the simulation.

Static (class) variables

Another important feature of this definition is the use of the `static` variable `number` to assign each customer a unique ID number. Remember that a `static` variable belongs to the class itself, not to its instances. Therefore each `Customer` that is created can share this variable. By incrementing it and assigning its new value as the `Customer`'s ID, we guarantee that each customer has a unique ID number.

JAVA LANGUAGE RULE **Static (Class) Variables.** Static variables are associated with the class itself and not with its instances.

Figure 13–11 Definition of the `Customer` class, version 1.

```
public class Customer extends Thread {

    private static int number = 10000;      // Initial ID number
    private int id;
    private TakeANumber takeANumber;

    public Customer( TakeANumber gadget ) {
        id = ++number;
        takeANumber = gadget;
    }
    public void run() {
        try {
            sleep( (int)(Math.random() * 1000 ) );
            System.out.println("Customer " + id + " takes ticket " + takeANumber.nextNumber());
        } catch (InterruptedException e) {
            System.out.println("Exception " + e.getMessage());
        }
    } // run()
} // Customer
```

EFFECTIVE DESIGN: Unique IDs. Static variables are often used to assign a unique ID number or a unique initial value to each instance of a class.

13.5.5 The `Clerk` Class

Simulating the clerk

The `Clerk` thread should simulate the behavior of serving the next customer in line, so the `Clerk` thread will repeatedly access `TakeANumber.nextCustomer()` and then serve that customer. For the sake of this simulation, we'll just print a message to indicate which customer is being served. Because there's only one clerk in this simulation, the only variable in its internal state will be a reference to the `TakeANumber` object. In addition to the constructor, all we really need to define for this class is the `run()` method. This leads to the definition of `Clerk` shown in Figure 13–12. In

Figure 13–12 Definition of `Clerk`, version 1.

```
public class Clerk extends Thread {
    private TakeANumber takeANumber;

    public Clerk(TakeANumber gadget) {
      takeANumber = gadget;
    }
    public void run() {
        while (true) {
            try {
                sleep( (int)(Math.random() * 50));
                System.out.println("Clerk serving ticket " + takeANumber.nextCustomer());
            } catch (InterruptedException e) {
                System.out.println("Exception " + e.getMessage() );
            }
        } //while
    } //run()
} // Clerk
```

Figure 13–13 Definition of the Bakery class.

```
public class Bakery {
    public static void main(String args[]) {
        System.out.println( "Starting clerk and customer threads" );
        TakeANumber numberGadget = new TakeANumber();
        Clerk clerk = new Clerk(numberGadget);
        clerk.start();
        for (int k = 0; k < 5; k++) {
            Customer customer = new Customer(numberGadget);
            customer.start();
        }
    } // main()
} // Bakery
```

this case the `sleep()` method is necessary to allow the `Customer` threads to run. The `Clerk` will sit in an infinite loop serving the next customer on each iteration.

13.5.6 The `Bakery` Class

The main program

Finally, `Bakery` is the simplest class to design. It contains the `main()` method, which gets the whole simulation started. As we said, its role will be to create one `Clerk` thread and several `Customer` threads, and get them all started (Figure 13–13). Notice that the `Customer`s and the `Clerk` are each passed a reference to the shared `TakeANumber` gadget.

Problem: Nonexistent Customers

Testing and debugging

Now that we have designed and implemented the classes, let's run several experiments to test that everything works as intended. Except for the `synchronized` `nextNumber()` method, we've made little attempt to make sure that the `Customer` and `Clerk` threads will work together cooperatively, without violating the real-world constraints that should be satisfied by the simulation. If we run the simulation as it is presently coded, it will generate five customers and the clerk will serve all of them. But we get something like the following output:

```
Starting clerk and customer threads
  Clerk serving ticket 1
  Clerk serving ticket 2
  Clerk serving ticket 3
  Clerk serving ticket 4
  Clerk serving ticket 5
Customer 10004 takes ticket 1
Customer 10002 takes ticket 2
  Clerk serving ticket 6
Customer 10005 takes ticket 3
  Clerk serving ticket 7
  Clerk serving ticket 8
  Clerk serving ticket 9
  Clerk serving ticket 10
Customer 10001 takes ticket 4
Customer 10003 takes ticket 5
```

Obviously, our current solution violates an important real-world constraint: You can't serve customers before they enter the line! How can we ensure that the clerk doesn't serve a customer unless there's actually a customer waiting?

Problem: The clerk thread doesn't wait for customer threads

The wrong way to address this issue would be to increase the amount of sleeping that the `Clerk` does between serving customers. Indeed, this would allow more customer threads to run, so it might appear to have the desired effect, but it doesn't truly address the main problem: A clerk cannot serve a customer if no customer is waiting.

The correct way to solve this problem is to have the clerk check that there are customers waiting before taking the next customer. One way to model this would be to add a `customerWaiting()` method to our `TakeANumber` object. This method would return `true` whenever `next` is greater than `serving`. That will correspond to the real-world situation in which the clerk can see customers waiting in line. We can make the following modification to `Clerk.run()`:

The clerk checks the line

```
public void run() {
    while (true) {
        try {
            sleep((int)(Math.random() * 50));
            if (takeANumber.customerWaiting())
                System.out.println("Clerk serving ticket " + takeANumber.nextCustomer());
        } catch (InterruptedException e) {
            System.out.println("Exception " + e.getMessage() );
        }
    } // while
} // run()
```

And we add the following method to `TakeANumber`:

```
public boolean customerWaiting() {
    return next > serving;
}
```

In other words, the `Clerk` won't serve a customer unless there are customers waiting — that is, unless `next` is greater than `serving`. Given these changes, we get the following type of output when we run the simulation:

```
Starting clerk and customer threads
Customer 10003 takes ticket 1
  Clerk serving ticket 1
Customer 10005 takes ticket 2
  Clerk serving ticket 2
Customer 10001 takes ticket 3
  Clerk serving ticket 3
Customer 10004 takes ticket 4
  Clerk serving ticket 4
Customer 10002 takes ticket 5
  Clerk serving ticket 5
```

This example illustrates that in designing applications that involve cooperating threads, the algorithm used must ensure the proper cooperation and coordination among the threads.

EFFECTIVE DESIGN: Thread Coordination. When two or more threads must behave cooperatively, their interaction must be carefully coordinated by the algorithm.

13.5.7 Problem: Critical Sections

Thread interruptions are unpredictable

It is easy to forget that thread behavior is asynchronous. You can't predict when a thread might be interrupted or might have to give up the CPU to another thread. In designing applications that involve cooperating threads, it's important that the design incorporate features to guard against problems caused by asynchronicity. To illustrate this problem, consider the following statement from the `Customer.run()` method:

```
System.out.println("Customer " + id + " takes ticket " + takeANumber.nextNumber());
```

Even though this is a single Java statement, it breaks up into several Java bytecode statements. A `Customer` thread could certainly be interrupted between getting the next number back from `TakeANumber` and printing it out. We can simulate this by breaking the `println()` into two statements and putting a `sleep()` in their midst:

```
public void run() {
    try {
        int myturn = takeANumber.nextNumber();
        sleep( (int)(Math.random() * 1000 ) );
        System.out.println("Customer " + id + " takes ticket " + myturn);
    } catch (InterruptedException e) {
        System.out.println("Exception " + e.getMessage());
    }
} // run()
```

If this change is made in the simulation, you might get the following output:

```
Starting clerk and customer threads
  Clerk serving ticket 1
  Clerk serving ticket 2
  Clerk serving ticket 3
Customer 10004 takes ticket 4
  Clerk serving ticket 4
  Clerk serving ticket 5
Customer 10001 takes ticket 1
Customer 10002 takes ticket 2
Customer 10003 takes ticket 3
Customer 10005 takes ticket 5
```

Because the Customer threads are now interrupted in between taking a number and reporting their number, it looks as if they are being served in the wrong order. Actually, they are being served in the correct order. It's their reporting of their numbers that is wrong!

The problem here is that the Customer.run() method is being interrupted in such a way that it invalidates the simulation's output. A method that displays the simulation's state should be designed so that once a thread begins reporting its state, that thread will be allowed to finish reporting before another thread can start reporting its state. Accurate reporting of a thread's state is a critical element of the simulation's overall integrity.

Problem: An interrupt in a critical section

A **critical section** is any section of a thread that should not be interrupted during its execution. In the bakery simulation, all of the statements that report the simulation's progress are critical sections. Even though the chances are small that a thread will be interrupted in the midst of a println() statement, the faithful reporting of the simulation's state should not be left to chance. Therefore, we must design an algorithm that prevents the interruption of critical sections.

Creating a Critical Section

The correct way to address this problem is to treat the reporting of the customer's state as a critical section. As we saw earlier when we discussed the concept of a monitor, a synchronized method within a shared object ensures that once a thread starts the method, it will be allowed to finish it before any other thread can start it. Therefore, one way out of this dilemma is to have the TakeANumber object report which customer is next (Figure 13–14). In this version all of the methods are synchronized, so all the actions of the TakeANumber object are treated as critical sections.

Making a critical section uninterruptible

Figure 13–14 Definition of the TakeANumber class, version 2.

```
public class TakeANumber {
    private int next = 0;     // Next place in line
    private int serving = 0;  // Next customer to serve

    public synchronized int nextNumber(int custId) {
        next = next + 1;
        System.out.println( "Customer " + custId + " takes ticket " + next );
        return next;
    }

    public synchronized int nextCustomer() {
        ++serving;
        System.out.println("  Clerk serving ticket " + serving );
        return serving;
    }

    public synchronized boolean customerWaiting() {
        return next > serving;
    }
} // TakeANumber
```

Note (Figure 13–14) that the reporting of both the next number and the next customer to be served are now handled by `TakeANumber`. Because the methods that handle these actions are `synchronized`, they cannot be interrupted by any threads involved in the simulation. This guarantees that the simulation's output will faithfully report the simulation's state.

Given these changes to `TakeANumber`, we must make the following changes to the `run()` methods in `Customer`:

```
public void run() {
    try {
        sleep((int)(Math.random() * 2000));
        takeANumber.nextNumber(id);
    } catch (InterruptedException e) {
        System.out.println("Exception: " + e.getMessage() );
    }
} // run()
```

and in `Clerk`:

```
public void run() {
    for (int k = 0; k < 10; k++) {
        try {
            sleep( (int)(Math.random() * 1000));
            if (takeANumber.customerWaiting())
                takeANumber.nextCustomer();
        } catch (InterruptedException e) {
            System.out.println("Exception: " + e.getMessage());
        }
    } // for
} // run()
```

Rather than printing their numbers, these methods now just call the appropriate methods in `TakeANumber`. Given these design changes, our simulation now produces the following correct output:

```
Starting clerk and customer threads
Customer 10001 takes ticket 1
  Clerk serving ticket 1
Customer 10003 takes ticket 2
Customer 10002 takes ticket 3
  Clerk serving ticket 2
Customer 10005 takes ticket 4
Customer 10004 takes ticket 5
  Clerk serving ticket 3
  Clerk serving ticket 4
  Clerk serving ticket 5
```

Preventing undesirable interrupts

The lesson to be learned from this is that in designing multithreaded programs, it is important to assume that if a thread can be interrupted at a certain point, it will be interrupted at that point. The fact that an interrupt is unlikely to occur is no substitute for the use of a critical section. This is something like "Murphy's Law of Thread Coordination."

EFFECTIVE DESIGN: The Thread Coordination Principle. Use critical sections to coordinate the behavior of cooperating threads. By designating certain methods as synchronized, you can ensure their mutually exclusive access. Once a thread starts a synchronized method, no other thread will be able to execute the method until the first thread is finished.

In a multithreaded application, the classes and methods should be designed so that undesirable interrupts will not affect the correctness of the algorithm.

PROGRAMMING TIP: Critical Sections. Java's monitor mechanism will ensure that while one thread is executing a synchronized method, no other threads can gain access to it. Even if the first thread is interrupted, when it resumes execution again it will be allowed to finish the synchronized method before other threads can access synchronized methods in that object.

SELF-STUDY EXERCISES

EXERCISE 13.10 Given the changes we've described, the bakery simulation should now run correctly regardless of how slow or fast the `Customer` and `Clerk` threads run. Verify this by placing different sized sleep intervals in their `run()` methods. (*Note*: You don't want to put a `sleep()` in the synchronized methods because that would undermine the whole purpose of making them `synchronized` in the first place.)

13.5.8 Using `wait/notify` to Coordinate Threads

The examples in the previous sections were designed to illustrate the issues of thread asynchronicity and the principles of mutual exclusion and critical sections. Through the careful design of the algorithm and the appropriate use of the `synchronized` qualifier, we have managed to design a program that correctly coordinates the behavior of the `Customers` and `Clerk` in this bakery simulation.

The Busy-Waiting Problem

One problem with our current design of the Bakery algorithm is that it uses **busy waiting** on the part of the `Clerk` thread. This is wasteful of CPU time, and we should modify the algorithm.

Busy waiting

As it is presently designed, the `Clerk` thread sits in a loop that repeatedly checks if there's a customer to serve:

```
public void run() {
    for (int k = 0; k < 10; k++) {
        try {
            sleep( (int)(Math.random() * 1000));
            if (takeANumber.customerWaiting())
                takeANumber.nextCustomer();
        } catch (InterruptedException e) {
            System.out.println("Exception: " + e.getMessage());
        }
    } // for
} // run()
```

Producer/consumer

A far better solution would be to force the `Clerk` thread to wait without using the CPU until a customer arrives. As soon as a `Customer` becomes available, the `Clerk` thread can be notified and enabled to run. Note that this description views the customer/clerk relationship as one-half of the producer/consumer relationship. The customer's taking of a number *produces* a customer in line that must be served (that is, *consumed*) by the clerk.

This is only half the producer/consumer relationship because we haven't placed any constraint on the size of the waiting line. There's no real limit to how many customers in line can be produced. If we did limit the line size, customers might be forced to wait before taking a number if, say, the tickets ran out, or the bakery filled up. In that case customers would have to wait until the line resource became available and we would have a full-fledged producer/consumer relationship.

The `wait/notify` *Mechanism*

So, let's use Java's `wait/notify` mechanism to eliminate busy waiting from our simulation. As noted in Figure 13–9, the `wait()` method puts a thread into a waiting state, and `notify()` takes a thread out of waiting and places it back in the ready queue. To use these methods in this program we need to modify the `nextNumber()` and `nextCustomer()` methods. When the `Clerk` calls the `nextCustomer()` method, if there is no customer in line, the `Clerk` should be made to `wait()`:

```
public synchronized int nextCustomer() {
    try {
        while (next <= serving)
            wait();
    } catch(InterruptedException e) {
        System.out.println("Exception: " + e.getMessage());
    } finally {
        ++serving;
        System.out.println("  Clerk serving ticket " + serving);
        return serving;
    }
}
```

A waiting thread gives up the CPU

Note that the `Clerk` still checks whether there are customers waiting. If there are none, the `Clerk` calls the `wait()` method. This removes the `Clerk` from the CPU until some other thread notifies it, at which point it will be ready to run again. When it runs again, it should check that there is in fact a customer waiting before proceeding. That's why we use a while loop here. In effect, the Clerk will wait until there's a customer to serve. But this is not busy waiting because the Clerk thread loses the CPU and must be notified each time a customer becomes available.

When and how will the Clerk be notified? Clearly, the Clerk should be notified as soon as a customer takes a number. Therefore, we put a notify() in the nextNumber() method:

```
public synchronized int nextNumber( int custId) {
    next = next + 1;
    System.out.println("Customer " + custId + " takes ticket " + next);
    notify();
    return next;
}
```

Thus, as soon as a Customer thread executes the nextNumber() method, the Clerk will be notified and allowed to proceed.

If we use this model of thread coordination, we no longer need to test customerWaiting() in the Clerk.run() method. It is to be tested in the TakeANumber.nextCustomer(). Thus the Clerk.run() can be simplified to

```
public void run() {
    while (true) {
        try {
            sleep((int)(Math.random() * 1000));
            takeANumber.nextCustomer();
        } catch (InterruptedException e) {
            System.out.println("Exception: " + e.getMessage() );
        }
    } // while
} // run()
```

The Clerk thread may be forced to wait when it calls the nextCustomer method.

Because we no longer need the customerWaiting() method, we end up with the new definition of TakeANumber shown in Figure 13–15. Given this version of the program the following kind of output will be generated:

```
Starting clerk and customer threads
Customer 10004 takes ticket 1
Customer 10002 takes ticket 2
  Clerk serving ticket 1
  Clerk serving ticket 2
Customer 10005 takes ticket 3
Customer 10003 takes ticket 4
  Clerk serving ticket 3
Customer 10001 takes ticket 5
  Clerk serving ticket 4
  Clerk serving ticket 5
  Clerk waiting
```

In this particular run, the customers get served as soon as they enter the line. The reason for this is because the Clerk() thread sleeps for up to just 1000 milliseconds on each iteration, while the Customer threads sleep for up to 2000 milliseconds.

Figure 13–15 The TakeANumber class, version 3.

```
public class TakeANumber {

    private int next = 0;
    private int serving = 0;

    public synchronized int nextNumber(int custId) {
        next = next + 1;
        System.out.println( "Customer " + custId + " takes ticket " + next );
        notify();
        return next;
    } // nextNumber()

    public synchronized int nextCustomer() {
        try {
            while (next <= serving) {
                System.out.println("  Clerk waiting ");
                wait();
            }
        } catch(InterruptedException e) {
            System.out.println("Exception " + e.getMessage() );
        } finally {
            ++serving;
            System.out.println("  Clerk serving ticket " + serving );
            return serving;
        }
    } // nextCustomer()
} // TakeANumber
```

PROGRAMMING TIP: Busy Waiting. Java's wait/notify mechanism can be used effectively to eliminate busy waiting from a multithreaded application.

EFFECTIVE DESIGN: Producer/Consumer. The producer/consumer model is a useful design for coordinating the wait/notify interaction.

SELF-STUDY EXERCISES

EXERCISE 13.11 An interesting experiment to try is to make the Clerk a little slower by making it sleep for up to 2000 milliseconds. Take a guess at what would happen if you ran this experiment. Then run the experiment and observe the results.

The wait/notify *Mechanism*

Wait/notify go into synchronized methods

There are a number of important restrictions that must be observed when using the wait/notify mechanism:

- Both wait() and notify() are methods of the Object class, not the Thread class. This enables them to lock objects, which is the essential feature of Java's monitor mechanism.
- A wait() method can be used within a synchronized method. The method doesn't have to be part of a Thread.

- You can only use `wait()` and `notify()` within `synchronized` methods. If you use them in other methods, you will cause an `IllegalMonitorStateException` with the message "current thread not owner."
- When a `wait()` [or a `sleep()`] is used within an `synchronized` method, the lock on that object is released, allowing other methods access to the object's `synchronized` methods.

DEBUGGING TIP: Wait/Notify. It's easy to forget that the `wait()` and `notify()` methods can only be used within `synchronized` methods.

13.6 CASE STUDY: The Spider and Fly Threads

Another good use for threads is to simulate the behavior of two independent entities in an application. Let's design a Java applet that simulates the interaction between two or more `CyberPets`. One `CyberPet` will be the spider that we introduced in Chapter 2. In addition to eating and sleeping, however, this version will also be able to dream big dreams and will be able to catch buzzing flies as well as flies already trapped in its web.

Problem statement

The second type of `CyberPet` will be a fly, which, for this simulation, will buzz around just outside the reach of the spider's web. In its frustration, the spider begins wishing that it was a frog so that it could capture the fly with its sticky tongue. And, lo and behold, in its dream state the spider magically transforms into a frog and captures the buzzing fly (Figure 13–16). To see how this all looks, you may wish to run the demo program at

```
http://www.prenhall.com/morelli/cyberpet/
```

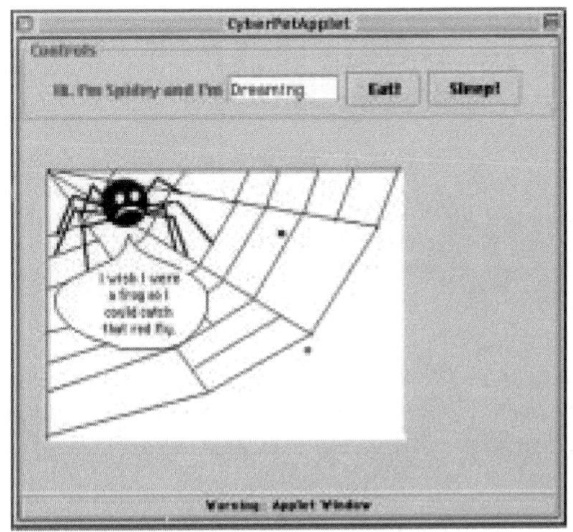

Figure 13–16 The Spider and the Fly.

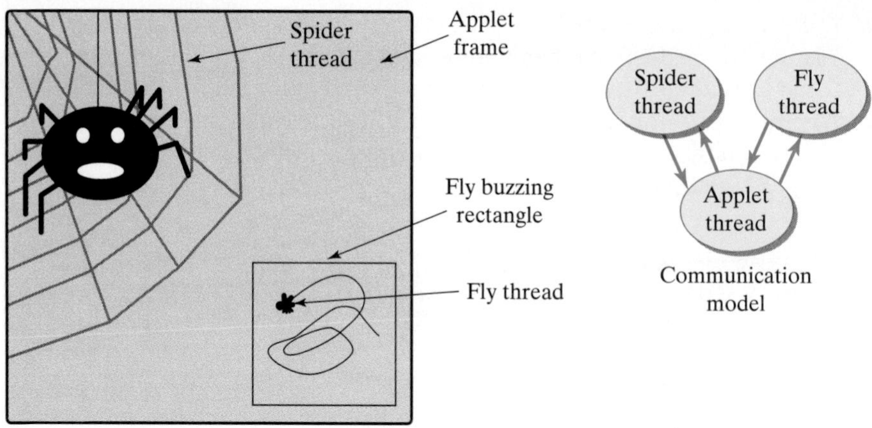

Figure 13–17 Design of the GUI for the spidey/fly applet.

13.6.1 Problem Decomposition

What objects do we need?

For this simulation we want to represent the spider and the fly as separate classes: `Spider` and `Fly`. It will also be necessary that `Spider` and `Fly` be independent threads. A third class, an applet, will provide a GUI interface, displaying the animated images of the characters, and will also serve as the their intermediary. For example, the applet will make it possible for the `Spider` to "see" the `Fly` and eat the `Fly` (Figure 13–17). In order to refer to the applet, both `Spider` and `Fly` will need references to it.

One possible design is to define `Fly` and `Spider` as `Thread` subclasses. However, this design presents certain problems. Because a class can have only one immediate superclass, if `Fly` and `Spider` are `Threads`, they can't also be `CyberPets`.

A better design would be to define `Spider` and `Fly` as subclasses of `CyberPet` and have each of them implement the `Runnable` interface. This design uses a limited form of *multiple inheritance*. As subclasses of `CyberPet` both `Spider` and `Fly` inherit their shared characteristics, such as the state variable, the `eat()` and `sleep()` method, and so on. But as `Runnable` objects, they inherit the basic characteristics of a thread. This leads to the following basic definitions:

```
public class Fly extends CyberPet implements Runnable { ... }
public class Spider extends CyberPet implements Runnable { ... }
```

Given this class hierarchy (Figure 13–18), to make `Spiders` and `Flys` into independent threads, we need only define their respective `run()` methods.

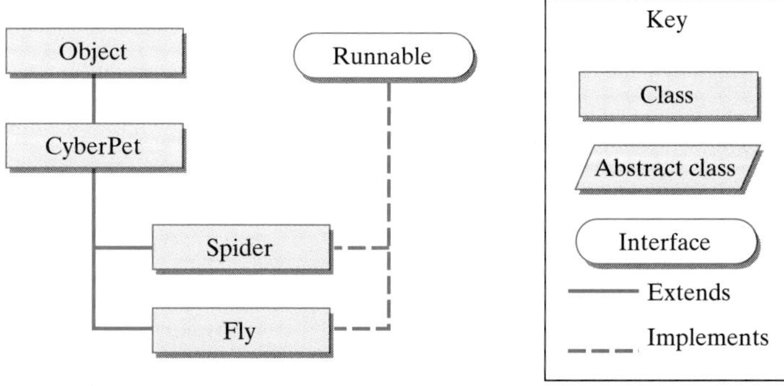

Figure 13–18 Hierarchy of the classes used in the Spider/Fly simulation.

EFFECTIVE DESIGN: Multiple Inheritance. Java interfaces provide a limited form of multiple inheritance, because they allow a class to inherit methods from more than one superclass.

13.6.2 The Revised CyberPet Class

Given the revised definition of CyberPet as a subclass of Thread, and our definition of Spider as a subclass of CyberPet, we have to make several design changes in the CyberPet class (Figure 13–19).

What data do we need?

First, the CyberPet's internal state has been expanded to include the DREAMING, DEAD, and FLYING states as possible state values. As in previous versions of CyberPet, these are defined as class constants. Second, the state variables, state and name, must now be declared protected, instead of private, so they can be inherited by the Spider and Fly subclasses.

Finally, the other major change is that we have removed all but the minimal functionality from the various public methods that define the CyberPet's behavior. For example, the eat() method in this version simply changes CyberPet's state to EATING:

```
public void eat() {
    state = EATING;
}
```

Superclass/subclass design

In previous versions of this class the eat(), sleep(), think(), and dream() methods also displayed images of the CyberPet's current state. That part of a CyberPet's functionality must now be handled by its subclasses — by Spider and Fly — so the images will be appropriate to the type of CyberPet. Although the default versions of these methods will suffice for the Fly class, we have to override them in the Spider class. For example,

Figure 13–19 The revised CyberPet class.

```
public class CyberPet {
    protected int state;
    protected String name;
    public static final int DEAD = -1;
    public static final int EATING = 0;
    public static final int SLEEPING = 1;
    public static final int THINKING = 2;
    public static final int DREAMING = 3;
    public static final int FLYING = 4;     // For flying cyberpets

    public CyberPet ( ) {
        state = EATING;
        name = "no name";
    }

    public CyberPet (String str) {
        name = str;
        state = EATING;
    }

    public CyberPet (String str, int inState) {
        state = inState;
        name = str;
    }

    public String getState() {
        if (state == EATING)
            return "Eating";
        else if (state == SLEEPING)
            return "Sleeping";
        else if (state == THINKING)
            return "Thinking";
        else if (state == DREAMING)
            return "Dreaming";
        return "Error in State";
    } // getState()

    public void setPetName(String name) { this.name = name;   }
    public String getPetName()          { return name;        }

    // The next four methods can be overridden in subclasses

    public void eat()                   { state = EATING;     }
    public void sleep()                 { state = SLEEPING;   }
    public void think()                 { state = THINKING;   }
    public void dream()                 { state = DREAMING;   }

    protected void delay(int N) {       // delay for N milliseconds
       try {
           Thread.sleep(N);
       } catch (InterruptedException e) {
           System.out.println(e.toString());
       }
    } // delay()
} // CyberPet
```

```
public void sleep() {
    Graphics g = applet.getGraphics();
    int choice = (int)(Math.random() * 3);
    if (choice == 2)                        // i.e., 1 in 3 chance
        g.drawImage(image[NOT_SLEEPY_IMG], 20, 100, applet);
    else {
        state = SLEEPING;
        g.drawImage(image[SLEEPING_IMG], 20, 100, applet);
    }
} // sleep()
```

Note how the reference to the `applet` enables the `Spider` to use the applet's `Graphics` object to do the drawing. Also, as in previous versions of `CyberPet`, the `Spider` sometimes sleeps and sometimes doesn't when it is told to sleep. This functionality is now defined in the `Spider` class, as a `Spider` behavior, not in the `CyberPet` class, as a behavior that is common to all `CyberPet`s.

Referring to a shared object

EFFECTIVE DESIGN: Inheritance. The higher you place methods and variables in an inheritance hierarchy, the more broadly they can be shared. Features that should be shared by subclasses should be defined in their superclass. Those that make a particular subclass unique, should be defined in the particular subclass.

13.6.3 The Fly Thread

The `Fly` thread is simple to design, because the `Fly`'s only action will be to buzz around just outside the reach of the spider's web. Let's define a collection of class constants to demarcate the fly's buzzing area. These are the minimum and maximum values of the fly's x- and y-coordinates on the display:

What data does `Fly` need?

```
private static final int XMIN = 225;
private static final int XMAX = 300;
private static final int YMIN = 245;
private static final int YMAX = 305;
private static final int SIDE = 5;          // Size of fly rectangle
private static final int MAX_RANGE = 15;  // Max and min change of location
private static final int MIN_DELTA = -10;
```

Next let's design the `Fly`'s state. In addition to the variables it inherits from `CyberPet`, a `Fly` needs instance variables to keep track of its current location on the applet window:

```
private CyberPetApplet applet;    // Reference to the simulation's interface
private Point location;           // The fly's coordinates within the applet
```

The `Fly()` constructor method can be defined as follows:

```
public Fly (CyberPetApplet app) {
    applet = app;
    location = new Point(XMAX, YMAX);  // Starting location
    state = FLYING;
}
```

Thus, when a `Fly` is constructed, it is given a reference to the applet where its image will be displayed and an initial location within the applet.

Next let's design the `Fly`'s `buzzaround()` method. Suppose the buzzing fly will be represented by a colored rectangle drawn directly onto the applet. The animation can be carried out by a three-step algorithm:

1. Erase the current image of the fly.
2. Move the fly to a new location.
3. Draw the fly at the new location.

Simulating random motion

To simulate the fly's random motion, the new coordinates for its location will be generated randomly. Finally, we will use if/else statements to ensure that the random locations we generate stay within the boundaries of its buzzing rectangle (Figure 13–17). These design considerations lead to the definition shown in Figure 13–20. Note that because this method changes the fly's state, we want to define it as a critical method. Hence we declare it to be `synchronized`. This will insure that it can't be interrupted by the spider.

PROGRAMMING TIP: Animation. Animation can be implemented by repeatedly drawing, erasing, and moving an image. A delay may be necessary between these steps to achieve the desired appearance.

Thread Communication

What methods do we need?

In order to simulate the `Spider` eating the `Fly`, the `Spider` will need to know the `Fly`'s location. Therefore, let's give `Fly` a `public` method that reports its location:

```
public Point getLocation() {
    return location;
}
```

Since `Fly`s will occasionally get eaten, we need a method to simulate this:

```
public synchronized void die() {
    state = DEAD;
}
```

Figure 13–20 The Fly's buzzaround() method.

```
public synchronized void buzzaround() {
    state = FLYING;
    Graphics g = applet.getGraphics();

                                  // Erase current image
    g.setColor(Color.white);
    g.fillRect(location.x, location.y, SIDE, SIDE);

                                  // Calculate new location
    int dx = (int)(MIN_DELTA +  Math.random() * MAX_RANGE);
    int dy = (int)(MIN_DELTA + Math.random() * MAX_RANGE);

    if (location.x + dx >= XMIN)  location.x = location.x + dx;
    else                          location.x = XMIN;

    if (location.y + dy >= YMIN)  location.y = location.y + dy;
    else                          location.y = YMIN;

    if (location.x + dx <= XMAX)  location.x = location.x + dx;
    else                          location.x = XMAX;
    if (location.y + dy <= YMAX)  location.y = location.y + dy;
    else                          location.y = YMAX;

                                  // Draw new image at new location
    g.setColor(Color.red);
    g.fillRect(location.x, location.y, SIDE, SIDE);
} // buzzaround()
```

The `die()` method simply sets the `Fly`'s state to DEAD. Given the above definitions, the `Fly`'s run algorithm is very simple to define. The fly will simply `buzzaround()` until it is `DEAD`:

```
public void run() {
    while (state != DEAD) {
        buzzaround();
        delay(125);
  }//while
} // run()
```

Note the use of the `delay(N)` method to make the `Fly`'s buzzing seem more realistic. This method was defined in the `CyberPet` class, so that it can be used to provide a delay for both the `Spider` and the `Fly`. It simply calls the `Thread.sleep()` method. The complete definition of the `Fly` class is shown in Figure 13–21.

Delaying the animation

Figure 13–21 The `Fly` class.

```
import java.awt.*;          // Import the GUI components

public class Fly extends CyberPet implements Runnable {

    // The image is 283 x 210 and its top left edge
    // is at (20,100). We want the fly to buzz around
    // just outside the spider's web.
```

Figure 13–21 *Continued*

```
    private static final int XMIN = 225;
    private static final int XMAX = 300;
    private static final int YMIN = 245;
    private static final int YMAX = 305;
    private static final int SIDE = 5;         // Size of fly rectangle
    private static final int MAX_RANGE = 15;  // Max and min change of location
    private static final int MIN_DELTA = -10;

    private CyberPetApplet applet;   // Reference to the simulation's interface
    private Point location;          // The fly's coordinates within the applet

    public Fly (CyberPetApplet app) {
        applet = app;
        location = new Point(XMAX, YMAX); // Starting Location
        state = FLYING;
    }

    public Point getLocation() {
        return location;
    }

    public synchronized void buzzaround() {
        state = FLYING;
        Graphics g = applet.getGraphics();

                                         // Erase current image
        g.setColor(Color.white);
        g.fillRect(location.x, location.y, SIDE, SIDE);

                                         // Calculate new location
        int dx = (int)(MIN_DELTA +  Math.random() * MAX_RANGE);
        int dy = (int)(MIN_DELTA + Math.random() * MAX_RANGE);

        if (location.x + dx >= XMIN)  location.x = location.x + dx;
        else                          location.x = XMIN;

        if (location.y + dy >= YMIN)  location.y = location.y + dy;
        else                          location.y = YMIN;

        if (location.x + dx <= XMAX)  location.x = location.x + dx;
        else                          location.x = XMAX;
        if (location.y + dy <= YMAX)  location.y = location.y + dy;
        else                          location.y = YMAX;

                                        // Draw new image at new location
        g.setColor(Color.red);
        g.fillRect(location.x, location.y, SIDE, SIDE);
    } // buzzaround()

    public synchronized void die() {
        state = DEAD;
     }

    public void run() {
        while (state != DEAD) {
            buzzaround();
            delay(125);
      }//while
    } // run()
} // Fly
```

13.6.4 The Spider Thread

The `Spider` thread should behave more or less the same as in its previous incarnation as `CyberPet`. It should respond to eat and sleep commands issued through the applet, but it should occasionally (randomly) ignore the commands. It should decide autonomously when it wants to eat, sleep, or think. Also, for this simulation it should contain a fourth state, DREAMING, during which it will magically transform into a frog and catch the buzzing fly. Since dreaming is a state that might well apply to other kinds of `CyberPets`, let's define it in `CyberPet`, thereby making it inheritable by all `CyberPets`. (Maybe some day `Flys` will learn to dream!)

Simulating the spider

The `Spider`'s run method should generate one of four possible actions and then simply take that action:

```
public void run() {
    while (true) {
        int choice = (int)(Math.random() * 4);
        if (choice == 0)
            autoeat();
        else if (choice == 1)
            autosleep();
        else if (choice == 2)
            think();
        else
            dream();
        delay(5000);
    } //while
} // run()
```

On each iteration of its infinite loop, the `Spider` alternates randomly between eating, sleeping, thinking, and dreaming. The `Math.random()` method is used to ensure that each activity is done approximately one-fourth of the time. To make the animation more realistic looking, the `Spider` delays for a relatively long interval — up to 5000 milliseconds — on each iteration.

As noted earlier, the `Spider` will occasionally eat the `Fly`. This will happen in the `dream()` method. The basic script for the dream is that the `Spider` first wishes it could be a frog, and then it magically transforms into one, and catches the fly with its sticky tongue (Figure 13–22).

The transformation to a frog is done by changing the images that are displayed on the applet. A sequence of three images is used, with appropriate delays. The first image shows the spider wishing it were a frog. The second shows a frog. And the third shows a happy frog saying "yum, yum," after just having eaten the `Fly`.

Eating the buzzing fly is simulated by drawing a line from the frog's tongue to the `Fly`'s current location. Note how the applet is used as an intermediary object here to get the `Fly`'s location:

Spider/fly interaction

```
flyLocation = applet.getFlyLocation();      // Look at the fly
```

Figure 13–22 The Spider's dream() method.

```
public synchronized void dream() {
    state = DREAMING;
    applet.updateStateField();
    Graphics g = applet.getGraphics();          // Draw dreaming image
    g.drawImage(image[DREAMING_IMG], 20, 100, applet);
    delay(5000);
    g.drawImage(image[FROG], 20, 100, applet);  // Transform to a frog
    delay(5000);
    flyLocation = applet.getFlyLocation();      // Look at the fly
    g.setColor( Color.pink);
    g.drawLine(FROG_X, FROG_Y, flyLocation.x, flyLocation.y);  // Eat the fly
    g.drawLine(FROG_X + 1, FROG_Y + 1, flyLocation.x + 1, flyLocation.y + 1);
    g.drawLine(FROG_X + 2, FROG_Y + 2, flyLocation.x + 1, flyLocation.y + 1);
    g.drawLine(FROG_X + 3, FROG_Y + 3, flyLocation.x + 1, flyLocation.y + 1);
    applet.eatFly();
    delay(250);
    g.drawImage(image[HAPPY_FROG], 20, 100, applet);
    delay(5000);
    applet.newFly();
} // dream()
```

As soon as the line is drawn, the `Fly` thread must stop and the `Fly` must disappear. Stopping the `Fly` thread is done by calling `applet.eatFly()` method, which in turn calls `Fly`'s `die()` method, which causes the fly thread to exit.

```
public void eatFly() {
    pest.die();
}
```

Making the `Fly` disappear from the screen is done by displaying the image of the happy frog. Then, after a suitable delay, the `applet.newFly()` method is invoked, which causes a new buzzing fly to be created:

```
public void newFly() {
    pest = new Fly(this);
    new Thread(pest).start();
}
```

It's important to note that the reason the `Fly` disappears from the display is twofold: First, since it is `DEAD`, it no longer buzzes around redrawing itself at a new location. In fact, it exits its `run()` method which kills that thread instance. Second, the `Spider` displays a new image. This causes the lingering image of the `Fly` to disappear. Of course, this happens so quickly, that it gives a reasonably convincing animation of a frog eating the fly. The complete implementation of the `Spider` class is shown in Figures 13–23 and 13–24.

Figure 13–23 The Spider class, part I.

```
import java.awt.*;                        // Import the GUI components

public class Spider extends CyberPet implements Runnable {
    protected int nImageFiles =  13;
    protected String imageFileName = "spiderweb";
    protected Image image[] = new Image[nImageFiles];

    protected CyberPetApplet applet ;          // Spider's interface
    static int currentImg = 0;

    private static final int SLEEPING_IMG = 5;
    private static final int NOT_HUNGRY_IMG = 6;
    private static final int NOT_SLEEPY_IMG = 7;
    private static final int LIKE_FLY = 8;
    private static final int NO_ESCAPE = 9;
    private static final int DREAMING_IMG = 10;
    private static final int FROG = 11;
    private static final int HAPPY_FROG = 12;

    private static final int FROG_X = 60;
    private static final int FROG_Y = 125;

    private Point flyLocation;

    public Spider(String name, CyberPetApplet app) {
        super(name);                               // Construct a CyberPet
        applet = app;
    }

    public void getImages() {
        Graphics g = applet.getGraphics();
        for (int k = 0; k < nImageFiles; k++) {
            image[k] = applet.getImage(applet.getDocumentBase(),imageFileName + (k+1) + ".gif");
            g.drawImage(image[k],20,100,applet);
        }
    } // getImages()

    public void eat() {
        Graphics g = applet.getGraphics();
        int choice = (int) ( Math.random() * 3 );
        if ( choice == 2 )         // i.e., 1 in 3 chance
            g.drawImage(image[NOT_HUNGRY_IMG], 20, 100, applet);
        else {
            state = EATING;
            for (int k = 0;  k < SLEEPING_IMG; k++) {
                g.drawImage(image[k], 20, 100, applet);
                delay(200) ;
            }
        } // else
    } // eat()

    private void autoeat() {
        Graphics g = applet.getGraphics();
        state = EATING;
        applet.updateStateField();
        for (int k = 0;  k < SLEEPING_IMG; k++) {
            g.drawImage(image[k], 20, 100, applet);
            delay(200) ;
        }
    } // autoeat()
```

Figure 13–24 The Spider class, part II.

```
public void sleep() {
    Graphics g = applet.getGraphics();
    int choice = (int)(Math.random() * 3);
    if (choice == 2)                       // i.e., 1 in 3 chance
        g.drawImage(image[NOT_SLEEPY_IMG], 20, 100, applet);
    else {
        state = SLEEPING;
        g.drawImage(image[SLEEPING_IMG], 20, 100, applet);
    }
} // sleep()

private void autosleep() {
    Graphics g = applet.getGraphics();
    state = SLEEPING;
    applet.updateStateField();
    g.drawImage(image[SLEEPING_IMG], 20, 100, applet);
} // autosleep()

public void think() {
    state = THINKING;
    applet.updateStateField();
    Graphics g = applet.getGraphics();
    int choice = (int)(Math.random() * 2);
    if (choice == 1)                       // i.e., 1 in 2 chance
        g.drawImage(image[NO_ESCAPE], 20, 100, applet);
    else {
        g.drawImage(image[LIKE_FLY], 20, 100, applet);
    }
} // think()

public synchronized void dream() {
    state = DREAMING;
    applet.updateStateField();
    Graphics g = applet.getGraphics();           // Draw dreaming image
    g.drawImage(image[DREAMING_IMG], 20, 100, applet);
    delay(5000);
    g.drawImage(image[FROG], 20, 100, applet);  // Transform to a frog
    delay(5000);
    flyLocation = applet.getFlyLocation();       // Look at the fly
    g.setColor( Color.pink);
    g.drawLine(FROG_X, FROG_Y, flyLocation.x, flyLocation.y);  // Eat the fly
    g.drawLine(FROG_X + 1, FROG_Y + 1, flyLocation.x + 1, flyLocation.y + 1);
    g.drawLine(FROG_X + 2, FROG_Y + 2, flyLocation.x + 1, flyLocation.y + 1);
    g.drawLine(FROG_X + 3, FROG_Y + 3, flyLocation.x + 1, flyLocation.y + 1);
    applet.eatFly();
    delay(250);
    g.drawImage(image[HAPPY_FROG], 20, 100, applet);
    delay(5000);
    applet.newFly();
} // dream()

public void run() {
    while (true) {
        int choice = (int)(Math.random() * 4);
        if (choice == 0)      autoeat();
        else if (choice == 1) autosleep();
        else if (choice == 2) think();
        else                  dream();
        delay(5000);
    }//while
} // run()
} // Spider
```

Figure 13–25 The `CyberPetApplet` class.

```
import java.awt.*;                                  // Import the GUI components
import java.awt.event.*;                            // Import event classes
import javax.swing.*;                               // Import Swing classes

public class CyberPetApplet extends JApplet implements ActionListener {
    private Spider spidey = new Spider ("Spidey", this);  // Create a Pet
    private Fly pest = new Fly(this);                      //  and a Fly
                                                       // GUI Components
    private JLabel nameLabel = new JLabel("Hi.  I'm "
                         + spidey.getPetName() +  " and I'm");
    private JTextField stateField = new JTextField(8);
    private JButton eatButton = new JButton("Eat!");
    private JButton sleepButton = new JButton("Sleep!");
    private JPanel controls = new JPanel();

    public void init() {
        eatButton.addActionListener(this);   // Initialize the interface
        sleepButton.addActionListener(this);
        controls.add(nameLabel);
        controls.add(stateField);
        controls.add(eatButton);
        controls.add(sleepButton);
        controls.setBorder(BorderFactory.createTitledBorder("Controls"));
        this.getContentPane().add(controls, "North");
        this.setSize(425,350);

        stateField.setText(spidey.getState()); // Init spidey's state
        showStatus("Loading image files");     //  and loads its images
        spidey.getImages();

        new Thread(spidey).start();      // Start spidey thread
        new Thread(pest).start();        // Start the fly thread
    } // init()

    public void eatFly() {
        pest.die();
    }
    public void newFly() {
        pest = new Fly(this);
        new Thread(pest).start();
    }
    public Point getFlyLocation() {
        return pest.getLocation();
    }
    public void updateStateField() {
        stateField.setText( spidey.getState() ); // Display state
    }
    public void actionPerformed (ActionEvent evt) {
        if (evt.getSource() == eatButton)   // If eatButton clicked
            spidey.eat();                   //     tell spidey to eat
        else                                // If sleepButton clicked
            spidey.sleep();                 //     tell spidey to sleep
        updateStateField();                 // Display state
    } // actionPerformed()
} // CyberPetApplet
```

13.6.5 The `CyberPetApplet` Class

The applet serves as an intermediary

The final component of the simulation is the applet class, which is shown in its entirety in Figure 13–25. The applet is where we instantiate the `Spider` and `Fly` objects and start their independent threads:

```
private Spider spidey = new Spider ("Spidey", this);  // Create a Pet
private Fly pest = new Fly(this);                     //  and a Fly
...
new Thread(spidey).start();     // Start spidey thread (in init())
new Thread(pest).start();       // Start the fly thread (in init())
...
```

The only other changes required from previous incarnations of this applet are the public methods used to coordinate the interaction between the `Spider` and the `Fly`:

```
public void eatFly() {
    pest.die();
}
public void newFly() {
    pest = new Fly(this);
    new Thread(pest).start();
}
public Point getFlyLocation() {
    return pest.getLocation();
}
```

As we discussed, these methods are invoked from the `Spider` and `Fly` threads and serve to mediate the interaction between these two, otherwise independent, threads.

OBJECT-ORIENTED DESIGN: Inheritance and Polymorphism

The Spider and Fly simulation provides a good example of how the object-oriented principles of inheritance and polymorphism contribute to the design of extensible code. First, we've used inheritance in our design by defining `Spider` and `Fly` as subclasses of `CyberPet`. This required several fairly minimal changes to `CyberPet` itself—such as, changing its `private` instance variables to `protected` and defining some new `static, final` class constants. The largest change was that the public methods that define a `CyberPet`'s actions — `eat()` and `sleep()` — were given simple, default implementations in `CyberPet`, with the intention that they would be overridden, if necessary, in `Spider` and `CyberPet` subclasses. This way, different kinds of `CyberPet` could implement these actions in ways that were appropriate.

Using inheritance to share methods

One advantage of this design is that it allows us to locate shared methods and variables within the superclass. Thus the `getState()` and `delay()` methods are shared by all subclasses of `CyberPet`. The default versions of `eat()`, `sleep()`, and so on, are also available to all subclasses.

Another advantage of this design is its generality and extensibility. We can easily add `Dog`, `Cat`, and other subclasses to the `CyberPet` hierarchy and give them distinguishing characteristics. Each new subclass will inherit the functionality now defined in the `CyberPet` class.

The use of polymorphism in this example occurs in the way that a thread's `run()` method is implemented. Within the `runnable` interface class the `run()` method is defined as an abstract method — that is, a method without a body. By implementing `run()` in each of our `CyberPet` subclasses, we are creating a polymorphic method — that is, a method that behaves differently depending upon the object that invokes it. This is seen most clearly in the fact that nowhere in our program do we actually call our thread's `run()` method directly. Instead we run a thread by invoking its `start()` method. As you would expect, the `Thread.start()` method invokes `run()`:

```
public synchronized void start() {
  // Do some system-related stuff
    run();
}
```

Because Java's thread system depends for its implementation on features of the particular operating system platform, it is necessary to incorporate all threads into a preexisting system. This is done by the `start()` method before the thread's `run()` method is invoked. The `run()` method itself is inherently polymorphic, because you *have* to override it.

Using polymorphism to extend built-in functionality

IN THE LABORATORY: THE SPIDER, THE FLY, AND THE BEE

The main purpose of this lab is to extend the Spider/Fly animation so that it incorporates a buzzing bee, as a third independent `CyberPet` thread. This is not hard, but it requires that you understand the concepts of *inheritance* and `threads`, as they were discussed in this chapter. The objectives of the lab are

- To define a `Bee` subclass of `CyberPet`.
- To incorporate a `Bee` instance into the spider/fly animation.
- To understand appropriate uses of inheritance in object-oriented design.

Problem Description

Define a `Bee` class as a subclass of `CyberPet`. A `Bee` is very similar to a `Fly`. For example, both fly around in the same rectangular area of the display. However, a `Bee` has the following differences:

- `Bee`s are magenta, whereas `Fly`s are red.
- `Bee`s are bigger than `Fly`s.
- New `Bee`s start from a different location than `Fly`s.
- `Bee`s make a beep-beep sound when they die.

Object-Oriented Design

What objects do we need?

There are different ways to design the Bee class. You could define Bee as a direct subclass of CyberPet. According to this design, the Bee class would be very similar, in its details, to the Fly subclass. Thus, you could simply copy the Fly class and then modify some of its details and save it as the Bee class.

This cut and paste approach is probably the poorest design alternative, with the least flexibility and the most redundancy. For example, both the Bee and Fly class will have almost identical declarations and method definitions. Why should all the CyberPet subclasses that fly around have to duplicate the buzzaround() code? Surely this is not a good example of code reuse.

Alternatively, you could define Bee as a subclass of Fly. This model would require that you make certain changes to Fly before extending it. For example, instead of defining the Fly's size as a class constant, you would want to make it a variable that can be set in both the Fly and Bee constructors. You'd want to make similar changes to accommodate their differences in color and initial location. Also, you would want to redesign the buzzaround() method, so that it will work for both Bees and Flys.

According to this model, a Bee is a kind of Fly. An important advantage of this model is that it could easily be extended to define, say, a Wasp. And it cuts down on the amount of redundant code. For example, all subclasses of Fly could use its buzzaround() method. This model would also be easier to maintain. If there's a change in the design of buzzaround(), it needs to be made only once and it will be inherited by all Fly subclasses.

Using an abstract *class*

A third model would define an abstract class, FlyingInsect, and make both Fly and Bee its direct subclasses. This abstract class would implement those methods common to all flying insects, leaving as abstract those methods which distinguish one type of flying insect from another. For example, because all flying insects will buzz around, it would be useful to implement the buzzaround() method in the FlyingInsect class. For most subclasses, this method could be used as is.

Similarly, because all flying insects eventually die, it would be useful to implement the die() method in FlyingInsect. However, suppose that all flying insects make some kind of distinct noise when they die, ranging from the Bee's beep-beep to the Wasp's peep, and so on. The Fly's silence, of course, could be treated as a special case, or we could modify it and make it beep when it dies. One way to design this feature would be to define an abstract lastGasp() method, which is called in die(), but implemented in the subclasses. That way it can be given an implementation that is appropriate to that particular subclass.

The lastGasp() *method is polymorphic*

This is the most economical and most extensible design. It gets the most mileage from code reuse. And, to define a new subclass of FlyingInsect, you need only implement its lastGasp() method and distinguish its color and size. Let's adopt this design for this project (Figure 13–26).

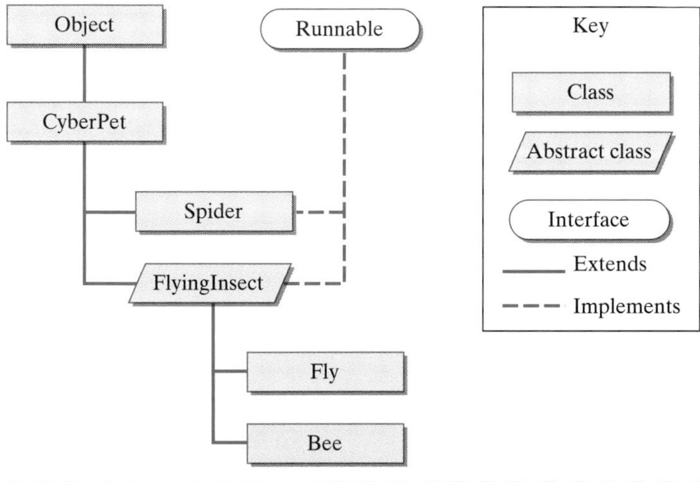

Figure 13–26 Hierarchy of classes for this lab.

The `FlyingInsect` Class

The `FlyingInsect` class will now absorb most of the constants, variables, and methods that were previously defined in the `Fly` class. Here's a list of things that should be incorporated into the definition of `FlyingInsect`:

- In order to allow `FlyingInsects` to have different colors, sizes, and starting locations, it will be necessary to use variables, rather than class constants, for these values.
- In addition to the constructor that was defined in the `Fly` class, you should define a constructor that allows a `FlyingInsect`'s color, size, and initial location to be set. An appropriate signature for this method would be

```
FlyingInsect (CyberPetApplet app, Color col, int siz, Point loc);
```

- The `getLocation()` and `run()` methods can be adopted from the previous version of `Fly`.
- Modify the implementations of the `buzzaround()` and `die()` methods so they will work with any `FlyingInsect` subclass. For example, `buzzaround()` should display the right color and size of the insect. And `die()` must call the `lastGasp()` method.
- Define the `abstract` method `lastGasp()`. Its implementation will be left up to the subclasses.

The Fly and Bee Classes

The revised Fly class will now be a subclass of FlyingInsect. To illustrate how simple this class becomes, we provide its full definition in Figure 13–27. Note how it uses the super keyword to call FlyingInsect's constructor method. Note also how the Toolkit.beep() method is used to generate a sound during the lastGasp() method. The Bee class will be a simple variant of this definition.

Figure 13–27 Definition of the Fly class.

```
import java.awt.*;     // IMPORT the GUI components

public class Fly extends FlyingInsect implements Runnable{

    public Fly ( CyberPetApplet app ) {
        super(app);
    }

    public void lastGasp(){
        Toolkit.getDefaultToolkit().beep();
    }
} // Fly
```

The CyberPetApplet Class

The applet as intermediary object

To incorporate a second buzzing insect into the simulation, several changes must be made to the applet class. First, you need to create a Bee instance in the applet and start() it running. The most interesting design issue here is how the applet will serve as an intermediary now that there are two buzzing insects. This will require changes to the following methods:

- getFlyLocation(): Which fly's location should be returned by this method, the Bee's or the Fly's? One way to "finesse" this issue would be to return one or the other at random. You could use Math.random() and if its value is greater than 0.5, you could return Fly's location; otherwise, you return Bee's location. Because the frog will eat the insect whose location is returned, it will be necessary to remember which insect was picked. Therefore, you'll want to create an instance variable of type CyberPet and assign it a reference to either the Bee or the Fly, depending on which one was picked:

  ```
  currentPest = (Bee) bee;
  ```

  Note the use of the cast operator, (Bee), to convert a Bee reference into (a more general) Cyberpet reference.
- eatFly(): The change to this method should just make use of the currentPest reference to decide which insect should die.
- newFly(): Similarly, if you killed the Bee during eatFly(), you should make a new Bee in this method, again making use of currentPest.

Resources

In order to animate your simulation, you will need the same set of images that were used in CyberPet animation in this chapter. These are available on the course Web site.

CHAPTER SUMMARY

Technical Terms

asynchronous	blocked	busy waiting
concurrent	critical section	deadlock
starvation	dispatched	fetch-execute-cycle
lock	monitor	multithreaded
multitasking	mutual exclusion	priority scheduling
producer/consumer model	quantum	queue
ready queue	round-robin scheduling	thread
time slicing	thread life cycle	

Java Keywords

abstract	catch	extends
private	protected	static
super	synchronized	try/catch

Java Classes

ActionListener	Thread	Toolkit
Button	Applet	BorderLayout
IllegalMonitorState Exception	Canvas	Graphics
	Object	TextField

Java Library Methods

actionPerformed()	init()	notify()
print()	println()	run()
setPriority()	sleep()	start()
stop()	wait()	

Programmer-Defined Classes

Bakery	Bee	Clerk
Customer	CyberPetApplet	CyberPet
Dotty	Fly	FlyingInsect
NumberThread	Numbers	RandomDotApplet
Spider	TakeANumber	

Programmer-Defined Methods

buzzaround()	clear()	customerWaiting()
delay(N)	die()	draw()
dream()	eat()	eatFly()
getFlyLocation()	getLocation()	getState()
lastGasp()	newFly()	nextCustomer()
nextNumber()	takeANumber()	

Summary of Important Points

- *Multitasking* is the technique of executing several tasks at the same time within a single program. In Java we give each task a separate *thread of execution*, thus resulting in a *multithreaded* program.
- A *sequential* computer with a single *Central Processing Unit (CPU)* can execute only one machine instruction at a time. A *parallel* computer uses multiple CPUs operating simultaneously to execute more than one instruction at a time.
- Each CPU uses a *fetch-execute cycle* to retrieve the next machine instruction from memory and execute it. The cycle is under the control of the CPU's internal clock, which typically runs at several hundred *megahertz* — where 1 megahertz (MHz) is one million cycles per second.
- *Time slicing* is the technique whereby several threads can share a single CPU over a given time period. Each thread is given a small slice of the CPU's time under the control of some kind of scheduling algorithm. In *round-robin scheduling*, each thread is given an equal slice of time, in a first-come-first-served order. In *priority scheduling*, higher-priority threads are allowed to run before lower-priority threads are run.
- There are generally two ways of creating threads in a program. One is to create a subclass of `Thread` and implement a `run()` method. The other is to create a `Thread` instance and pass it a `Runnable` object — that is, an object that implements `run()`.
- The `sleep()` method removes a thread from the CPU for a determinate length of time, giving other threads a chance to run.
- The `setPriorty()` method sets a thread's priority. Higher-priority threads have more and longer access to the CPU.
- Threads are *asynchronous*. Their timing and duration on the CPU is highly sporadic and unpredictable. In designing threaded programs, you must be careful not to base your algorithm on any assumptions about the threads' timing.
- To improve the responsiveness of interactive programs, you could give compute-intensive tasks, such as drawing lots of dots, to a lower-priority thread or to a thread that sleeps periodically.
- A thread's life cycle consists of ready, running, waiting, sleeping, and blocked states. Threads start in the ready state and are dispatched to the CPU by the scheduler, an operating system program. If a thread performs an I/O operation, it blocks until the I/O is completed. If it voluntarily sleeps, it gives up the CPU.
- In *round-robin* scheduling, each thread gets a fixed amount of time on the CPU, before being forced to give it up.
- According to the *producer/consumer* model, two threads share a resource, one serving to produce the resource and the other to consume the resource. Their cooperation must be carefully synchronized.

- An object that contains `synchronized` methods is known as a *monitor*. Such objects ensure that only one thread at a time can execute a synchronized method. The object is *locked* until the thread completes the method or voluntarily sleeps. This is one way to ensure mutually exclusive access to a resource by a collection of cooperating threads.
- The `synchronized` qualifier can also be used to designate a method as a *critical section*, whose execution should not be preempted by one of the other cooperating threads.
- In designing multithreaded programs it is useful to assume that if a thread *can* be interrupted at a certain point, it *will* be interrupted there. Thread coordination should never be left to chance.
- One way of coordinating two or more cooperating threads is to use the `wait/notify` combination. One thread waits for a resource to be available, and the other thread notifies when a resource becomes available.
- In the Spider/Fly example, inheritance is used to implement the shared elements of the `Spider` and `Fly` classes. By implementing the runnable interface, both `Spider` and `Fly` can be implemented as independent threads. Each can provide its own implementation of the `run()` method.

ANSWERS TO SELF-STUDY EXERCISES

EXERCISE 13.1

```
public class PrintOdds implements Runnable{
  private int bound;
  public PrintOdds( int b ) {
   bound = b;
  }

  public void print() {
    if (int k = 1; k < bound; k+=2)
      System.out.println( k );
  }

  public void run() {
    print();
  }
}
```

EXERCISE 13.2 On my system the experiment yielded the following output, if each thread printed its number after every 100,000 iterations:

```
1111112222222211111111333333332222222211111113333333
22222444444444333333344444445555555554444455555555555
```

This suggests that round-robin scheduling is being used.

EXERCISE 13.3 If each thread is given 50 milliseconds of sleep on each iteration, they tend to run in the order in which they were created:

```
123451234512345...
```

EXERCISE 13.4 The garbage collector runs whenever the available memory drops below a certain threshold. It must have higher priority than the application, since the application won't be able to run if it runs out of memory.

EXERCISE 13.5 If the JVM were single-threaded, it wouldn't be possible to break out of an infinite loop, because your program's loop would completely consume the CPU's attention.

EXERCISE 13.6 If round-robin scheduling is used, each thread will be get a portion of the CPU's time, so the applet thread will eventually get its turn. But you don't know how long it will be before the applet gets its turn, so there may still be an unacceptably long wait before the user's actions are handled. Thus to *guarantee* responsiveness, it is better to have the drawing thread sleep on every iteration.

EXERCISE 13.7 If `Dotty`'s priority is set to 1, a low value, this does improve the responsiveness of the interface, but it is significantly less responsive than using a `sleep()` on each iteration.

EXERCISE 13.8 To improve the responsiveness of an interactive program, the system could give a high priority to the threads that interact with the user and a low priority to those that perform noninteractive computations, such as number crunching.

EXERCISE 13.9 In a real bakery only one customer at a time can take a number. The take-a-number gadget "enforces" mutual exclusion by virtue of its design: There's room for only one hand to grab the ticket and there's only one ticket per number. If two customers got "bakery rage" and managed to grab the same ticket, it would rip in half and neither would benefit.

EXERCISE 13.10 One experiment to run would be to make the clerk's performance very slow by using large sleep intervals. If the algorithm is correct, this should not affect the order in which customers are served. Another experiment would be to force the clerk to work fast but the customers to work slow. This should still not affect the order in which the customers are served.

EXERCISE 13.11 You should observe that the waiting line builds up as customers enter the bakery, but the clerk should still serve the customers in the correct order.

EXERCISES

1. Explain the difference between the following pairs of terms.

    a. *Blocked* and *ready*.
    b. *Priority* and *round-robin* scheduling.
    c. *Producer* and *consumer*.
    d. *Monitor* and *lock*.
    e. *Concurrent* and *time slicing*.
    f. *Mutual exclusion* and *critical section*.
    g. *Busy* and *nonbusy* waiting.

2. Fill in the blank:

   a. _____ happens when a CPU's time is divided among several different threads.
   b. A method that should not be interrupted during its execution is known as a _____.
   c. The scheduling algorithm in which each thread gets an equal portion of the CPU's time is known as _____.
   d. The scheduling algorithm in which some threads can preempt other threads is known as _____.
   e. A _____ is a mechanism that enforces mutually exclusive access to a synchronized method.
   f. A thread that performs an I/O operation may be forced into the _____ state until the operation is completed.
   g. Two threads could become _____ if each one is holding a resource that the other one needs.

3. Describe the concept of *time slicing* as it applies to CPU scheduling.
4. What's the difference in the way concurrent threads would be implemented on a computer with several processors and on computer with a single processor.
5. Why are threads put into the *blocked* state when they perform an I/O operation?
6. What's the difference between a thread in the sleep state and a thread in the ready state?
7. Suppose you have a four-way intersection and that cars are entering the intersection from each branch. Describe the problems of *deadlock* and *starvation* in terms of the intersection.
8. Describe an algorithm that drivers can use to avoid creating a deadlock in a four-way intersection.
9. Use the `Runnable` interface to define a thread that repeatedly generates random numbers in the interval 2 through 12.
10. Use the `Runnable` interface to convert `CyberPet` into a thread. For its `run()` method, have the `CyberPet` alternate endlessly between eating, sleeping, and thinking.
11. Create a version of the `Bakery` program that uses two clerks to serve customers.
12. Modify the `Numbers` program so that the user can interactively create `NumberThreads` and assign them a priority. Modify the `NumberThreads` so that they print their numbers indefinitely (rather than for a fixed number of iterations). Then experiment with the system by observing the effect of introducing threads with the same, lower, or higher priority. How do the threads behave when they all have the same priority? What happens when you introduce a higher-priority thread into the mix? What happens when you introduce a lower-priority thread into the mix?
13. Create a bouncing ball simulation in which a single ball (thread) bounces up and down in a vertical line. The ball should bounce off the bottom and top of the enclosing frame.
14. Modify the simulation in the previous exercise so that more than one ball can be introduced. Allow the user to introduce new balls into the simulation by pressing the space bar or clicking the mouse.
15. Modify your solution to the previous problem by having the balls bounce off the wall at a random angle.

16. **Challenge:** One type of producer/consumer problem is the *reader/writer* problem. Create a subclass of `JTextField` that can be shared by threads, one of which writes a random number to the text field, and the other of which reads the value in the text field. Coordinate the two threads so that the overall effect of the program will be that it will print the values from 0 to 100 in the proper order. In other words, the reader thread shouldn't read a value from the text field until there's a value to be read. The writer thread shouldn't write a value to the text field until the reader has read the previous value.
17. **Challenge:** Create a streaming banner thread that moves a simple message across a panel. The message should repeatedly enter at the left edge of the panel and exit from the right edge. Design the banner as a subclass of `JPanel` and have it implement the `Runnable` interface. That way it can be added to any user interface. One of its constructors should take a `String` argument that let's the user set the banner's message.
18. **Challenge:** Create a slide show applet, which repeatedly cycles through an array of images. The displaying of the images should be a separate thread. The applet thread should handle the user interface. Give the user some controls that let it pause, stop, start, speed up, and slow down the images.
19. **Challenge:** Create a horse race simulation, using separate threads for each of the horses. The horses should race horizontally across the screen, with each horse having a different vertical coordinate. If you don't have good horse images to use, just make each horse a colored polygon or some other shape. Have the horses implement the `Drawable` interface, which we introduced in Chapter 10.
20. **Challenge:** The game of Pong was the rage in the 1970s. It consists of a ball that moves within a rectangular region, as in a previous exercise, and a single paddle, which is located at the right boundary, which can be moved up and down by the user. When the ball hits the paddle, it bounces off at a random angle. When it hits the wall, it just reverses direction. The ball should be one thread and the user interface (and paddle) should be the other.

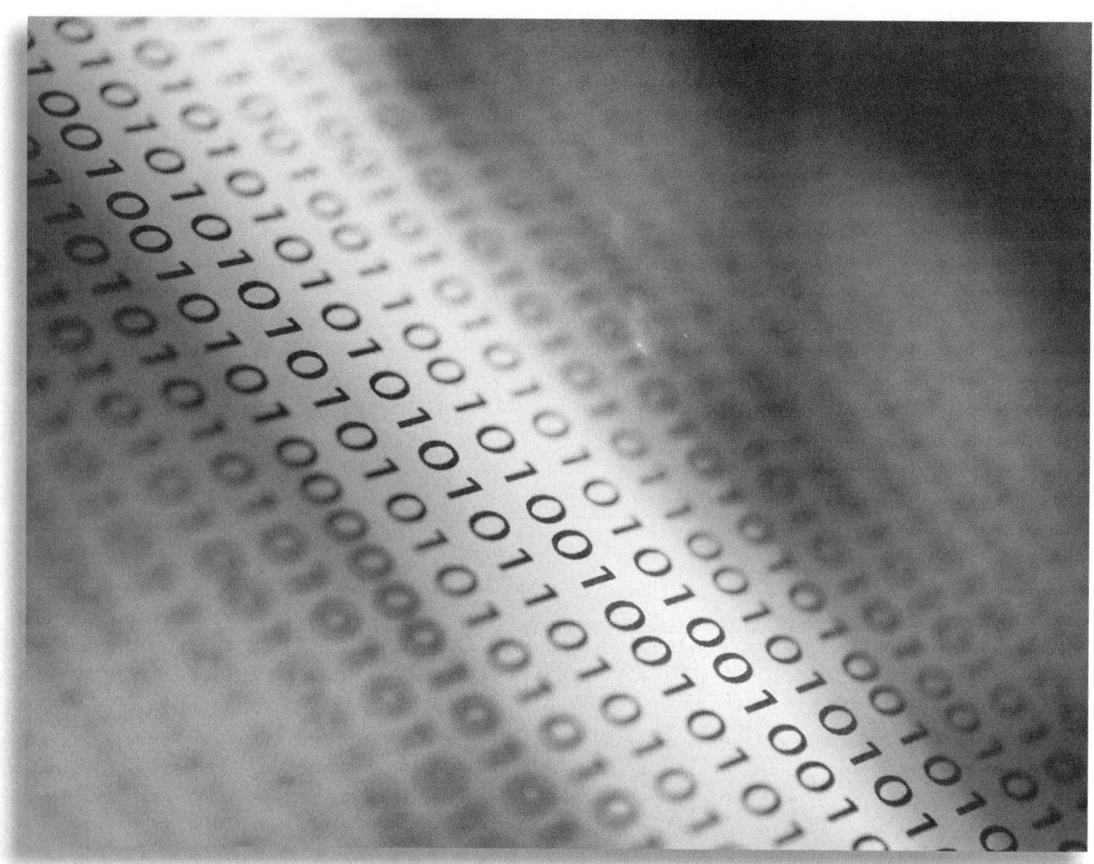

Photograph courtesy of Nick Koudis, PhotoDisc, Inc.

14

Files, Streams, and Input/Output Techniques

OBJECTIVES

After studying this chapter, you will

- Be able to read and write text files.
- Know how to read and write binary files.
- Understand the use of `InputStreams` and `OutputStreams`
- Be able to design methods for performing input and output.
- Know how to use the `File` class.
- Be able to use the `JFileChooser` class.

OUTLINE

14.1 Introduction

Input refers to *reading* information or data from some external source into a running program. Up to this point, whenever our programs have input data, they have come from the keyboard or from a `JTextField` in a GUI interface. These external sources are *transitory* in that they exist only while the program is running. `JTextField`s reside in the computer's primary memory, in an area that is temporarily assigned to the program that created them. They cease to exist when the program stops running.

Output refers to *writing* information or data from the running program to some external destination. Up to this point, whenever our programs have produced output, it has been sent to the Java console, to a text area, or to some other GUI component. All of these destinations are transitory, in the sense that they too reside in the computer's primary memory and exist only so long as the program is running.

A *file* is a collection of data that's stored on a disk or on some other relatively permanent storage medium. A file's existence does not depend on a running program. In this chapter we will learn how to create files and how to perform input and output operations on their data.

14.2 Streams and Files

I/O streams

All Input and Output (I/O) in Java, whether it be file I/O or I/O involving the keyboard and the screen, is accomplished through the use of streams. A **stream** is an object that delivers information to and from another object. A stream is like a pipe or a conduit that connects a source of information and its destination. For example, `System.out` and `System.in` are two streams that we have used (Figure 14–1. `System.out` connects your program (source) to the screen (destination).

More generally, `System.out` is an **output stream** that connects a program to the *standard output device*. When you perform a `System.out.println()` statement, information flows from the program, through `System.out`

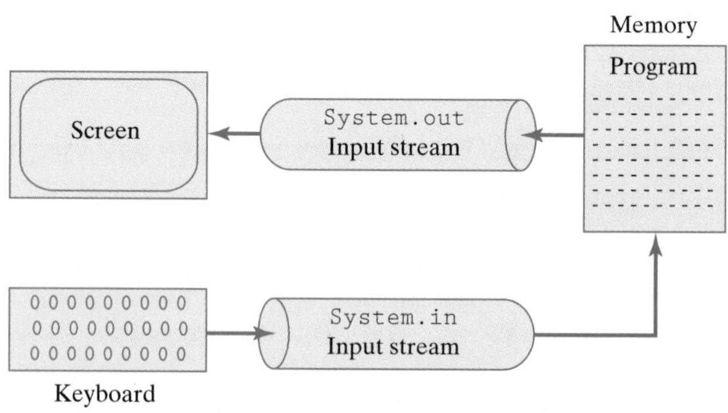

Figure 14–1 A stream serves like a pipe through which data flow.

to the screen. Similarly, `System.in` usually connects the keyboard (source) to the running program (destination). As an **input stream**, it connects a *standard input device* to a running program. When you perform a `System.in.read()` operation, information flows from the keyboard, through `System.in` to the program.

System.in and System.out streams

14.2.1 The Data Hierarchy

What flows through a Java stream, and what is stored in a file, is information or data. All data are comprised of binary digits or *bits*. A bit is simply a 0 or a 1, or rather the electronic states that correspond to these values. A bit is the smallest unit of data.

However, it would be tedious if a program had to work with data in units as small as bits. Therefore, most operations involve various sized aggregates of data such as an 8-bit `byte`, a 16-bit `short`, a 16-bit `char`, a 32-bit `int`, a 64-bit `long`, a 32-bit `float`, or a 64-bit `double`. As we know, these are Java's primitive numeric types. In addition to these aggregates, we can group together a sequence of `char` to form a `String`.

It is also possible to group data of different types into objects. A **record**, which corresponds closely to a Java object, can have **fields** that contain different types of data. For example, a student record might contain fields for the student's name and address (`Strings`), expected year of graduation (`int`), and current grade point average (`double`). Collections of these records are typically grouped into **files**. For example, your registrar's office may have a separate file for each of its graduating classes. These are typically organized into a collection of related files, which is called a **database**.

The data hierarchy

Taken together, the different kinds of data that are processed by a computer or stored in a file can be organized into a **data hierarchy** (Figure 14–2).

It's important to recognize that while we, the programmers, may group data into various types of abstract entities, the information flowing through an input or output stream is just a sequence of bits. There are no natural boundaries that mark where one byte (or one `int` or one record) ends and the next one begins. Therefore, it will be up to us to provide the boundaries as we process the data.

14.2.2 Binary Files and Text Files

There are two types of files in Java: binary files and text files. Both kinds store data as a sequence of bits — that is, a sequence of 0's and 1's. Thus the difference between the two types of files lies in the way they are interpreted by the programs that read and write them. A **binary file** is processed as a sequence of bytes, whereas a **text file** is processed as a sequence of characters.

Binary vs. text file

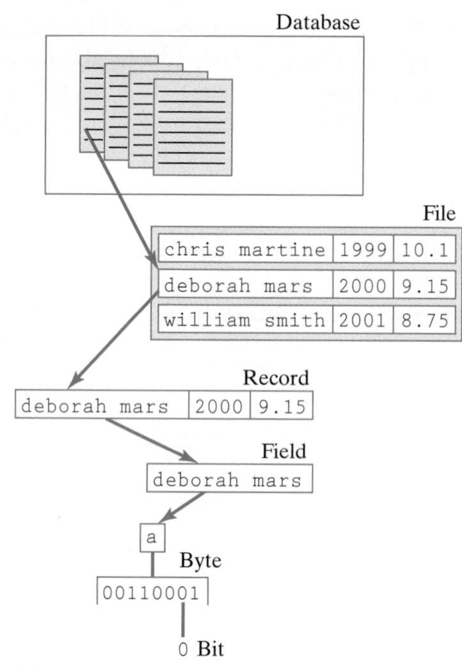

Figure 14–2 The data hierarchy.

Text files are portable

Text editors, and other programs that process text files, interpret the file's sequence of bits as a sequence of characters — that is, as a string. Your Java source programs (`*.java`) are text files, and so are the HTML files that populate the World Wide Web. The big advantage of text files is their portability. Because their data are represented in the ASCII code (Table 5–11), they can be read and written by just about any text processing program. Thus a text file created by a program on a Windows/Intel computer can be read by a Macintosh program.

In a binary file, data are stored as bytes, and the representation used varies from computer to computer. Binary data stored in a file have the same representation as binary data stored in the computer's memory. Thus binary data are not very portable. A binary file of integers created on a Macintosh cannot be read by a Windows/Intel program.

Binary files are platform dependent

One reason for the lack of portability is that each type of computer uses its own definition for how an integer is defined. On some systems it may be 16 bits, and on others it may be 32 bits, so even if you know that a Macintosh binary file contains integers, that still won't make it readable by Windows/Intel programs. Another problem is that even if two computers use the same number of bits to represent an integer, they may use different representation schemes. Thus, on some computers, 10000101 is used as the 8-bit representation of the number 133, whereas on other computers, the reverse, 10100001, is the used to represent 133.

The good news for us is that Java's designers have made its binary files *platform independent* by carefully defining the exact size and representation that must be used for integers and all other primitive types. Thus binary files created by Java programs can be interpreted by Java programs on any platform.

JAVA LANGUAGE RULE **Platform independence.** Java binary files are platform independent. They can be interpreted by any computer that supports Java.

14.2.3 Input and Output Streams

Java has a wide variety of streams for performing I/O. They are defined in the `java.io` package, which must be imported by any program that does I/O. They are generally organized into a hierarchy (Figure 14–3). We will cover only a small portion of the hierarchy. Generally speaking, binary files are processed by subclasses of `InputStream` and `OutputStream`. Text files are processed by subclasses of `Reader` and `Writer`, both of which are streams, despite their names. Table 14–1 gives a brief description of the most commonly used input and output streams.

I/O streams

`InputStream` and `OutputStream` are abstract classes that serve as the root classes for reading and writing binary data. Their most commonly used subclasses are `DataInputStream` and `DataOutputStream`, which are used for processing `String` data and data of any of Java's primitive types — `char`, `boolean`, `int`, `double`, and so on. The analogues of these classes for processing text data are the `Reader` and `Writer` classes, which serve as the root classes for all text I/O.

PROGRAMMING TIP: Choosing a Stream. In choosing an appropriate stream for an I/O operation, `DataInputStreams` and `Data OutputStreams` are normally used for binary I/O. `Reader` and `Writer` streams are normally used for text I/O.

The various subclasses of these root classes perform various specialized I/O operations. Thus, `FileInputStream` and `FileOutputStream` are used for performing binary input and output on files. The `PrintStream` class contains methods for outputting various primitive data — integers, floats, and so forth — as text. The `System.out` stream, one of the most widely used output streams, is an object of this type. The `PrintStream` class has been deprecated in JDK 1.2 and has been superseded by the `PrintWriter` class, which is designed to support platform independence and internationalized I/O.

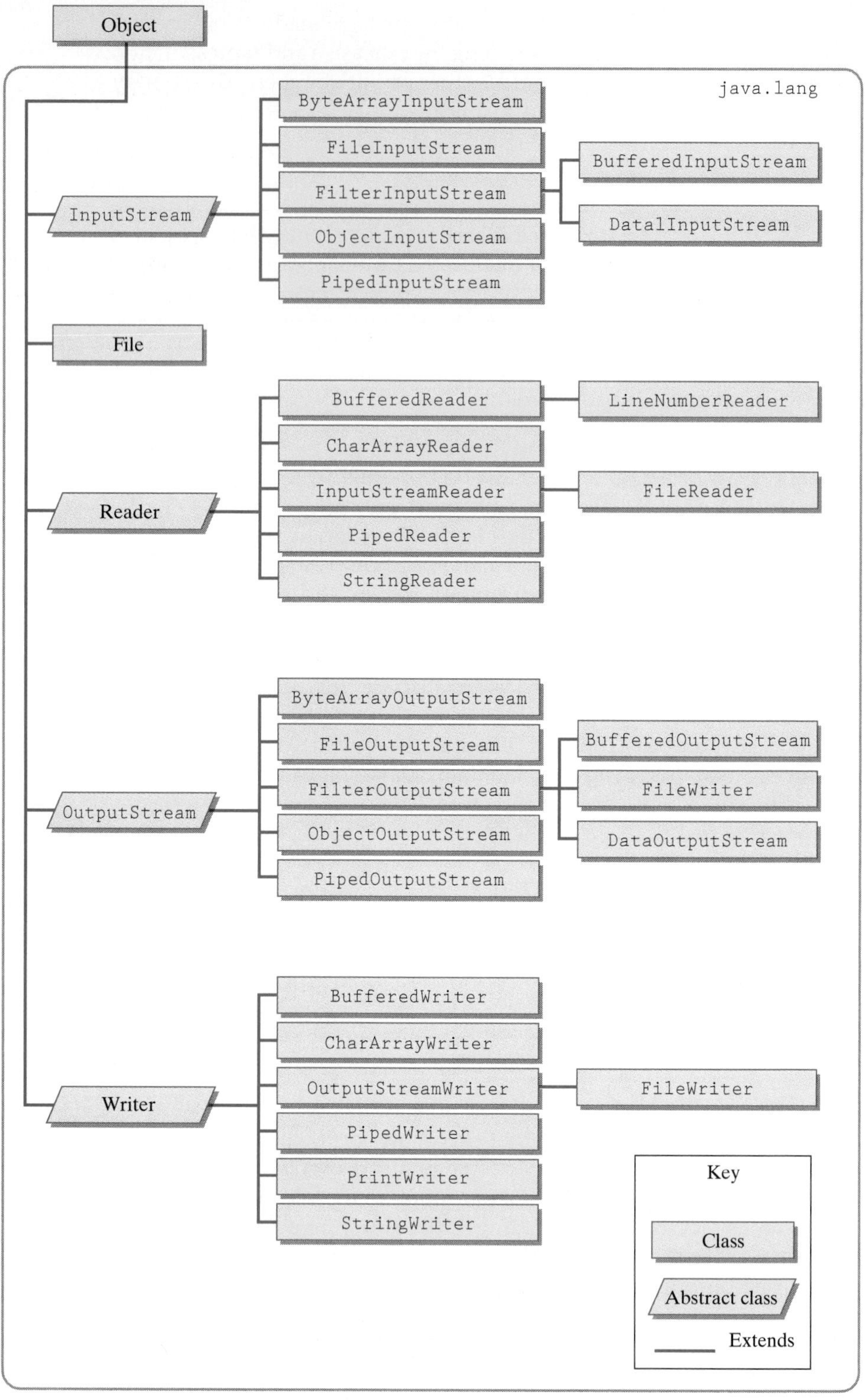

Figure 14–3 Java's stream hierarchy.

Table 14.1. Description of some of Java's important stream classes

Class	Description
`InputStream`	Abstract root class of all binary input streams
`FileInputStream`	Provides methods for reading bytes from a binary file
`FilterInputStream`	Provides methods required to filter data in various ways
`BufferedInputStream`	Provides input data buffering for reading large files
`ByteArrayInputStream`	Provides methods for reading an array as if it were a stream
`DataInputStream`	Provides methods for reading Java's primitive data types
`PipedInputStream`	Provides methods for reading piped data from another thread
`OutputStream`	Abstract root class of all binary output streams
`FileOutputStream`	Provides methods for writing bytes to a binary file
`FilterOutputStream`	Provides methods required to filter data in various ways
`BufferedOutputStream`	Provides output data buffering for writing large files
`ByteArrayOutputStream`	Provides methods for writing an array as if it were a stream
`DataOutputStream`	Provides methods for writing Java's primitive data types
`PipedOutputStream`	Provides methods for writing piped data to another thread
`PrintStream`	Provides methods for writing primitive data as text
`Reader`	Abstract root class for all text input streams
`BufferedReader`	Provides buffering for character input streams
`CharArrayReader`	Provides input operations on `char` arrays
`FileReader`	Provides methods for character input on files
`FilterReader`	Provides methods to filter character input
`StringReader`	Provides input operations on `Strings`
`Writer`	Abstract root class for all text output streams
`BufferedWriter`	Provides buffering for character output streams
`CharArrayWriter`	Provides output operations to `char` arrays
`FileWriter`	Provides methods for output to text files
`FilterWriter`	Provides methods to filter character output
`PrintWriter`	Provides methods for printing binary data as characters
`StringWriter`	Provides output operations to `Strings`

The various methods defined in `PrintWriter` are designed to output a particular type of primitive data. Here are the signatures of some of its methods:

```
public void print(int i);          public void println(int i);
public void print(long l);         public void println(long l);
public void print(float f);        public void println(float f);
public void print(double d);       public void println(double d);
public void print(String s);       public void println(String s);
public void print(Object o);       public void println(Object o);
```

As you would expect, there is both a print() and println() method for each kind of data that one wishes to output.

Filtering refers to performing operations on data while they are being input or output. Methods in the FilterInputStream and FilterReader classes can be used to filter binary and text data during input. Methods in the FilterOutputStream and FilterWriter can be used to filter output data.

These classes serve as the root classes for various filtering subclasses. They can also be subclassed to perform customized data filtering. All of these classes are declared abstract, and are meant to be subclassed.

Buffering

One type of filtering is *buffering*, which is provided by several buffered streams, including BufferedInputStream and BufferedReader, for performing binary and text input, and BufferedOutputStream and BufferedWriter, for buffered output operations. A **buffer** is a relatively large region of memory used to temporarily store data while it is being input or output. When buffering is used, rather than reading one byte at a time from the relatively slow input device, the program will transfer a large number of bytes into the buffer and then transfer these to the program as each read operation is performed. The transfer from the buffer to the program's memory is very fast.

Similarly, when buffering is used during output, rather than writing one byte at a time (or one integer or one float), data are transferred directly to the buffer and then written to the disk when the buffer fills up or when the flush() method is called.

PROGRAMMING TIP: Buffering. Buffered streams can be used to improve a program's overall efficiency by reducing the amount of time it spends accessing relatively slow input or output devices.

Filtering data

You can also define your own data filtering subclasses to perform customized filtering. For example, suppose you want to add line numbers to a text editor's printed output. To perform this task, you could define a FilterWriter subclass and override its write() methods to perform the desired filtering operation. Similarly, to remove the line numbers from such a file during input, you could define a FilterReader subclass. In that case you would override its read() methods to suit your own purposes.

The various piped streams consist of methods used to transfer data between threads, rather than files. A *pipe* is simply a type of communication channel between two threads. Once a pipe has been established, methods of the PipedInputStream and PipedOutputStream classes can be used to perform binary I/O between the two threads. Similarly, methods of the PipedReader and PipedWriter classes can be used for text I/O between two threads.

There are several classes that provide I/O-like operations on various internal memory structures. Thus, ByteArrayInputStream and Byte

ArrayOutputStream and CharArrayReader and CharArrayWriter are classes that take input from or send output to arrays in the program's memory. Methods in these classes may be useful for performing various operations on data during input or output. For example, suppose a program reads an entire line of integer data from a binary file into a ByteArray. It might then transform the data by, say, computing the remainder modulo *N* of each value. These transformed data can then be read by the program by treating the byte array as an input stream. A similar example would apply for some kind of output transformation.

The StringReader and StringWriter classes provide methods for treating Strings and StringBuffers as I/O streams. These methods are sometimes useful for performing certain data conversions.

PROGRAMMING TIP: Integer/String Conversion. An integer can be converted to a String by writing it to a StringBuffer, which can then be output as an entire line of text. StringReader methods can be used to read integer data from an ordinary String object.

14.3 CASE STUDY: Reading and Writing Text Files

Suppose you are writing a simple text editor, as we will be doing in the laboratory project for this chapter. One of the subtasks of this project is to be able to read and write data to and from a text file. Thus, let's develop a set of methods to perform I/O on text files. To help us test our methods, we'll write a frame-based application.

GUI design

The GUI for this application will contain a JTextArea, where text file data may be input and displayed, and a JTextField, where the user can enter the file's name. It will also contain two JButtons, one for reading a file into the JTextArea, and the other for writing the data in the JTextArea into a file (Figure 14–4). Note that even this simple interface will let the user create new files and rename existing files.

14.3.1 Text File Format

The end-of-file character

A text file consists of a sequence of characters divided into zero or more lines and ending with a special **end-of-file** character. When you open a new file in a text editor, it contains zero lines and zero characters. After typing a single character, it would contain one character and one line. The following would be an example of a file with four lines of text:

```
one\ntwo\nthree\nfour\eof
```

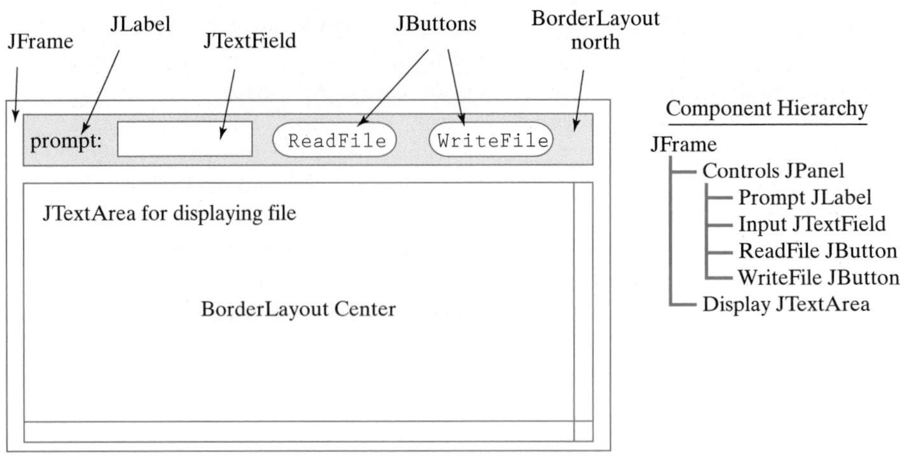

Figure 14–4 The GUI design for a program that reads and writes text files.

Note the use of the end-of-line character, `\n`, to mark the end of each line, and the use of the end-of-file character, `\eof`, to mark the end of the file. As we'll see, the I/O methods for text files use these special characters to control reading and writing loops. Thus, when the file is read by appropriate Java methods, such as the `BufferedReader.readLine()` and `BufferedReader.read()` methods, one or more characters will be read until either an end-of-line or end-of-file character is encountered. When a line of characters is written using `println()`, the end-of-line character is appended to the characters themselves.

14.3.2 Writing to a Text File

Let's see how to write to a text file. In this program we write the entire contents of the `JTextArea()` to the text file. In general, writing data to a file requires three steps:

1. Connect an output stream to the file.
2. Write text data into the stream, possibly using a loop.
3. Close the stream.

Output stream

As Figure 14–1 shows, connecting a stream to a file is like doing a bit of plumbing. The first step is to connect an output stream to the file. The output stream serves as a conduit between the program and a named file. It opens the file and gets it ready to accept data from the program. If the file already exists, then opening the file will destroy any data it previously contained. If the file doesn't yet exist, then it will be created from scratch.

Once the file is open, the next step is to write the text to the stream, which passes it on to the file. This step may require a loop which outputs one line of data on each iteration. Finally, once all the data have been written to the file, the stream should be closed. This also has the effect of closing the file itself.

EFFECTIVE DESIGN: Writing a file. Writing data to a file requires a three-step algorithm: (1) connect an output stream to the file, (2) write the data, and (3) close the file.

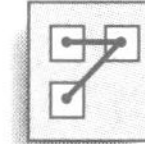

Code Reuse: Designing an Output Method

Now let's see how these three steps are done in Java. Suppose the text we want to write is contained in a `JTextArea`. Thus we want a method that will write the contents of a `JTextArea` to a named file.

Choosing an output stream

What output stream should we use for the task of writing a `String` to a named file? To decide this, we need to use the information in Figure 14–3 and Table 14–1. As we pointed out earlier, because we're writing a text file, we would use a `Writer` subclass. But which subclass should we use? The only way to decide this is to look at the methods available in the various subclasses. Ideally, we would like to be able to create an output stream just given the name of the file, and we would like to be able to write a `String` to the file.

One likely candidate is the `FileWriter` class. Its name and description (Table 14–1) suggest that it's designed for writing text files. And indeed it contains the kind of constructor we need — that is, one that takes the file's name as a parameter:

```
public class FileWriter extends OutputStreamWriter {
    public FileWriter(String fileName) throws IOException;
    public FileWriter(String fileName, boolean append) throws IOException;
}
```

Note that by taking a `boolean` parameter, the second constructor allows us to append data to a file, rather than rewrite the entire file, which is the default case.

Inheritance

However, `FileWriter` doesn't directly define a `write()` method. This doesn't necessarily mean that it doesn't contain such a method. It might have inherited one from its superclasses, so let's look at its `OutputStream Writer` and `Writer` superclasses (Figure 14–3). Both of these classes have methods that write `Strings`, but the `Writer` class contains a method whose signature suggests that it is ideally suited for our task:

```
public void write( String s) throws IOException;
```

Having decided on a FileWriter stream, the rest of the task of designing our method is simply a matter of using FileWriter methods in an appropriate way:

```
private void writeTextFile(JTextArea display, String fileName) {
    FileWriter outStream = new FileWriter(fileName); // Create stream & open file
    outStream.write(display.getText());              // Write the entire display text
    outStream.close();                               // Close the output stream
}
```

We use the FileWriter() to create an output stream to the file whose name is stored in fileName(). In this case, the task of writing data to the file is handled by a single write() statement, which writes the entire contents of the JTextArea in one operation.

Finally, once we have finished writing the data, we close() the output stream. This also has the effect of closing the file. The overall effect of this method is that the text contained in display has been output to a file, named fileName, which is stored on the disk.

PROGRAMMING TIP: Closing a File. Even though Java will close any files and streams left open when a program terminates normally, it is good programming practice to close the file yourself with a close() statement. It also reduces the chances of damaging the file if the program terminates abnormally.

Because so many different things can go wrong during an I/O operation, most I/O operations generate some kind of *checked exception*. Therefore it is necessary to embed them within a try/catch statement. In this example, the FileWriter() constructor, the write() method, and the close() method may each throw an IOException. Therefore the entire body of this method should be embedded within a try/catch block that catches the IOException (Figure 14–5).

Figure 14–5 A method to write a text file.

```
private void writeTextFile(JTextArea display, String fileName) {
    try {
        FileWriter outStream
            = new FileWriter (fileName);
        outStream.write (display.getText());
        outStream.close();
    } catch (IOException e) {
        display.setText("IOERROR: " + e.getMessage() + "\n");
        e.printStackTrace();
    }
} // writeTextFile()
```

14.3.3 Code Reuse: Designing Text File Output

The `writeTextFile()` method provides a simple example of how to write data to a text file. More importantly, its development illustrates the kinds of choices necessary to design effective I/O methods. Two important design questions we asked and answered were

- What methods do we need to perform the desired task?
- What streams contain the desired methods?

As in so many other examples we've considered, designing a method to perform a task is often a matter of finding the appropriate methods in the Java class hierarchy.

EFFECTIVE DESIGN: Code Reuse. Developing effective I/O routines is primarily a matter of choosing the right library methods. Start by asking yourself, "What methods do I need?" and then find a stream class that contains the appropriate methods.

As you might expect, there is more than one way to write data to a text file. Suppose we decided that writing text to a file is like printing data to `System.out`. And suppose we chose to use a `PrintWriter` object as our first candidate for an output stream (Figure 14–3 and Table 14–1). This class contains a wide range of `print()` methods for writing different types of data as text:

```
public class PrintWriter extends Writer {
   // Constructor methods
    public PrintWriter(Writer out);
    public PrintWriter(OutputStream out);
   // Instance methods
    public void close(); // Implements Writer method
    public void flush(); // Implements Writer method
    public print(int i); // print() methods for each data type & object
    ...
    public print(String s);
    public println(int i); // println() methods for each data type & object
    ...
    public println(String s);
}
```

So it has exactly the kind of method we need: `print(String)`. However, this stream does not contain a constructor method that allows us to create a stream from the name of a file. Its constructors require either a `Writer` object or an `OutputStream` object.

This means that we can use a `PrintWriter` to print to a file, but only if we can first construct either an `OutputStream` or a `Writer` object to the file. So we must go back to searching Figure 14–3 and Table14–1 for an appropriate candidate. Fortunately, the `FileOutputStream` class has just the constructors we want:

```
public class FileOutputStream extends OutputStream {
   // Constructors
    public FileOutputStream(String name) throws IOException;
    public FileOutputStream(String name, boolean append) throws IOException;
}
```

We now have an alternative way of coding the `writeTextFile()` method, this time using a combination of `PrintWriter` and `FileOutputStream`:

```
PrintWriter outStream =                              // Create an output stream
    new PrintWriter(new FileOutputStream(fileName)); // And open the file
outStream.print ( display.getText() );               // Write the entire display text
outStream.close();                                   // Close the output stream
```

Parameter agreement

Note how the output stream is created in this case. First we create a `FileOutputStream` using the file name as its argument. Then we create a `PrintWriter` using the `FileOutputStream` as its argument. The reason we can do this is because the `PrintWriter()` constructor takes a `FileOutputStream` parameter. This is what makes the connection possible.

To use the plumbing analogy again, this is like connecting two sections of pipe between the program and the file. The data will flow from the program through `PrintWriter`, through the `OutputStream`, to the file. Of course, you can't just arbitrarily connect one stream to another. They have to "fit together," which means that their parameters have to match.

EFFECTIVE DESIGN: Stream/Stream Connections. Two different kinds of streams can be connected if a constructor for one stream takes the second kind of stream as a parameter. This is often an effective way to create the kind of object you need to perform an I/O task.

The important lesson here is that we found what we wanted by searching through the `java.io.*` hierarchy. This same approach can be used to help you to design I/O methods for other tasks.

SELF-STUDY EXERCISES

EXERCISE 14.1 Is it possible to perform output to a text file using a `PrintWriter` and a `FileWriter` stream in combination? If so, write the Java code.

14.3.4 Reading from a Text File

Let's now look at the problem of inputting data from a text file. In general, there are three steps to reading data from a file:

1. Connect an input stream to the file.
2. Read the text data using a loop.
3. Close the stream.

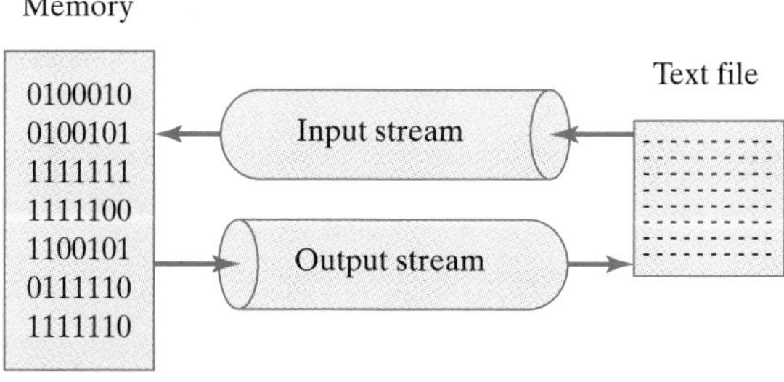

Figure 14–6 A stream serves as a pipe through which data flow.

As Figure 14–6 shows, the input stream serves as a kind of pipe between the file and the program. The first step is to connect an input stream to the file. Of course, in order to read a file, the file must exist. The output stream serves as a conduit between the program and the named file. It opens the file and gets it ready for reading. Once the file is open, the next step is to read the file's data. This will usually require a loop that reads data until the end of the file is reached. Finally, once all the data are read, the stream should be closed.

EFFECTIVE DESIGN: Reading data from a file requires a three-step algorithm: (1) connect an input stream to the file, (2) read the data, and (3) close the file.

Now let's see how these three steps are done in Java. Suppose that we want to put the file's data into a `JTextArea`. Thus we want a method that will be given the name of a file and a reference to a `JTextArea`, and it will read the data from the file into the `JTextArea`.

Choosing an input stream

What input stream should we use for this task? Here again we need to use the information in Figure 14–3 and Table 14–1. Because we're reading a text file, we should use a `Reader` subclass. A good candidate is the `FileReader`, whose name and description suggest that it might contain useful methods.

What methods should we use?

What methods do we need? As in the previous example, we need a constructor method that connects an input stream to a file, given the name of the file. And, ideally, we'd like to have a method that will read one line at a time from the text file. The `FileReader` class has the right kind of constructor:

```
public class FileReader extends InputStreamReader {
    // CONSTRUCTORS
    public FileReader( String fileName ) throws FileNotFoundException;
}
```

However, it contains no `readLine()` methods itself. Searching upward through its superclasses, we find that `InputStreamReader`, its immediate parent class, has a method that reads `int`s:

```
public int read() throws IOException();
```

This method turns out to be an override of the `read()` method defined in the `Reader` class, the root class for text file input streams. Thus, there are no `readLine()` methods in the `Reader` branch of the hierarchy.

One class that does contain a `readLine()` method is `BufferedReader`. Can we somehow use it? Fortunately, the answer is yes. `BufferedReader` contains the following method:

```
public class BufferedReader extends Reader {
   // Constructors
    public BufferedReader(Reader instream);
   // Public instance methods
    public String readLine() throws IOException;
}
```

Its constructor takes a `Reader` object as a parameter. But a `FileReader` *is* a `Reader` — that is, it is a descendant of the `Reader` class. So, to use our plumbing analogy again, to build an input stream to the file, we can join together a `BufferedReader` and a `FileReader`:

```
BufferedReader inStream
     = new BufferedReader(new FileReader(fileName));
```

Given this sort of connection to the file, the program can use `BufferedReader.readLine()` to read one line at a time from the file.

Using the end-of-file character

So we have a method that reads one line at a time. Now we need an algorithm that will read the entire file. Of course, this will involve a loop, and the key will be to make sure we get the loop's termination condition correct. An important fact about `readLine()` is that it will return `null` as its value when it reaches the end of the file. Recall that text files have a special end-of-file character. When `readLine()` encounters this character, it will return `null`. Therefore we can specify the following `while` loop:

```
String line = inStream.readLine();
while (line != null) {
    display.append(line + "\n");
    line = inStream.readLine();
}
```

We begin (outside the loop) by attempting to read a line from the file. If the file happens to be empty (which it might be), then `line` will be set to `null`; otherwise it will contain the `String` that was read. In this case we append the line to a `JTextArea`. Note that `readLine()` *does not* return the end-of-line character with its return value. That's why we add a `\n` before we append the line to the `JTextArea`.

Figure 14–7 A method for a text file.

```
private void readTextFile(JTextArea display, String fileName) {
    try {
        BufferedReader inStream                            // Create and
            = new BufferedReader (new FileReader(fileName));// Open the stream
        String line = inStream.readLine();                 // Read one line
        while (line != null) {                             // While more text
            display.append(line + "\n");                   // Display a line
            line = inStream.readLine();                    // Read next line
        }
        inStream.close();                                  // Close the stream
    } catch (FileNotFoundException e) {
        display.setText("IOERROR: File NOT Found: " + fileName + "\n");
        e.printStackTrace();
    } catch ( IOException e ) {
        display.setText("IOERROR: " + e.getMessage() + "\n");
        e.printStackTrace();
    }
} // readTextFile()
```

PROGRAMMING TIP: End of Line. Remember that `readLine()` does not return the end-of-line character, `\n`, as part of the text it returns. If you want to print the text on separate lines, you must append `\n`.

The last statement in the body of the loop attempts to read the next line from the input stream. If the end of file has been reached, this attempt will return `null` and the loop will terminate. Otherwise, the loop will continue reading and displaying lines until the end of file is reached. Taken together these various design decisions lead to the definition for `readTextFile()` shown in Figure 14–7.

Note that we must catch both the `IOException`, thrown by `readLine()` and `close()`, and the `FileNotFoundException`, thrown by the `FileReader()` constructor. It's important to see that the read loop has the following form:

`IOException`

```
try to read one line of data and store it in line    // Loop initializer
while ( line is not null ) {                         // Loop entry condition
    process the data
    try to read one line of data and store it in line  // Loop updater
}
```

When it attempts to read the *end-of-file* character, `readLine()` will return `null`.

EFFECTIVE DESIGN: Reading Text. In reading text files, the `readLine()` method will return `null` when it tries to read the end-of-file character. This provides a convenient way of testing for the end of file.

EFFECTIVE DESIGN: Reading an Empty File. Loops designed for reading text files are designed to work even if the file is empty. Therefore the loop should attempt to read a line *before* testing the loop entry condition. If the initial read returns `null` that means the file is empty and the loop body will be skipped.

SELF-STUDY EXERCISES

EXERCISE 14.2 What's wrong with the following loop for reading a text file and printing its output on the screen?

```
String line = null;
do {
    line = inStream.readLine();
    System.out.println ( line );
} while (line != null);
```

14.3.5 Code Reuse: Designing Text File Input

Our last example used `BufferedReader.readLine()` to read an entire line from the file in one operation. But this isn't the only way to do things. For example, we could have used the `FileReader` stream directly if we were willing to do without the `readLine()` method. Let's design an algorithm that will work in this case.

As we saw earlier, if you use a `FileReader` stream, then you must use the `InputStreamReader.read()` method. This method reads bytes from an input stream and translates them into Java Unicode characters. The `read()` method, for example, returns a single Unicode character as an `int`:

```
public int read() throws IOException();
```

Of course, we can always convert this to a `char` and concatenate it to a `JTextArea`, as the following algorithm illustrates:

```
int ch = inStream.read();           // Initializer: try to read the next character
while (ch != -1) {                  // Loop-entry-condition: while there are characters to read
    display.append((char)ch + ""); // Append the character
    ch = inStream.read();           // Updater: try to read the next character
}
```

Although the details are different, the structure of this loop is the same as if we were reading one line at a time.

The loop variable in this case is an `int` because `InputStreamReader.read()` returns the next character as an `int`, or it returns −1 if it encounters the `end-of-file` character. Because `ch` is an `int` we must convert it to a `char` and then to a `String` in order to `append()` it to the display.

Data conversion

A loop to read data from a file has the following basic form:

```
try to read data into a variable       // Loop initializer
while ( read was successful ) {        // Loop entry condition
    process the data
    try to read data into a variable    // Loop updater
}
```

EFFECTIVE DESIGN: Read Loop Structure. The `read()` and `readLine()` methods have different ways to indicate when a read attempt fails. This will affect how the loop-entry condition is specified, but the structure of the read loop is the same.

PROGRAMMING TIP: Read versus Readline. Unless it is necessary to manipulate each character in the text file, reading a line at a time is more efficient, and therefore preferable.

Reusing existing code

It is worth noting again the point we made earlier: Designing effective I/O routines is largely a matter of searching the `java.io` package for appropriate classes and methods. The methods we've develop can serve as suitable models for a wide variety of text I/O tasks, but if you find that they aren't suitable for a particular task, you can design your own method. Just find the stream classes that contain methods you can use to perform the desired task. The basic reading and writing algorithms will be pretty much the same no matter which particular read or write method you use.

SELF-STUDY EXERCISES

EXERCISE 14.3 What's wrong with the following loop for reading a text file and printing its output on the screen?

```
int ch;
do {
    ch = inStream.read();
    System.out.print((char)ch);
}  while (ch != -1) {
```

14.3.6 The `TextIO` Application

In order to complete this application, we need only set up its GUI and write its `actionPerformed()` method. Given that we have defined methods to handle the text I/O, the `actionPerformed()` method is quite short:

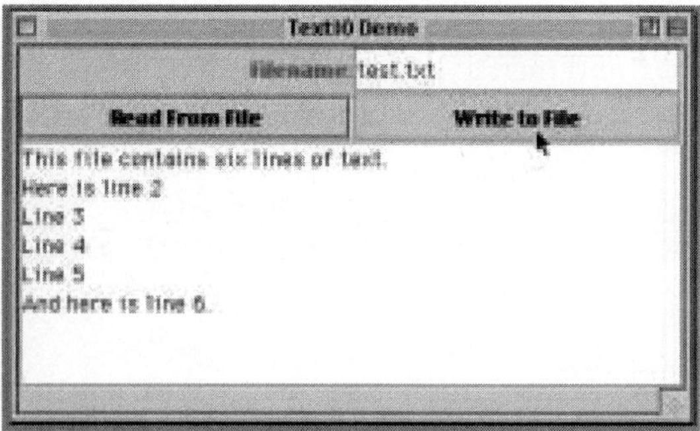

Figure 14–8 An application that performs simple text I/O.

```
public void actionPerformed(ActionEvent evt) {
    String fileName = nameField.getText();
    if (evt.getSource()  == read) {
        display.setText("");
        readTextFile(display, fileName);
    }
    else writeTextFile(display, fileName);
} // actionPerformed()
```

Setting up the GUI for this application is straightforward. The details are shown in Figure 14–9, and Figure 14–8 shows how the finished product looks.

Figure 14–9 TextIO() illustrates simple input and output from a text file.

```
import javax.swing.*;        // Swing components
import java.awt.*;
import java.io.*;
import java.awt.event.*;

public class TextIO extends JFrame implements ActionListener{
    private JTextArea display = new JTextArea();
    private JButton read = new JButton("Read From File"),
                    write = new JButton("Write to File");
    private JTextField nameField = new JTextField(20);
    private JLabel prompt = new JLabel("Filename:",JLabel.RIGHT);
    private JPanel commands = new JPanel();

    public TextIO() {                       // Constructor
        super("TextIO Demo");               // Set window title
        read.addActionListener(this);
        write.addActionListener(this);
        commands.setLayout( new GridLayout(2,2,1,1));  // Control panel
        commands.add(prompt);
        commands.add(nameField);
        commands.add(read);
        commands.add(write);
        display.setLineWrap(true);
        this.getContentPane().setLayout(new BorderLayout());
        this.getContentPane().add("North", commands);
        this.getContentPane().add( new JScrollPane(display));
        this.getContentPane().add("Center", display);
    } // TextIO
```

Figure 14–9 *Continued*

```
    private void readTextFile(JTextArea display, String fileName) {
        try {
            BufferedReader inStream                          // Create and
                = new BufferedReader (new FileReader(fileName));//Open the stream
            String line = inStream.readLine();               // Read one line
            while (line != null) {                           // While more text
                display.append(line + "\n");                 // Display a line
                line = inStream.readLine();                  // Read next line
            }
            inStream.close();                                // Close the stream
        } catch (FileNotFoundException e) {
            display.setText("IOERROR: File NOT Found: " + fileName + "\n");
            e.printStackTrace();
        } catch (IOException e) {
            display.setText("IOERROR: " + e.getMessage() + "\n");
            e.printStackTrace();
        }
    } // readTextFile

    private void writeTextFile(JTextArea display, String fileName) {
        try {
            FileWriter outStream =  new FileWriter (fileName);
            outStream.write (display.getText());
            outStream.close();
        } catch (IOException e) {
            display.setText("IOERROR: " + e.getMessage() + "\n");
            e.printStackTrace();
        }
    } // writeTextFile()

    public void actionPerformed(ActionEvent evt) {
        String fileName = nameField.getText();
        if (evt.getSource()  == read) {
            display.setText("");
            readTextFile(display, fileName);
        }
        else writeTextFile(display, fileName);
    } // actionPerformed()

    public static void main(String args[]) {
        TextIO tio = new TextIO();
        tio.setSize(400, 200);
        tio.setVisible(true);
        tio.addWindowListener(new WindowAdapter() {       // Quit the application
            public void windowClosing(WindowEvent e) {
                System.exit(0);
            }
        });
    } // main()
}//TextIO
```

14.4 The File Class

As we've seen, an attempt to create a `FileReader` stream may throw a `FileNotFoundException`. The only way this can happen is if the user has provided a name for a file that doesn't exist or that isn't located where its name says it should be located. Is there any way we can detect these kinds of errors before attempting to read the file?

The `java.io.File` class provides methods that we can use for this task. The `File` class provides a representation of the computer's file and directory information in a platform-independent manner. As you know, a **file** is a collection of data, whereas a **directory** is a collection of files. (Actually, a directory is a file that stores its files' names and attributes, not the files themselves.)

Files and directories

14.4.1 Names and Paths

The file hierarchy

File systems are organized into a hierarchy. A **path** is a description of a file's location in the hierarchy. For example, consider the hierarchy of files in Figure 14–10. Assume that your Java program is named `MyClass.class`. When a program is running, the program's directory is considered the `current directory`. Any files located in the current directory can be referred to by name alone — for example, `MyClass.java`. To refer to a file located in a subdirectory of the current directory, you would provide the name of the subdirectory and the file: `datafiles/data.txt`. In this case we are assuming a Unix file system, so we are using the / as the separator between the name of the directory (`datafiles`) and the name of the file (`data.txt`).

File path names

When a file is specified in relation to the current directory, this is called a **relative path name**. Alternatively, a file can be specified by its **absolute path name**. This would be a name whose path starts at the root directory of the file system. For example, `/root/java/examples/datafiles/data.txt` would be the absolute path name for the file named `data.txt` on a Unix system. When you supply the name of a file to one of the stream constructors, you are actually providing a *path* name. If the path consists of just a name, such as `data.txt`, Java assumes that the file is located in the same directory as the program itself.

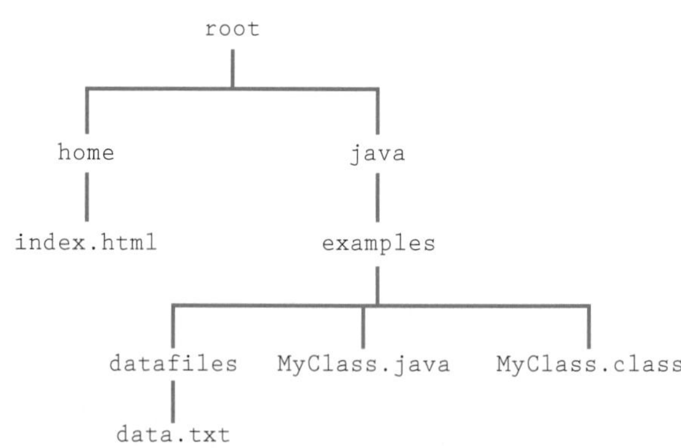

Figure 14–10 A simple hierarchy of directories and files.

14.4.2 Validating File Names

The File class provides platform-independent methods for dealing with files and directories. It contains methods that list the contents of directories, determines a file's attributes, and renames and deletes files:

```
public class File extends Object implements Serializable {
   // Constants
    public static final String pathSeparator;
    public static final char pathSeparatorChar;
    public static final String separator;
    public static final char separatorChar;
   // Constructors
    public File(String path);
    public File(String path, String name);
   // Public instance methods
    public boolean canRead();           // Is the file readable?
    public boolean canWrite();          // Is the file writeable?
    public boolean delete();            // Delete the file
    public boolean exists();            // Does the file exist?
    public String getName();            // Get the file's name
    public String getParent();          // Get the file or directory's parent
    public String getPath();            // Get the file's path
    public boolean isDirectory();       // Is the file a directory ?
    public boolean isFile();            // Is the file a file ?
    public long lastModified();         // When was the file last modified?
    public long length();               // How many bytes does it contain?
    public String[] list();             // List the contents of this directory
    public boolean renameTo(File f);    // Rename this file to f's name
}
```

Note the several static constants provided. These allow path names to be specified in a platform-independent way. For example, on a Unix system, the File.separator character will be the / and on a Windows system it will be the \,backslash. File.separator will be initialized to the appropriate separator for the particular system being used.

PROGRAMMING TIP: File Separators. To make your programs platform independent, use the File.separator constant instead of a literal value whenever you are specifying a path name.

As an example of how you might use some of File's methods, let's write a method that tests whether the file name entered by the user is the name of a valid, readable file.

Method design

A file may be unreadable for a number of reasons. It may be owned by another user and readable only by that user. Or, it may be designated as not readable by its owner. We'll pass the method the name of the file (a String), and the method will return true if a readable file with that name exists. Otherwise the method will throw an exception and return false:

```
private boolean isReadableFile(String fileName) {
    try {
        File file = new File(fileName);
        if (!file.exists())
            throw (new FileNotFoundException("No such File:" + fileName));
        if (!file.canRead())
            throw (new IOException("File not readable: " + fileName));
        return true;
    } catch (FileNotFoundException e) {
        System.out.println("IOERROR: File NOT Found: " + fileName + "\n");
        return false;
    } catch (IOException e) {
        System.out.println("IOERROR: " + e.getMessage() + "\n");
        return false;
    }
} // isReadableFile
```

The method simply creates a `File` instance and uses its `exists()` and `canRead()` methods to check whether its name is valid. If either condition fails, an exception is thrown. The method handles its own exceptions, printing an error message and returning false in each case.

Before attempting to write data to a file, we might want to check that the file has been given an appropriate name. For example, if the user leaves the file name blank, we should not write data to the file. Also, a file might be designated as unwriteable in order to protect it from being inadvertently overwritten. We should check that the file is writeable before attempting to write to it:

```
private boolean isWriteableFile(String fileName) {
    try {
        File file = new File (fileName);
        if (fileName.length() == 0)
            throw (new IOException("Invalid file name: " + fileName));
        if (file.exists() && !file.canWrite())
            throw (new IOException("IOERROR: File not writeable: " + fileName));
        return true;
    } catch (IOException e) {
        display.setText("IOERROR: " + e.getMessage() + "\n");
        return false;
    }
} // isWriteableFile()
```

The first check in this code tests that the user has not forgotten to provide a name for the output file. It is unlikely that the user wants to name the file with the empty string. We use the `exists()` method to test whether the user is attempting to write to an existing file. If so, we use the `canWrite()` method to test whether the file is writeable. Both kinds of errors result in `IOException`s.

SELF-STUDY EXERCISES

EXERCISE 14.4 The other methods of the `File` class are just as easy to use. Write a method that takes the name of file as its single parameter and prints the following information about the file: its absolute path, its length, and whether it is a directory or a file.

14.5 Example: Reading and Writing Binary Files

Although text files are extremely useful and widespread, they can't be used (and shouldn't be used) for every data processing application. For example, your college's administrative data system undoubtedly uses files to store student records. Because your student record contains a variety of different types of data — `Strings`, `ints`, `doubles` — it cannot be processed as text. Similarly, a company's inventory files, which include data of a wide variety of types, cannot be processed as text. Files such as these must be processed as binary data.

Suppose you are asked to write an application that involves the use of a company's employee records. Recall that a **record** is a structure that combines different types of data into a single entity. It's like an object with no methods, just instance variables.

A binary file is a sequence of bytes. Unlike a text file, which is terminated by a special end-of-file marker, a binary file consists of nothing but data. A binary file doesn't have an end-of-file character because any such character would be indistinguishable from a binary datum.

DEBUGGING TIP: End of Binary File. Because a binary file does not have an end-of-file character, it would be an error to use the same loop-entry conditions we used in the loops we designed for reading text files.

Generally speaking, the steps involved in reading and writing binary files are the same as for text files:

1. Connect a stream to the file.
2. Read or write the data, possibly using a loop.
3. Close the stream.

The difference between text and binary file I/O resides in the Java streams that we use.

14.5.1 Writing Binary Data

Let's begin by designing a method that will output employee data to a binary file. As the developer of this program, one thing you'll have to do is build some sample data files. These can't easily be built by hand — remember you can't use a text editor to create them — so you'll want to develop a method that can generate some random data of the sort your application will have to process.

Generating binary data

EFFECTIVE DESIGN: I/O Design. When designing file I/O applications, it is good to design the input and the output methods together. This is especially important for binary I/O.

The first thing we need to know is exactly what the data look like. Let's assume that each record contains three individual pieces of data — the employee's name, age, and pay rate. For example, the data in a file containing four records might look like this, once the data are interpreted:

```
Name0 24 15.06
Name1 25 5.09
Name2 40 11.45
Name3 52 9.25
```

As you can see, these data look as if they were randomly generated, but they resemble the real data in the important respects: They are of the right type — `String`, `int`, `float` — and have typical values. Of course when these data are stored in the file, or in the program's memory, they just look like one long string of 0's and 1's.

Our approach to designing this output method will be the same as the approach we used in designing methods for text I/O. That is, we start with two questions:

- What stream classes should I use?
- What methods can I use?

And we find the answers to these by searching through the `java.io` package (Figure 14–3 and Table 14–1).

Choosing an output stream

Because we are performing binary output, we need to use some subclass of `OutputStream`. Because we're outputting to a file, one likely candidate is `FileOutputStream`. This class has the right kind of constructors, but it only contains `write()` methods for writing `int`s and `byte`s:

```
public class FileOutputStream extends OutputStream {
   // Constructors
    public FileOutputStream(String filename) throws IOException;
    public FileOutputStream(String filename, boolean append) throws IOException;
   // Instance methods
    public void write(int b) throws IOException;
    public void write(byte b[]) throws IOException;
}
```

We need to be able to write `String`s and `double`s as well as `int`s. These kinds of methods are found in `DataOutputStream`, which contains a `write()` method for each different type of data:

```
public class DataOutputStream extends FilterOutputStream {
   // Constructor
    public DataOutputStream( OutputStream out );
   // Public instance methods
    public void flush()                      throws IOException;
    public final void writeBoolean(boolean b) throws IOException;
    public final void writeByte(byte b)       throws IOException;
    public final void writeBytes(String s)    throws IOException;
    public final void writeChar(int c)        throws IOException;
    public final void writeChars(String s)    throws IOException;
    public final void writeDouble(double d)   throws IOException;
    public final void writeFloat(float f)     throws IOException;
    public final void writeInt(int i)         throws IOException;
    public final void writeLong(long l)       throws IOException;
    public final void writeShort(short s)     throws IOException;
    public final void writeUTF(String s)      throws IOException;
}
```

As you can see, there's one method for each primitive type. However, note that the `writeChar()` takes an `int` parameter, which indicates that the character is written in binary format rather than as a ASCII or Unicode character. Although you can't tell by just reading its method signature, the `writeChars(String)` method also writes its data in binary format, rather than as a sequence of characters. This is the main difference between these `write()` methods and the ones defined in the `Writer` branch of Java's I/O hierarchy.

We've now found the classes and methods we need. To construct a stream to use in writing employee records, we want to join together a `DataOutputStream` and a `FileOutputStream`. The `DataOutputStream` gives us the output methods we need, and the `FileOutputStream` lets us use the file's name to create the stream:

Connecting two streams

```
DataOutputStream outStream
      = new DataOutputStream(new FileOutputStream (fileName));
```

The program will write data to the `DataOutputStream`, which will pass them through the `FileOutputStream` to the file itself. That settles the first question.

To develop the output algorithm, we need some kind of loop which involves calls to the appropriate methods. In this case, because we are generating random data, we can use a simple for loop to generate, say, five records of employee data. We need one `write()` statement for each of elements in the employee record: the name (`String`), age (`int`), and pay rate (`double`):

```
for (int k = 0; k < 5; k++) {                   // Output 5 data records
    outStream.writeUTF("Name" + k);                           // Name
    outStream.writeInt((int)(20 + Math.random() * 25)); // Random age
    outStream.writeDouble(Math.random() * 500);         // Random payrate
}
```

Within the loop body we have one output statement for each data element in the record. The names of the methods reflect the type of data they write. Thus we use `writeInt()` to write an `int`, and `writeDouble()` to write a `double`. But why do we use `writeUTF` to write the employee's name, a `String`?

The Unicode Text Format (UTF)

There is no `DataOutputStream.writeString()` method. Instead `Strings` are written using the `writeUTF()` method. **UTF** stands for *Unicode Text Format*. It is a coding scheme for Java's Unicode character set. Recall that Java uses the Unicode character set instead of the ASCII set. As a 16-bit code, Unicode can represent 8-bit ASCII characters plus a huge variety of Asian and other international characters. However, Unicode is not a very efficient coding scheme if you aren't writing an international program. If your program just uses the standard ASCII characters, which can be stored in 1 byte, you would be wasting 1 byte per character if you stored them as straight Unicode characters. Therefore, for efficiency purposes, Java uses the more efficient UTF format. UTF encoding can still represent all of the Unicode characters, but it provides a more efficient way of representing the ASCII subset.

ASCII vs. Unicode

It's now time to combine these separate elements into a single method (Figure 14–11). The `writeRecords()` method takes a single `String` parameter that specifies the name of the file. This is a `void` method. It will output data to a file, but it will not return anything to the calling method: The method follows the standard output algorithm: Create an output stream, write the data, close the stream. Note also that the method includes a `try/catch` block to handle any `IOExceptions` that may be thrown.

14.5.2 Reading Binary Data

The steps involved in reading data from a binary file are the same as for reading data from a text file: Create an input stream and open the file, read

Figure 14–11 A method to write a binary file consisting of five randomly constructed records.

```
private void writeRecords( String fileName ) {
    try {
        DataOutputStream outStream
            = new DataOutputStream(new FileOutputStream(fileName)); // Open stream
        for (int k = 0; k < 5; k++) {                      // Output 5 data records
            String name = "Name" + k;
            outStream.writeUTF("Name" + k);                         // Name
            outStream.writeInt((int)(20 + Math.random() * 25));     // Age
            outStream.writeDouble(5.00 + Math.random() * 10);       // Payrate
        } // for
        outStream.close();                                 // Close the stream
    } catch (IOException e) {
        display.setText("IOERROR: " + e.getMessage() + "\n");
    }
} // writeRecords()
```

the data, close the file. The main difference lies in the way you check for the end-of-file marker in a binary file.

Let's design a method to read the binary data that was output by the `writeRecords()` method. We'll call this method `readRecords()`. It too will consist of a single `String` parameter, which provides the name of the file to be read. And it too will be a void method. It will just display the data on `System.out`.

Choosing an input stream

What stream classes should we use, and what methods should we use? For binary input, we need an `InputStream` subclass (Figure 14–3 and Table 14–1). As you've probably come to expect, the `FileInputStream` class contains constructors that let us create a stream from a file name:

```
public class FileInputStream extends InputStream {
   // Constructors
    public FileInputStream( String filename ) throws FileNotFoundException;
}
```

However, it does not contain useful `read()` methods. Fortunately, the `DataInputStream` class contains the input counterparts of the methods we found in `DataOutputStream`:

```
public class DataInputStream extends FilterInputStream {
   // Instance methods
    public final boolean readBoolean() throws IOException;
    public final byte readByte() throws IOException;
    public final char readChar() throws IOException;
    public final double readDouble() throws IOException;
    public final float readFloat() throws IOException;
    public final int readInt() throws IOException;
    public final long readLong() throws IOException;
    public final short readShort() throws IOException;
    public final String readUTF() throws IOException;
}
```

Therefore, our input stream for this method will be a combination of `DataInputStream` and `FileInputStream`:

```
DataInputStream inStream
     = new DataInputStream(new FileInputStream(file));
```

Designing the read loop

Now that we have identified the classes and methods we'll use to read the data, the most important remaining issue is designing a read loop that will terminate correctly. Unlike text files, binary files do not contain a special end-of-file marker. Therefore the read methods can't see anything in the file that tells them they're at the end of the file. Instead, when a binary read method attempts to read past the end of the file, an end-of-file exception `EOFException` is thrown. Thus, the binary loop is coded as an infinite loop that's exited when the `EOFException` is raised:

```
try {
    while (true) {                                     // Infinite loop
        String name = inStream.readUTF();                 // Read a record
        int age = inStream.readInt();
        double pay = inStream.readDouble();
        display.append(name + "   " + age + "   " + pay + "\n");
    } // while
} catch (EOFException e) {}                         // Until EOF exception
```

An expected exception

The read loop is embedded within a `try/catch` statement. Note that the `catch` clause for the `EOFException` does nothing. Recall that when an exception is thrown in a `try` block, the block is exited for good, which is precisely the action we want to take. That's why we needn't do anything when we catch the `EOFException`. We have to catch the exception; otherwise Java will catch it and terminate the program. This is one example of an expected exception.

EFFECTIVE DESIGN: `EOFException`. An attempt to read past the end of a binary file will cause an `EOFException` to be thrown. Catching this exception is the standard way of terminating a binary input loop.

Note also the `read()` statements within the loop are mirror opposites of the `write()` statements in the method that created the data. This will generally be true for binary I/O routines: The statements that read data from a file should "match" those that wrote the data in the first place.

EFFECTIVE DESIGN: Matching Input to Output. The statements used to read binary data should match those that wrote the data. If a `writeX()` method were used to write the data, a `readX()` should be used to read it.

To complete the method, the only remaining task is to `close()` the stream after the data are read. The complete definition is shown in Figure 14–12.

It's important that a `close()` statement be placed after the `catch EOFException` clause. If it were placed in the `try` block, it would never get executed. Note also that the entire method is embedded in an outer `try` block which catches the `IOException`, thrown by the various `read()` methods, and the `FileNotFoundException`, thrown by the `FileInputStream()` constructor. These enlarge the method, but it is nicely self-contained.

PROGRAMMING TIP: The `finally` Block. In coding a binary read loop, the try block is exited as soon as the `EOFException` is raised. Therefore, the `close()` statement must be placed in the `finally` clause, which is executed after the `catch` clause.

Figure 14–12 A method for reading binary data.

```
private void readRecords( String fileName ) {
    try {
        DataInputStream inStream
           = new DataInputStream(new FileInputStream(fileName)); // Open stream
        display.setText("Name    Age Pay\n");
        try {
            while (true) {                            // Infinite loop
                String name = inStream.readUTF();          // Read a record
                int age = inStream.readInt();
                double pay = inStream.readDouble();
                display.append(name + "    " + age + "    " + pay + "\n");
            } // while
        } catch (EOFException e) {                   // Until EOF exception
        } finally {
            inStream.close();                          // Close the stream
        }
    } catch (FileNotFoundException e) {
        display.setText("IOERROR: File NOT Found: " + fileName + "\n");
    } catch (IOException e) {
        display.setText("IOERROR: " + e.getMessage() + "\n");
    }
} // readRecords()
```

EFFECTIVE DESIGN: Nested try/catch. Nested try blocks must be used to perform binary I/O correctly. The outer block encapsulates statements that throw `IOExceptions`. The inner block encapsulates the read loop and catches the `EOFException`. No particular action need be taken when the `EOFException` is caught.

SELF-STUDY EXERCISES

EXERCISE 14.5 Identify the error in the following method, which is supposed to read a binary file of `ints` from a `DataInputStream`.

```
public void readIntegers(DataInputStream inStream) {
    try {
        while (true) {
            int num = inStream.readInt();
            System.out.println(num);
        }
        inStream.close();
    } catch (EOFException e) {
    } catch (IOException e) {
    }
} // readIntegers
```

14.5.3 The `BinaryIO` application

The `BinaryIO` program in Figure 14–14 incorporates both `readRecords()` and `writeRecords()` into a complete Java program. The program sets up the same interface we used in the text file example (Figure 14–13). It allows the user to specify the name of a data file to read or write. One button allows the user to write random employee records to a binary file, and the other allows the user to display the contents of a file in a `JTextArea`.

Figure 14–13 A program to read and write binary files.

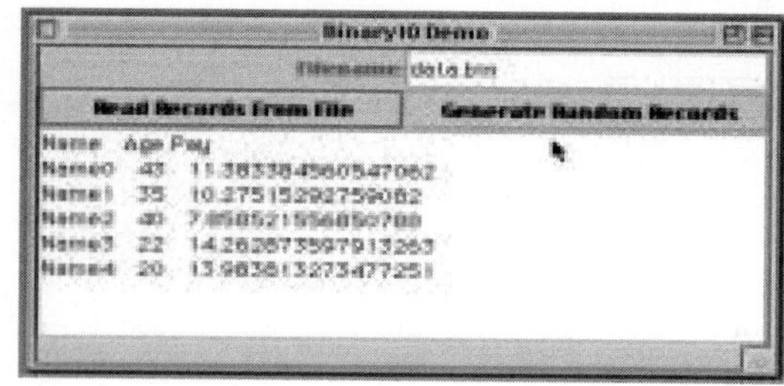

Figure 14–14 BinaryIO() illustrates simple input and output from a binary file.

```
import javax.swing.*;          // Swing components
import java.awt.*;
import java.io.*;
import java.awt.event.*;

public class BinaryIO extends JFrame implements ActionListener{
    private JTextArea display = new JTextArea();
    private JButton read = new JButton("Read Records From File"),
                    write = new JButton("Generate Random Records");
    private JTextField nameField = new JTextField(10);
    private JLabel prompt = new JLabel("Filename:", JLabel.RIGHT);
    private JPanel commands = new JPanel();

    public BinaryIO() {
        super("BinaryIO Demo");                    // Set window title
        read.addActionListener(this);
        write.addActionListener(this);
        commands.setLayout(new GridLayout(2,2,1,1));  // Control panel
        commands.add(prompt);
        commands.add(nameField);
        commands.add(read);
        commands.add(write);
        display.setLineWrap(true);
        this.getContentPane().setLayout(new BorderLayout () );
        this.getContentPane().add("North", commands);
        this.getContentPane().add( new JScrollPane(display));
        this.getContentPane().add("Center", display);
    } // BinaryIO()

    private void readRecords( String fileName ) {
        try {
            DataInputStream inStream
               = new DataInputStream(new FileInputStream(fileName)); // Open stream
            display.setText("Name   Age Pay\n");
            try {
                while (true) {                         // Infinite loop
                    String name = inStream.readUTF();      // Read a record
                    int age = inStream.readInt();
                    double pay = inStream.readDouble();
                    display.append(name + "   " + age + "   " + pay + "\n");
                } // while
            } catch (EOFException e) {                 // Until EOF exception
            } finally {
                inStream.close();                      // Close the stream
            }
        } catch (FileNotFoundException e) {
            display.setText("IOERROR: File NOT Found: " + fileName + "\n");
        } catch (IOException e) {
            display.setText("IOERROR: " + e.getMessage() + "\n");
        }
    } // readRecords()
```

Figure 14–14 *Continued*

```
    private void writeRecords( String fileName )  {
        try {
            DataOutputStream outStream
                  = new DataOutputStream(new FileOutputStream(fileName)); // Open stream
            for (int k = 0; k < 5; k++) {                         // Output 5 data records
                String name = "Name" + k;
                outStream.writeUTF("Name" + k);                           // Name
                outStream.writeInt((int)(20 + Math.random() * 25));       // Age
                outStream.writeDouble(5.00 + Math.random() * 10);         // Payrate
             } // for
             outStream.close();                                   // Close the stream
        } catch (IOException e) {
             display.setText("IOERROR: " + e.getMessage() + "\n");
        }
    } // writeRecords()

    public void actionPerformed(ActionEvent evt) {
        String fileName = nameField.getText();
        if (evt.getSource()  == read)
            readRecords(fileName);
        else
            writeRecords(fileName);
    } // actionPerformed()

    public static void main(String args[]) {
        BinaryIO bio = new BinaryIO();
        bio.setSize(400, 200);
        bio.setVisible(true);
        bio.addWindowListener(new WindowAdapter() {       // Quit the application
            public void windowClosing(WindowEvent e) {
                System.exit(0);
            }
        });
    } // main()
} // BinaryIO
```

14.5.4 Abstracting Data from Files

It's important to recognize that the method to read a binary file must exactly match the method that wrote the binary file in the relative order in which the write and read statements are placed. If the file contains records that consist of a `String` followed by an `int` followed by a `double`, then they must be written by a sequence consisting of

```
writeUTF();
writeInt():
writeDouble();
```

And they must thereafter be read by a sequence consisting of

```
readUTF();
readInt():
readDouble();
```

Attempting to do otherwise would make it impossible to interpret the data in the file.

Portability

This point should make it evident why binary files are not portable whereas text files are. With text files, each character consists of 8 bits, and each 8-bit chunk can be interpreted as an ASCII character, so, even though a text file consists of a long sequence of 0's and 1's, we know how to find the boundaries between each character. That's why any text editor can read a text file, no matter what program created it.

On the other hand, binary files are also just a long sequence of 0's and 1's, but we can't tell where one data element begins and another one ends. For example, the following 64-bit sequence

```
010100110011001001010100110011000001010011001100101101010011001100
```

could represent two 32-bit `int`s or two 32-bit `float`s or one 64-bit `double` or four 16-bit `char`s or a single `String` of 8 ASCII characters. We can't tell what data we have unless we know exactly how the data were written.

DEBUGGING TIP: Interpreting Binary Data. The fact that you can read the data in a binary file is no guarantee that you are interpreting it correctly. To interpret it correctly, you must read it the same way it was written.

EFFECTIVE DESIGN: Data Abstraction. Binary data are "raw." They have no inherent structure. It is only the programs that read and write the data that provide them with structure. A string of 64 0's and 1's can be interpreted as two `int`s or one `long` or even as some kind of object, so an `int`, `long` or an object is an abstraction imposed upon the data by the program.

14.6 Reading and Writing Objects

The examples in the previous sections showed how to do I/O operations on simple binary data or text. The `java.io` package also provides methods for reading and writing objects, a process known as *object serialization*.

Objects can be *serialized* using the `ObjectOutputStream` class, and they can be *deserialized* using the `ObjectInputStream` class. Here is a summary of their relevant methods:

```
public class ObjectOutputStream extends OutputStream implements ObjectOutput {
    public final void writeObject(Object obj) throws IOException;
}

public class ObjectInputStream extends InputStream implements ObjectInput {
    public final Object readObject() throws IOException,
                                            ClassNotFoundException;
}
```

Figure 14–15 The *serializable* Student class.

```
import java.io.*;

public class Student implements Serializable {
    private String name;
    private int year;
    private double gpr;

    public Student() {}

    public Student (String nameIn, int yr, double gprIn) {
        name = nameIn;
        year = yr;
        gpr = gprIn;
    }

    public void writeToFile(FileOutputStream outStream) throws IOException{
        ObjectOutputStream ooStream = new ObjectOutputStream(outStream);
        ooStream.writeObject(this);
        ooStream.flush();
    } // writeToFile()

    public void readFromFile(FileInputStream inStream) throws IOException, ClassNotFoundException {
        ObjectInputStream oiStream = new ObjectInputStream(inStream);
        Student s = (Student)oiStream.readObject();
        this.name = s.name;
        this.year = s.year;
        this.gpr = s.gpr;
    } // readFromFile()

    public String toString() {
        return name + "\t" + year + "\t" + gpr;
    }
} // Student
```

Despite the complexity of the serialization/deserialization processes, these methods make the task just as easy as reading and writing primitive data.

Object serialization

To illustrate object serialization, let's begin by defining a Student class (Figure 14–15). In order to serialize an object, it must be a member of a class that implements the Serializable interface. The Serializable interface is a *marker interface*, an interface that doesn't define any methods or constants but just serves to designate whether an object can be serialized or not.

The Student class contains its own I/O methods, readFromFile and writeToFile. This is an appropriate object-oriented design. The Student class encapsulates all the relevant information needed to read and write its data.

EFFECTIVE DESIGN: I/O Design. If an object is going to be input and output to and from files, it should define its own I/O methods. An object contains all the relevant information needed to perform I/O correctly.

Note the definition of the `writeToFile()` method, which performs the output task. This method's `FileOutputStream` parameter is used to create an `ObjectOutputStream`, whose `writeObject()` method is used to write the object into the file. To output a `Student` object, we merely invoke the `writeObject()` method. This method writes out the current values of all the object's public and private fields. In this case the method would write a `String` for the object's `name`, an `int` for the object's `year`, and a `double` for the object's `gpr`.

Although our example doesn't require it, the `writeObject()` method can also handle fields that refer to other objects. For example, suppose our `Student` object contained a field for `courses` that contained a reference to an array of objects, each of which described a course the student has taken. In that case the `writeObject()` method would recursively serialize the array and all its objects (assuming they are serializable). Thus when a complex object is serialized the result would be a complex structure that contains all the data linked to that root object.

Object deserialization

Object deserialization, as shown in the `readFromFile()` method, is simply the reverse of the serialization process. The `readObject()` method reads one serialized object from the `ObjectInputStream`. Its result type is `Object`, so it is necessary to cast the result into the proper type. In our example we use a local `Student` variable to store the object as it is input. We then copy each field of the local object to `this` object.

Note that the `readFromFile()` method throws both the `IOException` and `ClassNotFoundException`. An `IOException` will be generated if the file you are attempting to read does not contain serialized objects of the right type. Objects that can be input by `readObject()` are those that were output by `writeObject()`. Thus, just as in the case of binary I/O, it is best to design an object's input and output routines together so that they are compatible. The `ClassNotFoundException` will be thrown if the `Student` class cannot be found. This is needed to determine how to deserialize the object.

PROGRAMMING TIP: Object Serialization. Java's serialization classes, `ObjectOutputStream` and `ObjectInputStream`, should be used whenever an object needs to be input or output from a stream.

The `ObjectIO` *Class*

Given the `Student` class, let's now write a user interface that can read and write `Student` objects. We can use the same interface we used in the `BinaryIO` program. The only things we need to change are the `writeRecords()` and `readRecords()` methods. Everything else about this program will be exactly the same as in `BinaryIO`.

The `writeRecords()` method will still write five random records to the data file. The difference in this case is that we will call the `Student.writeToFile()` method to take care of the actual output operations. The revised algorithm will create a new `Student` object, using randomly generated data for its name, year, and GPA and then invoke its `writeToFile()` to output its data:

```
private void writeRecords(String fileName) {
    try {
        FileOutputStream outStream = new FileOutputStream(fileName); // Open a stream
        for (int k = 0; k < 5; k++) {                       // Generate 5 random objects
            String name = "name" + k;                          // Name
            int year = (int)(2000 + Math.random() * 4);        // Class year
            double gpr = Math.random() * 12;                   // GPA
            Student student = new Student(name, year, gpr); // Create the object
            display.append("Output: " + student.toString() +  "\n"); //  and display it
            student.writeToFile(outStream) ;                //  and tell it to write data
        } //for
        outStream.close();
    } catch (IOException e) {
        display.append("IOERROR: " + e.getMessage() + "\n");
    }
} // writeRecords()
```

Note how a `FileOutputStream` is created and passed to the `Student.writeToFile()` method.

The `readRecords()` method will read data from a file containing serialized `Student` objects. To do so, it first creates a `Student` object and then invokes its `readFromFile()` method, passing it a `FileInputStream`. Note how the `FileInputStream` is created, and note that unlike in `BinaryIO`, the inner try block is exited by an `IOException` rather than an `EOFException`:

```
private void readRecords(String fileName) {
    try {
        FileInputStream inStream = new FileInputStream(fileName);  // Open a stream
        display.setText("Name\tYear\tGPR\n");
        try {
            while (true) {                                  // Infinite loop
                Student student = new Student();               // Create a student instance
                student.readFromFile(inStream);                //  and have it read an object
                display.append(student.toString() +  "\n"); //  and display it
            }
        } catch (IOException e) {                           // Until IOException
        }
        inStream.close();                                   // Close the stream
    } catch (FileNotFoundException e) {
        display.append("IOERROR: File NOT Found: " + fileName + "\n");
    } catch (IOException e) {
        display.append("IOERROR: " + e.getMessage() + "\n");
    } catch (ClassNotFoundException e) {
        display.append("ERROR: Class NOT found " + e.getMessage() + "\n");
    }
} // readRecords()
```

These are the only changes necessary to change the `BinaryIO` program into one that reads `Student` objects. Figure 14–16 provides the full definition of the `ObjectIO` class.

Figure 14–16 ObjectIO() provides an interface to reading and writing files of Students.

```
import javax.swing.*;          // Swing components
import java.awt.*;
import java.io.*;
import java.awt.event.*;

public class ObjectIO extends JFrame implements ActionListener{
    private JTextArea display = new JTextArea();
    private JButton read = new JButton("Read From File"),
                    write = new JButton("Write to File");
    private JTextField nameField = new JTextField(10);
    private JLabel prompt = new JLabel("Filename:",JLabel.RIGHT);
    private JPanel commands = new JPanel();

    public ObjectIO () {
        super("ObjectIO Demo");                    // Set window title
        read.addActionListener(this);
        write.addActionListener(this);
        commands.setLayout( new GridLayout(2,2,1,1));  // Control panel
        commands.add(prompt);
        commands.add(nameField);
        commands.add(read);
        commands.add(write);
        display.setLineWrap(true);
        this.getContentPane().setLayout(new BorderLayout () );
        this.getContentPane().add("North",commands);
        this.getContentPane().add( new JScrollPane(display));
        this.getContentPane().add("Center", display);
     } // ObjectIO

     private void readRecords(String fileName) {
         try {
             FileInputStream inStream = new FileInputStream(fileName);  // Open a stream
             display.setText("Name\tYear\tGPR\n");
             try {
                 while (true) {                             // Infinite loop
                     Student student = new Student();            // Create a student instance
                     student.readFromFile(inStream);             //  and have it read an object
                     display.append(student.toString() +  "\n"); //  and display it
                 }
             } catch (IOException e) {                      // Until IOException
             }
             inStream.close();                              // Close the stream
         } catch (FileNotFoundException e) {
             display.append("IOERROR: File NOT Found: " + fileName + "\n");
         } catch (IOException e) {
             display.append("IOERROR: " + e.getMessage() + "\n");
         } catch (ClassNotFoundException e) {
             display.append("ERROR: Class NOT found " + e.getMessage() + "\n");
         }
    } // readRecords()

    private void writeRecords(String fileName) {
        try {
            FileOutputStream outStream = new FileOutputStream( fileName ); // Open a stream
            for (int k = 0; k < 5 ; k++) {                 // Generate 5 random objects
                String name = "name" + k;                      // Name
                int year = (int)(2000 + Math.random() * 4);    // Class year
                double gpr = Math.random() * 12;               // GPA
                Student student = new Student(name, year, gpr); // Create the object
                display.append("Output: " + student.toString() +  "\n"); //  and display it
                student.writeToFile(outStream) ;            //  and tell it to write data
            } //for
            outStream.close();
        } catch (IOException e) {
            display.append("IOERROR: " + e.getMessage() + "\n");
        }
    } // writeRecords()
```

Figure 14–16 *Continued*

```
    public void actionPerformed(ActionEvent evt) {
        String fileName = nameField.getText();
        if (evt.getSource() == read)
            readRecords(fileName);
        else
            writeRecords(fileName);
    } // actionPerformed()

    public static void main(String args[]) {
        ObjectIO io = new ObjectIO();
        io.setSize( 400,200);
        io.setVisible(true);
        io.addWindowListener(new WindowAdapter() {  // Quit the application
            public void windowClosing(WindowEvent e) {
                System.exit(0);
            }
        });
    } // main()
} // ObjectIO
```

SELF-STUDY EXERCISES

EXERCISE 14.6 Given the following definition, would a binary file consisting of several `SomeObject`s be readable by either the `BinaryIO` or the `ObjectIO` programs? Explain.

```
public class SomeObject {
    private String str;
    private short n1;
    private short n2;
    private long  n3;
}
```

From the Java Library: `JFileChooser`

The `javax.swing.JFileChooser` class is a useful class for dealing with files and directories in a GUI environment. You are probably already familiar with `JFileChooser`s, although you may not have known them by that name. A `JFileChooser` provides a dialog box that enables the user to select a file and a directory when opening or saving a file. Figure 14–17 shows an example.

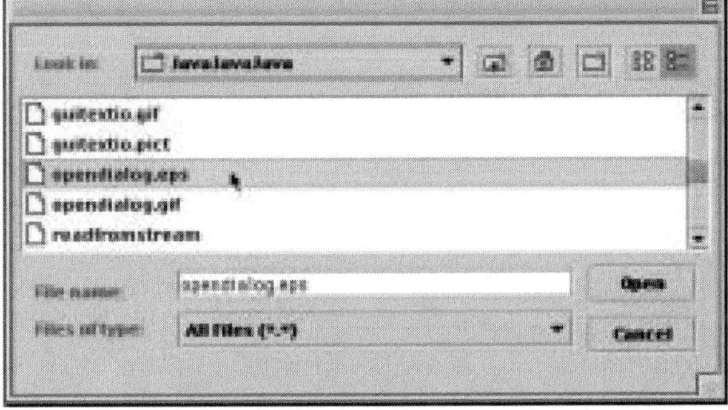

Figure 14–17 The *Open File* dialog window.

A `JFileChooser` is designed primarily to be used in conjunction with menu-based programs:

```
public class javax.swing.JFileChooser extends javax.swing.JComponent {
  // Constants
    public static final int APPROVE_OPTION; // Dialog approved
    public static final int CANCEL_OPTION;   // Dialog cancelled
  // Constructors
    public JFileChooser();
    public JFileChooser(File currentDirectory);
    public JFileChooser(String currentDirectoryPath);
  // Instance methods
    public File getCurrentDirectory();   // Get the selected file's directory
    public File getSelectedFile();       // Get the selected file's name
    public File[] getSelectedFiles();    // Get an array of selected files
    public int showOpenDialog(Component parent);  // Pops up an ''open file'' dialog
    public int showSaveDialog(Component parent);  // Pops up an ''save file'' dialog
    public void setCurrentDirectory(File dir);
}
```

The `JFileChooser` class contains methods that support the *Open File* and *Save As* menu options. We've used `JMenus` and `JDialogs` in Chapter 9, so you should already be familiar with their general functioning.

The laboratory for this chapter will involve writing a simple text editing program using a `JFileChooser` to help manage files, so in this section we just provide the basics for how to use a `JFileChooser`.

A `JFileChooser` is not itself the dialog window but rather the object that manages the dialog. After creating a `JFileChooser` instance, its `showOpenDialog()` or `showSaveDialog()` methods are used to open a dialog window. Note that these methods require a `Component` parameter. This is usually a `JFrame` or a `JApplet`. Thus `JFileChooser`s can be used only in GUI applications and applets.

To illustrate how to use a `JFileChooser`, let's consider the case where the user has selected the *Open File* menu item. In this case we want to present an "Open File" dialog:

```
JFileChooser chooser = new JFileChooser();
int result = chooser.showOpenDialog(this);

if (result == JFileChooser.APPROVE_OPTION) {
    File file = chooser.getSelectedFile();
    String fileName = file.getName();
    display.setText("You selected " + fileName);
} else
    display.setText("You cancelled the file dialog");
```

We begin by creating a `JFileChooser` and then telling it to `showOpenDialog()`. If we were saving a file, rather than opening one, we would tell it to `showSaveDialog()`. In either case a dialog window will pop up on the screen. The dialog assists the user in navigating through the file system and selecting a file (Figure 14–17).

Opening a file

The dialog contains two buttons, one labeled "Open" and the other labeled "Cancel." If the user selects a file, that corresponds to the `APPROVE_OPTION`. If the user cancels the dialog, that corresponds to the

CANCEL_OPTION. After opening a dialog, the code should check which option resulted. In this case, if the user opened a file, the code gets a reference to the file and then simply uses that to print the file's path name.

Using Command-Line Arguments

File dialogs are useful for GUI applications. However, what if your application uses a *command-line* interface, as in many Unix systems? One way to handle file specifications would be to allow the user to input them as **command line arguments**. Command-line arguments are strings, separated by blank spaces, that follow the name of the application program on the command line. For example, suppose you had a FileCopy application that copies one file to another. One way to specify the names of the two files would be

Command line arguments

```
java FileCopy file.txt newfile.txt
```

In this case, file.txt is the original file and newfile.txt is a copy that will be made by the program. They both serve as command-line arguments to the FileCopy program. These arguments are passed to the main() (by the system) as an array of String. As you know, every main() method takes an array of String as a parameter. The purpose of this array is to store the command-line arguments, where they can be accessed by the program.

For example, in FileCopy, supposed main()'s parameter is named args[]. Given the above command line, the following array would be passed to CopyFile:

```
file.txt newfile.txt
```

That is, the first array element, args[0], contains the first command-line argument, file.txt, and the second array element, args[1], contains the second command-line argument, newfile.txt. If there were additional arguments, they would be contained in args[2], args[3], and so on.

In order to use the command-line arguments in your program, you must extract them from args and then pass them to the I/O methods. For example, suppose the copy program is named FileCopy and it contains a public fileCopy() method, which takes the name of the source and destination files as String parameters. The following main() could be used:

```
public static void main(String args[]) {
    FileCopy fc = new FileCopy();
    if (args.length >= 2)
        fc.fileCopy(args[0], args[1]);
    else {
        System.out.println("Usage: java FileCopy srcFile destFile");
        System.exit(1);
    }
} // main()
```

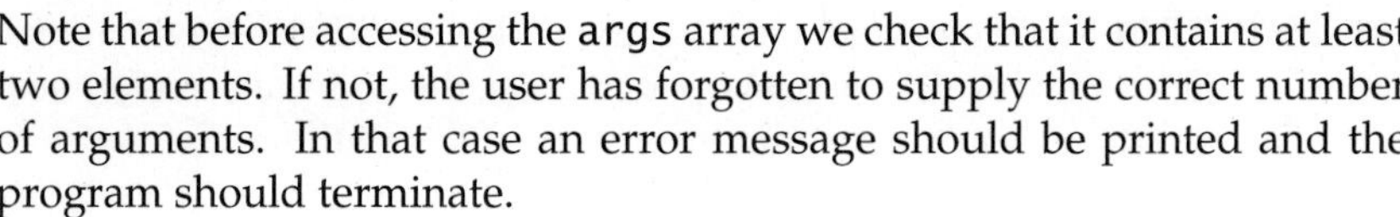

Note that before accessing the `args` array we check that it contains at least two elements. If not, the user has forgotten to supply the correct number of arguments. In that case an error message should be printed and the program should terminate.

SELF-STUDY EXERCISES

EXERCISE 14.7 Write the `fileCopy()` method used in the above example. To be as general as possible you should treat file copying as a binary I/O task. Use `DataInputStream` and `DataOutputStream` and the `readByte()` and `writeByte()` methods in your solution.

IN THE LABORATORY: THE `TextEdit` PROGRAM

The main purpose of this lab is to develop a simple text editor application with a GUI interface. The program will let the user create and edit text files that can then be saved, renamed, or reedited. In terms of programming techniques, this lab will provide practice in designing code that uses `Files` and `Streams`. The objectives are

- To develop a text editing application by extending the `SimpleTextEditor` editing application developed in Figure 9–23.
- To develop appropriate I/O routines using Java's stream hierarchy.
- To develop an appropriate GUI that makes use of Java's `JFileChooser` and `JMenu` classes.

Problem Description

Problem specification

Write a Java GUI application that implements a simple *text editor*. The application should enable the user to open and save existing text files, and to create and save new files. It should enable the user to edit a file's text data by either cutting, copying, and pasting the text, or by simply typing in new text. Your implementation should make use of the techniques, methods, and classes that were introduced in this chapter.

Object-Oriented Design

An appropriate design for this problem would define a single class, let's call it `TextEditor`, which will implement both the file handling and edit functions of the application. This should be a Java application, rather than an applet, because Java applets are restricted, for security reasons, from performing most types of file I/O. Because the program will perform file I/O, it must import the `java.io.*` package. The following is an appropriate outline for the `TextEditor` class:

Databases and Personal Privacy

During a typical day we all come in contact with lots of electronic databases that store information about us. If you use a supermarket discount card, every purchase you make is logged against your name in the supermarket's database. When you use your bank card at the ATM machine, your financial transaction is logged against your account. When you charge gasoline, or buy dinner, those transactions are logged against your credit card account. If you visit the doctor or dentist, a detailed record of your visit is transmitted to your medical insurance company's database. If you receive a college loan, detailed financial information about you is entered into several different credit service bureaus. And so on.

Should we be worried about how this information is used? Many privacy advocates say yes. With the computerization of medical records, phone records, financial transactions, driving records, and many other records, there is an enormous amount of personal information held in databases. At the same time, there are pressures from a number of sources for access to this information. Law enforcement agencies want to use this information to monitor individuals. Corporations want to use it to help them market their products. Political organizations want to use it to help them market their candidates.

Recently there has been pressure from government and industry in the United States to use the Social Security Number (SSN) as a unique identifier. Such an identifier would make it easy to match personal information across different databases. Right now the only thing your bank records, medical records, and supermarket records may have in common is your name, which is not a unique identifier. If all on-line databases were based on your SSN, it would be much simpler to create a complete profile. While this might be improve services and reduce fraud and crime, it might also pose a significant threat to our privacy.

The creation and use of on-line databases serve many useful purposes. They help fight crime and reduce the cost of doing business. They help improve government and commercial services that we have come to depend on. On the other hand, the databases can be and have been misused. They can be used by unauthorized individuals or agencies, or in unauthorized ways. When they contain inaccurate information, they can cause personal inconvenience or even harm.

There are a number of organizations that have cropped up to address the privacy issues raised by on-line databases. If you're interested in learning more about this issue, a good place to start would be the Web site maintained by the Electronic Privacy Information Center (EPIC) at http://www.epic.org/.

```
import javax.swing.*;
import java.awt.*;
import java.awt.event.*;
import java.io.*;

public class TextEdit extends JFrame implements ActionListener {

    public void actionPerformed(ActionEvent e) { }
}
```

EFFECTIVE DESIGN: Applications versus Applets. Programs that perform file I/O should be designed as Java applications, not applets. Applets have too many security restrictions to permit their effective use for file I/O.

An appropriate GUI interface for a text editor will make use of Java menus, which were discussed in Chapter 9. And, an appropriate approach to designing and coding this application would extend the program shown in Figure 9–23, which provides a suitable framework for a menu-based, editing application. The program in Figure 9–23 implements an *Edit* menu, which supports copying, cutting, and pasting of the text in the application's `JTextArea`. An appropriate extension of that program will involve the following additions and modifications:

- Modify and rename the `quitMenu` so that it becomes a full-fledged `fileMenu`. As such it should contain menu items for the *Open*, *Save*, *Save As*, *Quit* functions.
- Modify the `actionPerformed()` method to incorporate the code needed to implement the new menu items.
- Design and write a method named `openFile(String)` which takes a single `String` parameter, representing the full path name for a file. This method should create a `BufferedReader` input stream to the file that was named as its parameter. It should then read the entire contents of the file into the program's `JTextArea`. (See Figures 14–9 and 14–14 for ideas on how to design this method.)
- Design and write a method named `saveFile(String)` which takes a single `String` parameter, representing the full path name for a file. This method should create a `FileWriter` output stream to the file that was named as its parameter. It should then write the entire contents of the `JTextArea` to the file. (See Figures 14–9 and 14–14 for ideas on how to design this method.)

Algorithm Design

The algorithms used in the methods of this application are simple variations of the algorithms used in the programs shown in Figures 14–9 and 14–14. You should be able to modify and adapt that code to suit the requirements of this application.

Testing and Using the Text Editor

As always, you should use the stepwise refinement approach to implementing your application. The individual steps should correspond pretty closely to the individual items listed in the previous section.

Despite its simplicity, this text editor has quite a wide range of functionality. It could easily be useful as an editor for creating Java programs, or HTML files, or other simple editing tasks. To convince yourself of its usefulness, once you have completed the implementation, use the program to carry out each of the following tasks:

- Create from scratch a new file named `file1.txt` on your computer's desktop.
- Open `file1.txt` and make several editing changes to it, and save it as `file2.txt` on your computer's desktop.
- Create from scratch a new file named `file3.txt` and save it on your computer's desktop.
- Merge the contents of `file1.txt` and `file3.txt` into a new file named `file4.txt`. (*Hint*: Copy the contents of one file onto the clipboard before opening the other file.)

CHAPTER SUMMARY

Technical Terms

absolute path name
binary file
data hierarchy
field
input stream
platform independent
serialization
UTF
buffering
command-line argument
directory
file
output stream
record
stream
buffer
database
end-of-file character
filtering
path
relative path name
text file

New Java Keywords

null

Java Classes

```
JButton
JTextArea()
StringBuffer
System.out.println()
BufferedInputStream
DataOutputStream
File
FileOutputStream
IOException
PrintWriter
JFrame
JTextArea
String
System.out
BufferedReader
EOFException
FileInputStream
FileReader
InputStream
Menu
JTextField
System.in
System
DataInputStream
JFileChooser
FileNotFoundException
FileWriter
OutputStream
```

Java Library Methods

actionPerformed()	canWrite()	close()
exists()	getFile()	show()
fileName()	openFile()	print()
println()	read()	readLine()
show()	toString()	write()
writeChar()	writeInt()	writeString()
writeUTF()		

User-Defined Classes

BinaryIO	ObjectIO	Student
TextEdit	TextIO	

User-Defined Methods

readRecords()	readFromFile()	readTextFile()
saveFile()	saveFile(String)	writeRecords()
writeTextFile()	writeToFile()	TextIO()

Summary of Important Points

- A *file* is a collection of data stored on a disk. A *stream* is an object that delivers data to and from other objects. An `InputStream` is a stream that delivers data to a program from an external source — such as the keyboard, or a file. `System.in` is an example of an `InputStream`. An `OutputStream` is a stream that delivers data from a program to an external destination — such as the screen, or a file. `System.out` is an example of an `OutputStream`.
- Data can be viewed as a hierarchy. From highest to lowest, a *database* is a collection of files. A *file* is a collection of records. A *record* is a collection of fields. A *field* is a collection of bytes. A *byte* is a collection of 8 bits. A *bit* is one binary digit, either 0 or 1.
- A *binary file* is a sequence of 0's and 1's that is interpreted as a sequence of bytes. A *text file* is a sequence of 0s and 1s that is interpreted as a sequence of characters. A text file can be read by any text editor. A binary file cannot. `InputStream` and `OutputStream` are abstract classes that serve as the root classes for reading and writing binary data. `Reader` and `Writer` serve as root classes for text I/O.
- *Buffering* is a technique in which a *buffer*, a temporary region of memory, is used to store data while they are being input or output.
- A text file contains a sequence of characters divided into lines by the `\n` character and ending with a special *end-of-file* character.
- The standard algorithm for performing I/O on a file consists of three steps: (1) Open a stream to the file, (2) perform the I/O, (3) close the stream.

- Designing effective I/O routines proceeds by answering two questions: (1) What streams should I use to perform the I/O? and (2) What methods should I use to do the reading or writing?
- To prevent damage to files when a program terminates abnormally, streams should be closed when they are no longer needed.
- Most I/O operations generate an `IOException` which should be caught in the I/O methods.
- Text input uses a different technique to determine when the end of a file has been reached. Text input methods return `null` or `-1` when they attempt to read the special end-of-file character. Binary files don't contain an end-of-file character, so binary read methods throw a `EOFException` when they attempt to read past the end of the file.
- The `java.io.File` class provides methods that enable a program to interact with a file system. Its methods can be used to check a file's attributes, including its name, directory, path.
- Streams can be joined together if necessary to perform I/O. For example, a `DataOutputStream` and a `FileOutputStream` can be joined to perform output to a binary file.
- A binary file is "raw" in the sense that it contains no markers within it that allow you to tell where one data element ends and another begins. The interpretation of binary data is up to the program that reads or writes the file.
- Object serialization is the process of writing an object to an output stream. Object deserialization is the reverse process of reading a serialized object from an input stream. These processes use the `java.io.ObjectOutputStream` and `java.io.ObjectInputStream` classes.
- The `JFileChooser` class provides a dialog box that enables the user to select a file and directory when opening or saving a file.

ANSWERS TO SELF-STUDY EXERCISES

EXERCISE 14.1 Because `FileWriter` contains a constructor that takes a filename argument, `FileWriter(String)`, it can be used with `PrintWriter` to do output to a text file:

```
PrintWriter outStream =                          // Create an output stream
    new PrintWriter(new FileWriter(fileName)); // And open the file
outStream.print (display.getText());           // Write the entire display text
outStream.close();                               // Close the output stream
```

EXERCISE 14.2 This loop doesn't worry about the possibility that the file might be empty. If the file is empty, it will print a `null` line. The test `line != null`, should come right after the `readLine()`, as it does in the `while` loop.

EXERCISE 14.3 This loop won't work on an empty text file. In that case, `ch` would be set to −1, and the attempt to cast it into a `char` would cause an error.

EXERCISE 14.4

```
public String getFileAttributes(String fileName) {
    File file = new File (fileName);
    System.out.println(filename);
    System.out.println("absolute path:" + file.getAbsolutePath());
    System.out.println("length:" + file.length());
    if (file.isDirectory())
        System.out.println("Directory");
    else
        System.out.println("Not a Directory");
} // getFileAttributes()
```

EXERCISE 14.5 The `inStream.close()` statement is misplaced in `readIntegers`. By placing it inside the same `try/catch` block as the read loop, it will get skipped and the stream will not be closed. The `EOFException` should be caught in a separate `try/catch` block from other exceptions, and it should just cause the read loop to exit.

EXERCISE 14.6 Yes, a binary file containing several `SomeObjects` would be "readable" by the `BinaryIO` program because the program will read a `String` followed by 64 bytes. However, `BinaryIO` would misinterpret the data, because it will assume that `n1` and `n2` together comprise a single `int`, and `n3` (64 bits) will be interpreted as a `double`. A file of `SomeObjects` could not be read by the `ObjectIO` program, because `SomeObject` does not implement the `Serializable` interface.

EXERCISE 14.7

```
public void fileCopy(String src, String dest) {
    try {
        DataInputStream inStream
              = new DataInputStream(new FileInputStream(src));
        DataOutputStream outStream
              = new DataOutputStream(new FileOutputStream(dest));
        try {
            while (true) {
                byte data = inStream.readByte();
                outStream.writeByte(data);
            } // while
        } catch (EOFException e) {
        } finally {
            inStream.close();
            outStream.close();
        }
    } catch (IOException e) {
        System.out.println("IOERROR: " + e.getMessage());
    }
} // fileCopy()
```

EXERCISES

1. Explain the difference between each of the following pairs of terms:
   a. `System.in` and `System.out`
   b. *File* and *directory*.
   c. *Buffering* and *filtering*.
   d. *Absolute* and *relative path name*.
   e. *Input stream* and *output stream*.
   f. *File* and *database*.
   g. *Record* and *field*.
   h. *Binary file* and *text file*.
   i. *Directory* and *database*.
2. Fill in the blanks:
   a. Unlike text files, binary files do not have a special ----- character.
   b. In Java, the `String` array parameter in the `main()` method is used of -----.
   c. ----- files are portable and platform independent.
   d. A ----- file created on one computer can't be read by another computer.
3. Arrange the following kinds of data into their correct hierarchical relationships: `bit`, `field`, `byte`, `record`, `database`, `file`, `String`, `char`.
4. In what different ways can the following string of 32 bits be interpreted?

```
00010101111000110100000110011110
```

5. When reading a binary file, why is it necessary to use an infinite loop that's exited only when an exception occurs?
6. Is it possible to have a text file with 10 characters and 0 lines? Explain.
7. In reading a file, why is it necessary to attempt to read from the file before entering the read loop?
8. When designing binary I/O, why is it especially important to design the input and output routines together?
9. What's the difference between ASCII code and UTF code?
10. Could the following string of bits possibly be a Java object? Explain.

```
00010111000111101010101010000111001000100
11010010010101010010101001000001000000111
```

11. Write a method, which could be added to the `TextIO` program, that reads a text file and prints all lines containing a certain word. This should be a `void` method that takes two parameters: the name of the file and the word to search for. Lines not containing the word should not be printed.
12. Write a program that reads a text file and reports the number of characters and lines contained in the file.
13. Modify the program in the previous exercise so that it also counts the numbers of words in the file. (*Hint*: The `StringTokenizer` class might be useful for this task.)
14. Modify the `ObjectIO` program so that it allows the user to designate a file and then input `Student` data with the help of a GUI. As the user inputs data, each record should be written to the file.
15. Write a program that will read a file of `int`s into memory, sort them in ascending order, and output the sorted data to a second file.

16. Write a program that will read two files of `ints`, which are already sorted into ascending order, and merge their data. For example, if one file contains 1, 3, 5, 7, 9, and the other contains 2, 4, 6, 8, 10, then the merged file should contain 1, 2, 3, 4, 5, 6, 7, 8, 9, 10.
17. Suppose you have file of data for a geological survey, such that each record consists of a longitude, a latitude, and an amount of rainfall, all represented by `doubles`. Write a method to read this file's data and print them on the screen, one record per line. The method should be `void` and it should take the name of the file as its only parameter.
18. Suppose you have the same data as in the previous exercise. Write a method that will generate 1000 records of random data and write them to a file. The method should be void and should take the file's name as its parameter. Assume that longitudes have values in the range +/− 0 to 180 degrees, latitudes have values in the range +/− 0 to 90 degrees, and rainfalls have values in the range 0 to 20 inches.
19. Design and write a file copy program that will work for either text files or binary files. The program should prompt the user for the names of each file and copy the data from the source file into the destination file. It should not overwrite an existing file, however. (*Hint*: read and write the file as a file of `byte`.)
20. Design a class, similar to `Student`, to represent an `Address`, consisting of street, city, state and zip code. This class should contain its own `readFromFile()` and `writeToFile()` records.
21. Using the class designed in the previous exercise, modify the `Student` class so that it contains an `Address` field. Modify the `ObjectIO` program to accommodate this new definition of `Student` and test your program.
22. Write a program called `Directory`, which provides a listing of a directory. This program should use an optional command-line argument, so that it will have the following command line:

```
java Directory [ dirName ]
```

The brackets here indicate that `dirName` is an optional argument. If no `dirName` is given, the program should print a directory listing of the current directory. If a directory name is given, it should print a listing of that directory. The listing should contain the following information: the full path name of the directory, and then for each file, the file name, length, and last modified date, and a read/write code. The read/write code should be an 'r' if the file is readable and a 'w' if the file is writeable, in that order. Use a '-' to indicate not readable or not writeable. For example, a file that is readable but not writable will have the code "r-". Here's an example listing:

```
Listing for directory: myfiles
  name          length modified   code
  index.html    548    129098     rw
  index.gif     78     129190     rw
  me.html       682    128001     r-
  private.txt   1001   129000     --
```

Note that the `File.lastModified()` returns a `long`, which gives the modification time of the file. This number can't easily be converted into a date, so just report its value.

23. **Challenge:** In Unix systems there's a program named `grep` that can be used to list the lines in a text file that contain a certain string. It has the following command line:

```
grep "search string" filename
```

Write a Java version of this program.

24. **Challenge:** Write the following command-line program in Java. The program's name is `Copy` and its purpose is to copy one file into another. So its command line will be as follows:

```
java Copy filename1 filename2
```

Both `filename1` and `filename2` must exist or the program should throw a `FileNotFoundException`. Although `filename1` must be the name of a file (not a directory), `filename2` may be either a file or a directory. If `filename2` is a file, then the program should copy `filename1` to `filename2`. If `filename2` is a directory, then the program should simply copy `filename1` into `filename2`. That is, it should create a new file with the name `filename1` inside the `filename2` directory. Copy the old file to the new file, and then delete the old file.

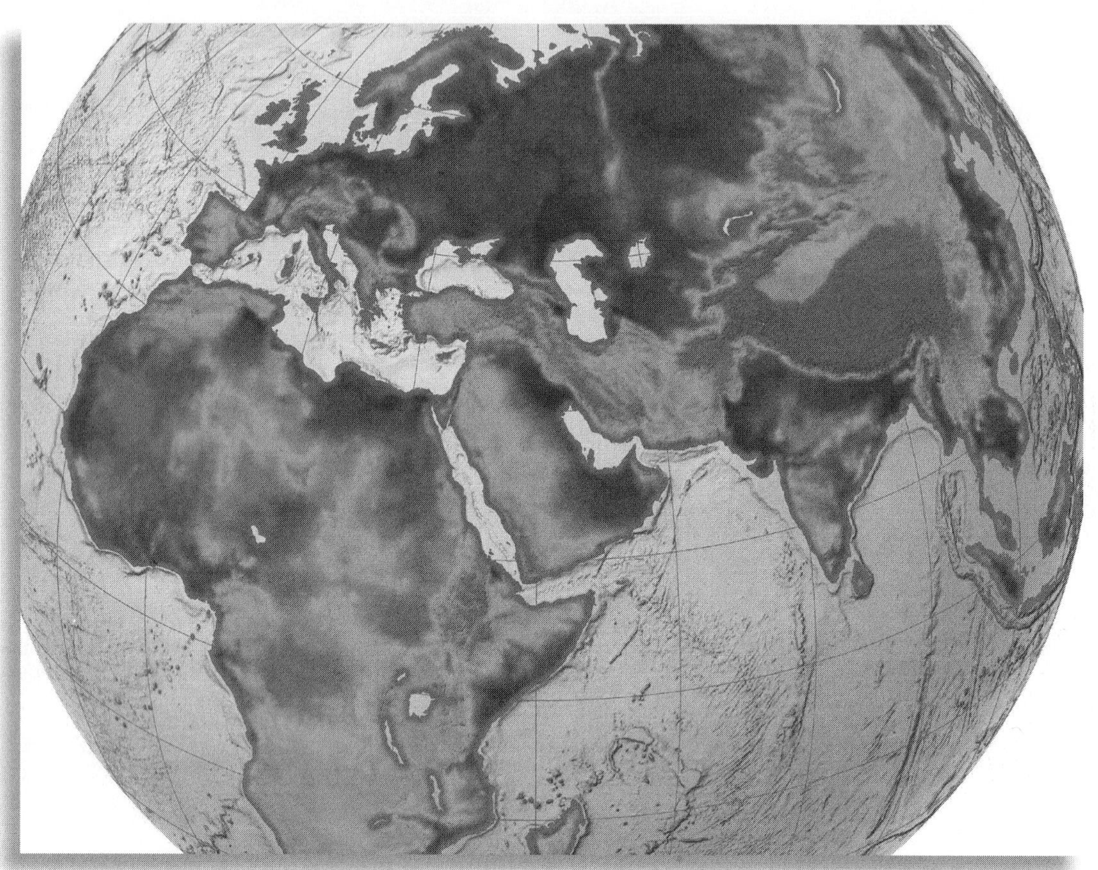

Photograph courtesy of Cartesla, PhotoDisc, Inc.

15

Sockets and Networking

OBJECTIVES

After studying this chapter, you will

- Understand some basic facts about networks.
- Know how to use Java's `URL` class to download network resources from an applet or application.
- Be able to design networking applications using the client/server model.
- Understand how to use Java's `Socket` and `ServerSocket` classes.

OUTLINE

15.1 Introduction

Suppose you want to turn CyberPet into an Internet Pet? For example, can we get it to retrieve stock quotes for us from an Internet stock quote server?

One of the key strengths of Java is the support it provides for the Internet and client/server programming. In the previous chapter, we saw how to make Java programs transfer information to and from external files. Although files are external to the programs that process them, they are still located on the same computer. In this chapter we learn how to transfer information to and from files that reside on a network. This enables programs to communicate with programs running on other computers. With networking, we can communicate with computers anywhere in the world. With networking, we can "train" CyberPet to fetch our Internet newspaper for us!

15.2 An Overview of Networks

Networking is a broad and complex topic. In a typical computer science curriculum, it is covered in one or more upper-level courses. Nevertheless, in this chapter you can learn enough about networking to be able to use network resources and to design simple Java networking applications.

15.2.1 Network Size and Topology

Computer networks come in a variety of sizes and shapes. A *local area network (LAN)* is usually a privately owned network located within a single office or a single organization. Your campus network would be an example of a LAN. A *Wide Area Network (WAN)* spans a wide geographical distance like a country or a continent. It may use a combination of public, private, and leased communication devices. Some of the large commercial networks, such as MCI and Sprint, are examples of WANs.

Network topology

The computers that make up a network can be arranged in a variety of **topologies**, or shapes, some of the most common of which are shown in Figures 15–1 and 15–2. As you would expect, different topologies use different techniques for transmitting information from computer to computer.

In a star network (Figure 15–1), a central computer functions as a hub, with every other computer in the network connected to the hub. Each computer can communicate with the others, but only through the hub. The bus topology doesn't have a hub computer. Instead, the network passes data from one computer to another in a sequence, just like bus picking up and letting off passengers along a bus route. Information passes through the network only in this predefined sequence.

A ring network (Figure 15–1) also has no host, and the computers are connected in a loop, through which they exchange information. The tree topology (Figure 15–2) is organized into a hierarchy, with each level (trunk

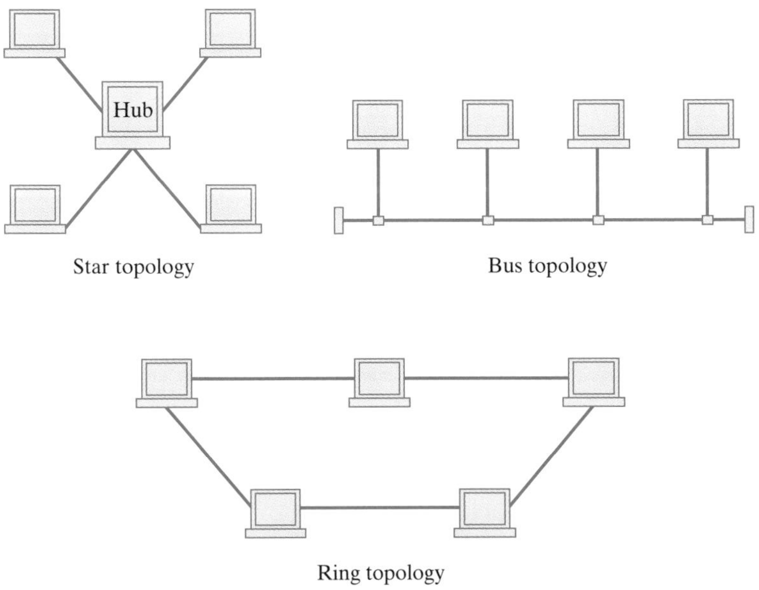

Figure 15–1 Star, bus, and ring topologies.

of the tree, major branch of the tree) controlled by a hub. The fully connected mesh network directly connects all points to all points, eliminating the "middleman." Here there is no need to go through one or more other computers in order to communicate with a particular computer in the network.

Network topologies differ quite a bit in the expense of the wiring they required, their efficiency, their susceptibility to failure, and the types of protocols they use. These differences are beyond the scope of this chapter.

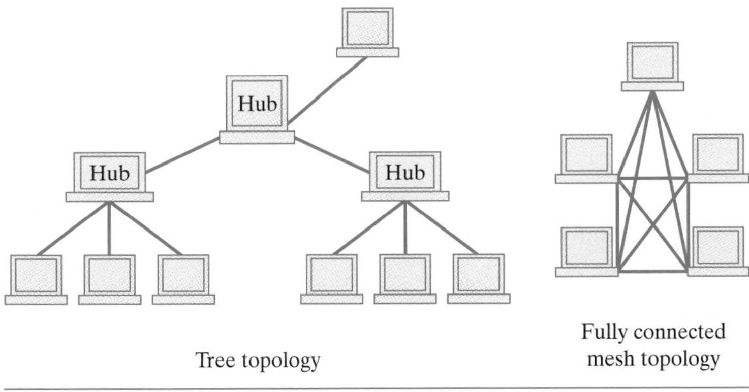

Figure 15–2 Tree and fully connected mesh topologies.

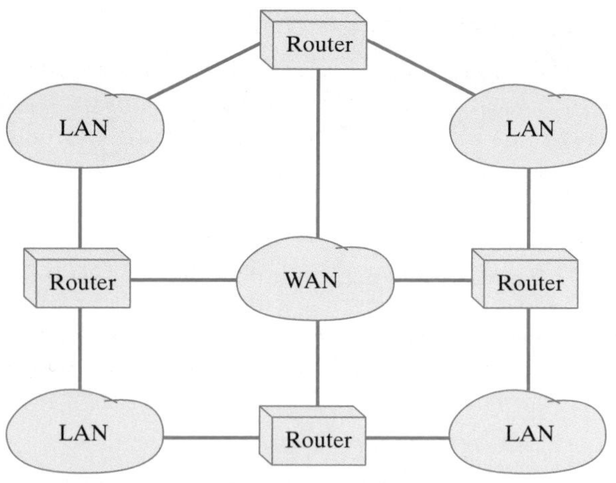

Figure 15–3 An internet is a collection of distinct networks joined together by routers.

15.2.2 Internets

An internet vs. the Internet

An **internet** (lowercase *i*) is a collection of two or more distinct networks, joined by devices called *routers* (Figure 15–3). An internet is like a meeting of the United Nations. Each country sends a delegation, all of whose members speak that country's language. A national delegation is like a single computer network. Language interpreters take on the task of translating one language to another so that any two delegations, say the United States and China, can communicate. The routers play a similar translation role within an internet. The UN conference, comprised of communicating delegations from all the different countries of the world, is like a world wide internet.

The United Nations is an apt analogy for **the Internet** (uppercase *I*), which is an example of a particular world wide internet. Internets, in the generic sense, shouldn't be confused with the Internet. It's quite likely that your campus LAN is itself an internet, comprised of several, smaller networks, each of which uses its own "language."

SELF-STUDY EXERCISES

EXERCISE 15.1 In a network of ten computers, which topology would require the most cables?

EXERCISE 15.2 Which topology would be most resistant to having one of its computers crash?

EXERCISE 15.3 Which topology would be least resistant to having one of its computers crash?

15.2.3 Network Protocols

A **protocol** is a set of rules that governs the communication of information. For example, the World Wide Web is based on the *HyperText Transfer Protocol (HTTP)*. HTTP describes how information is to be exchanged between a Web browser, such as Internet Explorer or Netscape Navigator, and a Web server, which stores an individual's or company's Web pages. Web pages are encoded in the *HyperText Markup Language (HTML)*. Among other things, the HTTP protocol is able to interpret HTML pages.

Network protocols

Similarly, the *Simple Mail Transfer Protocol (SMTP)* is a set of rules that governs the transfer of *E-mail*. And the *File Transfer Protocol (FTP)* is the protocol that governs the transfer of files across the Internet.

Application Protocols

These three examples — HTTP, SMTP, and FTP — are examples of application protocols. They are relatively high-level protocols that support and govern a particular network application, such as E-mail or WWW access. Among the things they govern are how one addresses different computers on the network. For example, the HTTP protocol specifies Web addresses by using a **Uniform Resource Locator (URL)**. A URL specifies three necessary bits of information: the method used to transfer information (e.g., HTTP or FTP), the address of the host computer (e.g., `www.prenhall.com`), and the path describing where the file is located on the host (`/morelli/index.html`):

```
METHOD://HOST/PATH
HTTP://www.prenhall.com/morelli/index.html
```

Similarly, an E-mail address is specified by the SMTP protocol to consist of a local mailbox address (`Bill.Clinton`) followed by the address of the computer (`mail.whitehouse.gov`):

```
LOCAL_MAILBOX@COMPUTER
Bill.Clinton@mail.whitehouse.gov
```

Another good example of an application protocol is the Internet's **Domain Name System (DNS)**, which is the system that governs how names, such as `whitehouse.gov` and `troy.trincoll.edu`, can be translated into numeric addresses. In the DNS each host computer on the Internet is identified with a unique host name, for example, `mail`, `troy`, which is usually made up by the network administrator whose job it is to manage an organization's network. The DNS divides the entire Internet into a hierarchy of *domains* and *subdomains*. The generic domains are names like `com`, `edu`, and `mil`, which refer to the type of organization — commercial, educational, and military, respectively. In addition to these there are country domains, such as `fr`, `au`, and `nz`, for France, Australia, and New Zealand. Finally, individuals and organizations can buy their own domain names, such as `whitehouse`, `microsoft`, and `trincoll`.

Internet domain names

What makes the whole system work is that certain computers within the network are designated as DNS servers. It is their role to translate names such as `troy.trincoll.edu` to numeric addresses whenever they are requested to do so by clients such as the SMTP or the HTTP server. Also, the DNS servers must communicate among themselves to make sure that their databases of names and addresses are up to date.

SELF-STUDY EXERCISES

EXERCISE 15.4 What's the URL of the Web server at Prentice Hall? Identify its component parts — host name, domain name, Internet domain.

15.2.4 Client/Server Applications

The HTTP, FTP, SMTP, and DNS protocols are examples of **client/server** protocols, and the applications they support are examples of client/server applications. In general, a client/server application is one in which the task at hand has been divided into two subtasks, one performed by the client and one performed by the server (Figure 15–4).

E-mail client/server

For example, in the HTTP case, the Web browser plays the role of a client by requesting a Web page from a Web (HTTP) server. A Web server is just a computer that runs HTTP software — a program that implements the HTTP protocol. For E-mail, the program you use to read your E-mail — Eudora, Pine, or Outlook — is an E-mail client. It requests certain services, such as send mail or get mail, from an E-mail (SMTP) server, which is simply a computer that runs SMTP software. In the FTP case, to transfer a program from one computer to another, you would use an FTP client, such as Fetch. Finally, in the DNS case, the DNS servers handle requests for name to address translations that come from HTTP, FTP, and SMTP servers, acting in this case like clients.

So we can say that a client/server application is one that observes the following protocol:

```
Server: Set up a service on a particular host computer.
Client: Contact the server and request the service.
Server: Accept a request from a client and provide the service.
```

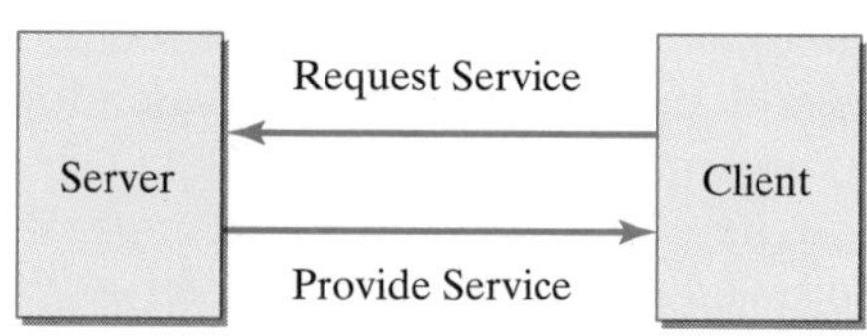

Figure 15–4 Client/server application.

As these examples illustrate, many Internet applications are designed as client/server applications.

EFFECTIVE DESIGN: Divide and Conquer The client/server protocol is an example of the effective use of the divide-and-conquer strategy.

SELF-STUDY EXERCISES

EXERCISE 15.5 Lots of our everyday interactions fit into the client/server model. Suppose you are the client in the following services. Identify the server and then describe the basic protocol.

- Buying a piece of software at a bookstore.
- Buying a piece of software over the phone.
- Buying a piece of software over the Internet.

15.2.5 Lower-Level Network Protocols

Modern computer networks, such as the Internet, are organized into a number of levels of software and hardware. Each level has its own collection of protocols (Figure 15–5).

The application level, which contains the HTTP, FTP, SMTP, and DNS protocols, is the highest level. Underlying the application level protocols are various *transmission protocols*, such as the *Transfer Control Protocol (TCP)* and the *User Datagram Protocol (UDP)*. These protocols govern the transfer

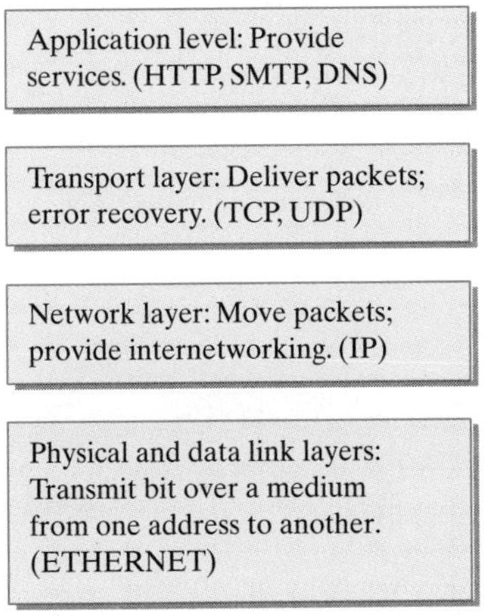

Application level: Provide services. (HTTP, SMTP, DNS)

Transport layer: Deliver packets; error recovery. (TCP, UDP)

Network layer: Move packets; provide internetworking. (IP)

Physical and data link layers: Transmit bit over a medium from one address to another. (ETHERNET)

Figure 15–5 Levels of network protocols.

of large blocks of information, or **packets**, between networked computers. All of the applications we mentioned — WWW, E-mail, and file transfer — involve data transmission and therefore rely on one or more of the transmission protocols.

Packet transfer

At the very lowest end of this hierarchy of protocols are those that govern the transmission of bits or electronic pulses over wires, and those that govern the delivery of data from node to node. Most of these protocols are built right into the hardware — the wires, connectors, transmission devices — that networks use. On top of these are protocols, such as the **ethernet protocol** and *token ring protocol*, that govern the delivery of packets of information on a local area network. These too may be built right into the network hardware.

Disparate protocols

As you might expect, these lower-level protocols are vastly different from each other. An ethernet network cannot talk directly to a token ring network. How can we connect such disparate networks together? Think again of our United Nations analogy. How do we get Greek-speaking networks to communicate with English-speaking networks? The answer supplied by the Internet is to use the **Internetworking Protocol (IP)** which governs the task of translating one network protocol to a common format (Figure 15–6).

The Internet protocol

To push the UN analogy a bit further, the Internet's IP is like a universal language built into the routers that transmit data between disparate networks. On one end of a transmission, a router takes a Greek packet of information, received from one of the delegates in its network. The router translates the Greek packet into an IP packet, which it then sends on through the network to its destination. When the IP packet gets close to its destination, another router takes it and translates it into an English packet before sending it on to its destination on its network.

15.2.6 The `java.net` Package

As we have seen, networks are glued together by a vast array of protocols. Most of these protocols are implemented in software that runs on general-

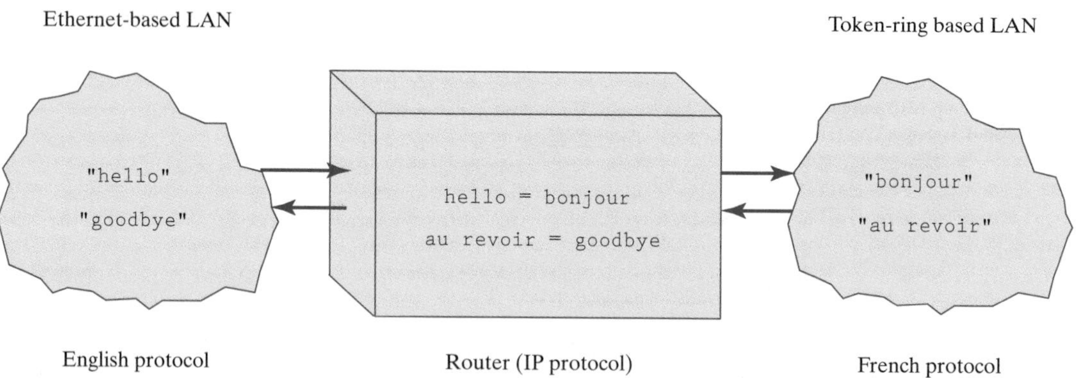

Figure 15–6 Routers between individual networks use the IP protocol to translate one network protocol to another.

purpose computers. You can install software on your personal computer to turn it into a Web server, an FTP server, or an E-mail server. Some of the lower-level protocols are implemented in software that runs on special-purpose computers, the routers. Still other protocols, such as the ethernet protocol, are implemented directly in hardware.

Fortunately, we don't have to worry about the details of even the highest-level protocols in order to write client/server applications in Java. The `java.net` (Figure 15–7) package supplies a powerful and easy-to-use set of classes that support network programming.

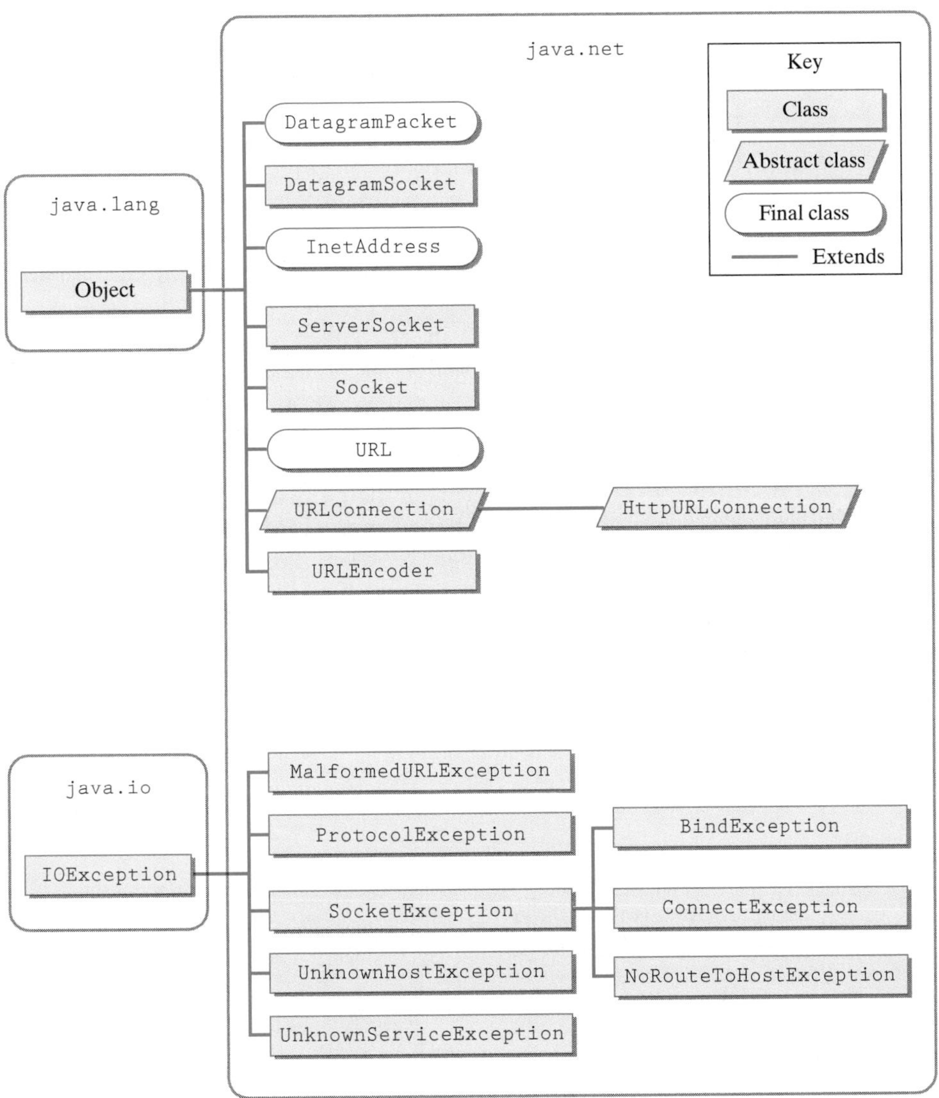

Figure 15–7 The `java.net` package.

`java.net.*`

The `java.net.URL` class provides a representation of the Internet's uniform resource locator that we described earlier. We'll show how to use its methods to download WWW pages. We'll also look at an example that uses a URL and an input stream so that files stored on the Web can be used as input files to a Java applet or application program.

The `Socket` and `ServerSocket` classes provide methods that let us develop our own networking applications. They enable us to make a direct connection to an Internet host, and read and write data through `InputStreams` and `OutputStreams`. As we will see, this is no more difficult than reading and writing data to and from files. The `DatagramPacket` and `DatagramSocket` classes provide support for even lower-level networking applications, based on Internet packets.

15.3 Using Network Resources from an Applet

Problem statement

Suppose you want to write an applet that will automatically display a slide show consisting of images or documents that you've prepared and stored on your Web site. Perhaps you can use such an applet to give people who visit your site a tour of your campus (Figure 15–8). Or perhaps a company might use such an applet to advertise its products. In addition to making the slide show available through its main Web site, you can imagine it running continuously on a computer kiosk in the company's lobby.

Specifying Web resources

In order to solve this problem we have to be able to download and display Web resources. As you know, Web resources are multimedia. That is, they could be documents, images, sounds, video clips, and so on. All Web resources are specified in terms of their **Uniform Resource Locators (URLs)**. Thus, to download an image (or an HTML file or a audio clip), we usually type its URL into a Web browser. We want our program to know beforehand the URLs of the images it will display, so there won't be any need for inputting the URL. We want to implement something like the following algorithm:

```
repeat forever
    Generate the URL for the next slide.
    Use the URL to download the image or document.
    Display the image or document.
```

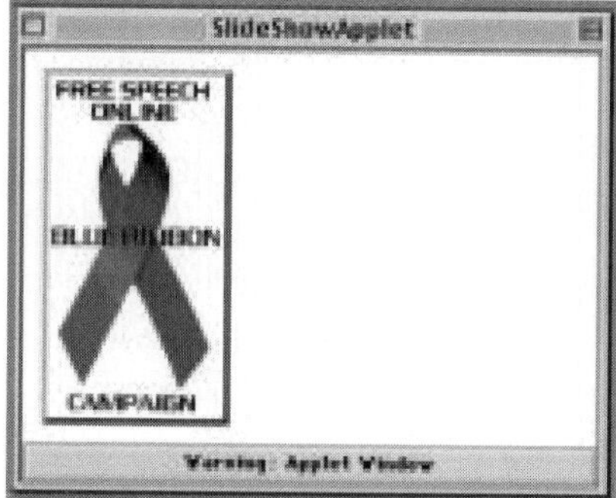

Figure 15–8 An applet that continuously displays slides downloaded from the Web.

A URL specification is just a String, such as,

```
http://www.prenhall.com:80/morelli/applets/slideshow/slide1.gif
```

which describes how to retrieve the resource. First, it specifies the protocol or method that should be used to download the resource (http). Next, it provides the domain name of the server that runs the protocol and the port number where the service is running (www.prenhall.com:80). Next, the URL specifies the resource's file name (morelli/applets/slideshow/slide1.gif).

From the Java Library: java.net.URL

Given such a URL specification, how can we download its associated resource? Are there Java classes that can help us solve this problem? Fortunately, there are. First, the java.net.URL class contains methods to help retrieve the resource associated with a particular URL:

```
public final class URL extends Object {
  // Constructor
    public URL( String urlSpec ) throws MalformedURLException;
  // Public instance methods
    public URLConnection openConnection() throws IOException;
    public final InputStream openStream() throws IOException;
}
```

The URL class represents a uniform resource locator. The URL() constructor shown here (there are others) takes a URL specification as a String, and assuming it specifies a valid URL, it creates a URL object. If the URL specification is invalid, a MalformedURLException is thrown. A URL might be invalid if the protocol were left off or if it is not a known protocol. The following simple code creates a URL for the home page of our companion Web site:

```
URL url;
try {
    url = new URL("http://www.prenhall.com:80/morelli/index.html");
} catch (MalformedURLException e) {
    System.out.println("Malformed URL: " + url.toString()) ;
}
```

Note how we catch the MalformedURLException when we create a new URL.

Once we have a valid URL instance, it can be used to download the data or object associated with it. There are different ways to do this. The openConnection() method creates a URLConnection, which can then be used to download the resource. You would only use this method if your application required extensive control over the download process. A much

URLs and streams

simpler approach would use the `openStream()` method. This method will open an `InputStream`, which you can then use to read the associated URL data the same way you would read a file. This method is especially useful for writing Java applications (rather than applets). As you might guess, downloading Web resources is particularly easy from a Java applet. So let's search around for other methods that we can use.

Code Reuse: The `java.applet.Applet` Class

The `java.applet.Applet` class itself contains several useful methods for downloading and displaying Web resources. These methods are inherited by `javax.swing.JApplet`.

```
public class Applet extends Panel {
    public AppletContext getAppletContext();
    public AudioClip getAudioClip(URL url);
    public Image getImage(URL url);
    public void play(URL url);
    public void showStatus(String msg);
}
```

As you see, both the `getImage()` and `getAudioClip()` methods use a URL to download a resource. An `AudioClip` is a sound file encoded in `AU` format, a special type of encoding for sound files. The `getImage()` method can return files in either `GIF` or `JPEG` format, two popular image file formats. The `play()` method does the downloading and playing of an audio file in one easy step. For example, to download and play an audio clip within an applet requires just two lines of code:

```
URL url;
try {
    url = new URL("http://www.prenhall.com/morelli/sounds/sound.au");
    play(url);
} catch (MalformedURLException e) {
    System.out.println("Malformed URL: " + url.toString()) ;
}
```

Similarly, to download (and store a reference to) an image is just as simple:

```
URL url;
try {
    url = new URL("http://www.prenhall.com/morelli/gifs/demo.gif") ;
    imgRef = getImage(url);
} catch (MalformedURLException e) {
    System.out.println( "Malformed URL: " + url.toString()) ;
}
```

What methods can we use?

So, it looks as if we've found the methods we need to implement our slide show applet. We'll use the `URL()` constructor to create a URL from a `String`, and we'll use the `Applet.getImage(URL)` method to retrieve the images from the Web.

15.4 The Slide Show Applet

Problem Specification

Let's suppose our slide show will repeatedly display a set of images named "demo0.gif," "demo1.gif," and "demo2.gif." Suppose these images are stored on a Web site on `www.prenhall.com` and are stored in a directory named `/morelli/applets/slideshow`. This means our program will have to load the following three URLs:

```
http://www.prenhall.com/morelli/applets/slideshow/demo0.gif
http://www.prenhall.com/morelli/applets/slideshow/demo1.gif
http://www.prenhall.com/morelli/applets/slideshow/demo2.gif
```

We want our show to cycle endlessly through these images, leaving around 5 seconds between each slide.

User Interface Design

The user interface for this applet doesn't contain any GUI components. It just needs to display an image every 5 seconds. It can use a simple `paint()` method to display an image each time it is repainted:

```
public void paint(Graphics g) {
    if (currentImage != null)
        g.drawImage(currentImage, 10, 10, this);
}
```

The assumption here is that the `currentImage` instance variable will be set initially to `null`. Each time an image is downloaded, it will be set to refer to that image. Because `paint()` is called before the applet starts downloading the images, it is necessary to guard against attempting to draw a `null` image, which would lead to an exception.

Problem Decomposition

Delaying between slides

One problem we face with this applet is getting it to pause between each slide. One way to do this is to set up a loop that does nothing for around 5 seconds:

```
for (int k = 0; k < 1000000; k++ ) ;// Busy waiting
```

However, this isn't a very good solution. As we saw in Chapter 13, this is a form of *busy waiting* which monopolizes the CPU, making it very difficult to break out of the loop. Another problem with this loop is we don't really know how many iterations to do to approximate 5 seconds of idleness.

A much better design would be to use a separate timer thread, which can `sleep()` for 5 seconds between each slide. So our program will have two classes: one to download and display the slides, and one to serve as a timer.

1. `SlideShowApplet` — This `Applet` subclass will take care of downloading and displaying the images and starting the timer thread.
2. `Timer` — This class will implement the `Runnable` interface so it can run as a separate thread. It will repeatedly sleep for 5 seconds and then tell the applet to display the next side.

EFFECTIVE DESIGN: Busy Waiting. Instead of busy waiting, a thread that sleeps for a brief period on each iteration is a better way to introduce a delay into an algorithm.

15.4.1 The `SlideShowApplet` class

What should we do with the images we download? Should we repeatedly download and display them, or should we just download them once and store them in memory? The second of these alternatives seems more efficient. If an image has already been downloaded, it would be wasteful to download it again.

EFFECTIVE DESIGN: Network Traffic. In general, a design that minimizes network traffic is preferable.

What data do we need?

So we'll need an array to store the images. Our slide show will then consist of retrieving the next image from the array and displaying it. To help us with this task, let's use a `nextImg` variable as an array index to keep track of the next image. Even though it isn't absolutely necessary, we could use a third variable here, `currentImage`, to keep track of the current image to be displayed. Thus, our applet needs the following instance variables:

```
private static final int NIMGS = 3;
private Image[] slide = new Image[NIMGS];
private Image currentImage = null;
private int nextImg = 0;
```

Method design

Given these variables, let's now write a method to take care of choosing the next slide. Recall that the `paint()` method takes care of displaying `currentImage`, so all this method needs to do is to update both `currentImage` and `nextImage`. This method should be designed so that it can be called by the `Timer` thread whenever it is time to display the next slide. So it should be a `public` method. It can be a `void` method with no parameters, because the applet already contains all the information needed to display the next slide. Thus there's no need for information to be passed back and forth between `Timer` and this method:

```
public void nextSlide() {
    currentImage = slide[nextImg];
    nextImg = (nextImg + 1) % NIMGS;
    repaint();
}// nextSlide()
```

The method's algorithm is very simple. It sets `currentImage` to whatever `slide` is designated by `nextImg` and it then updates `nextImg`'s value. Note here the use of modular arithmetic to compute the value of `nextImg`. Given that NIMGS is 3, this algorithm will cause `nextImg` to take on the repeating sequence of values 0, 1, 2, 0, 1, 2, and so forth. Finally, the method calls `repaint()` to display the image.

PROGRAMMING TIP: Modular Arithmetic. Modular arithmetic (x % N) is useful for cycling repeatedly through the values `0, 1, ..., N-1, 0, 1,...,N-1`.

The applet's `init()` method will have two tasks:

1. Download and store the images in `slide[]`.
2. Start the `Timer` thread.

As we discussed, downloading Web resources requires the use of `URL()` and `getImage()`. Here we just place these method calls in a loop:

```
URL url = null;
try {
    for (int k=0; k < NIMGS; k++) {
        url = new URL( "http://troy.trincoll.edu/jjj/gifs/demo" + k + ".gif" ) ;
        slide[k] = getImage(url);
    }
} catch (MalformedURLException e) {
    System.out.println("ERROR: Malformed URL: " + url.toString());
}
```

Note here how we convert the loop variable *k* into a `String` and concatenate it right into the URL specification. This allows us to have URLs containing "demo0.gif," "demo1.gif," and "demo2.gif." This makes our program easily extensible should we later decide to add more slides to the show. Note also the use of the class constant NIMGS as the loop bound. This too adds to the program's extensibility.

PROGRAMMING TIP: Concatenation. Concatenating an integer value (k) with a string lets you create file names of the form `file1.gif`, `file2.gif`, and so on.

The task of starting the `Timer` thread involves creating an instance of the `Timer` class and calling its `start()` method:

```
Thread timer = new Thread(new Timer(this));
timer.start();
```

Note that `Timer` is passed a reference to `this` applet. This enables `Timer` call the applet's `nextSlide()` method every 5 seconds. This programming technique is known as *callback* and the `nextSlide()` method is an example of a *callback method*.

PROGRAMMING TIP: Callback. Communication between two objects can often be handled using a callback technique. One object is passed a reference to the other object. The first object uses the reference to call one of the public methods of the other object.

This completes our design and development of `SlideShowAplet`, which is shown Figure 15–9.

15.4.2 The `Timer` Class

The timer thread

The `Timer` class is a subclass of `Thread`, which means it must implement the `run()` method. Recall that we never directly call a thread's `run()` method. Instead we call its `start()` method, which automatically calls `run()`. This particular thread has a very simple and singular function. It should call the `SlideShowApplet.nextSlide()` method and then sleep for 5 seconds. So its main algorithm will be

```
while (true) {
    applet.nextSlide();
    sleep( 5000 );
}
```

However, recall that `Thread.sleep()` throws the `InterruptedException`. This means that we'll have to embed this while loop in a `try/catch` block.

Note also that in order to call the applet's `nextSlide()` method, we need a reference to the SlideShowApplet, so we need to give it such a reference as an instance variable, as well as a constructor that allows the applet to pass `Timer` a reference to itself.

Given these design decisions, the complete implementation of `Timer` is shown in Figure 15–10. To see how it works, download it from the *Java, Java, Java* Web site and run it.

SELF-STUDY EXERCISES

EXERCISE 15.6 Describe the design changes you would make to `SlideShowApplet` if you wanted to play a soundtrack along with your slides. Assume that the sounds are stored in a sequence of files, "sound0.au", sound1.au", and so forth, on your Web site.

Figure 15–9 The SlideShowApplet class.

```
import java.awt.*;
import javax.swing.*;
import java.net.*;

public class SlideShowApplet extends JApplet  {
    public static final int WIDTH=300, HEIGHT=200;
    private static final int NIMGS = 3;
    private Image[] slide = new Image[NIMGS];
    private Image currentImage = null;
    private int nextImg = 0;

    public void paint(Graphics g) {
        g.setColor(getBackground());
        g.fillRect(0, 0, WIDTH, HEIGHT);
        if (currentImage != null)
        g.drawImage(currentImage, 10, 10, this);
    }//paint()

    public void nextSlide() {
        currentImage = slide[nextImg];
        nextImg = (nextImg + 1) % NIMGS;
        repaint();
    }// nextSlide()

    public void init() {
        URL url = null;
        try {
            for (int k=0; k < NIMGS; k++) {
                url = new URL("http://www.prenhall.com/morelli/gifs/demo" + k + ".gif") ;
                slide[k] = getImage( url );
            }
        } catch (MalformedURLException e) {
            System.out.println("ERROR: Malformed URL: " + url.toString() );
        }

        Thread timer = new Thread(new Timer(this));
        timer.start();
        setSize( WIDTH, HEIGHT );
    }// init()
}// SlideShowApplet
```

Figure 15–10 The Timer class.

```
public class Timer implements Runnable {
    private SlideShowApplet applet;

    public Timer( SlideShowApplet app ) {
        applet = app;
    }

    public void run() {
        try {
            while ( true ) {
                applet.nextSlide();
                Thread.sleep( 5000 );
            }
        } catch (InterruptedException e) {
            System.out.println(e.getMessage());
        }
    }// run()
}// Timer
```

15.5 Using Network Resources from an Application

Applet restrictions

The `SlideShowApplet` illustrates the ease of downloading Web resources from an applet. However, applets have limited use in this regard, because they come with rather severe security restrictions that would make them a poor choice for most networking applications (see Section 15.8). For example, applets cannot save files that they download, because they cannot access the host computer's file system. Similarly, an applet can only download files from the same host from which it was downloaded. This wouldn't be a problem for the slide show applet, since we can simply store the slides in the same directory as the applet itself. So, we want to learn how to download Web resources from a Java application. The next example illustrates a solution to this problem.

Problem Specification

Problem statement

Suppose a realtor asks you to write a Java application that will let its customers view pictures and descriptions of homes from its on-line database. The application should allow the customer to select a home and should then display both an image of the home and a text description of its features, such as square footage, asking price, and so on.

Suppose that the database of image and text files is kept at a fixed location on the Web, but the names of the files themselves may change. This will enable the company to change the database as it sells the homes. As input to this program the company will provide a text file that contains the names of the files for the current selection of homes. To simplify matters, both image and text files have the same name, but different extensions — for example, `ranch.txt` and `ranch.gif`. The data file will store just the names of the files, one per line, giving it the following format:

```
beautifulCape
handsomeRanch
lovelyColonial
```

15.5.1 Downloading a Text File from the Web

This application requires us to solve three new problems:

1. How do we download a text file of names and use them as menu items?
2. How do we download a text file and display it in a `JTextArea`?
3. How do we download and display an image file?

The third problem is very similar to the problem we solved in `SlideShowApplet`, but here we can't use the `Applet.getImage()` method. However, as we shall see, we can find a Java library method to perform this task for us.

Understanding the problem

Therefore, the most challenging part of this program is the task of downloading a Web file and using its data in the program. For this program we must make use of two types of data downloaded from the Web.

The first will be the names of the image and document files. We'll want to read these names and use them as menu items that the user can select. Second, once the user has selected a house to view, we must download and display an image and a text description of the house. Downloading the text is basically the same as downloading the file of names. The only difference is that we need to display this text in a JTextArea. Downloading the image file can be handled in more or less the same way that it was handled in the SlideShowApplet — by using a special Java method to download and display the image file.

Clearly the problems of downloading a file from the Web and reading a file from the disk are quite similar. Recall that for reading disk files, we used *streams* to handle the I/O operations. The various InputStream and OutputStream classes contained the read() and write() methods needed for I/O. The situation is exactly the same for downloading Web files.

File download algorithm

Recall that the URL class contains the openStream() method, which opens an InputStream to the resource associated with the URL. Once the stream has been opened, you can read data from the stream just as if it were coming from a file. The program doesn't care whether the data are coming from a file on the Internet or a file on the disk. It just reads data from the stream. So, to download a data file from the Internet, regardless of whether it's a text file, image file, audio file, or whatever, you would use the following general algorithm:

```
URL url;
InputStream data;
try {
    url = new URL(fileURL);             // Create a URL
    data = url.openStream();            // Open a stream to the URL
  // READ THE FILE INTO MEMORY          // Read the data
    data.close();                       // Close the stream
} catch (MalformedURLException e) {     // May be thrown by URL()
    System.out.println(e.getMessage());
} catch( IOException e ) {              // May be thrown by read or close
    System.out.println(e.getMessage());
}
```

The algorithm consists of four basic steps.

1. Create a URL instance.
2. Open an InputStream to it.
3. Read the data.
4. Close the stream.

Step 3 of this algorithm — read the data — involves many lines of code and has therefore been left as a subtask suitable for encapsulation within a method.

Reading the Data

Text or binary data?

As we saw in the previous chapter, the algorithm for step 3 will depend on the file's data. If it's a text file, we would like to read one line at a time, storing the input in a `String`. If it's an image or an audio file, we would read one `byte` at a time.

What library methods can we use?

Because our data are contained in a text file, we want to read one line at a time. The `BufferedReader` class contains a `readLine()` method that returns either a `String` storing the line or the value `null` when it reaches the end of file. The following method shows how you would read a text file into the program's `JTextArea`, which is named `display`:

```
private void readTextIntoDisplay(URL url) throws IOException {
    BufferedReader data
        = new BufferedReader(new InputStreamReader(url.openStream()));

    display.setText("");               // Reset the text area
    String line = data.readLine();
    while (line != null)  {            // Read each line
        display.append(line + "\n");   // And add it to the display
        line = data.readLine();
    }
    data.close();
}// readTextIntoDisplay()
```

The method is passed the file's URL and it uses the `URL.openStream()` method to open the input stream. Note that the method `throws IOException`, which means that any I/O exceptions that get raised will be handled by the calling method.

I/O Exceptions

The input algorithm reads each line of the file and adds it to the `display`. For our real estate application, this method could be called from `itemStateChanged()` to display a description of one of the homes selected by the user. The same basic algorithm can be used to read the names of the data files and store them in a menu that can be used to make selections. For example, if we use a `Choice` box menu named `homeChoice`, we would simply add each line to it:

```
String line = data.readLine();
while (line != null) {
    homeChoice.addItem(line);
    line = data.readLine();
}
```

15.5.2 Code Reuse: The `java.awt.Toolkit` Class

How do we read and display an image file? Recall that in the `SlideShowApplet` we were able to find the `Applet.getImage()` method to retrieve an image from the Web. Is there a similar method that we could use for applications?

Fortunately, there is. It's located in the `java.awt.Toolkit` class, which contains the following useful methods:

```
public abstract class Toolkit {
  // Class methods
    public static Toolkit getDefaultToolkit();
  // Instance methods
    public abstract void beep();
    public abstract Image getImage(String filename);
    public abstract Image getImage(URL url);
}
```

The `Toolkit` class implements various platform-dependent methods to support the Java GUI `Components`. The `getDefaultToolkit()` method is used to retrieve the toolkit that's being used by a particular platform. To use a `Toolkit` method, you first must first retrieve the default kit and then use it as reference to the method you wish to use. For example, to use the `beep()` method, which causes an audible beep to be emitted, you would type:

```
Toolkit.getDefaultToolkit().beep();
```

The `beep()` method might be useful as an alternative to a printed error message when the user mistypes something during input.

The `getImage(String)` and `getImage(URL)` method inputs an image from a disk file and from a URL, respectively. The use of `Toolkit.getImage()` will greatly simplify the task of downloading and displaying an image. Without it, we could easily manage downloading the image file, but how would we convert it into an `Image` object that could be used by the program? With this method, our task is simplified to

```
Image currentImage = Toolkit.getDefaultToolkit().getImage(url);
```

15.5.3 The `RealEstateViewer` Application

Now that we have figured out how to download and use Web resources in an application, let's design our `RealEstateViewer` application.

Interface Design

The interface for this application is very important. It should provide some means to display a text file and an image. The text file can be displayed in a `JTextArea`, and the image can be drawn on a `JPanel`.

In terms of the controls, the customer should be allowed to select a home to view from a menu of options. Because the program will have the list of available homes, it can provide the options in a `Choice` box.

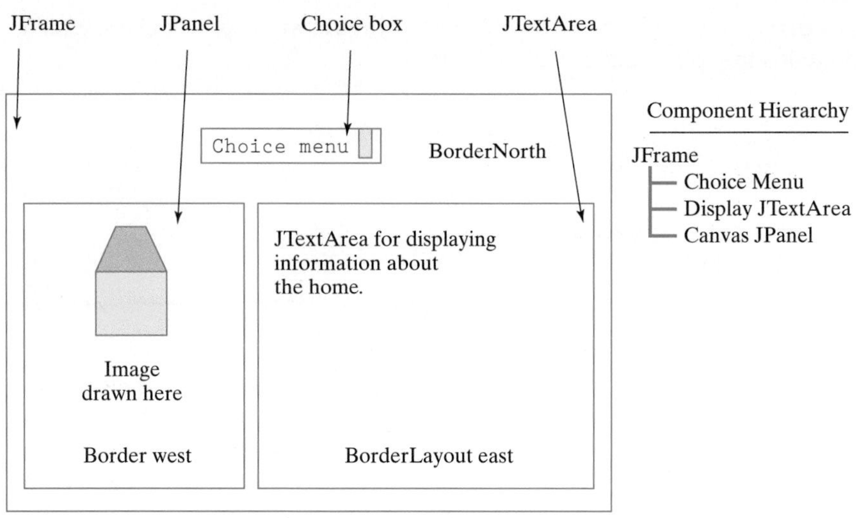

Figure 15–11 User interface design for the real estate application.

Interface layout

In terms of an appropriate layout, we want to make sure that the controls, the image, and `JTextArea` all have their own region of the application's window. This suggests a `BorderLayout`, which is the default layout for a `JFrame`. We can put the `Choice` menu at the "North" border, and the image and text on the "West" and "East" borders, respectively. Figure 15–11 summarizes these various design decisions.

Problem Decomposition: `RealEstateViewer`

What classes do we need?

The task of downloading and displaying information from the Internet is best handled by two separate classes: one to perform the downloading and user interface tasks, and the other to take care of displaying the image.

The task of downloading the image and text files from the Web can be handled by program's main class, the `RealEstateViewer`, which will also handle the user interface. As the application's top-level window, `RealEstateViewer` will be a subclass of `JFrame`. Because its controls will include a `Choice`, it must implement the `itemStateChanged()` method of the `ItemListener` interface.

What components and other instance variables will we need for this class? According to our interface design, it will need a `Choice`, a `JTextArea`, and the `ImagePanel`. Because it will be downloading images, it will need an `Image` variable.

What data do we need?

In terms of constants used by this application, the URL string for the data file should be defined as a constant. Also, because all the images and data files will start with the same prefix — `http://troy.trincoll.edu/jjj/applets/homes/` — we should make this a constant in the program. These preliminary decisions lead to the initial version of `RealEstateViewer`

Figure 15–12 The RealEstateViewer, version 1.

```
import java.awt.*;
import java.awt.event.*;
import java.net.*;
import java.io.*;
import javax.swing.*;

public class RealEstateViewer extends JFrame implements ItemListener {
    public static final int WIDTH=400,HEIGHT=200;
    private final String dataFileURL = "http://troy.trincoll.edu/~jjj/applets/homes/homes.txt";
    private final String baseURL = "http://troy.trincoll.edu/~jjj/applets/homes/";
    private JTextArea display = new JTextArea(20,20);
    private JComboBox homeChoice = new JComboBox();
    private ImagePanel imagePanel = new ImagePanel(this);
    public Image currentImage = null;

    public RealEstateViewer () {}                        // Constructor
    public void itemStateChanged( ItemEvent evt ) { }    // ItemListener

    public static void main(String args[]) {
        RealEstateViewer viewer = new RealEstateViewer();
        viewer.setSize(viewer.WIDTH,viewer.HEIGHT);
        viewer.setVisible(true);
        viewer.addWindowListener(new WindowAdapter() {    // Quit the application
            public void windowClosing(WindowEvent e) {
                System.exit(0);
            }
        });
    }// main()
}// RealEstateViewer
```

shown in Figure 15–12. Note that the `main()` method merely creates an instance of the application and shows it. Note also that the `currentImage` variable is declared `public`. This will let the `ImagePanel` have direct access to `currentImage` whenever it needs to display a new image.

The `ImagePanel` *Class*

We'll use a second class, the `ImagePanel`, to handle the displaying of the image (Figure 15–13). The reason we use a separate class for this task is that we want the image to appear in its own panel (which appears on the West border of the main window). Besides its constructor, the only method needed in this class is the `paintComponent()` method. This method will be called automatically whenever the main window is repainted. Its task is simply to get the current image from its parent frame and display it. Note that a reference to the parent frames is passed to the object in its constructor.

Overriding `paintComponent()`

Method Decomposition

The stub methods listed in the initial version of `RealEstateViewer` (Figure 15–12) outline the main tasks required by the application. Some of these methods are very simple and even trivial to implement. Others should be broken up into subtasks.

Figure 15–13 The ImagePanel class.

```
import javax.swing.*;
import java.awt.*;

public class ImagePanel extends JPanel {

    private RealEstateViewer frame;

    public ImagePanel(RealEstateViewer parent) {
        frame = parent;
    }

    public void paintComponent(Graphics g) {
        if (frame.currentImage != null)
            g.drawImage(frame.currentImage, 0, 0, this);
    }
}// ImagePanel
```

The constructor method should be responsible for creating the user interface, most of which will involve the routine tasks of registering a listener for the `Choice` menu and setting up an appropriate layout that implements the design we developed for the user interface:

```
public RealEstateViewer () {
    super("Home Viewer Application");    // Set the window title
    homeChoice.addItemListener( this);
    this.getContentPane().add("North",homeChoice);
    this.getContentPane().add("East",display);
    this.getContentPane().add("Center",imagePanel);
    display.setLineWrap(true);
    initHomeChoices();                   // Set up the choice box
    showCurrentSelection();              // Display the current home
}
```

Note the last two statements of the method. The first sets up the `Choice` by reading its contents from a file stored in the company's database. Because that task will require several statements, we define it as a separate method, `initHomeChoices()`, and defer its development for now. Similarly, the task of displaying the current menu choice has been organized into the `showCurrentSelection()` method, whose development we also defer for now.

ItemListener

The `itemStateChanged()` method is called automatically when the user selects a home from the `Choice` menu. Its task is to download and display information about the current menu selection. So it can simply call the `showCurrentSelection()` method:

```
public void itemStateChanged(ItemEvent evt) {
    showCurrentSelection();
}
```

Downloading the Menu Items

Recall that according to our specification, the real estate firm stores its current listing of homes in a text file, one home per line. The `initHomeChoices()` method downloads the text and uses its contents to set up the items in the `Choice` menu:

```
private void initHomeChoices() {
    try {
        URL url = new URL(dataFileURL);
        BufferedReader data = new BufferedReader(new InputStreamReader(url.openStream()));
        String line = data.readLine();
        while (line != null) {
            homeChoice.addItem(line);
            line = data.readLine();
        }
        data.close();
    } catch (MalformedURLException e) {
        System.out.println( "ERROR: " + e.getMessage()) ;
    } catch (IOException e) {
        System.out.println( "ERROR: " + e.getMessage()) ;
    }
}// initHomeChoices()
```

It uses the algorithm we developed above for downloading a text file. Each line of the text file represents a menu item, so, as each line is read, `readLine(data)`, it is added to the `Choice` menu.

Downloading and Displaying Home Information

The `showCurrentSelection()` method is responsible for downloading and displaying images and text files whenever the user selects a home to view. Recall that our specification called for using the name of the menu item as a basis for constructing the name of its corresponding text file and image file. Therefore the basic algorithm we need is

1. Get the user's home choice.
2. Create a URL for the associated text file.
3. Download and display the associated text file.
4. Create a URL for the associated gif file.
5. Download and display the image.

Method decomposition

Because downloading a text document requires stream processing, we should handle that in a separate method. The task of downloading an image file is also a good candidate for a separate method. Both of these methods will use a URL, so we can leave that task up to `showCurrentSelection()` itself. The `showCurrentSelection()` method will create the URLs and then invoke the appropriate methods to download and display the resources:

Figure 15–14 An application for downloading images and documents off the Web.

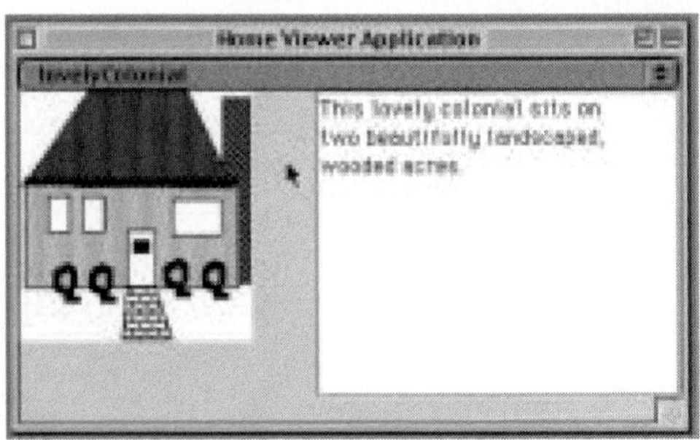

```
private void showCurrentSelection() {// throws IOException {
    URL url = null;
    String choice = homeChoice.getSelectedItem().toString();      // Get user's choice
    try {
        url = new URL(baseURL + choice + ".txt") ;                // Create url
        readTextIntoDisplay(url);                                 // Download and display text file
        url = new URL(baseURL + choice + ".gif");                 // Create url
        currentImage = Toolkit.getDefaultToolkit().getImage(url);// Download image
        Toolkit.getDefaultToolkit().beep();                       // Alert the user
        repaint();
    } catch (MalformedURLException e) {
        System.out.println( "ERROR: " + e.getMessage()) ;
    } catch (IOException e) {
        System.out.println("ERROR: " + e.getMessage()) ;
    }
}// showCurrentSelection()
```

Note that we have also elected to handle both the `MalformedURLException` and `IOException` in this method. The advantage of this design is that separates exception handling from the normal algorithm and organizes it into one method. Finally, note how string concatenation is used to build the URL specifications, each of which consists of three parts: the `baseURL`, the user's `choice`, and the file extension.

The task of reading the text file and displaying its contents has been encapsulated into the `readTextIntoDisplay()` method. This `private` utility method performs a standard file reading algorithm using the `readLine()` method that we developed earlier. Figure 15–15 provides the complete implementation of this program. Figure 15–14 provides a view of the program's appearance as it is displaying information to a user.

Figure 15–15 The `RealEstateViewer` class.

```
import java.awt.*;
import java.awt.event.*;
import java.net.*;
import java.io.*;
import javax.swing.*;

public class RealEstateViewer extends JFrame implements ItemListener {
    public static final int WIDTH=400,HEIGHT=200;
    private final String dataFileURL = "http://troy.trincoll.edu/jjj/applets/homes/homes.txt";
    private final String baseURL = "http://troy.trincoll.edu/jjj/applets/homes/";
    private JTextArea display = new JTextArea(20,20);
    private JComboBox homeChoice = new JComboBox();
    private ImagePanel imagePanel = new ImagePanel(this);
    public Image currentImage = null;
```

Figure 15–15 *Continued*

```
    public RealEstateViewer () {
        super("Home Viewer Application");    // Set the window title
        homeChoice.addItemListener( this);
        this.getContentPane().add("North",homeChoice);
        this.getContentPane().add("East",display);
        this.getContentPane().add("Center",imagePanel);
        display.setLineWrap(true);
        initHomeChoices();                   // Set up the choice box
        showCurrentSelection();              // Display the current home
    }
    private void initHomeChoices() {
        try {
            URL url = new URL(dataFileURL);
            BufferedReader data = new BufferedReader(new InputStreamReader(url.openStream()));
            String line = data.readLine();
            while (line != null) {
                homeChoice.addItem(line);
                line = data.readLine();
            } data.close();
        } catch (MalformedURLException e) {
            System.out.println( "ERROR: " + e.getMessage()) ;
        } catch (IOException e) {
            System.out.println( "ERROR: " + e.getMessage()) ;
        }
    }// initHomeChoices()
    private void readTextIntoDisplay(URL url) throws IOException {
        BufferedReader data
            = new BufferedReader(new InputStreamReader(url.openStream()));
        display.setText("");                // Reset the text area
        String line = data.readLine();
        while (line != null)  {             // Read each line
            display.append(line + "\n");    // And add it to the display
            line = data.readLine();
        } data.close();
    }// readTextIntoDisplay()
    private void showCurrentSelection() {// throws IOException {
        URL url = null;
        String choice = homeChoice.getSelectedItem().toString();     // Get user's choice
        try {
            url = new URL(baseURL + choice + ".txt") ;                // Create url
            readTextIntoDisplay(url);                                 // Download and display text file
            url = new URL(baseURL + choice + ".gif");                 // Create url
            currentImage = Toolkit.getDefaultToolkit().getImage(url);// Download image
            Toolkit.getDefaultToolkit().beep();                       // Alert the user
            repaint();
        } catch (MalformedURLException e) {
            System.out.println( "ERROR: " + e.getMessage()) ;
        } catch (IOException e) {
            System.out.println("ERROR: " + e.getMessage()) ;
        }
    }// showCurrentSelection()
    public void itemStateChanged(ItemEvent evt) {
        showCurrentSelection();
    }
    public static void main(String args[]) {
        RealEstateViewer viewer = new RealEstateViewer();
        viewer.setSize(viewer.WIDTH,viewer.HEIGHT);
        viewer.setVisible(true);
        viewer.addWindowListener(new WindowAdapter() {      // Quit the application
            public void windowClosing(WindowEvent e) {
                System.exit(0);
            }
        });
    }// main()
}// RealEstateViewer
```

15.5.4 Reusing Code

As in other examples we have developed, our discovery and use of the `Toolkit.getImage()` method, and other classes from the Java class library, illustrate an important principle of object-oriented programming.

EFFECTIVE DESIGN: Code Reuse. Before writing code to perform a particular task, search the available libraries to see if there is already code that performs that task.

An important step in designing object-oriented programs is making appropriate use of existing classes and methods. In some cases you want to directly instantiate a class and use its methods to perform the desired tasks. In other cases it is necessary to create a subclass (inheritance) or implement an interface (inheritance) in order to gain access to the methods you need.

Of course, knowing what classes exist in the libraries is something that comes with experience. There's no way that a novice Java programmer would know about, say, the `Toolkit.getImage()` method. However, one skill or habit of mind that you should try to develop is always to ask yourself the question: "Is there a method that will do what I'm trying to do here?" That question should be the first question on your search through the libraries and reference books.

15.6 Client/Server Communication via `Sockets`

As we said earlier, many networking applications are based on the client/server model. According to this model, a task is viewed as a service that can be requested by clients and handled by servers. In this section we develop a simple client/server framework based on a socket connection between the client and the server.

A **socket** is a simple communication channel through which two programs communicate over a network. A socket supports two-way communication between a client and a server, using a well-established protocol. The protocol simply prescribes rules and behavior that both the server and client must follow in order to establish two-way communication.

Sockets and ports

According to this protocol, a server program creates a socket at a certain port and waits until a client requests a connection. A **port** is a particular address or entry point on the host computer, which typically has hundreds of potential ports. It is usually represented as a simple integer value. For example, the standard port for an HTTP (Web) server is 80. Once the connection is established, the server creates input and output streams to the socket and begins sending messages to and receiving messages from the client. Either the client or the server can close the connection, but it's usually done by the client.

DEBUGGING TIP: Reserved Port Numbers. Port numbers below 1024 are reserved for system use and should not be used by an application program.

Client/server protocol

To help clarify this protocol, think of some service performed by a human using a telephone connection. The "server" waits for the phone to ring. When it rings, the server picks it up and begins communicating with the client. A socket, combined together with input and output streams, is something like a two-way phone connection.

From the client's side, the protocol goes as follows. The client creates a socket and attempts to make a connection to the server. The client has to know the server's URL and the port at which the service exists. Once a connection has been established, the client creates input and output streams to the socket, and begins exchanging messages with the server. The client can close the connection when the service is completed.

Think again of the telephone analogy. A human client picks up the phone and dials the number of a particular service. This is analogous to the client program creating a socket and making a connection to a server. Once the service agent answers the phone, two-way communication between the client and the server can begin.

Sockets and channels

Figure 15–16 provides a view of the client/server connection. Note that a socket has two channels. Once a connection has been established between a client and a server, a single two-way channel exists between them. The client's output stream is connected to the server's input stream. The server's output stream is connected to the client's input stream.

PROGRAMMING TIP: Socket streams. Each socket has two streams, one for input and one for output.

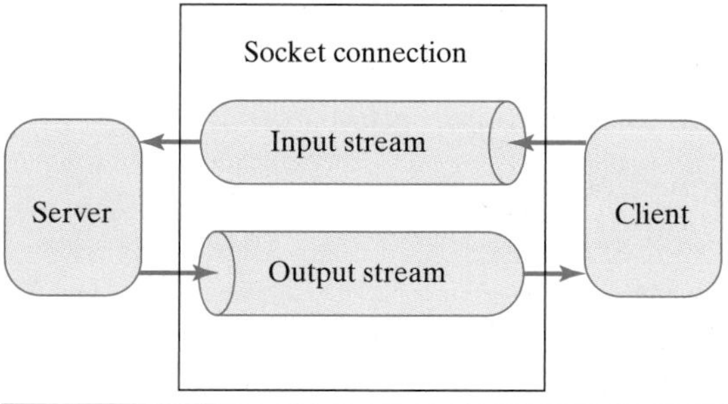

Figure 15–16 A socket is a two-channel communication link.

Figure 15–17 Template for the server protocol.

```
Socket socket;          // Reference to the socket
ServerSocket port;      // The port where the server will listen
try {
    port = new ServerSocket(10001, 5);    // Create a port
    socket = port.accept();               // Wait for the client to call

   // Communicate with the client

    socket.close();
} catch (IOException e) {
    e.printStackTrace();
}
```

15.6.1 The Server Protocol

Let's now see how a client/server application would be coded in Java. The template in Figure 15–17 shows the code that is necessary on the server side. The first step the server takes is to create a `ServerSocket`. The first argument to the `ServerSocket()` method is the port at which the service will reside. The second argument specifies the number of clients that can be backlogged, waiting on the server, before a client will be refused service. If more than one client at a time should request service, Java would establish and manage a waiting list, turning away clients when the list is full.

Waiting for client requests

The next step is to wait for a client request. The `accept()` method will *block* until a connection is established. The Java system is responsible for waking the server up when a client request is received.

Once a connection is established, the server can begin communicating with the client. As we have suggested, a socket connection is like a two-way telephone conversation. Both the client and server can "talk" back and forth to each other. The details of this step are not shown here. As we will see, the two-way conversation is managed by connecting both an input and an output stream to the socket.

Once the conversation between client and server is finished — once the server has delivered the requested service — the server can close the connection by calling `close()`. Thus there are four steps involved on the server side:

1. Create a `SocketServer` and establish a port number.
2. Listen for and accept a connection from a client.
3. Converse with the client.
4. Close the socket.

What distinguishes the server from the client is that the server establishes the port and accepts the connection.

Figure 15–18 Template for the client protocol.

```
Socket connection;      // Reference to the socket
try {
    connection = new Socket("troy.cs.trincoll.edu", 10001);//Request a connection

   // Carry on a two-way communication

    connection.close();         // Close the socket
} catch (IOException e ) {
    e.printStackTrace();
}
```

15.6.2 The Client Protocol

The client protocol (Figure 15–18) is just as easy to implement. Indeed, on the client side there are three steps involved. The first step is to request a connection to the server. This is done in the `Socket()` constructor by supplying the server's URL and port number. Once the connection is established, the client can carry out two-way communication with the server. This step is not shown here. Finally, when the client is finished, it can simply `close()` the connection. Thus, from the client side, the protocol involves just three steps:

Initiating a request

1. Open a socket connection to the server, given its address.
2. Converse with the server.
3. Close the connection.

What distinguishes the client from the server is that the client initiates the two-way connection by requesting the service.

15.6.3 A Two-way Stream Connection

Now that we have seen how to establish a socket connection between a client and server, let's look at the actual two-way communication that takes place. Because this part of the process will be exactly the same for both client and server, we develop a single set of methods, `writeToSocket()` and `readFromSocket()`, that may be called by either.

The `writeToSocket()` method takes two parameters, the `Socket` and a `String`, which will be sent to the process on the other end of the socket:

Output routine

```
protected void writeToSocket(Socket sock, String str) throws IOException {
    oStream = sock.getOutputStream();
    for (int k = 0; k < str.length() ; k++)
        oStream.write(str.charAt(k));
}// writeToSocke()
```

If `writeToSocket()` is called by the server, then the string will be sent to the client. If it is called by the client, the string will be sent to the server.

Protected methods

The method is declared `protected` because we will define it in a superclass so that it can be inherited and used by both the client and server classes. Note also that the method declares that it throws an `IOException`. Because there's no way to fix an `IOException`, we'll just let this exception be handled elsewhere, rather than handling it within the method.

In order to write to a socket we need only get the socket's `OutputStream` and then write to it. For this example, `oStream` is an instance variable of the client/server superclass. We use the `Socket.getOutputStream()` method to get a reference to the socket's output stream. Note that we are not creating a new output stream here. We are just getting a reference to an existing stream, which was created when the socket connection was accepted. Note also that we do not close the output stream before exiting the method. This is important. If you close the stream, you will lose the ability to communicate through the socket.

JAVA LANGUAGE RULE **Socket Streams.** When a socket is created, it automatically creates its own streams. To use it you just need to get a reference to it.

DEBUGGING TIP: Socket Streams. After writing to or reading from a socket I/O stream, do not close the stream. That would make the socket unusable for subsequent I/O.

Given the reference to the socket's output stream, we simply write each character of the string using the `OutputStream.write()` method. This method writes a single `byte`. Therefore, the input stream, on the other side of the socket, must read bytes and convert them back into characters.

EFFECTIVE DESIGN: Designing a Protocol. In designing two-way communication between a client and a server, you are designing a protocol that each side must use. Failure to design and implement a clear protocol will cause the communication to break down.

Input routine

The `readFromSocket()` method takes a `Socket` parameter and returns a `String`:

```
protected String readFromSocket(Socket sock) throws IOException {
    iStream = sock.getInputStream();
    String str="";
    char c;
    while (  ( c = (char) iStream.read() ) != '\n')
        str = str + c + "";
    return str;
}
```

It uses the `Socket.getInputStream()` method to obtain a reference to the socket's input stream, which has already been created. So here, again, it is important that you don't close the stream in this method. A socket's input and output streams will be closed automatically when the socket connection itself is closed.

The `InputStream.read()` method reads a single byte at a time from the input stream until an end-of-line character is received. For this particular application, the client and server will both read and write one line of characters at a time. Note the use of the cast operator, `(char)`, in the `read()` statement. Because `bytes` are being read, they must be converted to `char` before they can be compared to the end-of-line character or concatenated to the `String`. When the read loop encounters an end-of-line character, it terminates and returns the `String` that was input.

DEBUGGING TIP: Bytes and Chars. It is a syntax error to compare a `byte` and a `char`. One must be converted to the other using an explicit cast operator.

15.7 CASE STUDY: Generic Client/Server Classes

Problem statement

Suppose your boss asks you to set up generic client/server classes that can be used to implement a number of related client/server applications. One application that the company has in mind is a query service, in which the client would send a query string to the server, and the server would interpret the string and return a string that provides the answer. For example, the client might send the query "Hours of service," and the client would respond with the company's business hours.

Another application the company wants will have the client fill out an order form and transmit it as a string to the server. The server will interpret the order, fill it, and return a receipt, including instructions as to when the customer will receive the order.

All of the applications to be supported by this generic client/server will communicate via strings, so something very much like the `readFromSocket()` and `writeToSocket()` methods can be used for their communication. Of course, you want to design classes so they can be easily extended to support byte-oriented, two-way communications, should that type of service become needed.

The echo service

In order to test the generic models, we will subclass them to create a simple echo service. This service will echo back to the client any message that the server receives. For example, we'll have the client accept keyboard input from the user and then send the user's input to the server and simply report what the server returns. The following shows the output generated by a typical client session.

```
CLIENT: connected to 'troy.cs.trincoll.edu'
SERVER: Hello, how may I help you?
CLIENT: type a line or 'goodbye' to quit
INPUT: hello
SERVER: You said 'hello'
INPUT: this is fun
SERVER: You said 'this is fun'
INPUT: java java java
SERVER: You said 'java java java'
INPUT: goodbye
SERVER: Goodbye
CLIENT: connection closed
```

On the server side, the client's message will be read from the input stream and then simply echoed back (with a some additional characters attached) through the output stream. The server doesn't display a trace of its activity other than to report when connections are established and closed. We will code the server in an infinite loop so that it will accept connections from a (potentially) endless stream of clients. In fact, most servers are coded in this way. They are designed to run forever, and must be restarted whenever the host that they are running needs to be rebooted. The output from a typical server session is as follows:

```
Echo server at troy.cs.trincoll.edu/157.252.16.21 waiting for connections
Accepted a connection from troy.cs.trincoll.edu/157.252.16.21
Closed the connection

Accepted a connection from troy.cs.trincoll.edu/157.252.16.21
Closed the connection
```

EFFECTIVE DESIGN: Infinite Loop. A server is an application that's designed to run in an infinite loop. The loop should be exited only when some kind of exception occurs.

15.7.1 Object-Oriented Design

A suitable solution for this project will make extensive use of object-oriented design principles. We want `Server` and `Client` classes that can easily be subclassed to support a wide variety of services. The solution should make appropriate use of *inheritance* and *polymorphism* in its design. Perhaps the best way to develop our generic class is first to design the echo service, as a typical example, and then generalize it.

The Threaded Root Subclass: `ClientServer`

One lesson we can draw at the outset is that both clients and servers use basically the same socket I/O methods. Thus, as we've seen, the `readFromSocket()` and `writeToSocket()` methods could be used by both clients and servers. Because we want all clients and servers to inherit these methods, they must be placed in a common superclass. Let's name this the `ClientServer` class.

Where should we place this class in the Java hierarchy? Should it be a direct subclass of `Object`, or should it extend some other class that would give it appropriate functionality? One feature that would make our clients and servers more useful is if they were independent threads. That way they could be instantiated as part of another object and given the subtask of communicating on behalf of that object. For example, if we give our `CyberPet` a `Client` object, the `CyberPet` could use it to communicate with a server.

The class hierarchy

Therefore, let's define the `ClientServer` class as a subclass of `Thread`. Recall from Chapter 13 that the typical way to derive functionality from a `Thread` subclass is to override the `run()` method. The `run()` method will be a good place to implement the client and server protocols. Because they are different, we'll define `run()` in both the `Client` and `Server` subclasses.

Inheritance

For now, the only methods contained in `ClientServer` (Figure 15–19) are the two I/O methods we designed. The only modification we have made to the methods occurs in the `writeToSocket()` method, where we have added code to make sure that any strings written to the socket are terminated with an end-of-line character.

This is an important enhancement, because the read loop in the `readFromSocket()` method expects to receive an end-of-line character. Rather than rely on those who implement specific clients to guarantee that their strings end with `\n`, our design takes care of this problem for them. This

Figure 15–19 The `ClientServer` class serves as the root class for a client and server applications.

```
import java.io.*;
import java.net.*;

public class ClientServer extends Thread {

    protected InputStream iStream;           // Instance variables
    protected OutputStream oStream;

    protected String readFromSocket(Socket sock) throws IOException {
        iStream = sock.getInputStream();
        String str="";
        char c;
        while (  ( c = (char) iStream.read() ) != '\n')
            str = str + c + "";
            return str;
        }

    protected void writeToSocket(Socket sock, String str) throws IOException {
        oStream = sock.getOutputStream();
        if (str.charAt( str.length() - 1 ) != '\n')
            str = str + '\n';
        for (int k = 0; k < str.length() ; k++)
            oStream.write(str.charAt(k));
    }// writeToSocket()
}// ClientServer
```

ensures that every communication that takes place between one of our clients and servers will be line oriented.

EFFECTIVE DESIGN: Defensive Design. Code that performs I/O, whether it be across the network or otherwise, should be designed to anticipate and remedy common errors. This will lead to more robust programs.

15.7.2 The `EchoServer` Class

What data do we need?

Let's now develop a design for the echo server. This class will be a subclass of `ClientServer`. As we saw in discussing the server protocol, one task that echo server will do is create a `ServerSocket` and establish a port number for its service. Then it will wait for a `Socket` connection, and once a connection is accepted, it will then communicate with the client. This suggests that our server needs at least two instance variables. It also suggests that the task of creating a `ServerSocket` would be an appropriate action for its constructor method. This leads to the following initial definition:

```
import java.net.*;
import java.io.*;

public class EchoServer extends ClientServer {

    private ServerSocket port;
    private Socket socket;

    public EchoServer( int portNum, int nBacklog)  {
        try {
            port = new ServerSocket (portNum, nBacklog);
        } catch (IOException e) {
            e.printStackTrace();
        }
    }

    public void run() { }  // Stub method
}// EchoServer
```

Note that the constructor method catches the `IOException`. Note also that we have included a stub version of `run()`, which we want to define in this class.

The server algorithm

Once `EchoServer` has set up a port, it should issue the `port.accept()` method and wait for a client to connect. This part of the server protocol belongs in the `run()` method. Most servers are designed to run in an infinite loop. That is, they don't just handle one request and then quit. Instead, once started (usually by the system), they repeatedly handle requests until deliberately stopped by the system. This leads to the following run algorithm:

```
public void run() {
    try {
        System.out.println("Echo server at "
                         + InetAddress.getLocalHost() + " waiting for connections ");
        while(true) {
            socket = port.accept();
            System.out.println("Accepted a connection from " + socket.getInetAddress());
            provideService(socket);
            socket.close();
            System.out.println("Closed the connection\n");
        }
    } catch (IOException e) {
        e.printStackTrace();
    }
}// run()
```

Note that for simplicity we are printing the server's status messages on `System.out`. Ordinarily these should go to a log file. Note also that the details of the actual service algorithm are hidden in the `provideService()` method.

The `provideService()` method consists of writing a greeting to the client, and then repeatedly reading a string from the input stream and echoing it back to the client via the output stream. This is easily done using the `writeToSocket()` and `readFromSocket()` methods we developed. The implementation of this method is shown, along with the complete implementation of `EchoServer` in Figure 15–20.

The protocol used by `EchoServer.provideService()` starts by saying "hello" and loops until the client says "goodbye." When the client says "goodbye," the server responds with "goodbye." In all other cases it responds with "You said X," where X is the string that was received from the client. Note the use of the `toLowerCase()` method to convert client messages to lowercase. This simplifies the task of checking for "goodbye."

EFFECTIVE DESIGN: Defensive Design. Converting I/O to lowercase helps to minimize miscommunication between a client and server and leads to a more robust protocol.

This completes the design of the `EchoServer`. We have deliberately designed it in a way that will make it easy to convert into a generic server. Hence the motivation for using `provideService()` as the name of function that provides the echo service. In order to turn `EchoServer` into a generic `Server` class, we can simply make `provideService()` an abstract method, leaving its implementation to the `Server` subclasses. We'll discuss the details of this change below.

Designing for extensibility

EFFECTIVE DESIGN: Encapsulation. Encapsulating a portion of the algorithm into a separate method makes it easy to change the algorithm by overriding the method.

Figure 15–20 The service provided by EchoServer is simply to echo the client's message.

```
import java.net.*;
import java.io.*;

public class EchoServer extends ClientServer {

    private ServerSocket port;
    private Socket socket;

    public EchoServer( int portNum, int nBacklog)  {
        try {
            port = new ServerSocket (portNum, nBacklog);
        } catch (IOException e) {
            e.printStackTrace();
        }
    }

    public void run() {
        try {
            System.out.println("Echo server at "
                              + InetAddress.getLocalHost() + " waiting for connections ");
            while(true) {
                socket = port.accept();
                System.out.println("Accepted a connection from " + socket.getInetAddress());
                provideService(socket);
                socket.close();
                System.out.println("Closed the connection\n");
            }
        } catch (IOException e) {
             e.printStackTrace();
        }
    }// run()

    protected void provideService (Socket socket) {
        String str="";
        try {
            writeToSocket(socket, "Hello, how may I help you?\n");
            do {
                str = readFromSocket(socket);
                if (str.toLowerCase().equals("goodbye"))
                    writeToSocket(socket, "Goodbye\n");
                else
                    writeToSocket( socket, "You said '" + str + "'\n");
            }  while (!str.toLowerCase().equals("goodbye"));
        } catch (IOException e) {
            e.printStackTrace();
        }
    }// provideServer()

    public static void main(String args[]) {
        EchoServer server = new EchoServer(10001,3);
        server.start();
    }// main()
}// EchoServer
```

15.7.3 The EchoClient Class

The EchoClient class is just as easy to design. It too will be a subclass of ClientServer. It needs an instance variable for the Socket that it will use, and its constructor should be responsible for opening a socket connection to a particular server and port. The main part of its protocol should be placed in the run() method. Its initial definition is as follows:

```
import java.net.*;
import java.io.*;

public class EchoClient extends ClientServer {

    protected Socket socket;

    public EchoClient(String url, int port) {
        try {
            socket = new Socket(url, port);
            System.out.println("CLIENT: connected to " + url + ":" + port);
        } catch (Exception e) {
            e.printStackTrace();
            System.exit(1);
        }
    }// EchoClient()

   public void run() { }// Stub method
}// EchoClient
```

The constructor method takes two parameters that specify the URL and port number of the echo server. By making these parameters, instead of hard coding them within the method, we give the client the flexibility to connect to servers on a variety of hosts.

As with other clients, EchoClient's run() method will consist of requesting some kind of service from the server. Our initial design called for EchoClient to repeatedly input a line from the user, send the line to the server, and then display the server's response. Thus, for this particular client, the service requested consists of the following algorithm:

The client algorithm

```
Wait for the server to say "hello".
Repeat
    Prompt and get and line of input from the user.
    Send the user's line to the server.
    Read the server's response.
    Display the response to the user.
until the user types "goodbye"
```

With an eye toward eventually turning EchoClient into a generic client, let's encapsulate this procedure into a requestService() method, which we can simply call from the run() method. This method will take a Socket parameter and perform all the I/O for this particular client:

```
protected void requestService(Socket socket) throws IOException {
    String servStr = readFromSocket(socket);          // Check for "Hello"
    System.out.println("SERVER: " + servStr);         // Report the server's response
    System.out.println("CLIENT: type a line or 'goodbye' to quit");// Prompt the user
    if (servStr.substring(0,5).equals("Hello")) {
        String userStr = "";
        do {
            userStr = readFromKeyboard();                  // Get input from user
            writeToSocket(socket, userStr + "\n");         // Send it to server
            servStr = readFromSocket(socket);              // Read the server's response
            System.out.println("SERVER: " + servStr);      // Report the server's response
        } while (!userStr.toLowerCase().equals("goodbye"));// Until user says 'goodbye'
    }
}// requestService()
```

Although this method involves several lines, they should all be familiar to you. Each time client reads a message from the socket, it prints it on `System.out`. The first message it reads should start with the substring "Hello." This is part of its protocol with the client. Note how the `substring()` method is used to test for this. After the initial greeting from the server, the client begins reading user input from the keyboard, writing it to the socket, then reading the server's response, and displaying it on `System.out`.

Note that the task of reading user input from the keyboard has been made into a separate method, which is one we've used before:

```
protected String readFromKeyboard( ) throws IOException {
    BufferedReader input = new BufferedReader(new InputStreamReader(System.in));
    System.out.print("INPUT: ");
    String line = input.readLine();
    return line;
}// readFromKeyboard()
```

The only method remaining to be defined is the `run()`, which is shown together with the complete definition of `EchoClient` in Figure 15–21. The `run()` method can simply call the `requestService()` method. When control returns from the `requestService()` method, `run()` closes the socket connection. Because `requestService()` may throw an `IOException`, the entire method must be embedded within a `try/catch` block that catches that exception.

Testing the Echo Service

Both `EchoServer` and `EchoClient` contain `main()` methods (Figures 15–20 and 15–21). In order to test the programs, you would run the server on one computer and the client on another computer. (Actually they can both be run on the same computer, although they wouldn't know this and would still access each other through a socket connection.)

The `EchoServer` must be started first, so that its service will be available when the client starts running. It has pick a port number. In this case it picks 10001. The only constraint on its choice is that it cannot use one of the privileged port numbers — those below 1024 — and it cannot use a port that's already in use.

```
public static void main(String args[]) {
    EchoServer server = new EchoServer(10001,3);
    server.start();
}// main()
```

When an `EchoClient` is created, it must be given the server's URL (`troy.trincoll.edu`) and the port that the service is using:

Figure 15–21 The EchoClient class prompts the user for a string and then sends it to the EchoServer, which simply echoes it back.

```
import java.net.*;
import java.io.*;

public class EchoClient extends ClientServer {

    protected Socket socket;

    public EchoClient(String url, int port) {
        try {
            socket = new Socket(url, port);
            System.out.println("CLIENT: connected to " + url + ":" + port);
        } catch (Exception e) {
            e.printStackTrace();
            System.exit(1);
        }
    }// EchoClient()

    public void run() {
        try {
            requestService(socket);
            socket.close();
            System.out.println("CLIENT: connection closed");
        } catch (IOException e) {
            System.out.println(e.getMessage());
            e.printStackTrace();
        }
    }// run()

    protected void requestService(Socket socket) throws IOException {
        String servStr = readFromSocket(socket);          // Check for "Hello"
        System.out.println("SERVER: " + servStr);         // Report the server's response
        System.out.println("CLIENT: type a line or 'goodbye' to quit");// Prompt the user
        if (servStr.substring(0,5).equals("Hello")) {
            String userStr = "";
            do {
                userStr = readFromKeyboard();                   // Get input from user
                writeToSocket(socket, userStr + "\n");          // Send it to server
                servStr = readFromSocket(socket);               // Read the server's response
                System.out.println("SERVER: " + servStr);       // Report the server's response
            } while (!userStr.toLowerCase().equals("goodbye"));// Until user says 'goodbye'
        }
    }// requestService()

    protected String readFromKeyboard( ) throws IOException {
        BufferedReader input = new BufferedReader(new InputStreamReader(System.in));
        System.out.print("INPUT: ");
        String line = input.readLine();
        return line;
    }// readFromKeyboard()

    public static void main(String args[]) {
        EchoClient client = new EchoClient("troy.trincoll.edu",10001);
       client.start();
    }// main()
}// EchoClient
```

```
public static void main(String args[]) {
    EchoClient client = new EchoClient("troy.trincoll.edu",10001);
    client.start();
}// main()
```

As they are presently coded, you will have to modify both EchoServer and EchoClient to provide the correct URL and port for your environment. In testing this program, you may wish to experiment by trying to introduce various errors into the code and observe the results. When you run the service, you should observe something like the following output on the client side.

```
CLIENT: connected to troy.trincoll.edu:10001
SERVER: Hello, how may I help you?
CLIENT: type a line or 'goodbye' to quit
INPUT: this is a test
SERVER: You said 'this is a test'
INPUT: goodbye
SERVER: Goodbye
CLIENT: connection closed
```

15.7.4 Abstracting the Generic Server

This completes the design and testing of the generic echo service. It is based on a common root class, ClientServer, a subclass of Thread. Both EchoServer and EchoClient extend the root class, and each implements its own version of run(). How can we turn this design into one that can be used to support a wide range of services?

Designing for extensibility

The answer lies in being able to distinguish what is common to all servers and clients and what is particular to the echo service and client. Clearly, the general server and client protocols, as defined here in their respective run() methods, is something that all servers and clients have in common. What differs from one application to another is the particular service provided and requested, as detailed in their respective provideService() and requestService() methods.

Abstract service methods

Therefore, the way to generalize this application is to define the run() method in the generic Server and Client classes. This method calls provideService() and requestService(), respectively, so these methods must be declared as abstract methods in the Server and Client classes, respectively. Any class that contains an abstract method must itself be declared abstract. This leads to the definition of Server shown in Figure 15–22. Note that provideService() is left unimplemented. Servers such as EchoServer can implement provideService() in a way that is appropriate for that particular service.

EFFECTIVE DESIGN: Polymorphism Defining a method as abstract within a superclass, and implementing it in various ways in subclasses, is an example of polymorphism. Polymorphism is a powerful object-oriented design technique.

Figure 15–22 The abstract `Server` class.

```
import java.net.*;
import java.io.*;

public abstract class Server extends ClientServer {

    protected ServerSocket port;
    protected Socket socket;

    public Server(int portNum, int nBacklog)  {
        try {
            port = new ServerSocket (portNum, nBacklog);
        } catch (IOException e) {
            e.printStackTrace();
        }
    }// Server()

    public void run() {
        try {
            System.out.println("Server at " + InetAddress.getLocalHost() + " waiting for connections ");
            while (true) {
                socket = port.accept();
                System.out.println("Accepted a connection from " + socket.getInetAddress());
                provideService(socket);
                socket.close();
                System.out.println("Closed the connection\n");
            }// while
        } catch (IOException e) {
            e.printStackTrace();
        }
    }// run()

    protected abstract void provideService(Socket socket);  // Implemented in server subclasses

}// Server
```

Extensibility

Given the abstract definition of the `Server` class, defining a new service is simply a matter of extending `Server` and implementing `provideService()`, as the new definition of `EchoServer` illustrates (Figure 15–23). Note that `EchoServer` contains a `main()` method. This will enable us to test it, but this would be omitted if `EchoServer` were to be used as part of another application.

Creating new clients

The same points apply to the relationship between the abstract `Client` class (Figure15–24) and its extension in `EchoClient` (Figure 15–25). The `requestService()` method is called by `Client.run()`. It is implemented in `EchoServer`. In this way any number of clients can be derived from `Client` by simply implementing their own `requestService()` method. Note that we have left the `readFromKeyboard()` method in the `Client` class. This is a useful, general method that can be used by a large variety of clients, so it is best if they don't have to redefine it themselves.

Figure 15–23 The EchoServer class.

```
import java.net.*;
import java.io.*;

public class EchoServer extends Server {

    public EchoServer( int port, int backlog) {
        super(port,backlog);
    }

    protected void provideService (Socket socket) {
       String str="";
       try {
           writeToSocket(socket, "Hello, how may I help you?\n");
           do {
               str = readFromSocket(socket);
               if (str.toLowerCase().equals("goodbye"))
                   writeToSocket(socket, "Goodbye\n");
               else
                   writeToSocket(socket, "You said '" + str + "'\n");
           }  while (!str.toLowerCase().equals("goodbye"));
       } catch (IOException e) {
           e.printStackTrace();
       }
    }// provideService()

    public static void main(String args[]) {
        EchoServer server = new EchoServer(10001,5);
        server.start();
    }// main()
}// EchoServer
```

Figure 15–24 The abstract Client class.

```
import java.net.*;
import java.io.*;

public abstract class Client extends ClientServer {

    protected Socket socket;

    public Client(String url, int port) {
        try {
            socket = new Socket(url,port);
            System.out.println("CLIENT: connected to " + url + ":" + port);
        } catch (Exception e) {
            e.printStackTrace();
            System.exit(1);
        }
    }// Client()

    public void run() {
        try {
            requestService(socket);
            socket.close();
            System.out.println("CLIENT: connection closed");
        } catch (IOException e) {
            System.out.println(e.getMessage());
            e.printStackTrace();
        }
    }// run()

    protected abstract void requestService(Socket socket) throws IOException;

    protected String readFromKeyboard( ) throws IOException {
        BufferedReader input = new BufferedReader ( new InputStreamReader (System.in) );
        System.out.print("INPUT: ");
        String line = input.readLine();
        return line;
    }// readFromKeyboard()
}// Client
```

Figure 15–25 The derived `EchoClient` class.

```
import java.net.*;
import java.io.*;

public class EchoClient extends Client {

    public EchoClient( String url, int port ) {
        super(url,port);
    }

    protected void requestService(Socket socket) throws IOException {
        String servStr = readFromSocket(socket);          // Check FOR "Hello"
        System.out.println("SERVER: " + servStr);         // Report the server's response
        System.out.println("CLIENT: type a line or 'goodbye' to quit");// Prompt the user
        if ( servStr.substring(0,5).equals("Hello") ) {
            String userStr = "";
            do {
                userStr = readFromKeyboard();                 // Get input from user
                writeToSocket(socket, userStr + "\n");        // Send it to server
                servStr = readFromSocket(socket);             // Read the server's response
                System.out.println("SERVER: " + servStr);     // Report the server's response
            } while(!userStr.toLowerCase().equals("goodbye"));// Until user says 'goodbye'
        }
    }// requestService()

    public static void main(String args[]) {
        EchoClient client = new EchoClient("troy.trincoll.edu", 10001);
        client.start();
    }// main()
}// EchoClient
```

The overall design of the echo service consist of five classes organized into the hierarchy shown in Figure 15–26. At the root of the hierarchy is the ClientServer class, which contains nothing but I/O methods used by both clients and servers. The abstract `Server` and `Client` classes contain implementations of the `Thread.run()` method, which defines the basic protocols for servers and clients. Finally, the details of the particular service are encoded in the `provideService()` and `requestService()` methods.

EFFECTIVE DESIGN: Inheritance By placing as much functionality as possible into a generic client/server superclass, you can simplify the creation of new services. This is an effective use of Java's inheritance mechanism.

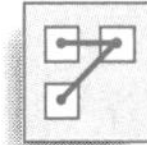

SELF-STUDY EXERCISES

EXERCISE 15.7 The design of the client/server hierarchy makes it easy to create a new service by extending both the `Server` and `Client` classes. Describe how you would implement the scramble service using this model. The scramble service is useful for people trying to solve the daily scramble puzzles given in many newspapers. Given a string of letters, the scramble service will return a string containing all possible permutations of the letter. For example, given "cat," the scramble service will return "act atc cat cta tac tca."

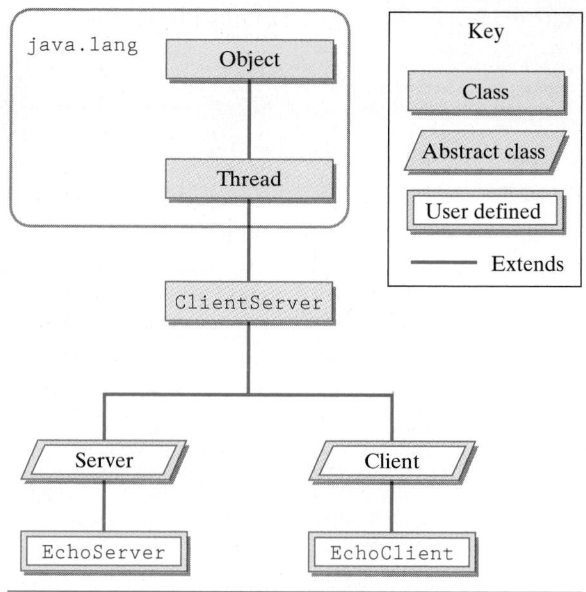

Figure 15–26 The Echo Service classes.

15.7.5 Testing the Echo Service

Testing the revised version of the echo service will be no different than for the original version. The service will work exactly the same way as in the original version, even though we have given it a different implementation. The advantage of our new design is not in its functionality, but in the fact that it can be easily extended to create other services.

To test the service, you want to run both `EchoServer` and `EchoClient` at the same time, and preferably on different computers. As they are presently coded, you will have to modify both `EchoServer` and `EchoClient` to provide the correct URL and port for your environment.

SELF-STUDY EXERCISES

EXERCISE 15.8 Describe what happens when each of the following errors is introduced into the `EchoClient` or `EchoServer` programs.

- Specify the wrong host name when running `EchoClient`.
- Specify the wrong port number when running `EchoClient`.
- Remove the reference to `\n` in the `writeToSocket()` call in `requestService()`.

15.8 Java Network Security Restrictions

One of the most attractive features of Java is that extensive effort has been made to make it a *secure* language. This is especially important for a language that makes it so easy to implement networking applications. After all, nobody wants to download a Java applet that proceeds to erase the hard disk. Such an applet might be written by a cyber terrorist, deliberately aiming to cause severe damage, or it might be written by a cyberdoofus, who inadvertently writes code that does severe damage.

Code verification

What are some of Java's techniques for guarding against either deliberately or inadvertently insecure code? One level of security is Java's *bytecode verification* process which the Java Virtual Machine performs on any "untrusted" code that it receives. Java checks every class that it loads into memory to make sure it doesn't contain illegal or insecure code. Another line of defense is the so-called **sandbox model**, which refers to the practice of restricting the kinds of things that certain programs can do. For example, the "sandbox" environment made available to Java applets restricts them from having any access whatsoever to the local file system.

Limited privileges

Limited network access

Another restriction imposed on applets is to limit their networking capabilities. For example, a Java applet cannot create a network connection to any computer except the one from which its code was downloaded. Also, a Java applet cannot listen for, or accept, connections on privileged ports — those numbered 1024 or lower. Together, these two restrictions severely limit the kinds of client/server programs that can be build as applets.

Java sets aside certain locations as repositories for **trusted code**. For example, the Java class libraries would be placed in such a location, as would the directories where your Java programs are stored. Any class loaded from some other directory is considered *untrusted*. By this definition, applets downloaded over the Internet would be considered untrusted code.

Trusted code

In addition to the above restrictions for applets, which apply to all untrusted code, Java defines a number of other limitations:

- Untrusted code cannot make use of certain system facilities, such as `System.exit()`, and classes in the `java.security` package.
- Untrusted code cannot make use of certain AWT methods, such as methods that access the system clipboard. Another AWT restriction is that any window created by untrusted code must display a message informing the user that it is untrusted. You may have seen such messages on windows opened from applets.
- Untrusted code is limited to the kinds of threads it can create.

New security enhancements introduced in JDK 1.2 are based on the concepts of "permission" and "policy." Code is assigned "permissions" based on the security policy currently in effect. Each permission specifies the type of access allowed for a particular resource (such as "read" and "write" access to a specified file or directory, "connect" access to a given host and port, etc.). The policy that controls permissions can be initialized from an external configurable policy file. Unless a permission is explicitly granted to code, it cannot access the resource that is guarded by that permission. These new enhancements offer a more fine-grained and extensible approach to security for both applets and applications.

As this brief overview illustrates, the Java Virtual Machine is designed with security as one of its primary issues. This doesn't guarantee 100 percent security, but it is a big improvement over some of the languages and systems that preceded Java. Moreover, security is an ongoing concern of the Java development process. Flaws in the existing security system are fixed very quickly. Advanced methods are constantly being developed and incorporated into the system. One such enhancement is the use of encryption to guarantee the integrity of classes transferred over the network.

IN THE LABORATORY: THE INTERNET CyberPet

The purpose of this lab is to develop a stock market quote service by extending the generic client/server model developed in the generic client/server example. As the interface to this service, the client will use our familiar CyberPet interface. The objectives of this lab are

- To extend the `Server` and `Client` class to define a new client/server application.
- To write a method that reads a file of stock quotes.
- To incorporate the client object within a CyberPet object.

Problem Description

Stock quote service

Design and implement a stock market quote service by extending the client/server model developed in the generic client/server. The stock market quotes will be stored in a tab delimited text file that is accessible to the server—for example, in the directory of the server itself. The service works as follows: The client prompts the user for the stock's symbol. It then sends the symbol, as a query, to the quote server. The quote server looks up the stock in the file and returns, as a single line, the stock symbol, name, and current price. If the server can't find the stock, it should return a line which reports `"ERROR: Stock not found."` The client should report this error as `"Sorry, the stock you requested cannot be found. Please make sure your symbol is correct and try again."`

The quote file stores the stock data as tab delimited text, with one stock per line. That is, there is a tab character, `\t`, between each field in the line:

```
AppleC    Apple Computer    45.0
Cisco     Cisco Systems     103.58
Intel     Intel             129.25
MCSFT     Microsoft         150.50
Netscpe   Netscape          63.87
SunMic    Sun Microsystems  89.75
```

User Interface

The Graphical User Interface (GUI) should contain a `JTextField` into which the user can enter the stock's symbol, and a `JTextArea` where the client can report the stock quotes. It is not necessary to clear the `JTextArea` after every quote. For example, Figure 15–27 shows an appropriate design for a simple client interface.

Privacy and the Internet

The Intel Corporation was recently awarded an "Orwell Award" by the London-based privacy advocacy group, Privacy International. The awards recognize government or private groups that have done the most to invade personal privacy in the United States. The award was announced at a "Big Brother Awards" ceremony, scheduled to coincide with the fiftieth anniversary of the publication of George Orwell's classic novel, *1984*.

Intel was cited for its controversial Pentium III chip, which includes a Processor Serial Number (PSN). According to Intel, the purpose of the PSN is to help identify and authenticate users in electronic commerce and other Internet applications. Its intended goal is to make the Internet more secure and reliable as a medium for business and commerce. Privacy advocates worry that the PSN, which can be accessed remotely across the Internet, will be used by mass marketers and others to link users' Internet transactions and further encroach on their privacy.

In some ways the PSN would function like a universal *cookie*. As you may know, a cookie is an identifier that's placed on your PC by a remote Web site. It helps the Web site identify you in future transactions so that it can customize its services to you. Browsers are programmed to ask your permission before storing cookies on your system. However, most browsers allow you to give blanket permission, after which any Web site can simply store cookies on your system without your necessarily being aware of it. One problem with cookies is that they differ in format and content from site to site. However, representatives of the marketing industry have been pushing for standardization of cookies so that consumer information can be more easily shared.

In addition to viewing it as a potential threat to consumer privacy, Intel's PSN has also come under criticism from computer security professionals who believe that the software designed to access the PSN would not be completely protected from hackers intent on forging the PSN.

The Intel/PSN controversy serves to illustrate the basic tension that exists between two conflicting needs: the need to ensure that commerce and financial transactions can be performed securely, and the need to guard the consumer's right to privacy. While this particular controversy may pass, it will undoubtedly be followed by similar issues. If you are interested in this and related issues, a good place to start your search would be by visiting the Electronic Freedom Foundation (EFF) Web site at `http://www.eff.org/`.

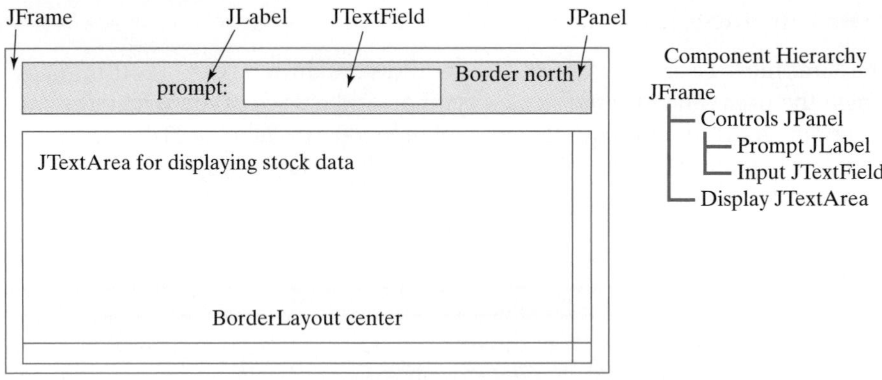

Figure 15–27 A GUI design for the stock quote application.

Designing the Stock Quote Service

It is important that the user interface for this application be kept distinct from the client itself. That will make it possible for the client part of the service to be attached to other interfaces — for example, a CyberPet interface.

Problem Decomposition

What objects do we need?

Our goal is to develop a client/server application to provide stock quotes. Given that we want the interface to be kept separate from the client, this suggests that we need three separate classes:

1. `StockServer` will supply stock quotes.
2. `StockClient` will request stock quotes on behalf of the user.
3. `ClientInterface` will get the user input and pass it along to the `StockClient` object.

Design: `StockServer`

The `StockServer` class should be derived from the generic `Server` class. You should use the `EchoServer` (Figure 15–23) as a model. What's new in `StockServer` is that it has to be able to read stock data from a file in order to supply answers to the queries it will receive. One strategy that the server could use is to read the entire file of quotes into some sort of memory structure when it starts up and then just look them up from there as needed. However, because it's important that the stock quotes be up to date, it's probably a better idea to search the quote file itself each time a query is received.

What methods do we need?

One method that the StockServer must implement is the provide Service() method. Once a proper connection is established with the client, this method should carry out something like the following algorithm:

1. Read a stock symbol from the client [readFromSocket()].
2. Look up the symbol's record in stock file.
3. Write a reply to the client writeToSocket().

What methods does the StockServer need, in addition to provideService()? Steps 1 and 3 of the above algorithm should be simple method calls. However, step 2 will require several statements, and possibly even additional methods. Therefore, let's design a method, named getQuoteBySymbol(), to handle this task.

The getQuoteBySymbol() method

According to our specification, the server should receive a symbol string from the client and return a string to the client. This suggests that the getQuoteBySymbol() method should take a String parameter, the stock symbol, and return a String result, the complete stock quote, as described in the specification. Because this method will be used only within this class, it should be declared private.

Algorithm design

In terms of an algorithm for this method, have we already solved the problem of reading data from a text file? Yes. The following algorithm from Chapter 14 can easily be adapted to read the stock file:

```
BufferedReader inStream =                    // Create an input stream
    new BufferedReader (new FileReader(fileName)); // And open the file
String line = inStream.readLine();           // Read one line
while (line != null) {                       // As long as there are more lines
    display.append(line + "\n");             //  Display the current line
    line = inStream.readLine();              //  Read the next line
}
inStream.close();                            // close the input stream
```

What sort of adaptations will we need to make? One change is that it may not be necessary to read every line of the file. If we find the stock we're searching for before the end of the file, we can just execute a return statement, thereby exiting the while loop before the end of file. Some of the other design questions you should think about in designing this method are

- How will you break apart the input line into the individual fields? (*Hint*: Use the StringTokenizer class.)
- What if the symbol passed by the client is in uppercase, but the stock symbol in the file is lowercase?
- How will you handle the case where the stock is not found in the file?

The StockClient Class

The StockClient class should be derived from Client (Figure 15–24). Therefore, it must implement the requestService() method. What's new in this class is that we want to separate its communication functions from its interface functions. Recall that EchoClient used a method named readFromKeyBoard() to get the user's query. We want StockClient to get its input — a stock symbol — from the interface. Another difference is that StockClient should respond to the user's initiatives, rather than simply run through a loop that prompts the user on each iteration. How can these changes be done?

Service duration?

Another design issue for StockClient concerns how long it should keep open the connection. The user will initiate queries, so it would not be good design to keep the connection open if the user hasn't even requested a stock quote. To do so would prevent other clients from accessing the server. A better strategy would be to create a new StockClient each time the user initiates a query, have the client make one query, and then say goodbye.

Algorithm design

It looks as if we don't want our StockClient to run() in a loop at all. To prevent this we just won't call its start() method. Instead, we want to be able to call a method (from the interface class) that causes the StockClient to send a query to the StockServer. Thus, we need a public method that takes a String parameter, a stock symbol, and returns a String, the stock quote. An appropriate algorithm for the getQuote() method would be

```
public String getQuote( String symbol ) {
    String replyStr = "";
  // write the symbol to the socket
  // read the server's reply
  // say "goodbye" to the server
   return replyStr;
}
```

Given this design for getQuote(), each time the user initiates a query through the interface, the interface class would execute something like the following code:

```
StockClient sc = new StockClient( host, port );
String result = sc.getQuote( symbol );
```

What about the requestService() method? How would our design make use of it? It looks as if we don't even need to use this method, so we can just implement it as a stub method — that is, we can leave its body empty. In other words, this subclass of client will not use the run() or the requestService() methods.

Design: Client/Server Communication

Protocol design

In designing a client/server application, you must take care that both the server and the client know each other's protocol. For example, after the connection is made, will the server say "hello" rather than just waiting for a query from the client? If so, then the client must read the "hello" before sending a query. Similarly, how will the client indicate that it is done? The server must be aware of how the client says "goodbye" so that it can close the connection. The important point is that both the client and server must agree upon the protocol they will use for communication. Otherwise communication will inevitably break down.

Design: `ClientInterface`

Develop a simple frame-based interface to test your client. This class should implement the GUI described earlier.

Debugging and Testing

Testing a client/server application presents a real challenge because there are so many different kinds of things that can go wrong. That's why it is especially important to develop your application in stages using stepwise refinement. Here's a stepwise development plan that you might wish to follow:

Stepwise refinement

1. Test that `StockServer` successfully waits for a connection.
2. Test that `StockServer` can find a symbol in the data file.
3. Test that `StockClient` successfully makes a connection to `StockServer`
4. Test that `StockServer` and `StockClient` can successfully communicate an appropriate "hello" and "goodbye" protocol.
5. Test that `StockClient` can send an appropriately formatted query to `StockServer`.
6. Test that `StockServer` returns the correct result.

One advantage of using a tab-delimited text file, instead of a binary file, is that you can easily type in some test data.

The Stock Quoting CyberPet (Optional)

Once you have successfully tested the stock quote service using the simple frame-based interface, incorporate a `StockClient` into a `CyberPet` interface. There are a number of interesting ways you might do this:

- Have CyberPet give up eating, sleeping, or thinking in favor of making stock quotes!
- Have CyberPet make autonomous recommendations based on the stock quotes — "Apple Computer is currently 60.5. You should buy some."
- Create your own images for a CyberStockPet and make stock quoting its only activity.

CHAPTER SUMMARY

Technical Terms

block, domain name, ethernet, command-line argument, Internet protocol, packet, Internet, protocol, router, port, server, socket, sandbox security model, Uniform Resource Locator (URL), stream, busy waiting, client

New Java Keywords

`abstract`, `null`, `private`, `protected`, `public`, `try/catch`

Java Classes

`AudioClip`, `DatagramPacket`, `DatagramSocket`, `IOException`, `Image`, `InputStream`, `InterruptedException`, `ItemListener`, `JComponent`, `JApplet`, `JButton`, `JTextField`, `JFrame`, `JTextArea`, `ServerSocket`, `MalformedURLException`, `OutputStream`, `Thread`, `Socket()`, `System`, `Toolkit`, `URL`

Java Library Methods

`accept()`, `actionPerformed()`, `beep()`, `close()`, `getAudioClip()`, `getImage()`, `init()`, `itemStateChanged()`, `openConnection()`, `openStream()`, `paint()`, `play()`, `read()`, `write()`, `readLine()`, `repaint()`, `run()`, `sleep()`, `start()`

User-Defined Classes

`Client`, `ClientInterface`, `ClientServer`, `CyberPet`, `EchoClient`, `EchoServer`, `RealEstateViewer`, `Server`, `SlideShowAplet`, `StockClient`, `StockServer`, `Timer`

User-Defined Methods

`currentImage()`, `getQuote()`, `getQuoteBySymbol()`, `initHomeChoices()`, `nextImage()`, `nextSlide()`, `readFromKeyboard()`, `readFromSocket()`, `provideService()`, `requestService()`, `run()`, `writeToSocket()`

Summary of Important Points

- An *internet* is a collection of two or more distinct networks joined by *routers*, which have the task of translating one network's language to the other's. The *Internet* is an internet which uses the *Internet Protocol (IP)* as the translation medium.
- A *protocol* is a set of rules that control the transfer of information between two computers in a network. The *HyperText Transfer Protocol (HTTP)* governs information exchange on the World Wide Web (WWW). The *Simple Mail Transfer Protocol* controls mail service on the Internet. The *File Transfer Protocol (FTP)* controls the transfer of files between Internet computers. The *Domain Name System (DNS)* governs the use of names on the Internet.
- A *client/server* application is one that divides its task between a client, which requests service, and a server, which provides service. Many Internet applications and protocols are based on the client/server model.
- Lower-level protocols, such as the *ethernet protocol* and *token ring protocol*, govern the transmission of data between computers on a single network. The *Internet Protocol (IP)* translates between such protocols.
- A *Uniform Resource Locator (URL)* is a standard way of specifying addresses on the Internet. It consists of several parts separated by slashes and colons: METHOD://HOST:PORT/PATH/FILE. The `java.net.URL` class is used to represent URLs.
- Files of text or data (images, audio files) on the Internet or Web can be downloaded using the same `InputStreams` and `OutputStreams` as files located on a disk. To read or write a resource located on a network, you need to connect its URL to an input or output stream.
- The `java.awt.Toolkit` class contains useful methods for downloading `Images` into an application.
- A *socket* is a two-way communication channel between two running programs on a network. The `java.net.Socket` class can be used to set up communication channels for client/server applications. The *server* process listens at a socket for requests from a client. The *client* process requests service from a server listening at a particular socket. Once a connection exists between client and server, input and output streams are used to read and write data over the socket.

ANSWERS TO SELF-STUDY EXERCISES

EXERCISE 15.1 The fully connected mesh topology requires the most cables.

EXERCISE 15.2 The fully connected mesh topology would have the most potential to use alternate routes if one of the host computers crashed.

EXERCISE 15.3 The star topology would be rendered completely useless if its central hub crashed.

EXERCISE 15.4 Prentice Hall's Web server is located at `http://www.prenhall.com`. The protocol is `http`. The host computer is named `www`. Prentice Hall's domain name is `prenhall`, and it is part of the `com` (commercial) Internet domain.

EXERCISE 15.5

- For buying a piece of software at a bookstore, the server would be the sales clerk. The protocol would be to select the software from off the shelf, bring it to the checkout counter, give the sales clerk the money, and get a receipt.
- For buying a piece of software over the phone, the server would be the telephone sales clerk. The protocol would be to select from a catalog, provide the sales clerk with your credit card information, and say goodbye.
- For buying a piece of software over the Internet, the server would be the computer which handles the transaction. The protocol would be to select the item from a Web-based form, provide the form with personal and payment information, and click on the "buy" button.

EXERCISE 15.6 To play sounds along with slides in the `SlideShowApplet`, you would make the following modifications to the code. Declare an array of `URL`s to store the URLs of the audio files you want to play:

```
private URL soundURL[] = new URL[NIMGS];
```

Assign URLs to the array at the same time you input the images:

```
for (int k=0; k < NIMGS; k++) {
    url = new URL( "http://troy.trincoll.edu/~jjj/gifs/demo" + k + ".gif" ) ;
    slide[k] = getImage( url );
    soundURL[k] = new URL("http://troy.trincoll.edu/~jjj/sounds/demo" + k + ".au");
}
```

Each time an image is displayed in `paint()`, play the corresponding sound by using the URL from the array:

```
public void paint(Graphics g) {
    if (currentImage != null) {
        g.drawImage(currentImage,10,10,this);
        play( soundURL[ currentImage] );
    }
}
```

EXERCISE 15.7 The scramble service would be implemented by defining two new classes: The `ScrambleServer` class is a subclass of `Server`, and the `ScrambleClient` class is a subclass of `Client`. The `ScrambleClient` would implement the `requestService()` method and the `ScrambleServer` would implement the `provideService()` method.

EXERCISE 15.8

- If you specify the wrong host name or port, you will get the following exception: `java.net.ConnectException: Connection refused`.
- If you leave off the `\n` in the `writeToSocket()` call, nothing will go wrong because the `writeToSocket()` method will catch this error and add the end-of-line character to the string before sending it to the server. The server reads lines from the client, so every communication must end with `\n` or the protocol will break down.

EXERCISES

1. Explain the difference between each of the following pairs of terms:

   a. *Stream* and *socket*.
   b. *Internet* and *internet*.
   c. *Domain name* and *port*.
   d. *Client* and *server*.
   e. *Ethernet* and *Internet*.
   f. *URL* and *domain name*.

2. What is a *protocol*. Give one or two examples of protocols that are used on the Internet.
3. What service is managed by the HTTP protocol?
4. Give examples of client applications that use the HTTP protocol.
5. Why is it important that applets be limited in terms of their network and file system access. Describe the various networking restrictions that apply to Java applets.
6. What does the `Internet Protocol` do? Describe how it would be used to join together an Ethernet and a token ring network.
7. Describe one or two circumstances under which a `ConnectException` would be thrown.
8. Modify the `SlideShowApplet` so that it plays an audio file along with each slide.
9. Design and implement a Java applet that downloads a random substitution cryptogram and provides an interface that helps the user try to solve the cryptogram. The interface should enable the user to substitute an arbitrary letter for the letters in the cryptogram. The cryptogram files should be stored in the same directory as the applet itself.
10. Design and implement a Java application that displays a random message (or a random joke) each time the user clicks a `GetMessage` button. The messages should be stored in a set of files in the same directory as the applet itself. Each time the button is clicked, the applet should download one of the message files.
11. Write a client/server application of the message or joke service described in the previous exercise. Your implementation should extend the `Server` and `Client` classes.
12. Write an implementation of the scramble service. Given a word, the scramble service will return a string containing all possible permutations of the letters in the word. For example, given "man," the scramble service will return "amn, anm, man, mna, nam, nma." Use the `Server` and `Client` classes in your design. (See the Self-Study Exercises for a description of the design.)
13. **Challenge:** Design a Nim server that plays a two-person game of Nim. There are many versions of Nim but here's a simple one. The game starts with 21 sticks being thrown on the table. The players take turns picking up sticks. On each turn the player must pick 1, 2, or 3 sticks. The player who picks up the last stick wins the game. The server should start the game and then let the client have the first move. The server should also announce who won the game. (The server should be a good sport and shouldn't gloat too much when it wins!)
14. **Challenge:** Modify the previous program so that the client and server can negotiate the rules of the game, including how many sticks, how many pick-ups per turn, and who goes first.

15. **Challenge:** Design a CyberPet protocol and use it to establish a two-way conversation between two CyberPets. One pet will have to play the role of the server and the other the role of the client. Use the protocol to let two CyberPets carry on a simple exchange of information — what is their favorite food.
16. **Challenge:** CyberPets need a registry to help them select food gifts for each other. Design and implement a registry service. The service should let a CyberPet register itself by giving its name and its favorite food. A CyberPet can also request the server to tell it another CyberPet's favorite food. Design a client program that acts as an interface to the registry server.

Photograph courtesy of Andrew Olney, Tony Stone Images.

16

Data Structures: Lists, Stacks, and Queues

OBJECTIVES

After studying this chapter, you will

- Understand the concept of a dynamic data structure.
- Be able to create and use dynamic data structures such as linked lists.
- Grasp the concept of an Abstract Data Type (ADT).
- Understand the stack and queue ADTs.
- Know how to use inheritance to define extensible data structures.

OBJECTIVES

16.1 Introduction

A **data structure** is a construct used to organize information to make it easy and efficient to access and process. An *array* is an example of a data structure in which all of the data are of the same type or class, and in which individual elements are accessed by their position (index or subscript) within the structure. An array is an example of a **static structure**, because its size is fixed for the duration of the program's execution. (This is a different meaning of "static" than the Java keyword `static`).

A **vector** is another example of a data structure. Like an array, individual vector elements are accessed by their position. However, unlike arrays, a vector is an example of a **dynamic structure** — that is, one that can grow and shrink during a program's execution.

These are only two of the many data structures developed by computer scientists. For more advanced problems, it is often necessary to develop specialized structures to store and manipulate information. Some of these structures — linked lists, stacks, queues — have become classic objects of study in computer science. This chapter describes how to implement a linked list, and how to use inheritance to extend the list to implement the stack and queue structures.

16.2 The Linked List Data Structure

Static vs. dynamic

As we said, a **static** data structure is one whose size is fixed during a program's execution — its memory is allocated at compile time — while a **dynamic** structure is one that can grow and shrink as needed. In this section we will develop a dynamic list structure. A **list** is a data structure whose elements are arranged in a linear sequence. There is a first element in the list, a second element, and so on. Lists are quite general and have a broad range of applications. Depending on how elements are inserted and removed from a list, they can be used for a range of specialized purposes.

16.2.1 Using References to Link Objects

Referring to objects

As you know from earlier chapters, when you create an object using the `new` operator you get back a *reference* to the object, which you can assign to a reference variable. In the following example, *b* is a reference to a `JButton`:

```
JButton b = new JButton();
```

We have defined many classes that contained references to other objects:

```
public class CyberPet {
    private String name;
}
```

In this example, `name` is a reference to a `String` object.

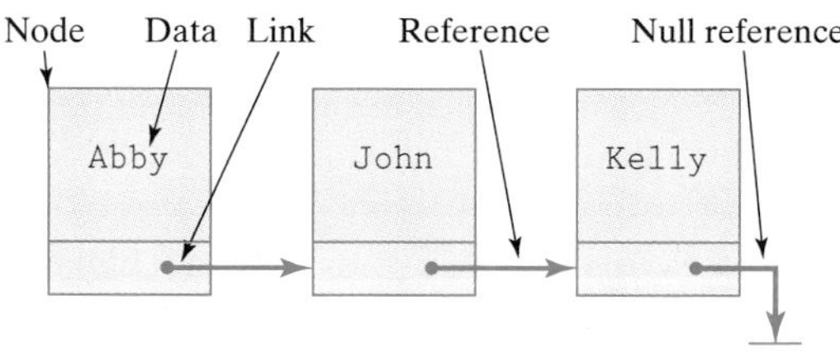

Figure 16–1 A linked list of Nodes terminated by a null link.

Self-referential objects

To make a linked list, we will define a class of self-referential objects. A **self-referential object** is one that contains a reference to an object of the same class. The convention is to name these objects Nodes:

```
public class Node {
    private String name;
    private Node next;
}
```

Linking objects together

In addition to the reference to a String object, each Node object contains a reference to another Node object. The next variable is often called a **link** because it is used to link together two Node objects. For example, Figure 16–1 provides an illustration of a linked list of Nodes.

By assigning references to the next variables in each Node, we can chain together arbitrarily long lists of objects. Therefore, we will want to add methods to our Node class that enable us to manipulate a Node's next variable. By assigning it a reference to another Node, we can link two Nodes together. By retrieving its value, we can find the next Node in the list.

JAVA LANGUAGE RULE **Self-referential Object.** A *self-referential* object is one that contains an instance variable that refers to an object of the same class.

In addition to the link variable, each Node stores some data. In this example, the data is a single String. But there's no real limit to the amount and type of data that can be stored in a linked list. Therefore, in addition to methods that manipulate a Node's link, we will also want methods to manipulate its data. These points suggest the following basic design for a Node:

```
public class Node {
    private Object data;
    private Node next;

    public Node(Object obj);          // Constructor

    public void setData(Object obj);  // Data access
    public Object getData();

    public void setNext(Node link);   // Link access
    public Node getNext();
} // Node
```

Note that we have defined the `Node`'s data in the most general possible way: as a reference to an `Object`. Because the `Object` class is the root of Java's entire class hierarchy, an `Object` can encompass any kind of data. By using Java's wrapper classes, such as `Integer` and `Double`, a `Node`'s data can even include primitive data.

Divide and conquer

The important point is that regardless of its type of data, a `Node` will have data access methods and link access methods. The data access methods differ, depending on the type of data, but the link access methods will generally be the same.

EFFECTIVE DESIGN: Link versus Data. Making a clear distinction between an object's data and those elements used to manipulate the object is an example of the divide-and-conquer principle.

SELF-STUDY EXERCISES

EXERCISE 16.1 Write a statement to create a new `Node` whose data consist of the `String` "Hello."

EXERCISE 16.2 Write a statement to create a new `Node` whose data consist the `CyberPet` named "Socrates."

16.2.2 Example: The Dynamic Phone List

Let's define a `PhoneListNode` class that can be used to implement a phone list. This definition will be a straightforward specialization of the generic `Node` list defined in the previous section. Each element of the phone list will consist simply of a person's name and phone number. These will be the node's data and can be stored in two `String` variables. To access these data, we will provide a constructor and a basic set of access methods. Thus we have the definition shown in Figure 16–2.

Accessing a list's data

The constructor and data access methods should be familiar to you. Note that the constructor sets the initial value of `next` to `null`, which means that it refers to no object.

DEBUGGING TIP: Null Reference. A common programming error is the attempt to use a `null` reference to refer to an object. This usually means the reference has not been successfully initialized.

Manipulating a list's nodes

Let's discuss the details of the link access methods — the `setNext()` and `getNext()` methods — which are also quite simple to implement. Because this is a `PhoneListNode`, these methods take `PhoneListNode` as a parameter and return type, respectively. Given a reference to a `PhoneListNode`, the `setNext()` method simply assigns it to `next`. The `getNext()` method simply returns the value of its `next` link.

Figure 16–2 The PhoneListNode class.

```
public class PhoneListNode {
    private String name;
    private String phone;
    private PhoneListNode next;

    public PhoneListNode(String s1, String s2) {
        name = s1;
        phone = s2;
        next = null;
    } // PhoneListNode()

    public void setData(String s1, String s2) {
        name = s1;
        phone = s2;
    } // setData()

    public String getName() {
        return name;
    } // getName()

    public String getData() {
        return name + " " + phone;
    } // getData()

    public String toString() {
        return name + " " + phone;
    } // toString()

    public void setNext(PhoneListNode nextPtr) {
        next = nextPtr;
    } // setNext()

    public PhoneListNode getNext() {
        return next;
    } // getNext()
} // PhoneListNode
```

Let's now see how we would use these methods to construct a list. The following statements create three nodes:

```
PhoneListNode node1 = new PhoneListNode("Roger M", "090-997-2918");
PhoneListNode node2 = new PhoneListNode("Jane M", "090-997-1987");
PhoneListNode node3 = new PhoneListNode("Stacy K", "090-997-9188");
```

The next two statements chain the nodes together into the list shown in Figure 16–3.

```
node1.setNext(node2);
node2.setNext(node3);
```

If we wanted to add a fourth node to the end of this list, we could use the following statements:

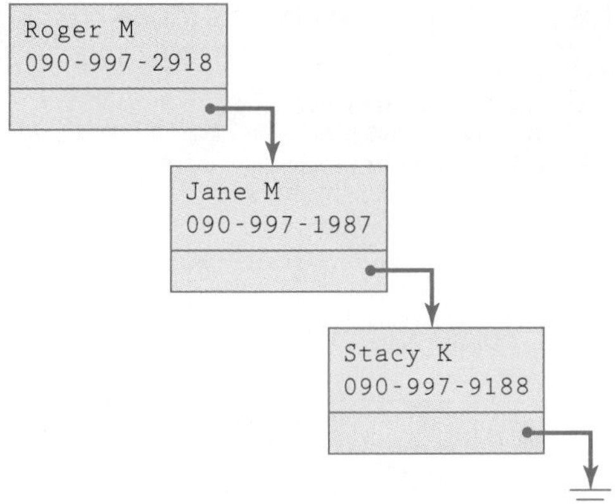

Figure 16–3 The phone list: A linked list of nodes, each which contains a person's name and phone number.

```
PhoneListNode node4 = new PhoneListNode("gary g","201-119-8765");
node3.setNext(node4);
```

Although this example illustrates the basic technique for inserting nodes at the end of the list, it depends too much on our knowledge of the list. In order to be truly useful we will have to develop a more general set of methods to create and manipulate a list of nodes.

EFFECTIVE DESIGN: Generality. In a well-designed list data structure you should be able to manipulate its elements without knowing anything about its data.

SELF-STUDY EXERCISES

EXERCISE 16.3 Suppose you know that `nodeptr` is a reference to the last element of a linked list of `PhoneListNode`s. Create a new element for "Bill C" with phone number "111–202–3331" and link it into the end of the list.

16.2.3 Manipulating the Phone List

In addition to the `Node`s that make a list, we must define a class containing methods to manipulate the list. This class will include the insert, access, and remove methods. It must also contain a reference to the list itself. This leads to the following basic design:

```
public class PhoneList {

    private PhoneListNode head;

    public PhoneList() {
        head = null;          // Start with empty list
    }

    public boolean isEmpty() {  // Defines an empty list
        return head == null;
    }

    public void insert(PhoneListNode node) { }

    public String getPhone(String name) { }

    public String remove(String name) { }

    public void print() { }
} // PhoneList
```

Because this is a list of `PhoneListNode`s we need a `PhoneListNode` reference to point to the list, which is the purpose of the `head` variable. When a new `PhoneList` instance is constructed, `head` is initialized to `null`, meaning the list is initially empty. Since we will frequently want to test whether the list is empty, we define the `boolean isEmpty()` method for that purpose. As you can see, its definition says that a list is empty when the reference to the `head` of this list is `null`.

An empty list

PROGRAMMING TIP: The `null` Reference. A `null` reference is useful for defining limit cases, such as an empty list or an uninstantiated object.

Inserting Nodes into a List

The `insert()` method will have the task of inserting new `PhoneListNode`s into the list. There are a number of ways to do this. The node could be inserted at the beginning or at the end of the list, or in alphabetical order, or possibly in other ways. As we'll see, it is easiest to insert a new node at the head of the list. But for this example, let's develop a method that inserts the node at the end of the list.

Insertion algorithm

There are two cases we need to worry about for this algorithm. First, if the list is empty, we can insert the node by simply setting `head` to point to the node [Figure 16–4(a)]. Second, if the list is not empty, we must **traverse** down the links of the list until we find the last node and insert the new node after it [Figure 16–4(b)]. In this case, we want to set the `next` variable of the last node to point to the new node. This gives us the following algorithm:

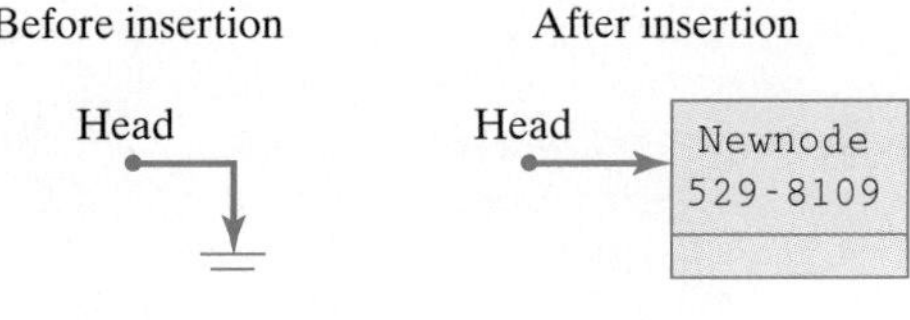

(a) Insertion into empty list

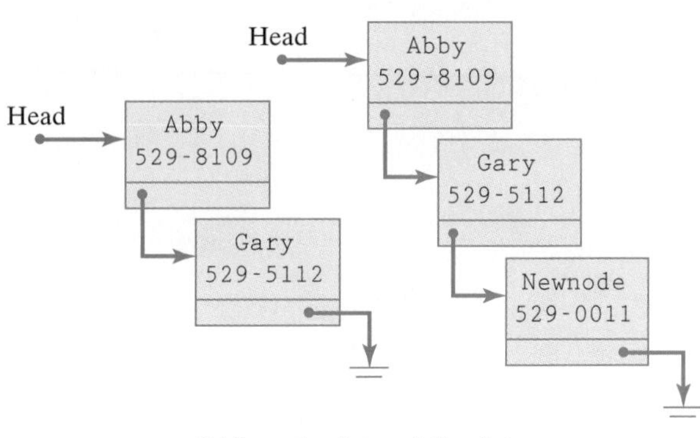

(b) Insertion into existing list

Figure 16–4 Two cases. (a) The list is empty before the insertion, which takes place at head. (b) The list is not empty, so the insertion takes place at the end of the list.

```
public void insert(PhoneListNode newNode) {
    if (isEmpty())
        head = newNode;                     // Insert at head of list
    else {
        PhoneListNode current = head;       // Start traversal at head
        while (current.getNext() != null) // While not at the last node
            current = current.getNext();  //   go to the next node
        current.setNext( newNode );         // Do the insertion
    }
} // insert()
```

Recall that when nodes are linked together, their `next` variables are non-`null`. So when a node's `next` variable is `null`, that indicates the end of the list — there's no next node. Thus, our algorithm begins by checking if the list is empty. If so, we assign `head` the reference to `newNode`, the `PhoneListNode` that's being inserted.

Traversing a list

If the list is not empty, then we need to find the last node. In order to traverse the list, we will need a temporary variable, `current`, which will always point to the current node. It's important to understand the while loop used here:

```
PhoneListNode current = head;       // Initializer
while (current.getNext() != null)   // Entry condition
    current = current.getNext();    // Updater
```

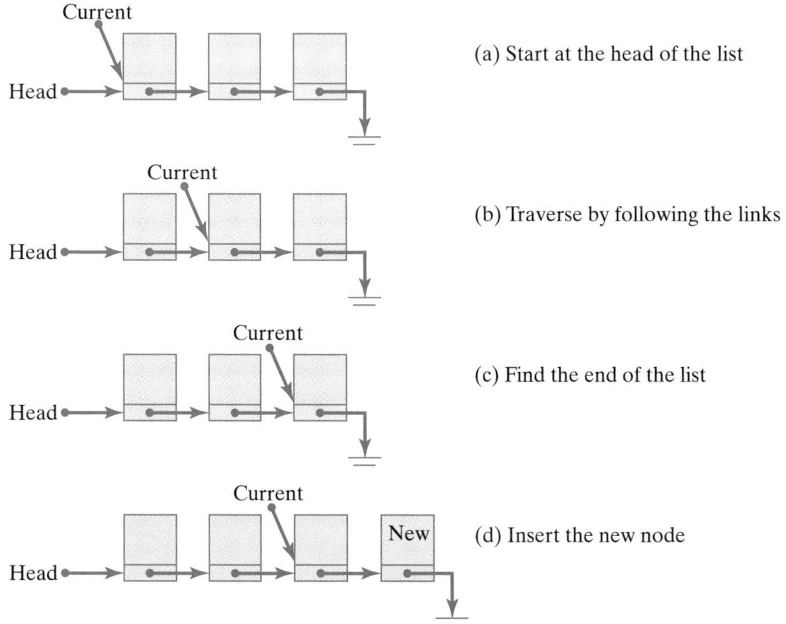

Figure 16–5 The temporary variable `current` is used to traverse the list to find its end.

The loop variable, `current` is initialized by setting it to point to the head of the list. The entry condition tests whether the `next` link, leading out of `current` is `null` (Figure 16–5). That is, when the link coming out of a node is `null`, then that node is the last node in the list [Figure 16–5(c)]. Inside the while loop, the update expression simply assigns the next node to `current`. In that way, `current` will point to each successive node until the last node is found. It's very important that the loop exits when `current.next` is `null`. That way `current` is pointing to the last node, and can be used to set its `next` variable to the node being inserted [Figure 16–5(d)]. Thus, after the loop is exited, `current` still points to the last node. At that point, the `setNext()` method is used to link `newNode` into the list as the new last node.

Loop exit condition

DEBUGGING TIP: List Traversal. A common error in designing list traversal algorithms is an erroneous loop entry or loop exit condition One way to avoid this error is to hand trace your algorithm to make sure your code is correct.

Printing the Nodes of a List

The `print()` method also uses a traversal strategy to print the data from each node of the list. Here again, it is necessary to test whether the list is empty. If so, we must print an error message. (This would be a good place to throw a programmer-defined exception, such as an `EmptyListException`.) If the list is not empty, then we use a temporary variable to traverse the list, printing each node's data along the way:

List traversal

```
public void print() {
    if (isEmpty())
        System.out.println("Phone list is empty");
    PhoneListNode current = head;                  // Start traversal at head
    while (current != null) {                      // While not at end of list
        System.out.println( current.toString() ); //   print node's data
        current = current.getNext();               //   go to the next node
    }
} // print()
```

Note the differences between this while loop and the one used in the insert() method. In this case we exit the loop when current becomes null; there's no action to be taken after the loop is exited. The printing takes place within the loop. Thus in this case the entry condition, (current != null), signifies that the task has been completed.

PROGRAMMING TIP: Terminating a Traversal. In designing list traversal algorithms where the reference, *p*, points to the nodes in the list, if you need to refer to the last node in the list after the traversal loop exits, then your exit condition should be p.next == null. If you have finished processing the nodes when the loop exits, your exit condition should be p == null.

Looking up a Node in a List

List traversal

The traversal strategy must also be used to look up someone's phone number in the PhoneList. Here again, we start at the head of the list, and traverse down the next links until we find the node containing the desired phone number. This method takes the name of the person as a parameter. There are three cases to worry about: (1) The list is empty; (2) the normal case where the person named is found in the list; and (3) the person named is not in the list. Because the method returns a String, we can return error messages in the first and third cases:

```
public String getPhone(String name) {
    if (isEmpty())                                 // Case 1: empty list
        return "Phone list is empty";
    else {
        PhoneListNode current = head;
        while ((current.getNext() != null) && (!current.getName().equals(name)))
            current = current.getNext();
        if (current.getName().equals(name))  // Case 2: found the name
            return current.getData();
        else                                       // Case 3: no such person
            return ("Sorry.  No entry for " + name);
    }
} // getPhone()
```

Compound exit condition

Note the while loop in this case. As in the insert() method, when the loop exits, we need a reference to the current node, so we can print its phone number [current.getData()]. But here there are three ways to exit the loop: (1) We reach the end of the list without finding the named person; (2) we find the named person in the interior of the list; or (3) we find the named person in the last node of the list. In either case, after the loop is exited, it is necessary to test whether the name was found or not. Then appropriate action can be taken.

SELF-STUDY EXERCISES

EXERCISE 16.4 What if the exit condition for the while loop in `getPhone()` were stated as `((current.getNext() != null) || (!current.getName().equals(name)))`?

Removing a Node From a List

Node removal algorithm

By far the most difficult task is that of removing a node from a list. In the `PhoneList` we use the person's name to identify the node, and we return a `String`, which can be used to report either success or failure. There are four cases to worry about in designing this algorithm: (1) The list is empty; (2) the first node is being removed, (3) some other node is being removed, and (4) the named person is not in the list. The same traversal strategy we used in `getPhone()` is used here, with the same basic while loop for cases 3 and 4.

As Figure 16–6 shows, the first two cases are easily handled. If the list is empty we just return an error message. We use `current` as the traversal variable. If the named node is the first node, we simply need to set `head` to `current.getNext()`, which has the effect of making `head` point to the second node in the list [Figure 16–7(a)]. Once the node is cut out from the chain of links, there will be no further reference to it. In this case Java will recapture the memory it uses when it does garbage collection.

JAVA LANGUAGE RULE **Garbage Collection.** Java's garbage collector handles the disposal of unused objects automatically. This helps to simplify linked list applications. In languages such as C++ the programmer would have to *dispose* of the memory occupied by the deleted node.

Figure 16–6 The `remove()` method.

```
public String remove(String name) { // Remove an entry by name
    if (isEmpty())                              // Case 1: empty list
        return "Phone list is empty";
    PhoneListNode current = head;
    PhoneListNode previous = null;
    if (current.getName().equals(name)) {       // Case 2: remove first node
        head = current.getNext();
        return "Removed " + current.toString() ;
    }
    while ((current.getNext() != null) && (!current.getName().equals(name)))  {
        previous = current;
        current = current.getNext();
    }
    if (current.getName().equals(name)) {       // Case 3: remove named node
        previous.setNext(current.getNext());
        return "Removed " + current.toString();
    } else
        return ("Sorry.  No entry for " + name); // Case 4: node not found
} // remove()
```

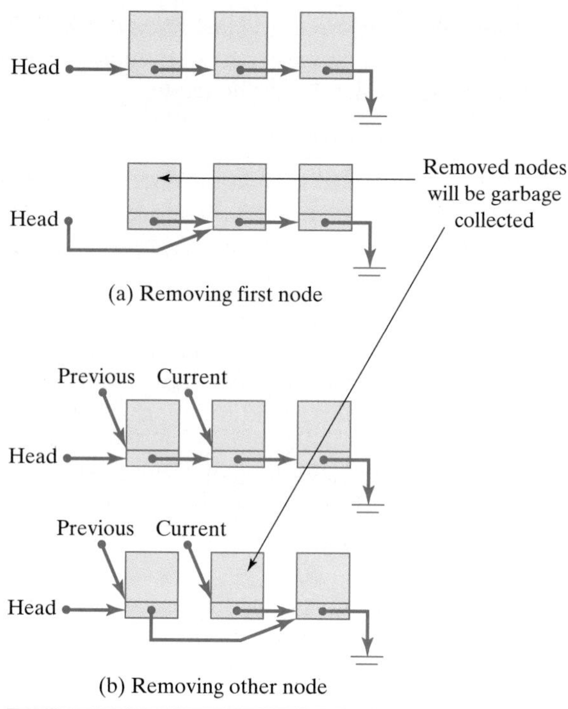

Figure 16–7 Removing different nodes from a linked list.

Tandem traversal

In order to remove some other node besides the first, two traversal variables are needed: `previous` and `current`. And they proceed in tandem down the list, with `previous` always pointing to the node just before the `current` node. The reason, of course, is that to remove the `current` node, you need to adjust the link pointing to it contained in the `previous` node [Figure 16–7(b)]. That is, the new value of `previous.next` will be the current value of `current.next`. We use the `getNext()` and `setNext()` methods to effect this change:

```
previous.setNext(  current.getNext() );
```

Testing the List

Designing test data

In developing list processing programs, it is very important to design good test data. As we have seen, the insertion and removal operations each involves several distinct cases. Proper testing of these methods would ideally test every possible case. Of course, there are often so many combinations of list operations that exhaustive testing may not be feasible. At the very least you should design test data that test each of the different conditions identified in your algorithms. For example, in testing removals from a list, you should test all four cases that we discussed. In testing insertions or lookups, you should test all three cases that were identified.

Figure 16–8 A `main()` method containing a set of tests for the `PhoneList` class.

```
public static void main(String argv[]) {
                              // Create list and insert some nodes
    PhoneList list = new PhoneList();
    list.insert( new PhoneListNode("Roger M", "997-0020"));
    list.insert( new PhoneListNode("Roger W", "997-0086"));
    list.insert( new PhoneListNode("Rich P", "997-0010"));
    list.insert( new PhoneListNode("Jane M", "997-2101"));
    list.insert( new PhoneListNode("Stacy K", "997-2517"));

                              // Test whether insertions worked
    System.out.println( "Phone Directory" );
    list.print();
                              // Test whether lookups work
    System.out.println("Looking up numbers by name");
    System.out.println(list.getPhone("Roger M"));
    System.out.println(list.getPhone("Rich P"));
    System.out.println(list.getPhone("Stacy K"));
    System.out.println(list.getPhone("Mary P"));
    System.out.println(list.remove("Rich P"));

    System.out.println("Phone Directory");
    list.print();
            // Test removals, printing list after each removal
    System.out.println(list.remove("Roger M"));
    System.out.println("Phone Directory");
    list.print();
    System.out.println(list.remove("Stacy K"));
    System.out.println("Phone Directory");
    list.print();
    System.out.println(list.remove("Jane M"));
    System.out.println("Phone Directory");
    list.print();
    System.out.println(list.remove("Jane M"));
    System.out.println("Phone Directory");
    list.print();
    System.out.println(list.remove("Roger W"));
    System.out.println("Phone Directory");
    list.print();
    System.out.println(list.remove("Roger W"));
    System.out.println("Phone Directory");
    list.print();
} // main()
```

EFFECTIVE DESIGN: Test Data. Test data for validating list processing algorithms should (at least) test each of the cases identified in each of the removal and insertion methods.

The `main()` program in Figure 16–8 illustrates the kinds of tests that should be performed. This method could be incorporated directly into the `PhoneList` class, or it could be made part of a separate class.

SELF-STUDY EXERCISES

EXERCISE 16.5 Trace through the `main()` method line by line and predict its output.

EXERCISE 16.6 Design a test of `PhoneList` that shows that new elements can be inserted into a list after some or all of its previous nodes have been removed.

OBJECT-ORIENTED DESIGN: The List Abstract Data Type (ADT)

The PhoneList example from the previous section illustrates the basic concepts of the linked list. Keep in mind that there are other implementations that could have been described. For example, some linked lists use a reference to both the first and last elements of the list. Some lists use nodes that have two pointers, one to the next node and one to the previous node. This enables traversals in two directions: front to back and back to front. So the example we showed was intended mainly to illustrate the basic techniques involved in list processing.

A generic list structure

Also, the PhoneList example is limited to a particular type of data — namely, a PhoneListNode. Let's develop a more general linked list class and a more general node class that can be used to store and process lists of any kind of data.

An **Abstract Data Type (ADT)** involves two components: the data that are being stored and manipulated, and the methods and operations that can be performed on those data. For example, an int is an ADT. The data are the integral whole values ranging from some MININT to some MAXINT. The operations are the various integer operations: addition, subtraction, multiplication, and division. These operations prescribe the ways that ints can be used. There are no other ways to manipulate integers.

Information hiding

Moreover, in designing an ADT, it's important to hide the implementation of the operations from the users of the operations. Thus our programs have used all of these integer operations on ints, but we have no real idea how they are implemented — that is, what exact algorithm they use.

Objects can be easily designed as ADTs, because we can easily distinguish an object's use from its implementation. Thus the private parts of an object — its instance variables and private methods — are hidden from the user while the object's interface — its public methods — are available. As with the integer operators, the object's public methods prescribe just how the object can be used.

Design specifications

So let's design a list ADT. We want it to be able to store any kind of data and we want to prescribe the operations that can be performed on those data — the insert, delete, and so on. Also, we want to design the ADT so that it can be easily extended to create more specialized kinds of lists.

The Node Class

EFFECTIVE DESIGN: Generalizing a Type. An effective strategy for designing an abstract data type is to start with a specific list and generalize it. The result should be a more abstract version of the original list.

Our approach will be to generalize the classes we created in the PhoneList example. Thus the PhoneListNode will become a generic Node that can store any kind of data (Figure 16–9). Some of the changes are merely

Figure 16–9 The Node class is a more abstract version of the PhoneListNode class.

```
public class Node {
    private Object data;        // Stores any kind of data
    private Node next;

    public Node(Object obj) {  // Constructor
        data = obj;
        next = null;
    }
                              // Data access methods
    public void setData(Object obj) {
        data = obj;
    }

    public Object getData() {
        return data;
    }

    public String toString() {
        return data.toString();
    }
                              // Link access methods
    public void setNext( Node nextPtr ) {
        next = nextPtr;
    }

    public Node getNext() {
        return next;
    }
} // Node
```

name changes. Thus wherever we had `PhoneListNode`, we now have just `Node`. The link access methods have not changed significantly. What has changed is that instead of instance variables for the name, phone number, and so on, we now have just a single data reference to an `Object`. This is as general as you can get, because, as we pointed out earlier, `data` can refer to any object whatsoever, even to primitive data.

Note that the data access methods, `getData()` and `setData()`, use references to `Object` for their parameter and return type. Note also how we've defined the `toString()` method. It just invokes `data.toString()`. Because `toString()` is defined in `Object`, every type of data will have this method. And because `toString()` is frequently overridden in defining new objects, it is very useful here.

The `List` Class

Let's now generalize the `PhoneList` class. This class will still contain a reference to the `head` of the list, which will now be a list of `Node`s. It will still define its constructor, its `isEmpty()`, and its `print()` methods in the same way as in the `PhoneList`.

Generic list methods

However, in generalizing the `PhoneList` class, we want to design some new methods, particularly because we want to use this class as the basis for more specialized lists. The `PhoneList.insert()` method was used to insert nodes at the end of a list. In addition to this method, let's design a method that inserts at the head of the list. Also, PhoneList had a method to remove nodes by name. However, now that we have generalized our data, we don't know if the list's Objects have a name field, so we'll scrap this method in favor of two new methods that remove a node from the beginning or end of the list, respectively.

We already know the basic strategies for implementing these new methods, which are shown in the definition in Figure 16–10. We have renamed the insertAtRear() method which otherwise is very similar to the PhoneList.insert() method. The key change is that now its parameter must be an Object, because we want to be able to insert any kind of object into our list. At the same time, our list consists of Nodes, so we have to use the Object to create a Node in our insert methods:

```
head = new Node( newNode );
```

Recall that the Node constructor takes an Object argument and simply assigns it to the data reference. So when we insert an Object into the list, we make a new Node and set its data variable to point to that Object. Note that this method assumes that the list is not empty — that is, that it has a first element.

```
List l = new List();
l.insertAtRear( new Integer(5) );
l.insertAtRear( new String( "hello") );
```

The new insertAtFront() method is very simple to implement, as no traversal of the list is necessary. Therefore, you simply need to update head to point to the newNode and you have to make newNode.next point to the previous head of the list [Figure 16–4(a)]. Of course, we must use the setNext() method to access the newNode.next variable.

The new removeFirst() method is also quite simple to implement. In this case you want to return a reference to the Object that's being removed. But you also want to adjust head so that it points to whatever the previous head.next was pointing to before the removal. This requires the use of a temporary variable, as shown in the method. Note that this method assumes that the list is not empty — that is, it has a first element.

The new removeLast() method is a bit more complicated, but no more so than the PhoneList.remove() method. It handles three cases: (1) the empty list case, (2) the singleton list, and (3) all other lists. If the list is empty, it merely returns null. Obviously, it shouldn't even be called in this case. In designing subclasses of List we will first invoke isEmpty() before attempting to remove a node.

If the list contains a single node, we treat it as a special case and simply set head to null, thus resulting in an empty list. In the typical case, case 3, we traverse the list to find the last node, using again the strategy of maintaining both a previous and a current pointer. When we find the last node, we must adjust previous.next so that it no longer points to it.

Figure 16–10 The `List` ADT.

```
public class List {
    private Node head;

    public List() {
        head = null;
    }

    public boolean isEmpty() {
        return head == null;
    }

    public void print() {
        if (isEmpty())
            System.out.println("List is empty");
        Node current = head;
        while (current != null) {
            System.out.println(current.toString());
            current = current.getNext();
        }
    } // print()

    public void insertAtFront( Object newNode ) {
        Node current =  new Node( newNode );
        current.setNext( head );
        head = current;
    }

    public void insertAtRear( Object newNode ) {
        if (isEmpty())
            head = new Node( newNode );
        else {
            Node current = head;                     // Start at head of list
            while (current.getNext() != null)        // Find the end of the list
                current = current.getNext();
            current.setNext(new Node(newNode));      // Insert the newNode
        }
    } // insertAtRear()

    public Object removeFirst() {
        Node first = head;
        head = head.getNext();
        return first;
    } // removeFirst()

    public Object removeLast() {
        if (isEmpty())  // empty list
            return null;

        Node current = head;
        if (current.getNext() == null) {         // Singleton list
            head = null;
            return current;
        }

        Node previous = null;                    // All other cases
        while (current.getNext() != null) {
            previous = current;
            current = current.getNext();
        }
        previous.setNext(null);
        return current;
    } // removeLast()
} // List
```

Figure 16–11 A series of tests for the `List` ADT.

```
public static void main( String argv[] ) {
                // Create list and insert heterogeneous nodes
    List list = new List();
    list.insertAtFront(new PhoneRecord("Roger M", "997-0020"));
    list.insertAtFront(new Integer(8647));
    list.insertAtFront(new String("Hello World"));
    list.insertAtRear(new PhoneRecord("Jane M", "997-2101"));
    list.insertAtRear(new PhoneRecord("Stacy K", "997-2517"));

                // Print the list
    System.out.println("Generic List");
    list.print();
                // Remove objects and print resulting list
    Object o;
    o = list.removeLast();
    System.out.println(" Removed " + o.toString());
    System.out.println("Generic List:");
    list.print();
    o = list.removeLast();
    System.out.println(" Removed " + o.toString());
    System.out.println("Generic List:");
    list.print();
    o = list.removeFirst();
    System.out.println(" Removed " +o.toString());
    System.out.println("Generic List:");
    list.print();
} // main()
```

Testing the List ADT

Heterogeneous lists

Testing the list ADT follows the same strategy used in the `PhoneList` example. However, one of the things we want to test is that we can indeed create lists of heterogeneous types — lists that include `Integers` mixed with `Floats`, mixed with `CyberPets`, and so on. The `main()` method in Figure 16–11 illustrates this feature.

The list we create here involves various types of data. The `PhoneRecord` class is scaled down version of the `PhoneListNode` we used in the previous example. Its definition is shown in Figure 16–12. Note in `main()` how we use an `Object` reference to remove objects from the list. We use the `Object.toString()` method to display the object that was removed.

EFFECTIVE DESIGN: The `List` ADT. One advantage of defining a `List` ADT is that it let's you avoid having to write the relatively difficult list processing algorithms each time you need a list structure.

SELF-STUDY EXERCISES

EXERCISE 16.7 Trace through the `main()` method line by line and predict its output.

EXERCISE 16.8 Design a test of the `List` program that shows that it is possible to insert new elements into a list after some or all of its previous nodes have been removed.

Figure 16–12 A PhoneRecord class.

```
public class PhoneRecord {
    private String name;
    private String phone;

    public PhoneRecord(String s1, String s2) {
        name = s1;
        phone = s2;
    }

    public String toString() {
        return name + " " + phone;
    }

    public String getName( ) {
        return name;
    }

    public String getPhone( ) {
        return phone;
    }
} // PhoneRecord
```

16.3 The Stack ADT

A **stack** is a special type of list which limits insertions and removals to the front of the list. It therefore enforces **Last-In-First-Out (LIFO)** behavior on the list. Think of a stack of dishes at the salad bar, which is probably where the term "stack" came from. When you put a dish on the stack, it goes onto the top of the stack. When you remove a dish from the stack, it comes from the top of the stack. These operations are conventionally called *push*, for insert, and *pop*, for remove, respectively (Figure 16–13). Thus, the stack ADT stores a list of data and supports the following operations:

Stack operations

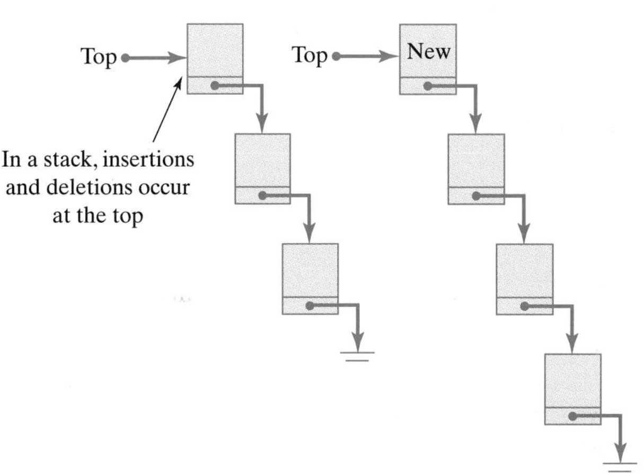
Top
Top
New
In a stack, insertions and deletions occur at the top

Figure 16–13 A stack is a list that permits insertions and removals only at its top.

- Push — insert an object onto the top of the stack.
- Pop — remove the top object from the stack.
- Empty — returns true if the stack is empty.
- Peek — retrieve the top object without removing it.

Stack applications

Stacks are useful for a number of important computing tasks. For example, during program execution, method call and return happens in a LIFO fashion. The last method called is the first method exited. Therefore, a stack — sometimes called the runtime stack — is used to manage method calls during program execution. When a method is called, an activation block is created, which includes the method's parameters, local variables, and return address. The activation is pushed onto the stack. When that method call returns, the return address is retrieved from the activation block and the whole block is popped off the stack. The `Exception.printStackTrace()` method makes use of the runtime stack to print a trace of the method calls that led up to an exception.

16.3.1 The `Stack` Class

Given our very general definition of `List` and `Node`, it is practically trivial to define the stack ADT as a subclass of `List`. We can simply use the `insertAtFront()` and `removeFirst()` methods for the push and pop operations, respectively (Figure 16–14). Because the `isEmpty()` method is defined in `List`, there's no need to override it in `Stack`. In effect, the `push()` and `pop()` methods merely rename the `insertAtFront()` and `removeFirst()` methods.

Protected methods are inherited

Do we have to make any changes to the `List` class in order to use it this way? Yes. We want to change the declaration of `head` from `private` to `protected`, so it can be accessed in the `Stack` class. And we want to declare `List`'s `public` access methods, such as `insertAtFront()` and `removeFirst()`, as `protected`. That will allow them to be used in `Stack`,

Figure 16–14 The `Stack` ADT.

```
public class Stack extends List {

    public Stack() {
        super();
    }

    public void push( Object obj ) {
        insertAtFront( obj );
    }

    public Object pop() {
        return removeFirst();
    }
} // Stack
```

and in any classes that extend `List`, but not by other classes. This is essential. Unless we do this we haven't really restricted the stack operations to push and pop, and therefore we haven't really defined a stack ADT. Remember, an ADT defines the data and the operations on the data. A stack ADT must restrict access to the data to just the push and pop operations.

JAVA LANGUAGE RULE **Protected Elements.** An object's `protected` elements are hidden from all other objects except instances of the same class or its subclasses.

EFFECTIVE DESIGN: Information Hiding. Use the `private` and `protected` qualifiers to hide an ADT's implementation details from other objects. Use `public` to define the ADT's interface.

SELF-STUDY EXERCISES

EXERCISE 16.9 Define the `peek()` method for the `Stack` class. It should take no parameters and return an `Object`. It should return the `Object` on the top of the stack.

16.3.2 Testing the `Stack` Class

A stack can be used to reverse the letters in a `String`. The algorithm is this: Starting at the front of the `String`, push each letter onto the stack until you reach the end of the `String`. Then pop letters off the stack and concatenate them, left to right, into another `String`, until the stack is empty (Figure 16–15).

Reversing a string

Figure 16–15 A method to test the `Stack` ADT.

```
public static void main( String argv[] ) {
    Stack stack = new Stack();
    String string = "Hello this is a test string";

    System.out.println("String: " + string);
    for (int k = 0; k < string.length(); k++)
        stack.push(new Character( string.charAt(k)));

    Object o = null;
    String reversed = "";
    while (!stack.isEmpty()) {
        o  = stack.pop();
        reversed = reversed + o.toString();
    }
    System.out.println("Reversed String: " + reversed);
} // main()
```

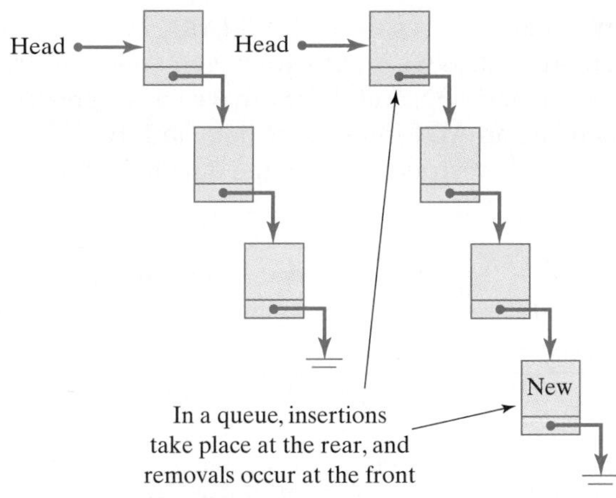
Head
Head
New
In a queue, insertions take place at the rear, and removals occur at the front

Figure 16–16 A queue is a list that permits insertions at the rear and removals at the front only.

Note that because our `Node`s store `Objects`, we must convert each `char` into a `Character`, using the wrapper class. Note also that we can use the `toString()` method to convert from `Object` to `String` as we are popping the stack.

16.4 The Queue ADT

A **queue** is a special type of list which limits insertions to the rear and removals from the front of the list. It therefore enforces **First-In-First-Out (FIFO)** behavior on the list. Think of the waiting line at the salad bar. You enter the line at the rear and you leave the line at the front. These operations are conventionally called *enqueue*, for insert, and *dequeue*, for remove, respectively (Figure 16–16). Thus, the stack ADT stores a list of data and supports the following operations:

Queue operations

- Enqueue — insert an object onto the rear of the list.
- Dequeue — remove the object at the front of the list.
- Empty — return true if the queue is empty.

Queues are useful for a number of computing tasks. For example, the ready, waiting, and blocked queues used by the CPU scheduler all use a FIFO protocol. Queues are also useful in implementing certain kinds of simulations. For example, the waiting line at a bank or a bakery can be modeled using a queue.

16.4.1 The `Queue` Class

The `Queue` class is also trivial to derive from `List`. Here we just restrict operations to the `insertAtRear()` and `removeFirst()` methods (Figure 16–17). To test the methods of this class we replace the `push()` and

Figure 16–17 The Queue ADT.

```
public class Queue extends List {

    public Queue() {
        super();
    }

    public void enqueue(Object obj) {
        insertAtRear( obj );
    }

    public Object dequeue() {
        return removeFirst();
    }
}// Queue
```

pop() operations of the last example to enqueue() and dequeue(), respectively (Figure 16–18). In this case the letters of the test string will come out of the queue in the same order they went in — FIFO.

SELF-STUDY EXERCISES

EXERCISE 16.10 Define a peekLast() method for the Queue class. It should take no parameters and return an Object. It should return the last Object in the list without removing it.

EFFECTIVE DESIGN: ADTs. ADTs encapsulate and manage the difficult tasks involved in manipulating the data structure. But because of their extensibility, they can be used in a wide range of applications.

Figure 16–18 A method to test the Queue ADT.

```
public static void main(String argv[]) {
    Queue queue = new Queue();
    String string = "Hello this is a test string";
    System.out.println("String: " + string);
    for (int k = 0; k < string.length(); k++)
        queue.enqueue( new Character(string.charAt(k)));
    System.out.println("The current queue:");
    queue.print();

    Object o = null;
    System.out.println("Dequeuing:");
    while (!queue.isEmpty()) {
        o  = queue.dequeue();
        System.out.print( o.toString() );
    }
} // main()
```

From the Java Library: java.util.Stack

The Java class library contains implementations of some of the abstract data types that we discussed earlier. The Java utility package, `java.util.*`, contains a `Stack` class, implemented as a subclass of the `java.util.Vector` class. It contains the following methods:

```
public class Stack extends Vector {
    public boolean empty();
    public Object peek();
    public Object pop();
    Object push(Object item);
    int search(Object o);     // Returns o's location in the stack
}
```

For the most part, these methods provide the same functionality as the methods we developed.

The `java.util.LinkedList` is an implementation of a linked list. Like our implementation, it contains methods that can easily be used to define the standard stack and queue methods. Many of the standard list processing methods are defined as part of the `List` interface:

```
public class LinkedList extends AbstractSequentialList implements List {
    public void add(int index, Object o); Inserts o index position
    public void addFirst(Object o); // Inserts o at the beginning of the list
    public void addLast(Object o);  // Appends o to the end of the list
    public Object get(int index);   // Returns the list element at index
    public Object getFirst();       // Returns the first element in the list
    public Object getLast();        // Returns the last element in list.
    public Object removeFirst();    // Removes and returns the first element
    public Object removeLast();     // Removes and returns the last element
```

The advantage of defining list operations as an interface is that it can be attached to a wide range of sequential structures. For example, you could define a stack or a queue class that stored its objects in an array rather than a linked list. By implementing the `List` interface, this design would still function the same way as the class we defined or as Java's `java.util.Stack` class.

EFFECTIVE DESIGN: Code Reuse. Given the relative difficulty of writing correct and efficient list processing algorithms, applications that depend on lists should make use of library classes whenever possible.

IN THE LABORATORY: CAPITAL GAINS

Problem Statement

Suppose your accountant asks you to write a program that will help him calculate the capital gain or loss for a stock account. As you may know, accountants have two ways of accounting for such transactions: *LIFO accounting* and *FIFO accounting*.

The LISP Language

One of the very earliest computer languages, and the one that's most often associated with Artificial Intelligence (AI), is LISP, which stands for *LISt Processor*. The earliest (pure) versions of LISP had no control structures and the only data structure they contained were the list structure. Repetition in the language was done by recursion.

Lists are used for everything in LISP, including for LISP programs themselves. LISP's unique syntax is very simple. A LISP program consists of symbols, such as *5* and *x*, and lists of symbols, such as *(5)*, *(1 2 3 4 5)*, and *((this 5) (that 10))*, where a list is simply anything enclosed within parentheses. The null list is represented by `()`.

Programs in LISP are like mathematical functions. For example, here's a definition of a function to compute the square of two numbers:

```
(define (square x) (* x x) )
```

The expression *(square x)* is a list giving the name of the function and its parameter. The expression *(* x x)* gives the body of the function. LISP uses *prefix notation* in which *(* x x)* is equivalent to *(x * x)* in Java's *infix notation*. To run this program, you would simply input an expression like *(square 25)* to the LISP interpreter, and it would evaluate it to 625.

LISP provides three basic list operators. The expression *(car x)* returns the first element of the (nonempty) list x. The expression *(cdr x)* returns the tail of the list x. Finally, *(cons z x)* constructs a list by making *z* the head of the list and *x* its tail. For example, if *x* is the list *(1 3 5)*, then *(car x)* is 1, *(cdr x)* is *(3 5)*, and *(cons 7 x)* is *(7 1 3 5)*.

Given these basic list operators, it is practically trivial to define a stack in LISP:

```
(define (push x stack) (cons x stack))
(define (pop stack) (setf stack (cdr stack)) (car stack))
```

The push operation creates a new stack by forming the *cons* of the element *x* and the previous version of the stack. The pop operation returns the *car* of the stack, but first changes the stack (using `setf`) to the tail of the original stack.

These simple examples show that you can do an awful lot of computation using just a simple list structure. The success of LISP, particularly its success as an AI language, shows the great power and generality inherent in recursion and lists. LISP has been used to build programs for human learning, natural language processing, chess playing, human vision processing, and a wide range of other applications.

In LIFO accounting, the order of buys and sells are taken in a last-in-first-out manner — as if they were stored in a stack. In FIFO accounting, the order of buys and sells are taken in a last-in-first-out manner — as if they were stored in a queue.

For example, suppose you bought 100 shares of a particular stock in each of the months of January, February, and May, for prices of \$10, \$15, \$3, respectively. And suppose you sold 100 shares in March when the price per share was \$20. So you presently hold 200 shares of the stock. In calculating your gain or loss you wouldn't count those shares.

FIFO accounting

If you use FIFO accounting, your capital gain or loss would be calculated by using the March transaction as income. You would match it against the expense of the 100 shares you bought in January. Your total capital gain would be calculated as $100 \times 20 - 100 \times 10 = 1000$. So you would have a gain of \$1000.

LIFO accounting

If you use LIFO accounting, your capital gain or loss would be calculated by using your March transaction as income again. But this time it would be matched against the 100 shares you bought in May. Using this form of accounting your total capital gain would be calculated as $100 \times 20 - 100 \times 3 = 1700$. So you would have a gain of \$1700.

Of course, if you're interested in minimizing your tax liability, you would want to use FIFO accounting in this case. According to that method, you made less money.

Specifications

Problem statement

Design and write a Java application that lets the user input a sequence of stock transactions, either purchases or sales, and then calculates the capital gain or loss using both LIFO and FIFO accounting. The user should be able to input several transactions and then press a button to process the transactions and compare the results of the two accounting methods. After one batch of transactions is processed, the user should be able to input another batch.

GUI Design

User interface

For each transaction, the user has to enter three items of data: the price of the stock, the number of shares, and whether the transaction is a sale or a purchase. `JTextField`s can be used for inputting the price and number of shares. A good way to input the type of transaction would be to use a set of `JRadioButton`s, since the transaction must be either a purchase or a sale.

What controls are needed for this application? The user will be taking two kinds of actions: entering data for a transaction, and asking the program to do the accounting for the current set of transactions. This suggests two `JButton` controls: an "Insert Transaction" button and a "Calculate" button.

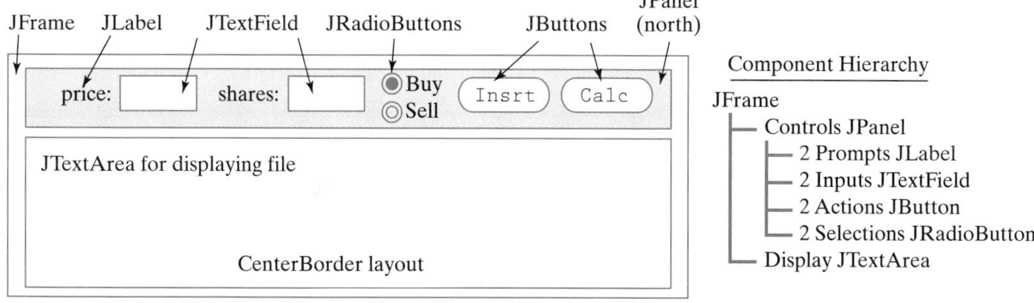

Figure 16–19 GUI design for the accounting application.

In terms of the program's layout, we can use a `JFrame` for the top-level window. As we have done in other programs, we can place a control, containing the buttons and textfields at the top border of the window, and a `JTextField` at the center. This suggests the layout shown in Figure 16–19.

Problem Decomposition

What objects do we need?

In addition to the GUI components used in the interface, this project requires several objects to help with the computation. First, we'll need an `JFrame` object to serve as the top-level window and handle the user interface tasks.

The transactions that the user inputs should be represented as individual objects of the `Transaction` class. We also need an `Accountant` object to serve as the accountant expert. This object will do all the accounting tasks for the application.

The `Accountant` object will need `Queue`s and `Stack`s to store the stock transactions. Because these objects depend for their definition on the `List` and `Node` classes, our project must also include definitions for these two classes. This gives us the following list of classes, each of which must be included in the project.

Class	Task Description
`AccountantFrame`	Top-level window; user interface
`Accountant`	FIFO/LIFO accounting expert
`Transaction`	Stock transaction object
`Queue`	FIFO queue of transactions
`Stack`	LIFO stack of transactions
`List`	Superclass of `Queue` and `Stack`
`Node`	Data element of `List`

The Transaction Class

What data do we need?

Each Transaction contains three pieces of data: the price of the stock, the number of shares, and whether it is a purchase or sale transaction. So these elements will have to be defined as instance variables. The constructor method for this class should let the user pass the values for these variables when a Transaction is instantiated.

What methods do we need?

In terms of the methods needed for this class, it's always useful to have a toString() method. This lets you display the object's value, which can be useful during program development as well as part of the program's output. It will also be convenient if each transaction would calculate its total value. This is done by multiplying the number of shares by the price per share. If the transaction is a sale, the transaction amount would be positive (income). If the transaction is a purchase, the amount would be negative (an expense). These design decisions lead to the following initial definition of the Transaction class:

A transaction's value

```
public class Transaction {
    public static final boolean BUY = true, SELL=false;
    public double pricePerShare;
    public double nShares;
    public boolean transType;      // Buy or sell

    public Transaction(double price, double shares, boolean type) {}
    public String toString() {}
    public double getValue() {}
}
```

The Accountant Class

The Accountant class is responsible for calculating capital gains and losses using the FIFO and LIFO accounting methods. How will this be done?

The accounting algorithm

Capital gains (or losses) are triggered by the sale of stock, because a sale transaction generates income. Each sale of *X* shares of stock must be balanced against a corresponding purchase of *X* shares. (To simplify this algorithm, let's assume that all purchases and sales happen in blocks of *X* shares.)

For a given sale transaction, the difference between the FIFO and LIFO models lies in how they choose the matching purchase transaction. FIFO chooses by starting at the first purchase made. LIFO chooses by starting at the last purchase made. For example, the following algorithm calculates capital gains using FIFO accounting:

```
// Algorithm for FIFO calculation of capital gain
Set capital gain to zero.
For each sale transaction in the Sales Queue
    Add the amount of the sale transaction to capital gain.
    Get the next purchase in the Purchases Queue.
    Add the amount of the purchase transaction to capital gain.
```

What data do we need?

Note that the algorithm uses two queues, one to store the sales and the second to store the purchases. One important condition for this problem is that the length of the sales queue must always be less than or equal to the length of the purchases queue. You can't sell stock that you don't have.

A similar algorithm for the LIFO calculation would use two stacks to store purchases and sales, respectively. Given these considerations we have the following initial definition of the Accountant class:

```
public class Accountant {
    private Queue buyQueue, sellQueue;
    private Stack buyStack, sellStack;

    public Accountant() { }
    public void insert (Transaction trans) { } // Insert a transaction.
    public double lifoAccounting() { }         // Return capital gain(loss)
    public double fifoAccounting() { }         // Return capital gain(loss)
}
```

The constructor should create instances of the four data structures. The `insert()` method should insert one transaction record into the queues and stacks. In order to be able to compare FIFO and LIFO accounting, it will be necessary to insert the transaction in two lists, either in the two sell structures, if it's a sale, or in the two buy structures, if it's a purchase. Finally, the `lifoAccounting()` and `fifoAccounting()` methods are responsible for calculating capital gain or loss.

What methods do we need?

The AccountantFrame Class

The `AccountantFrame` class is responsible for managing the user interface. Figure 16–19 shows a design for the interface. `JRadioButtons` are used to designate the transaction as a purchase or sale. Remember that radio buttons must be added to a `ButtonGroup` object, which will manage their mutual selection.

The `AccountantFrame` must implement the `ActionListener` interface. The way it should work is that the user should input the transaction data and then click on the "Insert" button. This will cause the transaction to be inserted in the `Accountant` object. After entering several transactions — remember there must always be more purchases than sales — the user will click on the "Calculate" button. At this point the program will print a comparison of the two accounting methods in the display area.

Figure 16–20 shows a sample calculation. You can use the data shown there to test your own program.

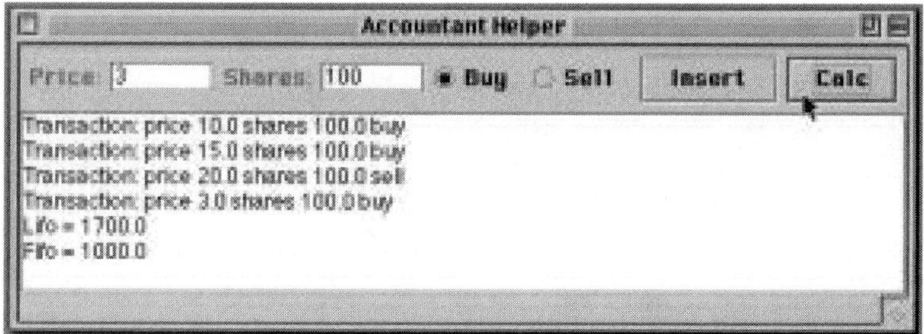

Figure 16–20 An example calculation of capital gains.

CHAPTER SUMMARY

Technical Terms

Abstract Data Type (ADT)	data structure	dequeue
dynamic structure	link	linked list
pop	queue	reference
self-referential object	stack	static structure
traverse	vector	

Important Java Keywords

`null`	`private`	`protected`
`public`	`static`	

Java Classes

`Button`	`Integer`	`Float`
`Object`	`String`	`Vector`

Java Library Methods

`main()`	`toString()`

User-Defined Classes and Methods

`EmptyListExeption`	`List`	`Node`
`PhoneListNode`	`PhoneList`	`Queue`
`Stack`		

User-Defined Methods

`dequeue()`	`enqueue()`	`getData()`
`setData()`	`getNext()`	`getPhone()`
`insert()`	`insertAtFront()`	`removeFirst()`
`insertAtRear()`	`isEmpty()`	`peek()`
`peekLast()`	`print()`	`pop()`
`push()`	`removeFirst()`	`removeLast()`
`setNext()`		

Summary of Important Points

- A *data structure* is a construct used to organize data and make them more efficient to process. An array is an example of a *static structure*, since its size does not change during a program's execution. A vector is an example of a *dynamic structure*, one whose size can grow and shrink during a program's execution.
- A *linked list* is a linear structure in which the individual nodes of the list are joined together by references. A *reference* is a variable that refers to

an object. Each node in the list has a *link* variable which refers to another node. An object that can refer to the same kind of object is said to be *self-referential*.

- The Node class is an example of a self-referential class. It contains a link variable that refers to a Node. By assigning references to the link variable, Nodes can be chained together into a linked list. In addition to their link variables, Nodes contain data variables, which should be accessible through public methods.
- Depending on the use of a linked list, nodes can be inserted at various locations in the list: at the head, the end, or in the middle of the list.
- Traversal algorithms must be used to access the elements of a singly linked list. To traverse a list you start at the first node and follow the links of the chain until you reach the desired node.
- Depending on the application, nodes can be removed from the front, rear, or middle of a linked list. Except for the front node, traversal algorithms are used to locate the desired node.
- In developing list algorithms, it is important to test them thoroughly. Ideally, you should test every possible combination of insertions and removals that the list can support. Practically, you should test every independent case of insertions and removals that the list supports.
- An *Abstract Data Type (ADT)* is a concept that combines two elements: a collection of data, and the operations that can be performed on the data. For the list ADT, the data are the nodes that make up the list, and the operations are insertion, removal, and tests of whether the list is empty.
- In designing an ADT, it's important to provide a public interface which can be used to access the ADT's data. The ADT's implementation details should not matter to the user and should therefore be hidden. A Java class definition, with its public and private aspects, is perfectly suited to implement an ADT.
- A *stack* is a list that allows insertions and removals only at the front of the list. A stack insertion is called a *push* and a removal is called a *pop*. The first element in a stack is usually called the top of the stack. The Stack ADT can easily be defined as a subclass of List. Stacks are used for managing the method call and return in most programming languages.
- A *queue* is a list that only allows insertions at the rear and removals from the front of a list. A queue insertion is called *enqueue*, and a removal is called *dequeue*. The Queue ADT can easily be defined as a subclass of List. Queues are used for managing the various lists used by the CPU scheduler — such as, the ready, waiting, and blocked queues.

ANSWERS TO SELF-STUDY EXERCISES

EXERCISE 16.1

```
Node node = new Node(new String("Hello"));
```

EXERCISE 16.2

```
Node node = new Node(new CyberPet("Socrates"));
```

EXERCISE 16.3

```
PhoneListNode newNode = new PhoneListNode("Bill C", "111-202-3331");
nodeptr.setNext(newNode);
```

EXERCISE 16.4 The condition `((current.getNext() != null)||(!current.getName().equals(name)))` is too general. It will cause the loop to exit as soon as a nonnull node is encountered, whether or not the node matches the one being sought.

EXERCISE 16.5 The `PhoneList` program will generate the following output, which has been edited slightly to improve its readability:

```
Phone Directory
---------------
Roger M 997-0020        Roger W 997-0086        Rich P  997-0010
Jane M  997-2101        Stacy K 997-2517
Looking up numbers by name
  Roger M 997-0020
  Rich P 997-0010
  Stacy K 997-2517
  Sorry. No entry for Mary P
Removed Rich P  997-0010
Phone Directory
---------------
Roger M 997-0020        Roger W 997-0086        Jane M  997-2101
Stacy K 997-2517
Removed Roger M 997-0020
Phone Directory
---------------
Roger W 997-0086        Jane M  997-2101        Stacy K 997-2517
Removed Stacy K 997-2517
Phone Directory
---------------
Roger W 997-0086        Jane M  997-2101
Removed Jane M  997-2101
Phone Directory
---------------
Roger W 997-0086
Sorry. No entry for Jane M
Phone Directory
---------------
Roger W 997-0086
Removed Roger W 997-0086
Phone Directory
---------------
Phone list is empty
```

EXERCISE 16.6 Executing the following method calls will test whether it is possible to insert items into a list after items have been removed.

```
        // Create and insert some nodes
PhoneList list = new PhoneList();
list.insert(new PhoneListNode("Roger M", "997-0020"));
list.insert(new PhoneListNode("Roger W", "997-0086"));
System.out.println(list.remove("Roger M") );
list.insert(new PhoneListNode("Rich P", "997-0010"));
System.out.println(list.remove("Roger W"));
list.insert(new PhoneListNode("Jane M", "997-2101"));
list.insert(new PhoneListNode("Stacy K", "997-2517"));
System.out.println(list.remove("Jane M"));
System.out.println(list.remove("Stacy K"));
list.print();
        // List should be empty
```

EXERCISE 16.7 The List ADT program will produce the following output:

```
Generic List
---------------
Hello World
8647
Roger M 997-0020
Jane M 997-2101
Stacy K 997-2517
 Removed Stacy K 997-2517
Generic List:
Hello World
8647
Roger M 997-0020
Jane M 997-2101
 Removed Jane M 997-2101
Generic List:
Hello World
8647
Roger M 997-0020
 Removed Hello World
Generic List:
8647
Roger M 997-0020
```

EXERCISE 16.8 Executing the following method calls will test whether it is possible to insert items into a a `List` after items have been removed.

```
        // Create and insert some nodes
List list = new List();
list.insertAtFront(new PhoneRecord("Roger M", "997-0020"));
list.insertAtFront(new PhoneRecord("Roger W", "997-0086"));
System.out.println("Current List Elements");
list.print();
Object o = list.removeLast();   // Remove last element
list.insertAtFront(o);         // Insert at the front of the list
System.out.println("Current List Elements");
list.print();
o = list.removeFirst();
System.out.println("Removed " + o.toString());
o = list.removeFirst();
System.out.println("Removed " + o.toString());
list.insertAtRear(o);
System.out.println("Current List Elements");
list.print();                   // List should have one element
```

EXERCISE 16.9 The peek() method should just return the first node without deleting it:

```
public Object peek() {
    return head;
}
```

EXERCISE 16.10 The peekLast() method can be modeled after the List.removeLast() method:

```
public Object peekLast() {
    if (isEmpty())
        return null;
    else {
        Node current = head;                    // Start at head of list
        while (current.getNext() != null)       // Find the end of the list
            current = current.getNext();
        return  current;                        // Return last node
    }
} // peekLast()
```

EXERCISES

1. Explain the difference between each of the following pairs of terms:

   a. *Stack* and *queue*.
   b. *Static structure* and *dynamic structure*.
   c. *Data structure* and *abstract data type*.
   d. *Push* and *pop*.
   e. *Enqueue* and *dequeue*.
   f. *Linked list* and *node*.

2. Fill in the blanks:

   a. An *abstract data type* consists of two main parts: _____ and _____.
   b. An object that contains a variable that refers to an object of the same class is a _____.
   c. One application for a _____ is to manage the method call and returns in a computer program.
   d. One application for a _____ is to balance the parentheses in an arithmetic expression.
   e. A _____ operation is one that starts at the beginning of a list and processes each element.
   f. A vector is an example of a _____ data structure.
   g. An array is an example of a _____ data structure.
   h. By default the initial value of a reference variable is _____.

3. Add an insertAt() method to the List class to return the object at a certain index location in the list. This method should take an int parameter, specifying the object's position in the list, and it should return an Object.
4. Add a removeAt() method to the List class that will insert an object at a certain position in the list. This method should take two parameters, the Object to be inserted, and an int to designate where to insert it. It should return a boolean to indicate whether the insertion was successful.

5. Add a `removeAll()` method to the `List` class. This `void` method should remove all the members of the list.

6. Write an `int` method named `size()` that returns the number of elements in a `List`

7. Write an `boolean` method named `contains(Object o)` that returns `true` if its `Object` parameter is contained in the list.

8. The *head* of a list is the first element in the list. The *tail* of a list consists of all the elements except the head. Write a method named `tail()` that returns a reference to the tail of the list. Its return value should be `Node`.

9. Write a program that uses the `List` ADT to store a list of 100 random floating-point numbers. Write methods to calculate the average of the numbers.

10. Write a program that uses the `List` ADT to store a list of `Student` records, using a variation of the Student class defined in Chapter 14. Write a method to calculate the average grade point average for all students in the list.

11. Write a program that creates a copy of a `List`. It is necessary to copy each node of the list. This will require that you create new nodes that are copies of the nodes in the original list. To simplify this task, define a copy constructor for your node class and then use that to make copies of each node of the list.

12. Write a program that uses a `Stack` ADT to determine if a string is a palindrome — spelled the same way backwards and forwards.

13. Design and write a program that uses a `Stack` to determine whether a parenthesized expression is well formed. Such an expression is well formed only if there is a closing parenthesis for each opening parenthesis.

14. Design and write a program that uses `Stacks` to determine whether an expression involving both parentheses and square brackets is well formed.

15. Write a program that links two lists together, appending the second list to the tail of the first list.

16. Design a `Stack` class that uses a `Vector` instead of a linked list to store its elements. This is the way Java's `Stack` class is defined.

17. Design a `Queue` class that uses a `Vector` instead of a linked list to store its elements.

18. **Challenge:** Design a `List` class, similar in functionality to the one we designed in this chapter, that uses an *array* to store the list's elements. Set it up so that the middle of the array is where the first element is put. That way you can still insert at both the front and rear of the list. One limitation of this approach is that unlike a linked list, an array has a fixed size. Allow the user to set the initial size of the array in a constructor, but if the array becomes full, don't allow any further insertions.

19. **Challenge:** Add a method to the program in the previous exercise that lets the user increase the size of the array used to store the list. You may want to review the In the Laboratory section of Chapter 11.

20. **Challenge:** Recursion is a useful technique for list processing. Write recursive versions of the `print()` method and the lookup-by-name method for the `PhoneList`. (*Hint*: The base case in processing a list is the empty list. The recursive case should handle the head of the list and then recurse on the tail of the list. The tail of the list is everything but the first element.)

21. **Challenge:** Design an `OrderedList` class. An ordered list is one that keeps its elements in order. For example, if it's an ordered list of integers, then the first integer is less than or equal to the second, the second is less than or equal to the third, and so on. If it's an ordered list of employees, then perhaps the employees are stored in order according to their social security numbers. The `OrderedList` class should contain an `insert(Object o)` method that inserts its object in the proper order. One major challenge in this project is designing your class so that it will work for any kind of object. (Hint: Define an `Orderable` interface that defines an abstract `precedes()` method. Then define a subclass of `Node` that implements `Orderable`. This will let you compare any two `Nodes` to see which one comes before the other.)

APPENDIX A

Coding Conventions

This appendix covers various aspects of programming style and coding conventions. It follows the conventions suggested in the Java Language Specification (`http://java.sun.com/docs/books/jls`), which is summarized on Sun's Java Website (`http://java.sun.com/docs`). The conventions have been modified somewhat to fit the needs of an academic programming course. For further details see

```
http://java.sun.com/docs/codeconv/index.html
```

Coding conventions improve the readability and maintainability of the code. Because maintenance is often done by programmers who did not have a hand in designing or writing the original code, it is important that the code follow certain conventions. For a typical piece of commercial software, much more time and expense are invested in maintaining the code than in creating the code.

Comments

Java recognizes two types of comments: *C-style* comments use the same syntax found in C and C++. They are delimited by /* ... */, and //. The first set of delimiters is used to delimit a multiline comment. The Java compiler will ignore all text that occurs between /* and */. The second set of delimiters is used for a single-line comment. Java will ignore all the code on the rest of the line following a double slash (//). C-style comments are called *implementation comments* and are mainly used to describe the implementation of your code.

Documentation comments are particular to Java. They are delimited by /** ... */. These are used mainly to describe the specification or design of the code, rather than its implementation. When a file containing documentation comments is processed by the *javadoc* tool that comes with the Java Development Kit (JDK), the documentation comments will be incorporated into an HTML document. This is how on-line documentation has been created for the Java library classes.

Implementation Commenting Guidelines

Implementation (C-style) comments should be used to provide an overview of the code and to provide information that is not easily discernible from the code itself. They should not be used as a substitute for poorly written or poorly designed code.

In general, comments should be used to improve the readability of the code. Of course, readability depends on the intended audience. Code that's easily readable by an expert programmer may be completely indecipherable to a novice. Our commenting guidelines are aimed at someone who is just learning to program in Java.

Block Comments

A *block comment* or *comment block* is a multiline comment that is used to describe files, methods, data structures, and algorithms:

```
/*
 * Multiline comment block
 */
```

Single-Line Comments

A single-line comment can be delimited either by // or by `/* ... */`. The // is also used to *comment out* a line of code that you want to skip during a particular run. The following example illustrates these uses:

```
/* Single line comment */
System.out.println("Hello");          // End of line comment
// System.out.println("Goodbye");
```

Note that the third line is commented out and would be ignored by the Java compiler.

In this text we generally use slashes for single-line and end-of-line comments. And we frequently use end-of-line comments to serve as a running commentary on the code itself. The types of comments serve a pedagogical purpose — to teach you how the code works. In a "production environment" it would be unusual to find this kind of running commentary.

Java Documentation Comments

Java's on-line documentation has been generated by the `javadoc` tool that comes with the Java Development Kit (JDK). To conserve space, we use documentation comments only sparingly in the programs listed in this textbook itself. However, `javadoc` comments are used more extensively to document the on-line source code that accompanies the textbook.

Documentation comments are placed before classes, interfaces, constructors, methods, and fields. They generally take the following form:

```
 /**
  * The Example class blah blah
  * @author J. Programmer
  */
public class Example { ...
```

Note how the class definition is aligned with the beginning of the comment. `Javadoc` comments use special tags, such as *@author* and *@param*, to identify certain elements of the documentation. For details on `javadoc`, see:

```
http://java.sun.com/products/jdk/1.2/docs/tooldocs/tools.html
```

Indentation and White Space

The use of indentation and white space helps to improve the readability of the program. *White space* refers to the use of blank lines and blank space in a program. It should be used to separate one program element from another, with the goal being to draw attention to the important elements of the program.

- Use a blank line to separate method definitions and to separate a class's instance variables from its methods.
- Use blank spaces within expressions and statements to enhance their readability.
- Be consistent in the way you use white space in your program.

Code should be indented in a way that shows the logical structure of the program. You should use a consistent number of spaces as the size of the indentation tab. The Java Language Specification recommends 4 spaces.

In general, indentation should represent the *contained in* relationships within the program. For example, a class definition contains declarations, for instance variables and definitions of methods. The declarations and definitions should be indented by the same amount throughout the class definition. The statements contained in the body of a method definition should be indented:

```
public void instanceMethod() {
    System.out.println("Hello");
    return;
}
```

An if statement contains an if clause and an else clause, which should be indented.

```
if (condition)
    System.out.println("If part");   // If clause
else
    System.out.println("Else part"); // Else clause
```

The statements contained in the body of a loop should be indented:

```
for (int k = 0; k < 100; k++) {
    System.out.println("Hello " + 'k'); // Loop body
}
```

Finally, indentation should be used whenever a statement or expression is too long to fit on a single line. Generally, lines should be no longer than 80 characters.

Naming Conventions

The choice of identifiers for various elements within a program can help improve the readability of the program. Identifiers should be descriptive of the element's purpose. The name of class should be descriptive of the class's role or function. The name of a method should be descriptive of what the method does.

The way names are spelled can also help improve a program's readability. Table 1 summarizes the various conventions recommended by the Java Language Specification and followed by professional Java programmers.

Table A.1. Naming rules for Java identifiers.

Identifier Type	Naming Rule	Example
Class	Nouns in mixed case with the first letter of each internal word capitalized.	CyberPet TextField
Interfaces	Same as class names. Many interface names end with the suffix "able."	Drawable ActionListener
Method	Verbs in mixed case with the first letter in lowercase and the first letter of internal words capitalized.	actionPerformed() sleep() insertAtFront()
Instance Variables	Same as method names. The name should be descriptive of how the variable is used.	maxWidth isVisible
Constants	Constants should be written in uppercase with internal words separated by _.	MAX_LENGTH XREF
Loop Variables	Temporary variables, such as loop variables, may have single character names: i, j, k.	int k; int i;

Use of Braces

Curly braces { } are used to mark the beginning and end of a block of code. They are used to demarcate a class body, a method body, or simply to combine a sequence of statements into a single code block. There are two conventional ways to align braces and we have used both in the text. The opening and closing brace may be aligned in the same column with the enclosed statements indented:

```
public void sayHello()
{
    System.out.println("Hello");
}
```

This is the style that's used in the first part of the book, because it's easier for someone just learning the syntax to check that the braces match up.

Alternatively, the opening brace may be put at the end of the line where the code block begins, with the closing brace aligned under the beginning of the line where the code block begins:

```
public void sayHello() {
   System.out.println("Hello");
}
```

This is the style that's used in the last two parts of the book, and it seems the style preferred by professional Java programmers.

Sometimes even with proper indentation, it it difficult to tell which closing brace goes with which opening brace. In those cases you should put an end-of-line comment to indicate what the brace closes:

```
public void sayHello() {
    for (int k=0; k < 10; k++) {
        System.out.println("Hello");
    }//for loop
}// sayHello()
```

File Names and Layout

Java source files should have the `.java` suffix, and Java bytecode files should have the `.class` suffix.

A Java source file can only contain a single `public` class. Private classes and interfaces associated with a public class can be included in the same file.

Source File Organization Layout

All source files should begin with a comment block that contains important identifying information about the program, such as the name of the file, author, date, copyright information, and a brief description of the classes in the file. In the professional software world, the details of this "boilerplate" comment will vary from one software house to another. For the purposes of an academic computing course, the following type of comment block would be appropriate:

```
/*
 * Filename: Example.java
 * Author: J. Programmer
 * Date:  April, 20 1999
 * Description: This program illustrates basic coding conventions.
 */
```

The beginning comment block should be followed by any package and import statements used by the program:

```
package java.mypackage;
import java.awt.*;
```

The *package* statement should only be used if the code in the file belongs to the package. None of the examples in this book use the package statement. The *import* statement allows you to use abbreviated names to refer to the library classes used in your program. For example, in a program that imports `java.awt.*` we can refer to the `java.awt.Button` class as simply `Button`. If the import statement were omitted, we would have to use the fully qualified name .

The `import` statements should be followed by the class definitions contained in the file. Figure 1 illustrates how a simple Java source file should be formatted and documented.

Statements

Declarations

There are two kinds of declaration statements: field declarations, which include a class's instance variables, and local variable declarations.

- Put one statement per line, possibly followed by a end-of-line comment if the declaration needs explanation.
- Initialize local variables when they are declared. Instance variables are given default initializations by Java.
- Place variable declarations at the beginning of code blocks in which they are used rather than interspersing them throughout the code block.

Figure A–1 A sample Java source file.

```
/*
 * Filename: Example.java
 * Author: J. Programmer
 * Date:  April, 20 1999
 * Description: This program illustrates basic coding conventions.
 */

import java.awt.*;

/**
 * The Example class is an example of a simple class definition.
 *
 * @author J. Programmer
 */
public class Example {

    /** Doc comment for instance variable, var1 */
    public int var1;

    /**
     * Constructor method documentat comment describes
     *   what the constructor does.
     */
    public Example () {
     // ... method implementation goes here
    }

    /**
     *  An instanceMethod() documentation comment describes
     *   what the method does.
     *  @param N is a parameter than ....
     *  @return This method returns blah blah
     */
    public int instanceMethod( int N ) {
     // ... method implementation goes here
    }
}// Example
```

The following class definition illustrates these points:

```
public class Example {
    private int size = 0;          // Window length and width
    private int area = 0;          // Window's current area

    public void myMethod() {
       int mouseX = 0;             // Beginning of method block

       if (condition) {
           int mouseY = 0;         // Beginning of if block
       ...
       }
    }// myMethod()
}// Example
```

Executable Statements

Simple statements, such as assignment statements, should be written one per line and should be aligned with the other statements in the block. Compound statements are those that contain other statements. Examples would include if statements, for statements, while statements, and do-while statements. Compound statements should use braces and appropriate indentation to highlight the statement's structure. Here are some examples of how to code several kinds of compound statements:

```
if (condition) {          // A simple if statement
    statement1;
    statement2;
}

if (condition1) {         // An if-else statement
    statement1;
} else if (condition2) {
    statement2;
    statement3;
} else {
    statement4;
    statement5;
}

for (initializer; entry-condition; updater) { // For statement
    statement1;
    statement2;
}

while (condition) {            // While statement
    statement1;
    statement2;
}

do {                           // Do-while statement
    statement1;
    statement2;
} while (condition);
```

Preconditions and Postconditions

A good way to design and document loops and methods is to specify their preconditions and postconditions. A *precondition* is a condition that must be true before the method (or loop) starts. A *postcondition* is a condition that must be true after the method (or loop) completes. Although the conditions can be represented formally — using boolean expressions — this is not necessary. It suffices to give a clear and concise statement of the essential facts before and after the method (or loop).

Chapter 6 introduces the use of preconditions and postconditions and Chapters 6 through 8 provide numerous examples of how to use them. It may be helpful to reread some of those examples and model your documentation after the examples showed there.

Sample Programs

For specific examples of well-documented programs used in the text, see the online source code which is available on the accompanying Web site at:

```
http://www.prenhall.com/morelli
```

APPENDIX B

The Java Development Kit

The Java Development Kit (JDK), version 1.2, is a set of command-line tools for developing Java programs. It is available for free in versions for Microsoft Windows and Solaris (Sun Microsystems). Download information is available at

```
http://java.sun.com/products/jdk/1.2/
```

Sun's Website provides extensive documentation for JDK at

```
http://java.sun.com/products/jdk/1.2/docs/tooldocs/tools.html
```

This appendix summarizes some of the primary tools available in the JDK. For more detailed information you should consult Sun's Web site.

Table B.1 provides a summary of some of the JDK tools.

The Java Compiler: `javac`

The Java compiler (`javac`) translates Java source files into Java bytecode. A Java source file must have the `.java` extension. The `javac` compiler will

Table B.1. Tools included in the Java Development Kit.

Tool Name	Description
javac	Java compiler. Translates source code into bytecode.
java	Java interpreter. Translates and executes bytecode.
javadoc	Java documentation generator. Creates HTML pages from documentation comments embedded in Java programs.
appletviewer	Appletviewer. Used instead of a browser to run Java applets.
jar	Java archive manager. Manages Java archive (JAR) files.
jdb	Java debugger. Used to find bugs in a program.
javap	Java disassembler. Translates bytecode into Java source code.

create a bytecode file with the same name but with the .class extension. The javac command takes the following form:

```
javac    [ options ]    sourcefiles    [ @files ]
```

The brackets in this expression indicate optional parts of the command. Thus, *options* is an optional list of options, and *@files* is an optional list of files, each of which contains a list of Java source files. The *@files* option would be used if you were compiling a very large collection of files, too large to list each file individually on the command line.

Most of the time you would simply list the *sourcefiles* you are compiling immediately after the word javac, as in the following example:

```
javac MyAppletClass.java MyHelperClass.java
```

Given this command, javac will read class definitions contained in MyAppletClass.java and MyHelperClass.java and translate them into bytecode files named MyAppletClass.class and MyHelperClass.class.

If a Java source file contains inner classes, these would be compiled into separate class files. For example, if MyAppletClass.java contained an inner class named Inner, javac would compile the code for the inner class into a file named MyAppletClass$Inner.class.

If you are writing a program that involves several classes, it is not necessary to list each individual class on the command line. You must list the main class — that is, the class where execution will begin. The compiler will perform a search for all the other classes used in the main class. For example, if MyAppletClass uses an instance of MyHelperClass, you can compile both classes with the following command:

```
javac MyAppletClass.java
```

In this case, javac will perform a search for the definition of MyHelperClass.

How Java Searches for Class Definitions

When compiling a file, javac needs a definition for every class or interface that's used in the source file. For example, if you are creating a subclass of java.applet.Applet, javac will need definitions for all of Applet's superclasses, including Panel, Container, and Component. The definitions for these classes are contained in the java.awt package. Here's how javac will search for these classes.

Javac will first search among its library files. This is where it should find definitions for library classes, such as `Applet` and `Panel`. Next, `javac` will search among the files and directories listed on the user's *class path*. The class path is a system variable that lists all the user directories and files that should be searched when compiling a user's program. The class path can be set either by using the environment variable CLASSPATH or by using the `-classpath` option when invoking `javac`. Because the details for setting the class path are system dependent, it's best to consult the on-line documentation to see exactly how this is done on your system.

During a successful search, `javac` may find a source file, a class file, or both. If it finds a class file but not source file, `javac` will use the class file. This would be the case for Java library code. If `javac` finds a source file but not a class file, it will compile the source and use the resulting class file. This would be the case for the first compilation of one of your source programs. If `javac` finds both a source and a class file, it determines whether the class file is up to date. If so, it uses it. If not, it compiles the source and uses the resulting class file. This would be the case for all subsequent compilations of one of your source programs.

As noted earlier, if your application or applet uses several source files, you need only provide `javac` with the name of the main application or applet file. It will find and compile all the source files, as long as they are located in a directory that's listed in the class path,

The Java Interpreter: `java`

The `java` interpreter launches a Java application. This command takes one of the following forms:

java	[*options*]	classname	[*argument* ...]	
java	[*options*]	**-jar**	file.jar	[*argument* ...]

If the first form is used, `java` starts a Java runtime environment. It then loads the specified *classname* and runs that class's `main()` method, which must be declared as follows:

```
public static void main(String args[])
```

The `String` parameter `args[]` is an array of strings, which is used to pass any *arguments* listed on the command line. Command-line arguments are optional.

If the second form of the `java` command is used, `java` will load the classes and resources from the specified *Java archive (JAR)*. In this case the special `-jar` option flag must be specified.

The appletviewer

The appletviewer tool lets you run Java applets without using a Web browser. This command takes the following form:

appletviewer [*threads flag*] [*options*] url ...

The optional *threads flag* tells Java which of the various threading options to use. This is system dependent. For details on this feature and the command line *options*, refer to Sun's Web site.

The appletviewer will connect to one or more HTML documents specified by their *Uniform Resource Locators (URLs)*. It will display each applet referenced in those documents in a separate window. Some example commands would be:

```
appletviewer http://www.domain.edu/account/myapplet.html
appletviewer myapplet.html
```

In the first case, the document's full path name is given. In the second case, since no host computer is mentioned, appletviewer will assume that the applet is located on the local host and will search the class path for myapplet.html.

Once appletviewer retrieves the HTML document, it will find the applet by looking for either the object, embed or applet tags within the document. The appletviewer ignores all other HTML tags. It just runs the applet. If it cannot find one of these tags, the appletviewer will do nothing. If it does locate an applet, it starts a runtime environment, loads the applet, and then runs the applet's init() method. The applet's init() must have the following method signature:

```
public void init()
```

The applet Tag

The applet tag is the original HTML 3.2 tag used for embedding applets within an HTML document. If this tag is used, the applet will be run by the browser, using the browser's own implementation of the Java Runtime Environment (JRE).

Note, however, that if your applet uses the latest Java language features and the browser is not using the latest version of JRE, the applet may not run correctly. For example, this might happen if your applet makes use of Swing features that are not yet supported in the browser's implementation of the JRE. In that case, your applet won't run under that browser.

To ensure that the applet runs with the latest version of the JRE — the one provided by Sun Microsystems — you can also use the `object` or the `embed` tags. These tags are used to load the appropriate version of the JRE into the browser as a *plugin* module. A plugin is a helper program that extends the browser's functionality.

The `applet` tag takes the following form:

```
<applet
    code="yourAppletClass.class"
    object="serializedObjectOrJavaBean"
    codebase="classFileDirectory"
    width="pixelWidth"
    height="pixelHeight"
>
   <param name="..." value="...">
   ...
   alternate-text
</applet>
```

You would use only the `code` or `object` attribute, not both. For the programs in this book, you should always use the `code` tag. The `code` tag specifies where the program will begin execution — that is, in the applet class.

The optional `codebase` attribute is used to specify a relative path to the applet. It may be omitted if the applet's class file is in the same directory as the HTML document.

The `width` and `height` attributes specify the initial dimensions of the applet's window. The values specified in the applet tag can be overridden in the applet itself by using the `setSize()` method, which the applet inherits from the `java.awt.Component` class.

The `param` tags are used to specify arguments that can be retrieved when the applet starts running (usually in the applet's `init()` method). The methods for retrieving parameters are defined in the `java.applet.Applet` class.

Finally, the `alternative-text` portion of the applet tag provides text that would be displayed on the Web page if the appletviewer or browser is unable to locate the applet.

Here's a simple example of an applet tag:

```
<applet
    code="HelloWorldApplet.class"
    codebase="classfiles"
    width="200"
    height="200"
>
    <param name="author" value="Java Java Java">
    <param name="date" value="May 1999">

    Sorry, your browser does not seem to be able to
    locate the HelloWorldApplet.
</applet>
```

In this case the applet's code is stored in a file name `HelloWorldApplet.class`, which is stored in the `classfiles` subdirectory — that is, a subdirectory of the directory containing the HTML file. The applet's window will be 200 × 200 pixels. And the applet is passed the name of the program's author and date it was written. Finally, if the applet cannot be located, the "Sorry . . . " message will be displayed instead.

The `object` Tag

The `object` tag is the HTML 4.0 tag for embedding applets and multimedia objects in an HTML document. It is also an Internet Explorer (IE) 4.x extension to HTML. It allows IE to run a Java applet using the latest JRE plugin from Sun. The `object` tag takes the following form:

```
<object
    classid="name of the plugin program"
    codebase="url for the plugin program"
    width="pixelWidth"
    height="pixelHeight"
>
    <param name="code" value="yourClass.class">
    <param name="codebase" value="classFileDirectory">
     ...
    alternate-text
</object>
```

Note that parameters are used to specify your applet's code and codebase. In effect, these are parameters to the plugin module. An example tag that corresponds to the `applet` tag for the `HelloWorldApplet` might be as follows:

```
<object
    classid="clsid:8AD9C840-044E-11D1-B3E9-00805F499D93"
    codebase="http://java.sun.com/products/plugin/1.1/jinstall-11-win32.cab#Version=1,1,0,0"
    width="200"
    height="200"
>
    <param name="code" value="HelloWorldApplet.class">
    <param name="codebase" value="classfiles">
    <param name="author" value="Java Java Java">
    <param name="date" value="May 1999">

    Sorry, your browser does not seem to be able to
    locate the HelloWorldApplet.
</object>
```

For further details on how to use the `object` tag, see Sun's plugin site at

```
http://java.sun.com/products/plugin/1.1.1/docs/tags.html
```

The embed Tag

The embed tag is Netscape's version of the `applet` and `object` tags. It is included as extension to HTML 3.2. It can be used to allow a Netscape 4.x browser to run a Java applet using the latest Java plugin from Sun. It takes the following form:

```
<embed
    type="Type of program"
    code="yourAppletClass.class"
    codebase="classFileDirectory"
    pluginspage="location of plugin file on the web"
    width="pixelWidth"
    height="pixelHeight"
>
    <noembed>
    Alternative text
    </noembed>
</embed>
```

The `type` and `pluginspage` attributes are not used by the appletviewer, but they are necessary for browsers. They would just be ignored by the appletviewer.

For example, an `embed` tag for `HelloWorldApplet` would be as follows:

```
<EMBED
    type="application/x-java-applet;version=1.1"
    width="200"
    height="200"
    code="HelloWorldApplet.class"
    codebase="classfiles"
    pluginspage="http://java.sun.com/products/plugin/1.1/plugin-install.html">

   <NOEMBED>
       Sorry.  This page won't be able to run this applet.
   </NOEMBED>
</EMBED>
```

It is possible to combine the `applet`, `embed`, and `object` tags in the same HTML file. And Sun even provides code that should enable an applet to use the correct Java plugin no matter what browser runs the applet. For details see Sun's plugin page:

```
http://java.sun.com/products/plugin/1.1.1/docs/tags.html
```

The Java Archiver jar Tool

The `jar` tool can be used to combine multiple files into a single JAR archive file. Although the `jar` tool is a general-purpose archiving and compression tool, it was designed mainly to facilitate the packaging of Java applets and applications into a single file.

The main justification for combining files into a single archive and compressing the archive is to improve download time. The jar command takes the following format:

jar	[*manifest*] destination-file	input-file	[input-files]

For an example of its usage, lets use it to archive the files involved in the AnimatedCyberPet example in Chapter 6. This is an applet that uses several images to animate the pet. We want to allow users to download the applet via a browser. To improve download times we want to combine all the .class files and the .gif files into a single jar file. Here's list of the files we want to archive.

```
AnimatedCyberPet.class
CyberPet.class
eatImage.gif
eat2Image.gif
happyImage.gif
sleepImage.gif
```

The command we use is as follows:

```
jar cf animated.jar *.class *.gif
```

In this case the cf options specify that we are creating a jar file named animated.jar that will consist of all the files having the .class and .gif suffixes.

Once we have created the jar file, we need to specify it in the applet tag. For example, the HTML file for the animated pet applet now becomes

```
<html>
    <head><title>CyberPet Applet</title></head>
    <body>
    <applet
        archive="animated.jar"
        code="AnimatedCyberPet.class"
        width=350 height=350
    >
        <parameter name="author" value="Java Java Java">
        <parameter name="date" value="February 1999">
    </applet>
    </body>
</html>
```

When specified in this way, the browser will take care of downloading the archive file and extracting the individual files needed by the applet. Note that the code attribute must still designate the file where the program will start execution.

The Java Documentation Tool: javadoc

The javadoc tool parses the declarations and documentation comments in a Java source file and generates a set of HTML pages that describe the following elements: public and protected classes, inner classes, interfaces, constructors, methods, and fields.

The javadoc tool can be used on a single file or an entire package of files. Recall that a Java documentation comment is one that begins with /** and ends with */. These are the comments that are parsed by javadoc.

The javadoc tool has many features, and it is possible to use Java *doclets* to customize your documentation. For full details on using the tool, it is best to consult Sun's Web site. To illustrate how it might be used, let's just look at a simple example.

The TimerApplet program from Chapter 1 contains documentation comments. It was processed using the following command:

```
javadoc TimerApplet.java
```

javadoc generated the following HTML documents:

```
TimerApplet.html -The main documentation file
AllNames.html    -Details on the names used in TimerApplet
tree.html        -A tree showing TimerApplet's place in the class hierarchy
packages.html    -Details on the packages used in TimerApplet
```

To see how the documentation appears, review the TimerApplet.java source file and the documentation it generated. Both are available at

```
http://www.prenhall.com/morelli/
```

APPENDIX C

The ASCII and Unicode Character Sets

Java uses version 2.0 of the Unicode character set for representing character data. The Unicode set represents each character as a 16-bit unsigned integer. It can therefore represent $2^{16} = 65{,}536$ different characters. This enables Unicode to represent characters from not only English but also a wide range of international languages. For details about Unicode see

```
http://www.unicode.org
```

Unicode supersedes the ASCII character set (American Standard Code for Information Interchange). The ASCII code represents each character as a 7-bit or 8-bit unsigned integer. A 7-bit code can represent only $2^7 = 128$ characters. In order to make Unicode backwards compatible with ASCII, the first 128 characters of Unicode have the same integer representation as the ASCII characters.

Table C.1 shows the integer representations for the *printable* subset of ASCII characters. The characters with codes 0 through 31 and code 127 are *nonprintable* characters, many of which are associated with keys on a standard keyboard. For example, the delete key is represented by 127, the backspace by 8, and the return key by 13.

Table C.1. ASCII codes for the printable characters

Code	32	33	34	35	36	37	38	39	40	41	42	43	44	45	46	47
Char	SP	!	"	#	$	%	&	'	(	)	*	+	,	-	.	/

Code	48	49	50	51	52	53	54	55	56	57
Char	0	1	2	3	4	5	6	7	8	9

Code	58	59	60	61	62	63	64
Char	:	;	<	=	>	?	@

Code	65	66	67	68	69	70	71	72	73	74	75	76	77
Char	A	B	C	D	E	F	G	H	I	J	K	L	M

Code	78	79	80	81	82	83	84	85	86	87	88	89	90
Char	N	O	P	Q	R	S	T	U	V	W	X	Y	Z

Code	91	92	93	94	95	96
Char	[	\	]	^	_	`

Code	97	98	99	100	101	102	103	104	105	106	107	108	109
Char	a	b	c	d	e	f	g	h	i	j	k	l	m

Code	110	111	112	113	114	115	116	117	118	119	120	121	122
Char	n	o	p	q	r	s	t	u	v	w	x	y	z

Code	123	124	125	126
Char	{	|	}	~

APPENDIX D

Java Keywords

The words shown in Table D.1 are reserved for use as Java *keywords* and cannot be used as identifiers. The keywords `const` and `goto`, which are C++ keywords, are not actually used in Java. They were included mainly to enable better error messages to be generated when they are mistakenly used in a Java program.

The words `true`, `false`, and `null` may look like keywords but are technically considered *literals*. They also cannot be used as identifiers.

Table D.1. The Java keywords cannot be used as names for identifiers.

abstract	default	if	private	throw
boolean	do	implements	protected	throws
break	double	import	public	transient
byte	else	instanceof	return	try
case	extends	int	short	void
catch	final	interface	static	volatile
char	finally	long	super	while
class	float	native	switch	
const	for	new	synchronized	
continue	goto	package	this	

APPENDIX E

Operator Precedence Hierarchy

Table E.1 summarizes the precedence and associativity relationships for Java operators. Within a single expression, an operator of order m would be evaluated before an operator of order n if $m < n$. Operators having the same order are evaluated according to their association order. For example, the expression

```
25 + 5 * 2 + 3
```

would be evaluated in the order shown by the following parenthesized expression:

```
(25 + (5 * 2)) + 3   ==> (25 + 10) + 3 ==> 35 + 3  ==> 38
```

In other words, because * has higher precedence than +, the multiplication operation is done before either of the addition operations. And because addition associates from left to right, addition operations are performed from left to right.

Table E.1. Java operator precedence and associativity table

<table>
<tr><th>Order</th><th>Operator</th><th>Operation</th><th>Association</th></tr>
<tr><td>0</td><td>( )</td><td>Parentheses</td><td></td></tr>
<tr><td>1</td><td>++ -- .</td><td>Postincrement Postdecrement Dot Operator</td><td>L to R</td></tr>
<tr><td>2</td><td>++ -- + - !</td><td>Preincrement Predecrement</td><td>R to L</td></tr>
<tr><td></td><td></td><td>Unary plus Unary minus Boolean NOT</td><td></td></tr>
<tr><td>3</td><td>(type) new</td><td>Type Cast Object Instantiation</td><td>R to L</td></tr>
<tr><td>4</td><td>* / %</td><td>Multiplication Division Modulus</td><td>L to R</td></tr>
<tr><td>5</td><td>+ - +</td><td>Addition Subtraction String Concatenation</td><td>L to R</td></tr>
<tr><td>6</td><td>< > <= >=</td><td>Relational Operators</td><td>L to R</td></tr>
<tr><td>7</td><td>== !=</td><td>Equality Operators</td><td>L to R</td></tr>
<tr><td>8</td><td>^</td><td>Boolean XOR</td><td>L to R</td></tr>
<tr><td>9</td><td>&&</td><td>Boolean AND</td><td>L to R</td></tr>
<tr><td>10</td><td>||</td><td>Boolean OR</td><td>L to R</td></tr>
<tr><td>11</td><td>= += -= *= /= %=</td><td>Assignment Operators</td><td>R to L</td></tr>
</table>

Most operators associate from left to right, but note that assignment operators associate from right to left. For example, consider the following code segment:

```
int i, j, k;
i = j = k = 100;      // Equivalent to i = (j = (k = 100));
```

In this case, each variable will be assigned 100 as its value. But it's important that this expression be evaluated from right to left. First, *k* is assigned 100. Then it's value is assigned to *j*. And finally *j*'s value is assigned to *i*.

For expressions containing mixed operators, it's always a good idea to use parentheses to clarify the order of evaluation. This will also help avoid subtle syntax and semantic errors.

APPENDIX F

Advanced Language Features

This appendix describes some of the basic features of some advanced elements of the Java language. As for many language features, there are details and subtleties involved in using these features that are not covered here. For further details, you should consult Sun's on-line references or other references for a more comprehensive description.

Inner Classes

Inner classes were introduced in Java 1.1. This features lets you define a class as part of another class, just as fields and methods are defined within classes. Inner classes can be used to support the work of the class in which they are contained.

Java defines four types of inner classes. A *nested top-level* class or interface is a *static* member of an enclosing top-level class or interface. Such classes are considered top-level classes by Java.

A *member class* is a nonstatic inner class. It is not a top-level class. As a full-fledged member of its containing class, a member class can refer to the fields and methods of the containing class, even the `private` fields and methods. Just as you would expect for the other instance fields and methods of a class, all instances of a member class are associated with an instance of the enclosing class.

A *local class* is an inner class that's defined within a block of Java code, such as within a method or within the body of a loop. Local classes have local scope — they can only be used within the block in which they are defined. Local classes can refer to the methods and variables of its enclosing classes. They are used mostly to implement *adapters*, which are used to handle events.

When Java compiles a file containing a named inner class, it creates separate class files for them with names that include the nesting class as a qualifier. For example, if you define a inner class named `Metric` inside a top-level class named `Converter`, the compiler will create a class file named `Converter$Metric.class` for the inner class. If you wanted to access the inner class from some other class (besides `Converter`), you would use a qualified name: `Converter.Metric`.

An *anonymous class* is a local class whose definition and use are combined into a single expression. Rather than defining the class in one statement and using it in another, both operations are combined into a single expression. Anonymous classes are intended for one-time use. Therefore they don't contain constructors. Their bytecode files are given names like `ConverterFrame$1.class`.

Nested Top-Level versus Member Classes

The `Converter` class (Figure F–1) shows the differences between a nested top-level class and a member class. The program is a somewhat contrived example that performs various kinds of metric conversions. The outer `Converter` class serves as a container for the inner classes, `Distance` and `Weight`, which perform specific conversions.

The `Distance` class is declared `static`, so it is a top-level class. It is contained in the `Converter` class itself. Note the syntax used in `ConverterUser.main()` to create an instance of the `Distance` class:

```
Converter.Distance distance = new Converter.Distance();
```

Figure F–1 A Java application containing a top-level nested class.

```
public class Converter {
    private static final double INCH_PER_METER = 39.37;
    private final double LBS_PER_KG = 2.2;

    public static class Distance {              // Nested Top-level class
        public double metersToInches(double meters) {
            return meters * INCH_PER_METER;
        }
    }// Metric

    public class Weight {                        // Member class
        public double kgsToPounds(double kg) {
            return kg * LBS_PER_KG;
        }
    }//Weight
}//Converter

public class ConverterUser {

    public static void main(String args[]) {
        Converter.Distance distance = new Converter.Distance();
        Converter converter = new Converter();
        Converter.Weight weight = converter.new Weight();

        System.out.println( "5 m = " + distance.metersToInches(5) + " in");
        System.out.println( "5 kg = " + weight.kgsToPounds(5) + " lbs");
    }
}// ConverterUser
```

A fully qualified name is used to refer to the `static` inner class via its containing class.

The `Weight` class is not declared `static`. It is therefore associated with *instances* of the `Converter` class. Note the syntax used to create an instance of the `Weight` class:

```
Converter converter = new Converter();
Converter.Weight weight = converter.new Weight();
```

Before you can create an instance of `Weight`, you have to declare an instance of `Converter`. In this example we have used two statements to create the `weight` object, which requires using the temporary variable, `converter`, as a reference to the `Converter` object. We could also have done this with a single statement by using the following syntax:

```
Converter.Weight weight = new Converter().new Weight();
```

Note that in either case the qualified name `Converter.Weight` must be used to access the inner class from the `ConverterUser` class.

There are a couple of other noteworthy features in this example. First, an inner top-level class is really just a programming convenience. It behaves just like any other top-level class in Java. One restriction on top-level inner classes is that they can only be contained within other top-level classes, although they can be nested one within the other. For example, we could nest additional converter classes within the `Distance` class. Java provides special syntax for referring to such nested classes.

Unlike a top-level class, a member class is nested within an instance of its containing class. Because of this, it can refer to instance variables (`LBS_PER_KG`) and instance methods of its containing class, even to those declared `private`. By contrast, a top-level inner class can only refer to class variables (`INCH_PER_METER`) — that is, to variables that are declared `static`. So you would use a member class if it were necessary to refer to instances of the containing class.

There are many other subtle points associated with member classes, including special language syntax that can be used to refer to nested member classes and rules that govern inheritance and scope of member classes. For these details you should consult the *Java Language Specification*, which can be accessed on-line at

```
http://java.sun.com/docs/books/jls/html/index.html
```

Local and Anonymous Inner Classes

As we have seen, Java's event handling model uses predefined interfaces, such as the `ActionListener` interface, to handle events. When a separate class is defined to implement an interface, it is sometimes called an *adapter* class. Rather than defining adapter classes as top-level classes, it is often more convenient to define them as local or anonymous classes. In the `ConverterFrame` class (Figure F–2) a local class is used to create an `ActionEvent` handler for the application's two buttons.

Figure F–2 The use of a local class as an `ActionListener` adapter.

```
public class ConverterFrame extends JFrame {

    private Converter converter = new Converter();        // Reference to app
    private JTextField inField = new JTextField(8);
    private JTextField outField = new JTextField(8);
    private JButton metersToInch;
    private JButton kgsToLbs;

    public ConverterFrame() {
        metersToInch = createJButton("Meters To Inches");
        kgsToLbs = createJButton("Kilos To Pounds");

        getContentPane().setLayout( new FlowLayout() );
        getContentPane().add(inField);
        getContentPane().add(outField);
        getContentPane().add(metersToInch);
        getContentPane().add(kgsToLbs);
    }

    private JButton createJButton(String s) {     // A method to create a JButton
        JButton jbutton = new JButton(s);

        class ButtonListener implements ActionListener { // Local class

            public void actionPerformed(ActionEvent e) {
                double inValue = Double.valueOf(inField.getText()).doubleValue();
                JButton button = (JButton) e.getSource();
                if (button.getLabel().equals("Meters To Inches"))
                    outField.setText(""+ converter.new Distance().metersToInches(inValue));
                else
                    outField.setText(""+ converter.new Weight().kgsToPounds(inValue));
            }
        }// ButtonListener

        ActionListener listener = new ButtonListener();// Create a listener
        jbutton.addActionListener(listener);             // Register buttons with listener
        return jbutton;
    }// createJButton()

    public static void main(String args[]) {
        ConverterFrame frame = new ConverterFrame();
        frame.setSize(200,200);
        frame.setVisible(true);
    }// main()
}// ConverterFrame
```

The key feature of the ConverterFrame program is the createJButton() method. This method is used instead of the JButton() constructor to create buttons and to create action listeners for the buttons:

```
private JButton createJButton(String s) {      // A method to create a JButton
    JButton jbutton = new JButton(s);

    class ButtonListener implements ActionListener { // Local class

        public void actionPerformed(ActionEvent e) {
            double inValue = Double.valueOf(inField.getText()).doubleValue();
            JButton button = (JButton) e.getSource();
            if (button.getLabel().equals("Meters To Inches"))
                outField.setText(""+ converter.new Distance().metersToInches(inValue));
            else
                outField.setText(""+ converter.new Weight().kgsToPounds(inValue));
        }
    }// ButtonListener

    ActionListener listener = new ButtonListener();// Create a listener
    jbutton.addActionListener(listener);           // Register buttons with listener
    return jbutton;
}// createJButton()
```

The createJButton() method takes a single String parameter for the button's label. It begins by instantiating a new JButton, a reference to which is passed back as the method's return value. After creating an instance button, a local inner class named ButtonListener is defined.

The local class merely implements the ActionListener interface by defining the actionPerformed method. Note how actionPerformed() uses the containing class's converter variable to acquire access to the metersToInches() and kgsToPounds() methods, which are inner class methods of the Converter class (Figure F–1). A local class can use instance variables, such as converter, that are defined in its containing class.

After defining the local inner class, the createJButton() method creates an instance of the class (listener) and registers it as the button's action listener. When a separate object is created to serve as listener in this way, it is called an *adapter*. It implements a listener interface and thereby serves as adapter between the event and the object that generated the event. Any action events that occur on any buttons created with this method will be handled by this adapter. In other words, for any buttons created by the createJButton() method, a listener object is created and assigned as the button's event listener. By using local classes, the code for doing this is much more compact and efficient.

Local classes have some important restrictions. Although an instance of a local class can use fields and methods defined within the class itself or inherited from its superclasses, it cannot use local variables and parameters defined within its scope unless these are declared final. The reason for this restriction is that final variables receive special handling by the Java compiler. Because the compiler knows that the variable's value won't change, it can replace uses of the variable with their values at compile time.

Anonymous Inner Classes

An anonymous inner class is just a local class without a name. Instead of using two separate statements to define and instantiate the local class, Java provides syntax that let's you do it in one expression. The following code illustrates how this is done:

```
private JButton createJButton(String s) {// A method to create a JButton
    JButton jbutton = new JButton(s);

    jbutton.addActionListener( new  ActionListener() {     // Anonymous class
        public void actionPerformed(ActionEvent e) {
            double inValue = Double.valueOf(inField.getText()).doubleValue();
            JButton button = (JButton) e.getSource();
            if (button.getLabel().equals("Meters To Inches"))
                outField.setText("" + converter.new Distance().metersToInches(inValue));
            else
                outField.setText("" + converter.new Weight().kgsToPounds(inValue));
        }// actionPerformed()
    });
    return jbutton;
}// createJButton()
```

Note that the body of the class definition is put right after the `new` operator. The result is that we still create an instance of the adapter object, but we define it on the fly. If the name following `new` is class name, Java will define the anonymous class as a subclass of the named class. If the name following `new` is an interface, the anonymous class will implement the interface. In this example, the anonymous class is an implementation of the `ActionListener` interface.

Local and anonymous classes provide an elegant and convenient way to implement adapter classes that are intended to be used once and have relatively short and simple implementations. The choice of local versus anonymous should largely depend on whether you need more than one instance of the class. If so, or if it's important that the class have a name for some other reason (readability), then you should use a local class. Otherwise, use an anonymous class. As in all design decisions of this nature, you should use whichever approach or style makes your code more readable and more understandable.

APPENDIX G

Java Resources

Reference Books

- **Kim Topley,** *Java Foundation Classes*, **Prentice Hall, 1998.** Part of the Prentice Hall core series, this book provides a comprehensive introduction to the JFC, especially the Swing components.
- **David Flanagan,** *Java in a Nutshell, 2d Ed.*, **O'Reilly and Associates 1997.** Part of the O'Reilly Java series, this book provides a concise desktop reference to Java and the API.
- **James Gosling, Bill Joy, and Guy Steele,** *The Java Language Specification*, **Addison-Wesley, 1996**. This book, which is part of Addison-Wesley's Java Series, provides a detailed description of the Java language. An online version is available at `http://java.sun.com/docs/books/jls`.

On-line References

- `http://java.sun.com` is one of Sun Microsystems' Java Web sites. From this link you can find information about Java documentation, products, demonstrations, and links to other interesting Java sites.
- `http://java.sun.com/products/jdk/1.2/docs/` is the root page for all documentation on version 1.2 of the Java Development Kit.
- `http://java.sun.com/products/jdk/1.2/docs/api/index.html` is the root page for all documentation on the application programming interface, including detailed and up-to-date specifications for all classes in all API packages.
- `http://java.sun.com/products/jdk/1.2/docs/guide/awt/index.html` is the root page for all documentation pertaining to the Abstract Window Toolkit. It is complete and up to date.
- `http://java.sun.com/products/jdk/1.2/docs/guide/swing/index.html` provides detailed documentation about the Swing component set.
- `http://java.sun.com/docs/codeconv/index.html` provides a description of coding conventions suggested by the *Java Language Specification* and followed by the Java programming community. (These are summarized in Appendix A.)
- `http://www.javasoft.sun` is another of Sun Microsystems' Java Web sites. This one specializes in Java technology, including news, training programs, conferences, and product information.
- `http://www.javasoft.sun/tutorial` provides an on-line Java tutorial.

- `http://www.gamelan.com` is an extensive on-line Java resource center. Billed as "The Official Java Directory," this site includes reference information, free downloads, lots of demonstration programs, discussion groups, a glossary, and a directory to other Java sites.
- `http://www.javaworld.com` is the on-line version of *Java World* magazine.
- `news:comp.lang.java` is the Java on-line newsgroup.
- `www.JARS.com` is another Gamelan site that provides reviews and ratings of the best Java applets.
- `http://www.digitalfocus.com/faq/` is a frequently asked (Java) questions site maintained by Digital Focus, Inc. Most of the answers consist of snippets of actual Java code.

Index

A

B

D

E

F

H

I

J

K

L

N

O

Q

R

T

License Agreement and Limited Warranty

READ THE FOLLOWING TERMS AND CONDITIONS CAREFULLY BEFORE OPENING THIS SOFTWARE PACKAGE. THIS LEGAL DOCUMENT IS AN AGREEMENT BETWEEN YOU AND PRENTICE-HALL, INC. (THE "COMPANY"). BY OPENING THIS SEALED SOFTWARE PACKAGE, YOU ARE AGREEING TO BE BOUND BY THESE TERMS AND CONDITIONS. IF YOU DO NOT AGREE WITH THESE TERMS AND CONDITIONS, DO NOT OPEN THE SOFTWARE PACKAGE. PROMPTLY RETURN THE UNOPENED SOFTWARE PACKAGE AND ALL ACCOMPANYING ITEMS TO THE PLACE YOU OBTAINED THEM FOR A FULL REFUND OF ANY SUMS YOU HAVE PAID.

1. GRANT OF LICENSE: In consideration of your purchase of this book, and your agreement to abide by the terms and conditions of this Agreement, the Company grants to you a nonexclusive right to use and display the copy of the enclosed software program (hereinafter the "SOFTWARE") on a single computer (i.e., with a single CPU) at a single location so long as you comply with the terms of this Agreement. The Company reserves all rights not expressly granted to you under this Agreement.
2. OWNERSHIP OF SOFTWARE: You own only the magnetic or physical media (the enclosed media) on which the SOFTWARE is recorded or fixed, but the Company and the software developers retain all the rights, title, and ownership to the SOFTWARE recorded on the original media copy(ies) and all subsequent copies of the SOFTWARE, regardless of the form or media on which the original or other copies may exist. This license is not a sale of the original SOFTWARE or any copy to you.
3. COPY RESTRICTIONS: This SOFTWARE and the accompanying printed materials and user manual (the "Documentation") are the subject of copyright. The individual programs on the media are copyrighted by the authors of each program. Some of the programs on the media include separate licensing agreements. If you intend to use one of these programs, you must read and follow its accompanying license agreement. You may not copy the Documentation or the SOFTWARE, except that you may make a single copy of the SOFTWARE for backup or archival purposes only. You may be held legally responsible for any copying or copyright infringement which is caused or encouraged by your failure to abide by the terms of this restriction.
4. USE RESTRICTIONS: You may not network the SOFTWARE or otherwise use it on more than one computer or computer terminal at the same time. You may physically transfer the SOFTWARE from one computer to another provided that the SOFTWARE is used on only one computer at a time. You may not distribute copies of the SOFTWARE or Documentation to others. You may not reverse engineer, disassemble, decompile, modify, adapt, translate, or create derivative works based on the SOFTWARE or the Documentation without the prior written consent of the Company.
5. TRANSFER RESTRICTIONS: The enclosed SOFTWARE is licensed only to you and may not be transferred to any one else without the prior written consent of the Company. Any unauthorized transfer of the SOFTWARE shall result in the immediate termination of this Agreement.
6. TERMINATION: This license is effective until terminated. This license will terminate automatically without notice from the Company and become null and void if you fail to comply with any provisions or limitations of this license. Upon termination, you shall destroy the Documentation and all copies of the SOFTWARE. All provisions of this Agreement as to warranties, limitation of liability, remedies or damages, and our ownership rights shall survive termination.
7. MISCELLANEOUS: This Agreement shall be construed in accordance with the laws of the United States of America and the State of New York and shall benefit the Company, its affiliates, and assignees.
8. LIMITED WARRANTY AND DISCLAIMER OF WARRANTY: The Company warrants that the SOFTWARE, when properly used in accordance with the Documentation, will operate in substantial conformity with the description of the SOFTWARE set forth in the Documentation. The Company does not warrant that the SOFTWARE will meet your

requirements or that the operation of the SOFTWARE will be uninterrupted or error-free. The Company warrants that the media on which the SOFTWARE is delivered shall be free from defects in materials and workmanship under normal use for a period of thirty (30) days from the date of your purchase. Your only remedy and the Company's only obligation under these limited warranties is, at the Company's option, return of the warranted item for a refund of any amounts paid by you or replacement of the item. Any replacement of SOFTWARE or media under the warranties shall not extend the original warranty period. The limited warranty set forth above shall not apply to any SOFTWARE which the Company determines in good faith has been subject to misuse, neglect, improper installation, repair, alteration, or damage by you. EXCEPT FOR THE EXPRESSED WARRANTIES SET FORTH ABOVE, THE COMPANY DISCLAIMS ALL WARRANTIES, EXPRESS OR IMPLIED, INCLUDING WITHOUT LIMITATION, THE IMPLIED WARRANTIES OF MERCHANTABILITY AND FITNESS FOR A PARTICULAR PURPOSE. EXCEPT FOR THE EXPRESS WARRANTY SET FORTH ABOVE, THE COMPANY DOES NOT WARRANT, GUARANTEE, OR MAKE ANY REPRESENTATION REGARDING THE USE OR THE RESULTS OF THE USE OF THE SOFTWARE IN TERMS OF ITS CORRECTNESS, ACCURACY, RELIABILITY, CURRENTNESS, OR OTHERWISE.

IN NO EVENT, SHALL THE COMPANY OR ITS EMPLOYEES, AGENTS, SUPPLIERS, OR CONTRACTORS BE LIABLE FOR ANY INCIDENTAL, INDIRECT, SPECIAL, OR CONSEQUENTIAL DAMAGES ARISING OUT OF OR IN CONNECTION WITH THE LICENSE GRANTED UNDER THIS AGREEMENT, OR FOR LOSS OF USE, LOSS OF DATA, LOSS OF INCOME OR PROFIT, OR OTHER LOSSES, SUSTAINED AS A RESULT OF INJURY TO ANY PERSON, OR LOSS OF OR DAMAGE TO PROPERTY, OR CLAIMS OF THIRD PARTIES, EVEN IF THE COMPANY OR AN AUTHORIZED REPRESENTATIVE OF THE COMPANY HAS BEEN ADVISED OF THE POSSIBILITY OF SUCH DAMAGES. IN NO EVENT SHALL LIABILITY OF THE COMPANY FOR DAMAGES WITH RESPECT TO THE SOFTWARE EXCEED THE AMOUNTS ACTUALLY PAID BY YOU, IF ANY, FOR THE SOFTWARE.

SOME JURISDICTIONS DO NOT ALLOW THE LIMITATION OF IMPLIED WARRANTIES OR LIABILITY FOR INCIDENTAL, INDIRECT, SPECIAL, OR CONSEQUENTIAL DAMAGES, SO THE ABOVE LIMITATIONS MAY NOT ALWAYS APPLY. THE WARRANTIES IN THIS AGREEMENT GIVE YOU SPECIFIC LEGAL RIGHTS AND YOU MAY ALSO HAVE OTHER RIGHTS WHICH VARY IN ACCORDANCE WITH LOCAL LAW.

ACKNOWLEDGMENT

YOU ACKNOWLEDGE THAT YOU HAVE READ THIS AGREEMENT, UNDERSTAND IT, AND AGREE TO BE BOUND BY ITS TERMS AND CONDITIONS. YOU ALSO AGREE THAT THIS AGREEMENT IS THE COMPLETE AND EXCLUSIVE STATEMENT OF THE AGREEMENT BETWEEN YOU AND THE COMPANY AND SUPERSEDES ALL PROPOSALS OR PRIOR AGREEMENTS, ORAL, OR WRITTEN, AND ANY OTHER COMMUNICATIONS BETWEEN YOU AND THE COMPANY OR ANY REPRESENTATIVE OF THE COMPANY RELATING TO THE SUBJECT MATTER OF THIS AGREEMENT.

Should you have any questions concerning this Agreement or if you wish to contact the Company for any reason, please contact in writing at the address below.

Robin Short
Prentice Hall PTR
One Lake Street
Upper Saddle River, New Jersey 07458

Authorized Book Publisher License Statement and Limited Warranty for Inprise Products

IMPORTANT — READ CAREFULLY

This license statement and limited warranty constitutes a legal agreement ("License Agreement") for the software product ("Software") identified above (including any software, media, and accompanying on-line or printed documentation supplied by Inprise) between you (either as an individual or a single entity), the Book Publisher from whom you received the Software ("Publisher"), and Inprise International, Inc. ("Inprise").

BY INSTALLING, COPYING, OR OTHERWISE USING THE SOFTWARE, YOU AGREE TO BE BOUND BY ALL OF THE TERMS AND CONDITIONS OF THE LICENSE AGREEMENT. If you are the original purchaser of the Software and you do not agree with the terms and conditions of the License Agreement, promptly return the unused Software to the place from which you obtained it for a full refund.

Upon your acceptance of the terms and conditions of the License Agreement, Inprise grants you the right to use the Software solely for educational purposes, in the manner provided below. No rights are granted for deploying or distributing applications created with the Software.

This Software is owned by Inprise or its suppliers and is protected by copyright law and international copyright treaty. Therefore, you must treat this Software like any other copyrighted material (e.g., a book), except that you may either make one copy of the Software solely for backup or archival purposes or transfer the Software to a single hard disk provided you keep the original solely for backup or archival purposes.

You may transfer the Software and documentation on a permanent basis provided you retain no copies and the recipient agrees to the terms of the License Agreement. Except as provided in the License Agreement, you may not transfer, rent, lease, lend, copy, modify, translate, sublicense, time-share or electronically transmit or receive the Software, media or documentation. You acknowledge that the Software in source code form remains a confidential trade secret of Inprise and/or its suppliers and therefore you agree not to modify the Software or attempt to reverse engineer, decompile, or disassemble the Software, except and only to the extent that such activity is expressly permitted by applicable law notwithstanding this limitation.

Though Inprise does not offer technical support for the Software, we welcome your feedback.

This Software is subject to U.S. Commerce Department export restrictions, and is intended for use in the country into which Inprise sold it (or in the EEC, if sold into the EEC).

LIMITED WARRANTY

The Publisher warrants that the Software media will be free from defects in materials and workmanship for a period of ninety (90) days from the date of receipt. Any implied warranties on the Software are limited to ninety (90) days. Some states/jurisdictions do not allow limitations on duration of an implied warranty, so the above limitation may not apply to you.

The Publisher's, Inprise's, and the Publisher's or Inprise's suppliers' entire liability and your exclusive remedy shall be, at the Publisher's or Inprise's option, either (a) return of the price paid, or (b) repair or replacement of the Software that does not meet the Limited Warranty and which is returned to the Publisher with a copy of your receipt. This Limited Warranty is void if failure of the Software has resulted from accident, abuse, or misapplication. Any replacement Software will be warranted for the remainder of the original warranty period or thirty (30) days, whichever is longer. Outside the United States, neither these remedies nor any product support services offered are available without proof of purchase from an authorized non-U.S. source.

TO THE MAXIMUM EXTENT PERMITTED BY APPLICABLE LAW, THE PUBLISHER, INPRISE, AND THE PUBLISHER'S OR INPRISE'S SUPPLIERS DISCLAIM ALL OTHER WARRANTIES AND CONDITIONS, EITHER EXPRESS OR IMPLIED, INCLUDING, BUT NOT LIMITED TO, IMPLIED WARRANTIES OF MERCHANTABILITY, FITNESS FOR A PARTICULAR PURPOSE, TITLE, AND NON-INFRINGEMENT, WITH REGARD TO THE SOFTWARE, AND THE PROVISION OF OR FAILURE TO PROVIDE SUPPORT SERVICES. THIS LIMITED WARRANTY GIVES YOU SPECIFIC LEGAL RIGHTS. YOU MAY HAVE OTHERS, WHICH VARY FROM STATE/JURISDICTION TO STATE/JURISDICTION.

LIMITATION OF LIABILITY

TO THE MAXIMUM EXTENT PERMITTED BY APPLICABLE LAW, IN NO EVENT SHALL THE PUBLISHER, INPRISE, OR THE PUBLISHER'S OR INPRISE'S SUPPLIERS BE LIABLE FOR ANY SPECIAL, INCIDENTAL, INDIRECT, OR CONSEQUENTIAL DAMAGES WHATSOEVER (INCLUDING, WITHOUT LIMITATION, DAMAGES FOR LOSS OF BUSINESS PROFITS, BUSINESS INTERRUPTION, LOSS OF BUSINESS INFORMATION, OR ANY OTHER PECUNIARY LOSS) ARISING OUT OF THE USE OF OR INABILITY TO USE THE SOFTWARE PRODUCT OR THE PROVISION OF OR FAILURE TO PROVIDE SUPPORT SERVICES, EVEN IF INPRISE HAS BEEN ADVISED OF THE POSSIBILITY OF SUCH DAMAGES. IN ANY CASE, INPRISE'S ENTIRE LIABILITY UNDER ANY PROVISION OF THIS LICENSE AGREEMENT SHALL BE LIMITED TO THE GREATER OF THE AMOUNT ACTUALLY PAID BY YOU FOR THE SOFTWARE PRODUCT OR U.S. $25; PROVIDED, HOWEVER, IF YOU HAVE ENTERED INTO A INPRISE SUPPORT SERVICES AGREEMENT, INPRISE'S ENTIRE LIABILITY REGARDING SUPPORT SERVICES SHALL BE GOVERNED BY THE TERMS OF THAT AGREEMENT. BECAUSE SOME STATES AND JURISDICTIONS DO NOT ALLOW THE EXCLUSION OR LIMITATION OF LIABILITY, THE ABOVE LIMITATION MAY NOT APPLY TO YOU.

HIGH RISK ACTIVITIES

The Software is not fault-tolerant and is not designed, manufactured or intended for use or resale as on-line control equipment in hazardous environments requiring fail-safe performance, such as in the operation of nuclear facilities, aircraft navigation or communication systems, air traffic control, direct life support machines, or weapons systems, in which the failure of the Software could lead directly to death, personal injury, or severe physical or environmental damage ("High Risk Activities"). The Publisher, Inprise, and their suppliers specifically disclaim any express or implied warranty of fitness for High Risk Activities.

U.S. GOVERNMENT RESTRICTED RIGHTS

The Software and documentation are provided with RESTRICTED RIGHTS. Use, duplication, or disclosure by the Government is subject to restrictions as set forth in subparagraphs (c)(1)(ii) of the Rights in Technical Data and Computer Software clause at DFARS 252.227–7013 or subparagraphs (c)(1) and (2) of the Commercial Computer Software-Restricted Rights at 48 CFR 52.227–19, as applicable.

GENERAL PROVISIONS

This License Agreement may only be modified in writing signed by you and an authorized officer of Inprise. If any provision of this License Agreement is found void or unenforceable, the remainder will remain valid and enforceable according to its terms. If any remedy provided is determined to have failed for its essential purpose, all limitations of liability and exclusions of damages set forth in the Limited Warranty shall remain in effect.

This License Agreement shall be construed, interpreted and governed by the laws of the State of California, U.S.A. This License Agreement gives you specific legal rights; you may have others which vary from state to state and from country to country. Inprise reserves all rights not specifically granted in this License Agreement.

Sun Microsystems, Inc. Binary Code License Agreement

READ THE TERMS OF THIS AGREEMENT AND ANY PROVIDED SUPPLEMENTAL LICENSE TERMS (COLLECTIVELY "AGREEMENT") CAREFULLY BEFORE OPENING THE SOFTWARE MEDIA PACKAGE. BY OPENING THE SOFTWARE MEDIA PACKAGE, YOU AGREE TO THE TERMS OF THIS AGREEMENT. IF YOU ARE ACCESSING THE SOFTWARE ELECTRONICALLY, INDICATE YOUR ACCEPTANCE OF THESE TERMS BY SELECTING THE "ACCEPT" BUTTON AT THE END OF THIS AGREEMENT. IF YOU DO NOT AGREE TO ALL THESE TERMS, PROMPTLY RETURN THE UNUSED SOFTWARE TO YOUR PLACE OF PURCHASE FOR A REFUND OR, IF THE SOFTWARE IS ACCESSED ELECTRONICALLY, SELECT THE "DECLINE" BUTTON AT THE END OF THIS AGREEMENT.

1. LICENSE TO USE. Sun grants you a non-exclusive and non-transferable license for the internal use only of the accompanying software and documentation and any error corrections provided by Sun (collectively "Software"), by the number of users and the class of computer hardware for which the corresponding fee has been paid.
2. RESTRICTIONS Software is confidential and copyrighted. Title to Software and all associated intellectual property rights is retained by Sun and/or its licensors. Except as specifically authorized in any Supplemental License Terms, you may not make copies of Software, other than a single copy of Software for archival purposes. Unless enforcement is prohibited by applicable law, you may not modify, decompile, reverse engineer Software. Software is not designed or licensed for use in on-line control of aircraft, air traffic, aircraft navigation or aircraft communications; or in the design, construction, operation or maintenance of any nuclear facility. You warrant that you will not use Software for these purposes. No right, title or interest in or to any trademark, service mark, logo or trade name of Sun or its licensors is granted under this Agreement.
3. LIMITED WARRANTY. Sun warrants to you that for a period of ninety (90) days from the date of purchase, as evidenced by a copy of the receipt, the media on which Software is furnished (if any) will be free of defects in materials and workmanship under normal use. Except for the foregoing, Software is provided "AS IS." Your exclusive remedy and Sun's entire liability under this limited warranty will be at Sun's option to replace Software media or refund the fee paid for Software.
4. DISCLAIMER OF WARRANTY. UNLESS SPECIFIED IN THIS AGREEMENT, ALL EXPRESS OR IMPLIED CONDITIONS, REPRESENTATIONS AND WARRANTIES, INCLUDING ANY IMPLIED WARRANTY OF MERCHANTABILITY, FITNESS FOR A PARTICULAR PURPOSE, OR NON-INFRINGEMENT, ARE DISCLAIMED, EXCEPT TO THE EXTENT THAT THESE DISCLAIMERS ARE HELD TO BE LEGALLY INVALID.

5. LIMITATION OF LIABILITY. TO THE EXTENT NOT PROHIBITED BY LAW, IN NO EVENT WILL SUN OR ITS LICENSORS BE LIABLE FOR ANY LOST REVENUE, PROFIT OR DATA, OR FOR SPECIAL, INDIRECT, CONSEQUENTIAL, INCIDENTAL OR PUNITIVE DAMAGES, HOWEVER CAUSED REGARDLESS OF THE THEORY OF LIABILITY, ARISING OUT OF OR RELATED TO THE USE OF OR INABILITY TO USE SOFTWARE, EVEN IF SUN HAS BEEN ADVISED OF THE POSSIBILITY OF SUCH DAMAGES. In no event will Sun's liability to you, whether in contract, tort (including negligence), or otherwise, exceed the amount paid by you for Software under this Agreement. The foregoing limitations will apply even if the above stated warranty fails of its essential purpose.

6. Termination. This Agreement is effective until terminated. You may terminate this Agreement at any time by destroying all copies of Software. This Agreement will terminate immediately without notice from Sun if you fail to comply with any provision of this Agreement. Upon Termination, you must destroy all copies of Software.

7. Export Regulations. All Software and technical data delivered under this Agreement are subject to US export control laws and may be subject to export or import regulations in other countries. You agree to comply strictly with all such laws and regulations and acknowledge that you have the responsibility to obtain such licenses to export, re-export, or import as may be required after delivery to you.

8. U.S. Government Restricted Rights. Use, duplication, or disclosure by the U.S. Government is subject to restrictions set forth in this Agreement and as provided in DFARS 227.7202–1 (a) and 227.7202–3(a) (1995), DFARS 252.227–7013 (c)(1)(ii)(Oct 1988), FAR 12.212 (a) (1995), FAR 52.227–19 (June 1987), or FAR 52.227–14(ALT III) (June 1987), as applicable.

9. Governing Law. Any action related to this Agreement will be governed by California law and controlling U.S. federal law. No choice of law rules of any jurisdiction will apply.

10. Severability. If any provision of this Agreement is held to be unenforceable, This Agreement will remain in effect with the provision omitted, unless omission would frustrate the intent of the parties, in which case this Agreement will immediately terminate.

11. Integration. This Agreement is the entire agreement between you and Sun relating to its subject matter. It supersedes all prior or contemporaneous oral or written communications, proposals, representations and warranties and prevails over any conflicting or additional terms of any quote, order, acknowledgment, or other communication between the parties relating to its subject matter during the term of this Agreement. No modification of this Agreement will be binding, unless in writing and signed by an authorized representative of each party.

For inquiries please contact: Sun Microsystems, Inc. 901 San Antonio Road, Palo Alto, California 94303

Java? 2 SDK, Standard Edition, Version 1.2.2 Supplemental License Terms

These supplemental terms ("Supplement") add to the terms of the Binary Code License Agreement ("Agreement"). Capitalized terms not defined herein shall have the same meanings ascribed to them in the Agreement. The Supplement terms shall supersede any inconsistent or conflicting terms in the Agreement.

1. Limited License Grant. Sun grants to you a non-exclusive, non-transferable limited license to use the Software without fee for evaluation of the Software and for development of Java? applets and applications provided that you: (i) may not re-distribute the Software in whole or in part, either separately or included with a product. (ii) may not create, or authorize your licensees to create additional classes, interfaces, or supplicates that are contained in the "java" or "sun" packages or similar as specified by Sun in any class file naming convention; and (iii) agree to the extent Programs are developed which utilize the Windows 95/98 style graphical user interface or components contained therein, such

applets or applications may only be developed to run on a Windows 95/98 or Windows NT platform. Refer to the Java 2 Runtime Environment Version 1.2.2 binary code license (http:// java.sun.com/products/jdk/1.2/jre/LICENSE) for the availability of runtime code which may be distributed with Java applets and applications.

2. Java Platform Interface. In the event that Licensee creates an additional API(s) which: (i) extends the functionality of a Java Environment; and, (ii) is exposed to third party software developers for the purpose of developing additional software which invokes such additional API, Licensee must promptly publish broadly an accurate specification for such API for free use by all developers.
3. Trademarks and Logos. This Agreement does not authorize Licensee to use any Sun name, trade-mark or logo. Licensee acknowledges as between it and Sun that Sun owns the Java trademark and all Java-related trademarks, logos and icons including the Coffee Cup and Duke ("Java Marks") and agrees to comply with the Java Trademark Guidelines at http://java.sun.com/trademarks.html.
4. High Risk Activities. Notwithstanding Section 2, with respect to high risk activities, the following language shall apply: the Software is not designed or intended for use in on-line control of air-craft, air traffic, aircraft navigation or aircraft communications; or in the design, construction, operation or maintenance of any nuclear facility. Sun disclaims any express or implied warranty of fitness for such uses.
5. Source Code. Software may contain source code that is provided solely for reference purposes pursuant to the terms of this Agreement.

NetBeans? DeveloperX2 2.1 Binary Code License Agreement

PLEASE READ THIS DOCUMENT CAREFULLY. BY DOWNLOADING THE SOFTWARE, YOU ARE AGREEING TO BECOME BOUND BY THE TERMS OF THIS AGREEMENT. IF YOU DO NOT AGREE TO THE TERMS OF THE AGREEMENT, PLEASE DO NOT DOWNLOAD THE SOFTWARE.

This is a legal Agreement between you and NetBeans, Inc. ("NetBeans"). This Agreement states the terms and conditions upon which NetBeans offers to license the software together with all related documentation and accompanying items including, but not limited to, the executable programs, drivers, libraries and data files associated with such programs (collectively, the "Software").

1. LICENSE. NetBeans grants to you ("Licensee") a nonexclusive, nontransferable, world-wide, royalty-free license to use this version of the Software for non-commercial and educational purposes.
2. COPYRIGHT. The Software is owned by NetBeans and is protected by United States copyright laws and international treaty provisions. You may not remove the copyright notice from any copy of the Software or any copy of the written materials, if any, accompanying the Software.
3. ONE ARCHIVAL COPY. You may make one (1) archival copy of the machine-readable portion of the Software for backup purposes only in support of your use of the Software on a single computer, provided that you reproduce on the copy all copyright and other proprietary rights notices included on the originals of the Software.
4. TRANSFER OF LICENSE. You may not transfer your license of the Software to a third party.
5. DECOMPILING, DISASSEMBLING, OR REVERSE ENGINEERING. You acknowledge that the Software contains trade secrets and other proprietary information of NetBeans and its licensors. Except to the extent expressly permitted by this Agreement or by the laws of the jurisdiction where you are located, you may not decompile, disassemble or otherwise reverse engineer the Software, or engage in any other activities to obtain underlying information that is not visible to the user in connection with normal use of the Software. In particular, you agree not for any purpose to transmit the Software or display the Software's object code on any computer screen or to make any hard copy memory dumps

of the Software's object code. If you believe you require information related to the interoperability of the Software with other programs, you shall not decompile or disassemble the Software to obtain such information, and you agree to request such information from NetBeans. Upon receiving such a request, NetBeans shall determine whether you require such information for a legitimate purpose and, if so, NetBeans will provide such information to you within a reasonable time and on reasonable conditions. In any event, you will notify NetBeans of any information derived from reverse engineering or such other activities, and the results thereof will constitute the confidential information of NetBeans that may be used only in connection with the Software.

6. TERMINATION. The license granted to you is effective until terminated. You may terminate it at any time by destroying the Software (including any portions or copies thereof) currently in your possession or control. The license will also terminate automatically without any notice from NetBeans if you fail to comply with any term or condition of this Agreement. You agree upon any such termination to destroy the Software (including any portions or copies thereof). Upon termination, NetBeans may also enforce any and all rights provided by law. The provisions of this Agreement that protect the proprietary rights of NetBeans will continue in force after termination.

7. NO WARRANTY. ANY USE BY YOU OF THE SOFTWARE IS AT YOUR OWN RISK. THE SOFTWARE IS PROVIDED FOR USE "AS IS" WITHOUT WARRANTY OF ANY KIND. TO THE MAXIMUM EXTENT PERMITTED BY LAW, NetBeans DISCLAIMS ALL WARRANTIES OF ANY KIND, EITHER EXPRESS OR IMPLIED, INCLUDING, WITHOUT LIMITATION, IMPLIED WARRANTIES OR CONDITIONS OF MERCHANTABILITY AND FITNESS FOR A PARTICULAR PURPOSE.

   NetBeans does not warrant that the functions contained in the Software will meet your requirements or that the operation of the Software will be uninterrupted or error-free. Any representation, other than the warranties set forth in this Agreement, will not bind NetBeans. You assume full responsibility for the selection of the Software to achieve your intended results, and for the downloading, use and results obtained from the Software. You also assume the entire risk as it applies to the quality and performance of the Software.

   This warranty gives you specific legal rights, and you may also have other rights which vary from country/state to country/state. Some countries/ states do not allow the exclusion of implied warranties, so the above exclusion may not apply to you.

8. NO LIABILITY FOR DAMAGES, INCLUDING WITHOUT LIMITATION CONSEQUENTIAL DAMAGES.

   In no event shall NetBeans or its Licensors be liable for any damages whatsoever (including, without limitation, incidental, direct, indirect, special or consequential damages, damages for loss of business profits, business interruption, loss of business information, or other pecuniary loss) arising out of the use or inability to use this Software, even if NetBeans or its Licensors have been advised of the possibility of such damages. Because some states/ countries do not allow the exclusion or limitation of liability for consequential or incidental damages, the above limitation may not apply to you.

9. INDEMNIFICATION BY YOU. If you distribute the Software in violation of this Agreement, you hereby indemnify, hold harmless and defend NetBeans from and against any and all claims or lawsuits, including attorney's fees and costs that arise, result from or are connected with the use or distribution of the Software in violation of this Agreement.

10. GENERAL. This Agreement is binding on you as well as your employees, employers, contractors and agents, and on any successors and assignees. Neither the Software nor any information derived therefrom may be exported except in accordance with the laws of the U.S. or other applicable provisions. This Agreement is governed by the laws of the Czech Republic. This Agreement is the entire Agreement between you and NetBeans and you agree that NetBeans will not have any liability for any untrue statement or representation made by its agents or anyone else (whether innocently or negligently) upon which you relied upon entering this Agreement, unless such untrue statement or representation was made fraudulently. This Agreement supersedes any other understandings or agreements, including, but not limited to, advertising, with respect to the Software.

If any provision of this Agreement is deemed invalid or unenforceable by any country or government agency having jurisdiction, that particular provision will be deemed modified to the extent necessary to make the provision valid and enforceable, and the remaining provisions will remain in full force and effect.

For questions concerning this Agreement, please contact NetBeans at info@netbeans.com